W9-BRT-964

The Canadian
Atlas
LIMITED EDITION

Nº 3781

FIRST PRINTING
JULY 2004

The Canadian Atlas

OUR NATION, ENVIRONMENT AND PEOPLE

READER'S DIGEST / MONTRÉAL

ACKNOWLEDGMENTS

Reader's Digest Canada / Canadian Geographic
The Canadian Atlas

THE READER'S DIGEST ASSOCIATION (CANADA) LTD.	CANADIAN GEOGRAPHIC ENTERPRISES
PRESIDENT AND CEO: Pierre Dion	CEO AND PUBLISHER: John L. Thomson
VICE PRESIDENT, BOOKS & HOME ENTERTAINMENT: Deirdre Gilbert	EDITOR: Rick Boychuk
ART DIRECTOR: John McGuffie	ART DIRECTOR: Stephen Hanks, Design Matters

PROJECT TEAM

PROJECT EDITOR: Andrew R. Byers	MANAGING EDITOR: Eric Harris
DESIGNER: Andrée Payette	CARTOGRAPHER: Steven Fick
COPY EDITOR: Gilles Humbert	CONTRIBUTING EDITOR: Wendy Simpson-Lewis
PRODUCTION COORDINATOR: Susan Wong	
ADMINISTRATOR: Elizabeth Eastman	

THE CANADIAN ATLAS ADVISORY BOARD
Dr. Mark Graham; Bruce Amos; Jean-Marie Beaulieu;
Helen Kerfoot; Dr. Brian S. Osborne; Peter Puxley;
Dr. Frank Quinn; Dr. Joan Schwartz

CONSULTANTS: Ed Cowell, Richard Loreto
CONTRIBUTING EDITORS: Robert Ronald, Philomena Rutherford
RESEARCHER: Martha Plaine
PICTURE RESEARCHER: Rachel Irwin
COPY EDITOR: Judy Yelon
IMAGE TREATMENT: Yves Lachance

MAPS

MAPMEDIA Corp.

MAPS PRODUCED AND COPYRIGHT BY: MAPmedia
© MAPmedia Corporation, Toronto, Ontario

SATELLITE IMAGES

WorldSat

© WorldSat International Inc. 2004, All Rights Reserved

Published in Canada in 2004 by

THE READER'S DIGEST ASSOCIATION (CANADA) LTD.	CANADIAN GEOGRAPHIC
1125 Stanley Street, Montréal, Quebec H3B 5H5	39 McArthur Ave., Ottawa, Ontario K1L 8L7

For information about this and other products
or to request a catalogue, please contact these 24-hour
Customer Service hotlines:

Reader's Digest at 1-800-465-0780. | Canadian Geographic at 1-800-267-0824.

You can also visit these websites:

Reader's Digest at www.rd.ca. | Canadian Geographic at www.canadiangeographic.ca.

Copyright © 2004 The Reader's Digest Association (Canada) Ltd.

All rights reserved. No part of this publication may be reproduced, stored in a retrieval system,
or transmitted in any form or by any means, electronic, mechanical,
photocopying, recording or otherwise, without permission of the copyright holders.

National Library of Canada Cataloguing in Publication Data

The Canadian atlas [cartographic material]:
our nation, environment and people.

Includes index.
ISBN 0-88850-770-4

1. Canada—Maps. 2. Canada—Gazetteers.
I. Reader's Digest Association (Canada).
G1115.C37 2004   912.71   C2004-901790-X

Reader's Digest and the Pegasus logo are registered trademarks of
The Reader's Digest Association, Inc.

Printed in Canada
04 05 06 07 / 5 4 3 2 1

FOREWORD

The Canadian Atlas encapsulates the complexity and majesty of our vast nation in the early years of the 21st century. This new and comprehensive visual reference work is the happy result of a collaborative effort between two of Canada's major publishers, Reader's Digest and Canadian Geographic. This atlas blends text, maps, images, charts, and tables in a way that provides informed understanding of all things Canadian. It offers a superb collection of up-to-date maps of virtually every part of the country, plus information-packed thematic spreads on issues of timely relevance and concern, with particular emphasis on sustainability. These illuminate aspects of many essential matters: the diversity of our natural regions, the abundance of our resource riches, our remarkable human past, the startling changes in our social values, and the dynamic drive of our ever-expanding urban centres. But *The Canadian Atlas* is more than just an inventory of national possessions and trends. It goes beyond the boundaries of the traditional atlas to explore many of the challenges that Canada faces today and tomorrow. True to this editorial vision, Reader's Digest and Canadian Geographic have created a truly unique reference work of matchless scope and insight, which they jointly present as a gift to Canada.

The Editors

Table of Contents

ASPECTS OF OUR NATION: A THEMATIC OVERVIEW

CANADA NOW   **8**
Key facts and sustainability questions relating
to our people, cities, land, resources, and water

CANADA'S MANY FACES   **10**
Landforms: Cordillera, Interior Plains, Arctic, Canadian
Shield, Great Lakes–St. Lawrence Lowlands, Appalachian
- **Rocks and fossils:** Geologic map and timeline; how rocks and
minerals are formed; plate tectonics, fossils—the record of life.
The forces that build mountains; a timeline of life-forms

THIS WATER-RICH LAND   **12**
Our most bountiful resource; the major drainage basins; water sources
and uses; harnessing water power
- **Rivers of ice:** the impact of glaciation past and present
- **A Natural Balance:** combating prairie drought

EXTREMES OF WEATHER   **14**
Forces that shape Canada's weather; when air masses collide; where
our weather begins; thunderstorms, ice storms, tornadoes, hurricanes;
record-breaking weather events
- **Climate zones and graphs**
- **A Natural Balance:** developing wind power

SIX NATURAL REGIONS   **16**
Arctic and Taiga, Pacific and Western Mountains, Central Plains, Boreal
Shield, Mixedwood Plains, Atlantic Region. Map: the six regions,
the national parks, RAMSAR and World Heritage sites
- **Canada's wetlands:** marshes, swamps, and bogs

THE FAR NORTH: ARCTIC AND TAIGA   **18**
Northern climatic and environmental extremes; the two poles;
permafrost and ice; the harvesting cycle; diamonds, oil, minerals
- **Ecozone overview:** Arctic Cordillera, Northern Arctic, Southern
Arctic, Taiga Plains, Taiga Shield, Hudson Plains, Arctic Basin,
and Arctic Archipelago
- **A Natural Balance:** "Circumpolar Protection"

PACIFIC AND WESTERN MOUNTAINS   **20**
A scenic, resource-rich region; mountain zones; how the "rain shadow"
affects the weather; fisheries, farms, and forests of British Columbia
- **A Natural Balance:** "Green Getaways"—the ecotourism approach
- **Ecozone overview:** Pacific Maritime, Montane Cordillera,
Boreal Cordillera, Taiga Cordillera, and Pacific Marine

CENTRAL PLAINS 22

A region of plains and boreal forests; rural depopulation; prairie crops; resource riches beneath the Prairies—potash, oil and natural gas production, the Alberta tar sands
● **A Natural Balance:** "The Pelican Project"
■ **Ecozone overview:** the Prairies—grassland and parkland; the Dry and Fertile Belts; Boreal Plains

BOREAL SHIELD 24

Canada's largest ecozone; mining and forest production; the impact of acid precipitation; clear-cutting concerns
● **A Natural Balance:** "The Greening of Sudbury"— reclaiming land devastated by industry and mining
■ **Ecozone overview:** natural hazards—fires and pests

MIXEDWOOD PLAINS 26

Canada's populous industrial powerhouse; the Great Lakes and the St. Lawrence Seaway; what the farms produce; where the people live; what the cities produce
● **A Natural Balance:** "Protecting the Oak Ridges Moraine"— safeguarding a significant natural area
■ **Ecozone overview**

ATLANTIC REGION 28

A region of fisheries, farms, and forests; the collapse of the cod fishery; the Hibernia oil project
● **A Natural Balance:** "A Model Forest"—ensuring the sustainability of Canada's forests
■ **Ecozone overview:** Atlantic Maritime, Atlantic and Northwest marine ecozones

FIRST PEOPLES 30

A diversity of aboriginal cultures—peoples of the Arctic, Subarctic, Pacific Northwest, Plateau, Plains, Eastern Woodlands; the arrival of the first peoples
■ **Aboriginals Today:** land treaties past and present; the growing population
▲ **Timeline:** 40,000 B.C.–A.D. 1400

SETTLING CANADA 32

Major explorers; the human tide—Vikings, Portuguese; French; Loyalists; Red River settlers; Irish; Asians, Eastern Europeans; interprovincial migration
■ **The New Mosaic:** how immigration is changing the fabric of Canadian society; visible minorities
▲ **Timeline:** 1487–1857

BUILDING CANADA 34

The nation's territorial evolution; the results of Canadian federal elections, 1867–2000; where bills become laws; governing Canada
■ **Provinces and Territories:** capitals, populations, areas
▲ **Timeline:** 1867–1999

CONNECTING CANADA 36

Communications: the Internet, satellites, cellular superlatives Transportation networks: highways and byways, waterways, railways, and airways

WHO WE ARE 38

A social profile of Canadians: births, languages, religions, education, marriage and divorce, family life, work and income, health, life expectancy
● **A Natural Balance:** "Caring for an Aging Population"
■ **Changing population patterns**

WHERE WE LIVE 40

Urban Canada; census metropolitan regions; city/regions; how to measure urban innovation; rural decline; suburban expansion; comparing amenities in five Canadian centres
● **A Natural Balance:** "Revitalizing Canada's Cities"
■ **Metro Canada:** populations, areas, densities

CANADA 2050 42

Future challenges: population, global warming, lifestyle and work; health; manufacturing, farming, and energy

MAPS OF CANADA 44

Relief map 46
Key map 48

CITY MAPS 134

MAP INDEX 150

Thematic subjects index 152

CREDITS 192

ASPECTS OF
THE NATION

Below: *A saltwater marsh where
the Fox River empties into Minas Channel,
just west of Parrsboro, New Brunswick. Visible
on the far shore is Cape Blomidon, Nova Scotia.*

Canada now

The challenge for Canada in the 21st century is no longer about wresting natural resources from a harsh and unpredictable environment. Today, Canada faces a different challenge—that of seeking "sustainability." This challenge embraces two main objectives: preserving resources while creating a buoyant long-lasting economy. With more area than any other country in the world except Russia, Canada is generously, if unevenly, endowed with raw materials. This resource base supports today's highly diversified Canadian economy, firmly centred in services and manufacturing, and the expanding urban scene where eight out of ten Canadians live and work. Canada is a country of complex interconnections, where the abuse of resources—the rampant exploitation of fisheries, forests, and mines, for example—may have serious widespread consequences. Achieving sustainability involves balancing our competing environmental, economic, and social concerns, some of which are surveyed on these pages. How such concerns will be resolved in the future is difficult to discern. When decisions are taken, however, the well-being of Canadians is of paramount importance. Canada ranks as one of the world's most desirable countries in which to live. Thinking of our concerns in the context of sustainability may ensure that it remains so.

KEY FACTS / SUSTAINABILITY QUESTIONS

Key facts about Canada appear to the right. **Sustainability questions** direct readers to pages where *The Canadian Atlas* explores questions about present and future social and environmental issues

THE LAND AND THE PEOPLE

Key facts: At 9,984,670 km², Canada is the world's second largest country. But, with 31,752,842 people (in 2004), it has only 0.5 percent of the world's 6 billion. By world standards, Canada's growth rate—1.06 percent a year—is low. Moreover, its population is aging. According to the 2001 census, the average median age was 37.6 years—up from 35.3 years in 1996.
Sustainability questions: Will population growth continue to slow? Given Canada's aging population, can we sustain health care, pensions, and other benefits? Will immigration reverse this trend? See pages 30–31, 33, 42–43

CITIES

Key facts: Urban Canada is driving the country's affluent high-tech post-industrial economy. From 1996 to 2001, the nation's largest centres—Toronto, Montréal, Vancouver, and the Calgary-Edmonton corridor—grew 7.6 percent and seem set to expand indefinitely.
Sustainability questions: Can Canada's cities, currently underfunded, be revitalized? What steps have been taken to curb urban sprawl? What will urban Canada look like 50 years from now? See pages 40–41, 42–43

CLIMATE AND WEATHER

Key facts: Global warming's impact is already evident in Canada. In the Northwest Territories, warmer-than-usual weather is melting the permafrost and drier conditions are causing more forest fires. Other changes—for example, coastal flooding and droughts—are predicted. But experts are divided on global warming's eventual outcome.
Sustainability questions: How rapidly will global warming occur? Is it possible that this climate trend will be slower than expected? See pages 14–15, 42–43

ENERGY

Key facts: Canada abounds in energy sources—oil, natural gas, coal, hydroelectric, and nuclear. But it also uses more energy than most other countries, ranking sixth among the world's energy consumers. Demand has risen steadily since the 1960s and is expected to continue unabated, increasing pollution levels and heightening global warming.
Sustainability questions: Can Canada sustain a high level of energy consumption? In future, will we choose to use existing energy sources more efficiently, or will we turn to alternative energy sources? See pages 12–13, 22–23, 42–43

FARMS

Key facts: Seven percent of Canada's land area—roughly 680,000 km²—is used for agriculture. Dominating this sector are several trends: a shift toward more diverse crop outputs, a decline in the number of farms, and rural depopulation.
Sustainability questions: How have Canada's various agricultural regions responded to these trends? Will technology and new agricultural methods change the farms of the future? See pages 21, 22–23, 27, 29, 40, 42

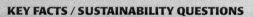

FISHERIES

Key facts: Overfishing—the result of escalating world and domestic demand—reduced Atlantic and Pacific species. Canada's fisheries remain in constant flux—sometimes for the worse, sometimes for the better. From 1990 to 2001, the tonnage of fish caught in all fisheries fell 37 percent, while the value of the catch rose by 43 percent.
Sustainability questions: Will there be future declines in fishing stocks? How can such a scenario be avoided? See pages 21, 28, 42–43

FORESTS

Key facts: Canada's forests cover 4.2 million square kilometres— 45 percent of the land area—and shelter two-thirds of the country's bird and animal species. In 2001, the timber-productive forests consisted of 2.45 million square kilometres. About a million hectares—only 0.4 percent of this area—is harvested annually. Since 1978, Canada's forest-product exports have increased almost fourfold, reaching $33.7 billion in 2002.
Sustainability questions: Will the profitable harvesting of Canada's productive forests destroy or seriously disrupt wildlife habitats? What steps are being taken to ensure Canada's forests remain sustainable? See pages 21, 25, 29

MINES

Key facts: Canada is a leading producer of potash, uranium, zinc, nickel, copper, platinum, cobalt, silver, and gold. Diamond production in the Far North is the latest Canadian mining success story. Output from new discoveries at Voiseys Bay in Labrador may some day rival those of the mineral-rich Sudbury region.
Sustainability questions: What have been the social and environmental consequences for mine-dependent communities when deposits run out or cease to be profitable? Will future technology disclose new extraction venues? See pages 16–17, 20–21, 23, 27

WATER

Key facts: Canada's freshwater is a renewable resource that most of the world would like to have. The average Canadian household, assured of a safe water supply, uses up 340 litres a day—an extravagant level when compared with other countries. In future, limiting water consumption may become imperative. Some experts predict that water will be "the oil of the 21st century." The export of Canada's water is already raising environmental concerns.
Sustainability questions: How well distributed is Canada's water supply? What is being done to save Canada's wetlands, a major natural asset? See pages 12–13, 16, 42–43

THE ECOZONE APPROACH

The Canadian Atlas adopts an "ecozone approach" to describe the complexity of the natural environment. The prefix "eco," from the Greek "oikos" for "home" or "household," is a reminder that ecozones are where we live—our home. Canada possesses 20 major ecozones: 15 terrestrial (land) and 5 marine (oceanic) ecozones, arranged under the headings of six natural regions (see pages 16 to 29). This approach provides a unique and timely perspective from which to explore some of the interconnections and relationships that exist between environmental and economic conditions. Sidebars give overviews of each ecozone's geographical and climatic characteristics, some of its plant and animal species, and human activities. "Natural Balance" features, identified by the globe (*below*), pinpoint regional sustainability success stories.

Canada's many faces

Viewed by satellite, the face of Canada reveals six clearly defined landform regions: Cordillera, Interior Plains, Canadian Shield, Great Lakes–St. Lawrence Lowlands, Appalachian, and Arctic Lands. All these regions occupy significant portions of Canada's vast expanse. Each possesses similar geologic structures, physical features, climatic conditions, soils, and vegetation. Considered as a whole, Canada's landforms encompass an unrivaled diversity of landscapes: spectacular mountain ranges, sweeping plains, rocky uplands, temperate lowlands, and frigid tundra. The forces of nature—our daily weather, for example—actively shape landforms. Some forces level landforms, others rebuild them. Over time, the impact of water, ice, and wind slowly and steadily reduce the mighty Rockies to rubble, while rivers bear away sediments to deltas and seabeds where new landforms wait to be born.

- Precambrian
- Paleozoic
- Mesozoic
- Cenozoic
- Mixed Paleozoic, Mesozoic, and Cenozoic

Geologists break down the earth's long history into comprehensible intervals of time. The longest intervals—eons—are divided into eras (Paleozoic, Mesozoic, Cenozoic), which are themselves divided into periods such as the Quaternary (*see timeline below*). The periods are further subdivided into epochs such as the Holocene—our own time. The geologic map of Canada (*above*) locates the underlying rock formations dating from the four major eras; the timeline identifies present-day landform regions supported by these formations.

TIMELINE: GEOLOGY

Era	Time (millions of years ago)	Landform regions
Precambrian	4,600 to 600	Canadian Shield, Arctic (Baffin Island)
Paleozoic	600 to 250	Interior Plains (northern), Canadian Shield (Hudson Bay Lowlands), Great Lakes–St. Lawrence Lowlands, Appalachian, Arctic, and Innuitian
Mesozoic	250 to 65	Interior Plains (southern)
Cenozoic Quaternary*	65 to today	Cordillera Arctic (Mackenzie River delta), Cordillera (Fraser River delta)

* The Quaternary period includes the most recent epochs: the Pleistocene, or Ice Age, and Holocene (the present time)

ROCKS AND MINERALS

A jumble of ceaselessly recycled igneous, sedimentary, and metamorphic rocks makes up the earth's surface. Igneous rock (granite, gneiss) forms when molten rock cools. The Canadian Shield's igneous base abounds in copper, gold, iron, and nickel. Sedimentary rock (sandstone, limestone) consists of hardened layers of rock particles. Beneath the Prairies, sedimentary layers store oil, gas, and coal. Mineral-rich metamorphic rock, baked or compressed igneous or sedimentary rock, shows up in the Shield and Cordillera.

PLATE TECTONICS

Canada rides on one of 30 or so tectonic plates, or slabs, which underlie the earth's continents and oceans. The plates—each tens of kilometres thick—move in different directions, possibly in response to currents of molten material below the earth's crust. When plates collide, earthquakes and volcanic activity occur. In geological time, collisions uplift mountain chains. (See *Building Mountains,* facing page.) Canada's west coast is situated in one of the world's most active collision zones, where the westbound North American plate overrides the Pacific plate.

FOSSILS

The record of life is found in fossils, plant and animal remains preserved in rock. Yet some 90 percent of the record is missing. Geological forces have erased virtually all fossils from the Cryptozoic eon (Greek for "hidden life")—the earth's first 4 billion years. The Phanerozoic eon ("evident life") dawns with Paleozoic era, which left behind fossils revealing an explosion of life forms. One of the world's important Paleozoic finds is the Burgess Shale Site in Yoho National Park. (See *Timeline: Life Forms,* facing page.)

CORDILLERA

The towering peaks and plateaus of the Cordillera took shape millions of years ago, when the westward moving North American tectonic plate collided with the Pacific plate. The collision uplifted mountain chains in British Columbia and the Yukon. In the last 20,000 years, weathering, erosion, and glaciation have carved the sharp relief of Rocky Mountain peaks such as Rampart Mountain in Banff National Park (*left*). The westward movement of the North American plate continues unabated, exposing British Columbia's populous coastal lowlands to an ever-present threat of earthquakes.

CANADA'S LANDFORM REGIONS

1. Cordillera
2. Interior Plains
3. Canadian Shield
4. Great Lakes–St. Lawrence Lowlands
5. Appalachian
6. Arctic Lands

BUILDING MOUNTAINS

Mountains are often found along coastlines where continental and ocean plates meet. The collision sets off a process in which the ocean plate slides underneath the continental plate, buckling it and uplifting mountains. As the surface buckles, volcanoes force up fiery rock in fractures (faults) and wavy folds.

Mountain building is measured in millions of years. Some 250 million years ago, the collision of the North American plate with Europe and Africa built up the Appalachian and Laurentian mountains. Canada's east coast is relatively calm now, but its west coast lies on the Pacific's earthquake-prone "ring of fire." The North American plate began creeping westward 80 to 40 million years ago, eventually colliding with the Pacific plate. The collision compressed sedimentary rocks, thrusting up highly faulted and folded parallel chains from the Rockies to the Coast Mountains. It also created British Columbia's Interior Plateau, now the eroded remnant of another ancient range. In the Yukon's St. Elias Mountains, uplift continues, pushing up Canada's youngest, loftiest peaks, including its highest—5,959-m Mount Logan.

TIMELINE: LIFE FORMS

3,500 TO 600 MILLION YEARS AGO

PRECAMBRIAN The first life—algae, bacteria, and soft-bellied marine creatures—develops in the depths of primeval seas more than 3 billion years ago. Canada's oldest known evidence of life: 2.5-billion-year-old algae fossils, discovered at Steep Rock Mine, Ont.

600 TO 250 MILLION YEARS AGO

PALEOZOIC (Greek for "ancient life") The age of fishes begins about 400 million years ago. The first plants, descended from algae, have already taken root on land. As vegetation spreads across the bare rock, insects flourish in conifer forests. By the late Paleozoic era, amphibians and reptiles invade the land.

250 TO 65 MILLION YEARS AGO

MESOZOIC ("middle life") Reptiles, particularly dinosaurs, dominate this era. Broadleaved trees and flowering plants replace conifers. Birds take wing, and small mammals appear. According to a prevailing view, dinosaurs die out in a global environmental disaster triggered by the impact of a huge asteroid.

65 MILLION YEARS AGO TO THE PRESENT

CENOZOIC ("recent life") The demise of the dinosaurs clears the way for a proliferation of mammals: horses, whales, and large carnivores. Grasslands develop. The Quaternary, starting about 2 million years ago, sees the arrival of the first known humans.

INTERIOR PLAINS

About 500 million years ago, shallow seas covered the Interior Plains. Rivers flowing into these waters deposited sediments, which were transformed into layer upon layer of sedimentary rock. In the southern part of the Interior Plains lie grasslands. The sedimentary materials here provide fertile soils for the patchwork of prairie farms. In the northern part, aspen parkland dwindles into sparsely treed taiga. Over time, weathering and erosion have cut deeply into the soft rock in parts of Alberta and Saskatchewan. At Horseshoe Canyon (left), near Drumheller, Alta., these processes have exposed multicolored layers from the Mesozoic era when dinosaurs roamed this region.

ARCTIC LANDS

Covering roughly 25 percent of Canada's landmass, the Arctic Lands embrace two distinct regions: Arctic and Innuitian. The land, permanently frozen to varying depths, supports only a thin surface mat of vegetation, which peters out completely in the high polar latitudes. The Arctic region includes the Yukon's narrow coastal plain, Banks and Victoria islands, and Baffin Island's lowlands. The Innuitian region runs along Baffin Island's rugged eastern upland, where sheer cliffs on Borden Peninsula overlook the ice-clogged waters of Lancaster Sound (left). This upland extends into Ellesmere Island, home of ice-capped mountain ranges, where elevations reach 1,500 m and higher. The island's loftiest pinnacle is 2,616-m-high Barbeau Peak.

CANADIAN SHIELD

Lion's Head (left), a wave-lashed arch of stone on the Lake Superior shores of Ontario's Sleeping Giant Provincial Park, exemplifies the Canadian Shield's rugged beauty. This region of rocks, lakes, and forests, also known as the Precambrian Shield, occupies more than half of Canada. Its enduring bedrock provides the geological foundation for adjacent regions, such as the Interior Plains. The capacious Shield includes the Hudson Bay Lowlands, one of the world's largest wetlands, the Torngat Mountains—Eastern Canada's highest peaks—and the uplands of central Baffin Island. Some 3 billion years ago, the Shield was a land of huge mountains and volcanoes. In the last ice age, glaciers stripped away the region's surface, exposing the world's oldest bedrock just east of Great Slave Lake.

GREAT LAKES–ST. LAWRENCE LOWLANDS

Stretching from Windsor to the city of Québec, this narrow plain is Canada's smallest landform region, but by far the most populous. East of Kingston, the Thousand Islands—an intrusion of the Canadian Shield—divides southern Ontario's lowlands from the St. Lawrence River valley. Around lakes Erie and Ontario, the bedrock is sedimentary, visible in the limestone strata of the Niagara Escarpment (left). An overlay of glacial debris, deposited during the last ice age, created southern Ontario's flat to rolling terrain. Along the St. Lawrence, the retreating ice-age Champlain Sea left behind a fertile riverine plain.

APPALACHIAN

The Appalachian Mountains, this region's dominant feature, extend from Newfoundland into the eastern United States. Once higher than the Rockies, these uplands formed 500 million years ago. Over time, weathering eroded the peaks. Except for Prince Edward Island's fertile fields, the interior is a land of rounded hills and narrow river valleys. Bold headlands rear up in the Gaspé Peninsula, shown left near Percé, Que. Along Nova Scotia's coast, the bays have long served as fishing ports and harbours.

This water-rich land

Canada's freshwater lakes and rivers cover 755,000 km², a bountiful 7.6 percent portion of the country. This abundance of water, flowing through an interconnecting network of waterways, has spurred Canada's development. Water provided the early routes for exploration, transportation, settlement, and trade. It is still put to myriad uses: hydroelectric power, shipping, irrigation, fishing, and recreation. Yet any undue future demand may overextend this resource. Many worry our water-rich land may one day export some of its supply to the United States. An overview of Canada's water already reveals a resource unevenly distributed and under threat. Whether a given region has an abundance or shortage of water is due in part to variations in precipitation. The rainy Pacific Coast enjoys a copious flow of water to the sea, while parched prairie drylands struggle with water deficits. These disparities aside, the pressure from industry and shipping along the Great Lakes and elsewhere pose ever-present pollution concerns.

Glaciers are flowing rivers of land ice, which originate with the accumulation and compression of snow. In the arctic climate of Ellesmere Island (*above*), glaciers overlay the land as they once did when they covered all of Canada. During the last 2 million years, ice swept over Canada four times. The ice retreated during warmer periods, including our present time. At the zenith of the last advance, 18,000 years ago, the Laurentide ice sheet extended beyond the Canadian Shield to depths of 3 km. In the West, the Cordilleran ice sheet stretched from the Rockies to the Pacific. The slow but relentless movement of ice scoured the face of Canada, leaving behind landmarks such as drumlins, eskers, and moraines (*below*). The only remnant from the distant icy past is the 100,000-year-old Barnes Ice Cap on Baffin Island. Today, three-quarters of Canada's glaciers cloak parts of the eastern arctic islands. The remaining glaciers cap the alpine summits of the Rockies and the West Coast ranges. In all, Canada's glaciers cover 200,000 km²—roughly half the area of Newfoundland and Labrador.

18,000 years ago | Today

DURING GLACIATION

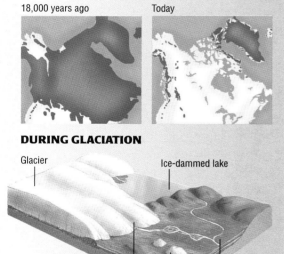

Glacier | Ice-dammed lake
Tunnel | Outwash plain with till deposits
Ice block

Some 12,000 years ago, meltwater of a glacier and an ice-dammed lake flowed from tunnels into streams, depositing mud, sand, and gravel. This debris, known as till, spread over the outwash plain where ice blocks fill steep-sided potholes.

AFTER GLACIATION

Drumlin shaped by overriding glacier | Esker
Moraine
Kettle lake

The glacial-lake bottom is now fertile land. Drumlins are hills composed of till; eskers, long or oval mounds that were the banks of the meltwater streams. Moraines mark the glacier's limit. Kettle lakes fill the potholes after the ice blocks melt.

Canada has five ocean drainage basins. The largest by far is the Hudson Bay basin; the smallest, situated in the southern Prairies, flows via the Missouri and Mississippi rivers into the Gulf of Mexico. Within each basin lie smaller subbasins. Drainage divides separate the basins. The best known of these is the Continental Divide of the Rockies, which separates rivers flowing westward to the Pacific from rivers flowing to the Arctic and Hudson Bay. The map at left locates Canada's five basins and main rivers, and lists figures for areas and streamflow to the sea.

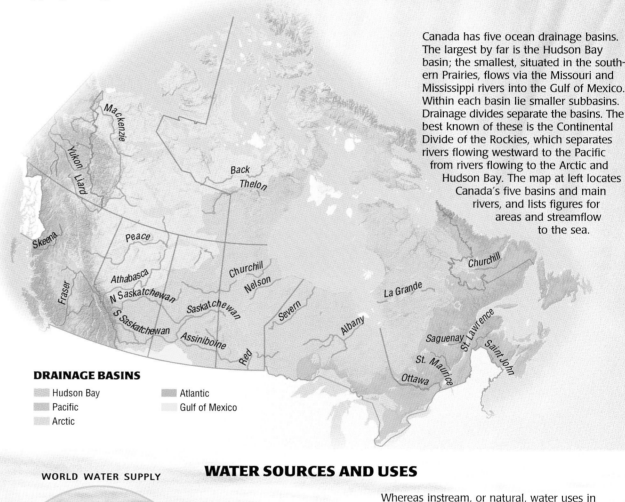

Mackenzie · Yukon · Liard · Back · Thelon · Skeena · Peace · Churchill · Nelson · Churchill · La Grande · Fraser · Athabasca · N Saskatchewan · Saskatchewan · Severn · Albany · Saguenay · St. Maurice · St. Lawrence · Saint John · S Saskatchewan · Assiniboine · Red · Ottawa

DRAINAGE BASINS

- Hudson Bay
- Pacific
- Arctic
- Atlantic
- Gulf of Mexico

WATER SOURCES AND USES

WORLD WATER SUPPLY
Salt water 97.2%
Freshwater 2.8%

FRESHWATER
Ice 2.15%
Surface water 0.03%
Groundwater 0.62%

SURFACE WATER

Whereas instream, or natural, water uses in Canada include hydroelectric power generation, shipping, and fisheries, withdrawal uses involve less than 3 percent of our freshwater, used for domestic and industrial purposes and irrigation. Most of Canada draws its freshwater from rivers and lakes, but some smaller communities and farms depend on groundwater. The chart below identifies the major withdrawal users. Thermal and nuclear power plants, which use water to cool condensers and to drive generators, withdraw more than all the other users combined. Industry reuses the same water twice; mining, more than twice. Annual withdrawals involve 1.3 percent of Canada's water supply. The water returned to natural sources is less that the amount withdrawn, and it has usually been degraded through use. Agriculture returns the least water to natural sources.

SURFACE WATER: FIVE MAIN WITHDRAWAL USES

Thermal power generation	Manufacturing	Municipal	Agriculture	Mining
64%	14%	12%	9%	1%

COMBATING DROUGHT

Most severe droughts occur in regions where farms depend on a limited water supply. One such region is the Prairie Dry Belt (*see map below*), where annual precipitation varies from less than 400 mm in southern Alberta to a high of 550 mm in southwestern Manitoba. Recent longer-than-usual summers and higher evaporation rates in this region have dried up soil moisture. It has revived fears of drought, dust storms, and crop failures that occurred in the 1930s. Some experts speculate the dry spell may be a foretaste of global warming; others see it as part of the recurrent cycle of wet and dry years. The dry years of the 1930s caused a drought that led to extensive topsoil erosion and drove 225,000 farm dwellers off the land. In response to this disaster, government drought-alleviation programs, such as the Prairie Farm Rehabilitation Administration (PFRA), were successfully introduced. Since the 1950s, PFRA-sponsored irrigation projects have revitalized the dry belt. Saskatchewan's Lake Diefenbaker irrigates 21,000 ha of farmland. Alberta's St. Mary and Waterton dams and reservoirs serve the 132,000-ha St. Mary Irrigation District, Canada's largest. The 466,000 ha of irrigated land in southern Alberta represents only 4 percent of the province's arable land. Yet this land supports 5,800 irrigation farms in a region where only 1,000 dryland wheat farms and ranches might normally thrive on existing water supplies. Moreover, these farms produce 18 percent of Alberta's agricultural output.

AT-A-GLANCE FACTS: WATER FRESH AND FROZEN

● The world's water supply measures 1.36 billion cubic kilometres. Water, as liquid, ice, or vapour in the atmosphere, constantly circulates from the oceans to the land, and back again

● 97.2% of the world's water is found in oceans, but salty oceanic water is unsuitable for drinking or farming

● 2.8% of the world's water supply is fresh, but 2.15% is locked up, often for centuries, in ice sheets and glaciers

● 0.62% of the world's freshwater is groundwater; only 0.03% exists in lakes and rivers, and in the soil

● With 7% of the world's renewable freshwater, Canada ranks fourth among the league of water-rich nations, after Brazil (18%), China (9%), and the United States (8%)

● 755,000 km² of Canada is covered by freshwater lakes and rivers

● Roughly 60% of all Canada's rivers and streams flow northward

● One in three Canadians depend on the Great Lakes for water

● In glacial coverage, Canada ranks third in the world, after Antarctica and Greenland

● Canada has 25% of the world's wetlands, which occupy 16% of its area

● Two-thirds of Canada's irrigated farmland is found in Alberta

AB   SK   MB

Edmonton
Calgary •Lloydminster
FERTILE BELT

DRY BELT •Winnipeg
•Lethbridge •Regina

HARNESSING THE WATERS

More than 60 percent of Canada's energy needs are supplied by water power. Several factors can influence a region's hydroelectric development: high precipitation, sloping landforms, and the proximity to markets. The Atlantic drainage basin was the site of the first hydroelectric power plants, built in the early 1900s at Niagara Falls, Trois-Rivières, and Shawinigan. But most hydroelectric production is found within the Canadian Shield area of the Hudson Bay basin. This area offers ideal conditions: Canada's highest streamflow, sudden drops in land elevation, and mighty rivers. The rivers of the Pacific basin, with the second highest streamflow (due to high precipitation along the coast), have also been extensively harnessed.

By the 1960s, virtually all the power sites close to markets had been developed. Since then, major hydroelectric power plants have been situated at remote northern sites such as Quebec's Manicouagan River (*left*). Canada's largest hydroelectric generating stations and their capacity include: LG-2 on La Grande Rivière, Que. (5,328 MW); Churchill Falls on the Churchill River, Nfld. (5,225 MW); and Gordon M. Shrum on the Peace River, B.C. (2,416 MW), the arctic drainage basin's only major hydroelectric development. To date, only 40 percent of Canada's hydroelectric potential has been realized.

Niagara Falls is the world's greatest waterfall by volume. Canada's Horseshoe Falls (above), largest of the fall's two cataracts, is 670 m wide, 54 m high, with a flow of 155,000 liters per minute. Its power was first tapped in 1893 by an electric tramway company. Sir Adam Beck No. 1 and No. 2 power stations, opened in 1922 and 1954 respectively, were built downstream from the falls to fully exploit its potential. Today's torrent is spectacular but less so than it once was. A 1950 Canada–United States treaty reduced the visible flow to a minimum, setting aside the rest for the hydroelectric production.

Extremes of weather

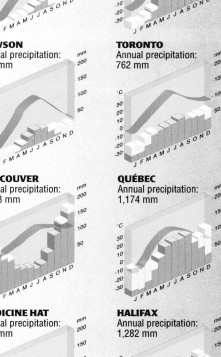

Pacific
Cordillera
Prairie
Great Lakes–St.
Lawrence Lowlands
Atlantic
Subarctic
Arctic

Climate is a region's weather over a long period. Within its vast expanse, Canada embraces seven climatic zones (*see map above*). Each of the zones depends on conditions such as proximity to large bodies of water, altitude, and latitude. Southern Ontario enjoys warm, humid summers and short, cold winters, because of the moderating influence of the Great Lakes. The mountainous interior of British Columbia and the Yukon Territory support glaciers on the summits and semideserts in the valleys. Latitude—the distance north or south of the equator—influences whether a climate is cold or hot. The midlatitude Prairies experience continental extremes: cold winters and hot, dry summers. The high-latitude Arctic endures intensely dry and frigid conditions. The largest zone by far is the Subarctic, which knows short, cool summers and long, cold winters, and low precipitation. All of southern Canada is classified as "temperate"— that is, it has four seasons. Winter touches all zones, save the Pacific, where warm winds promote a mild, rainy climate year-round. By contrast, the prevailing west-to-east winds moving across central Canada bring cool, humid summers and short, cool winters to Atlantic Canada.

CLIMATE GRAPHS

These show average temperatures and average snowfall and rainfall for each climatic zone. The growing season typically begins above 5°C.

■ Average monthly temperature
□ Average snowfall
▨ Average rainfall

RESOLUTE
Annual precipitation: 131 mm

WINNIPEG
Annual precipitation: 526 mm

DAWSON
Annual precipitation: 306 mm

TORONTO
Annual precipitation: 762 mm

VANCOUVER
Annual precipitation: 1,113 mm

QUÉBEC
Annual precipitation: 1,174 mm

MEDICINE HAT
Annual precipitation: 348 mm

HALIFAX
Annual precipitation: 1,282 mm

A combination of the sun's heat and the earth's rotation powers the movement of winds carrying weather systems across the globe—and across the length and breadth of Canada. The temperature differences between the poles and the equator provide the energy that drives atmospheric circulation: low-pressure polar air sinks and migrates to the equator while high-pressure warm air from the tropics rises and moves to the poles. This global circulation system is the mechanism that drives Canada's daily weather. In low-pressure areas, warm air rises and cools, forming clouds, which bring rain, fog, snow, hail, and thunderstorms. In high-pressure areas, cold air descends and, as it falls, it is compressed and heats up, generally bringing clear, warm, and settled weather. Canada's vast size and varied landscape also influence day-to-day conditions, some of which include the record-breaking weather extremes described below.

WHEN AIR MASSES COLLIDE

In a cold front, the leading edge of an advancing cold air mass meets less dense warm air and forces it up sharply like a blade, causing instability. Typically associated with low-pressure weather systems, cold fronts develop rapidly, often producing large cumulus and cumulonimbus clouds and triggering heavy rain and thunderstorms (*below*). Rainfall and winds are heaviest along the front.

In a warm front, the leading edge of a mass of warm air meets a stationary, cold air mass and gradually rises above it along a slope that can stretch for hundreds of kilometres. As the warm air rises, it cools, forming cirrus clouds. If higher clouds form, condensation will follow, causing widespread precipitation accompanied by strong winds.

COLD FRONT

WARM FRONT

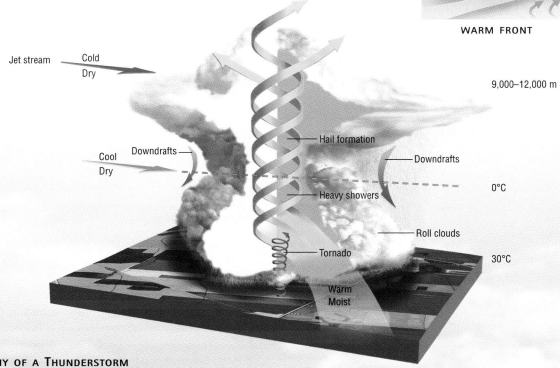

Jet stream · Cold Dry · 9,000–12,000 m · Hail formation · Downdrafts · Cool Dry · Downdrafts · Heavy showers · 0°C · Roll clouds · Tornado · 30°C · Warm Moist

ANATOMY OF A THUNDERSTORM

Thunderstorms begin when a parcel of warm, moist air begins to rise. As the air expands and cools, the water vapour within it condenses and forms a cloud. If there is sufficient atmospheric instability, the heat released by condensation will keep the air inside the cloud warmer than the air surrounding it, enabling it to grow larger and higher. The power of the rising air, or updraft, keeps millions of water droplets in suspension until they become so heavy they fall as rain. Above the freezing line (typically 12,000 to 15,000 m above the ground in summer), the droplets form supercooled ice crystals that can grow into hailstones. When the thundercloud reaches the cumulonimbus stage and hits the tropopause (where temperature stops

decreasing with height, around 12,000 m in summer), the jet stream tugs the cloud into its famous "anvil" shape, and the rising air in the cloud falls back to earth in cool, dry currents of air surrounding the warm, moist core of the storm. These downdrafts can pool at the bottom of the thunderstorm and create microbursts—brief, violent gusts of wind and rain. When the static buildup between the clashing air masses in a thunderstorm (the downdrafts carry a positive charge; the updrafts a negative one) triggers an electrical discharge, lightning forks through the sky at 145,000 km/s. The lightning heats the surrounding air, which expands at supersonic speeds, creating the mighty crashes we recognize as thunder.

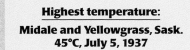

Highest temperature:	Lowest temperature:	Coldest month:	Greatest precipitation in one year:
Midale and Yellowgrass, Sask. 45°C, July 5, 1937	**Snag, Y.T. −63°C, Feb. 3, 1947**	**Eureka, N.W.T. −47.9°C, Feb. 1979**	**Henderson Lake, B.C. 9,479 mm, 1997**

WINTER AIR MASSES

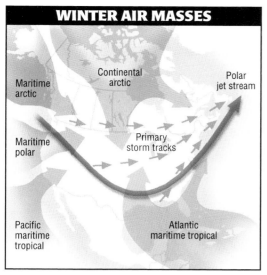

Maritime arctic — Continental arctic — Polar jet stream — Maritime polar — Primary storm tracks — Pacific maritime tropical — Atlantic maritime tropical

SUMMER AIR MASSES

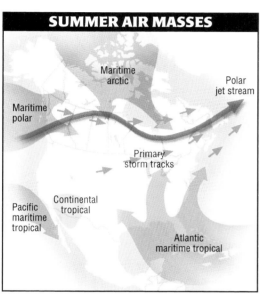

Maritime arctic — Polar jet stream — Maritime polar — Primary storm tracks — Pacific maritime tropical — Continental tropical — Atlantic maritime tropical

WHERE OUR WEATHER BEGINS

Five air masses affect Canada's weather: continental arctic, maritime arctic, maritime polar, maritime tropical, and continental tropical. Winds carry these great bodies of air across the country. Each air mass, extending hundreds or thousands of kilometres, has uniform temperature and moisture conditions, acquired from the underlying landmass or ocean where they developed. The very cold, dry continental arctic air mass, the source of Canada's bitter winters, originates over snow-covered barrens. In summer, its cool winds sweep south, bringing a welcome respite from heat waves. The maritime arctic air mass, traveling over large open bodies of water, is mild and moist. The maritime polar air masses of the Pacific and Atlantic soak coastal areas with rain, fog, and snow. The Atlantic maritime tropical air mass from the Gulf of Mexico scorches Eastern Canada with summer heat and humidity. By contrast, the Pacific maritime tropical has a cooling influence. The continental tropical air mass rarely reaches Canada because its hot, dry impact disappears as it moves north. The maps (*left*) show winter and summer air-mass movements. All weather changes are related to the interaction of these air masses along what are called fronts (*see opposite page*). The polar jet stream forms perhaps the biggest front, an ever-changing boundary where the cool winds from the north meet the warm winds from the south. In spring, the clashing air masses produce severe thunderstorms and tornadoes.

ride the WIND! the C-train is now 100% emissions-free Calgary Transit

RIDING ON AIR

Wind power is the world's fastest growing power source. In 2000, the capacity of the world's wind-power facilities grew by 32 percent to 17,700 megawatts (MW); two years later, capacity exceeded 31,000 MW. In Canada, wind-power capacity increased by about 20 percent in 2002 to about 250 MW, and is expected to surpass 3,000 MW in 2005. Canada lags in wind-power development because of the lack of subsidies and research grants given to other energy utilities such as oil and natural gas. Yet, experts estimate Canada's wind-power potential is about 30,000 MW, sufficient for 15 percent of the country's electricity needs. Canada's winter winds are a plus factor. Winds are strongest in winter; in northern latitudes, they grow stronger, particularly during the day. So, Canada could expect wind power to meet demand at peak periods. Quebec, Alberta, and Saskatchewan are Canada's wind-power leaders; Ontario, Prince Edward Island, and the Yukon have entered the field with new plants. Canada's largest wind-power producer is the Le Nordais project in the Gaspé Peninsula. In 2003, a 95-m-high direct-drive wind turbine went into operation at Toronto's waterfront Exhibition Place. Its owners are the Toronto Renewable Energy Co-operative (TREC), a group of about 650 individuals, businesses, and organizations that sells the wind-powered output to Toronto Hydro Energy. Calgary Transit's "Ride the Wind" program uses coaches (*above*) run on power from wind farms at Pincher Creek, Alta. (*below*).

(vertical text:) A NATURAL BALANCE

ICY AGONY

Freezing rain, precipitation that falls through a shallow layer of freezing temperatures before melting and then freezing upon impact, makes regular, transitory appearances during Canadian winters. But, on Jan. 5, 1998, freezing rain began to fall and continued for six days without letup, crippling eastern Ontario, southern Quebec, and the Maritimes. Trees snapped, roofs collapsed, and high-voltage towers crumpled under the weight of a 5-to-7.5-cm veneer of ice. The electrical system failed, leaving 4 million people in frozen darkness for at least 36 hours. Thousands took refuge in emergency shelters where many stayed for weeks. In the largest peacetime troop deployment in Canadian history, the army was called in to help. Storm-related claims totaled at least $2 billion. The ice storm caused 22 deaths in Quebec and 4 in Ontario.

TERRIFYING TWISTERS

All regions of Canada except the Arctic experience tornadoes, or twisters. Tornadoes occur from March to late October, peaking in early summer, with the most frequently affected areas being southern Ontario and the Prairie provinces. Forming in thunderstorms (*see opposite page*) rotated by high winds, a tornado occurs when a downward-spinning column of air inside the thunderstorm touches the ground, creating a funnel-shaped twister that can cut a path up to 1.6 km wide and 3.2 to 8 km long. Winds range from weak (65 km/h) to devastating (500 km/h). The 1912 Regina twister, Canada's deadliest, took 28 lives and destroyed the downtown area. Almost as destructive, the 1987 Edmonton tornado killed 27 people, injured over 200, and caused an estimated $250 million in damage.

HORRIFYING HURRICANES

A hurricane is a cyclical storm of tropical origin thousands of square kilometres across with speeds between 65 and 240 knots (120–445 km/h). Canada's east coast is often visited by hurricanes between August and October, although most dissipate and are downgraded to gale force (34–47 knots or 65–90 km/h) storms by the time they reach our shores. Some hurricanes, however, have left their horrifying mark:
● On Aug. 24–25, 1927, a hurricane swept through Atlantic Canada, washing out roads, filling basements, and swamping boats. In Newfoundland, 56 people died at sea.
● On Oct. 15, 1954, Hurricane Hazel dumped an estimated 300 million tonnes of rain on Toronto, obliterating streets and washing out bridges. In all, 83 people died.
● On Sept. 11, 1995, the QE2 ocean liner was struck by a 30-m wave during Hurricane Luis off the coast of Newfoundland, the largest measured wave height in the world.
● On Sept. 28, 2003, Hurricane Juan walloped Nova Scotia with winds in excess of 150 km/h (*below*). The storm killed 2 people, beached boats, uprooted hundreds of trees, and left thousands without power for days.

Wind farm at Pincher Creek, Alta. Situated in foothills country, this prairie community captures energy from winds that reach more than 150 km/h between October and March.

Least annual precipitation:	**Greatest seasonal snowfall:**	**Greatest one-day snowfall:**	**Highest winds:**	**Heaviest hailstone:**
Arctic Bay, N.W.T. 12.7 mm, 1949	Revelstoke/Mount Copeland, B.C. 2,446.5 cm, 1971–72	Tahtsa Lake, B.C. 145 cm, Feb. 11, 1999	Cape Hopes Advance (Quaqtaq), Que. 201.1 km/h, Nov. 18, 1931	Cedoux, Sask. 290 g, Aug. 27, 1973

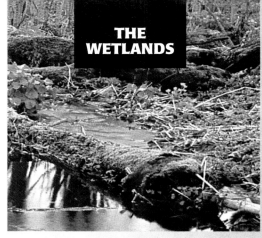

THE WETLANDS

REALMS OF REFUGE AND RECREATION

Wetlands such as marshes, swamps, and bogs (see below) host animals ranging from amphibians and fish to large mammals. Birds, wetlands' most conspicuous creatures, use these refuges for nesting, permanent homes, and stopovers during migration.

Wetlands also aid human endeavour. They trap nutrients and purify water by filtering out pollutants. They store rainfall and runoff, preventing flooding and shoreline erosion. Wetlands provide food (wild rice, cranberries, fish, wildfowl), energy (peat, wood, charcoal), and building material (lumber). Finally, wetlands are valued for recreation.

Wetlands cover 6 percent of the world's surface. Canada holds a quarter of these wetlands, which occupy 1.27 million square kilometres, an area surpassed only by Russia's 1.5 million square kilometres. Wetlands exist in all provinces and territories, but the greatest number dot the Boreal Shield and Hudson Bay Lowlands. Here, bogs (also called muskeg) absorb carbon dioxide, storing it in thick layers of peat. This counters the impact of greenhouse gases produced by humans. An estimated 25 percent of the world's carbon may be locked up in the peat bogs of Canada's boreal forests.

MARSHES are the most biologically rich and diverse wetlands, characterized by mineral soils and by plant life dominated by grasses. Marshes occur at the mouths of rivers or in open shallows, where water flows sluggishly. Marsh beds have no distinct peat layer as organic materials decay rapidly and drain away to adjacent water bodies.

SWAMPS are low-lying areas of dense forest that are waterlogged or seasonally flooded. The boreal forest swamps host cedars and spruces; swamps in southern Canada have red and silver maples, ash, and yellow birch. Swamps are oxygen-rich and encourage plant growth. Because they also stimulate the rapid decomposition of organic matter, only thin peat layers form on swamp beds.

BOGS are poorly drained basins, blanketed by waterlogged, spongy sphagnum-moss mats. Bogs cannot break down organic materials. Instead, these materials collect in thick peat layers on bog floors, eventually building up and filling the space beneath the mats.

PROTECTING THE WETLANDS

In Canada, wetlands are in retreat. Most losses are due to agricultural expansion. Wetland areas hardest hit include the Fraser River delta (80 percent gone), the Prairies potholes region (71 percent), the lower Great Lakes and the St. Lawrence Valley (70 percent), and Atlantic coastal marshes (65 percent). In 1981, Canada entered into the Ramsar Convention, an international accord on wetlands protection, to stem further losses. Across Canada, 36 Ramsar sites protect 13 million hectares of wetlands.

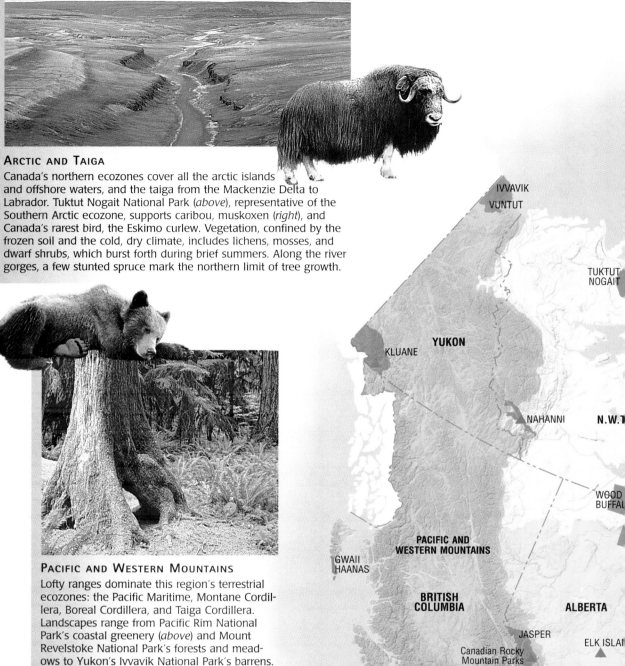

ARCTIC AND TAIGA

Canada's northern ecozones cover all the arctic islands and offshore waters, and the taiga from the Mackenzie Delta to Labrador. Tuktut Nogait National Park (above), representative of the Southern Arctic ecozone, supports caribou, muskoxen (right), and Canada's rarest bird, the Eskimo curlew. Vegetation, confined by the frozen soil and the cold, dry climate, includes lichens, mosses, and dwarf shrubs, which burst forth during brief summers. Along the river gorges, a few stunted spruce mark the northern limit of tree growth.

PACIFIC AND WESTERN MOUNTAINS

Lofty ranges dominate this region's terrestrial ecozones: the Pacific Maritime, Montane Cordillera, Boreal Cordillera, and Taiga Cordillera. Landscapes range from Pacific Rim National Park's coastal greenery (above) and Mount Revelstoke National Park's forests and meadows to Yukon's Ivvavik National Park's barrens. The rugged mainland coast is home to the grizzly bear (top). Pacific Rim, a typical Pacific Maritime area, comprises surf-pounded beaches, seal-inhabited islands, and the wind-tangled woods of the West Coast Trail. Offshore lie the teeming waters of the Pacific Marine ecozone.

CENTRAL PLAINS

Riding Mountain National Park lies in a belt between this region's two ecozones: the cropland of the southern Prairies and the forests of the Boreal Plains. Rising 500m above the surrounding expansive farmland, Riding Mountain contains prairie meadows (above) and a mix of conifers and hardwoods. No part of Canada has been altered as much as the Prairies. The largest remnant survives in Grasslands National Park. In the Boreal Plains ecozone, Wood Buffalo National Park shelters whooping cranes (left) and small herds of bison, once the monarchs of the grasslands.

BOREAL SHIELD

Largest of Canada's terrestrial ecozones, the Boreal Shield is one vast ecozone stretching from northern Alberta to Newfoundland's eastern coast. It superimposes a mantle of evergreens over much of the Canadian Shield, imperfectly hiding a rugged landscape still showing the scars of glacial assault and retreat. Pukaskwa National Park (above) on Lake Superior's northeastern shore sums up many of this region's essentials: rocky headlands, sand and cobble beaches, a dense forest of spruce and fir, rock-ringed lakes, and rolling rivers. Beaver and loons, ubiquitous denizens of the Shield, thrive here. Other typical wildlife include rare woodland caribou, moose, wolf, and black bear.

Six natural regions

Canada is a mosaic of natural regions, or ecozones, distinguished by their iconic features: the rain forest of the Pacific Coast, the flat-to-rolling horizon of the prairie, the ever-green wilderness of the Canadian Shield, and the polar barrens of the Arctic. A network of shared properties—geologic, vegetative, climatic, landforms and water, and human input—define the essence of each natural region. This network also encloses countless eco-systems—significant natural units such as wetlands. Altogether, Canada contains 15 terrestrial and 5 maritime ecozones, arranged here as follows: Arctic and Taiga, Pacific and Western Mountains, Central Plains, Boreal Shield, Mixed-wood Plains, and Atlantic. The natural regions vary in size and shape. The Boreal Shield ecozone stretches across Canada; the Mixed-wood Plains region lies along a narrow plain in the southern parts of Ontario and Quebec. The natural regions also vary in biodiversity. The spacious Central Plains are less abun-dant in plant and animal species than the Pacific ecozone, where rich layers of life ascend from ocean tidal pools to alpine mountain summits. The past and present impact of human endeavour, specifically agricultural devel-opment, resource exploitation, and urbanization, has radically altered the ecozones. Our national park system provides enclaves where their essence survives untouched. But a chal-lenge for our time is learning to sustain our quality of life without straining their capacities further.

Map labels

QUTTINIRPAAQ

NORTHERN BATHURST ISLAND

AULAVIK

SIRMILIK

AUYUITTUQ

Queen Maud Gulf Migratory Bird Sanctuary

Dewey Soper Migratory Bird Sanctuary

ARCTIC AND TAIGA

UKKUSIKSALIK (WAGER BAY)

EAST ARM OF GREAT SLAVE LAKE

NUNAVUT

- ▲ National Parks
- ▲ Proposed National Parks
- ▲ Ramsar Sites (selected)
- ▲ World Heritage Sites (selected)
- ▲ National Marine Parks

WAPUSK

SASKATCHEWAN

MANITOBA

Polar Bear Provincial Park

PRINCE ALBERT

MANITOBA LOWLANDS

CENTRAL PLAINS

Quill Lakes
Last Mountain Lake National Wildlife Area

BOREAL SHIELD

RIDING MOUNTAIN

Oak Hammock Marsh

GRASSLANDS

ONTARIO

PUKASKWA

BRUCE PENINSULA

FATHOM FIVE

GEORGIAN BAY ISLANDS

MIXEDWOOD PLAINS

Long Point

POINT PELEE

TORNGAT MOUNTAINS

MEALY MOUNTAINS

NFLD. AND LAB.

ARCTIC AND TAIGA

TERRA NOVA

GROS MORNE

NFLD. AND LAB.

QUEBEC

MINGAN ARCHIPELAGO

FORILLON

CAPE BRETON HIGHLANDS

BOREAL SHIELD

Miguasha

N.B.

P.E.I. PRINCE EDWARD ISLAND

SAGUENAY-ST. LAWRENCE

KOUCHIBOUGUAC

Chignecto National Wildlife Area

Cap Tourmente National Wildlife Area

ATLANTIC REGION

FUNDY

N.S.

LA MAURICIE

KEJIMKUJIK

Lac Saint-François National Wildlife Area

ST. LAWRENCE ISLANDS

MIXEDWOOD PLAINS

This ecozone, encompassing the lower Great Lakes and the St. Lawrence River valley, is Canada's industrial heartland, a region radical-ly altered by the impact of human activity. Three of Canada's smaller national parks pre-serve distinctive pockets of the region's varied vegetation and wildlife. Point Pelee boasts rare trees of the Carolinian type, such as shagbark hickory, sassafras, and hackberry, whose ranges extend far to the south. The park's mix of forest, field, and marshland (*left*) is a destina-tion for hundreds of birds and monarch butter-flies (*above left*) on their biannual migrations. Bruce Peninsula National Park is an area of rare orchids, limestone cliffs, and strange eroded rock formations, while Georgian Bay Islands National Park is situated in a transition zone with the northern Boreal Shield.

ATLANTIC REGION

Six national parks—Forillon, Kouchibouguac, Fundy, Prince Edward Island, Cape Breton Highlands, and Kejimkujik—preserve this region's coastal areas. Forillon, a domain of boreal forest and sheer cliffs, is home to bird and marine life. Prince Edward Island National Park, a seashore of shifting sand, is the habitat for many birds, including the endangered piping plover. Situated in central Nova Scotia, the inland portion of Kejimkujik National Park (*left*) safeguards a primeval forest (mixed forest covers 90 per-cent of this region), island-studded lakes, and smooth-flowing rivers. The park is a refuge for the Blanding's turtle (*below left*), found only in this part of the Maritimes.

Harp seal

ARCTIC CORDILLERA

Landforms: Canada's most mountainous region outside the Rockies. Ice caps, glaciers, deep fjords

Climate: Very cold, dry, and windy

Vegetation: Arctic flowers and some ground-hugging shrubs flourish in the southern areas

Wildlife: Arctic hare, northern fulmar

Resources and industries: Hunting, tourism

NORTHERN ARCTIC

Landforms: Barren plains, some rocky outcrops

Climate: Cold and dry, with September-to-June snow cover

Vegetation: Herb-lichen tundra

Wildlife: Peary caribou, musk ox, red-throated loon, greater snow goose

Resources and industries: Hunting, mining

Arctic fox

SOUTHERN ARCTIC

Landforms: Plains, hills, and cold, clear lakes

Climate: Cold, dry; continuous permafrost

Vegetation: Shrublands, wet sedge meadows

Wildlife: Barren-ground caribou, wolf, arctic fox, arctic loon, snowy owl

Resources and industries: Hunting, trapping, tourism, mineral development

TAIGA PLAINS

Landforms: Plains bordering the Mackenzie River

Climate: Cold, semiarid to moist

Vegetation: Dense to open mixed forest

Wildlife: Moose, woodland caribou, wolf, black bear, red squirrel, northern shrike, spruce grouse

Resources and industries: Hunting, trapping, tourism, oil and gas development

TAIGA SHIELD

Landforms: Plains, some hills

Climate: Cold, moist to semiarid

Vegetation: Lichen-shrub tundra; evergreen-deciduous forest rests on the bedrock of the Canadian Shield

Wildlife: Barren-ground caribou, snowshoe hare, red-necked phalarope

Resources and industries: Tourism and recreation, mining, hunting, trapping

HUDSON PLAINS

Landforms: One of the world's largest wetlands

Climate: Cold to mild; discontinuous permafrost

Wildlife: Marten, arctic fox, Canada goose

Resources and industries: Hunting, trapping, recreation

ARCTIC BASIN

Landforms: Most of the northern polar waters. Water depths more than 2,000 m; year-round sea ice up to 2 m thick over 90 percent of the surface

Sealife: Virtually devoid of life

ARCTIC ARCHIPELAGO

Landforms: Arctic islands; Hudson and James bays

Sealife: In the northern parts, marine life occurs near polynyas and shoreleads; in the southern Arctic, a great diversity of bird and animal life

Resources and industries: Oil and gas, some fishing and hunting

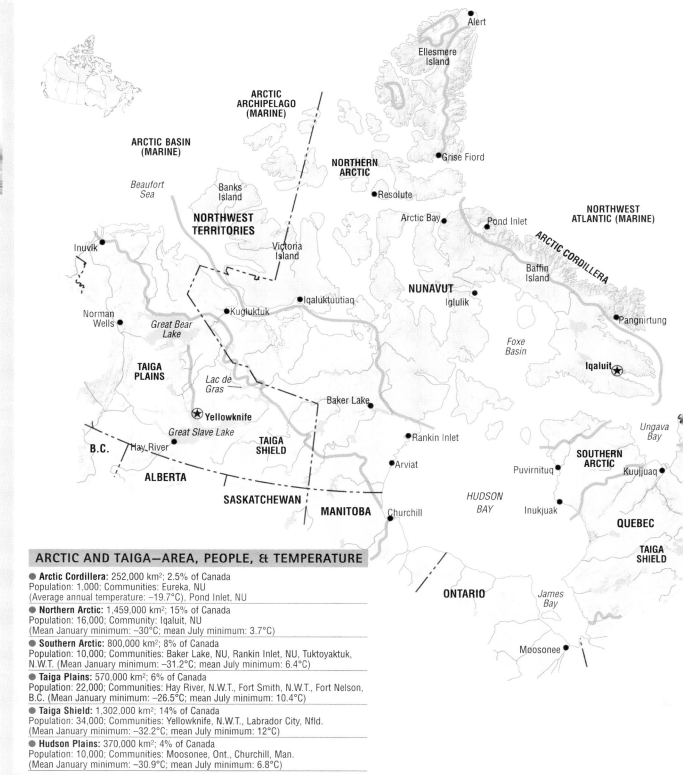

ARCTIC AND TAIGA—AREA, PEOPLE, & TEMPERATURE

- **Arctic Cordillera:** 252,000 km²; 2.5% of Canada
Population: 1,000; Communities: Eureka, NU
(Average annual temperature: –19.7°C), Pond Inlet, NU
- **Northern Arctic:** 1,459,000 km²; 15% of Canada
Population: 16,000; Community: Iqaluit, NU
(Mean January minimum: –30°C; mean July minimum: 3.7°C)
- **Southern Arctic:** 800,000 km²; 8% of Canada
Population: 10,000; Communities: Baker Lake, NU, Rankin Inlet, NU, Tuktoyaktuk, N.W.T. (Mean January minimum: –31.2°C; mean July minimum: 6.4°C)
- **Taiga Plains:** 570,000 km²; 6% of Canada
Population: 22,000; Communities: Hay River, N.W.T., Fort Smith, N.W.T., Fort Nelson, B.C. (Mean January minimum: –26.5°C; mean July minimum: 10.4°C)
- **Taiga Shield:** 1,302,000 km²; 14% of Canada
Population: 34,000; Communities: Yellowknife, N.W.T., Labrador City, Nfld.
(Mean January minimum: –32.2°C; mean July minimum: 12°C)
- **Hudson Plains:** 370,000 km²; 4% of Canada
Population: 10,000; Communities: Moosonee, Ont., Churchill, Man.
(Mean January minimum: –30.9°C; mean July minimum: 6.8°C)

LAND OF THE TWO POLES

The Arctic boasts a geographic north pole and a north magnetic pole. The former, the earth's northernmost point, lies about 725 km north of Ellesmere Island in the Arctic Ocean. Year-round ice covers the north pole. Recently, open water was observed there, possibly a sign of global warming. The north magnetic pole is more than 1,600 km south of the geographic pole. Like its southern counterpart in Antarctica, this is the site where the earth's magnetic field reaches maximum intensity. It is the point toward which all compasses point, and it is constantly moving—at an average rate of 15 km a year. The map (left) traces its ever-shifting path. In the 1990s, the magnetic pole was located on Ellef Ringnes Island, Nunavut; by 2001, it had moved on to 80° North 110° West; and by 2004 it was located at 82.3° North 113.4° West.

THE POWER OF PERMAFROST

Permafrost is made up of two layers: a thin "active" upper layer that melts in summer, and a thick underlying base of frozen ground that never melts. The Arctic and the Taiga lie within zones of continuous, discontinuous, or sporadic permafrost. (Alpine permafrost, another type of permafrost, is found primarily in the Rockies and the Coast Mountains.) The permafrost varies in depth and extent from zone to zone. In the eastern Arctic, where 80 percent of the ground is frozen, permafrost is continuous and half a kilometre thick. In the northern Taiga, where frozen ground ranges from 30 to 80 percent, discontinuous permafrost occurs. In the southern Taiga, permafrost is sporadic, reaching depths of only a few centimetres below the active level (see illustration). Permafrost is formed when annual mean ground temperature—determined by air temperature, soil, drainage, and snow cover—remains below zero. The thawing of the "active" layer creates boggy conditions because the unyielding frozen layer hinders water drainage. Permafrost impedes mineral exploration and extraction. Thawing permafrost can undermine road surfaces, which require insulating layers of sand and gravel. Buildings must be steadied by supports capable of withstanding ground shifting. But thawing permafrost can be beneficial for it provides the mix of soil and water essential for the brief outburst of summer vegetation in the Canadian North.

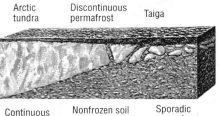

Arctic tundra · Discontinuous permafrost · Taiga · Continuous permafrost · Nonfrozen soil · Sporadic permafrost

The Far North: Arctic and Taiga

Half of Canada lies within the Arctic and Taiga ecozones, which manifest some of the nation's many climatic and environmental extremes. The Arctic is characterized by treeless tundra, carpeted with low-lying vegetation of mosses, lichens, herbs, and dwarf shrubs; and the Taiga, by sticklike forests of spruce and fir, interspersed with immense wetlands. The region's marine ecozones—the Arctic and the Arctic Archipelago, including Hudson and James bays—are as vast and complex as the terrestrial ecozones. Given the immensity of these regions, few generalizations can be made about them that are totally valid. Yet, one thing is sure: the environment of these ecozones is fragile, slow to change, and easy to disturb. In earlier times, Europeans hunted for whales, seals, and furs; today, developers search for minerals, gas, and oil in a rich—but vulnerable—environment. Politically, these regions encompass Canada's most sparsely populated regions: Nunavut, the Northwest Territories, the Yukon's coastal strip, and the northern parts of six provinces. The indigenous people who have long survived here are now reasserting control over their traditional domain.

Nain
Voiseys Bay
Davis Inlet

NEWFOUNDLAND AND LABRADOR

A NATURAL BALANCE

CIRCUMPOLAR PROTECTION

Developing policies that safeguard the Arctic and promote Inuit rights is a priority of the Inuit Circumpolar Conference (ICC). Working with the United Nations and other international forums, the organization represents some 155,000 Inuit living in Canada, Alaska, Greenland, Russia, and Scandinavia (*see map above*). In 2001, the ICC was instrumental in 151 countries signing the Stockholm Convention to reduce and eventually eliminate certain persistent organic pollutants (POPs), including chlordane, DDT, and other pesticides, industrial chemicals such as PCBs, and combustion by-products such as dioxins.

Although POPs have never been used or manufactured in the Arctic, tests show high levels of DDT, PCBs, dioxins, and other POPs in Inuit blood, lipid tissue, and breast milk samples. This happens because POPs travel long distances on air and in water, return to earth in precipitation, and enter the food chain. Accumulations are especially high in whales and seals, the traditional Inuit diet. Pregnant and nursing mothers in the Arctic are now advised to avoid marine mammals and fat, and to replace them with caribou meat and arctic char, which are low in POPs.

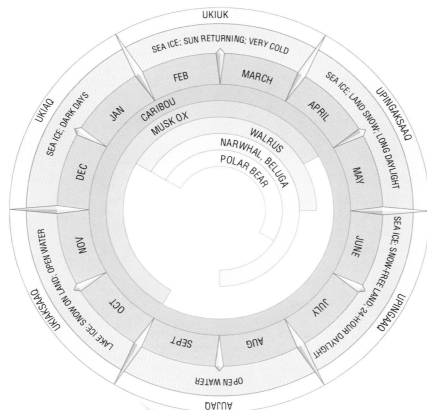

HARVESTING CYCLE

The aboriginal peoples of the Canadian North are strongly attached to "country food"—that is, meat and fish obtained by hunting. This food is more than just an alternative to store-bought foods. It is an intrinsic feature of aboriginal culture, where hunting lies at the heart of traditional community, family, and personal values. Country food is so important that the aboriginals have made wildlife a key issue in land-claim negotiations. The year-round harvesting cycle, above, depicts the changing conditions in weather and wildlife availability confronting the Inuit of Lancaster Sound in the Arctic.

RICHES OF THE NORTH

Major sites of mineral development in the Arctic and Taiga ecozone stretch from the oil and gas-fields of Norman Wells on the Mackenzie River (*above*) to the newly discovered reserves of nickel, copper and cobalt at Voiseys Bay in Labrador. But it is the northern diamond mines that have stirred the greatest excitement. In 1991, diamonds with economic potential were discovered in diamond-bearing kimberlite rock at Lac de Gras, some 300 km northeast of Yellowknife. The discovery precipitated an exploratory rush unprecedented in Canadian mining history. The Ekati diamond mine at Lac de Gras began operating in 1998. Other sites may be mined in the future. The recovery of the diamonds from vast quantities of waste rock takes place in a processing plant. Cutting and polishing takes place at Yellowknife. In 2000, the Ekati mine reported total sales at $430 million worth of diamonds. Another mine—Diavik—is also operating in the Lac de Gras area. The money, jobs, and investment have boosted the northern economy. By 2003, Canada ranked third among the world's diamond producers.

ICEBOUND SEAS

In the Arctic, sea ice is land-like for part of the year; in many areas, for all of it. For the Inuit, the ice can be used to travel a region without roads. Even as ice melts or drifts away, it is replaced by other drifting ice, or by the new ice that forms in the autumn. In the southern Arctic, the sea freezes slowly; in the high Arctic, the sea ices over with startling rapidity, virtually overnight. In winter, ice envelops the arctic islands and coastlines, which remain ice-locked from October to June. Polynyas (open water areas) and shoreleads (long, linear cracks) appear in the midst of the sea ice. Created by strong winds or upwelling warm water, these openings serve as oases of sea life. Sea ice comes in many shapes. Initially, it is called brash, slush, or pancake. But as it grows stronger and thicker, ice collects in floes or packs. Icebergs, calved from Greenland's glaciers, float in Davis Strait, off Baffin Island. The south-flowing Labrador Current moves the icebergs toward Newfoundland and the Grand Banks. "Iceberg Alley," as these waters are called, is not ice-free until July.

Left: The polar bear, the king of arctic mammals, spends its life at sea on the ice floes, searching for seals, which make up its winter diet. In summer, when the sea ice breaks up, the bears head for land where they feast on waterfowl, berries, and marine vegetation.

Pacific and Mountains

Resource-rich and breathtakingly beautiful, the Pacific and Western Mountains region is made up of four land ecozones: the Pacific Maritime coastal strip of mountain, rain forest, and fjord; and the three rugged Cordilleran zones: Montane Cordillera, Boreal Cordillera, and Taiga Cordillera. A fifth ecozone—the Pacific Marine—encompasses Canada's waters of the Pacific Ocean. The land zones comprise British Columbia and the Yukon Territory, but also include parts of Alberta and the Northwest Territories. Blessed with a diverse wildlife and vegetation, parts of this natural region—particularly the Pacific Maritime ecozone—are under pressure from rapid population growth, urban development, and resource exploitation.

PACIFIC MARITIME

Landscape: Mountainous coast, marine islands

Climate: More than 2,500 mm of precipitation a year along the coast. Average temperatures range from 4°C to 6°C (January) to 12°C to 18°C (July)

Vegetation: Coastal forests host western hemlock, western red cedar, Sitka spruce. In the rain-shadow areas, Douglas fir, mountain hemlock; on the Gulf Islands, rare Garry oak, arbutus

Cougar

Wildlife: Black and grizzly bears, cougar, Roosevelt deer (found only on Vancouver Island). Typical seabirds: black oystercatcher, tufted puffin

Resources and industries: Forestry, fish processing, agriculture, tourism. Construction in the lower mainland, the Gulf Islands, and Victoria, where three-quarters of all British Columbians live

MONTANE CORDILLERA

Landscape: Mountain chains, interior plateaus. Large, deep lakes, major river systems

Climate: Over 600 mm of precipitation a year at Prince George; well below 500 mm in the Okanagan Valley. Average temperatures at Kamloops range from −2.1°C (January) to 28.5°C (July)

Vegetation: Alpine shrubs, evergreen forests, sagebrush, grasslands

Wildlife: Mountain goat, Dall sheep inhabit the mountain heights; wapiti, woodland caribou, mule deer, bighorn sheep, and bobcat dwell in dense forests. Typical birds: black-billed magpie, blue grouse, golden eagle, Steller's jay

Resources and industries: Forestry, agriculture, mining, hydroelectricity, tourism

Mountain goat

BOREAL CORDILLERA

Landscape: Some of Canada's highest peaks, as well as plateaus and wide valleys

Climate: Over 1,000 mm of precipitation a year above the treeline; 500 mm at lower elevations. Average temperatures at Whitehorse: −14.4°C (January); 22.6°C (July)

Vegetation: White and black spruce, lodgepole pine at low levels; subalpine fir higher up

Ptarmigan

Wildlife: Moose, black and grizzly bears, Dall sheep, mountain goat, woodland caribou. Birds: ptarmigan, spruce grouse

Resources and industries: Forestry, mining, hunting and trapping, tourism

TAIGA CORDILLERA

Landscape: Some areas escaped ice-age glaciers. Flat-topped, ramplike mountains; broad valleys

Climate: At Old Crow, Y.T., the mean precipitation reaches 248 mm a year. Average temperatures: −36.7°C (January); 8.1°C (July)

Vegetation: In the south, forests host white and black spruce, dwarf birch, willow. In the north, only alpine plants thrive on partially frozen soil

Wildlife: Large migrating Porcupine caribou herd, Canada's most numerous wolverine population

Resources and industries: Trapping, hunting, mining, tourism and recreation, oil and gas

PACIFIC MARINE

Extent: Pacific Ocean basin and continental shelf

Climate: The Alaska Current creates the mild, moist coastal climate and drives west-to-east winds across southern Canada. Coastal sea ice is absent, except in sheltered bays and inlets

Sealife: Five species of salmon; clams, Dungeness crab. Marine animals: Steller sea lion, sea otter, northern fur seal, killer and gray whales

Industries: Commercial fishing, tourism

Old Crow

TAIGA CORDILLERA

Dawson

YUKON

N.W.T.

Whitehorse

BOREAL CORDILLERA

Watson Lake

PACIFIC OCEAN

BRITISH COLUMBIA

Stewart

Queen Charlotte Islands (Haida Gwaii)

Prince Rupert

Prince George

PACIFIC MARITIME

MONTANE CORDILLERA

COAST MTNS

ROCKY MOUNTAINS

Williams Lake

Jasper

Kamloops

Banff

Nanaimo

Vancouver

Kelowna

Cranbrook

PACIFIC MARINE

Alpine zone. From the icy rock terrain on the mountaintop to the treeline: lichens, mosses, shrubs, sedges

Subalpine zone. From the treeline to the lower slopes: alpine fir, Engelmann spruce

Montane zone. On the densely forested lower slopes: lodgepole pine, Douglas fir, Douglas maple. At the mountain base lie the Parkland and Prairie zones

MOUNTAIN ZONES AND BOUNDARIES

Mountain slopes host a great variety of trees and plants according to elevation, as shown above. Zone elevations move downward in cold, northern locations. In southern B.C., the alpine-subalpine boundary, discernible at the treeline, is found at the 1,800-m level; in the Yukon, it lies near the foot of the mountain.

"GREEN GETAWAYS": THE NEW TOURISM

Outdoor recreation and tourism generate over $9 billion a year for British Columbia. But the annual tourist influx—22.6 million visitors in 2002—places heavy pressures on the province's much-visited natural attractions and affects local communities as well. In the 1980s, the adverse impact of large-scale tourism became a crucial issue for environmentalists, the tourism industry, and governments, both in Canada and abroad. In response to this issue, ecotourism has since evolved as a possible solution. Ecotourism promotes ideas of exploring, developing, and sustaining natural habitats in ways least likely to cause environmental damage or disruption. This "green getaways" approach may also produce beneficial spinoffs such as support for local environmental efforts and employment for guides or interpreters of local cultural traditions. Ecotours include wildlife and wilderness expeditions, whale-watching excursions (*above*), and aboriginal ecotours, which mix natural and cultural features.

A NATURAL BALANCE

Coast Range   Interior B.C.   The Rockies

Wood products
(by value)

Europe 2.6%
Other 1.9%
U.S.A. 59%
Japan 14.4%
Canada 22.1%

IN THE RAIN SHADOW: WHERE LUSH FORESTS GIVE WAY TO PARCHED LANDSCAPES

Parts of the Pacific Coast get 2,500 mm of rain and snow in a year; others, barely 500 mm. The Coast Range is responsible for these variations. When warm, moisture-laden ocean air hits the range and is forced upward, the rising air cools, losing its ability to retain moisture. This results in heavy rainfall that feeds lush forests on the western slopes. On the eastern slopes, the descending air becomes warmer and retains moisture. This effect, called the "rain shadow," creates the parched landscape of interior B.C. Moving eastward, the air recovers moisture, which falls as snow on the Rockies. If the air is moisture-starved for long periods, the result may be forest fires in the dry mountain valleys and drought on the Prairies.

Pulp, paper,
paperboard
(by volume)

Asia 39.2%
Europe 24.7%
U.S.A. 24.5%
Rest of Canada 7.7%
Other 3.9%

FISHERIES: WILD VERSUS FARMED

British Columbia's commercial coastal and river fisheries harvest over 80 different kinds of fish and other species. Salmon is the most commercially valuable fish species, followed by herring, shellfish, and groundfish. The Pacific fishery has become more important since Atlantic groundfish catches declined around 1990. Pacific groundfish—hake, cod, rockfishes, halibut—represent the largest harvest by volume. Yet, the fishery faces declining catches. Excessive harvests have reduced fish stocks and, in turn, the number of fish caught. Other factors contributing to this decline include the growth in the size of the fishing fleets, and the use of radar and sonar equipment. Aquaculture, or fish farming, has expanded rapidly as catches declined. The fish farms, situated around Vancouver Island, keep fish (including nonindigenous Atlantic salmon) in net cages floating in seawater. Some experts claim aquaculture threatens the marine environment, citing the sea lice from fish farms that fatally infested wild pink salmon in the Broughton Archipelago. The debate over wild versus farmed fish intensified in September 2002, when B.C. lifted a seven-year moratorium on fish-farm expansion.

Halibut

FARM CASH RECEIPTS	
	in millions $
Floriculture & Nursery	394
Dairy	364
Cattle & Calves	348
Potatoes & Vegetables	335
Poultry & Eggs	331
Berries & Grapes	92
Tree Fruit	64
Grains & Oilseeds	52
Hogs	50
Ginseng	27
Other	155
Total	**2,212**

FARMING: PRODIGIOUS OUTPUT

Only 3 percent of British Columbia is suitable for farming. Most activity occurs in the lower Fraser River and Okanagan valleys, where much of the farmland, often ideal for fruit-growing, has been lost to urban sprawl. B.C. produces 5 percent of Canada's agricultural output by value. Some of this output, unique to this region, is prodigious. B.C. produces 18.4 kg of berries, kiwifruit, and grapes for every resident. The agricultural sector has introduced specialities such as ginseng and greenhouse peppers. The lower Fraser River valley has almost half of B.C.'s farms and generates over half of B.C.'s farm revenue of $1.8 billion. Dairy products, vegetables, berries, floriculture, and nursery products are its top commodities. The Okanagan Valley, second in output and revenue, is renowned as a top fruit-growing area. Ranching is centred in the Cariboo, Thompson-Nicola, and Kootenay regions.

FORESTRY: REGULATING LOGGING

British Columbia's forests cover 60 million hectares—64 percent of the province's land area. The coastal forests nourish 60-m-high Douglas firs and century-old western hemlocks. But interior B.C., with a diverse range of softwood trees, is the most timber-productive region. Coastal forests provide 32 percent of the timber harvest; the interior forest, 68 percent. In the 1980s, the B.C. forestry industry came under criticism for its clear-cutting of old-growth forest and its damaging logging practices. In response to the outcry of environmentalists, the B.C. government, owner of 95 percent of the forests, imposed regulations on logging. About 36 million hectares are now protected in parks or can never be touched; the remainder is open to logging. The B.C. forestry industry itself has improved its production, cutting, and reforestation practices. The annual cut of 190,000 ha represents a third of 1 percent of B.C.'s forest lands. B.C. produces most of Canada's plywood, half its softwood lumber, 15 percent of both its newsprint and its paper and paperboard. In 2000, the value of B.C. forest products abroad reached $16.8 billion.

Newsprint
(by volume)

U.S.A. 47.6%
Asia 28.6%
Rest of Canada 13.9%
Europe 3%
Other 6.9%

VALUE OF B.C. CATCHES

Farmed salmon $292 million
Wild and farmed shellfish $120 million
Wild salmon $52 million
Herring $45 million
Groundfish $133 million
Other $26 million

Male sockeye salmon

▼ Waterton Lakes National Park

In the Okanagan Valley (above), a hot, dry, sunny climate and fertile, well-irrigated soil create bountiful crops. The valley's northern sector produces dairy products and vegetables, while orchards in the dry southern sector grow more than 95 percent of B.C.'s fruit-tree output. Valley vineyards supply all the premium wine grapes in the province.

B.C. TIMBER HARVEST BY SPECIES

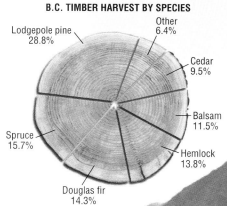

Lodgepole pine 28.8%
Other 6.4%
Cedar 9.5%
Balsam 11.5%
Hemlock 13.8%
Douglas fir 14.3%
Spruce 15.7%

Central Plains

Wheat fields, grain elevators, and remote farmsteads on the rolling prairie endure as persistent images of the Central Plains. But, on close inspection, this natural region presents a more varied and complex geographic and economic picture. The Central Plains consists of two distinct ecozones: the Prairies and the Boreal Plains, which cover much of the three Prairie provinces, as well as parts of British Columbia and the Northwest Territories. The Prairies, roughly triangular in shape, rolls westward from Winnipeg to the Rocky Mountain foothills, with Edmonton marking this ecozone's northern apex. The Boreal Plains to the north is an arc of boreal forest twice the size of the Prairies. Of all Canada's natural regions, the Prairies ecozone is the most greatly altered, largely through agriculture development. The long dominance of agriculture is now being challenged and transformed by resource extraction and industrial production that promise a more secure economic foundation for the Central Plains. Nowhere is this change more apparent than in Calgary, Edmonton, Saskatoon, Regina, and Winnipeg, which increasingly reflect more diversified economies and employment opportunities.

THE PRAIRIES: GRASSLAND

Landforms: Flat or rolling plains, some hills

Climate: Long, cold winters; short, hot summers. The Rockies frequently block eastbound moisture-bearing clouds from reaching the Prairies. As a result, low precipitation, combined with a high evaporation rate, causes periodic droughts

Pronghorn

Vegetation: Short-to-tall grasses

Wildlife: Prairie dog, pronghorn, coyote, Richardson's ground squirrel, northern pocket gopher. Birds: ferruginous hawk, greater prairie chicken, sharp-tailed grouse, burrowing owl (endangered)

Resources and industries: Grain farming, ranching operations by the foothills and on the dry plains. Oil and gas extraction and refining

THE PRAIRIES: PARKLAND

Vegetation: This belt of land, separating grasslands from the boreal forest, is sometimes called "aspen parkland" for its most prevalent tree species. In western Manitoba and eastern Saskatchewan, the parkland supports bur oak. Mosses, willow shrubs, and tamarack thrive in the sloughs and marshes that dot the landscape

Coyote

Wildlife: The farmland perimeter is frequented by large mammal species: white-tailed deer, moose, black bear, coyote, wolf, red fox, caribou, beaver, elk. Myriad wetlands support one of the highest bird populations in North America, including ducks and geese

FARMING BELTS: THE DRY AND THE FERTILE

Soils, climate, and natural grassland vegetation define the two prairie agricultural zones. Most grassland soils are black, dark brown, and brown soils, all classified as chernozemic (Russian for "black earth"). The tall grasses that thrive on black or dark-brown humus-rich soils have fibrous roots that absorb water and nutrients from moist clays in the subsoil. The tallgrass zone extends from southwestern Manitoba to Edmonton and north to the prairie parkland. This zone—the Fertile Belt ❶—is ideal for crops and livestock. South of this belt, evaporation rates increase, transforming the land from tallgrass to short-grass prairie. Short grass is characteristic of this semiarid region—the Dry Belt ❷—that stretches across the southern Prairies from Estevan, Sask., to the Alberta foothills, and almost reaches Saskatoon. Here, brown, sandy, humus-poor soil is a half-metre deep. Beyond this point, roots and rainwater rarely penetrate, and the subsoil is permanently dry. But in recent years, irrigation has overcome this obstacle and made possible the cultivation of potatoes and lentils, crops new to this region.

BOREAL PLAINS

Landforms: Plains, foothills in western Alberta. Over 80 percent is forest; the rest is farmland. About 7 percent of the ecozone is covered by fresh water. The largest bodies of water are lakes Winnipeg and Winnipegosis

Climate: Harsh, cold winters; short, warm summers. High precipitation, plus low evaporation, creates moister conditions than exist on the plains

Vegetation: A mixed forest of conifers (white and black spruce, jack pine, tamarack, balsam fir) and deciduous species (poplar, trembling aspen, balsam poplar, white birch)

Wildlife: Woodland caribou, mule deer, moose, wapiti, black bear, beaver, muskrat. Small herds of bison, once dominant wildlife, are confined to park reserves. Birds: boreal and great horned owl, gray jay, white-tailed sparrow, rose-breasted and evening grosbeaks, Franklin's gull, brown-headed cowbird. Fish: walleye, northern pike, burbot

Bison

Resources and industries: Agriculture in Peace River country (Canada's most extensive northern agricultural area); forestry, pulp and paper, oil and gas development, hydro-electric production

RESOURCE RICHES BENEATH THE PLAINS

Since the 1960s, development of resources such as oil, gas, and potash has moved the Central Plains in new economic directions. The 1990s saw fast-growing prairie cities move aggressively into high-tech and industrial enterprises. This trend offset the dampening effect of the crisis in agriculture. Although the agricultural economy is still vital, it is changing fast. The 1995 cancellation of the Crow Benefit, designed to allow farmers to ship their products by rail at a reduced rate, initiated an ongoing agricultural restructuring.

Europe 1.5%
United States 55%
Australia 3.5%
Latin America 11%
Asia 29%

SASKATCHEWAN—THE WORLD'S PREMIER POTASH PRODUCER

Saskatchewan boasts the world's largest and highest-quality potash deposit. More than 95 percent of Canada's potash comes from a belt stretching from the central to south-central parts of the province. The deposit, found about a kilometre below the surface of the prairie, lies in neatly arranged horizontal bands 2 to 3 m thick. Its thickest extent is around Saskatoon, where six of the province's nine potash mines are located. They consist of immense chambers and pillars, with corridors that stretch for hundreds of kilometres. Potash is used largely in fertilizers, while small amounts are used in soaps, glass, ceramics, dyes, drugs, water softeners, and explosives. In the late 1990s, Saskatchewan alone supplied 32 percent of the global output of potash and met 95 percent of the national demand. Canada exports 95 percent of its production to more than 30 countries. The United States is the major importer, buying 55 percent of Canada's exports.

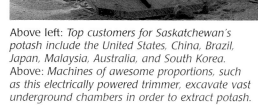

Above left: *Top customers for Saskatchewan's potash include the United States, China, Brazil, Japan, Malaysia, Australia, and South Korea.* Above: *Machines of awesome proportions, such as this electrically powered trimmer, excavate vast underground chambers in order to extract potash.*

Leaving Prairie Farms—Rural Outflow, Urban Growth

Across Canada, the number of farms is falling rapidly. According to the 2001 census, farm numbers dropped 11 percent after the 1996 census—the biggest percentage decline since 1971. This means that 3 of every 10 farmers counted in 1996 had left farming in only five years. The steepest declines were recorded on the Prairies, where farms shrank in number, yet grew in size. Getting out or getting bigger is the choice facing prairie farmers who have been pressed by falling profits, rising production and transportation costs, and decade-long dry growing conditions. Farmers who stayed expanded their operations and produced more through the use of mechanization and technological innovation. As a result, fewer people are needed to work on farms. Rural migrants now head for Edmonton, Calgary, Winnipeg, and other burgeoning prairie cities, where jobs in service and high-technology industries are abundant. With the resulting depopulation, the small rural communities built to serve local needs struggle to survive.

Gross value of prairie crops, 1997
(in millions of dollars)

- Oats 3.5% ($258)
- Flaxseed 4.5% ($333)
- Barley 12% ($920)
- Canola 26% ($1,975)
- Wheat 54% ($4,127)

Prairie crop areas, 1996
(in millions of hectares)

- Wheat 49% (12)
- Barley 20% (4.8)
- Canola 14% (3.5)
- Alfalfa 10% (2.6)
- Oats 7% (1.9)

Diversifying Prairie Crops

Grains have long been the traditional crops on the Central Plains. The Prairie provinces produce most of Canada's grain output, which represents 5 percent of the world's supply of wheat, 9.9 percent of its barley, and 14 percent of its oats. But in recent decades, prairie farmers have diversified considerably, moving away from grains to more profitable oilseeds, dominated by canola, and specialty crops such as peas and lentils, mustard, and sunflower and canary seeds. The diversification has been prompted by low grain prices, rising costs of shipping grain by rail, the loss of the grain rail subsidy, and much higher grain subsidies in Europe and the United States. High-value canola, primarily used for salad oil and margarine, is now Canada's second major crop after wheat. From 1976 to 2001, the total area used for canola production increased more than five times to 3.5 million hectares, representing 10 percent of Canada's total agricultural land. By the late 1990s, Canada was responsible for 43 percent of the world's canola oil exports. Besides alternative crops, prairie farmers have turned to livestock and hog production. One of the most significant increases shown by the 2001 census was the 26-percent increase in hog numbers since 1996. International demand, from the United States, Japan, and new markets such as Mexico, helped to spur the increase.

A NATURAL BALANCE

THE PELICAN PROJECT

What started as a nonprofit project to protect a colony of 900 to 1,100 pairs of white pelicans in Saskatchewan's Redberry Lake Migratory Bird Sanctuary became a UNESCO Biosphere Reserve in 2001. Biosphere status confirmed that the project, with the support of the local community of Hafford, had committed to sustainability principles such as conserving biological diversity and creating opportunities for education and research. From the outset, the project has promoted sustainable viewing programs. The interpretative centre's programs and tours encourage knowledgeable appreciation of the area's varied wildlife. The 6,000-ha lake is a stopover for more than 200 migrating bird species, including threatened and endangered whooping cranes and peregrine falcons. The lake project uses a mobile satellite and computer telecommunications system to watch over its resident pelican colony. In recent years, Hafford has broadened its sustainability vision to deal with rural depopulation.

To stem outward migration, community plans call for enhancing the region's traditional agricultural mainstays of wheat and livestock and developing more sustainable farming methods, new markets, crops, and tourism-related activities.

Brightly painted, wooden grain elevators like these near Webb, Sask., have long dominated the prairie horizon. However, they are slowly disappearing and being replaced by large cylinder-shaped concrete terminals. Saskatchewan once possessed more than 3,000 traditional grain elevators. By 2001, fewer than 300 were left standing.

OIL PRODUCTION
Thousand cubic metres

90	97	110	114	118	124	128	122
1980	1983	1986	1989	1992	1995	1998	2001

NATURAL GAS PRODUCTION
Million cubic metres

99	129	139	148	154	156	161	163
1980	1983	1986	1989	1992	1995	1998	2001

Left: Canada's petroleum output, 1980–2001.

Below: The main oil and natural gas pipelines to markets in eastern Canada and the U.S.A.

- ▪▪ Oil pipeline
- ▪▪ Gas pipeline
- ○ Oil refinery
- ◉ Oil/gas well

Alberta

Saskatchewan

Manitoba

Edmonton

Calgary

Regina

Winnipeg

Alberta—Treasure of the Tar Sands

The most valuable resources on the Central Plains are its oil and natural gas deposits. The ecozone holds over 70 percent of Canada's oil reserves. Alberta sits on 65 percent of the oil—followed by Saskatchewan (12 percent)—and 82 percent of the natural gas. Pipelines carry western oil and gas to eastern Canada and the United States. In addition to these reserves, some 2.5 trillion barrels of oil, 300 billion of which is recoverable, are locked up in northern Alberta's tar sands. This oil-and-sand mixture, known as bitumen, lies in four different deposits over an area the size of New Brunswick. The tar sands put Canada after Saudi Arabia in proven oil reserves. At Fort McMurray, site of the largest deposit, bitumen is extracted from one of the world's largest open-pit mines (*right*). Once mined, bitumen is heated to separate oil from the sand. Although the tar-sands project has followed provincial environmental guidelines, its long-term effect is problematic. Already, Fort McMurray's two oil-sands plants are Canada's fourth largest source of carbon dioxide. In economic terms, the future is assured: by 2025, an estimated 70 percent of Canada's oil will come from the tar sands.

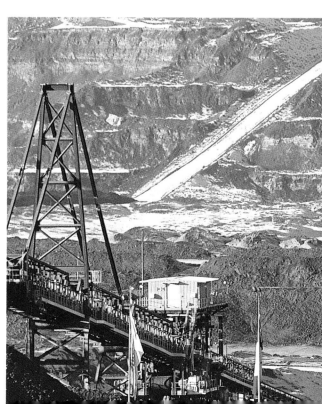

Boreal Shield

Otter

"SHIELD COUNTRY"

Landforms: Uplands and hills composed of Precambrian rock, exposed by repeated advances of ice-age glaciers. This rugged ecozone is strewn with lakes, rivers, streams, and wetlands, which form 20 percent of the Shield

Climate: Cold winters, warm to hot summers, with moderate precipitation in the heart of the ecozone. At Thunder Bay, the average monthly temperatures range from −8.9°C (January) to 24.4°C (July), while the average annual precipitation is 704 mm. At St. John's, temperatures are slightly lower, but precipitation much higher: 1,482 mm

Vegetation: White spruce, black spruce, and balsam fir create the uniform evergreen mass covering most of the Boreal Shield. Black spruce, the most northerly growing tree, fades out where the Boreal Shield borders the Hudson Bay Lowlands and the Taiga. Alder, birch, poplar, and willow are deciduous species found along river edges or in burnt-out clearings and cut-over areas. Tamarack grows in wetland areas; jack pine, in rocky clefts. Along its southeastern margins, evergreens blend with the deciduous species of the Mixedwood Plains ecozone. Here, maples enliven the landscape with brilliant splashes of colour in the fall

Lynx

Wildlife: The various natural settings of the boreal forest provide habitats for different animals. Woodland caribou seek out mature forests, which have an abundance of its favourite food, lichens. Ponds and swamps host creatures such as beaver, muskrat, and otter, as well as the mighty moose and predators such as the wolf and the lynx. Clear-cut areas attract the black bear, the porcupine, the striped skunk, and the white-tailed deer. Birds include the loon (a species adversely affected by the acidification of lakes), the boreal owl, the gray jay, and the woodpecker. Half a billion warblers, songsters of the forests, nest in this region from spring to fall. Boreal lakes host Brook char, lake trout, northern pike, perch, muskellunge, and walleye

Striped skunk

Loon

Resources and Industries:
Forestry, mining, pulp and paper production, tourism and recreation, hunting and trapping. Farming, limited by thin soil, is confined to a small number of fertile enclaves, including the Clay Belt near Cochrane, in north-central Ontario, and around Lac Saint-Jean in Quebec

NATURAL HAZARDS: FIRES AND PESTS

Across Canada, 9,000 to 12,000 forest fires occur annually, burning 2 to 7 million hectares. Wildfire is an inescapable aspect of the forest cycle, periodically removing overmature trees to clear the way for vigorous new growth. Many plants flourish in direct sunlight and the mineral-rich soil left by fire. In the Boreal Shield, fire benefits poplar and birch, which spread seeds widely after a conflagration. Although most fires result from human carelessness—an untended campfire or a smoldering cigarette—85 percent of the forest area burned annually is caused by lightning strikes. In built-up areas, fire suppression is essential to protect property and commercial timber stands. Firefighting may involve clearing fire lines and trenches to halt the fire, or using airplanes to douse a blaze with water.

Insect infestation is also a major forest menace. Spruce budworm, the dominant infestation of the Boreal Shield, takes hold in about 10 million hectares annually. According to some estimates, insects cause nine times more damage than fire.

S ituated where an evergreen forest overlies the Canadian Shield, the Boreal Shield is the largest of Canada's terrestrial ecozones. This natural region—popularly known as "shield country"—extends 3,800 km from Saskatchewan to Newfoundland and Labrador. It covers 1.8 million square kilometres and encompasses almost 20 percent of Canada's landmass; its myriad rivers and lakes account for 22 percent of Canada's freshwater surface area. The Boreal Shield's rich supply of minerals and lumber plays a major role in fueling the economy of the "heartland" of southern Ontario and Quebec. Its bare rock, thin soils, and muskeg have restricted development to resource exploitation. Some major communities—Chicoutimi-Jonquière, Sudbury, Elliot Lake, and Thunder Bay—have successfully diversified their economic base, while other one-industry centres have experienced significant declines in population and primary-resource activity. Although less than 10 percent of Canadians reside here, the Boreal Shield's beauty attracts outdoor enthusiasts from urban centres in the south.

A NATURAL BALANCE

Sudbury area before 1990

Sudbury area after 1990

MINING IN THE SHIELD

Ancient geological upheavals formed the bounty of minerals in the Boreal Shield. In the 1880s, the building of the CPR across northern Ontario first revealed the region's deposits of gold, silver, copper, nickel, cobalt, and zinc. The output of this region's mines (*see below*) ensures Canada's position as a leading mineral producer. Mining is the mainstay for more than 80 communities in the Shield. The map identifies some of the main mining centres. Although the mining industry is dominant in this region, its operations cover only 5,500 km² —or about 0.03 percent of this vast ecozone. Ontario and Quebec are the leaders in terms of the value of production. In the 1990s, for example, the annual value of Ontario's mineral production, based entirely in the Boreal Shield, was about $4 billion. The focus of uranium production, once dominated by Ontario, has moved to Rabbit Lake and other sites in northern Saskatchewan.

Lake Athabasca

Wollaston Lake

Reindeer Lake

SASKATCHEWAN

Churchill River

Nelson River

La Ronge

Flin Flon

Thompson

MANITOBA

Norway House

Lake Winnipeg

■ Forestry-dependent communities
▲ Mining-dependent communities

ONTARIO

Pine Falls

Lake Nipigon

Kenora Dryden

Fort Frances

Thunder Bay

Marathon

Lake Superior

Wawa

Sault Ste. Marie

SHIELD MINING OUTPUT
(in tonnes)

Iron ore
35,149,000

Gold 117

Nickel 181,139

Silver 364

Copper 341,779

Cobalt 2,022

Zinc 367,478

Uranium 9,921

DAMAGING DELUGE

Smelting and refining of sulfur-bearing metal ores and the combustion of fossil fuels for transportation, power generation, and heating produce sulfur dioxide and nitrogen oxide. These emissions combine with atmospheric water vapour to produce corrosive nitric and sulfuric acid, which fall as rain, fog, or snow, or spread as gases and particles. Acid precipitation has long been a problem in the Boreal Shield, particularly in Ontario and Quebec, where rock, water, and soil cannot neutralize acid. The fallout damages forests, and kills lakes and streams. Winds waft emissions far from their sources, as the illustration to the right suggests. Some acid rain that falls in Canada comes from industries in the midwestern United States. Canada, however, sends some of its acid rain to the eastern United States. In 1991, the two countries signed an accord to cut emissions. But a decade later, experts claimed 56 percent of Canada's lakes were still acidified; 11 percent were in worse condition. By 2010, about 800,000 km² in eastern Canada may still receive harmful levels of acid rain.

Labels on illustration: Atmosphere · Acid snow · Acid rain · Wind · Cloudwater · Nitric acid emission · Sulfuric acid emission · Nitrogen oxide emission · Sulfur dioxide emission · Fossil fuel · Lake acidification · Watercourse · Leaching · Water table · Soil

THE GREENING OF SUDBURY

Sudbury is the site of Canada's largest mining and smelting complex, the processor of one of the world's most valuable deposits of nickel. Situated in the heart of a 1,600-km² mineral-rich geological basin—possibly created by meteorite impact—the city developed after the construction of the CPR mainline in the 1880s. By the early 20th century, it had become the major mining centre. But the impact of its activities on the local environment was devastating. By the 1970s, decades of mining and smelting had left soils on local sites so acidic that nothing would grow. Some 10,000 hectares had been reduced to desolation. With Laurentian University and Inco Ltd., Sudbury embarked on land reclamation through reforestation.

Reclamation involves adding limestone to neutralize the soil, followed by fertilizer and special seed mix to increase nutrient levels. Once vegetation is established, the site is planted with pine seedlings. Much of the work, undertaken in some cases by student volunteers, is done by hand. Inco grows and supplies thousands of pine seedlings. The firm uses the warm and protective conditions of abandoned mine shafts to grow seedlings, which are brought to the surface every spring. As a result of success in land reclamation, Sudbury is now a world centre for environmental science issues relating to mining.

Map labels: Cartwright · NEWFOUNDLAND AND LABRADOR · ATLANTIC OCEAN · Bonavista · Grand Falls-Windsor · Gander · St. John's · Corner Brook · Havre-St-Pierre · Anticosti I. · GULF OF ST. LAWRENCE · Réservoir Manicouagan · Sept-Îles · Baie-Comeau · QUEBEC · Dolbeau-Mistassini · Saguenay R. · Lac St-Jean · Alma · Chicoutimi-Jonquière · Réservoir Gouin · St-Maurice River · Iroquois Falls · Timmins · Rouyn-Noranda · Val-d'Or · Kirkland Lake · Sudbury · Lake Nipissing · North Bay · Ottawa River · Ottawa · Manitoulin I. · Lake Huron

Tree Species in the Shield

Poplar 8% · Birch 7% · Cedar 3% · Maple 5% · Fir 5% · Pine 19% · Other 15% · Spruce 38%

WEALTH OF THE WOODLANDS

The Boreal Shield ecozone contains much of Canada's largest forest: a belt of spruce and balsam fir some 1,000 km wide in places, stretching from northern Saskatchewan to Newfoundland and Labrador. Almost 70 percent of the ecozone's forest—some 106 million hectares—is timber-productive land, which amounts to almost half of the Canadian total. The bulk of this land lies in Quebec and Ontario, which together have 40 percent of Canada's commercial forest. Across the Boreal Shield ecozone, the forestry industry harvests some 400,000 ha of timber a year. In terms of volume of wood cut, Quebec and Ontario rank second and third after British Columbia. This wood is turned into lumber and sawmill products, but the greatest portion is reserved for pulp and paper production. In Quebec, most of the productive forest of the Boreal Shield extends as far as 52° North, while the pulp and paper industry is based along the St. Lawrence, Ottawa, and Saguenay rivers. In Ontario, the productive forest is concentrated north of Lake Superior, where pulp and paper mills provide the only economic base for many communities.

CLEAR-CUTTING CONCERNS

Decades of harvesting spruce and balsam fir—the best sources of wood pulp for paper manufacturing—have had an effect on the landscape. In the Boreal Shield, roughly 90 percent of the harvest is carried out by clear-cutting. With this method, all commercially usable trees in a block of forest—as large as 60 ha—are felled at once (*right*). After cutting, the ground is prepared for new growth. Renewing the forest—by letting it reseed naturally, or through replanting by hand or machine—does not always guarantee the growth of commercially valuable species. Careless clear-cutting can cause environmental disruption, notably soil erosion and the loss of wildlife habitats. Extensive use of clear-cutting poses another threat. It puts such pressure on the boreal forest that original species disappear. As a result, the fabric of the boreal forest is changing. Broadleaf species such as poplar and birch now usurp a domain once predominantly spruce and pine.

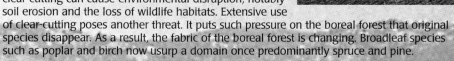

Left: George Lake, Killarney Provincial Park, Ontario, embodies the distinctive essence of the Boreal Shield landscape

Mixedwood Plains

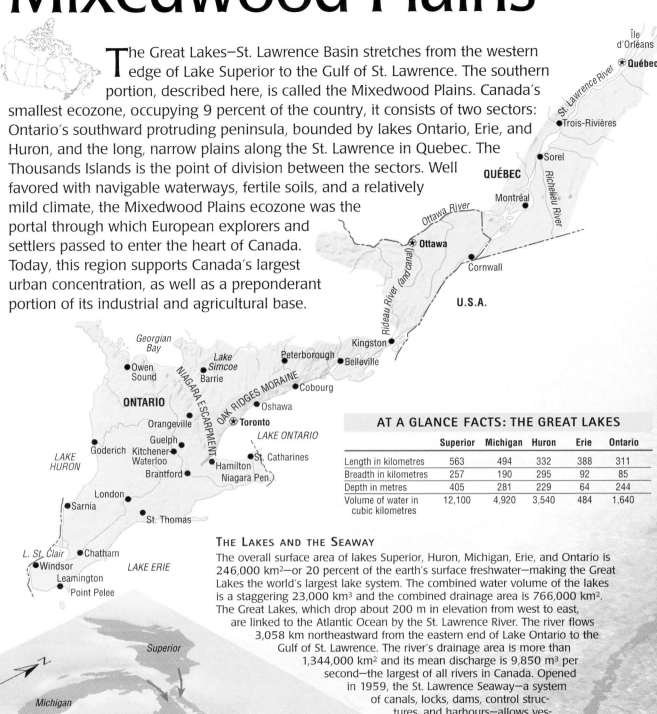

The Great Lakes–St. Lawrence Basin stretches from the western edge of Lake Superior to the Gulf of St. Lawrence. The southern portion, described here, is called the Mixedwood Plains. Canada's smallest ecozone, occupying 9 percent of the country, it consists of two sectors: Ontario's southward protruding peninsula, bounded by lakes Ontario, Erie, and Huron, and the long, narrow plains along the St. Lawrence in Quebec. The Thousands Islands is the point of division between the sectors. Well favored with navigable waterways, fertile soils, and a relatively mild climate, the Mixedwood Plains ecozone was the portal through which European explorers and settlers passed to enter the heart of Canada. Today, this region supports Canada's largest urban concentration, as well as a preponderant portion of its industrial and agricultural base.

Landforms: A relatively flat landscape with some hills. The thick and fertile claybed of eastern Ontario and southern Quebec is the legacy left by the Champlain Sea, which covered this area 10,000 years ago. In southern Ontario, moraines and other ice-age remnants lend a gently rolling aspect to the land. The outstanding physical features include the Oak Ridges Moraine (*see opposite page*), the Niagara Escarpment, and the Niagara Peninsula, famed for its fruit and wines. Another feature of interest is Point Pelee, the most southerly tip of the Canadian mainland. This 18-km-long peninsula is composed of a 70-m-thick deposit of sand, which sits on a submerged limestone ridge. Jutting into Lake Erie, Point Pelee lies at the same latitude as Northern California. In southern Quebec, the Monteregian Hills near Montréal are the most distinctive features in an otherwise flat-lying region

Climate: Cool to cold winters, warm to hot summers, moderate rainfall. Mean daily temperatures range from −3°C to −12°C in January to 18°C to 22°C in July; precipitation ranges from 720 mm to 1,000 mm annually. In southwestern Ontario, agriculture benefits from the moderating effect of the Great Lakes. Changeable weather throughout the region is caused by an alternating flow of air masses, such as the warm, humid air from the Gulf of Mexico and cold, dry air from the Arctic

Vegetation: The forests contain a mixture of deciduous and evergreen species. Little of the original woodland survives in this heavily urbanized and agricultural region. Deciduous species include beech and maple in mature forests; red and white oak, and walnut in younger woodlands. Conifers interspersed throughout the deciduous stands include white and red pine, and western hemlock. Southwestern Ontario is the northern limit of the Carolinian forest, where rich soil and a warm climate support a wide variety of colourful tree species, such as sassafras, hackberry, and shagbark hickory, as well as sycamore and tulip tree

Wildlife: Gray squirrel, groundhog, opossum, otter, raccoon, red fox, and woodchuck are typical woodland denizens. Large mammals such as the white-tailed deer and black bear, once found here, have largely disappeared due to human encroachment. Birds include blue jay, whippoorwill, Baltimore oriole, and red-headed woodpecker. More than 200 bird species pass over Point Pelee, where two major North American migratory routes—the Mississippi and Atlantic flyways—intersect. In the fall, the monarch butterfly also pauses here

Resources and Industries: Manufacturing and service industries, commerce and finance, construction, agriculture, tourism, and recreation

AT A GLANCE FACTS: THE GREAT LAKES

	Superior	Michigan	Huron	Erie	Ontario
Length in kilometres	563	494	332	388	311
Breadth in kilometres	257	190	295	92	85
Depth in metres	405	281	229	64	244
Volume of water in cubic kilometres	12,100	4,920	3,540	484	1,640

THE LAKES AND THE SEAWAY

The overall surface area of lakes Superior, Huron, Michigan, Erie, and Ontario is 246,000 km² —or 20 percent of the earth's surface freshwater—making the Great Lakes the world's largest lake system. The combined water volume of the lakes is a staggering 23,000 km³ and the combined drainage area is 766,000 km². The Great Lakes, which drop about 200 m in elevation from west to east, are linked to the Atlantic Ocean by the St. Lawrence River. The river flows 3,058 km northeastward from the eastern end of Lake Ontario to the Gulf of St. Lawrence. The river's drainage area is more than 1,344,000 km² and its mean discharge is 9,850 m³ per second—the largest of all rivers in Canada. Opened in 1959, the St. Lawrence Seaway—a system of canals, locks, dams, control structures, and harbours—allows vessels up to 222.5 m long, 23.2 m wide, and loaded to a maximum draft of 7.9 m, to sail 3,800 km from Montréal to the head of Lake Superior. There are six canals with a total length of 97 km on the Seaway. The canals have 19 locks, eight of which are on the Welland Canal, which bypasses the 99.5-m drop on the Niagara River— including 54-m-high Niagara Falls—which connects lakes Erie and Ontario. Overall, about 200 million tonnes of cargo move through the Seaway every year.

❶

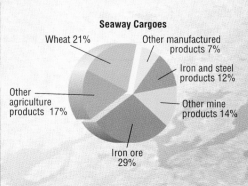

Seaway Cargoes

- Wheat 21%
- Other manufactured products 7%
- Iron and steel products 12%
- Other mine products 14%
- Iron ore 29%
- Other agriculture products 17%

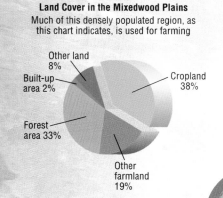

This view shows the St. Lawrence River as it flows northeastward from Lake Ontario to the Gulf of St. Lawrence. Along its 1,197-km course, the mighty river narrows or widens at different points (from bottom to top): ❶ the Thousand Islands; ❷ the junction of the Ottawa and St. Lawrence rivers in the lakes and rivers around Montréal; ❸ Lac Saint-Pierre, fed by the waters of the Richelieu River; ❹ the city of Québec and Île d'Orléans; and ❺ the estuary, where fresh and salt waters meet and the river is more than 50 km wide.

Land Cover in the Mixedwood Plains
Much of this densely populated region, as this chart indicates, is used for farming

- Other land 8%
- Built-up area 2%
- Forest area 33%
- Other farmland 19%
- Cropland 38%

A NATURAL BALANCE

PROTECTING THE OAK RIDGES MORAINE

In 2002, the Ontario government issued a plan to ensure the sustainability of the Oak Ridges Moraine. The plan was intended to resolve a clash between developers and environmentalists over a proposed housing scheme on moraine land at Richmond Hill, just north of Toronto. The moraine is a conspicuous height of land—some 160 km long and up to 24 km wide—that extends from the Niagara Escarpment to Rice Lake. A popular recreational spot, the moraine supports a delicate environment of woods and wetlands. Beneath its surface lies Canada's largest aquifer, which feeds waterways such as the River Rouge (*above*). The plan divides the moraine into four zones. Natural Core Areas, occupying 38 percent of the moraine, get maximum environmental protection. The plan permits agriculture and recreation in Countryside Areas (30 percent) and more intensive development in Settlement Areas (8 percent). About a quarter of the moraine is set aside for a network of corridors, at least 2 km wide, which provide for the movement of wildlife. Although environmentalists debate the plan, some hail it as offering a significant degree of protection.

WHAT THE FARMS PRODUCE

The Mixedwood Plains' fertile soil, hot summers, plus an abundant water supply, provide ideal conditions for ample livestock and agricultural production. Roughly 37 percent of Canada's agricultural production comes from this ecozone.

■ Fodder crops, particularly hay and corn, support a livestock industry of cattle, sheep, pigs, and poultry in the St. Lawrence River valley.

■ The Niagara Peninsula—or the Fruit Belt—just east of Hamilton grows cherries, pears, peaches, and numerous other fruits in abundance. The area also grows grapes and is the centre of a vibrant wine industry.

■ Ontario's southwestern Essex and Kent counties—the province's Vegetable Belt—enjoys the warmest year-round climate in eastern Canada. The area produces the bulk of the nation's greenhouse cucumbers and tomatoes.

Industrial Profiles: Windsor to Québec

- ■ Nonmetallic minerals and miscellaneous
- Rubber, plastic, petroleum, coal, and chemicals
- Primary metals and metal fabricating
- Machinery, transport equipment, and electrical products
- Wood furniture, paper, publishing, and printing
- Leather, textiles, knitting, and clothing
- Food and beverages

Windsor
London
Kitchener
Hamilton
St. Catharines/Niagara
Toronto
Oshawa
Ottawa
Montréal
Trois-Rivières
Québec

0 10 20 30 40 50 60 70 80 90 100%

WHERE THE PEOPLE LIVE

■ Canada's most highly urbanized concentration is located around the lower Great Lakes and along the St. Lawrence. According to the 2001 census, 12 of Canada's 27 census metropolitan areas (CMAs)—that is, urban areas with core centres of more than 100,000 people—are located here.

■ Population density is over 100 persons per square kilometre—10 times higher than anywhere else in Canada.

■ Ontario's population accounts for 38 percent of the Canadian total. More than 93 percent of the province's 12 million people live in the Mixedwood Plains.

■ Quebec has 24 percent of Canada's population. About 80 percent of the province's population is concentrated in three centres: Montréal, Québec, and Trois-Rivières, all of which lie in the Mixedwood Plains.

WHAT THE CITIES PRODUCE

The Mixedwood Plains is the site of Canada's industrial powerhouse. Ontario's part of this region produces over 40 percent of the country's goods; the Quebec portion, 22 percent.

■ No other region in Canada can match southern Ontario's advantages favourable to industry: a large labour force and consumer market, proximity to the United States, abundant supplies of raw materials and energy, and superior rail, road, and water transportation links. Toronto, with its many investment and insurance companies, and its bank and corporate head offices, is the city with the most diversified industrial base.

■ Around the western end of Lake Ontario, stretching from St. Catharines–Niagara to Oshawa, is the "Golden Horseshoe," an industrial concentration, which embraces St. Catharines–Niagara, Hamilton, Oakville, and Oshawa. This concentration extends westward from Toronto to Windsor and includes Brantford, Guelph, Kitchener, London, and Chatham-Kent.

■ Southern Quebec boasts a strong, diversified industrial base, with Montréal dominating high-technology fields such as aerospace, biotechnology, fiber optics, and computers. Quebec's industries also excel in clothing design and manufacturing, metal refining, printing, textiles, and transport equipment.

■ The chart (*left*) indicates the importance of different types of manufacturing in key industrial centres along the Windsor-Québec corridor.

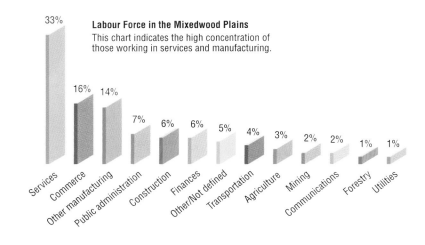

Labour Force in the Mixedwood Plains
This chart indicates the high concentration of those working in services and manufacturing.

- Services 33%
- Commerce 16%
- Other manufacturing 14%
- Public administration 7%
- Construction 6%
- Finances 6%
- Other/Not defined 5%
- Transportation 4%
- Agriculture 3%
- Mining 2%
- Communications 2%
- Forestry 1%
- Utilities 1%

ATLANTIC MARITIME

Eastern bluebird

Landforms: Uplands, coastal lowlands

Climate: The Gulf Stream creates a temperate climate. Cool to cold winters, warm to hot summers, moderate to heavy precipitation

Vegetation: A mix of conifer (softwood) and deciduous (hardwood) species. Red and black spruce and balsam fir flourish along the coastlines and in the highlands of Cape Breton and the Gaspé

Wildlife: White-tailed deer, moose, black bear, raccoon, blue jay, eastern bluebird

Resources and industries: Forestry, agriculture, fish processing, tourism/recreation

ATLANTIC ECOZONE

Extent: The chief feature of this marine ecozone is the continental shelf that spreads 500 km east from Newfoundland and 200 km southeast of Nova Scotia. Dozens of undersea plateaus, known as banks, lie across the shelf. Water depths over the banks are generally less than 100 m. They create an excellent environment for fish reproduction and growth. The largest, the Grand Banks of Newfoundland and the Georges Bank in the Gulf of Maine, have long been vital fishing areas

Climate: The Gulf Stream brings equatorial waters to the Maritimes before crossing the Atlantic to Europe. The waters off Nova Scotia and in the Bay of Fundy, also part of this ecozone, are temperate and ice-free

Fish: Capelin, cod, flounder, hake, haddock, herring, plaice, pollock, redfish, turbot; lobster and scallop; mackerel and Atlantic salmon

Seabirds: Great and double-crested cormorant, Atlantic puffin, common and thick-billed murre, black guillemot, razorbill

Marine mammals: Seals, whales, porpoises, dolphins

Resources and industries: Important commercial fisheries, oil and gas development

Humpback whale

NORTHWEST ATLANTIC

Extent: This marine ecozone stretches from the mouth of Lancaster Sound in the southern Arctic ecozone to the Grand Banks, where the frigid south-flowing Labrador Current merges with the Gulf Stream. It encompasses the southern Baffin Island Shelf, Hudson Strait, the Labrador Shelf, and the northern Newfoundland Shelf, and extends into the Gulf of St. Lawrence

Wildlife: More than 20 whale species, notably humpback, bluefin, and minke, are found in this ecozone. Harp seals thrive on an abundant marine food supply available along the Labrador coast

Resources and industries: Fishing, tourism

Razorbills

Atlantic Region

The Atlantic Maritime ecozone covers 2 percent of Canada's area. Within its embrace are Nova Scotia, New Brunswick, and Prince Edward Island, bound together by fisheries and forests. This ecozone extends to parts of Quebec: the Appalachian highlands and the Gaspé Peninsula. A diversity of physical features—wooded uplands, fertile lowlands, and an 11,200-km-long shoreline—endow this ecozone with incomparable beauty. Offshore lie the Atlantic and Northwest Atlantic Marine ecozones, which the Maritime provinces and Quebec share with Newfoundland. In the 20th century, the Atlantic provinces faltered with slow economic and population growth. Yet, as a new century dawns, offshore oil and gas development promises to quicken the economic pace.

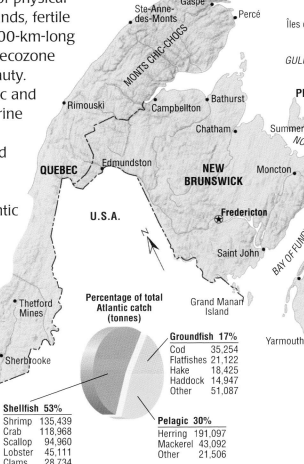

Percentage of total Atlantic catch (tonnes)

Shellfish 53%
Shrimp 135,439
Crab 118,968
Scallop 94,960
Lobster 45,111
Clams 28,734
Other 24,116

Groundfish 17%
Cod 35,254
Flatfishes 21,122
Hake 18,425
Haddock 14,947
Other 51,087

Pelagic 30%
Herring 191,097
Mackerel 43,092
Other 21,506

Newfoundland is part of the Boreal Shield, yet dependent on the fisheries of the Atlantic marine ecozone. This map locates the region's major fishing banks: Funk Island ❶; Grand Banks ❷; St. Pierre ❸; Banquerau ❹; Sable Island ❺; and Georges Banks ❻. Also shown, the Hibernia oil site. The White Rose deposit lies north of Hibernia; Terra Nova is situated to the south.

ATLANTIC FISHERIES

The Maritime provinces, Newfoundland and Labrador, and Quebec account for roughly 75 percent of Canada's total fish catch. In the Atlantic Maritime, Nova Scotia and Prince Edward Island fishers ply the waters where they find a variety of fish, including cod, grey sole, flounder, redfish, and shellfish. Nova Scotia is the leading producer of fish (about 30 percent of total production), followed by Newfoundland and Labrador and the Pacific Coast fishery of British Columbia (each about 20 percent). In terms of value, the same rankings apply. Along the Atlantic coast, some 1,000 communities mainly depend on the fisheries and related industries such as fish processing plants and shipbuilding. Any change in the fishery industry exerts a powerful effect on the communities that support it.

Before the 1992 ban, Newfoundlanders depended mostly on cod. They still fish in the Grand Banks, where cod and other groundfish congregate in the shallow waters of the continental shelf. But focus on different fish and fishing techniques has superseded the onetime dependence on cod fishing, and has resulted in a rejuvenation of the Newfoundland and Labrador economy. Sales of snow crab and northern shrimp, whose catches require fishing farther from shore and in deeper waters, have increased dramatically since 1992. Increased production of crab and shrimp has opened new markets and has resulted in the construction and operation of new processing plants. Of the 30,000 fishers who lost their jobs in 1992, more than half are again employed.

Atlantic cod

COD CALAMITY

For over 500 years, Atlantic Canada had one of the world's richest commercial fisheries. The Grand Banks were long a major source of cod, one of the world's leading food fishes. From the 1950s on, new fishing technologies—including dragnet fishing—and expanding markets for seafood caused overfishing. In 1977, Canada intervened to protect dwindling stocks and the Atlantic fishery by extending the offshore limit to 370 km (200 nautical miles). But by the late 1980s, groundfish stocks (fish living near the ocean floor, such as cod and halibut) were seriously depleted. In 1992, the steep decline in cod and other groundfish prompted Canada to curtail cod fishing off eastern Newfoundland and Labrador. What was originally a two-year government moratorium has since been extended indefinitely. Unfortunately, some foreign trawlers continue to overfish outside Canada's 200-mile protective limit.

Redfish

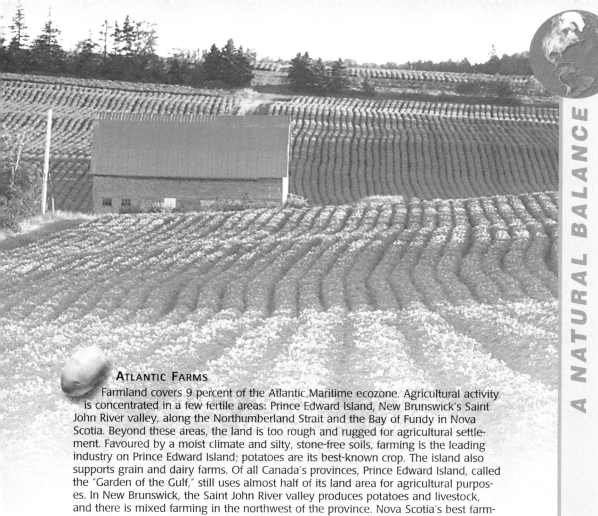

A MODEL FOREST

Model forests—there are 11 in Canada—enable individuals and groups to work together to maximize social and economic benefits from a forest region in ways that best sustain the forest. The Fundy Model Forest, for example, is a 34-member partnership, which occupies some 420,000 ha in southeastern New Brunswick. It embraces Moncton, Fredericton, and Saint John, many communities, most of Fundy National Park (*above*), 3,500 privately owned woodlots, and major forestry operations.

The forest supports maple sugar products; woodcraft industries; Christmas trees—wreath production alone is worth more than $670,000 annually; firewood worth about $2 million a year to 40 percent of the region's households. Fishing brings in about $2.2 million a year; snowmobiling, cycling, downhill and cross-country skiing, and hunting (deer, moose, and bear) are all booming. Some 270,000 people visit Fundy National Park annually. Serving this tourist influx are 15 campgrounds and 31 motels, hotels, and bed-and-breakfasts.

To balance businesses' needs with forest survival, the model forest works with government, university, and industry researchers and scientists. As a result, loggers know that certain quantities of debris are needed to shelter small animals and provide nutrients for regrowth. Rather than working in isolation, woodlot owners jointly plan harvesting to make sure animal habitats and the watershed are preserved.

ATLANTIC FARMS

Farmland covers 9 percent of the Atlantic Maritime ecozone. Agricultural activity is concentrated in a few fertile areas: Prince Edward Island, New Brunswick's Saint John River valley, along the Northumberland Strait and the Bay of Fundy in Nova Scotia. Beyond these areas, the land is too rough and rugged for agricultural settlement. Favoured by a moist climate and silty, stone-free soils, farming is the leading industry on Prince Edward Island; potatoes are its best-known crop. The island also supports grain and dairy farms. Of all Canada's provinces, Prince Edward Island, called the "Garden of the Gulf," still uses almost half of its land area for agricultural purposes. In New Brunswick, the Saint John River valley produces potatoes and livestock, and there is mixed farming in the northwest of the province. Nova Scotia's best farmland is located along the Bay of Fundy and the Northumberland Strait, where the main agriculture activity revolves around dairy farming and poultry production. Nova Scotia's Annapolis Valley is renowned for its output of fruit—particularly apples. In the Atlantic Maritime region, as elsewhere across the country, farm size is increasing and the number of farms is decreasing.

Atlantic abundance
(crops per thousand hectares)

Tame hay and fodder	
Potatoes	
Barley	
Alfalfa	

0   50   100   150   200

ATLANTIC FORESTS

In the Atlantic Maritime ecozone, forests make up 90 percent of the total land cover. About half of this area is a mixed forest—a distinctive blend of deciduous (hardwood) and coniferous (softwood) species. Forestry has a long history here, longer than anywhere else in Canada. Old-growth hardwoods once covered much of the fertile land, but today only a few pockets of the true old-growth remain. In the early 1990s, it was estimated that more than 13 percent of the area harvested had been replanted or seeded several times. Unlike other regions, the Atlantic Maritime has a large proportion of privately owned forestland, totaling 90 percent in Prince Edward Island, 75 percent in Nova Scotia, and 50 percent in New Brunswick. In some rural areas, forestry may be the sole source of employment and the chief reason for a community's existence. The pulp and paper industry is the largest consumer of wood, using 65 percent of the annual harvest. About 24 percent is sawn into lumber. The Atlantic Maritime ecozone has two working-scale model forests—the Fundy and the Lower St. Lawrence—whose objective is the implementation of sustainable forest development. The Fundy Model Forest is described above.

The 16 teeth of Hibernia's platform can resist the impact of a 1-million-tonne iceberg

Hibernia's Topsides was placed on barges, then towed into position in the Atlantic

WEALTH FROM THE SHELF

Oil and gas developments hold the promise of revitalizing the economy of Atlantic Canada. Two oil projects in Newfoundland and Labrador have proved to be great successes: Hibernia and Terra Nova, in production since 1997 and 2002; a third major project, White Rose, is slated to begin production in 2005. Hibernia, located 315 km east of St. John's, Newfoundland, is a deposit of over 3 billion barrels of oil, lying underneath the Grand Banks—80 m below the water surface. The project required the construction of a specially designed 111-m-high storm- and iceberg-proof Gravity Based Structure (GBS). Atop this structure sits Topsides: two oil drill shafts, a riser shaft, and a utility shaft—each 17 m in diameter. By 2000, Hibernia accounted for 12 percent of Canada's oil output. Hibernia also holds a vast reserve of natural gas, which may be extracted in the future. The first offshore natural gas development in Canadian history was Nova Scotia's Sable project. Over 17 million cubic metres of gas are produced every day. In New Brunswick, oil and gas have been produced since the early 20th century.

Advocate Bay on Minas Channel, Nova Scotia, where the world's highest tides have been recorded

WHO WERE THE EARLIEST ARRIVALS?

The traditional theory holds that North America's first arrivals were Northeast Asian hunters of Mongoloid stock who followed mastodons across the Bering land bridge ❶ or sailed along the ice-free Pacific coast ❷. Some experts now think that ice-age Europeans known as Solutreans may have been the first arrivals. This new theory is based on the discovery of Solutrean-type spear points on the Atlantic coast. Extinct for 19,000 years, Solutreans came from France, Spain, and Portugal, and may have sailed to eastern North America along the ice-sheet edge ❸, subsisting on seals and seabirds. Skeletal remains from other archeological digs have given rise to another tantalizing hypothesis: that first arrivals were southern Asians, possibly Polynesians, who journeyed to North America via Australia, the Pacific, and South America.

ARCTIC PEOPLES

With no edible vegetation, and driftwood their only wood, the Arctic peoples—the Inuit—led a precarious life in the Far North. They hunted seals, whales, and walruses along the coastline, and followed the caribou inland. Birds, birds' eggs, and small mammals were other food sources. Blubber, fish, and meat were eaten raw. Dog teams pulled the snow sleds they made from driftwood, whalebone, and caribou antlers. Because of their keen sense of beauty, even everyday objects were fashioned with extraordinary care. All adornments had animal motifs. Groups of up to 100 wintered in snow house villages. Shamans and medicine men were highly regarded by these deeply spiritual people.

This 1901 photograph shows a long-abandoned Haida village on the Queen Charlotte Islands. Epidemics devastated the rich culture of the Haida as a result of contact with European traders in the late 1800s.

PACIFIC NORTHWEST

Salmon-swarming rivers, a bountiful sea, and the majestic rain forest gave power and wealth to the Haida and Coast Salish, the trading Tsimshian, the Nuu-chah-nulth (Nootka) whalers, the Tlingit, the Kwakwaka'wakw, and the Nuxalk (Bella Coolas). Food was varied and abundant. Towering red cedars yielded rot-resistant beams and framing for their fine homes, logs for their 22-m-long canoes, and rain-resistant bark for clothing and blankets. Renowned carvers of totems, masks, bowls, and helmets, they revered shamans for their links to the spirit world. The potlatch, a communal ritual of feasting, storytelling, dancing, and gift-giving, was all-important.

A DIVERSITY OF CULTURES

A network of independent native nations was spread across what is now Canada when the Europeans arrived. The nations spoke 55 languages and occupied vastly different environments. Their social and trading rituals, religious beliefs, and political structures were quite varied. Nevertheless, they could be classified into six major cultural groups (*see below*). They all shared a profound respect for nature, and all lacked immunity to smallpox, measles, and other imported diseases that would later all but wipe out the native population.

Right: An Inukshuk, "likeness of a person" in Inuktitut, is a cairn of stone used by the Inuit of the Arctic to show directions to travelers, or to mark a place of respect.

GWICH'IN (KUTCHIN)
HARE
INUVIALUIT
INUIT
TUTCHONE
DOGRIB
ARCTIC
TAHLTAN
DENE-THAH (SLAVEY)
HAIDA
TSIMSHIAN
SUBARCTIC
CHIPEWYAN
NUXALK
DAKELH-NE (CARRIER)
DUNNE-ZA (BEAVER)
NORTH-WEST COAST
CREE
NUU-CHAH-NULTH
SHUSWAP
SARCEE
CREE
PLATEAU
PLAINS CREE
CREE
KOOTENAY
PLAINS
BLACKFOOT
ASSINIBOINE
OJIBWA

PLATEAU

Fishing and foraging were mainstays of the Carrier, Lillooet, Okanagan, Shuswap, and other small tribes living between the Coast and Rocky mountains. They had great diversity of dress, religious beliefs, and language. They spoke dialects of four major language groups. Most wintered in semi-underground dwellings they entered through the roof; in summer they built bulrush-covered wooden lodges. The Columbia and Fraser rivers were their travel and trade routes and source of fish. Other foods were berries, wild vegetables, and game. The Plateau people fashioned canoes from the area's pine and cottonwood, and traded copper, jadeite, herbs, and oolichan oil to the coast Indians for otter pelts and decorative baskets.

c. 40,000–9000 B.C.
Waves of Asian hunters tracking mammoths cross over to North America via the Beringia land bridge

Some Asian migrants skirt the Pacific coast in small boats

c. 9000–6000 B.C.
Hunters' descendants, Paleo-Indians, occupy southern areas of what is now mainland Canada

c. 6000 B.C.
After mammoths become extinct, aboriginals hunt buffalo, caribou, small game, fish, and forage for fruit, nuts, roots, and berries

Ontario sites have yielded tools, axes, knives, and spear points from this era

c. 3000 B.C.
Paleo-Eskimos (the Denbigh people), coming from Siberia, via Alaska, settle in the Arctic. The Dorset People, their descendants, develop a technology suitable for the Arctic

Tools of this era have been found on Ellesmere Island

c. 500 B.C.–A.D. 1000
The dominance of the Dorset Culture peoples in the Arctic region

First Peoples

Aboriginal is the Canadian Constitution's collective term for our indigenous Indian, Inuit, and Métis peoples, now comprising more than 1.3 million (4.4 percent) of our population. Some 62 percent are native Indian, 30 percent are Métis, 5 percent are Inuit, and others belong to more than one aboriginal group. About one in five lives either in Ontario (22 percent) or British Columbia (19 percent). Less than half (47 percent) live on reserves, with the remainder in urban areas; half the aboriginal community is under 25 years of age. They may see their people's long struggle for land, resources, and self-government realized in their lifetimes because negotiations with the federal government and many provincial governments, more frequent and more fruitful in recent years, continue today. One of the most historic of hundreds of land settlements, ongoing since the 1970s, is the Inuit homeland, Nunavut. Ruling one-fifth of Canada's landmass, its legislature is the first in North America to be run by an aboriginal government.

SUBARCTIC

This culture encompassed mobile bands of Algonquian-speaking Cree and Innu east of Hudson Bay, and Athabascan-speaking Chipewyans, Dogrib, Hare, Dene-thah (Slavey), Dunne-za (Beaver), Gwich'in (Kutchin), Tutchone, Tahltan, and Dakelh-ne (Carrier) to the west. Skilled hunters, they occupied the taiga and boreal forests from Yukon to Newfoundland and Labrador. Caribou was their staple and this animal provided most of their necessities. Each summer, groups joined forces to socialize, pick berries, make canoes and snowshoes, and tan hides.

Right: *A shaman of the Western Subarctic once used this mask to enter the spirit world.*

PLAINS

The Plains Culture encompassed the nomadic Assiniboine, Blackfoot, Sarcee, and Plains Cree. Other than water and poles for their tepees, the buffalo met all their needs. Its meat was eaten at every meal. Hooves were boiled into glue; sinew became thread; stomachs served as pots; horns and bones were fashioned into tools and utensils; ribs became sled runners; hides made teepee covers, clothing, moccasins, and sleeping robes; buffalo hair made comfy cradle boards. Before horses, buffalo were hunted by herding them into enclosures or over cliffs. The arrival of horses in the early 1700s gave the hunters a distinct advantage and horses became a kind of currency on the Prairies. The Plains women played important roles in religious rituals.

EASTERN WOODLANDS

Two major language groups dominated this culture. Algonquian-speaking Ojibwa, Algonquins, Mi'kmaq, and Malaseet occupied land from Lake Superior to the Atlantic. The Iroquoian-speaking tribes included the Huron, located in southern Ontario, and the Iroquois, the Mohawk and others who lived in villages south of the Great Lakes and the St. Lawrence. Iroquoian speakers had a warring tradition. Men hunted and fished; women cultivated beans, maize, squash, and tobacco. When the soil was depleted in one place, they moved to new sites. The Algonquian speakers' lives were governed by the seasons: hunting in fall and winter; harvesting roots and berries in summer.

Left: *A 1965 recreation of a Plains Cree war bonnet. The eagle feathers on these elaborate headdresses traditionally represented acts of bravery in battle.*

TREATIES: PAST AND PRESENT

Historic Indian treaties encompass several agreements made between 1725 and 1923 by the Crown with various Indian tribes. Included were "peace and friendship" agreements in the East, and the "numbered" (1 to 11) treaties covering vast tracts in the West and North. Many tribes in Atlantic Canada, British Columbia, and Quebec were still without treaties when this phase ended.

In the 1970s, courts began ruling that aboriginal title rights exist in law. This prompted Ottawa to begin a flurry of modern treaties, the first being the 1975 James Bay and Northern Quebec Agreement with the Cree and Inuit. Another Inuit agreement in 1993 led to Nunavut's creation six years later.

Hundreds of modern treaties have now been made. Of 60 to 70 still in negotiation, some 50 are in British Columbia. An agreement with the Nisga'a in 2000 marked that province's first modern treaty. Negotiations elsewhere include Innu territory in Quebec, an Ottawa River valley claim by the Algonquin, and a Mississauga claim for compensation for some 102,000 ha on which Toronto and many of its suburbs sit.

Modern treaties as of 2001
Outstanding claims
Areas without treaties

Gwich'in (Kutchin) Inuvialuit
Yukon Sahtu (Dene) Deh Cho North Slavey Nunavut South Slavey
Nisga'a Nunavut James Bay

Above: *Aboriginal land claims as of 2000. The map identifies aboriginal claims resolved by treaty, outstanding claims, and areas without treaties.*

A GROWING POPULATION

"We shall live again," proclaimed a ghost-dance song in the late 1800s, a time when many considered the aboriginal population a dying race. Data from the 2001 census affirms the song: at just over 1.3 million (4.4 percent of the total population, compared to 3.8 percent five years earlier), Canada's aboriginal population is on the rise. The upturn is most dramatic in the Métis community, which increased 43 percent in five years because of an increased fertility rate and better enumeration of community members.

The aboriginal community overall increased sevenfold in the second half of the 20th century, during which time Canada's general population merely doubled. This is all the more surprising since native birthrates have declined from 4 times to 1.5 times those of the general population.

Births, however, are only part of the picture. Lower infant death rates were a major factor, and about half the increase resulted from better reporting. More reserves were also better enumerated this time around (although some 30 were still not counted), and people were more willing than previously to acknowledge their aboriginal roots. Researchers attribute this to esteem-nurturing events such as the Royal Commission on Aboriginal People, court rulings on aboriginal rights, and the creation of Nunavut.

One-third of today's aboriginal population is 14 years or younger. In Nunavut, the median age is 19.1. Across the country, the median aboriginal age is 24.7—13 years younger than the mean age (37.7) for the general population.

A.D. 300–500
Eastern Woodland tribes cultivate beans, maize, squash. Villages develop

A Dorset mask (*right*), dating back 1,000 years, was likely used in rituals by shamans

C. A.D. 1000
Thule whalers from Alaska, ancestors of today's Inuit, displace the Dorset Culture population in most of the Arctic

Ivory bow drill (*right*) with depictions of Thule life

C. A.D. 1142
Iroquois Confederacy frames its constitution Gayanashagowa, or Great Binding Law, which remains in force today

An Iroquois vase (*right*)

C. A.D. 1400
West Coast tribes establish vast trading network

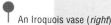

Settling Canada

Aboriginal peoples were here for thousands of years before France planted a toehold on the Atlantic in 1605. When Britain acquired New France (1763), the toehold was a foothold on what are now the Atlantic provinces, Quebec, and Ontario. Loyalists arrived and a tradition began: people fleeing poverty, prejudice, and famine would be given refuge. In 1812, evicted Scottish farmers came to what is now Manitoba. Germans and Scandinavians, as well as persecuted Hutterites, Jews, and Mennonites, were among the million or so prairie pioneers who arrived between 1875 and 1914. To open the West, Canada bought Rupert's Land and made treaties with native peoples. In the 1880s, Chinese immigrants helped build a transcontinental railway.

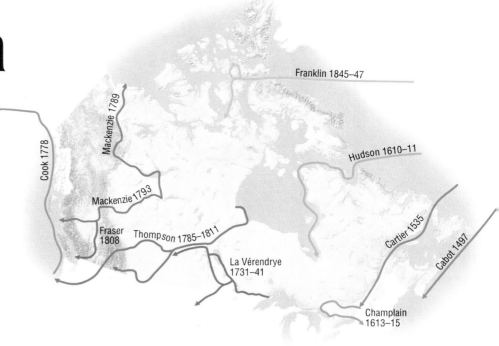

Far in advance of settlers came myriad explorers whose expeditions into unknown territories and seas gradually unveiled the vastness of Canada. The map right outlines routes taken by major explorers of Canada between the 15th and 19th centuries.

■ John Cabot	1497		■ James Cook	1778
■ Jacques Cartier	1535		■ David Thompson	1785–1811
■ Henry Hudson	1610–11		■ Alexander Mackenzie	1789–93
■ Samuel de Champlain	1613–15		■ Simon Fraser	1808
■ Pierre de La Vérendrye	1731–41		■ John Franklin	1845–47

In the late 1890s, Canada opened the Prairies to eastern Europeans. Among the new arrivals, this Doukhobor family from Grandview, Manitoba, posed for their photograph in 1900.

To escape discrimination in British Columbia, the Chinese moved to the Prairies, then to Ontario and Quebec. This photograph of four Chinese in Calgary dates from 1910.

Dutch immigrants of the 1920s await departure from the Canadian Railways Terminal, Halifax. In the palmy twenties, many Dutch headed for Ontario, where jobs were plentiful.

VIKINGS

Africans, Britons, and Irish may have reached what is now Canada at various times between 500 B.C. and A.D. 500. The first confirmed European settlement, built about A.D. 1000, was the Viking enclave at L'Anse aux Meadows at the tip of Northern Peninsula in Newfoundland and Labrador. Discovered in 1960, the site has been reconstructed and declared a World Heritage Site. When occupied, it contained eight sod houses and an iron smelter. This might be the Vinland of Norse sagas, which describe encounters with an unknown people, possibly Dorset or Beothuk.

PORTUGUESE

Although Portuguese did not settle here in large numbers until the 1950s, place names such as Fundy (*Fundo*) and Labrador (*Lavrador*) are reminders of earlier visits. It is believed that they explored eastern Canada in 1452, 1470, and 1493, and Gaspar Corte-Real landed in Labrador in 1501. Portuguese fishermen hunted whales in the Arctic and fished the Grand Banks for cod for the next 200 years. Cod especially was in great demand in Europe where Catholics of the day abstained from meat on Fridays.

FRENCH

Jacques Cartier's voyages and discovery of the Gulf of St. Lawrence paved the way for settlement; first tiny colonies in present-day Nova Scotia (Port Royal, 1605) and present-day Québec (Champlain's fort, 1608), then other frail settlements on the Gulf. Jesuits preached to the Hurons, and *coureurs de bois* roamed inland in search of furs. Despite early hardships and Iroquois wars, a flourishing fur trade kept the colony alive. By 1688, New France had 10,000 inhabitants and extended from Hudson Bay to the Gulf of Mexico, and from Newfoundland to the Prairies.

LOYALISTS

British supporters in the American Revolution called themselves Loyalists. But in the fledgling United States many were beaten and lynched as traitors; 50,000 fled north between 1776 and 1783. Some settled in the St. Lawrence River valley and Great Lakes region. Most took refuge in what is now New Brunswick. Privation marked the early years but eventually they prospered, farming on land grants of 100 to 5,000 acres, lumbering, sawmilling, and trading with former enemies. The Loyalists were the first mass influx of English-speaking people into what is now Canada.

RED RIVER SETTLERS

The West's first European settlers were impoverished Highland Scots. They were brought there by Thomas Douglas, Earl of Selkirk, who owned a vast tract of the Red and Assiniboine river valleys. The first farmers arrived in 1812, occupying land the Métis considered theirs. Fearing disruption of the fur trade, the North West Company incited the Métis to resist. When 21 settlers were killed at Seven Oaks in 1816, the others abandoned the colony. Lord Selkirk hired a private army, rebuilt the settlement, and brought the settlers back. Ensuing court battles impoverished the Nor'Westers who were taken over by the Hudson's Bay Company in 1821.

1497
John Cabot lands in eastern Canada

1534–36
Jacques Cartier charts the Gulf of St. Lawrence (1534); overwinters at what is now Québec (1535–36)

1608
Samuel de Champlain builds a fort at present-day Québec

1635
Champlain dies at Québec on Christmas Day

1642
Paul de Chomedey, Sieur de Maisonneuve, founds Montréal

1670
Newly founded Hudson's Bay Company granted all lands draining into Hudson Bay

H.B.C.

1713
Treaty of Utrecht cedes Hudson Bay, Newfoundland, and mainland Acadia to Britain

1749–55
1749: Halifax founded by British
1755: Britain deports Acadians

1763
New France ceded to Britain by the Treaty of Paris

INTERPROVINCIAL MIGRATION: UPROOTING AND RELOCATION

More than a million Canadians move every year, mostly within their immediate environs. Roughly one in five relocates to larger centres in other provinces, prompted by economic considerations. Migrants may leave remote or rural communities because they lack jobs or services. Between 1954 and 1972, Newfoundland uprooted 27,000 people from outports (*above*) in a bid to deliver better health care and education. In recent years, there has been an outflow from farms and resource-based communities. During the 1977–81 oil boom, Alberta was the top destination for Canadians from other provinces. When the oil boom dissipated in the 1980s, Alberta was replaced as the choice location by Ontario and, then, by British Columbia in the early 1990s. The chart (*right*) shows the inward and outward flow of interprovincial migration from 1996 to 2001, with Ontario and Alberta again on top.

Net internal migrants by province (1996–2001)

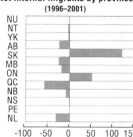

(Chart showing provinces NU, NT, YK, AB, SK, MB, ON, QC, NB, NS, PE, NL with scale from -100 to 150)

CANADA'S CHANGING FACE

Canada's commitment to immigration is producing a rich ethnic mosaic. More immigrants came in the 1990s than in any decade in the last 100 years. The 2001 census shows 18.4 percent of the population was born outside Canada. Since the 1960s, there has been a major shift in where our immigrants come from. Unlike their predecessors, today's arrivals are choosing urban over rural lives, as the following charts show.

TOP 10 COUNTRIES OF BIRTH IN CANADA

1961		2001	
1. United Kingdom	24.3%	1. China	10.8%
2. Italy	16.5%	2. India	8.5%
3. Germany	10.8%	3. Philippines	6.7%
4. Netherlands	8.9%	4. Hong Kong	6.5%
5. Poland	5.0%	5. Sri Lanka	3.4%
6. United States	3.9%	6. Pakistan	3.2%
7. Hungary	3.1%	7. Taiwan	2.9%
8. Ukraine	2.4%	8. United States	2.8%
9. Greece	2.3%	9. Iran	2.6%
10. China	1.8%	10. Poland	2.4%

TOP 10 DESTINATIONS OF IMMIGRANTS IN 2001

1. Toronto, Ont.	111,564	6. Edmonton, Alta.	4,225
2. Montréal, Que.	32,998	7. Winnipeg, Man.	3,810
3. Vancouver, B.C.	29,922	8. Hamilton, Ont.	3,078
4. Calgary, Alta.	9,038	9. London, Ont.	1,709
5. Ottawa, Ont.	7,151	10. Québec, Que.	1,335

MINORITIES GAINING VISIBILITY

At Confederation, 61 percent of Canadians were of British, Irish, or Scottish origin; 31 percent were French; and the remaining 8 percent were aboriginals and other groups. Immigration patterns throughout the next century preserved this composition: some 90 percent of new Canadians were European-born, compared to about 3 percent from Asia.

Beginning in the 1960s, immigration patterns changed. Newcomers from southern Europe surpassed those from western and northern Europe. During the 1970s, Asians and Middle Easterners began arriving in larger numbers. Today, 58 percent of immigrants are Chinese, Indian, and other Asians; only 20 percent are European.

One result is a soaring number of visible minorities, Canada's term for people who are neither aboriginal or white. Because most new immigrants come from China, Canada's ethnic Chinese population now exceeds a million. One-third live in Vancouver. Other than Winnipeg, where they are outnumbered by a Filipino population, the Chinese are the largest visible minority in every city in western Canada. Minorities account for 16 percent of Calgary's population and 14 percent of Edmonton's.

Left: Many immigrants to Canada crossed the Atlantic on liners in conditions less ideal than this welcoming poster suggests. Between 1928 and 1971, over a million of these newcomers first set foot in this country at Halifax's Pier 21, now a national historic site

Today's immigrants head to major centres such as Toronto, Vancouver, and Montréal. In some cities, visible minorities are on their way to being the majority. Toronto, at 42.8 percent, has the largest visible minority, mostly Chinese, South Asians, and Blacks. Blacks are the largest visible minority in the Ottawa-Gatineau area, followed by Arabs, Southwest Asians, Chinese, and South Asians. Among provinces, British Columbia, at 18 percent, has the largest visible minority population, followed by Ontario (less than 16 percent), Alberta (10 percent), Manitoba (7 percent), and Quebec (7 percent).

Among the 40,000 war brides that arrived in Canada at the end of World War II was this happy group with their offspring.

After the early 1970s, most newcomers to Canada were of non-European ancestry, as reflected in this mixed group of new citizens, receiving language instruction in 2002.

IRISH

In the 1700s, Irish crewmen on British ships often stayed behind in Newfoundland. Also, Irish people comprised some 5 percent of New France's population (Riel—Reilly—is one of many French-Canadian corruptions of Irish names). Mass immigration, however, did not occur until the 1840s, when some 500,000 "Famine Irish" arrived—a pool of cheap labour that drove the economic expansion of the 1850s–60s. By 1871, Irish-Canadians accounted for more than 24 percent of Canada's population. Discriminated against because of their extreme poverty (much of what they earned was sent to their starving relatives), thousands migrated to the United States.

ASIANS

In the 1860s, the Chinese came to British Columbia to work on the Cariboo Road and in the goldfields. Many of the 15,000 who arrived between 1880 and 1885 worked on the railway, often assigned the most dangerous jobs and paying with their lives. Chinese- and Japanese-Canadians constantly faced discrimination. In Vancouver, mobs attacked their homes. They could not vote, practice law, or be elected to public office. With many subsisting on $20 monthly, an immigration head tax of up to $500 was implemented to restrict their numbers. To escape the hostility, many moved east to prairie towns, and to Ontario and Quebec.

EASTERN EUROPEANS

A "stalwart peasant in a sheepskin coat, born on the soil . . . with a stout wife and a half-dozen children is good quality," Minister of the Interior Sir Clifford Sifton told his critics. The majority of Canadians wanted only British and French homesteaders on the Prairies. Sifton disagreed, and paid recruiters $5 for each East European farmer, plus $2 for each family member, they signed up. Finns, Poles, Russian Doukhobors, Germans, and Ukrainians flocked to the West in 1885–1914. Place-names such as Valhalla, Gimli, and Steinbach signpost the communities where they settled. Ukrainians, in particular, became politically active and many, such as former Governor General Ray Hnatyshyn, have held prominent government posts.

1778
Capt. James Cook, anchors in Nootka Sound, on the west coast of Vancouver Island

1779–83
1779: North West Company established
1783: Canada-U.S. boundary fixed from the Atlantic to Lake of the Woods

1784
The first United Empire Loyalist refugees arrive at Saint John, N.B.

1792
David Thompson begins a 28-year career as a surveyor and mapmaker that sees him cover a distance of over 88,000 km

1793
York, present-day Toronto, is founded

1812
Britain and United States go to war
Red River Settlement is founded

Medal of 1813 proclaiming the successful defence of Upper Canada against United States

1818
49th parallel chosen as the boundary between Canada and United States, from Lake of the Woods to the Rocky Mountains

1821
Agreement to merge the North West Company and Hudson's Bay Company

1841
Upper Canada and Lower Canada united into Province of Canada

1857
Ottawa is named Canada's capital by Queen Victoria

Building Canada

From the time of Confederation in 1867 to the establishment of Nunavut more than 130 years later, Canada evolved from a scattering of provinces and communities to a transcontinental nation that has become a leader in the global economy. Yet the building of the nation was not without its struggles. The Canada of 1867 was far from complete. Prince Edward Island and Newfoundland refused to join Confederation. Vast, unsettled plains and mountain wilderness stood between the fledgling nation and British Columbia. It would take nearly 50 years for most of the provinces and territories to assume their present-day boundaries. The completion of the Canadian Pacific Railway in 1885 opened up the West. Over time, Hudson's Bay Company land was carved into new provinces and territories. Drafting boundaries was sometimes a straightforward matter of following lines of latitude and longitude; at other times, the source of dispute.

1867

1882

1895

1905

On July 1, 1867, New Brunswick, Nova Scotia, and the Province of Canada unite to form the Dominion of Canada. The Province of Canada is divided into Ontario and Quebec. In 1870, Canada acquires the North-West Territories from the Hudson's Bay Company, and Manitoba becomes Canada's fifth province.

In 1871, British Columbia joins Confederation as the sixth province, followed in 1873 by Prince Edward Island as the seventh. In 1876, the District of Keewatin is created from part of the North-West Territories. In 1880, British rights to the arctic islands pass to Canada. In 1881, the boundaries of Manitoba are extended eastward, an expansion that is contested by Ontario.

In 1895, the districts of Ungava, Mackenzie, Yukon, and Franklin join the existing districts in the North-West Territories. The creation of the Franklin District acknowledges the inclusion of the arctic islands in Canada. Three years later, the District of Yukon becomes a territory.

Alberta and Saskatchewan become the eighth and ninth provinces. The District of Keewatin is transferred back to the North-West Territories. The boundaries of the renamed Northwest Territories are redefined one year later.

FEDERAL ELECTION RESULTS, 1867 TO 2000

- Liberal Party
- Conservative Party
- New Democratic Party (CCF)
- Alliance Party (Reform)
- Bloc Québécois
- Social Credit
- Others

100%
80%
60%
40%
20%
0%

1867 1882 1900 1917 1930 1949 1962 1972 1984 2000

POLITICAL PING-PONG

Throughout its history, Canada's laws, policies, and domestic and international affairs have been steered by one of two major political parties, the Conservatives or the Liberals. The chart above shows their fluctuating fortunes as reflected in the popular vote at every federal election since Confederation. Left-wing parties like the Prairie Co-operative Commonwealth Federation (the forerunner of today's New Democratic Party) have often run a distant third, yet have distinguished themselves by weaving the first strands of Canada's "social safety net," championing social services such as Medicare, family allowance, and unemployment insurance. In 1993, disaffected Quebecers and westerners voiced their frustration with the ruling Conservatives by voting in large numbers for two new regional parties, the Bloc Québécois and the western-based Reform Party, reducing the Tories to two seats in the House of Commons. After years of vote splitting, the Alliance (Reform) and Progressive Conservative parties united to form the Conservative Party of Canada in 2003.

WHERE BILLS BECOME LAW

Parliament Hill in Ottawa (right) is home to both Canada's House of Commons and the Senate, and is where bills become law. To be adopted into law, a bill must first gain a majority of votes from MPs in the House, then be approved by the Senate before receiving royal assent from the Governor General. The Gothic Revival structure was built between 1859 and 1866. A devastating fire in 1916 leveled the centre block, which was rebuilt by 1922 to a new design that included the 93-m Peace Tower.

1867
Confederation: Four of Canada's colonies are united as the Dominion of Canada on July 1 by the British North America Act

1870
Manitoba Act establishes province of Manitoba

1871
British Columbia joins Confederation

1873
Prince Edward Island joins Confederation

The North-West Mounted Police, forerunner of the RCMP, is established by an Act of Parliament

1878
A secret ballot is used for the first time in a federal election

1885
Last spike driven in the Canadian Pacific Railway at Craigellachie, B.C.

1898
Yukon Territory established

1905
Provinces of Alberta and Saskatchewan established

1910–1929
1914: Canada enters World War I
1919: Winnipeg General Strike
1921: A Canadian coat of arms is established

1929–1939
The Depression years
1931: Statute of Westminster gives Canada complete autonomy
1939: Canada declares war on Germany

1999

A third territory, Nunavut, is created by absorbing the eastern mainland portion of the Northwest Territories and most of the northern arctic islands.

1949

After a series of closely contested referendums to decide its political future, Newfoundland enters Confederation as the tenth province of Canada.

1912

Ontario and Manitoba attain their present boundaries. Quebec's northern boundary is extended to Hudson Bay and Hudson Strait. In 1927, the boundary dispute between Quebec and Labrador is settled when Labrador is ceded to Newfoundland. The dispute began in 1902 when Newfoundland started lumber operations along the Churchill River.

GOVERNING CANADA

Canada is both a constitutional monarchy, with a governor general (the Queen of England's representative in Canada) as the head of state, and a self-governing democracy, represented by 301 Members of Parliament (MPs) who sit in the House of Commons and 104 appointed representatives who sit in the Senate. Citizens across the country elect an MP for their riding; the number of seats in the House per province is calculated by a formula that takes into account population distribution, with the more populous provinces retaining more seats (*right*). Senators representing the provinces are appointed by the Governor General on advice of the Prime Minister.

Number of Seats in the House of Commons	
Ontario	103
Quebec	75
British Columbia	34
Alberta	26
Manitoba	14
Saskatchewan	14
Nova Scotia	11
New Brunswick	10
Newfoundland and Labrador	7
Prince Edward Island	4
Northwest Territories	1
Nunavut	1
Yukon	1

BRITISH COLUMBIA
Joined Confederation July 20, 1871
Capital: Victoria
Population (2002): 4,118,141
Area: 994,735 km² (9.46% of Canada)

ALBERTA
Joined Confederation September 1, 1905
Capital: Edmonton
Population (2002): 3,101,561
Area: 661,848 km² (6.63% of Canada)

SASKATCHEWAN
Joined Confederation September 1, 1905
Capital: Regina
Population (2002): 1,001,224
Area: 651,036 km² (6.52% of Canada)

MANITOBA
Joined Confederation July 15, 1870
Capital: Winnipeg
Population (2002): 1,150,038
Area: 647,797 km² (6.49% of Canada)

ONTARIO
Joined Confederation July 1, 1867
Capital: Toronto
Population (2002): 11,977,360
Area: 1,076,395 km² (10.78% of Canada)

QUEBEC
Joined Confederation July 1, 1867
Capital: Québec
Population (2002): 7,432,005
Area: 1,542,056 km² (15.44% of Canada)

NEW BRUNSWICK
Joined Confederation July 1, 1867
Capital: Fredericton
Population (2002): 756,939
Area: 72,908 km² (0.73% of Canada)

NOVA SCOTIA
Joined Confederation July 1, 1867
Capital: Halifax
Population (2002): 943,497
Area: 55,284 km² (0.55% of Canada)

PRINCE EDWARD ISLAND
Joined Confederation July 1, 1873
Capital: Charlottetown
Population (2002): 135,294
Area: 5,660 km² (0.06% of Canada)

NEWFOUNDLAND AND LABRADOR
Joined Confederation March 31, 1949
Capital: St. John's
Population (2002): 531,820
Area: 405,212 km² (4.06% of Canada)

NUNAVUT
Became Territory April 1, 1999
Capital: Iqaluit
Population (2002): 29,016
Area: 2,093,190 km² (20.96% of Canada)

NORTHWEST TERRITORIES
Became Territory July 15, 1870
Capital: Yellowknife
Population (2002): 40,071
Area: 1,346,106 km² (13.48% of Canada)

YUKON
Became Territory June 13, 1898
Capital: Whitehorse
Population (2002): 29,552
Area: 482,443 km² (4.83% of Canada)

1940–1950
1947: Canadian citizenship begins
1949: Newfoundland enters Canada as the tenth province
1959: Opening of the St. Lawrence Seaway

1965
Canada adopts the Maple Leaf flag
1970: FLQ kidnaps James Cross and Pierre Laporte, initiating the October Crisis

1980
Quebec votes no in a historic referendum on separation

1982
New Constitution and Charter of Rights and Freedoms comes into effect
1987: The "loonie" one-dollar coin is introduced as a cost-saving measure

1992
North American Free Trade Agreement (NAFTA) signed between Canada, United States, and Mexico

1995
Second Quebec referendum on sovereignty narrowly defeated

1999
Territory of Nunavut established

Connecting Canada

Canada's vastness has long posed a challenge for the exchange of materials and information. Yet, despite its expanse, Canada is solidly connected by ribbons of steel and asphalt, and invisibly crisscrossed by webs of airline routes and satellites. These interlocking networks form a system of telecommunications and transportation (*see facing page*) admired throughout the world. Canada's success in the competitive telecommunications field ensures the nation benefits from ongoing cutting-edge research and development. A paramount goal of Canada's communications system—from the establishment of the earliest telegraph line in 1846 to the launching of Anik F2 in 2004—is to provide a reliable and consistent flow of information to a population widely separated by vast distances and many time zones.

CANADA ONLINE

Vancouver author William Gibson coined the term "cyberspace" in 1984 to describe the netherworld inside a futuristic worldwide network of computers. Within a decade this science fiction fantasy would become a reality with the birth of the Internet.

Today the Internet is used daily by Canadian schools, libraries, governments, hospitals, police, and businesses large and small. According to Statistics Canada, 60 percent of Canadian households had at least one Internet user in 2001.

British Columbia and Alberta are the provinces with the highest proportion of households with at least one Internet user, at 65.3 percent. Ottawa remains Canada's most wired city, with 67 percent of households having at least one Internet user.

The different uses of the Internet are shown in the graph at right. Shopping on the Internet is becoming big business; in 2001, 2.2 million households spent almost $2 billion shopping online.

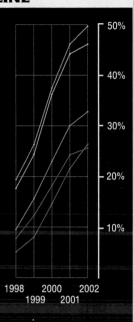

50%
40%
30%
20%
10%

1998   2000   2002
   1999   2001

■ E-mail
■ General browsing
■ Medical/health information
■ Electronic banking
■ Playing games

CELLULAR SUPERLATIVES
● Canadians send 800,000 text messages via their cell phones every day.
● The longest cellular corridor in the world is between Windsor and Québec.
● The wireless industry employs approximately 25,000 Canadians.
● Wireless revenues in Canada totaled $6.4 billion in 2001.

WIRELESS NATION
The introduction of the wireless or cellular phone in 1985 gave people a new life of mobility. Canadians were early adopters as cell phones became one of the fastest growing consumer products in history. As of 2003, over 12 million Canadians subscribed to a mobile phone service. By 2005, it is estimated that more than half of all Canadians will be cell phone users.

Scheduled to remain in a geosynchronous—or stationary—orbit 35,850 km above the Earth in 2004, Anik F2 will handle millions of cell phone calls and wireless Internet connections daily.

CANADA'S EYES IN THE SKY
With the launch of atmospheric studies satellites Alouette I in 1962 and Alouette II in 1965, Canada officially entered the space age. Our first telecommunications satellite, Anik A1, launched in 1972, made live television broadcasts possible. Today, six satellites orbiting the Earth allow Canadians to call, fax, e-mail, surf, and watch the information superhighway: Anik F1 (*pictured*) and Anik E2 carry all of Canada's television broadcasts; Nimiq 1 and Nimiq 2 carry hundreds of pay-per-view television channels; MSat, a communications satellite, is used by people in remote locations; and RADARSAT, Canada's first remote sensing satellite, was launched in 1995 to aid in scientific and geographical research.

Map Labels

YUKON
Whitehorse

NORTHWEST TERRITORIES
Yellowknife

NUNAVUT
Iqaluit

BRITISH COLUMBIA

ALBERTA
Edmonton
Calgary

Vancouver
1,148 TEUs*

SASKATCHEWAN

MANITOBA
Churchill

ONTARIO
Winnipeg
Thunder Bay

QUEBEC
Québec

NEWFOUNDLAND AND LABRADOR
Gander
St. John's

P.E.I.
N.B.
N.S.
Halifax
501 TEUs*

Montréal
919 TEUs*
OTTAWA
Toronto

OUR SHRINKING COUNTRY

Technology has shrunk Canada's vast distances to the blink of an eye. The illustration above shows the ever-dwindling time it takes a letter to travel coast to coast.

- 1893: Steam train, 115 hours
- 1935: Steam train, 90 hours
- 1971: Diesel train, 60 hours
- 1930: Propeller-driven aircraft, 18 hours
- 1981: Jet aircraft, 5 hours
- ✱ 2004: Internet, 30 seconds

Legend

- Major highways
- Major railways
- ✈ Major airports
- ⚓ Major ports
- * Volume of container cargo by port (in twenty-foot equivalent units)

HIGHWAYS AND BYWAYS

Canada has more than 1.4 million kilometres of two-lane-equivalent roads serving some 24 million motor vehicles. Most are classed as urban streets or local roads, with freeways and primary and secondary highways accounting for only 217,000 km. Over two-thirds of Canada's road system lies west of the Atlantic

CANADA'S PUBLIC ROADS

	Two-lane-equivalent kilometres
Saskatchewan	250,000
Ontario	230,600
Quebec	228,300
Alberta	205,300
British Columbia	204,800
Manitoba	104,500
New Brunswick	76,600
Nova Scotia	48,700
Newfoundland and Labrador	27,100
Yukon	16,100
Northwest Territories & Nunavut	10,200
Prince Edward Island	6,500
Total	1,408,700

provinces (see above). Canada's longest road, the Trans-Canada Highway, is also the longest national highway in the world, spanning some 7,821 km and passing through 10 provinces. Canada's roads form a major backbone of our transportation network, with trucks moving 234 million tonnes of goods in 1998, everything from live animals to steel, consumer goods to cars, chemicals to forest products.

WATERWAYS

Goods transported along Canada's navigable waterways are generally bulk commodities of relatively low value per tonne, such as coal, ore, grain, and salt. Water transportation may be separated into three areas: ocean, inland water, and coastal transportation. Ocean transportation is vitally important to Canada, as about one-third of what Canada produces is exported. Much of this export traffic is carried overseas in containers by large, oceangoing vessels.

CONTAINER CARGO BY COMMODITY

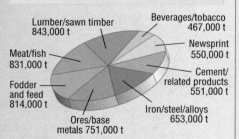

- Lumber/sawn timber 843,000 t
- Beverages/tobacco 467,000 t
- Newsprint 550,000 t
- Cement/related products 551,000 t
- Iron/steel/alloys 653,000 t
- Ores/base metals 751,000 t
- Fodder and feed 814,000 t
- Meat/fish 831,000 t

Almost one-third of all of these exports move through Vancouver, the largest port in Canada. (Tonnage handled by major Canadian ports is indicated on the chart above.) The Great Lakes and the St. Lawrence Seaway provide inland water transportation of grain, coal, and iron ore to and from the heartland of Canada on vessels called lakers. Coastal water transportation is important on the West Coast, where logs, lumber, chemicals, and other bulk commodities are moved by barge in British Columbia's coastal waters.

RAILWAYS

With 73,000 km of track, Canada's rail network is the world's third longest, after those of the U.S.A. and Russia. Canada's two major railways, Canadian National and Canadian Pacific, move millions of passengers and millions of tonnes of goods annually. The railways transport large quantities of bulk commodities over long distances at relatively low cost, so that our coal, potash, and lumber reach world markets efficiently and profitably.

RAIL CARGO BY COMMODITY

	Tonnes (000s)
Forest products (logs, pulpwood, newsprint)	42,121
Coal	39,522
Iron ore	39,063
Grain (barley, corn, oats, wheat)	30,619
Fertilizer materials (potash, sulfur)	21,928
Containers on flat car	18,075
Trailers on flat car	1,869
Other	91,566
Total	284,763

Movement by rail container is growing in importance. Most finished goods are now transported by this method. Until 2001, passenger traffic on Canadian railways declined because of airline deregulation and competition from other types of transport. In 1983, the number of rail passengers topped 7 million. In 1998, this figure fell to 3.9 million. Most of the passenger traffic was along the Windsor-Québec corridor. Since 2001, however, passenger traffic has increased by 1.4 percent.

AIRWAYS

Canada has 1,149 airports linked by 130,000 km of controlled airways. Of these, 26 major airports handle 94 percent of all airline passengers. Air transport also moves a wide variety of consumer goods and freight. In 2000, 853,110 tonnes of cargo were flown to and from Canada on domestic (61 percent), transborder (12 percent), and international routes (27 percent). Major airline routes are shown on the map above. Since deregulation in 1985, Canada's airways have been dominated by Air Canada. The airline industry has been struggling for survival since the terrorist attacks on the United States on September 11, 2001. In 1999, 85.3 million passengers boarded or deplaned at Canadian airports. This dropped to 80.1 million after 2001.

CANADA'S BUSIEST AIRPORTS

	Enplaned and deplaned passengers (000s)
Pearson International, Toronto	26,690
Vancouver International	15,137
Pierre Elliott Trudeau International, Montréal	8,188
Calgary International	8,102
Edmonton International	3,829
Macdonald-Cartier International, Ottawa	3,210
Halifax International	2,893
Winnipeg International	2,748
Mirabel International, Montréal	1,218
Total	72,015

Who we are

Canada is aging: our fastest-growing population group is 80 and over, and expected to number 1.3 million within a decade. Eighty percent of the population lives in large urban areas, half in the greater metropolitan areas of Vancouver, Edmonton-Calgary, Toronto, and Montréal. Our future growth will be determined by the influx of immigrants from 210 countries, increasingly Asian. Women are outpacing men in education and sometimes in the workplace; 66.6 percent of Alberta's workforce, for example, is female. Our 3.9 million 20-year-olds, 13 percent of the population, are the most educated generation ever. On the debit side, nearly 17 percent of Canadians live in poverty. The income gap between rich and poor is growing in every province, with the biggest gap in Alberta. And even though national crime rates are declining, 29 percent of women feel unsafe alone in their homes at night.

MARRIAGE AND DIVORCE

1981
Average age: 26.2
Average age: 28.8
190,082 marriages
67,671 divorces

2001
Average age: 31.9
Average age: 34.4
146,618 marriages
71,783 divorces

Fewer couples are marrying, and are doing so later in life. Common-law unions are on the increase. Such couples are twice as prevalent in Canada as in the United States. Of 1.1 million Canadian common-law couples, 44 percent live in the province of Quebec.
■ First unions increasingly are common-law, but most such couples will eventually marry.
■ On average, brides are aged 31.9 years; bridegrooms, 34.4.
■ People in their late 20s are the most likely to divorce.

LANGUAGES

1. English
2. French
3. Chinese
4. Italian
5. German
6. Punjabi
7. Spanish
8. Portuguese
9. Polish
10. Arabic

EDUCATION

Levels of educational attainment
(population aged 25 and over)

College 16%
Trades 12%
High school 23%
University 20%
Less than high school 29%

Of Canadians 15 years and older, 51 percent have post-secondary qualifications. Among 25- to 34-year-olds, the figure is 61 percent. One-quarter of Ontarians, ages 25 to 64, have a university degree.

TOP FIELDS OF STUDY

1. Education
2. Engineering
3. Business
4. Finance
5. Psychology
6. Nursing
7. Computer science
8. Law
9. Economics
10. Medicine

■ The risk of divorce is greatest after five years of marriage. Based on current rates, one out of three married couples will divorce; two out of three marriages will endure.
■ Intermarriage between couples with different ethnic and cultural backgounds is on the rise. In Vancouver, 13 percent of all pairs in their 20s are mixed couples.

BIRTHS

Natural increase
(in thousands of persons)

300
250
200
150
100
50
0
−50
1976 1981 1986 1991 1996 2001

Despite a slight upturn in 2001, the Canadian birthrate continues to slide downward, as shown in the chart above. Of the 333,744 babies born that year, Ontario couples welcomed nearly one in three births.
■ The fertility rate (the average number of children a woman will have in her lifetime) is 1.5, well below the 2.1 children per woman needed to maintain the population. If present trends continue, natural increase (births minus deaths) will be at zero in 2030, and immigration will be the only way the population can grow.
■ The number of children born per 1,000 women during their child-bearing years peaked in 1959 at 3,935 births. Today, the number is less than 1,500.
■ In remote regions and northern areas with large aboriginal populations, infant mortality rates are up to 3.1 times higher than the national rate (5.7 deaths for boys, 4.8 for girls, per 1,000 live births).
■ For aboriginal infants, the death rate from accidental injuries is four times the national rate.
■ Canada's current population growth is about three-quarters that of the United States. Eighteen percent of Canada's population was born outside the country.

One in 6 Canadians (and 4 in 10 Torontonians) are allophones whose mother tongue is neither English nor French. Allophones comprise 18 percent of the population; anglophones 59.1 percent, and francophones, 22.9 percent. The rate of English-French bilingualism increased 8.1 percent in the five years ending 2001.
■ Chinese is Canada's leading nonofficial language, as indicated in the top-ten list above. In the late 1990s, the use of Punjabi and Arabic increased 32.7 percent; Urdu, 50 percent; and Tagalog (the official language of the Philippines), 26.3 percent. Dravidian languages (spoken in India, Sri Lanka, and Pakistan) and Pashto (an Iranian language) are among the hundred other different mother tongues of new Canadians.
■ Only about 25 percent of aboriginal peoples can speak their own language, and many Native languages are endangered. Some aboriginal languages, such as Inuktitut, which is spoken by 9 out of 10 Inuit, is flourishing.

Selected religions

Muslim 2%
Jewish 1%
Buddhist 1%
Hindu 1%
Sikh 1%
Others 1%

Other religions 7%
Other Christians 4%
No religion 16%
Protestant 29%
Catholic 44%

RELIGIONS

One in 3 British Columbians, 1 in 4 Albertans, and 4 in 10 Yukoners are among the 4.8 million Canadians (representing 16 percent of the population) belonging to no organized religion.
■ Seven out of every 10 Canadians are Roman Catholic or Protestant. Catholics make up roughly 44 percent of the population: Protestants, 29 percent. Both groups are declining.
■ Islam, Hinduism, Sikhism, and Buddhism are up substantially in Canada, a shift consistent with changing immigration patterns.
■ People of Muslim faith, the second most reported religion among 20-year-olds, have more than doubled—from 253,300 in 1991 to 579,600 in 2001. Of 1.8 million immigrants in the 1990s, Muslims accounted for 15 percent, Hindus, almost 7 percent, and Buddhists and Sikhs, 5 percent each.
■ Greek and Ukrainian Orthodox church memberships are declining, while Serbian and Russian Orthodox memberships have more than doubled in the last decade.
■ Some 1 percent of the population is of the Jewish faith.
■ Having lost much of their congregations, some Christian churches are increasingly being converted to day-care centres, food banks, and other uses.

Among 25- to 64-year-olds in the working population, 1.1 million have doctorates, master's degrees, and qualifications above the bachelor's degree level.
■ Fifty-one percent of all working-age university graduates, and 59 percent of all college graduates, are women.
■ Male university students are leaning to technology, females to education, and both to business and finance. At the college level, men choose computer science; women, finance and business.
■ Trades are dominated by men; 63 percent of all 2001 working-age trade graduates were male.
■ Building and construction lead in trades' studies, but data processing and computer science studies are increasing for men. Women are still drawn to beauty care and hairdressing.
■ More young people in every province are finishing high school.
■ More than 1 in 4 Canadians participate in adult education and training programs.

Household size declining

Legend: 1981, 1991, 2001

Household size (persons): 1, 2, 3, 4, 5+

FAMILY LIFE

Over three decades, the size of the Canadian family has decreased from 3.7 to 3 persons.
■ Four times more children live with common-law parents than 20 years ago. About 19 percent of all children live with single parents, mostly mothers.
■ Step-families are on the rise. Half have only the female spouse's children; 1 in 10 has only the male's.
■ In what has become known as the "skip generation," nearly 1 percent of all grandparents, mostly women, are raising or living with children without the involvement of either of the child's parents.
■ Roughly 15 percent of female same-sex couples live with children, compared with only 3 percent of male same-sex couples.
■ Ottawa-Gatineau and Vancouver have the highest proportion of same-sex couples.
■ The number of childless couples and "empty nesters" is increasing.
■ More people, seniors especially, are living alone. In Quebec, Manitoba, Saskatchewan, British Columbia, and the Yukon, 3 out of 10 are one-person households. In Alberta, one-person households are increasing at double the national rate.

A NATURAL BALANCE

CARING FOR AN AGING POPULATION

Thirteen percent of today's population is 65 or older. By 2020, seniors will number 6.7 million, about 19 percent of the population. Federal and provincial governments are already working on strategies to ensure this senior overload will not cripple either the health care system or the Canada/Quebec pension plans.

Seniors will need accessible public transit and safe, affordable places to live, so more funding for transportation and affordable housing may be in order. As older people are increasingly rejecting homes for the aged in favour of living alone, more home-care services are a must.

Serving the needs of retirees offers businesses a host of opportunities. Senior lifestyle communities, recreational clubs, and tour packages are just a few of the possible needs to fill. Some businesses may even find it advantageous to relocate to areas with large elderly populations.

With one-quarter of the population about to retire, and the ratio of younger to older workers declining, analysts predict shortages of doctors, nurses, professors, pipefitters, carpenters, bricklayers, plumbers, and electricians. Public and private sectors need to develop strategies to attract skilled workers to fill such jobs, possibly immigrants with young families. This would entail providing affordable housing, parks, schools, and day-care centres for the newcomers.

WORK AND INCOME

Seventy-four percent of Canada's labour force is in services; 15 percent, in manufacturing; and 6 percent, in farming, forestry, and other primary industries.
■ Three of the fastest growing jobs are service jobs such as call centre customer service workers, childcare workers, and financial planners.
■ Truck driving, the top job for men, increased 29 percent in the last decade. The demand for secretaries (excluding legal and medical) declined 35 percent over 10 years. Even so, it remains the second most common job for women after salesperson.
■ Half the country's 15.6 million workers have a postsecondary degree or diploma.
■ The median family income is $55,016. With average annual incomes of slightly more than $185,000, the top 10 percent of families earn 28 percent of total family income. Average income of the bottom tenth is $10,341.

Rate of disease onset
(1994–97)

High blood pressure
Cataracts
Bronchitis/ emphysema
Urinary incontinence
Stomach/ intestinal ulcers

Legend: Women, Men

Cases per 100 population aged 12+
1 2 3 4 5 6

LIFE EXPECTANCY

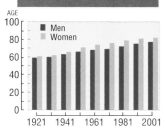

AGE
100
80
60
40
20
0
1921 1941 1961 1981 2001

Legend: Men, Women

Canada ranks third in life expectancy, after Switzerland and Japan.
■ A woman's life expectancy is now 81.7 years; a man's, 76.3 years.
■ People in southern urban areas in and west of Ontario live longer. Mortality rates in these areas are 10 percent lower for all causes than the national average.
■ Life expectancy is four years less than the national average in remote parts of the country.
■ Life expectancy increases as the rate of unemployment decreases and the level of education increases.

HEALTH

Compared to many countries, Canadians live longer and suffer fewer chronic illnesses and disabilities. People with higher incomes can expect to live longer and be healthier than those earning less. University educated people tend to have better health than those with little education. Single mothers often have poorer health than other groups.
■ Alcohol, smoking, unprotected sex, and inactivity reduce the quality of many lives. Obesity is on the rise for all age and sex groups—except women 20 to 34—and in all provinces, particularly Alberta.
■ Accidental injuries are a major cause of hospitalization and premature death. Cancer, heart disease, and stroke are the three top killers overall.

WHERE WE WORK

1. Sales and service
2. Business, finance, and administration
3. Trade and transport
4. Management
5. Manufacturing/ utilities
6. Natural and applied sciences
7. Social science, education, government
8. Health
9. Primary industries
10. Art, culture, recreation, sport

In the early years of the 21st century, Canada's population was 31,414,000, of which 25.9 percent was under 19 years old; 61.1 percent was 20 to 64 years; and 13 percent was 65 years and older. There were 75 senior men for every 100 senior women. As more and more young people flocked to large urban centres in search of jobs, small towns across Canada became communities of older people. This was particularly true in eastern Canada, but less so in western Canada, where, apart from British Columbia, the provinces and territories had the youngest populations. Of all the provinces, Alberta had the youngest in the country; Quebec had some of the oldest. Based on census statistics and demographic trends evident since the 1970s, statisticians projected how this population would most likely evolve.

Canada's age pyramid, 1900
Population: 5.3 million

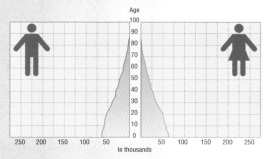

Canada's age pyramid, 2000
Population: 30 million

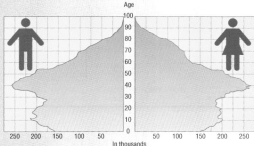

Above: *The shape of Canada's populations in 1900 and 2000. The middle-age bulge in the 2000 age pyramid represents the baby-boomer generation.*

FUTURE TRENDS

According to one scenario, Canada will continue growing for some 25 years, but at a decelerated rate. Due to a combination of an increased senior population and continued low fertility levels, by 2016, for the first time ever in Canadian history, people 65 years and over—10 million strong—will outnumber those 14 years and younger.

By 2026, some 8 million Canadians will be 65 or older; 1 in every 5 will be a senior (compared to 1 in 8 in 2000). With deaths exceeding births, the population will be in decline by 2046–50. By 2050, the median age in Canada will be 46.2; in 2000 it was 36.8. According to this scenario, the population decline in Canada could be as early as the 2030s.

All projections show the working population increasing up to 2016, then beginning to go into a decline. Such a decline would affect what is known as the "dependency ratio," the proportion of children and elderly to the working population. In 2003, there were some 100 people of working age per 46 children and seniors. Without the working-age people to replace future retirees, the children/seniors segment ratio will range from 55 to 60 as early as 2026.

Imbalance between old and young affects the "potential support ratio," the number of working-age people per senior. This will continue to spiral downward. In 2000, there were more than five working-age persons per senior; by 2026, it will be three per senior.

Immigration will be essential for growth and current immigration patterns offer some clues as to where this will occur. Up to 2026, some population gain is likely to occur in all provinces and territories, except Newfoundland and Labrador, New Brunswick, and Saskatchewan. Populations in Atlantic Canada, Quebec, Manitoba, and Saskatchewan will eventually decline. Alberta, British Columbia, and Ontario, already the fast-growing provinces, will continue to expand.

REVITALIZING CANADA'S CITIES

A survey of 205 cities worldwide ranks Vancouver (*above*) third for the overall quality of life. (Toronto, Ottawa, and Montréal also appear in the top 25.) Unfortunately, this quality of life is not available to all Canadian city dwellers.

Our cities' rapid growth is partly to blame. Affordable rental housing for low-income families is at an all-time low. Poor neigh-bourhoods are growing faster than cities overall, and the income gap between the affluent and the poor is widening. On a broader scale, the explosion in city populations has strained aging roads, bridges, and water and waste disposal systems. Compounding the gravity of the situation is the significant decline in federal and provincial funding for cities.

Revitalizing Canada's neglected cities has become the hot topic of the decade. Unlike in other countries, our cities are largely depen-dent on property taxes. Some municipal councils say they need user fees and additional tax tools to survive. Canada's big city may-ors met in 2004 and sent a message to the federal government: funding at the national level is essential—even with provincial contribution. (Constitutionally, cities are a provincial responsibility.)

In early 2004, the federal Liberal Party set up a committee to explore urban issues. Under discussion was the possibility of giving municipalities a permanent share of gas and diesel-fuel taxes.

Bohemian Index
1 Vancouver
2 Toronto
3 Victoria

Mosaic Index
1 Toronto
2 Vancouver
3 Hamilton

Talent Index
1 Ottawa
2 Halifax
3 Toronto

TechPole
1 Montréal
2 Toronto
3 Ottawa-Hull

MEASURING INNOVATION

Cities recognize that innovation is as vital to the urban economy as raw materials. Measuring innovation, which involves surveying artistic creativity and social attitudes, has been used to predicate growth potential. A recent study of some Canadian cities, using the four innovation indexes: the Bohemian (the size of the cre-ative community); the Mosaic (the numbers of foreign-born—an indicator of openness and diversity); the Talent (university-educat-ed numbers); and the TechPole (level of high-tech employment). Top scorers in each index are shown at left.

Vancouver, with almost 10 per 1,000 population in the Bohemian category, led all others, followed by Toronto, Victoria, and Montréal. Toronto, where 42 percent of the population is foreign-born, dominated the Mosaic Index, followed by Vancouver, with just under 35 percent. The Ottawa area leads the Talent Index, with 23 percent of all adults educated at university, followed by Halifax and Toronto, each scoring 20 percent. Montréal dominates the TechPole Index. High-tech workers repre-sent about 37 percent of all employment, largely due to the city's aerospace industry. Toronto follows at roughly 33, Ottawa-Hull at about 17, and Vancouver at about 12.

RURAL RETREAT

Statistics Canada defines "rural" in various ways: an area with 150 persons per square kilometre; an area with less than 1,000 population; or all territory outside urban areas. Another benchmark (and the basis for the figures that follow) is to define as rural any area, including small towns, out-side an urban centre with a population of 10,000 or more. In 1996, such rural areas were home to 21.5 percent of Canadians. By 2001, this percentage had fallen to 20.3 percent or about 6.1 million people. Only Ontario, Manitoba, and Alberta

Urban and rural population

Rural — Urban

100%, 80%, 60%, 40%, 20%, 0% — NORTH, B.C., ALTA., SASK., MAN., ONT., QUE., N.B., N.S., P.E.I., NFLD.

bucked the trend. (Areas that grew generally had more than 1 in 3 residents commut-ing to larger centres.) Resource-rich communities of Northern Ontario (Greenstone, Kirkland Lake, and Elliott Lake) and British Columbia (Mackenzie, Prince Rupert, and Comox-Strathcona) were especially hard hit, with losses exceeding 12 percent of their populations.

Below: In a time of rapid urban growth, Norton, New Brunswick, is a reminder of the enduring charm of many rural Canadian communities

COMMUTING TO WORK

The journey to the job is on average a 62-minute daily chore for 11.4 million Canadians. Although 7 km is the average commute, 1 in 6 workers in population-dense Toronto, Montréal (*above*), and Vancouver travel 20 km or more. Driving is the preferred method everywhere except Nunavut. In 2001, 5.6 million men and 4.3 million women drove to work; 77 percent overall were alone in their cars. Drivers average 58 minutes on the road, compared to 100 minutes for bus/sub-way riders. And despite flexible work hours, traffic patterns still show 8 a.m. and 5 p.m. as the busiest times on the road.

Quebecers, Ontarians, and Manitobans led in public transit use, of which women and young adults are top users. A handful of workers walk to work (mostly women) or bike (mostly men).

Where we live

Canadians, inhabitants of the world's second largest country, are moving by the thousands from rural areas into urban settings. In 2001, 79.4 percent—four out of five Canadians—lived in communities of 10,000 people or more. Some 64 percent resided in 27 regions called "census metropolitan areas"—or CMAs—where core populations are 100,000 or more. Two-thirds of Canadians live in city/regions—urban agglomerations of a million or more. Eight such urban entities exist: Ontario's Golden Horseshoe, centred around Toronto; Vancouver-Victoria; the Calgary-Edmonton corridor; Montréal and adjacent regions; Halifax-Dartmouth; Ottawa-Hull; Québec; and Winnipeg. The first four hold 51 percent of the Canadian population. All city/regions contain sizable proportions of provincial populations: almost 60 percent of Ontarians live around the Greater Toronto area and 72 percent of Albertans in the Calgary-Edmonton corridor. More than 70 percent of immigrants make their homes in Toronto, Montréal, and Vancouver. With immigration becoming the driving force behind Canada's population increase, the growth of these three areas seems certain.

EXPANSION AT THE EDGES

The "donut effect" is the term used to describe the sprawling suburbs and municipalities encircling the stagnant or declining cores of many CMAs. According to the 2001 census, Saskatoon and Regina exemplify this phenomenon. Between 1996 and 2001, Saskatoon's core population grew by 1.6 percent, while its surroundings grew by 14.6 percent. In this same period, Regina's core declined by 1.2 percent; its surroundings increased by 10 percent. A few exceptions are Abbotsford, B.C., and the Ottawa-Gatineau area, where the reverse applies: the core is outstripping surroundings.

People-scarce city cores have been part of the Canadian urban scene since the 1960s. Until then, many chose to live downtown to be near work. Immigrants settled in central districts where services for newcomers were available. Decades of suburban flight—accelerated by widespread car ownership and extensive expressway construction—have left many city cores empty and inhospitable. Many of the expanding outlying areas have severed connections with the core. These self-sufficient units are part of "the donut" that is just getting bigger. Between 1996 and 2001, immigrants to the Toronto city/region swelled the population of 4 of the 10 fastest-growing municipalities: Vaughan, a 37.3 percent increase; Barrie, 31 percent; and Richmond Hill, 29.8 percent. Interprovincial migration fueled the growth in communities along the Calgary-Edmonton corridor, the location of 5 of the 10 fastest-growing Canadian municipalities: Cochrane, a 58.9 percent increase; Sylvan Lake, 44.5 percent; Strathmore, 43.4 percent; Okotoks, 36.8 percent; and Rocky View No. 44, 31.6 percent.

Suburbs encircle Edmonton, expanding across the open prairie on the city's periphery.

Above: *Toronto's cluster of downtown towers symbolizes urban Canada's vitality*

URBAN AMENITIES: A COMPARISON OF FIVE CITIES

This chart ranks a handful of Canadian cities against amenities likely to influence where people choose to live and work. Affordability and safety are basic concerns. So is clean air. Most people appreciate convenient public transit, and ready access to cultural and recreational facilities. Such services, however, may mean higher taxes.

RANK IN CANADA	1	2	3	4	5
Availability of affordable housing	Regina	Saint John	Halifax-Dartmouth	Edmonton	Montréal
Green spaces	Edmonton	Vancouver	Winnipeg	Halifax	Regina
Cultural & recreational facilities	Toronto	Montréal	Vancouver	Ottawa	Calgary
Mass public transit network	Montréal	Toronto	Vancouver	Calgary	Ottawa
Air quality	Québec	St. John's	Winnipeg	Saint John	Regina
Low tax rate	Calgary	Halifax	Ottawa	Toronto	Montréal
Low crime rate	Québec	Toronto	Ottawa	Montréal	St. John's

CMA POPULATIONS—2003 ESTIMATES

1.	Toronto, Ont.	4,907,000
2.	Montréal, Que.	3,511,400
3.	Vancouver, B.C.	2,099,400
4.	Ottawa-Hull, Ont.-Que.	1,108,500
5.	Calgary, Alta.	969,600
6.	Edmonton, Alta.	954,100
7.	Québec, Que.	694,000
8.	Winnipeg, Man.	684,300
9.	Hamilton, Ont.	680,000
10.	Kitchener, Ont.	431,200
11.	London, Ont.	425,200
12.	St. Catharines–Niagara, Ont.	391,000
13.	Halifax, N.S.	359,100
14.	Victoria, B.C.	319,900
15.	Windsor, Ont.	313,700
16.	Oshawa, Ont.	304,600
17.	Saskatoon, Sask.	231,500
18.	Regina, Sask.	198,300
19.	St. John's, Nfld.	176,400
20.	Chicoutimi-Jonquière, Que.	158,800
21.	Sudbury, Ont.	157,900
22.	Sherbrooke, Que.	155,000
23.	Abbotsford, B.C.	147,370
24.	Kingston, Ont.	146,838
25.	Trois-Rivières, Que.	141,200
26.	Saint John, N.B.	127,300
27.	Thunder Bay, Ont.	125,700

METRO AREA (KM²)

1.	Edmonton, Alta.	9,419
2.	Toronto, Ont.	5,903
3.	Halifax, N.S.	5,496
4.	Ottawa-Hull, Ont.-Que.	5,318
5.	Saskatoon, Sask.	5,192
6.	Calgary, Alta.	5,083
7.	Winnipeg, Man.	4,151
8.	Montréal, Que.	4,047
9.	Sudbury, Ont.	3,536
10.	Regina, Sask.	3,408

POPULATION GROWTH—1996–2001

1.	Calgary, Alta.	15%
2.	Oshawa, Ont.	10%
3.	Vancouver, B.C.	8%
4.	Edmonton, Alta.	8%
5.	Kitchener, Ont.	8%
6.	Vancouver, B.C.	8%
7.	Abbotsford, B.C.	7%
8.	Windsor, Ont.	7%
9.	Hamilton, Ont.	6%
10.	Ottawa-Hull, Ont.-Que.	6%

DENSITY—POPULATION PER SQUARE KILOMETRE, 2002

1.	Montréal, Que.	847
2.	Toronto, Ont.	793
3.	Vancouver, B.C.	690
4.	Kitchener, Ont.	501
5.	Victoria, B.C.	499
6.	Hamilton, Ont.	438
7.	Oshawa, Ont.	328
8.	Windsor, Ont.	301
9.	St. Catharines–Niagara, Ont.	268
10.	Abbotsford, B.C.	235

Canada 2050

For Canadians, the journey to the world of 2050 holds many challenges. Some of these emerged in the last decades of the 20th century, when it became apparent that the land and its resources were neither limitless nor endlessly exploitable. Faced with stark realities as diverse as global warming and disappearing wetlands, a consensus developed around concepts of sustainability, which have been touched on throughout the preceding pages of *The Canadian Atlas.* These final pages speculate on how Canadians may live 50 years hence. Of all its resources, Canada's own people are its greatest asset. Whatever path they take, they are likely to ensure the country remains stable, dynamic, full of promise, and a welcoming destination for newcomers eager to experience the adventure of meeting Canada's future challenges.

HOW HOT WILL IT GET?

■ The world's climate will continue to get warmer. Industrial activity is responsible for the increase of greenhouse gases, such as carbon dioxide, in the atmosphere. But experts differ about the outcome of global warming. Some predict changes will come with savage suddenness within decades. Others believe that global warming will be slower than expected and that dramatic environmental changes will take hundreds of years. In 2050, "green methods" of manufacturing and greater use of alternative energy may have reduced greenhouse gas emissions. By that time, scientists may also have learned to purge air pollution, ending the threat of global warming.

HOW MANY OF US WILL THERE BE?

■ By 2050, Canada's population is expected to reach 40 million—give or take 5 million. Between now and then, population growth will have slowed due to continued low fertility levels, a measure of the number of children women have over their childbearing years. The population could level off at 35 million if the present low birthrate is not offset by a high rate of immigration.

■ At 1 senior to 8 working-age persons, the proportion of seniors in Canada was less than in many other industrialized countries as this century began. But in coming decades, the Canadian population will age more rapidly as baby boomers—those born in the two decades after World War II—reach the age of 65. By 2026, some 8 million Canadians, 1 person in every 5, will be 65 or older. By 2050, seniors may number 10 million, roughly 25 percent of the projected population.

■ Immigration from Asia, Africa, and Latin America will continue to drive Canada's population growth. Some analysts expect the newcomers will adopt the prevailing social values. They also believe Canada will move from a "mosaic" embracing a diversity of cultures and groups toward a homogenous society akin to the American "melting pot" model. Only aboriginals will resist assimilation and assert social and economic positions appropriate to their traditional values.

WHAT MAJOR CHANGES CAN WE EXPECT BY 2050?

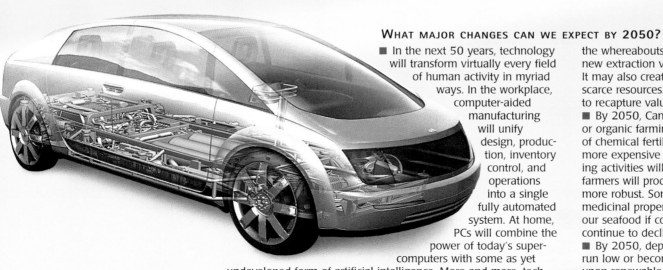

■ In the next 50 years, technology will transform virtually every field of human activity in myriad ways. In the workplace, computer-aided manufacturing will unify design, production, inventory control, and operations into a single fully automated system. At home, PCs will combine the power of today's supercomputers with some as yet undeveloped form of artificial intelligence. More and more, technology will be brought into play to ensure the sustainability of resources. Technology—combined with exploration—may reveal the whereabouts of mineral reserves in new extraction venues such as seabeds. It may also create new materials to replace scarce resources. "Green methods" of manufacturing will be used to recapture valuable by-products from industrial wastes.

■ By 2050, Canadian farmers will have incorporated alternative or organic farming techniques with traditional methods. The use of chemical fertilizers and pesticides will decline as they become more expensive and less effective. Computerized control of farming activities will be commonplace. With technological advance, farmers will produce crops that grow faster, resist disease, and are more robust. Some produce may have been engineered to provide medicinal properties. Improved aquaculture may provide much of our seafood if commercial fish species depleted by overfishing continue to decline.

■ By 2050, dependence on fossil fuels will decline as reserves run low or become more difficult to access. Canadians will call upon renewable sources—geothermal, hydroelectric, tidal, and wind—to meet our energy needs. Solar power may produce electricity at costs comparable to conventional sources.

Left: *Towers massed on a man-made island: a visionary model of a 21st-century high-density urban centre from famed Canadian architect Arthur Erickson*

HOW WILL WE LIVE AND WORK?

■ In 2050, there will be fewer building starts, and more recycling of existing structures. Older buildings will be massively retrofitted with the latest technological innovations. New homes and workplaces will be smarter, built for energy efficiency and ease of maintenance. They will be constructed with self-repairing "intelligent materials," capable of responding to environmental changes. Home and business energy requirements will be supplied by wind and solar power, or by fuel cell or photovoltaic devices.

■ Urban sprawl, already infringing on Canada's first-rate farmland, will be halted by mid-century. A general awareness of the environmental impact and expense of building and maintaining highways and other infrastructures may diminish the appeal of the suburban, commuting lifestyle. By 2050, many people may have returned to the cities, where urban spaces will be extensively redeveloped for business and residential purposes. In city cores, moreover, there will be a high proportion of people living on their own, particularly young singles, widows, or widowers.

■ The city-bound flow will increase urban densities. Today more than 12 million Canadians live and work in Toronto, Montréal, Vancouver, and the Edmonton-Calgary corridor. Within 50 years, 8 to 10 million more will be concentrated in these centres.

■ By 2050, virtually all homes will have an entertainment centre, which combines interactive television, telephone, and computing capacity. Household robots will be commonplace. Garages will house small, quiet, nonpolluting battery-powered vehicles with ceramic engines and recycled plastic bodies. For the most part, products will be created from recycled materials. At least half of all products will be purchased through the use of the computer.

■ In 2050, Canadians will be better educated, constantly renewing skills to keep up with rapid changes in information and technology. Technological advances will enable most people to work at home. Retirement will be an outmoded concept. Many seniors will opt to work as long as their health, and their desire to do so, holds out.

■ The 2050 economy may be driven by the knowledge-intensive jobs (design work, for example), administration, education, social work, tourism, leisure, and the cultural field. Only a few will work in the primary sector (farms, fisheries, forests, and mines). Automation will mean small staffs in the manufacturing sector, which will produce high-quality goods that will be inexpensive. Some experts say most manufacturing may be sent "offshore"—a trend increasingly apparent in today's global economy. Whether some manufacturing is retained here or goes abroad will depend on comparative production costs.

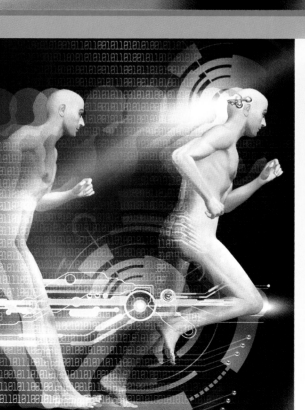

HOW HEALTHY WILL WE BE?

■ More Canadians in 2050 will be better fed, and live longer and healthier lives than ever before. This will be the result of improvements in lifestyle, nutrition, and medicine. By 2041, life expectancy at birth in Canada is expected to reach 81 years for men and 86 years for women.

■ In coming decades, aging baby boomers untouched by conditions such as Alzheimer's disease and cancer may find their quality of life challenged by some form of disability. A less active post-baby-boomer generation may, however, impose its burdens on the health-care system. According to some experts, the latter will experience a high incidence of diabetes and cardiovascular disease.

■ New and unpredictable diseases—caused by the cross-transmission of viruses from animals and birds to human—will mutate more rapidly as the world shrinks through air travel.

■ By 2050, a better understanding of life and living organisms will provide greater control over disease and disability. Treatments will involve more biochemical and engineered solutions. Computers and automated laboratory equipment will refine diagnostic capabilities and create new, purer pharmaceuticals. Such developments will reduce health-care costs and possibly overcome a decline in health-care personnel. By 2050, the number of doctors is projected to fall to two-thirds of the present level. Half of this reduction may occur as baby-boomer doctors reach retirement.

MAPS OF CANADA

Below: *A grizzly bear patrols the placid river shore in the Khutzeymateen Grizzly Bear Sanctuary, located north of Prince Rupert, British Columbia.*

Next page: *A satellite image of Canada*

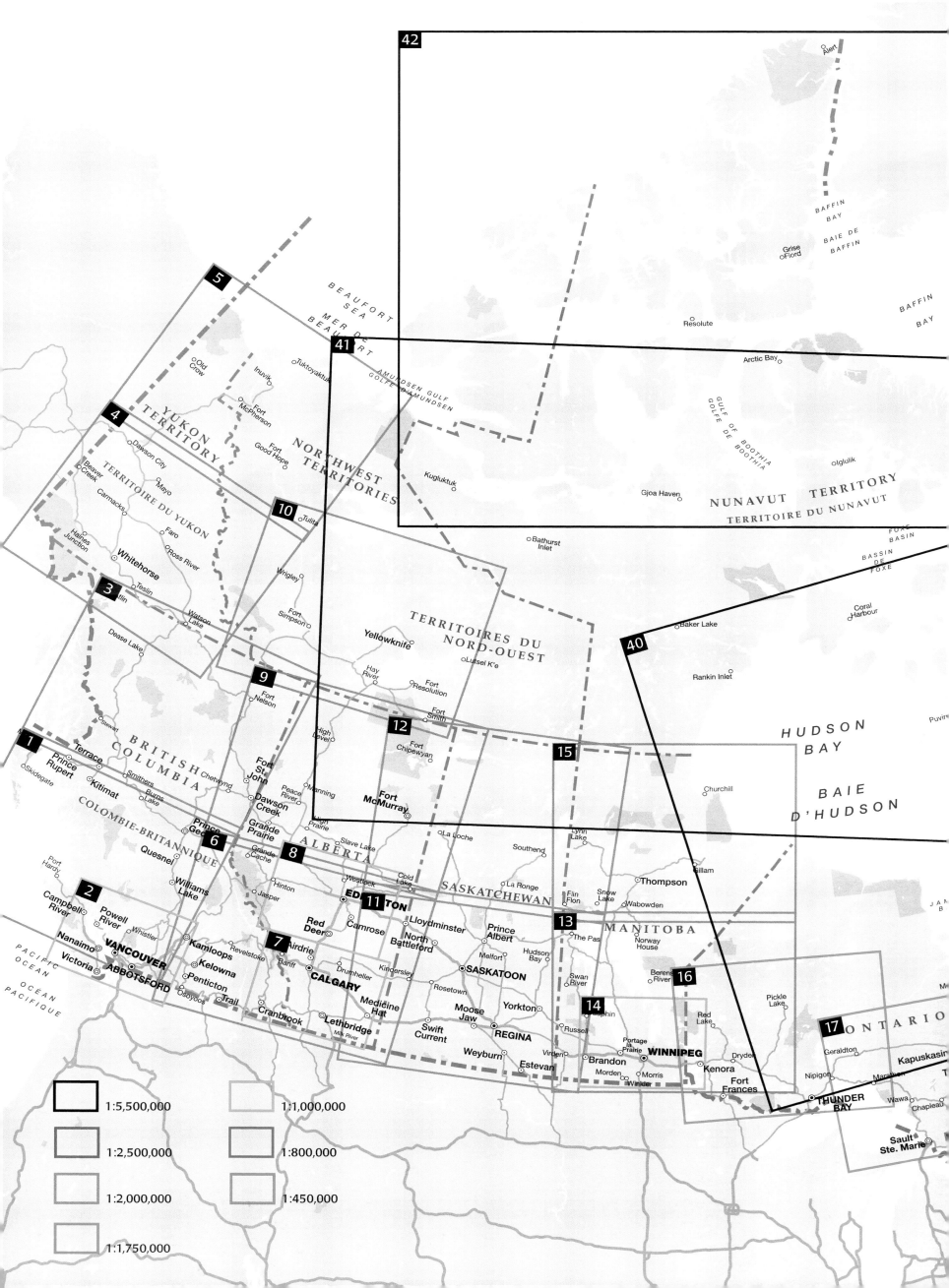

Key map

1 Western British Columbia
2 Southwestern British Columbia
3 Northern British Columbia
4 Southern Yukon
5 Yukon / Northwest Territories
6 Southeastern British Columbia / Southern Alberta
7 Southeastern British Columbia / Southern Alberta
8 Central Alberta
9 Northern Alberta
10 Northwest Territories
11 Southern Prairies
12 Northern Prairies
13 Southern Manitoba / Northwestern Ontario
14 Southern Manitoba
15 Northern Manitoba
16 Northwestern Ontario
17 Northeastern Ontario
18 Western Ontario
19 Southwestern Ontario
20 South Central Ontario
21 Southeastern Ontario
22 Northeastern Ontario / Northwestern Quebec
23 Northwestern Quebec
24 Southeastern Ontario / Southwestern Quebec
25 Central Quebec
26 Central Quebec
27 Southern Quebec
28 Lac Saint-Jean, Quebec
29 Gaspé Peninsula, Quebec / Northern New Brunswick
30 Gaspé Peninsula, Quebec
31 Southeastern New Brunswick
32 Southern New Brunswick / Central Nova Scotia
33 Western Nova Scotia
34 Eastern Nova Scotia
35 Prince Edward Island
36 Southwestern Newfoundland
37 Eastern Newfoundland
38 Northern Newfoundland
39 North Shore, Quebec / Newfoundland and Labrador
40 Northeastern Canada
41 North Central Canada
42 Arctic Islands

Map symbols

28	Provincial highway	🅢	Expressway service centre area
10	Ontario county highway	198	Interchange number
16	Yellowhead Highway	▾ 37	Kilometre distance
◪	Crowsnest Highway	▾ 78	Cumulative kilometres distance
⬯	Trans-Canada Highway	○	Native community

Dot indicative of population size
○ Hay Lakes, AB
○ Vanderhoof, BC
◉ Flin Flon, MB
◉ Kenora, ON
◉ Shawinigan, QC
● St. John's, NL

⊟ Provincial tourism welcome centre

● Point of interest

● Spot height

▲ Mountain peak

🦫 Parks Canada facility

🛖 Organized park – camping

🛖 Organized park – no camping

⛺ Unorganized park – camping

⛺ Unorganized park – no camping

▲ Campground (inside large park)

▲ Interest area (inside large park)

🅒 Ontario conservation area (camping)

🅒 Ontario conservation area (no camping)

🦅 National wildlife facility

👁 Provincial wildlife facility

🕸 24-hour border crossing

🎿 Major ski centre

○ Toll expressway full interchange

◎ Toll expressway partial interchange

○ Expressway full interchange

◎ Expressway partial interchange

○ Highway full interchange

◎ Highway partial interchange

✈ Major airport

✛ Minor airport

✛ Remote access airport

🅡 Expressway rest area

══ Controlled access expressway (4 lane/divided)

── Controlled access expressway (2 lane/undivided)

══ Controlled access toll expressway (4 lane/divided)

🔄 Expressway interchange

─○─ Primary 2-lane highway with interchange

══ Multilane highway

══ Secondary highway

── Local road

── Winter road

══ Scenic parkway (limited access)

── Scenic roadway

─ ─ Auto ferry

── Passenger ferry

🔺 International boundary

🔺 Provincial boundary

🔺 County/district/ MRC boundary

─ Reorganized city boundary

── Railway

── Major walking trail

•••• Time zone boundary

▨ Urban built-up area

⊂⊃ National Capital Commission facility

▨ Park

▢ Wildlife area

GEOGRAPHICAL NAMES SOURCES

For bilingual forms of geographical names, the following sources were used:

Ontario: the Ontario Ministry of Natural Resources OnTerm GeoNames, Index (www.onterm.gov.on.ca/geo), and the Ontario Ministry of Tourism and Recreation *Guide touristique de l'Ontario*

New Brunswick: the official road map *New Brunswick Travel Map* and the New Brunswick Department of Tourism and Parks *Guide touristique du Nouveau-Brunswick*

Nunavut: Nunavut Tourism

Northwest Territories: the official *Explorers Map*

National Parks and World Heritage Sites: Parks Canada

National Wildlife Areas and National Migratory Bird Sanctuaries: Canadian Wildlife Service, Environment Canada

General source:

Geographical Names Board of Canada: This federal/provincial/ territorial committee, coordinated by Natural Resources Canada, is the primary source of Canadian geographical names. For further information, see http://geonames.nrcan.gc.ca.

Dixon Entrance
Détroit de Dixon

Langara Point
Cape Knox
Langara Island
Klashwun Point
Wiah Point
McIntyre Bay
Rose Point
Rose Spit
White Point
Morgan Point
Haida
Masset
Agate Beach
Naikoon
Naden Harbour
Pure Lake Provincial Park

Museum of Northern British Columbia
Metlakatla
Melville I.
Prince Rupert
Port Edward
Prudhomme Lake Prov. Park
Terrace
Kitsumkaylum
Creek Provincial Park
Exchamsiks River Provincial Park
Lakelse Lake Provincial Park

A

GRAHAM ISLAND
ÎLE GRAHAM

Tian Head
Port Louis
Athlow Bay
Seal Inlet
Hippa Island
Juskatla
Port Clements
Cape Ball
Misty Meadows
Tlell
Dead Tree Point

SKEENA-QUEEN CHARLOTTE

Stephens
Prescott I.
Diana Lake Prov. Park
Port Essington
Kitson Island Prov. Marine Park

Porcher Island
Oona River
Kitkatla
Goschen Island
Cape George
Baird Point
McCauley Island
Browning Entrance
Pitt Island
Kitimat
Kitimat Centennial Museum
Kitamaat Village
Kildala Arm

KITIMAT RANGES

Eagle Peak 2093m
Barrett Lake
Houston
Topley

Andesite Peak 2379m
Burns Lake
Chesink
Franço
Noralee
Wistaria Provincial Park
Tatalrose
Takы
Little Andrews Bay Provincial Marine Park
Ootsa Lake

B

Kindakun Point
Cone Head
Hunter Point
Chaatl Island
Kano Inlet
Queen Charlotte City
Skidegate
Sandspit

ÎLES DE

LA REINE-

Cumshewa Head
Skedans Point
Bonilla Island
Cliff Point
Kelp Point
Banks Island
Estevan Group

CHARLOTTE

Union Passage Provincial Marine Park
Hartley Bay
Gribbell Island
Farrant
Grief Point
Gil Island
Princess Royal Island

Green Inlet Provincial Marine Park
Fiordland Conservancy Provincial Recreation Area
Kitlope Heritage
Kemano
Mt. Dubose 2734m
Powell Pk. 2012m
Kimsquit

BRITI
COLUM

North Tweedsmuir
Tweedsmuir North Provincial Recreation Area
Whitesail Lake
Eutsuk Lake
Provincial
Park

QUEEN
CHARLOTTE
ISLANDS

Moresby Camp
MORESBY ISLAND
ÎLE MORESBY
Hibben Island
Sewell Inlet
Louise Island
Talunkwan Island
Tanu I.
Kunga I.
Lyell I.
Ramsay

GWAII HAANAS NATIONAL MARINE RESERVE (Proposed)

Rennison Island
Aristazabal Island
Campania Group
Caamaño Sound
Surf Inlet
Laredo Sound
Sarah Island
Pooley Island
Roderick Island

Comet Mountain 2018m

Kalone Peak 2557m
Thunder Mountain 2681m
Firvale
Bella Coola
Hagensborg

CO
BRI

South Tweedsm
Provincia

C

GWAII HAANAS NATIONAL PARK RESERVE AND HAIDA HERITAGE SITE

Darwin Sound
Huxley Island
Burnaby Island
Skincuttle Inlet
Ikeda Point
Carpenter Bay
Benjamin Point

RÉSERVE DE PARC NATIONAL ET SITE DU PATRIMOINE HAIDA GWAII HAANAS

RÉSERVE D'AIRE MARINE NATIONALE GWAII HAANAS (Projet)

Klemtu
Swindle Island
Price I.
Dowager I.
Lady Douglas I.
Athlone I.
Oliver Cove Provincial Marine Park
Waglisla-McLoughlin Bay
Bella Bella
Denny I.
Shearwater
Campbell Island
Hunter Island

Jackson Narrows Provincial Marine Park
Roscoe Inlet
Sir Alexander Mackenzie Provincial Park
Ocean Falls
Bella Coola Historic Museum
Codville Lagoon Provincial Marine Park
Kwakwa
Mount Saugstad 2908m

Nagas Point
Nan Sdins National Historic Site/
Lieu historique national de Nan Sdins
SGaang Gwaii (Anthony Island)/
SGaang Gwaii (île Anthony)
Luxana Bay
Kunghit Island
Cape St. James
Goose Island
Namu
Hakai Provincial Recreation Area

Moose Inlet
Fish Inlet
Rivers Inlet

Monarch
Icefield

Silverthrone

D

PACIFIC

OCEAN

Queen Charlotte Sound

Bassin de la Reine-Charlotte

Herbert Inlet
Calvert Island
Dawsons Landing
Good Hope
Penrose Island Provincial Marine Park
Cape Calvert
Greaves
Smith Sound
Cape Caution
Burnett Bay
Bramham I.
Belize Inlet

Silverthrone Mountain 2896m

MOUNT WADDINGTON

Seymour Inlet
Wakeman Sound
Kingcome Inlet

COAST
CHAÎNE

E

OCÉAN

PACIFIQUE

Scott Islands
Lanz I.
Cox
Cape Scott
Scott Islands Provincial Park
Scott Islands Provincial Marine Park
San Josef
Holberg
Cape Sutil
Tsulquate
Bear Cove
Port Hardy
Port Hardy Historic Museum
Kippase
Malcolm Island
Sointula
Port McNeill
Alert Bay
Beaver Cove
Telegraph Cove

God's Pocket Provincial Marine Park
Sullivan Bay
Broughton I.
Echo Bay Provincial Marine Park
Gilford Island
Cracroft I.
Minstrel Island
Port Neville
Kelsey Bay
White River Prov. Park

VANCOUVER
ISLAND

Winter Harbour
Quatsino
Port Alice
Marble River Prov. Park
Kokish
Nimpkish Lake Prov. Park
Lower Tsitika River Prov. Park
Woss
Mount Cain 1840m
Schoen Lake Provincial Park
Loveland Bay

Cape Parkins
Lawn Point
Lawn Point Provincial Park
Brooks Peninsula
Brooks Peninsula Prov. Park
Nimpkish Lake
Claud Elliott Lake Prov. Park

F

Cape Cook
Clerke Point
Chamiss Bay
Kyuquot
Fair Harbour
Artlish Caves Prov. Park
Woss Lake Provincial Park
Victoria Pk 2163m
Waymer Cr.

Big Bunsby Marine Prov. Park
Zeballos
Tahsis
Esperanza
Ceepeecee
Hecate
Gold Muchalat PPP

VANCOUVER

ÎLE DE
VANCOUVER

Nuchatlitz Provincial Park
Nootka Island
Ferrer Point
Bligh Island Prov. Park
Yuquot
Bajo Point
White Ridge PPP
Gold River
Mowachaht
Santa Boca Provincial Park

Hesquiat Peninsula Provincial Park
Maquinna Provincial Park
Flores Island Provincial Park
Gibson Provincial Marine Park
Hesquiat
Sydney Inlet Prov. Park
Stewardson Inlet
Ahousat
Markos
Flores I.
Vargas Island Provincial Park
Tofino
Vargas I.
Dawley Passage Provincial Marine Park
Esowista

PACIFIC RIM NATIONAL PARK RESERVE
RÉSERVE DE PARC NATIONAL PACIFIC

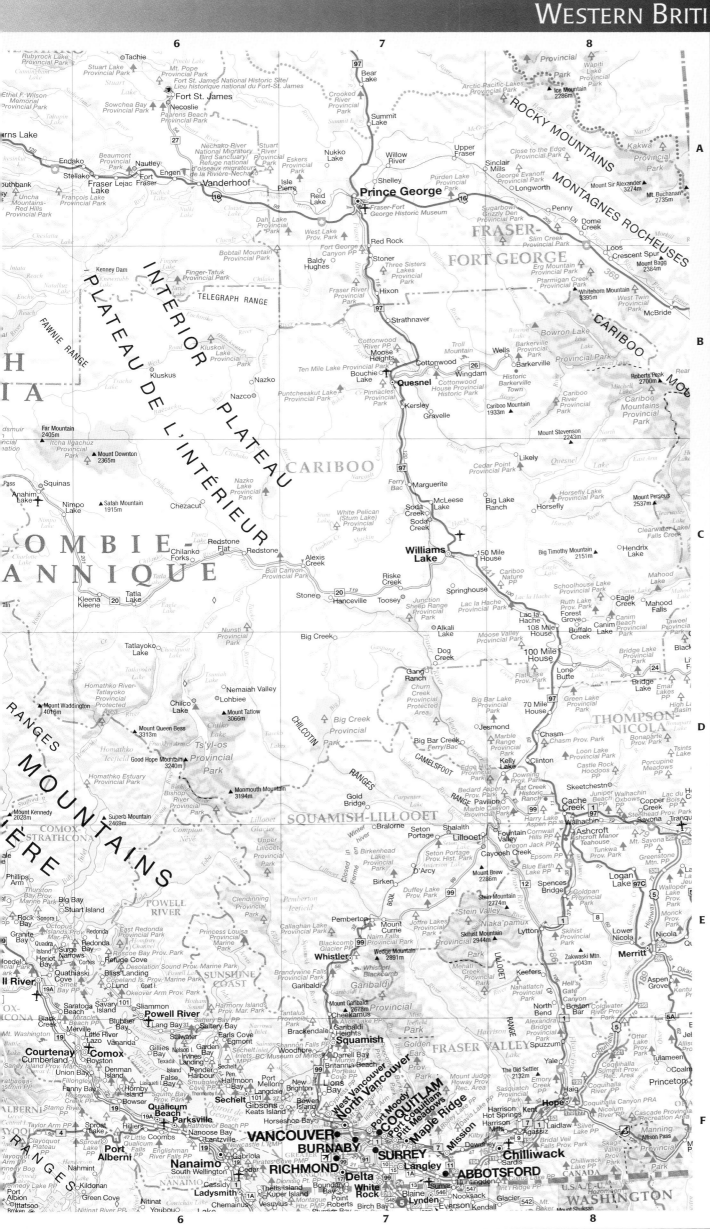

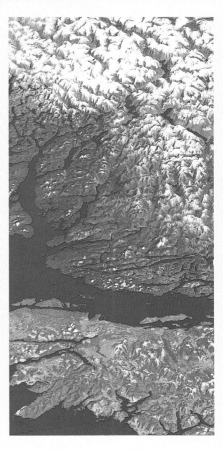

FJORDS AND MOUNTAINS

This view shows Quatsino Sound on northwestern Vancouver Island, Queen Charlotte Strait, and the mountainous, fjord-indented coastline of mainland British Columbia. Calvert, Hecate, and Hunter islands in Queen Charlotte Sound (left centre) lie at the entrance to Burke Channel. This spectacular fjord extends 130 km inland to the small saltwater port of Bella Coola. Beyond the coastal strip rise the Coast Mountains, some of which are more than 2,500 m high. Moist westerly Pacific winds, forced upward by this mountain chain, deluge the slopes and peaks with rain and snow.

Other points of interest

■ British Columbia's coastline extends 22,894 km, nearly three times as long as the Canada-United States border.

■ Canada's most powerful recorded earthquake, measuring 8.1 on the Richter Scale, occurred off the Queen Charlotte Islands [A1-C2] on Aug. 22, 1949.

■ Canada's wettest place is Ocean Falls [C4], where the average annual precipitation is 4,826 mm.

■ Glacier-fed Chilko Lake [D6], 80 km long and covering an area of 158 km², is North America's largest natural, high-elevation (1,171 m) freshwater lake.

■ At 948,597 km², British Columbia is nearly four times the size of Great Britain, 2.5 times larger than Japan, and larger than any American state except Alaska.

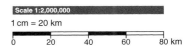

Scale 1:2,000,000

1 cm = 20 km

0   20   40   60   80 km

COAST MOUNTAINS CHAÎNE CÔTIÈRE

PACIFIC RANGES

COAST RANGES

MT WADDINGTON

SQUAM...

POWELL RIVER

BRITISH COLUMBIA

VANCOUVER ISLAND

ISLAND RANGES

COMOX-STRATHCONA

SUNSHINE COAST

ALBERNI-CLAYOQUOT

NANAIMO

COWICHAN VALLEY

ÎLE DE VANCOUVER

GREATER VANCOUVER

CAPITAL

PACIFIC OCEAN

OCÉAN PACIFIQUE

WASHINGTON

Kingcome Inlet, Thompson Sound, Mount Kennedy 2028m, Superb Mountain 2469m, Good Hope Mountain 3240m, Monmouth Mountain 3194m, Homathko Estuary Provincial Park, Ts'il-os Provincial Park, Bishops River Provincial Park

Viscount I., Glendale Cove, Minstrel Island, Port Neville, Hardwicke Island, Kelsey Bay, Sayward, West Thurlow I., East Thurlow I., Blind Channel, Sonora Island, Big Bay, Stuart Island, Rock Bay, Phillips Arm, Phillips Lake, Clendinning Provincial Park, Pemberton, Upper Lillooet Provincial Park

Granite Bay, Quadra Island, Bloedel, Heriot Bay, Read Island, Cortes, Redonda Bay, East Redonda I., West Redonda I., Refuge Cove, Roscoe Bay Provincial Park, Desolation Sound Provincial Marine Park, Powell Lake, Emerald Estates, Whistler, Garibaldi, Brandywine Falls Provincial Park

Victoria Peak 2163m, Elk Falls Provincial Park, Campbell River, Quathiaski Cove, Quinsam, Smelt Bay Provincial Park, Mansons Landing, Hernando Island, Copeland Islands Provincial Marine Park, Savary I., Lund, Okeover Arm, Powell River, Harmony Islands Provincial Marine Park, Cheekamus, Mount Garibaldi 2678m, Brackendale, Garibaldi Heights

Gold River, White Ridge Provincial Park, Buttle Lake, Strathcona Provincial Park, Saratoga Beach, Miracle Beach Provincial Park, Williams Beach, Kitty Coleman Provincial Park, Bates Beach, Blubber Bay, Pebble Beach, Paradise Valley, Saltery Bay, Earls Cove, Egmont, Skookumchuck Narrows Provincial Park, Squamish, Woodfibre, Darrell Bay, Shannon Falls Provincial Park, Stawamus Chief PP

Mowachaht, Golden Hinde 2200m, Black Creek, Merville, Grantham, Little River, Kin Beach Provincial Park, Lazo, Courtenay, Comox, Royston, Vananda, Lang Bay, Stillwater, Saltery Bay Provincial Park, Nelson I., Musket Island Provincial Marine Park, Sechelt, Garden Bay, Irvines Landing, Madeira Park, Pender Harbour, Halfmoon Bay, Wilson Creek, Langdale, Gibsons, Horseshoe Bay, Lions Bay, West Vancouver, North Vancouver

Cumberland, Union Bay, Denman I., Fanny Bay, Hornby Island, Denman Island, Fillongley Provincial Park, Tribune Bay PP, Helliwell Provincial Park, Bowser, Qualicum, Qualicum National Wildlife Area, Qualicum Beach, Parksville, Coombs, Errington, Hilliers, Lantzville, Wellington, Nanoose Bay, Nanaimo, Newcastle Island PMP, Gabriola Island, Gabriola Sands PP, UBC Museum of Anthropology, VANCOUVER, BURNABY, RICHMOND, Delta (Ladner), Tsawwassen, Port Moody

Strathcona-Westmin Provincial Park, Sproat Lake, Port Alberni, Stamp River Provincial Park, Taylor Arm Provincial Park, Home Lake Provincial Park, Spider Lake Provincial Park, MacMillan Provincial Park, Englishman River Falls Provincial Park, Petroglyphs PP, South Wellington, Cedar, Cassidy, Gulf Islands National Park Reserve / Réserve de parc national des Îles-Gulf, Thetis Island, Kuper Island, Ladysmith, Saltair, Chemainus, North Cowichan, Crofton, Vesuvius, Saltspring Island, Ganges, Maple Bay, Duncan, Glenora, GREATER VANCOUVER

Tofino, Clayoquot Arm Provincial Park, Pacific Rim National Park Reserve (Long Beach Unit), Réserve de parc national Pacific Rim (Secteur de la plage Long), Green Point, Esowista, Ucluelet, Amphitrite Point, Port Albion, Ittatsoo, Broken Group Islands, Pacific Rim National Park Reserve (Broken Group Islands Unit), Réserve de parc national Pacific Rim (Secteur l'archipel Broken Group), Sarita, Bamfield, Anacla, Cape Beale, Nitinat River Provincial Park, Caycuse, Youbou, Lake Cowichan, Honeymoon Bay, Mesachie Lake, Cowichan River Provincial Park, Cowichan Bay, Shawnigan Lake, Mill Bay, Sidney, North Saanich, Central Saanich, Saanichton

Pacific Rim National Park Reserve (West Coast Trail Unit), Réserve de parc national Pacific Rim (Secteur sentier de la Côte-Ouest), Clo-oose, Carmanah Walbran Provincial Park, Ditidaht, Nitinat, Pachena Point, Port Renfrew, Strait of Juan de Fuca, Détroit de Juan de Fuca, French Beach Provincial Park, Jordan River, Sooke, Milnes Landing, Metchosin, Sooke Potholes Provincial Park, Gowlland Tod Provincial Park, Goldstream Provincial Park, Malahat, Highlands, View Royal, Langford, Colwood, Esquimalt, Victoria, SAANICH, Oak Bay, Race Rocks Marine Protected Area / Zone de protection marine de Race Rocks

Neah Bay, Cape Flattery, Flattery Rocks National Wildlife Refuge, CANADA, U.S.A./É.-U.

San Juan Island, Friday Harbor, Roche Harbor, Orcas Island, Lopez Island, Eastsound

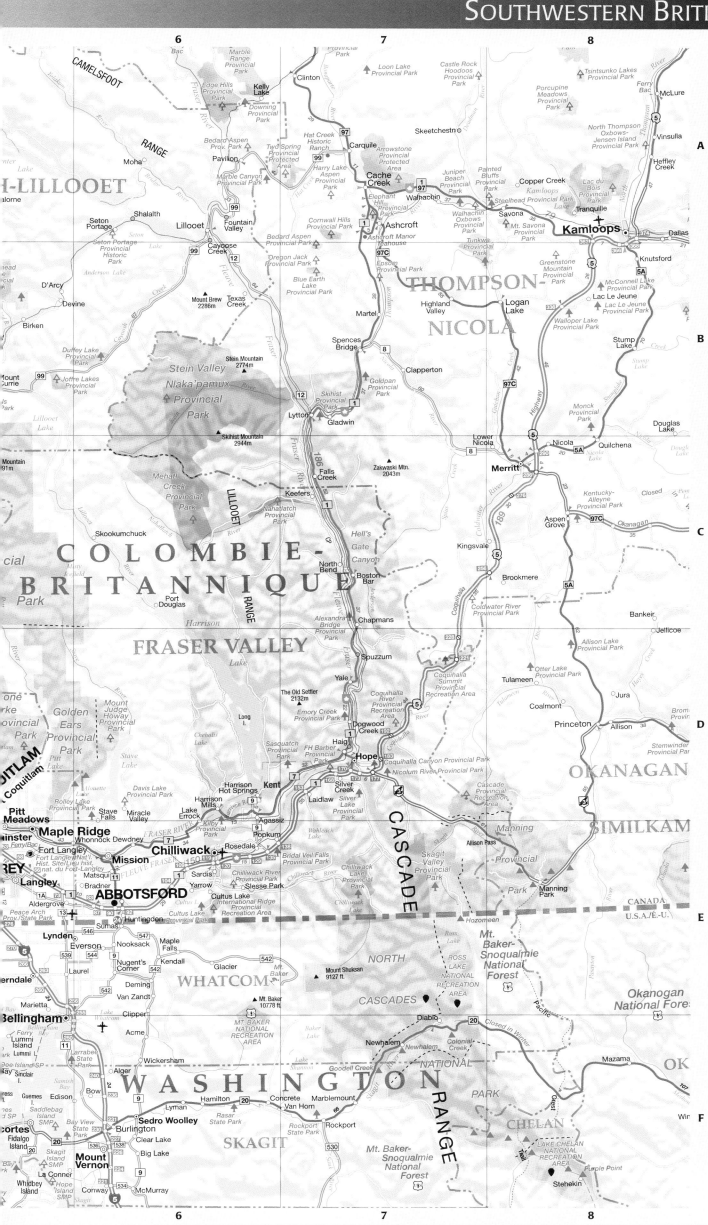

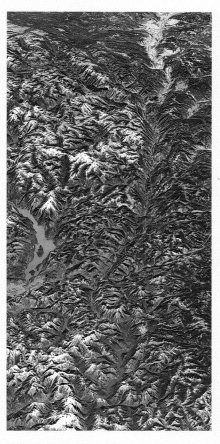

RIVER AND CANYON

The Thompson River (upper right) passes through British Columbia's arid interior plateau as it flows toward its junction with the Fraser River. South of the junction, near Lytton, the Fraser River is tightly constricted by the Coast Mountains to the west, and by the Cascade Mountains to the east. This 100-km stretch is the Fraser Canyon, where walls rise 1,000 m in some places. At Hell's Gate, the canyon narrows to a 30-m gap, through which the raging river rushes at 7 m a second. At its southern end, near Hope, the Fraser turns west abruptly and travels tamely through level farmland to the Pacific. Along this stretch, waters from the 65-km-long Harrison Lake (left centre) and other tributaries feed the river.

Other points of interest

■ Vancouver Island has more than 1,000 known caves. The Upana Caves, a network of caverns near Gold River [C1], have 15 entrances and a combined length of 450 m.

■ At 440 m, Della Falls is Canada's highest waterfall. It lies just south of Buttle Lake in Strathcona Provincial Park [C1-D1].

■ The Carmanah Giant, over 95 m high, is the world's largest Sitka spruce. More than 400 years old, this mighty tree may also be the world's oldest specimen. It is located in Carmanah Walbran Provincial Park [F3].

■ Volcanic formations are outstanding natural features of 1,958 km² Garibaldi Provincial Park [C5]. A notable example is 2,678-m Black Tusk Mountain, the eroded remains of an ancient volcanic core, which is located just north of Garibaldi Lake.

Scale 1:1,000,000

1 cm = 10 km

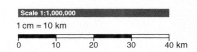

0   10   20   30   40 km

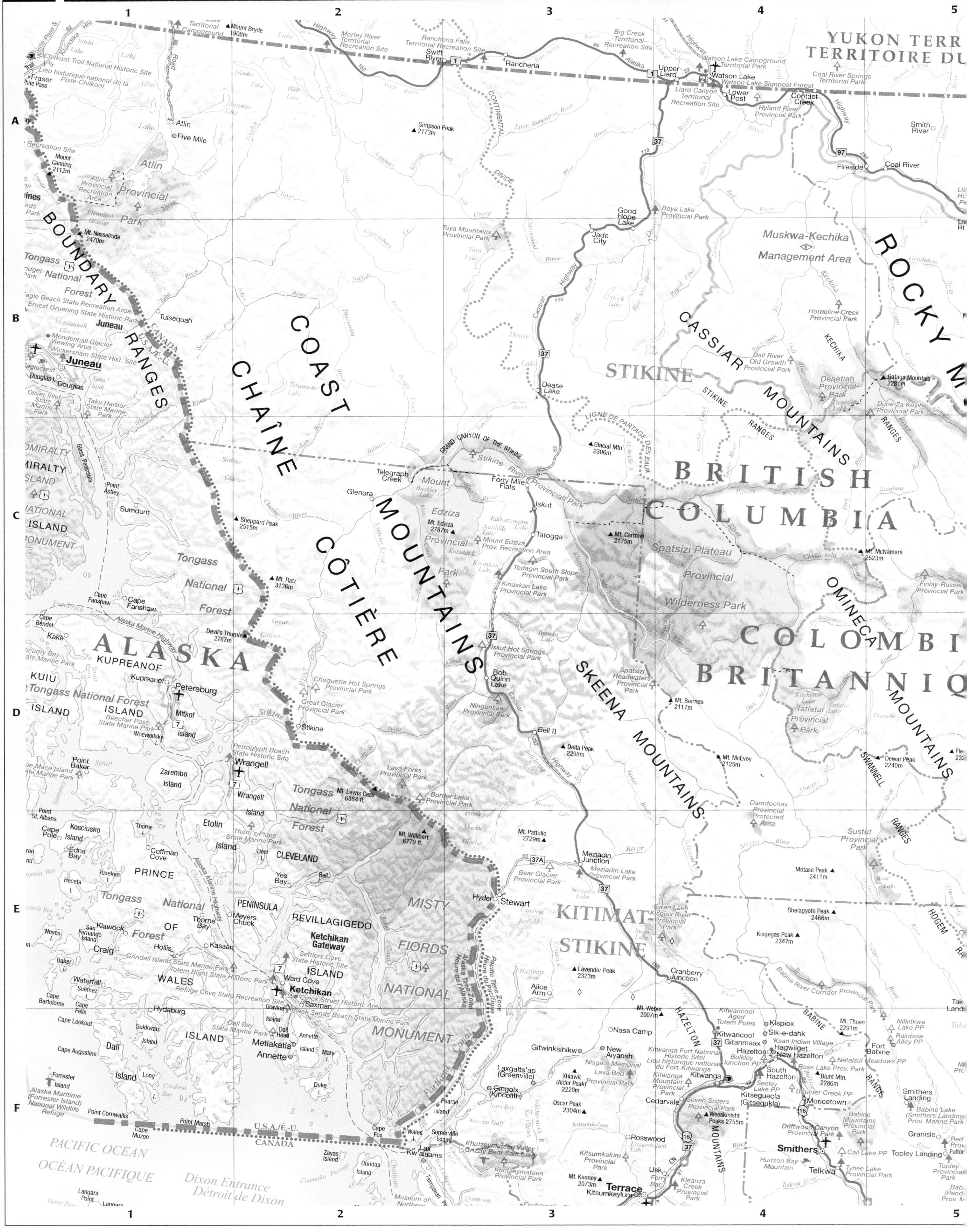

YUKON TERR
TERRITOIRE DU

BRITISH
COLUMBIA

COLOMBIE
BRITANNIQUE

ROCKY M

ALASKA

COAST
CHAÎNE
MOUNTAINS
CÔTIÈRE

BOUNDARY RANGES

CASSIAR MOUNTAINS
RANGES

STIKINE

SKEENA MOUNTAINS

OMINECA
MOUNTAINS

SWANNELL RANGES

HOGEM RANGES

BABINE RANGES

KITIMAT-STIKINE

Muskwa-Kechika
Management Area

Spatsizi Plateau
Provincial
Wilderness Park

PACIFIC OCEAN
OCÉAN PACIFIQUE

Dixon Entrance
Détroit de Dixon

U.S.A./É.-U.
CANADA

Juneau
Petersburg
Wrangell
Ketchikan
Atlin
Watson Lake
Dease Lake
Telegraph Creek
Stewart
Hyder
Smithers
Terrace
Hazelton
New Hazelton
Kitwanga
Moricetown
Telkwa

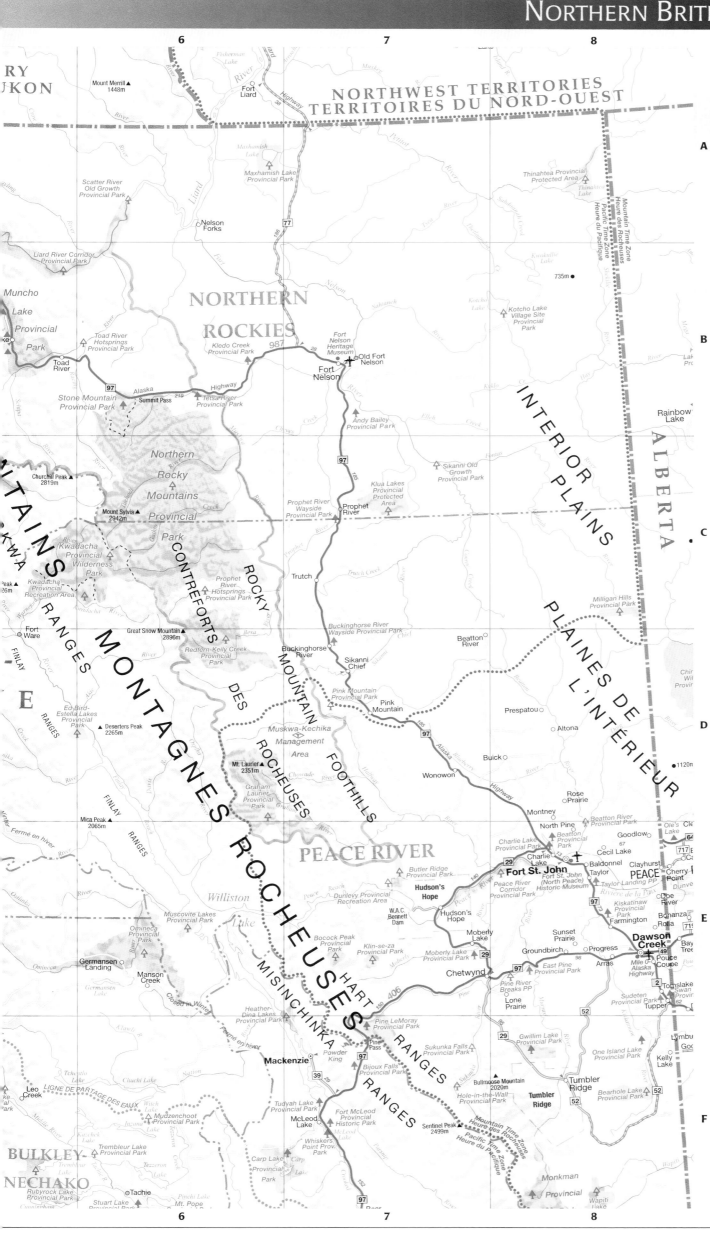

VOLCANO COUNTRY

The Frank Mackie Glacier (left centre) in British Columbia's Coast Mountains is the source of the Unuk River (lower left). This remote river crosses the Canada-United States border and flows into Behm Canal, a coastal waterway of the Misty Fiords National Monument in the Alaska panhandle. Just north of the Unuk River, Lava Forks Provincial Park preserves the site of what is believed to be Canada's youngest volcano, which erupted in 1904.

Other points of interest

■ Dease Lake [B3] is one of the world's biggest producers of nephrite jade. This gemstone was first discovered here in 1965. Another high-quality deposit, roughly 50 km east of the community, was found in the 1990s.

■ Mount Edziza Provincial Park [C2-C3], covering some 2,300 km^2, preserves a spectacular region that has seen volcanic eruptions, probably within the last three hundred years. The park's dominant features are some 30 cinder cones, the largest of which is 2,787-m Mount Edziza, which towers over the surrounding 640-km^2 lava plain.

■ Within 2,170-km^2 Stikine River Provincial Park [C2-C5] lies one of Canada's most awesome sites, the 80-km-long Grand Canyon of the Stikine. Through the canyon flows the unruly 539-km Stikine River. The canyon has been carved by relentless river erosion. Its walls, up to 300 m high, are tinted gray, green, pink, and purple by various minerals. In the canyon depths, the width of the Stikine River ranges from 200 m across to a tiny 2-m gap through which the river tumbles.

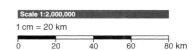

Scale 1:2,000,000

1 cm = 20 km

0   20   40   60   80 km

1 2 3 4 5

ALASKA

YUKON TERRITORY / TERRITOIRE DU YUKON

PACIFIC OCEAN / OCÉAN PACIFIQUE

BRITISH COLUMBIA / COLOMBIE

Column 1 / Row A
Liberty
Clinton Creek
Mount Warbelow 5553ft
Taylor Mountain 5059ft
Chicken
Jack Wade
Boundary
Top of The World Highway
Prindle Volcano 5125ft
Mount Hart 1621m
Mount Fairplay 5541ft

Row A–B (central)
Harper 1874m
Fortymile
Forty Mile, Fort Cudahy and Fort Constantine Historic Site
Tombstone Territorial Park
Tombstone
Klondike Historic Complex National Historic Site / Lieu historique national du Complexe-historique-de-Dawson
Dawson City
Bear Creek
Henderson Corner
Hunker Creek Rd.
Bonanza Creek Rd.
Gold Dredge #4 National Historic Site / Lieu historique national de la Drague-Numéro-Quatre
Discovery Claim National Historic Site / Lieu historique national de la concession Discovery
Klondike River Territorial Campground
Klondike Highway
Reindeer Mountain 1578m
Australia Mountain 1593m
McQuesten
Red Mountain 1762m

Castle Mountain 2098m
Steamboat Mountain 1120m
Rusty Mountain 1861m
Mount Patterson 2088m
Elsa
Keno
Keno City Mining Museum
Mount Ortell 2063m
Mount Joy 2235m
Mt. Edwards 2088m
Five Mile Lake Territorial Campground
Mayo Lake Rd.
South McQuesten Rd.
Hanson Lake Rd.

Row B
Stewart
Mount Stewart 1244m
Stewart Crossing
Moose Creek Territorial Campground
Ethel Lake Territorial Campground
Silver Trail
Mayo
Ddhaw Gro Habitat Protection Area
Horseshoe Slough Territorial Habitat Protection Area
Mount Armstrong 2159m
RUSSEL RANGE
ILESS RIVER

Northway Junction
Northway
Tetlin National Wildlife Refuge
Coffee Creek
Isaac Creek
High Cache
YUKON
Selwyn
Fort Selkirk
Fort Selkirk Territorial Historic Site
Pelly Crossing
L'hutsaw Wetland Territorial Habitat Protection Area
WILKINSON RANGE
Mt. McKenzie 1784m
1986m
Mount Selous 2176m

Row C
Beaver Creek
Wellesley Mountain 4966ft
Needle Peak 7586ft
Dry Creek 974m
NUTZOTIN MOUNTAINS
Koidern
Mount Baker
Snag
Donjek
Lynx City
Wellesley Lake
Snag Junction Territorial Campground
Pickhandle Lake Territorial Recreation Site
Lake Creek Territorial Campground
NISLING RANGE
Mount Cockfield 1890m
Mount Pitts 1592m
Mount Apex
Mt. Prospector 1976m
Minto
McCabe Creek
1435m
Mt. Klaza 1939m
Mt. Nansen
Mt. Nansen Rd.
Carmacks
Ta'tla Mun Special Territorial Management Area
GLENLYON RANGE
Glenlyon Peak 2190m
Tatchun Lake Territorial Campground
Tatchun Creek Territorial Campground
TATCHUN HILLS
Truitt Peak 2072m
Little Salmon River
Nunatuk Territorial Campground
Five Finger Rapids Territorial Recreation Site
Frenchman Tatchun Campground
Frenchman Lake Territorial Campground
Mt. Mye 2061m
Faro
Johnson Lake Territorial Campground
ANVIL RANGE
Little Salmon Lake Territorial Campground
Drury Creek Territorial Campground
Mount Lokken 1835m
PELLY RANGE
Lapie Canyon Territorial Campground

Row D
Mount Natazhat 13435ft
WRANGELL-ST. ELIAS NATIONAL PARK
Mount Tittmann 9400ft
Kluane Wildlife Sanctuary
2292m
Mount Constantine
ST. ELIAS
CENTENNIAL RANGE
Mount Wood 4840m
Burwash Landing
Destruction Bay
Mount Lucania 5226m
Kluane
KLUANE NATIONAL PARK AND RESERVE
Congdon Creek Territorial Campground
Sheep Mountain Visitors Centre
Kluane Lake
KLUANE RANGE
RUBY RANGE
Talbot Creek
1935m
Aishihik
Aishihik Lake
Otter Falls Territorial Recreation Site
Aishihik Lake Territorial Campground
Kingston Mountain
Fox Lake Territorial Campground
Mount Anticline 1362m
NORDENSKIOLD
Nordenskiold Wetland Habitat Protection Area
Twin Lakes Territorial Campground
Mount Packers 1446m
Big Salmon
Hootalinqua
1848m
Mount Caribou
SEMENOF HILLS
Livingstone Creek
Mount St.Cyr 2050m
Twin Mount
Pass Peak 2162m
BIG SALMON RANGE
Quiet Lake Territorial Recreation Site

Row E
King Peak
Table Mount 9360ft
Mount Logan 5959m
Mount Queen Mary 3886m
Mt. Cairnes 2783m
Mount Archibald
Spruce Beetle Trail Territorial Recreation Site
Haines Junction
Kluane/Wrangell-St. Elias/Glacier Bay/Tatshenshini-Alsek
PARC NATIONAL ET RÉSERVE KLUANE
MOUNTAINS
Mount St. Elias 5489m
Mount Augusta 4289m
Mount Vancouver 4785m
Mount Cook 4194m
Snowshoe Peak
Mount Bratnober
Kathleen Lake
Pine Lake Territorial Campground
Haines Junction Visitors Centre
Canyon Creek
Champagne
162
Ibex Valley
Takhini Hotspring
Takhini
Takhini River Territorial Campground
Takhini
Crestview
Porter Creek
WHITEHORSE
S.S. Klondike National Historic Site / Lieu historique national S.S. Klondike
Beringia
MacRae
Mt. Arkell
Kusawa Lake Territorial Recreation Site & Campground
Kookatsoon Lake Ter. Rec. Site
Wolf Creek Territorial Campground
Marsh Lake Territorial Campground
Mount Cap 1801m
1898m
Mount Byng
Mount Murphy
State Mount
Quiet Lake Territorial Campground
Nisutlin River Territorial Recreation Site
Mount Streak
Johnsons Crossing
Brooks Brook

Mount Hendrickson 4590ft
WRANGELL-ST. ELIAS NATIONAL PRESERVE
Malaspina Glacier
Kluane/Wrangell-St. Elias/Glacier Bay/Tatshenshini-Alsek
Mount Seattle 3072m
Goatherd Mountain
Dezadeash Lake
Beloud Post
Klukshu
Kusawa Lake
Dalton Post
Shawshe (Dalton Post) Territorial Campground
Million Dollar Falls Territorial Campground
2259m
2382m
Mount Skukum
Robinson
Mt. Lorne
Mount Granger 2035m
Mount Lorne
Tagish Bridge Terr. Rec. Site
Carcross
Tagish
Carcross Desert
Squanga Lake Territorial Campground
Jake's Corner
Hayes Peak
Tagish Territorial Campground
Snafu Lake Territorial Campground
Teslin Lake Territorial Campground
Tarfu Lake Territorial Campground
Mount Bryde 1908m
Teslin
Nisutlin National Reserve / Réserve nationale du Delta de la rivière

Row F
Knight I.
Point Manby
Yakutat Bay
Mount Wade 7960ft
Mount Armour 8770ft
Khantaak I.
Ocean Cape
Yakutat
Situk
Mount Reaburn
Mount Root 12860ft
Fairweather Mount
Tongass National Forest
Crescent National 4770ft
Mount Ruhamah 5620ft
ALSEK RANGES
Tatshenshini-Alsek Provincial Wilderness Park
256
Highway Subject to Periodic Winter Closings / Route parfois fermée en hiver
Chilkoot Pass National Historic Site / Lieu historique national de la Piste-Chilkoot
Mt. Foster 2173m
Chilkat Pass
Mosquito Lake State Park
Alaska Chilkat Bald Eagle Preserve
Pleasant Camp
Fraser
White Pass
Carcross/Tagish
Klondike Gold Rush National Historical Park
Dyea
Skagway
Klukwan
Chilkat State Park
Haines
Chilkat Inlet
Portage Cove State Park
GLACIER BAY NATIONAL PARK
GLACIER BAY NATIONAL PRESERVE
COAST MOUNTAINS / CHAÎNE CÔTIÈRE
Atlin
Atlin Lake
Atlin Provincial Park
Five Mile
Mount Canning 2112m
Surprise Lake
BRITISH COLUMBIA / COLOMBIE

Alaska Time Zone / Heure de l'Alaska
Pacific Time Zone / Heure du Pacifique

1 2 3 4 5

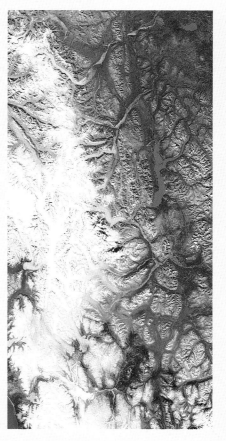

PEAKS AND ICEFIELDS

At 22,015 km², Kluane National Park and Reserve is Canada's second largest park and the site of the country's highest and largest mountains, the St. Elias. The mountains are split into two ranges—the Icefield (left) and the Kluane (centre). The Icefield ranges have more than 20 peaks higher than 4,200 m, including 5,959-m Mount Logan and 5,226-m Mount Lucania (upper right). The park contains the world's largest nonpolar icefields, which, as this view shows, spread glaciers from the heights into the valleys. The Kluane ranges, about 2,500 m on average, are visible from the Alaska Highway, which runs between the park's eastern boundary and Kluane Lake (upper right). Kluane is a World Heritage Site.

Other points of interest

■ The 3,185-km-long Yukon River system [A1-E4] rises in Tagish Lake on the British Columbia border and empties into the Bering Sea. It flows north and northwest across 1,149 km of rugged terrain in Canada, draining water from 65 percent of the Yukon Territory. The river continues 2,036 km through Alaska. The Yukon—from the Loucheux Indian word for "big river"—is North America's fifth longest river.

■ Gold may have been discovered near Dawson City [A2] in 1896, but today's mining activity in this area centers on asbestos, copper, lead, silver, and zinc.

■ Beaver Creek [C1] is the westernmost community in Canada.

■ Carcross [E4] boasts that it is the site of the "World's Smallest Desert," which consists of 260 ha of sand dunes, all that remains of an ancient glacial lake.

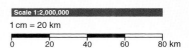

Scale 1:2,000,000

1 cm = 20 km

0   20   40   60   80 km

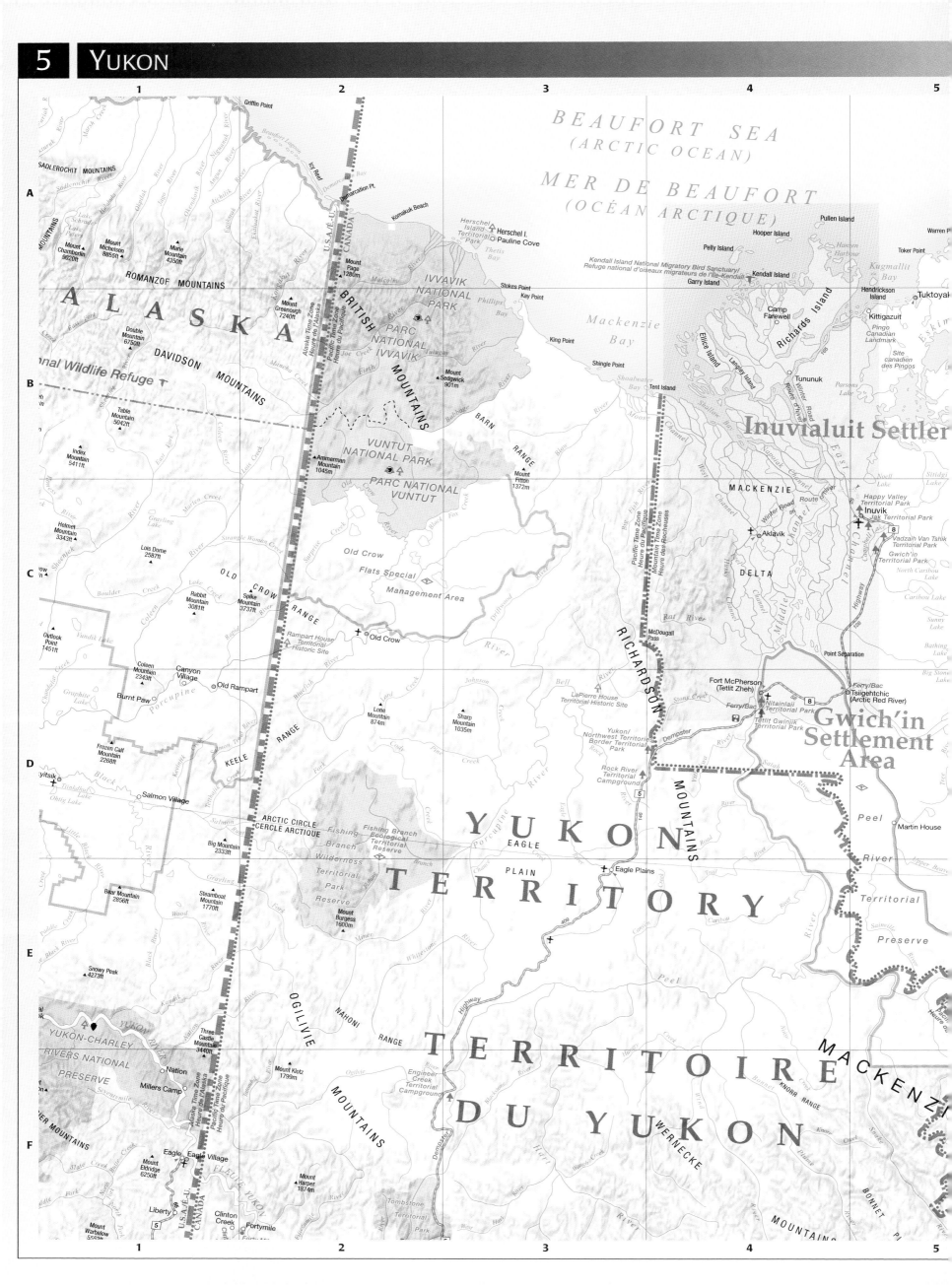

BEAUFORT SEA
(ARCTIC OCEAN)

MER DE BEAUFORT
(OCÉAN ARCTIQUE)

Griffin Point

SADLEROCHIT MOUNTAINS

Mount
Chamberlin
9020ft
Mount
Michelson
8855ft
Marie
Mountain
4350ft

ROMANZOF MOUNTAINS

A L A S K A

DAVIDSON MOUNTAINS

nal Wildlife Refuge

Double
Mountain
6750ft

Mount
Greenough
7240ft

Table
Mountain
5042ft

Index
Mountain
5411ft

Helmet
Mountain
3343ft

Lois Dome
2587ft

OLD

Rabbit
Mountain
3081ft

Spike
Mountain
3737ft

CROW

RANGE

Outlook
Point
1451ft

Coleen
Mountain
2343ft

Canyon
Village

Old Rampart

Burnt Paw

Frozen Calf
Mountain
2268ft

KEELE

RANGE

Syitsik

Salmon Village

ARCTIC CIRCLE
CERCLE ARCTIQUE

Big Mountain
2333ft

Bear Mountain
2856ft

Steamboat
Mountain
1770ft

Snowy Peak
4273ft

YUKON

YUKON-CHARLEY

RIVERS NATIONAL

PRESERVE

Nation

Millers Camp

Three
Castle
Mountain
3440ft

Mount Klotz
1799ft

OGILVIE

MOUNTAINS

Mount Eldridge
6250ft

Eagle   Eagle Village

Liberty

Mount Harper
1874m

Mount
Warbelow
5552ft

Clinton
Creek

Fortymile

Tombstone

Territorial

Park

BRITISH

MOUNTAINS

IVVAVIK
NATIONAL
PARK

PARC
NATIONAL
IVVAVIK

Mount
Page
1280m

Demarcation Pt.

Icy Reef

Komakuk Beach

Herschel
Island
Territorial
Park

Herschel I.
Pauline Cove

Thetis
Bay

Mount
Sedgwick
901m

VUNTUT
NATIONAL
PARK

Ammerman
Mountain
1045m

PARC NATIONAL
VUNTUT

BARN

RANGE

Mount
Fitton
1372m

Old Crow

Flats Special

Management Area

Rampart House
Territorial
Historic Site

Old Crow

Lone
Mountain
874m

Sharp
Mountain
1035m

Fishing

Branch

Fishing Branch
Ecological
Territorial
Reserve

Branch

Wilderness

Territorial

Park

Reserve

Mount
Burgess
1600m

Y U K O N

T E R R I T O R Y

EAGLE

PLAIN

Eagle Plains

Stokes Point

Kay Point

King Point

Phillips
Bay

Shingle Point

Mackenzie

Bay

Shoalwater
Bay

Tent Island

Shallow

McDougall
Pass

Bell

LaPierre House
Territorial Historic Site

Yukon/
Northwest Territories
Border Territorial
Park

Rock River
Territorial
Campground

Kendall Island National Migratory Bird Sanctuary/
Refuge national d'oiseaux migrateurs de l'Île-Kendall

Garry Island

Kendall Island

Pelly Island

Hooper Island

Pullen Island

Warren P

Hansen
Harbour

Toker Point

Kugmallit
Bay

Eskim

Hendrickson
Island

Tuktoyak

Kittigazuit

Pingo
Canadian
Landmark

Site
canadien
des Pingos

Camp
Farewell

Richards Island

Ellice Island

Langley Island

Tununuk

Parsons
Lake

Winter
Road

Noell
Lake

Sitidgi
Lake

MACKENZIE

DELTA

Inuvialuit Settler

Aklavik

Happy Valley
Territorial Park

Inuvik

Jak Territorial Park

Vadzaih Van Tshik
Territorial Park

Gwich'in
Territorial Park

North Caribou
Lake

Caribou

Bathing
Lake

Big Stone

Point Separation

Fort McPherson
(Tetlit Zheh)

Ferry/Bac

Tsiigehtchic
(Arctic Red River)

Nitainlaii
Territorial Park

Tetlit Gwinjik
Territorial Park

RICHARDSON

MOUNTAINS

Gwich'in
Settlement
Area

Peel

Martin House

River

Territorial

Preserve

T E R R I T O I R E

D U   Y U K O N

WERNECKE

TERRITOIRE

MACKENZI

KNORR RANGE

MOUNTAINS

BONNET

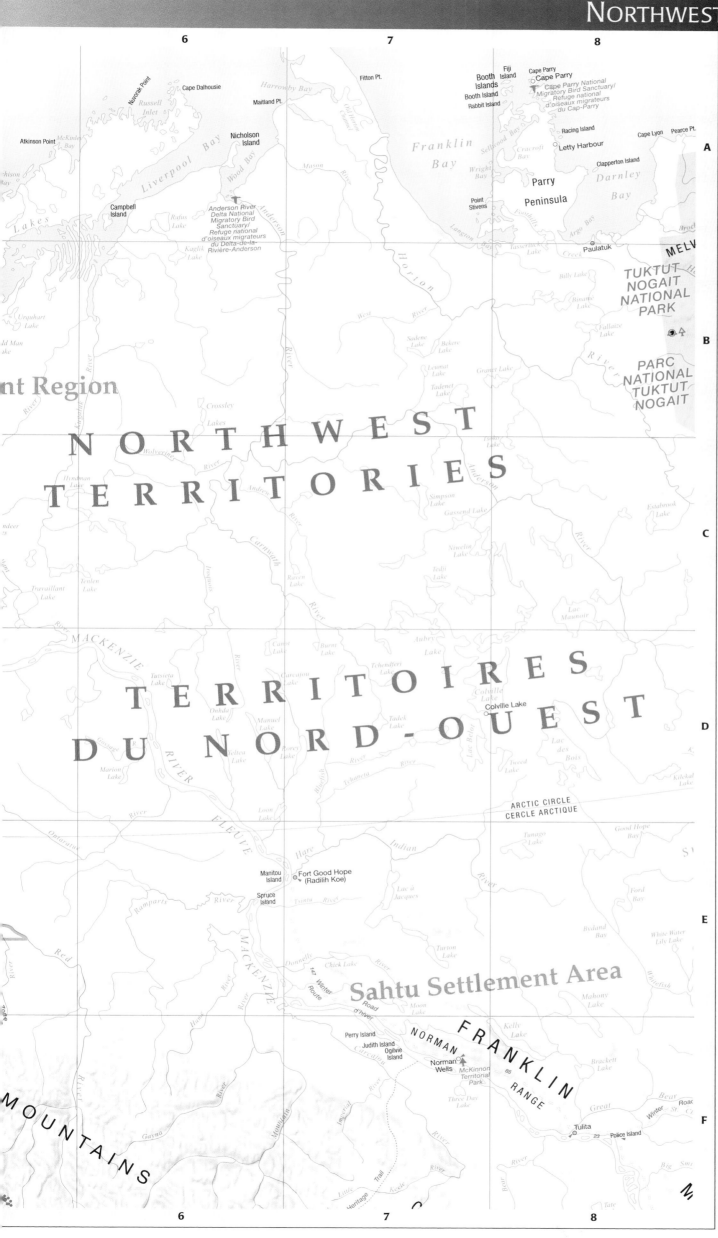

Map labels (Northwest Territories / Territoires du Nord-Ouest):

6 **7** **8**

Nuvorak Point · Cape Dalhousie · Russell Inlet · Harrowby Bay · Fitton Pt. · Booth Islands · Fiji Island · Cape Parry · Cape Parry National Migratory Bird Sanctuary / Refuge national d'oiseaux migrateurs du Cap-Parry · Booth Island · Rabbit Island · Maitland Pt. · Nicholson Island · Atkinson Point · McKinley Bay · Liverpool Bay · Wood Bay · Mason · River · Franklin Bay · Wright Bay · Racing Island · Letty Harbour · Cape Lyon · Pearce Pt. · Clapperton Island · **A**

Campbell Island · Rufus Lake · Anderson River Delta National Migratory Bird Sanctuary / Refuge national d'oiseaux migrateurs du Delta-de-la-Rivière-Anderson · Kaglik Lake · Point Stivens · Parry Peninsula · Darnley Bay · Argo Bay · Brock · Langton · Horton · MELV · Paulatuk · Tasserluck Lake · Creek ·

Lakes · Urquhart Lake · nt Region · Old Man Lake · West · River · Billy Lake · Iliname Lake · TUKTUT NOGAIT NATIONAL PARK · Fullaxe Lake · River · **B** · Sadene Lake · Bekere Lake · Leumat Lake · Granet Lake · Tadenet Lake · PARC NATIONAL TUKTUT NOGAIT

N O R T H W E S T   T E R R I T O R I E S

Crossley Lakes · Wolverine · River · Niwelin Lake · Tesjii Lake · Estabrook Lake · Carnwath · River · Raven Lake · Lac Maunoir · **C**

Henderman Lake · Travaillant Lake · Tenlen Lake · Simpson Lake · Gassend Lake · Anderson · River · Joaquin · River ·

T E R R I T O I R E S   D U   N O R D - O U E S T

MACKENZIE · Camp Lake · Burnt Lake · Tchendjeri Lake · Aubry Lake · Tutsieta Lake · Carcamon · River · Colville Lake · Colville Lake · Tadek Lake · Tweed Lake · Lac des Bois · Kilekal Lake · **D** · Onhal Lake · Manuel Lake · Bistcho · River · Tchaneta · River · Marion Lake · Tussisse Lake · Beltea Lake · Roary Lake · Loon Lake · Lac à Jacques ·

ARCTIC CIRCLE CERCLE ARCTIQUE · Tunago Lake · Good Hope Bay · **S** · Ontaratue · River · FLEUVE · Igre · River · Indian · River ·

MOUNTAINS · Red · River · Manitou Island · Fort Good Hope (Radilih Koe) · Lac à Jacques · Ford Bay · Bedami Bay · White Water Lily Lake · **E** · Spruce Island · Tsinta · River · Ramparts · River · Turton Lake ·

Donnells · River · Chick Lake · 147 Winter Route · Moon Lake · Mahony Lake · Whitefish · River · **Sahtu Settlement Area** · Kelly Lake ·

Perry Island · Judith Island · Ogilvie Island · **NORMAN** · **FRANKLIN** · Brackett Lake · MOUNTAINS · Gayna · River · Norman Wells · McKinnon Territorial Park · 85 · **RANGE** · Bear · River · Winter · St. · Road · **F** · Three Day Lake · Great · Big · Sm · Tulita · 23 · Police Island · Keele · River · Trail · Heritage · Trail · Little · Tate ·

6 **7** **8**

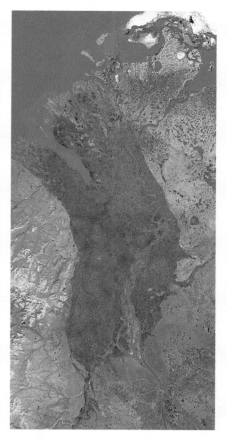

AN ARCTIC DELTA

The Mackenzie River, about one to two kilometres wide, flows majestically and placidly until it meets the Peel River (lower right). At this point, the broad stream dissolves into the labyrinthine Mackenzie Delta (centre), which extends 210 km to Mackenzie Bay and the Beaufort Sea in the Arctic Ocean (top). At 12,272 km², the Mackenzie Delta is the largest coastal delta in Canada. It contains some 20,000 lakes and ponds, and an intricate network of channels thousands of kilometres long. The Middle Channel, visible above, is the largest of three main waterways that flow through the delta and are used for navigation purposes. The natural curiosities of this region are pingoes—cone-shaped, ice-hills that rise up to 50 m. The delta has roughly 1,450 pingoes.

Other points of interest

■ In Ivvavik National Park [A2-B3] lies part of a region that escaped the impact of ice-age glaciation. More than 90 percent of this 10,168-km² park is dominated by the British Mountains, where some of the peaks reach 1,800 m. This is Canada's only non-glaciated range. South of Ivvavik, Vuntut National Park [B2-C3] is the site of an important waterfowl habitat.

■ Opened in 1979, the Dempster Highway [F2-C4] is the northernmost public highway in Canada, and the only one to traverse the Arctic Circle. Its construction took 20 years in often inhospitable conditions. It stretches from Dawson City to Inuvik, a distance of 720 km. Most of the highway had to be elevated on gravel "berms" to insulate the road from permafrost and prevent excess thawing.

Scale 1:2,000,000

1 cm = 20 km

0   20   40   60   80 km

1 2 3 4 5

A

FRASER-
FORT GEORGE

Upper
Fraser
Sinclair
Mills
George Evanoff
Provincial Park
Longworth
Penny
Ice Mountain
2286m
Mount Sir Alexander
3274m
Mt. May 2450m
Intersection Mountain
2461m
Nose
Lake
Twin
Lakes
Kakwa
Provincial
Park
Kakwa
Wildland
Provincial
Park
Smoky
River
South
Grande
Cache
Kakwa
River
Bison
Flats
Sheep
Creek
Southview
Fox Creek
Iosegun
Lake
Freeman
River
Fort Assiniboine
Sandhills Wildland
Provincial Park
Trapper
Lea's
Whitecourt
Carson-
Pegasus
Provincial
Park
Lone
Pine
Blue
Ridge
Tiger Lily
Green
Court
Thunder Lake
Prov. Park
Camp
Barrhead

B

Wells
Bowron Lake
Provincial Park
Barkerville
Historic
Barkerville
Town
Cariboo Mountain
1933m
Slim Creek
Provincial Park
Erg Mountain
Provincial Park
Ptarmigan Creek
Provincial Park
Dome
Creek
Loos
Crescent Spur
Mount Bagg
2384m
Whitehorn Mountain
3395m
Mount De Veber
2577m
Resthaven Mountain
3098m
Mount Chown
3331m
McBride
Dunster
Croydon
Station
Roberts Peak
2700m
Tête Jaune Cache
Mount Robson
3954m
The Ranee
2939m
Jasper House National Historic Site/
Lieu historique national Jasper House
JASPER NATIONAL PARK
Pocahontas
Miette Hot
Springs
Hinton
Brûlé
Entrance
Marlboro
Edson
Robb
Coalspur
Cadomin
Foothills
Drayton
Valley
Mayerthorpe

C

Cariboo Mountain
1933m
Mount Stevenson
2243m
Likely
Horsefly Lake
Provincial Park
Horsefly
BRITISH
COLUMBIA
Mount Perseus
2537m
Wells Gray
Provincial Park
Azure Mountain
2495m
Hallam Peak
3219m
Mica
Creek
ROCKY MOUNTAINS
Mount
Columbia
3747m
Mount Amery 3329m
Columbia
Icefield
Athabasca Glacier
Viewing Area
Saskatchewan
River Crossing
Howse
Pass
Mt. Wilson
3261m
FOOTHILLS
Rocky Mountain House
Nordegg
Chambers

D

COLUMBIA-
SHUSWAP
MONASHEE MOUNTAINS
SELKIRK MOUNTAINS
Adamant Mountain
3355m
Mt. Sir Sandford
3522m
Blackwater Mountain
2732m
Rogers Pass National Historic Site/
Lieu historique national du Col-Rogers
GLACIER
NATIONAL
PARK
PARC
NATIONAL
DES GLACIERS
Donald
Golden
YOHO
NATIONAL
PARK
Field
Lake Louise
Castle
Mountain
BANFF NATIONAL PARK
PARC NATIONAL BANFF
Canmore
Banff

E

Merritt
Nicola
Quilchena
Logan
Lake
Kamloops
Salmon
Arm
Vernon
Kelowna
Lumby
Cherryville
COLOMBIE-
BRITANNIQUE
Nakusp
Kaslo
New
Denver
Silverton
Kimberley
EAST KOOTENAY
Elkford
MONTAGNES ROCHEUSES
RANGES
Radium Hot
Springs
Invermere
Windermere
Fairmont Hot
Springs
Canal Flats

F

Manning
Provincial
Park
Princeton
Summerland
Penticton
Keremeos
Oliver
Osoyoos
WASHINGTON
Grand
Forks
Greenwood
BOUNDARY
KOOTENAY
CENTRAL
KOOTENAY
Castlegar
Trail
Rossland
Fruitvale
Montrose
Salmo
Nelson
Creston
Cranbrook
Fort Steele
Moyie
Fernie
ROCHEUSES
IDAHO
U.S.A./É.-U.
CANADA

1 2 3 4 5

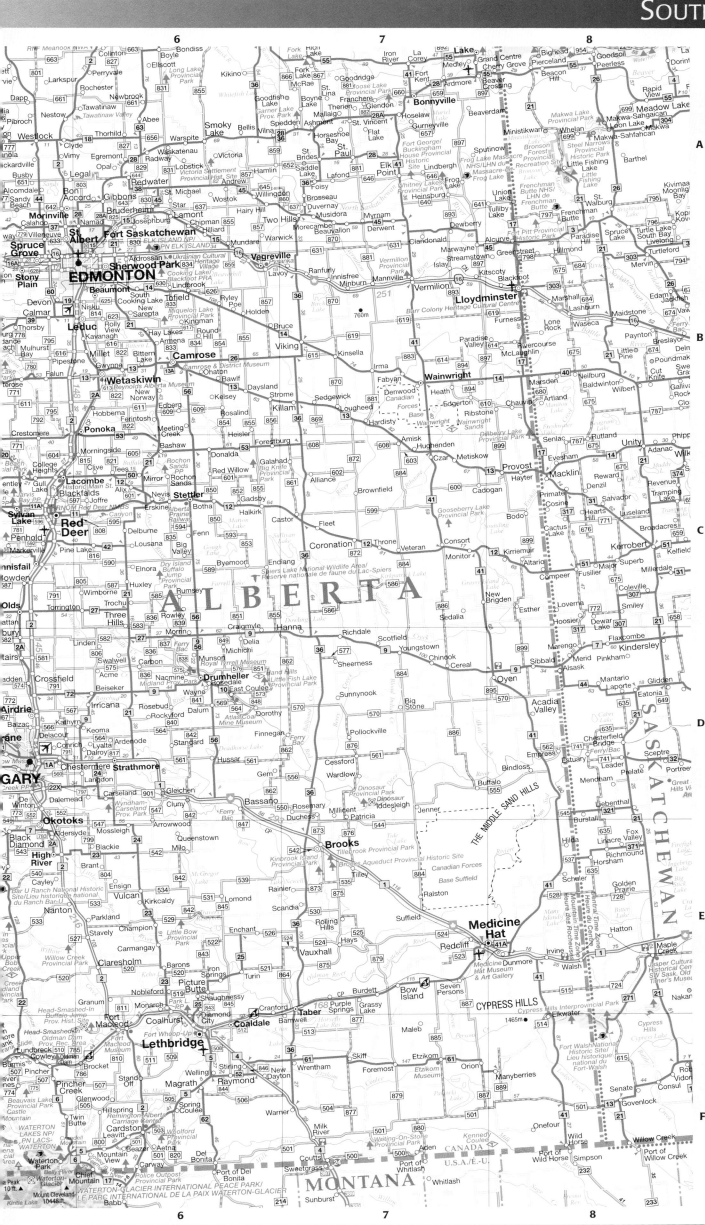

LAKES IN THE TRENCH

The Rocky Mountain Trench is a 1,600-km-long valley, which extends through British Columbia from just below the Canada-United States border into the Yukon. The damming of rivers to produce hydroelectric power covered large areas of the valley with long, linear lakes, such as Kinbasket Lake (shown above). Williston Lake, farther north, is also a trench lake. Kinbasket Lake lies behind Mica Dam, which confines the flow of Columbia River (lower left). Towering over Kinbasket Lake are the Columbia (left) and Rocky Mountains. The Rocky Mountain Trench marks the Rockies' western boundary.

Other points of interest

■ Banff, Jasper, Kootenay, and Yoho are the four national parks [B2-E4] that make up the Canadian Rocky Mountain Parks, a United Nations World Heritage Site. Also part of this site are three adjacent B.C. provincial parks: Hamber [C3], Mount Assiniboine [D4], and Mount Robson [B2].

■ The Columbia Icefield [C3], covering an area of 230 km² at a depth of up to 365 m, is the largest accumulation of glacial ice in the Rocky Mountains. It is called "the mother of rivers" because its meltwaters feed the North Saskatchewan, Columbia, Athabasca, and Fraser river systems. It contains some 30 glaciers. The Athabasca Glacier [C3], adjacent to the Icefields Parkway in Jasper National Park, is one of the largest.

■ In Yoho National Park [D4], the Burgess Shale Site preserves the fossils of some 120 species of marine creatures, dating back 515 million years. The site was discovered in 1909 by American paleontologist Charles Walcott.

Scale 1:2,000,000

1 cm = 20 km

0 20 40 60 80 km

BANFF NATIONAL PARK

YOHO NATIONAL PARK / PARC NATIONAL YOHO

KOOTENAY NATIONAL PARK / PARC NATIONAL KOOTENAY

Mount Willingdon 3873m
Wapiti Mountain 3028m
Panther Mountain 2943m
Mount St. Bride 3316m
Crowfoot Glacier
Mosquito Creek
Twin Falls Tea House National Historic Site / Lieu historique national du Salon-de-Thé-des-Chutes-Twin
Kicking Horse Pass National Historic Site / Lieu historique national du Col-Kicking-Horse
Canadian Rocky Mountain Parks / Parcs des montagnes Rocheuses canadiennes
Skoki Ski Lodge National Historic Site / Lieu historique national de l'Auberge-de-Ski-Skoki
Lake Louise
Field
Abbot Pass Refuge Cabin Nat'l. Hist. Site / Lieu hist. nat. du Refuge-du-Col-Abbot
Moraine Lake
Deltaform Mtn. 3424m
Mount Goodsir 3581m
Hoodoo Creek
Wapta Falls
Monarch
Marble Canyon
Paint Pots
Protection Mountain
Castle Mountain
Johnston Canyon
Banff Park Museum National Historic Site / Lieu historique national du Musée-du-Parc-Banff
Mt. Brett 2984m
Cave & Basin National Historic Site / lieu historique national Cave & Basin
Vermilion Crossing
Mt. Norquay
Tunnel Mountain
Banff
Canmore
Canmore Nordic Centre Provincial Park
Sunshine Village
Mount Assiniboine Provincial Park / Parc National
Mt. Assiniboine 3618m
Mt. Allan 2816m
Nakiska
Kananaskis Village
Mt. Sir Douglas 3406m
Mt. King George 3457m
Fisher Peak 3063m
Elbow-Sheep Wildland Provincial Park
Peter Lougheed Provincial Park
Mt. Marconi 3106m
Mt. Fisher 2846m
Mt. Taylor 2250m
Mt. Haig 2611m
Gilnockie Mtn.
Yahk Mtn. 2180m
Teepee Mtn. 2797m

ROCKY MOUNTAIN FOOTHILLS / CONTREFORTS

ROCKY MOUNTAINS / MONTAGNES ROCHEUSES DES ROCHEUSES

PURCELL MOUNTAINS

Continental Divide / Ligne de partage des eaux
Height of the Rockies Provincial Park

BRITISH COLUMBIA / COLOMBIE-BRITANNIQUE
EAST KOOTENAY

ALBERTA

Kananaskis Country

Kootenay Valley Viewpoint

Castledale
Harrogate
Spillimacheen
Brisco
Edgewater
Radium Hot Springs
Redstreak
Dry Gulch Provincial Park
Wilmer
Athalmer
Invermere
Windermere
Panorama
Toby Creek
Mt. Toby 3212m
Fairmont Hot Springs
Columbia Lake Provincial Park
Thunder Hill Provincial Park
Canal Flats
James Chabot Provincial Park
Windermere Lake
Crooks Meadow
Dolly Varden
McLeod Meadows
Shuswap
Skookumchuck
Premier Lake Provincial Park
Whiteswan Lake Provincial Park
Top Of The World Provincial Park
Elkford
Tornado Mountain 3099m
Oldman River North
Upper Bob Creek
Bob Creek Wildland Provincial Park
Racehorse Creek
Maycroft
Dutch Creek
Wasa Lake Provincial Park
Ta Ta Creek
Wasa
Kimberley
Marysville
Meachen
Wycliffe
Fort Steele
Fort Steele Turn-of-the-Century Town
Canadian Mus. of Rail Travel
Jimsmith Lake Provincial Park
Norbury Lake Provincial Park
Mount Fernie Provincial Park
Sparwood
Natal
Michel
Chinook
Crowsnest Provincial Park
Island Lake
Hosmer
Corbin
Fernie
Baker
Bull River
Cranbrook
Lumberton
Moyie Lake Provincial Park
Wardner
Wardner Provincial Park
Jaffray
Galloway
Morrissey
Morrissey Provincial Park
Caithness
Elko
Lumberton
Kianuko Provincial Park
Moyie
Kikomun Creek Provincial Park
Baynes Lake
Grasmere
Newgate
Roosville
Flathead
Wynndel
Arrow Creek
Kitchener
Ryan
Goatfell
Erickson
Canyon
Curzon
Glenlily
Yahk
Yahk Provincial Park
Ryan Provincial Park
Lister
Kingsgate
Eastport
IDAHO

McGILLIVRAY RANGE
MacDONALD RANGE
BORDER RANGES

Crowsnest Pass
Coleman
Frank
Lee
Blairmore
Bellevue
Hillcrest Mines
Burmis
Cowley
Lundbreck
Lundbreck Falls
Frank Slide Prov. Hist. Site
Leitch Collieries Provincial Historic Site
Castle River
Beaver Mines
Pincher
Pincher Creek
Gladstone Valley
Beaver Mines Lake
Beauvais Lake Provincial Park
Castle Mountain
Mt. Haig
Waterton Lakes National Park / Parc National les Lacs-Waterton
Akamina-Kishinena Provincial Recreation Area
First Oil Well in Western Canada National Historic Site / Premier Puits de Pétrole dans l'Ouest Canadien
Waterton-Glacier International Peace Park / Le Parc International de la Paix Waterton-Glacier
Crandell
Waterton Park
Townsite
Police Outpost Provincial Park

CANADA
U.S.A. / É.-U.

Sundre
Sundre Pioneer Village Museum
Olds
Westward Ho
Harmattan
Minaret
Bearberry
Mound
Eagle Hill
Mayton
Torrington
Curlew
Trochu
Equity
Three Hills
Wimborne
Westerdale
Shantz
Elkton
Didsbury
Neapolis
Sunnyslope
Linden
Swalwell
Acme
Bircham
Grainger
Cremona
Garfield
Carstairs
Crump
Stirlingville
Water Valley
Dogpound
Madden
Crossfield
Collicutt
Kersey
Beiseker
Bottrell
Waiparous
Big Hill Springs Provincial Park
Airdrie
Irricana
Craigdu
Kathyrn
Keoma
Nightingale
Tudor
Dalroy
Ardenode
Waterton
North Ghost
Ghost River Provincial Wilderness Area
Ghost River
Ghost Lake
Morleyville
Morley
Mitford
Cochrane
Cochrane Ranche Provincial Historic Site
Glenbow
Symons Valley
Olympic Park
Balzac
Delacour
Lyalta
Interlake
Conrich
CALGARY
Glenbow Museum
Chestermere
Cheadle
Strathmore
Namaka
Langdon
Indus
Shepard
Redwood Meadows
Bragg Creek
Bragg Creek Provincial Park
Elk Valley
Priddis
Brown Lowery Provincial Park
Fish Creek Provincial Park
Academy
De Winton
Dalemead
Carseland
Strangmuir
Stobart
Wyndham-Carseland Provincial Park
Millarville
Turner Valley
Turner Valley Gas Plant Provincial Historic Site
Black Diamond
Hartell
Sheep River Provincial Park
Bluerock Wildland Provincial Park
Okotoks
Aldersyde
Gladys
Mossleigh
Mazeppa
Blackie
Herronton
Arrowwood
Longview
High River
Brant
Azure
Ensign
Don Getty Wildland Provincial Park
Highwood House
Mount Burke 2540m
Plateau Mountain
Pekisko
Cayley
Vulcan
Bar U Ranch National Historic Site / Lieu historique national du Ranch-Bar-U
Nanton
Durward
Parkland
Champion
Chain Lakes Provincial Park
Forestry Trunk Road
Livingstone Falls
Willow Creek Provincial Park
Stavely
Claresholm
Woodhouse
Granum
Furman
Head-Smashed-In Buffalo Jump Provincial Historic Site
Spring Point
Fort Macleod
Fort Macleod Museum
Oldman River Reservoir
Oldman Dam Provincial Recreation Area
Oldman Dam
Brocket
Brockio
Pincher Creek
Ardenville
Pearce
Orton
Kirkcaldy
Durward
Nanton
Twin Butte
Pecten
Fishburn
Glenwood
Hartleyville
Hillspring
Parkbend
Mountain View
Leavitt
Aetna
Beazer
Cardston
Carway
Remington-Alberta Carriage Centre
St. Mary Reservoir
Raley

Highways: 93, 95, 95A, 1, 1A, 1X, 40, 68, 66, 22, 2, 3, 5, 6, 27

IN THE BADLANDS

For some 300 km, the windswept, weathered, and eroded terrain of the Alberta Badlands flanks the Red Deer River. In this view, the river snakes through a section of the arid, barren valley just west of Drumheller. Little Fish Lake Provincial Park (upper right) and the Finnegan Field Wetlands (lower left) brighten the scene with patches of vegetation. Once the domain of dinosaurs, this Badlands region abounds with the remains of these ancient creatures. Drumheller's famed Royal Tyrrell Museum of Palaeontology reveals fine examples, unearthed locally.

Other points of interest

■ Waterton Lakes National Park [F4], with an area of 525 km², embraces different natural environments ranging from rolling grasslands to snowcapped peaks, almost 3,000 m high. Its features include the three Waterton lakes. Upper Waterton Lake, at a depth of more than 150 m, is the deepest in the Rockies.

■ Big Rock, 7 km west of Okotoks [C4], is the world's largest glacial erratic. This 18,000-tonne quartzite boulder, measuring 40 x 18 x 9 m, was thought to have been carried from Jasper by advancing glaciers during the last ice age.

■ More than 500 skeletal remains of 50 dinosaur species have been discovered in Dinosaur Provincial Park [C7]. The park's most ancient fossil find dates back 77 million years.

■ Once described by Rudyard Kipling as the "City With All Hell for a Basement," Medicine Hat [D8] sits atop a natural gas field occupying 390 km². This field produces over 5 million cubic meters of natural gas daily.

Scale 1:1,000,000

1 cm = 10 km

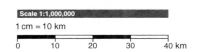

0   10   20   30   40 km

1   **2**   **3**   **4**   **5**

SWAN HILLS

A

Forestry Trunk Road

Iosegun Lake

Smoke Lake

Fox Creek

Kaybob

Freeman Lake

Swan Hills

33

Freeman River

Trapper Lea's

32

Freeman River

661

Dori

Fort Assir Sandhills Provincia

Fort Assinboine

658

Lone Pine

33

763

Tiger Lily

B

43

947

341

43

32

Whitecourt

43

55

Lonira

658

Blue Ridge

Connor Creek

Peavine

Mystery Lake

655

Tiger Lake

18

763

Car

Thunder Lake Provincial Park

18

Benbow Junction

Benbow

Glenister

Green Court

16

18

757

Mayerthorpe

654

Cosmo

Mea

Mahaska

32

Rochfort Bridge

Pembridge

Ba

Haddock

Highway

Anselmo

647

Sangudo

43

764

Lisburn

Cherhill

Gle

C

Little Sundance Creek

Sundance Provincial Park

Pioneer

McLeod Valley

Hattonford

22

Rangeton

757

Stanger

Park Court

748

748

FerryBac

Rosevear

Peers

Niton

MacKay

Ravine

Pembina River Provincial Park

633

Darwel

Obed

Obed Lake Provincial Park

75

Marlboro

Wolf Creek

Yates

Carrot Creek

59

Nojack

Chip Lake

Evansburg

16A

Magnolia

Gainford

Rock Lake

Obed

16

Hargwen

Galloway

Bickerdike

Edson

32

16

366

Niton Junction

Nojack

Wildwood

Entwistle

22

31

Seba Beach

William A. Switzer Provincial Park

Pedley

McLeod River

753

Moon Lake

759

Horen

Water's Edge

Rock Lake-Solomon Creek Wildland Provincial Park

40

A L B E R T A

D

Entrance

Hinton

Fickle Lake

Erith

627

Brûlé

47

Weald

Minnow Lake

Tomahawk

Northleigh

624

Lambert Creek

McLeod River

Wolf Lake West

Cynthia

621

Round Valley

Rocky Rapids

759

Lindale

Pocahontas

Pocahontas

40

Robb

Coalspur

Coalspur

Poplar Ridge

Drayton Valley

39

Jasper House Nat'l Hist. Site/ Lieu hist. nat. Jasper House

16

Miette Hot Springs

Mercoal

Coal Branch Historic Area

22

Carnwood

Watson Creek

Violet Grove

620

Luscar

Lovett River

Pembina

Buck Creek

616

Snaring River

Henry House National Historic Site/ Lieu historique national/Henry House

Cadomin

78

Fidler

40

Foothills

Lodgepole

620

761

Buck Calhoun Bay

Jasper Park Information Centre National Historic Site/ Lieu historique national du Centre d'Accueil-du-Parc-Jasper

Whitehorse Wildland Provincial Park

Fairfax Lake

Pembina Forks

Brazeau Reservoir

Buck Lake

761

Per

id ain n

Jasper

Mountain Park

Elk River

Brazeau Dam

Brazeau Reservoir

Alder Flats

13

E

Whistlers

Wapiti

Sirdar Mountain 2804m

Medicine Lake

Brazeau River

22

93

JASPER NATIONAL PARK

R O C K Y

Basin

Wabasso

93A

Mt. Balinhard 3130m

Brazeau Canyon Wildland Provincial Park

Brown Creek

Medicine Lake

Mt. Edith Cavell 3363m

Malingne Lake

Canadian Rocky Mountain Parks/ Parcs des montagnes Rocheuses canadiennes

Marshybank

1151m

C O N T R E F O R T S

Willesde Green

Mt. Kerkeslin

PARC NATIONAL JASPER

Blackstone

734

Mt. Fryatt 3361m

Honeymoon Lake

Mt. Brazeau 3470m

Upper Shunda Creek

Harlech

Shunda Viewpoint

Jackfish Lake

Highway

Crimson Lake Provincial Park

Frisco

Sunwapta Falls

93

Thompson

Beaverdam

11

12

R O C K Y   M O U N T A I N S

Highway Subject to Periodic Winter Closings

Jonas Creek

Fish Lake

Nordegg

Saunders

Chambers Creek

Crimson Lake

Bingley

M O U N T A I N

Goldeye Lake

David

Horburg

756

Codner

598

Stanley Falls

11

Dry Haven

Aylmer

Horburg

Rocky Mountain House

11A

Ferrier

Garth

Alhambra

F

M O N T A G N E S   R O C H E U S E S

Athabasca Pass National Historic Site/ Lieu historique national/Col-Athabasca

Crescent Falls

D E S

Rocky Mountain House National Historic Site/ Lieu historique national Rocky Mountain House

752

Dovercourt

Hamber Provincial Park

Mount Alberta 3619m

White Goat Provincial Wilderness Area

Abraham Lake

734

North Ram River

Prairie Creek

Congresbury

22

Columbia Icefield

Mount Michener 2337m

South Fork

Mitchell Lake

Cheddarville

Cummins Lake Provincial Park

Clemenceau Icefield

Mount Columbia 3747m

Athabasca Glacier Viewing Area Columbia Icefield

F O O T H I L L S

Swan Lake

BRITISH COLUMBIA

Tsar Mountain 3424m

93

Mount Amery 3329m

Kootenay Plains

Ram Falls

Phyllis Lake

Caroline

22

COLOMBIE-BRITANNIQUE

Rampart Creek

229

11

Kootenay Plains

Peppers Lake

Elk Creek

Seven Mile

591

Tay River

Kinbasket Lake

Saskatchewan River Crossing

Saskatchewan River Crossing

Thompson Creek

Limestone Mountain 2252m

Crammond

Mistaya Canyon

Siffleur Provincial Wilderness Area

734

Jar

Waterfowl Lake

1   **2**   **3**   **4**

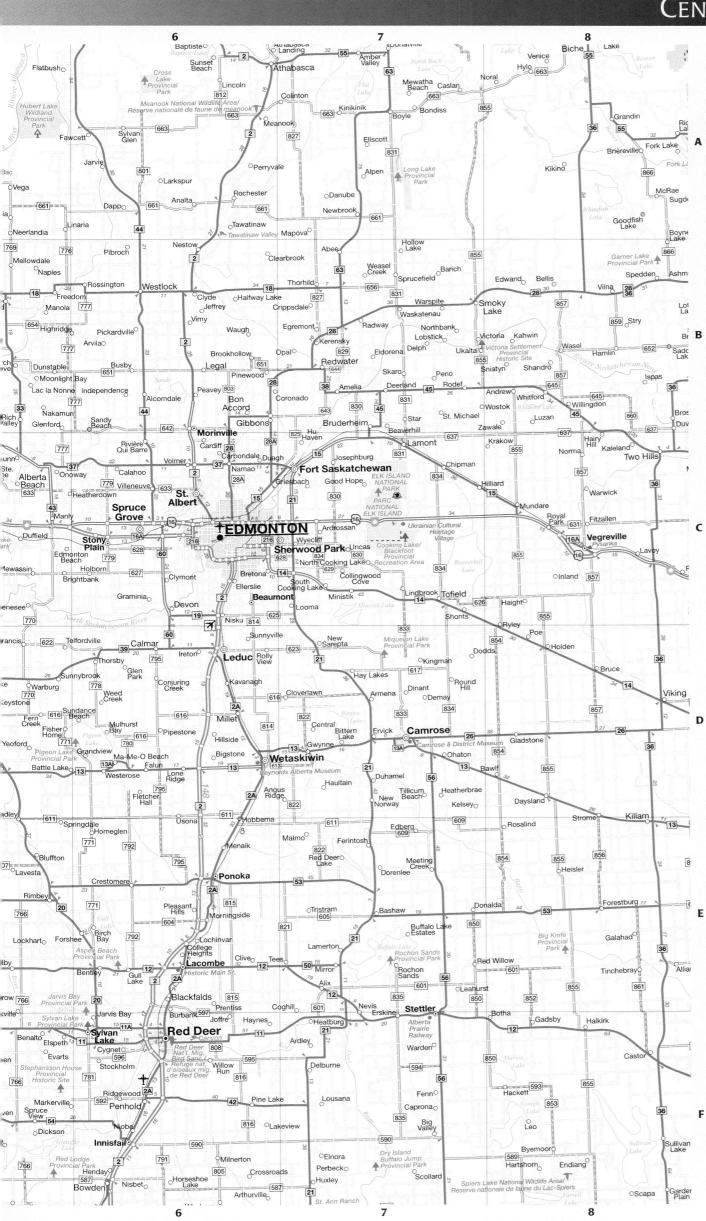

FROM PARK TO PRAIRIE

This view of Jasper National Park shows the wide scenic valley just north of the park townsite. The Trans-Canada Yellowhead Highway (Highway 16) runs between Jasper and Talbot lakes (lower right) and, farther on, along the banks of the Athabasca River. At the gap in the Rockies, the Yellowhead exits the park, passes Brulé Lake (left), and heads toward the horizon on the Prairies. The bold shape of Roche Miette (right centre) hides Fiddle Valley, where a road leads to one of Jasper's popular attractions, the Miette Hot Springs.

Other points of interest

■ Elk Island National Park [C7] is a 194-km² wildlife refuge. It is the only national park completely surrounded by a fence. The fenced boundary prevents park animals—elk, bison, moose, and deer—from straying, and stops predators—wolves and bears—from entering. Because the elk population increases at a rate of 20 percent per year, the management of the herd involves relocating excess numbers to other parts of Canada and the United States. Elk Island also preserves a remnant of Alberta's Beaver Hills.

■ On Feb. 13, 1947, "black gold" gushed from the Leduc No. 1 Oilwell site, located several kilometres north of Leduc [D6]. The Imperial Oil crew drilled 133 dry wells before it struck oil at a depth of 1,771 m, finally tapping the 300-million-barrel Leduc oil field. A plaque at the site commemorates the event. The oil derricks are long since gone as oilmen seek new sources underground or in Alberta's oil-rich tar sands.

Scale 1:1,000,000

1 cm = 10 km

0 10 20 30 40 km

NORTHWEST TERRITORIES — TERRITOIRES DU NO

60th Parallel Territorial Park

BRITISH COLUMBIA

COLOMBIE-BRITANNIQUE

INTERIOR PLAINS — PLAINES DE L'INTÉRIEUR

CAMERON HILLS

Indian Cabins

Steen River

Lutose

Caribou Mountains Wildland Provincial Park

CARIBOU MOUNTAINS

Zama City

Slavey Creek

Meander River

Mackenzie

•1022m

Thinahtea Provincial Protected Area

Pacific Time Zone Heure du Pacifique
Mountain Time Zone Heure des Rocheuses

Kotcho Lake Village Site Provincial Park

•735m

Fort Nelson Heritage Museum
Old Fort Nelson
Fort Nelson

Andy Bailey Provincial Park

97

Sikanni Old Growth Provincial Park

Klua Lakes Provincial Protected Area

Prophet River

Habay

Hay-Zama Lakes Wildland Provincial Park

Chateh (Assumption)

Tugate
Hutch Lake
35
High Level
MacKenzie Crossroads Museum

Rocky Lane
North Vermilion
Fort Vermilion
Boyer
58

John D'or Prairie

Fox

Rainbow Lake

58

Machesis Lake

La Crete

88

Milligan Hills Provincial Park

Horse River Provincial Park

Beatton River

Pink Mountain

•1082m

Paddle Prairie
Ferry Bac
Buffalo Head Prairie

Keg River
695
Carcajou

Prespatou

Altona

Chinchaga Wildland Provincial Park

Kemp River
128

Twin Lakes
35
Twin Lakes
692
Notikewin Provincial Park

BUFFALO HEAD HILLS

•738m

97

Buick

Wonowon

•1120m

CLEAR HILLS

Running Lake

Sulphur Lake

Hotchkiss
741

Notikewin
691
Manning

North Star
Deadwood
690
35

88

ALBE

Rose Prairie

Montney
North Pine

Beatton Provincial Park
Beatton River Provincial Park

Worsley

Eureka River
730
726

Dixonville
743

Chinook Valley

Cadotte Lake
986
Little Buffalo

Red Earth Creek
Loon Lake
Trout Lake

Peerl Lake
686

Charlie Lake Provincial Park
29
Charlie Lake
Fort St. John
Baldonnel
Cecil Lake

Hudson's Hope

Peace River Corridor Historic Museum

Taylor
Clayhurst

Goodlow
Cleardale
Ole's Lake
64
717
Bear Canyon
Silver Valley
120

Hines Creek
64
685

Queen Elizabeth Provincial Park
737
986

Peace River
2A
688
Grimshaw
St. Isidore
684
685
Berwyn

Greene Valley Provincial Park

Atikameg
Gift Lake
Atikamisis Lake

Hudson's Hope

Moberly Lake

PEACE RIVER VALLEY

Cherry Point
729
735
732
Whitelaw
Bluesky
2
Brownvale
683
Marie-Reine
Nampa
744
Reno

Jean Côté

Doe River
681
Silver Valley
725
Blueberry Mountain
680
Dunvegan
Historic Fort Dunvegan
64A
Fairview
740

Moberly Lake Provincial Park
29

Sunset Prairie
Farmington

Bonanza
Rolla

Moonshine Lake Provincial Park

Dunvegan Provincial Park

Chetwynd
97
East Pine Provincial Park
Arras
Progress
Groundbirch
Dawson Creek
49
719
Gordondale
105
727
Rycroft
Spirit River
739
Tangent
Girouxville
Falher
750

Eaglesham
Watino
49
McLennan
2
Donnelly

Pouce Coupe
Bay Tree
1033m
Wanham
104

Heart River
Salt Prairie
Big Prairie
Grouard Mission
Native Culture Arts Museum
Lesser Slave Lake

Pine River Breaks PP
Lone Prairie
52
2
Tomslake
731
Woking
733
Peoria
744
Guy
Kathleen
679
Grouard
Marten Beach

Tupper
Demmitt
Valhalla Centre
724
677
677
676
49
2A
High Prairie
88

Sudeten Provincial Park
59
La Glace
Buffalo Lake
Teepee Creek
2
Enilda
Winagami Lake Provincial Park
Joussard
Canyon Creek
Widewater

43
Hythe
672
Sexsmith
674
733
676
DeBolt
747
Kinuso

Lymburn
Goodfare
671
723
Saskatoon Island PP
Clairmont
670
Goodwin Corner
Bezanson
736
New Fish Creek
669
Driftpile
Faust
Slave Lake

Gwillim Lake Provincial Park
One Island Lake Provincial Park
Kelly Lake
667
Beaverlodge
Huallen
2
Grande Prairie
43
Ridgevalley
Crooked Creek
Young's Point Provincial Park
Sunset House
Valleyview
33

Bearhole Lake Provincial Park
52
Elmworth
722
Wembley
Flyingshot
668
Grande Prairie Pioneer Museum
Sturgeon Heights
Williamson Provincial Park
Calais
665
43
747
Grizzly Ridge Wildland Provincial Park

Tumbler Ridge

Bullmoose Mountain 2020m

Hole-in-the-Wall Provincial Park

Grovedale
666
O'Brien Provincial Park

House Mtn. 1067m

Wallace Mountain 1259m

Monkman Provincial Park

Arctic-Pacific Lakes Provincial Park
Wapiti Lake Provincial Park
Ice Mountain 2286m

40
Musreau Lake
Kakwa River

Little Smoky

Goose Mountain

SWAN HILLS
Freeman Lake
Swan Hills
32

Chrystina Lake

Hubert Lake Wildla

Sentinel Peak 2499m

Mountain Time Zone Heure des Rocheuses
Pacific Time Zone Heure du Pacifique

Nose Lake

Twin Lakes

Bison Flats

245

Waskahigan River

Joseguri Lake

Trapper Lea's

Fort Assiniboine Sandhills Wildland Provincial Park

Fox Creek
211
Lone
661
Fort

AN INLAND DELTA

The Peace-Athabasca Delta occupies an area of 3,200 km², which contains meadows, marshes, and lakes. This sprawling wetland is the world's largest inland delta. Much of it lies within the southeastern corner of Wood Buffalo, Canada's largest national park, which covers 44,802 km². This view shows parts of the region's largest lakes, Claire (left) and Athabasca (right). The Peace-Athabasca Delta really consists of three deltas—those of the Peace, Athabasca, and Birch rivers. The Peace River delta is the river's junction with the Slave River (top). The largest delta, the Athabasca, has filled the west end of Lake Athabasca. Before reaching the delta, the Athabasca River winds past dunes (lower left) and Richardson Lake. The delta of the Birch River [B6] expands into Lake Claire, which, in turn, empties into Lake Athabasca. The Peace-Athabasca Delta is a key intersection of North America's four migratory bird flyways.

Other points of interest

■ Athabasca Dunes [A7-B8] and Richardson River Dunes Wildland Provincial Park [B7-C7] contain the largest area of actively migrating sand in Alberta, and are part of Canada's largest dune field. The dunes, said to be 8,000 years old, are 7 km long and 1.5 km wide. Some of the dunes reach heights of 35 m. The dunes are moving in a southeast direction at a rate of 1.5 m per year.

■ Near Fort McMurray [D7], the Athabasca Oil Sands is one of the world's great oil deposits. The oil sands cover some 77,000 km², equivalent to the area of New Brunswick. Reserves are estimated to be about 300 billion barrels.

Scale 1:2,000,000

1 cm = 20 km

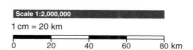

0   20   40   60   80 km

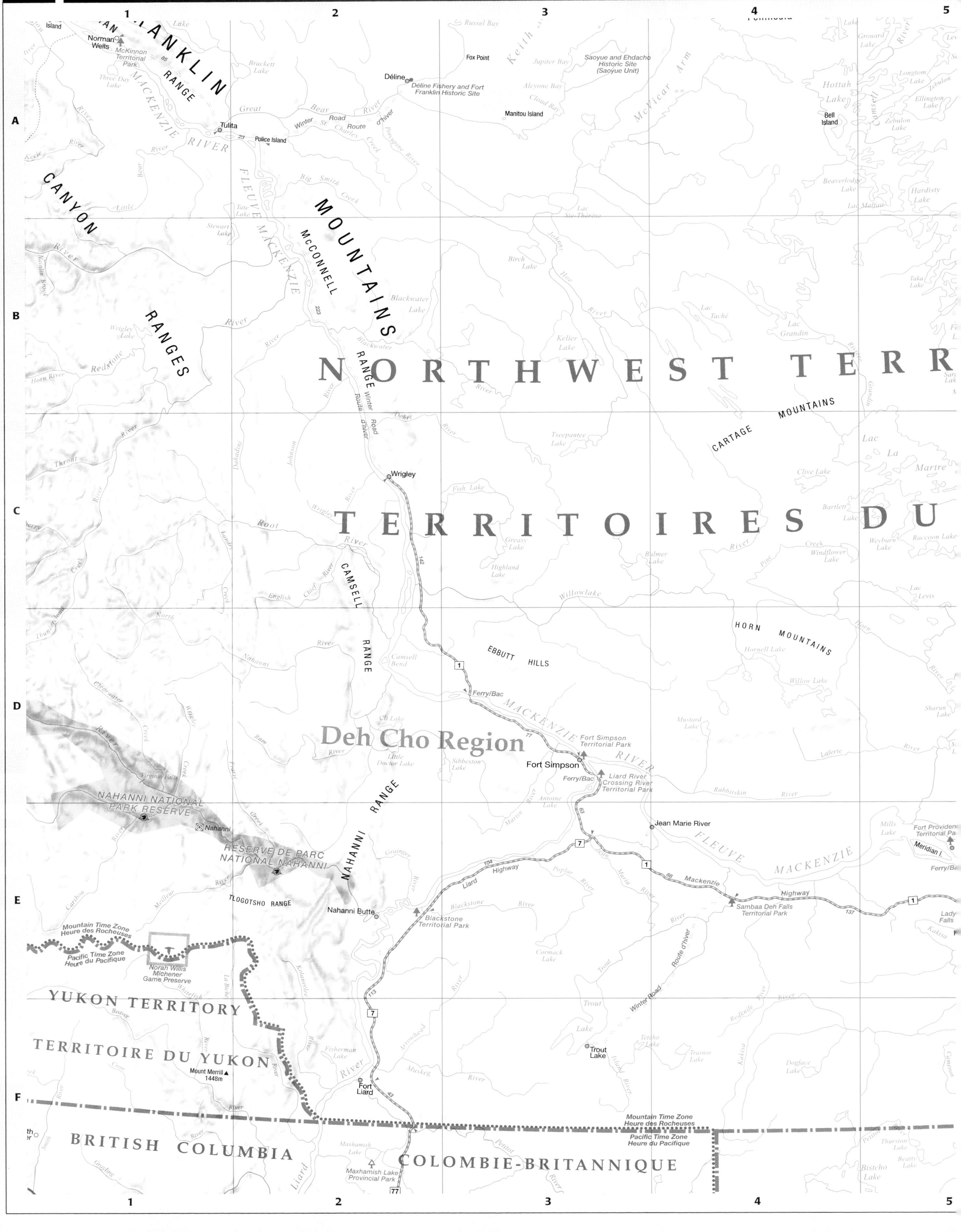

NORTHWEST TERR

TERRITOIRES DU

Deh Cho Region

FRANKLIN RANGE

MACKENZIE RANGE

CANYON RANGES

McCONNELL MOUNTAINS

FLEUVE MACKENZIE

CARTAGE MOUNTAINS

HORN MOUNTAINS

CAMSELL RANGE

EBBUTT HILLS

NAHANNI NATIONAL PARK RESERVE

RÉSERVE DE PARC NATIONAL NAHANNI

TLOGOTSHO RANGE

NAHANNI RANGE

Norah Willis Michener Game Preserve

Mountain Time Zone
Heure des Rocheuses

Pacific Time Zone
Heure du Pacifique

YUKON TERRITORY

TERRITOIRE DU YUKON

Mount Merrill
1448m

BRITISH COLUMBIA

COLOMBIE-BRITANNIQUE

Maxhamish Lake
Provincial Park

Mountain Time Zone
Heure des Rocheuses

Pacific Time Zone
Heure du Pacifique

MACKENZIE RIVER

FLEUVE MACKENZIE

Island

Norman Wells

McKinnon Territorial Park

Three Day Lake

Tulita

Police Island

Brackett Lake

Great Bear Lake

Déline

Déline Fishery and Fort Franklin Historic Site

Fox Point

Russel Bay

Jupiter Bay

Alcyone Bay

Cloud Bay

Manitou Island

Saoyue and Ehdacho Historic Site (Saoyue Unit)

Keith

McVicar Arm

Hottah Lake

Bell Island

Beaverlodge Lake

Lac Maunoir

Hardisty Lake

Winter Road
Route d'hiver

Smith Creek

Tate Lake

Stewart Lake

Wrigley Lake

Redstone River

Horn River

Little

Blackwater Lake

Birch Lake

Keller Lake

Lac Taché

Lac Grandin

Blackwater River

Fish Lake

Wrigley

Greasy Lake

Highland Lake

Bulmer Lake

Windflower Lake

Clive Lake

Bartlet Lake

Weyburn Lake

Raccoon Lake

Lac Levis

Throat River

English River

Camsell River

North River

Nahanni River

Willowlake River

Hornell Lake

Willow Lake

Ferry/Bac

Camsell Bend

Old Lake

MACKENZIE RIVER

Mustard Lake

Sharun Lake

Fort Simpson Territorial Park

Fort Simpson

Little Doctor Lake

Sibbeston Lake

Ferry/Bac

Liard River Crossing River Territorial Park

Antoine Lake

Laferte River

Rabbitskin River

Jean Marie River

Mills Lake

Fort Providence Territorial Park

Meridian I.

Ferry/Bac

Virginia Falls

Nahanni

Grainger River

Martin River

Mackenzie Highway

Sambaa Deh Falls Territorial Park

Lady Falls

Blackstone Territorial Park

Nahanni Butte

Liard Highway

Blackstone River

Poplar River

Cormack Lake

Trout Lake

Trout River

Fisherman Lake

Arrowhead River

Muskeg River

Trout Lake

Teetoo Lake

Tronnor Lake

Dogface Lake

Fort Liard

La Biche River

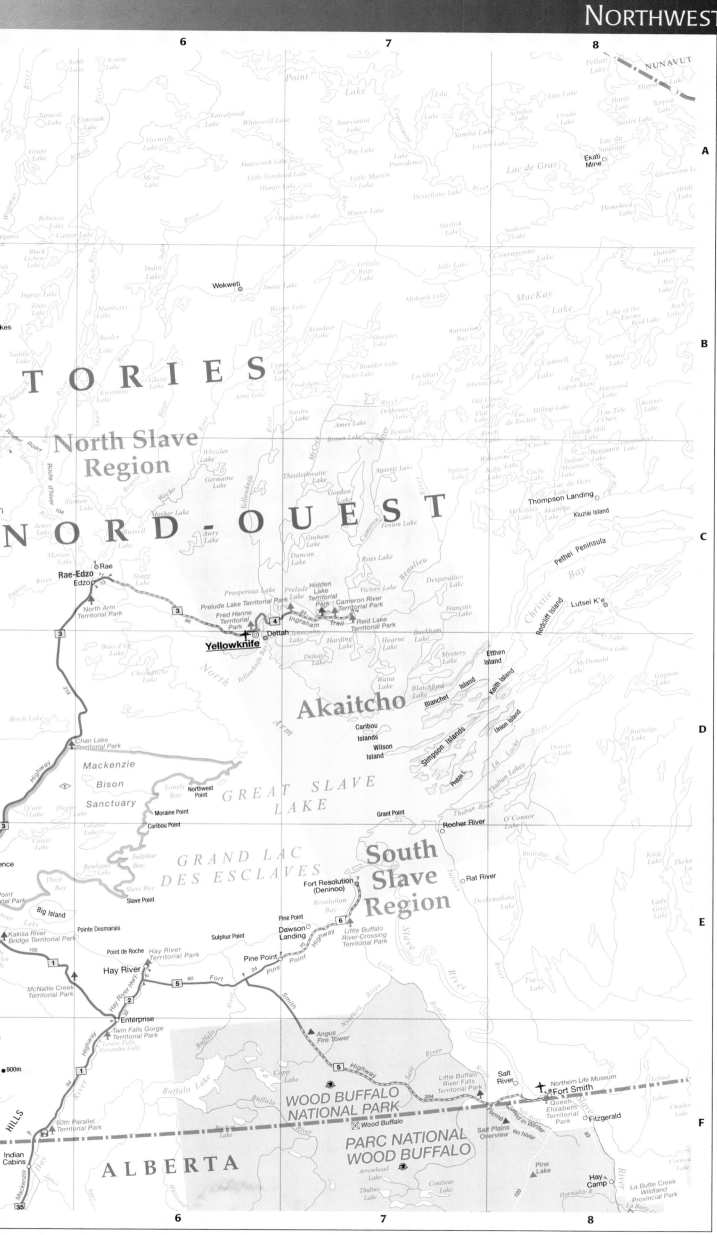

THE DEEPEST LAKE

At 28,568 km², Great Slave Lake is Canada's fourth largest and the world's eleventh largest lake. It is also Canada's deepest lake, reaching a maximum depth of 614 m. The forests of the Boreal Shield extend as far as the southern shore of the lake. But most of the region around the lake is a transition zone where the Shield gives way to the sparser vegetation of the taiga. This view shows island-congested Christie Bay at the entrance to the East Arm (right), which has been proposed as the site of a national park. Yellowknife, the capital of the Northwest Territories and its largest city, is visible at the head of Yellowknife Bay on the North Arm (upper left). In the jumble of lakes and woods northwest of Yellowknife lie the world's most ancient rocks—granites that formed more than 3.96 billion years ago.

Other points of interest

■ The 320-km-long South Nahanni River runs through 4,700-km² Nahanni National Park Reserve [D1-E2]. The turbulent river rushes through three huge canyons more than 1,000 m deep and plunges over 90-m Virginia Falls. Other natural features of this remote park include hot springs and icy caves.

■ In 1985, geologists found kimberlites—ancient volcanic formations containing diamonds—at Lac de Gras [A8] in the treeless tundra of the Northwest Territories. Six years later, Ekati Mine, the first Canadian diamond mine, announced the discovery of substantial deposits in this region. The news started one of the largest staking rushes in Canadian history. Ekati Mine now produces between 3 million and 5 million carats of diamonds per year.

Scale 1:2,000,000

1 cm = 20 km

0   20   40   60   80 km

1
2
3
4
5
A
B
C
D
E
F
ALBERTA
SASKATCH
MONTANA
CANADA
U.S.A./É.-U.
TOOLE
LIBERTY
Lloydminster
North Battleford
SASKATOON
Prince Albe
Swift Current
Medicine Hat
Moose Jaw
Brooks
Vegreville
Wainwright
Kindersley
Rosetown
Biggar
Maple Creek
Shaunavon
Assiniboia
Gravelbourg
Oyen
Hanna
Coronation
Vermilion
Meadow Lake
Bonnyville
Unity
Outlook
PRINCE ALBERT NATIONAL PARK
PARC NATIONAL DE PRINCE ALBERT
GRASSLANDS NATIONAL PARK/
PARC NATIONAL DES PRAIRIES
CYPRESS HILLS
THE GREAT SAND HILLS
THE MIDDLE SAND HILLS
COTEAU HILLS
BAD HILLS
Canadian Forces Base Suffield
Mountain Time Zone
Heure des Rocheuses
Central Time Zone
Heure du Centre

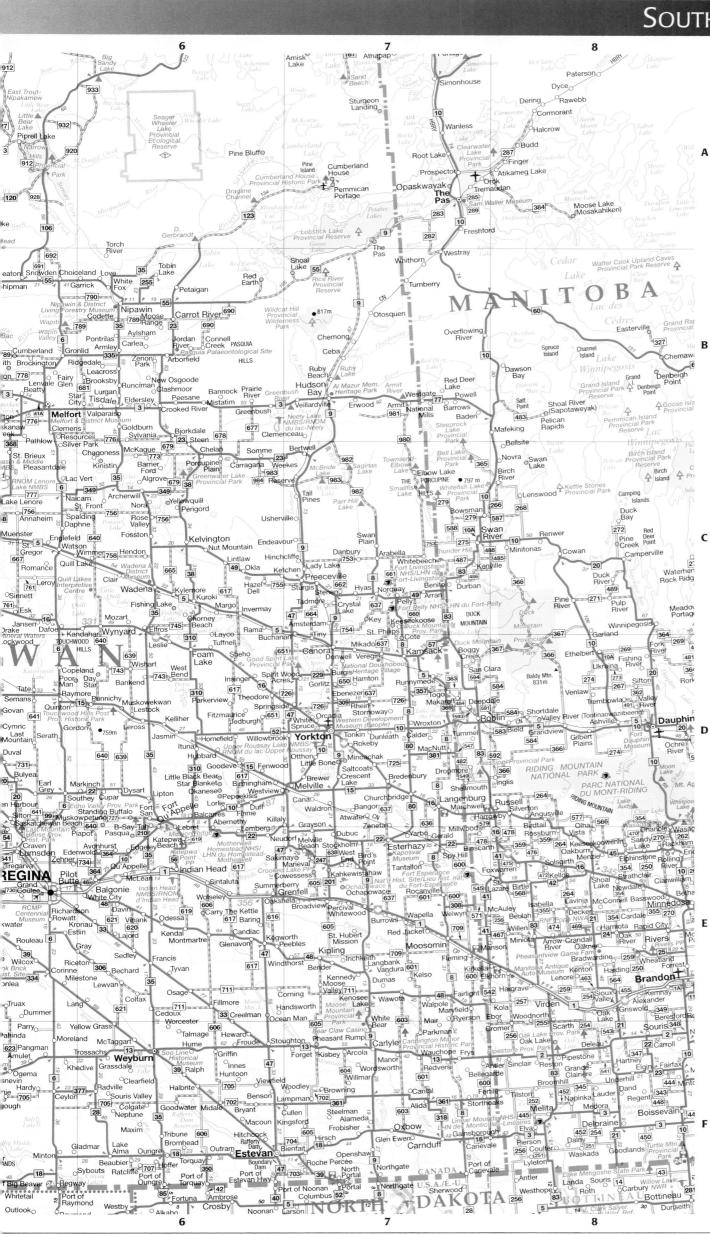

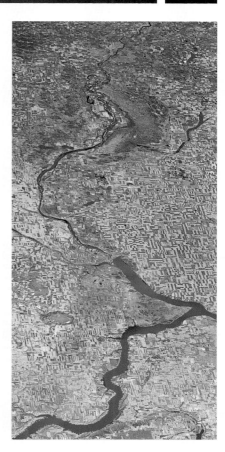

A PRAIRIE RESERVOIR

The serpentine shape of Lake Diefenbaker, some 220 km long but never more than 2 to 3 km wide, stands out indelibly in the patchwork prairie landscape of south-central Saskatchewan. This man-made reservoir, the fifth largest in Canada, stores 94 million cubic metres of water, collected from the east-flowing South Saskatchewan River. The earth-fill Gardiner Dam, 5 km wide and 64 m high, is clearly visible at the top of Lake Diefenbaker's north arm. The dam generates hydroelectric power, supplies 45 percent of Saskatchewan's drinking water, and irrigates some 43,000 ha of the farmland in this semiarid region. North of the Gardiner Dam, the South Saskatchewan River resumes a narrow course northward toward Saskatoon.

Other points of interest

■ Lloydminster [B2] is the only city in Canada that is divided between two provinces: the 110th meridian of longitude—which forms the boundary between Alberta and Saskatchewan—runs down the middle of Main Street.

■ Little Manitou Lake [D5], the remnant of an ancient glacial lake, has a salinity level of 12 percent, making it 3.5 times saltier than sea water. It also has a specific gravity of 1.06. This statistic indicates that Little Manitou Lake is denser than the Dead Sea in the Middle East.

■ Estevan [F6], the "Sunshine Capital of Canada," averages 2,500 hours of sunshine per year, more than any other city in the country. Estevan has also the highest annual number of hours per year with clear skies: 2,979 hours.

Scale 1:2,000,000

1 cm = 20 km

0 20 40 60 80 km

NORTHWEST TERRITORIES Mountain Time Zone / Heure des Rocheuses
Central Time Zone / Heure du centre

WOOD BUFFALO

NATIONAL PARK

PARC NATIONAL

WOOD BUFFALO

ALBERTA

SASKATCHEWAN

BIRCH MOUNTAINS

Birch Mountains Wildland Provincial Park

Fort MacKay

Wood Buffalo

Fort McMurray Oil Sands Discovery Centre

Fort McMurray

Saprae Creek Estates

Gregoire Lake Provincial Park

Gipsy Lake Wildland Provincial Park

Anzac

Stony Mountain Wildland Provincial Park

CHEECHAM HILLS

Mariana Lake

Pelican

Crow Lake Provincial Park

Chard

Conklin

Christina Lake

Wandering River

Breynat

Grassland

Imperial Mills

Sir Winston Churchill Provincial Park

Plamondon

Lac la Biche

Lakeland Provincial Park

Lakeland Provincial Recreation Area

Beaver Lake

Atmore

Mewatha Beach

Hylo

Caslan

Bondiss

Ellscott

Long Lake Provincial Park

Kikino

Fork Lake

Rich Lake

Iron River

La Corey

Wolf Lake

Cold Lake Provincial Park

Cold Lake

Ethel Lake

Crane Lake

COLD LAKE AIR WEAPONS RANGE

Primrose Lake Provincial Ecological Reserve

Primrose Lake

MOSTOOS HILLS

McCusker Lake Provincial Ecological Reserve

Canoe Lake

Cole Bay

Jans Bay

Canoe Narrows

La Plonge

Beauval

Île-à-la-Crosse

Île-à-la-Crosse South Bay

Fort Black

Patuanak

Dipper Lake

Primeau Lake

Knee Lake

Elak Dase

Gordon Lake

Pinehouse Lake

Morin Lake

Little Hills

La Ronge

Kitsakie

Dore Lake

Michel Point

Sled Lake

Green Lake

THUNDER HILLS

Montreal River

Weyakwin

Molanosa

Smoky Lake

Waskatenau

Warspite

Vilna

Bellis

Spedden

Ashmont

St. Vincent

Glendon

Bonnyville

Hoselaw

Beaver Crossing

Ardmore

Fort Kent

Medley

Grand Centre

Cherry Grove

Pierceland

Beacon Hill

Goodsoil

Peerless

Dorintosh

Meadow Lake Provincial Park

Waterhen Lake

Glaslyn

Flat Valley

Barnes

Lavallée

WOOD BUFFALO NATIONAL PARK

Fort Smith Visitors Centre

Fitzgerald

La Butte Creek Wildland Provincial Park

Hay Camp

Pine Lake

Salt Plains en hiver Overview

Peace Point

Sweetgrass Landing

Wood Buffalo National Park Fort Chipewyan Visitors Centre

Fort Chipewyan

Fort Chipewyan Bicentennial Museum

Colin-Cornwall Lakes Wildland Provincial Park

Cypress Point

Fidler Point

Egg Island

Burntwood Island

Bustard Island

Richardson Lake National Migratory Bird Sanctuary / Refuge national d'oiseaux migrateurs du Lac-Richardson

Maybelle River Wildland Provincial Park

Athabasca Dunes

Richardson River Dunes Wildland Provincial Park

Marguerite River Wildland Provincial Park

Whitemud Falls Wildland Provincial Park

Lake Athabasca

Lac Athabasca

Athabasca Sand Dunes Wilderness Provincial Park

Camsell Portage

Uranium City

Beaver Lodge

Eldorado

Fond-du-Lac

Stony Rapids

Stony Lake

Black Lake

Cluff Lake Mine

Descharme Lake

Clearwater River Provincial Park

Big C

La Loche West

La Loche

Black Point

Garson Lake

Turnor Lake

Bear Creek

Michel

Buffalo River

St. George's Hill

Dillon

Buffalo Narrows

Churchill Lake

Dipper Lake

Cree Lake

Key Lake

GRIZZLY BEAR HILLS

Waskwei Island

Kazan Lake

Landing

COLD LAKE

PRIMROSE LAKE

Route numbers: 63, 69, 881, 858, 855, 866, 867, 882, 660, 659, 897, 892, 950, 954, 55, 28, 36, 41, 28A, 831, 141, 430, 663, 55, 909, 955, 956, 962, 964, 966, 155, 925, 908, 918, 903, 904, 919, 941, 951, 224, 914, 909, 910, 935, 165, 917, 929, 938, 921, 939, 916, 924, 922, 923, 969, 965, 905

A LAKE THAT FLOWS TWO WAYS

At 2,681 km², Wollaston Lake is Canada's 19th largest lake, where waters drain in two directions. The lake flows northwest through Hatchet Lake (upper left) and the Fond du Lac River into Lake Athabasca and the Mackenzie River; and northeast, past Usam Island (upper right) via the Cochrane River into Reindeer Lake and Churchill River. With a 4,300-km shoreline and myriad islands, the lake is a sports fishing destination, renowned for its trophy-size catches of northern pike, lake trout, walleye, and arctic grayling. The road visible on Wollaston Lake's west side (left centre) leads to Rabbit Lake Mine, one of northern Saskatchewan's major uranium operations.

Other points of interest

■ Clearwater Wilderness Provincial Park [C3-D3] encompasses much of the 280-km Clearwater River, which flows west to join the Athabasca River at Fort McMurray [Plate 9, D7]. Along the river lie canyons and waterfalls. Once a fur-trade route, the Clearwater has been designated a Canadian Heritage River.

■ In 1,600-km² Meadow Lake Provincial Park [F2-F3] lie forests, meadows, and marshes. A significant park feature is a chain of 25 lakes linking Cold Lake [F2] with Waterhen Lake [F3].

■ A cairn at Montréal River [F5] marks the geographical centre of Saskatchewan. To the north lies 1,414-km² Lac La Ronge and Lac La Ronge Provincial Park [E5-F5]. At 3,345 km², the park is a popular year-round recreational destination. Farther north is Saskatchewan's oldest building, the Holy Trinity Anglican Church (built in the 1850s) situated at Stanley Mission.

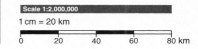

Scale 1:2,000,000

1 cm = 20 km

0   20   40   60   80 km

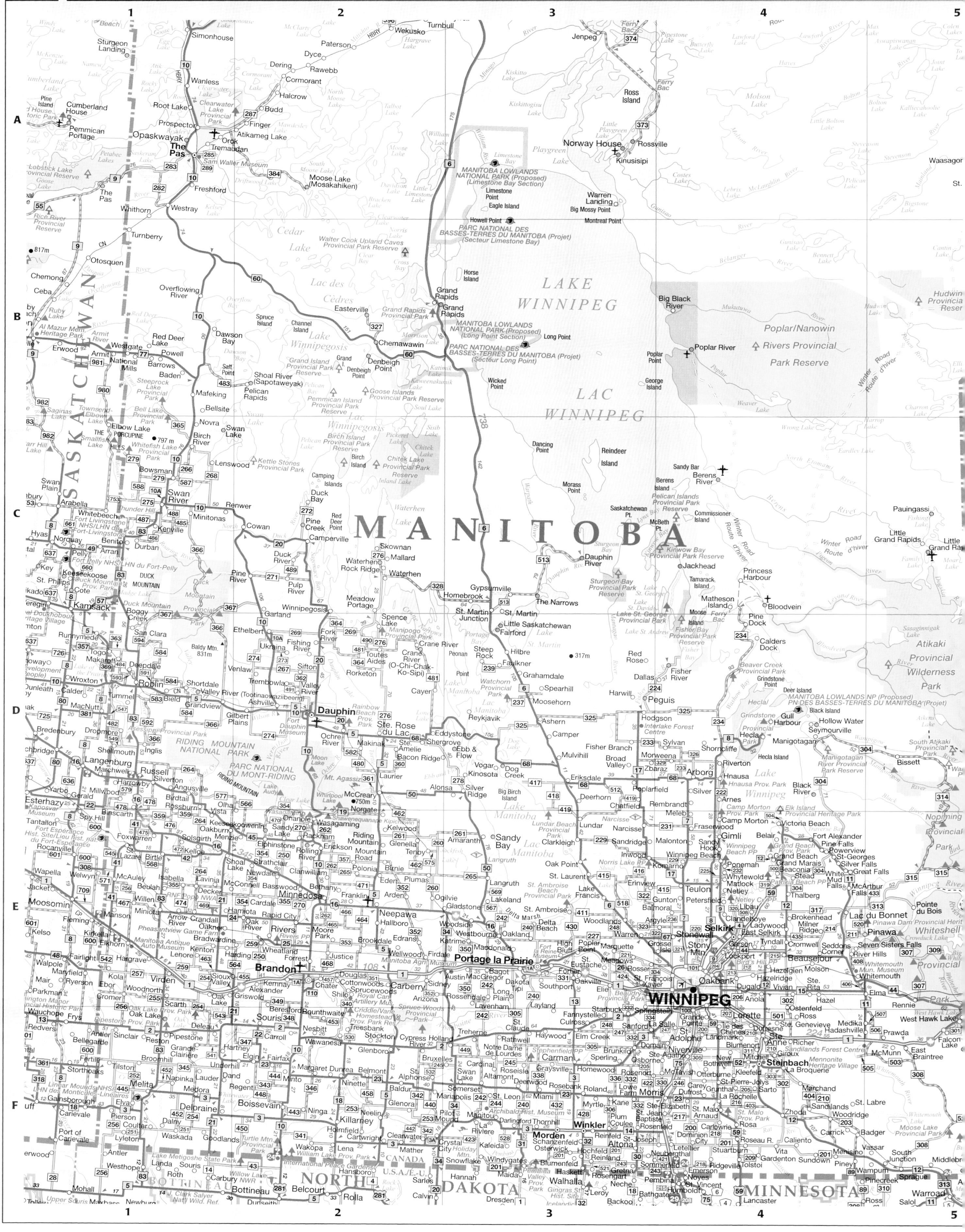

1 2 3 4 5

SASKATCHEWAN

MANITOBA

LAKE WINNIPEG

LAC WINNIPEG

Lake Winnipegosis

Lac Winnipegosis

Lac Manitoba

NORTH DAKOTA

MINNESOTA

CANADA

U.S.A./É.U.A.

BOTTINEAU

Major places:

The Pas · Opaskwayak · Grand Rapids · Norway House · Rossville · Kinusisipi · Poplar River · Berens River · Dauphin · Swan River · Roblin · Kamsack · Russell · Minnedosa · Neepawa · Brandon · Virden · Portage la Prairie · Selkirk · Stonewall · Gimli · Teulon · Beausejour · Pinawa · Lac du Bonnet · WINNIPEG · Steinbach · Morris · Carman · Winkler · Morden · Altona · Emerson · Killarney · Boissevain · Melita · Deloraine · Souris · Moosomin · Esterhazy

CONTRASTING SHORES

Lake Winnipeg, with lakes Manitoba and Winnipegosis, dominates central Manitoba. At 24,400 km², Lake Winnipeg is Canada's sixth largest, but it is relatively shallow, with a maximum depth of 18 m. The view above shows its northern expanse, from Sturgeon Bay (lower right) to Big Mossy Point (upper right), where the lake flows northward through Playgreen Lake into the Nelson River and, eventually, Hudson Bay. Lake Winnipeg presents contrasting shores: the eastern shore has the granite outcrops of the Canadian Shield; and the western shore, the level landscape of the Manitoba Lowlands, where a proposed national park would include Limestone Stone Bay (upper left) and Long Point Peninsula (left centre).

Other points of interest

■ The southeastern corner of Duck Mountain Provincial Park [C1] is the site of Manitoba's highest point, 831-m Baldy Mountain [D1].

■ Lake of the Woods [F5-F6], shared by Ontario, Manitoba, and Minnesota, has 104,000 km of shoreline and contains 14,000 islands.

■ Manitoba's 100,000 lakes hold most of the 900 trillion litres of surface water covering 16 percent of the province.

Scale 1:2,000,000

1 cm = 20 km

0   20   40   60   80 km

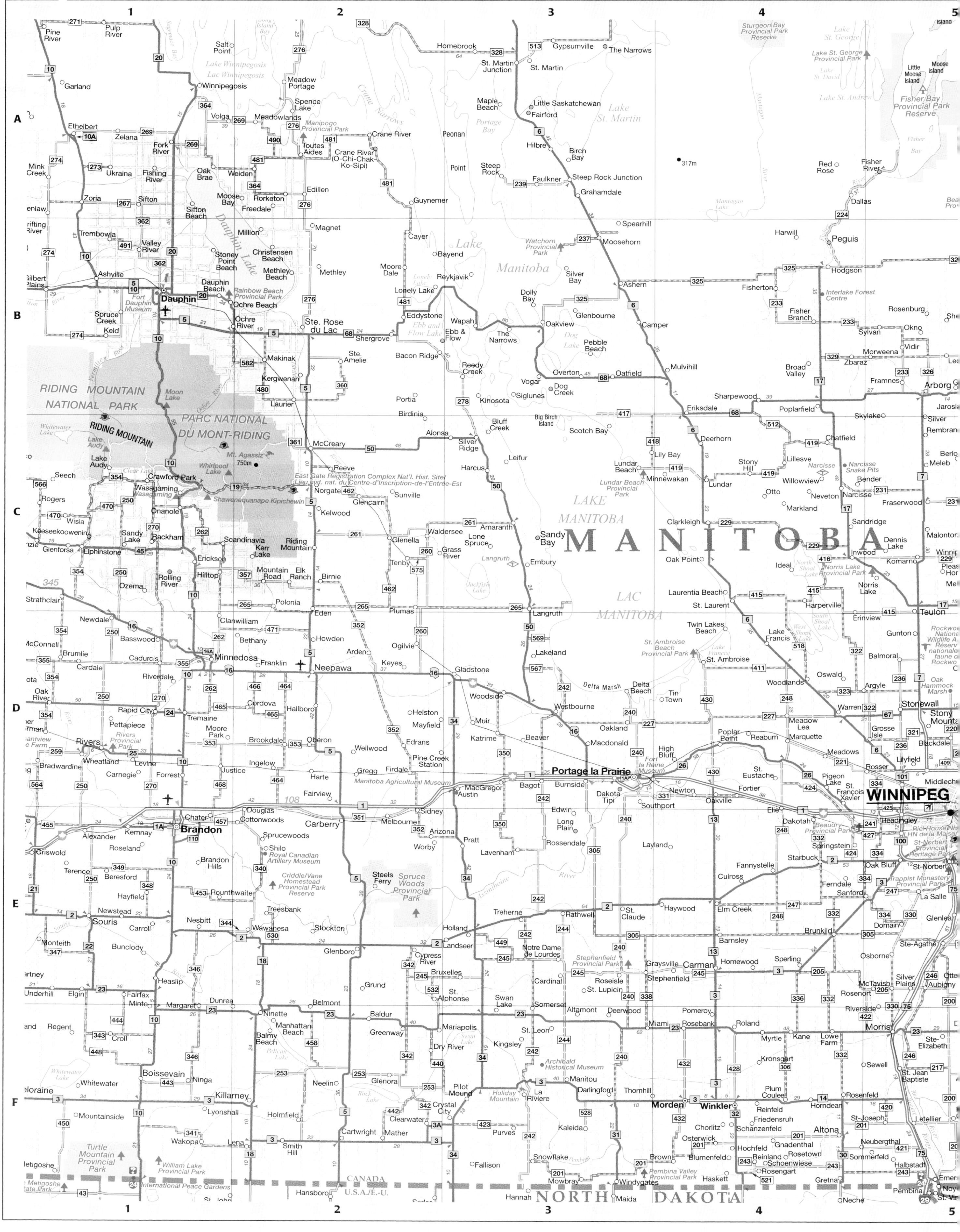

MANITOBA

WINNIPEG

Dauphin

Brandon

Portage la Prairie

Morden · Winkler · Morris

RIDING MOUNTAIN NATIONAL PARK
PARC NATIONAL DU MONT-RIDING

Lake Winnipegosis / Lac Winnipegosis

Lake Manitoba

LAKE MANITOBA / LAC MANITOBA

Lake St. Martin

Fisher Bay Provincial Park Reserve

Turtle Mountain Provincial Park

Spruce Woods Provincial Park

CANADA
U.S.A./É.-U.
NORTH DAKOTA

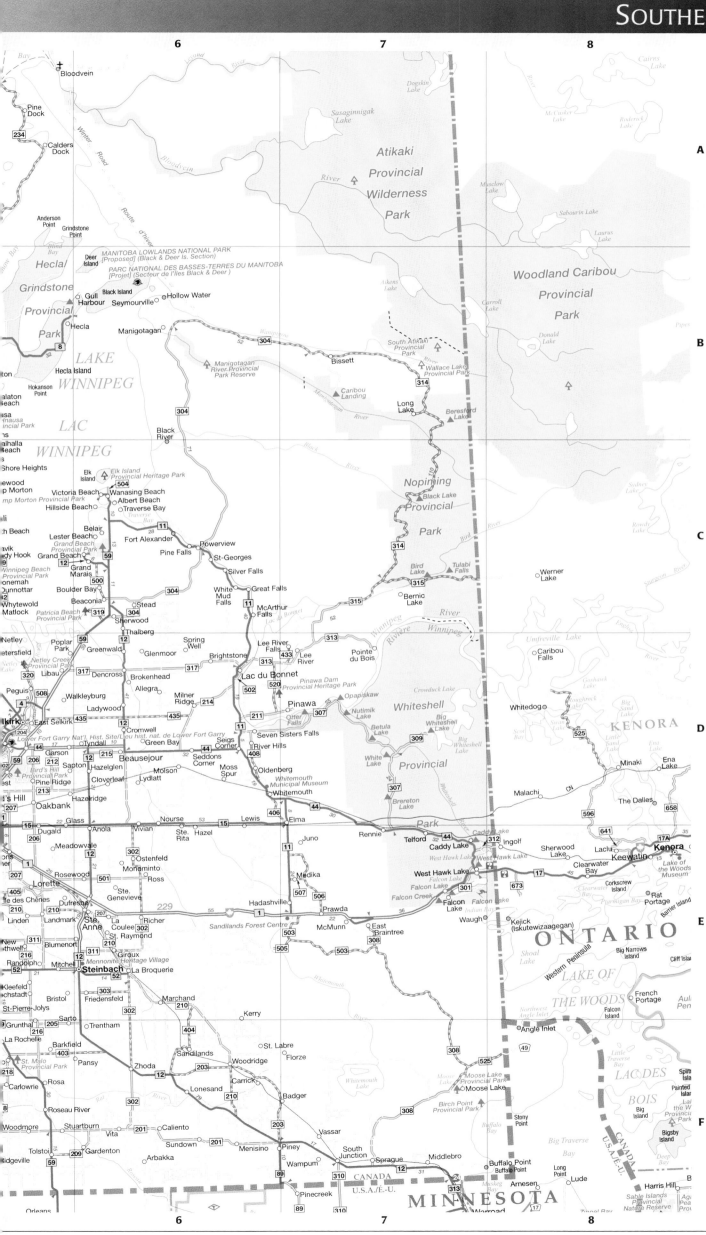

A PRAIRIE ESCARPMENT

This view shows the dark green plateau of Riding Mountain National Park (centre) and the bright, blue waters of Dauphin Lake (upper centre). Riding Mountain National Park is situated on the Manitoba Escarpment—a series of uplands that angle northwest through Manitoba and Saskatchewan. The park's northern boundary, sharply defined above, rises 450 m above a landscape checkered with farm fields. Within its 3,000 km², the park contains boreal and deciduous forest, aspen parkland, open grassland, and meadows. Also visible above is Clear Lake at Riding Mountain's southern entrance. Dauphin Lake, like larger Winnipeg, Winnipegosis, and Manitoba lakes, is a remnant of Lake Agassiz, which covered much of southern Manitoba 12,000 years ago.

Other points of interest

■ South of Carberry, Spruce Woods Provincial Park [E2] preserves an untamed desert formed thousands of years ago when this region was once the delta of an ancient river. Spruce Woods has two natural curiosities: Spirit Sands, a 5-km tract of shifting dunes towering 30 m above the prairie, and The Devil's Punchbowl, a sunken pit created by currents in an underground stream.

■ The 877-km-long Red River [C5-F5] may flood when its headwaters in the United States thaw before the river in Manitoba is ice-free. This has caused disastrous floods twice: in 1950 and 1997. During the last flood, more than 8,600 members of the Canadian Forces called in to control the rising waters. It was Canada's largest military operation since the Korean War.

Scale 1:1,000,000
1 cm = 10 km

0   10   20   30   40 km

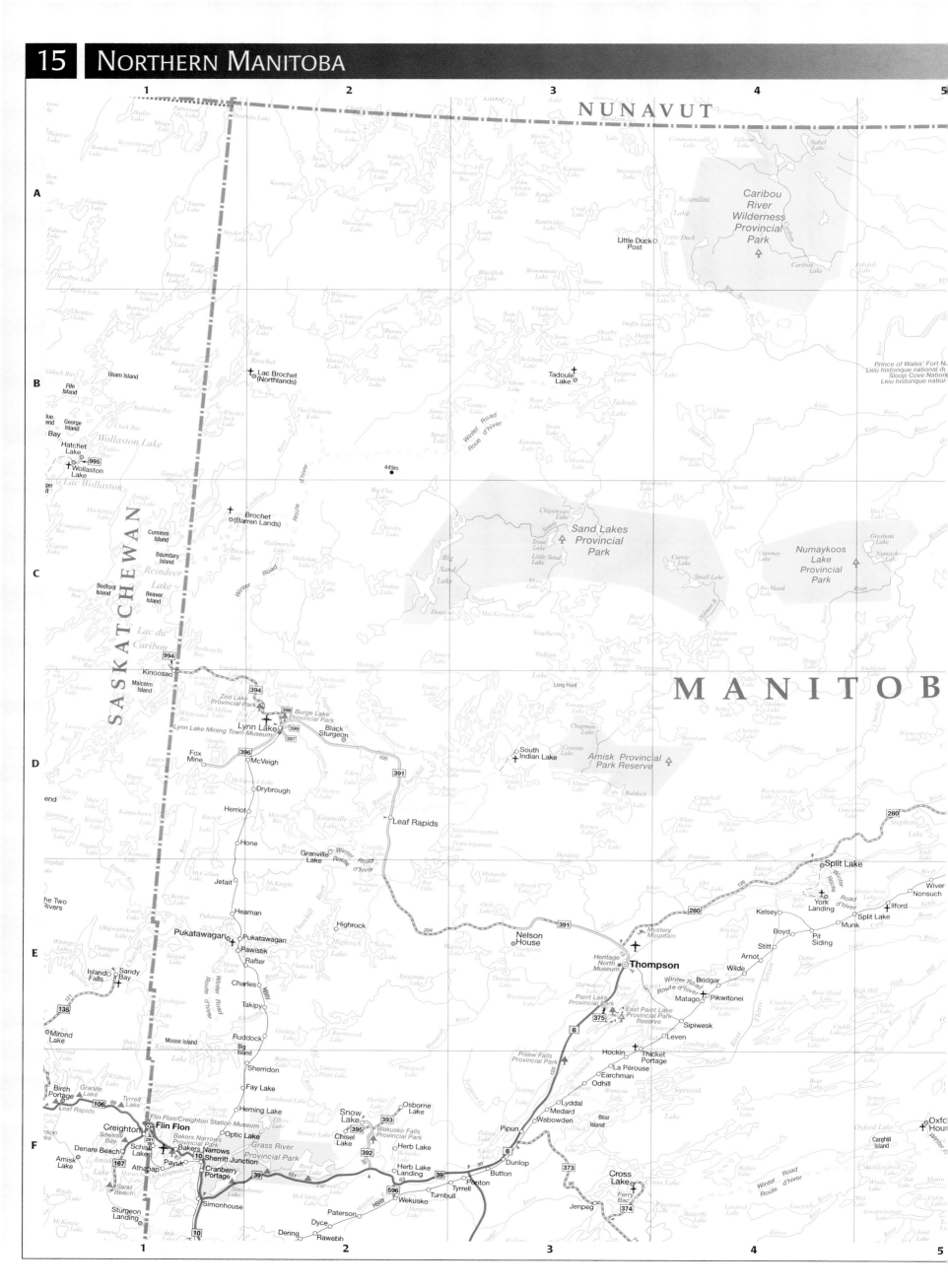

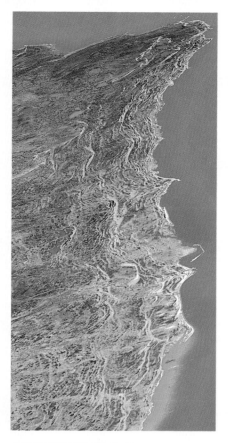

A NORTHERN WETLAND

Hudson Bay's cold waves crash on the beaches of Wapusk National Park, where Cape Churchill (top) is the northernmost promontory. Canada's eighth largest park, Wapusk protects an 11,475-km² portion of the Hudson Bay Lowlands, which stretch along Hudson Bay shoreline from the Manitoba-Nunavut boundary to James Bay. The lowlands—Canada's largest wetland region and the world's third largest wetland—occupy an area of 300,000 km². In Wapusk National Park, about half the surface is covered with lakes, bogs, fens and streams, and rivers. Along the coast, the park is a treeless tundra, carpeted with willows, sedges, and other low arctic vegetation. The beach ridges—the shorelines of earlier times—indicate the slow coastal rebound (at about a metre per century) from the last ice age's immense glacial weight.

Other points of interest

■ Churchill [B5], Canada's only seaport on the Arctic Ocean, is open only three months a year for navigation.

■ Hudson Bay is an immense inland sea, covering 822,324 km² and penetrating deeply into northern Canada. Its maximum length is 1,500 km; its greatest width is 830 km. The Hudson Bay Lowlands form the southwestern shore, but the remaining coast is mainly part of the Canadian Shield. Many rivers enter the bay, among them the Thelon, Churchill, Nelson, Severn, La Grande, and Eastmain. The total area of the Hudson Bay drainage is 3.8 million square kilometres. The bay is shallow, mostly between 100 and 200 m deep. The bay's floor is slowly rising, exposing more and more of the coastline.

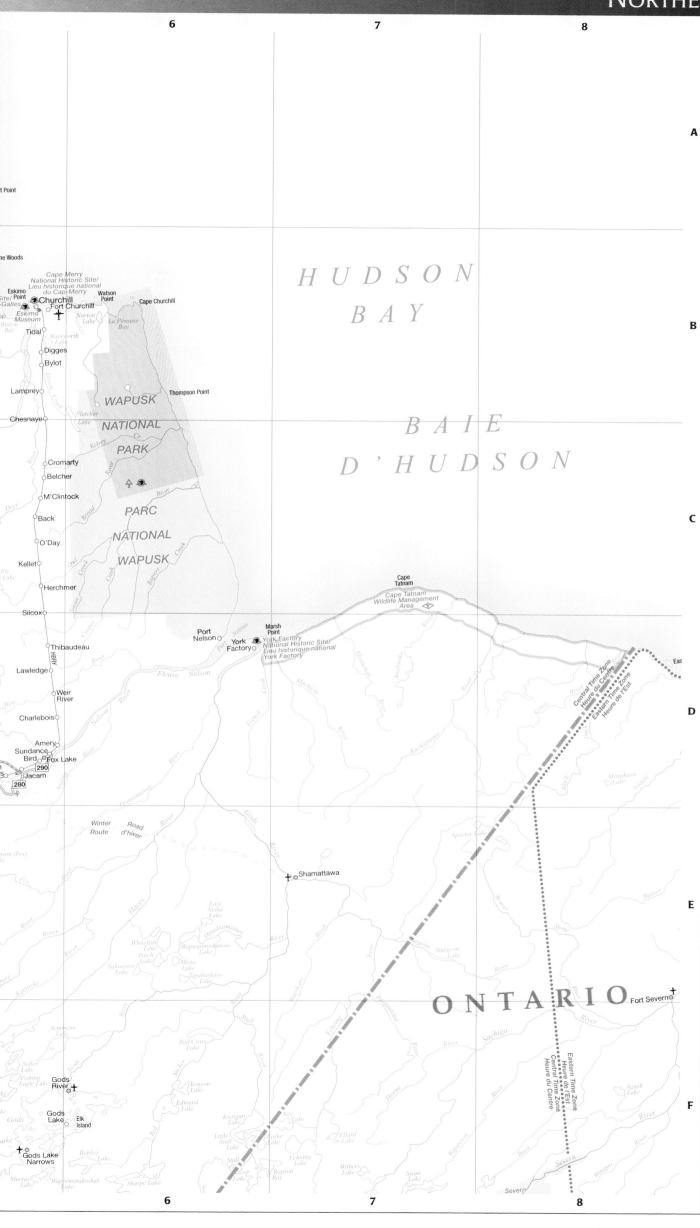

HUDSON BAY

BAIE D'HUDSON

ONTARIO

Scale 1:2,000,000

1 cm = 20 km

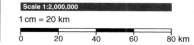

0   20   40   60   80 km

MANITOBA

ONTA...
ONTARIO

MINNESOTA

KENORA

RAINY RIVER

KOOCHICHING

BELTRAMI

LAKE OF THE WOODS

LAKE OF THE WOODS

LAC DES BOIS

VOYAGEURS NATIONAL PARK

Quetico Provincial Park

Parc provincial

Woodland Caribou Provincial Park

Parc provincial Pakwash Provincial Park

Atikaki Provincial Wilderness Park

Whiteshell Provincial Park

Nopiming Provincial Park

Central Time Zone / Heure du Centre — Eastern Time Zone / Heure de l'Est

Places:
Lewis Lake, Carr-Harris Lake, Pauingassi, Little Grand Rapids, Family Lake, Winter Deer Lake, Deer Lake, Poplar Hill, North Spirit Lake, North Caribou Lake, MacDowell, 462m, Pikangikum, Cat Lake, Bissett, 304, 314, 315, 313, 307, 309, Caribou Falls, Whitedog (Wabasseemoong), Werner Lake, Mckenzie Island, Cochenour, Balmertown, Red Lake, Madsen, Starratt-Olsen, 125, 618, 13, 105, Snake Falls, Bruce Lake, South Bay, Slate Falls, Pickle Lake, Central P, Mishkeegogamang (New Osnaburgh), 599, Ear Falls, 804, Goldpines, 657, 186, Kenora, St. Raphael Provincial Park, Wabauskang, Perrault Falls, Lac Seul, 516, 434m, Savant Lake, Allan Water, 664, 599, Camp Robinson, 105, 609, Red Lake Road, McIntosh, Amesdale, Sioux Lookout, Superior Junction, Ghost River, Hudson, Sam Lake, Richan, 601, 665, 72, 642, O'Briens Landing, Minaki, Redditt, Jones, 671, Quibell, Willard Lake, 647, Vermillion Bay, Eton-Rugby, Minnitaki, 605, Dryden, 603, Umfreville, Silver Dollar, Malachi, Ochiichagwe'babigo'ining, 596, 658, Ingolf, Sherwood Lake, 641, Laclu, 17A, Jaffray Melick, Longbow Lake, 505m, Keewatin, Eagle River, Oxdrift, Wabigoon, Dinorwic, Dyment, West Hawk Lake, 44, 312, 1, 17, Clearwater Bay, Kenora, Musee Lake of the Woods Museum, Eagle Lake, Wabigoon Lake, Borups Corners, 502, Falcon Lake, 673, Kejick (Iskutewizaagegan), Wauzhushk Onigum, East Braintree, Waugh, 306, Shoal Lake, Gold Rock, 622, Ignace, Sandbar Lake Provincial Park, 249, Moose Lake Prov. Park, 525, 49, Angle Inlet, 308, Birch Point Prov. Park, Aulneau Peninsula, Sioux Narrows, Whitefish Bay, 71, 138, Bonheur River Kame Provincial Nature Reserve, Martin, English River, 498m, Graham, Middlebro, Buffalo Point, 2, 24, Big I., Morson, Bigsby I., Crow Lake, Nestor Falls, Caliper Lake, Turtle River, White Otter Castle, 71, 502, Upsala, 31, Arnesen, Lude, Minahico, Bergland, North Branch, Burditt Lake, Northwest Bay, Government Landing, 622, 11, Warroad, 600, 621, Arbor Vitae, Gameland, 619, 617, 615, Off Lake Corner, Black Hawk, CN, Glenorchy, Crilly, Calm Lake, Flanders, Atikokan, 11B, Sapawe, Kawene, CN, Seine River Village, 623, 633, Kashabowie, 5, Swift, Roosevelt, Williams, 6, Rainy River, 621, Sleeman, Pinewood, 613, 611, Rocky Inlet, 11, Mine Centre, 116, 288, 11, 802, Shebandowan, 586, Pitt, 172, 53, Stratton, Barwick, Emo, La Vallee, 611, Couchiching, Fort Frances, International Falls, 332, Sandpoint Island Provincial Park, Burchell Lake, 11, 18, Baudette, Clementson, 411, Birchdale, 59, Indus, Devlin, 611, 602, Pelland, 71, Loman, Ericsburg, 53, Ray, 217, 122, 50, 129, Ash River, Kabetogama, Crane Lake, Hunter Island, Saganaga Lake, 588, Little Greenwater Lake Provincial Nature Reserve, Matawin River Provincial Park, Fourtown, 89, Waskish, Upper Red Lake, Lower Red Lake, Big Falls, Grand Falls, Ash Lake, Nett Lake, Quetico, Pickerel Lake, Dawson Trail, Greenwater Lake, 802, Castle Creek PNR, Divide Ridge Prov. Nat. Res., Ponemah, Saum, Kelliher, Gemmell, Margie, 71, 35, Big Falls, Bois Fort, Cusson, Buyck, 116, Arrowhead Peninsula PNR, Lac la Croix, Agnes Lake, Verendrye, Redlake, Redby, Shooks, Mizpan, Northome, 6, 5, Greaney, Linden, 169, Snowbank Lake, 12, Pigeon, Castle Danger

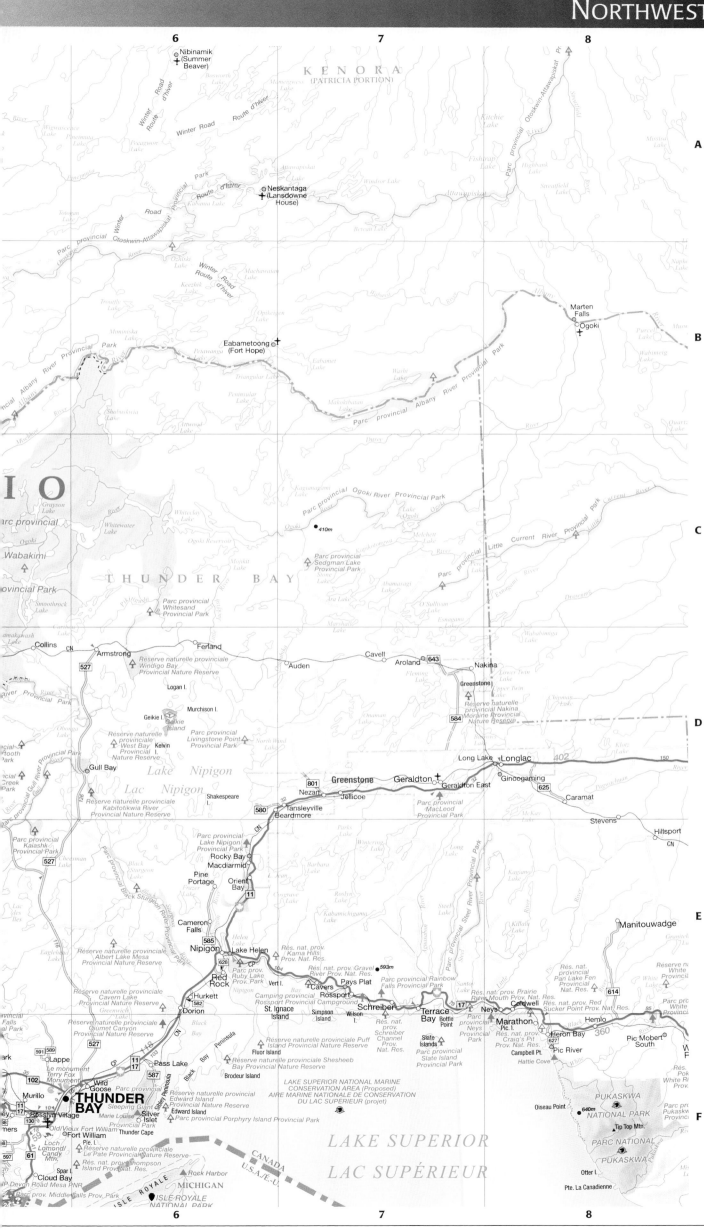

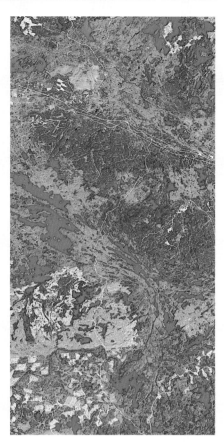

IN SHIELD COUNTRY

In northwestern Ontario, the Trans-Canada Highway has two sections: Highway 17 (Kenora-Thunder Bay) and Highway 11 (Fort Frances-Thunder Bay). The road at the top of the view is a section of Highway 17, just east of Dyment, Ontario. The road south is Provincial Highway 622, a secondary route linking up with Highway 11 at Atikokan. In this view, the 622 threads through rugged Shield country [E3], where blocks of clear-cut forest are visible.

Other points of interest

■ Sleeping Giant Provincial Park [F6] covers most of Sibley Peninsula. At the southwest corner of the 243-km² park lies the Sleeping Giant, a cluster of mesas rising 300 m high. From Thunder Bay, some 25 km away, the mesas resemble a huge recumbent figure.

■ Ouimet Canyon Provincial Nature Reserve [F6] preserves a 5-km-long, 150-m-wide gorge where sheer cliffs plunge 100 m to the canyon floor.

■ Lake Nipigon [D6], the fourth largest in Ontario, drains south into Lake Superior through the Nipigon River. The lake receives water from the Albany River [B5-B7], via the Ogoki River and Reservoir [B8-C6]. This diverted water increases the lake's capacity and allows hydroelectric generation at three plants along the Nipigon River.

■ In 1981, Hemlo, Ontario [F8], was the site of a major gold discovery. Within 10 years, Hemlo had become the largest source of gold in Canada. Its development revived the importance of gold to Canada's economy. Hemlo's three mines produce 25 percent of Canada's supply.

Scale 1:1,725,000
1 cm = 17.25 km

0 10 20 30 40 50 60 70 km

1 2 3 4 5

A

410m

Ogoki Reservoir

Parc provincial Sedgman Lake Provincial Park

Parc provincial Whitesand Provincial Park

Murchison I.

Ferland

Auden

Cavell

Aroland 643

Nakina

Greenstone

584

Reserve naturelle provincial Nakina Moraine Provincial Nature Reserve

Pagwa River

Parc provincial Fushimi Lake Provincial Park

COCHRANE

B

Long Lake

Greenstone

801

Geraldton

Geraldton East

Longlac

402

Ginoogaming

625

Constance Lake 663 Calstock 63

Lac-Ste-Thérèse

Hearst

Hallebourg

Mattice

Nezah

Jellicoe

Caramat

150

11

Jogues

Coppell

Val Côté

Lowther

ONR

Shakespeare

580

Tansleyville Beardmore

Stevens

631

Mead 583

Parc provincial Lake Nipigon Provincial Park

Rocky Bay

Macdiarmid

Hillsport

CN

Parc provincial Nagagami Lake Provincial Park

Parc provincial Nagagamisis Provincial Park

ACR

Parc provincial Missinaibi Provincial Park

Pine Portage

Orient Bay

11

Lac Nipigon

Horsepayne

MacDuff

ONT

585

Lake Helen

Manitouwadge

Oba

628

Red Rock

Parc provincial Ruby Lake Prov. Park

593m

Rés. nat. prov. Kama Hills Prov. Nat. Res.

Rés. nat. prov. Gravel River Prov. Nat. Res.

Rés. nat. prov. Pichogen River Prov. Nat. Res.

Fire River

ALGOMA

C

Burkett

Cavers

Rossport

Schreiber

Terrace Bay

Neys

Coldwell

614

631

Argolis

Chapleau Crown Game Preserve

St. Ignace Island

Simpson Island

Wilson I.

Bottle Point

Marathon

Hemlo

360

85

Parc provincial White Lake Provincial Park

Peterbell

Peninsula

Fluor Island

Réserve naturelle provinciale Puff Island Provincial Nature Reserve

Réserve naturelle provinciale Sheesheb Bay Provincial Nature Reserve

Brodeur Island

Parc provincial Slate Island Provincial Park

Slate Islands

Rés. nat. prov. Prairie River Mouth Prov. Nat. Res.

Heron Bay

627

Campbell Pt.

Pic River

Pic Mobert South

White River

Rés. nat. prov. Red Sucker Point Prov. Nat. Res.

Amyot

Franz

D

LAKE SUPERIOR NATIONAL MARINE CONSERVATION AREA (Proposed) AIRE MARINE NATIONALE DE CONSERVATION DU LAC SUPÉRIEUR (projet)

Porphyry Island Provincial Park

Oiseau Point

640m

Top Top Mtn.

PUKASKWA NATIONAL PARK

PARC NATIONAL PUKASKWA

Parc provincial Pukaskwa River Provincial Park

Parc provincial Obatanga Provincial Park

Rés. nat. prov. Pokei Lake / White River Wetlands Prov. Nat. Res.

Dubreuilville

519

Lochalsh

Missanabie

Goudreau

Dalton

CP

Parc provincial Missinaibi Provincial Park

Réserve de chasse de la Couronne Chapleau

Nicholson

101

CANADA U.S.A./É.-U.

LAKE SUPERIOR LAC SUPÉRIEUR

Otter I.

Pte. La Canadienne

547 Hawk Junction

Michipicoten

Michipicoten River

Wawa

Perry

High Falls Chutes High

Rés. nat. prov. Potholes Provincial Nature Reserve

651

101

Chapleau

129

Nemegos

602m

E

Copper Harbor

Fort Wilkins State Park

26

Central

Lac La Belle

44

Keweenaw Pt.

Bete Grise

Pt. Isabelle

Keweenaw Peninsula

Gay

Traverse Bay

Linden

Michipicoten Island

Parc provincial Michipicoten Island Provincial Park

Cape Gargantua

Rabbit Blanket Lake

17

Parc provincial Lake Superior Provincial Park

Musée Centennial Chapleau Centennial Museum

Duck Lake

667

Parc provincial Five Mile Lake Provincial Park

Kormak

Leach Island

315

Agawa Bay

Frater

Algoma Central Railway Agawa Canyon/ Canyon Agawa

Parc provincial Wenebegon River Provincial Park

Parc pro Wakami Provincia

F

Point Abbaye

Huron Bay

Huron River Pt.

Huron Mountain

Big Bay

Thoney Pt.

Montreal Island

Montreal River

Parc provincial Montreal River Provincial Park

ACR

653m

Parc provincial Batchawana River Provincial Park

Parc provincial Algoma Headwaters Provincial Park

Parc provincial Aubinadong River Provincial Park

Parc provincial Saymo-Aubinadong-Gong Provincial Park

563

Batchawana Bay

Parc provincial Pancake Bay Provincial Park

Parc provincial Batchawana Bay Provincial Park

Rés. nat. prov. Sandy Islands Sanley Islands Prov. Nat. Res.

Waboo

Karalash Corners

532

Searchmont

556

Ranger Lake

129

Parc provincial Goulais River Provincial Park

Parc provincial Aubrey Falls Provincial Park

ALGOMA

Craig Lake State Park

MARQUETTE

Nestoria

Three Lakes

28

Diorite

10

Trowbridge Park

GRAND ISLAND NATIONAL RECREATION AREA

Grand

PICTURED ROCKS NATIONAL LAKESHORE

Grand Marais

Muskallonge Lake State Park

Deer Park

H58

Crisp Point

Whitefish Point

Whitefish Point

Paradise

Goulais Bay

Goulais River

552

Searchmont

ACR

Kirbys Corner

Island Lake

Heyden

170

Hilton Beach

638

Little White River Provincial Park

Champion

41

94

Marquette

North Lake

Ishpeming

553

Sand River

Au Train

Christmas

H58

5

Melstrand

H37

Lower Falls

Upper Falls

Tahquamenon Falls State Park

Red Rock

Gros Cap

Sault Ste. Marie

Canal de Sault Canal

550

Garden River

Echo Bay

Leeburn

Poplar Dale

Dunns Valley

Musée minier Rock Lake

638

Wharncliffe

554

Nestoria

95

Negaunee

Republic

35

Palmer

Gwinn

New Swanzy

Princeton

Little Lake

41

Kiva

Munising

Eben Junction

67

Forest Lake

Skandia

Dukes

Diffin

94

Traunik

Wetmore

Shingleton

28

94

Seney

McMillan

Germfask

77

H44

Logging Museum

Hulbert

123

Eckerman

Raco

Strongs

28

WC

Dafter

Brimley

Pointe aux Pins

Payment

Sault Ste. Marie

17

Rosedale

129

Desbarats

Bruce Bank

Rock Lake

548

Sowerby

Iron Bridge

Mississippi River

Thessalon

MICHIGAN

DICKINSON

Channing

Ralph

Sagola

Arnold

Northland

35

Rock

H38

Felch Mountain

Trombly

H13

H40

123

Curtis

117

Blaney Park

Gould

Naubinway

Engadine

Rexton

Garnet

Gilchrist

Corinne

Stalwart

75

129

Pickford

Fibre

Kentvale

Kinross

Cottage Park

Trout Lake

MACKINAC

RNOM St. Joseph's I. NMBS

Fort St. Joseph Nat'l. Hist. Site

St. Joseph Island

Blind

North Shore Waterway

Delta Pt.

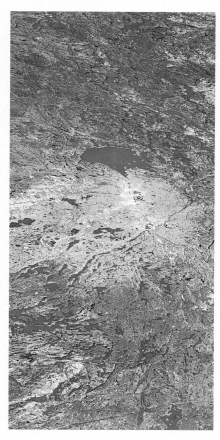

A BASIN OF MINERALS

Wanapitei Lake (centre) lies northeast of Greater Sudbury, the leading regional centre in northeastern Ontario. Nickel Centre is the site of the Falconbridge smelter. It is situated in the brown and yellow circular area below the lake. The colour here and elsewhere in this view shows where the forest cover is thin as a result of pollution. The city of Sudbury itself is visible just below Nickel Centre. Greater Sudbury is situated in a 60 x 27-km oval-shaped geological basin, possibly created either by the impact of a meteor or volcanic eruption. Whatever the cause, it endowed the region with a wealth of minerals: gold, silver, cobalt, platinum, and the world's largest known deposit of nickel. Since the 1980s, the reclamation of the local landscape, ravaged by a century of mining and industrial pollution, has been remarkably successful.

Other points of interest

■ Wawa [D3] supplies iron ore for the steel mills at Sault Ste. Marie [F4], Canada's second largest steel-producing center (after Hamilton). South of Wawa is High Falls, a 25-m-high, 40-m-wide waterfall on the Magpie River.

■ Pukaskwa National Park [C2-D3] occupies 1,878 km² of land on Lake Superior. Its natural features include sheer cliffs along the Lake Superior shoreline and 640-m Tip-Top Mountain inland. Lake Superior Provincial Park [D3-E4] is the site of towering granite headlands such as Cape Gargantua.

■ In 1903, the world's richest silver vein was discovered at Cobalt [E8]. Since then, Cobalt has produced more than 500 million ounces of silver.

Scale 1:1,725,000
1 cm = 17.25 km

0 10 20 30 40 50 60 70 km

1   2   3   4   5

A

Dunns Valley
Wharncliffe
Kynoch
546
129
554
Parkinson
546
Little Rapids
Sowerby
Day Mills
Patton
17
29
Thessalon Point
Thessalon
Iron Bridge
HCR
Dean Lake
Mississagi River
Algoma Mills
Spragge
17
538
Pronto East
Blind River
Sandford Island
Turnbull Island
John Island
Serpent River
Cutler
Spanish
Walford
Massey
17
Webbwood
McKerrow
Espanola
6
639
Musée minier et nucléaire d' Elliot Lake Mining & Nuclear Museum
Elliot Lake
108
553
557
ALGOMA
High Falls
Worthington
Turbine
Whitefish
4
17
10
144
69
Dowling
Phelans
Larchwood
Nairn Centre

B

Drummond Island
MICHIGAN
Cockburn Island
Tolsmaville
Meldrum Bay
Sheshegwaning
540
The Queen Elizabeth The Queen Mother M'Nidoo M'Nissing Provincial Park
Greene Island
Silver Water
Burnt Island
Barrie Island
540A
540B
Gore Bay
Kagawong
540
Tobacco Lake
542
Honora
West Bay
540
Long Bay
NORTH CHANNEL
CHENAL NORTH
MANITOULIN
Aird Island
Eagle Island
Fox I.
Croker Island
Amedroz Island
Bedford
E. Rous I.
Darch Island
Innes Island
Clapperton Island
McBean Harbour
Sagamok
La Cloche
Whitefish Falls
Birch Island
Great La Cloche Island
Sucker Creek
Little Current
Strawberry Island
Badgeley Pt.
Northeastern Manitoulin and the Islands
6
Sheguiandah
Heywood
Mudge Bay
Pike I.
Big Burnt I.
Mountains
McGregor Bay
SUDBURY
Parc provincial Killarney Provincial Park
South La Cloche Mountains
Killarney
637
Killarney
George Island
Edward Island
Parc provincial Killarney Coast & Islands Provincial Park

C

Western Duck Island
Réserve naturelle provinciale Misery Bay Provincial Nature Reserve
Elizabeth Bay
Evansville
Poplar
Britainville
Grimsthorpe
542
Spring Bay
Mindemoya
551
Providence Bay
551
Tehkummah
542A
6
Michael's Bay
Parc provincial Blue Jay Creek Provincial Park
South Baymouth
Perivale
542
Sandfield
Manitowaning
Kaboni
Wikwemikong
Musée Assiginack Museum
Buzwah
Wikwemikonsing
MANITOULIN ISLAND
ÎLE MANITOULIN
Great Duck Island
Outer Duck Island
Squaw Island
Rabbit Island
Wall Island
Club Island
Lonely Island
GEORGIAN

D

Thompson's Harbour State Park
North Point
Old Presque Isle Lighthouse
Presque Isle
PRESQUE ISLE
24
Besser
23
Middle Island
Cathro
LAKE HURON
Fitzwilliam Island
Yeo Island
Flewpot Channel
Main Channel
PARC MARIN NATIONAL FATHOM FIVE NATIONAL MARINE PARK
Rés. nat. prov. Little Cove Prov. Nat. Res.
Cove Island
Flowerpot Island
Bears Rump Island
Russel Island
Tobermory
Cape Hurd
Singing Sands
ONTARIO
BRUCE PENINSULA
PÉNINSULE
BRUCE PENINSULA NATIONAL PARK/ PARC NATIONAL DE LA PÉNINSULE-BRUCE
Cabot Head
Réserve naturelle provinciale Cabot Head Provincial Nature Reserve

E

Alpena Lighthouse
ALPENA
32
5
Alpena
MICHIGAN
Ossineke
Michigan Islands National Wildlife Refuge
Spruce
23
Black River
F41
Huron National Forest
Alcona
ALCONA
Lincoln
Negwegon State Park
South Point
Sturgeon Point
Thunder Bay Island
North Point
Thunder Bay
LAC HURON
Dyer's Bay
Cape Chin
Réserve naturelle provinciale Smokey Head-White Bluff Provincial Nature Reserve
Eagle Point
St. Edmunds
Parc provincial Johnston Harbour Pine Tree Point Provincial Park
Miller Lake
Pine Tree Point
Northern Bruce Peninsula
110
Parc provincial Ira Lake Provincial Park
Clarke's Corners
Stokes Bay
Ferndale
Lion's Head
9
Barrow Bay
Hope Bay
Pike Bay
Howdenvale
Red Bay
Mar
9
Greenough Point
Réserve naturelle provinciale McMaster Island Provincial Nature Reserve
Lyal Island
Parc provincial Black Creek Provincial Park

F

72
17
Harrisville
Harrisville State Park
F41
F30
Mikado
Greenbush
35
23
Oscoda Au Sable
IOSCO
Tuttle Marsh
Au Sable Point
Tawas
East
IOSCO
Wiarton
13
South Bruce Peninsula
Oliphant
Chiefs Point
Sauble Falls
Parc provincial Sauble Falls Provincial Park
Sauble Beach North
Sauble Beach
8
Hepworth
14
Park Head
Sauble Beach South
13
Scotch Settlement
Allenford
10
Chippawa Hill
Elsinore
Southampton
Chantry Island National Migratory Bird Sanctuary/ Refuge national d'oiseaux migrateurs de l'Île-Chantry
3
Arkwright
17
Tara
Port Elgin
Saugeen Shores
17
Burgoyne
Arran-Elderslie
Dobbinton
Parc provincial MacGregor Point Provincial Park
Brucedale
North Bruce
40
Saugeen

1   2   3   4

PENINSULA AND ISLAND

In this view, the Bruce Peninsula points northwest across Main and Fitzwilliam channels toward Manitoulin Island (top). The peninsula's northern tip is the site of Bruce Peninsula National Park (still under development), as well as Fathom Five National Marine Park (Canada's first marine park), which protects Cove, Flowerpot, and other islands visible offshore in Lake Huron (left) and Georgian Bay (right). "The Bruce" is part of Ontario's 725-km-long Niagara Escarpment. This height of land runs from the Niagara Peninsula to Manitoulin Island and beyond. At 2,700 km², Manitoulin is the world's largest island in a freshwater lake. Beyond Manitoulin on the far shore of the North Channel lies La Cloche Provincial Park.

Other points of interest

■ Located on the southern edge of the Canadian Shield, 345-km² Killarney Provincial Park [B4-B5] contains rock formations more than 2 billion years old. Its rugged beauty inspired the Group of Seven painter A. Y. Jackson. It was through his efforts that this area became a park.

■ The 110-km-long French River [B6-B7] connects Lake Nipissing to Georgian Bay. Fur traders once plied its maze of channels and secluded bays, and portaged its rapids and falls. It has been designated as one of Canada's most historic waterways.

■ At 832 km², Lake Nipissing is the fifth largest lake in Ontario—excluding the Great Lakes. The lake connects the Ottawa and French rivers, part of the historic route of the early explorers and fur traders heading westward.

Scale 1:800,000

1 cm = 8 km

0   10   20   30 km

LAKE HURON / LAC HURON

MICHIGAN

OHIO

LAKE ST. CLAIR / LAC SAINTE-CLAIRE

Major places:

- DETROIT
- WINDSOR
- LONDON
- Sarnia
- Port Huron
- Chatham-Kent / Chatham
- Goderich
- St. Thomas
- Sterling Heights
- Warren
- Rochester Hills
- Troy
- Royal Oak
- Southfield
- Wyandotte
- Amherstburg
- Leamington
- Kingsville
- Essex
- Strathroy
- Exeter
- St. Marys
- Wingham
- Huron East
- South Huron
- West Elgin
- Dutton/Dunwich

POINT PELEE NATIONAL PARK / PARC NATIONAL DE LA POINTE-PELÉE

Parc provincial Wheatley Provincial Park

Parc provincial Rondeau Provincial Park

Pelee Island

Put-in-Bay

PERRY VICTORY AND INT'L PEACE MEMORIAL

Geneva-On-The-Lake

Mentor-On-The-Lake

Painesville

LAKES AND FARMLANDS

Southwestern Ontario is bounded by three lakes: Huron (top), St. Clair (centre), and Erie (bottom). At 1,114 km², Lake St. Clair is "the smallest of the Great Lakes." It is connected to Lake Huron to the north by the St. Clair River and empties into Lake Erie to the south by the Detroit River. The delta of the St. Clair River is visible on the lake's north shore. The Thames River, which enters at the lake's south end, flows through some of Canada's best farmland. This view shows the highly productive fields in Ontario's Essex and Chatham-Kent counties. The 18-km-long triangular spit jutting into Lake Erie is Point Pelee, the site of the second smallest of Canada's national parks, after St. Lawrence Islands, and mainland Canada's southernmost point.

Other points of interest

■ At 59,600 km², Lake Huron is the second largest of the Great Lakes, and the world's fifth largest. The Canadian portion occupies 36,000 km².

■ Lake Erie is the shallowest of the Great Lakes, with a maximum depth of 64 m, and also the smallest by volume (484 km³). The Canadian portion occupies slightly less than half of the lake's 25,700 km². Erie's waters fall 100 m to Lake Ontario; roughly half of the drop occurs at Niagara Falls.

■ Uninhabited Middle Island [F2] is Canada's southernmost bit of territory.

■ Oil Springs, Ont. [C3], is the site of North America's first commercial oil well, which James Miller Williams put into production in 1857. A museum near the site traces the history of oil production in this region. In 1999, southern Ontario still produced crude oil valued at $44 million.

Scale 1:800,000

1 cm = 8 km

0   10   20   30 km

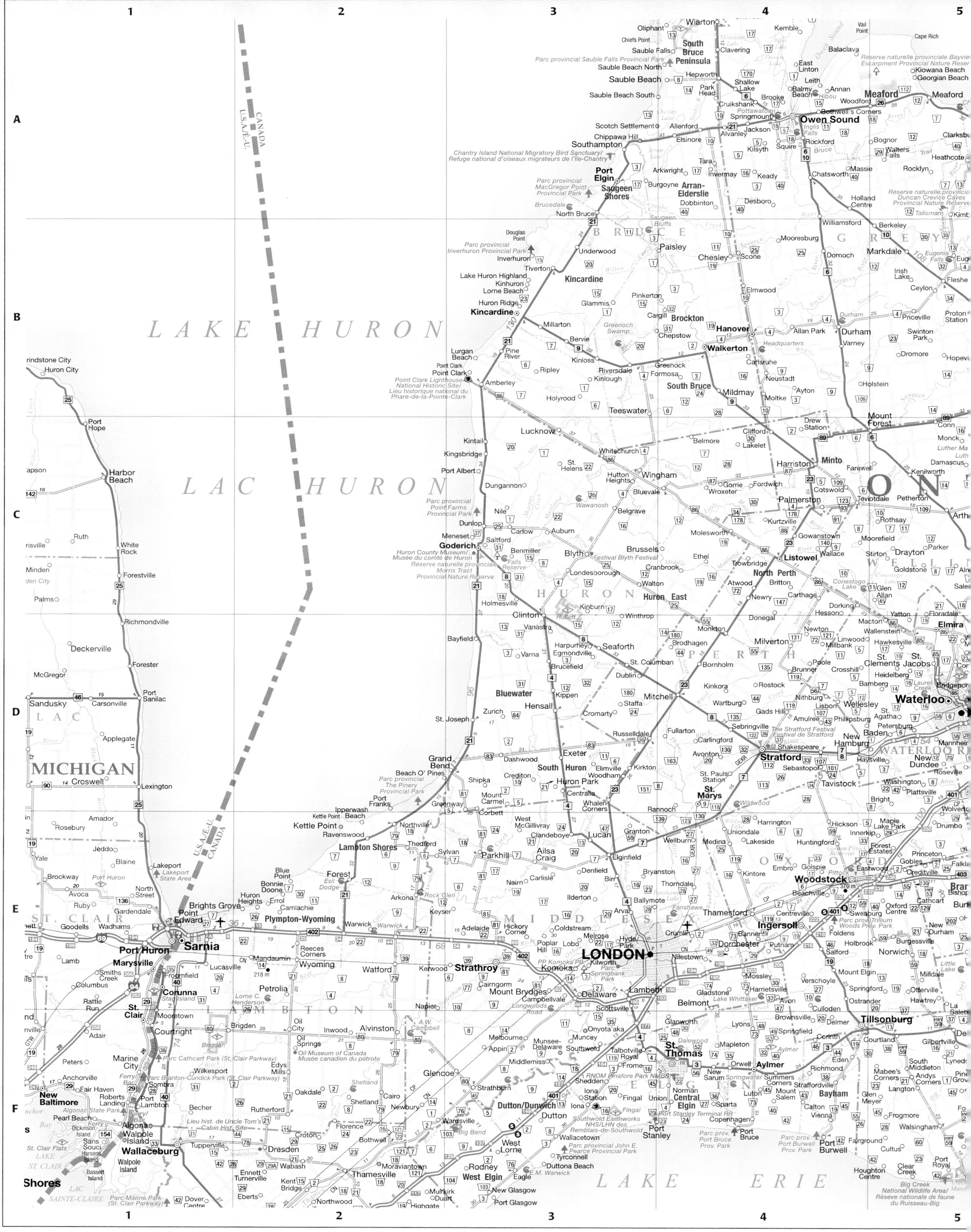

LAKE HURON

LAC HURON

MICHIGAN

LAKE ST. CLAIR / LAC SAINTE-CLAIRE

LAKE ERIE

BRUCE

GREY

HURON

PERTH

WELLINGTON

MIDDLESEX

OXFORD

LAMBTON

ELGIN

ST. CLAIR

Owen Sound, Meaford, Port Elgin, Saugeen Shores, Southampton, Kincardine, Walkerton, Hanover, Goderich, Stratford, Waterloo, Listowel, London, St. Thomas, Woodstock, Ingersoll, Tillsonburg, Sarnia, Port Huron, Marysville, Strathroy, Aylmer, Wallaceburg, St. Marys

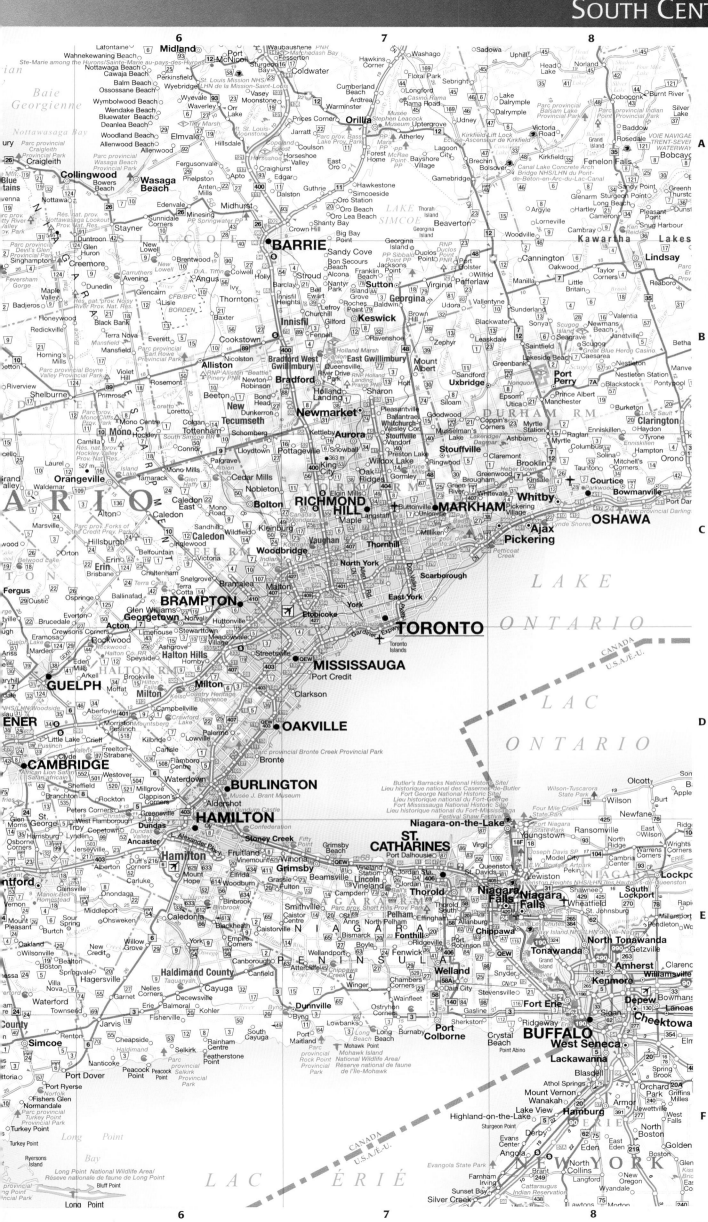

ONTARIO'S GOLDEN HORSESHOE

The Golden Horseshoe wraps around the western end of Lake Ontario from St. Catharines to Toronto and beyond. With almost 7 million inhabitants, the region has Canada's densest population cluster. The area takes its name from the lake's horseshoe-like curve, as well as the good fortune bestowed by its industrial and financial activities. Some of its features visible above include: Port Weller Harbour, the gateway to the Welland Canal east of St. Catharines (lower right); central Hamilton and the Skyway Bridge (lower left); and the expanse of Metro Toronto, lying just north of its two lakeshore harbours. Pickering—the site of a nuclear power station—sits on the promontory at the far right. At the top of this view is Cook's Bay on Lake Simcoe.

Other points of interest

■ Long Point National Wildlife Area [F5-F6] is a 32-km-long spit of sand dunes and marshland. Some 237 bird species—roughly 75 percent of all species recorded in Ontario—have been spotted at Long Point. It is an important stopover for migrating waterbirds, bats, and butterflies.

■ Niagara Falls [E8] is the world's greatest by volume (2,832 m³). The Canadian, or Horseshoe, Falls is 54 m high, 675 m wide, and flows at a rate of 155 million litres per minute. Some 12,500 years ago, as the last ice age was ending, Niagara Falls was born when Lake Erie plunged over the edge of Niagara Escarpment. At that time, the cataract began retreating at the rate of 1.2 m a year. It is now more than 11 km from its birthplace at Queenston.

Scale 1:800,000

1 cm = 8 km

0　　10　　20　　30 km

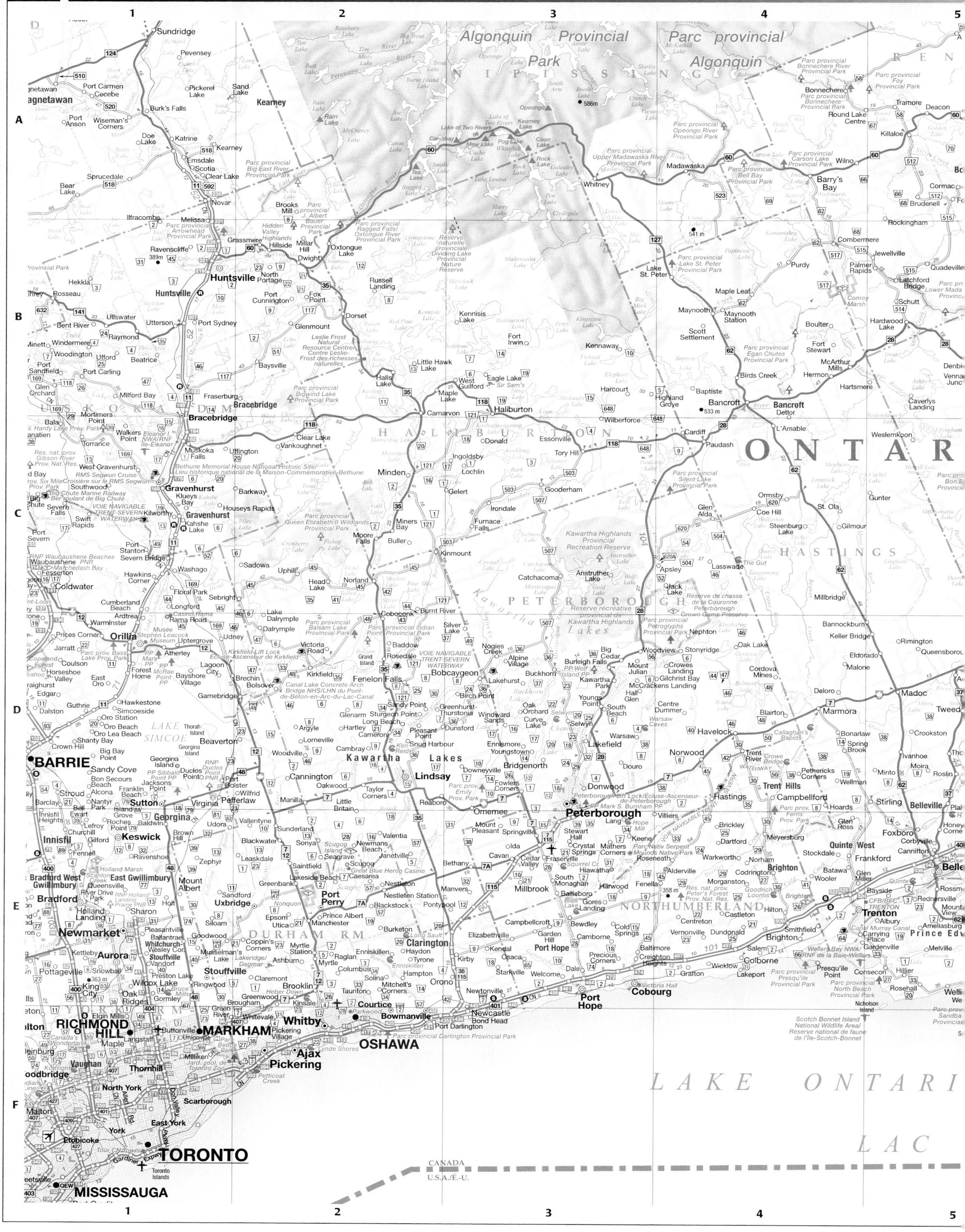

Algonquin Provincial Park / Parc provincial Algonquin

ONTARIO

LAKE ONTARIO / LAC ONTARIO

CANADA
U.S.A./É.-U.

TORONTO
MISSISSAUGA
MARKHAM
OSHAWA
Pickering
Ajax
Whitby
RICHMOND HILL
Newmarket
Aurora
BARRIE
Orillia
Gravenhurst
Bracebridge
Huntsville
Peterborough
Lindsay
Cobourg
Port Hope
Bowmanville
Clarington
Bancroft
Haliburton
Minden
Bobcaygeon
Fenelon Falls
Uxbridge
Stouffville
Keswick
Sutton
Beaverton
Cannington
Brighton
Trenton
Quinte West
Belleville
Campbellford
Hastings
Norwood
Lakefield
Madoc
Marmora
Stirling
Bancroft
Barry's Bay
Madawaska
Whitney
Killaloe
Combermere

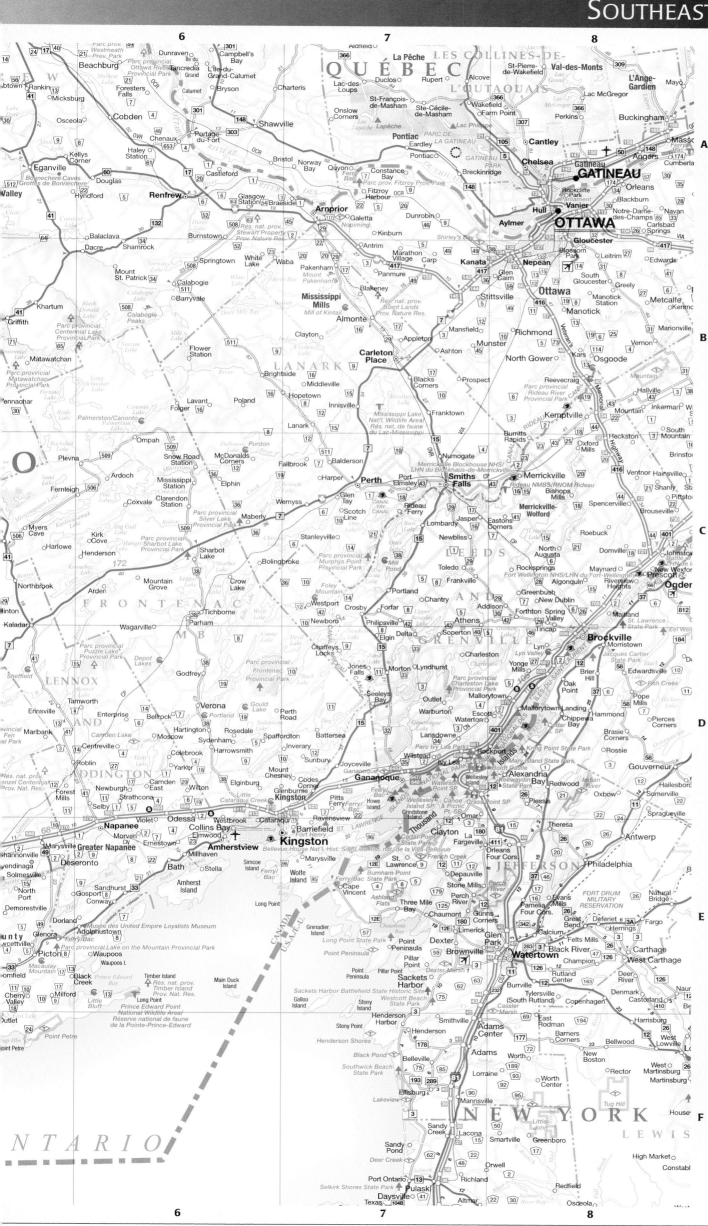

ISLANDS IN THE RIVER

This view of the Thousand Islands on the St. Lawrence River shows the section from Gananoque to just beyond Mallorytown Landing. The Thousand Islands—summits of ancient hills now submerged by the St. Lawrence—are formed by the Frontenac Axis, an 80-km-wide belt of granite that connects the Canadian Shield with the Adirondack Mountains in New York State. Visible (left to right) are the tips of Howe and Wolfe islands, and Grenadier Island on Canada's side of the river; Grindstone and Wellesley islands, on the American side. North of the St. Lawrence lies Shield country, where a string of lakes (top) links the 202-km-long Rideau Canal that connects Kingston and Ottawa.

Other points of interest

■ Kawartha Lakes [D2-D4], a chain of 14 lakes, forms a boundary between southern Ontario's rolling farmland and the Canadian Shield. The Kawarthas— "bright waters and happy lands" in the Huron language—are connected by the canals and locks of the Trent-Severn waterway. The 388-km-long waterway begins at Trenton [E4] and uses Rice Lake, the Kawarthas, and Lake Simcoe to reach Port Severn on Georgian Bay. A major link in the waterway is the Lift Lock at Peterborough [D3].

■ At Sandbanks Provincial Park [E5-F5], dunes up to 25 m high stretch 10 km along the shores of Lake Ontario.

■ Lake on the Mountain Provincial Park [E5], situated 62 m above the Bay of Quinte, has a turquoise-coloured lake. Its source was long a mystery until divers discovered that it is fed by underground streams flowing through subterranean layers of limestone.

Scale 1:800,000

1 cm = 8 km

0   10   20   30 km

11
65
Témiscamingue
Notre-Dame-du-Nord
Dymond
New Liskeard
558
Haileybury
North Cobalt
11B
Cobalt
Latchford
Parc prov. W.J.B. Greenwood Prov. Park
567
St-Bruno-de-Guigues
101
382
391
Laverlochère
382
Lorrainville
Ville-Marie
Lieu historique national du Fort-Témiscamingue/ Fort Témiscamingue National Historic Site
Béarn
391
Fabre
Angliers
Quinze
Moffet
Laforce
Belleterre
Winneway
R0815
R0816
R0817

A

Timiskaming
Lac
Témiscamingue
R0814
R0829
Laniel
122
Hunter's Point
TÉMISCAMINGUE
ZEC Kipawa
Lac Kipawa
R0812
R0812
R0813
R0704

B

11
Réserve de Chasse de la Couronne Nipissing Crown Game Reserve
Temagami
Parc provincial Finlayson Point Provincial Park
64
Marten River
Réserve nat. prov. Kenny Forest Prov. Nat. Reserve
Parc prov. Marten River Prov. Park
ONR
101
Kebaowek
Kipawa
Tee Lake
Thorne
Témiscaming
R0819
R0819
R0852
ZEC Restigo
QUÉ

C

Tilden Lake
NIPISSING
63
Eldee
Balsam Creek
Redbridge
533
656
ZEC Maganasipi
Dumoine
526m
Rapides-des-
R0706
R0834
R0834

17
CFB North Bay
North Bay
11B
344
Manitou Islands
Parc prov. Manitou Islands Prov. Park
94
Corbeil
531
17
Rutherglen
Mattawa
Deux Rivières
Bac/Ferry
17
Joachims
ZEC St-

D

Beaucage Point
Jocko Point
Cross Point
Deepwater Point
Callander
Nosbonsing
Bonfield
Eau Claire
Parc provincial Samuel de Champlain Provincial Park
Bissett Creek
Stonecliffe
Parc provincial Driftwood Provincial Park
Rapides-des-Joachims (Da Swisha)
635
Patric

654
Parc prov. South Bay Prov. Park
Astorville
11
Himsworth
Powassan
534
Restoule
PP Restoule PP
534
524
Nipissing
630
Parc provincial Amable du Fond Provincial Park
Kiosk
Parc provincial Bissett Creek Provincial Park
Parc provincial Grant's Creek Provincial Park
Mackey
Rolphton
Point Alexander
Deep River
17

E

522B
Trout Creek
522
Commanda
Brent
Algonquin Provincial Park
NIPISSING
Chalk River
CFB/BFC PETAWAWA
Parc provincial Barron River Provincial Park
Petawawa
Black Bay
28

PARRY SOUND
Parc prov. Mikisew Prov. Park
South River
Sundridge
510
124
Magnetawan
Port Carmen
Cecebe
11
Pickerel Lake
520
Burk's Falls
Katrine
Parc provincial Algonquin
Parc provincial Bonnechere Provincial Park
Parc prov. Bonnechere Prov. Park
58
REN

F

Bear Lake
518
Sprucedale
518
592
Emsdale
Scotia
Kearney
Novar
Melissa
Ravenscliffe
2
45
Parc provincial Arrowhead Provincial Park
Parc provincial J. Albert Bauer Provincial Park
8
Millar Hill
60
Parc provincial Oxtongue River-Ragged Falls Provincial Park
60
Smoke Lake
Whitney
Madawaska
Parc provincial Opeongo River Provincial Park
Parc provincial Upper Madawaska River Provincial Park
Parc provincial Carson Lake Provincial Park
Bonnechere
Round Lake Centre
58
Barry's Bay
60
Wilno
Tramore
Deacon
Killaloe
512
Brudenell
Cormac
523
Parc provincial Bell Bay Provincial Park
62

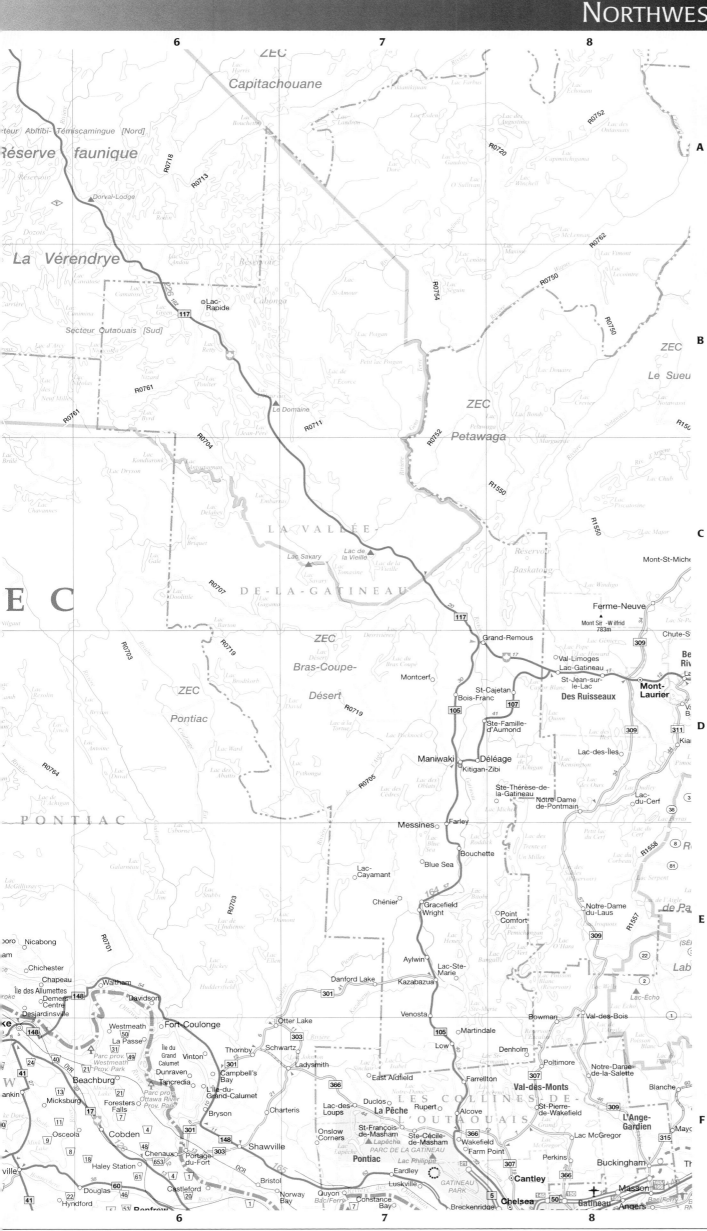

UPSTREAM ON THE OTTAWA

The 1,271-km-long Ottawa River originates in a chain of Quebec lakes and reservoirs: Réservoir Dozois, Grand Lac Victoria, Lac Granet, Réservoir Decelles, Lac Simard, and Lake Timiskaming (see also Plate 23, F5, F4, F3, and F1). South of Lake Timiskaming, the Ottawa—which stretches diagonally across this view—becomes a wide, powerful river, and a natural boundary between Quebec (right) and Ontario. Highway 101, visible on the Quebec side, runs parallel to the river until it reaches the pulp-and-paper town of Témiscaming. Here, travelers cross the river to reach Highway 63 in Ontario. The X-shaped expanse of water on the Quebec side is Lac Kipawa; just below it is Lac Beauchêne.

Other points of interest

■ Algonquin Provincial Park [E2-E4, F2-F4], covering 7,723 km² of Shield country contains some 2,500 lakes. Wildlife includes deer, moose, and wolves, as well as 240 species of birds. Established in 1893, it is Canada's oldest and still one of the largest of provincial parks.

■ The 13,615-km² Réserve Faunique La Vérendrye [A4-A7, B4-B7, C6-C7] has more than 4,000 lakes and rivers, including Réservoir Dozois, a source of the Ottawa River. This wildlife reserve, once the domain of the Algonquin Indians, fur trappers, and lumberjacks, was created in 1939. In 1950, it was renamed to commemorate the 200th anniversary of the death of French explorer La Vérendrye.

Scale 1:800,000

1 cm = 8 km

0   10   20   30 km

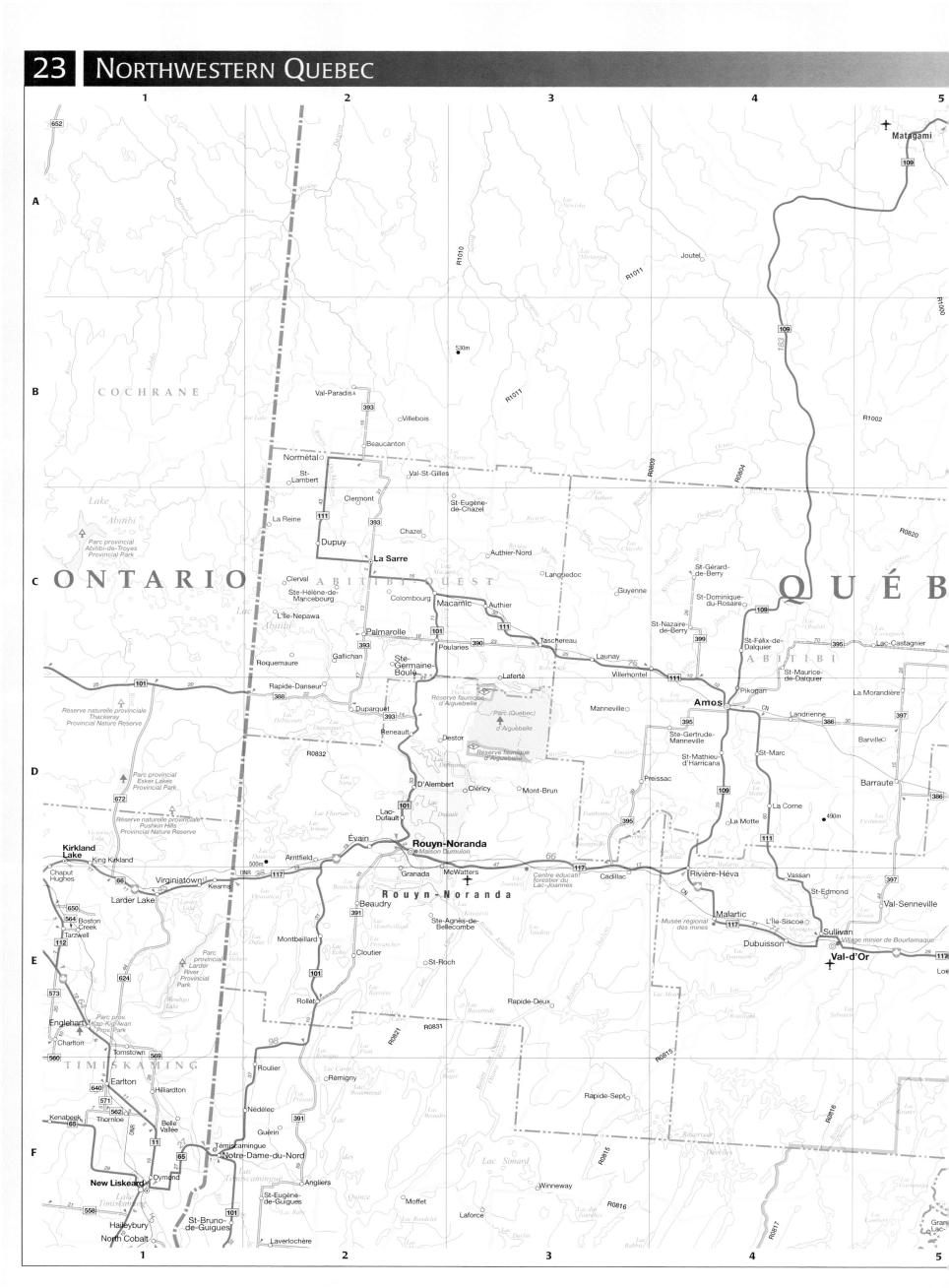

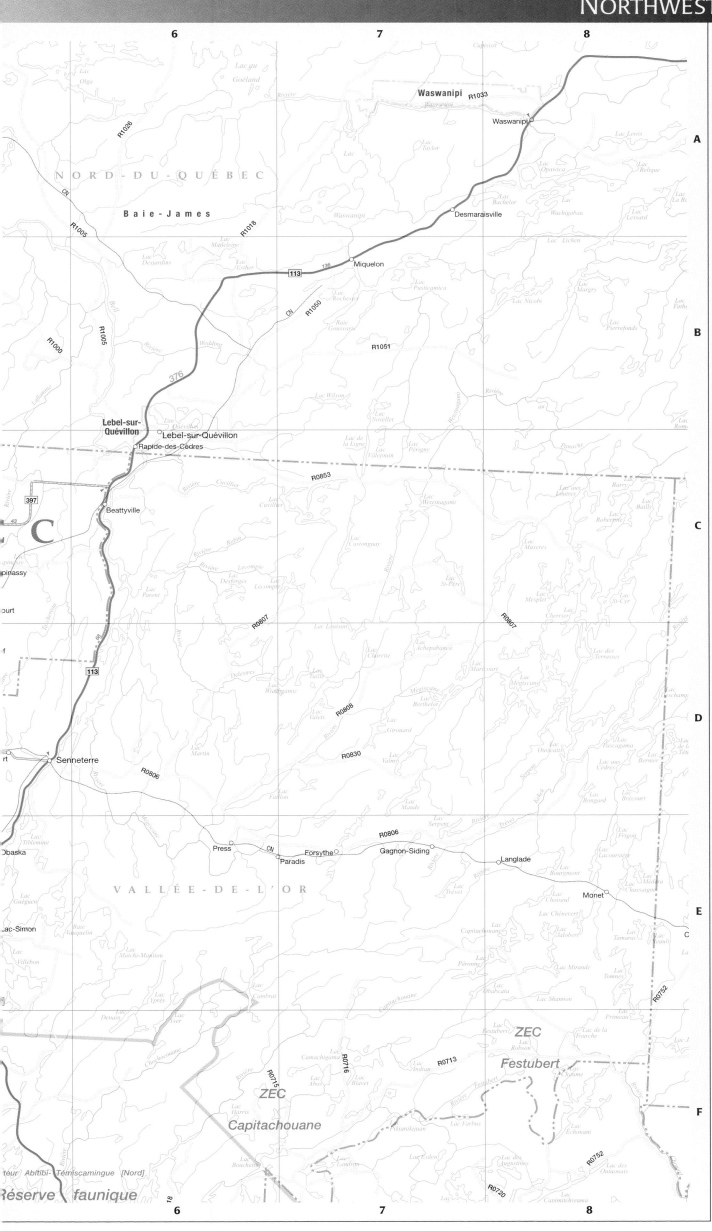

THE ROUYN-NORANDA REGION

The view looks northeast across the mining region of Rouyn-Noranda toward Lac Dufault (centre) and Lac Dufresnoy (top). Rich copper and gold deposits were discovered in this part of the Canadian Shield in the mid-1920s. The prosperity of Rouyn-Noranda (the latter name combines the words "Nor[th]" and "[C]an[a]da") still rests on smelting and processing ore from the region's many mines. Rouyn-Noranda is located on Lac Osisko (far right, just below Lac Dufault). The junction of the region's two major provincial highways, 117 and 101, is visible just east of the city.

Other points of interest

■ In 1912, the prospector Harry Oakes discovered the gold that sparked the growth of Kirkland Lake [D1]. Although none of the original mines are still active, the opening of new mines in the vicinity, and the processing of old mine tailings, have helped revive the city's fortunes.

■ Abitibi-de-Troyes Provincial Park [C1], located on the southern shore of Lake Abitibi, is a mixture of forest and swamp. One of the park's natural features is a 12-km-long peninsula jutting into the lake.

Scale 1:800,000

1 cm = 8 km

0   10   20   30 km

ZEC Bras-Coupé-Désert
DE-LA-GATINEAU
LA-VALLÉE
ANTOINE-LABELLE
de la Maison-de-Pierre
Réserve faunique Rouge-Matawin
QUÉ

Grand-Remous
Val-Limoges
Lac-Gatineau
St-Jean-sur-le-Lac
Des Ruisseaux
Mont-Laurier
Beaux-Rivages
Lac-des-Écorces
Guénette
Val-Barrette
Ste-Véronique
L'Ascension
Montcert
St-Cajetan Bois-Franc
Ste-Famille-d'Aumond
Maniwaki
Déléage
Kitigan-Zibi
Ste-Thérèse-de-la-Gatineau
Notre-Dame-de-Pontmain
Kiamika
Nominingue
L'Annonciation
Bellerive-sur-le-Lac
La Macaza
Labelle
Messines
Farley
Bouchette
Blue Sea
Lac-Cayamant
Chénier
Gracefield Wright
Point Comfort
Notre-Dame-du-Laus
La Minerve
Mont-Tremblant
Mont-Tremblant Village
Mont-Tremblant-Supérieur
St-Faustin-Lac-Carré
Val-des-Lacs
Lantier
Ste-Lucie
Doncaster
Aylwin
Lac-Ste-Marie
Kazabazua
Danford Lake
Réserve faunique
Labelle
St-Rémi-d'Amherst
Barkmere
Ste-Agathe-des-Monts
Val-David
Val-Morin
LAURENTIDES
Otter Lake
Venosta
Bowman
Val-des-Bois
Duhamel
St-Émile-de-Suffolk
Huberdeau
Arundel
Weir
St-Adolphe-d'Howard
Ste-Adèle
Schwartz
Ladysmith
East Aldfield
Martindale
Low
Denholm
Namur
Chénéville
Vinoy
Boileau
Lac-des-Seize-Îles
Lakeview
Montfort
St-Sauveur-des-Monts
Thornby
Charteris
Lac-des-Loups
La Pêche
Duclos
Rupert
Alcove
Poltimore
Notre-Dame-de-la-Salette
Blanche
Ripon
Notre-Dame-de-la-Paix
Montpellier
Lac-Grosleau
Kilmar
Pine Hill
Harrington
Lost River
Rivington
Laurel
Lac-Marois
Mille-Isles
Shawville
Onslow Corners
St-François-de-Masham
Ste-Cécile-de-Masham
Wakefield
Farm Point
Perkins
Buckingham
Mayo
St-Sixte
St-André-Avellin
ARGENTEUIL
Dalesville
Brownsburg
Louisa
Lakefield
St-Colomban
Pontiac
Eardley
Luskville
Breckenridge
Cantley
Chelsea
GATINEAU
Masson
Angers
Thurso
Clarence
Rockland
Wendover
Montebello
Papineauville
Plaisance
Fassett
Pointe-au-Chêne
Grenville
Hawkesbury
L'Orignal
Calumet
St-Philippe-d'Argenteuil
Lachute
Bristol
Norway Bay
Quyon
Constance Bay
Dunrobin
Aylmer
Hull
OTTAWA
Orleans
Cumberland
Clarence Creek
St-Pascal
Plantagenet
Curran
Pleasant Corners
Vankleek Hill
St-Eugene
Ste-Anne-de-Prescott
Rigaud
Hudson
Braeside
Arnprior
Galetta
Kinburn
Antrim
Carp
Kanata
Nepean
Gloucester
Navan
Sarsfield
Hammond
Pendleton
Riceville
St-Bernardin
Fournier
Dalkeith
Ste-Marthe
Ste-Justine-de-Newton
White Lake
Pakenham
Blakeney
Appleton
Carleton Place
Almonte
Clayton
Middleville
Hopetown
Innisville
Lanark
Franktown
Richmond
Munster
Stittsville
Ottawa
Ashton
Manotick
Kars
Osgoode
North Gower
Glen Cairn
Greely
Russell
Embrun
Limoges
Casselman
Maxville
Greenfield
Moose Creek
Green Valley
Alexandria
Dunvegan
Lochiel
Glen Robertson
Dalhousie Mills
St-Polycarpe
Les Coteaux
Coteau
Rivière-Beaudette
STORMONT, DUNDAS AND GLENGARRY
PRESCOTT AND RUSSELL
ONTARIO
Metcalfe
Kenmore
Marionville
Vernon
Morewood
Berwick
Crysler
Finch
Newington
Monkland
Apple Hill
North Lancaster
St. Raphaels
Bainsville
Williamstown
Lancaster
South Gloucester
Manotick Station
Mountain
Winchester
Chesterville
Winchester Springs
Inkerman
South Mountain
Williamsburg
Hallville
Harrisons Corner
St. Andrews
Summerstown
Port Lewis
Kemptville
Burritts Rapids
Oxford Mills
Heckston
Brinston
Hainsville
Osnabruck Centre
Ingleside
Long Sault
Lakeview Heights
Cornwall
Fort Covington
Massena
Morrisburg
Louisville
Helena
Bombay
Westville Center
Constable
Burke
Merrickville
Bishops Mills
Shanly
Stampville
Waddington
Chase Mills
Raymondville
Brasher Falls
North Lawrence
Malone
Perth
Smiths Falls
Jasper
Lombardy
Merrickville-Wolford
Spencerville
Brouseville
Iroquois
Cardinal
Norfolk
Brookdale
Winthrop
Bangor
Balderson
Harper
Newbliss
Roebuck
Domville
Madrid
Chipman
North Bangor
Lawrenceville
Stanleyville
Westport
Crosby
Forfar
Chantry
Greenbush
New Dublin
Maynard
Johnstown
Lisbon
Bucks Bridge
Madrid
Springs
Morley
West Potsdam
Hopkinton
Potsdam
LEEDS AND GRENVILLE
Newboro
Elgin
Delta
Soperton
Athens
Toledo
Frankville
Algonquin
Rocksprings
Forthton
Spring Valley
Prescott
Ogdensburg
Brockville
Morristown
Lyn
NEW YORK
ST. LAWRENCE
FRANKLIN

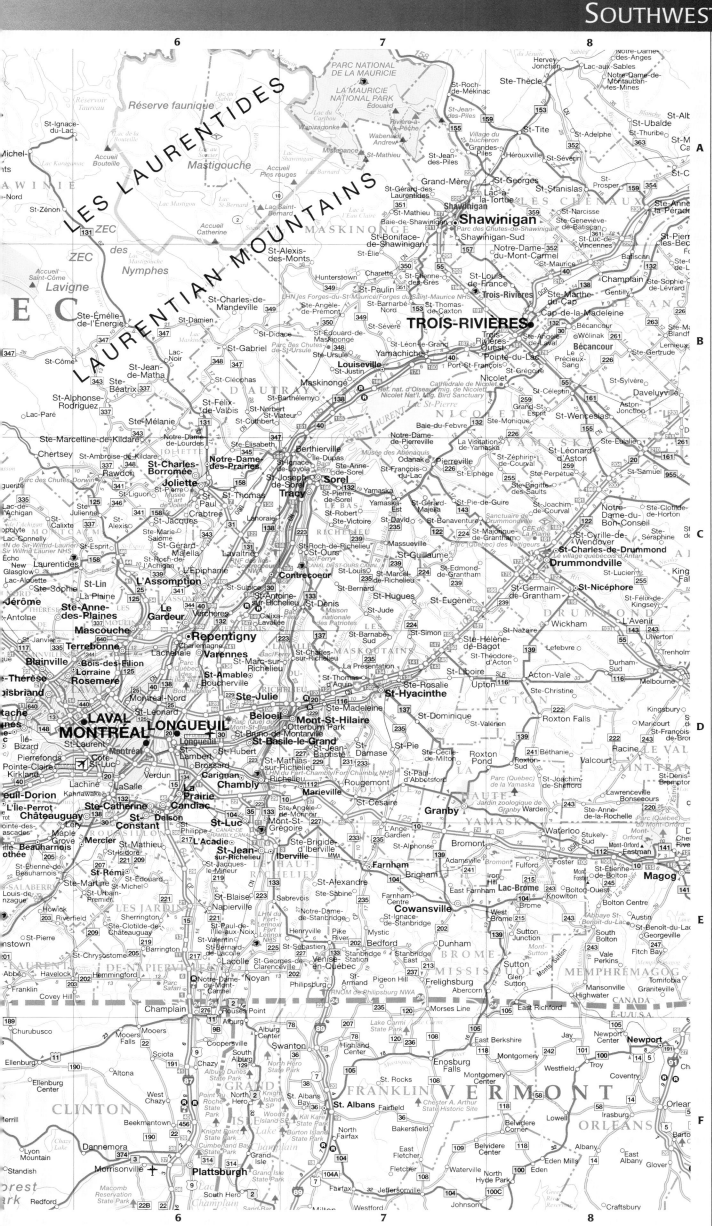

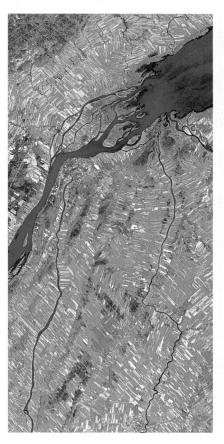

A LAKE IN THE ST. LAWRENCE

In New France, seigneurs parceled out farmland in long, thin strips to ensure their tenants had river frontage. The persistence of this land pattern is clearly evident in this view of the southern Quebec region where the Richelieu, Yamaska, and Saint-François rivers (left to right) flow north into the St. Lawrence River. At the mouth of the Richelieu lies the industrial city and seaport of Sorel. At this point, the St. Lawrence River widens to form Lac Saint-Pierre, a shallow, sluggish reach of water some 10 km across at its widest point. Île Dupas, Île aux Ours, and other low, mud-banked islands clog the entrance to the lake.

Other points of interest

■ Gatineau Park [D1-D2] encompasses 35,600 ha of forest, swamp, peat bogs, and lakes. Rich in flora and fauna, the park is home to 1,000 plants and 40 species of trees. The park supports 54 mammal species, including a population of 2,000 white-tailed deer, as well as 230 bird species.

■ The Laurentian Mountains form a 100- to 200-km-wide belt across the southern edge of the Canadian Shield in Quebec. This highland region stretches from the Gatineau Park in the west to the Saguenay River in the east—a distance of roughly 550 km. Geologically, the Laurentians were formed more than a billion years ago. Originally rising to much greater heights, they have been worn down into rounded hills.

Scale 1:800,000

1 cm = 8 km

0   10   20   30 km

1　　2　　3　　4　　5

A

R0830
Lac Valmy
Lac Maude
Lac aux Cèdres
Lac Bernier
Lac Têtê
Lac Lapage
ss
CN
R0806
Forsythe
Paradis
Gagnon-Siding
Langlade
Ouareau
Lac Bongard
Lac Brésourt
Lac Frigon
Lac Lacoursière
Lac Tessier
Lac Echouo
Lac Sultèe
Lac Huguenin
Lac Garamciève
Lac des Cinq Milles
E - L ' O R
Lac Trévet
Lac Chênevert
Lac Mistern
Lac Chassang
Lac Jaux
Lac Oskélanéo
Lac Benjamin
Lac Francœur
Lac Delâge
Lac Peter
LE HAUT-SA
R0400
Lac Choiseul
Monet
Lac Butes
Lac du Gros Ours
Lac Capitachouane
Lac Jaloubert
Lac Tamara
Clova
Oskélanéo
Lac Parker
Lac Carme
CN
Parent
R0405

B

Lac Péronne
Lac Mirande
Lac des Neiges
Lac du Brouillard
Lac Lorette
Lac Décelle
Lac Bérard
Lac Obabcata
Lac Shannon
Lac Tommey
Lac Primeau
Lac Jeune
Fortier
Lac des Dix Milles
Lac Mauser
Lac Dumas
Lac Gnetelin
ZEC
R0716
R0713
Lac Festubert
Lac Robson
Lac Indian
Festubert
Lac de la Fourche
Lac Gosselin
Lac Thaumur
Lac Choquette
R1502
Lac Landry
Lac Niverville
Lac Capintt
Casey
R0
R0715
ZEC
R0716
Capitachouane
Rivière Festubert
Pikanikigan
Lac Farbus
Lac Echouani
Bivers
Lac Dandurand

C

Lac Bouchette
Lac Landron
Lac des Augustines
R0752
Lac des Outaouais
Lac Pierre
Lac Long
ZEC
Lac Adonis
Lac à L
Nemotocachingue
Kempt
Lac
R0720
Lac Gaudon
Lac Capimitchigama
Lac Gircno
Lac Nasigon
Lac Lehan
Lac Busquet
QUÉB
Lac Doré
Lac O'Sullivan
Lac Winchell
Lac Lajoue
Lac De La Bulière
Lac Duchastel
Lac Turnball
ZEC
Normandie
Réservoir
R0762
Lac McLennan
R0750
Lac Maxime
Lac Lenoire
Lac Vimont
Lac Lecontre
Lac Mitchinamécus
R1502
Mitchinamécus
Cabonga

D

St-Amour
R0754
Lac Séguin
Lac Déplessis
Lac Badajoz
Lac Waterloo
Lac Tourbi
Lac Pongan
Petit lac Pongan
Lac Domaire
Lac Crèvier
Lac Notawassi
Lac Dieppe
R1502
Lac Sproule
Manawan
Lac Repas
ZEC
Le Sueur
ZEC
Le Domaine
R0711
Lac Petawaga
R0752
Petawaga
Lac Marguerite
Lac Bondy
R1503
Lac Châpin
Lac Gorman
Lac Lemgin
Lac Rupert
R1555
Mazana
R1500
R1450
ZEC
Boulé
Lac Jean-Pére
Riv. d'Argent
Lac des Polomas
Lac Revelstoke
R1501
Lac Sunset
Lac Ronge
Lac Napoléon

E

LA VALLÉE-
Lac de l'Écorce
Lac Chub
R1550
Lac Piscatteine
Lac Tapano
Beauregard
Lac de la Maison de Pierre
Lac Antoine
Lac Matawin
R1500
Réserve faunique
63
Lac Embarras
Lac Savary
Lac de la Vieille
Réservoir Baskatong
R1550
Lac Major
Ste-Anne-du-Lac
309
Lac de la Hache
47
ZEC
de la
Maison-
576
Lac Croze
63
Lac Gagama
Lac Tomasine
Lac Windigo
ANTOINE-LABELLE
Mont-St-Michel
R1555
Poissant
Lac St-Paul
Lac Frandière
Rouge-Matawin
63
DE-LA-GATINEAU

F

Mont Sir-Wilfrid 783m
Lac St-Paul
Val-Viger
de-
57
51
117
R719
ZEC
Lac Desrivières
Lac du Bras Coupe
Grand-Remous
17
Val-Limoges
Ferme-Neuve
309
Chute-St-Philippe
Pierre
47
45
4
Bras-Coupe-
Montcerf
Lac Pope
Lac-Gatineau
17
Beaux-Rivages
Lac-St-Paul
Lac-des-Écorces
L'Ascension
6
41
Désert
St-Cajetan
Bois-Franc
107
St-Jean-sur-le-Lac
Des Ruisseaux
Mont-Laurier
Guénette
Ste-Véronique
117
42
4
Parc (Québec) du Mont-Tremblant
28
R0719
105
Ste-Famille-d'Aumond
41
Val-Barrette
Lac-Saguay
321
L'Annonciation
Secteur de La Diable
Maniwaki
Déléage
309
311
Kiamika
Nominingue
Belleriée-sur-le-Lac
La Macaza
Secteur de La Pimbina
Accueil Saint-Do
Kitigan-Zibi
Lac-des-Îles
Lac-Monroe
Lac-Provost
Ste-Thérèse-de-la-Gatineau
Notre-Dame-de-Pontmain
Lac-du-Cerf
38
3
La Minerve
Labelle
Centre de services du Lac-Monroe Lac-Chat
125
St-Donat
Messines
Farley
Réserve faunique
Lac Joinville
Lac-Désert
Mont Tremblant 968m
329
Notre-Dame-de-la-Mer
Bouchette
Blue Sea
R1558
8

1　　2　　3　　4

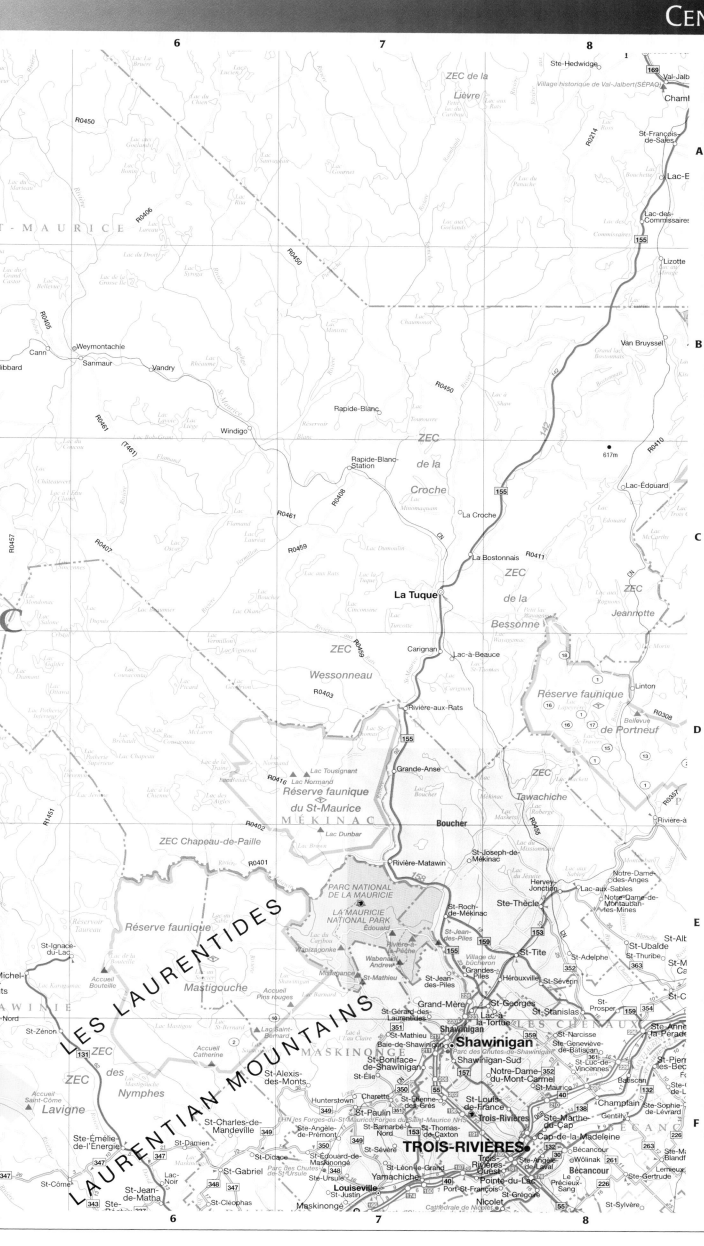

LA MAURICIE

Downstream from Lac Saint-Pierre, the St. Lawrence River resumes a fairly regular channel some two and a third kilometres wide. Trois-Rivières (lower right), where the 563-km-long St. Maurice River flows into the St. Lawrence, is halfway between Montréal and Québec. Founded in 1634, Trois-Rivières is Canada's second oldest city after Québec. This region, known as La Mauricie, provides logs and hydroelectric power for saw- and pulp-and-paper mills. La Mauricie National Park is located at the upper right of this view. Shawinigan, situated just before the bend in the river (left centre), processes metals and minerals, and produces chemicals.

Other points of interest

■ Parc du Mont-Tremblant [F4-F5] covers 1,500 km² of rugged Laurentian wilderness, encompassing some 500 lakes, seven rivers, and many streams and waterfalls. Mont Tremblant—at 986 m, the park's highest peak—is a favourite with skiers. The park's wildlife includes moose, white-tailed deer, black bear, and fox. Originally established as a forest reserve in 1894, Mont-Tremblant is Quebec's oldest provincial park and one of Canada's most popular.

■ The 549-km² La Mauricie National Park [E7] is divided into sectors. The southern sector has been developed for campers; the northern sector is still a rugged wilderness. Lac Wapizagonke is a favourite with canoeists and sailing enthusiasts.

Scale 1:800,000

1 cm = 8 km

0   10   20   30 km

1 **2** **3** **4** **5**

A

B

C

D

E

F

Réserve fa
Lacs-Albane
et-Wae

Lac du
Sauvage

R1031
(Route du Nord)

Lac
Chevrillon

R1029

R1000

Chibougamau

167

Chibougamau

CN

167

Lac
Omo

Lac
Dumas

Lac des
Petites
Plages

Lac
Caupichigau

Lac
L'Eau Noire

Lac
McDonald

Lac La
Ribourde

Lac
Michwacho

Lac de
la Chaleur

Chibougamau

Lac
Barlow

Lac
Bourbeau

Lac
Gwillim

Lac Inconnu

Lac des Deux
Orignaux

Lac
Opemisca

Lac Capisisit

113   125

Waswanipi   R1033

Lac
Méchamegus

Lac
Scott

Lac
Simon

Lac
Cavan

Chapais

Chapais

Lac Anville

Lac de la
Presqu'île

R1013

Lac à
l'Eau
Jaune

Lac du
Presqu'île

Lac
Trenholme

Lac
Goudreau

Waswanipi

Lac
Taylor

Lac Lewis

Lac
Dickson

Lac
Merrill

Lac
Sébastien

La Belle
Royer

R1018

Lac
Opatagaman

Lac de
la Baie

Lac
Verneuil

Lac
Bachelor

Lac
Opawica

Lac
Relique

Lac
La Ronde

Rivière

Lac
Irène

Lac en
Travers ce

Lac du Bras
Coupé

B E C

Waswanipi

Lac
Wachigabau

Lac
Laussard

Lac
Caopatina

Desmaraisville

R1009

Lac
Mannaud

Lac en
Malo

Lac Father

Rivière

Lac
du

Lac
Malo

R1050

Lac
Puskacamica

Lac
Nicabu

Lac
Margry

Lac
des Vents

Lac
d'Eau

Rivière

Miquelon

113   136

Lac
Rochester

Baie
Gouvarin

Lac de la
Surprise

Lac
Rouilli

CN

Lac
Pierrefonds

Lac Father

Lac Doda

Lac de la
Surprise

Lac
Pambrun

Lac
Crisafy

Lac
Gabriel

R0461

R1051

Lac
Hébert

Lac
Nézic

R1032

Lac
Monaco

Lac
Nemegosse

Q U É B E

illon

Lac Wilson

Lac
Novellet

Rivière

Lac
Roméo

Petit
lac Hébert

Panache

Lac
Oliva

Lac
Compton

Lac
Beaucours

Lac
Pesquites

Lac Robert

Lac
de la
Ligne

Lac
Villejoin

Lac
Péroux

R0853

Lac
Cuvillier

Lac aux
Loutres

Barry

Lac
Lacmon

Lac
Augusti

Lac
Ventadour

R0212

QUÉBE

villier

Lac
Cuvillier

Lac
Metemagami

Lac
Bailly

Lac
Baptiste

Lac
Nairn

Lac
Robin

Lac
Castonguay

Lac
Robertson

Lac
Pfister

Lac
Normandin

Lac
Lecompte

Lac
Desforges

Lac
Lecompte

Lac
St-Père

Lac
Mascère

Lac
Perrier

Lac
Duvois

Lac
Beauvivier

R0451

D

Lac
St-Cyr

Lac
Froid

Lac
Principal

R0807

Lac
Leuison

Lac
Achépabanca

Lac
Mesplès

Lac
Cherrier

Lac de la
Rencontre

Lac
Mathieu

R0807

Lac
Belisle

Deleares

Lac
Charme

Lac
Maricourt

Lac
Megiscand

Obedjiwan

Lac Lindsay

Lac
Wastigamic

Lac
Tuells

Lac
Megiscand

Reservoir   Gouin

Bel

R0808

Mégiscane

Lac
Berthelot

Lac
du

R0808

Lac
Valets

Lac
Girouard

Lac
Måle

Lac du
Déserteur

R0830

Lac
Valmy

E

Lac
Ouiscatis

Lac
Pascaguma

Lac
Bernier

Lac
Lepage

Lac
Faillon

Lac
Maude

Lac aux
Cèdres

Lac de
la Tête

Lac
Vauton

Rivière

Serpent

Lac
Bongard

Lac
Brennan

Lac
Garancereet

Lac des
Cinq Milles

Lac
Frigon

Lac
Sulte

Lac
Huguenin

R0806

Lac
Lacourvieve

Lac
Tessier

Lac
Francon, j

Lac
Leblanc

SS   CN   Forsythe   Gagnon-Siding

Langlade

Lac
Médeva

Lac
Jaux

Lac
Eclintre

Lac
Delage

Paradis

Lac
Chassaigne

Lac
Beaumain

Lac
Tassé

E - L' O R

Lac
Trévet

Lac
Bourgmont

Monet

Lac
Choseul

Lac
Bures

Lac
Oskélanéo

Lac du
Castor

LE HAUT-SA

Lac
Capitachouane

Lac
Chonevert

Lac
Dalobert

Clova

Oskélanéo

Lac
Carmen

R0400

R0405

F

Lac
Cambrai

Lac
Péronny

Lac
Mirandy

Lac
Tommy

Lac
Nevgus

Lac du
Brouillard

Parker

Lac de
l'Ours
Blanc

Lac
Lorette

Lac
Gaston

R0752

Lac
Obabcata

Lac
Shannon

Lac
Primeau

Lac
Jeanne

CN   Parent

ZEC

Lac
Festubert

Lac de
la Fourche

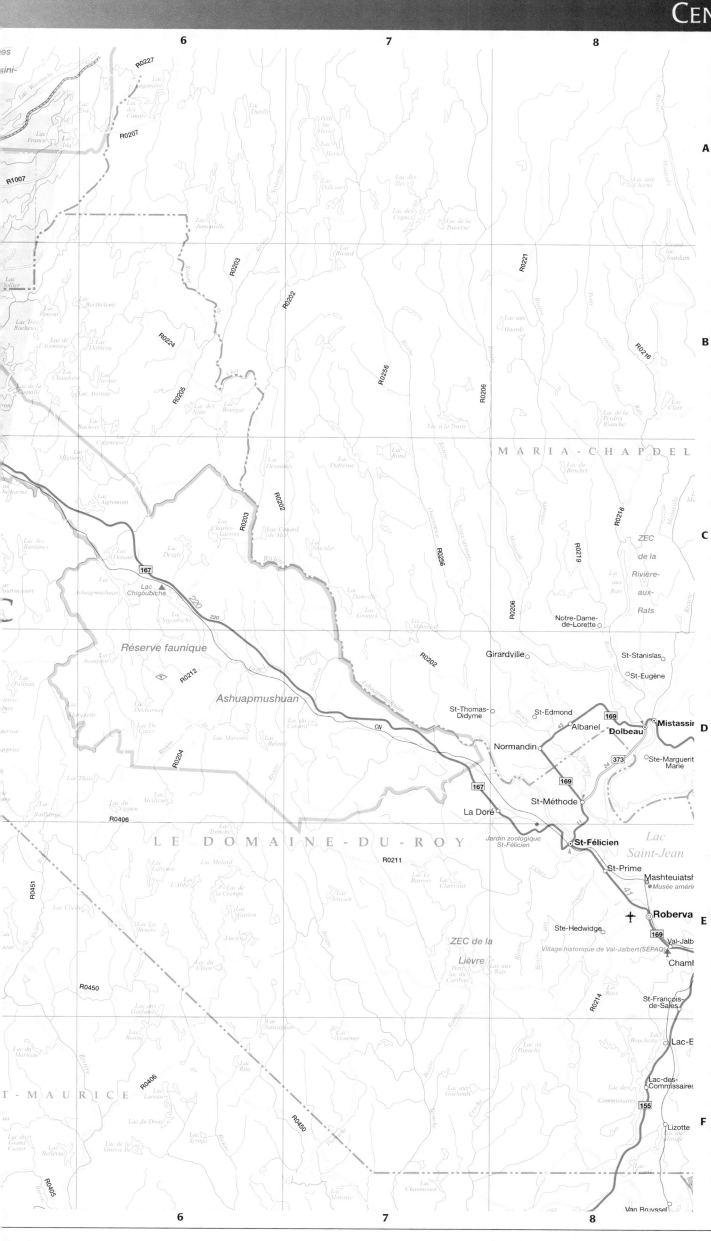

AROUND LAC CHIBOUGAMAU

In this view, the large expanse of water is Lac Chibougamau (top right). Just to the south of the lake, Highway 167 leads to the isolated mining town of Chibougamau, situated west of the lake. The townspeople work in the many copper and zinc mines located in this forested region. North of Lac Chibougamau, the Réserve Faunique des Lacs-Albanel-Mistassini-et-Waconichi has more than 5,000 lakes within its area of 28,285 km².

Other points of interest

■ The 4,500-km² Réserve Faunique Ashuapmushuan [C6, D6-D7] takes its name from the Montagnais "the place where the moose are seen." Black bear, fox, wolf, and hare inhabit this wildlife park. Brook trout, walleye, and northern pike abound in the park's 1,200 lakes. The park has two forest zones: firs and hardwoods dominate the southern sector; black spruce and jack pine, the northern sector.

■ Réservoir Gouin [D4, E3-E5] is a 1,570-km² artificial lake, accessible to visitors only by water and air. It was completed in 1918 as part of a hydroelectric project to control the flow of water in the Upper Mauricie River.

Scale 1:800,000

1 cm = 8 km

0   10   20   30 km

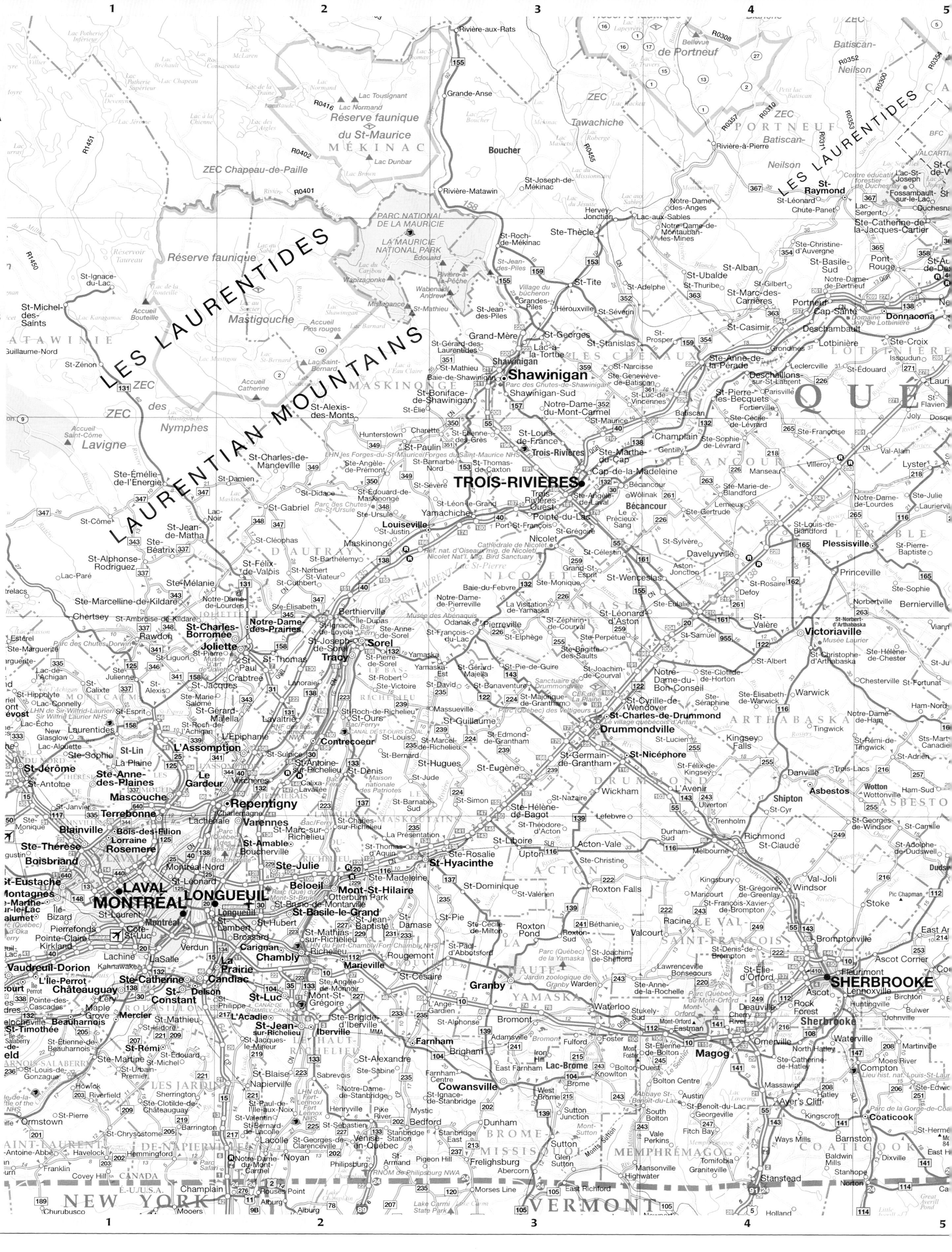

LES LAURENTIDES

LAURENTIAN MOUNTAINS

Réserve faunique du St-Maurice

MÉKINAC

ZEC Chapeau-de-Paille

PARC NATIONAL DE LA MAURICIE / LA MAURICIE NATIONAL PARK

Réserve faunique

Mastigouche

MASKINONGE

Shawinigan

Shawinigan-Sud

TROIS-RIVIÈRES

Trois-Rivières-Ouest

Louiseville

Maskinongé

Nicolet

Bécancour

Plessisville

Victoriaville

Joliette

Sorel

Tracy

Drummondville

St-Jérôme

L'Assomption

Mascouche

Terrebonne

Blainville

Rosemère

Boisbriand

Repentigny

Varennes

Ste-Julie

Beloeil

Mont-St-Hilaire

St-Hyacinthe

LAVAL

MONTRÉAL

LONGUEUIL

St-Laurent

Verdun

Lachine

LaSalle

La Prairie

Chambly

Candiac

St-Luc

Marieville

Granby

Bromont

SHERBROOKE

Magog

Coaticook

Cowansville

Farnham

Lac-Brome

St-Jean-sur-Richelieu

Vaudreuil-Dorion

Châteauguay

St-Rémi

Napierville

NEW YORK

VERMONT

CANADA / É.-U./U.S.A.

BROME-MISSISQUOI

MEMPHRÉMAGOG

NICOLET

BÉCANCOUR

YAMASKA

ARTHABASKA

DRUMMOND

ACTON

LES LAURENTIDES

PORTNEUF

St-Raymond

Donnacona

Deschambault

WHERE A MIGHTY RIVER NARROWS

This view looks northward toward Québec, visible on 98-m-high Cap Diamant above the St. Lawrence. At Québec, high cliffs narrow the river to a width of a kilometre. The bridge downstream from Québec (right centre) connects the north shore of the St. Lawrence with the picturesque 193-km² Île d'Orléans, the second largest island in the St. Lawrence after the island of Montréal. The island marks the tidal zone of the St. Lawrence where the river's freshwater currents meet and mix with saltwater tides. Other north-shore sites: Lac Saint-Charles (top left) and the Rivière Montmorency (centre right), east of the bridge leading to the Île d'Orléans. South of the St. Lawrence, the Rivière Chaudière flows north through the farmland of the serene Beauce region.

Other points of interest

■ The 200-m-high Mont Royal in the heart of Montréal [E1] is one of 10 Monteregian Hills, which rise abruptly from agricultural lowlands of southern Quebec. Geologists believe the hills were formed when igneous rock thrust into layers of sedimentary rock below the earth's surface. Millions of years of erosion wore down the sedimentary rock, eventually exposing the hills.

■ The 400-m-high Mont Saint-Hilaire [E2], the highest of Monteregian Hills, is the site of a McGill University conservation area, which is a well-known bird sanctuary and Canada's first UNESCO biosphere reserve.

Scale 1:800,000
1 cm = 8 km
0   10   20   30 km

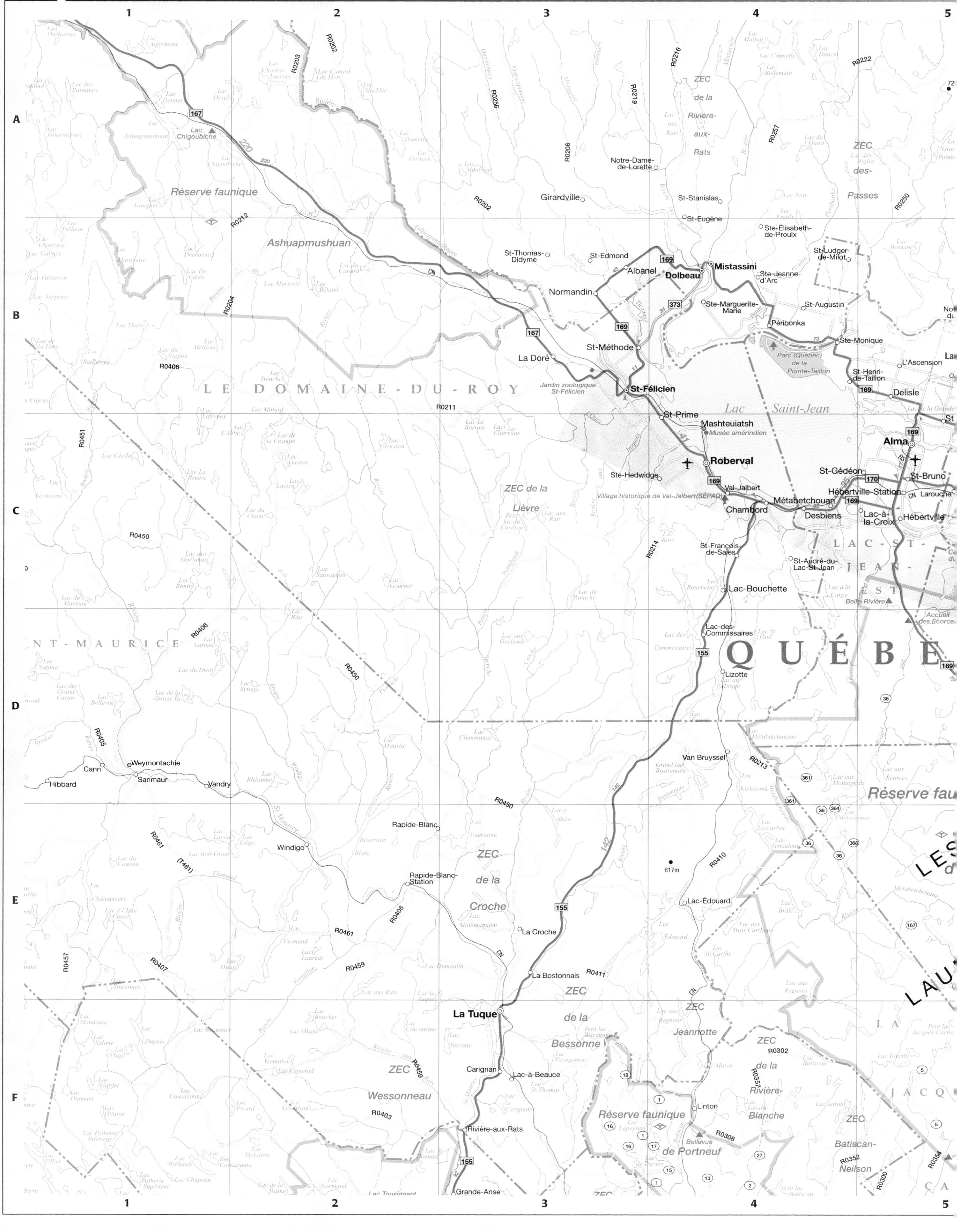

Réserve faunique Ashuapmushuan

LE DOMAINE-DU-ROY

ZEC de la Rivière-aux-Rats

ZEC de la Lièvre

ZEC de la Croche

ZEC de la Bessonne

ZEC Wessonneau

Réserve faunique de Portneuf

QUÉBEC

LAC-ST-JEAN-EST

Places:
Notre-Dame-de-Lorette, Girardville, St-Stanislas, St-Eugène, Ste-Élisabeth-de-Proulx, St-Thomas-Didyme, St-Edmond, St-Ludger-de-Milot, Albanel, Dolbeau, Mistassini, Ste-Jeanne-d'Arc, St-Augustin, Normandin, Ste-Marguerite-Marie, Péribonka, Ste-Monique, St-Méthode, L'Ascension, La Doré, Parc (Québec) de la Pointe-Taillon, St-Henri-de-Taillon, Delisle, Jardin zoologique St-Félicien, St-Félicien, St-Prime, Lac Saint-Jean, Mashteuiatsh, Musée amérindien, Alma, Roberval, Ste-Hedwidge, St-Gédéon, St-Bruno, Village historique de Val-Jalbert (SÉPAQ), Val-Jalbert, Métabetchouan, Hébertville-Station, Larouche, Chambord, Desbiens, Lac-à-la-Croix, Hébertville, St-François-de-Sales, St-André-du-Lac-St-Jean, Lac-Bouchette, Lac-des-Commissaires, Lizotte, Van Bruyssel, Weymontachie, Cann, Hibbard, Sanmaur, Vandry, Rapide-Blanc, Windigo, Rapide-Blanc-Station, La Croche, Lac-Édouard, La Bostonnais, La Tuque, Carignan, Lac-à-Beauce, Linton, Rivière-aux-Rats, Grande-Anse

ST-MAURICE

Réserve faunique

Lac Saint-Jean

Highways: 167, 169, 170, 373, 155, 220, 36, 361, 364, 368, 18, 16, 17, 27, 15, 13, 5

Roads: R0202, R0203, R0204, R0206, R0211, R0212, R0214, R0216, R0219, R0222, R0250, R0256, R0257, R0302, R0308, R0351, R0352, R0354, R0403, R0405, R0406, R0407, R0408, R0410, R0411, R0450, R0451, R0457, R0459, R0461, R0213

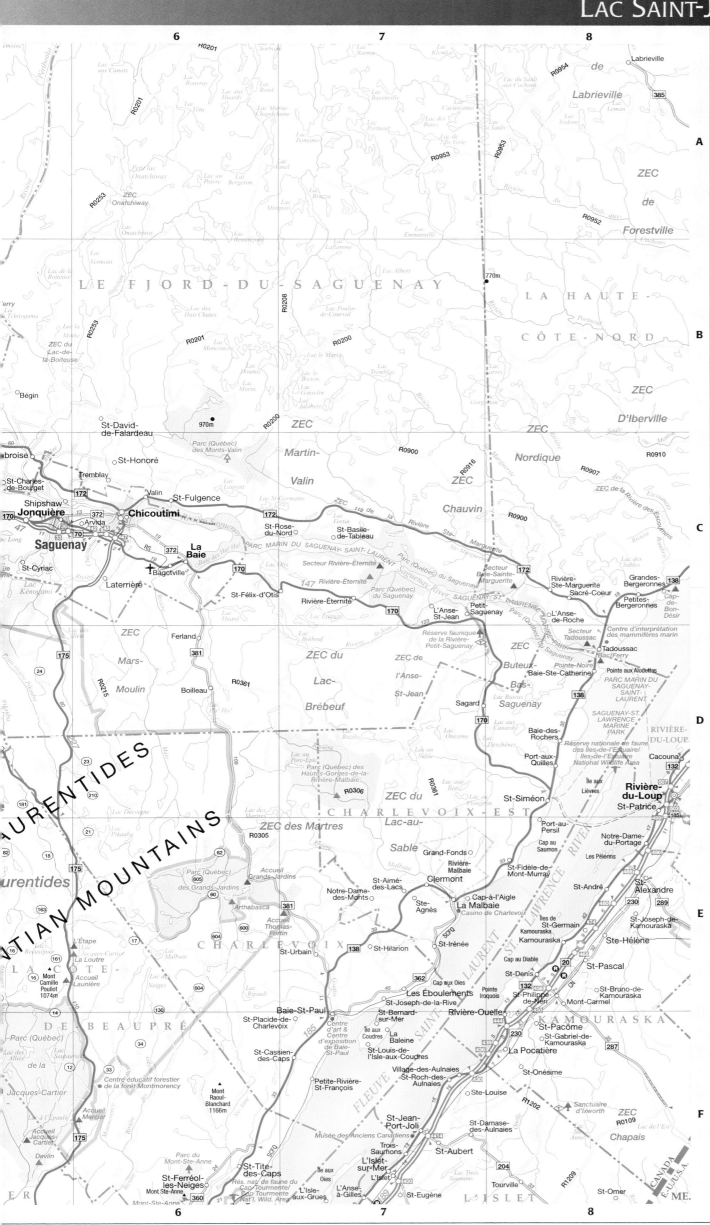

A LAURENTIAN "KINGDOM"

Prosperous farmland and rugged Laurentian Highlands encircle the 1,002-km² Lac Saint-Jean. The many rivers that feed the lake originate in the surrounding highlands, including the Ashuapmushuan and Mistassini (top left and right), which flow into the lake from the west, and the Péribonka (right), which enters from the north. Lac Saint-Jean is drained by the Saguenay River (right), which flows east through a majestic 150-km-long fjord to the St. Lawrence. The overall length of the Saguenay to its source at the head of the Péribonka in the Laurentian Highlands is 698 km. The populous but remote Lac-Saint-Jean–Saguenay region is often called the "Kingdom of the Saguenay."

Other points of interest

■ The 1,138-km² Saguenay–St. Lawrence Marine Park [C6-D8], a federal-provincial park, protects the waters of the Saguenay and St. Lawrence, which support seal and porpoises, as well as minke, beluga, and blue whales.

■ The 228-km² Parc du Saguenay [C7-D8], a provincial park, occupies strips of land on either side of the Saguenay River. It overlooks the Saguenay fjord, carved from the Precambrian rock by glaciers during the last ice age. This majestic inlet, 2 km wide and 250 m deep, is flanked by cliffs up to 500 m high. The southernmost of Canada's fjords, the Saguenay is unique in that it flows into a larger river, not into the ocean as is usual elsewhere.

Scale 1:800,000

1 cm = 8 km

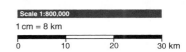

0   10   20   30 km

Column numbers: 1 2 3 4 5

Row letters: A B C D E F

LES LAURENTIDES

LAURENTIAN MOUNTAINS

LA HAUTE

CÔTE-NORD

MANICOUAGAN

Labrieville

R0954

Labrieville

Lac Leman

Lac Isidore

de

385

Labrieville-Sud

Lac Lessard

R0952

Forestville

Lac McDonald

385

R0912

R0908

R0901

Barrage Manic-Deux

389

Franquelin

Godbout

Pointe-des-

Secteur Mingan (Hauterive) 21

Pointe St-Pancrace

Pointe à la Croix

Chute-aux-Outardes

Barrage Manic-Un

Secteur Marquette

Baie-Comeau

Les Buissons

Pointe-Lebel

Pointe de Manicouagan

Péninsule de Manicouagan

Raguenau

Ruisseau-Vert

138

Pointe-aux-Outardes

Parc régional de Pointe-aux-Outardes

Papinachois

Betsiamites

Rivière-Bersimis

Pointe de Betsiamites

Les Îlets-Jérémie

193

Colombier

Cap Colombier

St-Marc-de-Latour

R0952

Forestville

FLEUVE SAINT-LAURENT

ST. LAWRENCE RIVER

ST. LAWRENCE

Ste-Anne-de-Portneuf

Matane

Petit-Matane

L'Anse-à-la-Croix

Ste-Félicité

Grosses-

132

St-Ulric

31

St-Léandre

St-Luc

St-Ad

195

St-René-de-

ZEC de la Rivière-

Baie-des-Sables

64

Métis-sur-Mer

Les Boules

Ste-Paule

297

Réserve faunique de la Rivière-Matane

Centre d'interprétation du saumon Atlantique

Jardins de Métis

Grand-Métis

St-Damase

Ste-Flavie

St-Octave-de-Métis

St-Vianney

Accueil Jc

Pointe-à-Boisvert

61

Pointe à Boisvert

Price

St-Noël

Lac Matapédia

St-Paul-du-Nord

Mont-Joli

St-Joseph-de-Lepage

234

St-Moïse

132

Sayabec

Val-Brillant

Sault-au-Mouton

Ste-Luce

Padoua

19

73

195

Baie-des-Bacon

Lieu historique national du Phare-de-Pointe-au-Père/

Pointe-au-Père Lighthouse National Historic Site

Pointe-au-Père

Luceville

St-Donat

Ste-Angèle-de-Mérici

Ste-Jeanne-d'Arc

St-Tharcisiu

Réserve nationale de faune de Pointe-au-Père/Pointe-au-Père National Wildlife Area

298

St-Cléophas

25

Ste-Odile

St-Anaclet

234

St-Gabriel

La Rédemption

Ste-Irène

Amqui

Les Escoumins

Essipit

Rimouski-Est

Neigette

298

Lac-au-Saumon

St-Alex-des-L

Musée régional de Rimouski

Île St-Barnabé

Rimouski

• 907m

QUEBEC

Sacré-Coeur

Île du Bic

Cap à l'Original

132

20

600

Ste-Blandine

Les Hauteurs

St-Charles-Garnier

Lac Inférieur

195

Petites-Bergeronnes

Parc (Québec) du Bic

Le Bic

St-Valérien

232

Mont-Lebel

St-Marcellin

LA MÉTIS

Lac-Humqui

St-Léon-le-Grand

172

Cap de Bon-Désir

St-Fabien-sur-Mer

St-Narcisse-de-Rimouski

Albertville

138

Cap de Bon-Désir

St-Fabien

St-Eugène-de-Ladrière

232

Ste-Florence

Grandes-Bergeronnes

Pointe Sauvage

61

Lac Taché

R0114

CVM

arc (Québec) du Saguenay

Centre d'interprétation des mammifères marins

St-Simon

St-Mathieu

ZEC

Bas-

Parc (Québec) du Saguenay

PARC MARIN DU SAGUENAY - SAINT-LAURENT

RIMOUSKI-

NOTRE-DAME

Tadoussac

Île aux Basques

NEIGETTE

St-Sifroi

LES

Pointe-Noire

Réserve Duchénier

La Trinité-des-Monts

1

15

12

Laurent

Pointe aux Alouettes

Trois-Pistoles

Ste-Françoise

Esprit-Saint

14

Lac Mistigougèche

R0115

Baie-Ste-Catherine

Rivière-Trois-Pistoles

296

St-Médard

46

Réserve faunique de Rimouski

124

R0104

138

Réserve nationale de faune de la Baie-de-l'Isle-Verte/Baie-de-l'Isle-Verte National Wildlife Area

Île Verte

St-Éloi

293

St-Jean-de-Dieu

296

232

A2

142

R0115

SAGUENAY-ST. LAWRENCE MARINE PARK

Notre-Dame-des-Sept-Douleurs

L'Isle-Verte

St-Paul-de-la-Croix

La Société

Lac-des-Aigles

31

Accueil Biencourt

Réserve faunique de la Rivière-Patapédia

Réserve national de faune des Îles-de-l'Est/Îles-de-l'Estuaire National Wildlife Area

St-Georges-de-Cacouna

Cacouna

St-Clément

Ste-Rita

295

Lac-Rimouski

A2

St-François-d'A

St-Jean-de-Matapédia

Île aux Lièvres

20

291

St-Arsène

St-Épiphane

St-François-Xavier-de-Viger

293

St-Cyprien

296

Biencourt

1

211

L'Ascension-de-Patapédia

Rivière-du-Loup

Musée du Bas-St-Laurent

St-Modeste

553

St-Hubert

232

Squatec

Réserve faunique de Kedgwick

St-Patrice

132

RIVIÈRE

Lamy

R0108

Kedgwick Game Refuge

Mennev

Notre-Dame-du-Portage

185

DU-LOUP

St-Pierre-de-Lamy

ZEC

Les Pèlerins

St-Antonin

291

St-Honoré

232

Auclair

Owen

NEW

St-André

20

Whitworth

Fort Ingall

185

Lejeune

Lac Toulad

Bac/Ferry

Grand lac Squatec

St-Alexandre

230

289

St-Joseph-de-Kamouraska

Cabano

St-Juste-du-Lac

295

Lots-Renversés

Whites

BRUNSWI

Ste-Hélène

KAMOURASKA

Sanctuaire du Parke

R0113

St-Elzéar

TÉMISCOUATA

Notre-Dame-du-Lac

Kedgwick River

265

St-Martin-de-Restigouche

260

Pohénégamook

Dégelis

185

17

St-Éleuthère

Lac Pohénégamook

St-Eusèbe

232

Packington

R0108

MADAWASKA

St-Quentin

Five Fingers

180

289

Estcourt

Sully

Pied-du-Lac

Moulin-Morneault

St-Joseph-de-Madawaska

VICTORIA

St-Athanase

Rivière-Bleue

St-Jean-de-la-Lande

Parc provincial des Jardins de la République/Provincial Park

St-Jacques

Musée des automobiles d'autrefois/Antique Automobile Museum

287

St-Marc-du-Lac-Long

289

2

Edmundston

G-109

ZEC Lac de l'Est

144

St-Basile

Chapais

Lac-Baker

120

Verret

144

Baker Brook

Madawaska

St-Hilaire

St. David

Grand Isle

Rivière-Verte

Notre-Dame-de-Lourdes

AROOSTOOK

215

Caron Brook

Quisibis

St-François-de-Madawaska

Clair

Frenchville

1

2

Ste-Anne-de-Madawaska

161

Fort Kent St. Historic Site

Fort Kent

St. Agatha

Lille

Notre Dame

Connors

205

Wheelock

Fort Kent Mills

Ste-Anne-de-Madawaska

161

Daigle

162

Keegan

Siegas

St-Léonard

St-Armand

255

MAINE

Dickey

161

St. John

11

161

10

Sinclair

Van Buren

St-Léonard-Parent

St-André

Bradbury

Ouellette

Long Lake

Bellefleur

1A

St. Francis

Soldier Pond

Guerette

1

Wallagrass

Plaisted

Allagash

Eagle Lake State Reserve

CANADA

U.S.A.

CANADA

É.U./U.S.A.

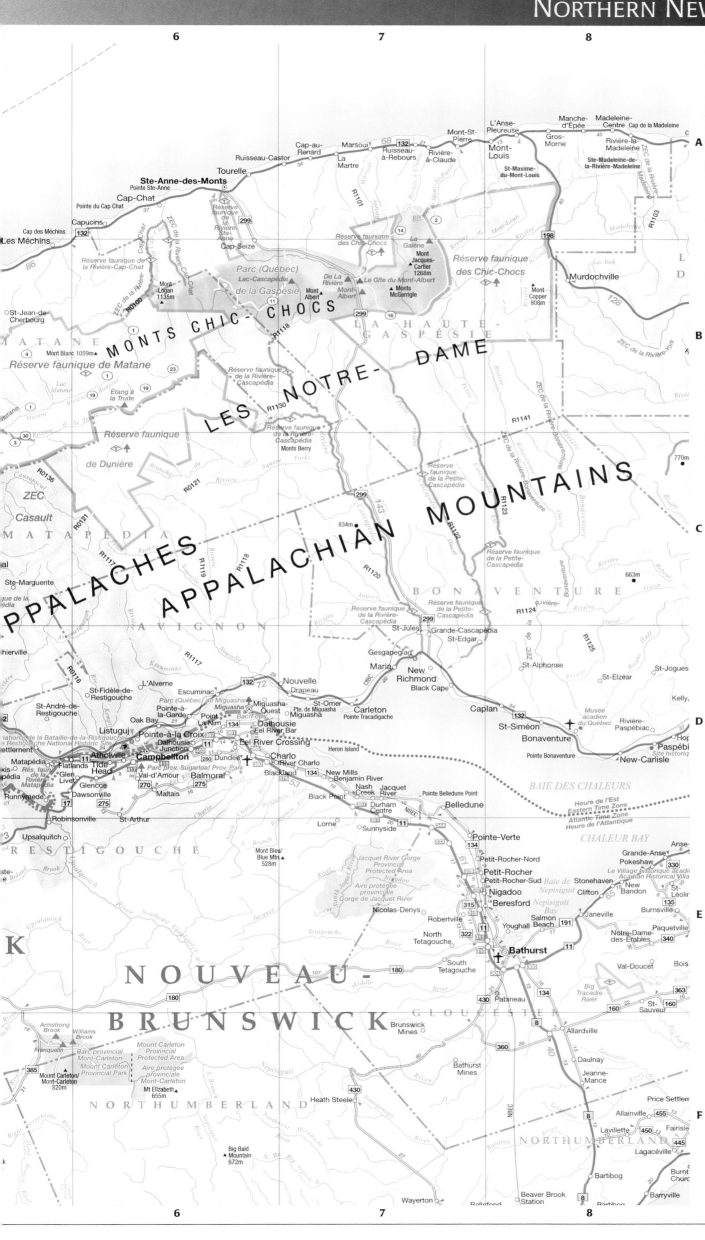

RESTIGOUCHE AND MATAPÉDIA

This view shows the wide estuary of the 200-km-long Restigouche River, which is slightly pinched where it empties into the waters of Chaleur Bay (right bottom). The Restigouche, with the Patapédia [Plate 31, A3], forms part of the boundary between Quebec and New Brunswick. One of its tributaries is the Rivière Matapédia, whose confluence with the Restigouche is clearly visible above (left bottom). The Matapédia flows south from the Notre Dame Mountains and through the Appalachians. Both are part of the Appalachian mountain system that extends from the eastern United States into this region.

Other points of interest

■ Réserve Faunique de Matane [B6-C5] is a 1,300-km² wilderness park with one of the highest concentrations of moose in Quebec. The terrain changes from rolling hills in the south to 1,000-m-high peaks of the Chic-Chocs in the north. Popular with hikers, the reserve contains a 72-km stretch of the International Appalachian Trail. Wildlife includes white-tailed deer, black bear, fox, and coyote, as well as 150 species of birds.

■ The 174-km² Mount Carleton Provincial Park [F5-F6] is named for its most outstanding physical feature, Mount Carleton—at 820 m, the highest mountain peak in the Maritimes. The remote park is renowned for its hiking trails and salmon spawning grounds.

Scale 1:800,000

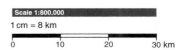

1 cm = 8 km

0   10   20   30 km

Réserve faunique
SÉPAQ
Anticosti
ÎLE
Cap Ottawa
•320m
M
Détroit d'Honguedo
Strait of Honguedo
Baie des Sables
Rivière-Chicotte
Eastern Time Zone
Heure de l'Est

A

Manche-d'Épée
Madeleine-Centre
Cap de la Madeleine
Gros-Morne
45
Rivière-la-Madeleine
Cap Barré
Grande-Vallée
Petite-Vallée
Pointe-à-la-Frégate
Ste-Madeleine-de-la-Rivière-Madeleine
Cap de la Madeleine
Petite-Anse
Cloridorme
St-Yvon
27
Maxime-ont-Louis
198
40
R1103
170
132
Pointe à la Renommée

L'Anse-à-Valleau
Pointe-Jaune
St-Maurice-de-l'Échouerie
Petit-Cap
Petit-Rivière-au-Renard
Rivière-au-Renard
L'Anse-à-Fugère
197
Centre d'accueil
Pointe Nord-Ouest
L'Anse-au-Griffon
132

B

Mont Copper 808m
Murdochville
LA CÔTE-DE-GASPÉ
R1140
128
R1126
R1138
Morris
18
PARC NATIONAL FORILLON
FORILLON NATIONAL PARK
Centre d'accueil
Jersey Cove
Cap des Rosiers
Cap-des-Rosiers
St-Majorique
Penouille
Cap-aux-Os
Des-Rosiers
Cap-Bon-Ami
Gaspé
Musée de la Gaspésie
Sandy Beach
Petit-Gaspé
Grande-Grave
198
Wakeham
York Centre
Haldimand
Douglastown
Cap de Gaspé
ZEC de la Rivière-York
R1102
ZEC York-Baillargeon
44
Baie de Gaspé

C

R1141
ZEC de la Rivière-York
Réserve faunique de la Rivière-St-Jean
R1102
Réserve faunique de la Rivière-St-Jean
QUÉBEC
132
Cap du Bois Brûlé
Fort-Prével
St-Georges-de-Malbaie
Belle-Anse
Pointe-St-Pierre
Pointe Verte
770m
R1151
Barachois
Bridgeville
Coin-du-Banc
ROCHER PERCÉ
Percé
Cannes-de-Roches
R1150
Rameau
Percé
Val-d'Espoir
Cap Blanc
Parc (Québec) de l'Île-Bonaventure-et-du-Rocher-Percé
Rocher Percé
Île Bonaventure
L'Anse-à-Beaufils
Parc de la Baie-de-Percé
663m
St-Isidore
Cap-d'Espoir
Cap d'Espoir
Grande-Rivière
Ste-Thérèse-de-Gaspé
Petite-Rivière-Ouest
44
Petit Pabos
ZEC des Anses
Lac des Sept Iles
R1128

D

R1124
R1125
Pabos
Chandler
Pabos Mills
Pointe de Newport
Réserve faunique de Port-Daniel
Newport
St-Alphonse
St-Jogues
Clemville
Pointe au Maquereau
132
L'Anse-aux-Gascons
St-Elzéar
Port-Daniel
Baie de Port-Daniel
Pointe de l'Ouest
170
85
Kelly
Marcil
Musée acadien du Québec
Shigawake
32
St-Godefroi
Rivière-Paspébiac
Hope Town
37
iméon
Bonaventure
Paspébiac
Site historique du Banc-de-Paspébiac
Pointe Bonaventure
New-Carlisle
113
Île Miscou
Miscou Island

BAIE DES CHALEURS

Heure de l'Est
Eastern Time Zone
Atlantic Time Zone
Heure de l'Atlantique
Miscou Centre
Pte. Sandy Pt.
Miscou Harbour
18
CHALEUR BAY
Petite-Rivière-de-l'Île
Petit-Shippagan
313
Ste-Cécile
Pigeon Hill

E

er-Nord
cher
Anse-Bleue
320
Île Caraquet I.
Île Pokesudie
Grande-Anse
303
Maisonnette
113
310
Île Lamèque
Lameque Island
Pokeshaw
330
11
Le Village historique acadien/
Acadian Historical Village
Caraquet
Petite-Lamèque
305
Lamèque
Pokeoudie
Stonehaven
New Bandon
145
Bas-Caraquet
Ste-Marie-St-Raphaël
Clifton
St-Léolin
135
Bertrand
335
Shippagan
Salmon Beach
Janeville
Burnsville
325
Haut-Pokemouche
St-Simon
113
Aquarium and Marine Centre
L'Aquarium et Centre Marin
191
Maltampec
345
Le Goulet
ghall
Paquetville
Pokemouche
11
Notre-Dame-des-Érables
350
217
Inkerman
Val-Doucet
340
Rang-St-Georges
355
135
Bois-Blanc
11
134
athurst
NEW
Pont-Landry
160
BRUNSWICK
Big Tracadie River
363
St-Isidore
Losier Settlement
160
St-Sauveur
160
365
Tracadie
8
Allardville
St-Irénée
Tracadie-Sheila
Sheila
Parc provincial Val Comeau Provincial Park

F

NOUVEAU
Pont-Lafrance
370
Val-Comeau
Daulnay
Rivière-du-Portage
Jeanne-Mance
460
Brantville
BRUNSWICK
Wishart Point
Price Settlement
Tabusintac
Tabusintac Lagoon
8
Allainville
455
445
11
Lavillette
450
Fairisle
NORTHUMBERLAND
445
Neguac
Plage Neguac Beach
Lagacéville

GO
SAINT

1 2 3 4 5

Map labels

6 7 8

arc (Québec)
d'Anticosti

G A N I E

Rivière

Rivière aux Saumons

Anse Harvey

Pointe Joseph

ANTICOSTI

UÉBEC

Baie Prinsta

Cap de la Table

Baie du Renard

A

NTICOSTI ISLAND

Lac du Renard

Baie du Renard

Baie-du-Renard

40

Rivière

Priveau

Rivière

Réserve faunique SÉPAQ Anticosti

Pointe de l'Est

Rivière-de-la-Chaloupe

Pointe du Sud

Pointe au Cormoran

Pointe Heath

Baie du Naufrage

B

E   D U

A U R E N T

C

G U L F   O F

L A W R E N C E

D

Refuge national d'oiseaux migrateurs des Rochers-aux-Oiseaux/ Bird Rocks National Migratory Bird Sanctuary

Rochers aux Oiseaux

Refuge écologique de l'Île-Brion

Île Brion

E

Grosse-Île-Nord

Réserve nationale de faune de la Pointe-de-l'Est/ Pointe de l'Est National Wildlife Area

La Grosse-Île

Grosse-Île [199] Île de l'Est

Old Harry

Île de la Grande Entrée

Pointe-aux-Loups

Grande-Entrée

Les Îles-de-la-Madeleine

Île Shag

ÎLES DE LA MADELEINE

QUÉBEC

Île du Havre aux Maisons

Fatima

Les Caps

Havre-aux-Maisons

L'Étang-du-Nord

Cap-aux-Meules

La Vernière

Île du Cap aux Meules

Gros-Cap

Île-d'Entrée

F

[199]

Baie de Plaisance

Île du Havre Aubert

L'Île-d'Entrée

Étang-des-Caps

Cap du Sud-Ouest

Havre-Aubert

Bassin

L'Anse-à-la-Cabane

6 7 8

HEADLANDS OF THE GASPÉ

The 3,200-km-long Appalachian mountain system reaches a terminus at the end of the Gaspé Peninsula. This view shows the prominent bays and high headlands (top to bottom): Cap de Gaspé (the site of Forillon National Park), Baie de Gaspé, Pointe Verte, La Malbaie, Cap Blanc, and Cap d'Espoir. Just beside Cap Blanc, the shape of famed Percé Rock can be glimpsed. Some 3.5 km farther offshore lies Île Bonaventure, home of one of the world's largest colonies of seabirds.

Other points of interest

■ At the northern tip of the Gaspé Peninsula, 240-km² Forillon National Park [B2-B3] embraces limestone cliffs, pebble beaches, sandy coves, and a boreal inland forest.

■ At the entrance of Chaleur Bay lies 64-km² Miscou Island [D2-E2], New Brunswick's "Land's End," a picturesque spot with white sand beaches and saltwater lagoons.

■ At 8,000 km², Anticosti Island [A4-A7] is larger than Prince Edward Island, but its population is only 300 people. Its physical features include sheer limestone cliffs, deep river canyons, and offshore reefs. In 1895, the wealthy French chocolate manufacturer Henri Menier purchased Anticosti for use as his own sports preserve. The island's 100,000 white-tailed deer are the descendants of the 220 that Menier introduced to the island.

■ Îles de la Madeleine [E8-F7], an archipelago of 16 islands, islets, and reefs in the Gulf of St. Lawrence, is some 100 km long, and has more than 300 km of sandy beaches.

Scale 1:800,000

1 cm = 8 km

0   10   20   30 km

QUÉBEC

NEW BRUNS

NOUVE

BRUNSW

MAINE

AROOSTOOK

CARLETON

VICTORIA

RESTIGOUCHE

MADAWASKA

TÉMISCOUATA

LES BASQUES

RIMOUSKI-NEIGETTE

LA MITIS

LA MATAPÉDIA

AVIGNON

YORK

LES NOTRE-DAME

Réserve faunique de la Rivière-Matapédia

Réserve Duchénier

Réserve faunique de Rimouski (SÉPAQ)

Parc (Québec)

Parc prov. Sugarloaf Prov. Pa

Kedgwick Provincial Wildlife Management Area
Unité provinciale d'aménagement de la faune Kedgwick

Eastern Time Zone / Heure de l'Est
Atlantic Time Zone / Heure de l'Atlantique

Lieu historique national de la Bataille-de-la-Ristigouche
Battle of the Restigouche National Historic Site
Réserve faunique de la Rivière-Ristigouche

Parc provincial Les Jardins de la République Provincial Park
Antique Automobile Museum/Musée des automobiles d'autrefois

Mount Carleton Provincial Park
Parc provincial Mont-Carleton

Mount Carleton Provincial Protected Area
Aire protégée provinciale Mont-Carleton

Mount Carleton/Mont-Carleton 820 m

Plaster Rock-Renous Provincial Game Area

Zone de conservation provi
Kennedy Lakes Wilderness
Provincial Conservation A
Aire pro
Ke
Provin

Deboullie Mountain 1981 ft.
Deboullie State Reserve

Eagle Lake State Reserve

Aroostook State Park

Squa Pan State Reserve

Scraggly Lake State Reserve

Baxter State

The Traveler 3543 ft.

Saddleback Mountain 1695 ft.

Bald Peak 636m

Fort Kent State Historic Site

Longest Covered Bridge/Le plus long pont couvert

Beaverbrook Art Gallery
Galerie d'art Beaverbrook

CANADA U.S.A./É.-U.

Cities and towns:

St-Eugène-de-Ladrière, St-Mathieu, St-Médard, St-Jean-de-Dieu, Ste-Françoise, istoles, Société, Ste-Rita, St-Cyprien, St-Pierre-de-Lamy, ert, St-Louis-du Ha!Ha!, Cabano, St-Juste-du-Lac, Elzéar, Notre-Dame-du-Lac, Packington, Pied-du-Lac, Rivière-Bleue, St-Eusèbe, Dégelis, St-Marc-du-Lac-Long, Lac-Baker, Baker Brook, Caron Brook, St-François-de-Madawaska, Clair, St-Jean-de-la-Lande, Connors, Wheelock, St.John, Bradbury, St. Francis, Fort Kent, Fort Kent Mills, Soldier Pond, Wallagrass, Plaisted, Allagash

St-Guy, La Trinité-des-Monts, Esprit-Saint, Biencourt, Squatec, Lac-des-Aigles, Auclair, Lejeune, St-Louis

Duchénier, Rimouski

Ciquart, Rang-des-Bosse, St-Joseph-de-Madawaska, Moulin-Morneault, St-Jacques, Verret, Edmundston, Madawaska, St-Hilaire, St. David, Grand Isle, Frenchville, Upper Frenchville, Lille, St. Agatha, Cleveland, Notre Dame, Daigle, Sinclair, Ouellette, Guerette, St-Basile, Rivière-Verte, Quisibis, Notre-Dame-de-Lourdes, Ste-Anne-de-Madawaska, Siegas, Keegan, Van Buren, St-Léonard, St-Léonard-Parent, St-Amand, St-André, Balleflem

Kedgwick River, Kedgwick, Thibault, St-Martin-de-Restigouche, Five Fingers, St-Quentin, Whites Brook, St-Jean-Baptiste-de-Restigouche, Menneval, Glenwood, Upsalquitch, Robinsonville, St-Arthur, McKendrick, Maltais, Val-d'Amour, Glencoe, Campbellton, Atholville, Tide Head, Listuguj, Dalhousie Junction, Oak Bay, Pointe-à-la-Croix, Pointe-à-la-Garde, Escumina, L'Alverne, Routhierville, Ste-Florence, St-André-de-Restigouche, St-Fidèle-de-Restigouche, St-Alexis-de-Matapédia, St-François-d'Assise, St-Jean-de-Matapédia, L'Ascension-de-Patapédia, Mann Settlement, Matapédia, Flatlands, Glen Levit, Dawsonville

Armstrong Brook, Williams Brook, Franquelin, Nictau, Riley Brook

Stockholm, Jemtland, Connor, North Lyndon, Sweden, New Sweden, Hanford, Barrett, Woodland, Spaulding, Perham, Carson, North Wade, Washburn, Crouseville, State Road, Mapleton, Brennan, Maple Grove, Chapman, Fairmount, Easton Center, Easton, Presque Isle, Caribou, Grimes Mills, Four Falls, Aroostook, Tilley, Four Corners, Anderson Road, Three Brooks, St. Almo, Wapske, Plaster Rock, Sisson Ridge, Hazeldean, Anfield, Lake Edward, Limestone, Ortonville, New Denmark, Drummond, Grand Falls/Grand-Sault, Hamlin, Everett, Oxbow, Gillespie Settlement, Rowena, Currie, Red Rapids, Odell, Arthurette, Tobique Narrows, Malicet, Carlingford, Perth-Andover, Hillandale, Kintore, Bon Accord, Kilburn, Kincardine, River de Chute, Johnville, Holmesville, Juniper, Juniper Station, Argyle, Hayesville, Bloomfield Ridge, Parker Ridge, Napadogan, Maple Grove, Williamsburg, Cross Creek, Stanley, Tay Creek, McGivney, Williamstown, Mars Hill, Blaine, Robinsons, Tracey Mills, Bristol, Glassville, Gordonsville, Fielding, Florenceville, Knowlesville, Bridgewater, Centreville, Riverbank, Mount Pleasant, Windsor, Stickney, Lower Windsor, Bloomfield, Lakeville, Simonds, Peel, Coldstream, Monticello, Somerville, Hartland, Victoria Corner, Cloverdale, Lindsay, Becaguimec, Littleton, Jacksonville, Newburg, Belleville, Grafton, Woodstock, Richmond Corner, Green Road, Houlton, Debec, Clarkville, Millville, Lower Hainesville, Upper Hainesville, Temperance Vale, Maple Ridge, Zealand, Keswick Ridge, Kingsley, Burtts Corner, Hamtown Corner, Nackawic, Springfield, Rossville, Campbell Settlement, Benton, Marys

Deboullie Mountain, Quimby, Winterville, Portage, Ashland, Sheridan, Squa Pan, Masardis, Oxbow, Shin Pond, Hersey, Smyrna Mills, Ludlow, New Limerick, Oakfield, Dyer Brook, Hodgdon, Linneus, Crystal, Island Falls, Patten

Fish River Lake, Munsungan Lake, Millnocket Lake, Grand Lake Metagamon, Grand Lake Seboeis, Eagle Lake, Square Lake, Long Lake, Cross Lake, Glazier Lake, Lac Témiscouata, Grand lac Squatec, Lac Touladi, Lac Méruimticook

Nashwaak, Miramichi

THE NORTHUMBERLAND SHORE

The shallow, warm waters of Northumberland Strait lap the gently sloping shoreline of eastern New Brunswick. The main sites on the 60-km-long stretch of the Northumberland shore shown above include (top to bottom): the Richibucto River estuary, Richibucto Cape, Baie de Buctouche, Cocagne Harbour, and Shediac Bay. Just north of Richibucto River lies Kouchibouguac National Park, which encloses the region's characteristic natural features: mixed forests inland, and sand dunes, lagoons, and beaches along the coast.

Other points of interest

■ The Saint John River rises in the forests of northern Maine and runs along the southern edge of New Brunswick's Madawaska County [C1], where it forms the boundary between Canada and the United States. At Edmundston [C2], the 673-km river turns southeast. From Grand Falls [D3], the Saint John flows through prosperous farming country and widens as it approaches the Bay of Fundy. The 23-m-high Grand Falls [D3] has been tamed for hydroelectric power. Hartland [F3] is the site of the world's longest covered bridge.

■ The Miramichi River flows 217 km from Juniper [E4] across central New Brunswick to the Gulf of St. Lawrence [D7]. The river is the offspring of the Southwest and Northwest Miramichi branches, which connect near Newcastle [D6]. The Miramichi, long one of Canada's major salmon rivers, has suffered through overfishing and pollution.

Scale 1:800,000

1 cm = 8 km

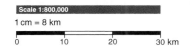

0   10   20   30 km

NEW BRUNSWICK

NOUVEAU BRUNSWICK

MAINE

WASHINGTON

CARLETON

YORK

SUNBURY

QUEENS

KINGS

CHARLOTTE

ST. JOHN

THE FUNDY ISLES

LES ÎLES DE FUNDY

BAY OF FUNDY

GULF OF MAINE

GOLFE DU MAINE

CANADA / U.S.A. / É.-U.

Fredericton

Saint John

Woodstock

Houlton

St. Stephen

Oromocto

Quispamsis

Grand Manan

GRAND MANAN ISLAND / ÎLE DU GRAND MANAN

Perth-Andover · Currie · Red Rapids · Carlingford · Blackville · Coughlan · Rogersville · Pleasant Ridge · Acadie Siding · Howard · Upper Blackville · Weaver Siding · Blissfield · Doaktown · Priceville · McNamee · Ludlow · Carrolls Crossing · Grand Lake Road · New Bandon · Hayesville · Holtville · Porter Cove · Bloomfield Ridge · Parker Ridge · Taxis River · Boiestown · Astle · Maple Grove · Napadogan · McGivney · Williamsburg · Cross Creek · Stanley · Nashwaak Bridge · Taymouth · Durham Bridge · Marysville · St. Marys · Gaspereau Forks · Salmon Creek · Duffys Corner · Humphrey Corner · Chipman · Coal Creek · Newcastle Bridge · Newcastle Creek · The Range · Minto · New Zion · Canaan Forks · Cumberland Bay · Penniac · Ripples · Princess Park · Youngs Cove · Coles Island · Cody's · Cambridge-Narrows · Long Creek · Carsonville · Head of Millstream · Pearsonville · Centreville · Berwick · Collina · Belleisle Creek · Roachville · Sussex · Youngs Cove Road · Douglas Harbour · Waterborough · Scotchtown · Whites Cove · Mill Cove · Jemseg · Gagetown · Lower Jemseg · Queenstown · McDonalds Point · Shannon · Hatfield Point · Carpenter · Springfield · Searsville · Apohaqui · Wickham · Hampstead · Evandale · Long Point · Kingston · Bloomfield · Hillsdale · Norton · Hampton · Titusville · Hanford Brook · Oak Point · Browns Flat · Long Reach · Nauwigewauk · Barnesville · Glenwood · Gondola Point · Upham · Welsford · Greenwich Hill · Fairvale · Rothesay · Baxters Corner · Morrisdale · Nerepis · Westfield · Hardings Point · Quispamsis · East Riverside-Kingshurst · Shanklin · West Quaco · Grand Bay · Bayswater · Summerville · Renforth · Ben Lomond · Loch Lomond · Garnett Settlement · Prince of Wales · Red Head · Mispec · Lorneville · Musquash · Black Beach · Chance Harbour · Dipper Harbour · Maces Bay · Pocologan · Pennfield · New River Beach · Beaver Harbour · Lepreau · Letang · Blacks Harbour · Back Bay · Lambertville · Leonardville · Fairhaven · Wilsons Beach · Welshpool · North Head · Castalia · Woodwards Cove · Grand Harbour · Ross Island · Seal Cove · White Head · St. George · St. Andrews · L'Etete · Deer Island · Campobello Island · Eastport · Lubec · South Lubec · West Lubec · North Lubec · Whiting · Jacksonville · East Machias · Machias · Machiasport · Marshfield · Whitneyville · Centerville · Roque Bluffs · Jonesboro · Jonesport · Beals · South Addison · Milbridge · Cherryfield · Columbia Falls · Addison · Indian River · West Jonesport · Sealand · Wyman

St. Croix · McAdam · Vanceboro · Brookton · Forest City · Topsfield · Codyville · Baillie · Dumbarton · Pomeroy · Honeydale · Moores Mills · Oak Bay · Waweig · Elmsville · Rollingdam · Bonny River · Utopia · Pennfield Ridge · Digdeguash · Chamcook · Bocabec · Baring · Calais · Red Beach · Robbinston · St. Stephen · The Ledge · Milltown · Upper Mills · Bayside · Woodland · Princeton · West Princeton · Grand Lake Stream · Waite · Eaton · Forest Station · Lambert Lake · Brockway · Lawrence Station · Pleasant Ridge · Tweedside · Harvey · Acton · Cork · Manners Sutton · Coburn · York Mills · Thomaston Corner · Upper Brockway · Magaguadavic · Tracy · Fredericton Junction · Upper Tracy · Central Blissville · Blissville · Hoyt · Patterson · Enniskillen · Wirral · Petersville · Clarendon · Greenwich Hill

Fort Anne & Scots Fort National Historic Site / Lieu historique national du Fort-Anne & du Fort-Scots
Melanson Settlement National Historic Site / Lieu historique national de l'Établissement Melanson
Port-Royal National Historic Site / Lieu historique national de Port-Royal
New Brunswick Museum / Musée du Nouveau-Brunswick
Carleton Martello Tower National Historic Site / Lieu historique national de la Tour-Martello-de-Carleton
Reversing Falls / Chutes réversibles
Point Lepreau Nuclear Generating Station / Station nucléaire Point Lepreau
Roosevelt-Campobello International Park / Parc international Roosevelt-Campobello
Machias Seal Island National Migratory Bird Sanctuary / Refuge national d'oiseaux migrateurs de l'Île-Machias-Seal
Grand Manan National Migratory Bird Sanctuary / Refuge nationale d'oiseaux migrateurs Grand Manan
St. Croix Island International Historic Site / Lieu historique international de l'Île-Sainte-Croix
St. Andrews Blockhouse NHS / LHN du Blockhaus-de-St-Andrews
Kings Landing Historical Settlement / Village historique de Kings Landing
Beaverbrook Art Gallery / Galerie d'art Beaverbrook
Longest Covered Bridge / Le plus long pont couvert

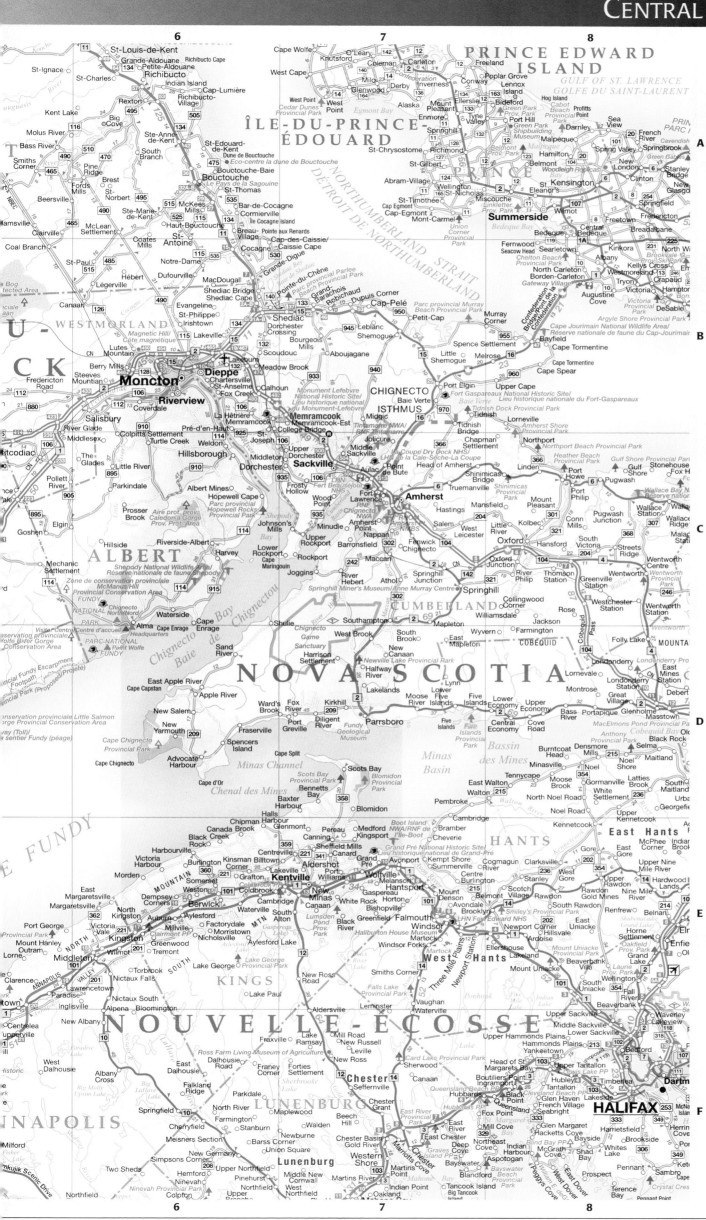

BAYS AND CHANNELS

The eastern end of the deep and narrow Bay of Fundy is indented with smaller bays and channels (clockwise, from top to bottom): Chignecto Bay and its two arms, Shepody Bay and Cumberland Basin on the New Brunswick side, and Minas Channel and Minas Basin on the Nova Scotia side. Minas Basin is the site of the world's highest tides, which can reach as high as 16 m. Moncton is located at the bend in the Petitcodiac River (top); Fundy National Park lies just beyond Cape Enrage (centre left). The upland that rims the Bay of Fundy's southern shore provides a protective shield for the apple orchards of Nova Scotia's Annapolis Valley (bottom).

Other points of interest

■ Grand Manan Island is one of three major islands at the entrance to the Bay of Fundy. The 24-km-long and 10-km-wide island is frequented by more than 400 species of migratory birds. Offshore waters are visited by humpback, minke, and other whales.

■ On Campobello Island [E2-F2], the centrepiece of the Roosevelt-Campobello International Park is the 34-room mansion, where U.S. President Franklin D. Roosevelt spent his summers until 1921, when he was stricken with polio. Off Deer Island [E2] lies Old Sow, the world's second largest whirlpool (after Norway's Maelstrom).

■ Fundy National Park [C6-D6] contains 206 km² of wooded hills, deep valleys, and 13 km of craggy Fundy shoreline. The spruce-fir forest on the coast and the birch-maple forests of the interior of the park support beaver, bobcat, coyote, and moose, as well as peregrine falcons and migrating shorebirds.

Scale 1:800,000
1 cm = 8 km

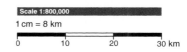

0   10   20   30 km

1 **2** **3** **4** **5**

A

Hatfield Point
Hampstead
Wickham
Norton
Jeffries Corner
Poodiac
Long Point
Bloomfield
Hammondvale
Waterside
Cape Enrage
Alma
Cape Enrage
Headquarters
Shulie
Southampton
Mapleton
South Brook
New Maplefo
Petersville
Evandale
Oak Point
Hampton
Upham
Hillsdale
Zone de conservation Point Wolfe River Gorge Provincial Conservation Area
Point Wolfe
PARC NATIONAL FUNDY
West Brook
New Canaan
Newville Lake Provincial Park
Halfway River
Wirral
Glenwood
Browns Flat
Long Reach
Kingston
Moss Glen
Titusville
Hanford Brook
East Apple River
Cape Capstan
Apple River
Ward's Brook
Fox River
Kirkhill
Parrsboro
Lakelands
Moose River
Five Islands
Clarendon
Welsford
Greenwich Hill
Morrisdale
Fairvale
Rothesay
Baxters Corner
Barnesville
New Salem
New Yarmouth
Spencers Island
Fraserville
Port Greville
Diligent River
Fundy Geological Museum
Five Islands
Petersburg
ST. JOHN
Parc provincial Fundy Fundy Escarpment Footpath
Advocate Harbour
Cape Chignecto Provincial Park
Cape Split
Minas Channel
Scots Bay Provincial Park
Blomidon Provincial Park
Minas Basin
Nerepis
Westfield
Bayswater
Hardings Point
Renforth
East Riverside-Kingshurst
Summerville
Shanklin
Fairfield
St. Martins
West Quaco
Quaco Bay
Cape d'Or
Chenal des Mines
Scots Bay
Bennetts Bay
Baxter Harbour
Blomidon
Pembroke
Grand Bay
Saint John
Ben Lomond
Loch Lomond
Garnett Settlement
Gardner Creek
Halls Harbour
Chipman Brook
Glenmont
Pereau
Kingsport
Boot Island
Medford
Canning
Canard
Grand Pré National Historic Site
Kempt Shore
Summerville
Reversing Falls/Chutes réversibles
New Brunswick Museum/Musée du Nouveau-Brunswick
Carleton Martello Tower National Historic Site
Black River
Red Head
Black Creek
Harbourville
Burlington
Centreville
Sheffield Mills
Canard
Avonport
Hantsport
Mount Denson
Aire protégée provinciale Loch Alva Provincial Protected Area
Prince of Wales
Mispec
Cape Spencer
Victoria Harbour
Morden
Kinsman Corner
Billtown
Lakeville
Port Williams
New Minas
Wolfville
Melanson
Grand Pré
Horton
Bishopville
Windsor
Musquash
Lorneville
Black Beach
Morristown
North Kingston
Auburn
Aylesford
Waterville
Cambridge
Coldbrook
Berwick
Kentville
Grafton
Cambridge
White Rock
Greenfield
Falmouth
Windsor Forks
Chance Harbour
Dipper Harbour
NEW BRUNSWICK NOUVEAU-BRUNSWICK
BAIE DE FUNDY
BAY OF FUNDY
Dempsey Corners
Somerset
Weston
Factorydale
Tremont
Wilmot
Middleton
Nictaux
South Alton
Lumsden Pond Prov. Park
Black River
Smiths Corner
Newport Station
Point Lepreau Nuclear Generating Station/Station nucléaire Point Lepreau
Cottage Cove Provincial Park
Port George
Margaretsville
Mount Hanley
Port Lorne
Kingston
Victoria Vale
Clairmont PP
Morristown
Nicholsville
Aylesford Lake
Lake George Provincial Park
New Ross Road
Haliburton House Museum
Martock
WEST HANTS
Port Wade
Prim Point
Ste. Croix Cove
Hampton
Phinney Cove
Young's Cove
Clarence
Paradise
Lawrencetown
Inglisville
Nictaux South
Bloomington
Alpena
New Albany
Lake Paul
Aldersville
Leminster
Waterville
Vaughan
Parkers Cove
Hillsburn
Litchfield
Granville Centre
Belleisle
Centrelea
Bridgetown
Tupperville
Round Hill
New Albany
Fraxville
Lake Ramsay
Mill Road
New Russell
Leville
Sherwood
Card Lake Provincial Park
Delaps Cove
Granville Ferry
Annapolis Royal
Leguille
Upper Clements
Lake La Rose
Annapolis Royal Historic Gardens
Dalhousie East
Dalhousie Road
Franey Corner
Forties Corner
New Ross
Sherbrooke
Fort Anne & Scots Fort National Historic Site
Melanson Settlement National Historic Site
Port-Royal National Historic Site
Port Royal
Karsdale
Upper Clements Provincial Park
Greywood
West Dalhousie
Albany Cross
Falkland Ridge
Parkdale
Chester Grant
Canaan
Chester
Seffernville
Queenslan
Hubba
Culloden
Victoria Beach
Deep Brook
Clementsport
Cornwallis
Springfield
North River
Maplewood
Chester Basin
Prim Point
Smiths Cove
Digby
Clementsvale
Milford
South Milford
Cherryfield
Farmington
Stanburn
Newburne
Walden
Beech Hill
Chester Basin
Gold River
Graves
Point
Bayswater
Gulliver's Cove
Rossway
Waterford
Brighton
Barton
Acaciaville
Marshalltown
Hillgrove
Bloomfield
Hainsfield
Bear River
Greenland
Hemford
New Germany
Simpsons Corner
Union Square
Pinehurst
Middle New Cornwall
West Northfield
Blockhouse
Oakland
Indian Point
Mahone Bay
Tancook
Big Tancook
Trout Cove
Centreville
Gilbert Cove
New Edinburgh
Plympton
Plympton Station
Doucetteville
South Range
Morganville
Northfield
Two Sheds
Ninevah
Ninevah Provincial Park
Colpton
Branch LaHave
Newburne
Newcombville
Dayspring
Upper LaHave
Lunenburg
Stonehurst West
Blue Rocks
Sandy Cove
Mink Cove
Little River
Tiddville
St. Bernard
Belliveau Cove
Weymouth North
Weymouth
Sissiboo Falls
Weymouth Falls
Danvers
Riverdale
Southville
DIGBY
Kempt
Maitland Bridge
KEJIMKUJIK NATIONAL PARK
New Grafton
Harmony Mills
West Brookfield
North Brookfield
Pleasant River
Lower Branch
Baker Settlement
Wileville
Bridgewater
Pleasantville
Conquerall Mills
West LaHave
East LaHave
Dublin Shore
Kingsburg
East Ferry
Tiverton
Freeport
Grosses Coques
Church Point
Concession
Havelock
New Tusket
Corberrie
St. Joseph
CLARE
Bangor
KEJIMKUJIK NATIONAL HISTORIC SITE
New France (Electric City) Historic Site
Tobeatic Wilderness Area
Low Landing
Whiteburn Mines
Hibernia
West Caledonia
Molega
Chelsea
Waterloo
Hebbs Cross
Lapland
Buckfield
Italy Cross
Crousetown
Middlewood
Petite Rivière
Crescent Beach
Rissers Beach Provincial Park
Central Grove
Central Grove Provincial Park
Westport
Brier Island
Whipple Point
Comeauville
Saulnierville
Meteghan River
Meteghan
Meteghan Station
Maxwelton Station
Richfield
Hectanooga
North Kemptville
East Kemptville
Kemptville
Tobeatic Wilderness Area
Tobeatic Wildlife Management Area
Luc Rossignol
Indian Gardens
Pleasantfield
Bangs Falls
Greenfield
Middlefield
Charleston
East Medway
Riversdale
Voglers Cove
Broad Cove
Green Bay
Cape LaHave Island
Bush Island Provincial Park
St. Martins
Bear River
St. Alphonse
Mavillette
Cape St. Mary
Mavillette Beach Provincial Park
Norwood
Lake Annis
NOUVELLE-ÉCOSSE
Ten Mile Lake Provincial Park
Medway
Port Medway
Eagle Head
West Berlin
Beach Meadows
Andrews Head
Medway Harbour
Pollock Point
Cherry Hill
Salmon River
Bartletts Beach
Beaver River
YARMOUTH
Lake George
Carleton
Milton
Brooklyn
Liverpool
Western Head
Port Maitland Beach Provincial Park
Port Maitland
Brenton
Deerfield
Quinan
Upper Ohio
Ohio
Middle Ohio
Shelburne
Beech Hill
Summerville Centre
Hunts Point
Summerville Beach Provincial Park
White Point
GULF OF MAINE
Darling Lake
Sandford
Hebron
South Ohio
Ellenwood Lake Provincial Park
Upper Clyde River
SHELBURNE
Port Mouton
Haley Lake National Migratory Bird Sanctuary/Refuge national d'oiseaux migrateurs du Lac-Haley
KEJIMKUJIK NATIONAL PARK (Seaside Adjunct)/PARC NATIONAL KEJIMKUJIK (A
Port Joli National Migratory Bird Sanctuary/Refuge national d'oiseaux migrateurs de Port Joli
Port l'Hébert National Migratory Bird Sanctuary/Refuge national d'oiseaux migrateurs de Port Hébe
Thomas H. Raddall Provincial Park
Chegoggin
Pembroke Shore
Dayton
Yarmouth
Belleville
Ste. Anne du Ruisseau
Middle Ohio
Lower Ohio
Jordan Falls
Welshtown
Sable River
Sable River Provincial Park
Port l'Hébert
East Port l'Hébert
Little Port l'Hébert
Sable River National Migratory Bird Sanctuary/Refuge national d'oiseaux migrateurs de la Rivière-de-Sable
Firefighters Museum of Nova Scotia
Overton
Sand Beach
Kelley Cove
Arcadia
Plymouth
Glenwood Provincial Park
Glenwood
Central Argyle
Argyle
The Islands Provincial Park
Shelburne
East Jordan
Allendale
Louis Head
Rockland
Little Harbour
Chebogue Point
Chebogue
Little River Harbour
Comeau Hill
GOLFE DU MAINE
Sand Pond National Wildlife Area/Réserve nationale de faune de l'Étang-Sand
Lower Eel Brook
Surette's Island
Lower Argyle
Wedgeport
West Pubnico
Lower Wedgeport
Churchover
Sandy Point
West Green Harbour
Jordan Bay
Lockeport
East Green Harbour
Gunning Cove
Clyde River
Port Clyde
Port Saxon
Roseway
Round Bay
West Pubnico
Middle West Pubnico
Lower West Pubnico
Middle East Pubnico
Barrington
Thomasville
Cape Negro
North East Point
East Point
Cape Negro Island
Western Head
Tusket Island
St. Ann Point
Lower East Pubnico
Charlesville
Upper Woods Harbour
Woods Harbour
Forbes Point
Lower Woods Harbour
Mud Island
Oak Park
Barrington
Doctors Cove
Crowell
Barrington Passage
Port La Tour
Blanche
Baccaro
Smithville
Baccaro Point
West Baccaro
Shag Harbour
Archelaus Smith Museum
Outer Island
Newellton
Centreville
South Side
Clark's Harbour
The Hawk
Seal Island
Cape Sable
Ingomar
East Point Island
Blanche

1 **2** **3** **4** **5**

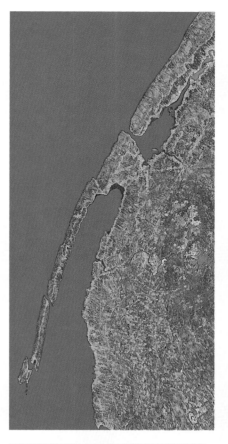

DIGBY NECK & THE FRENCH SHORE

At the western end of the Bay of Fundy, Brier and Long islands and the 45-km-long Digby Neck shelter St. Mary's Bay. Across the bay lies the "French Shore," where picturesque Acadian villages line Highway 101 along the Gulf of Maine. Away from the coast are the mixed forests typical of inland Nova Scotia. The fishing port of Digby—a popular tourist destination—is situated on the west side of Annapolis Basin (top). A ferry service connects Digby with Saint John, N.B., 50 km across the Bay of Fundy.

Other points of interest

■ Lake Rossignol [D3], 26 km by 16 km, is Nova Scotia's largest freshwater lake. It drains into the Atlantic by way of the Mersey River.

■ Cape Sable Island [F2], Nova Scotia's most southerly point, is a haven for the white ibis and other exotic birds. A 1,200-m causeway connects the island with Barrington Passage. Clark's Harbour, the island's largest community, is the 1907 birthplace of the 12-m-long Cape Island boat, still used (now with inboard motors) by inshore fishermen.

■ Kejimkujik National Park consists of two inland and seashore sectors. The 380-km² interior [D3] contains island-dotted lakes, low-lying hills, and one of Nova Scotia's finest forests. More than 500 species of plants, including many different types of ferns, orchids, and aquatic plants, are found here. The park's Seaside Adjunct [E4] serves as a migratory bird sanctuary.

■ Shubenacadie Provincial Wildlife Park [B6] shelters North American wildlife, such as lynx, moose, and reindeer.

Scale 1:800,000

1 cm = 8 km

0   10   20   30 km

1 2 3 4 5

GULF OF ST. LAWRENCE

GOLFE DU SAINT-LAURENT

PRINCE EDWARD ISLAND
ÎLE- DU- PRINCE- ÉDOUARD

PRINCE EDWARD ISLAND NATIONAL PARK
PARC NATIONAL DE L'ÎLE-DU-PRINCE-ÉDOUARD

PRINCE EDWARD ISLAND NP
(Greenwich Dune Systems)
PN ÎLE-DU-PRINCE ÉDUARD
(Complexe dunaire de Greenwich)

A

North Cape
Seacow Pond
Norway
Cross Pond
Tignish
Anglo Tignish
Tignish Shores
Fisherman's Haven Provincial Park
St. Roch
Kildare Capes
Greenmount
Cape Kildare
Kildare
Montrose
Jacques Cartier Provincial Park
Alberton
Northport
Elmsbank
Cascumpec Bay
Mill River East
Cascumpec
Mill River Provincial Park

B

Carleton
Freeland
Conway
Poplar Grove
Lennox Island
Inverness
Mount Pleasant
Ellerslie
Bideford
Enmore
Port Hill
Tyne Valley
Springhill
Hamilton
Malpeque
Hog Island
Profitts Point
Sea View
Darnley
French River
Springbrook
Cavendish
Stanley Bridge
New London
Clinton
Mayfield
North Rustico
Rustico
Stanhope
Brackley Beach
Savage Harbour
Greenwich
St. Peters Bay
Campbell's Cove Provincial Park
Priest Pond
Hermanville
Monticello
Lakeville
North Lake
East Point
Elmira

Richmond
St-Gilbert
Kensington
St-Nicholas
Wellington
Miscouche
Linkletter Prov. Park
Timothee
Mont-Carmel
Summerside
Bedeque Bay
Wilmot
Springfield
Fredericton
Breadalbane
Hunter River
Ebenezer
Brookfield
Milton
Oyster Bed Bridge
Pleasant Grove
Tracadie Cross
Fort Augustus
Peakes
Mount Stewart
Bangor
Dingwells Mills
St. Georges
Bear River
New Zealand
Fortune Bridge
Eglington
Howe Point
Little Pond
Souris
Red Point
Basin Head Fisheries Museum
Black Pond National Migratory Bird Sanctuary /
Refuge national d'oiseaux migrateurs de Black Pond

C

Charlottetown
Province House NHS
Stratford
Cornwall
New Haven
New Dominion
DeSable
Argyle Shore
Canoe Cove
Nine Mile Creek
Mermaid
Donagh
Clarkin
Vernon River
Millview
Cherry Valley
Orwell
Orwell Corner Historic Village
New Perth
Summerville
Rosebank
Newport
Montague
Valleyfield
Eldon
Iona
St Marys Road
Pinette
Caledonia
Georgetown
Brudenell River Provincial Park
Panmure Island
Panmure Island Provincial Park
Gaspereaux
Alliston
Murray Harbour North
Murray Head
Murray Harbour
White Sands
High Bank

Parc provincial Murray Beach Provincial Park
Petit-Cap
Murray Corner
Spence Settlement
Melrose
Bayfield
Cape Tormentine
NEW BRUNSWICK
NOUVEAU-BRUNSWICK
Cape Spear
Northumberland Strait
Détroit de Northumberland

D

Port Elgin
Upper Cape
Fort Gaspareaux National Historic Site /
Lieu historique nationale du Fort-Gaspareaux
Tidnish Dock Provincial Park
Tidnish Bridge
Chapman Settlement
Lorneville
Northport
Linden
Port Howe
Pugwash
Gulf Shore
Stonehouse
Fox Harbour
Wallace Bay National Wildlife Area /
Réserve nationale de faune de Wallace Bay
North Shore
Malagash
Sandville
Brule
River John
Hodson
Caribou River
Caribou
Pictou Island
Waterside Beach Provincial Park
Seafoam
Toney River
Doctors Brook
Malignant Cove
Livingstone Cove
Cape George
Ballantynes Cove
Georgeville
Lakevale
Crystal Cliffs
Morristown
Arisaig
Arisaig Provincial Park
Knoydart
Lismore
Antigonish

Amherst
Truemanville
Mansfield
Mount Pleasant
Port Philip
Pugwash Junction
Wallace Station
Wallace
Wallace Ridge
Maladash Station
Bayhead
Tatamagouche
Denmark
Meadowville
Welsford
Lyons Brook
Pictou
Pictou Landing
Hector Heritage Quay
Powells Point
Melmerby Beach Provincial Park
Merigomish
Barneys River
Marshy Hope
Lower Barneys River
Bailey Brook
Clydesdale
North Grant
Pomquet Beach
Pomquet
Afton
South River

E

Mapleton
Wyvern
Farmington
Williamsdale
Jackson
Rose
Westchester Station
Folly Lake
COBEQUID MOUNTAINS
Wentworth
Wentworth Centre
Wentworth Station
Greenville Station
West New Annan
Balmoral Mills
Balmoral Mills Provincial Park
East Earltown
Earltown
North Earltown
The Falls
West Branch River John
Durham
Loganville
Central West River
Green Hill
Salt Springs Provincial Park
Salt Springs
Scotsburn
Alma
New Glasgow
Stellarton
Westville
Thorburn
Sutherlands River
French River
Kenzieville
Addington Forks
Glen Road
St. Andrews
Ashdale
Fraser Mills
Caledonia Mills
Roman Valley
Glencoe

Springhill Junction
Springhill
Murray Centre
River Philip
Thomson Station
Collingwood Corner
Oxford Junction
Oxford
Hansford
South Victoria
Streets Ridge
Kolbec
Conn Mills
Little River
West Leicester
Salem
Hastings
COLCHESTER
Londonderry
Londonderry Prov. Park
Great Mines Station
Belmont
North River
Onslow
Bible Hill
Truro
Valley
Union
Greenfield
Riversdale
Lansdowne
Lorne
Glengarry
Eden Lake
Sunny Brae
Willowdale
Rocky Mountain
East River St. Marys
New Town
Denver
Lochiel Lake Provincial Park
PICTOU
Blue Mountain
Garden of Eden
Greens Brook
Churchville
Rocklin
Riverton
Hopewell
Springville
Gairloch
Watervale
West River Station
Bridgeville
ANTIGONISH
Beaver Mountain Provincial Park
Rossfield
St. Joseph
McPhersons Mills
Glen Alpine
North Lochaber
Upper South River
Lower South River
Goshen
Eight Island Lake
Forest Hill

F

Cobequid Bay
Old Barns
Central Onslow
Masstown
Glenholme
Debert
MacElmons Pond Provincial Park
Cobequid Bay
Five Islands
Lower Five Islands
Economy
Upper Economy
Lower Economy
Bass River
Portapique
Highland Village
Great Village
Central Economy
Cove Road
Five Islands Provincial Park
Bassin des Mines
Minas Basin
Burntcoat Head
Noel
Noel Shore
Maitland
Selma
Princeport
Green Oaks
South Maitland
Urbania
Georgefield
Brookfield
Middle Stewiacke
Upper Stewiacke
Dean
Chaplin
Newton Mills
Stewiacke Cross Road
Governor Lake
Cameron Settlement
Caledonia
Trafalgar
St. Mary's
Liscomb Game Sanctuary
Smithfield
Gleneig
Crows Nest
Waternish
Aspen
GUYSBOROUGH
Stillwater
Jordanville
Sherbrooke Village
Sherbrooke
Sherbrooke Provincial Park
Goldenville
St. Mary's River
Sonora
Country Harbour
Melrose
Indian Harbour Lake
Port Hilford
Wine Harbour

Minasville
Tennycape
Noel Road
Walton
East Walton
Pembroke
Cambridge
Bramber
Kempt Shore
Summerville
Centre Burlington
Cogmagun
Clarksville
West Gore
Stanley
Upper Nine Mile River
Gore
East Gore
McPhee Corner
Indian Brook
Shubenacadie
Shubenacadie Provincial Wildlife Park
West St. Andrews
Wittenburg
Coldstream
Chaswood
Milford
Middle Musquodoboit
Upper Musquodoboit
Pleasant Valley
Higginsville
Murchyville
Moose River Gold Mines
Moose River
Elderbank
Elderbank Provincial Park
Mooseland
Lochaber Mines
Marinette
Caribou Gold Mines
South Branch
Centre Musquodoboit
Upper Musquodoboit
Spanish Ship Bay
Liscomb Mills
St. Mary's River
Marie Joseph
Moser River
Necum Teuch
Malay Falls
Mooshead
Ecum Secum
Liscomb
Liscomb Island
Liscomb Point

Windsor
Fort Edward NHS
Martock
Newport Corner
Hillsville
Ardoise
Mount Denson
Avondale
Cheverie
Brooklyn
Scotch Village
South Rawdon
Rawdon Gold Mines
Upper Rawdon
Smiley's Provincial Park
Nine Mile River
Hardwood Lands
Renfrew
Belnan
Horne Settlement
Oakfield
Enfield
Elmsdale
Wyse Corner
Antrim
Cooks Brook
Gays River
Halifax
West Sheet Harbour
Sheet Harbour
Watt Section
Port Dufferin
East Quoddy
Harrigan Cove
Barren Island

NOUVELLE-ÉCOSSE

HANTS
East Hants
COLCHESTER
PICTOU
ANTIGONISH
GUYSBOROUGH

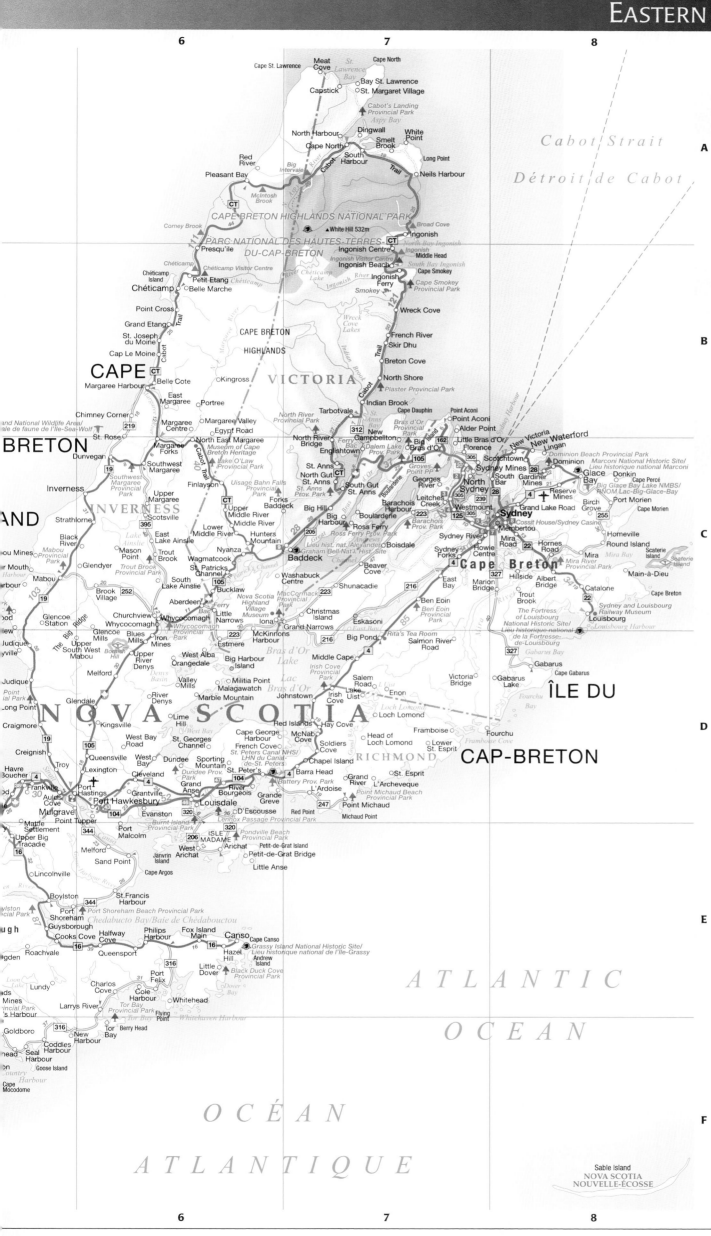

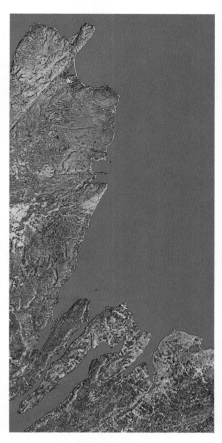

THE HIGHLANDS OF CAPE BRETON

This view sweeps across northeastern Cape Breton Island. Along the curve of the coast facing Cabot Strait lie these sites (counterclockwise, top to bottom): Cape North, the island's uppermost tip; Aspy Bay, just north of the site of Cape Breton Highlands National Park; North and South Ingonish bays (separated by a small peninsula); St. Anns Bay; Great Bras d'Or and St. Andrews channels, which lie north and south of Boularderie Island. The industrial city of Sydney (bottom right) is visible at the east side of Sydney Harbour.

Other points of interest

■ Bras d'Or Lake is an arm of the Atlantic Ocean, covering 1,098 km² and almost dividing Cape Breton Island in two. At its north end, Great Bras d'Or and St. Andrews are natural channels linking "the lake" to the Atlantic Ocean. At the south end, the St. Peter's Canal is another—man-made—channel that cuts through a kilometre-wide isthmus. Built between 1854 and 1869, the ship continues to provide a shortcut through Cape Breton Island that is safer than the route around the island.

■ Sable Island [F8], 35 km long and 1.6 km wide, is an exposed tip of the eastern continental shelf. Wind and water constantly change the shape of its shifting sandy terrain. The island is famed for its bands of wild horses, whose numbers vary from 175 to 450. It was thought the horses were shipwreck survivors, but recent evidence suggests they may have arrived during an ill-advised attempt to create an island settlement. Lying 300 km east of Halifax, the island is now the focus of offshore natural gas exploration.

Scale 1:800,000

1 cm = 8 km

0   10   20   30 km

GULF OF ST.

GOLFE DU SAINT

PRINCE

ÎLE-

DU-

EDWARD

PRIN

PRINCE EDWARD ISLAND NATIONAL P
PARC NATIONAL DE L'ÎLE-DU-PRINCE-ED

NORTHUMBERLAND STRAIT

NEW
BRUNSWICK

NOUVEAU-
BRUNSWICK

WESTMORLAND

CUMBERLAND

NOVA SCOTIA

NOUVELLE-ÉCOSSE

DÉTROIT DE NORTHUMBERLAND

North Cape
North Cape Interpretive Centre/ Aquarium
Elephant Rock
Seacow Pond
Nail Pond
Norway
Christopher Cross
Anglo Tignish
Skinners Pond
Ascension
Waterford
Peterville
Pleasant View
Léoville
Judes Point
Tignish Shore
Fisherman's Haven Provincial Park
St. Felix
Tignish
Cape Gage
Palmer Road
St. Louis
St. Roch
Kildare Capes
Kildare Capes Red Sandstone Cliffs
Miminegash
St. Edward
Greenmount
Cape Kildare
Kildare
Alma
Montrose
Jacques Cartier Provincial Park
St. Lawrence
Huntley
Roseville
Elmsdale
Alberton
Alberton Museum & Genealogy Centre
Alberton Harbour
Brockton
Rosebank
Campbellton
Piusville
Mill River East
Northport (Alberton South)
Burton
Bloomfield
Cascumpec Sand Hills
Seal Point
Bloomfield Corner
Duvar
Bloomfield Provincial Park
Howlan
Cascumpec
Cascumpec Bay
Cape Wolfe
Haliburton
Mill River Provincial Park
Unionvale
Knutsford
O'Leary
O'Leary Museum
West Cape
Mount Royal
Carleton
Roxbury
Foxley River
Murray Road
Springfield West
Milburn
Coleman
West Cape
Glenwood
Milo
West Devon
Freeland
Conway
Poplar Grove
West Point Lighthouse Museum
West Point
Derby
Inverness
McNeills Mills
East Bideford
Cedar Dunes Provincial Park
Indian Point Sand Hills
Brae Harbour
North Enmore
Ellerslie
Bideford
Lennox Island
Hog Island
PRINCE
Alaska
Enmore
Mount Pleasant
Tyne Valley
Mi'kmaq Cultural Centre
Green Park Provincial Park
Shipbuilding Museum & Yeo House
Grande Digue Point
Mossy Point
Port Hill
Gillis Point
Red Point
Fish Island
Egmont Bay
Victoria West
Springhill
Northam
Birch Hill
Malpeque Harbour
Profitts Point
Saint-Chrysostome
Harmony
Arlington
Winchester Cape
Courtin Island
Cabot Beach Provincial Park
Saint-Philippe
Bayside
Malpeque
Sea View
L.M. Montgomery Heritage Museum
Baie-Egmont
Saint-Gilbert
Richmond
South West Lot 16
Belmont
Darnley
Baltic
Spring Valley
French River
Springbrook
Cavendish
Orby Head
Abram-Village
Urbanville
Wellington
Central Lot 16
Beech Point
Hamilton
Indian River
Margate
Long River
Woodleigh Replicas & Gardens
New London
Green Gables House/ Maison Green Gables
Maximeville
Saint-Timothée
Saint-Raphaël
Central Museum/ Le musée acadien
Burnt Point
Clermont
Kensington
Clinton
Stanley Bridge
Mayfield
North Rustico
Cap-Egmont
Acadian Pioneer Village
Saint-Nicholas
Miscouche
St. Eleanors
Sherbrooke
New Annan
Norboro
Grahams Road
New Glasgow
South Rustico
Oyster Bed Bridge
Brackley Beach
Stanhope
Mont-Carmel
Union Corner
Linkletter
Sunbury Cove
Summerside
Wilmot Valley
Kelvin Grove
Summerfield
Millvale
St. Ann
New Glasgow
Wheatley River
Winsloe North
Covehead Road
Union Corner Provincial Park
MacCallums Point
North Bedeque
Lower Bedeque
Springfield
Stanley Bridge
South Granville
Fredericton
Glen Valley
Greenvale
Harrington
Ebenezer
Dunstaffnage
Bedeque Bay
Graham Head
Central Bedeque
Freetown
Breadalbane
Newton
Highest Point on PEI (142m)
Brookfield
North Milton
Union Road
York
Suffolk
Fernwood
Seacow Head
Bedeque
South Freetown
Kinkora
Shamrock
Stanchel
Hartsville
Springvale
Warren Grove
QUEENS
Chelton
Chelton Beach Provincial Park
Middleton
Searletown
Maple Plains
Brookvale Provincial Ski Park
North Wiltshire
Milton
Brackley
Marshfie
North Carleton
Gordon Point
Albany
Westmoreland
Kellys Cross
Loyalist
Kingston
Emyvale
Charlotte
Carleton Cove
Gateway Village
Carleton
North Tryon
Tryon
Crapaud
South Melville
Riverdale
Bonshaw
New Haven
Clyde River
Elmwood
Cornwall
Stratford
Borden
Cape Traverse
Bells Point
Augustine Cove
Victoria
Richard Point
Tryon Head
Hampton
DeSable
Macvors Point
Black Point
Argyle Shore
Argyle Shore Provincial Park
Strathgartney Provincial Park
Meadow Bank
New Dominion
Port-la-Joye/ Fort Amherst National Historic Site/ Lieu historique national de Port-la-Joye/Fort-Amherst
York Point
Province House NHS
Ardgowan NHS
Confederation Bridge (Toll)
Pont de la Confédération (Péage)
Passage Abegweit Passage
Canoe Cove
Rice Point
Nine Mile Creek
Hillsborough Bay
Cape Jourimain National Wildlife Area/ Réserve nationale de faune du Cap-Jourimain
Île Jourimain
Bayfield
Cape Tormentine
Cape/Cap Tormentine
Spence Settlement
Cape Spear
Cape/Cap Spear
St. Peters Island
Governors Island
Cap-de-Cocagne
Cap de Cocagne
Cap-des-Caissie/ Caissie Cape
Bourgeois
Pointe de Grande-Digue Point
Shediac Island
Parc provincial Parlee Beach Provincial Park
Cap-Brûlé
Barachois
Cap Pelé Cape
Pointe Fagan Point
Bourgeois Mills
Cormier-Village
Robichaud
Cap-Pelé
Trois-Ruisseaux
Haute-Aboujagane
St-André-de-Shediac
Leblanc
Gallant Settlement
Botsford Portage
Basse-Aboujagane
Shemogue
Petit-Cap
Cap Shemogue Head
Pointe Cadman Point
Parc provincial Murray Beach Provincial Park
Murray Corner
Anderson Settlement
Mates Corner
Cadman Corner
Chapmans Corner
Murray Road
Woodside
Little Shemogue
Melrose
Malden
Cape/Cap Tormentine
Cookville
Centre Village
Timber River
Hardy
Upper Cape
Cape/Cap St-Laurent
Coburg
Port Elgin
Bayside
Point Prim
Baie Verte
Baie Verte Road
Parc linéaire Tantramar Rail Trail
Brooklyn Road
Brooklyn
Midgic
Tidnish
Tintamarre National Wildlife Area/ Réserve national de faune Tintamarre
Halls Hill
Tidnish Dock Provincial Park
Seagrove
Lorneville
Mount View
Ward
Upper Point de Bute
Jolicure
Tidnish Bridge
Beecham Settlement
Amherst Shore
Chapman Settlement
Coldspring Head
Amherst Shore Provincial Park
Woodhurst
Fairfield
Mount Allison University
Upper Sackville
Middle Sackville
Ogden Mill
Point de Bute
Amherst Head
Lower Shinimicas
Northport
Northport Beach Provincial Park
Birch Head
Cherry Burton
Sackville
West Whatley
Shinimicas Bridge
East Linden
Linden
West Linden
Upper Linden
Heather Beach Provincial Park
Upper Gulf Shore
Lower Gulf Shore
West Sackville
Westcock
Aulac
Fort Beauséjour National Historic Site/ Lieu historique national du Fort-Beauséjour
Mount Whatley
La Coupe Dry Dock National Historic Site/ Lieu historique national de la Coupe-Sèche-de-La Coupe
Fort Gaspareaux National Historic Site/ Lieu historique national du Fort-Gaspareaux
Tintamarre National Wildlife Area
Punqwash Harbour

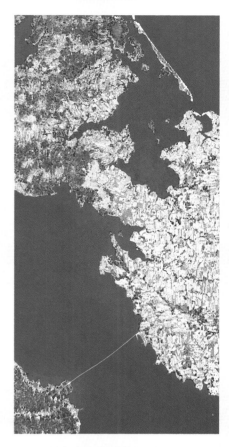

THE BAYS AND THE BRIDGE

The capes and coves of Malpeque Bay lie north of the isthmus connecting Prince (left) and Queens (right) counties on Prince Edward Island. At the entrance to the bay, Hog Island acts as a slender barrier against the shivery waters of the Gulf of St. Lawrence. On the south side of the isthmus is Summerside, P.E.I.'s second largest community, which is visible on Bedeque Bay. The patchwork of farms is a reminder that P.E.I. is Canada's smallest, most densely populated province, with the highest proportion of the people still living on farms. What looks like a slender thread stretched across Northumberland Strait is the 13-km-long multispan Confederation Bridge linking P.E.I. and New Brunswick.

Other points of interest

■ Prince Edward Island National Park [D4-D6], a mere 18 km², preserves a 40-km coastal strip of sand, bluffs, and wetlands along the province's northern shore. The notable features include red sandstone cliffs—rising up to 30 m— and some of the finest beaches in North America. The deep, stringy roots of marram grass (*Ammophila arenaria*, meaning "sand loving") anchor the fragile dune system against wind and salt spray. Great white heron and piping plover frequent the saltwater marshes and freshwater ponds.

■ Basin Head [D8] is the site of a fisheries museum that recounts the history of inshore commercial fishery in Prince Edward Island.

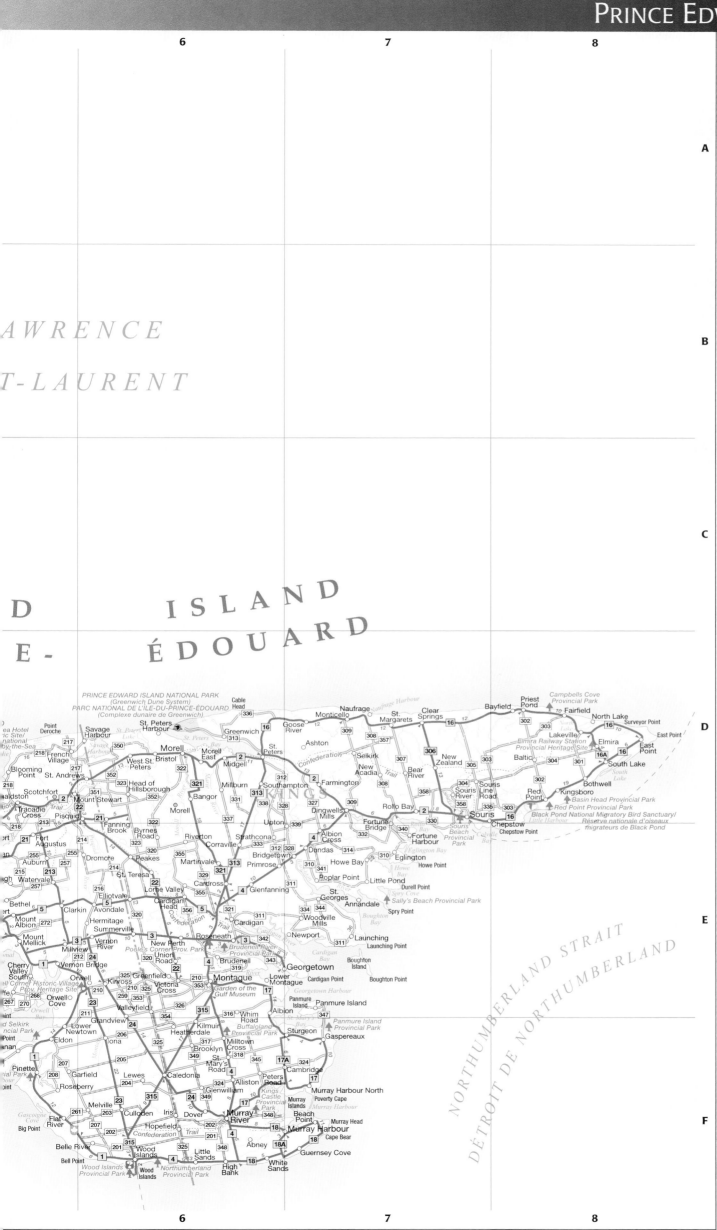

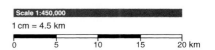

Scale 1:450,000

1 cm = 4.5 km

0   5   10   15   20 km

GULF OF
ST. LAWRENCE

GOLFE DU
SAINT-LAURENT

St. George's Bay

ATLANTIC

OCEAN

OCÉAN

ATLANTIQUE

Cabot Strait
Détroit de Cabot

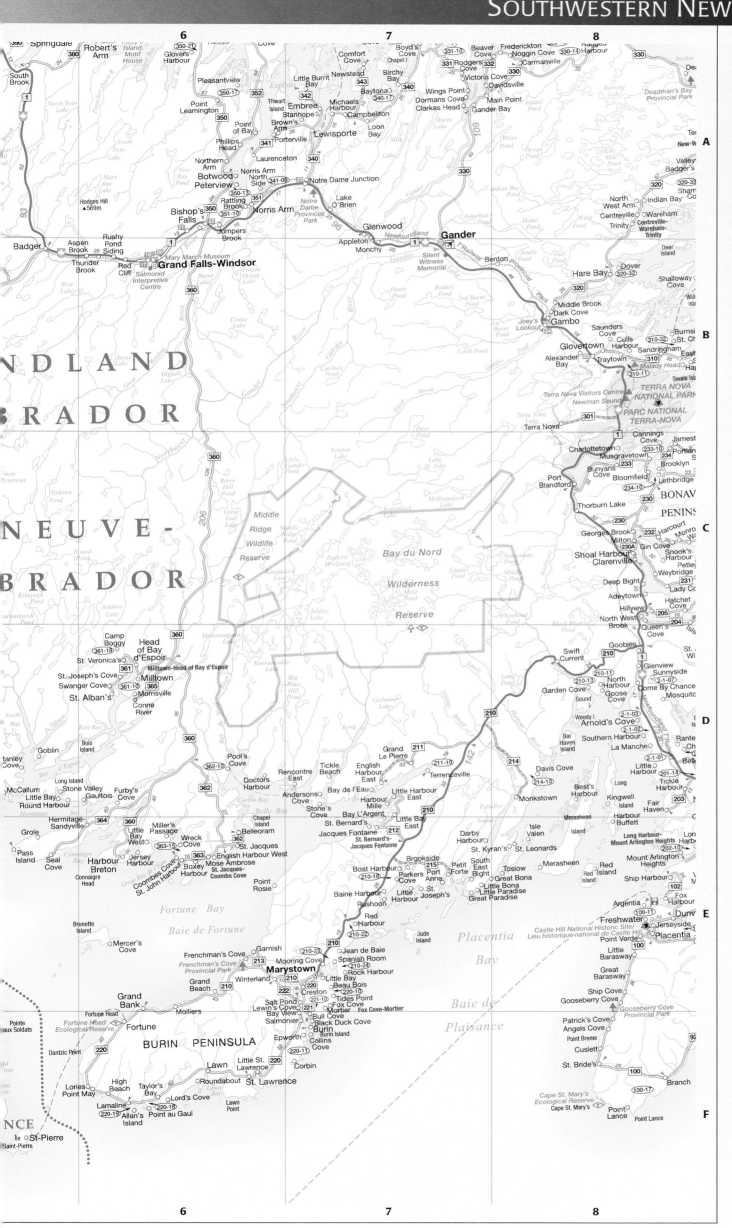

A GATEWAY TO THE ISLAND

Southwestern Newfoundland is a wind-swept land of coastal barrens, bold headlands, placid wilderness lakes, and densely forested mountains. Channel-Port aux Basques (bottom) connects the island to the rest of Canada by ferry (via North Sydney, Nova Scotia) and by highway. The Trans-Canada Highway starts here and continues to St. John's some 850 km away. The Long Range Mountains (right bottom), part of the Appalachian mountain system (see also Plates 29, 30, and 38), run the full length of western Newfoundland. Cape Anguille (bottom left) is the westernmost point on the island of Newfoundland.

Other points of interest

■ At 344 km², Grand Lake [B3-A4] is the largest lake on the island of Newfoundland. It is accessible from Deer Lake [A3] by way of T'Railway Provincial Park, Newfoundland's portion of the Trans Canada Trail.

■ At 2,895 km², Bay du Nord Wilderness Reserve has ample roaming room for a herd of 15,000 caribou, the largest on the island of Newfoundland. The reserve encompasses a variety of environments: bogs, fens, and barrens, and forests of black spruce, balsam fir, and trembling aspen. It can be accessed by challenging canoe routes and hiking trails. (A provincial travel permit required.) The Bay du Nord River, flowing south into Fortune Bay, is a Canadian Heritage River, whose rapids and lower reaches require expert skill.

■ Fortune [F6] provides a ferry service to the French-controlled islands of Saint-Pierre and Miquelon [E5-F5].

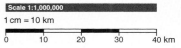

Scale 1:1,000,000

1 cm = 10 km

0 10 20 30 40 km

1 2 3 4 5

A

The Shoal Brook
Birchy Head
Winter House Brook
Lomond
Glenburnie
Glenburnie-
Birchy Head-
Shoal Brook
Wiltondale
Wiltondale
Pioneer Village
Bonne Bay Big Pond
Trout River Pond
Tablelands
Adies Pond
Little Falls
Big Falls
Sir Richard Squires Memorial Provincial Park
Sheppardville
Upper Indian Pond
Springdale
Robert's Arm
Glovers Harbour
Comfort Cove
Newstead
Cormack
South Brook
West Pond
Little Burnt Bay
Pleasantview
Embree
Stanhope
Michaels Harbour
Bayto
Campbell
Nicholsville
Reidville
Howley
Birchy Lake
Sheffield Lake
West Brook Ecological Reserve
Point Leamington
Point of Bay
Phillips Head
Brown's
Porterville
Lewisporte
Deer Lake
Junction Brook
Main Dam
Howley
Mizzen Topsail 555m
Main Topsail 536m
Great Gull Lake
South Twin Lake
North Twin Lake
Hodges Hill
Northern Arm
Botwood
Peterview
Norris Arm North Side
Notre Dame Junction
Spillway
St. Judes
Pynn's Brook
Little Harbour
Lobster House 584m
Mary Ann Lake
Dawes Pond
Hinds Brook
Bishop's Falls
Rattling Brook
Norris Arm
Lake O'Brien
Notre Dame Provincial Park
Glen
Cox's Cove
McIver's
Gillams
Meadows
Hughes Brook
Little Rapids
Pasadena
Humber Village
Steady Brook
Irishtown
Summerside
Millertown Junction
Badger
Aspen Brook
Rushy Pond Siding
Grand Falls-Windsor
Jumpers Brook
Appleton
Monch
ner Brook
Massey Drive
Marble Mountain
Thunder Brook
Red Cliff
Mary March Museum
Salmonid Interpretive Centre

B

Glover Island
Corner Brook Pond
Indian Pond
Buchans Lake
Buchans Junction
Buchans
Millertown
Exploits
West Lake
Crowe Lake
Burnt Pond
Frozen Ocean Lake
Caribou Pond

NEWFOUNDLAND

Red Indian Lake
Tally Pond
Miguels Lake
Gander Lake
Great Rattling Brook
Southwest River
Star Lake
Island Pond
Little Grand Lake
Hare Hill 596m

AND LABRADOR

MOUNTAINS
ANNIEOPSQUOTCH
Lloyds Lake
Long Lake
Quinn Lake
Rogerson Lake
Redcross Lake
Wilding Lake
Sandown Pond
Upper Salmon Reservoir
Salmon River
Victoria Lake
Newton Lake
Little Gander Lake
Berry Hill Pond
Great Gull Lake
Middle Ridge
Newton Lake

C

King George IV Ecological Reserve
King George IV Lake
Spruce Pond
Scotts Lake
Rocky Ridge Pond
Middle Lake
Burnt Pond
White Bear Lake
Dollard Pond
Granite Lake
Maelpaeg Reservoir
Cold Spring Pond
Round Pond
Kikupegh Pond
Jeddore Lake

TERRE-NEUVE-

Koskaecodde Lake
Ahwachanjeesh Pond
Wolf Lake

ET- LABRADOR

Middle Ridge Wildlife Reserve
Big Blue Hill Pond
Little Blue Hill Pond
Maximeagtik Lake
Jubilee Lake

BLUE HILLS OF COUTEAU
Peter Snout 515m
Top Pond
Camp Boggy
Head of Bay d'Espoir
St. Veronica's
Milltown-Head of Bay d'Espoir
St. Joseph's Cove
Milltown
Swanger Cove
Morrisville
St. Alban's
Conne River

D

Otter Point
Muddy Hole Point
Sandbanks Provincial Park
Burgeo
Burgeo Islands
Deer Island
Fox Island Harbour
Grey River
Bay de Loup
Ramea
Ramea Islands
White Bear Bay
North East Arm
Dolland Bight
Hare Bay
Lock's Cove
Mosquito
McCallum
Stone Valley
Gaultois
Furby's Cove
Little Bay Round Harbour
Long Island
Goblin
Stanley Cove
Bois Island
Roti Bay
Brent Cove
North Bay
Cape la Hune
François
Rencontre West
Hermitage-Sandyville
Grole
Miller's Passage
Wreck Cove
Little Bay West
Jersey Harbour
Harbour Breton
Pool's Cove
Doctors Harbour
Rencontre East
Tickle Beach
Bay de l'Eau
Andersons Cove
Stone's Cove
Belle Bay
Harbr Hill
Bay L'Arge
Corbin Bay
St. Bernard's
Jacques Fontaine
St. Bernar
Jacques Fc
Boat Ha
English Harbour East
English Harbour West
Mose Ambrose
St. Jacques-Coombs Cove
Point Rosie
St. Jacques
Boxey
Harbour
Coombes Cove
St. John Harbour
Connaigre Head
Seal Cove
Pass Island

E

Penguin Islands
Brunette Island
Mercer's Cove
Fortune Bay
Baie de Fortune
Garnish
Frenchman's Cove
Frenchman's Cove Provincial Park
Mooring Cove
Jean de Ba
Spanish Roc
Rock Hai
Baine Harbou
Rusho
Red Harbo
Marystown
Newfoundland Time Zone
Heure de Terre-Neuve
Atlantic Time Zone
Heure de l'Atlantique
Winterland
Little Bay
Beau Bois
Creston
Tides Point
Fox Cove
Mortier
Cap du Nid à l'Aigle
Baie du Miquelon
Pointe aux Soldats
Grand Beach
Grand Bank
Bull Cove
Bay View
Salmonier
Lewin's Cove
Burin
Black Duck Cove
Burin Island
Collins Cove
Epworth
Miquelon
Molliers
Fortune Head
Fortune
Fortune Head Ecological Reserve
Fortupe Head
BURIN PENINSULA

F

ATLANTIC
Grande Miquelon
Isthme de Langlade
Anse à Phoque
Grand Barachois
Petite Miquelon
Pointe Plate
Anse du Sud-Ouest
FRANCE
Pointe de l'Ouest
Île
Saint-Pierre
St-Pierre
Dantzic Point
Lories Point May
Lamaline
Allan's Island
Point au Gaul
High Beach
Taylor's Bay
Lord's Cove
Lawn Point
Roundabout
St. Lawrence
Corbin
Little St. Lawrence
Lawn

OCEAN

A T L A N T I C

O C E A N

A T L A

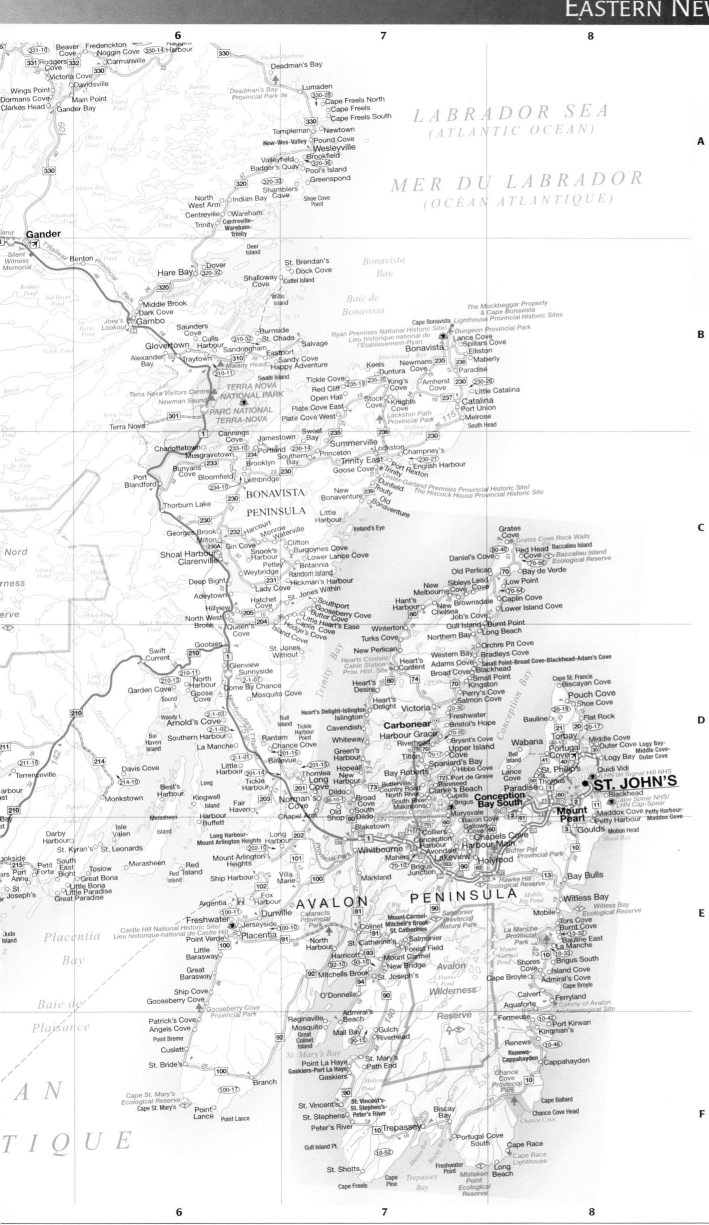

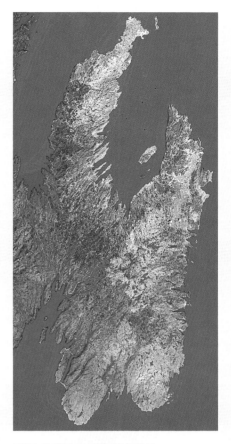

THE AVALON PENINSULA

The bulky coastal cliffs of Newfoundland's 10,360-km² Avalon Peninsula confront the cold, turbulent waters of the North Atlantic. Four capacious bays (clockwise, top to bottom)—Trinity, Conception, Trepassey, and St. Mary's—shelter myriad tiny fishing ports from the unruly ocean. The narrow, almost landlocked, harbour of St. John's can be detected just above the bulge of Cape Spear, Canada's easternmost point (upper right).

Other points of interest

■ The natural features of 296-km² Terra Nova National Park [B6-C6] include towering headland and tranquil beaches along the coast of Bonavista Bay. Inland are gently rolling hills and forests with ponds, streams, and bogs. The landscape of Terra Nova—Canada's most easterly national park—was created by ice-age glacial activity. Until midsummer, icebergs borne along by the icy Labrador Current drift offshore in the Atlantic's "Iceberg Alley."

■ Cape St. Mary's Ecological Reserve [F6], at the southwest tip of the Avalon Peninsula, is accessible by a 16-km road from Route 100. The outstanding natural attraction is 76-m-high Bird Rock, which is linked to the shore by a land bridge. More than 50,000 seabirds—gannets, murres, and kittiwakes—gather on the mighty rock and the coastal cliffs.

Scale 1:1,000,000

1 cm = 10 km

0   10   20   30   40 km

1   2   3   4   5

QUÉBEC

LABRADOR
NEWFOUNDLAND AND LABRADOR
TERRE-NEUVE-ET-LABRADOR

Barge Bay

Trans Labrador Highway

510 Red Bay
Red Bay National Historic Site
Lieu historique national de Red Bay

Pinware

Pinware River Provincial Park

Cap Diable
L'Anse-au-Loup
L'Anse-au-Diable

Boat Harbour

Wild Bight

Burnt Cape Ecological Reserve
Cook's Harbour
Ship
Raleigh

Rivière-Saint-Paul
Middle Bay   138
Brador
Blanc-Sablon
510
Forteau
L'Anse-Amour
510-11
Amour Point
Anse-au-Clair

Lourdes-de-Blanc-Sablon

Vieux-Fort
Salmon Bay

Strait of Belle Isle
Détroit de Belle Isle

Watts Point Calcareous Ecological Reserve

Big Brook

435
18
430
437

Green Island Cove
Green Island Brook
134

Île Greenly

Refuge national d'oiseaux migrateurs de la Baie-Brador/--Brador Bay National Migratory Bird Sanctuary

Savage Cove
Nameless Cove
Flower's Cove
430
Sandy Cove

Seal Bay

Grenfell Ho

432
Hare Bay
Hare Bay Islands Ecological Reserve

Deadman's Cove
Anchor Point
St. Barbe
St. Barbe
Black Duck Cove
Forresters Point   Pigeon Cove
430-52
Main Brook

Maiden Point

Shekatika

Saint-Augustin
Pakuashipi

Île Bayfield

Île de la Grande Passe

Pond Cove
Blue Cove
Brig Bay
430-46
Plum Point
432

Grandois
438
St. Juli
Croque

Îles-Monger

New Ferolle
New Ferolle Peninsula
Shoal Cove
Bird Cove
Reef's Harbour
430-36
Bartletts Harbour
430-32
433
Crouse
Cape Rouge

Baie-des-Ha! Ha!

Roddickton
434
Conche

La Tabatière

St. John
Island
Flat Island
Barr'd Harbour

Castors River
430
St. John Bay
433-10
Bide Arm

Mutton Bay

Refuge national d'oiseaux migrateurs de Gros-Mécatina/ Gros-Mecatina National Migratory Bird Sanctuary

Eddies Cove West

NEWFOUNDLAND AND LABRADOR

Englee
Fren

Port au Choix National Historic Site
Lieu historique national de Port au Choix
Port au Choix
Gargamelle
430-28
Point Riche
Port Saunders

NORTHERN PENINSULA

Hooping Harbour

Ingornachoix Bay

Hawke's Bay

Williamsport
Granite Point

GULF OF ST. LAWRENCE

River of Ponds
River of Ponds Lake

Eastern Blue Pond

Blue Mountain
▲649m

Western Blue Pond

Harbour Deep

430
Bateau Cove
Deer Cove

TERRE-NEUVE-ET-LABRADOR

Table Point Ecological Reserve
Bellburns

Lake Michel

LONG RANGE MOUNTAINS

Daniel's Harbour

Spudgels Cove

Horse
Western Island
Islands

GOLFE DU SAINT-LAURENT

Portland Creek
Portland Creek Pond

Gros Pate
673m

Partridge Point

Fleur de Lys

The Arches Provincial Park
136

Parson's Pond
Parsons Pond

Coachman's Cove
410-10
Cape Corbin
410
Ming's Bight
417
Packet

Three Mile Rock

Wild Cove
Lobster Cove
Baie Verte
419
418
Woodstock
Harbour Round

Belldowns Point
Shallow Bay
Cow Head

Jackson's Arm
412
Seal Cove
414

BAIE VERTE PENINSULA

St. Paul's
St. Pauls Inlet

Back Cove
411-11
Bear Cove
Western Arm
411
Snooks Arm
415

430
Western Brook Pond

GROS MORNE NATIONAL PARK PARC NATIONAL DU GROS-MORNE

Sop's Arm
Sop's Island
420
Westport
Purbeck's Cove
413-10
Smith's Harbour

Burlington

Sally's Cove

Green Point
Berry Hill
Bakers Brook
Lobster Cove
Bear Cove
Gros Morne
806m
Rocky Harbour
430-15
Gros Morne Visitor Centre
Gros Morne/Gros-Morne

Pollards Point
420-10
Middle Arm
Jackson's Cove

King's Cove
Harry's Harbour

Brown's Cove

Beachside
391
Little Bay
Suley Ann's Cove

Western Head
Wild Cove
Curzon Village
Norris Point
Woody Point
Neddy Harbour
Winter House Brook
Lomond

Rattling Brook
391-10
King's Point
St. Patricks
Coffee Cove
Miles Cove
Port Anson
392
381
Pilley's

Trout River
The Shoal Brook
Birchy Head
431
Glenburnie
Glenburnie-Birchy Head-Shoal Brook
431

Hampden
Bayside
421

Springdale
390
380
Robert's Arm

Trout River Pond
Tablelands

Wiltondale
Wilfondale Pioneer Village

Little Falls
Big Falls
420

Sheppardville

South Brook
1

Cape St. Gregory

Mount St. Gregory
▲674m
North Head

Cormack
422
430

Sir Richard Squires Memorial Provincial Park

10
73

West Brook Ecological Reserve

Tweed Island
Guernsey Island

Pearl Island

Reidville
1
45

West Brook
Main Topsail 536m

Mizzen Topsail 555m

Main Dam
401
Howley

Pynn's Brook

Deer Lake
Nicholsville
Junction Brook
Spillway
St. Judes

Lobster Pond
Big Pond 584m

Hodges Hill
▲569m

Bottle Cove
Lark Harbour
Innismara
Woods Island
Cox's Cove
Little Harbour

Blow Me Down Provincial Park
Frenchman's Cove
York Harbour
McIver's

Millertown

A WORLD HERITAGE SITE

Along western Newfoundland's Northern Peninsula, the Long Range Mountains rise dramatically above a low coastal plain. The coastline is deeply indented with fjords and bays (top to bottom): Parsons Pond, St. Pauls Inlet, Western Brook Pond, and Bonne Bay. Gros Morne National Park, covering 1,943 km², encircles Bonne Bay. Its terrain was formed by continental collision 450 million years ago, but its present landscape was shaped by ice-age glaciers. Among its sites are Western Brook Pond (centre)–a fjordlike lake–and 806-m-high Gros Morne Mountain, visible above the point where Bonne Bay splits into two arms. Because of its intriguing geological history and formations, the park has been recognized as a World Heritage Site.

Other points of interest

■ L'Anse aux Meadows National Historic Site [A5] preserves the remains of a Viking settlement, established here about A.D. 1000. The site contains eight structures discovered by a team of Norwegian archeologists in 1960. L'Anse aux Meadows was declared a World Heritage Site in 1978.

■ At St. Anthony [B5], the Grenfell Hospital Mission serves the remote ports of northern Newfoundland and southern Labrador. The Grenfell House Museum recounts the work of Dr. Wilfred Grenfell, who founded the mission in 1893.

■ Port au Choix Historic Site [C3] was unearthed in the late 1960s. The site is a reminder of the "red paint people" who lived in this vicinity some 5,000 years ago. Relics belonging to these aboriginal peoples are displayed here.

Scale 1:1,000,000

1 cm = 10 km

0   10   20   30   40 km

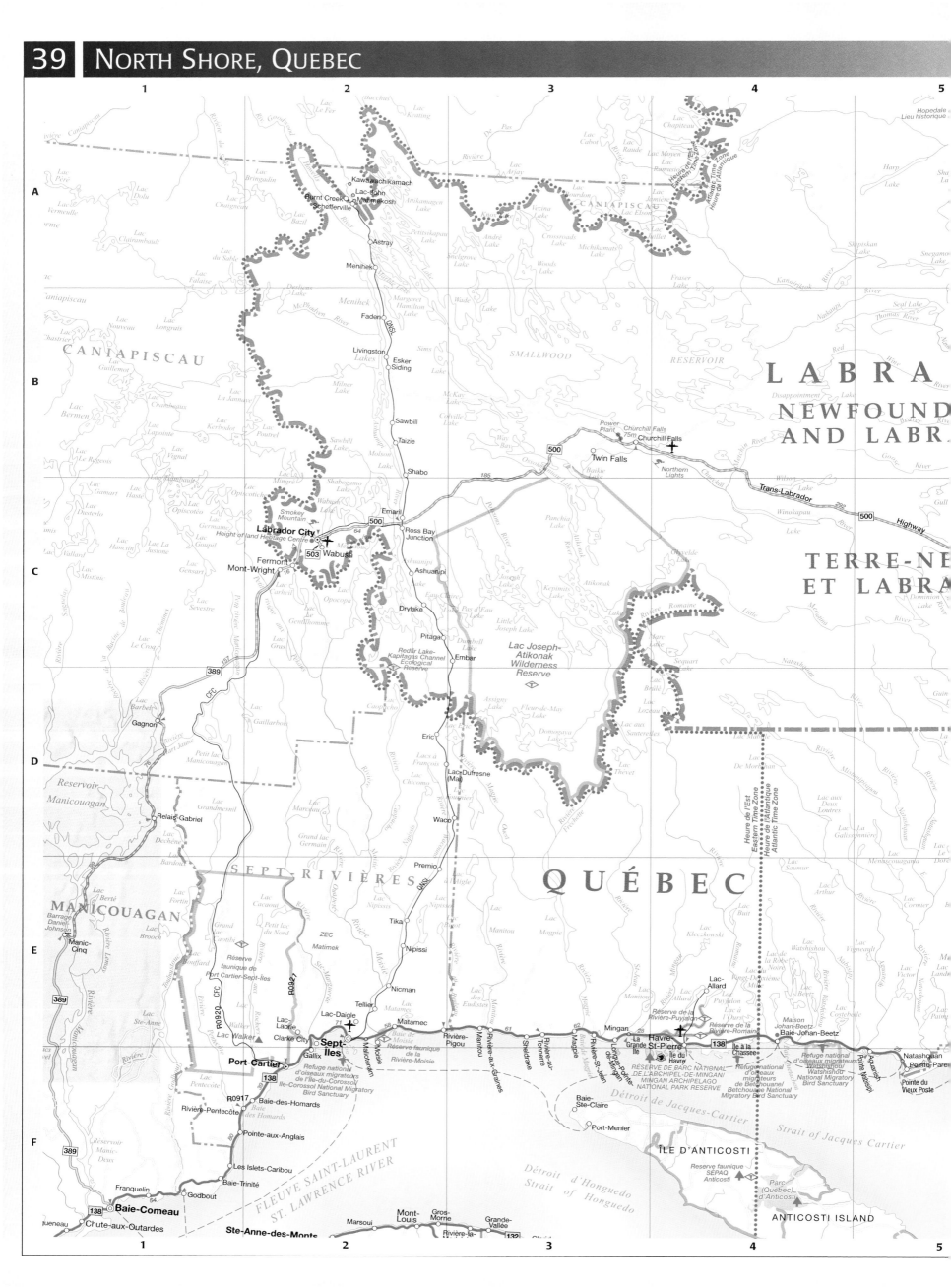

ÎLE D'ANTICOSTI

ANTICOSTI ISLAND

LABRA

NEWFOUND
AND LABRA

TERRE-NE
ET LABRA

QUÉBEC

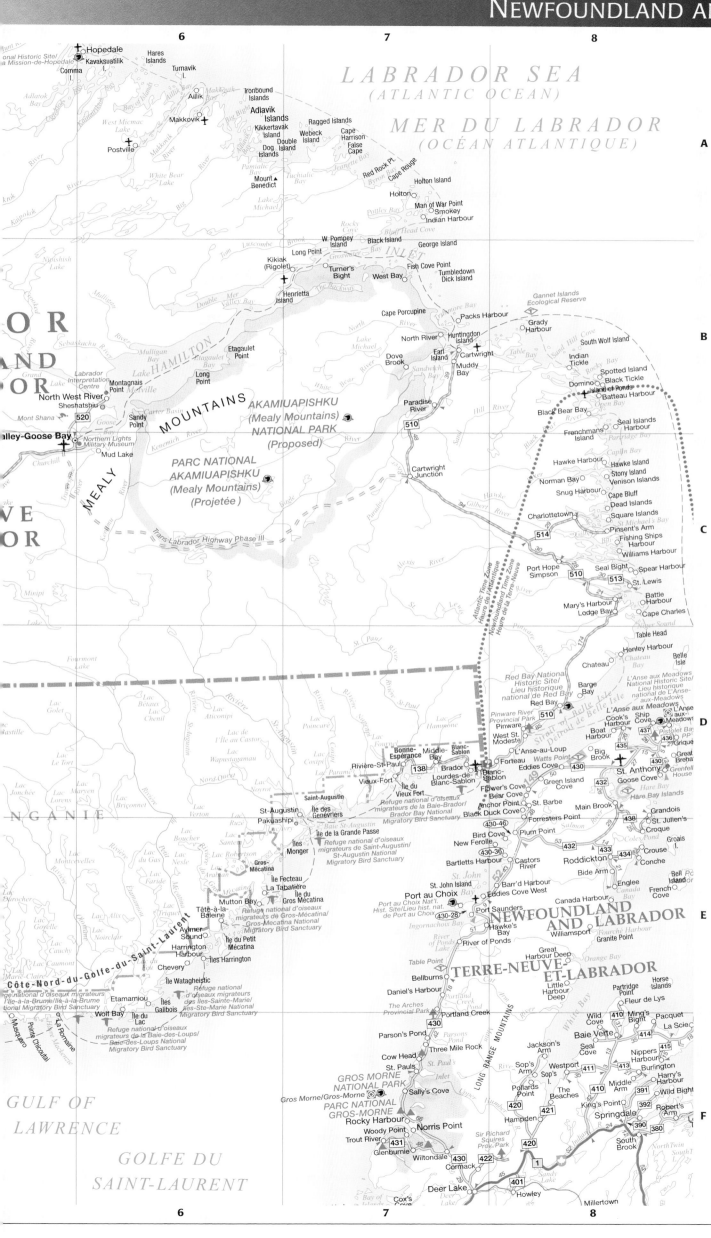

A LAKE OF METEORITE ORIGIN

Réservoir Manicouagan, Quebec's second largest natural lake after Lac Mistassini (Plate 40, F5), was created by the impact of a meteorite millions of years ago. At the centre of the lake lies Île René-Levasseur, capped by 952-m-high Mont de Babel. The waters of the lake flow south to the St. Lawrence by way of Rivière Manicouagan (centre left). The hydroelectric development of the river followed the 1971 opening of the Daniel Johnson Dam (Manic 5). The dam, one of the world's largest, is located some 40 km downstream from the lake.

Other points of interest

■ With an area of 6,423 km², Réserve faunique de Port-Cartier–Sept-Îles [E1-E2], with over 1,000 lakes and 15 rivers, is prized for Quebec red and brook trout, and Atlantic salmon.

■ Labrador's Mealy Mountains [B6-C7] are the site of the proposed Akamiuapishku National Park, which embraces several environments—tundra, boreal forest, and wetland. The region is a haven for caribou, moose, osprey, and harlequin duck.

Scale 1:2,175,000

1 cm = 21.75 km

0   20   40   60   80 km

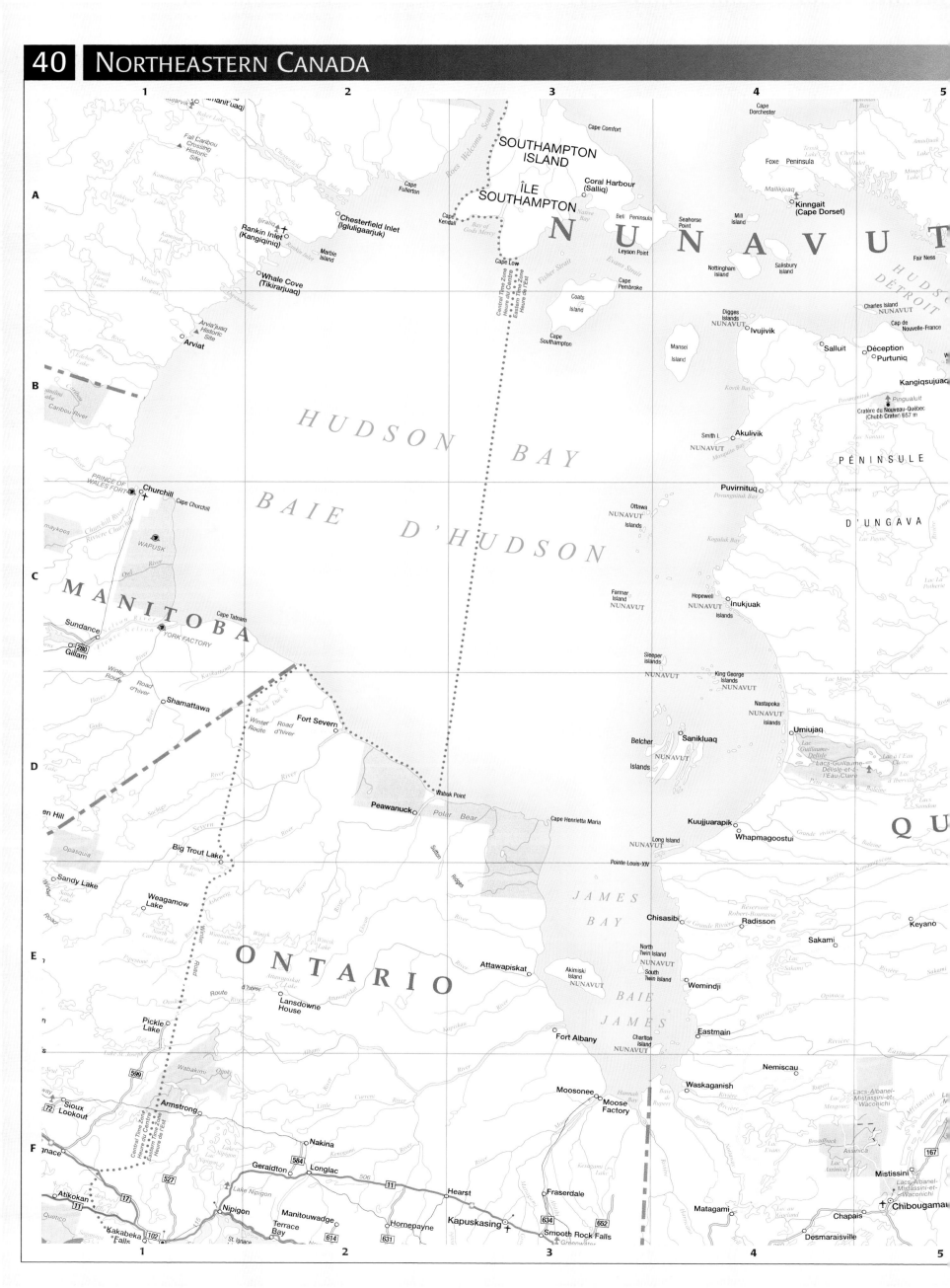

Bujarivik
'manit'uaq
Baker Lake

Fall Caribou
Crossing
Historic
Site

Kommuniak

Kazan

SOUTHAMPTON
ISLAND

Cape Comfort

Cape Dorchester

Foxe Peninsula

Mallikjuaq

Kinngait
(Cape Dorset)

Chesterfield Inlet

Cape
Fullerton

ÎLE
SOUTHAMPTON

Coral Harbour
(Salliq)

Ijiralik
Rankin Inlet
(Kangiqiniq)

Cape
Kendall

Cape Low

Bay of
Gods Mercy

Bell Peninsula

Seahorse
Point

Fair Ness

Marble
Island

Leyson Point

N U N A V U T

Charles Island
NUNAVUT

Cap de
Nouvelle-France

Whale Cove
(Tikirarjuaq)

Fisher Strait

Evans Strait

Nottingham
Island

Salisbury
Island

Salluit

Déception
Purtuniq

Arvia'juaq
Historic
Site

Central Time Zone
Heure du Centre
Eastern Time Zone
Heure de l'Est

Cape
Pembroke

Digges
Islands
NUNAVUT

Ivujivik

Kangiqsujuaq

Arviat

Cape
Southampton

Coats
Island

Mansel
Island

Pingualuit
Cratère du Nouveau-Québec
(Chubb Crater) 657 m

Smith I.
NUNAVUT

Akulivik

PÉNINSULE

H U D S O N   B A Y

Kovik Bay

Mosquito Bay

D'UNGAVA

B A I E   D ' H U D S O N

Puvirnituq
Povungnituk Bay

Churchill
PRINCE OF
WALES FORT

Cape Churchill

Churchill River
Rivière Churchill

Ottawa
NUNAVUT
Islands

Kogaluk Bay

maykoos

WAPUSK

Cape Tatnam

Farmer
Island
NUNAVUT

Hopewell
NUNAVUT
Islands

Inukjuak

M A N I T O B A

Sundance

280

Gillam

YORK FACTORY

Sleeper
Islands
NUNAVUT

King George
Islands
NUNAVUT

Winter
Route
Road
d'hiver

Nastapoka
NUNAVUT
Islands

Umiujaq

Lac
Guillaume-
Delisle

Lacs-Guillaume-et-
Delisle-et-à-
l'Eau-Claire

Lac à l'Eau
Claire

Shamattawa

Winter
Route
Road
d'hiver

Fort Severn

Belcher
NUNAVUT
Islands

Sanikluaq

en Hill

Wabuk Point

Opasquia

Peawanuck

Polar Bear

Cape Henrietta Maria

Kuujjuarapik

Q U

Big Trout Lake

Sutton

Long Island
NUNAVUT

Whapmagoostui

Sandy Lake

Ridges

Pointe Louis-XIV

Weagamow
Lake

J A M E S

B A Y

Chisasibi

Radisson

Keyano

O N T A R I O

Sakami

Pickle
Lake

Lansdowne
House

Attawapiskat

Akimiski
Island
NUNAVUT

North
Twin Island
NUNAVUT

Wemindji

Eastmain

South
Twin Island
NUNAVUT

B A I E

599

Fort Albany

Charlton
Island
NUNAVUT

Nemiscau

Waskaganish

Armstrong

Central Time Zone
Heure du Centre
Eastern Time Zone
Heure de l'Est

Wabakimi

Moosonee

Moose
Factory

Lacs-Albanel-
Mistassini-et-
Waconichi

Sioux
Lookout

72

Nakina

167

Mistissini

527

584

Longlac

Geraldton

Fraserdale

Matagami

Lacs-Albanel-
Mistassini-et-
Waconichi

Chibougamau

Atikokan

17

11

506

11

Hearst

634

652

Chapais

Desmaraisville

Nipigon

Manitouwadge

Hornepayne

Kapuskasing

Smooth Rock Falls

Kakabeka
Falls

102

Terrace
Bay

614

631

Greenwater

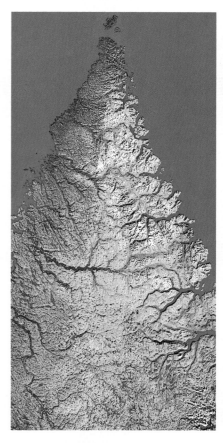

PEAK AND PLATEAU

The Labrador Peninsula has two distinct regions: the George Plateau in Quebec (left) and the Torngat Mountains, largely in Labrador (right). The George Plateau is a flat, rocky plain, cut deeply by rivers flowing into Ungava Bay. The Torngats, the highest peaks east of the Rockies, rise up 900 m from the frigid Labrador Sea. Along this coast, fjords extend some 30 to 80 km inland. Visible in this view (right centre) are Nachvak Fiord, Saglek Bay, and the inner reaches of Hebron Fiord. At 1,676 m, Cirque Mountain is the region's highest. Its snowy summit is visible just south of the Nachvak Fiord. At the very tip of the peninsula are Killiniq and the Button Islands of Nunavut. A national park has been proposed for this spectacular region.

POINTS OF INTEREST

■ James Bay [E3-E4] is 160 km wide between Cape Henrietta Maria and Pointe Louis-XIV. The heart of Quebec's James Bay Project is Réservoir Robert-Bourassa [E4], which receives water diverted from the Eastmain and other rivers. Nunavut administers Akimiski and all the other islands in the bay.

■ At 6,527 km², Smallwood Reservoir [D7-E7] is Canada's tenth largest freshwater body, created by the damming of the Churchill River for hydroelectric power production. Smallwood Reservoir is one of the world's largest man-made lakes.

■ Mingan Archipelago National Park Reserve [F7] comprises 40 islands, myriad islets, and reefs that extend more than 150 km. Spectacular rock formations—the products of erosion by winds and waves—are among the outstanding features of this park.

Scale 1:5,600,000

1 cm = 56 km

0   50   100   150   200 km

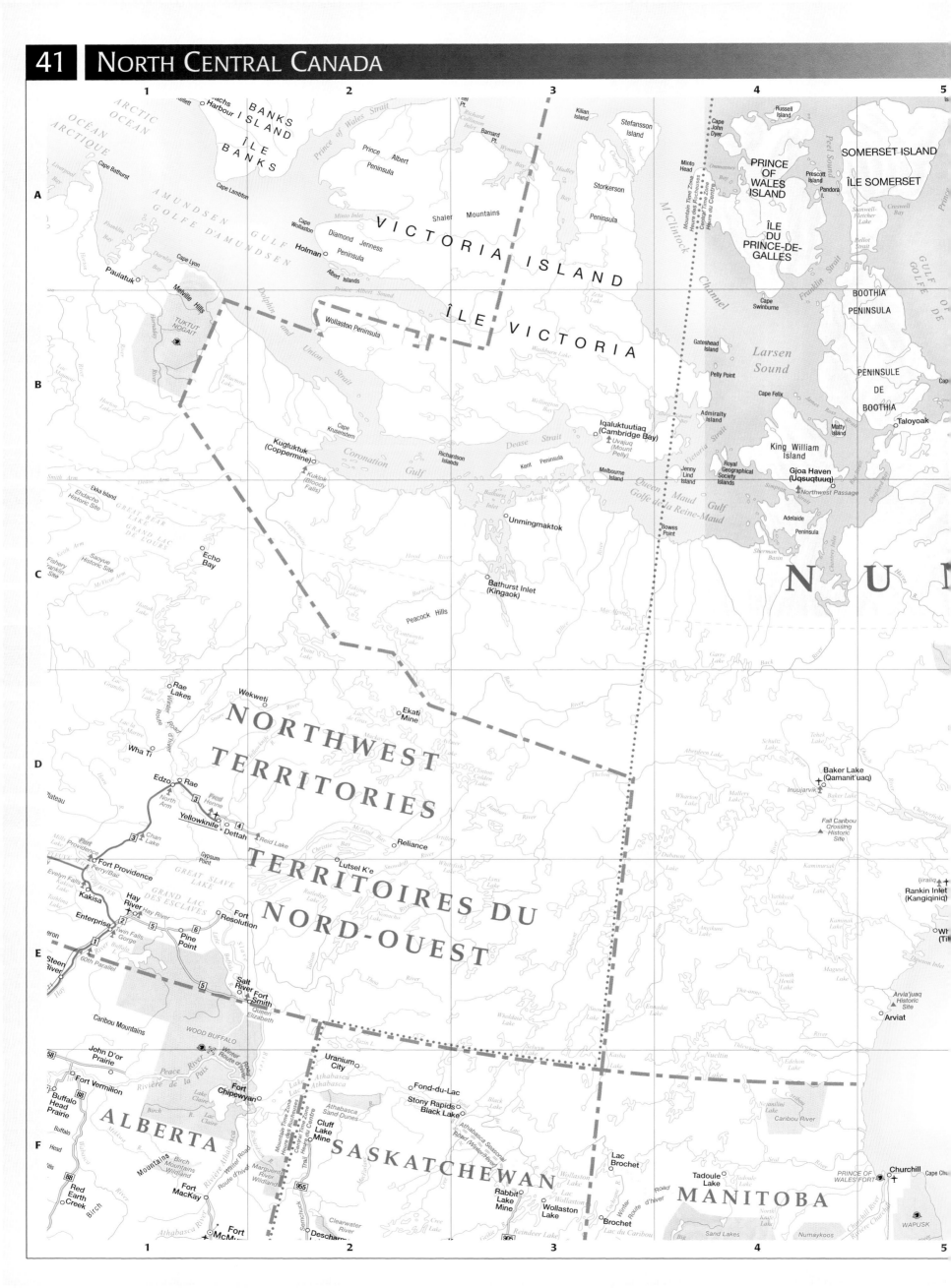

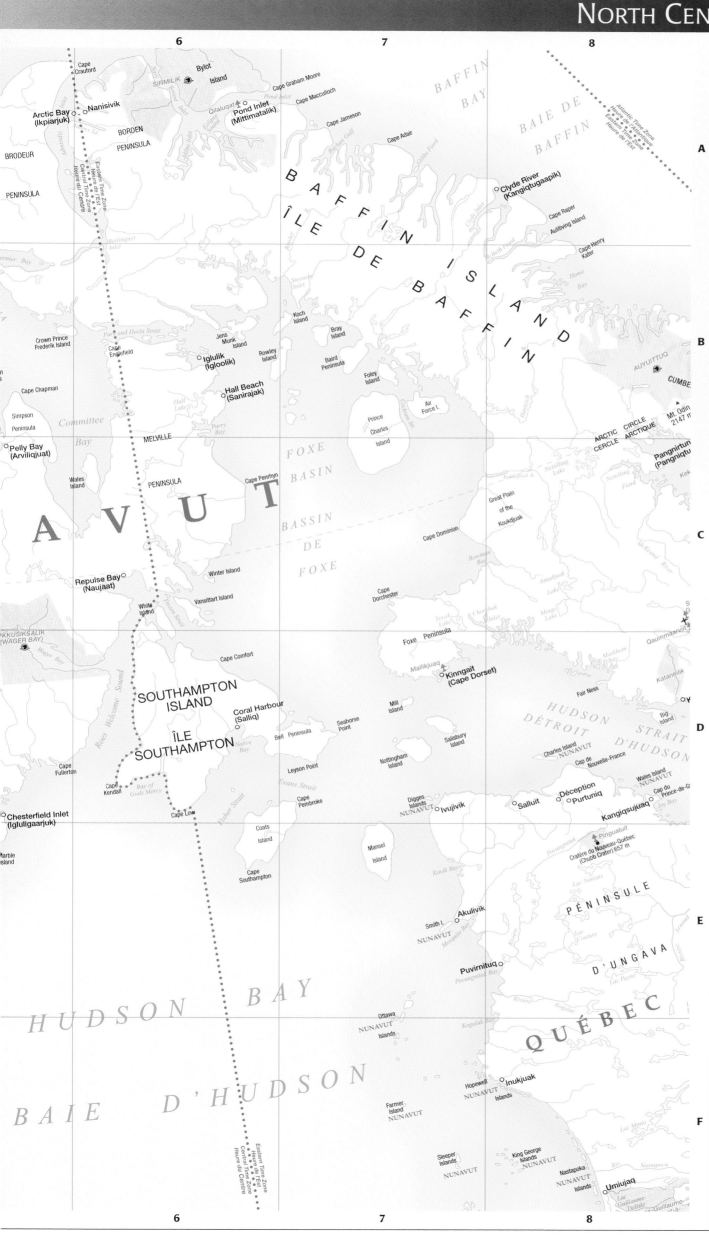

AT THE END OF THE CONTINENT

Icebound Boothia Peninsula (centre right) is North America's northernmost point. It is connected to the continent by a 40-km isthmus and separated from Somerset Island (top right) by Bellot Strait, only 2 km wide but clearly visible above. In 1831, James C. Ross discovered the magnetic north pole on the west side of the peninsula. (Since then, the pole has migrated farther north.) At 24,786 km², Somerset Island is ninth largest in the Arctic Archipelago; Prince of Wales Island (top left), at 33,339 km², ranks eighth. King William Island (bottom left) is associated with Sir John Franklin, whose search for the Northwest Passage ended in disaster and mystery. Franklin is known to have died on June 11, 1847.

POINTS OF INTEREST

■ Arviat [E5], Nunavut, is the geographical centre of Canada.

■ At 22,200 km², Sirmilik National Park [A6] encompasses three distinct environments: Bylot Island, which has a landscape of mountains, glaciers, and coastal lowlands; Borden Peninsula, which is cut deeply by broad river valleys; and a narrow fjord named Oliver Sound. Bylot Island supports a vast seabird colony.

■ When 21,469-km² Auyuittuq National Park [B8] was established in 1976, it was the world's first park above the Arctic Circle. In 1988, it was joined by Sirmilik (see above); in 1992, by 12,200-km² Aulavik National Park on Banks Island [Plate 42, D1]; and 37,775-km² Quttinirpaaq National Park, on Ellesmere Island [Plate 42, A5].

Scale 1:5,600,000

1 cm = 56 km

0   50   100   150   200 km

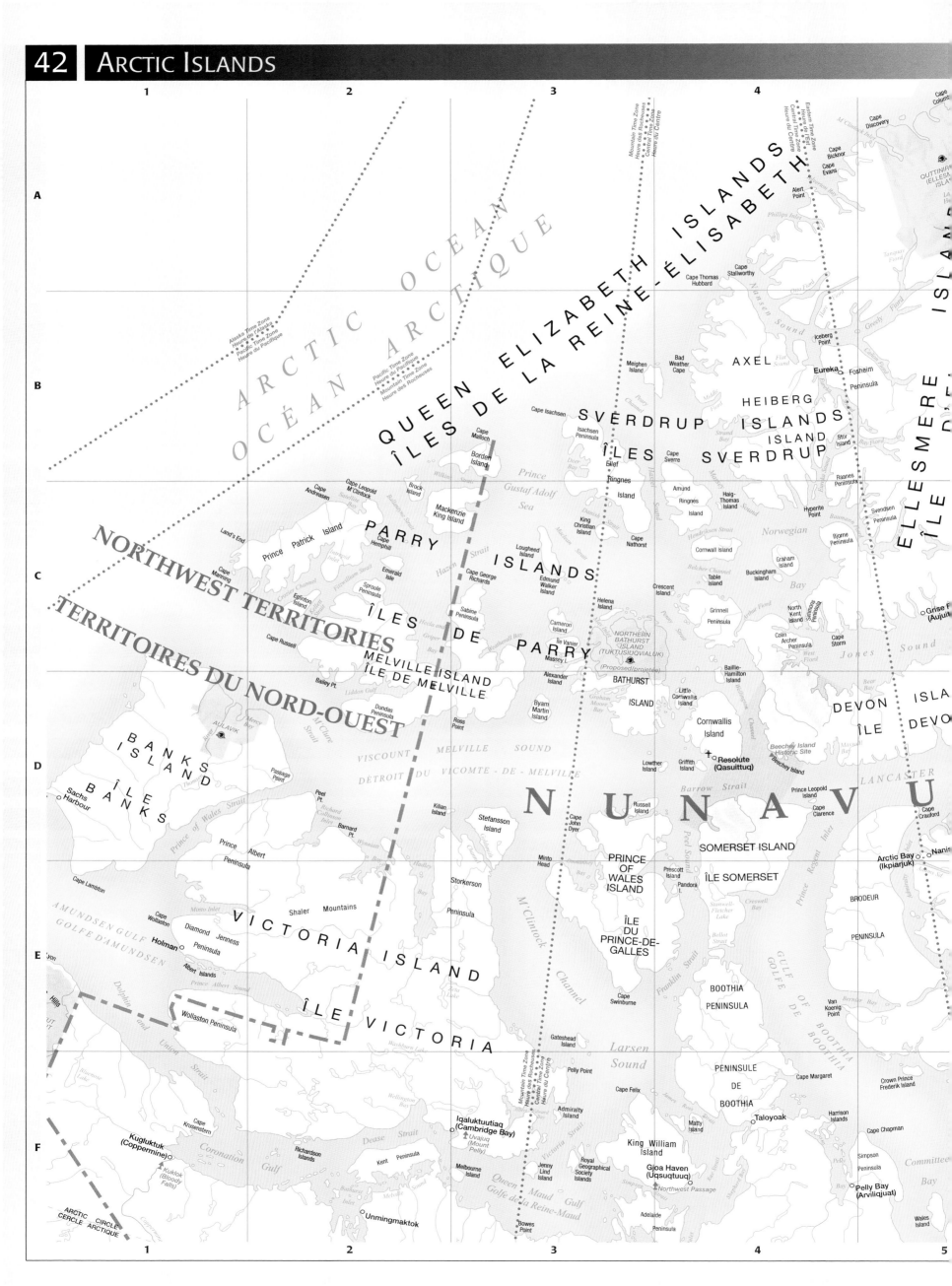

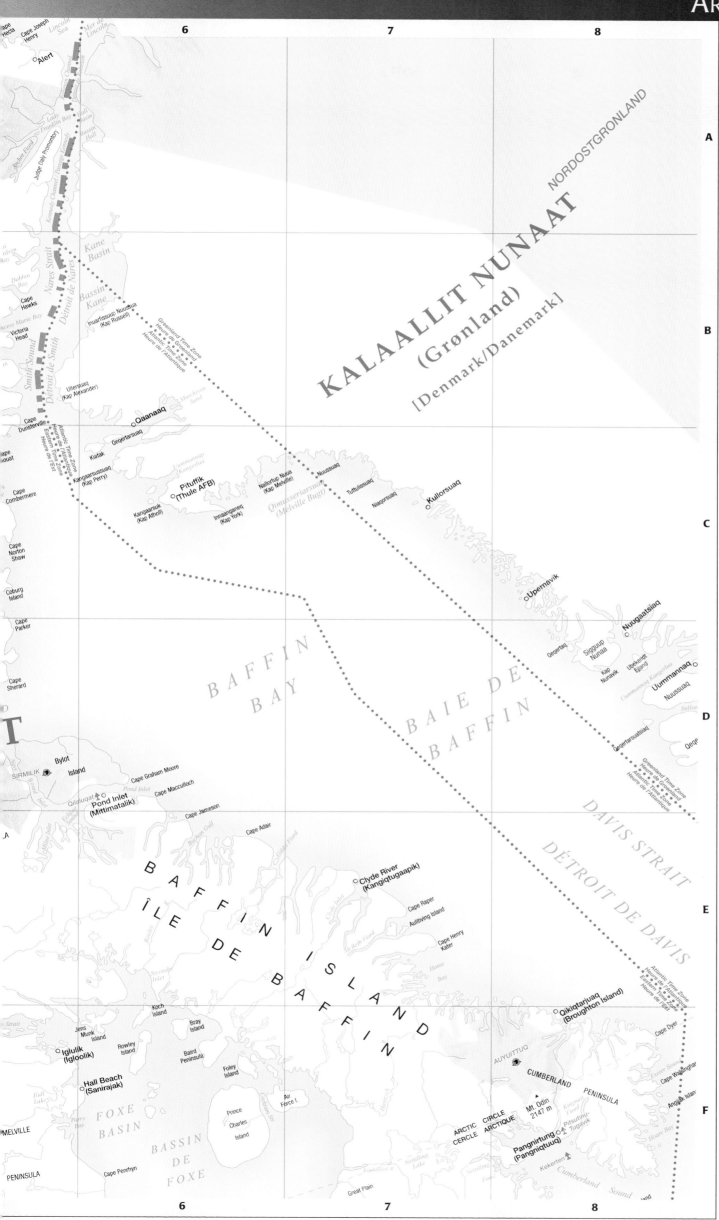

A MARS LANDSCAPE IN THE ARCTIC

The three Arctic islands shown above are Devon (top right), Cornwallis (centre left) and the northern shore of Somerset Island (bottom). Devon Island is the site of the Haughton Crater—the light-blue circular shape visible top right. More than 20 km in diameter, the crater was formed by the impact of an asteroid or a comet some 23 million years ago. In 1997, NASA, the United States National Research Council, and the Geological Survey of Canada chose the crater as a simulation site for the study of missions to Mars. Experts say the crater resembles conditions on Mars: the landscape is a cold, dry, and rocky desert, virtually unvegetated and drenched in ultraviolet light in summer. Tiny Beechey Island is visible in Lancaster Sound just south of Devon Island. The island served as a base for the ill-fated Franklin expedition and, later, for others who came in search of Franklin after his disappearance.

Other points of interest

■ The remote Canadian outpost of Alert [A5] is the world's northernmost community, closer to Moscow than it is to Toronto. A population of less than 100 inhabitants works at the weather station or the Canadian military base.

■ In 1985, paleontologists from the Geographical Survey of Canada discovered the fossils of a 40-million-year-old forest at the Geodetic Hills on Axel Heiberg Island [B4]. The fossils include swamp cypress, dawn redwood, and other semitropical trees, some of which reached as high as 35 m.

Scale 1:5,600,000

1 cm = 56 km

0   50   100   150   200 km

CITY MAPS

Below: *Edmonton's downtown towers add their glow to a winter evening.*

VANCOUVER BC

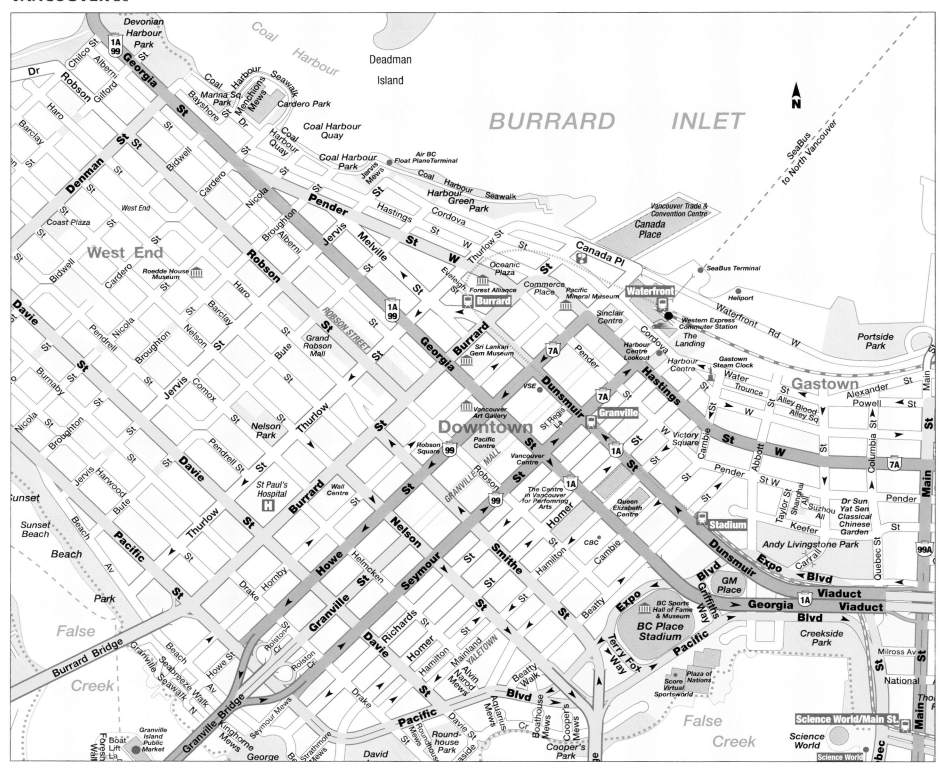

CALGARY AB

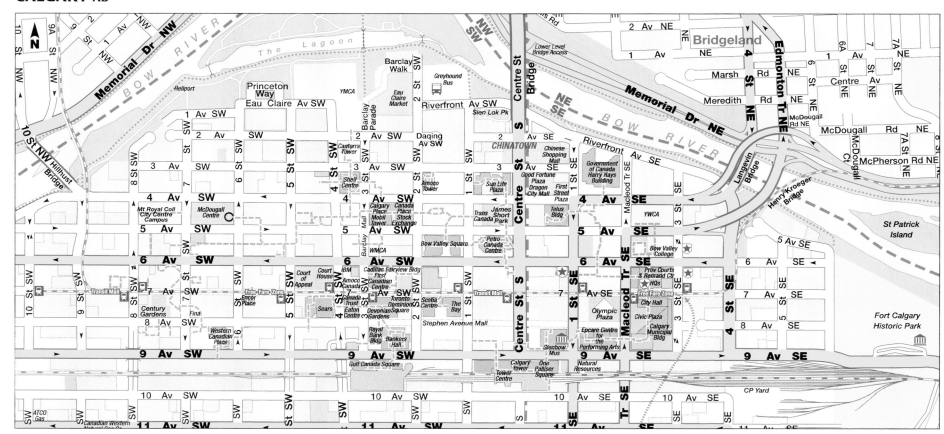

YELLOWKNIFE NT

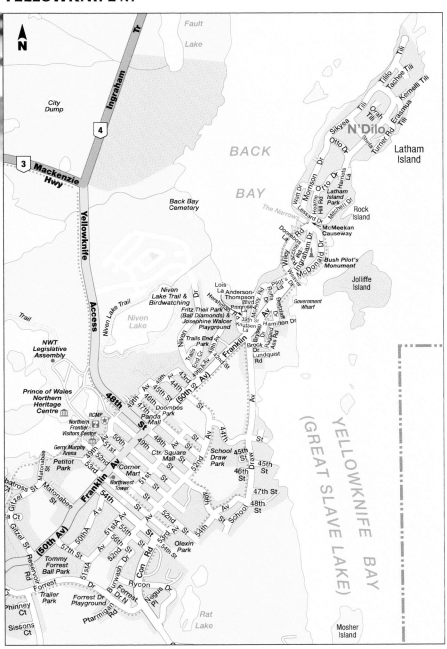

WHITEHORSE YT

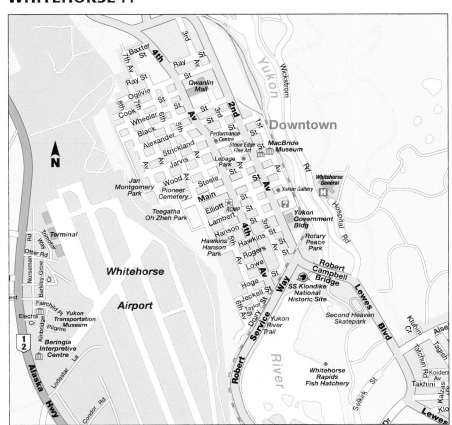

EDMONTON AB

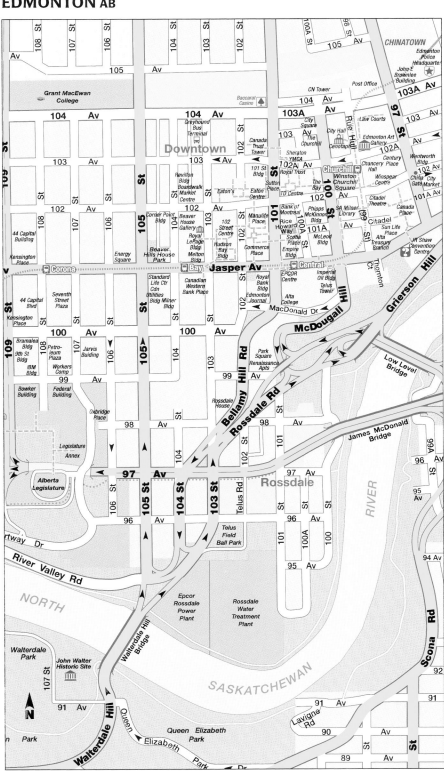

VICTORIA BC

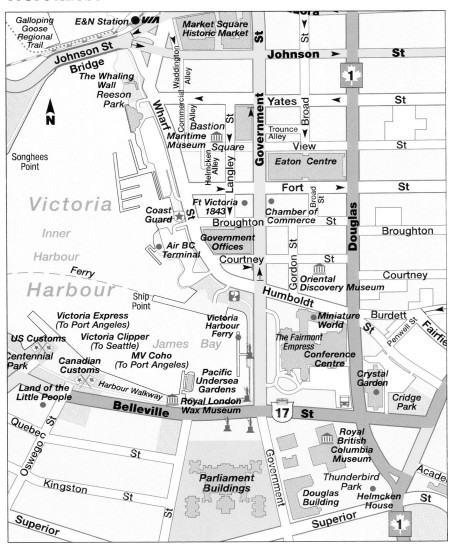

REGINA SK

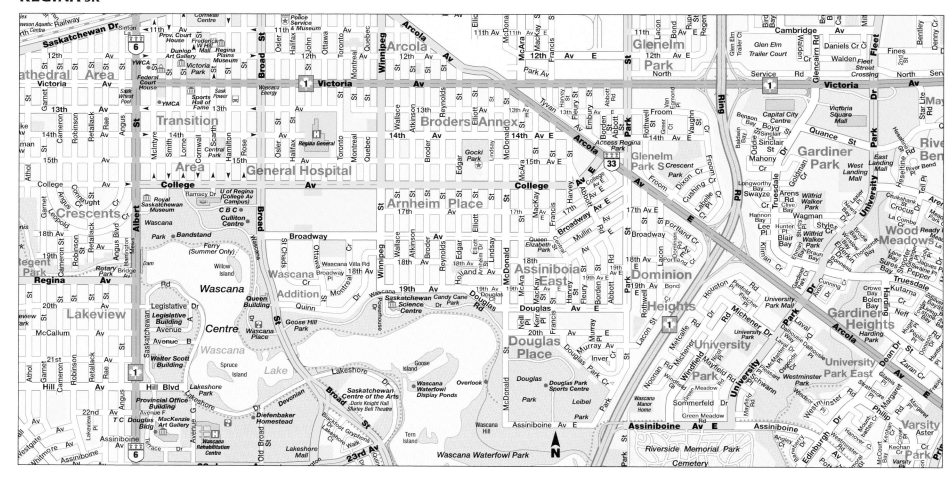

WINNIPEG MB

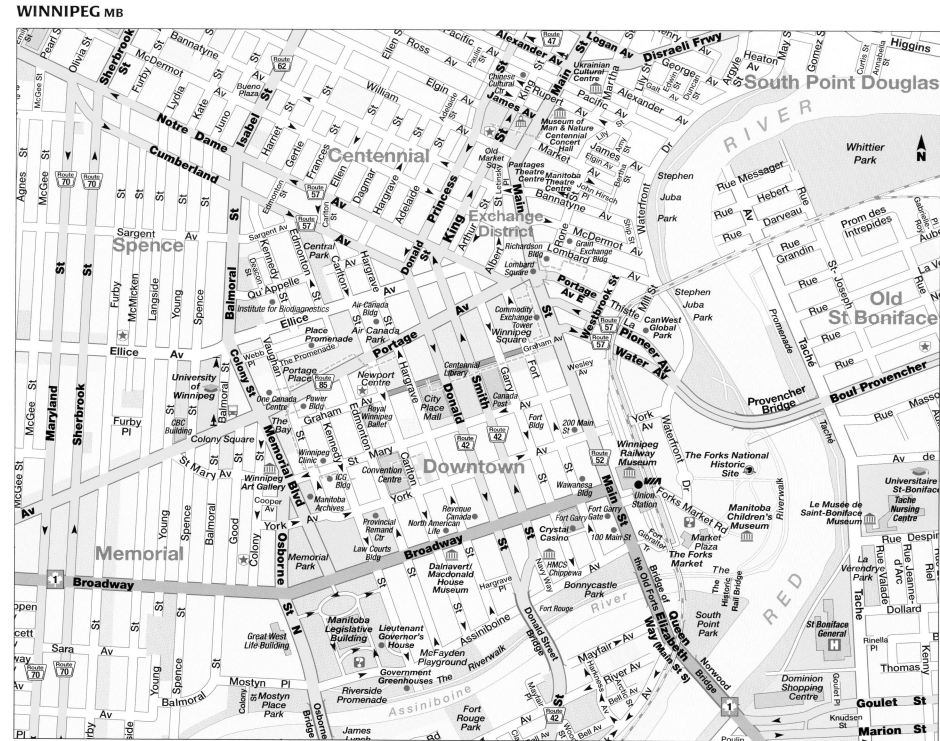

SASKATOON SK

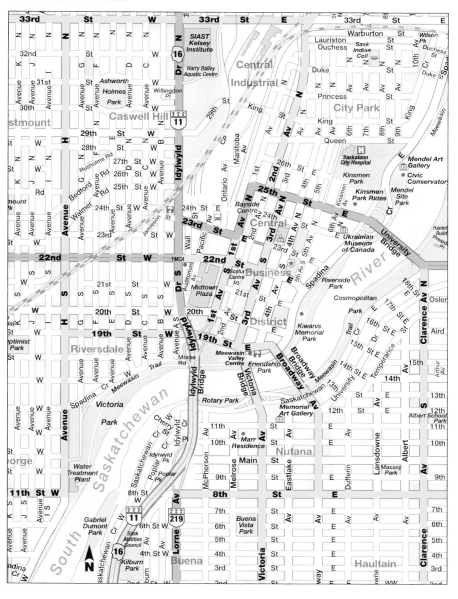

THUNDER BAY ON

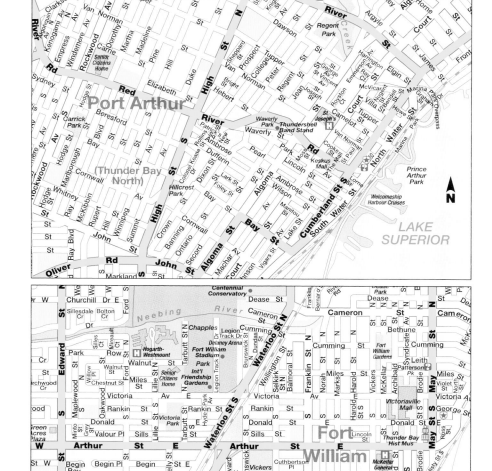

SUDBURY ON

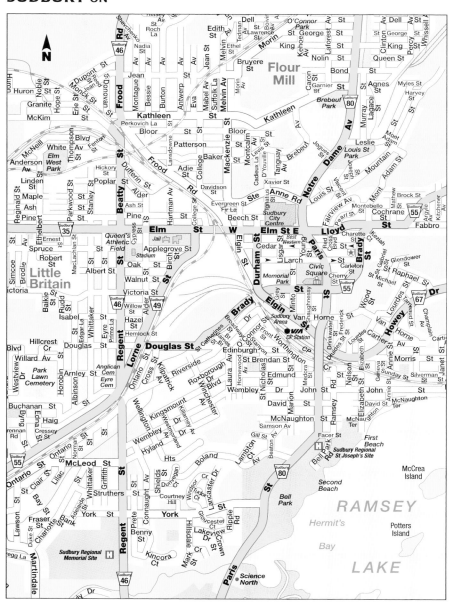

WINDSOR ON

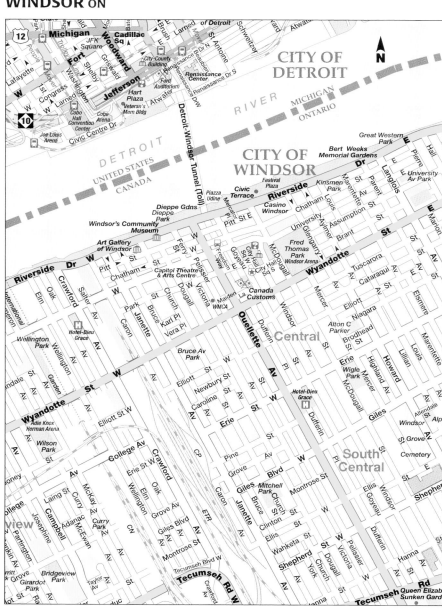

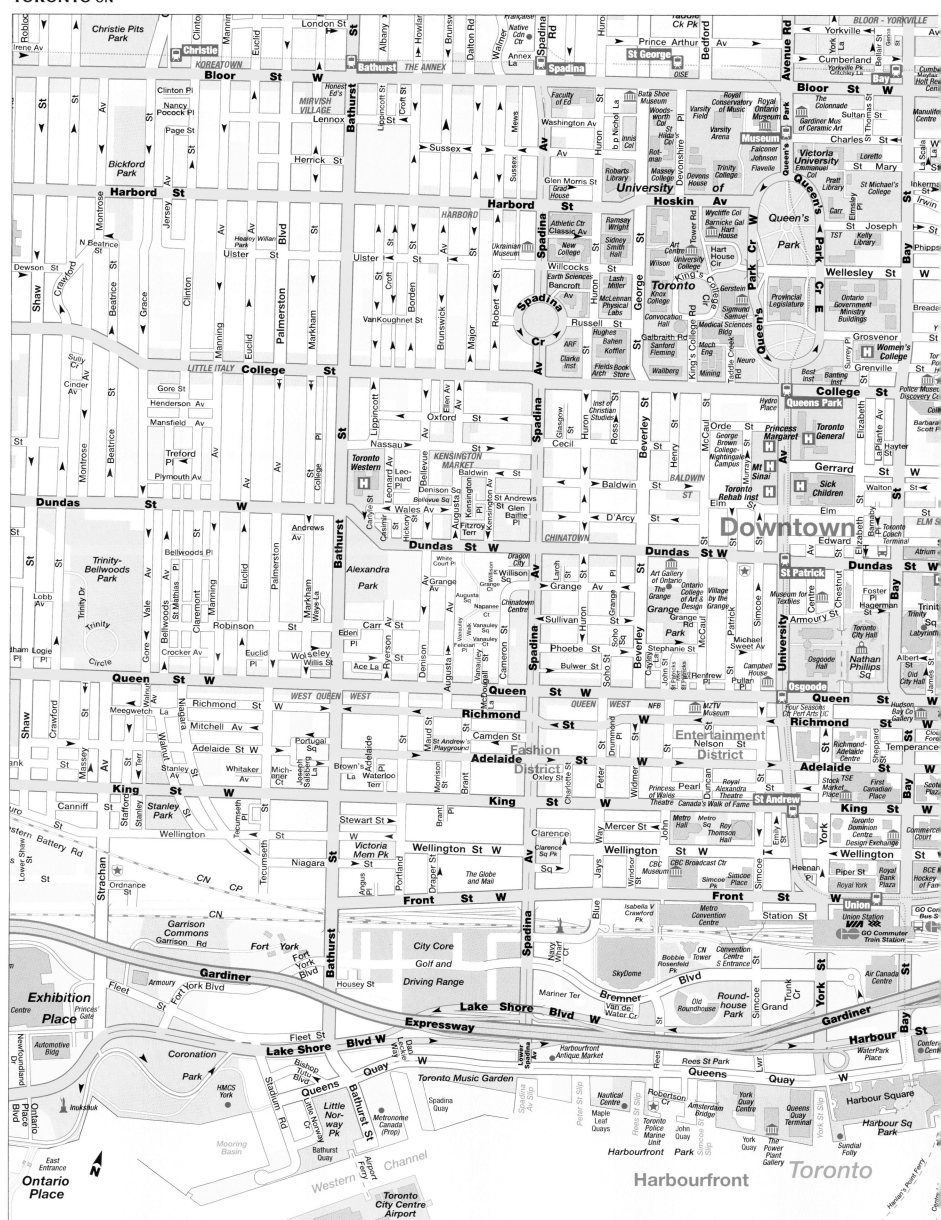

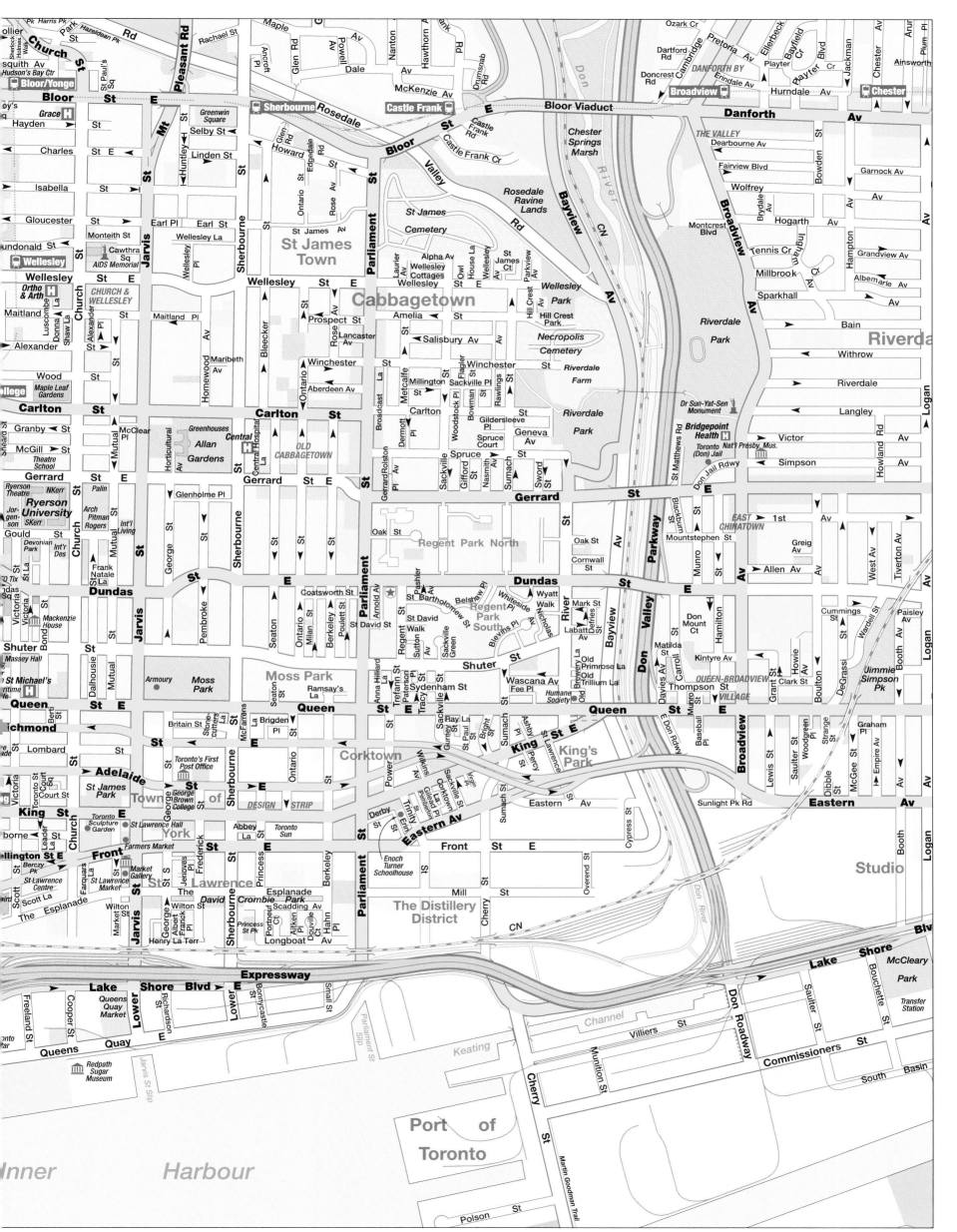

LONDON ON

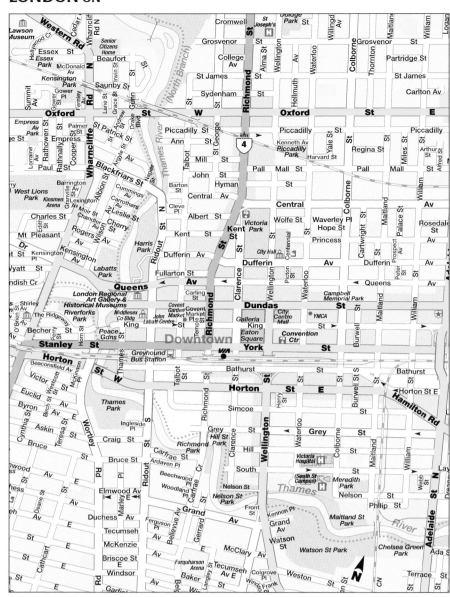

KITCHENER/WATERLOO ON

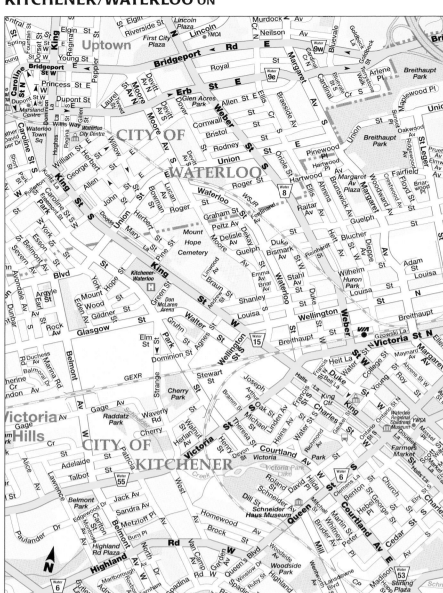

ST. CATHARINES ON

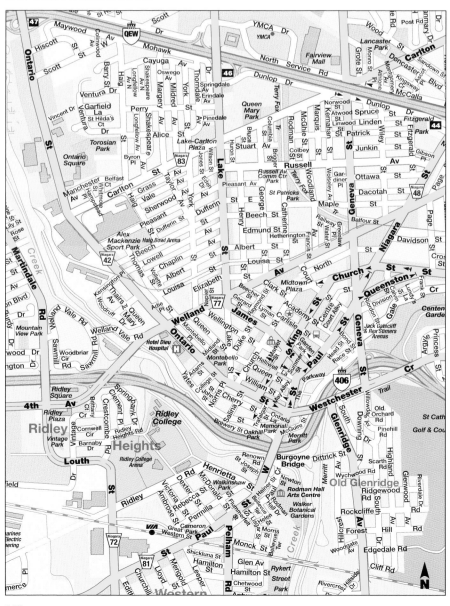

HAMILTON ON

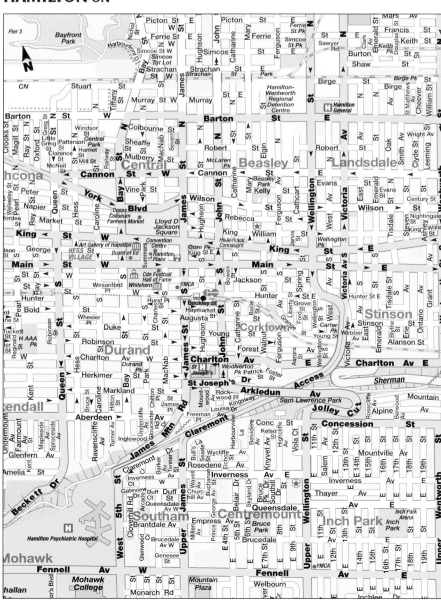

OTTAWA/GATINEAU ON/QC

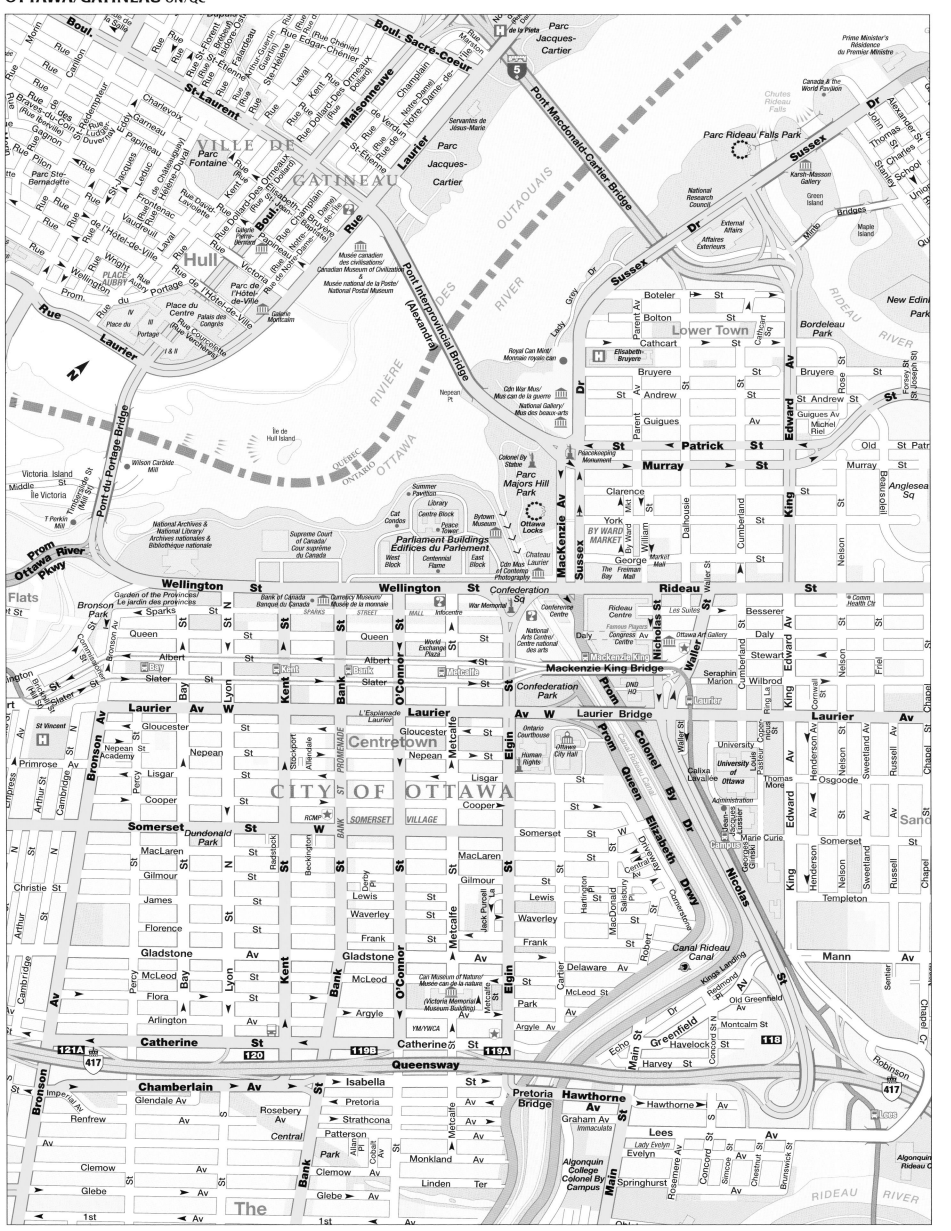

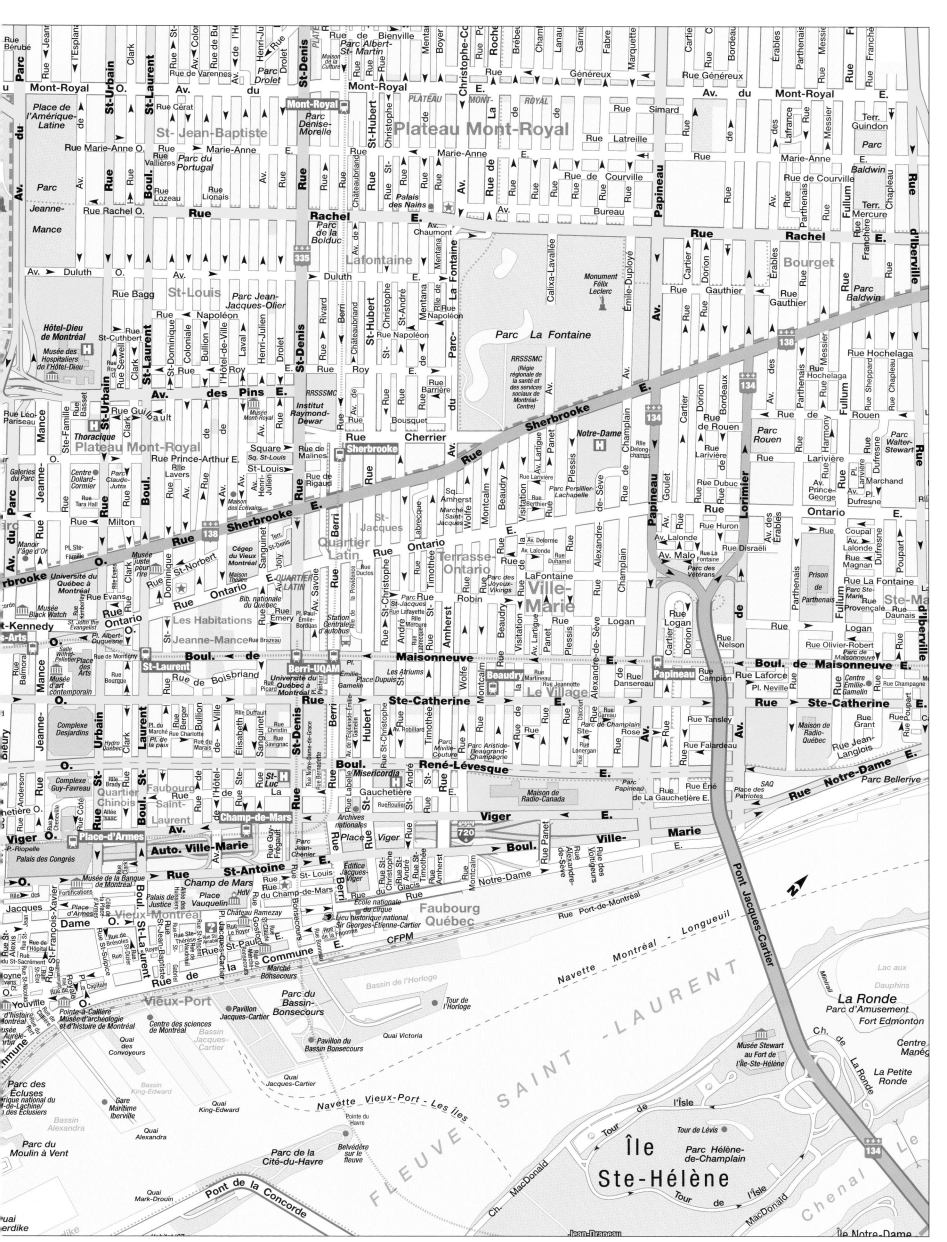

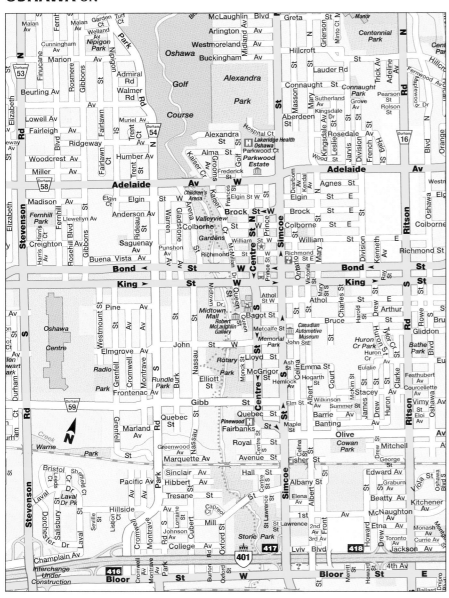

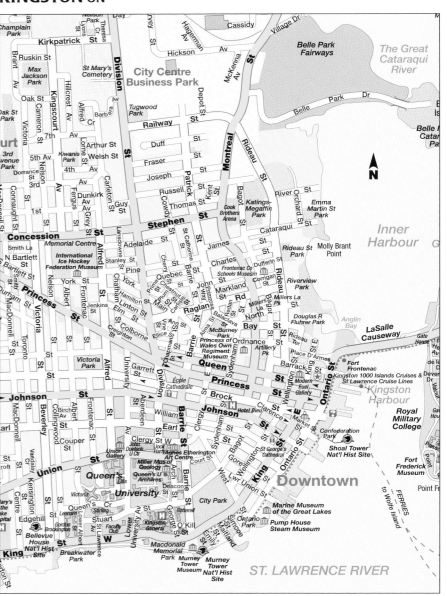

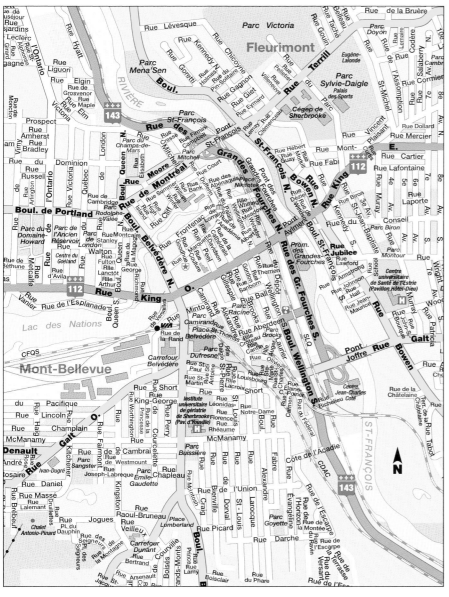

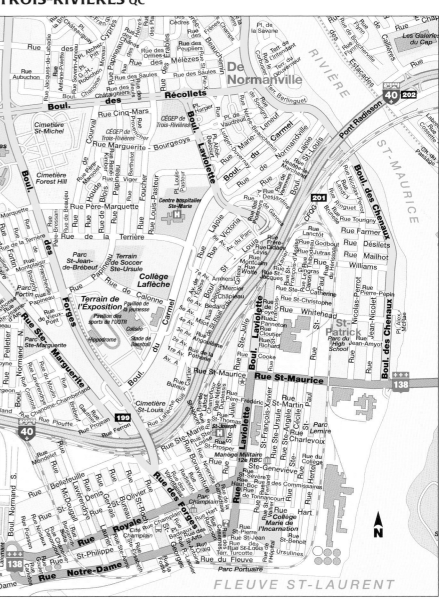

QUÉBEC QC

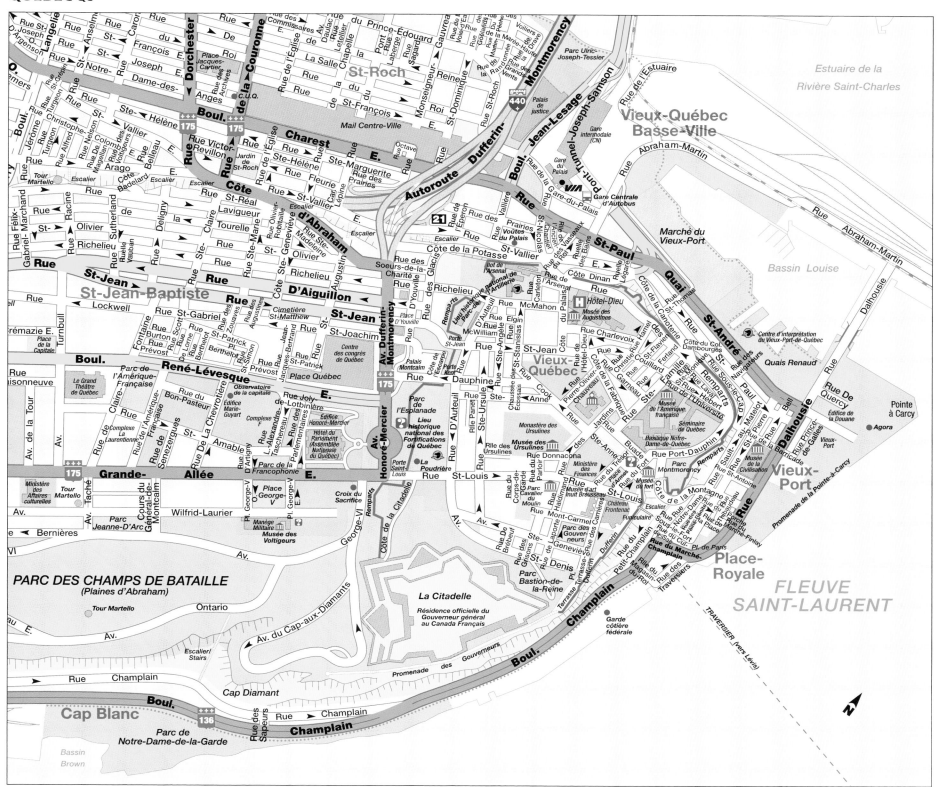

SAGUENAY QC

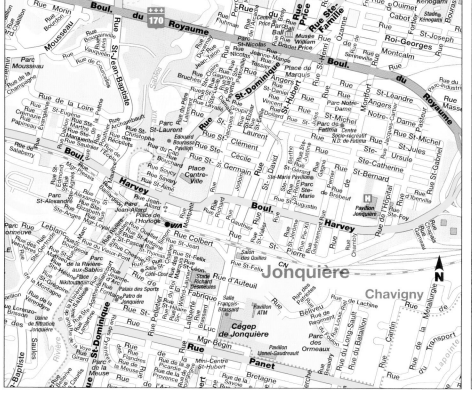

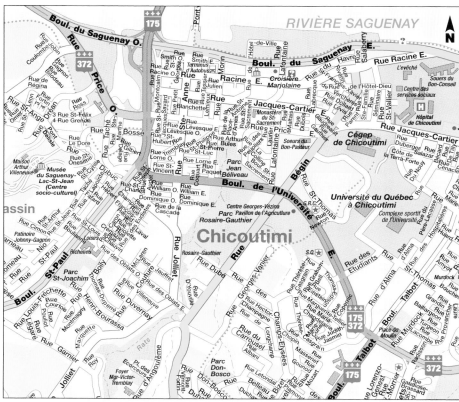

FREDERICTON NB

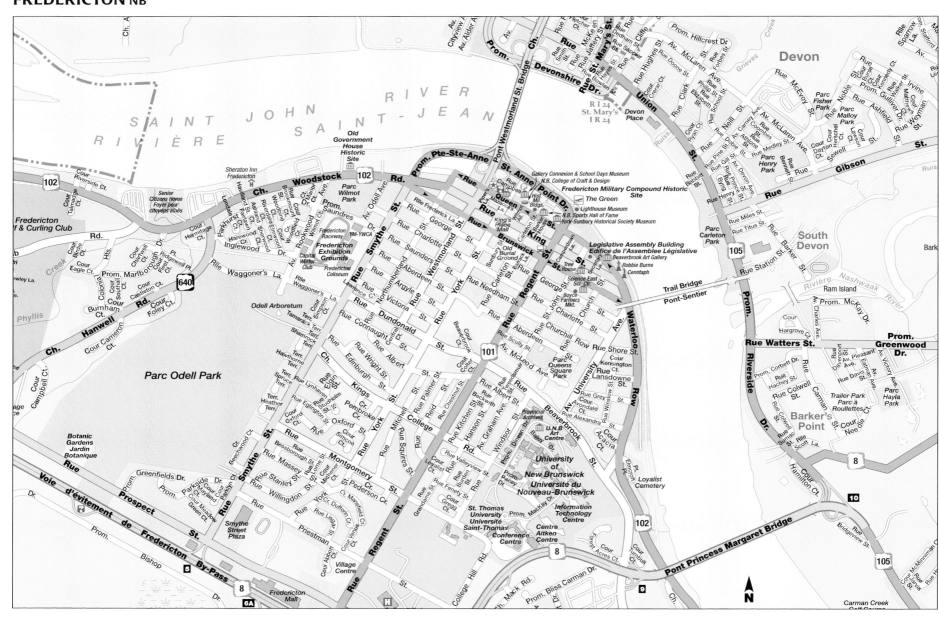

CHARLOTTETOWN PE

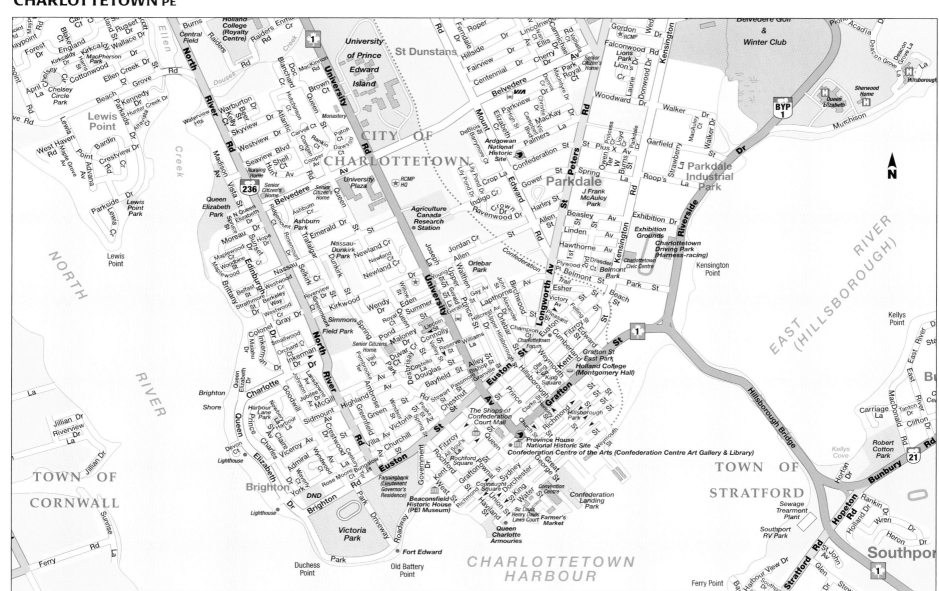

IQALUIT NU

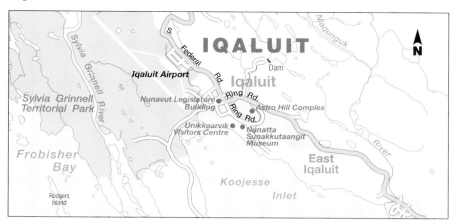

HALIFAX NS

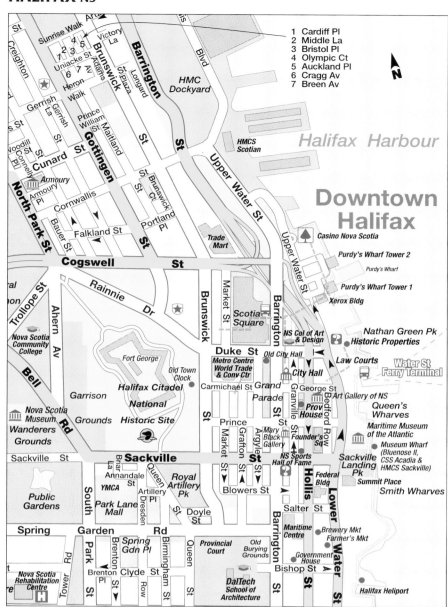

MONCTON NB

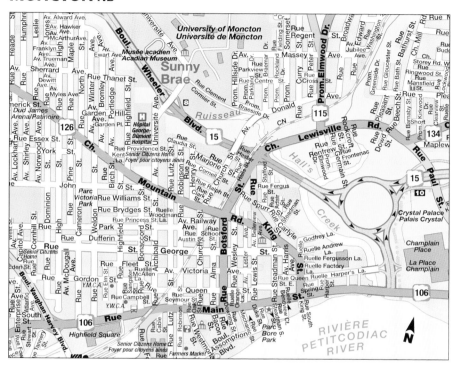

ST. JOHN'S NL

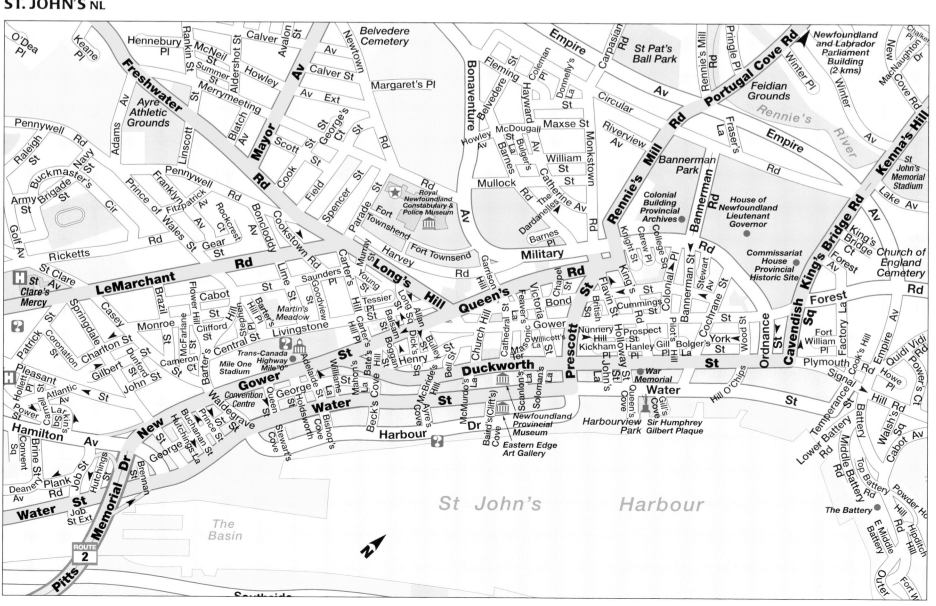

THEMATIC SUBJECT INDEX

Aboriginal peoples, 30–31
acid precipitation, 25
air masses, 14–15
airways, 37
Appalachian (landform), 11
Arctic and Taiga, 16, 18–19
Arctic Archipelago (ecozone), 18
Arctic Basin (ecozone), 18
Arctic Cordillera (ecozone), 18
Arctic Lands (landform), 11
Atlantic (ecozone), 28
Atlantic Region (ecozone), 17
Bering land bridge, 30
births, 38
bogs, 16
Boreal Cordillera (ecozone), 20
Boreal Plains (ecozone), 22
Boreal Shield (ecozone), 16, 24–25
British Columbia, 20–21
Canada, territorial evolution, 34–35
Canadian Shield (landform), 11
Census Metropolitan Regions, 43
Central Plains (ecozone), 16, 22–23
Circumpolar Conference, 19
cities, 8, 27, 40–41, 43
climate and weather, 8, 14–15, 42
climate graphs, 16
climate zones, 14
cod fishery, 28
communications, 36
commuting, 41
container cargoes, 37
Cordillera (landform), 10
diamonds, 19
"Donut Effect," 41
drainage basins, 12
Dry Belt, 13, 22
ecotourism, 20
ecozones, 9, 16–29
education, 38
elections (federal), 34
energy, 8, 13, 15, 41
explorers, 32
family life, 39
farms, farming, 8, 21, 22–23, 27, 29, 42
Fertile Belt, 13, 22
fisheries, 9, 21, 28
forest fires, 24
forestry, 9, 21, 24, 29
fossils, 10
geological eras (timeline), 10
glaciers, glaciation, 12
global warming, 8, 42
government (federal), 35
Grand Banks, 28
Grasslands (ecozone), 22
Great Lakes, 26
Great Lakes–St. Lawrence Lowlands (landform), 11
greenhouse gases, 42
harvesting cycle, 18
health, 39, 41
Hibernia oil project, 29
highways, 37
hogs, 23
Hudson Bay Lowlands (landform), 11

Hudson Plains, 18
hurricanes, 15
hydroelectricity, 13
ice, 12, 19, 30
Ice ages, 12
icesheets, 12, 30
ice storms, 15
immigration, 8, 32–33, 42
Indian treaties, 31
innovation, measuring, 40
Interior plains (landform), 11
Internet, 36
interprovincial migration, 33
Inuit, 18–19, 30
irrigation, 13
land claims, 31
landform regions, 10–11
land reclamation, 25
languages, 38
life expectancy, 39
life forms (timeline), 11
Magnetic Pole, 18
Model Forests, 29
livestock, 23
marriage and divorce, 38
marshes, 16
mines, minerals, 9, 10, 19, 22, 24, 42
Mixedwood Plains (ecozone), 17, 26–27
Montane Cordillera (ecozone), 20
mountain building, 11
mountain zones, 20
muskeg, 16
national marine parks, 16–17
national parks, 16–17
natural regions, 16–17
Niagara Falls, 13
Northern Arctic (ecozone), 18
Northwest Atlantic (ecozone), 28
Oak Ridges Moraine, 27
oil and gas, 27
Pacific and Western Mountains (ecozone), 16, 20–21
Pacific Marine (ecozone), 20
Pacific Maritime (ecozone), 16, 20–21
Parkland (ecozone), 22
Pelican Project, 23
permafrost, 18
plate tectonics, 10
population, 8, 27, 31, 38–43
ports, 37
potash, 22
provinces, 35
rail cargo, 37
railways, 37
Ramsar sites, 16–17
religions, 38
rural decline, 40
St. Lawrence Seaway, 26, 37
satellites, 36
settlers, 32–33
Sudbury (land reclamation), 25
swamps, 16
Taiga Cordillera, 20
Taiga Plains, 18
Taiga Shield, 18
territories, 35
thunderstorms, 14
timelines, 30–35
tornadoes, 15
transportation, 37
urban amenities, 41
urban growth, 40–41
water, 9, 12–13
wetlands, 16
wind power, 15
work and income, 39, 41
World Heritage Sites, 16–17

HOW TO USE THE MAP INDEX

This index lists the names of more than 33,000 populated places, physical features, and other points of interest that appear on the preceding map plates. Each name is followed by a bold figure (the map plate number) and the map coordinates—the numbers at the top and bottom of the map plate, and the letters at each side of the map plate. When searching for a specific place name, use the coordinates to find the appropriate area on the map plate, then scan the area for the name. Aberdeen *NS*, for example, has the following references: **34** C6. After noting the references, go to Map Plate 34 and use the coordinates C6 to pinpoint the map area where Aberdeen appears.

ABBREVIATIONS

Provinces and Territories

AB	Alberta
BC	British Columbia
MB	Manitoba
NB	New Brunswick
NL	Newfoundland and Labrador
NS	Nova Scotia
NT	Northwest Territories
NU	Nunavut
ON	Ontario
PE	Prince Edward Island
QC	Quebec
SK	Saskatchewan
YT	Yukon

Other abbreviations used in the map index

APP	aire protégée provinciale	PP	Provincial Park/parc provincial
CA	Conservation Area	PPA	Provincial Protected Area
HS	Historic Site		
LHN	lieu historique national	PRA	Provincial Recreation Area
MPP	Marine Provincial Park	PRS	Provincial Recreation Site
NHS	National Historic Site	PWP	Provincial Wilderness Park
NMBS	National Migratory Bird Sanctuary	RF	réserve faunique
NMP	National Marine Park	RNF	réserve nationale de faune
NP	National Park		
NPR	National Park Reserve	RNOM	refuge national d'oiseaux migrateurs
NWA	National Wildlife Area	RNP	réserve naturelle provinciale
PCA	Provincial Conservation Area	RPN	réserve de parc national
PGA	Provincial Game Area	SH	site historique
PHS	Provincial Historic Site	TP	Territorial Park
		WMA	Wildlife Management Area
PMN	parc marin national	ZCP	zone de conservation provinciale
PMP	Provincial Marine Park	ZEC	zone d'exploitation contrôlée
PN	parc national	ZPF	zone provinciale de faune
PNR	Provincial Nature Reserve		

A

Aaron, lac *QC*	**28**	F4
Aaron PP *ON*	**13**	E7
Aaron PP *ON*	**16**	D3
Abamasagi Lake *ON*	**16**	C7
Abamasagi Lake *ON*	**17**	A2
Abattis, lac des *QC*	**22**	D6
Abbey *SK*	**11**	D3
Abbot Pass Refuge Cabin NHS *AB*	**7**	A-B1
Abbotsford *BC*	**1**	F7-8
Abbotsford *BC*	**2**	E6
Abee *AB*	**6**	A6
Abee *AB*	**8**	B7
Abegweit, passage *PE*	**35**	E3
Abegweit Passage *PE*	**35**	E3
Abenakis *QC*	**27**	B6
Abercorn *QC*	**24**	E7
Abercorn *QC*	**27**	F3
Aberdeen *NS*	**34**	C6
Aberdeen *SK*	**11**	C4
Aberdeen Lake *NU*	**40**	A1
Aberdeen Lake *NU*	**41**	D4
Aberfoyle *ON*	**19**	B7
Aberfoyle *ON*	**20**	D6
Abernethy *SK*	**11**	D-E6
Abino, Point *ON*	**20**	F8
Abitibi, lac *ON*	**17**	C7-8
Abitibi, lac *QC*	**23**	C1-2
Abitibi, lake *ON*	**17**	C7
Abitibi, Lake *ON*	**23**	C1
Abitibi Canyon *ON*	**17**	B6
Abitibi-de-Troyes PP *ON*	**17**	C7
Abitibi-de-Troyes PP *ON*	**23**	C1
Abney *PE*	**35**	F6
Abos, lac *QC*	**23**	F7
Abos, lac *QC*	**25**	B1
Aboujagane *NB*	**32**	B2
Abraham Lake *AB*	**6**	C4
Abraham Lake *AB*	**8**	F3
Abrahams Cove *NL*	**36**	C1
Abram-Village *PE*	**32**	A7
Abram-Village *PE*	**35**	D2
Acaciaville *NS*	**32**	F4-5
Acaciaville *NS*	**33**	C2
Academy *AB*	**7**	C4
Acadia Valley *AB*	**6**	D8
Acadia Valley *AB*	**11**	D2
Acadie, rivière l' *QC*	**27**	F1-2
Acadie Siding *NB*	**31**	E7
Acadie Siding *NB*	**32**	A5
Acadieville *NB*	**31**	D7
Acadieville *NB*	**32**	A5
Acasta Lake *NT*	**10**	A8
Acasta River *NT*	**10**	A5-6
Achapuskow Lake *MB*	**12**	F7
Achapuskow Lake *MB*	**15**	F1
Acheninni Lake *SK*	**11**	A6
Acheninni Lake *SK*	**12**	F6
Achepabanca, lac *QC*	**23**	D7
Achepabanca, lac *QC*	**26**	D1-2
Achigan, lac de l' *QC*	**22**	D5
Achigan, lac de l' *QC*	**22**	D8
Achigan, lac de l' *QC*	**24**	C5
Achigan, lac de l' *QC*	**24**	B2
Achigan, lac de l' *QC*	**26**	C5
Achigan, lac de l' *QC*	**27**	D1
Achigan, rivière de l' *QC*	**24**	C5-6

Achigan, rivière de l' *QC*	**27**	D1
Achilles Lake *NT*	**10**	A8
Achintre, lac *QC*	**25**	A3
Achintre, lac *QC*	**26**	F3
Acme *AB*	**6**	D6
Acme *AB*	**7**	A4-5
Aconi, Point *NS*	**34**	B7
Actinolite *ON*	**21**	D5
Acton *NB*	**32**	C2
Acton *ON*	**19**	A7
Acton *ON*	**20**	C-D6
Acton Vale *QC*	**24**	D8
Acton Vale *QC*	**27**	E3
Adair, Cape *NU*	**41**	A7
Adair, Cape *NU*	**42**	E6
Adam, rivière *QC*	**29**	B2
Adamant Mountain *BC*	**6**	C3
Adam Creek, RNP *ON*	**17**	A5
Adam Creek PNR *ON*	**17**	A5
Adam River *BC*	**1**	E5
Adam River *BC*	**2**	B1
Adams Cove *NL*	**37**	D7
Adams Lake *BC*	**6**	D2
Adams Lake *BC*	**6**	D2
Adams Lake PP *BC*	**6**	D1-2
Adams River *BC*	**6**	C-D2
Adams Sound *NU*	**41**	A5-6
Adams Sound *NU*	**42**	E5
Adamsville *NB*	**31**	E7
Adamsville *NB*	**32**	A5
Adamsville *ON*	**18**	E5
Adamsville *QC*	**24**	E7
Adamsville *QC*	**27**	F3
Adanac *SK*	**6**	C8
Adanac *SK*	**11**	D2
Addington Forks *NS*	**34**	E4
Addison *ON*	**21**	C7-8
Addison *ON*	**24**	F1-2
Adelaide *ON*	**19**	C4
Adelaide *ON*	**20**	E3
Adelaide Peninsula *NU*	**41**	C4
Adelaide Peninsula *NU*	**42**	F3-4
Aden *AB*	**6**	D2
Aden *AB*	**7**	F7-8
Aden *AB*	**11**	F1
Adeytown *NL*	**36**	C8
Adeytown *NL*	**37**	C6
Adies Pond *NL*	**36**	A4
Adies Pond *NL*	**37**	A2
Adies Pond *NL*	**38**	F3
Adlatok Bay *NL*	**39**	A5
Adlavik Bay *NL*	**39**	A6
Adlavik Islands *NL*	**39**	A6-7
Admiral *SK*	**11**	F3
Admiral Rock *NS*	**33**	B6
Admiral Rock *NS*	**34**	F2
Admiral's Beach *NL*	**37**	E-F7
Admiral's Cove *NL*	**37**	E8
Admiralty Inlet *NU*	**41**	B5
Admiralty Inlet *NU*	**42**	D-E5
Admiralty Island *NU*	**41**	B4
Admiralty Island *NU*	**42**	D5
Adolphus Beach *ON*	**21**	E6
Adolphustown *ON*	**21**	E6
Adonis, lac *QC*	**25**	C4
Adstock, mont *QC*	**27**	D6
Advocate Harbour *NS*	**32**	D6
Advocate Harbour *NS*	**33**	A3-4
Aerofoil Lake *ON*	**16**	C3
Aetna *AB*	**6**	F6
Aetna *AB*	**7**	F5
Afridi Lake *NT*	**10**	A8
Afton *NS*	**34**	D5

Afton (IR) *NS*	**34**	D-E5
Agassiz *BC*	**1**	F8
Agassiz *BC*	**2**	D6-7 E6-7
Agassiz Lake *NT*	**10**	C7
Agassiz Peatlands, RNP *ON*	**16**	E1
Agassiz Peatlands PNR *ON*	**16**	E1
Agawa Bay *ON*	**17**	E3-4
Agawa Bay *ON*	**17**	E3-4
Agawa River *ON*	**17**	E4
Agimak Lake *ON*	**16**	E4
Agnes Lake *ON*	**16**	F4
Agnew Lake *ON*	**17**	F6
Agnew Lake *ON*	**18**	A4
Aguanish *QC*	**39**	F5
Aguanish *QC*	**40**	F7-8
Aguanish, rivière *QC*	**39**	E5
Aguanus, rivière *QC*	**40**	E-F7
Aguasabon River *ON*	**16**	E7
Aguasabon River *ON*	**17**	C2
Aguathuna *NL*	**36**	B2
Agusk Lake *ON*	**15**	F8
Ahmic Harbour *ON*	**18**	C7
Ahmic Lake *ON*	**18**	C8
Ahmic Lake *ON*	**21**	A1
Ahmic Lake *ON*	**22**	F1
Ahousat *BC*	**1**	F5
Ahousat *BC*	**2**	D1
Ahtahakoop *SK*	**11**	B4
Ahwachanjeesh Pond *NL*	**36**	C-D5
Ahwachanjeesh Pond *NL*	**37**	C-D3
Aigle, lac à l' *QC*	**39**	E2-3
Aigle, lac de l' *QC*	**22**	E8
Aigle, lac de l' *QC*	**24**	B3
Aigle, rivière de l' *QC*	**22**	D-E7
Aigle, rivière de l' *QC*	**24**	B1
Aigle, rivière de l' *QC*	**25**	F1
Aigle, rivière de l' *QC*	**26**	C3
Aigles, lac des *QC*	**25**	D6
Aigles, lac des *QC*	**27**	A2
Aigles, lac des *QC*	**28**	A4-5
Aigles, lac des *QC*	**28**	A1
Aigremont, lac *QC*	**26**	C6
Aigremont, lac *QC*	**28**	A1
Aiguebelle, parc d' *QC*	**17**	C8
Aiguebelle, parc d' *QC*	**23**	D3
Aiguebelle, RF d' *QC*	**23**	D2-3 D3
Aikens Lake *MB*	**13**	D5
Aikens Lake *MB*	**14**	B7
Aikens Lake *MB*	**16**	B1
Aillik *NL*	**39**	A6
Ailsa Bay *NL*	**39**	A6
Ailsa Craig *ON*	**19**	B-C4
Ailsa Craig *ON*	**20**	E3
Ainslie, Lake *NS*	**34**	C6
Ainsworth Hot Springs *BC*	**6**	F3
Aird Island *ON*	**18**	B3
Airdrie *AB*	**6**	D5
Airdrie *AB*	**7**	B4
Air Force Island *NU*	**41**	B7
Air Force Island *NU*	**42**	F6-7
Air Ronge *SK*	**12**	F5
Aishihik *NL*	**4**	D2-3
Aishihik Lake *YT*	**4**	D3
Aishihik River *YT*	**4**	D3
Ajax *ON*	**20**	C8
Ajax *ON*	**21**	F2
Ajax Lake *NT*	**10**	A8
Akaitcho Lake *NT*	**10**	C8
Akaiyesseh Lake *NT*	**10**	A6-7

Akamina-Kishenena PRA *BC*	**6**	F5
Akamina-Kishenena PRA *BC*	**7**	F3-4
Akamiuapishku NP (proposed/projeté) *NL*	**39**	B6-7 C6-7
Akamiuapishku NP (proposed/projeté) *NL*	**40**	D-E8
Akie River *BC*	**3**	D6
Akimiski Island *NU*	**40**	E3
Aklavik *NT*	**5**	C4
Akpatok Island *NU*	**40**	B4
Akulivik *QC*	**40**	A3
Akulivik *QC*	**41**	E7
Akwesasne *QC*	**24**	E4
Alameda *SK*	**11**	F7
Alaska *PE*	**32**	A7
Alaska *PE*	**35**	C2
Alban *ON*	**17**	F7
Alban *ON*	**18**	B6
Albanel *QC*	**26**	D8
Albanel *QC*	**28**	B2
Albanel, lac *QC*	**40**	F5
Albany *PE*	**32**	B8
Albany *PE*	**34**	C1-2
Albany Cross *NS*	**3**	D1
Albany Cross *NS*	**32**	F4
Albany River *ON*	**16**	B5-6
Albany River *ON*	**16**	B8
Albany River *ON*	**40**	E-F2
Albany River PP *ON*	**16**	B5-6
Albany River PP *ON*	**16**	B7-8
Albert, lac *QC*	**28**	B7
Albert, mont *QC*	**29**	B7
Alberta, Mount *AB*	**6**	C3
Alberta, Mount *AB*	**8**	E1-2 F1-2
Alberta, Mount *AB*	**2**	C-D7
Alberta Beach *AB*	**6**	A-B5
Alberta Beach *AB*	**8**	C5
Albert Beach *MB*	**14**	C6
Albert Bridge *NS*	**34**	C8
Albert Edward Bay *NU*	**41**	B4
Albert Edward Bay *NU*	**42**	F3
Albert Islands *NT*	**41**	A2
Albert Islands *NT*	**42**	E1
Albert Lake Mesa, RNP *ON*	**16**	E6
Albert Lake Mesa PNR *ON*	**16**	E6
Albert Mines *NS*	**32**	C6
Alberton *ON*	**19**	C7
Alberton *ON*	**20**	E6
Alberton *PE*	**34**	B1
Alberton *PE*	**35**	B2
Alberton Harbour *PE*	**35**	B2
Albertville *SK*	**29**	C5
Albertville *SK*	**11**	B5
Albion *PE*	**35**	E-6-7
Albion Cross *PE*	**35**	E7
Albion Hills CA *ON*	**20**	C6
Albreda *BC*	**6**	B-C2
Albury *ON*	**21**	E5
Alcida *NB*	**31**	B6
Alcomdale *AB*	**6**	A5
Alcomdale *AB*	**8**	B6
Alcona *ON*	**20**	B7
Alcona *ON*	**21**	D1
Alcove *QC*	**21**	A7
Alcove *QC*	**24**	C2
Alcurve *AB*	**6**	A-B8
Alcurve *AB*	**11**	A-B2

Alderdale *ON*	**17**	F8
Alderdale *ON*	**18**	B8
Alder Flats *AB*	**6**	B5
Alder Flats *AB*	**8**	D4-5
Aldergrove *BC*	**2**	E5
Alder Point *NS*	**34**	B7-8
Aldershot *NS*	**32**	E7
Aldershot *NS*	**33**	B4
Aldershot *ON*	**19**	B7
Aldershot *ON*	**20**	D6
Aldersville *NS*	**32**	E-F7
Aldersville *NS*	**33**	C4
Aldersyde *AB*	**6**	E5-6
Aldersyde *AB*	**7**	C4
Alderville *ON*	**21**	E4
Alert *NU*	**42**	A5
Alert Bay *BC*	**1**	E4
Alert Point *NU*	**42**	A4
Alex, lac *QC*	**28**	A5
Alex, rivière *QC*	**28**	A-B5
Alexander *MB*	**11**	E8
Alexander *MB*	**13**	E2
Alexander *MB*	**14**	E1
Alexander Bay *NL*	**36**	B8
Alexander Bay *NL*	**36**	B8
Alexander Bay *NL*	**37**	B6
Alexander Bay *NL*	**37**	B6
Alexander-Graham-Bell, LHN *NS*	**34**	C7
Alexander Graham Bell NHS *NS*	**34**	C7
Alexander Island *NU*	**42**	D3
Alexander Lake Forest PP *ON*	**17**	F8
Alexandra *PE*	**35**	E5
Alexandra Bay *PE*	**35**	E5
Alexandra Bridge PP *BC*	**1**	F8
Alexandra Bridge PP *BC*	**2**	E6
Alexandra Falls *NT*	**10**	F6
Alexandria *ON*	**24**	E3
Alexis Creek *BC*	**1**	C7
Alexis River *NL*	**39**	C7
Alfred *ON*	**24**	D3
Algoma Headwaters PP *ON*	**17**	E4
Algoma Mills *ON*	**17**	F5
Algoma Mills *ON*	**18**	A-B2
Algonquin *ON*	**21**	C3
Algonquin *ON*	**24**	F2
Algonquin PP *ON*	**21**	A3
Algonquin PP *ON*	**22**	E3-4
Algrove *SK*	**11**	C6
Alhambra *AB*	**6**	C5
Alhambra *AB*	**8**	F5
Alice *ON*	**21**	A5
Alice *ON*	**22**	F5
Alice Arm *BC*	**3**	E-F3
Alice Arm *BC*	**3**	E3
Alice Beach *SK*	**11**	D5
Alice Creek *BC*	**9**	C6
Alice Creek *AB*	**12**	B1
Alida *SK*	**11**	F7
Alingly *SK*	**11**	B4-5
Alix *AB*	**6**	C6
Alix *AB*	**8**	E7
Alix, lac *QC*	**39**	E6
Alkali Creek *AB*	**6**	D7
Alkali Creek *AB*	**7**	B8
Alkali Creek *AB*	**11**	D2
Alkali Lake *BC*	**1**	C-D7
Allainville *NB*	**29**	F3
Allainville *NB*	**30**	F1
Allainville *NB*	**31**	C7
Allan *SK*	**11**	C4
Allan, Mount *AB*	**6**	D4-5

Allan, Mount *AB*	**7**	B2
Allanburg *ON*	**19**	C8
Allanburg *ON*	**20**	E7
Allan Creek *YT*	**4**	E7
Allan Park *ON*	**20**	B4
Allan's Island *NL*	**36**	F6
Allan's Island *NL*	**37**	F4
Allan Water *ON*	**13**	E8
Allan Water *ON*	**16**	D5
Allan Water Ogoki River *ON*	**16**	C5-6 D5
Allard, lac *QC*	**39**	E4
Allardville *NB*	**29**	F8
Allardville *NB*	**30**	F1
Allardville *NB*	**31**	C7
Allardville East *NB*	**31**	B-C7
Allegra *MB*	**14**	C3
Allendale *NS*	**33**	E-F3
Allenford *ON*	**18**	F5
Allenford *ON*	**20**	A4
Allen Lake *ON*	**18**	B6
Allenwood *ON*	**18**	F7
Allenwood *ON*	**20**	A6
Allenwood Beach *ON*	**18**	F7
Allenwood Beach *ON*	**20**	A6
Alliance *AB*	**6**	C7
Alliance *AB*	**11**	C1
Alliés, lac des *QC*	**28**	F5
Alligator Lake *YT*	**4**	E3-4
Allingham *AB*	**7**	A4
Allison *BC*	**2**	D8
Allison Lake PP *BC*	**2**	D8
Allison Lake PP *BC*	**6**	F1
Allison Pass *BC*	**1**	F8
Allison Pass *BC*	**2**	E7-8
Allison Pass *BC*	**6**	F1
Alliston *ON*	**20**	B6
Alliston *PE*	**34**	C3
Alliston *PE*	**35**	F6
Alliston "Beattie" Pinery, RNP *ON*	**20**	B6
Alliston "Beattie" Pinery PNR *ON*	**20**	B6
Allumettes, île des *QC*	**22**	E5
Alma *NB*	**32**	C-D6
Alma *NS*	**33**	A7
Alma *NS*	**34**	E3
Alma *ON*	**19**	A6
Alma *ON*	**20**	C5
Alma *PE*	**35**	B2
Alma *QC*	**28**	C5
Almonte *ON*	**21**	B7
Almonte *ON*	**24**	E1
Alonsa *MB*	**13**	D2-3
Alonsa *MB*	**14**	C2-3
Alpen *AB*	**8**	A7
Alpena *NS*	**32**	E-F6
Alpena *NS*	**33**	A7
Alpine Village *ON*	**21**	D3
Alsask *SK*	**6**	D8
Alsask *SK*	**11**	D2
Alsek Ranges *BC*	**4**	F3
Alsek River *BC*	**4**	F2
Alsek River *YT*	**4**	E2
Alsever Lake *ON*	**22**	F4
Alsike *AB*	**6**	B5
Alsike *AB*	**8**	D5
Alstead River *SK*	**12**	E4
Alston Creek *MB*	**15**	B5
Altamont *MB*	**13**	F3
Altamont *MB*	**14**	F3
Altario *AB*	**6**	C8

Altario *AB* **11** C2
Alticane *SK* **11** B4
Alton *NS* **33** B6
Alton *NS* **34** F2
Alton *ON* **19** A7
Altona *BC* **3** D8
Altona *BC* **9** D1-2
Altona *BC* **13** F3
Altona *MB* **14** F4
Alvanley *ON* **18** F5
Alvanley *ON* **20** A4
Alvena *SK* **11** C4-5
Alvinston *ON* **19** C3
Alvinston *ON* **20** F2
Amable du Fond PP *ON* **22** D-E2
Amable du Fond River *ON* **22** D-E2
Amable du Fond River PP *ON* **17** E8
Amadjuak Lake *NU* **40** A5
Amadjuak Lake *NU* **41** C8
Amaranth *MB* **13** E3
Amaranth *MB* **14** C3
Amateewakea River *ON* **18** A-B6
Amazon *SK* **11** D5
Amberley *ON* **20** B3
Amber River *AB* **9** A-B2
Amber Valley *AB* **8** A7
Amedroz Island *ON* **18** B3
Amelia *AB* **8** B7
Ameliasburg *ON* **21** E5
Amery *MB* **15** D5
Amery, Mount *AB* **6** C3
Amery, Mount *AB* **8** F2
Amesdale *ON* **13** E6
Amesdale *ON* **16** D3
Ames Lake *NT* **10** B7
Amherst *NS* **32** C7
Amherst Cove *NL* **37** B7
Amherst Cove *PE* **35** E3
Amherst Head *NS* **35** F2
Amherst Island *ON* **21** E6
Amherst Island *NS* **32** C7
Amherst Point *NS* **32** C7
Amherst Point, RNOM *NS* **32** C7
Amherst Point NMBS *NS* **32** C7
Amherst Pointe *ON* **19** E1
Amherst Shore *NS* **35** F2
Amherst Shore PP *NS* **32** B-C8
Amherst Shore PP *NS* **34** D1
Amherst Shore PP *NS* **35** F2-3
Amherstview *ON* **21** E6
Amisk *AB* **6** C7
Amisk *AB* **11** B1-2
Amisk Lake *SK* **11** A7
Amisk Lake *SK* **12** F7
Amisk Lake *SK* **12** F7
Amisk Lake *SK* **15** F1
Amisk Lake *SK* **15** F1
Amisk PP Reserve *MB* **15** D3-4
Amisk River *AB* **6** A6
Amisk River *AB* **8** A8
Amisk River *AB* **9** F6
Amisk River *AB* **12** F1
Ammerman Mountain *YT* **5** B-C2
Amos *QC* **23** D4
Amour Point *NL* **38** A3
Amphitrite Point *BC* **1** F5
Amphitrite Point *BC* **2** E1
Amqui *QC* **29** C4-5
Amsterdam *SK* **11** C7
Amulet *SK* **11** F5
Amulree *ON* **19** B5
Amulree *ON* **20** D4
Amund Ringnes Island *NU* **42** C4
Amundsen, golfe d' *NT* **41** A1-2
Amundsen, golfe d' *NT* **42** E1
Amundsen Gulf *NT* **41** A1-2
Amundsen Gulf *NT* **42** E1
Amyot *ON* **17** C-D3
Anabusko River *MB* **15** D7
Anacla *BC* **2** E2
Anagance *NB* **32** C5
Anaharea Lake *ON* **17** C3-4
Anahim Lake *BC* **1** C5
Analta *AB* **8** A6
Ancaster *ON* **19** B7
Ancaster *ON* **20** D8
Anchor Harbour *NL* **37** A6-7
Anchor Point *NL* **38** B4
Anchor Point *NL* **39** D7-8
Anctil, lac *QC* **26** D5
Anderson Bay PMP *BC* **2** D3
Anderson Creek *YT* **4** D6-7
Anderson Lake *BC* **1** E7
Anderson Lake *BC* **2** B6
Anderson Point *MB* **14** A5
Anderson River *BC* **2** C-D7
Anderson River *NT* **5** A6-B7
Anderson River *NT* **5** C7-8
Anderson River Delta NMBS *NT* **5** A6-7
Anderson Road *NB* **31** D3
Andersons Cove *NL* **36** D6-7
Andersons Cove *NL* **37** D4-5
Anderson Settlement *NB* **35** E1
Andesite Peak *BC* **1** A4

Andou, lac *QC* **22** B6
Andreasen, Cape *NT* **42** C2
André Lake *NL* **39** A3
Andrew *AB* **6** A6
Andrew *AB* **8** B8
Andrew *AB* **11** A1
Andrew Island *NS* **34** E6
Andrew Lake *AB* **9** D7
Andrew Lake *AB* **12** A2-3
Andrew River *NT* **5** C6-7
Andrews Head *NS* **33** E4
Andys Corners *ON* **19** D6
Andys Corners *ON* **20** F5
Aneroid *SK* **11** F4
Anfield *NB* **31** D3
Angekum Lake *ON* **13** B6
Angels Cove *NL* **36** F8
Angels Cove *NL* **37** F6
Angers *QC* **21** A8
Angers *QC* **24** D2-3
Angers, rivière *QC* **29** C-D7
Angikuni Lake *NU* **41** E4
Anglais, rivière des *QC* **24** E5-6
Anglais, rivière des *QC* **27** F1
Anglemont *BC* **6** D2
Angliers *QC* **17** E8
Angliers *QC* **22** A2
Angliers *QC* **23** F2
Anglin Lake *SK* **11** A4-5
Anglin Lake PRS *SK* **11** A4-5
Anglo Tignish *PE* **34** A1
Anglo Tignish *PE* **35** A2
Angus *ON* **20** B6
Angus Ridge *AB* **8** D6-7
Angusville *MB* **11** D8
Angusville *MB* **13** D1
Anicet, lac *QC* **24** A5
Anicet, lac *QC* **25** E5
Anima Nipissing Lake *ON* **17** E7
Anishinabi Lake *ON* **16** C2
Anjigami Lake *ON* **17** D4
Anmore *BC* **2** D5
Annaheim *SK* **11** C5
Annan *ON* **18** F5-6
Annan *ON* **20** A4
Annandale *PE* **34** C4
Annandale *PE* **35** E7
Annapolis Basin *NS* **32** E-F5
Annapolis Basin *NS* **32** F5
Annapolis Basin *NS* **33** C2
Annapolis River *NS* **33** B-C3
Annapolis Royal *NS* **32** F5
Annapolis Royal *NS* **33** C2-3
Annapolis Valley *NS* **32** E5-6
Annapolis Valley *NS* **33** B-C3
Annie Lake *ON* **21** A3
Annieopsquotch Mountains *NL* **37** C1-2
Annieoqsquotch Mountains *NL* **36** C3-4
Anola *MB* **13** E4
Anola *MB* **14** E6
Anselmo *AB* **8** B4
Anse-Bleue *NB* **30** E1
Anse-Bleue *NB* **31** B7
Anses, ZEC des *QC* **30** C2
Anse-Saint-Jean, ZEC de l' *QC* **28** D7
Anse Sloop, LHN de l' *MB* **15** B5
Anson Creek *ON* **21** C2
Anstruther Lake *ON* **21** C3
Anstruther Lake *ON* **21** C3
Anten Mills *ON* **18** F7
Anten Mills *ON* **20** A6
Anthony *ON* **17** C7
Anthony PP *NS* **32** D8
Anthony PP *NS* **33** A5-6
Anthony PP *NS* **34** E1-2
Anticline, Mount *YT* **4** D3-4
Anticosti, île d' *QC* **30** A5-6
Anticosti, île d' *QC* **39** F4
Anticosti, parc d' *QC* **30** A5
Anticosti, parc d' *QC* **39** F4
Anticosti, RF *QC* **30** A4-5
Anticosti, RF *QC* **30** A7
Anticosti Island *QC* **30** A5-6
Anticosti Island *QC* **40** F7
Antigonish *NS* **34** D4-5
Antigonish Harbour *NS* **34** D5
Antique, lac *QC* **24** A5
Antique, lac *QC* **25** E5
Antler *SK* **11** F7-8
Antler *SK* **13** F1
Antler River *SK* **11** F7
Antoine, lac *QC* **22** B6
Antoine Creek *ON* **22** D2
Antoine Lake *NT* **10** D-E3
Antonid *AB* **7** F7
Antostagnan, lac *QC* **22** C6
Antrim *NS* **33** B6
Antrim *NS* **34** F2
Antrim, lac de l' *QC* **22** F8

Antrim *ON* **21** B7
Antrim *ON* **24** D1
Anville, lac *QC* **26** B3
Anvil Range *YT* **4** C4
Anzac *AB* **9** D7
Anzac *AB* **12** D2
Apeganau Lake *MB* **12** E8
Apeganau Lake *MB* **15** E2
Apex, Mount *YT* **4** C2
Apodaca PP *BC* **2** D4
Apohaqui *NB* **32** C5
Appalaches, monts *QC* **29** C6-8
Appalachian Mountains *QC* **29** C6-8
Appin *ON* **19** C-D4
Appin *ON* **20** F3
Appin Road *PE* **35** E4
Applegrove *BC* **6** E-F3
Apple River *BC* **2** A2
Apple River *NS* **32** D6
Apple River *NS* **33** A4
Appleton *NL* **36** B7
Appleton *NL* **37** B5
Appleton *ON* **21** B7
Appleton *ON* **24** E1
Apps Lake *ON* **16** A2
Apsley *ON* **21** C4
Apto *ON* **18** F7
Apto *ON* **20** A6
Aquadeo *SK* **11** B3
Aquaforte *NL* **37** E8
Arabella *SK* **11** C7
Arabella *SK* **13** C1
Arabian, lac *QC* **39** E6
Araignées, lac aux *QC* **27** E6-7
Ara Lake *ON* **16** C7
Ara Lake *ON* **17** A1
Arbakka *MB* **14** F6
Arborfield *SK* **11** B6
Arborg *MB* **13** D4
Arborg *MB* **14** B5
Arbor Vitae *ON* **13** F6
Arbor Vitae *ON* **16** E1-2
Arbuthnot *SK* **11** E4
Arbutus Grove PP *BC* **2** D-E3
Arcadia *NS* **32** F3
Archambault, lac *QC* **24** B5
Archambault, lac *QC* **25** F5
Archer Fiord *NU* **42** A3
Archerwill *SK* **11** C6
Archibald *NB* **31** D8
Archibald, Mount *YT* **4** E2
Archibald Lake *SK* **9** A-B8
Archibald Lake *SK* **12** B3
Archipel-de-Mingan, LHN de l' *QC* **40** F7
Archipel-de-Mingan, RPN de l' *QC* **39** F3-4
Arcola *SK* **11** F7
Arctic Bay *NU* **42** D-E5
Arctic Circle *NT* **5** D8
Arctic Circle *YT* **5** D2
Arctic Ocean *NT* **41** A1
Arctic Ocean *NU* **42** A2-3 B1-2
Arctic Ocean *NU* **42** A2-3 B1-3
Arctic Ocean *NU* **5** A3-4
Arctic Pacific Lakes PP *BC* **1** A7-8
Arctic Pacific Lakes PP *BC* **1** A7-8
Arctic Red River *NT* **5** E5 F6
Arctic Red River *NT* **5** D4-5
Arctique, cercle *NT* **5** D-E8
Arctique, cercle *YT* **5** D2
Arctique, océan *NT* **41** A1
Arctique, océan *NT* **42** A3 B1-3
Arctique, océan *NU* **42** A3 B1-3
Arctique, océan *NU* **5** A3-4
Ardath *SK* **11** D4
Ardbeg *MB* **13** E2
Ardbeg *MB* **14** D2
Arden *MB* **13** E2
Arden *ON* **21** C6
Ardenode *AB* **6** D6
Ardenode *AB* **7** B5
Ardenville *AB* **7** E4-5
Ardgowan, LHN *PE* **34** C2-3
Ardgowan, LHN *PE* **35** E4-5
Ardgowan NHS *PE* **34** C2-3
Ardill *SK* **11** E4-5
Ardley *ON* **8** F7
Ardmore *AB* **6** A7
Ardmore *AB* **9** F7
Ardmore *AB* **11** A2
Ardmore *AB* **12** F2
Ardoise *NS* **32** E8
Ardoise *NS* **33** B5
Ardoise *NS* **34** F1
Ardrossan *AB* **6** B6
Ardrossan *AB* **8** C7
Ardtrea *ON* **18** F8
Ardtrea *ON* **20** A7
Ardtrea *ON* **21** D1
Arelee *SK* **11** C3-4
Argent, rivière d' *QC* **24** D2-3
Argent, rivière d' *QC* **25** D2-3
Argenta *BC* **6** E3-4
Argentia *NL* **36** E8
Argentia *NL* **37** E6
Argile, lac de l' *QC* **22** F8

Argile, lac de l' *QC* **24** C2
Argo Bay *NT* **5** A8
Argolis *ON* **17** C4
Argonaut Mountain *BC* **6** C2-3
Argos, Cape *NS* **34** E6
Argyle *MB* **13** E3-4
Argyle *MB* **14** D4-5
Argyle *NB* **31** E3
Argyle *NB* **32** A2
Argyle *NS* **33** E2
Argyle *ON* **20** A8
Argyle *ON* **21** D2
Argyle Shore *PE* **34** C2
Argyle Shore *PE* **35** E4
Argyle Shore PP *PE* **32** B8
Argyle Shore PP *PE* **34** C1-2
Argyle Shore PP *PE* **35** E4
Arichat *NS* **34** E6
Arisaig *NS* **34** D4
Arisaig PP *NS* **34** D4
Ariss *ON* **19** A6
Ariss *ON* **20** D3
Aristazabal Island *BC* **1** B-C3
Aristote, lac *QC* **26** B5-6
Arizona *MB* **13** E2
Arizona *MB* **14** E2-3
Arjay, lac *QC* **39** A3
Arkell *ON* **19** B7
Arkell *ON* **20** D6
Arkell, Mount *YT* **4** E3
Arkona *ON* **19** C3
Arkona *ON* **20** E2
Arkwright *ON* **18** F5
Arkwright *ON* **20** A3-4
Arlington *PE* **35** C2
Arlington *NB* **32** A2
Arlington Beach *SK* **11** D5
Arm River *SK* **11** D5
Armada *AB* **7** C5-6
Armagh *QC* **27** B7
Armagh, rivière *QC* **27** B7
Armena *AB* **8** B6
Armena *AB* **8** D7
Armi Lake *NT* **10** B6
Armit *SK* **11** B7
Armit *SK* **13** B1
Armit River *MB* **11** B7
Armit River *MB* **13** B1
Armley *SK* **11** B6
Armstrong *BC* **6** E2
Armstrong *ON* **16** D6
Armstrong *ON* **40** F1
Armstrong *QC* **27** D7
Armstrong, lac *QC* **24** B3
Armstrong, lac *QC* **25** F3
Armstrong, Mount *YT* **4** B5
Armstrong Lake *MB* **15** E4
Arnaud *MB* **13** F4
Arnaud *MB* **14** F5
Arnaud, rivière *QC* **40** C5
Arnaud, rivière *QC* **41** A8
Arnes *MB* **13** D4
Arnes *MB* **14** B5
Arnold's Cove *NL* **36** D8
Arnold's Cove *NL* **37** D6
Arnot *MB* **15** E4
Arnoux, lac *QC* **23** D2
Arnprior *ON* **21** A7
Arnprior *ON* **24** D1
Arnstein *ON* **18** B7
Arntfield *QC* **17** D8
Arntfield *QC* **23** D2
Aroland *ON* **16** D7
Aroland *ON* **17** A2
Aroma Lake *NS* **11** C3
Aroostook *NB* **31** D3
Arran *SK* **11** C7
Arran *SK* **13** C1
Arran-Elderslie *ON* **18** F5
Arran-Elderslie *ON* **20** A4
Arran Lake *ON* **18** F5
Arran Lake *ON* **20** A3-4
Arras *BC* **3** E8
Arras *BC* **9** E1-2
Arrow Creek *BC* **6** F1
Arrowhead Lake *AB* **9** A5
Arrowhead Lake *AB* **10** F7
Arrowhead Lake *AB* **12** A1
Arrowhead Peninsula, RNP *ON* **16** F4
Arrowhead Peninsula PNR *ON* **16** F4
Arrowhead PP *ON* **18** D8
Arrowhead PP *ON* **21** B1
Arrowhead PP *ON* **21** F1-2
Arrowhead River *NT* **10** E3 F2
Arrow Lake *ON* **16** F5
Arrow Lake PP *ON* **16** F4-5
Arrow Lakes PP *BC* **6** E3
Arrow Park *BC* **6** E3
Arrow River *MB* **11** E8
Arrow River *MB* **13** E1
Arrowstone PPA *BC* **2** A7
Arrowwood *AB* **6** D6
Arrowwood *AB* **7** C5
Arthur *ON* **19** A6
Arthur *ON* **20** C5
Arthur, lac *QC* **39** E4
Arthurette *NB* **31** D3
Arthur Fiord *NU* **42** C4
Arthurville *AB* **8** F6
Artillery Lake *NT* **41** D2-3
Artland *SK* **6** B8
Artland *SK* **11** B2
Artlish Caves PP *BC* **1** E4
Arundel *QC* **24** C4
Arva *ON* **19** C4

Arva *ON* **20** E3
Arvia'juaq HS *NU* **41** E5
Arviat *NU* **40** B1
Arviat *NU* **41** E5
Arvida *QC* **28** C6
Arvilla *AB* **8** B6
Arviliquit *NU* **41** C5
Arviliquit *NU* **42** F4-5
Asbestos *QC* **27** D4
Ascension *PE* **35** A2
Ascot, rivière *QC* **27** F5
Ascot *QC* **27** E4
Ascot Corner *QC* **27** E5
Asessippi PP *MB* **11** D7-8
Asessippi PP *MB* **13** D1
Ashburn *ON* **20** C8
Ashburn *ON* **21** E2
Ashby Lake *ON* **21** B5
Ash Creek *BC* **3** A-B3
Ash Creek *BC* **4** F6
Ashcroft *BC* **1** E8
Ashcroft *BC* **2** A7
Ashcroft *BC* **6** D1
Ashdale *NS* **34** E4-5
Ashern *MB* **13** D3
Ashern *MB* **14** B3
Asheweig River *ON* **40** E1-2
Ashgrove *ON* **19** A7
Ashgrove *ON* **20** D6
Ashmont *AB* **6** A7
Ashmont *AB* **11** A1
Ashmont *AB* **12** F1
Ashnola River *BC* **2** E8
Ash River *BC* **2** D2
Ashton *PE* **35** D7
Ashton *ON* **21** B7
Ashton *ON* **24** E1-2
Ashville *MB* **11** D8
Ashville *MB* **13** D2
Ashville *MB* **14** B1
Asipoquobah Lake *ON* **13** A7
Aspen *SK* **34** E4
Aspen Beach PP *AB* **6** C5
Aspen Beach PP *AB* **8** E5-6
Aspen Brook *NL* **37** B3-4
Aspen Cove *NL* **38** E-F7
Aspen Grove *BC* **2** C8
Aspen Grove *BC* **6** E1
Aspotogan *NS* **32** F8
Aspotogan *NS* **33** C5
Aspy Bay *NS* **34** A7
Asquith *SK* **11** C4
Assaikwatamo River *MB* **15** D4
Assean Lake *MB* **15** E4
Assemetquagan, rivière *QC* **29** C6 D5-6
Assigny Lake *NL* **39** D3
Assiniboia *SK* **11** F4-5
Assiniboine, Mount *AB* **6** D4
Assiniboine, Mount *AB* **7** C2
Assiniboine River *MB* **13** F2-3
Assiniboine River *MB* **14** E3
Assinica, lac *QC* **40** F4-5
Assinica, parc *QC* **40** F4-5
Assomption, rivière l' *QC* **24** B5-6
Assomption, rivière l' *QC* **27** C1-2
Astle *NB* **31** E5
Astle *NB* **32** A3
Aston-Jonction *QC* **24** B8
Aston-Jonction *QC* **27** C4
Astorville *ON* **17** F7
Astorville *ON* **18** B8
Astorville *ON* **22** D1-2
Astray *NL* **39** A2
Aswapiswanan Lake *MB* **13** A5
Aswapiswanan Lake *MB* **15** F5
Athabasca *AB* **8** A6-7
Athabasca *AB* **9** F6
Athabasca, lac *AB* **41** F2
Athabasca, lac *SK* **9** A8
Athabasca, lac *SK* **41** F2
Athabasca, Lake *AB* **12** A3 B2
Athabasca, Lake *AB* **41** F2
Athabasca, Lake *SK* **9** A-A7
Athabasca, Lake *SK* **12** A3 B2
Athabasca, Lake *SK* **41** F2
Athabasca, rivière *AB* **6** A4
Athabasca, rivière *AB* **8** A3
Athabasca, rivière *AB* **9** B5
Athabasca, rivière *AB* **12** C2
Athabasca, rivière *AB* **12** D1
Athabasca, rivière *AB* **41** F1
Athabasca Landing *AB* **8** A6-7

Athabasca Landing *AB* **9** F6
Athabasca Pass NHS *AB* **6** C3
Athabasca Pass NHS *AB* **8** E1
Athabasca River *AB* **6** A3
Athabasca River *AB* **6** A4
Athabasca River *AB* **8** A5
Athabasca River *AB* **8** B2
Athabasca River *AB* **9** B-C6
Athabasca River *AB* **9** E6
Athabasca River *AB* **12** C1-2
Athabasca River *AB* **41** F1
Athabasca Sand Dunes PP *SK* **41** F2
Athabasca Sand Dunes PWP *SK* **9** A-B8
Athabasca Sand Dunes PWP *SK* **12** B3
Athabasca Sand Dunes PWP *SK* **9** A-B8
Athalmer *BC* **6** E4
Athalmer *BC* **7** C1
Athapap *MB* **11** A7
Athapap *MB* **12** F7
Athapap *MB* **15** F1
Athelstan *QC* **24** E5
Athenia Lake *NT* **10** B7-8
Athens *ON* **21** C7
Athens *ON* **24** F1-2
Atherley *ON* **18** F8
Atherley *ON* **20** A7
Atherley *ON* **21** D1
Athlone Island *BC* **1** C3
Athlow Bay *BC* **1** A1
Athol *NS* **32** C7
Athol Bay *ON* **21** F5
Atholville *NB* **29** D6
Atholville *NB* **31** A4
Aticonipi, lac *QC* **39** D6
Atikaki PWP *MB* **13** D5
Atikaki PWP *MB* **14** A7
Atikaki PWP *MB* **16** B1
Atikameg *AB* **9** E4
Atikameg Lake *MB* **11** A8
Atikameg Lake *MB* **13** A2
Atikamisis Lake *AB* **9** E4
Atik Lake *MB* **11** A7
Atik Lake *MB* **13** A1
Atik Lake *MB* **15** E-F5
Atikokan *ON* **16** E3-4
Atikokan *ON* **40** F1
Atikonak Lake *NL* **39** C3
Atikonak Lake *NL* **40** E7
Atikonak River *NL* **39** C3
Atik River *MB* **15** E5
Atikwa Lake *ON* **13** F6
Atikwa Lake *ON* **16** D-E2
Atkinson (Fox) Lake *MB* **15** E5
Atkinson Point *NT* **5** A4
Atlantic Ocean **36** E2-3 F2-3
Atlantic Ocean *NL* **37** F1-2
Atlantic Ocean *NS* **32** F4
Atlantic Ocean *NS* **33** D6-7 E6-7
Atlantic Ocean *NS* **34** E7-8 F7-8
Atlantique, océan **36** F3-4
Atlantique, océan *NL* **37** F4-6
Atlantique, océan *NL* **37** E7 F6-8
Atlantique, océan *NS* **33** E7 F6-8
Atlantique, océan *NS* **34** F6-7
Atlee *AB* **7** B-C8
Atlin *BC* **3** A1
Atlin *BC* **4** F4
Atlin Lake *BC* **3** A1
Atlin Lake *BC* **4** F4
Atlin PP *BC* **3** A1-2
Atlin PP *BC* **4** F4
Atlin PRA *BC* **3** A1
Atlin PRA *BC* **4** F4
Atmore *AB* **9** F6
Atmore *AB* **12** F1
Attawapiskat *ON* **40** E3
Attawapiskat Lake *ON* **16** A7
Attawapiskat Lake *ON* **40** E2
Attawapiskat River *ON* **16** A7-8
Attawapiskat River *ON* **40** E3
Attercliffe *ON* **19** B7
Attercliffe *ON* **20** E7
Attica *SK* **11** C5
Attihamagen Lake *NL* **40** D6
Attikamagen Lake *NL* **39** A2
Attikamagen Lake *NL* **40** D6
Attwood Lake *ON* **16** B-C6
Atwater *SK* **11** D7
Atwood *ON* **19** A5
Atwood *ON* **20** C4
Atwoods Brook *NS* **33** F2
Auberge-de-Ski-Skoki, LHN de l' *AB* **6** D4-5
Auberge-de-Ski-Skoki, LHN de l' *AB* **7** A1-2
Aubichon Arm *SK* **12** E3
Aubigny *NB* **14** E5
Aubinadong River PP *ON* **17** E4-5
Aubrey Falls PP *ON* **17** E4-5
Aubry Lake *NT* **5** D7
Azilda *ON* **17** F6
Azilda *ON* **18** A5
Azure *AB* **7** C4

Auburn *PE* **35** E5
Auclair *QC* **29** E2-3
Auclair *QC* **31** B1
Auden *ON* **16** D7
Auden *ON* **17** A1
Audet *QC* **27** E6-7
Augusta, lac *QC* **26** D4
Augusta, Mount *YT* **4** E1
Augustine Cove *PE* **32** B8
Augustine Cove *PE* **34** C1
Augustine Cove *PE* **35** E3
Augustines, lac des *QC* **22** A8
Augustines, lac des *QC* **23** F8
Augustines, lac des *QC* **25** C2
Aujuittuq (Grise Fiord) *NU* **42** C5
Aulac *QC* **32** C7
Aulac *NB* **35** F1
Aulavik NP *NT* **42** D1
Aulds Cove *NS* **34** D5
Aulitiving Island *NU* **41** A8
Aulitiving Island *NU* **42** E7
Aulneau Peninsula *ON* **13** F5-6
Aulneau Peninsula *ON* **16** E1-2
Aumont, lacs *QC* **22** C5
Aupaluk *QC* **40** C5
Aurora *ON* **20** B-C7
Aurora *ON* **21** E1
Austin *MB* **13** E3
Austin *MB* **14** D3
Austin *ON* **24** E8
Austin *ON* **27** F4
Australia Mountain *YT* **4** B3
Authier *ON* **17** C8
Authier *QC* **23** C3
Authier, lac *QC* **23** C3
Authier-Nord *QC* **17** C8
Authier-Nord *QC* **23** C3
Auyuittuq NP *NU* **41** B8
Auyuittuq NP *NU* **42** F7-8
Avalon Peninsula *NL* **37** E-F7
Avalon Wilderness Reserve *NL* **37** E-F7
Avauguor, lac *QC* **26** D6
Avaugour, lac *QC* **28** A1
Avening *ON* **20** B6
Aventure, lac de l' *QC* **36** E3
Aviron Point *NL* **36** E4
Aviron Point *NL* **37** E2-3
Avola *BC* **6** C2
Avon *ON* **19** C5
Avon *ON* **20** E4
Avondale *NL* **37** E7
Avondale *NS* **32** F4
Avondale *NS* **33** B5
Avondale *NS* **34** E4
Avondale *PE* **35** E6
Avonhurst *SK* **11** E6
Avonlea *SK* **11** E5
Avonmore *ON* **24** E3
Avonport *NS* **32** E7
Avonport *NS* **33** B5
Avon River *NS* **32** E7
Avon River *NS* **33** B-C5
Avon River *NS* **34** F1
Avon River *ON* **19** B5
Avon River *ON* **20** D4
Avonton *ON* **19** B5
Avonton *ON* **20** D4
Awenda PP *ON* **18** E7
Awenda PP *ON* **20** A6
Awry Lake *NT* **10** D8
Axe Lake *ON* **18** D8
Axe Lake *ON* **21** A-B1
Axe Lake *ON* **22** F1
Axel Heiberg Island *NU* **42** B4
Ayer's Cliff *QC* **27** F4
Aylen Lake *ON* **21** A4
Aylen Lake *ON* **22** F4
Aylesbury *SK* **11** D5
Aylesford *NS* **32** E6
Aylesford *NS* **33** B4
Aylesford Lake *NS* **32** E6
Aylesford Lake *NS* **33** B4
Aylmer *ON* **19** D5
Aylmer *ON* **20** F4
Aylmer, lac *QC* **27** D5
Aylmer, Mount *AB* **6** D4-5
Aylmer Lake *NT* **41** D2-3
Aylsham *SK* **11** B6
Aylwin *QC* **22** E7
Aylwin *QC* **24** C1
Ayr *ON* **19** B6
Ayr *ON* **20** D5
Ayton *ON* **20** B4
Azilda *ON* **17** F6
Azilda *ON* **18** A5
Azure *AB* **7** C4
Azure Lake *BC* **6** C2
Azure Mountain *BC* **6** C2

B

Babbage River *YT* **5** B3
Babine Lake *BC* **3** F5
Babine Lake (Pendleton Bay) PMP *BC* **1** A5
Babine Lake (Pendleton Bay) PMP *BC* **3** F5
Babine Lake (Smithers Landing) PMP *BC* **1** A5
Babine Lake (Smithers Landing) PMP *BC* **3** F5
Babine Mountains PP *BC* **3** F4-5
Babine Range *BC* **3** F4-5
Babine River *BC* **3** F4
Babine River Corridor PP *BC* **3** E4-5 F5
Baby, lac *QC* **22** A2
Baby, lac *QC* **23** F2
Baccaro *NS* **33** F2-3
Baccaro Island *NL* **37** C8
Baccaro Point *NS* **33** F2-3
Bachelor, lac *QC* **23** A8
Bachelor, lac *QC* **26** B2
Bachois, lac *QC* **26** B5-6
Back Bay *NB* **32** E2
Backbone Ranges *NT* **4** A6 B7
Back Cove *NL* **38** E4
Back Harbour *NL* **38** E6
Back Lake *NT* **10** B8
Back River *NL* **41** C4
Back River *NU* **41** D3
Backus CA *ON* **19** D6
Backus CA *ON* **20** F6
Bacon Cove *NL* **37** E7-8
Bacon Ridge *MB* **13** D2
Bacon Ridge *MB* **14** B2
Badajoz, lac *QC* **25** D4
Baddeck *NS* **34** C7
Baddow *ON* **20** A8
Baddow *ON* **21** D2
Baden *MB* **11** B7
Baden *ON* **19** B5-6
Baden *ON* **20** D4-5
Badesdawa Lake *ON* **16** B5
Badger *MB* **13** F4-5
Badger *MB* **14** F7
Badger *NL* **36** B5
Badger *NL* **37** B3
Badger Bay *NL* **38** A6
Badger Bay *NL* **37** A4
Badger's Corners *ON* **18** B4
Badger's Quay *NL* **37** A6-7
Badger's Quay *NL* **38** B7
Bad Hills *SK* **11** D3
Badjeros *ON* **20** B5
Bad Lake *SK* **11** D3
Badwater River *SK* **12** E3
Bad Weather Cape *NU* **42** B2
Baezaeko River *BC* **1** B6
Baffin, baie de *NU* **41** A8
Baffin, baie de *NU* **42** D6-7 F7
Baffin, île de *NU* **40** A5-6
Baffin, île de *NU* **41** A7-8 B7-8
Baffin, île de *NU* **42** E6-7 F7
Baffin Bay *NU* **41** A8
Baffin Bay *NU* **42** D6-7
Baffin Island *NU* **40** A5-6
Baffin Island *NU* **41** A7-8 B7-8
Baffin Island *NU* **42** E6-7 F7
Bagg, Mount *BC* **1** B8
Bagg, Mount *BC* **6** A-B1
Bagot *MB* **13** E3
Bagot *MB* **14** D3
Bagotville *QC* **28** C6
Baie, lac de la *QC* **26** B4
Baie-Brador, RNOM de la *QC* **38** B3
Baie-Brador, RNOM de la *QC* **39** D-E7
Baie-Comeau *QC* **29** A3-4
Baie-Comeau *QC* **39** F1
Baie-Comeau *QC* **40** F6
Baie-de-l'Isle-Verte, RNF de la *QC* **29** D1
Baie de l'Isle-Verte NWA *QC* **29** D1
Baie-de-Percé, parc de la *QC* **30** C3
Baie-des-Bacon *QC* **29** C1-2
Baie-des-Ha! Ha! *QC* **38** C1
Baie-de-Shawinigan *QC* **24** A7
Baie-de-Shawinigan *QC* **25** F7
Baie-de-Shawinigan *QC* **27** B2-3
Baie-des-Homards *QC* **39** F2
Baie-des-Loups, RNOM de *QC* **39** F6
Baie-des-Loups NMBS *QC* **39** F6
Baie-des-Rochers *QC* **29** B6
Baie-des-Sables *QC* **29** B4
Baie-du-Febvre *QC* **24** B7
Baie-du-Febvre *QC* **27** C3
Baie-du-Renard *QC* **30** A5
Baie-Egmont *PE* **35** D7
Baie-James *QC* **17** B8
Baie-Johan-Beetz *QC* **39** F4
Baie-Johan-Beetz *QC* **40** F7

Baies, lac des *QC* **22** B4
Baies, lac des *QC* **28** A7
Baies, lac des *QC* **31** D8
Baie-Sainte-Anne *NB* **31** D8
Baie-Sainte-Catherine *QC* **28** D8
Baie-Sainte-Catherine *QC* **29** D1
Baie-Sainte-Claire *QC* **39** F3
Baie-Saint-Paul *QC* **28** E-F7
Baie-Trinité *QC* **39** F1-2
Baie-Trinité *QC* **40** F6
Baie Verte *NB* **32** B7
Baie Verte *NB* **34** D1
Baie Verte *NS* **35** F2
Baie Verte *NL* **38** E4
Baie Verte *NL* **39** F8
Baie Verte Peninsula *NL* **38** E4-5
Baie Verte Road *NB* **35** F2
Baie-Wellers, RNF de la *ON* **21** E4-5
Baikie Lake *NL* **39** B-C3
Bailey Brook *NS* **34** D4
Bailey Creek *ON* **20** B-C6
Bailey Lake *SK* **12** A6
Bailey Lake *SK* **15** A1
Bailey Point *NT* **42** D2
Bailieboro *ON* **21** E3
Baillairgé, lac *QC* **28** B1
Baillargé, lac *QC* **26** D5
Baillie *NB* **32** D2
Baillie-Hamilton Island *NU* **42** C-D4
Bailly, lac *QC* **23** C8
Bailly, lac *QC* **26** D3
Baine Harbour *NL* **36** E7
Baine Harbour *NL* **37** E5
Bain Lake *MB* **12** A-B8
Bain Lake *MB* **15** B3
Bainsville *ON* **24** E4
Baird Peninsula *NU* **41** B7
Baird Peninsula *NU* **42** F6
Baird Point *BC* **1** A2
Bajo Point *BC* **1** F4
Baker *BC* **7** E2
Baker, lac *NB* **29** F3
Baker, Mount *YT* **4** C1
Baker Brook *NB* **29** F3
Baker Brook *NB* **31** C1
Baker Creek *BC* **1** B7
Baker Lake *NU* **40** A1
Baker Lake *NU* **41** D4
Baker Lake (Qamanit'uaq) *NU* **41** D4-5
Bakers Brook *NL* **38** D2
Baker Settlement *NS* **34** C7
Bakers Narrows *MB* **12** F7
Bakers Narrows *MB* **15** F1
Bakers Narrows PP *MB* **12** F7
Bakers Narrows PP *MB* **15** F1
Bala *ON* **18** E8
Bala *ON* **21** C1
Balaclava *ON* **18** F5-6
Balaclava *ON* **20** A4
Balaclava *ON* **21** A-B6
Balaton Beach *MB* **14** B5
Balcarres *SK* **11** D6
Balderson *ON* **21** C7
Balderson *ON* **24** E1
Baldock Lake *MB* **15** D3
Baldonnel *BC* **3** E8
Baldonnel *BC* **9** D1-2
Bald Peak *NB* **29** F5
Bald Peak *NB* **31** C4
Baldur *MB* **13** F2
Baldur *MB* **14** F2
Baldwin *ON* **20** B7
Baldwin *ON* **21** E1
Baldwin Mills *QC* **27** F4
Baldwinton *SK* **6** B8
Baldwinton *SK* **11** B2-3
Baldy Hughes *BC* **1** B7
Baldy Mountain *MB* **11** D8
Baldy Mountain *MB* **13** D1
Baleine, rivière à la *QC* **40** C-D6
Balfour *BC* **6** F3
Balgonie *SK* **11** E6
Balijennie *SK* **11** C3
Balinhard, Mount *AB* **6** B3
Balinhard, Mount *AB* **8** E1-2
Ball, Cape *BC* **1** A1-2
Ballantine *AB* **8** B5
Ballantrae *ON* **20** B7
Ballantrae *ON* **21** E1
Ballantyne Bay *SK* **12** F6
Ballantyne River *SK* **11** A6
Ballantyne River *SK* **12** F6
Ballantynes Cove *NS* **34** D5
Ballantyne Strait *NT* **42** A7
Ballard, Cape *NL* **37** F8
Ballinafad *ON* **19** A7
Ballinafad *ON* **20** C6
Ballingall Islets Nature PP *BC* **2** E4
Ball's Falls CA *ON* **19** C8
Ball's Falls CA *ON* **20** E7
Ballymote *ON* **19** C4-5
Ballymote *ON* **20** E3-4
Balm Beach *ON* **18** F7
Balm Beach *ON* **20** A6
Balmertown *ON* **13** D6
Balmertown *ON* **16** C2
Balmoral *MB* **13** E3-4
Balmoral *MB* **14** D5
Balmoral *NB* **29** D6
Balmoral *NB* **31** A5
Balmoral *ON* **19** C7
Balmoral *ON* **20** E6
Balmoral Mills *NS* **34** D-E2

Balmoral Mills PP *NS* **34** E2-3
Balmy Beach *MB* **14** F2
Balmy Beach *ON* **18** F5
Balmy Beach *ON* **20** A4
Balsam Creek *ON* **17** F8
Balsam Creek *ON* **22** D2
Balsam Lake *ON* **20** A8
Balsam Lake *ON* **21** D2
Balsam Lake PP *ON* **20** A8
Balsam Lake PP *ON* **21** D2
Baltic *PE* **34** B4
Baltic *PE* **35** C-D3
Baltic *PE* **35** D8
Baltimore *ON* **21** E3-4
Balzac *AB* **6** D5
Balzac *AB* **7** B4
Bamaji Lake *ON* **13** D7
Bamaji Lake *ON* **16** B-C4
Bamberg *ON* **19** B5-6
Bamberg *ON* **20** D4-5
Bamberton PP *BC* **2** F4
Banc-de-Paspébiac, SH du *QC* **30** D1-2
Bancroft *ON* **21** B4
Banff *AB* **6** D4
Banff *AB* **7** B2
Banff, PN *AB* **6** D4
Banff, PN *AB* **7** A1-2 B2
Banff NP *AB* **6** D4
Banff NP *AB* **7** A1
Banff Park Museum NHS *AB* **7** B1-2
Bangall, lac *QC* **22** E7-8
Bangall, lac *QC* **24** C2
Bangle Lake *MB* **12** A8
Bangle Lake *MB* **15** A3
Bangor *NS* **33** D1
Bangor *PE* **34** C3
Bangor *PE* **35** D6
Bangor *SK* **11** D7
Bangs Falls *NS* **33** D4
Bankier *BC* **2** C8
Bankier *BC* **6** E1
Bankend *SK* **11** D6
Banner *ON* **19** C5
Banner *ON* **20** E4
Bannock *SK* **11** B6
Bannockburn *ON* **21** D4
Bannock Lake *SK* **12** B6
Bannock Lake *SK* **15** B1
Banning Lake *NL* **36** A8
Banning Lake *NL* **37** A6
Banting Lake *NB* **38** F7
Bantry *AB* **7** C7
Bapaume *SK* **11** B3-4
Baptiste *ON* **21** B4
Baptiste, lac *QC* **26** D4
Baptiste Lake *AB* **8** A6
Baptiste Lake *ON* **21** B4
Barachois *NB* **35** E1
Barachois *SK* **30** C3
Barachois Brook *NL* **36** C2
Barachois Harbour *NS* **34** C7
Barachois Pond PP *NL* **36** C2
Barachois PP *NS* **34** C7
Baralzon Lake *MB* **15** A3
Barbara Lake *ON* **16** F7
Barbara Lake *ON* **17** B1
Barbel, lac *QC* **39** D1
Barber Lake *SK* **11** D3
Barbers Bay *ON* **17** C7
Barclay *ON* **20** B6-7
Barclay *ON* **21** D1
Bardanes, lac des *QC* **26** C5
Bardanes, lac des *QC* **28** A1
Bar-de-Cocagne *NB* **31** E8
Bar-de-Cocagne *NB* **32** A6-7
Bardoux, lac *QC* **39** D-E1
Bareneed *NL* **37** D7
Barge Bay *NL* **38** A4
Barge Bay *NL* **39** D8
Bar Haven Island *NL* **36** D6
Bar Haven Island *NL* **37** D6
Barich *AB* **8** B7
Baril Lake *AB* **9** B6
Baril Lake *AB* **12** B2
Baring *NL* **11** E6
Barkerville *BC* **1** B8
Barkerville *BC* **6** B1
Barkerville PP *BC* **1** B8
Barkerville PP *BC* **6** B1
Barkfield *MB* **14** F5-6
Bark Lake *ON* **17** E5
Bark Lake *ON* **21** A4
Bark Lake *ON* **21** C3
Bark Lake *ON* **22** F1
Barkley Sound *BC* **2** E1-2
Barkmere *QC* **24** C4
Barkway *ON* **21** C2
Bar Lake *SK* **12** E4
Barlow, lac *QC* **26** A4
Barma, lac *QC* **28** A7
Barnaby River *NB* **31** D-E7
Barnaby River *NB* **33** A1
Barnard, lac *QC* **24** A7
Barnard, lac *QC* **25** E7
Barnard, lac *QC* **26** C5
Barnard Point *NT* **41** A3
Barnard Point *NT* **42** D2
Barnes Crossing *SK* **11** A3
Barnes Lake *MB* **15** D3
Barnesville *NB* **32** D4-5

Barnesville *NB* **33** A2
Barneys Brook *NL* **36** A5
Barneys Brook *NL* **37** A3
Barneys Brook *NB* **38** F4
Barneys River *NS* **34** E4
Barn Range *YT* **5** B3
Barnston *QC* **27** F4-5
Barnumville *ON* **18** F5
Barnwell *AB* **6** A4
Barnwell *AB* **7** E6
Barons *AB* **6** A6
Barons *AB* **7** D5
Barra Head *NS* **34** D7
Barraute *QC* **23** D5
Barr'd Harbour *NL* **38** C3
Barr'd Harbour *NL* **39** E8
Barr'd Islands *NL* **38** E7
Barre, cap *QC* **30** A1
Barrel Lake *ON* **13** E-F7
Barren Island *NS* **34** F5
Barrett Lake *BC* **1** A4
Barrhead *AB* **6** A5
Barrhead *AB* **8** B5
Barrie *ON* **20** B6-7
Barrie *ON* **21** D1
Barriefield *ON* **21** E7
Barrie Island *ON* **18** D2
Barriere *BC* **6** D1-2
Barrière, lac *QC* **23** E2
Barrière, lac *QC* **24** C3
Barrier Ford *SK* **11** C6
Barrier Islands *ON* **14** E8
Barrington *NS* **33** F2
Barrington *ON* **24** E6
Barrington *ON* **27** F1-2
Barrington Lake *MB* **12** D8
Barrington Lake *MB* **15** D2
Barrington Passage *NS* **33** F2
Barrington River *MB* **12** D8
Barrington River *MB* **15** D2
Barron Lake *ON* **22** E4
Barron River *ON* **22** E4-5
Barron River PP *ON* **22** E4-5
Barronsfield *NS* **32** C7
Barrow Bay *ON* **18** E5
Barrow Bay *ON* **18** E5
Barrows *MB* **11** B7
Barrows *MB* **13** B1
Barrow Strait *NU* **42** D4
Barry, lac *QC* **23** C2
Barry, lac *QC* **26** D2
Barrydowne *ON* **18** A5-6
Barry's Bay *ON* **21** A4
Barrys Bay *ON* **21** A4
Barry's Bay *ON* **22** F4
Barry's Bay *ON* **22** F4
Barryvale *ON* **21** B6
Barryville *NB* **29** F8
Barryville *NB* **31** C7
Barss Corner *NS* **32** F6-7
Barss Corner *NS* **33** C4
Barthel *SK* **6** A8
Barthel *SK* **11** A3
Barthélémy, lac *QC* **26** B5-6
Bartholomew River *NB* **31** E5-6
Bartholomew River *NB* **32** A4
Bartibog *NB* **29** F8
Bartibog *NB* **31** C7
Bartibog Bridge *NB* **31** C7
Bartibog River *NB* **29** F8
Bartibog River *NB* **31** C6-7
Bartlett Lake *NT* **10** C4-5
Bartletts Beach *NS* **33** E1
Bartletts Harbour *NB* **38** B3
Bartletts Harbour *NL* **39** E7-8
Barton *NS* **32** F4
Barton *NS* **33** C2
Barton, lac *QC* **22** C6
Barton Lake *ON* **13** C6
Barton Lake *ON* **16** A2
Bar U Ranch NHS *AB* **6** E5-6
Bar U Ranch NHS *AB* **7** C-D4
Barville *ON* **23** D5
Barwick *ON* **16** E-F2
Bas-Caraquet *NB* **30** E2
Bas-Caraquet *NB* **31** B8
Bashaw *AB* **6** C6
Bashaw *AB* **8** E7
Basin & Middle Lakes, RNOM *SK* **11** C5
Basin & Middle Lakes NMBS *SK* **11** C5
Basin Head *PE* **34** B4-5 C4-5
Basin Head PP *PE* **35** D8
Basin Lake *SK* **11** C5
Baskatong, réservoir *QC* **22** C8
Baskatong, réservoir *QC* **24** A2
Baskatong, réservoir *QC* **25** E2
Basket Lake *ON* **16** D3
Basler Lake *NT* **10** B6
Basques, lac aux *QC* **29** D1
Bas-Saint-Laurent, ZEC *QC* **29** C3 D4
Basse-Aboujagane *NB* **35** E1
Basserode, lac *QC* **23** E3
Basses-Terres-du-Manitoba (projet), PN des *MB* **13** D4-5

Basses-Terres-du-Manitoba (projet), PN des *MB* **14** B6-7
Bassett Island *ON* **19** D2
Bassett Island *ON* **20** F1
Bassin *QC* **30** F7
Bass Lake *ON* **18** B3-4
Bass Lake *ON* **18** F5
Bass Lake *ON* **20** A4
Bass Lake *ON* **21** C7
Bass Lake *ON* **24** F1
Bass Lake PP *ON* **18** F8
Bass Lake PP *ON* **20** A7
Bass Lake PP *ON* **21** D1
Bass River *NB* **31** B-C6
Bass River *NB* **31** E7
Bass River *NS* **32** A5
Bass River *NS* **32** D8
Bass River *NS* **33** A5
Bass River *NS* **34** E1
Basswood *MB* **11** E8
Basswood *MB* **13** E2
Basswood *MB* **14** D1
Basswood Lake *ON* **18** A1
Basswood Ridge *NB* **32** D1-2
Bastille, lac *QC* **39** D5
Bat, lac *QC* **23** F2
Bataille-de-Fish Creek, LHN de la *SK* **11** C4
Bataille-de-la-Châteauguay, LHN de la *QC* **24** E5
Bataille-de-la-Ristigouche, LHN de la *QC* **29** D5-6
Bataille-de-la-Ristigouche, LHN de la *QC* **31** A3-4
Bataille-du-Moulin-à-Vent, LHN de la *ON* **24** F2-3
Batawa *ON* **21** E4
Batchawana Bay *ON* **17** F3-4
Batchawana Bay *ON* **17** E3-4
Batchawana Bay PP *ON* **17** E3-4
Batchawana River *ON* **17** E4
Batchawana River PP *ON* **17** E4
Bateau Cove *NL* **38** D2-3
Bateau Island *ON* **18** D6
Bateman *NL* **11** E4
Bates Beach *BC* **2** C2
Bates Lake *YT* **4** E2
Bath *NB* **31** E3
Bath *NB* **32** A1
Bath *ON* **21** E6
Bathing Lake *NT* **5** C5
Bathurst *NB* **29** E8
Bathurst *NB* **31** B6-7
Bathurst, Cape *NT* **41** A1
Bathurst Inlet *NU* **41** C3
Bathurst Inlet *NU* **42** F7
Bathurst Inlet (Kingaok) *NU* **41** C3
Bathurst Island *NU* **42** D3
Bathurst Mines *NB* **29** F7
Bathurst Mines *NB* **31** C6
Batiscan *QC* **24** B8
Batiscan *QC* **25** F8
Batiscan *QC* **27** B-C4
Batiscan, lac *QC* **28** F4
Batiscan, rivière *QC* **25** D-E8
Batiscan, rivière *QC* **27** A4
Batiscan-Neilson, ZEC *QC* **28** F4-5
Batiscan-Neilson, ZEC *QC* **27** A4
Batoche, LHN de *SK* **11** C4-5
Batoche NHS *SK* **11** C4-5
Batteau Harbour *NL* **39** B8
Battersea *ON* **21** D7
Battery PP *NS* **34** D6-7
Battle Creek *SK* **6** F8
Battle Creek *SK* **11** F2
Battleford *SK* **11** B3
Battle Harbour *NL* **38** C8
Battle Lake *AB* **8** D5
Battle of Fish Creek NHS *SK* **11** C4
Battle of the Chateauguay NHS *QC* **24** E5
Battle of the Restigouche NHS *QC* **29** D5-6
Battle of the Restigouche NHS *QC* **31** A3-4
Battle of the Windmill NHS *ON* **24** F2-3
Battle River *AB* **6** B6 C6-7
Battle River *AB* **11** B-C1
Battle River *SK* **6** B8
Battle River *SK* **11** B2-3
Battrum *SK* **11** E4
Batty Lake *MB* **12** F7-8
Batty Lake *MB* **15** F2
Baude, lac *QC* **25** D6
Baude, lac *QC* **27** A2
Bauline *NL* **37** D8
Bauline East *NL* **37** E8
Baumann Fiord *NU* **42** C4-5
Bawlf *AB* **6** B6
Bawlf *AB* **8** D7-8
Bawlf *AB* **11** B1
Baxter *ON* **20** B6
Baxter Harbour *NS* **32** D6-7
Baxter Harbour *NS* **33** B4
Baxters Corner *NB* **32** D3
Baxters Corner *NB* **33** A1
Bay, lac *QC* **22** A3-4
Bayard *SK* **11** E5
Bay Bulls *NL* **37** E8

Bay de l'Eau *NL* **36** D7
Bay de l'Eau *NL* **37** D5
Bay de loup Brook *NL* **36** D3
Bay de loup Brook *NL* **37** D1
Bay de Verde *NL* **37** C8
Bay du Nord River *NL* **36** D7
Bay du Nord River *NL* **37** D4
Bay du Nord Wilderness Reserve *NL* **36** C7
Bay du Nord Wilderness Reserve *NL* **37** C5
Bay du Vin *NB* **31** D7
Bay du Vin Island, ZCP *NB* **31** C7-8 D7-8
Bay du Vin Island PCA *NB* **31** C7-8 D7-8
Bay du Vin River *NB* **31** D7
Bayend *NB* **14** B2-3
Bayeuville, lac *QC* **28** A7
Bayfield *NB* **32** B8
Bayfield *NB* **34** C1
Bayfield *NB* **35** E3
Bayfield *NS* **34** D5
Bayfield *ON* **19** A4
Bayfield *ON* **20** D3
Bayfield *PE* **35** D7-8
Bayfield, île *QC* **38** B1-2
Bayfield Beach PP *NS* **34** D5
Bayfield River *ON* **19** A-B4
Bayfield River *ON* **20** D3
Bayfield Inlet *ON* **18** C6
Bayfield Inlet *ON* **21** A1
Bayfield Sound *ON* **18** B2
Bayham *ON* **19** D5
Bayham *ON* **20** F4
Bayhead *NS* **34** D2
Bay L'Argent *NL* **36** D-E7
Bay L'Argent *NL* **37** D-E5
Bayly Lake *MB* **15** F5
Baynes Lake *BC* **7** F2
Bayonne, rivière *QC* **24** B-C6
Bayonne, rivière *QC* **27** C2
Bay Roberts *NL* **37** D7
Bays, Lake of *ON* **13** E7
Bays, Lake of *ON* **16** D4
Bays, Lake of *ON* **21** B2
Bay Shore Heights *MB* **14** C5
Bayshore Village *ON* **18** F6-7
Bayshore Village *ON* **20** A7
Bayshore Village *ON* **21** D1
Bayside *NB* **32** E2
Bayside *NB* **35** F2
Bayside *NB* **38** F3-4
Bayside *NS* **32** F8
Bayside *NS* **33** C5-6
Bayside *PE* **35** C2
Baysville *ON* **21** B2
Bayswater *NB* **32** D4
Bayswater *NB* **33** A1
Bayswater *NS* **32** F7
Bayswater *NS* **33** C5
Bayswater Beach PP *NS* **32** F8
Bayswater Beach PP *NS* **33** C-D5
Baytona *NL* **36** A7
Baytona *NL* **37** A5
Baytona *NL* **38** F6
Bay Trail *SK* **11** C5
Bay Tree *AB* **3** E8
Bay Tree *AB* **9** E2
Bay View *NL* **36** F7
Bay View *NL* **37** F5
Bayview *NL* **38** E6
Bayview Escarpment, RNP *ON* **18** F6
Bayview Escarpment, RNP *ON* **20** A4-5
Bayview Escarpment PNR *ON* **18** F6
Bayview Escarpment PNR *ON* **20** A4-5
Bazil, lac *QC* **39** A2
Bazile, lac *QC* **28** D7
Bazin, rivière *QC* **25** B4 C3-4
Bazinet, lac *QC* **24** B8
Beach Meadows *NS* **33** E4
Beachburg *ON* **21** A6
Beachburg *ON* **22** F5-6
Beach O'Pines *ON* **19** B3
Beach O'Pines *ON* **20** D2
Beach Point *PE* **34** D4
Beach Point *PE* **35** F7
Beach Point *NB* **32** B7
Beachside *NL* **38** E5
Beachville *ON* **19** C5
Beachville *ON* **20** E4
Beacon Hill *SK* **6** A8
Beacon Hill *SK* **9** F8
Beacon Hill *SK* **11** A2
Beacon Hill *MB* **12** F7
Beaconia *MB* **13** E4
Beadle *SK* **11** D3
Beadle, Cape *BC* **2** E1
Bealton *ON* **19** C6-7
Bealton *ON* **20** E5-6
Beamsville *ON* **19** C8
Beamsville *ON* **20** E7
Bear Bay *NU* **42** D5
Bearberry *AB* **6** C5
Bearberry *AB* **7** A3
Bearbone Lake *ON* **13** A7
Bear Canyon *AB* **3** E7
Bear Canyon *AB* **9** D2-3
Bear Cove *BC* **1** D-E4
Bear Cove *NL* **38** E2

Bear Cove *NL* **38** E4
Bear Cove *NL* **39** D7-8
Bear Cove *NS* **33** C-E1
Bear Creek *ON* **18** A7
Bear Creek *ON* **19** C3
Bear Creek *ON* **20** E2
Bear Creek *SK* **9** D8
Bear Creek *SK* **12** D3
Bear Creek *YT* **4** A2
Bear Creek PP *BC* **6** E1-2
Beardmore *ON* **16** D6-7
Beardmore *ON* **17** B1
Beardy's & Okemasis *SK* **11** B4
Bear Glacier PP *BC* **3** E3
Bear Head *NB* **36** A-B2
Bearhead Creek *AB* **9** E4
Bear Head Lake *MB* **16** E1 ?

Bear Head Lake *MB* **14** E1
Bearhole Lake PP *BC* **3** F8
Bearhole Lake PP *BC* **9** F1-2
Bear Island *MB* **15** F3
Bear Island *ON* **17** E7
Bear Lake *BC* **1** A7
Bear Lake *BC* **3** E5
Bear Lake *MB* **15** F4
Bear Lake *ON* **18** B4-5
Bear Lake *ON* **18** D8
Bear Lake *ON* **21** A1
Bear Lake *ON* **22** F1
Bear Lake *ON* **22** F1
Bear River *AB* **9** B-C4
Bear River *NS* **32** F5
Bear River *PE* **34** B4
Bear River *PE* **35** D7
Bear River *SK* **11** A5-6
Bear River *SK* **12** F5-6
Bear River (IR) *NS* **32** F5
Bear River (IR) *NS* **33** C2
Bearskin Lake *ON* **13** A7
Bearskin Lake *ON* **13** A7
Bears Rump Island *ON* **18** D4
Beatrice *ON* **18** D8
Beatrice *ON* **21** B1
Beatton PP *BC* **3** E8
Beatton *BC* **9** D1
Beatton River *BC* **3** D8
Beatton River *BC* **9** C-D1
Beatton River *BC* **9** C1
Beatton River PP *BC* **3** D-E8
Beatton River PP *BC* **9** D1-2
Beatty *SK* **11** B5
Beatty Creek *BC* **3** B2
Beatty Lake *AB* **9** A3
Beatty Lake *AB* **10** F5
Beattyville *QC* **23** C6
Beaubier *SK* **11** F6
Beau Bois *NL* **36** E7
Beau Bois *NL* **37** E5
Beaucage Point *ON* **22** D1
Beaucanton *QC* **17** C8
Beaucanton *QC* **23** B2
Beauceville *QC* **27** C6
Beauchamp, lac *QC* **23** D4
Beauchastel, lac *QC* **23** E2
Beauchêne, lac *QC* **17** F8
Beauchêne, lac *QC* **22** C2
Beaucours, lac *QC* **26** C4
Beaudry *QC* **17** D8
Beaudry, lac *QC* **23** E2
Beaudry, lac *QC* **17** D8
Beaudry PP *MB* **13** E3
Beaudry PP *MB* **14** E4
Beaufield *SK* **11** C3
Beaufort (océan Arctique), mer de *YT* **5** A3-4
Beaufort Sea (Arctic Ocean) *YT* **5** A3-4
Beauharnois *QC* **24** E5
Beauharnois *QC* **27** F1
Beaulac *QC* **27** D5
Beau Lac *QC* **29** F2
Beaulieu, rivière *QC* **24** D6
Beaulieu, rivière *QC* **29** C1
Beaulieu River *NT* **10** C7
Beaumesnil, lac *QC* **25** C6
Beaumier, lac *QC* **25** C6
Beaumier, lac *QC* **28** F1-2
Beaumont *AB* **8** B6
Beaumont *NL* **38** E5
Beaumont *QC* **27** A-B6
Beaumont PP *BC* **1** A6
Beaumont PP *BC* **2** A6
Beaumont Unit (Gulf Islands NPR) *BC* **2** F4-5
Beauport *QC* **27** A6
Beaupré *QC* **27** A6
Beaupré Lake *SK* **11** A4
Beaupré Lake *SK* **12** F4
Beauregard, lac *QC* **25** D4 E3-4
Beaurivage, rivière *QC* **27** B5 C5-6
Beausejour *MB* **13** E4
Beauséjour *MB* **14** D6
Beauséjour, lac *QC* **24** A-B6
Beausoleil Island *ON* **18** E7
Beaussier, lac *QC* **26** D5
Beauvais Lake PP *AB* **6** F5
Beauvais Lake PP *AB* **7** D3
Beauval *SK* **12** F4
Beauvallon *AB* **8** B7
Beauvallon *AB* **6** A7

Beauvallon *AB* **11** A1
Beaux-Rivages *QC* **24** A3
Beaux-Rivages *QC* **25** E3
Beaver *AB* **14** D3
Beaverbank *NS* **32** E-F8
Beaverbank *NS* **33** C6
Beaverbank Villa *NS* **32** E8
Beaverbank Villa *NS* **33** B5-6
Beaver Brook *NL* **38** B4
Beaver Brook *NS* **33** A6
Beaver Brook *NB* **34** E-F2
Beaver Brook Station *NB* **29** F8
Beaver Brook Station *NB* **31** C6-7
Beaver Cove *BC* **1** E4
Beaver Cove *NL* **36** A7-8
Beaver Cove *NL* **37** A5-6
Beaver Cove *NS* **34** C7
Beaver Creek *ON* **21** C5-6
Beaver Creek *ON* **21** C-D4
Beaver Creek *YT* **4** C1
Beaver Creek PP *MB* **13** D4
Beaver Creek PP *MB* **14** A5
Beaver Crossing *AB* **6** A7-8
Beaver Crossing *AB* **8** A8
Beaver Crossing *AB* **11** A2
Beaver Crossing *AB* **12** F2
Beaverdam *AB* **6** A7-8
Beaverdam *AB* **11** A2
Beaver Dam *NB* **32** C2-3
Beaverdell *BC* **6** F2
Beaver Harbour *NB* **32** E3
Beaver Harbour *NS* **33** B8
Beaver Harbour *NS* **33** B8
Beaver Harbour *NS* **32** C2
Beaver Island *SK* **15** C1
Beaver Lake *AB* **8** A8
Beaver Lake *AB* **9** F7
Beaver Lake *AB* **12** F1
Beaver Lake *NT* **10** E5
Beaver Lake *ON* **21** D6
Beaver Lake *SK* **9** A8
Beaver Lake *SK* **12** A3
Beaverlodge *AB* **9** E-F2
Beaverlodge Lake *NT* **10** A4-5
Beaverlodge Lake *SK* **12** A3-4
Beaver Mines *AB* **6** F5
Beaver Mines *AB* **7** E-F4
Beaver Mountain PP *NS* **34** A8
Beaver Mountain PP *NS* **34** E4
Beaver River *AB* **9** A6-7
Beaver River *AB* **9** F6-7
Beaver River *AB* **12** F1
Beaver River *AB* **39** B5
Beaver River *ON* **20** A-B5
Beaver River *ON* **21** D-E2
Beaver River *SK* **11** A3
Beaver River *SK* **12** F3
Beaver River *YT* **4** A4
Beaver River *YT* **11** F1-2
Beaverstone Bay *ON* **18** B5
Beaver Stone River *ON* **39** D8
Beaver Valley *SK* **11** C3
Beazer *AB* **6** F6
Beazer *AB* **7** F5
Bécancour *QC* **24** B8
Bécancour *QC* **27** C3-4
Bécancour, rivière *QC* **27** C5
Bechard *SK* **11** E6
Becher *ON* **19** D2
Becher *ON* **20** F1
Beckett Creek, RNOM de *ON* **24** D3
Beckett Creek NMBS *ON* **24** D3
Beckwith Island *ON* **18** E7
Bedard Aspen PP *BC* **1** D7-8
Bedard Aspen PP *BC* **2** A6
Bedard Aspen PP *BC* **2** A6-7 B6-7
Bede Creek *AB* **9** B3-4
Bedeque *PE* **34** C1
Bedeque *PE* **35** D3
Bedeque Bay *PE* **34** C1
Bedeque Bay *PE* **35** D2
Bedford *NS* **32** F8
Bedford *NS* **33** C6
Bedford *QC* **27** F2-3
Bedford Island *NS* **18** B3
Bedford Island *NS* **12** C6
Bedford Island *NS* **15** C1
Bedwell River *BC* **2** D1
Bedwell Sound *BC* **1** F5
Bedwell Sound *BC* **2** C1
Beecham Settlement *NS* **35** F2

Beechey Island HS *NU* **42** D4
Beech Hill *NS* **32** F7
Beech Hill *NS* **33** C4
Beech Hill *NS* **33** E4
Beech Point *PE* **35** D3
Beechwood *NB* **31** E3
Beechwood *NB* **32** A1
Beechy *SK* **11** D3-4
Beersville *NB* **31** E7
Beersville *NB* **32** A5
Beeton *ON* **20** B6
Beetz, lac *QC* **39** E4
Begbie, Mount *BC* **6** D3
Bégin *QC* **28** B5
Beirnes, Mount *BC* **3** D4
Beirnes Lake *NT* **10** B8
Beiseker *AB* **6** D6
Beiseker *AB* **7** A4
Bekanon *ON* **18** C6
Bekere Lake *NT* **5** B7
Belair *NB* **13** E4
Belair *MB* **14** C6
Béland, lac *QC* **26** D6-7
Béland, lac *QC* **28** B8
Béland, rivière *QC* **29** B8
Béland, rivière *QC* **30** B1
Bélanger Bay *ON* **18** B1-2
Bélanger River *NB* **13** B4
Bélanger River *SK* **12** E4-5
Belbutte *SK* **11** B3-4
Belcarra *BC* **2** D5
Belcher *MB* **15** C5-6
Belcher Channel *NU* **42** C4
Belcher Islands *NU* **40** E6
Belcourt *QC* **23** D5
Belfountain *ON* **19** A7
Belfountain *ON* **20** C6
Belgrave *ON* **19** A4
Belgrave *ON* **20** C4
Belinge, rivière *QC* **22** A-B7
Belinge, rivière *QC* **25** C1-2
Belisle, lac *QC* **26** D5
Belize Inlet *BC* **1** D4
Bell, rivière *QC* **23** A5 B6
Bell, rivière *QC* **30** A6
Bella Bella *BC* **1** C4
Bella Coola *BC* **1** C4-5
Bella Coola River *BC* **1** C5
Bella Lake *ON* **21** A2
Bella Lake *ON* **22** F2
Bell Bay PP *ON* **21** A4
Bell Bay PP *ON* **22** F4
Bellburns *NL* **38** D2-3
Bellburns *NL* **39** E7
Belldowns Point *NL* **38** D2
Belle-Anse *QC* **30** C3
Belledune *NB* **29** D7
Belledune *NB* **31** A6
Belledune, pointe *NB* **29** D7
Belledune, pointe *NB* **31** A6
Belledune Point *NB* **29** D7
Belledune Point *NB* **31** A6
Bellefeuille *QC* **24** C5
Bellefleur *NB* **29** F4
Bellefleur *NB* **31** D2
Bellefond *NB* **31** C6
Bellegarde *SK* **11** F7-8
Bellegarde *SK* **13** F1
Belle Isle *NL* **38** A4
Belleisle *NS* **32** F5
Belleisle *NS* **33** C2-3
Belle Isle, détroit de *NL* **38** A4
Belle Isle, détroit de *NL* **39** D8
Belle Isle, Strait of *NL* **38** A4
Belle Isle, Strait of *NL* **39** D8
Belleisle Bay *NB* **32** C-D4
Belleisle Bay *NB* **33** A3
Belleisle Creek *NB* **32** C4
Belle Marche *NS* **34** B6
Bellemare, lac *QC* **26** E6
Belleoram *NL* **36** E6
Belleoram *NL* **37** E4
Belle Plaine *SK* **11** E5
Belle River *ON* **19** E2
Belle River *ON* **19** E2
Belle River *PE* **34** D3
Belle River *PE* **35** F5-6
Belleterre *QC* **17** E8
Belleterre *QC* **22** A3
Belle Vallée *ON* **17** D8
Belle Vallée *ON* **23** F1
Belleville *NB* **31** F3
Belleville *NB* **32** B1
Belleville *ON* **21** E5
Belleville *ON* **21** E5
Bellevue *AB* **6** F5
Bellevue *AB* **7** E3
Bellevue *NL* **37** D6-7
Bellevue, lac *QC* **25** B5
Bellevue, lac *QC* **26** F5
Bellevue, lac *QC* **28** D1
Bellevue House NHS *ON* **21** E6-7
Bell Ewart *ON* **20** B7
Bell Ewart *ON* **21** D-E1
Bellhouse PP *BC* **2** E4-5
Bell-Irving River *BC* **3** D3
Bellis *AB* **6** A6
Bellis *AB* **8** B8
Bellis *AB* **11** A1
Bellis *AB* **12** F1
Bell Island *NL* **37** D8

Bell Island *NL* **38** C5
Bell Island *NL* **39** E8
Bell Island *NT* **11** A4
Belliveau *NS* **33** D1-2
Belliveau Cove *NS* **33** D1
Bell Lake *ON* **16** D4
Bell Lake PP *MB* **11** C7
Bell Lake PP *MB* **13** B-C1
Bellmans Cove *NL* **36** B-C2
Bellot Strait *NU* **41** A4-5
Bellot Strait *NU* **42** E4
Bell Peninsula *NU* **40** A3
Bell Peninsula *NU* **41** D6-7
Bell Point *YT* **5** D3
Bellrock *ON* **21** D6
Bellsite *MB* **11** C8
Bellsite *MB* **13** B1
Bells Point *PE* **35** E3
Bell II *BC* **3** D3
Belly River *AB* **6** F6
Belly River *AB* **7** E5
Belmont *MB* **13** F2
Belmont *MB* **14** E-F2
Belmont *NS* **33** A6
Belmont *NS* **33** B5
Belmont *NS* **34** E2
Belmont *NS* **34** F1
Belmont *ON* **19** C5
Belmont *ON* **20** E4
Belmont *PE* **32** A8
Belmont *PE* **34** B1
Belmont *PE* **35** D3
Belmont Lake *ON* **21** D4
Belmont PP *PE* **32** A8
Belmont PP *PE* **34** B1
Belmont PP *PE* **35** C-D2
Belmore *ON* **19** C5
Belnan *NS* **33** B6
Belnan *NS* **34** F2
Belot, lac *NT* **5** D7
Beloud Post *YT* **4** E3
Belsham Lake *MB* **12** B8
Belsham Lake *MB* **15** B3
Belwood *ON* **19** A6
Belwood *ON* **20** C5
Belwood, Lake *ON* **19** A6
Belwood, Lake *ON* **20** C5
Belwood Lake CA *ON* **19** A6
Belwood Lake CA *ON* **20** C5
Benalto *AB* **6** C5
Benalto *AB* **8** F5
Benbow *AB* **8** B2-3
Benbow Junction *AB* **8** B3
Bender *MB* **14** C4-5
Bender *SK* **11** E7
Benedict, Mount **39** A6
Ben Eoin *NS* **34** C7
Ben Eoin PP *NS* **34** C7
Bengough *SK* **11** F5
Beniah Lake *NT* **10** B-C7
Benito *MB* **11** C7
Benito *MB* **13** C1
Benjamin, lac **25** A3-4
Benjamin, lac *QC* **26** F3-4
Benjamin Lake *NT* **10** C8
Benjamin Point *BC* **1** C2
Benjamin River *NB* **29** D6-7
Benjamin River *NB* **29** D7
Benjamin River *NB* **31** A5-6
Ben Lomond *MB* **32** D4
Ben Lomond *NB* **33** A1-2
Benmiller *ON* **19** A4
Benmiller *ON* **20** C3
Bennett *AB* **6** C5
Bennett *AB* **8** E6
Bennett Bay & Georgeson Island Unit (Gulf Islands NPR) *BC* **2** E4-5
Bennett Lake *MB* **13** D4
Bennett Lake *YT* **4** E4
Bennett Lake *ON* **21** C6-7
Bennetts Bay *NS* **32** D7
Bennetts Bay *NS* **33** A-B4
Benny *ON* **17** E5
Benoit's Cove *NL* **36** B2-3
Benoit's Cove *NL* **40** F8
Benson *SK* **11** F6
Benson Bay *MB* **13** A5-6
Bentick Cove *PE* **35** D2-3
Bentley *AB* **6** C5
Bentley *AB* **8** E6
Bentley Lake *SK* **12** B6
Bentley Lake *SK* **15** B1
Benton *NB* **32** C1
Benton *NL* **36** B7-8
Benton *NL* **37** B5-6
Bent River *ON* **18** D8
Bent River *ON* **21** B1
Bérard, lac *QC* **25** B5
Bérard, lac *QC* **26** F5
Berens Island *MB* **13** C3-4
Berens Lake *ON* **16** B2
Berens River *MB* **13** C4
Berens River *MB* **13** C4
Berens River *ON* **16** A1
Berens River *ON* **16** A-B2
Berens River *ON* **16** B2-3
Beresford *MB* **11** E8
Beresford *MB* **13** E-F2
Beresford *NB* **14** E1
Beresford *NB* **29** E8
Beresford *NB* **31** B6
Beresford Bay *BC* **1** A1
Berford Lake *ON* **18** E5
Bergen *AB* **6** D5
Bergen *AB* **7** A3
Bergeron, lac *QC* **28** A6
Bergland *ON* **13** F5-6
Bergland *ON* **16** E1-2
Berkeley *ON* **20** B5
Berland River *AB* **6** A3

Berland River *AB* **8** B1
Berlinguet, lac *QC* **26** E5
Berlinguet Inlet *NU* **41** A-B6
Berlinguet Inlet *NU* **42** A5
Berlo *MB* **14** C5
Bermen, lac *QC* **39** B1
Bernabé, lac *QC* **28** B5
Bernard Lake *ON* **18** C8
Bernard Lake *ON* **21** A1
Bernard Lake *ON* **22** E-F1
Bernic Lake *MB* **14** C7
Bernie, lac *QC* **23** D8
Bernier, lac *QC* **25** A3
Bernier, lac *QC* **26** E3
Bernier Bay *NU* **41** B5
Bernier Bay *NU* **42** E4-5
Bernierville *QC* **27** C5
Bernierville *QC* **29** C7
Berry, rivière *QC* **23** C4
Berry Creek *AB* **6** D7
Berry Creek *AB* **7** A-B7
Berry Creek *AB* **9** A-B5
Berry Creek *AB* **11** D1
Berry Head *NL* **36** B-C2
Berry Head *NS* **34** F6
Berry Hill Pond *NL* **36** C6
Berry Hill Pond *NL* **37** C4
Berry Mills *NB* **31** F7-8
Berry Mills *NB* **32** B6
Berté, lac *QC* **39** E1
Berthelot, lac *QC* **23** D7
Berthelot, lac *QC* **26** E1-2
Berthierville *QC* **24** C7
Berthierville *QC* **27** C2
Bertrand *NB* **30** E1-2
Bertrand *NB* **31** B7
Bertwell *SK* **11** C7
Bervie *ON* **20** B3
Berwick *NB* **32** C5
Berwick *NS* **32** E6
Berwick *NS* **33** B4
Berwick *ON* **24** E3
Berwyn *AB* **9** E3
Besace, lac de la *QC* **26** B5
Besnard Lake *SK* **12** E5
Bessonne, ZEC de la *QC* **25** C8
Bessonne, ZEC de la *QC* **28** E-F3
Best's Harbour *NL* **36** D8
Best's Harbour *NL* **37** D6
Bétaux, lac *QC* **39** D6
Betchouane, RNOM de *QC* **39** F4
Betchouane NMBS *QC* **39** F4
Beteau Lake *ON* **16** A7
Béthanie *QC* **24** D8
Béthanie *QC* **27** E3
Bethany *MB* **13** E2
Bethany *MB* **14** D2
Bethany *ON* **21** E2-3
Bethel *PE* **35** E5
Bethune *SK* **11** E5
Bethune Memorial House NHS *ON* **21** C1-2
Betsiamites *QC* **29** B3
Betsiamites, pointe de *QC* **29** B3
Betsiamites, rivière *QC* **29** A-B2
Betsiamites, rivière *QC* **40** F6
Beulah *MB* **11** E8
Beulah *MB* **13** E1
Beverley *SK* **11** E3
Bevin, lac *QC* **24** C4
Bevin Lake *ON* **18** A5
Bewdley *ON* **21** E3
Beynon *AB* **7** B5
Bezanson *AB* **9** E-F3
Bible Hill *NS* **33** A6
Bible Hill *NS* **34** A2
Bic, île du *QC* **29** C2
Bic, parc du *QC* **29** C2
Bic, rivière du *QC* **29** C2
Bickerdike *AB* **8** C3
Bickleigh *SK* **11** D3
Bicknor, Cape *NU* **42** A4
Bide Arm *NL* **38** C4
Bide Arm *NL* **39** E8
Bideford *PE* **32** A8
Bideford *PE* **34** B1
Bideford *PE* **35** C2
Bield *MB* **11** D8
Bield *MB* **13** D1
Biencourt *QC* **29** D2-3
Biencourt *QC* **31** A1
Bienfait *SK* **11** F6-7
Bienville, lac *QC* **40** D5
Big Bald Mountain *NB* **29** F6
Big Bald Mountain *NB* **31** C5
Big Bar Creek *BC* **1** D7
Big Bar Lake PP *BC* **1** D7-8
Big Bay *ON* **18** E5-6
Big Bay *BC* **2** B2
Big Bay *ON* **18** E5
Big Bay *ON* **21** E5
Big Bay Point *ON* **18** E5
Big Bay Point *ON* **20** A-B7
Big Bay Point *ON* **21** D1
Big Beaver *SK* **11** F5
Big Bend CA *ON* **19** D4
Big Bend CA *ON* **20** F3
Big Bight *NL* **39** A6
Big Birch Island *MB* **13** D3
Big Birch Island *MB* **14** C3
Big Black River *MB* **13** B8
Big Blue Hill Pond *NL* **36** D7
Big Blue Hill Pond *NL* **37** D5

Big Bras d'Or *NS* **34** C7
Big Brook *NL* **38** A4
Big Brook *NL* **39** D8
Big Bunsby MPP *BC* **1** E4
Big Burnt Island *ON* **18** B4
Big C *SK* **9** D8
Big C *SK* **12** D3
Big Campbell Creek *YT* **4** D6
Big Canyon Lake *ON* **16** D2
Big Caribou Lake *ON* **18** B7
Big Cedar *ON* **21** D3
Big Chute *ON* **18** E8
Big Cove *NB* **31** E8
Big Cove *NB* **32** A6
Big Creek *BC* **1** D1
Big Creek *BC* **1** D7
Big Creek *ON* **19** C-D6
Big Creek *ON* **19** C6
Big Creek *ON* **20** E-F5
Big Creek *YT* **4** C3
Big Creek Marsh *ON* **19** D6
Big Creek Marsh *ON* **20** F5
Big Creek NWA *ON* **19** D6
Big Creek NWA *ON* **20** F5
Big Creek Territorial Recreation Site *YT* **3** A3
Big Creek Territorial Recreation Site *YT* **4** E6-7
Big Crow Lake *ON* **22** E3
Big East River *ON* **21** A2
Big East River *ON* **22** F1-2
Big East River PP *ON* **21** A2
Big Falls *NL* **36** A4
Big Falls *NL* **37** A2
Big Falls *NL* **38** F3
Big Fish River *YT* **5** C3-4
Big Flat Lake *MB* **12** B-C8
Big Flat Lake *MB* **15** C2
Big Forks Brook *NB* **31** E6
Big Forks Brook *NB* **32** A4-5
Big Glace Bay Lake NMBS *NS* **34** C8
Big Grassy River *ON* **13** F6
Big Grassy River *ON* **16** E1-2
Big Gull Lake *ON* **21** C6
Big Harbour *NS* **34** C7
Big Harbour Island *NS* **34** D6
Bighead *SK* **6** A8
Bighead *SK* **9** F8
Bighead *SK* **11** A2-3
Bighead *SK* **12** F2-3
Bighead River *ON* **18** F6
Bighead River *ON* **20** A4-5
Big Hill *NS* **34** C7
Big Hill Springs PP *AB* **6** D5
Big Hill Springs PP *AB* **7** B3
Bighorn Wildland PRA *AB* **6** C4
Big Island *MB* **12** E-F7
Big Island *MB* **15** E1-2 F1-2
Big Island *NT* **10** E5
Big Island *NU* **40** B5
Big Island *NU* **41** D8
Big Island *ON* **13** F5
Big Island *ON* **14** F8
Big Island *ON* **16** E1
Big Island *ON* **18** A3
Big Jolicure, lac *NB* **35** F1
Big Jolicure Lake *NB* **35** F1
Big Kalzas Lake *YT* **4** B4
Big Knife PP *AB* **6** C6-7
Big Knife PP *AB* **8** E8
Big Knife PP *AB* **11** B-C1
Big LaHave Lake *NS* **32** F6
Big LaHave Lake *NS* **33** C5
Big Lake *AB* **6** B7
Big Lake *AB* **11** B1
Big Lake *NT* **10** B3
Big Lake *NT* **10** D5
Big Lake *ON* **13** D7
Big Lake *ON* **16** D6
Big Lake *ON* **17** F6
Big Lake *ON* **18** A3
Big Lake *SK* **11** B3
Big Lake *SK* **11** B3
Big Lake Ranch *BC* **1** C7-8
Big Marsh *SK* **34** D4-5
Big Mink Lake *ON* **21** B3
Big Molly Upsim Lake *NS* **32** F6
Big Molly Upsim Lake *NS* **33** C3
Big Moon Lake *ON* **18** A2
Big Mossy Point *MB* **13** A3
Big Muddy Badlands *SK* **11** F5
Big Muddy Lake *SK* **11** F5
Big Narrows Island *NS* **34** E8
Big Otter Creek *ON* **19** C-D5
Big Otter Creek *ON* **20** F4
Big Point *PE* **35** F5
Big Pond *NL* **37** E7
Big Pond *NS* **34** D7
Big Prairie *AB* **9** B5
Big Quill Lake *SK* **11** C5-6
Big Rideau Lake *ON* **21** C7
Big Rideau Lake *ON* **24** F1
Big River *NL* **39** A6
Big River *SK* **11** B4
Big River *SK* **11** A4
Big River (FN) *SK* **11** A-B4
Big Salmon *YT* **4** C3
Big Salmon Lake *YT* **4** D4-5
Big Salmon Range *YT* **4** D4 E4-5
Big Salmon River *NB* **32** D5
Big Salmon River *NB* **33** A2-3
Big Sand Lake *MB* **12** C8
Big Sand Lake *MB* **15** C2-3
Big Sand Lake *ON* **14** D8
Big Sandy Lake *SK* **11** A6

Big Sandy Lake *SK* **12** F6
Bigsby Island *ON* **13** F5
Bigsby Island *ON* **14** F8
Bigsby Island *ON* **16** E1
Big Shell *SK* **11** B4
Big Shell Lake *ON* **16** B1-2
Big Smith Creek *NT* **10** A2
Big Spruce River *MB* **15** A-B4
Big Stick Lake *SK* **9** D8
Big Stick Lake *SK* **11** E2
Big Stone *AB* **6** D7
Big Stone *AB* **7** B7
Bigstone *AB* **8** D6
Big Stone Lake *NT* **5** D5
Bigstone Lake *MB* **13** A5
Bigstone Lake *SK* **12** F5
Bigstone River *MB* **15** E5
Big Tancook Island *NS* **32** F7
Big Tancook Island *NS* **33** D5
Big Timber Creek *YT* **4** C5-6
Big Timothy Mountain *BC* **1** C8
Big Timothy Mountain *BC* **6** C1
Big Tracadie River *NB* **30** F1
Big Tracadie River *NB* **31** B-C7
Big Trout Lake *ON* **13** A8
Big Trout Lake *ON* **13** A8
Big Trout Lake *ON* **21** A2
Big Trout Lake *ON* **21** C2
Big Trout Lake *ON* **22** E-F2
Big Trout Lake *ON* **40** E1
Big Trout Lake *ON* **40** D1
Big Valley *AB* **6** C6
Big Valley *AB* **8** F7
Big Whiteshell Lake *MB* **13** E5
Big Whiteshell Lake *MB* **14** D7
Bigwood *ON* **17** F7
Bigwood *ON* **18** B6
Bijoux Falls PP *BC* **3** F7
Billings, Mount *YT* **4** D7
Billtown *NS* **32** E6
Billtown *NS* **33** B4
Billy Lake *NT* **5** B8
Binamé Lake *NT* **5** B8
Binbrook *ON* **19** C7
Binbrook *ON* **20** E6
Binbrook CA *ON* **19** C7
Binbrook CA *ON* **20** E6
Bindloss *AB* **6** D8
Bindloss *AB* **11** D2
Bingley *AB* **8** E5
Binscarth *MB* **11** E7-8
Binscarth *MB* **13** E1
Bircham *AB* **7** A5
Birch Bay *AB* **8** E6
Birch Cove *AB* **6** A5
Birch Cove *AB* **8** B5
Birch Grove *NS* **34** C8
Birch Head *NS* **35** F3
Birch Hill *PE* **35** C2
Birch Hills *SK* **11** B5
Birch Island *BC* **6** C-D2
Birch Island *MB* **11** C8
Birch Island *MB* **13** C2
Birch Island *NT* **10** A7
Birch Island *ON* **17** F6
Birch Island PP Reserve *MB* **11** C8
Birch Island PP Reserve *MB* **13** C2
Birch Lake *AB* **6** B7
Birch Lake *AB* **11** B1
Birch Lake *NT* **10** B3
Birch Lake *NT* **10** D5
Birch Lake *ON* **13** D7
Birch Lake *ON* **16** D6
Birch Lake *ON* **17** F6
Birch Lake *ON* **18** A3
Birch Lake *SK* **11** B3
Birch Lake *SK* **11** B3
Birch Mountains *AB* **9** C6
Birch Mountains *AB* **12** C1
Birch Mountains *AB* **12** C1
Birch Mountains Wildland *AB* **41** F1
Birch Mountains Wildland PP *AB* **9** C6
Birch Mountains Wildland PP *AB* **12** C1
Birch Point *ON* **21** D3
Birch Point PP *MB* **13** F5
Birch Point PP *MB* **14** F7
Birch Point PP *MB* **16** E1
Birch Portage *SK* **12** F6-7
Birch Portage *SK* **15** F1
Birch River *AB* **9** B-C5
Birch River *AB* **41** F1
Birch River *MB* **11** C8
Birch River *MB* **13** C1
Birchton *QC* **27** E5
Birchtown *NS* **33** F3
Birchy Bay *NL* **36** A7
Birchy Bay *NL* **38** F6
Birchy Head *NL* **36** A3
Birchy Head *NL* **37** A1
Birchy Head *NL* **38** F2
Birchy Lake *NL* **36** A4
Birchy Lake *NL* **37** A2
Birchy Lake *NL* **38** F4
Bird *MB* **15** D5
Bird Cove *NL* **38** B3
Bird Cove *NL* **39** E7-8
Birdinia *MB* **14** B-C2

Bird River *MB* **14** C7-8
Bird River *ON* **13** E5
Bird Rocks NMBS *QC* **30** E8
Bird's Hill *MB* **14** D5
Bird's Hill PP *MB* **13** E4
Bird's Hill PP *MB* **14** D5
Bird's Hill PP *MB* **14** D5
Bird's Point *SK* **11** E7
Birds Creek *ON* **21** B4
Birdtail *MB* **11** D-E8
Birdtail *MB* **13** D1
Birdtail Creek *MB* **11** D1
Birdtail Creek *MB* **13** D1
Birken *BC* **1** E7
Birken *BC* **2** B5
Birkenhead Lake PP *BC* **1** E7
Birkenhead Lake PP *BC* **2** B5
Birkenhead River *BC* **2** B5
Birmingham *SK* **11** D6
Birnie *MB* **13** E3
Birnie *MB* **14** C2
Birr *ON* **20** E3
Birsay *SK* **11** D4
Birtle *MB* **11** E8
Birtle *MB* **13** E1
Biscayan Cove *NL* **37** D8
Biscay Bay *NL* **37** F7
Biscay Bay *NL* **37** F7
Biscay Bay River *NL* **37** F7
Biscotasi Lake *ON* **17** E6
Biscotasi Lake PP *ON* **17** E5-6
Biscotasing *ON* **17** E6
Bishop River *BC* **1** D6
Bishop River *BC* **2** A3
Bishop River PP *BC* **1** D6
Bishop River PP *BC* **2** A3
Bishop's Falls *NL* **36** A6
Bishop's Falls *NL* **37** A4
Bishop's Falls *NL* **38** F5
Bishopsgate *ON* **19** C6
Bishopsgate *ON* **20** E5
Bishops Mills *ON* **21** C8
Bishops Mills *ON* **24** F2
Bishopton *QC* **27** E5
Bishopville *NS* **32** E7
Bishopville *NS* **33** B4-5
Bismarck *ON* **19** C8
Bismarck *ON* **20** E7
Bison Lake *AB* **9** D4
Bissett *MB* **13** D5
Bissett *MB* **14** B7
Bissett *MB* **16** B-C1
Bissett Creek *ON* **22** D-E3 D4
Bissett Creek *ON* **22** D3-4
Bissett Creek PP *ON* **22** E3
Bissett Lake *ON* **22** E3-4
Bistcho Lake *AB* **9** A3
Bistcho Lake *AB* **10** F5
Bitobi, lac *QC* **22** E7
Bitobi, lac *QC* **24** B2
Bitter Lake *SK* **6** E8
Bitter Lake *SK* **11** E2
Bittern Lake *AB* **6** B6
Bittern Lake *AB* **8** D7
Bittern Lake *AB* **8** D7
Bittern Lake *SK* **11** A5
Bittern Lake *SK* **11** A5
Bjorkdale *SK* **11** B6
Bjorne Peninsula *NU* **42** C4
Black, Mount *YT* **4** D4
Black Angus Creek *BC* **3** A4
Black Angus Creek *BC* **4** F7
Black Bank *ON* **20** B6
Black Bay *NL* **38** A4
Black Bay *ON* **16** F6
Black Bay *ON* **22** E5
Black Bay *SK* **9** A8
Black Bay *SK* **12** A3
Black Bay *SK* **12** E3
Black Bay Peninsula *ON* **16** F6
Black Bear Island Lake *SK* **12** E5
Black Bear Lake *ON* **13** A7
Black Bear River *NL* **39** B-C8
Blackbear River *NL* **13** A7-8
Black Birch Lake *NL* **16** A1
Black Birch Lake *SK* **12** D3-4
Blackburn *ON* **21** A8
Black Cape *QC* **29** D7
Black Cape *QC* **30** C3
Blackcomb Glacier PP *BC* **1** E7
Blackcomb Glacier PP *BC* **2** C5
Black Creek *BC* **1** E-F5
Black Creek *BC* **2** C2
Black Creek *ON* **19** B5
Black Creek *ON* **19** C3 D2
Black Creek *ON* **20** D4
Black Creek *ON* **20** F1-2
Black Creek *ON* **21** E5-6
Black Creek PP *ON* **18** F7
Blackdale *MB* **14** D5
Black Diamond *AB* **6** E5
Black Diamond *AB* **7** C4
Black Donald Lake *ON* **21** B6
Black Duck *NL* **36** B2
Black Duck Brook *NL* **36** B1-2
Black Duck Cove *NL* **36** F7
Black Duck Cove *NL* **37** F5
Black Duck Cove *NL* **38** B5

Black Duck Cove *NL* **39** D7-8
Black Duck Cove PP *NS* **34** E6
Black Duck River *ON* **13** B8
Black Duck River *AB* **40** D2
Blackfalds *AB* **6** C5-6
Blackfalds *AB* **8** E6
Blackfish Lake *MB* **12** A8
Blackfish Lake *MB* **15** A3
Blackfoot *AB* **6** B8
Blackfoot *AB* **11** B2
Blackhead *NL* **37** D8
Blackhead *NL* **37** D8
Blackhead Bay *NL* **37** B7
Blackheath *ON* **19** C7
Blackheath *ON* **20** E6
Blackie *AB* **6** E6
Blackie *AB* **7** C4
Black Island *MB* **13** D4
Black Island *MB* **14** C6
Black Island *NL* **39** A-B7
Black Lake *QC* **27** D5
Black Lake *SK* **12** A5
Black Lake *SK* **12** B5
Black Lake *SK* **41** F2-3
Black Lake *YT* **4** D6
Blackland *NB* **29** D6-7
Blackland *NB* **31** A6
Black Lichen Lake *NT* **10** D5
Black Point *NB* **29** D7
Black Point *NB* **31** A6
Black Point *NS* **32** F8
Black Point *NS* **33** C5
Black Point *PE* **35** E4
Black Point *SK* **9** D8
Black Point *SK* **11** E1
Black Pond, RNOM de *PE* **34** C4-5
Black Pond, RNOM de *PE* **35** D-E8
Black Pond NMBS *PE* **34** C4-5
Black Pond NMBS *PE* **35** D-E8
Blackpool *BC* **6** C-D1
Black River *MB* **13** D5
Black River *MB* **14** C7
Black River *MB* **14** B-C6
Black River *NB* **31** D7
Black River *NB* **32** D4
Black River *NB* **33** B2
Black River *NS* **32** E7
Black River *NS* **33** B4
Black River *NS* **34** C5-6
Black River *ON* **16** E-F8
Black River *ON* **17** C2
Black River *ON* **21** C5
Black River *ON* **21** E1
Black River *YT* **4** D6
Black River Lake *SK* **32** E7
Black River Lake *SK* **33** B4
Black River Pond *NL* **36** C-D8
Black River Pond *NL* **37** C-D6
Black River PPA *NB* **31** D7
Black Rock *NS* **33** A6
Black Rock *NS* **34** E2
Blacks Corners *ON* **21** B7
Blacks Corners *ON* **24** E1
Blacks Harbour *NB* **32** E3
Blackstock *ON* **20** B8
Blackstock *ON* **21** E2
Blackstone Lake *ON* **16** C4
Blackstone Lake *ON* **18** D7
Blackstone River *NT* **10** E3
Blackstone TP *NT* **10** E2-3
Blackstrap PP *SK* **11** C-D4
Black Sturgeon *MB* **15** D2
Black Sturgeon Lake *ON* **16** E6
Black Sturgeon River *ON* **16** E6
Black Sturgeon River PP *ON* **16** E6
Black Tickle *NL* **39** D6
Blackville *NB* **31** E6
Blackville *NB* **32** A4
Blackwater *ON* **20** B7-8
Blackwater *ON* **21** E2
Blackwater Lake *NT* **10** B2
Blackwater Mountain *BC* **6** D3
Blackwater River *NT* **10** B2-3
Bladworth *SK* **11** D4-5
Blaine Lake *SK* **11** B4
Blaine Lakes *SK* **11** B4
Blainville *QC* **24** D5
Blainville *QC* **27** E1
Blair *ON* **19** B6
Blair *ON* **20** D5
Blairmore *AB* **6** F5
Blairmore *AB* **7** E3
Blairton *ON* **21** D3
Blakeney *ON* **21** B7
Blaketown *NL* **37** E7
Blanc, lac *QC* **30** C3
Blanc, lac *QC* **29** A4-5
Blanc, mont *QC* **29** B5-6
Blanc, réservoir *QC* **25** B-C7
Blanc, réservoir *QC* **28** E2

Blanchard Road *NS* **33** A8
Blanchard Road *NS* **34** E4
Blanche *NS* **33** F3
Blanche **22** F8
Blanche *QC* **24** C3
Blanche, lac la *QC* **24** C3
Blanche, rivière *QC* **24** A8
Blanche, rivière *QC* **24** B8
Blanche, rivière *QC* **25** E8
Blanche, rivière *QC* **27** B4
Blanche, rivière *QC* **27** C4
Blanche River *ON* **23** E1
Blanchet Island *NT* **10** D7
Blanc-Sablon *QC* **38** A3
Blanc-Sablon *QC* **39** D7-8
Blanc-Sablon *QC* **40** E8
Blandford *NS* **32** F7-8
Blandford *NS* **33** D5
Blanket Creek PP *BC* **6** D-E3
Blatchford Lake *NT* **10** D7
Blavet, lac *QC* **23** B7
Blavet, lac *QC* **25** B1
Bleuets, rivière aux *QC* **29** E2
Bleuets, rivière aux *QC* **25** B-C3
Blevins Lake *MB* **12** A8
Blevins Lake *MB* **15** A3
Blezard Valley *ON* **17** F6
Bligh Island PP *BC* **1** F4-5
Blind Bay *BC* **6** D2
Blind Bay *MB* **14** A-B5
Blind Bay PP *NS* **32** F8
Blind Bay PP *NS* **33** C5
Blind Channel *BC* **1** E5
Blind Channel *BC* **2** B1-2
Blind Creek *YT* **4** C5
Blind River *ON* **17** F5
Blind River *ON* **18** A2
Blind River *ON* **18** B2
Blissfield *NB* **31** E6
Blissfield *NB* **32** A4
Bliss Landing *BC* **1** E6
Bliss Landing *BC* **2** C2-3
Blissville *NB* **32** D3
Blockhaus-de-Merrickville, LHN du *ON* **21** C7-8
Blockhaus-de-Merrickville, LHN du *ON* **24** F1-2
Blockhaus-de-St. Andrews, LHN du *NB* **32** E2
Blockhouse *NS* **33** D4
Bloedel *BC* **1** E5
Bloedel *BC* **2** C2
Blomidon *NS* **32** D7
Blomidon *NS* **33** B4
Blomidon PP *NS* **32** D7
Blomidon PP *NS* **33** A4-5
Blood Indian Creek *AB* **6** D7
Blood Indian Creek *AB* **7** B7
Blood Indian Creek *AB* **11** D1
Bloodsucker Lake *MB* **15** C3-4
Bloodsucker Lake *SK* **11** A6-7
Bloodvein *MB* **13** D4
Bloodvein *MB* **14** A5-6
Bloodvein River *MB* **13** D4-5
Bloodvein River *MB* **14** A6-7
Bloodvein River *MB* **16** B1
Bloody Falls (Kuklok) TP *NU* **41** B6
Bloody Falls (Kuklok) TP *NU* **42** F1
Bloomfield *NB* **31** F2-3
Bloomfield *NB* **32** B1
Bloomfield *NB* **32** D4-5
Bloomfield *NB* **33** A2
Bloomfield *NL* **36** C6
Bloomfield *NL* **37** C4
Bloomfield *ON* **21** E5
Bloomfield *PE* **35** D3
Bloomfield Corner *PE* **35** B1-2
Bloomfield PP *PE* **35** B1
Bloomfield Ridge *NB* **31** E5
Bloomfield Ridge *NB* **32** A3
Bloomingdale *ON* **19** B6
Bloomingdale *ON* **20** D5
Blooming Point *PE* **35** D4
Bloomington *NS* **32** E6
Bloomington *NS* **33** C3
Bloomsbury *AB* **8** B5
Blossom Park *ON* **21** B8
Blossom Park *ON* **24** D2
Blouin, lac *QC* **23** E5
Blow Me Down PP *NL* **36** B2
Blow Me Down PP *NL* **38** F1
Blow River *YT* **5** B3
Blubber Bay *BC* **1** E-F6
Blubber Bay *BC* **2** C2
Blue, Cape *NS* **34** D7
Blueberry Mountain *AB* **9** E2
Blueberry River *BC* **3** D7-8
Blueberry River *BC* **9** D1
Blue Cove *NL* **38** B3
Blue Earth Lake PP *BC* **1** E8
Blue Earth Lake PP *BC* **2** B7
Bluefish River *NT* **5** C2-3
Bluefish River *YT* **5** C-D2
Blue Hills of Couteau *NL* **36** D3
Blue Hills of Couteau *NL* **37** D1

Blue Island *SK* **12** B6
Blue Jay Creek *ON* **18** C3
Blue Jay Creek PP *ON* **18** C3
Blue Lake PP *ON* **13** E6
Blue Lake PP *ON* **16** D2
Blue Mountain *NB* **29** E7
Blue Mountain *NL* **38** D3
Blue Mountain *NS* **33** A8
Blue Mountain *NS* **34** E4
Bluenose Lake *NT* **41** B1
Bluenose Lake *NU* **42** F1
Blue Point *ON* **19** C3
Blue Point *ON* **20** D3
Blue Ridge *AB* **6** A4-5
Blue Ridge *AB* **8** B4
Blue River *BC* **3** A3
Blue River *BC* **4** F6
Blue River *BC* **6** C2
Blue River Black Spruce PP *BC* **6** C2
Blue River Pine PP *BC* **6** C2
Blue Rocks *NS* **33** D5
Blue Sea *QC* **22** E7
Blue Sea *QC* **24** B1
Blue Sea, lac *QC* **22** E7
Blue Sea, lac *QC* **25** F1-2
Bluesky *AB* **9** E3
Blues Mills *NS* **34** D6
Bluets, rivière aux *QC* **27** D6
Bluevale *ON* **19** A4-5
Bluevale *ON* **20** C3-4
Bluewater *ON* **19** B4
Bluewater *ON* **20** D3
Bluewater Beach *ON* **18** F7
Bluewater Beach *ON* **20** A6
Bluff, Cape *NL* **39** C8
Bluff Creek *MB* **14** D2
Bluff Head *NL* **36** B2
Bluff Head Cove *NL* **39** A7
Bluff Point *ON* **19** D7
Bluff Point *ON* **20** F6
Bluffton *AB* **6** B5
Blumenfeld *MB* **13** F3
Blumenfeld *MB* **14** F4
Blumenheim *SK* **11** C4
Blumenhof *SK* **11** E3-4
Blumenort *MB* **13** F4
Blumenort *MB* **14** E5-6
Blumenthal *SK* **11** C4
Blunt Mountain *NS* **3** F4
Blyth *ON* **19** A4
Blyth *ON* **20** C3
Blyth Brook *ON* **19** A4
Blyth Brook *ON* **20** C3
Blytheswood *ON* **19** E2
Boat Harbour *NL* **36** E7
Boat Harbour *NL* **37** E5
Boat Harbour *NL* **38** A4-5
Boat Harbour *NL* **39** D8
Boat Lake *ON* **18** F5
Boat Lake *ON* **20** A4
Bobby Cove *NL* **38** E5
Bobcaygeon *ON* **21** D2-3
Bob Creek Wildland PP *AB* **6** E5
Bob Creek Wildland PP *AB* **7** D3-4 E3-4
Bob-Grant, lac *QC* **25** B-C6
Bob-Grant, lac *QC* **26** F6
Bobinec *QC* **22** B3-4
Bobinet, lac *QC* **21** C2
Bob Quinn Lake *BC* **3** D3
Bobs Lake *ON* **21** C6
Bobtail Mountain *BC* **1** B6
Bocabec *NB* **32** E2
Bocock Peak PP *BC* **3** F4
Bodin *SK* **11** A4
Bodo *AB* **6** C8
Bodo *AB* **11** C2
Boggy Creek *MB* **11** D7
Boggy Creek *MB* **13** C-D1
Bognor *ON* **18** F6
Bognor *ON* **20** A5
Boharm *SK* **11** E5
Bohier, lac *QC* **39** E5
Bohn Lake *AB* **9** F7
Bohn Lake *AB* **12** F1
Boiestown *NB* **31** E5
Boiestown *NB* **32** A3
Boileau *QC* **24** C4
Boileau *QC* **28** D6
Bois, lac des *NT* **5** D8
Bois, lac des *NT* **13** F5
Bois, lac des *NT* **14** F8
Bois, lac des *NT* **16** E1
Bois, lac des *QC* **22** A2
Bois-Blanc *QC* **22** D7-8
Bois-Blanc *QC* **24** A2
Bois-Blanc *QC* **25** F2
Bois-Blanc Island Lighthouse NHS *ON* **19** E1
Boisbriand *QC* **24** D5
Boisbriand *QC* **27** E1
Bois Brûlé, cap du *QC* **30** C3
Boischatel *QC* **27** A5-6
Boisdale *NS* **34** C7
Bois-des-Filion *QC* **24** D6
Bois-des-Filion *QC* **27** E1
Bois-Franc *QC* **22** D7-8
Bois-Franc *QC* **24** A2
Bois-Franc *QC* **25** F2
Bois-Gagnon *NB* **31** B7

Boishébert, LHN NB
　31 D5-6
Boishébert NHS NB 31 D5-6
Bois Island NL　36 D6
Bois Island NL　37 D4
Boissevain MB　11 F8
Boissevain MB　13 F2
Boissevain MB　14 F1
Boisvert, lac QC　26 B5
Boisvert, pointe à QC 29 B2
Boiteuse, lac de la QC
　28 B5-6
Boland Brook NB　29 E5
Bolingbroke ON　21 C6-7
Bolney SK　11 B3
Bolsover ON　20 A7-8
Bolsover ON　21 D2
Bolton ON　19 A7-8
Bolton ON　20 C6
Bolton Centre QC　24 E8
Bolton Centre QC　27 F4
Bolton Creek ON　21 C6
Bolton Lake NB　13 A5
Bolton Lake MB　29 E5
Bolton-Ouest QC　24 E8
Bolton-Ouest QC　27 F3-4
Bolton River MB　13 A4-5
Bompas Lake SK　12 A5
Bon Accord AB　6 A5-6
Bon Accord AB　8 B6
Bon Accord AB　31 E3
Bon Accord NB　32 A1
Bonanza AB　3 E8
Bonanza AB　9 E2
Bonaparte Lake AB　1 D8
Bonaparte Lake BC　6 D1
Bonaparte AB　1 D8
Bonaparte PP BC　6 D1
Bonaparte River BC　1 D8
Bonaparte River BC　2 A7
Bonaparte River BC　6 D1
Bonar AB　1 D8
Bonarlaw ON　21 D4-5
Bonaventure QC　29 D8
Bonaventure QC　30 D1
Bonaventure QC　31 A7
Bonaventure, île QC　30 C3
Bonaventure, pointe QC
　29 D8
Bonaventure, pointe QC
　30 D1
Bonaventure, pointe QC
　31 A6-7
Bonaventure, rivière QC
　29 B-C8
Bonaventure, rivière QC
　30 C1
Bonaventure, rivière QC
　31 A6-7
Bonaventure-et-du-Rocher-
　Percé, parc QC　30 C3
Bonaventure Ouest, rivière
　QC　29 B-C8
Bonavista NL　37 B7
Bonavista, baie de NL
　37 B7
Bonavista, Cape NL　37 B7
Bonavista Bay NL　37 B7
Bonavista Peninsula NL
　37 C6-7
Bon-Désir, cap de QC 29 C1
Bond Head ON　20 B6
Bond Head ON　21 F3
Bondiss AB　6 A6
Bondiss AB　8 A7
Bondiss AB　9 F6
Bondiss AB　12 F1
Bond Sound BC　1 D5
Bond Sound BC　2 A1
Bondy, lac QC　22 B8
Bondy, lac QC　25 D2
Bon Echo PP ON　21 C5
Bonfield ON　17 F8
Bonfield ON　22 D2
Bongard, lac QC　23 D8
Bongard, lac QC　25 A2
Bongard, lac QC　26 E2
Bonheur River Kame, RNP
　ON　16 E4
Bonheur River Kame PNR
　ON　13 F8
Bonheur River Kame PNR
　ON　16 E4
Bonilla Island BC　1 B2
Bonin, lac QC　25 A6
Bonin, lac QC　26 F6
Bonin, lac QC　28 C1
Bonjour, rivière QC 29 B5-6
Bonne Bay NL　38 E2
Bonne Bay Big Pond NL
　36 A3
Bonne Bay Big Pond NL
　37 A1
Bonne Bay Big Pond NL
　38 F2
Bonnechere ON　21 A4
Bonnechere ON　22 F4
Bonnechere PP ON　21 A4
Bonnechere PP ON 22 F4-5
Bonnechere River ON
　21 A6
Bonnechere River ON
　22 F5-6
Bonnechere River PP ON
　22 F4
Bonnechere Valley ON
　21 A5
Bonne-Espérance QC 39 D7
Bonnet Plume Range YT
　4 A5
Bonnet Plume River YT
　5 F4-5

Bonnie Doone ON　19 C3
Bonnie Doone ON　20 E2
Bonny River NB　32 E2
Bonnyville AB　9 F7
Bonnyville AB　11 A2
Bonnyville AB　12 F1
Bonokoski Lake SK　12 A6
Bonokoski Lake SK　15 A1
Bonsecours QC　24 D8
Bonsecours QC　27 E4
Bon Secours Beach NB
　20 B7
Bon Secours Beach NB
　21 D1
Bonshaw PE　34 C2
Bonshaw PE　35 E4
Bonshaw PP PE　34 C2
Bonshaw PP PE　35 E4
Bonville ON　24 E4
Boom Creek ON　22 D3
Booth, lac QC　22 C3
Boothia, golfe de NU
　41 A-B5
Boothia, golfe de NU
　42 E-F4
Boothia, Gulf of NU
　41 A-B5
Boothia, Gulf of NU 42 E-F4
Boothia, péninsule de NU
　41 B4-5
Boothia, péninsule de NU
　42 F4
Boothia Peninsula NU
　41 B4-5
Boothia Peninsula NU
　42 F4
Booth Island NT　5 A7-8
Booth Islands NT　5 A7-8
Booth Lake MB　12 A8
Booth Lake MB　15 A3
Booth Lake ON　21 A3
Booth Lake ON　22 F3
Boot Island National
　Wilderness Area NS
　32 E7
Boot Island National
　Wilderness Area NS
　33 B5
Borden PE　35 E3
Borden SK　11 C4
Borden-Carleton PE　32 B8
Borden-Carleton PE　34 C1
Borden Island AB　42 B3
Borden Lake ON　17 D5
Borden Peninsula NU 41 A6
Borden Peninsula NU
　42 E5
Border Lake PP AB　3 D2-3
Border Ranges AB　6 F5
Border Ranges AB　7 F3
Bornholm ON　19 B5
Bornholm ON　20 D4
Borups Corners AB　13 F7
Borups Corners ON
　16 D-E3
Boston ON　19 C6
Boston ON　20 E5
Boston Bar BC　1 E8
Boston Bar BC　2 C7
Boston Creek ON　17 D7
Boston Creek ON　19 C6-7
Boston Creek ON　20 E5-6
Boston Creek ON　23 E1
Bostonnais, rivière QC
　25 B-C8
Bostonnais, rivière QC
　28 D4 E3
Boswarlos NL　36 B2
Boswell BC　6 F4
Boswell River YT　4 D4
Bosworth Lake ON　16 A6
Botha AB　6 C6
Botha AB　8 F8
Bothwell ON　19 D3
Bothwell ON　20 F2
Bothwell PE　35 D8
Bothwell's Corners ON
　18 F5-6
Bothwell's Corners ON
　20 A4-5
Botsford Portage NB
　35 E1-2
Bottle Cove NL　36 A2
Bottle Cove NL　38 F1
Bottle Point ON　16 F7
Bottle Point ON　17 C2
Bottrell AB　6 D5
Bottrell AB　7 A-B3
Botwood NL　36 A6
Botwood NL　37 A4
Botwood NL　38 F5
Boucher QC　25 D-E7
Boucher QC　27 A3
Boucher, lac QC　25 C6-7
Boucher, lac QC　27 A3
Boucher, lac QC　39 E6
Boucher, rivière QC 29 A2
Boucherville QC　24 D6
Boucherville QC　27 E2
Bouchette QC　22 F7-8
Bouchette QC　24 B2
Bouchette QC　35 F2
Bouchette, lac QC　22 A6
Bouchette, lac QC　23 F6
Bouchette, lac QC　25 A8
Bouchette, lac QC　25 C1
Bouchette, lac QC　26 F8
Bouchette, lac QC　28 C4
Bouchie Lake BC　1 B7
Bouctouche NB　31 E8
Bouctouche NB　32 A6

Bouctouche, dune de NB
　31 E8
Bouctouche, dune de NB
　32 A6
Boudreau NB　35 E1
Bouffard, lac QC　39 E1
Boughey Bay BC　2 B1
Boughton Bay PE　34 C4
Boughton Island PE　34 C4
Boughton Island PE　35 E7
Boughton Island PE　34 C4
Boughton Island PE　35 E7
Boughton Point PE　35 E7
Boughton River PE　35 E7
Boulain, lac QC　39 E5
Boulardie NS　34 C7
Boulardie Island NS
　34 B-C7
Boulder Creek PP BC　3 F4
Boulder Lake NT　10 B7
Bouleau, rivière au QC
　39 E3
Boullé, rivière QC　25 D-E5
Boulogne Lake NT　10 E6
Boulter ON　21 B4
Boundary Bay BC　1 F7
Boundary Bay BC　2 E5
Boundary Bay BC　2 E5
Boundary Creek PP BC　6 F2
Boundary Dam SK　11 F5
Boundary Dam SK　12 C7
Boundary Island SK　15 C1
Bounty SK　11 D4
Bourbeau, lac QC　26 A5
Bourbon, rivière QC
　27 C4-5
Bourdon, lac QC　39 A3
Bourgat, lac QC　26 B6
Bourgeois NB　35 D1
Bourgeois Mills NB　32 B7
Bourgeois Mills NB　35 E1
Bourget ON　24 D3
Bourgmont, lac QC　23 E8
Bourgmont, lac QC　25 A2
Bourgmont, lac QC　26 F2
Bourkes ON　17 D7
Bournemouth SK　11 B5
Bousso River NT　10 B-C6
Bouteille, lac de la QC
　24 A4
Bouteille, lac de la QC
　25 E6
Bouteille, lac de la QC
　27 B1
Bouteroute, lac QC　26 C5
Boutiliers Point NS 32 F7-8
Boutiliers Point NS　33 C5
Bow City AB　7 C6
Bowden AB　6 D5
Bowden AB　8 F5-6
Bowell AB　7 D8
Bowen Island BC　1 F7
Bowen Island BC　2 D4
Bowen Island BC　2 D4
Bowers Beach ON　18 F7
Bowers Beach ON　20 A6
Bowes Point NU　41 C4
Bowes Point NU　42 F3
Bowie Lake BC　1 B8
Bow Island BC　6 E7
Bow Island AB　7 E7
Bow Island AB　11 E1
Bowland's Bay ON　17 F7
Bowman QC　22 E-F8
Bowman QC　24 C2
Bowman Bay NU　40 A4-5
Bowman Bay NU　41 C7-8
Bowmanton AB　7 D8
Bowmanville ON　20 C8
Bowmanville ON　21 F2
Bowmanville Creek ON
　20 C8
Bowmanville Creek ON
　21 E2
Bowman Lake BC　1 B8
Bowron Lake BC　6 B1
Bowron Lake PP BC　1 B8
Bowron Lake PP BC　6 B1
Bowron River BC　1 A7 B8
Bowron River BC　6 A-B1
Bowser BC　1 F6
Bowser BC　2 D3
Bowser Lake BC　3 D-E3
Box Lake NT　10 B8
Box Lake SK　12 A4
Boya Lake PP BC　3 A-B4
Boya Lake PP BC　4 F7
Boyd AB　15 E4
Boyd's Cove NL　36 A7
Boyd's Cove NL　37 A5
Boyd's Cove NL　38 F6
Boyer AB　9 B4
Boyer, rivière QC　27 B6
Boyer River AB　9 B3-4
Boyle AB　6 A6
Boyle AB　8 A7
Boyle AB　9 F6

Boyle ON　19 C8
Boyle ON　20 E7
Boyle Point PP BC　2 D3
Boylston SK　34 E5-6
Boylston PP NS　34 E5
Boyne Lake AB　8 A-B8
Boyne Lake AB　11 A1
Boyne Lake AB　12 F1
Boyne River ON　20 B6
Boyne Valley PP ON
　20 B5-6
Brabant Lake SK　12 E6
Brabant Lake SK　12 E6
Bracebridge ON　21 B1-2
Bracebridge ON　21 C1-2
Bracken SK　11 F3
Brackendale BC　1 F7
Brackendale BC　2 C4-5
Brackendale BC　2 C4-5
Brackendale Eagles PP BC
　2 C4-5
Bracken Lake MB　11 A8
Bracken Lake MB　13 A2
Brackett Lake NT　5 F8
Brackett Lake NT　10 A2
Brackley PE　34 C2
Brackley PE　35 E5
Brackley Beach PE　34 C2
Brackley Beach PE　35 D4
Braddock SK　11 F3
Bradford ON　20 B6-7
Bradford ON　21 E1
Bradford West Gwillimbury
　ON　20 B6-7
Bradford West Gwillimbury
　ON　21 E1
Bradian AB　2 A5
Bradleys Cove NL　37 D7-8
Bradner BC　2 E6
Brador QC　38 A3
Brador QC　39 D7
Brador Bay NMBS QC 38 B3
Brador Bay NMBS QC
　39 D-E7
Bradshaw Lake MB　15 C5
Bradwardine MB　11 E8
Bradwardine MB　13 E1-2
Bradwardine MB　14 D1
Bradwell SK　11 C4
Brae Harbour PE　35 C1-2
Braeside ON　21 A6-7
Braeside ON　24 D1
Bragg Creek AB　6 D5
Bragg Creek AB　7 B3
Bragg Creek PP AB　6 D5
Bragg Creek PP AB　7 B3
Bralorne BC　1 E7
Bralorne BC　2 A5
Bramalea ON　19 A7
Bramalea ON　20 C6
Bramber NS　32 E7
Bramber NS　33 B5
Bramber NS　34 F1
Bramham Island BC　1 D4
Brampton ON　19 A7
Brampton ON　20 C6
Brancepeth SK　11 B5
Branch NL　36 B8
Branch NL　37 F6
Branchton ON　19 B6-7
Branchton ON　20 D5
Brandon MB　11 E8
Brandon MB　13 E2
Brandon MB　14 E1
Brandon Hills MB　14 E1
Brandywine Falls PP BC
　1 E6-7
Brandywine Falls PP BC
　2 C5
Brant AB　6 E6
Brant AB　7 C4
Brant CA ON　19 C6
Brant CA ON　20 E5
Brant County ON　19 C6
Brant County ON　20 E5
Brantford ON　19 C6
Brantford ON　20 E5
Branton-Cundick, parc ON
　19 D2-3
Branton-Cundick, parc ON
　20 F1-2
Branton-Cundick Park
　(St. Clair Parkway) ON
　19 D2-3
Branton-Cundick Park
　(St. Clair Parkway) ON
　20 F1-2
Brantville NB　30 F2
Brantville NB　31 C8
Bras, rivière le QC　27 B6
Brigham QC　24 E7
Bras Coupé, lac du QC
　22 D7
Bras Coupé, lac du QC
　24 A1
Bras Coupé, lac du QC
　25 E1
Bras-Coupe-Désert, ZEC QC
　22 D7
Bras-Coupe-Désert, ZEC QC
　24 A1
Bras-Coupe-Désert, ZEC QC
　25 E-F1
Bras d'Apic QC　27 A7-8
Bras d'Henri, rivière QC
　27 B5-6
Bras-d'Or, lac NS　34 D6-7
Bras d'Or Lake NT　10 D6
Bras d'Or PP NS　34 D7
Bray Island NU　41 B7

Bray Island NU　42 F6
Bray Lake ON　18 B8
Bray Lake ON　22 E1
Brazeau, Mount AB　6 C3
Brazeau, Mount AB　8 E2
Brazeau Canyon Wildland
　PP AB　6 B3-4
Brazeau Canyon Wildland
　PP AB　8 D-E2
Brazeau Dam AB　8 D4
Brazeau Reservoir AB　6 B4
Brazeau Reservoir AB　8 D4
Brazeau River AB　6 B4
Brazeau River AB　8 D-E3
Brazza QC　28 A7
Breadalbane PE　32 A8
Breadalbane PE　34 C2
Breadalbane PE　35 D3-4
Breakeyville QC　27 B6
Breau-Village NB　31 E8
Breau-Village NB　32 A-B6
Brébeuf QC　24 C4
Brébeuf, lac QC　28 D7
Brechin ON　20 A7-8
Brechin ON　21 D2
Breckenridge QC　24 D2
Breckinridge QC　21 A7-8
Brécourt, lac QC　23 D8
Brécourt, lac QC　25 A2-3
Brécourt, lac QC　26 F2-3
Bredenbury SK　11 D7
Bredenbury SK　13 D1
Breeches, lac QC　27 D5
Bréhault, lac QC　25 D6
Bréhault, lac QC　27 A1
Bréhault, lac QC　28 F1
Breme, Point QC　36 B8
Breme, Point QC　37 F6
Brennan Lake ON　16 C5
Brent ON　22 B3
Brent Cove NL　36 D5
Brent Cove NL　38 E5
Brenton NS　33 E1
Brent's Cove NL　38 E5
Brentwood ON　20 B6
Brésaylor SK　11 B3
Breslau ON　19 B6
Breslau ON　20 D5
Breslayor SK　6 B8
Bressani, lac QC　25 D3
Brest NB　31 E8
Brest NB　32 A6
Breton AB　6 B5
Breton AB　8 D5
Breton, Cape NS　34 C8
Bretona AB　8 C6
Brett, Mount AB　6 D4
Brett, Mount AB　7 B1
Brevoort Island NU　40 A6
Brew, Mount BC　1 E7-8
Brew, Mount BC　2 B6
Brewer SK　11 D7
Breynat QC　9 F6
Breynat AB　12 E1
Brick, rivière du QC　30 A4
Brickley ON　21 E4
Briçonnet, lac QC　39 D6
Bridal Veil Falls PP BC　1 F8
Bridal Veil Falls PP BC　2 E7
Bridesville BC　6 F2
Bridgar NB　15 E4
Bridge Creek BC　1 D8
Bridge Creek BC　6 C1
Bridgeford SK　11 D4
Bridge Lake BC　1 D8
Bridge Lake BC　6 D1
Bridge Lake PP BC　1 D8
Bridge Lake PP BC　6 C-D1
Bridgenorth ON　21 D3
Bridgeport NL　38 E6
Bridgeport ON　20 D5
Bridge River BC　1 D-E7
Bridge River BC　2 A4
Bridge River BC　2 A6
Bridgetown NS　32 E5
Bridgetown NS　33 C3
Bridgetown PE　34 C3
Bridgetown PE　35 E6-7
Bridgeville NS　33 A7
Bridgeville NS　34 E3
Bridgeville NS　30 C3
Bridgewater NS　33 D4
Briercrest SK　11 E5
Briereville AB　8 A8
Brier Island NS　33 D2
Brierly Brook NS　34 D-E4
Brig Bay NL　38 B3
Brigden ON　19 C2-3
Brigden ON　20 F1-2
Brigham QC　27 F3
Bright ON　19 B6
Bright ON　20 D5
Brightbank AB　8 C5-6
Bright Lake ON　18 A1
Brighton NL　38 E5
Brighton NS　32 F4
Brighton NS　33 C2
Brighton ON　21 E4
Brightsand Lake SK　6 A8
Brightsand Lake SK
　11 A-B3
Brightsand River PP ON
　16 D4-5 E4
Brights Grove ON　19 C2-3
Brights Grove ON　20 E1-2
Brightside ON　21 B6-7
Brightstone MB　14 D6
Brightwater Lake SK
　11 C-D4
Brigus NL　37 D7

Brigus Junction NL　37 E7
Brigus South NL　37 E8
Bringadin, lac QC　39 A2
Brinston ON　24 F2-3
Brion, île QC　30 E8
Brisbane ON　19 A7
Brisbane ON　20 C6
Brisay QC　40 E5
Brisco BC　6 D4
Brisco BC　7 C1
Bristol MB　14 E5
Bristol NB　31 E3
Bristol NB　32 A1
Bristol PE　35 D6
Bristol QC　21 A6-7
Bristol QC　22 F6
Bristol QC　24 D1
Bristol's Hope NL　37 D7-8
Britainville NL　18 C3
Britannia NL　37 C7
Britannia Beach BC　1 F7
Britannia Beach BC　2 D5
British Mountains YT　5 B2
Britt ON　18 C5
Britton ON　19 A5
Britton ON　20 C4
Britton Lake MB　12 F7
Britton Lake MB　15 E1
Broadacres SK　6 C8
Broadacres SK　11 C2-3
Broadback, rivière QC
　40 F4
Broad Cove NL　36 B2
Broad Cove NL　37 D7
Broad Cove NS　33 D4
Broad River NB　15 C6
Broad River NS　33 E3
Broad Valley MB　13 D3
Broad Valley MB　14 B4
Broadview SK　11 E7
Brochet, lac MB　12 B7
Brochet, lac MB　15 B2
Brochet, lac MB　41 F3
Brochet, lac du QC　26 C8
Brochet (Barren Lands) MB
　12 B7
Brochet (Barren Lands) MB
　15 C1-2
Brochet Bay MB　13 D3
Brochet Bay MB　15 C1-2
Brock SK　11 D3
Brocket AB　6 F6
Brocket AB　7 E4
Brock Island NT　42 C2
Brockton ON　20 B4
Brockton PE　35 B1
Brockville ON　21 D8
Brockville ON　24 F2
Brockway NB　32 D2
Broderick SK　11 D4
Brodeur Island ON　16 F6
Brodeur Island ON　17 C1
Brodeur Peninsula NU
　41 A5
Brodeur Peninsula NU
　42 E4-5
Brodhagen ON　19 A5
Brodhagen ON　20 D4
Brodtkorb, lac QC　22 D6
Brodtkorb, lac QC　24 A1
Brodtkorb, lac QC 25 E-F1
Brokenhead MB　13 E4
Brokenhead MB　14 D6
Broken Group Islands BC
　2 E2
Broken Skull River NT
　4 B-C7
Brome QC　27 F3
Brome, lac QC　24 E8
Brome, lac QC　27 F3
Bromhead SK　11 F6
Bromley Rock PP BC　6 F1
Bromont QC　24 E7
Bromont QC　27 F3
Brompton, lac QC　27 E4
Bromptonville QC　27 E4-5
Bronson Forest PRS ON
　6 A8
Bronson Forest PRS SK
　11 A2
Bronson Lake SK　6 A8
Bronson Lake SK　11 A2
Bronte ON　19 B7-8
Bronte ON　20 D5
Bronte Creek PP ON
　20 D6-7
Bronte Creek PP ON
　19 B7-8
Brooch, lac QC　39 E1
Brookdale MB　13 E2
Brookdale MB　14 D2
Brooke ON　20 A4
Brooke ON　18 F5
Brookdale AB　8 B6
Brookfield NL　38 F8
Brookfield NS　33 A6
Brookfield NS　34 F2
Brookfield PE　34 C2
Brookfield PE　35 D4
Brookhollow AB　8 B6
Brooklin ON　20 C8
Brooklin ON　21 E2
Brooklyn NB　35 F1
Brooklyn NS　36 C8
Brooklyn NL　37 C6
Brooklyn NS　32 E7-8
Brooklyn NS　33 B5
Brooklyn NS　33 E1
Brooklyn NS　33 D5
Brooklyn NS　34 F1

Brooklyn PE　35 F6
Brooklyn Road NB　35 F1
Brookmere BC　2 C8
Brooks AB　6 E7
Brooks AB　7 C7
Brooks AB　8 D1
Brooks Aqueduct PHS AB
　6 E7
Brooks Aqueduct PHS AB
　7 C7
Brooks Aqueduct PHS AB
　11 E1
Brooks Bay BC　1 E4
Brooks Brook YT　4 E5
Brooksby SK　11 B6
Brookside ON　36 E7
Brookside NL　37 E5
Brookside NS　32 F8
Brookside NS　33 C6
Brooks Mill ON　21 A2
Brooks Peninsula BC　1 E4
Brooks Peninsula PP BC
　1 E4
Brookvale Provincial Ski
　Park PE　32 B8
Brookvale Provincial Ski
　Park PE　34 C2
Brookvale Provincial Ski
　Park PE　35 E4
Brook Village NS　34 C6
Brookville ON　19 B7
Brookville ON　20 D6
Broomhill MB　11 F8
Broomhill MB　13 F1
Brooms Brook NL　36 B2
Brossard QC　24 D6
Brossard QC　27 E2
Brosseau AB　6 A7
Brosseau AB　11 A1
Brougham ON　20 C7-8
Brougham ON　21 E1-2
Broughton Archipelago
　PMP BC　1 D-E4
Broughton Island BC　1 D4
Broughton Island
　(Qikiqtarjuaq) NU
　42 E-F8
Broughton Station QC
　27 C6
Brouillard, lac du QC　25 E3
Brouillard, lac du QC　26 F3
Brouseville ON　21 C8
Brouseville ON　24 F2-3
Brown MB　14 F3-4
Brown, lac QC　25 E7
Brown, lac QC　27 A2
Brown Creek ON　19 C3
Brown Creek ON　20 E2
Brownell Lake SK　12 F6
Brownfield AB　6 C7
Brownfield AB　11 C1
Brown Hill ON　20 B7
Brown Hill ON　21 E1
Browning SK　11 F7
Browning Entrance BC　1 A2
Brown Lake NT　10 B-C7
Brown Lowery PP AB　6 D5
Brown Lowery PP AB　7 C3
Brown Passage BC　1 A2
Brown's Arm NL　36 A6-7
Brown's Arm NL　37 A4-5
Brown's Arm NL　38 F5
Brownsburg QC　24 D5
Brown's Cove NL　38 E3
Brownsdale NL　37 C7-8
Browns Flat NB　32 D3-4
Browns Flat NB　33 A1
Brownstone Lake MB 12 A8
Brownstone Lake MB 15 A3
Brownsville ON　19 C4-5
Brownsville ON　20 F4
Brownvale AB　9 E3
Broxburn AB　7 E5-6
Broye, Cape NL　37 E8
Bruce AB　6 B6-7
Bruce AB　8 D8
Bruce, lac QC　22 C5
Bruce, péninsule de ON
　18 D4-5 E5
Brucedale ON　20 C5
Brucedale CA ON　18 F4
Brucedale CA ON　20 A3
Brucefield ON　19 B4
Brucefield ON　20 D3
Bruce Lake NT　10 F6
Bruce Lake NT　41 E1
Bruce Lake ON　13 D6
Bruce Lake ON　16 C2
Bruce Mines ON　17 F4
Bruce Peninsula ON
　18 D-E5
Bruce Peninsula NP ON
　18 D4-5
Brudenell ON　21 A5
Brudenell PE　22 F5
Brudenell PE　35 E6
Brudenell River PP PE
　34 C3-4
Brudenell River PP PE 35 E6
Bruderheim AB　6 A6
Bruderheim AB　8 B7
Brule AB　6 B3
Brule AB　8 C1
Brule NS　34 D2
Brûlé, lac QC　22 C5
Brûlé, lac QC　24 C5
Brûlé, lac QC　28 E4

Brûlé, lac QC　39 D3-4
Brule Lake ON　21 B5
Brumlie MB　14 D1
Bruneau Lake MB　15 F3
Brunette Island NL 36 E5-6
Brunette Island NL 37 E3-4
Brunkild MB　13 F2-3
Brunkild MB　14 E4
Brunner ON　19 B5
Brunner ON　20 D4
Bruno SK　11 C5
Brunswick Lake ON　17 C4
Brunswick Mines NB 29 F7
Brunswick Mines NB 31 C6
Brussels ON　19 A4-5
Brussels ON　20 C3-4
Bruxelles MB　13 F2-3
Bruxelles MB　14 E2-3
Bryanston ON　19 C4-5
Bryanston ON　20 E3-4
Bryant SK　11 F6
Bryant's Cove NL　37 D7-8
Bryde, Mount YT　3 A1-2
Bryde, Mount YT　4 E-F5
Bryson QC　21 A6
Bryson QC　22 F6
Bryson, lac QC　22 D6
B-Say-Tah SK　11 D-E6
Buade, lac QC　26 C-D5
Buccaneer Bay PP BC　2 D5
Buchanan SK　11 D6-7
Buchanan, Mount BC　1 A8
Buchanan, Mount BC
　6 A1-2
Buchanan Bay NU　42 B5
Buchanan Point PE　35 F5
Buchan Gulf NU　41 A7
Buchan Gulf NU　42 E6
Buchan Lake AB　9 A4-5
Buchan Lake AB　10 F6
Buchans NL　36 B4
Buchans NL　37 B2
Buchans Junction NL 36 B5
Buchans Junction NL 37 B3
Buchans Lake NL　36 B4
Buchans Lake NL　37 B2
Buck Creek AB　8 B5
Buck Creek BC　8 D4-5
Buck Creek BC　1 A5
Buckfield NS　33 D4
Buckham Lake NT 10 C-D7
Buckhorn ON　21 D3
Buckhorn Lake ON　21 D3
Buckingham QC　21 A8
Buckingham QC　22 F8
Buckingham QC　24 D2-3
Buckingham Island NU
　42 C4
Buckinghorse River BC
　3 D6-7
Buckinghorse River
　Wayside PP BC　3 C-D7
Buck Lake AB　6 B5
Buck Lake AB　8 B5
Buck Lake AB　8 D5
Buck Lake ON　18 D8
Buck Lake ON　21 A1
Buck Lake ON　21 D7
Buck Lake ON　22 F1
Buckland QC　27 B7
Buckland Lake MB　15 F5
Bucklaw NS　34 C6
Buckley Lake BC　3 C2
Buckshot Lake ON　21 C5
Budd MB　11 A8
Budd MB　11 E5
Buena Vista SK　11 E5
Buffalo AB　6 D7-8
Buffalo AB　7 C8
Buffalo AB　11 D1-2
Buffalo Bay MB　13 F5
Buffalo Bay MB　14 F7-8
Buffalo Bay MB　16 E1
Buffalo Creek BC　1 C-D8
Buffalo Gap SK　11 F5
Buffalo Head Hills AB
　9 C-D4
Buffalo Head Prairie AB
　9 C4
Buffalo Head Prairie AB
　41 F1
Buffalo Lake AB　6 C6
Buffalo Lake AB　8 E7
Buffalo Lake AB　8 E7
Buffalo Lake NT　10 F6
Buffalo Lake NT　41 E1
Buffalo Lake Estates AB
　8 E7
Buffaloland PP PE　34 C3
Buffaloland PP PE　35 F6
Buffalo Narrows SK　9 E8
Buffalo Narrows SK　12 E3
Buffalo Point MB　13 F5
Buffalo Point MB　16 E1
Buffalo Pound Lake SK
　11 E5
Buffalo Pound PP SK　11 E5
Buffalo River NT　9 A5
Buffalo River NT　10 E-F6
Buffalo River NT　10 F6-7
Buffalo River NT　9 E7
Buffalo River NS　12 E5
Buffer Lake SK　11 C5
Bugaboo PP BC
　6 D3-4 E3-4
Buick BC　3 D7-8
Buick BC　9 D1
Buies, lac QC　25 A3
Buies, lac QC　26 F3
Buit, lac QC　39 E4
Bulkley Junction PP BC 3 F4

Bulkley River *BC* 3 F4
Bull Arm *NL* 36 D8
Bull Arm *NL* 37 D6
Bull Canyon PP *BC* 1 C6-7
Bull Cove *NL* 36 F7
Bull Cove *NL* 37 F5
Buller *ON* 21 C2
Bull Island *NL* 37 D6-7
Bullmoose Mountain *BC* 3 F7-8
Bullmoose Mountain *BC* 9 E-F1
Bullpond Creek *AB* 6 D7
Bullpond Creek *AB* 7 B6-7
Bullpound Creek *AB* 11 D1
Bull River *BC* 6 E-F5
Bull River *BC* 7 E2
Bull River *BC* 7 E2
Bullshead *AB* 7 D8
Bulmer Lake *NT* 10 C3-4
Bulstrode, rivière *QC* 27 C4-5 D5
Bulwer *QC* 27 E5
Bulyea *SK* 11 D5
Bulyea River *SK* 9 A8
Bulyea River *SK* 12 A4
Bummers Roost *ON* 18 C8
Bunclody *MB* 14 E1
Bunyans Cove *NL* 36 E8
Bunyans Cove *NL* 37 C8
Burbank *AB* 8 E-F6
Burchell Lake *ON* 16 F4
Burdett *AB* 6 D7
Burdett *AB* 7 E7
Burdett *AB* 11 E1
Burditt Lake *ON* 13 F6
Burditt Lake *ON* 13 F6
Burditt Lake *ON* 16 E2
Burford *ON* 19 C6
Burford *ON* 20 E5
Burge Lake PP *MB* 12 D7-8
Burge Lake PP *MB* 15 D2
Burgeo *NL* 36 D3
Burgeo *NL* 37 D1
Burgeo Islands *NL* 36 E3
Burgeo Islands *NL* 37 E1
Burges & James Gadsden PP *BC* 6 D3
Burgess, Mount *YT* 5 E2
Burgessville *ON* 19 C6
Burgessville *ON* 20 E5
Burgis *SK* 11 D7
Burgoyne *ON* 18 F5
Burgoyne *ON* 20 A3-4
Burgoynes Cove *NL* 37 C7
Burin *NL* 36 F6
Burin *NL* 37 F5
Burin Island *NL* 36 F7
Burin Island *NL* 37 F5
Burin Peninsula *NL* 36 F6
Burin Peninsula *NL* 37 F4
Burke, Mount *AB* 6 E5
Burke, Mount *AB* 7 D3
Burke Channel *BC* 1 C4
Burketon *ON* 20 B8
Burketon *ON* 21 E2
Burk's Falls *ON* 18 C8
Burk's Falls *ON* 21 A1
Burk's Falls *ON* 22 F1
Burleigh Falls *ON* 21 D3
Burlington *NL* 38 E4-5
Burlington *NL* 39 F8
Burlington *NS* 32 E6
Burlington *NS* 33 B4
Burlington *ON* 19 B7-8
Burlington *ON* 20 D6-7
Burman River *BC* 2 D1
Burmis *AB* 6 F5
Burmis *AB* 7 E3-4
Burnaby *BC* 1 F7
Burnaby *BC* 2 E4-5
Burnaby *ON* 19 C8
Burnaby *ON* 20 F7
Burnaby Island *BC* 1 C2
Burnett Bay *BC* 1 D4
Burnett Lake *SK* 12 B6
Burnett Lake *SK* 15 A1
Burnie Lake *MB* 12 B8
Burnie Lake *MB* 15 B2
Burnley Creek *ON* 21 E4
Burnside *MB* 14 D3
Burnside *NL* 37 B6-7
Burnside *NS* 33 A7
Burnside *NS* 34 E-F3
Burnside River *NU* 41 C2-3
Burns Lake *BC* 1 A5
Burns Lake *BC* 1 A5
Burns Lake PP *BC* 1 A5
Burnstown *ON* 21 A-B6
Burnsville *NB* 29 E8
Burnsville *NB* 30 E1
Burnsville *NB* 31 E1
Burnt Berry Brook *NL* 36 A5
Burnt Berry Brook *NL* 36 A5
Burnt Berry Brook *NL* 38 F4
Burntbush River *ON* 17 B7
Burntbush River *ON* 23 A1-2
Burnt Cape Ecological Reserve *NL* 38 A5
Burnt Church *NB* 31 C7
Burntcoat Head *NS* 32 D8
Burntcoat Head *NS* 33 A5
Burntcoat Head *NS* 34 E-F1
Burnt Cove *NL* 37 E8
Burnt Creek *NL* 39 A2
Burnt Flat *BC* 6 F3
Burnt Island *NL* 18 B7
Burnt Island *ON* 18 B-C2
Burnt Island Lake *ON* 21 A2
Burnt Island PP *NS* 34 D-E6
Burnt Islands *NL* 36 D-E1
Burnt Lake *NL* 36 A7
Burnt Lake *NL* 36 B6

Burnt Lake *NL* 37 A5
Burnt Lake *NL* 37 B4
Burnt Lake *NL* 38 F6-7
Burnt Lake *NT* 5 D7
Burnt Lands, RNP *ON* 21 B7
Burnt Lands Alvar PP *ON* 24 E1
Burnt Lands PNR *ON* 21 B7
Burnt Point *NL* 37 C-D8
Burnt Point *PE* 35 D3
Burnt Pond *NL* 36 C3
Burnt Pond *NL* 37 C1-2
Burnt River *ON* 20 A8
Burnt River *ON* 21 C2-3
Burnt River *ON* 21 C2-3
Burnt River *ON* 34 A7
Burntroot Lake *ON* 22 E2-3
Burntwood Island *AB* 9 B7
Burntwood Island *AB* 12 B2
Burntwood Lake *MB* 12 E8
Burntwood Lake *MB* 13 D5
Burpee, ZPF de *NB* 31 F5
Burpee, ZPF de *NB* 32 B-C3
Burpee PGA *NB* 31 F5
Burpee PGA *NB* 32 B3
Burr *SK* 11 C5
Burrage Creek *BC* 3 D3
Burrard Inlet *BC* 1 F7
Burrard Inlet *BC* 2 D4-5
Burritts Rapids *ON* 21 B-C8
Burritts Rapids *ON* 24 E2
Burrows *SK* 11 E7
Burrows Lake *ON* 16 D7-8
Burrows Lake *ON* 17 B2
Burstall *SK* 6 D-E8
Burstall *SK* 11 C2
Burstall Lake *AB* 9 A7
Burstall Lake *AB* 12 A2-3
Burtch *ON* 19 C6
Burtch *ON* 20 E5
Burton *BC* 6 E3
Burton *NB* 32 C3
Burton *PE* 35 B1
Burtonsville *AB* 8 C5
Burtts Corner *NB* 31 F4
Burtts Corner *NB* 32 B2
Burwash *ON* 17 F6-7
Burwash *ON* 18 A5-6
Burwash Lake *ON* 17 E6
Burwash Landing *YT* 4 D2
Bury *QC* 27 E5
Busby *AB* 6 A5
Busby *AB* 8 B6
Bushell Park *SK* 11 E5
Bushe River *AB* 9 B4
Bush Island PP *NS* 33 D4-5
Bustard Island *AB* 9 B7
Bustard Island *AB* 12 B2
Bustard Islands *ON* 18 B5
Bute Inlet *BC* 1 E5-6
Bute Inlet *BC* 2 B2
Buteux, lac *QC* 28 D8
Buteux-Bas-Saguenay, ZEC *QC* 28 D8
Butler Lake, RNP *ON* 16 D3
Butler Lake PNR *ON* 16 D3
Butler Lake PP *ON* 13 F6-7
Butler Ridge PP *BC* 3 E7
Butler Ridge PP *BC* 9 D1
Butler's Barracks NHS *ON* 20 D7-8
Butlerville *NL* 37 D7
Butnau River *MB* 15 E5
Butter Cove *NL* 37 C7
Butterfly Lake *MB* 13 A4
Butterfly Lake *MB* 15 F4
Butter Pot PP *NL* 37 E8
Button *ON* 21 A2
Butt Lake *ON* 22 F2
Buttle Lake *BC* 1 F5
Buttle Lake *BC* 2 C1
Button *MB* 15 F3
Button Bay *MB* 15 B5
Button Islands *NU* 40 B6
Buttonville *ON* 19 A8
Buttonville *ON* 20 C7
Buttonville *ON* 21 F1
Buttress *SK* 11 E5
Buzwah *ON* 18 C4
Byam Martin Island *NU* 42 D3
Bydand Bay *NT* 5 E8
Byemoor *AB* 6 C6
Byemoor *AB* 8 F8
Bylot *AB* 15 B5
Bylot Island *NU* 41 A6
Bylot Island *NU* 42 D5-6
Bynd, Mount *YT* 4 E4
Byng *ON* 19 C8
Byng *ON* 20 E-F7
Byng CA *ON* 19 C7-8
Byng CA *ON* 20 E6
Byng Inlet *ON* 18 C6
Byng Inlet *ON* 18 C6
Byrd, lac *QC* 22 B6
Byrnes Road *PE* 35 E6
Byron Bay *NL* 39 A7

C

Caamaño Passage *BC* 3 F2
Caamaño Sound *BC* 1 B3
Cabana *SK* 11 A3
Cabano *QC* 29 E2
Cabano *QC* 31 B1
Cabano, rivière *QC* 29 E2
Cabbage Island Unit (Gulf Islands NPR) *BC* 2 E5
Cabin Creek *YT* 4 E6
Cable Head *PE* 35 D6
Cabonga, réservoir *QC* 24 C6-7
Cabonga, réservoir *QC* 22 B6-7

Cabonga, réservoir *QC* 25 C-D1
Cabot, détroit de *QC* 39 A3
Cabot, détroit de *NS* 34 A8
Cabot, lac *QC* 39 A3
Cabot Beach PP *PE* 32 A8
Cabot Beach PP *PE* 34 B1
Cabot Beach PP *PE* 35 C3
Cabot Head *ON* 18 D5
Cabot Head, RNP *ON* 18 D4-5
Cabot Head PNR *ON* 18 D4-5
Cabot's Landing PP *NS* 34 A7
Cabot Strait *NL* 36 E1
Cabot Strait *NS* 34 A8
Cabri *SK* 11 E3
Cabri Lake *SK* 6 D8
Cabri Lake *SK* 11 D2
Cacaoui, lac *QC* 39 E2
Cache Bay *ON* 17 F7
Cache Bay *ON* 18 A7
Cache Creek *BC* 1 D8
Cache Creek *BC* 2 A7
Cache Creek *BC* 6 D1
Cache Creek *NT* 4 A6-7
Cache Lake *NT* 10 C8
Cache Lake *ON* 18 A7
Cache Lake *ON* 21 A3
Cacouna *QC* 28 D8
Cacouna *QC* 29 D1
Cactus Lake *SK* 6 C8
Cactus Lake *SK* 11 C2
Cacuscanus, lac *QC* 28 A7
Caddy Lake *MB* 14 E7
Cadillac *QC* 23 E3
Cadillac *SK* 11 F3
Cadillac, lac *QC* 23 D4
Cadman, pointe *NB* 35 E2
Cadman Corner *NB* 35 E2
Cadman Point *NB* 35 E2
Cadogan *AB* 6 C7-8
Cadogan *AB* 11 C2
Cadomin *AB* 6 B3
Cadomin *AB* 8 D1-2
Cadotte Lake *AB* 9 D4
Cadotte Lake *AB* 9 D4
Cadotte River *AB* 9 D3-4
Cadurcis *MB* 14 D1
Caen Lake *NT* 10 D5
Caesarea *ON* 20 B8
Caesarea *ON* 21 E2
Cain, Mount *BC* 1 E5
Cains River *NB* 31 E6
Cains River *NB* 32 A4
Cainsville *ON* 19 C6-7
Cainsville *ON* 20 E5-6
Caire, lac *QC* 23 E2
Cairn-de-Glengarry, LHN du *ON* 24 E4-5
Cairnes, Mount *YT* 4 E2
Cairngorm *ON* 19 C4
Cairngorm *ON* 20 E3
Cairns Lake *ON* 13 C5-6
Cairns Lake *ON* 14 A8
Cairns Lake *ON* 16 B2
Cairns Lake *SK* 12 C6
Cairns Lake *SK* 15 C1
Cairo *ON* 19 D3
Cairo *ON* 20 F2
Caissie Cape *NB* 32 B6-7
Caistor Centre *ON* 19 C8
Caistor Centre *ON* 20 E6-7
Caistorville *ON* 19 C7-8
Caistorville *ON* 20 E6-7
Caithness *BC* 7 F2
Cajeux, lac du *QC* 26 E5
Calabogie *ON* 21 B6
Calabogie Lake *ON* 21 B6
Calahoo *AB* 6 A5
Calahoo *AB* 8 C6
Calais *AB* 9 F3
Calais Lake *NT* 10 E5
Calder *SK* 11 D7
Calder *SK* 13 D1
Calderbank *SK* 11 E4
Calders Dock *MB* 13 D4
Calders Dock *MB* 14 A5
Caledon *ON* 19 A7
Caledon *ON* 20 C6
Caledon East *ON* 19 A7
Caledon East *ON* 20 C6
Caledonia *NS* 33 A8
Caledonia *NS* 33 D3
Caledonia *NS* 34 E4
Caledonia *ON* 19 C7
Caledonia *ON* 20 E6
Caledonia *PE* 34 C3
Caledonia *PE* 35 F6
Caledonia Gorge, APP *NB* 32 C6
Caledonia Gorge PPA *NB* 32 C6
Caledonia Mills *NS* 34 E5
Cale-Sèche-La Coupe, LHN de la *NB* 32 C7
Cale-Sèche-La Coupe, LHN de la *NB* 35 F1-2
Calgary *ON* 20 D5
Calgary *AB* 7 B3-4
Calhoun *NB* 31 F8
Calhoun *NB* 32 B6-7
Caliento *MB* 13 F4
Caliento *MB* 14 F6
Caligata Lake PP *BC* 6 C2
Caliper Lake *ON* 13 A8
Caliper Lake *ON* 16 E2
Caliper Lake PP *ON* 13 F6
Caliper Lake PP *ON* 16 E2
Calixa-Lavallée *QC* 24 C6-7
Calixa-Lavallée *QC* 27 D2

Callaghan Lake PP *BC* 1 E6-7
Callaghan Lake PP *BC* 2 B-C5
Callaghan's Rapids CA *ON* 21 D4
Callander *ON* 17 F8
Callander *ON* 18 B8
Callander *ON* 22 D1
Calling Lake *AB* 9 F5-6
Calling Lake *AB* 9 F6
Calling Lake PP *AB* 9 F5-6
Call Inlet *BC* 2 B1
Call Lake PP *BC* 3 F4-5
Callum *ON* 17 F7
Callum *ON* 18 A6
Calmar *AB* 6 B5
Calmar *AB* 8 D6
Calm Lake *ON* 13 F7
Calm Lake *ON* 16 E3
Calm Lake *ON* 16 E3
Calstock *ON* 17 B4
Calton *ON* 19 D5
Calton *ON* 20 F4
Calumet *QC* 24 D4
Calvert *NL* 37 E8
Calvert, Cape *BC* 1 D4
Calvert Island *BC* 1 D4
Camachigama, lac *QC* 23 F7
Camachigama, lac *QC* 25 B1
Camatose, lac *QC* 22 B6
Camborne *ON* 21 E3
Cambrai, lac *QC* 23 E6
Cambrai, lac *QC* 25 B1
Cambrai, lac *QC* 26 F1
Cambray *ON* 20 A8
Cambray *ON* 21 D2
Cambria *NS* 7 A6
Cambria Icefield *BC* 3 E3
Cambridge *NS* 32 E6-7
Cambridge *NS* 33 B4
Cambridge *NS* 34 F1
Cambridge *ON* 19 B6-7
Cambridge *ON* 20 D5-6
Cambridge *PE* 35 F7
Cambridge Bay (Iqaluktuutiaq) *NU* 41 B3-4
Cambridge Bay (Iqaluktuutiaq) *NU* 42 F3
Cambridge-Narrows *NB* 32 C4
Camden *NS* 33 A6-7
Camden *NS* 34 E2
Camden East *ON* 21 D6
Camden Lake *ON* 21 D6
Camelsfoot Range *BC* 1 D7
Camelsfoot Range *BC* 2 A5-6
Cameron *ON* 20 A8
Cameron *ON* 21 D2
Cameron, lac *QC* 24 B4
Cameron Creek *ON* 18 A3
Cameron Falls *ON* 16 E6
Cameron Hills *AB* 9 B3
Cameron Hills *AB* 10 F5
Cameron Island *NU* 42 C3
Cameron Lake *ON* 17 C4
Cameron River *BC* 2 E3
Cameron River *NT* 10 B-C7
Cameron River *NT* 10 F5
Cameron River TP *NT* 10 C7
Camerons Brook PP *NS* 33 D3-4
Cameron Settlement *NS* 33 A8
Cameron Settlement *NS* 34 E3-4
Camilla *ON* 20 C6
Camille Pouliot, mont *QC* 28 E5
Camlachie *ON* 19 C3
Camlachie *ON* 20 F2
Campania Island *BC* 1 B3
Campbellcroft *ON* 21 D4
Campbellford *ON* 21 D4
Campbell Island *BC* 1 C3-4
Campbell Island *NT* 5 A6
Campbell Lake *BC* 1 F5
Campbell Lake *BC* 2 C1-2
Campbell Lake *MB* 15 D4
Campbell Lake *NT* 5 C5
Campbell Lake *SK* 12 C5
Campbell Point *ON* 16 F8
Campbell Point *ON* 17 C2
Campbell's Bay *QC* 21 A6
Campbell's Bay *QC* 22 F6
Campbell's Cove PP *PE* 34 B4
Campbells Cove PP *PE* 35 D8
Campbells Creek *NL* 36 C1-2
Campbell Settlement *NB* 31 F3
Campbell Settlement *NB* 32 B-C1
Campbellton *NB* 29 D6
Campbellton *NB* 31 A5
Campbellton *NB* 36 A7
Campbellton *NL* 37 A5
Campbellton *NL* 38 F6
Campbellton *PE* 35 B1
Campbellvale *ON* 19 C6
Campbellvale *ON* 20 E3
Campbellville *ON* 19 B7
Campbellville *ON* 20 D6
Camp Boggy *NL* 36 D6
Camp Boggy *NL* 37 D4
Camp Creek *AB* 6 A5

Camp Creek *AB* 8 B5
Campden *ON* 19 C8
Campden *ON* 20 E7
Camper *MB* 13 D3
Camper *MB* 14 B3-4
Camperville *MB* 11 C8
Camperville *MB* 13 C2
Camp Farewell *NT* 5 B4
Camping Islands *MB* 11 C8
Camping Islands *MB* 13 C2
Camp Morton *MB* 13 E4
Camp Morton *MB* 14 C5
Camp Morton PP *MB* 13 D-E4
Camp Morton PP *MB* 14 C5-6
Camp Robinson *ON* 13 E6
Camp Robinson *ON* 16 D2-3
Campsie *AB* 8 B5
Camrose *AB* 6 B6
Camrose *AB* 8 D7
Camsell Bend *NT* 10 D2
Camsell Lake *NT* 10 B8
Camsell Portage *SK* 9 A7
Camsell Portage *SK* 12 A3
Camsell Range *NT* 10 C-D2
Camsell River *NT* 10 A5
Cana *SK* 11 D7
Canaan *NB* 31 F7
Canaan *NB* 32 B5-6
Canaan *NS* 32 F7
Canaan *NS* 33 B4
Canaan *NS* 33 C5
Canaan Bog PPA *NB* 31 F7
Canaan Bog PPA *NB* 32 B5
Canaan Forks *NB* 31 F6-7
Canaan Forks *NB* 32 B4-5
Canaan River *NB* 31 F6-7
Canaan River *NB* 32 B5
Canaan Road *NB* 31 F7
Canaan Road *NB* 32 B5
Canada Bay *NL* 38 C4
Canada Bay *NL* 39 E8
Canada Creek *NS* 32 E6
Canada Creek *NS* 33 B4
Canada Harbour *NL* 39 E8
Canadian Rocky Mountain Parks *AB* 6 C3-4
Canadian Rocky Mountain Parks *AB* 7 A1-2
Canadian Rocky Mountain Parks *AB* 8 E1-2
Canadian Rocky Mountain Parks *BC* 7 B1-2
Canairiktok River *NL* 40 D7
Canal-de-St. Peters, LHN du *NS* 34 D6-7
Canal Flats *BC* 6 E4
Canal Flats *BC* 7 D1
Canal Flats PP *BC* 6 E4
Canal Flats PP *BC* 7 D1-2
Canal Lake *ON* 20 A8
Canal Lake *ON* 21 D2
Canal Lake Concrete Arch Bridge NHS *ON* 20 A8
Canal Lake Concrete Arch Bridge NHS *ON* 21 D2
Canard *NS* 32 E7
Canard *NS* 33 B4
Canard, lac *QC* 24 B4
Canard, lac du *QC* 27 D5
Canard, lac du *QC* 28 B2
Canard de Mer, lac *QC* 26 C6-7
Canard de mer, lac *QC* 28 A2
Canards, lac aux *QC* 28 D8
Canborough *ON* 19 C7
Canborough *ON* 20 E6
Candiac *QC* 24 D6
Candiac *ON* 27 E1-2
Candiac *SK* 11 E6
Candle Lake *SK* 11 A5
Candle Lake *SK* 11 A5
Candle Lake PP *SK* 11 A5
Cando *SK* 11 C3
Canfield *ON* 19 C7
Canfield *ON* 20 E6
Caniapiscau, réservoir *QC* 40 E6
Caniapiscau, rivière *QC* 40 C-D6
Canim Beach PP *BC* 1 C-D8
Canim Beach PP *BC* 6 C1
CaniminA, lac *QC* 22 B5-6
Canim Lake *BC* 1 C8
Canim Lake *BC* 6 C1
Canim Lake *BC* 6 C1
Canmore *AB* 6 D4
Canmore *AB* 7 B2
Cann *QC* 25 B5
Cann *QC* 28 D1
Cannes-de-Roches *QC* 30 C2-3
Cannifton *ON* 21 E5
Canning *NS* 32 E7
Canning, Mount *BC* 3 A1
Canning, Mount *BC* 9 E3
Canning Lake *ON* 21 C2-3
Cannings Cove *NL* 36 C8
Cannings Cove *NL* 37 C6
Cannington *ON* 20 B8
Cannington *ON* 21 D2
Cannington Manor Provincial Historic Park *SK* 11 F7
Canoe *BC* 6 D2
Canoe Cove *PE* 34 C2

Canoe Cove *PE* 35 E4
Canoe Lake *ON* 21 A2
Canoe Lake *ON* 21 D6
Canoe Lake *SK* 12 F3
Canoe Lake *SK* 12 F3
Canoe Narrows *SK* 12 F3
Canoe Reach *BC* 6 B-C2
Canoe River *BC* 6 B2
Cañon Fiord *NU* 42 B5
Canonto Lake *ON* 21 B6
Canoose Flowage, APP *NB* 32 D1-2
Canoose Flowage PPA *NB* 32 D1-2
Canoose Lake *NB* 32 D2
Canopus *SK* 11 F4
Canora *SK* 11 D7
Canot, rivière du *QC* 25 C3
Canot Lake *NT* 5 D6-7
Canots, lac aux *QC* 28 A6
Canots, lac des *QC* 26 A6
Canso *NS* 34 E6
Canso, Cape *NS* 34 E6
Canso, Strait of *NS* 34 D5-6 E6
Cantal *SK* 11 F7
Cantara Bay *SK* 9 A8
Cantara Bay *SK* 12 A3
Canterbury *NB* 32 C1
Cantin Lake *MB* 13 B5
Cantley *QC* 21 A8
Cantley *QC* 22 F8
Cantley *QC* 24 D2
Cantuar *SK* 11 E3
Canuck *SK* 11 F3
Canwood *SK* 11 B4
Canyon *BC* 6 F4
Canyon *BC* 7 F1
Canyon Creek *AB* 9 E4-5
Canyon Creek *YT* 5 E3-4
Canyon Hot Springs *BC* 6 D3
Canyon Ranges *NT* 4 A7 A-B8
Canyon Ranges *NT* 10 A-B1
Caopacho, lac *QC* 39 D2
Caopacho, rivière *QC* 39 D2
Caopatina, lac *QC* 26 B4
Cap, Mount *YT* 4 A8
Cap-à-l'Aigle *QC* 28 E7-8
Cap-au-Renard *QC* 29 A7
Cap-aux-Meules *QC* 30 F7
Cap-aux-Os *QC* 30 F7
Cap-Breton, île du *NS* 34 D7-8
Cap-Brulé *NB* 35 E1
Cap-Chat *QC* 29 A6
Cap-Chat, pointe du *QC* 29 A6
Cap-Chat, rivière du *QC* 29 A-B6
Cap-de-la-Madeleine *QC* 24 B8
Cap-de-la-Madeleine *QC* 25 F8
Cap-de-la-Madeleine *QC* 27 C3-4
Cap-des-Caissie *NB* 32 B6-7
Cap-d'Espoir *QC* 30 C3
Cap-des-Rosiers *QC* 30 B3
Cape Anguille *NL* 36 D1
Cape Breton *NS* 34 C7-8
Cape Breton Highlands *NS* 34 B6-7
Cape Breton Highlands NP *NS* 34 B6-7
Cape Breton Island *NS* 34 B6 C5-6
Cape Broyle *NL* 37 E7-8
Cape Charles *NL* 39 C8
Cape Chignecto PP *NB* 32 D6
Cape Chignecto PP *NS* 33 A3
Cape Cove *NL* 37 C8
Cape Croker *ON* 18 E5
Cape Dorset (Kinngait) *NU* 40 A7
Cape Dorset (Kinngait) *NU* 41 F7
Cape Enrage *NB* 32 C-D6
Cape Enrage *NB* 35 A2
Cape Freels *NL* 37 A7
Cape Freels *NL* 38 F8
Cape Freels North *NL* 37 A7
Cape Freels North *NL* 38 F8
Cape Freels South *NL* 37 A7
Cape Freels South *NL* 38 F8
Cape George *NS* 34 D5
Cape George Harbour *NS* 34 D5
Cape Hurd *ON* 18 D4
Cape Jourimain NWA *NB* 34 C1-2
Cape Jourimain NWA *NB* 35 E3
Cape LaHave Island *NS* 33 D4-5
Cape la Hune *NL* 36 E4
Cape la Hune *NL* 37 D-E2
Cape Merry NHS *NB* 15 B5-6
Cape Negro Island *NS* 33 E4
Cape North *NS* 34 A7
Cape Onion *NL* 38 A5
Cape Parry *NT* 5 A8
Cape Parry NMBS *NT* 5 A8

Cape Race *NL* 37 F8
Cape Ray *NL* 36 D1
Cape St. George *ON* 36 C1
Cape St. George *NL* 40 F8
Cape St. Mary *NS* 33 E1
Cape St. Mary's Ecological Reserve *NL* 36 F6
Cape St. Mary's Ecological Reserve *NL* 37 F6
Cape Scott PP *BC* 1 D3-4
Cape Smokey PP *NS* 34 B7
Cape Spear *NB* 32 B8
Cape Spear *NB* 34 C1
Cape Spear *NB* 35 F3
Cape Spear NHS *NL* 37 D8
Cape Tatnam WMA *MB* 15 C7
Cape Tormentine *NB* 32 B8
Cape Tormentine *NB* 34 C1
Cape Tormentine *NB* 35 E3
Cape Traverse *PE* 35 E3
Cape Walsingham *NU* 42 F8
Cape Wolfe *NB* 32 A7
Cape Wolfe *PE* 35 B1
Capimit, lac *QC* 25 B5
Capitachouane, lac *QC* 22 A8
Capitachouane, lac *QC* 25 C2
Capitachouane, lac *QC* 23 E7-8
Capitachouane, lac *QC* 25 A2
Capitachouane, rivière *QC* 23 F6-7
Capitachouane, rivière *QC* 34 F3
Capitachouane, ZEC *QC* 23 F6-7
Capitachouane, ZEC *QC* 25 B1
Cap-Jourimain, RNF du *NB* 4 A7 A-B8
Cap-Jourimain, RNF du *NB* 34 C1-2
Cap-Jourimain, RNF du *NB* 35 E3
Caplan *QC* 29 D7-8
Caplan *QC* 31 A6
Cap Le Moine *NS* 34 B6
Caplin Bay *NL* 39 C8
Caplin Cove *NL* 37 C8
Caplin Cove *NL* 37 C-D7
Cap-Lumière *NB* 31 E8
Cap-Lumière *NB* 32 A6
Cap-Merry, LHN du *NB* 15 B5-6
Capot Blanc, lac *NT* 10 B8
Cappahayden *NL* 37 F8
Cap-Parry, RNOM du *NT* 5 A8
Cap-Pelé *NB* 32 B7
Cap-Pelé *NB* 35 E1
Cap River *YT* 5 E4
Capon *AB* 7 B8
Capreol *ON* 17 F6-7
Caprona *AB* 8 F7
Cap-Rouge *QC* 27 B5
Cap-Saint-Ignace *QC* 27 A7
Cap-Santé *QC* 27 B4-5
Cap-Seize *QC* 29 B6
Cap-Spear, LHN du *NL* 37 D8
Capstan, Cape *NS* 33 A3
Capstan, Cape *NS* 34 A7
Cap-Tourmente *QC* 27 A6
Cap-Tourmente, RNF du *QC* 27 A6-7
Cap-Tourmente, RNF du *QC* 28 F6-7
Cap Tourmente National Wilderness Area *QC* 27 A6-7
Cap Tourmente National Wilderness Area *QC* 28 F6-7
Capucins *QC* 29 A5-6
Caramat *ON* 16 D8
Caramat *ON* 17 B2
Caraquet *NB* 30 E1
Caraquet *NB* 31 B7
Caraquet, île *NB* 30 E1
Caraquet, rivière *NB* 31 B7
Caraquet Island *NB* 30 E2
Carberry *MB* 13 F4
Carberry *MB* 14 E2
Carbon *AB* 6 C6
Carbon *AB* 7 A5
Carbondale *AB* 8 C6
Carbonear *NL* 37 D7
Carcajou *AB* 9 C4
Carcajou Lake *NT* 5 D6-7
Carcajou River *NT* 5 F7
Carcross *YT* 4 E4
Cardale *MB* 11 E8
Cardale *MB* 13 E2
Cardiff *AB* 8 C6
Cardiff *ON* 21 C4
Cardigan *PE* 34 C3
Cardigan *PE* 35 E6
Cardigan Bay *PE* 35 C1
Cardigan Head *PE* 35 E6
Cardigan Point *PE* 35 E6
Cardigan River *PE* 35 E6-7
Cardinal *AB* 8 C5
Cardinal *MB* 14 E2
Cardinal *ON* 24 F3
Cardinal Lake *AB* 9 E3
Card Lake PP *NS* 32 F7
Card Lake PP *NS* 33 C5
Cardross *PE* 35 E6

Cardross *SK* 11 E5
Card's Harbour *NL* 38 F5
Cardston *AB* 6 F6
Cardston *AB* 7 F5
Careen Lake *SK* 9 D8
Careen Lake *SK* 12 F3
Carey *MB* 13 F4
Carey *MB* 14 E5
Carghill Island *MB* 15 F5
Cariboo Mountain *AB* 1 B8
Cariboo Mountain *BC* 6 B1
Cariboo Mountains *BC* 6 B1-2
Cariboo Mountains PP *BC* 1 B8
Cariboo Mountains PP *BC* 6 B1
Cariboo Nature PP *BC* 1 C8
Cariboo River *BC* 6 B1
Cariboo River *BC* 6 B1
Cariboo River PP *BC* 1 B8
Cariboo River PP *BC* 6 B1
Caribou, lac du *MB* 41 F3
Caribou, lac du *QC* 24 A7
Caribou, lac du *QC* 25 E7
Caribou, lac du *QC* 27 B2
Caribou, lac du *SK* 12 C7
Caribou, Mount *YT* 4 D4-5
Caribou Falls *ON* 13 E5
Caribou Falls *ON* 14 D8
Caribou Falls *ON* 16 C-D1
Caribou Gold Mines *NS* 33 B7
Caribou Gold Mines *NS* 34 F3
Caribou Island *NS* 34 D5
Caribou Islands *NT* 10 D7
Caribou Lake *MB* 15 A4
Caribou Lake *NT* 5 C5
Caribou Lakes *YT* 4 E5
Caribou Lake *ON* 16 C5-6 D5
Caribou Mountains *AB* 9 B4-5
Caribou Mountains *AB* 41 E1
Caribou Mountains Wildland PP *AB* 9 A-B5
Caribou-Munroe's Island PP *NS* 34 D3-4
Caribou Point *NT* 10 E6
Caribou Pond *NL* 36 B7
Caribou Pond *NL* 37 B5
Caribou River *MB* 15 A4-5
Caribou River *MB* 40 B1
Caribou River *NB* 41 F4
Caribou River *NS* 33 D2
Caribou River *NS* 34 D3
Caribou River *NT* 4 D8
Caribou River *NT* 10 E1
Caribou River *YT* 5 E4
Caribou River, PP *MB* 40 B1
Caribou River PP *MB* 40 B1
Caribou River PP *MB* 41 F1
Caribou River Wilderness PP *MB* 15 A4
Caricevale *SK* 11 F7-8
Caricevale *SK* 13 F1
Carignan *QC* 24 C6
Carignan *QC* 25 D7
Carignan *QC* 27 E2
Carignan *QC* 28 F3
Carignan, lac *QC* 25 D7
Carignan, lac *QC* 28 F3
Carleton, mont *NB* 29 F5-6
Carleton, mont *NB* 31 C4
Carleton, Mount *NB* 29 F5-6
Carleton, Mount *NB* 31 C4
Carleton Cove *PE* 35 E3
Carleton Martello Tower NHS *NB* 32 D4-5
Carleton Martello Tower NHS *NB* 33 B1-2
Carleton Place *ON* 21 B7
Carleton Place *ON* 24 E1
Carleton *NS* 33 E2
Carleton *PE* 32 A7
Carleton *PE* 35 C2
Carleton *PE* 35 E3
Carleton *QC* 29 D7
Carleton *QC* 31 A6
Carling *ON* 18 D7
Carlingford *NB* 31 E3
Carlingford *NB* 32 A1
Carlingford *ON* 19 B5
Carlingford *ON* 20 D4
Carlisle *ON* 19 C6
Carlisle *ON* 20 B6
Carlisle *ON* 20 C6
Carlisle *ON* 20 E3
Carlos *AB* 8 E5
Carlow *ON* 19 A4
Carlow *ON* 20 C3
Carlowrie *MB* 13 F4
Carlowrie *MB* 14 E6
Carlsbad Springs *ON* 21 B8
Carlsbad Springs *ON* 24 D2-3
Carlsruhe *ON* 19 C7
Carluke *ON* 20 E6
Carl Wilson Lake *ON* 22 E2-3

Carlyle SK 11 F7
Carmacks YT 4 C3
Carman MB 13 F3
Carman MB 14 E4
Carmanah Walbran PP BC 2 F2-3
Carmangay AB 6 E6
Carmangay AB 7 D5
Carmanville NL 36 A8
Carmanville NL 37 A6
Carmanville NL 38 F7
Carmel SK 11 E3
Carmen, lac QC 25 A3-4
Carmen, lac QC 26 F3-4
Carmichael SK 11 E3
Carnarvon ON 21 B2-3
Carnduff SK 11 F7
Carnegie MB 13 F3
Carnwath River NT 5 C6-7
Carnwood AB 6 B5
Carnwood AB 8 D5
Caroline AB 6 C5
Caroline AB 8 F5
Caron SK 11 E4-5
Caron, lac QC 23 E2-3
Caron, lac QC 23 F7
Caron Brook NB 29 F2
Caron Brook NB 31 C1
Caronport SK 11 E5
Carp ON 21 B7
Carp ON 24 D1
Carpe, lac à la QC 28 C4
Carpenter SK 11 C4-5
Carpenter Bay BC 1 C2
Carpenter Lake BC 1 D7
Carpenter Lake BC 2 A5
Carp Lake BC 3 F7
Carp Lake PP BC 3 F6
Carp River ON 24 D1-2
Carquile BC 2 A7
Carragana SK 11 C6
Carr-Harris Lake MB 16 A1
Carrick MB 13 F4
Carrick MB 14 F6
Carrière, lac QC 22 B5
Carroll MB 11 F8
Carroll MB 13 F2
Carroll MB 14 E1
Carroll Lake ON 13 D5
Carroll Lake ON 14 B7-8
Carroll Lake ON 16 B1
Carrolls Crossing NB 31 E5-6
Carrolls Crossing NB 32 A3-4
Carrot Creek AB 6 A-B4
Carrot Creek AB 8 C3
Carrot River SK 11 B6
Carruthers CA ON 20 B6
Carrying Place ON 21 E4-5
Carry The Kettle SK 11 E6
Carseland AB 6 D6
Carseland AB 7 C4-5
Carson BC 6 F3
Carson Lake ON 21 A4
Carson Lake ON 22 F4
Carson Lake PP ON 21 A4
Carson Lake PP ON 22 F4
Carson-Pegasus PP AB 6 A4
Carson-Pegasus PP AB 8 A-B4
Carsonville NB 32 C5
Carstairs AB 6 D5
Carstairs AB 7 A4
Carswell Lake MB 12 D7
Carswell Lake MB 15 D1
Carswell Lake SK 9 B7-8
Carswell Lake SK 12 B3
Cartage Mountains NT 10 B-C4
Carter Basin NL 39 B6
Carter's Cove NL 38 E6
Carthage ON 19 A5
Carthage ON 20 C4
Cartier ON 17 F6
Cartier, lac QC 22 D1
Cartier Lake ON 22 E4-5
Cartmel, Mount BC 3 C3
Cartwright MB 13 F2
Cartwright MB 14 F2
Cartwright NL 39 B7-8
Cartwright NL 40 D8
Cartwright Junction NL 39 C7
Cartwright Sound BC 1 B1
Cartyville NL 36 C2
Carway AB 6 F6
Carway AB 7 F5
Casault, lac QC 29 C5
Casault, ZEC QC 29 C5
Cascade BC 6 F3
Cascade Inlet BC 1 C4
Cascade PRA BC 6 F1
Cascade PRA BC 2 D7-8
Cascade PRA BC 6 F1
Cascade Range BC 2 D-F7
Cascapédia, branche du lac QC 29 B6-7 C6
Cascapédia, rivière QC 29 C5
Cascumpec PE 34 B1
Cascumpec PE 35 B2
Cascumpec Bay PE 34 B1
Cascumpec Bay PE 35 B2
Cascumpec Sand Hills PE 35 B2
Caserne-de-Carillon, LHN de la QC 24 D4-5
Casernes-de-Butler, LHN des ON 20 D7-8
Casey QC 25 B5
Cashel Lake ON 21 C5
Casimir ON 17 F7

Casimir ON 18 A6
Caslan AB 8 A7
Caslan AB 9 F6
Caslan AB 12 F1
Casselman ON 24 D-E3
Cassels Lake ON 22 B1
Cassiar Mountains BC 3 B-C4
Cassiar Mountains YT 4 E5-6
Cassidy BC 1 F6
Cassidy BC 2 E3-4
Cassils AB 7 C6
Castagnier, lac QC 23 C5
Castagnier, rivière QC 23 C5
Castalia NB 32 F3
Castalia PP NB 32 F3
Castelveyre, lac QC 25 D5
Castle Creek, RNP ON 16 F4-5
Castle Creek PNR ON 16 F4-5
Castledale BC 7 B1
Castleford ON 21 A6
Castleford ON 22 F6
Castlegar BC 6 F3
Castle Hill, LHN de NL 36 E8
Castle Hill, LHN de NL 37 E6
Castle Hill NHS NL 36 E8
Castle Hill NHS NL 37 E6
Castle Mountain AB 6 D4
Castle Mountain AB 7 B3-4
Castle Mountain YT 4 A4
Castle Rock Hoodoos PP BC 1 C7-8
Castle Rock Hoodoos PP BC 1 D8
Castle Rock Hoodoos PP BC 2 A7
Castle Rock Hoodoos PP BC 6 D1
Castleton ON 21 E4
Castonguay, lac QC 23 C7
Castonguay, lac QC 26 D1
Castor AB 6 C6-7
Castor AB 8 F8
Castor AB 11 C1
Castor Blanc, lac QC 22 D7
Castor Blanc, lac QC 24 A2
Castor Blanc, lac QC 25 F2
Castor Lake NT 10 A5-6
Castor River NL 24 E3
Castors River NL 38 C3-4
Castors River NL 38 C3
Castors River NL 39 E8
Catala Island PMP BC 1 E4
Catalina NL 37 B7-8
Catalone NS 34 C8
Cataract Lake ON 18 A1-2
Cataracts PP NL 37 E7
Cataraqui ON 21 E6-7
Cataraqui River ON 21 D7
Cat Arm NL 38 D3
Cat Arm River NL 39 E7-8 F8
Catchacoma ON 21 C3
Catchacoma Lake ON 21 C3
Cater SK 11 B3
Catfish Creek ON 19 D5
Catfish Creek ON 20 F4
Catfish Lake ON 22 E3
Cathcart ON 19 C6
Cathcart ON 20 E5
Cathcart, parc ON 19 D2-3
Cathcart, parc ON 20 F1-2
Cathcart Park (St. Clair Parkway) ON 19 D2-3
Cathcart Park (St. Clair Parkway) ON 20 F1-2
Cathedral PP BC 6 F1
Catherwood SK 11 C4
Cat Lake ON 13 C7
Cat Lake ON 13 C7
Cat Lake ON 16 B4
Cat River ON 16 B4
Cauchon Lake MB 14 E4
Cauchy, lac QC 39 E5
Caumont, lac QC 39 E5
Caupichagua, lac QC 26 A3
Causapscal QC 29 C5
Causapscal, rivière QC 29 C5
Caution, Cape BC 1 D4
Cavan ON 21 E3
Cavan, lac QC 26 B4
Cave and Basin, LHN QC 7 B1-2
Cave and Basin NHS AB 7 B1-2
Cavell ON 16 D7
Cavell ON 17 A1-2
Cavell SK 11 C3
Cavendish AB 7 C8
Cavendish NL 37 D7
Cavendish PE 34 B2
Cavendish PE 35 D4
Caverlys Landing ON 21 B5
Cavern Lake, RNP ON 16 E6
Cavern Lake PNR ON 16 E6
Cavers ON 16 E7
Cavers ON 17 C1
Cawaja Beach ON 18 F7
Cawaja Beach ON 20 A6
Cawasachouane, lac QC 22 A4
Cawatose, lac QC 22 B1
Cawston BC 2 E3
Caycuse BC 2 E3
Cayer MB 13 D2
Cayer MB 14 B2
Cayley AB 6 E5

Cayley AB 7 C4
Cayoose Creek BC 2 B6
Cayoosh Creek BC 1 E7-8
Cayoosh Creek BC 2 B6
Cayuga ON 19 C7
Cayuga ON 20 E6
Cazaville QC 24 E4-5
Cazeneuve, lac QC 26 B-C6
Ceba SK 11 B7
Ceba SK 13 B1
Cecebe ON 18 C8
Cecebe ON 21 A1
Cecebe ON 22 F1
Cecebe Lake ON 18 C8
Cecebe Lake ON 21 A1
Cecebe Lake ON 22 F1
Cecil AB 7 D7
Cecil Lake BC 3 E8
Cecil Lake BC 9 D2
Cécile, lac QC 26 E5-6
Cécile, lac QC 28 C1
Cedar BC 1 F6
Cedar BC 2 E4
Cedar Beach ON 19 F1
Cedar Beach CA ON 19 E1
Cedar Dunes PP PE 32 A6-7
Cedar Dunes PP PE 35 C1
Cedarhurst Park ON 19 F1-2
Cedar Lake MB 11 B8
Cedar Lake MB 13 B2
Cedar Lake ON 13 E6
Cedar Lake ON 22 E3
Cedar Mills ON 19 A7
Cedar Mills ON 20 C6
Cedar Point ON 18 E7
Cedar Point PP ON 1 C7-8
Cedar Springs ON 19 E3
Cedarvale BC 3 F3-4
Cedar Valley ON 21 E3
Cedoux SK 11 E6
Cèdres, lac aux QC 23 D8
Cèdres, lac aux QC 25 A2
Cèdres, lac aux QC 26 E2
Cèdres, lac des MB 11 B8
Cèdres, lac des MB 13 B2
Cèdres, lac des QC 22 D7
Cèdres, lac des QC 24 B1
Cèdres, lac des QC 25 F1
Cèdres, rivière des QC 29 B1
Ceepeecee BC 1 E4
Celista BC 6 D2
Centennial Lake ON 21 B5
Centennial Lake PP ON 21 B5-6
Central AB 8 D7
Central Argyle NS 33 E-F2
Central Bedeque PE 32 A8
Central Bedeque PE 34 C1
Central Bedeque PE 35 D3
Central Blissville NB 32 C-D3
Central Butte SK 11 D-E4
Central Economy NS 32 D8
Central Economy NS 33 A5
Central Economy NS 34 E1
Central Elgin ON 19 D5
Central Elgin ON 20 F4
Central Grove NS 33 D1
Central Grove PP NS 33 D1
Centralia ON 19 B4
Centralia ON 20 D2
Central Lot 16 PE 35 D2
Central Onslow NS 33 A6
Central Onslow NS 34 E2
Central Patricia ON 13 D8
Central Patricia ON 16 B5
Central Saanich BC 2 F4
Central West River NS 33 A7
Central West River NS 33 A4
Centre Burlington NS 32 E7
Centre Burlington NS 33 B5
Centre Burlington NS 34 E6
Centre-d'Accueil-du-Parc-Jasper, LHN du AB 8 D1
Centre-d'Inscription-de-l'Entrée-Est, LHN du MB 14 C2-3
Centre Dummer ON 21 D4
Centre Island ON 18 B4
Centrelea NS 32 F5
Centrelea NS 33 C3
Centre Musquodoboit NS 33 B7
Centre Musquodoboit NS 34 F2-3
Centre Napan NB 31 D7
Centreton ON 21 E4
Centre Village NB 35 F1
Centreville NB 31 E3
Centreville NB 32 A1
Centreville NL 32 C5
Centreville NL 36 A8
Centreville NL 37 A6
Centreville NL 38 F7
Centreville NS 32 E6-7
Centreville NS 33 B4
Centreville NS 33 F2
Centreville NS 33 C1
Centreville ON 19 C5
Centreville ON 20 E4
Centreville ON 21 D6
Centreville-Wareham-Trinity NL 36 A-B8
Centreville-Wareham-Trinity NL 37 A6
Cereal AB 6 D7
Cereal AB 7 A8
Cereal AB 11 D1-2
Cerf, lac du QC 22 E8

Cerf, lac du QC 24 B2-3
Cerf, lac du QC 25 F2-3
Cessford AB 6 D7
Cessford AB 7 B7
Cessford AB 11 D1
Ceylon ON 20 B5
Ceylon SK 11 F5
Chaatl Island BC 1 B1
Chachukew Lake SK 12 E6
Chaffeys Locks ON 21 D7
Chaffeys Locks ON 24 F1
Chagoness SK 11 C6
Chaigneau, lac QC 39 A1-2
Chain Lakes PP AB 6 E5
Chain Lakes PP AB 7 D4
Chaleur, lac de la QC 26 A3
Chaleur Bay QC 29 E8
Chaleur Bay QC 30 E1
Chaleur Bay QC 31 A6-7
Chaleurs, baie des QC 29 E8
Chaleurs, baie des QC 30 D8
Chaleurs, baie des QC 31 A6
Chalk River ON 22 E5
Chaloupe, rivière de la QC 30 A6
Chambeaux, lac QC 39 A6
Chambeaux, lac QC 40 A1-2
Chamberlain SK 11 D5
Chamberlain Settlement NB 31 B6
Chambers Corners ON 19 C8
Chambers Corners ON 20 E7
Chambly QC 24 D6
Chambly QC 27 E2
Chambord QC 28 C4
Chamcook NB 32 E2
Chamiss Bay BC 1 E4
Champagne YT 4 E3
Champdoré, lac QC 40 D6
Champion AB 6 E6
Champion AB 7 D5
Champion Lakes PP BC 6 F3
Champlain QC 24 B8
Champlain QC 25 F8
Champlain QC 27 C4
Champlain, lac QC 27 F2
Champlain, rivière QC 24 B8
Champlain, rivière QC 25 F8
Champlain, rivière QC 27 B3-4 C3
Champlain Park ON 18 B8
Champneuf QC 23 D5
Champney's NL 37 C7
Chance Cove NL 37 F8
Chance Cove NL 37 D6-7
Chance Cove Head NL 37 F8
Chance Cove PP NL 37 F8
Chance Creek YT 5 D-E3
Chance Harbour NB 32 E3-4
Chance Harbour NB 33 B1
Chancellor AB 7 B5
Chanceport NL 38 E6
Chandindu River YT 4 A2
Chandler QC 30 D2
Chandos Lake ON 21 C4
Change Island NL 38 E7
Change Islands NL 38 E7
Chan Lake TP NT 10 B5-6
Chan Lake TP NT 41 D1
Channel Island MB 11 B8
Channel Island MB 13 B2
Channel-Port aux Basques NL 36 E1
Chantrey Inlet NU 41 C4
Chantry ON 21 C7
Chantry ON 24 F1
Chantry Island NMBS ON 18 F4
Chantry Island NMBS ON 20 A3
Chapais QC 26 B4
Chapais QC 40 F4-5
Chapais, ZEC QC 28 F8
Chapais, ZEC QC 29 F1
Chapeau QC 22 E5
Chapeau, lac QC 25 D6
Chapeau, lac QC 27 A1
Chapeau, lac QC 28 F1
Chapeau-de-Paille, ZEC QC 25 E6
Chapeau-de-Paille, ZEC QC 27 A1-2
Chapel Arm NL 37 D7
Chapel Island NL 36 A7
Chapel Island NL 36 D-E6
Chapel Island NS 37 D-E4
Chapel Island NS 38 F6
Chapel Island NS 34 D7
Chapin Bay MB 13 A5
Chapiteau, lac QC 39 A4
Chapleau ON 17 D4
Chapleau, réserve de chasse de la Couronne ON 17 D4
Chapleau Crown Game Preserve ON 17 C4
Chapleau-Nemegosenda River PP ON 17 D5
Chapleau River ON 17 D5
Chaplin NS 33 A-B7
Chaplin SK 34 F1
Chaplin SK 11 E4
Chaplin Lake SK 11 E4

Chapman, Cape NU 41 B5
Chapman, Cape NU 42 F5
Chapman Lake MB 15 D3
Chapmans BC 2 C7
Chapmans Corner NB 35 E2
Chapman Settlement NS 32 C7-8
Chapman Settlement NS 34 D1
Chapman Settlement NS 35 F2
Chaput ON 23 E1
Chaput Hughes ON 17 D7
Charbonneau River QC 9 B8
Charbonneau River SK 12 B3
Charcoal Lake SK 12 B6-7
Charcoal Lake SK 15 B1
Chard AB 9 E7
Chard AB 12 E2
Charest, rivière QC 24 A8
Charest, rivière QC 25 E8
Charest, rivière QC 27 B4
Charette QC 24 B7
Charette QC 25 F7
Charette, lac QC 27 C2-3
Charette, lac QC 23 D7
Charette, lac QC 26 D-E1
Charing Cross ON 19 E3
Charland, lac QC 25 E5
Charlebois MB 15 D5
Charlemagne QC 24 D6
Charlemagne QC 27 D-E2
Charles MB 12 E7
Charles MB 15 E1-2
Charles Island NU 40 B5
Charles Island NU 41 D8
Charles Lake AB 9 A7
Charles Lake AB 10 F8
Charles Lake AB 12 A7
Charleston NS 33 D4
Charleston ON 21 D7-8
Charleston ON 24 F1
Charleston Lake ON 21 D7-8
Charleston Lake PP ON 21 D7-8
Charlesville NS 33 F2
Charlie Lake BC 3 E8
Charlie Lake BC 9 D1
Charlie Lake NU 12 A7
Charlie Lake NU 15 A2
Charlie Lake PP BC 3 E8
Charlie Lake PP BC 9 D1
Charlo NB 29 D6-7
Charlo NB 31 A5
Charlo River NB 29 D-E6
Charlo River NB 31 A-B5
Charlos Cove NS 34 E6
Charlotte, Lake NS 33 B7
Charlotte Lake BC 1 C5
Charlottetown NL 36 E8
Charlottetown NL 37 C6
Charlottetown NL 39 C8
Charlottetown PE 34 C2
Charlottetown PE 35 E5
Charlottetown Harbour PE 35 E5
Charlton ON 17 D7
Charlton ON 23 E1
Charlton Island NU 40 E3-4
Charny QC 25 B5-6
Charny QC 27 B5
Charon, lac QC 26 B5
Charron Lake MB 13 B-C5
Charteris QC 21 A6-7
Charteris QC 22 F6-7
Charteris QC 24 C-D1
Chartersville NB 31 F8
Chartersville NB 32 B6
Chartier Lake ON 18 C7
Chartierville QC 27 F6
Chase BC 6 D2
Chasm BC 1 D8
Chasm BC 6 D1
Chasm PP BC 1 D8
Chasm PP BC 6 D1
Chassaigne, lac QC 23 E8
Chassaigne, lac QC 25 A2-3
Chassaigne, lac QC 26 F2-3
Chasse, île à la QC 39 E-F4
Chassignolle, lac QC 23 D3
Chastrier, lac QC 39 B1
Chaswood NS 33 B6
Chaswood NS 34 F2
Chateau NL 39 D8
Chateau Bay NL 39 D8
Châteauguay QC 24 D5-6
Châteauguay QC 27 E1
Châteauguay, rivière QC 24 B8
Châteauguay, rivière QC 27 F1
Château-Richer QC 25 A7
Châteauvert, lac QC 25 C5
Châteauvert, lac QC 28 E1
Chateh (Assumption) AB 9 B3
Chater MB 13 E2
Chater MB 14 E1
Chatfield MB 13 D3
Chatfield MB 14 C4
Chatham ON 19 D2-3
Chatham (Miramichi East) NB 31 D7
Chatham Head NB 31 D7
Chatham-Kent ON 19 D2-3
Chatsworth ON 18 F5-6

Chatsworth ON 20 A4
Chatwin Lake MB 12 B7
Chatwin Lake MB 15 B2
Chaud, lac QC 24 B4
Chaud, lac QC 25 F4
Chaudière, lac QC 26 B5
Chaudière, rivière QC 25 B-C6
Chaudière, rivière QC 27 D7
Chaudière, rivière QC 27 D7
Chaume, lac QC 23 F8
Chaume, lac QC 25 B2
Chaumonot, lac QC 25 B7
Chaumonot, lac QC 26 F7
Chaumonot, lac QC 28 D3
Chauvin AB 6 B8
Chauvin AB 11 B2
Chauvin, ZEC QC 28 C7
Chavannes, lac QC 22 C5
Chazel QC 17 C8
Chazel QC 23 C2
Cheadle AB 7 B4-5
Cheapside ON 19 C7
Cheapside ON 20 F6
Chebogue Point NS 33 F1
Chebogue Point NS 33 E-F1
Checleset Bay BC 1 E4
Chedabucto Bay NS 34 E6
Chedabucto Lake NT 10 D6
Cheddarville AB 8 F4-5
Cheecham Hills AB 9 E7
Cheecham Hills AB 12 D-E2
Cheekamus BC 1 E-F7
Cheekamus BC 2 C5
Cheekamus River BC 2 C5
Cheesman Lake ON 16 E5-6
Chef, rivière du QC 26 A3
Chegoggin NS 33 E1
Chehalis Lake BC 2 D6
Chelan BC 11 C6
Chelaslie River BC 1 B5
Chelmsford NB 31 D6-7
Chelmsford ON 17 F6
Chelmsford ON 18 A5
Chelsea NS 33 D4
Chelsea ON 21 A8
Chelsea QC 22 F8
Chelsea QC 24 D2
Cheltenham ON 19 A7
Cheltenham ON 20 C6
Chelton PE 35 D3
Chelton Beach PP PE 32 A8
Chelton Beach PP PE 34 C1
Chelton Beach PP PE 35 E2-3
Chemainus BC 1 F6
Chemainus BC 2 E4
Chemainus River PP BC 2 E3-4
Chemawawin MB 13 B2
Chemong SK 11 B7
Chemong SK 13 B1
Chemong Lake ON 21 D3
Chenaux ON 21 A6
Chenaux ON 22 F6
Chêne, rivière du QC 27 B4-C5
Chênes, île des MB 13 F4
Chênes, île des MB 14 E4
Chênevert, lac QC 23 E8
Chênevert, lac QC 25 A2
Chênéville QC 24 C3
Chenil, lac QC 39 D6
Chenon, lac QC 22 A-B3
Chepstow ON 20 B3-4
Chepstow PE 34 C2
Chepstow PE 35 D-E8
Chepstow Point PE 35 E8
Cherhill AB 6 A5
Cherhill AB 8 C-5
Cherrier, lac QC 23 C8
Cherrier, lac QC 26 D2
Cherrington Lake ON 16 A1
Cherryfield NS 32 F6
Cherryfield NS 33 C3-4
Cherry Grove AB 9 F7-8
Cherry Grove AB 11 A2
Cherry Grove AB 12 F2
Cherry Hill NS 33 D4
Cherry Point AB 3 E8
Cherry Point AB 2 F4
Cherry River QC 27 E-F4
Cherry Valley ON 21 E5
Cherry Valley PE 34 C3
Cherry Valley South PE 35 E5
Cherryville BC 6 E2
Chertsey QC 27 C-D1
Chertsey QC 24 C3
Cheslatta Lake BC 1 A-B5
Chesley ON 20 B4
Chesley Lake ON 18 F5
Chesley SK 20 A3-4
Chesnaye MB 15 C5
Chester NS 32 F7
Chester NS 33 C4-5
Chester Basin NS 32 F7
Chester Basin NS 33 C4
Chesterfield Bridge SK 6 D8
Chesterfield Bridge SK 11 D2
Chesterfield Inlet NU 40 A2
Chesterfield Inlet NU 41 D5
Chesterfield Inlet (Igluligaarjuk) NU 40 A2

Chesterfield Inlet (Igluligaarjuk) NU 41 D-E5
Chester Grant NS 32 F7
Chester Grant NS 33 C4-5
Chestermere AB 6 D5-6
Chestermere AB 7 B4
Chesterville ON 24 E3
Chesterville ON 27 D5
Chéticamp NS 34 B6
Chéticamp Island NS 34 B6
Chéticamp River NS 34 B6-7
Chetwynd BC 3 E7
Chetwynd BC 9 E1
Cheverie NS 32 E7
Cheverie NS 33 B5
Cheverie NS 34 F1
Chevery QC 39 E6
Chevreuil, lac du QC 24 B-C3
Chevreuils, rivière aux QC 27 C5
Chevrillon, lac QC 26 A4-5
Chezacut BC 1 C6
Chiasson NB 31 B8
Chiblow Lake ON 17 F5
Chiblow Lake ON 18 A2
Chibouet, rivière QC 24 C7
Chibouet, rivière QC 27 D3
Chibougamau QC 26 A-B5
Chibougamau QC 40 F5
Chibougamau, lac QC 26 A-B5
Chibougamau, rivière QC 26 A3
Chic-Chocs, monts QC 29 B6-7
Chic-Chocs, RF des QC 29 B7-8
Chic-Chocs, RF des QC 29 A-B7
Chichester QC 22 B7
Chichester Cove PE 35 D3
Chicken Lake MB 12 D8
Chicken Lake MB 15 D2
Chick Lake NT 5 E7
Chicobi, lac QC 23 C3
Chicomo, lac QC 39 D2
Chicotte, rivière QC 30 A5
Chicoutai, pointe QC 39 F5
Chicoutimi QC 28 C6
Chicoutimi, rivière QC 28 C6
Chief Mountain AB 6 F5-6
Chief Mountain AB 7 F4
Chiefs Point ON 18 F4-5
Chiefs Point ON 20 A3
Chien, lac du QC 25 A6
Chien, lac du QC 26 E6
Chien, lac du QC 28 C2
Chienne, lac à la QC 25 D6
Chienne, lac à la QC 27 A1
Chiens, lac aux QC 26 A8
Chiganois River NS 33 A6
Chiganois River NS 34 E2
Chignecto, Cape NS 32 D6
Chignecto, Cape NS 32 C7
Chignecto Bay NB 32 C-D6
Chignecto Bay NB 33 A3-4
Chignecto Bay NS 33 A3-4
Chignecto Game Sanctuary NS 32 D7
Chignecto Game Sanctuary NS 33 A4
Chignecto Isthmus NB 32 B7
Chignecto National Wilderness Area NS 32 C7
Chignectou, baie de NB 32 C-D6
Chignectou, baie de NB 33 A3-4
Chignectou, baie de NS 33 A3-4
Chignectou, RNF NS 32 C7
Chignectou, RNF NS 32 D7
Chigoubiche, lac QC 28 A1-2
Chilako River BC 1 B6-7
Chilanko Forks BC 1 C6
Chilanko River BC 1 C6
Chilco Lake BC 1 D6
Chilcotin Ranges BC 1 D7
Chilcotin Ranges BC 1 C6
Chilkat Pass BC 4 F3
Chilko Lake BC 1 D6
Chilkoot Pass BC 4 F3-4
Chilkoot Trail NHS BC 3 A1
Chilkoot Trail NHS BC 4 F3-4
Chilko River BC 1 C6
Chilliwack BC 1 F8
Chilliwack BC 2 E6
Chilliwack Lake BC 2 E7
Chilliwack Lake BC 2 E7
Chilliwack Lake PP BC 2 E7
Chilliwack River PP BC 2 E6-7
Chimney Corner NS 34 B5-6
Chin AB 7 E6
Chin, Cape NU 18 D5
Chinchaga River AB 9 C3
Chinchaga Wildland PP AB 9 C-D2
Chiniguchi Lake ON 17 E7

Chin Lakes AB 6 F6-7
Chin Lakes AB 7 E6
Chinook AB 6 D7
Chinook AB 7 A8
Chinook Valley AB 9 D3
Chipewyan Lake AB 9 C5
Chipewyan Lake AB 9 D5
Chipewyan Lake MB 15 C3
Chip Lake AB 6 A4
Chip Lake AB 8 C4
Chip Lake AB 8 C4
Chipman AB 6 A6
Chipman AB 8 D6
Chipman NB 11 A1
Chipman NB 31 F6
Chipman NB 32 B4
Chipman Brook NS 32 E6
Chipman Brook NS 33 B4
Chipman Lake ON 16 B6
Chipman Lake ON 17 B2
Chipman River SK 12 A5
Chippawa ON 20 E7-8
Chippawa Creek CA ON 19 C8
Chippawa Creek CA ON 20 E7
Chippawa Hill ON 18 F4-5
Chippawa Hill ON 20 A3
Chiputneticook Lakes NB 32 C-D1
Chisasibi QC 40 E3-4
Chisel Lake MB 12 F8
Chisel Lake MB 15 F2
Chisholm AB 9 F5
Chiswick ON 17 F8
Chitek Lake MB 13 C2
Chitek Lake SK 11 A3
Chitek Lake SK 11 A3
Chitek Lake PP Reserve MB 13 C2
Chitek Lake PRS SK 11 A3-4
Chitek River SK 11 A3
Chochocouane, rivière QC 23 F5-6
Choelquoit Lake BC 1 C6
Choiceland SK 11 B5-6
Choiseul, lac QC 25 A2
Choiseul, lac QC 26 F2
Chokio AB 7 E4
Chopaka BC 6 F1-2
Chopin QC 25 B3
Choquette, lac QC 25 B3
Choquette Hot Springs PP BC 40 B4-5
Chorkbak Inlet NU 40 C8
Chorkbak Inlet NU 41 C7-8
Chorlitz MB 14 F4
Chorney Beach SK 11 C6
Chouart, rivière QC 23 F8
Chouart, rivière QC 25 B2-3 C3
Chowade River BC 3 D7
Chown, Mount BC 6 B2
Christensen Beach MB 14 B2
Christian Channel ON 18 E7
Christian Island ON 18 E7
Christian Island ON 18 E7
Christie Bay NT 10 C8
Christie Bay NT 41 D2
Christie Beach CA ON 18 F6
Christie Beach CA ON 20 A5
Christie CA ON 19 B7
Christie CA ON 20 D6
Christie Islet NMBS BC 2 C5
Christie Lake ON 21 C6-7
Christie Lake ON 21 C6-7
Christie Memorial PP BC 6 F2
Christie Pass NT 4 B6
Christina Beach AB 9 E7
Christina Lake AB 12 E2
Christina Lake BC 6 F2-3
Christina Lake BC 6 F2-3
Christina Lake PP BC 6 F2-3
Christina Range BC 9 F7
Christina River AB 9 E7
Christina River AB 12 E2
Christmas Island NS 34 C7
Christopher Cross PE 35 A2
Christopher Lake SK 11 B5
Chub, lac QC 22 C8
Chub, lac QC 25 C2
Chub Lake ON 18 A1
Chuchi Lake BC 3 D5
Chu Chua Cottonwood PP BC 6 D1-2
Chukachida River BC 3 B4
Churchbridge SK 11 D7
Churchill MB 15 B5-6
Churchill MB 40 C1
Churchill MB 41 C6
Churchill ON 20 B7
Churchill ON 21 E1
Churchill PE 35 E4
Churchill, Cape MB 15 B6
Churchill, Cape MB 40 C1
Churchill, Cape MB 41 C5
Churchill, fleuve NL 39 C5
Churchill, fleuve NL 40 D2
Churchill, rivière MB 12 D8
Churchill, rivière MB 15 C5

Churchill, rivière *MB* **15** D2
Churchill, rivière *MB* **40** C1
Churchill, rivière *MB* **41** F4-5
Churchill, rivière *SK* **12** E6-7
Churchill, rivière *SK* **15** E1
Churchill Falls *NL* **39** B3-4
Churchill Falls *NL* **40** E7
Churchill Lake *ON* **13** D7-8
Churchill Lake *ON* **16** C4
Churchill Lake *SK* **9** D-E8
Churchill Lake *SK* **9** D8
Churchill Lake *SK* **12** E3
Churchill Lake *SK* **12** D-E3
Churchill Peak *BC* **3** C5
Churchill River *MB* **12** E8
Churchill River *MB* **15** C4-5
Churchill River *MB* **15** E2
Churchill River *MB* **40** C1
Churchill River *MB* **41** F4-5
Churchill River *NL* **39** B-C4
Churchill River *NL* **40** E7
Churchill River *SK* **12** E6
Churchover *NS* **33** F2-3
Churchview *NS* **34** C6
Churchville *NS* **33** A7-8
Churchville *NS* **34** E3
Churn Creek PPA *BC* **1** D7
Chute-aux-Outardes *QC* **29** A3
Chute-aux-Outardes *QC* **39** F1
Chute-Panet *QC* **17** F5-6
Chutes PP *ON* **17** F5-6
Chutes PP *ON* **18** A3
Chute-Saint-Philippe *QC* **24** A3
Chute-Saint-Philippe *QC* **25** E3
Chutes-de-Saint-Ursule, parc des *QC* **25** F6-7
Chutes-de-Shawinigan, parc des *QC* **25** F7-8
Chutine River *BC* **3** C2
Cigar Lake Mine *SK* **12** C5
Cinconsine, lac *QC* **25** C7
Cinconsine, lac *QC* **26** E4
Cinnemousun Narrows PP *BC* **6** D2
Cinq Cerf River *NL* **36** D2-3
Cinq Cerf River *NL* **37** D1
Cinq Milles, lac des *QC* **25** A4
Cinq Milles, lac des *QC* **26** E4
Ciquart *NB* **31** B-C2
Circle River *ON* **23** B1
Cirque Mountain *NL* **40** C7
Clair *NB* **29** F2
Clair *NB* **31** C1
Clair *SK* **11** C6
Clair, lac *QC* **26** B8
Clairambault, lac *QC* **39** A1
Claire, lac *AB* **9** B6
Claire, lac *AB* **41** F1
Claire, Lake *AB* **9** B6
Claire, Lake *AB* **12** B1-2
Claire, Lake *AB* **41** F1
Claire Lake *YT* **4** D4
Clairmont *AB* **9** E2-3
Clairmont PP *NS* **32** E6
Clairmont PP *NS* **33** B3-4
Clairvaux, lac *QC* **26** E7
Clairvaux, lac *QC* **28** C3
Clairville *NB* **31** E7
Clairville *NB* **32** A5
Clam Bay *NS* **33** C7
Clam Harbour *NS* **33** C7
Clam Harbour Beach PP *NS* **33** C7
Clam Lake *SK* **12** E5
Clandeboye *MB* **13** E4
Clandeboye *MB* **14** D5
Clandeboye *ON* **19** B4
Clandeboye *ON* **20** E3
Clandonald *AB* **6** A-B7
Clandonald *AB* **11** A2
Clanwilliam *MB* **11** E8
Clanwilliam *MB* **13** E2
Clanwilliam *MB* **14** D1-2
Clapperton *BC* **2** B7
Clapperton Channel *ON* **18** B3
Clapperton Island *NT* **5** A8
Clapperton Island **18** B3
Clappison's Corners *ON* **19** B7
Clappison's Corners *ON* **20** D6
Clare *NS* **33** D1-2
Claremont *ON* **20** C7-8
Claremont *ON* **21** E2
Clarence *NS* **32** E5
Clarence *NS* **33** B3
Clarence *ON* **24** D3
Clarence, Cape *NU* **41** A5
Clarence, Cape *NU* **42** D4
Clarence Creek *ON* **24** D3
Clarence-Steepbank Lakes PWP *SK* **11** A5
Clarendon *NB* **30** D3
Clarendon Station *ON* **21** C6
Clarenville *NL* **36** C8
Clarenville *NL* **37** C7
Clare River *ON* **21** D5
Claresholm *AB* **6** E6
Claresholm *AB* **7** D4
Clarington *ON* **20** B8
Clarington *ON* **21** E2-3
Clark, Point *ON* **20** B2-3
Clark Bay *SK* **12** B6

Clark Bay *SK* **15** B1
Clarke Bridge *SK* **11** F5
Clarke City *QC* **39** E2
Clarke Lake *SK* **11** A4
Clarke Lake *SK* **12** F4
Clarke's Beach *NL* **37** D7
Clarke's Corners *ON* **18** E4
Clarkes Head *NL* **36** A7
Clarkes Head *NL* **37** A5
Clarkes Head *NL* **38** F6-7
Clarkin *PE* **34** C3
Clarkin *PE* **35** E5-6
Clarkleigh *MB* **13** E3
Clarkleigh *MB* **14** C4
Clarksburg *ON* **18** F6
Clarksburg *ON* **20** A5
Clarkson *NL* **19** B8
Clarkson *ON* **20** D7
Clarksville *NS* **32** E8
Clarksville *NS* **33** B5
Clarksville *NS* **34** F1
Clarkville *NB* **31** F3-4
Clarkville *NB* **32** B1-2
Clashmoor *SK* **11** B6
Claude, rivière à *QC* **29** A7
Claud Elliott Lake PP *BC* **1** E4
Clavering *ON* **18** F5
Clavering *ON* **20** A4
Clavet *SK* **11** C4
Claybank *SK* **11** E5
Claydon *SK* **11** F2-3
Clayhurst *BC* **3** E8
Clayhurst *BC* **9** D2
Clay Lake *BC* **13** E6
Clay Lake *ON* **16** D2
Clayoquot Arm *BC* **2** E1
Clayoquot Arm PP *BC* **1** F5
Clayoquot Arm PP *BC* **2** E1
Clayoquot Plateau PP *BC* **1** F5
Clayoquot Plateau PP *BC* **2** D1-2
Clayoquot Sound *BC* **1** F5
Clayoquot Sound *BC* **2** E1
Clayton *ON* **21** B7
Clayton *ON* **24** E1
Clayton *ON* **21** B7
Clayton Lake *ON* **24** E1
Clearbrook *BC* **8** B6-7
Clear Bay *MB* **11** B8
Clear Bay *MB* **13** B2
Clearbrook *AB* **9** D2
Cleardale *AB* **9** D2
Clearfield *SK* **11** F6
Clear Hills *AB* **9** D2
Clear Lake *MB* **11** D8
Clear Lake *MB* **13** D2
Clear Lake *MB* **14** C1
Clear Lake *ON* **21** B-D2
Clear Lake *ON* **21** A1-2
Clear Lake *ON* **21** C2
Clear Lake *ON* **21** C2
Clear River *AB* **9** D2
Clear Springs *PE* **35** D7
Clearwater *BC* **6** C1-2
Clearwater *BC* **3** C1-2
Clearwater *MB* **14** C2
Clearwater Bay *ON* **13** E5
Clearwater Bay *ON* **14** E8
Clearwater Bay *ON* **14** E8
Clearwater Bay *ON* **16** D1
Clearwater Brook *NB* **31** D-E4
Clearwater Creek *NT* **4** C-D8
Clearwater Creek *NT* **10** D1
Clearwater Lake *BC* **1** C8
Clearwater Lake *BC* **6** C1
Clearwater Lake *MB* **11** A7
Clearwater Lake *MB* **13** A1
Clearwater Lake *MB* **13** A-B2
Clearwater Lake PP *MB* **11** A7-8
Clearwater Lake PP *MB* **13** A1
Clearwater River *AB* **6** C5
Clearwater River *AB* **8** F4-5
Clearwater River *AB* **9** D7
Clearwater River *AB* **12** D2
Clearwater River *BC* **6** C1
Clearwater River *SK* **9** C8
Clearwater River *SK* **12** C-D3
Clearwater River PP *SK* **9** D8
Clearwater River PP *SK* **12** D3
Clearwater River PP *SK* **41** F2
Clearwater West Lake *ON* **13** F7
Clearwater West Lake *ON* **16** E3-4
Clemenceau *SK* **11** B6-7
Clemenceau Icefield *BC* **6** C3
Clemenceau Icefield *BC* **8** F1
Clemens *SK* **11** B5-6
Clementsport *SK* **32** F5
Clementsport *NS* **33** C2
Clementsvale *SK* **32** F5
Clementsvale *NS* **33** C2
Clemow Lake *ON* **22** E4
Clemville *QC* **30** D1-2
Clemville *QC* **31** A7

Cléricy *QC* **23** D3
Clerke Point *BC* **1** E4
Clermont *PE* **35** D3
Clermont *QC* **17** C8
Clermont *QC* **23** C2
Clermont *QC* **28** E7
Clerval *QC* **17** C8
Clerval *QC* **23** C2
Cleveland *NS* **34** D6
Cleveland Beach PP *NS* **32** F8
Cleveland Beach PP *NS* **33** C5
Clifford *ON* **20** C4
Cliff Point *BC* **1** B2
Clifton *NB* **29** E8
Clifton *NB* **30** E1
Clifton *NB* **31** B7
Clifton *NL* **37** C7
Clifton Lake *MB* **12** B8
Clifton Lake *MB* **15** B3
Cli Lake *NT* **10** D2
Climax *SK* **11** F3
Clinton *BC* **2** A7
Clinton *ON* **19** A4
Clinton *ON* **20** C-D3
Clinton *PE* **32** A8
Clinton *PE* **34** B-C2
Clinton *PE* **35** D3
Clinton-Colden Lake *NT* **1** E4
Clinton-Colden Lake *NT* **41** D3
Clinton Creek *YT* **4** A1
Clinton Creek *YT* **5** F1
Clisbako River *BC* **1** C6
Clive *AB* **6** C6
Clive *AB* **8** E6
Clive Lake *NT* **10** C4
Cloan *SK* **11** C3
Clode Sound *NL* **36** B-C8
Clode Sound *NL* **37** B-C6
Clo-oose *BC* **2** F2
Clore River *BC* **1** A4
Cloridorme *QC* **30** A2
Close Lake *SK* **12** C5
Close to the Edge PP *BC* **1** F5
Close to the Edge PP *BC* **6** A1
Cloud Bay *NT* **10** A3
Cloud Bay *ON* **16** F5
Cloud River *NL* **38** C4
Clouston *SK* **11** B4-5
Cloutier *QC* **17** D8
Cloutier *QC* **23** C2
Clova *QC* **25** A3
Clova *QC* **26** F3
Cloverdale *BC* **2** E5
Cloverdale *NB* **31** F3-4
Cloverdale *NB* **32** B2
Cloverdale *NS* **33** B6-7
Cloverdale *NS* **34** F2-3
Clover Lake *ON* **22** F4
Cloverlawn *AB* **8** D7
Cloverleaf *MB* **14** D6
Clowhom Lake *BC* **2** C4
Cloyne *ON* **21** C5
Club Island *ON* **18** C4
Cluculz Creek *BC* **1** A-B6
Cluculz Lake *BC* **1** A6
Cluff Lake Mine *SK* **9** B7-8
Cluff Lake Mine *SK* **41** F2
Cluny *AB* **6** D6
Cluny *AB* **7** C5
Clute *ON* **17** C6
Clyde *AB* **6** A5-6
Clyde *AB* **8** B6
Clyde *ON* **19** B6
Clyde *ON* **20** D5
Clyde River *AB* **9** E6-7
Clyde River *AB* **12** E1
Clyde River *NS* **33** F2
Clyde River *NS* **33** F2-3
Clyde River *NS* **34** F1
Clyde River *ON* **21** B6
Clyde River *PE* **35** E4
Clyde River (Kangiqtugaapik) *NU* **41** A8
Clyde River (Kangiqtugaapik) *NU* **42** E7
Clydesdale *NS* **34** D4
Clymont *AB* **8** D8
Coachman's Cove *NL* **38** D4-5
Coal Branch *NB* **31** E7
Coal Branch *NB* **32** B5
Coal Brook *NB* **36** D1
Coal Creek *NB* **31** F6
Coal Creek *NB* **32** B4
Coaldale *AB* **6** F6
Coaldale *AB* **7** E6
Coal Harbour *BC* **1** E4
Coalhurst *AB* **6** F6
Coalhurst *AB* **7** E5
Coalmont *AB* **2** D8
Coalmont *BC* **6** F1
Coal River *BC* **3** A5
Coal River *BC* **4** F8
Coal River *YT* **4** D-E7
Coal River Springs TP *YT* **3** A4-5
Coal River Springs TP *YT* **4** E7-8
Coalspur *AB* **6** B3-4
Coalspur *AB* **8** D2

Coast Mountains *BC* **2** A2-3 B3-4
Coast Mountains *BC* **3** B-C2 D3
Coast Mountains *BC* **4** F4
Coast Mountains *YT* **4** E3
Coates Creek *ON* **20** A-B6
Coates Mills *NB* **31** E8
Coates Mills *NB* **32** A-B6
Coaticook *QC* **27** F5
Coaticook, rivière *QC* **27** F4-5
Coats Island *NU* **40** B3
Coats Island *NU* **41** E6
Coatsworth *ON* **19** E2
Cobalt *ON* **17** E8
Cobalt *ON* **22** A1
Cobbs Arm *NL* **38** E6-7
Cobden *ON* **21** A6
Cobden *ON* **22** E1
Cobequid Bay *NS* **32** D8
Cobequid Bay *NS* **33** A6
Cobequid Bay *NS* **34** E2
Cobequid Mountains *NS* **32** D8
Cobequid Mountains *NS* **34** C-C8
Cobham River *MB* **13** B5-6
Coboconk *ON* **20** A8
Coboconk *ON* **21** C-D2
Cobourg *ON* **21** E3-4
Coburg *NS* **35** F2
Coburg Island *NU* **42** C5
Coburn *NB* **32** C2
Cocagne *NB* **31** E8
Cocagne *NB* **32** B6
Cocagne, île *NB* **31** E8
Cocagne, île *NB* **32** A6-7
Cocagne Island *NB* **31** E8
Cocagne Island *NB* **32** A6-7
Cocagne River *NB* **31** E8
Cocagne River *NB* **32** B6
Cochenour *NL* **13** D6
Cochenour *ON* **16** C2
Cochin *SK* **11** B3
Cochrane *AB* **6** D5
Cochrane *AB* **7** B3
Cochrane *ON* **17** C6
Cochrane Bay *MB* **13** A5
Cochrane Ranche PHS *BC* **6** D5
Cochrane Ranche PHS *BC* **7** B3-4
Cochrane River *MB* **12** B-C7
Cochrane River *MB* **15** B-C2
Cochrane River *MB* **41** F3
Cockburn Island *ON* **18** B1
Cockfield, Mount *YT* **4** A2
Cockram Strait *NU* **40** B7
Cockram Strait *NU* **42** F6
Coddles Harbour *NS* **34** F5
Coderre *SK* **11** E4
Codette *SK* **11** B6
Codette Lake *SK* **11** B5
Cod Island *NL* **40** C7
Codner *AB* **8** E5
Codrington *ON* **21** E4
Codroy *NL* **36** D1
Codroy Pond *NL* **36** C-D2
Codroy Valley Beach PP *NL* **36** D1
Codville Lagoon PMP *BC* **1** C4
Cody Caves PP *BC* **6** F3-4
Cody Creek *BC* **21** B7
Cody Creek *YT* **5** D7
Codys *NB* **32** C4
Cœur, lac en *QC* **24** C3
Coffee Cove *NL* **38** E6-7
Coffee Creek *YT* **4** B2
Coghill *AB* **8** E6-7
Coghlan Lake *YT* **4** D3
Cogmagun River *NS* **32** E7-8
Cogmagun River *NS* **33** B5
Cogmagun River *NS* **34** F1
Coin-du-Banc *QC* **30** B2
Col-Athabasca, LHN du *AB* **8** E1
Col-Athabasca, LHN du *BC*
Colborne *ON* **21** E4
Colchester *ON* **19** F1
Cold Brook *NB* **36** B2
Coldbrook *NS* **32** E6
Coldbrook *NS* **33** B4
Coldbrook PP *NS* **32** E6-7
Coldbrook PP *NS* **33** B4
Cold Creek *ON* **21** E4
Cold Lake *AB* **9** F7
Cold Lake *AB* **12** E2
Cold Lake *SK* **9** F8
Cold Lake *SK* **12** F2
Cold Lake PP *AB* **9** F7-8
Cold Lake PP *AB* **12** F2
Coldspring Head *NS* **35** F2-3
Cold Spring Pond *NL* **36** C5
Cold Spring Pond *NL* **37** C3
Cold Springs *ON* **21** E3
Coldstream *NB* **31** F3
Coldstream *NB* **32** B1
Coldstream *NS* **33** B6
Coldstream *NS* **34** E1
Coldstream *ON* **19** C4
Coldstream *ON* **20** E3
Coldwater *BC* **2** C7
Coldwater *QC* **20** A7
Coldwater *ON* **21** C1
Coldwater River *BC* **1** E8
Coldwater River *BC* **2** C7-8

Coldwater River *BC* **6** E1
Coldwater River PP *BC* **1** E-F8
Coldwater River PP *BC* **2** C7-8
Coldwater River PP *BC* **6** E1
Coldwell *ON* **16** E8
Coldwell *ON* **17** C2
Cole Bay *SK* **9** E8
Cole Bay *SK* **12** F3
Colebrook *ON* **21** D5
Coleman *AB* **6** F5
Coleman *AB* **7** E3
Coleman *PE* **32** A7
Coleman *PE* **35** C2
Coleman Lake *AB* **7** A6
Colen Lakes *AB* **15** F5
Colen Lakes *MB* **15** F5
Coleraine *QC* **27** D5-6
Coles Island *NB* **32** C4
Coles Pond *NL* **38** B4-5
Coles Pond *NL* **39** E8
Coleville *SK* **6** C8
Coleville *SK* **11** C2
Colfax *SK* **11** E6
Colgan *ON* **20** B6
Colgate *SK* **11** F6
Col-Howse, LHN du *AB* **6** C3-4
Colin Archer Peninsula *NU* **42** C4
Colin-Cornwall Lakes Wildland PP *AB* **9** A7
Colin-Cornwall Lakes Wildland PP *AB* **12** A2
Colinet *NL* **37** E7
Colinet River *NL* **37** E7
Colin Lake *AB* **9** A7
Colin Lake *AB* **12** A2-3
Colin Lake *SK* **12** E6
Colinton *AB* **6** A6
Colinton *AB* **8** B7
Colinton *AB* **9** F6
Col-Kicking Horse, LHN du *AB* **7** A1
College Bridge *NB* **32** B-C7
College Heights *AB* **6** C5
College Heights *AB* **8** E6
Collette *NB* **31** D7
Collicutt *AB* **7** B4
Collier *SK* **11** E7
Colliers *NL* **37** E7
Collin, ZEC *QC* **24** A5
Collin, ZEC *QC* **25** E5
Collina *NB* **32** C2
Colline Saddle *QC* **27** E6
Collingwood *ON* **18** F6
Collingwood *ON* **20** A5-6
Collingwood Corner *NS* **33** B3
Collingwood Corner *NS* **34** C1
Collingwood Cove *AB* **8** C7
Collins *ON* **16** D5
Collins, lac *NB* **35** F2
Collins Bay *ON* **21** E6
Collins Bay *SK* **12** B6
Collins Cove *NL* **36** F7
Collins Cove *NL* **37** F5
Collins Inlet *ON* **18** B5
Collins Lake *SK* **12** E2
Colombier *QC* **29** B2
Colombier, cap *QC* **29** B2
Colombourg *QC* **17** C8
Colombourg *QC* **23** C2
Colonel Roscoe Vanderwater CA *ON* **21** D5
Colonel Roscoe Vanderwater CA *ON* **20** E6-7
Colonsay *SK* **11** C5
Colpitts Settlement *NB* **31** F8
Colpitts Settlement *NB* **32** C5
Colpoys Bay *ON* **18** E5
Colpton *NS* **32** F6
Colpton *NS* **33** D3-4
Colton *NS* **32** F6
Columbia, Cape *NU* **42** A5
Columbia, fleuve *BC* **6** D-E3
Columbia, fleuve *BC* **7** C1
Columbia, Mount *AB* **8** F1
Columbia, Mount *BC* **6** C3
Columbia Icefield *AB* **8** F2
Columbia Icefield *BC* **6** C3
Columbia Lake *BC* **6** E4
Columbia Lake PP *BC* **6** E4
Columbia Lake PP *BC* **7** D1-2
Columbia Mountains *BC* **6** B-C2
Columbia Reach *BC* **6** D3
Columbia River *BC* **6** D4
Columbia River *BC* **7** B1
Columbus *ON* **21** E2
Columbus *ON* **20** C6
Colville Bay *PE* **35** E7-8
Colville Lake *NL* **39** B2-3
Colville Lake *NT* **5** D7-8
Colwell *ON* **20** B6
Colwood *BC* **2** F3
Col-Yellowhead, LHN du *AB* **6** B2-3
Comber *ON* **19** E2
Combermere *ON* **21** B4-5
Combermere, Cape *NU* **42** C5

Come By Chance *NL* **36** D8
Come By Chance *NL* **37** D6
Comeau Hill *NS* **33** F1
Comeauville *NS* **33** D1
Comet *ON* **19** E1
Comet Mountain *BC* **1** B4
Comfort, Cape *NU* **40** A3
Comfort, Cape *NU* **41** D6
Comfort Cove *NL* **37** A5
Comfort Cove *NL* **38** F6
Comma Island *NL* **39** A5-6
Commanda *ON* **18** B8
Commanda *ON* **22** E1
Commanda Creek *ON* **18** B-C8
Commanda Lake *ON* **18** B7-8
Commanda Lake *ON* **22** E1
Commissaires, lac des *QC* **25** A5
Commissaires, lac des *QC* **26** F8
Commissaires, lac des *QC* **28** A4
Commissioner Island *MB* **13** C4
Committee Bay *NU* **40** B3
Committee Bay *NU* **41** B5-6 C6
Committee Bay *NU* **42** F5
Commodore, Cape *NU* **18** E5-6
Commonwealth Lake **15** A4
Como *QC* **24** D5
Comox *BC* **1** E5
Comox *BC* **2** D2
Comox Lake *BC* **1** F5
Comox Lake *BC* **2** D2
Compass *NL* **11** A3
Compeer *AB* **6** C8
Compeer *AB* **11** C2
Complexe-Historique-de-Dawson, LHN du *YT* **4** A2
Compton *QC* **27** F5
Compton, lac *QC* **26** C4
Compton Névé *BC* **1** E6
Compton Névé *BC* **2** A3
Conception Bay *NL* **37** D8
Conception Bay South *NL* **37** D7-8
Conception Harbour *NL* **37** E7
Conception Harbour *NL* **37** E7
Concession *NS* **33** D1-2
Concession Discovery, LHN de la *YT* **4** A1-2
Conche *NL* **38** C5
Conche *NL* **39** E8
Concord *ON* **20** F4
Concession Lake *ON* **18** B-C3
Confederation CA *ON* **21** D5
Confederation CA *ON* **20** E6-7
Confederation Island *MB* **13** A5
Confederation Lake *ON* **13** D7
Confederation Lake *ON* **16** C-D3
Confusion Bay *NL* **38** D-E5
Congerville *SK* **11** F3
Congresbury *AB* **8** F4-5
Congress *SK* **11** F4
Conibear Lake *AB* **9** A5-6
Conibear Lake *AB* **12** A1
Coniston *ON* **18** A5-6
Coniston *ON* **18** A5-6
Conjuring Creek *AB* **8** D6
Conkle Lake PP *BC* **6** F2
Conklin *AB* **9** E7
Conklin *AB* **12** E2
Conn *ON* **20** C5
Connaigre Bay *NL* **36** E5-6
Connaigre Bay *NL* **37** E3-4
Connaigre Head *NL* **36** E5-6
Connaigre Head *NL* **37** E3-4
Connaught *ON* **17** C6
Connell Creek *SK* **11** A5
Connelly, lac *QC* **28** A4
Connemara *SK* **7** C-D4
Conne River *NL* **36** D6
Conne River *NL* **37** D4
Conn Mills *NS* **33** D1
Conn Mills *NS* **34** D1
Connor *ON* **20** C6
Connor Creek *AB* **8** B4
Connors *NB* **29** F2
Connors *NB* **31** C1
Conquerall Mills *NS* **33** D4
Conquest *SK* **11** D4
Conrad *AB* **7** E7
Conrad Beach/Island PP *NS* **33** C6-7
Conrich *AB* **6** D5-6
Conrich *AB* **7** B4
Conroy Creek *BC* **3** C7

Conroy Creek *BC* **9** C1
Consecon *ON* **21** E4-5
Consecon Lake *ON* **21** E5
Consort *AB* **6** C7
Consort *AB* **11** C2
Constance Bay *ON* **21** A7
Constance Bay *ON* **22** F7
Constance Bay *ON* **24** D1
Constance Lake *ON* **17** B4
Constant, Mount *YT* **4** D1
Constantine, Mount *YT* **4** D1
Constant Lake *ON* **21** A5-6
Consul *SK* **6** F8
Consul *SK* **11** F2
Contact Creek *BC* **3** A4
Contact Creek *BC* **4** F7
Contrecoeur *QC* **24** C6-7
Contrecoeur *QC* **27** D2
Contwoyto Lake *NU* **41** C2
Conway *NL* **21** E6
Conway *PE* **32** A7
Conway *PE* **34** B1
Conway *PE* **35** C2
Conway Narrows *PE* **35** C2
Cook, Cape *BC* **1** E4
Cook, Mount *YT* **4** E1
Cooking Lake/Blackfoot PRA *AB* **6** B6
Cooking Lake/Blackfoot PRA *AB* **8** C7
Cooks Brook *NS* **33** B6
Cooks Brook *NS* **34** F2
Cooks Cove *NS* **34** E5-6
Cook's Harbour *NL* **38** A5
Cook's Harbour *NL* **39** D5
Cookshire *QC* **27** E5
Cooks Mills *ON* **17** F8
Cooks Mills *ON* **18** A8
Cookstown *ON* **20** B6
Cookville *NB* **35** F1
Cookville PP *NS* **33** C4
Coombes Cove *NL* **36** E6
Coombes Cove *NL* **37** E4
Coombs *ON* **1** F6
Coombs *BC* **2** D3
Cooper Creek *MB* **15** C-D6
Corning *SK* **11** E6-7
Copeland *SK* **11** D5-6
Copeland Islands PMP *BC* **1** E6
Copeland Islands PMP *BC* **2** C2
Copeland Lake *MB* **12** A8
Copeland Lake *MB* **15** B3
Copenhagen *ON* **19** D5
Copenhagen *ON* **20** F4
Copetown *ON* **19** B7
Copetown *ON* **20** E6
Coppell *ON* **17** B4
Coppen *SK* **11** E4
Copper, mont *QC* **29** B8
Copper, mont *QC* **30** B1
Copper Bay *BC* **1** B1-2
Copper Cliff *ON* **17** F6
Copper Cliff *ON* **18** A5
Copper Creek *BC* **1** D8
Copper Creek *BC* **2** A8
Copper Creek *BC* **6** D1
Coppermine (Kugluktuk) *NU* **41** B2
Coppermine (Kugluktuk) *NU* **42** F1
Coppermine River *NT* **10** A7-8
Coppermine River *NU* **41** C2
Coppin's Corners *ON* **20** B7-8
Coppin's Corners *ON* **21** E2
Copp Lake *NT* **10** F6-7
Coquihalla Canyon PP *BC* **1** F7-8
Coquihalla Canyon PRA *BC* **6** F1
Coquihalla Canyon PRA *BC* **1** F8
Coquihalla River *BC* **2** D7
Coquihalla River PP *BC* **1** F8
Coquihalla River PP *BC* **6** F1
Coquihalla River PRA *BC* **2** D7
Coquihalla Summit PRA *BC* **1** F8
Coquihalla Summit PRA *BC* **2** D7
Coquihalla Summit PRA *BC* **6** F1
Coquitlam *BC* **1** F7
Coquitlam *BC* **2** E4
Coquitlam Lake *BC* **2** D5
Coral Harbour (Salliq) **40** A3
Coral Harbour (Salliq) *NU* **41** D6
Coral Rapids, RNP *ON* **17** A6
Coral Rapids PNR *ON* **17** A6
Corbeau, lac du *QC* **22** E8
Corbeau, lac du *QC* **24** D2
Corbeau, lac du *QC* **25** F2
Corbeil *ON* **18** A-B8
Corberrie *NS* **33** D2
Corbett *ON* **20** D-E3
Corbett Lake *MB* **12** A8
Corbett Lake *MB* **15** A3
Corbetton *ON* **20** B5
Corbin *BC* **6** F5
Corbin *NL* **37** F5
Corbin *NL* **36** F7
Corbin, Cape *NL* **38** D5

Corbin Bay *NL* **36** D8
Corbin Bay *NL* **37** D4
Corbyville *ON* **21** E5
Cordova *MB* **14** D2
Cordova Bay *BC* **2** F4
Cordova Mines *ON* **21** A7
Cordova Mines *ON* **21** D4
Coriander *SK* **11** F3-4
Corinne *SK* **11** E5
Corinth *ON* **19** C5
Corinth *ON* **20** F4
Cork *NB* **32** C2
Corkscrew Island *ON* **14** E8
Cormac *ON* **21** A5
Cormac *ON* **22** F5
Cormack *NL* **36** A3-4
Cormack *NL* **37** A1-2
Cormack *NL* **38** F3
Cormack *NL* **39** F7
Cormack Lake *NT* **10** E3
Cormier, lac *QC* **39** E5
Cormier-Village *NB* **35** E1
Cormierville *NB* **31** E8
Cormierville *NB* **32** A6
Cormoran, pointe au *QC* **30** B7
Cormorant *MB* **11** A8
Cormorant *MB* **12** F8
Cormorant *MB* **13** A2
Cormorant Channel PMP *BC* **1** E4-5
Cormorant Lake *MB* **11** A8
Cormorant Lake *MB* **13** A2
Corneille Lake *SK* **12** F6-7
Corneille Lake *SK* **15** F1
Cornelius Grinnell Bay *NU* **40** A6
Corner Brook *NL* **36** B2-3
Corner Brook Pond *NL* **36** B3
Corner Brook Pond *NL* **37** B1
Cornhill *NB* **32** C5
Corning *SK* **11** E6-7
Cornwall *ON* **24** E4
Cornwall *PE* **34** C2
Cornwall *PE* **35** E4-5
Cornwall Hills PP *BC* **1** E8
Cornwall Hills PP *BC* **2** C2
Cornwall Island *NU* **42** C4
Cornwall Lake *AB* **9** A7
Cornwall Lake *AB* **12** A2
Cornwallis *NS* **32** F5
Cornwallis *NS* **33** C2
Cornwallis Island *NU* **42** C4
Coronado *AB* **8** B6-7
Coronation *AB* **6** C7
Coronation *AB* **11** C1
Coronation Gulf *NU*
Coronation Gulf *NU* **42** F1-2
Corraville *PE* **35** E6
Cortes Island *NL* **1** E6
Cortes Island *BC* **2** C2
Corunna *ON* **19** C2
Corunna *ON* **20** E1
Cosgrave Lake *ON* **16** E6-7
Cosgrave Lake *ON* **16** E7
Cosine *SK* **6** C8
Cosine *SK* **11** C2
Cosmo *AB* **8** B5
Costebelle, lac *QC* **39** E4-5
Costello Lake *MB* **12** A8
Costello Lake *MB* **15** B2
Costes Lake *MB* **13** A4
Costigan Lake *SK* **12** C5
Coteau Beach *SK* **11** D8
Coteau-du-Lac *QC* **24** D5
Coteau-du-Lac, LHN de *QC* **24** E4-5
Côteau-du-Lac NHS *QC* **24** E4-5
Coteau Hills *SK* **11** D7
Coteau Lakes *SK* **11** F3
Côteau-Nord-du-Golfe-du-Saint-Laurent *QC* **38** B2
Côteau-Nord-du-Golfe-du-Saint-Laurent *QC* **39** E5-6
Côte-Saint-Luc *QC* **24** D5
Côte-Saint-Luc *QC* **27** E1
Côtière, chaîne *QC* **1** D4-5 E5
Côtière, chaîne *QC* **2** A3 B3
Côtière, chaîne *QC* **3** B-D2
Côtière, chaîne *QC* **4** F4
Cotswold *ON* **19** A5
Cotswold *ON* **20** C4
Cottage Cove PP *NS* **32** E5
Cottage Cove PP *NS* **33** B2-3
Cottage-Hawthorne, LHN du *NT* **3** D7
Cottam *ON* **19** E2
Cottam *ON* **19** F2
Cottel Island *NL* **37** B7
Cottle's Island *NL* **38** E-F6
Cottonwood *BC* **1** B7
Cottonwood House Provincial Historic Park *BC* **1** B7
Cottonwood River *BC* **1** B7
Cottonwood River *BC* **3** B3
Cottonwood River *BC* **4** F3
Cottonwood River PP *BC* **1** B7
Cottonwoods *MB* **13** E2
Cottonwoods *MB* **14** E2
Cottrell's Cove *NL* **38** F6
Couchiching *ON* **16** F2

Couchiching, Lake ON 18 F8
Couchiching, Lake ON 20 A7
Couchiching, Lake ON 21 C-D1
Coucou, lac du QC 25 C5-6
Coucou, lac du QC 28 E1
Coudres, île aux QC 28 F7
Coughlan NB 31 D-E6
Coughlan NB 32 A4
Coulonge, rivière QC 22 D-E6
Coulonge Est, rivière QC 22 D6
Coulson ON 18 F8
Coulson ON 20 A7
Coulson ON 21 D1
Coulter MB 11 F8
Coulter MB 13 F1
Countess AB 7 C6
Country Harbour NS 34 E5 F5
Country Harbour Cross Roads NS 34 E5
Country Harbour Mines NS 34 E5
Country Road NL 37 D7
Courageous Lake NT 10 B8
Courcelles QC 27 D6
Courtenay BC 1 F5
Courtenay BC 2 D2
Courtice ON 20 C8
Courtice ON 21 E2
Courtin Island PE 35 C-D3
Courtland ON 19 C5-6
Courtland ON 20 F4-5
Courtright ON 19 C2
Courtright ON 20 F1
Courval SK 11 E4
Cousacouta, lac QC 25 D6
Cousacouta, lac QC 28 F1
Cousins Lake MB 15 D3
Coutts AB 6 F7
Coutts AB 7 F7
Couture, lac QC 40 C4-5
Couture, lac QC 41 E8
Covedell NB 31 C7-8
Covehead Road PE 35 D5
Cove Island ON 18 D4
Coverdale NB 31 F8
Coverdale NB 32 B6
Cove Road NS 32 D8
Cove Road NS 33 A5
Cove Road NS 34 E1
Covey Hill QC 24 E5
Covey Hill QC 27 F1
Cowan MB 11 C8
Cowan MB 13 C2
Cowan Lake SK 11 A4
Cowan River SK 11 A3-4
Cowansville QC 24 E7
Cowansville QC 27 F3
Cow Bay NS 33 C6
Cowessess SK 11 E6-7
Cow Head NL 38 E2
Cow Head NL 39 F7
Cowichan Bay BC 2 F4
Cowichan Lake BC 1 F6
Cowichan Lake BC 2 E3
Cowichan River BC 2 E3-4
Cowichan River PP BC 2 E3-4 F3-4
Cowley AB 6 F5
Cowley AB 7 E4
Coxipi, lac QC 39 D7
Coxipi, rivière QC 39 D7
Cox Island BC 1 D3
Cox Point BC 1 F5
Cox Point BC 2 E1
Cox's Cove NL 36 A3
Cox's Cove NL 37 A1
Cox's Cove NL 38 F2
Cox's Cove NL 40 F8
Coxvale ON 21 C6
Crabb Brook NL 36 A2-3
Crabb Brook NL 38 F2
Crabbs River NL 36 C-D2
Crabtree QC 24 C6
Crabtree QC 27 D2
Cracroft Bay NT 5 A8
Cracroft Island BC 1 E5
Craddock AB 7 E6
Craigdu AB 7 B4-5
Craigellachie BC 6 D2-3
Craighurst ON 18 F7-8
Craighurst ON 20 A6-7
Craigleith ON 18 F6-7
Craigleith ON 20 A5
Craigleith PP ON 18 F6-7
Craigleith PP ON 20 A5
Craigmore NS 34 D5
Craigmyle AB 6 C-D6
Craigmyle AB 7 A6
Craig River BC 3 D2
Craig's Pit, RNP ON 16 F8
Craig's Pit, RNP ON 17 C2
Craig's Pit PNR ON 16 F8
Craig's Pit PNR ON 17 C2
Craik SK 11 D5
Crammond AB 8 F5
Crampe, lac de la QC 26 E6
Crampe, lac de la QC 28 C2
Cranberry Junction BC 3 E4
Cranberry Lake ON 21 C2
Cranberry Lake ON 21 C8
Cranberry Lake, RNP ON 16 E1
Cranberry Lake PNR ON 16 E1
Cranberry Portage MB 12 F7
Cranberry Portage MB 15 F1
Cranberry River BC 3 E-F4
Cranbrook BC 6 F4
Cranbrook BC 7 E2
Cranbrook ON 19 A4-5
Cranbrook ON 20 C3-4
Crandall MB 11 E8
Crandall MB 13 E1
Crane Lake SK 11 E2
Crane Narrows MB 13 C-D2
Crane Narrows MB 14 A2
Crane River MB 13 D2-3
Crane River MB 14 A2
Crane River (O-Chi-Chak-Ko-Sipi) MB 13 D2
Crane River (O-Chi-Chak-Ko-Sipi) MB 14 A2
Crane Valley SK 11 F5
Cranford AB 6 E6-7
Cranford AB 7 E6
Cranswick River NT 5 E-F5
Crapaud PE 32 B8
Crapaud PE 34 C2
Crapaud PE 35 E3
Crauford, Cape NU 41 A5-6
Crauford, Cape NU 42 D5
Craven SK 11 E5
Crawford Bay BC 6 F3-4
Crawford Lake CA ON 19 B7
Crawford Lake CA ON 20 D6
Crawford Park MB 14 C1
Crean Lake SK 11 A4
Crediton ON 19 B4
Crediton ON 20 D3
Credit River ON 19 A7
Credit River ON 20 C6
Creditville ON 19 C6
Creditville ON 20 E5
Creekland AB 8 D5
Cree Lake SK 12 C5
Cree Lake SK 12 C4
Cree Lake SK 41 F2
Creelman SK 11 E6
Creemore ON 20 B5-6
Cree River SK 12 B5 C4-5
Cree River SK 41 F2-3
Creighton SK 12 F7
Creighton SK 15 F1
Creighton Heights ON 21 E3-4
Creignish NS 34 D5
Cremona AB 6 D5
Cremona AB 7 A3
Crescent Beach NS 33 D4-5
Crescent Island NU 42 C3-4
Crescent Lake SK 11 D7
Crescent Spur BC 1 B8
Crescent Spur BC 6 A1
Crestomere AB 6 B-C5
Crestomere AB 8 E6
Creston BC 6 F4
Creston NL 36 E7
Creston NL 37 E5
Crestview YT 4 E4
Crestwynd SK 11 E5
Creswell Bay NU 41 A5
Creswell Bay NU 42 E4
Crevier, lac QC 22 B8
Crevier, lac QC 25 D2
Crewsons Corners ON 19 A6-7
Crewsons Corners ON 20 D5-6
Crichton SK 11 E-F3
Criddle/Vane Homestead PP Reserve MB 13 F2
Criddle/Vane Homestead PP Reserve MB 14 E2
Crieff ON 19 B7
Crieff ON 20 D6
Crilly ON 16 E3
Crimson Lake AB 8 E4
Crimson Lake PP AB 6 C4-5
Crimson Lake PP AB 8 E4
Crippsdale AB 8 B6-7
Crisafy, lac QC 26 C4
Cristal, lac QC 25 C-D5
Cristal, lac QC 28 F1
Croche, rivière QC 25 A-B7
Croche, rivière QC 28 D3
Croche, ZEC de la QC 25 B-C7
Croche, ZEC de la QC 28 E3
Crockets Corner NB 32 C5
Crofton BC 2 E4
Croil Lake MB 12 A8
Croil Lake MB 15 A3
Croix, lac à la QC 29 C4
Croix, lac en QC 24 A5
Croix, lac en QC 25 F5
Croix, lac la ON 16 F3
Croix, pointe à la QC 29 A4
Croker, Cape ON 18 E5
Croker Island ON 18 B3
Croll MB 14 F1
Cromarty MB 15 C5-6
Cromarty ON 19 B4
Cromarty ON 20 D3
Cromer MB 11 F7-8
Cromer MB 13 E1
Cromwell MB 13 E4
Cromwell MB 14 D6
Crooked Bay ON 18 E7-8
Crooked Creek AB 9 F3
Crooked Lake ON 16 F3-4
Crooked Lake ON 18 B6
Crooked Lake PP SK 11 E6-7
Crooked River NL 39 B5
Crooked River SK 11 B6
Crooked River PP BC 1 A7
Crookston ON 21 D5
Croque NL 38 B5
Croque NL 39 E8
Crosby ON 21 C7
Crosby ON 24 F1
Cross SK 11 E2
Cross Bay MB 11 B8
Cross Bay MB 13 B2
Cross Creek NB 31 F4-5
Cross Creek NB 32 B3
Crossfield AB 6 D5
Crossfield AB 7 A4
Crosshill ON 19 B5
Crosshill ON 20 D4
Cross Island NS 33 D5
Cross Lake MB 15 F3-4
Cross Lake MB 15 F3
Cross Lake ON 17 E7
Cross Lake ON 21 A-B4
Cross Lake PP AB 8 A6
Cross Lake PP AB 9 F5
Crossley Lakes NT 5 B6
Cross Point ON 22 D1
Crossroads AB 8 F6-7
Crossroads Lake NL 39 A3
Crotch Lake ON 21 A3
Crotch Lake ON 21 C6
Croton ON 19 D3
Croton ON 20 F2
Crouse NL 38 B5
Crouse NL 39 E8
Crousetown NS 33 D4
Crowduck Lake MB 13 E5
Crowduck Lake MB 14 D7
Crowe Bridge CA ON 21 D4
Crowe Lake NL 36 B6
Crowe Lake NL 37 B4
Crowe Lake ON 21 D4
Crowell NS 33 F2
Crowe River ON 21 C-D4
Crowe River ON 21 D4
Crowes Landing ON 21 D4
Crowfoot AB 7 C6
Crow Head NL 38 E6
Crow Lake ON 13 F6
Crow Lake ON 16 E2
Crow Lake ON 21 C6
Crow Lake ON 21 C6
Crow Lake PP AB 9 E6
Crow Lake PP AB 12 E1
Crown Hill ON 18 F8
Crown Hill ON 20 A7
Crown Hill ON 21 D1
Crown Lake ON 22 F2
Crown Point PE 35 E5
Crown Prince Frederik Island NU 41 B5
Crown Prince Frederik Island NU 42 F5
Crow River YT 3 A5-6
Crow River YT 10 F1
Crows Nest NS 33 A8
Crows Nest NS 33 D6
Crowsnest Pass AB 6 F5
Crowsnest Pass AB 6 F5
Crowsnest Pass AB 7 E3
Crowsnest Pass AB 7 E3
Crowsnest PP BC 6 F5
Crowsnest PP BC 7 E3
Croydon Station BC 6 B2
Crozier Channel NT 42 C2
Cruikshank ON 18 F5
Cruikshank ON 20 A4
Cruikshank SK 11 E3-4
Crumlin ON 19 C5
Crumlin ON 20 E4
Crump AB 7 A4
Crutwell SK 11 B4
Cry Lake BC 3 B3-4
Crysler ON 24 E3
Crystal Beach ON 20 F7-8
Crystal City MB 13 F2-3
Crystal City MB 14 F2-3
Crystal Cliffs NS 34 D5
Crystal Crescent Beach PP NS 33 D6
Crystal Falls ON 17 F7-8
Crystal Falls ON 18 A7
Crystal Lake ON 21 C3
Crystal Lake SK 11 C7
Crystal Springs ON 21 E3
Crystal Springs SK 11 B5
Cuddle Lake MB 15 E4
Cudworth SK 11 C5
Cullen SK 11 F6-7
Culloden NS 32 F4
Culloden NS 33 C2
Culloden ON 19 C5
Culloden ON 20 E4
Culloden PE 35 F6
Culls Harbour NL 36 B8
Culls Harbour NL 37 B6
Cull's Island NL 38 E5
Culotte, lac à la QC 25 C4
Culross MB 13 F3
Culross MB 14 E4
Cultus ON 19 D6
Cultus ON 20 F5
Cultus Lake BC 2 E6
Cultus Lake BC 2 E6
Cultus Lake PP BC 1 F8
Cultus Lake PP BC 2 E6
Cumberland BC 1 F5
Cumberland BC 2 D2
Cumberland ON 24 D3
Cumberland PE 35 E4-5
Cumberland SK 11 B5
Cumberland Basin NB 32 C7
Cumberland Basin NS 32 C7
Cumberland Bay NB 31 F6
Cumberland Bay NB 32 B4
Cumberland Beach ON 18 F8
Cumberland Beach ON 20 A7
Cumberland Beach ON 21 C1
Cumberland Cove PE 35 E3
Cumberland House SK 11 A7
Cumberland House SK 13 A1
Cumberland House Provincial Historic Park SK 11 A6-7
Cumberland Lake SK 11 A6-7
Cumberland Peninsula NU 42 F8
Cumberland Sound NU 42 F8
Cumines Island SK 12 C6-7
Cumines Island SK 15 C1
Cumins Lake SK 9 E8
Cumins Lake SK 12 E3
Cummings Lake ON 18 A1
Cummins Lake PP BC 6 C2-3
Cummins Lake PP BC 8 F1
Cumshewa Head BC 1 B2
Cumshewa Inlet BC 1 B1-2
Cunning Bay SK 12 B6
Cunningham Lake BC 1 A5
Cupar SK 11 D6
Cupids NL 37 D7
Curières, lac QC 24 A4
Curières, lac QC 25 E4
Curlew AB 7 A5
Curran ON 24 D3
Currie NB 31 D3
Currie NB 32 A1
Currie Lake MB 15 C4
Curve Lake ON 21 D3
Curzon BC 7 F1
Curzon Village NL 38 E2
Cushing QC 24 D4
Cuslett NL 36 F8
Cuslett NL 37 F6
Cutarm Creek SK 11 D-E7
Cutarm Creek SK 13 D-E1
Cutbank SK 11 D4
Cutbank River AB 9 F2
Cut Beaver Lake SK 11 A6
Cut Knife SK 6 B8
Cut Knife SK 11 B3
Cutler ON 17 F5
Cutler ON 18 A-B3
Cuvillier, lac QC 23 C6-7
Cuvillier, lac QC 26 D1
Cuvillier, rivière QC 23 C6
Cygnes, lac des QC 26 A7
Cygnet AB 8 F6
Cygnet Lake MB 15 D5
Cymric SK 11 D5
Cynthia AB 6 B4
Cynthia AB 8 D4
Cypress Hills AB 6 E7-8
Cypress Hills AB 7 E8
Cypress Hills AB 11 E1
Cypress Hills SK 11 F2
Cypress Hills Interprovincial Park AB 6 E-F8
Cypress Hills Interprovincial Park AB 11 E-F2
Cypress Hills Interprovincial Park SK 6 E-F8
Cypress Hills Interprovincial Park SK 11 E-F2
Cypress Lake SK 6 F8
Cypress Lake SK 11 F2
Cypress Point AB 9 A7
Cypress Point AB 12 A2-3
Cypress PP BC 1 F7
Cypress PP BC 2 D4-5
Cypress River MB 13 F2
Cypress River MB 14 E2
Cyril River MB 15 E5
Czar AB 6 C7
Czar AB 11 C2

D

Daaquam QC 27 B7-8
Dacre ON 21 B6
Dafoe SK 11 C5
Dafoe Lake MB 15 E4
Dafoe River MB 15 E4-5
Dagenais, rivière QC 23 C2
Daggitt Lake MB 15 B3
Dahadini River NT 4 A-B8
Dahadini River NT 10 B-C2
Dahinda SK 11 F5
Dahl Lake PP BC 1 A6-7
Dain City ON 19 C8
Dain City ON 20 E7
Dakota Tipi MB 13 E3
Dakota Tipi MB 14 D3
Dakotah MB 14 E4
Dalcourt, lac QC 26 A7
Dale ON 21 E3
D'Alembert QC 17 D8
D'Alembert QC 23 D2-3
Dalemead AB 6 D5-6
Dalemead AB 7 C4
Dalem Lake PP NS 34 C7
Dalesville QC 24 D4-5
Dalewood CA ON 19 C5
Dalewood CA ON 20 F4
Dalhousie NB 29 D6-7
Dalhousie NB 31 A5
Dalhousie, Cape NT 5 A6
Dalhousie Junction NB 29 D6
Dalhousie Junction NB 31 A5
Dalhousie Lake ON 21 C6
Dalhousie Mills ON 24 E4
Dalhousie Road NS 32 F6
Dalhousie Road NS 33 C4
Dalhousie Station ON 24 E4
Dalkeith ON 24 D4
Dallas BC 2 A8
Dallas MB 13 D3
Dallas MB 14 A4-5
Dall Mountain YT 4 B5
Dall River BC 3 B4
Dall River Old Growth PP BC 3 B4
Dalmeny SK 11 C4
Dalny MB 11 F8
Dalny MB 13 F1
Dalroy AB 6 D6
Dalroy AB 7 B4
Dalrymple ON 20 A8
Dalrymple ON 21 D2
Dalston ON 18 F8
Dalston ON 20 A6-7
Dalston ON 21 D1
Dalton ON 17 D4
Dalton Post YT 4 E2-3
Dalum AB 6 D6
Dalum AB 7 B5-6
Dalvay-by-the-Sea Hotel NHS PE 34 B2-3
Dalvay-by-the-Sea Hotel NHS PE 35 D5
Daly Lake SK 12 D5
Damascus ON 19 A6
Damascus ON 20 C5
Damdochax PPA BC 3 D-E4
Damville, lac QC 26 C7
Damville, lac QC 28 A2
Dana SK 11 C5
Dana-Jowsey Lakes PP ON 17 D6
Danbury SK 11 C7
Dancing Point MB 13 C3
Dand MB 11 F8
Dand MB 13 F1-2
Dandurand, lac QC 25 B4
Dane ON 17 D7
Danford Lake QC 22 E7
Danford Lake QC 24 C1
Daniel's Cove NL 37 C7-8
Daniel's Harbour NL 38 D2
Daniel's Harbour NL 39 E7
Danielson PP SK 11 D4
Danish Strait NU 42 C3
Dantzic Point NL 36 F5-6
Dantzic Point NL 37 F3-4
Danube AB 8 A7
Danvers NS 33 D2
Danville QC 27 D4
Daphne SK 11 C5-6
Dapp AB 6 A5
Dapp AB 8 A6
Dapp AB 8 D5
Darby Harbour NL 36 E7
Darby Harbour NL 37 E5
Darch Island ON 18 B3
D'Arcy BC 1 E7
D'Arcy BC 2 B5
D'Arcy SK 11 D3
D'Arcy, lac QC 22 B5
D'Arcy Island Unit (Gulf Islands NPR) BC 2 F4
Darfield BC 6 D1-2
Dark Cove NL 36 B8
Dark Cove NL 37 B6
Darke Lake PP BC 6 F1
Darlans, rivière QC 23 E3
Darlingford MB 13 F3
Darlingford MB 14 F3
Darling Lake NS 33 E1
Darlington PP ON 21 F2-3
Darmody SK 11 E4
Darnley PE 32 A8
Darnley PE 34 B1
Darnley PE 35 C3
Darnley Basin PE 35 C3
Darnley Bay NT 5 A8
Darnley Bay NT 41 A1
Darrell Bay BC 1 F7
Darrell Bay BC 2 D5
Dartford ON 21 E4
Dartmouth NS 33 C6
Dartmouth, rivière QC 30 B2
Dartmouth Point NS 33 D1
Darwell AB 6 A-B5
Darwell AB 8 C5
Darwin Sound BC 1 B1
Dashwood ON 19 B4
Dashwood ON 20 D3
Dashwood Pond NL 36 C-D2
Dasserat, lac QC 23 D2
D.A. Tiffin CA ON 20 B6
Daulnay NB 29 F8
Daulnay NB 30 F1
Daulnay NB 31 C7
Dauphin MB 11 D8
Dauphin MB 13 D2
Dauphin MB 14 B1
Dauphin, Cape NS 34 B7
Dauphin Beach MB 14 B1
Dauphin Lake MB 11 D8
Dauphin Lake MB 13 D2
Dauphin Lake MB 14 B1-2
Dauphin River MB 13 C3
Dauphin River MB 13 C3
D'Auteuil, lac QC 39 E5
Daveluyville QC 24 B8
Daveluyville QC 27 C4
David, lac QC 22 D7
David, lac QC 24 A1
David, lac QC 24 A3
David, lac QC 25 E3
David, lac QC 25 F1
David, rivière QC 24 B6
David, rivière QC 24 C7
David, rivière QC 25 F6
David, rivière QC 27 C1
David, rivière QC 27 D3
Davidson QC 22 E6
Davidson SK 11 D5
Davidson Lake MB 11 A8
Davidson Lake MB 13 A2
Davidsville NL 36 A7-8
Davidsville NL 37 A5-6
Davidsville NL 38 F7
Davin SK 11 E6
Davin Lake SK 12 D6
Davis SK 11 B5
Davis, détroit de NU 40 A7
Davis, détroit de NU 42 E8
Davis Cove NL 36 D8
Davis Cove NL 37 D6
Davis Inlet NL 40 D7
Davis Lake PP BC 1 F7-8
Davis Lake PP BC 2 D6
Davis River BC 3 D3
Davis Strait NU 40 A7-8
Davis Strait NU 42 D-E8
Davy, rivière QC 23 C4
Davy Lake SK 9 B8
Davy Lake SK 12 B3-4
Dawes Pond NL 36 A5
Dawes Pond NL 37 A3
Dawes Pond NL 38 F4
Dawley Passage PMP BC 1 F4-5
Dawley Passage PMP BC 2 D-E1
Dawson, Mount BC 6 D3
Dawson Bay MB 11 B8
Dawson Bay MB 11 B8
Dawson Bay MB 13 B1-2
Dawson Bay MB 13 B1-2
Dawson City YT 4 A2
Dawson Creek BC 3 E8
Dawson Creek BC 9 E2
Dawson Inlet NU 40 B1-2
Dawson Inlet NU 41 E5
Dawson Landing NT 10 E6-7
Dawson Range YT 4 C2-3
Dawson River ON 13 B6
Dawsons Landing BC 1 D4
Dawsonville NB 29 D5-6
Dawsonville NB 31 A4
Daylesford SK 11 C5
Day Mills ON 17 F5
Day Mills ON 18 A1
Dayohessarah Lake ON 17 C3
Day Point BC 1 C3
Daysland AB 6 B6
Daysland AB 8 D8
Daysland AB 11 B1
Dayspring NS 33 D4
Day Star SK 11 D6
Dayton NS 33 E1
Ddhaw Gro Habitat Protection Area YT 4 B3-4
Deacon ON 21 A5
Deacon ON 22 F5
Deacons Corner MB 14 E5
Deadhorse Lake AB 6 D6
Deadhorse Lake AB 7 B6
Dead Islands NL 39 C8
Deadman River BC 1 D8
Deadman River BC 2 A7
Deadman River BC 6 D1
Deadman's Bay NL 37 A6-7
Deadman's Bay NL 38 F8
Deadman's Bay PP NL 36 A8
Deadman's Bay PP NL 37 A6
Deadman's Bay PP NL 38 F7-8
Deadman's Cove NL 38 B3-4
Dead Tree Point BC 1 A-B1
Deadwood AB 9 D3
Deadwood River BC 3 B4
Deadwood River BC 4 F7
Dealtown ON 19 E3
Dean NS 33 B7
Dean NS 34 F3
Dean Channel BC 1 C4
Dean Lake ON 18 A1
Dean Lake ON 18 A1
Deanlea Beach ON 18 F7
Deanlea Beach ON 20 A6
Dean River BC 1 B5
Dease Arm NT 41 C1
Dease Lake BC 3 B3
Dease Lake BC 3 B3
Dease River BC 3 A4 B3
Dease River BC 4 F7
Dease Strait NU 41 B3
Dease Strait NU 42 F2
Deauville QC 27 E4
Debden SK 11 B4
Debec NB 31 F3
Debec NB 32 B1
Debert NS 32 D8
Debert NS 33 A6
Debert NS 34 E2
Debert River NS 33 A6
Debert River NS 34 E2
DeBolt AB 9 E-F3
De Cazes, lac QC 26 D6
De Cazes, lac QC 28 B1
Decelles, lac QC 25 B4-5
Decelles, lac QC 26 F4-5
Decelles, réservoir QC 23 F4
Déception QC 40 B5
Déception QC 41 D8
Deception Lake SK 12 D6
Decewsville ON 19 C7
Decewsville ON 20 E6
Décharnay, lac QC 26 D6
Décharnay, lac QC 28 B1
Dechêne, lac QC 39 D1
Decker MB 11 E8
Decker MB 13 E1
Decoigne, lac QC 28 D6
Deep Bay NL 38 E7
Deep Bay NT 10 E5
Deep Bay ON 14 F8
Deep Bay SK 12 D6
Deep Bay SK 15 D1
Deep Bight NL 36 C8
Deep Bight NL 37 C6
Deep Brook NS 32 F5
Deep Brook NS 33 C2
Deep Cove NS 32 F7
Deep Cove NS 33 C5
Deepdale MB 11 D7-8
Deepdale MB 13 D1
Deep River ON 22 E4-5
Deepwater Point ON 22 D1
Deer Bay NU 42 B3
Deer Bay ON 18 B6
Deerbrook ON 19 E2
Deer Cove NL 38 D2-3
Deerfield NS 33 E1-2
Deerhorn MB 13 D3
Deerhorn MB 14 C4
Deer Island MB 13 D4
Deer Island MB 14 B6
Deer Island NB 32 E2
Deer Island NL 36 B8
Deer Island NL 36 D3-4
Deer Island NL 37 B6
Deer Island NL 37 D1-2
Deer Lake NL 36 A3
Deer Lake NL 36 A3
Deer Lake NL 37 A1
Deer Lake NL 37 A1
Deer Lake NL 38 F2-3
Deer Lake NL 38 F2-3
Deer Lake NL 39 F7
Deer Lake NL 39 F7
Deer Lake ON 13 B5-6
Deer Lake ON 13 B-C6
Deer Lake ON 16 A2
Deer Lake ON 16 A2
Deer Lake ON 18 E8
Deer Lake ON 21 C1
Deer Lake ON 22 E1
Deerland AB 8 B7
Deer Pond NL 36 B-C7
Deer Pond NL 37 B-C5
Deer River MB 15 C5
Deerock Lake ON 21 C5
Deerwood MB 13 F3
Deerwood MB 14 F3
Defeat Lake NT 10 D7
Defoy QC 27 C4
Dégelis QC 29 E2-3
Dégelis QC 31 B1
De Grau NL 36 C1
De La Bidière, lac QC 25 C3
Delacour AB 6 D5
Delacour AB 7 B4
Delâge, lac QC 25 A4
Delâge, lac QC 26 F4
Delahey, lac QC 22 C6
Delaps Cove NS 33 C2
Delaronde Lake SK 11 A4
Delaware ON 19 C4
Delaware ON 20 E3
Delayee Lake YT 4 E4
Del Bonita AB 6 F6
Del Bonita AB 7 F5
Delburne AB 6 C6
Delburne AB 8 F7
Déléage QC 22 D7-8
Déléage QC 24 B2
Déléage QC 25 F2
Deleau MB 11 F8
Deleau MB 13 F1
DeLesseps Lake ON 13 D8
De Lesseps Lake ON 16 C4
Delestres, rivière QC 23 D6
Delhi ON 19 C6
Delhi ON 20 F5
Delia AB 6 D6
Delia AB 7 A6
Déline NT 10 A2
Déline Fishery and Fort Franklin HS NT 10 A2-3
Delisle QC 28 B5
Delisle SK 11 C4
Delisle, rivière QC 24 E4
Delmas SK 11 B3
Delmer ON 19 C5
Delmer ON 20 F4
Deloraine MB 11 F8
Deloraine MB 13 F1
Deloro ON 21 D4
Delph AB 8 B7
Delson QC 24 D6
Delson QC 27 E1-2
Delta BC 1 F7
Delta ON 21 D7
Delta ON 24 F1
Delta (Ladner) BC 2 E5
Delta Beach MB 13 E3
Delta Beach MB 14 D3
Delta-de-la-Rivière-Anderson, RNOM du NT 5 A-B6
Delta-de-la-Rivière-Nisutlin, RNF du YT 4 E5
Deltaform Mountain AB 6 D4
Deltaform Mountain AB 7 B1
Delta Marsh MB 13 E3
Delta Marsh MB 14 D3
Delta Peak BC 3 D3
Demaine SK 11 D4
Demarcation Point YT 5 A2
Demay AB 8 D7
Demers-Centre QC 22 E5
Demmitt AB 9 E2
De Montigny, lac QC 23 E4
De Morbihan, lac QC 39 D4
Demorestville ON 21 E5
Dempsey Corners NS 32 E6
Dempsey Corners NS 33 B3
Demuth BC 6 E-F1
Denain, lac QC 23 E-F6
Denare Beach SK 12 F7
Denare Beach SK 15 F1
Denaut, lac QC 26 C6
Denaut, lac QC 28 A1
Denbeigh Point MB 11 B8
Denbeigh Point MB 11 B8
Denbeigh Point MB 13 B2
Denbeigh Point MB 13 B2
Denbigh ON 21 B5
Dencross MB 14 D6
Denetiah Lake BC 3 B4
Denetiah PP BC 3 B4
Denfield ON 19 C4
Denfield ON 20 E3
Denholm QC 22 F8
Denholm QC 24 C2
Denholm SK 11 B-C3
Denman Island BC 1 F6
Denman Island BC 2 D2-3
Denman Island BC 2 D2
Denmark NS 34 D2-3
Dennis Lake MB 14 C5
Denny Island BC 1 C4
Dension Lake MB 12 C8
Dension Lake MB 15 C2-3
Densmore Mills NS 32 D8
Densmore Mills NS 33 A5-6
Densmore Mills NS 34 E1
Denver NS 33 A8
Denver NS 34 E4
Denwood AB 6 B7
Denwood AB 11 B1-2
Denys Basin NS 34 D6
Denzil SK 6 C8
Denzil SK 11 C2
Departure Lake ON 17 B6
De Pas, rivière QC 39 A3
Depot Lakes CA ON 21 D6
Derby NB 31 D6
Derby PE 32 A7
Derby PE 35 C1-2
Derby Junction NB 31 D6-7
Dering MB 11 A8
Dering MB 12 F8
Dering MB 13 A2
Dering MB 15 F2
Deroche, Point PE 35 D5
Derwent AB 6 A7
Derwent AB 11 A1-2
DeSable PE 32 B8
DeSable PE 34 C2
DeSable PE 35 E4
Desaulniers ON 17 F7
Désaulniers ON 18 A7
Desautels, lac QC 26 C6-7
Desbarats ON 17 F4
Desbiens QC 28 C4
Desboro ON 18 F5
Desboro ON 20 A4
Desboues, rivière QC 23 C4
Deschaillons-sur-Saint-Laurent QC 27 B4
Deschambault QC 27 B4-5
Deschambault Lake SK 12 F6
Deschambault Lake SK 12 F6
Deschambault River SK 12 F6
Deschamps, lac QC 26 E3
Descharme Lake SK 9 C-D8
Descharme Lake SK 12 C-D3
Descharme River SK 9 C8
Descharme River SK 12 C3
Deschênes, lac QC 21 A7-8 B8
Deschênes, lac QC 28 D7-8
D'Escousse NS 34 D6
Deseronto ON 21 E5-6
Désert, lac QC 22 D7
Désert, lac QC 24 A1
Désert, lac QC 25 E1
Deserters Peak BC 3 D6
Déserteur, lac du QC 26 E5
Desforges, lac QC 23 C6
Desforges, lac QC 26 D1
Desgly, lac QC 26 C6
Desgly, lac QC 28 A1-2
Desjardins, lac QC 23 B6
Desjardinsville QC 22 E5
Deskenatlata Lake NT 10 E7-8
Desliens Lake NL 39 A-B2
Desmarais, pointe NT 10 E6
Desmaraisville QC 23 A7-8
Desmaraisville QC 26 B2
Desmaraisville QC 40 F4-5
Des Méloizes, rivière QC 23 B-C2
Desolation Sound PMP BC 1 E6
Desolation Sound PMP BC 2 C3

des-Passes, ZEC QC 28 A4-5
Desperation Lake NT 10 C7
Despinassy QC 23 C5
Despinassy, lac QC 23 C5
Desrivières, lac QC 22 C-D7
Desrivières, lac QC 24 A1
Desrivières, lac QC 25 E1
Des Ruisseaux QC 22 D8
Des Ruisseaux QC 24 A2
Des Ruisseaux QC 25 F2
Desteffany Lake NT 10 A7
Destor QC 17 C8
Destor QC 23 D2-3
Destruction Bay YT 4 D2
Detlor ON 21 B4
Detroit River ON 19 E1
Dettah NT 10 D6-7
Dettah NT 41 D1
Deux Loutres, lac aux QC 39 D4
Deux-Montagnes QC 24 D5
Deux-Montagnes, lac des QC 24 D5
Deux Orignaux, lac des QC 26 A3
Deux Rivieres ON 22 D3
Devastation Channel BC 1 A3
De Veber, Mount AB 6 A2
Devenyns, lac QC 25 D5-6
Devenyns, lac QC 27 A1
Devil Lake ON 21 D7
Devil Lake ON 24 F1
Devil's Glen PP ON 20 B5
Devine ON 16 F2
Devlin ON 16 F2
Devlin, lac QC 22 A3
Devlin, lac QC 23 F3
Devon AB 6 B5
Devon AB 8 C6
Devon, île NU 40 D4-5
Devon Island NU 42 D4-5
Devon Road Mesa, RNP ON 16 F5-6
Devon Road Mesa PNR ON 16 F5-6
Dewar Lake SK 6 C-D8
Dewar Lake SK 11 D2
Dewar Peak BC 3 D5
Dewberry AB 6 A7
Dewberry AB 11 A2
Dewdney BC 1 F7-8
Dewdney BC 2 E6
De Winton AB 6 D5
De Winton AB 7 C4
Dewittville QC 24 E5
Dezadeash Lake YT 4 E3
Dezadeash River YT 4 E3
Diable, cap NL 38 A4
Diable, cap au QC 28 E8
Diable, rivière du QC 24 A-B8
Diable, rivière du QC 24 C4
Diable, rivière du QC 25 F4
Diamant, lac QC 25 D5
Diamant, lac QC 28 F1
Diamond City AB 6 E-F6
Diamond City AB 7 E5-6
Diamond Cove NL 36 D-E2
Diamond Jenness Peninsula NT 41 A2
Diamond Jenness Peninsula NT 42 E1
Diana Lake PP BC 1 A3
Dickey Lake ON 21 C4
Dickson AB 6 C5
Dickson AB 8 F5
Dickson, lac QC 26 A3
Dickson Lake ON 22 E-F3
Didsbury AB 6 D6
Didsbury AB 7 A3-4
Diefenbaker, Lake SK 11 D4
Dieppe NB 31 F8
Dieppe NB 32 B6
Dieppe, lac QC 24 A2
Dieppe Lake NT 10 D5-6
Digby NS 32 F4
Digby NS 33 C2
Digby NS 33 D2
Digby Neck NS 33 C-D1
Digdeguash NB 32 C6
Digdeguash River NB 32 D2
Digges MB 15 B5-6
Digges Islands NU 40 B4
Digges Islands NU 41 D7
Dildo NL 37 D7
Dildo Run PP NL 38 E6-7
Diligent River NS 32 F4
Diligent River NS 33 A4
Dilke NL 11 D5
Dillberry Lake PP AB 6 C7-8
Dillberry Lake PP AB 11 C2
Dillon ON 18 D6
Dillon SK 9 E8
Dillon SK 12 E3
Dillon Lake SK 9 E8
Dillon Lake SK 12 E2-3
Dillon River SK 9 E7-8
Dillon River SK 12 E2-3
Dinant AB 8 D7
Dingwall NS 34 A7
Dingwells Mills PE 34 C3-4
Dingwells Mills PE 35 D7
Dinorwic ON 13 F7
Dinorwic ON 16 D3
Dinorwic Lake ON 13 F7
Dinorwic Lake ON 16 D3
Dinosaur AB 6 D7
Dinosaur AB 7 C7
Dinosaur AB 11 D1
Dinosaur PP AB 6 D7
Dinosaur PP AB 7 C7
Dinosaur PP AB 11 D1

Dinsmore SK 11 D4
Dionisio Point PP BC 1 F6-7
Dionisio Point PP BC 2 E4
Dipper Harbour NB 32 E3
Dipper Harbour NB 33 B1
Dipper Lake SK 12 E4
Dipper Lake SK 12 E4
Disappointment Lake NL 39 B4
Discover Island PMP BC 2 F4-5
Discovery, Cape NU 42 A5
Discovery Claim NHS YT 4 A1-2
Discovery Passage BC 2 B-C2
Disley SK 11 E5
Disraeli QC 27 D5
Ditidaht BC 2 E3
Divide SK 11 F2
Divide Ridge, RNP ON 16 F5
Divide Ridge PNR ON 16 F5
Dividing Lake, RNP ON 21 B2-3
Dividing Lake PNR ON 21 B2-3
Dixie Cove PP BC 1 C4
Dix Milles, lac QC 22 C4
Dix Milles, lac des QC 25 B4
Dixon SK 11 C5
Dixon, détroit de BC 1 A1-2
Dixon, détroit de BC 3 F1-2
Dixon Entrance BC 1 A1-2
Dixon Entrance BC 3 F1-2
Dixonville AB 9 D3
Dixville QC 27 F5
Dizzy Creek AB 9 A4
Doak, lieu historique provincial NB 31 E6
Doak, lieu historique provincial NB 32 A4-5
Doak PHS NB 31 E6
Doak PHS NB 32 A4-5
Doaktown NB 31 E5
Doaktown NB 32 A3-4
Dobbin Bay NU 42 B5
Dobbinton ON 18 F5
Dobbinton ON 20 A4
Dobie Lake ON 17 D7-8
Dobie Lake ON 13 D8
Dobie River ON 13 C-D8
Dobie River ON 16 B4-5
Dobleau, lac QC 26 B6
Dock Cove NL 37 B7
Doctor Island NS 34 D3
Doctors Brook NS 34 D4
Doctors Cove NS 33 F2
Doctors Harbour NL 36 D6
Doctors Harbour NL 37 D4
Doda, lac QC 26 C3
Dodd Lake BC 2 D7
Dodds AB 8 D7-8
Dodge Lake SK 12 A5
Dodsland SK 11 C3
Doe Lake ON 18 C8
Doe Lake ON 18 C8
Doe Lake ON 21 A1
Doe Lake ON 21 A1
Doe Lake ON 22 F1
Doe River BC 3 E8
Doe River BC 9 E2
Dog Creek BC 1 D7-8
Dog Creek MB 13 D3
Dog Creek MB 14 B3
Dogface Lake NT 10 F4
Dog Islands NL 39 A6
Dog Lake MB 13 D3
Dog Lake MB 14 B3
Dog Lake ON 16 E5
Dog Lake ON 17 D4
Dog Lake ON 21 D7
Dogpound AB 7 A3
Dog River BC 16 E5
Dogskin Lake MB 14 A7
Dogskin Lake MB 13 D5
Dogskin River MB 13 C6
Dogtooth Lake ON 13 F6
Doig River BC 3 D8
Doig River BC 9 D2
Dokis ON 17 F7
Dokis ON 18 B7
Dokis Point ON 18 A7
Dolbeau QC 26 D8
Dolbeau QC 28 B4
Dolland Bight NL 36 D5
Dolland Bight NL 37 D3
Dolland Pond NL 36 D5
Dolland Pond NL 37 D3
Dollard SK 11 F3
Dollard Brook NL 36 D5
Dollard Brook NL 37 D3
Dollar Lake PP NS 33 B6
Dollars Lake NL 37 B8
Dollier, lac QC 26 B5
Dolly Bay NL 38 B3
Dolphin and Union Strait NT 41 B2
Dolphin and Union Strait NT 42 E-F1
Dolphin and Union Strait NU 41 B2
Dolphin and Union Strait NU 42 E-F1
Dolu, lac QC 39 A1
Domain MB 13 F3-4
Domain MB 14 E5
Dome ON 17 D6
Dome Creek BC 1 A8
Dome Creek BC 6 A1
Dominion NS 34 C8
Dominion, Cape NU 41 C7

Dominion Beach PP NS 34 C8
Dominion City MB 13 F4
Dominion City MB 14 F5
Dominion Lake NL 39 C5
Domino NL 39 B8
Domogaya Lake NL 39 D3
Domremy SK 11 B5
Domville ON 21 C8
Domville ON 24 F2
Donagh PE 34 C3
Donagh PE 35 E5
Donald BC 6 D3
Donald ON 21 C3
Donalda AB 6 C6
Donalda AB 8 E7-8
Donald Lake ON 13 D5
Donald Lake ON 14 B8
Donaldston PE 35 D5
Donavon SK 11 C4
Donegal ON 19 A5
Donegal ON 20 D4
Donegal SK 11 C2
Don Getty Wildland PP AB 6 D5
Don Getty Wildland PP AB 6 E5
Don Getty Wildland PP AB 7 A-B2
Don Getty Wildland PP AB 7 B-C3
Don Getty Wildland PP AB 7 C3
Don Getty Wildland PP AB 7 D3
Don Peninsula BC 1 C4
Donkin NS 34 C8
Donnacona QC 27 B5
Donnegana Lake ON 17 E6
Donnelly AB 9 E3-4
Donnelly Lake ON 16 A4
Donnelly River NT 5 E7
Donwell SK 11 D7
Donwood ON 21 D3
Doolittle, lac QC 22 C6
Doran Lake ON 13 D8
Dorcas Bay ON 18 D4
Dorchester NB 32 C6-7
Dorchester ON 19 C5
Dorchester ON 20 D5
Dorchester, Cape NU 40 A4
Dorchester, Cape NU 41 C7
Dorchester Crossing NB 31 F8
Dorchester Crossing NB 32 B6-7
Doré, lac QC 22 A7
Doré, lac QC 25 C1
Doré, Lake ON 21 A5
Doré, Lake ON 22 F5
Doré Lake SK 12 F4
Doré Lake SK 12 F4
Dorenlee AB 8 E7
Doré River SK 12 F3-4
Dorés, lac aux QC 26 A-B5
Dorintosh SK 11 A3
Dorintosh SK 12 F3
Dorion ON 16 E6
Doris AB 8 A5
Dorking ON 19 A5
Dorking ON 20 C4
Dorland ON 21 E5-6
Dormans Cove NL 36 A7
Dormans Cove NL 37 A5
Dormans Cove NL 38 F6-7
Dornoch ON 20 B4
Dorothy AB 6 D6-7
Dorothy AB 7 B6
Dorset ON 21 B2
Dory Point TP NL 10 E5
Dosquet QC 27 B-C5
Doting Cove NL 38 F7-8
Douaire, lac QC 22 B8
Douaire, lac QC 25 D2
Double Island NL 39 A6-7
Double Mer NL 39 B6
Doucet QC 28 A4
Doucet Lake NT 10 D8
Doucetteville NS 33 D2
Douglas MB 13 E2
Douglas MB 14 E2
Douglas NB 31 F4-5
Douglas NB 32 C3
Douglas ON 21 A6
Douglas ON 22 F6
Douglas Channel BC 1 A-B3
Douglas Harbour NB 32 C4
Douglas Lake BC 2 C8
Douglas Lake BC 2 B8
Douglas Lake BC 6 E1
Douglas PP SK 11 D4
Douglas River SK 9 D7
Douglas River SK 12 B3
Douglastown NB 31 D6-7
Douglastown QC 30 B3
Doumic, lac QC 28 B6
Douro ON 21 D3
Dove Brook NL 39 B7
Dover NL 36 B8
Dover NL 37 B6
Dover PE 35 F6
Dover Bay NS 34 E6
Dover Centre ON 19 D2
Dover Centre ON 20 F1
Dovercourt AB 8 F5
Dowager Island BC 1 C3
Dowling ON 17 F6
Dowling ON 18 A5
Dowling Lake AB 6 C7
Dowling Lake AB 7 A6
Dowling Lake AB 11 C1

Downe SK 11 C3
Downeyville ON 21 D3
Downing PP BC 2 A6
Downton, Mount BC 1 C6
Downton Lake BC 2 A5
Doyles NL 36 D1
Dozois, réservoir QC 22 A5
Drag Lake ON 21 B3
Drague-Numéro-Quatre, LHN de la YT 4 A1-2
Drake SK 11 C-D5
Draney Inlet BC 1 D4
Drapeau QC 29 D7
Drapeau QC 31 A5
Drayton ON 19 A6
Drayton ON 20 C5
Drayton Valley AB 6 B4-5
Drayton Valley AB 8 D4-5
Dredge No. 4 NHS YT 4 A1-2
Dresden ON 19 D3
Dresden ON 20 F2
Drew Station ON 20 C4
Drewry Point PP BC 6 F3-4
Driftpile AB 9 E4
Driftpile River AB 9 F4
Drift River NL 38 B4
Driftwood ON 17 C6
Driftwood Canyon PP BC 3 F4
Driftwood Lake ON 13 C4
Driftwood Lake MB 13 A1-2
Driftwood PP ON 22 D4
Driftwood River BC 3 E4-5
Driftwood River YT 5 C3
Drinkwater SK 11 E5
Driscol Lake SK 11 F3
Drizzle Lake ON 21 B3
Droit, lac du QC 25 B6
Droit, lac du QC 26 F6
Droit, lac du QC 28 D1
Drolet, lac QC 27 D6
Dromore ON 20 B5
Dromore PE 35 E6
Dropmore MB 11 D7
Dropmore MB 13 D1
Drowning River ON 17 A2-3
Droxford SK 11 E4
Druid SK 11 C3
Drumbeg PP BC 2 E4
Drumbo ON 19 B6
Drumbo ON 20 E5
Drumhead NS 34 F5
Drumheller AB 6 D6
Drumheller AB 7 A5-6
Drummond NB 31 D3
Drummondville QC 24 C8
Drummondville QC 27 D3-4
Drury Inlet BC 1 D4
Drury Lake YT 4 C4
Dryberry Lake ON 13 E7
Dryberry Lake ON 16 D2
Drybones Lake NT 10 B7
Dryden ON 13 E7
Dryden ON 16 D3
Dry Creek YT 4 C1
Dry Gulch PP BC 6 E4
Dry Gulch PP BC 7 C1-2
Dry Island Buffalo Jump PP AB 6 C6
Dry Island Buffalo Jump PP AB 8 F7
Drylake NL 39 C2
Dry River MB 14 F2-3
Dryson, lac QC 22 C6
Drywood AB 7 F4
Duagh AB 8 C6-7
Duart ON 19 D3-4
Duart ON 20 F2-3
Dubawnt NT 41 E3
Dubawnt Lake NU 41 D-E4
Dublin ON 19 B4
Dublin ON 20 D3
Dublin Shore NS 33 D4-5
Dubois, lac QC 26 D4-5
Duborne, lac QC 18 A2
Dubose, Mount 1 A-B4
Dubreuilville 17 D3-4
Dubuc SK 11 E7
Dubuisson QC 23 E4
Ducharme, lac QC 26 C5
Ducharme, lac QC 28 A1
Duchastel, lac QC 25 C3
Duchat, lac QC 23 D3
Duchenier, réserve QC 31 A1
Duchesnay QC 27 A5
Duchesnay Creek ON 18 A8
Duchess AB 6 D-E7
Duchess AB 11 D1
Duck Bay MB 11 C8
Duck Bay MB 13 C2
Duck Lake BC 6 E2
Duck Lake MB 15 F3
Duck Lake ON 17 D5
Duck Lake ON 18 C7
Duck Lake NS 34 B4
Duck Lake PP BC 2 C3
Duck Mountain MB 11 C7
Duck Mountain MB 13 D1
Duck Mountain PP MB 11 C-D8
Duck Mountain PP MB 13 C-D1
Duck Mountain PP SK 11 C7

Duck River MB 11 C8
Duck River MB 13 C2
Dunk River PE 35 D3
Duclos QC 21 A7
Duclos QC 22 F7
Duclos QC 24 C1
Duclos Point ON 20 B7
Duclos Point ON 21 D1
Duclos Point, RNP ON 20 B7
Duclos Point, RNP ON 21 D1
Duclos Point PNR ON 20 B7
Duclos Point PNR ON 21 D1
Dudley, lac QC 22 D8
Dudley, lac QC 24 B2-3
Dudley, lac QC 25 F2-3
Dudswell QC 27 E5
Dufault, lac QC 23 D2-3
Dufay, lac QC 23 E2
Duff SK 11 D6
Duffey Lake PP BC 1 E7
Duffey Lake PP BC 2 B5-6
Duffield AB 6 B5
Duffield AB 8 C5
Duffin Lake MB 15 B3
Duff Roblin PP MB 14 D5
Duff's Corners ON 20 E6
Duff's Corners ON 21 A7
Duffs Corner NB 32 B4
Dufourville NB 31 F8
Dufourville NB 32 B6
Dufresne MB 13 F4
Dufresne MB 14 E5-6
Dufresne, lac QC 26 C7
Dufresnoy, lac QC 23 D2-3
Dufrost MB 13 F4
Dufrost MB 14 F5
Dugald MB 13 E4
Dugald MB 14 E5
Du Gas, lac QC 39 E6
Duguayville NB 31 B7
Dugué, lac QC 25 A4
Dugué, lac QC 26 F4
Dugué, rivière QC 27 A8
Duhamel AB 8 D7
Duhamel QC 24 C3
Duke River YT 4 D2
Dulwich SK 11 B3
Dumais, lac QC 25 B4
Dumas SK 11 E7
Dumas, lac QC 26 A3-4
Dumbarton NB 32 D2
Dumbell Lake NL 39 C3
Dumfries NB 32 C2
Dummer SK 11 E5
Dumoine, lac QC 22 C4
Dumoine, rivière QC 22 C-D4
Dumoine, ZEC QC 22 D4
Dumond River ON 13 C8
Dumont, lac QC 22 E6-7
Dumont, lac QC 24 B-C1
Dumoulin, lac QC 25 C7
Dumoulin, lac QC 28 E2-3
Dunblane SK 11 D4
Duncairn SK 11 F3
Duncairn, RNOM de la réserve SK 11 F3
Duncairn Reserve NMBS SK 11 F3
Duncan BC 2 E4
Duncan, lac QC 22 E4
Duncan Crevice Caves, RNP ON 18 F6
Duncan Crevice Caves, RNP ON 20 A5
Duncan Crevice Caves PNR ON 18 F6
Duncan Crevice Caves PNR ON 20 A5
Duncan Lake BC 6 E3-4
Duncan Lake NT 10 C7
Duncan Lake ON 17 D6
Duncan River BC 6 D-E3
Dunchurch ON 18 C7
Dundalk ON 20 B5
Dundas ON 19 C7
Dundas ON 20 E6
Dundas PE 34 C3-4
Dundas PE 35 E5
Dundas, Cape NU 18 E5
Dundas Island BC 3 F2
Dundas Peninsula NT 42 E7
Dundas Valley CA ON 19 B7
Dundas Valley CA ON 20 E6
Dundee NB 31 A5
Dundee NS 34 D6
Dundee ON 24 E4
Dundee QC 24 E4
Dundee Centre QC 24 E4
Dundela ON 24 F3
Dundonald ON 17 C8
Dundurn SK 11 C4
Dunedin ON 20 B6
Dune Za Keyih PP BC 3 B-C5
Dunfield NL 37 C7
Dungannon ON 19 A4
Dungannon ON 20 C3
Dungarvon River NB 31 E5-6
Dungarvon River NB 32 A3-4
Dungeon PP NL 37 B7-8
Dunham QC 24 E7
Dunham QC 27 F3
Dunière, RF de QC 29 C6
Dunière, RF de QC 29 C6
Dunkerron ON 20 B6
Dunkirk SK 11 E5

Dunkirk River AB 9 D6
Dunkirk River AB 12 C-D1
Dunleath SK 11 D7
Dunlevy PRA BC 3 E7
Dunlop MB 15 F3
Dunlop ON 19 A4
Dunlop ON 20 C3
Dunlop Lake ON 18 A2
Dunmaglass NS 34 D4
Dunmore AB 6 E8
Dunmore AB 7 D8
Dunmore AB 11 E1-2
Dunraven QC 21 A6
Dunraven QC 22 F6
Dunrobin ON 21 A7
Dunrobin ON 24 D1
Dunrea MB 13 F2
Dunrea MB 14 E-F1
Dunsford ON 21 D2-3
Dunsheath Lake MB 12 D7-8
Dunsheath Lake MB 15 D2
Dunstable AB 8 B4
Dunstaffnage PE 35 D-E5
Dunster BC 6 B2
Dunsterville, Cape NU 42 B-C5
Duntroon ON 18 F7
Duntroon ON 20 A-B6
Duntura NL 37 B7
Dunvegan AB 9 E2-3
Dunvegan NS 34 C5-6
Dunvegan ON 24 D3
Dunvegan PP AB 9 E3
Dunvegan West Wildland PP AB 9 D-E2
Dunville NL 37 E6-7
Duparquet QC 17 C8
Duparquet QC 23 C2
Duparquet, lac QC 23 C2
Duperow SK 11 C3
Duplessis, lac QC 25 D3
DuPont, lac QC 26 F3-4
DuPont PNR ON 24 F3-4
Duport River NT 10 C5
Dupuis, lac QC 25 C6
Dupuis, lac QC 28 E1
Dupuis Corner NB 32 B7
Dupuy QC 17 C8
Dupuy QC 23 C2
Durban MB 11 C7
Durban MB 13 C1
Durell Point PE 35 E7
Durham NS 34 E3
Durham ON 20 B4
Durham Bridge NB 31 E5
Durham Bridge NB 32 B3
Durham CA ON 20 B4
Durham Centre NB 29 D7
Durham Centre NB 31 A8
Durham-Sud QC 24 D8
Durham-Sud QC 27 E4
Durocher, lac QC 39 E5
Durrell NL 38 E6
Durward AB 7 D8
Dusey River ON 16 B8
Dusterlo, lac QC 39 C1
Dusty River YT 4 E2
Dutch Valley NB 32 C5
Dutilly, lac QC 26 A6
Duti River BC 3 D4
Dutton ON 19 D4
Dutton ON 20 F3
Dutton Beach ON 19 D4
Dutton Beach ON 20 F3
Dutton/Dunwich ON 19 D4
Dutton/Dunwich ON 20 E6
Duval SK 11 D5
Duval, rivière QC 29 C-D8
Duval, rivière QC 30 D1
Duvar PE 35 B1
Duvernay AB 6 A7
Duvernay AB 11 A1
Dwight ON 21 B2
Dyce MB 11 A8
Dyce MB 13 A2
Dyce MB 13 A2
Dyer, Cape NU 42 F8
Dyer's Bay ON 18 D5
Dyke Lake NL 39 D7
Dyment ON 13 F7
Dyment ON 16 D4
Dymond ON 17 E7-8
Dymond ON 22 A1
Dymond ON 23 F1
Dysart SK 11 D6

E

Eabamet Lake ON 16 B7
Eabametoong (Fort Hope) ON 16 B6
Eades ON 17 C7
Eager Lake MB 12 D7
Eager Lake MB 15 D1
Eagle ON 19 D4
Eagle ON 20 F3

Eagle Bay BC 6 D2
Eagle Creek BC 1 C8
Eagle Creek BC 1 C8
Eagle Creek BC 6 C1
Eagle Creek BC 6 C1
Eagle Creek SK 11 C-D3 C4
Eagle-Dogtooth PP ON 13 E3
Eagle-Dogtooth PP ON 16 D2
Eagle Head NS 33 E4
Eaglehead Lake ON 16 E5
Eagle Island MB 13 A3
Eagle Island ON 18 B3
Eagle Lake AB 7 B5
Eagle Lake BC 1 C6
Eagle Lake BC 1 C8
Eagle Lake ON 13 F6
Eagle Lake ON 13 F6
Eagle Lake ON 16 C1
Eagle Lake ON 16 D2-3
Eagle Lake ON 18 C8
Eagle Lake ON 20 E7
Eagle Lake ON 21 B3
Eagle Lake ON 22 E1
Eagle Peak BC 1 A4
Eagle Plain YT 5 D-E3
Eagle Plains YT 5 E3-4
Eagle Point ON 18 A4
Eagle River BC 3 B3
Eagle River NL 39 C6-7
Eagle River NL 39 C6-7
Eagle River ON 13 E-F6
Eagle River ON 16 C1
Eagle River ON 16 D2
Eagle River YT 5 D-E3
Eaglesham AB 9 E3
Eagles Lake SK 11 A3-4
Eakin Creek Canyon PP BC 6 D1-2
Eakin Creek Floodplain PP BC 6 D1-2
Earchman MB 15 F3
Eardley QC 21 A7
Eardley QC 22 F7
Eardley QC 24 D1
Eardley Lake MB 13 C4-5
Ear Falls ON 13 E6
Ear Falls ON 16 C2
Earl Grey SK 11 D5
Earl Island NL 39 B7
Earl Rowe PP ON 20 B6
Earls Brook NS 33 E3-4
Earls Cove BC 2 C3-4
Earlton ON 17 D7
Earlton ON 23 F1
Earltown NS 33 A6
Earltown NS 34 E2
Earnscliffe PE 34 C2-3
Earnscliffe PE 35 E5
East Aldfield QC 22 F7
East Aldfield QC 24 D1
East Angus QC 27 E5
East Apple River NS 32 D6
East Apple River NS 33 A7-8
East Archibald Lake SK 9 A8
East Archibald Lake SK 12 A3
East Arm BC 1 C8
East Arm NS 34 C1
East Arm YT 4 D6
East Bay MB 36 D2-3
East Bay NS 34 C-D7
East Bay NS 34 C7
East Bideford PE 35 C2-3
East Braintree MB 13 F5
East Braintree MB 14 F7
East Braintree MB 16 D1
East Broughton QC 27 C6
East Castor River ON 24 E2-3
East Channel NT 5 B4 C4-5
East Chester NS 32 F7
East Chester NS 33 C5
East Chezzetcook NS 33 C6-7
East Clifton QC 27 F5
East Coulee AB 6 D6
East Coulee AB 7 B6
East Dalhousie NS 32 F6
East Dalhousie NS 33 C3-4
East Dover NS 33 C-D6
East Dover NS 34 F1
East Earltown NS 34 E2-3
East English River PP ON 16 D4
East Farnham QC 24 E7-8
East Farnham QC 27 F3
East Gate Registration Complex NHS MB 15 E3-4
East Gore NS 32 E8
East Gore NS 33 B6
East Gore NS 34 F2
East Grant Island NU 18 B1
East Green Harbour NS 33 F3
East Gwillimbury ON 20 B7
East Gwillimbury ON 21 E1

East Hants NS 32 E5-6
East Hants NS 33 B6
East Hants NS 34 F1-2
East Hereford QC 27 F5
East Jeddore NS 33 C7
East Jordan Station NS 33 E3
East Kemptville NS 33 E3
East LaHave NS 33 D4-5
East Lake ON 21 F5
East Linden NS 35 F4
East Linton NS 18 F5
East Linton ON 20 A4
Eastmain QC 40 E4
Eastmain, rivière QC 40 E4-5
Eastman QC 24 E8
Eastman QC 27 F3
East Mapleton NS 32 F7
East Mapleton NS 33 A5
East Mapleton NS 34 E1
East Margaretsville NS 32 E5-6
East Margaretsville NS 33 B3
East Medway NS 33 B3
East Medway NS 33 D4
East Mines Station NS 32 D8
East Mines Station NS 33 A6
East Mines Station NS 34 E2
East New Annan NS 34 E2
East Niska Lake MB 15 E6
Eastons Corners ON 21 C7-8
East Oro ON 18 F8
East Oro ON 20 A7
East Oro ON 21 D1
East Paint Lake PP Reserve MB 15 E3-4
East Pine PP BC 3 E8
East Pine PP BC 9 E1
East Point NS 33 F3
East Point PE 34 B4
East Point PE 34 B4
East Point PE 35 D8
East Point PE 35 D8
East Port l'Hébert NS 33 E3-4
East Prairie River AB 9 E-F4
East Quoddy NS 33 F2
East Quoddy NS 34 F4
East Redonda Island BC 2 B2-3
East Redonda PP BC 1 E6
East Redonda PP BC 2 B2-3
East River NL 38 C3
East River NL 39 B7
East River NS 32 F7
East River NS 33 A3-4
East River NS 34 E3-4
East River PP NS 32 F7
East River PP NS 33 C5
East River St. Marys NS 33 A3-4
East River St. Marys NS 33 A3-4
East River Sheet Harbour NS 33 B8
East River Sheet Harbour NS 34 E2
East Riverside-Kingshurst NB 32 D4
East Riverside-Kingshurst NB 33 A1-2
East Rous Island NB 33 B3
East Selkirk MB 13 E4
East Selkirk MB 14 E2-3
East Sister Island NT 5 B4 C4-5
East Sister Island PP ON 19 F1
East Thurlow Island BC 2 B2
East Trout Lake SK 11 A5
East Trout Lake SK 12 F6
East Uniacke NS 33 B5-6
East Uniacke NS 34 F1
Eastville NS 33 A7
Eastville NS 34 E2
East Walton NS 33 A5
East Walton NS 34 F1
Eastwood ON 19 C5-6
Eastwood ON 20 E4-5
East York ON 19 A4
East York ON 20 C7
East York ON 27 E5
Eaton QC 27 E5
Eaton, rivière QC 27 E5
Eatonia SK 6 D8
Eatonia SK 11 C2
Eaton Nord, rivière QC 27 E5
Eatonville ON 19 E3
Eau, lac d' QC 26 C4
Eau Claire ON 18 F7
Eau Claire ON 22 F1
Eau Claire, lac à l' QC 24 C2
Eau Claire, lac à l' QC 25 C5-6
Eau Claire, lac à l' QC 25 C2
Eau Claire, lac à l' QC 28 E1
Eau Claire, lac à l' QC 40 D5
Eau-Claire Lake NL 39 C2-3
Eau Jaune, lac à l' QC 26 A4

Eau Noire, lac à l' QC **26** A3-4
Ebb & Flow MB **13** D3
Ebb & Flow MB **14** B2-3
Ebb and Flow Lake MB **13** D2-3
Ebb and Flow Lake MB **14** B2
Ebbutt Hills NT **10** D3
Ebenezer PE **34** C2
Ebenezer PE **35** D4
Ebenezer SK **11** D7
Eberts ON **19** D3
Eberts ON **20** F2
Ebor MB **11** E7-8
Ebor MB **13** E1
Écarté, lac QC **25** E1
Écarté, lac QC **26** F8
Écarté, lac QC **28** D4
Écho, lac QC **22** E8
Écho, lac QC **23** E2
Écho, lac QC **24** C2
Echo Bay BC **1** E5
Echo Bay NT **41** C1
Echo Bay ON **17** F4
Echo Bay SK **11** B4
Echo Bay PMP BC **1** D-E5
Echoing Lake ON **13** A7
Echoing Lake ON **15** F7
Echoing River MB **15** E-F7
Echo Lake ON **33** C6
Echo Lake ON **17** F4
Echo Lake ON **21** B2
Echo Lake SK **11** C6
Echo Lake PP BC **6** E2
Échouani, lac QC **22** A8
Échouani, lac QC **23** F8
Échouani, lac QC **24** C8
Echo Valley PP SK **11** D5-6
Eckville BC **6** C5
Eckville AB **8** E-F5
Eclipse Sound NU **41** A6
Eclipse Sound NU **42** D-E5
Écorce, lac de l' QC **22** B7
Écorce, lac de l' QC **25** D1
Écorces, lac aux QC **22** A8
Écorces, lac aux QC **28** D5
Écorces, lac des QC **24** C4
Écorces, rivière aux QC **28** C-D5
Ecstall River BC **1** A3
Ecum Secum NS **33** B8
Ecum Secum NS **34** F4
Eda Lake NT **10** A7
Edam SK **6** B8
Edam SK **11** B3
Edberg AB **6** A6
Edberg AB **8** E7
Ed Bird-Estella Lakes PP BC **3** D5-6
Eddies Cove NL **38** A4
Eddies Cove NL **39** D8
Eddies Cove West NL **38** C7
Eddies Cove West NL **39** E7-8
Eddontenajon Lake BC **3** C3
Eddystone MB **13** D2-3
Eddystone MB **14** B2
Edehon Lake NU **40** B1
Edehon Lake NU **41** F4
Eden MB **13** E2
Eden ON **14** C-D2
Eden ON **19** D5
Eden ON **20** F4
Eden Lake MB **12** D8
Eden Lake MB **15** D2
Eden Lake NS **33** A8
Eden Lake NS **34** E4
Eden Mills ON **19** A-B7
Eden Mills ON **20** D5-6
Edenvale ON **18** F7
Edenvale ON **20** A6
Edenwold SK **11** E5-6
Edgar ON **18** F8
Edgar ON **20** A6-7
Edgar ON **21** D1
Edge Hills PP BC **1** D7-8
Edge Hills PP BC **2** A6
Edgeley SK **11** E6
Edgell Island NU **40** B1
Edgerton AB **6** B7
Edgerton AB **11** B2
Edgewater BC **6** E4
Edgewater BC **7** D1
Edgewood BC **6** E2-3 F2-3
Edillen MB **14** A2
Edith Cavell, Mount AB **6** B-C3
Edith Cavell, Mount AB **8** E1
Edmonton AB **6** B5-6
Edmonton AB **8** C6-7
Edmonton Beach AB **6** B5
Edmonton Beach AB **8** C5-6
Edmund Lake MB **15** F6
Edmundston NB **29** F3
Edmundston NB **31** C1-2
Edmund Walker Island NU **42** C3
Édouard, lac QC **25** C8
Édouard, lac QC **28** E4
Edrans MB **13** E2
Edrans MB **14** D2
Edson AB **6** B4
Edson AB **8** D3
Edwand AB **8** B8
Edward Island ON **16** F6
Edward Island, RNP ON **16** F6
Edward Island PNR ON **16** F6
Edwards ON **21** B8
Edwards ON **24** E2-3
Edwards, Mount YT **4** B4
Edwin MB **14** D-E3

Edys Mills ON **19** D3
Edys Mills ON **20** F2
Edziza, Mount BC **3** C2-3
Edzo NT **10** C5-6
Edzo NT **41** D1
Eel Ground NB **31** D6
Eel River NB **29** D6
Eel River Bar NB **29** D6-7
Eel River Bar NB **31** A5
Eel River Bridge NB **31** D7
Eel River Crossing NB **29** D6-7
Eel River Crossing NB **31** A5
Eels Creek ON **21** C3-4
Eels Lake ON **21** C3
Effingham ON **19** C8
Effingham ON **20** E7
Effingham Inlet BC **2** E2
Effingham Lake ON **21** C5
Egan Chutes PP ON **21** B4
Egan Creek ON **21** C4
Eganville ON **21** A5
Eganville ON **22** F5
Egenolf Lake MB **12** A8
Egenolf Lake MB **15** B2
Egerton NS **34** E3-4
Egg Lake MB **11** A7
Egg Lake MB **12** F7
Egg Lake MB **13** A1
Egg Lake MB **15** F1
Egg Lake SK **11** A7
Egg Lake SK **12** F7
Egg Lake SK **13** A1
Eglington NS **34** C4
Eglington PE **35** E7
Eglinton Island NT **42** C2
Eglinton Bay PE **35** E7
Egmondville ON **19** A-B4
Egmondville ON **20** D3
Egmont BC **1** F6
Egmont BC **2** C4
Egmont, cap PE **32** A7
Egmont Bay PE **32** A7
Egmont Bay PE **35** C1
Egremont AB **6** A6
Egremont AB **8** B7
Egypt Road NS **34** B6
Ehdacho HS NT **41** C1
Eholt BC **6** F2
Eighteen Mile Island ON **18** B6
Eight Island Lake NS **34** E5
Ekati Mine NT **10** A8
Ekati Mine NT **41** D2
Ekka Island NT **41** C1
Ekwan River ON **40** E2-3
Ekwi River NT **4** A-B7
Elak Dase SK **12** E4
Elbow SK **11** D4
Elbow Creek ON **18** A6
Elbow Lake MB **12** F8
Elbow Lake MB **15** F2
Elbow Lake SK **11** C7
Elbow Lake SK **13** A1
Elbow River AB **6** D-E5
Elbow River AB **7** F1
Elbow-Sheep Wildland PP AB **6** D-E5
Elbow-Sheep Wildland PP AB **7** F1
Elcan AB **7** E6
Eldee ON **17** F8
Eldee ON **22** C2
Elderbank NS **33** B6-7
Elderbank NS **34** F2
Elderbank PP NS **33** B6-7
Elderbank PP NS **34** F2
Eldersley SK **11** B6
Eldon PE **34** C3
Eldon PE **35** F5
Eldorado ON **21** D4-5
Eldorado SK **9** A8
Eldorado SK **12** A3-4
Eldorena AB **8** B7
Eldred SK **11** B4
Eleanor Island National Wilderness Area ON **18** E8
Eleanor Island National Wilderness Area ON **17** C1
Elephant Hill PP BC **2** A7
Elephant Lake ON **21** B3
Elfrida ON **19** C7
Elfrida ON **20** E6
Elfros SK **11** C6
Elgin MB **11** E8
Elgin MB **13** F2
Elgin MB **14** E1
Elgin NB **32** C5
Elgin NS **33** A7
Elgin NS **34** E3
Elgin ON **21** D7
Elgin ON **24** F1
Elgin, lac QC **27** D5-6
Elginburg ON **21** D6
Elginfield ON **19** C4
Elginfield ON **20** E3
Elgin Mills ON **19** A8
Elgin Mills ON **20** C7
Elgin Mills ON **21** F1
Elie MB **13** E3
Elie MB **14** D-E4
Elimville ON **19** B4
Elimville ON **20** D3
Elizabeth, Mount BC **29** F6
Elizabeth Bay ON **16** F6
Elizabeth Bay ON **18** B2
Elizabethville ON **21** C6
Elk Falls PP BC **1** E5
Elk Falls PP BC **2** C1-2

Elkford BC **6** E5
Elkford BC **7** D3
Elkhorn MB **11** E7-8
Elkhorn MB **13** E1
Elk Island MB **14** C6
Elk Island MB **15** F6
Elk Island, PN AB **6** A-B6
Elk Island AB **8** C7
Elk Island NP AB **6** A-B6
Elk Island NP AB **8** C7
Elk Island Provincial Heritage Park MB **13** D-E4
Elk Island Provincial Heritage Park MB **14** C6
Elk Lake ON **17** D7
Elk Lakes PP BC **6** E5
Elk Lakes PP BC **7** C2
Elko BC **6** F5
Elko BC **7** F2
Elk Point AB **6** A7
Elk Point AB **11** A2
Elk Ranch AB **14** C2
Elk River BC **6** E5
Elk River BC **7** D-E3
Elkton AB **6** D5
Elkton AB **7** A3
Elk Valley AB **7** B3
Elk Valley PP BC **6** F5
Elk Valley PP BC **7** E2-3
Elkwater AB **6** E-F8
Elkwater AB **11** F2
Ella Lake ON **18** A4
Ellard Lake ON **15** F7
Ellef Ringnes Island NU **42** B-C3
Elleh Creek BC **3** B7
Elleh Creek BC **9** B1
Ellen, lac QC **22** E6
Ellenwood PP NS **33** E1-2
Ellershouse NS **33** B5
Ellerslie AB **8** C6
Ellerslie PE **32** A7
Ellerslie PE **34** B1
Ellerslie PE **35** C2
Ellesmere, île d' NU **42** A-C5
Ellesmere Island NU **42** A-C5
Ellesmere Island (Quttinirpaaq) NP NU **42** A5
Ellice Island NT **5** B4
Ellice River NU **41** C3
Ellington Lake NT **10** A5
Elliot Lake ON **13** B5
Elliot Lake ON **17** F5
Elliot Lake ON **18** A2
Elliot Lake ON **18** A2-3
Elliotvale PE **35** E6
Ellison PP BC **6** E1-2
Elliston NL **37** B7-8
Ellscott AB **6** A6
Ellscott AB **8** A7
Ellscott AB **9** F6
Ellscott AB **12** F1
Ells River AB **9** C-D6
Ells River AB **12** C1
Ellwood, lac QC **25** B5
Ellwood, lac QC **26** F5
Elma MB **13** E5
Elma MB **14** D7
Elm Creek MB **13** F3
Elm Creek MB **14** E4
Elmira ON **19** A6
Elmira ON **20** D5
Elmira PE **34** B4
Elmira PE **35** D8
Elmira Railway Station Provincial Heritage Site PE **35** D8
Elmsdale NS **33** B6
Elmsdale NS **34** F2
Elmsdale PE **35** B2
Elmstead ON **19** E1
Elmsvale NS **33** B7
Elmsvale NS **34** F3
Elmsville NB **32** D2
Elmvale ON **18** F7
Elmvale ON **20** A6
Elmwood NB **31** F3
Elmwood NB **32** B1
Elmwood ON **20** B4
Elmwood ON **21** E6
Elmwood PE **35** E4
Elmworth AB **9** F2
Elnora AB **6** C6
Elnora AB **8** F7
Elora ON **19** A6
Elora ON **20** C5
Elora Gorge CA ON **19** A6
Elora Gorge CA ON **20** C5
Elphin ON **21** C6
Elphinstone MB **11** E8
Elphinstone MB **13** E2
Elphinstone MB **14** C1
Elrose SK **11** D3
Elsa YT **4** A-B4
Elsas ON **17** C5
Elsie Lake BC **2** D2
Elston, lac QC **39** A3
Elspeth BC **8** F1
Eltrut Lake ON **16** D1
Elva MB **11** F8
Elva MB **13** F1
Emaril NL **39** C2
Emar Lakes PP BC **1** D8
Emar Lakes PP BC **2** A7
Embar BC **9** C3
Embarras, lac QC **22** C6-7

Embarras, lac QC **25** E1
Embleton Lake MB **15** C-D5
Embree NL **36** A7
Embree NL **37** A5
Embree NL **38** F6
Embro ON **19** C5
Embro ON **20** E4
Embrun ON **24** E3
Embury MB **14** C3
Embury Lake MB **12** F7
Embury Lake MB **15** F1
Emerald PE **35** D3
Emerald Estates BC **2** C5
Emerald Isle NT **42** C2
Emerald Lake ON **18** A2
Emerson MB **13** F4
Emerson MB **14** F5
Emeryville ON **19** E1-2
Emile River NT **10** B6
Emile River NT **10** B-C5
Emily PP ON **21** D3
Emma Lake SK **11** B5
Emma Lake PRS SK **11** A4
Emmaline Lake SK **12** F4
Emmuraillé, lac QC **28** A-B7
Emo ON **16** E-F2
Emory Creek PP BC **1** F8
Emory Creek PP BC **2** D7
Empire Corners ON **19** C7
Empire Corners ON **20** E6
Empress AB **6** D8
Empress AB **11** D2
Emsdale ON **18** C8
Emsdale ON **21** A1
Emsdale ON **22** F1
E.M. Warwick CA ON **19** D4
E.M. Warwick CA ON **20** F3
Ena Lake ON **14** D8
Ena Lake ON **18** C4
Ena Lake ON **14** D8
Ena Lake SK **9** A8
Ena Lake SK **12** A4
Enatik Lake MB **12** C-D8
Enatik Lake MB **15** D2
Enchant AB **6** E6
Enchant AB **7** D6
Endako BC **1** A5-6
Endeavour SK **11** C6-7
Enderby BC **6** E2
Endiang AB **6** C6-7
Endiang AB **8** F8
Eneas Lakes PP BC **6** E1
Enemy, Lake of the NT **10** B8
Enfield NS **33** B6
Enfield NS **34** F2
Engemann Lake SK **12** C4
Engen BC **1** A6
Englee NL **38** C4-5
Englee NL **39** E8
Englefeld SK **11** C5-6
Englefield, Cape NU **41** B6
Englefield, Cape NU **42** F5
Englefield Bay BC **1** B1
Englehart ON **17** D7-8
Englehart ON **23** E1
Englehart R. Fine Sand Plain & Waterway PP ON **17** D7
Engler Lake SK **12** A-B2
English Chief River NT **10** C2
English Harbour NL **37** C7
English Harbour East NL **36** D7
English Harbour East NL **37** D5
English Harbour West NL **36** E6-7
English Harbour West NL **37** E4-5
English River Falls PP BC **1** F6
Englishman River Falls PP BC **2** C3
Englishmans Range YT **4** E5
English River ON **13** E5
English River ON **13** E6
English River ON **13** E-F7
English River ON **14** C-D8
English River ON **16** C-D1 D2
English River ON **16** D4
English River ON **16** D-E4
English River ON **20** E2
Englishtown NS **34** C7
Enilda AB **9** E4
Ennadai Lake NU **41** E3-4
Ennett Turnerville ON **19** D3
Ennett Turnerville ON **20** F1-2
Ennishone NB **31** D3
Enniskillen NB **32** D3
Enniskillen NB **33** A1
Enniskillen ON **20** B8
Enniskillen ON **21** E2
Enniskillen CA ON **20** C8
Enniskillen CA ON **21** E2
Ennismore ON **21** D3
Ennotville ON **19** A6
Ennotville ON **20** C5
Enon ON **21** C3
Enrage, Cape NB **32** C-D6
Enrage, Cape NB **33** A3-4
Ensign AB **6** E5

Ensign AB **7** C5
Enterprise NT **10** E-F6
Enterprise NT **41** E1
Enterprise ON **21** D6
Entiako PP BC **1** B5
Entiako River BC **1** B5
Entrance AB **6** B3
Entrance AB **8** C1
Entrelacs QC **24** B5
Entwistle AB **6** B5
Entwistle AB **8** C4
Environ SK **11** C4
Épaule, lac à l' QC **28** F5
Epper Passage PP BC **1** F5
Epper Passage PP BC **2** D1
Epsom ON **20** B8
Epsom ON **21** E2
Epsom PP ON **1** E8
Epsom PP ON **2** B7
Epworth NL **36** F6-7
Epworth NL **37** F4-5
Equity AB **7** A5
Erables Lake ON **22** E2
Eramosa ON **19** A6
Eramosa ON **20** D5
Eramosa River ON **19** A7
Eramosa River ON **20** C-D6
Erg Mountain PP NL **1** B8
Erg Mountain PP BC **6** A-B1
Eric QC **39** D2
Éric, lac QC **39** D2-3
Erickson BC **6** F4
Erickson BC **7** F1
Erickson MB **13** E2
Erickson MB **14** C1
Erie BC **6** F3
Erie ON **19** C7
Erie ON **20** E6
Erie, lac ON **19** E4-6
Erié, lac ON **20** F6-7
Erie, Lake ON **19** E5-6
Erie, Lake ON **20** F3-4
Erieau ON **19** E3
Erie Beach ON **19** E3
Erie Creek PP BC **6** F3
Eriksdale MB **13** D3
Eriksdale MB **14** B4
Erin ON **19** A7
Erin ON **20** C6
Erinferry SK **11** A4
Erinsville ON **21** D5
Erinview MB **13** E3
Erinview MB **14** D4-5
Erinville NS **34** E5
Erith AB **8** C2
Ermine SK **11** C3
Ernest BC **1** A5-6
Ernest SK **11** C3
Ernestown ON **21** E6
Ernfold SK **11** E4
Ernie SK **11** D4
Errington BC **2** D3
Errol ON **19** C3
Errol ON **20** E2
Erskine AB **6** C6
Erskine AB **8** E-F7
Ervick AB **8** D7
Erwood SK **11** B7
Erwood SK **13** B1
Escalier, réservoir l' QC **22** F8
Escalier, réservoir l' QC **24** C2
Esclaves, rivière des QC **9** A-B6
Esclaves, rivière des QC **12** A-B2
Escott ON **21** D7-8
Escoumins, rivière des QC **28** C8
Escoumins, rivière des QC **29** C1
Escuminac NB **31** D8
Escuminac NB **29** D6
Escuminac NB **31** A5
Escuminac, Point NB **31** D8
Escuminac, rivière QC **29** C-D6
Esden, lac QC **22** A8
Esden, lac QC **23** F7
Esden, lac QC **25** C1-2
Esk SK **11** C5
Eskasoni NS **34** C7
Eskbank SK **11** E4
Esker Lakes PP ON **17** D7
Esker Siding NL **39** B2
Eskers PP BC **1** C6
Eskimo Lakes NT **5** A-B5
Eskimo Point MB **15** B5
Esli Dodge CA ON **19** D4
Esli Dodge CA ON **20** E2
Esnagami Lake ON **16** C-D7
Esnagami River ON **16** C8
Esnagami River ON **17** C4
Esnagi Lake ON **17** C4
Esowista BC **1** F5
Esowista BC **2** E1
Esox Lake ON **13** F6
Esparto SK **11** F6
Espanola ON **18** A4
Esperanza Inlet BC **1** E-F4
Espinosa Inlet BC **1** E4
Espoir, Bay d' NL **36** E5
Espoir, Bay d' NL **37** D3-4
Esprit-Saint QC **29** D3
Esprit-Saint QC **31** A1
Essex ON **19** E1
Essipit QC **29** C1
Est, Île de l' QC **30** E8
Est, lac de l' QC **28** E8
Est, lac de l' QC **29** F1

Est, pointe de l' QC **30** A7
Estabrook Lake NT **5** C8
Estaire ON **18** A5
Estaire ON **18** A6
Estcourt QC **29** E1-2
Esten Lake ON **18** A2
Estérel QC **24** C5
Estérel QC **27** D1
Esterhazy SK **11** E7
Esterhazy SK **13** D1
Estevan SK **11** F6
Estevan Group BC **1** B3
Estevan Sound BC **1** B3
Esther AB **6** C8
Esther AB **11** C2
Esther, lac QC **23** B6
Esther, lac QC **26** B-C1
Estlin SK **11** E5-6
Estmere NS **34** D6
Eston SK **11** D3
Estuary SK **6** C8
Estuary SK **11** D2
Etamamiou, rivière QC **39** E6
Étamamiou QC **39** B6 C6-7
Etang-des-Caps QC **30** F7
Étang Morice NB **35** F1
Étang-Sand, RNF de l' NS **33** E2
Etawney Lake MB **15** C4
Etchemin, lac QC **27** C7
Etchemin, rivière QC **27** B6-7
Éternité, lac QC **28** C7
Ethel ON **19** A5
Ethel ON **20** C4
Ethelbert MB **11** D8
Ethelbert MB **13** D1-2
Ethelbert MB **14** A1
Ethel F. Wilson Memorial PP BC **1** A5
Ethel Lake YT **4** B3
Ethelton SK **11** B5
Etobicoke ON **19** A8
Etobicoke ON **20** C7
Etobicoke ON **21** F1
Etomami River SK **11** B7
Eton-Rugby SK **13** E6
Eton-Rugby SK **11** C5
Etter's Beach SK **11** D5
Etthen Island NT **10** D7-8
Ettington SK **11** E4-5
Etzikom AB **6** F7
Etzikom AB **7** E8
Etzikom AB **11** F1
Etzikom Coulee AB **6** F7
Etzikom Coulee AB **7** E-F7
Euchiniko River BC **1** B6
Euchu Reach BC **1** B5
Eudists, lac des QC **39** E3
Eugenia ON **20** B5
Eugenia Falls CA ON **20** B5
Eugenia Lake ON **20** B5
Eulas Lake SK **12** E5
Eureka NS **33** A7
Eureka NS **34** E3
Eureka NU **42** B4
Eureka River AB **9** D2-3
Eureka River AB **9** D2-3
Eureka Sound NU **42** B4
Eureka Sound NU **42** B-C4
Eutsuk Lake BC **1** B5
Éva, lac QC **26** A5-6
Évain QC **17** D8
Évain QC **23** D2
Eva Lake AB **9** B5
Evandale NB **32** D4
Evandale NB **33** A1
Evangeline NB **31** B8
Evangeline NB **31** F8
Evangeline NB **32** B6
Evans, Cape NU **42** A4
Evans, lac QC **40** F4
Evansburg AB **6** B4-5
Evansburg AB **8** C4
Evans Strait NU **40** A3
Evans Strait NU **41** D6-7
Evansville ON **18** A7
Evansville ON **18** C2
Evanston NS **34** D6
Evarts AB **8** F5
Everett NB **31** D3-4
Everett ON **20** B6
Evergreen AB **8** F5
Everton ON **19** A6-7
Everton ON **20** C5-6
Evesham SK **6** B8
Evesham SK **11** C2
Excel AB **7** A8
Exchamsiks River PP BC **1** A3
Exeter ON **19** B4
Exeter ON **20** D3
Exeter Lake NT **10** A7-8
Exeter Sound NU **42** F8
Exmouth Lake NT **10** A5-6
Expanse SK **11** E5
Exploits, Bay of NL **38** F6
Exploits Islands NL **38** E6
Exploits River NL **36** B5-6
Exploits River NL **37** B3-4
Exshaw AB **6** D4-5
Exshaw AB **7** B2
Eyapamikama Lake ON **13** B8
Eyebrow SK **11** D4-5

Eyehill Creek AB **6** B-C8
Eyehill Creek AB **11** B-C2
Eyrie Lake MB **12** C7
Eyrie Lake MB **15** C2

F

Faber Lake NT **10** B5
Faber Lake NT **41** D1
Fabre QC **17** E8
Fabre QC **22** B1-2
Fabyan AB **6** B7
Fabyan AB **11** B1
Factorydale NS **32** E6
Factorydale NS **33** B4
Faden NL **39** B2
Fagan, pointe NB **35** E1-2
Fagan Point NB **35** E1-2
Faguy, lac QC **26** E5
Faillon, lac QC **23** D6-7
Faillon, lac QC **25** A1
Faillon, lac QC **26** E1
Fairbairn Lake NT **10** D8
Fairbank NL **38** E6
Fairbank Lake ON **18** A4-5
Fairbank PP ON **17** F6
Fairbank PP ON **18** A4
Fairchild Creek ON **19** B6 C6-7
Fairchild Creek ON **20** E5-6
Fairfax ON **11** B8
Fairfax MB **13** F2
Fairfax MB **14** E1
Fairfield NB **32** D4-5
Fairfield NB **33** A2
Fairfield NB **35** F1
Fairfield PE **35** D8
Fairford MB **13** D3
Fairford MB **14** A3
Fairground ON **19** D5-6
Fairground ON **20** F4-5
Fair Harbour BC **1** E4
Fairhaven NB **32** E2
Fair Haven NL **36** D8
Fair Haven NL **37** D6
Fairholme ON **18** C7
Fairholme NB **11** B3
Fairisle NB **29** F8
Fairisle NB **30** F1
Fairisle NB **31** C7
Fairlight SK **11** E7
Fairlight SK **13** E1
Fairmont Hot Springs BC **6** E4
Fairmont Hot Springs BC **7** D1
Fair Ness NU **40** A5
Fair Ness NU **41** D8
Fairvale NB **32** D4
Fairvale NB **33** A1
Fairview AB **9** E3
Fairview ON **18** C7
Fairweather Lake YT **4** B5
Fairweather Mountain YT **4** F2
Fairy Glen SK **11** B5
Fairy Lake ON **21** B1-2
Falaise, lac QC **39** A1
Falaise Lake NT **10** E6
Falconbridge ON **17** F7
Falconbridge ON **18** A6
Falcon Island ON **14** E-F8
Falcon Lake MB **13** F5
Falcon Lake MB **14** E7
Falcon Lake ON **16** D1
Falher AB **9** E3
Falkland BC **6** E2
Falkland ON **19** C6
Falkland ON **20** E5
Falkland Ridge NS **32** F6
Falkland Ridge NS **33** C4
Fallaize Lake NT **5** B8
Fallbrook ON **21** C6
Fallbrook ON **24** E1
Fall Caribou Crossing HS NU **41** D3
Fallis AB **6** B5
Fallis AB **8** C4
Fallison MB **14** F3
Falloon Lake MB **15** A4
Fall River NS **32** E8
Fall River NS **33** C6
Fall River ON **21** C6
Falls Brook NB **29** E4
Falls Creek BC **2** C7
Falls Lake PP NS **32** E7
Falls Lake PP NS **33** C4-5
Falls Reserve CA ON **19** A4
Falls Reserve CA ON **20** C3
Falmouth NS **32** F7
Falmouth NS **33** B5
False Bay BC **1** F6
False Bay BC **2** C4
False Cape NL **39** A7
False Detour Channel ON **18** B1
Falun AB **6** B5
Falun AB **8** D6
Famham, Mount BC **6** E4
Family Lake MB **13** C5
Family Lake MB **16** A1
Famine, rivière QC **27** C7
Fancy Lake PP NS **33** D4
Fanning Brook PE **35** D-E6
Fanny Bay BC **1** F5-6
Fanny Bay BC **2** D2
Fannystelle MB **13** F3
Fannystelle MB **14** E4

Fanshawe CA ON **19** C5
Fanshawe CA ON **20** E4
Fanshawe Lake ON **19** C4-5
Fanshawe Lake ON **20** E3-4
Fanson Lake SK **12** C7
Fanson Lake SK **15** A1
Faraud Lake SK **12** A4
Farbus, lac QC **22** A7
Farbus, lac QC **23** F7
Farbus, lac QC **25** B2
Farewell NL **38** E7
Farewell ON **19** A5-6
Farewell ON **20** C4-5
Faride, lac QC **40** C5
Faride, lac QC **39** E6
Farley QC **24** B3
Farley QC **25** F2
Farmer Island NU **40** C3
Farmer Island NU **41** F7
Farmington BC **3** E8
Farmington BC **9** E2
Farmington NS **32** F6
Farmington NS **32** D8
Farmington NS **33** C4
Farmington NS **33** A5
Farmington NS **34** E1
Farmington PE **35** D7
Far Mountain BC **1** B5-6
Farm Point QC **21** A7-8
Farm Point QC **22** F7-8
Farm Point QC **24** D2
Farnham QC **24** C4
Farnham QC **27** F2-3
Farnham-Centre QC **24** C4
Farnham-Centre QC **27** F2-3
Faro YT **4** C4-5
Farrant Island BC **1** B5-6
Farrell Lake AB **6** C6
Farrellton QC **22** F7-8
Farrellton QC **24** C2
Farrow AB **7** C5
Farwell Lake MB **12** F8
Farwell Lake MB **15** F2
Fassett QC **23** D4
Fassifern NB **24** D4
Father, lac QC **26** C3
Fathom Five, PMN ON **18** D3-4
Fathom Five NMP ON **18** D3-4
Fatima QC **30** F7
Faucon, lac du QC **22** F8
Faucon, lac du QC **24** C3
Faulkner MB **13** D3
Faulkner MB **14** A3
Fauquier BC **6** E3
Fauquier ON **17** B6
Faust AB **9** E-F4
Favourable Lake ON **13** B6
Fawcett AB **8** A5-6
Fawcett AB **9** F5
Fawcett Lake AB **9** E-F5
Fawcett Lake AB **13** D7
Fawcett Lake ON **16** B4
Fawcett Lake ON **21** E5
Fawcettville ON **21** E5
Fawnie Range BC **1** B5-6
Fawn Lake NT **10** D5
Fawn River NT **40** D1-2
Fawn River PP ON **13** A8
Fay Lake MB **12** F7-8
Fay Lake MB **15** F2
Featherstone Point ON **19** D7
Fecteau, île QC **39** E6-7
Félix, Cape NU **41** B4
Félix, Cape NU **42** F3
Felix Cove NL **36** C2
Felton, rivière QC **27** D-E6
Feltz South NS **33** D4
Fenella ON **21** E3-4
Fenelon Falls ON **20** A8
Fenelon Falls ON **21** D2
Fenn AB **6** C6
Fenn AB **8** F7
Fennell ON **20** B7
Fennell ON **21** E1
Fenton SK **11** B5
Fenton Lake NT **10** C7
Fenwick NS **32** C7
Fenwick NS **34** D1
Fenwick ON **19** C8
Fenwick ON **20** E7
Fenwood SK **11** D6-7
Fergus ON **19** A6
Fergus ON **20** C5
Ferguson Creek MB **15** F3
Fergusonvale ON **18** F7
Fergusonvale ON **20** A6
Ferintosh AB **6** B6
Ferintosh AB **8** D7
Ferland ON **16** D6
Ferland ON **17** A1
Ferland SK **11** F4
Ferme MacDonald, lieu historique provincial NB **31** D7
Ferme-Neuve QC **22** C8
Ferme-Neuve QC **24** A2-3
Ferme-Neuve QC **25** D2-3
Fermeuse NL **37** E8
Fermont QC **39** C2
Fermont QC **40** E6
Fern Creek AB **8** D5
Ferndale ON **18** E5
Fernie BC **6** F5
Fernie BC **7** E2-3

Fernleigh ON **21** C5-6
Fernwood PE **32** B8
Fernwood PE **34** C1
Fernwood PE **35** D2-3
Ferré, lac QC **29** C-D3
Ferré, rivière QC **30** A4
Ferrier AB **8** E4
Ferris PP ON **21** D-E4
Ferryland NL **37** E8
Ferry Road NB **31** D7
Fertile SK **11** F7-8
Fertile SK **13** F1
Fesserton ON **18** F8
Fesserton ON **20** A6-7
Fesserton ON **21** C1
Festubert, lac QC **23** F7-8
Festubert, lac QC **25** B2
Festubert, lac QC **26** F2
Festubert, rivière QC
23 F7-8
Festubert, rivière QC **25** B2
Festubert, ZEC QC **23** F8
Festubert, ZEC QC **25** B2
Feu, lac du QC **39** E6
Feudal SK **11** C3
Feuilles, lac aux QC **40** C5
Feuilles, rivière aux QC
40 C5
Feuquières, lac QC **26** C5
Feversham ON **20** B5
Feversham Gorge CA ON
20 B5
F.H. Barber PP BC **2** D7
Fichot Islands NL **38** B5
Fidler AB **8** D2
Fidler Bay SK **12** B-C6
Fidler Bay SK **15** B1
Fidler-Greywillow Wildland
PP AB **9** A-B7
Fidler-Greywillow Wildland
PP AB **12** A-B2
Fidler Lake MB **15** D4
Fidler Point AB **9** A-B7
Fidler Point AB **12** A-B2
Fiedmont, lac QC **23** D5
Field BC **6** D4
Field BC **7** A-B1
Field ON **17** F7
Field ON **18** A7
Fielding NB **31** E3
Fielding NB **32** A1
Fielding SK **11** C3-4
Fife Island SK **12** B6
Fife Island SK **15** B1
Fifteenmile River YT **4** A2
Fifteenmile River YT **5** F2
Fifth Lake NB **32** C1
Fifty Point CA ON **19** B8
Fifty Point CA ON **20** E7
Fighting Ile ON **19** E1
Fiji Island NT **5** A8
Fildegrand, rivière QC
22 D4
File Lake MB **12** F8
File Lake MB **15** F2
Filkars, rivière QC **27** C5-6
Fillmore SK **11** E6
Fillongley PP BC **1** F5-6
Fillongley PP BC **2** D2-3
Filndt River ON **16** C5
Fil River MB **12** E-F8
Fil River MB **15** F2
Fils, lac du QC **22** C3-4
Finch ON **24** E3
Findlater SK **11** E5
Findlayson River YT **4** D6
Fingal ON **19** D4
Fingal ON **20** F3
Finger MB **11** A8
Finger MB **13** A2
Finger Lake BC **1** B6
Finger Lake ON **13** B6
Finger-Tatuk PP BC **1** B6
Finlay Ranges BC **3** D5
Finlay Ranges BC **3** D-E6
Finlay Reach BC **3** D-E6
Finlay River BC **3** C-D5
Finlay-Russel PP BC **3** C5
Finlay Island NS **34** C6
Finlayson Channel BC **1** C3-4
Finlayson Lake YT **4** D6
Finlayson Lake Territorial
Historic Site YT **4** D6
Finlayson Point PP ON
17 E7
Finlayson Point PP ON
22 B1
Finmark ON **16** F5
Finn Creek PP BC **6** C2
Finnegan AB **6** D6-7
Finnegan AB **7** B6
Finnie SK **11** D6
Finns MB **14** B-C5
Fintry PP BC **6** E1-2
Fiord, Bay NU **42** B4-5
Fiordland PRA BC **1** B4
Firdale MB **13** E2-3
Firdale MB **14** C2
Firebag River AB **9** C7
Firebag River AB **12** C2
Firefight Lake SK **6** E8
Firefight Lake SK **11** E2-3
Fire River ON **17** C4-3
Fireside BC **3** A4
Fireside BC **4** F7-8
Firesteel River BC **3** D4-5
Fir Island SK **12** A-B5
Fir Mountain SK **11** F4
Fir River SK **11** B7
1st Burnt Pond NL **36** B8
1st Burnt Pond NL **37** B6

First Eel Lake NB **32** C1
First Lac NB **29** E3
First Oil Well in Western
Canada NHS AB **7** F3-4
Firth River YT **5** B2
Firvale BC **1** C5
Fischells NL **36** C2
Fischells Brook NL **36** C2
Fishburn AB **7** F4
Fish Cove Point NL **39** B7
Fish Creek ON **6** D5
Fish Creek PP AB **7** B4
Fish Egg Inlet BC **1** C-D4
Fisher, Mount BC **6** F4
Fisher, Mount BC **7** E2
Fisher Bay MB **13** D4
Fisher Bay MB **14** A5
Fisher Bay PP Reserve MB
13 D4
Fisher Bay PP Reserve MB
14 A5
Fisher Branch MB **13** D3
Fisher Branch MB **14** B4
Fisher Channel BC **1** C4
Fisher Home AB **6** B5
Fisher Home AB **8** D5
Fisher Lake MB **32** F5
Fisher Lake NS **33** C3
Fisherman Lake NT **3** A6
Fisherman's Haven PP PE
34 A1
Fisherman's Haven PP PE
35 B2-3
Fisher Peak AB **6** D5
Fisher Peak AB **7** C2-3
Fisher River MB **13** D3-4
Fisher River MB **13** D4
Fisher River MB **14** A-B4
Fisher River MB **14** A4-5
Fishers Glen ON **19** D6
Fishers Glen ON **20** F5
Fisher Strait NU **40** A3
Fisher Strait NU **41** D-E6
Fisherton MB **14** B4
Fisherville ON **19** C7
Fisherville ON **20** E-F6
Fishing Branch YT **5** E2
Fishing Branch Ecological
Territorial Reserve YT
5 D2
Fishing Branch Wilderness
TP Reserve YT **5** D-E2
Fishing Eagle Lake MB
15 F5
Fishing Lake MB **13** C5
Fishing Lake MB **16** A1
Fishing Lake SK **11** C6
Fishing Lake SK **11** C6
Fishing River MB **11** D8
Fishing River MB **13** D2
Fishing River MB **14** A1
Fishing Ships Harbour NL
39 C8
Fish Island PE **35** C3
Fish Lake NT **10** C3
Fish Lake YT **4** E3-4
Fish Lake YT **4** E5
Fishog Lake ON **21** C2
Fish Point, RNP ON **19** F2
Fish Point PNR ON **19** F2
Fishtail Lake ON **21** B3
Fishtrap Lake ON **16** A7-8
Fiske SK **11** D3
Fitch Bay QC **24** E8
Fitch Bay QC **27** F4
Fitton, Mount YT **5** B-C3
Fitzallen AB **8** C8
Fitzgerald AB **9** A6
Fitzgerald AB **10** F8
Fitzgerald AB **12** A2
Fitz Hugh Sound BC **1** D4
Fitzmaurice SK **11** D6
Fitzroy Harbour ON **21** A5
Fitzroy Harbour ON **24** D1
Fitzroy PP ON **21** A7
Fitzroy PP ON **24** D1-2
Fitzwilliam Channel ON
18 D4
Fitzwilliam Island ON **18** D4
Fitzwilliam Strait NT **42** E4
Five Finger Rapids
Territorial Recreation
Site YT **4** C3
Five Fingers NB **29** E3
Five Fingers NB **31** B3-4
Five Islands NS **32** D7
Five Islands NS **32** D7
Five Islands NS **33** A5
Five Islands NS **34** E1
Five Islands NS **34** E1
Five Islands PP NS **32** D7
Five Islands PP NS **33** A5
Five Islands PP NS **34** E1
Five Mile BC **3** A1
Five Mile BC **4** F8
Five Mile Bay ON **18** D7
Five Mile Lake NS **32** E-F8
Five Mile Lake NS **33** C5
Five Mile Lake PP ON
17 E4-5
Flamand, lac QC **25** C6
Flamand, lac QC **28** E2
Flamand, rivière QC **25** C6
Flamand, rivière QC
28 E1-2
Flamboro Centre ON **19** B7
Flamboro Centre ON **20** D6
Flanagan Lake ON **12** E7
Flanagan Lake SK **15** E1
Flanagan River ON **13** B-C6
Flanagan River ON **16** A3

Flanders ON **16** E3
Flat Bay NL **36** C2
Flat Bay Brook NL **36** C2
Flatbush AB **8** A5
Flatbush AB **9** F5
Flat Creek ON **19** B4-5
Flat Creek ON **20** D3-4
Flathead BC **6** F5
Flathead BC **7** F3
Flat Island NL **38** C3
Flat Lake AB **6** A7
Flat Lake AB **8** A7
Flat Lake AB **9** F6
Flat Lake AB **11** A2
Flat Lake NT **10** B7
Flat Lake PP BC **1** D8
Flat River NT **4** D7
Flat River PE **34** D3
Flat River PE **35** F5
Flat Rock NL **37** D8
Flatrock Lake MB **12** E8
Flatrock Lake MB **15** E2
Flat Sound NU **42** B4
Flatstone Lake SK
12 D3-4 E4
Flat Valley NL **11** A3
Flat Valley SK **12** F3
Flavrian, lac QC **23** D2
Flaxcombe SK **6** D8
Flaxcombe SK **11** D2
Fleet AB **6** C7
Fleet AB **11** C1
Fleet Peak BC **3** D5
Fleming SK **11** E7
Fleming SK **13** E1
Fleming Lake ON **16** D7
Fleming Lake ON **17** A2
Flesherton ON **20** B5
Fletcher ON **19** E2
Fletcher Hall AB **8** D5
Fletcher Lake MB **15** B-C6
Fleur de Lys NL **38** D4-5
Fleur-de-May Lake NL
39 D3
Fleurimont QC **27** E4-5
Flin Flon MB **12** F7
Flin Flon MB **15** F1
Flintoft SK **11** F4
Flinton ON **21** C5
Floradale ON **19** A6
Floradale ON **20** C-D5
Floral SK **11** C4
Floral Park ON **18** F8
Floral Park ON **20** A7
Floral Park ON **21** C1
Florence NS **34** C7-8
Florence ON **19** D3
Florence ON **20** F2
Florence Lake ON **17** E7
Florenceville NB **31** E3
Florenceville NB **32** A1
Florencia Bay BC **2** E1
Flores Island BC **1** F5
Flores Island BC **2** D1
Flores Island PP BC **1** F4-5
Florimond, lac QC **26** C5
Florio, lac QC **22** C4
Florize MB **14** F7
Flotten Lake SK **9** F8
Flotten Lake SK **12** F3
Flowerpot Island ON **18** D4
Flower's Cove NL **38** B3-4
Flower's Cove NL **39** D7-8
Flower Station ON **21** B6
Flowing Well SK **11** E4
Fluery Bight NL **38** E5-6
Fluor Island ON **16** F6-7
Fluor Island ON **17** C1
Flying Dust SK **11** A3
Flying Point NS **34** E-F6
Flyingshot Lake AB **9** F2
Fly Lake MB **15** C5
Foam Lake SK **11** C-D6
Foam Lake SK **13** D1
Foch Lagoon BC **1** A3
Fogo NL **38** E7
Fogo, Cape NL **38** E7
Fogo Head NL **38** E7
Fogo Island NL **38** E7
Fogo Island Region NL
38 E7
Foins, lac aux QC **22** B4
Foisy AB **6** A7
Foisy AB **11** A1
Foldens ON **19** C5
Foldens ON **20** E4
Foleyet ON **17** D5
Foley Island NU **41** B7
Foley Island NU **42** F6
Foley Mountain CA ON
21 C7
Foley Mountain CA ON
24 F1
Folger ON **21** B6
Folly Lake NS **32** D8
Folly Lake NS **33** A6
Folly Lake NS **34** E1-2
Fond du Lac SK **12** A4
Fond du Lac SK **12** A4
Fond-du-Lac SK **41** F2-3
Fond du Lac River NL
12 A4-5
Fond du Lac River NL
12 B5-6
Fond du Lac River SK **41** F3
Fond du Lac River SK
11 B-C3
Fontainebleau QC **27** D-E5
Fontaine Lake SK **12** A4-5
Fontas River BC **9** C7-8
Fontas River BC **9** B1-2
Fontbonne, lac QC **23** D3
Fonteneau, lac QC **39** D5

Fonthill ON **19** C8
Fonthill ON **20** E7
Foothills AB **6** B4
Foothills AB **8** D2-3
Foothills Creek NT **5** A-B8
Footprint Lake MB **15** E3
Forant, lac QC **22** D5
Forbes, lac QC **24** A5
Forbes, lac QC **25** F5
Forbes Point NS **33** F2
Ford Bay NT **5** E8
Fords Mills NB **31** E7
Fords Mills NB **32** A5-6
Fordwich ON **19** A5
Fordwich ON **20** C4
Foremost AB **6** F7
Foremost AB **7** E7
Foremost AB **11** F1
Forest ON **19** C3
Forest ON **20** E2
Forestburg AB **6** C6-7
Forestburg AB **8** E8
Forestburg AB **11** B1
Forester Lake ON **16** A5
Forester Lake ON
12 D3-4 E4
Foresters Falls ON **21** A6
Foresters Falls ON **22** F6
Forest Estates ON **19** B-C6
Forest Estates ON **20** E4-5
Forest Field NL **37** E7
Forest Gate SK **11** B5
Forest Glen NS **33** B6
Forest Glen NS **34** F2
Forest Grove BC **1** C8
Forest Grove BC **6** C1
Forest Hill NS **34** E5
Forest Home ON **18** F8
Forest Home ON **20** A7
Forest Home ON **21** D1
Forest Mills ON **21** D5
Forestville ON **19** D6
Forestville ON **20** F5
Forestville QC **29** B2
Forestville, ZEC de QC
28 A8
Forestville, ZEC de QC
29 A1-2
Forfar ON **21** C7
Forfar ON **24** F1
Forgan SK **11** D3
Forges-du-Saint-Maurice,
LHN des QC **24** B7
Forges-du-Saint-Maurice,
LHN des QC **25** F7
Forges-du-Saint-Maurice,
LHN des QC **27** C2-3
Forges du Saint-Maurice
NHS QC **24** B7
Forges du Saint-Maurice
NHS QC **25** F7
Forges du Saint-Maurice
NHS QC **27** C2-3
Forillon, PN QC **40** F7
Forillon NP QC **40** F7
Fork Lake AB **6** A7
Fork Lake AB **8** A8
Fork Lake AB **9** F7
Fork Lake AB **12** F1
Fork River MB **11** D8
Fork River MB **13** D2
Fork River MB **14** A1
Forks Baddeck NS **34** C6-7
Forks Branch NB **29** E3
Forks of the Credit PP ON
19 A6-7
Forks of the Credit PP ON
20 C5-6
Formosa ON **20** B3-4
Forrest MB **11** E8
Forrest MB **13** E2
Forrest MB **14** D1
Forresters Point NL **38** B3
Forresters Point NL
39 D-E8
Forrest Lake SK **9** C8
Forrest Lake SK **12** C3
Forshee AB **8** E5-6
Forsythe QC **23** E7
Forsythe QC **25** A1
Forsythe QC **26** F1
Forsyth Lake SK **9** A8
Forsyth Lake SK **12** A4
Forsyth Lake SK **12** B5
Fort Albany ON **40** E3
Fort Alexander MB **13** E4
Fort Alexander MB **14** C6
Fort Anne & Scots Fort NHS
NS **32** F3-5
Fort Anne & Scots Fort NHS
NS **33** C1-2
Fort-Anne et du Fort-Scots,
LHN du NS **32** F3-5
Fort-Anne et du Fort-Scots,
LHN du NS **33** C1-2
Fort Assiniboine AB **8** A5
Fort Assiniboine AB **9** F5
Fort Assiniboine Sandhills
Wildland PP AB **6** A5
Fort Assiniboine Sandhills
Wildland PP AB **8** A5
Fort Assiniboine Sandhills
Wildland PP AB **9** F5
Fort Augustus PE **34** C3
Fort Augustus PE **35** E3
Fort-Battleford, LHN du SK
11 B-C3
Fort Battleford NHS SK
11 B-C3
Fort-Beauséjour, LHN du NB
32 C7
Fort-Beauséjour, LHN du NS
35 F1-2

Fort Beauséjour NHS NB
32 C7
Fort Beauséjour NHS NS
35 F1-2
Fort Black SK **12** E3-4
Fort Carlton Provincial
Historic Park SK **11** B4
Fort-Chambly, LHN du QC
24 D6-7
Fort-Chambly, LHN du QC
27 E2-3
Fort Chambly NHS QC
24 D6-7
Fort Chambly NHS QC
27 E2-3
Fort Chipewyan AB **9** B7
Fort Chipewyan AB **12** B2
Fort Chipewyan AB **41** F1-2
Fort Churchill NHS **15** B5-6
Fort-Coulonge QC **22** F6
Forteau NL **38** A3
Forteau NL **40** E8
Forteau Bay NL **38** A3
Forteau Brook NL **38** A3
Fort-Edward, LHN du NS
32 E7-8
Fort-Edward, LHN du NS
33 B5
Fort-Edward, LHN du NS
34 F1
Fort Edward NHS NS
32 E7-8
Fort Edward NHS NS **33** B5
Fort Edward NHS NS **34** F1
Fort Erie ON **20** E8
Fort-Espérance, LHN du SK
11 E7
Fort Espérance NHS SK
11 E7
Fort Frances ON **16** F2
Fort-Fraser, LHN du BC
1 A6-7
Fort Fraser BC **1** A6
Fort-Gaspareaux, LHN du
NB **32** B7-8
Fort-Gaspareaux, LHN du
NB **34** D1-2
Fort-Gaspareaux, LHN du
NB **35** F2-3
Fort Gaspareaux NHS NB
32 B7-8
Fort Gaspareaux NHS NB
34 D1
Fort Gaspareaux NHS NB
35 F2-3
Fort-George, LHN du ON
20 D7-8
Fort George/Buckingham
House PHS **6** A7
Fort George/Buckingham
House PHS AB **8** A7
Fort George Canyon PP BC
1 B7
Fort George NHS ON
20 D7-8
Fort Good Hope (Radilih
Koe) NT **5** E7
Forthton ON **21** C8
Forthton ON **24** F2
Fort Hope (Eabametoong)
ON **16** B6
Fortier MB **13** E3
Fortier MB **14** D4
Fortier, rivière QC **25** B3
Fortierville QC **27** B4
Forties Settlement NS
32 F7
Forties Settlement NS
33 C4
Fortin, lac QC **28** C7
Fortin, lac QC **39** E1
Fortin Lake YT **4** C-D6
Fort Irwin ON **21** B3
Fort Kent AB **6** A7
Fort Kent AB **9** F7
Fort Kent AB **11** A2
Fort Kent AB **12** F1
Fort-Kitwanga, LHN du BC
3 F3-4
Fort-Langley, LHN du BC
2 E5-6
Fort Langley BC **2** E5-6
Fort Langley NHS BC
2 E5-6
Fort Lawrence NS **32** C7
Fort-Lennox, LHN du QC
24 E6-7
Fort-Lennox, LHN du QC
27 F2
Fort Lennox NHS QC
24 E6-7
Fort Lennox NHS QC **27** F2
Fort Liard NT **3** A6
Fort Liard NT **10** F2
Fort-Livingstone, LHN du SK
11 C7
Fort-Livingstone, LHN du SK
13 C1
Fort Livingstone NHS SK
11 C7
Fort Livingstone NHS SK
13 C1
Fort William ON **16** F5-6
Fort William ON **22** E5
Fortymile YT **4** A2
Fortymile YT **4** C3
Forty Mile, Fort Cudahy and
Fort Constantine HS YT
4 A1-2
Forty Mile Flats BC **1** F7
Fortymile River YT **4** A1-2
Fosheim Peninsula NU
42 B4-5
Fossambault-sur-le-Lac QC
27 A5
Fossli PP BC **2** D-E2
Fosston SK **11** C6

Fort-Malden, LHN du ON
19 E1
Fort Malden NHS ON **19** E1
Fort-Mississauga, LHN du
ON **20** D7-8
Fort Mississauga NHS ON
20 D7-8
Fort Nelson BC **3** B7
Fort Nelson BC **9** B1
Fort Nelson River BC **3** B6-7
Fort-Pelly, LHN du QC
11 C7-8
Fort-Pelly, LHN du SK **13** C1
Fort Pelly NHS SK **11** C7-8
Fort Pelly NHS SK **13** C1
Fort Pitt Provincial Historic
Park SK **6** A-B8
Fort Pitt Provincial Historic
Park SK **11** A-B2
Fort Providence NT **10** E5
Fort Providence NT **41** D-E1
Fort Providence TP NT
10 E5
Fort Providence TP NT
41 D-E1
Fort Qu'Appelle SK **11** E6
Fort Resolution NT **41** E1-2
Fort Resolution (Deninoo)
NT **10** E7
Fortress of Louisbourg NHS
NS **34** C-D8
Fort Rodd Hill et du Phare-
de-Fisgard, LHN du BC
2 F4-5
Fort Rodd Hill & Fisgard
Lighthouse NHS BC
2 F4-5
Fort St. James BC **1** A6-7
Fort-St.-James, LHN du BC
1 A6-7
Fort St. James NHS BC
1 A6-7
Fort St. John BC **3** E8
Fort St. John BC **9** D1
Fort-St. Joseph, LHN du ON
17 F4-5
Fort St. Joseph NHS ON
17 F4-5
Fort San SK **11** D6
Fort Saskatchewan AB **6** A6
Fort Saskatchewan AB **8** C7
Fort Selkirk YT **4** C2-3
Fort Selkirk Territorial
Historic Site YT **4** C3
Fort Severn ON **15** F8
Fort Severn ON **40** D2
Fort Simpson NT **10** D3
Fort Simpson TP NT **10** D3
Fort Smith NT **9** A6
Fort Smith NT **10** F8
Fort Smith NT **41** E2
Fort Steele BC **6** F4
Fort Steele BC **7** E2
Fort Stewart ON **21** B4
Fort-Témiscamingue, LHN
du QC **17** E8
Fort-Témiscamingue, LHN
du QC **22** A1-2
Fort Témiscamingue NHS
QC **17** E8
Fort Témiscamingue NHS
QC **22** A1-2
Fortier MB **13** E3
Fortune NL **36** F6
Fortune NL **37** F4
Fortune, baie de NL **36** F6
Fortune, baie de NL **37** F4
Fortune Bay NL **36** F6
Fortune Bay NL **37** F4
Fortune Bridge PE **34** C4
Fortune Bridge PE **35** D-E7
Fortune Harbour NL **38** E6
Fortune Harbour PE **36** E7
Fortune Head NL **36** F6
Fortune Head NL **37** F4
Fortune Lake ON **21** B5
Fort Vermilion AB **9** B8
Fort Vermilion AB **41** F1
Fort-Walsh, LHN du SK **6** F8
Fort-Walsh, LHN du SK
11 F1-2
Fort Walsh NHS SK **6** F8
Fort Walsh NHS SK **11** F1-2
Fort Ware BC **3** C-D5
Fort-Wellington, LHN du ON
21 C8
Fort-Wellington, LHN du ON
24 F2
Fort Wellington NHS ON
21 C8
Fort Wellington NHS ON
24 F2
Fort William ON **16** F5-6
Fort William ON **22** E5

Foster QC **24** E8
Foster QC **27** F3
Foster, mont QC **24** E8
Foster, mont QC **27** F3
Foster, Mount BC **4** F3-4
Foster River SK **12** D-E5
Fosterton SK **11** E3
Fosterville NS **32** C1
Fountain Valley BC **1** E8
Fountain Valley BC **2** A6
Fourche, lac de la QC **23** E8
Fourche, lac de la QC **25** B2
Fourche, lac de la QC **26** F2
Fourché Harbour NL **39** E8
Fourches, lac des QC **22** A3
Fourches, lac des QC **23** F3
Fourchu NS **34** D7-8
Fourchu Bay NS **34** D7
Four Falls NB **31** D3
Fourmel, lac QC **38** A2
Four Mile Lake ON **20** A8
Four Mile Lake ON **21** C2
Four Mile River BC **3** B3
Fourmont Lake NL **39** D5-6
Fournel, lac QC **39** D7
Fournier ON **24** D3-4
Fournier, lac QC **39** D2-3
Fournier, lac QC **40** C5
Fournière, lac QC **39** D2-3
Four Roads NB **31** B8
Fowlers Corners ON **21** D5
Foxboro ON **21** E5
Fox Cove NL **36** E7
Fox Cove NL **37** E5
Fox Cove-Mortier NL
36 E-F7
Fox Cove-Mortier NL
37 E-F5
Foxe, bassin de NU **41** C6-7
Foxe, bassin de NU **42** F6
Foxe Basin NU **41** C7
Foxe Peninsula NU **40** A4
Foxe Peninsula NU **41** C-D7
Foxford SK **11** B5
Fox Harbour NL **36** E8
Fox Harbour NL **37** E6
Fox Harbour NS **34** D2
Fox Harbour PP NS **34** D2
Fox Island NB **31** C7-8
Fox Island ON **18** B3
Fox Island Harbour NL
36 D4
Fox Island Harbour NL
37 D2
Fox Island Main NS **34** E6
Fox Island River NL **36** B2
Fox Island River NL **36** B2
Fox Lake AB **9** B5
Fox Lake AB **15** D5-6
Fox Lake ON **18** D8
Fox Lake ON **21** B1
Foxley Bay PE **35** B-C2
Foxley River PE **35** C2
Fox Mine MB **12** D7
Fox Mine MB **15** D1
Fox Mount YT **4** D4-5
Fox Point NS **32** F7-8
Fox Point NT **10** A3
Fox Point ON **21** B2
Fox River BC **3** C5
Fox River MB **15** E5-6
Fox River MB **32** D7
Fox River NS **33** A4
Fox Roost NL **36** E1
Fox Valley SK **6** E8
Fox Valley SK **11** E2
Foxwarren MB **11** E7-8
Foxwarren MB **13** E1
Foymount ON **21** A5
Foy PP ON **21** A5
Foy PP ON **22** F5
France, lac QC **26** A5
Frances Lake YT **4** D6
Frances Lake Territorial
Campground & Historic
Site YT **4** D6-7
Frances River YT **4** E7
Franchere AB **6** A7
Franchère AB **9** F7
Franchère AB **11** A1-2
Franchère, lac QC **12** F1-2
Franchère, lac QC **24** A3-4
Franchère, lac QC **25** E3-4
Francis SK **11** E6
Francis, Lake MB **14** D6
Francis Lake ON **18** F5
Francis Lake ON **21** B4
Francis Point PP BC **2** D3
Francoeur, lac QC **25** A4
Francoeur, lac QC **26** F4
François NL **36** D-E4
François NL **37** D-E2
François, lac QC **24** B3

François, lac QC **25** E3
François, lac QC **27** F3
François, lacs à QC **39** D2
François Lake BC **1** A5
François Lake NT **10** C7
François Lake PP BC **1** A5-6
Franey Corner NS **32** F6
Franey Corner NS **33** C4
Frank AB **6** F5
Frank AB **7** E3
Frank Lake AB **7** C4
Frank Lake YT **4** D4
Frankford ON **21** E4-5
Franklin MB **13** E2
Franklin MB **14** D2
Franklin QC **24** E5
Franklin QC **27** F1
Franklin Bay NT **5** A7
Franklin Bay NT **41** A1
Franklin Beach ON **20** B7
Franklin Beach ON **21** D1
Franklin Island ON **18** D6
Franklin Lake SK **12** A6
Franklin Lake SK **15** A1
Franklin Strait NU **41** A-B4
Franklin Strait NU **42** E4
Franklyn Arm BC **1** D6
Frank Mackie Glacier BC
3 E3
Frank Slide PHS AB **7** E3-4
Franks Pond NL **37** E7
Franktown ON **21** B7
Franktown ON **24** E1-2
Frankville NS **34** D5
Frankville ON **21** C7
Frankville ON **24** F1
Franquelin QC **29** A4
Franquelin QC **39** F1
Franz ON **17** C-D4
Fraser BC **3** A1
Fraser BC **4** F4
Fraser, fleuve BC **1** D7
Fraser, fleuve BC **1** B7
Fraser, fleuve BC **1** B8
Fraser, fleuve BC **1** F8
Fraser, fleuve BC **2** B6
Fraser, fleuve BC **2** C-D7
Fraser, fleuve BC **2** E6
Fraser, fleuve BC **6** B1-2
Fraserburg ON **21** B1-2
Fraserdale ON **17** B6
Fraserdale ON **40** F3
Fraser Lake BC **1** A6
Fraser Lake NL **39** A-B4
Fraser Lake ON **21** B4
Fraser Mills NS **34** D5
Fraser River BC **1** A-B8
Fraser River BC **1** B7
Fraser River BC **1** D7
Fraser River BC **1** E8
Fraser River BC **2** A6
Fraser River BC **2** C7
Fraser River BC **2** E6
Fraser River BC **6** A-B1
Fraser River NL **40** C-D7
Fraser River PP BC **1** B7
Fraserville NS **32** D6
Fraserville NS **33** A4
Fraserville ON **21** B3
Fraserwood MB **13** E4
Fraserwood MB **14** C5
Frater ON **17** E4
Fraxville NS **32** F6-7
Fraxville NS **33** C4
Frazer Bay ON **18** C6
Frazer Lake ON **16** E6
Fréchette, rivière QC **39** D3
Frederick ON **17** C6
Frederick Arm BC **2** B2
Frederick House Lake ON
17 C6
Frederick House Lake, RNP
ON **17** C6
Frederick House Lake PNR
ON **17** C6
Frederick Lake YT **4** E3
Frederickton NL **36** A4
Frederickton NL **37** A6
Fredericton NB **32** B7
Fredericton NB **32** C2-3
Fredericton PE **34** C2
Fredericton PE **35** D4
Fredericton Junction NB
32 C3
Fredericton Road NB **31** F7
Fredericton Road NB **32** B5
Fred Henne TP NT **10** C6
Fred Henne TP NT **41** D1
Freedale MB **14** A2
Freedom AB **8** B5-6
Freeland PE **32** A7-8
Freeland PE **34** B1
Freeland PE **35** C2
Freels, Cape NL **37** F7
Freelton NL **19** B7
Freelton ON **20** D6
Freeman Lake MB **15** C4
Freeman River AB **6** A4-5
Freeman River AB **8** A4
Freeman River AB **9** F4-5
Freemont SK **11** B2
Freeport NS **33** D1
Freetown PE **34** C1-2
Freetown PE **35** D3
Frelighsburg QC **24** E7
Frelighsburg QC **27** F3
French Beach PP BC **2** F3
French Cove NS **38** C5
French Cove NL **39** E8
French Cove NS **34** D6
French Creek MB **15** D6

Frenchfort PE **35** E5
French Lake NB **32** C3
Frenchman Butte SK **6** A8
Frenchman Butte SK **11** A-B2
Frenchman Butte, LHN de SK **6** A8
Frenchman Butte, LHN de SK **11** A2
Frenchman Butte NHS SK **6** A8
Frenchman Butte NHS SK **11** A2
Frenchman River SK **11** F3-4
Frenchman's Cove NL **36** A2-3
Frenchman's Cove NL **36** E6
Frenchman's Cove NL **37** E4
Frenchman's Cove NL **38** F2
Frenchman's Cove PP NL **36** E6
Frenchman's Cove PP NL **37** E4
Frenchmans Island NL **39** B-C8
French Portage ON **13** F5
French Portage ON **14** E8
French River NS **34** B7
French River NS **34** E4
French River ON **17** F7
French River ON **17** F7
French River ON **18** B6
French River ON **18** B6
French River ON **18** B6
French River PE **32** A4
French River PE **34** B2
French River PE **35** D3
French River North Channel ON **18** B6
French River PP ON **18** B5-6
French River PP ON **18** B6-7
French River PP ON **18** B7
French Village NS **32** F8
French Village NS **33** C5
French Village PE **35** D5
Frenchville SK **11** F3
Freshfield Icefield BC **6** D3-4
Freshford MB **11** A7-8
Freshford MB **13** A1
Freshwater NL **36** E8
Freshwater NL **37** D7
Freshwater NL **38** B8
Freshwater Bay NL **36** B8
Freshwater Bay NL **37** B6
Freshwater Lake SK **6** B-C8
Freshwater Lake SK **11** C2
Freshwater Point NL **37** F7
Friars Cove NL **36** D1
Friedensfeld MB **14** E6
Friedensruh MB **14** F4
Frigon, lac QC **25** A2-3
Frigon, lac QC **26** E2-3
Frisco AB **8** E5
Froatburn ON **24** E3
Frobisher AB **11** F7
Frobisher Bay NU **40** A-B6
Frobisher Lake SK **12** D3-4
Frodsham Lake NT **10** B7
Frog Lake AB **6** A7
Frog Lake AB **11** A2
Frog Lake AB **11** A2
Frog Lake Massacre NHS AB **6** A7-8
Frog Lake Massacre NHS AB **11** A2
Frogmore ON **19** D6
Frogmore ON **20** F5
Frog River BC **3** C4
Froid, lac QC **24** A4
Froid, lac QC **25** E4
Froid, lac QC **26** D4
Frome ON **19** D4
Frome ON **20** F3
Frontenac QC **27** E6-7
Frontenac, lac QC **26** D5
Frontenac, lac QC **28** B1
Frontenac, parc de QC **27** D6-7
Frontenac PP ON **21** D6-7
Frontier SK **11** F3
Froomfield ON **19** C2
Froomfield ON **20** E1
Frosty Hollow NB **32** C7
Froude SK **11** F6
Frozen Ocean Lake NL **36** B6
Frozen Ocean Lake NL **37** B4
Frozen Strait NU **41** C6
Fruitland ON **19** B-C7
Fruitland ON **20** E6
Fruitvale BC **6** F3
Fryatt, Mount AB **6** C3
Fryatt, Mount AB **11** E1
Fry Lake ON **13** D7-8
Fry Lake ON **16** B4
Frys SK **11** F7
Frys SK **13** F1
Fugèreville QC **17** E8
Fugèreville QC **22** A2
Fulda SK **11** C5
Fulford QC **24** E8
Fulford QC **27** F3
Fulford Harbour BC **2** E-F4
Fullarton ON **19** B5
Fullarton ON **20** D4
Fullerton, Cape NU **40** A2
Fullerton, Cape NU **41** D5
Fulmore Lake BC **2** B1
Fulton ON **19** C7-8

Fulton ON **19** C7-8
Fulton ON **20** E6-7
Fulton River BC **3** F5
Fulton River Dam BC **3** F5
Fundy, baie de NB **32** E5-6
Fundy, baie de NB **33** B2-3
Fundy, Bay of NB **32** E-F4
Fundy, Bay of NB **33** B1-2 C1
Fundy, îles de NB **32** F3
Fundy, PN NB **32** D6
Fundy, PN NB **33** A3
Fundy (péage), route d'accès du sentier NB **32** D5
Fundy (péage), route d'accès du sentier NB **33** A2-3
Fundy Escarpment PP (proposed/projeté) NB **32** D5-6
Fundy Escarpment PP (proposed/projeté) NB **33** A3
Fundy NP NB **32** C-D6
Fundy Trail Parkway (toll) NB **32** D5
Fundy Trail Parkway (toll) NB **33** A2-3
Funk Island NL **38** E8
Funk Island Ecological Reserve NL **38** E8
Furby's Cove NL **36** D6
Furby's Cove NL **37** D4
Furman AB **7** D4
Furnace Falls ON **21** C3
Furness SK **6** B8
Furness SK **11** B2
Fury and Hecla Strait NU **42** F5
Fury and Hecla Strait NU **41** B6
Fushimi Lake PP ON **17** B4
Fusilier SK **6** C8
Fusilier SK **11** C2

G

Gabarus NS **34** D8
Gabarus, Cape NS **34** D8
Gabarus Bay NS **34** D8
Gabarus Lake NS **34** D8
Gable Mountain BC **6** F2
Gabriel, lac QC **26** C4
Gabriel Strait NU **40** B6
Gabriola BC **1** F6
Gabriola BC **2** E4
Gabriola Island BC **2** E4
Gabriola Sands PP BC **2** E4
Gadsby AB **6** C6
Gadsby AB **8** F8
Gadsby AB **11** C1
Gads Hill ON **19** B5
Gads Hill ON **20** D4
Gagamo, lac QC **22** C6
Gagamo, lac QC **24** A1
Gagamo, lac QC **25** E1
Gage, Cape PE **35** B1
Gagetown NB **32** C3-4
Gagnon QC **39** D1
Gagnon QC **40** E6
Gagnon, lac QC **24** B3
Gagnon Lake NT **10** D8
Gagnon-Siding QC **23** E7
Gagnon-Siding QC **25** A1-2
Gagnon-Siding QC **26** F1-2
Gaillarbois, lac QC **39** D2
Gainford AB **6** B5
Gainford AB **8** C5
Gainsborough SK **11** F7-8
Gainsborough SK **13** F1
Gairloch NS **33** A7
Gairloch NS **34** E3
Galahad AB **6** C6-7
Galahad AB **8** E8
Galahad AB **11** B1
Galarneau, lac QC **22** E6
Galarneauville AB **7** B6-7
Gale, lac QC **22** C6
Galeairy Lake ON **21** A3
Galeairy Lake ON **22** F3
Galena Bay BC **6** E3
Galetta ON **21** A7
Galetta ON **24** D1
Galeville NL **38** E4
Galiano Island BC **2** E4
Galibois, îles QC **39** E-F6
Galifet, lac QC **25** D5
Galifet, lac QC **28** F1
Galilee SK **11** E5
Galinée, lac QC **26** D5
Galinée, lac QC **28** B1
Gallants NL **38** A1
Gallas Point PE **34** C2-3
Gallas Point PE **35** E5
Gallet, lac QC **38** A1
Gallichan ON **17** C8
Gallichan QC **23** C2
Gallivan SK **11** B3
Gallix QC **39** F2
Galloway AB **6** F8
Galloway BC **6** F4-5
Galloway BC **7** F2
Gallows Cove NL **37** E7
Gamart, lac QC **39** C1
Gambier Island BC **2** D4
Gambo NL **36** B8
Gambo NL **37** B6
Gambo Pond NL **36** B7-8

Gambo Pond NL **37** B5-6
Gamebridge ON **20** A7
Gamebridge ON **21** D1-2
Gameland ON **16** E1
Gamsby River BC **1** B4
Gananoque ON **21** D7
Gananoque Lake ON **21** D7
Ganaraska River ON **21** E3
Gander NL **36** A-B7
Gander NL **37** A-B5
Gander Bay NL **36** A7-8
Gander Bay NL **37** A5-6
Gander Bay NL **38** E-F7
Gander Bay NL **38** F7
Gander Lake NL **36** B7
Gander Lake NL **37** B5
Gander River NL **36** A7
Gander River NL **37** A5
Gander River NL **38** F6-7
Ganges BC **2** E4
Gannet Islands Ecological Reserve NL **39** B8
Gaotanaga, lac QC **22** A5
Gaotanaga, lac QC **24** A7
Gap AB **7** B2
Garancières, lac QC **25** A4
Garancières, lac QC **26** E4
Garden Bay BC **1** F6
Garden Bay BC **2** D3-4
Garden Cove NL **36** D8
Garden Cove NL **37** D6
Garden Hill MB **13** A5
Garden Hill NL **38** E3
Garden Lake ON **16** E5
Garden of Eden NS **33** A8
Garden of Eden NS **34** E4
Garden Plain AB **8** F8
Garden River ON **17** F4
Garden River ON **17** F4
Garden River SK **11** A-B5
Gardenton MB **13** F4
Gardenton MB **14** F4
Garden Village ON **17** F7-8
Garden Village ON **18** A7
Gardiner ON **17** D3-4
Gardiner Dam SK **11** D4
Gardiner Lakes AB **9** C6
Gardiner Lakes AB **12** C1
Gardiner Mines NS **34** C8
Gardner, lac QC **22** B5
Gardner Canal BC **1** B4
Gardner Creek NB **32** D4-5
Gardner Creek NB **33** B2
Garfield AB **7** A3
Garfield PE **34** C3
Garfield PE **35** F5-6
Gargamelle NL **38** C3
Gargantua, Cape ON **17** E3
Garia Bay NL **36** D2
Garia Brook NL **36** D2
Garibaldi BC **1** E7
Garibaldi BC **2** C5
Garibaldi, Mount BC **1** E7
Garibaldi, Mount BC **2** C5
Garibaldi Heights BC **1** F7
Garibaldi Heights BC **2** C5
Garibaldi Lake BC **1** E7
Garibaldi Lake BC **2** C5
Garibaldi PP BC **1** E-F7
Garibaldi PP BC **2** C5
Garin, rivière QC **29** C8
Garin, rivière QC **30** D1
Garland ON **11** C-D8
Garland MB **13** C-D2
Garland MB **14** A1
Garner Lake PP AB **6** A6-7
Garner Lake PP AB **8** B8
Garner Lake PP AB **11** A1
Garner Lake PP AB **12** F1
Garnet ON **20** E6
Garnett Settlement NB **31** D2-3
Garnett Settlement NB **33** A2
Garnish NL **36** E6
Garnish NL **37** E4
Garrick SK **11** B5-6
Garrington AB **8** F5
Garrick Lake ON **13** A7-8
Garry Island NT **5** A-B4
Garry Lake NU **41** C4
Garson MB **13** E4
Garson MB **14** D5
Garson ON **17** F7
Garson ON **18** A5
Garson Lake AB **9** D7
Garson Lake AB **12** D2
Garson Lake SK **9** D7-8
Garson Lake SK **12** D2
Garth AB **8** E-F4
Gartly AB **7** A5-6
Gascoigne SK **11** E5
Gascoigne Cove PE **35** F5
Gaspard Creek BC **1** D7
Gaspé QC **30** B2
Gaspé QC **30** B2-3
Gaspé QC **40** F7
Gaspé, baie de QC **30** B-C3
Gaspé, cap de QC **30** B3
Gaspereau NS **32** F7
Gaspereau NS **33** B4-5
Gaspereau, rivière NB **35** E1-2 F2
Gaspereau Forks NB **31** F6
Gaspereau Forks NB **32** B4
Gaspereau Lake NS **32** E6-7

Gaspereau Lake NS **33** B4
Gaspereau River NB **31** E-F6
Gaspereau River NB **32** B4
Gaspereau River NB **35** E-F2
Gaspereaux PE **34** C4
Gaspereaux PE **35** F7
Gaspésie, parc de la QC **29** B6-7
Gassend Lake NT **5** C7
Gaston, lac QC **25** B4
Gaston, lac QC **26** E6
Gaston, lac QC **26** F4
Gaston, lac QC **28** C2
Gataga Mountain BC **3** B5
Gataga River BC **3** B-C5
Gatehead Island NU **41** B4
Gatehead Island NU **42** E3
Gathto Creek BC **3** C6
Gatineau QC **21** A8
Gatineau QC **22** F8
Gatineau QC **24** D2
Gatineau, parc de la QC **21** A7
Gatineau, parc de la QC **22** F7
Gatineau, parc de la QC **24** D1-2
Gatineau, rivière QC **21** A7-8
Gatineau, rivière QC **22** C-D7
Gatineau, rivière QC **22** F7-8
Gatineau, rivière QC **24** A-B2
Gatineau, rivière QC **24** C-D2
Gatineau, rivière QC **25** E-F2
Gatineau Park QC **21** A7-8
Gatineau Park QC **22** F7
Gatineau Park QC **24** D2
Gaudois, lac QC **22** A7
Gaudois, lac QC **25** C2
Gauer Lake MB **15** D3-4
Gaultois NL **36** D6
Gaultois NL **37** D4
Gauvin, lac QC **24** A3
Gauvin, lac QC **25** F3
Gayford ON **7** B5
Gayna River NT **5** F6
Gays River NS **33** B6
Gays River NS **34** F2
Gaythorne NB **31** C7
Geary NB **32** C3
Gegogan Harbour NS **34** F5
Gegogan Harbour NS **34** F5
Geikie Island ON **16** D6
Geikie River SK **12** C5-6
Gelert ON **21** C3
Gem AB **6** D6
Gem AB **7** B6
Genelle BC **6** F3
Genesee AB **6** B5
Genesee AB **8** C5
Genévriers, île des QC **39** D-E7
Génier, lac QC **22** D8
Génier, lac QC **24** A2
Génier, lac QC **25** E2
Gensart, lac QC **39** C1
Gens de Terre, rivière QC **22** B-C7
Gens de Terre, rivière QC **25** D1
Gentilly QC **24** B8
Gentilly QC **25** F8
Gentilly QC **27** C4
Geoffrion, lac QC **25** D6
Geoffrion, lac QC **28** F2
George, Cape BC **1** A2
George, Cape NS **34** D5
George, Lake NS **32** C2
George, rivière QC **39** A3
George, rivière QC **40** C-D6
George Evanoff PP BC **1** A8
George Evanoff PP BC **6** A1
Georgefield NS **33** B6
Georgefield NS **34** F2
George Island MB **13** B3-4
George Island NL **39** B7
George Island NL **38** A4
George Island SK **12** B6
George Island SK **15** B1
George Lake SK **12** D-E4
George Richards, Cape NU **42** C3
Georges Brook NL **36** B8
Georges Brook NL **37** C6
Georges Lake NL **36** B2-3
Georges Lake NL **38** B2
Georges River NS **34** C7
Georgetown ON **19** A7
Georgetown ON **20** C6
Georgetown PE **34** C3-4
Georgetown PE **35** E7
Georgetown Harbour PE **34** C3-4
Georgetown Harbour PE **35** E7
Georgeville NS **34** D5
Georgeville NS **34** E8
Georgeville QC **27** E4
Georgia, Strait of BC **1** F6
Georgia, Strait of BC **2** C-D3
Georgian Bay ON **18** C5
Georgian Bay ON **20** A5
Georgian Bay Islands NP ON **18** E6-7
Georgian Bay Islands NP ON **18** E7
Georgian Beach ON **18** F6

Georgian Beach ON **20** A5
Georgie, détroit de BC **1** F6
Georgie, détroit de BC **2** D3-4
Georgienne, baie ON **18** D5-6
Georgienne, baie ON **20** A5-6
Georgina ON **20** B7
Georgina ON **21** E1
Georgina Island ON **18** F8
Georgina Island ON **20** A7
Georgina Island ON **20** B7
Georgina Island ON **21** D1
Georgina Island ON **21** D1
Gerald ON **16** D7
Gerald SK **13** D1
Geraldton ON **17** B2
Geraldton ON **40** F2
Geraldton East ON **16** D7-8
Geraldton East ON **17** B2
Germaine, lac QC **39** C1
Germaine Lake NT **10** C6
Germansen Lake BC **3** E6
Germansen Landing BC **3** E6
Gesgapegiag QC **29** D7
Gesgapegiag QC **31** A6
Gesto QC **19** E1
Geyser MB **14** B5
Ghost Lake AB **6** D5
Ghost Lake AB **7** B3
Ghost Lake NT **10** B6
Ghost River ON **13** E7-8
Ghost River ON **16** D4
Ghost River ON **23** C-D1
Ghost River Provincial Wilderness Area AB **7** A-B2
Ghost River Wilderness Area AB **6** D4-5
Giant Lake NS **34** E5
Giants Tomb Island ON **18** E7
Gibbons AB **6** A6
Gibbons AB **8** B6
Gibbs Fiord NU **41** A7
Gibbs Fiord NU **42** E6-7
Gibraltar BC **3** B6
Gibraltar Rock PP Reserve NS **33** B6-7
Gibson Lake ON **18** E7-8
Gibson PMP BC **1** F4-5
Gibson River, RNP ON **18** E8
Gibson River, RNP ON **21** C1
Gibson River PNR ON **18** E8
Gibson River PNR ON **21** C1
Gibsons BC **1** F6
Gibsons BC **2** D4
Gift Lake AB **9** E4
Gilbert Bay NL **39** C8
Gilbert Cove NS **32** F4
Gilbert Plains MB **11** D1-2
Gilbert Plains MB **13** D3
Gilbert River NL **39** C7-8
Gilbertville ON **19** C5
Gilbertville ON **20** F5
Gilby AB **8** E5
Gilchrist Bay ON **21** D4
Giles Lake SK **12** B5
Gilford ON **20** B7
Gilford ON **21** E1
Gilford Island BC **1** E5
Gil Island BC **1** B3
Gillam MB **15** D5
Gillam MB **40** C1
Gillams NL **36** A3-B3
Gillams NL **37** A-B1
Gillespie Settlement NB **31** D2-3
Gillespie Settlement NB **33** A2
Gillies ON **17** E7
Gillies Bay BC **1** F6
Gillies Bay BC **2** D3
Gillis Point PE **35** C3
Gilmour ON **21** C4
Gilmour Lake ON **22** E3
Gilnockie PP BC **6** F4-5
Gilnockie PP BC **7** F2
Gilttoyees Inlet BC **1** A3
Gimli MB **13** E4
Gimli MB **14** C5
Gin Cove NL **36** C8
Gin Cove NL **37** D6
Gingolx (Kincolith) BC **3** F3
Ginoogaming ON **16** D8
Ginoogaming ON **17** B2
Gipsy Lake AB **9** D7
Gipsy Lake AB **12** D2
Gipsy Lake Wildland PP AB **9** D7
Gipsy Lake Wildland PP AB **12** D2
Girardville QC **26** D7-8
Girardville QC **28** A3
Girène, lac QC **25** C3
Girouard, lac QC **26** E1
Girouard, lac QC **29** B2
Giroux MB **13** F4
Giroux MB **14** E6
Giroux, lac QC **22** B5
Girouxville AB **9** E3
Girvin SK **11** D4-5
Gisborne Lake NL **36** D7
Gisborne Lake NL **37** D5
Gitanmaax BC **3** F4
Gitchie River ON **13** C8 D7
Gitnadoix River PRA BC **1** A3
Gitwinksihlkw BC **3** F3

Gjoa Haven (Uqsuqtuuq) NU **41** B-C4
Gjoa Haven (Uqsuqtuuq) NU **42** F3-4
Glace Bay NS **34** C8
Glacial Mountain BC **3** C3
Glacier BC **6** D3
Glacier Lake BC **3** C1
Glacier NP BC **6** D3
Glaciers, PN des BC **6** D3
Glade BC **6** F3
Gladmar SK **11** F5-6
Gladstone AB **8** D8
Gladstone MB **13** D3
Gladstone MB **14** D3
Gladstone ON **19** C5
Gladstone ON **20** E4
Gladstone Creek YT **4** B4
Gladstone PP BC **6** F2-3
Gladstone Valley AB **7** F3-4
Gladue Lake SK **11** A3
Gladue Lake SK **12** F3
Gladwin BC **2** B7
Gladys AB **7** C4
Gladys Lake BC **3** A2
Gladys Lake BC **4** F5
Gladys River BC **3** A2
Gladys River BC **4** F5
Glamis SK **11** D3
Glammis ON **20** B3
Glamor Lake ON **21** C3
Glanford ON **19** B6
Glanford ON **20** F4
Glasgow Station ON **21** A6
Glaslyn SK **11** B3
Glasnevin SK **11** F5
Glass MB **14** D5-6
Glassville NB **31** E3
Glassville NB **32** A1-2
Gledhow SK **11** C4
Gleichen AB **6** D6
Gleichen AB **7** C5
Glen Alda ON **21** C4
Glen Allan ON **19** A6
Glen Allan ON **20** C5
Glen Alpine NS **34** E4-5
Glenarm ON **20** A8
Glenarm ON **21** D2
Glen Becker ON **24** D3
Glenboro MB **13** F2
Glenboro MB **14** F2
Glenbourne MB **14** B3
Glenbow AB **7** B3
Glenburnie NL **36** A3
Glenburnie NL **37** A1
Glenburnie NL **38** F2
Glenburnie NL **39** F7
Glenburnie ON **21** D6-7
Glenburnie-Birchy Head-Shoal Brook NL **36** A3
Glenburnie-Birchy Head-Shoal Brook NL **37** A1
Glenburnie-Birchy Head-Shoal Brook NL **38** F2
Glenbush SK **11** B3
Glencairn MB **14** C2
Glencairn ON **20** B6
Glen Cairn ON **21** B8
Glen Cairn ON **24** E2
Glencoe NB **29** D6
Glencoe NB **31** A4
Glencoe NS **33** A8
Glencoe NS **34** E5
Glencoe ON **19** D3-4
Glencoe ON **20** F2-3
Glencoe Mills NS **34** C-D6
Glencoe Station NS **34** C5
Glendale NS **34** D5-6
Glendale Cove BC **1** E5
Glendale Cove BC **2** A-B1
Glendon AB **6** A7
Glendon AB **11** A2
Glendon AB **12** F2
Glendyer NS **34** C6
Glenelg NS **33** A8
Glenelg NS **34** E4
Glenella MB **13** E2
Glenella MB **14** D2
Glenevis AB **6** A5
Glenevis AB **8** C5
Glen Ewen SK **11** F7
Glenfanning PE **35** E6-7
Glenfinnan PE **35** E5
Glenford AB **8** B5
Glenforsa MB **14** C1
Glengarry NS **33** A7
Glengarry NS **34** E3
Glengarry Cairn NHS ON **24** E4-5
Glen Haffy CA ON **19** A7
Glen Haffy CA ON **20** C6
Glen Harbour SK **11** D5
Glen Haven NS **32** F8
Glen Haven NS **33** C5
Glenholme NS **32** D8
Glenholme NS **33** A6
Glen Huron ON **20** B6
Gleniffer Lake AB **8** F5-6
Glenister AB **8** B5
Glen Kerr SK **11** D3
Glenlea MB **14** E5
Glen Levit NB **29** D5-6
Glen Livet NB **31** C7
Glenlily QC **7** F1
Glenlyon Peak YT **4** C4
Glenlyon Range YT **4** C4
Glen McPherson SK **11** F3
Glen Margaret NS **32** F8
Glen Margaret NS **33** C5

Glen Meyer ON **20** F4-5
Glen Miller ON **21** E4-5
Glen Mont NS **32** E6-7
Glenmoor MB **14** D6
Glen Morris ON **19** B6
Glen Morris ON **20** D-E5
Glenmount ON **21** B2
Glen Nevis ON **24** E4
Glenora BC **2** E-F4
Glenora BC **3** C2
Glenora MB **13** F2
Glenora MB **14** F2
Glenora ON **21** E5
Glen Orchard ON **18** E8
Glen Orchard ON **21** B1
Glenorchy ON **16** E3
Glen Park AB **8** D6
Glen Road NS **34** C4-5
Glen Robertson ON **24** D4
Glen Ross ON **21** E4
Glenside SK **11** D4
Glen Sutton QC **24** E8
Glen Sutton QC **27** F3
Glen Tay ON **21** C7
Glen Tay ON **24** F1
Glen Valley PE **35** D4
Glenview MB **13** D6
Glenview NL **37** D6
Glen Walter ON **24** E4
Glenwilliam PE **35** F6
Glen Williams ON **19** A7
Glen Williams ON **20** C6
Glenwood AB **6** F5-6
Glenwood AB **7** F4-5
Glenwood NB **31** B4
Glenwood NB **32** D4
Glenwood NL **33** A1
Glenwood NL **36** A7
Glenwood NS **33** E2
Glenwood PE **32** A7
Glenwood PE **35** C1
Glenwood PP NS **33** E2
Glidden SK **6** D8
Glidden SK **11** D2-3
Gloucester ON **21** A-B8
Gloucester ON **24** D2
Gloucester Pond ON **18** E8
Gloucester Pond ON **21** C1
Glover Island NL **36** B3
Glover Island NL **37** B1
Glovers Harbour NL **36** A4
Glovers Harbour NL **37** A4
Glovers Harbour NL **38** F5
Glovertown NL **36** B8
Glovertown NL **37** B6
Glowworm Lake NT **10** A8
Glundebery Creek BC **3** B2
Glyvelde Lake NL **39** C4
Gnadenthal MB **14** F4
Goatfell BC **7** F1
Goatherd Mountain YT **4** F3
Goat Island BC **1** E6
Goat Island BC **2** C3
Goat Lake BC **2** C3
Goat Range PP BC **6** E3
Goat River BC **6** F4
Goat River BC **7** F1
Gobles ON **19** C6
Gobles ON **20** E5
Goblin NL **36** D5
Goblin NL **37** D3
Godbout QC **39** F1
Godbout QC **40** F6
Godbout, rivière QC **39** F1
Goderich ON **19** A3-4
Goderich ON **20** C2-3
Gods Lake MB **15** F5
Gods Lake MB **15** F5-6
Gods Lake Narrows MB **13** A5
Gods Lake Narrows MB **15** F5
Gods Mercy, Bay of NU **36** E-F8
Gods Mercy, Bay of NU **40** A3
Gods Mercy, Bay of NU **41** D6
God's Pocket PMP BC **1** D4
Gods River MB **15** E6-7
Gods River MB **15** F6
Gods River MB **40** D1
Goéland, lac au QC **22** A6
Goéland, lac au QC **23** A6
Goéland, lac au QC **26** A-B1
Goélands, lac aux QC **25** A4
Goélands, lac aux QC **25** A7
Goélands, lac aux QC **26** E4
Goélands, lac aux QC **26** F7
Goélands, lac aux QC **28** C1
Goélands, lac aux QC **28** D3
Goffs NS **33** B6
Gogama ON **17** D-E6
Go Home Lake ON **18** E7
Go Home Lake ON **18** E7
Go Home River ON **18** E7
Goldboro NS **34** F5
Gold Bridge BC **1** D7
Gold Bridge BC **2** A5
Goldburn SK **11** B6
Gold Centre ON **17** D6
Gold Creek BC **6** F4
Gold Creek BC **7** F2
Golden BC **6** D3-4
Golden Ears PP BC **1** F7
Golden Ears PP BC **2** D5-6
Golden Hinde BC **1** F5
Golden Hinde BC **2** C-D1
Golden Lake ON **21** A5
Golden Lake ON **22** F5

Golden Lake ON **22** F5
Golden Prairie SK **6** E8
Golden Prairie SK **11** E2
Goldenville NS **34** F4
Gold Lake ON **21** C3
Gold Muchalat PP BC **1** E5
Goldpan PP BC **2** B7
Goldpan PP BC **6** E1
Goldpines ON **13** E6
Goldpines ON **16** C2-3
Gold River BC **1** E5
Gold River BC **2** C1
Gold River NS **32** F7
Gold River NS **33** C4
Gold River NS **33** C4
Gold Rock ON **13** F7
Gold Rock ON **16** E3
Goldsand Lake MB **12** D1
Goldsand Lake MB **15** D2
Goldsmith Channel NU **41** A3
Goldsmith Channel NU **42** D-E3
Gold Spur AB **7** B8
Goldstone ON **19** A6
Goldstone ON **20** C5
Goldstream PP BC **2** F4
Golet, lac QC **39** D5
Goletas Channel BC **1** D4
Golspie ON **19** C5
Golspie ON **20** E4
Gondola Point NB **32** D4
Gondola Point NB **33** A1-2
Goobies NL **36** D8
Goobies NL **37** D6
Gooderham ON **21** C3
Goodeve SK **11** D6
Goodfare AB **9** E2
Goodfish Lake AB **6** A6-7
Goodfish Lake AB **8** A8
Goodfish Lake AB **9** F6-7
Goodfish Lake AB **11** A1
Goodfish Lake AB **12** F1
Good Hope BC **8** C7
Good Hope BC **1** D4
Good Hope Bay NT **5** E8
Good Hope Lake BC **3** A3
Good Hope Lake BC **4** F6-7
Good Hope Mountain BC **1** D6
Good Hope Mountain BC **2** A3
Goodlands MB **11** F8
Goodlands MB **13** F1-2
Goodlow BC **3** D1
Goodlow BC **9** D2
Goodrich Loomis CA ON **21** E4
Goodridge AB **6** A7
Goodridge AB **9** F7
Goodridge AB **11** A1-2
Goodridge AB **12** F1-2
Goodsir, Mount BC **6** D4
Goodsir, Mount BC **7** B1
Goodsoil SK **6** A8
Goodsoil SK **9** F8
Goodsoil SK **11** A3
Goodsoil SK **12** F3
Good Spirit Lake SK **11** D6-7
Good Spirit Lake PP SK **11** D6-7
Goodwater SK **11** F6
Goodwin Corner AB **9** F3
Goodwin Mill NB **31** B6-7
Goodwood ON **20** C7
Goodwood ON **21** E1
Goodwood, rivière QC **39** B-C6
Goose Bay NL **39** B-C6
Gooseberry Cove NL **36** E8
Gooseberry Cove NL **37** C7
Gooseberry Cove NL **37** E6
Gooseberry Cove PP NL **36** E-F8
Gooseberry Cove PP NL **37** E-F6
Gooseberry Lake PP AB **6** C7-8
Gooseberry Lake PP AB **11** C2
Goose Cove NL **36** D8
Goose Cove NL **37** D6
Goose Cove NL **38** D8
Goose Cove NL **39** D8
Goose Harbour River NL **34** E5-6
Goose Island BC **1** C3
Goose Island NS **34** F5
Goose Islands PP Reserve MB **13** B2
Goose Lake MB **11** B4
Goose Lake MB **12** F7
Goose Lake MB **13** A1
Goose Lake MB **13** A5
Goose Lake NU **15** A2
Goose Lake ON **13** C6
Goose Lake SK **16** B3
Goose Lake SK **11** A-B7
Goose Lake SK **11** C4
Goose Lake SK **13** A1
Goose Pond NL **36** A4
Goose Pond NL **37** A2
Goose Pond NL **38** A5
Goose River NL **39** B5
Goose River NL **37** E6
Gordon SK **11** D5-6
Gordon Bay ON **18** D7
Gordon Bay PP BC **1** F5

Gordondale AB 9 E2
Gordon Horne Peak BC 6 C-D2
Gordon Lake AB 9 D7
Gordon Lake AB 12 D2
Gordon Lake NT 10 C7
Gordon Lake SK 12 E4
Gordon Pittock Reservoir ON 19 B-C5
Gordon Pittock Reservoir ON 20 E4
Gordon Point PE 35 E3
Gordon River BC 2 E-F3
Gordonsville NB 31 E3
Gordonsville NB 32 A1
Gore NS 32 E8
Gore NS 33 B5-6
Gore NS 34 F1
Gore Bay ON 18 B3
Gore Bay ON 18 B3
Gores Landing ON 21 E3
Gorge de Jacquet River, APP NB 29 E7
Gorge de Jacquet River, APP NB 31 B5-6
Gorgotton, lac QC 28 B7-8
Gorlitz SK 11 D7
Gorman, lac QC 25 D3
Gormanville NS 32 D8
Gormanville NS 33 A5-6
Gormanville NS 34 F1-2
Gormley ON 19 A8
Gormley ON 20 C7
Gormley ON 21 E1
Gorrie ON 19 A5
Gorrie ON 20 C4
Goschen Island BC 1 A2
Gosford, mont QC 27 F6
Goshawk Lake ON 14 D8
Goshen NB 32 C5
Goshen NS 34 E5
Gosnell BC 6 C2
Gosport ON 21 E6
Gossage River NT 5 D6
Gosselin, lac QC 25 B3
Gosselin, lac QC 28 B7
Goudreau ON 17 D4
Goudreau, lac QC 26 B4
Gouffre, rivière du QC 28 E7
Gough Lake AB 6 C6
Gough Lake AB 8 F8
Gouin, réservoir QC 26 E3-4
Goulais Bay ON 17 F4
Goulais Point ON 18 A7
Goulais River ON 17 F4
Goulais River PP ON 17 E-F4
Gould QC 27 E5
Gould Lake CA ON 21 D6
Goulds NL 37 E8
Gouldtown SK 11 E4
Goulet Lake MB 15 E4
Gounamitz River NB 29 E4
Gounamitz River NB 31 B2-3
Goupil, lac QC 39 C1
Gourlay Lake ON 17 C3
Gournet, lac QC 25 A7
Gournet, lac QC 26 F7
Gournet, lac QC 28 C2
Gousvaris, baie QC 23 B7
Gousvaris, baie QC 26 C1
Gouverneur SK 11 E-F3
Govan SK 11 D5
Govenlock SK 6 F8
Govenlock SK 11 F2
Government Landing ON 16 E2
Governor Lake NS 33 A-B7
Governor Lake NS 34 F3
Governors Island PE 35 E5
Gowan River MB 15 E5
Gowanstown ON 19 A5
Gowanstown ON 20 C4
Gowgaia Bay BC 1 C1
Gowganda ON 17 D6-7
Gowganda Lake ON 17 D-E7
Gow Lake SK 12 D5
Gowlland Tod PP BC 2 F4
Goyelle, lac QC 39 E5
Gracefield QC 22 E7
Gracefield QC 24 B1-2
Grady Harbour NL 39 B8
Grafton NB 31 F3
Grafton NB 32 B1
Grafton NS 32 E6
Grafton NS 33 B4
Grafton ON 21 E4
Graham ON 13 F8
Graham ON 16 E4-5
Graham, île BC 1 A1
Graham Corner NB 32 C1
Grahamdale MB 13 D3
Grahamdale MB 14 A3
Graham Head PE 35 D2
Graham Island BC 1 A1
Graham Island NU 42 C4
Graham Lake AB 9 D5
Graham Lake NT 10 C7
Graham Lake ON 21 D8
Graham Lake ON 24 F2
Graham Laurier PP BC 3 D6
Graham Moore, Cape NU 41 A6-7
Graham Moore, Cape NU 42 D6
Graham Moore Bay NU 42 D3
Graham River BC 3 D6-7 E7
Grahams Road PE 35 D3-4
Grainfield NB 31 D6
Grainger AB 7 A5
Grainger River NT 10 E2
Graminia AB 8 C6
Granada QC 23 E2
Granary Lake ON 18 A2
Granby QC 24 D7
Granby QC 27 E3
Granby PP BC 6 E2-3
Granby River BC 6 F2
Grand, lac QC 21 A8
Grand, lac QC 22 F8
Grand, lac QC 24 D2
Grand Anse NS 34 D6
Grand Bank NL 36 E6
Grand Bank NL 37 E4
Grand-Barachois NB 32 B7
Grand Bay NB 32 D4
Grand Bay NB 32 D3-4
Grand Bay NB 33 A1
Grand Bay NB 33 A1
Grand Bay NL 36 D1
Grand Bay East NL 36 D-E1
Grand Beach MB 13 E4
Grand Beach MB 14 C5-6
Grand Beach NL 36 E6
Grand Beach NL 37 E4
Grand Beach PP MB 13 E4
Grand Beach PP MB 14 C5-6
Grand Bend ON 19 B3-4
Grand Bend ON 20 D2-3
Grand Bruit NL 36 D2
Grand Calumet, île du ON 21 A6
Grand Calumet, île du QC 22 F6
Grand Canyon of the Stikine BC 3 C2-3
Grand Castor, lac du QC 25 B5
Grand Castor, lac du QC 26 F5
Grand Castor, lac du QC 28 D1
Grand Centre AB 6 A7-8
Grand Centre AB 9 F7-8
Grand Centre AB 11 A2
Grand Centre AB 12 F2
Grand Coulee SK 11 E5
Grande-Aldouane NB 31 D-E8
Grande-Aldouane NB 32 A6
Grande-Anse NB 29 E8
Grande-Anse NB 30 E1
Grande-Anse NB 31 B7
Grande-Anse QC 25 D7
Grande-Anse QC 27 A3
Grande-Anse QC 28 F3
Grande Cache AB 6 A2
Grande-Cascapédia QC 29 D7-8
Grande-Cascapédia QC 31 A6
Grande-Clairière MB 11 F8
Grande-Clairière MB 13 F1
Grande Décharge, lac de la QC 28 B5
Grande-Digue NB 31 E-F8
Grande-Digue NB 32 B6-7
Grande Digue Point PE 35 C1-2
Grande-Entrée QC 30 F8
Grande Entrée, île de la QC 30 E-F8
Grande Greve NS 34 D6
Grande-Île QC 24 E5
Grande Île, la QC 39 E-F3
Grande Passe, île de la QC 38 B1
Grande Passe, île de la QC 39 E7
Grande Pointe MB 13 F4
Grande Pointe MB 14 E5
Grande Pointe ON 19 D2
Grande Prairie AB 9 F2-3
Grande Rivière NB 29 F4
Grande Rivière NB 31 C3
Grande Rivière QC 30 C2
Grande-Rivière QC 30 C2
Grande Rivière, la QC 40 E4
Grande Rivière, la QC 40 E5
Grande-Rivière, ZEC de la QC 30 C2
Grande rivière de la Baleine QC 40 D4-5
Grandes-Bergeronnes QC 28 C8
Grandes-Bergeronnes QC 29 C1
Grandes-Piles QC 24 A7-8
Grandes-Piles QC 25 E7-8
Grandes-Piles QC 27 B3
Grandes Pointes, lac aux QC 28 A5
Grand Etang NS 34 B6
Grande-Vallée QC 30 A1
Grande-Vallée QC 39 F3
Grande-Vallée QC 40 F7
Grand Falls NB 31 D3
Grand Falls-Windsor NL 36 B6
Grand Falls-Windsor NL 37 B4
Grand-Fonds QC 28 E7
Grand Forks BC 6 F2
Grand Harbour NB 32 F2-3
Grandin AB 8 A8
Grandin, lac NT 10 B4
Grandin, lac NT 41 D1
Grandin, rivière NT 10 B4-5
Grand Island MB 11 B8
Grand Island MB 13 B2
Grand Island ON 20 A8
Grand Island ON 21 D2
Grand Island PP Reserve MB 11 B8
Grand Island PP Reserve MB 13 B2
Grand Jardin NL 36 C1
Grand lac Bostonnais QC 25 B8
Grand lac Bostonnais QC 28 D4
Grand lac Caotibi QC 39 E1
Grand Lac de l'Ours NT 41 C1
Grand Lac des Esclaves NT 10 E6-7
Grand Lac des Esclaves NT 41 E1
Grand lac Germain QC 39 D2
Grand lac Jourdain QC 26 A-B8
Grand lac Squatec QC 29 E2-3
Grand lac Squatec QC 31 B1
Grand lac Victoria QC 22 A5
Grand-Lac-Victoria QC 22 A5
Grand-Lac-Victoria QC 23 F5
Grand Lake NB 31 F6
Grand Lake NB 32 B-C4
Grand Lake NB 32 C1
Grand Lake NL 36 A-B4
Grand Lake NL 37 A-B2
Grand Lake NL 39 B5
Grand Lake NL 40 D7-8
Grand Lake NS 32 E8
Grand Lake NS 33 B6
Grand Lake ON 22 E4
Grand Lake Meadows PPA NB 31 F5-6
Grand Lake Meadows PPA NB 32 B-C4
Grand Lake Road NB 31 E6
Grand Lake Road NB 32 A4
Grand Lake Road NS 34 C8
Grand Le Pierre NL 36 D7
Grand Le Pierre NL 37 D5
Grand Manan NB 32 F2-3
Grand Manan, chenal du NB 32 F2
Grand Manan, île du NB 32 F3
Grand Manan, RNOM NB 32 F3
Grand Manan Channel NB 32 F2
Grand Manan Island NB 32 F2-3
Grand Manan NMBS NB 32 F3
Grand Marais MB 13 E4
Grand Marais MB 14 C5-6
Grand-Mère QC 24 A7
Grand-Mère QC 25 E7
Grand-Mère QC 27 B3
Grandmesnil, lac QC 39 D1
Grand-Métis QC 29 B3-4
Grandmother's Bay SK 12 E5-6
Grand Mountain BC 6 D3
Grand Narrows NS 34 C-D7
Grandois NL 38 B5
Grandois NL 39 D8
Grandora SK 11 C4
Grand Pabos, rivière du QC 30 C1-2
Grand Pacific Glacier BC 4 F2
Grand Portage, rivière du QC 26 D6-7
Grand Portage, rivière du QC 28 A2 B1-2
Grand Pré NS 32 E7
Grand Pré NS 33 B4
Grand-Pré, LHN de NS 32 E7-8
Grand-Pré, LHN de NS 33 B4-5
Grand Pré NHS NS 32 E7-8
Grand Pré NHS NS 33 B4-5
Grand Rapids MB 13 B2-3
Grand Rapids (IR) MB 13 B2-3
Grand Rapids PP MB 13 B2
Grand Rapids Wildland PP AB 9 D-E6
Grand Rapids Wildland PP AB 12 D1
Grand-Remous QC 22 D7-8
Grand-Remous QC 24 A2
Grand-Remous QC 25 E2
Grand River NS 34 D7
Grand River NS 34 D7
Grand River ON 19 A-B6
Grand River ON 19 C7
Grand River ON 20 B5
Grand River ON 20 C-D5
Grand River ON 20 E6
Grand River PE 35 D2
Grand-Saint-Esprit QC 24 B8
Grand-Saint-Esprit QC 27 C3
Grand-Sault NB 31 D3
Grands-Jardins, parc des QC 28 E6
Grand Sudbury ON 17 F7
Grand Sudbury ON 18 A5
Grand Tracadie PE 35 D5
Grand Valley ON 19 A6
Grand Valley ON 20 C5
Grandview AB 8 D6
Grandview MB 11 D8
Grandview MB 13 D1
Grandview PE 35 E-F6
Grandys Brook NL 36 D3
Grandys Brook NL 37 D1
Granet, lac QC 23 F5
Granet Lake NT 5 B7-8
Granger, Mount YT 4 E3-4
Granger Lake SK 12 B5
Granisle BC 3 F5
Granite Bay BC 1 E5
Granite Bay BC 2 B2
Granitehill Lake ON 17 C3
Granite Lake NL 36 C4
Granite Lake NL 37 C2
Granite Point NL 38 C4
Granite Point NL 39 E8
Graniteville QC 24 E8
Graniteville QC 27 F4
Grantham AB 7 D6-7
Grantham BC 2 C2
Grant Lake NT 10 A5
Granton NS 34 E3
Granton ON 19 B4
Granton ON 20 E3
Grant Point NT 10 D7
Grant's Creek PP ON 22 E4
Grantville NS 34 D6
Granum AB 6 E6
Granum AB 7 E5
Granville Centre NS 32 F5
Granville Centre NS 33 C2
Granville Ferry NS 32 F5
Granville Ferry NS 33 C2
Granville Lake MB 12 D8
Granville Lake MB 12 D7-8
Granville Lake MB 15 D2
Granville Lake MB 15 D-E2
Gras, lac QC 39 C2
Gras, lac de NT 10 A8
Gras, lac de NT 41 D2
Grasmere BC 6 F5
Grasmere BC 7 F2-3
Grassberry River SK 11 A6
Grassdale SK 11 F6
Grassie ON 19 C7-8
Grassie ON 20 E6-7
Grassland AB 9 F6
Grassland AB 12 F1
Grasslands NP SK 11 F3-4
Grassmere ON 21 B1-2
Grass River MB 14 C2-3
Grass River MB 15 E3-4
Grass River PP MB 12 F7-8
Grass River PP MB 15 F2
Grassy Island Fort NHS NS 34 E6-7
Grassy Island Lake AB 6 C7-8
Grassy Island Lake AB 11 C2
Grassy Lake AB 6 E7
Grassy Lake AB 7 E7
Grassy Lake AB 11 E1
Grassy Narrows ON 13 E6
Grassy Narrows ON 16 D2
Grassy Plains BC 1 A5
Grassy River-Mond Lake Lowlands & Ferris Lake Uplands, RNP ON 17 D6
Grassy River-Mond Lake Lowlands & Ferris Lake Uplands PNR ON 17 D6
Grates Cove NL 37 C8
Gravelbourg SK 11 E4
Gravel Hill NB 31 A5
Gravel Hill ON 24 E3
Gravelle BC 1 B7
Gravel River, RNP ON 16 E7
Gravel River, RNP ON 17 C1
Gravel River PNR ON 16 E7
Gravel River PNR ON 17 C1
Gravenhurst ON 18 E8
Gravenhurst ON 20 A7
Graves Island PP NS 32 F7
Graves Island PP NS 33 C5
Gray SK 11 E5-6
Gray Creek BC 6 F4
Grayling Fork YT 5 E1-2
Grayling River BC 3 A5
Grayling River BC 10 F1
Grayson SK 11 D-E7
Grayson Lake ON 16 C5
Graysville MB 13 F3
Graysville MB 14 E3-4
Grease River SK 12 A4
Greasy Lake NT 10 C3
Great Barasway NL 36 E8
Great Barasway NL 37 E6
Great Barren Lake NS 33 E2
Great Bay de l'Eau NL 36 E6
Great Bay de l'Eau NL 37 E4
Great Bear Lake NT 41 C1
Great Bear River NT 5 F8
Great Bear River NT 10 A2
Great Bona NL 36 E8
Great Bona NL 37 E6
Great Bras d'Or NS 34 C7
Great Brehat NL 38 A5
Great Brehat NL 39 D8
Great Central Lake BC 1 F5
Great Central Lake BC 2 D2
Great Codroy NL 36 D1
Great Colinet Island NL 37 F7
Great Duck Island ON 18 C2
Greater Napanee ON 21 E6
Greater Sudbury ON 17 F6-7
Greater Sudbury ON 18 A5
Great Falls MB 13 E4-5
Great Falls MB 14 C6-7
Great Glacier BC 3 D2
Great Glacier PP BC 3 D2
Great Gull Lake NL 36 C6
Great Gull Lake NL 37 C4
Great Gull Pond NL 36 A5
Great Gull Pond NL 37 A3
Great Gull Pond NL 38 F4
Great Harbour Deep NL 39 E8
Great La Cloche Island ON 18 B4
Great Paradise NL 36 E7-8
Great Paradise NL 37 E5-6
Great Plain of the Koukdjuak NU 41 C7-8
Great Pubnico Lake NS 33 F2
Great Rattling Brook NL 36 B6
Great Rattling Brook NL 37 B4
Great Slave Lake NT 10 D6-7
Great Slave Lake NT 41 E1
Great Snow Mountain BC 3 D6
Great Village NS 32 D8
Great Village NS 33 A6
Great Village NS 34 E1-2
Greaves Island BC 1 D4
Greece's Point QC 24 D4
Greely ON 21 B8
Greely ON 24 E2
Greely Fiord NU 42 B5
Green, lac QC 22 B6
Green, Mount YT 4 D5
Green Acres SK 11 B5
Greenan SK 11 D3
Greenbank ON 20 B8
Greenbank ON 21 E2
Green Bay MB 14 D6
Green Bay NL 38 E5
Green Bay NS 33 D4
Greenbough Lake ON 22 D3
Greenbush ON 21 C8
Greenbush ON 24 F2
Greenbush SK 11 B6
Greenbush Lake ON 13 D8
Greenbush Lake ON 16 C5
Green Court AB 6 A5
Green Court AB 8 B4
Green Cove BC 1 F6
Green Cove BC 2 E2
Greene Island ON 18 B1
Greene Valley PP AB 9 E3-4
Greenfield NS 32 E7
Greenfield NS 33 A7
Greenfield NS 33 B4-5
Greenfield NS 33 D4
Greenfield NS 34 E2-3
Greenfield ON 24 E4
Greenfield PE 35 E6
Green Gables House PE 35 D4
Green Hill NS 33 A7
Green Hill NS 34 E3
Green Hill PP NS 34 E3
Greenhurst-Thurstonia ON 21 D2-3
Green Inlet PMP BC 1 B3-4
Green Island Brook NL 38 B4
Green Island Cove NL 38 B4
Green Island Cove NL 39 D8
Green Lake BC 1 D8
Green Lake BC 6 D1
Green Lake SK 11 A3
Green Lake SK 11 A3-4
Green Lake SK 12 F3-4
Green Lake PP BC 1 D8
Green Lake PP BC 6 D1
Greenland NS 32 F5
Greenland NS 33 C2
Green Lane ON 24 D4
Greenly, île QC 38 B3
Greenmount PE 34 A1
Greenmount PE 35 B2
Green Oaks NS 33 A6
Green Oaks NS 34 F2
Greenoch Swamp CA ON 20 B3
Greenock ON 20 B3-4
Greenough Point ON 18 E4
Green Park PP PE 32 A8
Green Park PP PE 34 B1
Green Park PP PE 35 C2-3
Green Point NS 33 F3
Green River BC 2 B-C5
Green River NB 29 E3
Green River NB 31 B2
Green River ON 19 A8
Green River ON 20 C7
Green River ON 21 E-F1
Green River YT 4 E7
Green Road NB 31 F3
Green Road NB 32 B1
Greens Brook NS 33 A8
Greens Brook NS 34 E4
Greens Corner ON 19 D6
Greens Corner ON 20 F5
Green's Harbour NL 37 D7
Greenspond NL 37 A7
Greenspond NL 38 F8
Greenstone ON 16 D7
Greenstone ON 16 D7-8
Greenstone ON 17 B1
Greenstone ON 17 A2
Greenstone Mountain PP BC 1 E8
Greenstone Mountain PP BC 2 B8
Greenstone Mountain PP BC 6 E1
Greenstreet SK 6 B8
Greenstreet SK 11 B2
Greensville ON 19 B7
Greensville ON 20 D6
Greenvale PE 35 D4
Green Valley ON 24 E4
Greenville Station NS 32 C8
Greenville Station NS 34 E1
Greenwald MB 14 D6
Greenwater Lake ON 16 F5
Greenwater Lake PP SK 11 C6
Greenwater PP ON 17 C6-7
Greenway MB 14 F2
Greenway ON 19 B3-4
Greenway ON 20 D2-3
Greenwich PE 34 B3
Greenwich PE 35 D6
Greenwich Hill NB 32 D3-4
Greenwich Hill NB 33 A1
Greenwich Lake ON 16 E-F6
Greenwood BC 6 F2
Greenwood NS 32 E6
Greenwood NS 33 B3-4
Greenwood ON 20 C7-8
Greenwood ON 21 E2
Gregg MB 14 D2
Gregoire Lake AB 9 D7
Gregoire Lake AB 12 D2
Gregoire Lake PP AB 9 D7
Gregoire Lake PP AB 12 D2
Grégoires Mill ON 17 B-C6
Grenfell SK 11 E6-7
Grenville QC 24 D4
Grenville Channel BC 1 A-B3
Grenville Lake NT 10 A6
Gresham Lake MB 15 C5
Gretna MB 13 F3
Gretna MB 14 F4
Grew Lake AB 9 D6
Grew Lake AB 12 C-D1
Grey Island SK 12 C4
Greys Islands NL 38 C5
Grey River NL 36 C-D4
Grey River NL 36 D4
Grey River NL 37 C-D2
Grey River NL 37 D2
Greywood NS 32 F5
Greywood NS 33 C2-3
Gribbell Island BC 1 B3
Grief Point BC 1 F6
Griesbach AB 8 C6-7
Griffin SK 11 F6
Griffith ON 21 B5
Griffith Island NU 42 D4
Griffith Island ON 18 E5
Grimes Lake MB 12 B8
Grimes Lake MB 15 B3
Grimsby ON 19 C7-8
Grimsby ON 20 E6-7
Grimsby Beach ON 19 B8
Grimsby Beach ON 20 E7
Grimshaw AB 9 E3
Grimsthorpe ON 18 C3
Grindrod BC 6 E2
Grindstone, lac QC 22 C2-3
Grindstone Point MB 13 D4
Grindstone Point MB 14 A5-6
Grinnell Peninsula NU 42 C4
Griquet NL 38 A5
Griquet NL 39 D8
Grise Fiord (Aujuittuq) NU 42 C5
Griswold MB 11 E8
Griswold MB 13 E1-2
Griswold MB 14 E1
Grizzle Bear Lake NT 10 B7
Grizzly Bear Hills SK 9 E8
Grizzly Bear Hills SK 12 E2-3
Grizzly Ridge Wildland PP AB 9 F5
Groais Island NL 38 B-C5
Groais Island NL 39 E8
Grog Brook NB 29 E5
Grohman Narrows PP BC 6 F3
Grole NL 36 E5
Grole NL 37 E3
Grollier Lake SK 12 A5
Grondines QC 27 B4
Gronick, lac QC 26 C7
Gronick, lac QC 28 A2
Gronlid SK 11 B5-6
Gros Cap ON 17 F3-4
Gros-Cap QC 30 F7
Gros-Mécatina QC 39 E6
Gros-Mécatina, île du QC 39 E6-7
Gros Mécatina, rivière du QC 39 E6
Gros-Mécatina, RNOM de QC 38 C1
Gros-Mécatina, RNOM de QC 39 E6-7
Gros-Mécatina NMBS QC 38 C1
Gros-Mécatina NMBS QC 39 E6-7
Gros Morne NL 38 E2
Gros Morne NL 38 E2-3
Gros Morne NL 39 F6-7
Gros-Morne NL 39 F6-7
Gros-Morne QC 29 A8
Gros-Morne QC 30 A1
Gros-Morne QC 39 F2-3
Gros-Morne, PN du NL 38 E2-3
Gros-Morne, PN du NL 39 F7
Gros Morne NP NL 38 E2-3
Gros Morne NP NL 39 F7
Gros Ours, lac du QC 25 A4-5
Gros Ours, lac du QC 26 F4-5
Gros Pate NL 38 D3
Grosse Île QC 27 A6
Grosse-Île QC 30 E7-8
Grosse Île, la QC 30 E7
Grosse Île, lac de la QC 25 B6
Grosse Île, lac de la QC 26 F6
Grosse Île, lac de la QC 28 D1
Grosse Île and the Irish Memorial NHS QC 27 A6-7
Grosse-Île-et-le-Mémorial-des-Irlandais, LHN de la QC 27 A6-7
Grosse-Île-Nord QC 30 E7-8
Grosse Isle MB 13 E3-4
Grosse Isle MB 14 D5
Grosses Coques NS 33 D1
Grosses-Roches QC 29 B5
Groswater Bay NL 39 B7
Groswater Bay NL 40 D8
Grouard AB 9 E4
Grouard Lake NT 10 A5
Grouard Mission AB 9 E4
Groulx, monts QC 40 E-F6
Groundbirch BC 3 E8
Groundbirch BC 9 E1
Groundhog River ON 17 B6
Groundhog River ON 17 D5-6
Groundhog River PP ON 17 C5
Grouse Island SK 9 A8
Grouse Island SK 12 A3
Grovedale AB 9 F2
Groves Point PP NS 34 C7
Gruenthal SK 11 C4
Grund MB 14 E2
Grundy Lake PP ON 18 B6
Grunthal MB 13 F4
Grunthal MB 14 F5
Guay, lac QC 22 B2
Gué, rivière du QC 40 D5
Guéguen, lac QC 23 E5
Guelph ON 19 B6-7
Guelph ON 20 D5-6
Guelph Lake CA ON 19 A6
Guelph Lake CA ON 20 D5
Guénette QC 24 A3
Guénette QC 25 F3
Guénette, lac QC 25 B5
Guérin QC 22 A1
Guérin QC 23 F2
Guernesé, lac QC 38 A2
Guernsey SK 11 C5
Guernsey Cove PE 35 F7
Guernsey Island NL 36 A2
Guernsey Island NL 38 F1
Guichon Creek BC 1 E8
Guichon Creek BC 2 B8
Guichon Creek BC 6 E1
Guilds ON 19 E3
Guillaume-Delisle, lac QC 40 D4
Guillemot, lac QC 39 B1
Guines Lake NL 39 D5
Guiquac River NB 31 D4
Gulch NL 37 F7
Gulch Cove NL 36 E4
Gulch Cove NL 37 E2
Gulf of Georgia Cannery, LHN BC 2 E4-5
Gulf of Georgia Cannery NHS BC 2 E4-5
Gulf Shore NS 32 C8
Gulf Shore NS 34 D2
Gulf Shore PP NS 32 C8
Gulf Shore PP NS 34 D1-2
Gulf Shore PP NS 35 F3
Gull River ON 16 D5
Gull Bay ON 16 D6
Gull Harbour MB 13 D4
Gull Harbour MB 14 B6
Gull Island NL 37 C-D7
Gull Island NL 40 E7
Gull Island Point NL 37 F7
Gulliver Lake ON 16 E4
Gullivers Cove NS 32 F4
Gullivers Cove NS 33 C1-2
Gull Lake AB 6 C5
Gull Lake AB 6 C5
Gull Lake AB 8 E6
Gull Lake AB 8 E6
Gull Lake MB 15 D-E5
Gull Lake NL 39 C5
Gull Lake ON 13 D7
Gull Lake ON 21 C2
Gull Lake SK 11 E3
Gull Pond NL 36 B8
Gull Pond NL 37 B6
Gull Pond NL 38 E4
Gull River ON 21 C2
Gull River PP ON 16 D5-6 E5
Gullrock Lake ON 13 D6
Gullrock Lake ON 16 C2
Gullwing Lake ON 13 E7
Gundahoo River BC 3 B5
Gundahoo River BC 4 F8
Gunisao Lake MB 13 B4
Gunisao River MB 13 A3-4 B4
Gunn AB 6 A5
Gunn AB 8 C5
Gunners Cove NL 38 A5
Gunning Cove NS 33 F3
Gunnworth SK 11 D3
Gunter ON 21 C5
Gunton MB 13 E3-4
Gunton MB 14 D5
Gurneyville AB 6 A7
Gurneyville AB 11 A2
Guthrie ON 18 F8
Guthrie ON 20 A7
Guthrie ON 21 D1
Guthrie Lake MB 12 E7-8
Guthrie Lake MB 15 E2
Guy AB 9 E3
Guyenne QC 23 C3
Guynemer MB 14 A2-3
Guysborough NS 34 E5
Guysborough NS 34 E5-6
Gwaii Haanas, RPN et site du patrimoine haïda BC 1 C1-2
Gwaii Haanas (projetée), réserve d'aire marine nationale BC 1 C2
Gwaii Haanas National Marine Reserve (proposed) BC 1 B-C2
Gwaii Haanas NPR and Haida Heritage Site BC 1 B1-2 C1-2
Gwich'in TP NT 5 C5
Gwillim, lac QC 26 A4-5
Gwillim Lake PP BC 3 F8
Gwillim Lake PP BC 9 E1
Gwynne AB 6 B6
Gwynne AB 8 D7
Gypsum Point NT 41 D-E1
Gypsumville MB 13 C3
Gypsumville MB 14 A3
Gyrfalcon Islands NU 40 C6

H

Habay AB 9 B3
Hache, lac de la QC 25 E3
Hache, lac la BC 1 C8
Hache, lac la BC 1 C8
Hache, lac la BC 6 C1
Hache, lac la BC 6 C1
Hackett AB 8 F8
Hackett, lac QC 25 D8
Hackett, lac QC 27 A3
Hacketts Cove NS 32 F8
Hacketts Cove NS 33 C5
Hadashville MB 13 F4
Hadashville MB 14 E6-7
Haddock AB 8 B3
Hadley Bay NU 41 A3
Hadley Bay NU 42 D-E2
Hafford SK 11 B4
Hagar ON 17 F7
Hagar ON 18 A6
Hagen SK 11 B5
Hagensborg BC 1 C5
Hagersville ON 19 C7
Hagersville ON 20 E6
Hague SK 11 C4
Hagwilget BC 3 F4
Ha! Ha!, baie des QC 28 C6
Ha! Ha!, lac QC 28 D6
Haida BC 1 A1
Haig BC 1 F8
Haig BC 2 D7
Haig, Mount BC 6 F5
Haig, Mount BC 7 F3
Haig Lake AB 9 D4
Haight AB 8 C8
Haig-Thomas Island NU 42 C4
Haileybury ON 17 E7-8
Haileybury ON 22 A1
Haileybury ON 23 F1
Haines Junction YT 4 E2-3
Haines Lake ON 18 D7
Hainsfield NS 32 F4
Hainsfield NS 33 C-D2
Hainsville ON 21 C8
Hainsville ON 24 F2-3
Hairy Hill AB 6 A6
Hairy Hill AB 8 C8
Hairy Hill AB 11 A1
Hakai Passage BC 1 C3-4
Hakai PRA BC 1 C3-4 D3-4
Halbrite SK 11 F6
Halbstadt MB 14 F5
Halcomb NB 31 D6
Halcrow MB 11 A8
Halcrow MB 13 A2
Haldimand QC 30 B3
Haldimand CA ON 19 C-D7
Haldimand CA ON 20 F6
Haldimand County ON 19 C7
Haldimand County ON 20 E6
Hale Lake MB 15 D4
Haley Lake NMBS NS 33 E3
Haley Station ON 21 A6
Haley Station ON 22 F6
Halfmoon Bay BC 1 F6
Halfmoon Bay BC 2 D4
Halfway Cove NS 34 E6
Halfway Lake AB 8 B6-7
Halfway Lake MB 15 F3
Halfway Lake PP ON 17 E6
Halfway Point NL 36 B2-3
Halfway Pond NL 37 B-C7
Halfway River BC 3 D-E7
Halfway River MB 15 F3
Halfway River NS 32 D7
Halfway River NS 33 A4-5

Haliburton ON 21 B3
Haliburton PE 35 B1
Haliburton Lake ON 21 B3
Halifax NS 32 F8
Halifax NS 33 B7
Halifax NS 33 C6
Halifax NS 34 F2-3
Halifax Harbour NS 33 C6
Halkett Bay PP BC 2 D4
Halkirk AB 6 C6
Halkirk AB 8 F8
Halkirk AB 11 C1
Hall, rivière QC 29 D8
Hall, rivière QC 30 D1
Hall, rivière QC 31 A7
Hallam Peak BC 6 C2
Hall Beach (Sanirajak) NU 41 B6
Hall Beach (Sanirajak) NU 42 F6
Hallboro MB 13 E2
Hallboro MB 14 D2
Hallebourg ON 17 B4-5
Hall Glen ON 21 D3
Hall Lake BC 3 A2
Hall Lake BC 4 F5
Hall Lake NU 41 B6
Hall Lake NU 42 F5
Hall Peninsula NU 40 A6
Halls Bay NL 38 E-F5
Halls Harbour NS 32 D6 E6-7
Halls Harbour NS 33 B4
Halls Hill NB 35 F2
Halls Lake ON 21 B2
Hallville ON 21 B8
Hallville ON 24 E2
Halton Hills ON 19 A7
Halton Hills ON 20 D6
Halvorgate SK 11 E4
Hamber PP BC 6 C3
Hamber PP BC 8 E1
Hamer Bay ON 18 D7
Hamill Creek BC 6 E4
Hamilton NB 19 B7
Hamilton ON 19 B-C7
Hamilton ON 20 D-E6
Hamilton ON 20 E6
Hamilton PE 32 A8
Hamilton PE 34 B1
Hamilton PE 35 D3
Hamilton, lac QC 22 C3
Hamilton Inlet NL 39 B6-7
Hamilton Inlet NL 40 D8
Hamilton Sound NL 38 E7
Hamiota MB 11 E8
Hamiota MB 13 E1-2
Hamlin AB 6 A6
Hamlin AB 8 B8
Hamlin AB 11 A1
Hammond ON 24 D3
Hammonds Plains NS 32 F8
Hammonds Plains NS 33 C5
Hammondvale NB 32 D5
Hammondvale NB 33 A2
Hammone, lac QC 38 A3
Hammone, lac QC 39 D7
Ham-Nord QC 27 D5
Hampden NL 38 E3
Hampden NL 39 F8
Hampstead NB 32 D4
Hampstead NB 33 A1
Hampton NB 32 D4
Hampton NB 33 A1-2
Hampton NS 32 E5
Hampton NS 33 B2-3
Hampton ON 20 C8
Hampton ON 21 E2
Hampton PE 32 B8
Hampton PE 34 C2
Hampton PE 35 E4
Hampton Lake ON 16 A2
Ham-Sud QC 27 D5
Hamton SK 11 D7
Hamtown Corner NB 31 F4-5
Hamtown Corner NB 32 B3
Hanbury River NT 41 D3
Hanceville BC 1 C7
Hanctin, lac QC 39 C1
Hand Branch River NB 29 F5
Hand Branch River NB 31 C-D4
Handel SK 11 C3
Handsworth SK 11 E6-7
Haneytown NB 32 C3
Hanford Brook NB 32 D5
Hanford Brook NB 33 A2
Hanley SK 11 D4
Hanmer ON 17 F7
Hanna AB 6 C6-7 D6-7
Hanna AB 7 A6
Hanna AB 11 C1
Hannah Bay ON 40 F3
Hannah Lake SK 12 B6
Hanover ON 20 B4
Hansen Harbour NT 5 A4-5
Hansford NS 32 C8
Hansford NS 34 D1
Hanson Lake SK 12 F6
Hant's Harbour NL 37 C7
Hantsport NS 32 E7
Hantsport NS 33 B4-5
Hantzsch River NU 41 B8
Hantzsch River NU 42 F7
Hanwell NB 32 C2-3
Happy Adventure NL 37 B6-7
Happy Isle Lake ON 22 F3
Happy Valley TP NT 5 C5
Happy Valley-Goose Bay NL 39 C5
Happy Valley-Goose Bay NL 40 E7-8
Hara Lake SK 12 A-B7
Hara Lake SK 15 A1
Harbour Breton NL 36 E6
Harbour Breton NL 37 E4
Harbour Buffett NL 36 D-E8
Harbour Buffett NL 37 D-E6
Harbour Deep NL 38 D4
Harbour Dudgeon Lakes PP BC 6 D2
Harbour Grace NL 37 D7
Harbour Le Cou NL 36 D2
Harbour Main NL 37 E7-8
Harbour Mille NL 36 D7
Harbour Mille NL 37 D5
Harbour Round NL 38 E5
Harbourview NS 34 C-D5
Harbourville NS 32 E6
Harbourville NS 33 B3-4
Harcourt NB 31 E7
Harcourt NB 32 A5
Harcourt NL 36 C8
Harcourt NL 37 C6
Harcourt ON 21 B3
Harcus MB 14 C3
Harding MB 11 E8
Harding MB 13 E1-2
Harding Lake MB 15 D-E3
Harding Lake NT 10 D7
Hardings Point NB 32 D3-4
Hardings Point NB 33 A1
Hardisty AB 6 B7
Hardisty AB 11 B1
Hardisty Lake NT 10 A5
Hardwicke NB 31 D7-8
Hardwicke Island BC 1 E5
Hardwicke Island BC 2 B1
Hardwood Lake ON 21 B5
Hardwood Lands NS 32 E8
Hardwood Lands NS 33 B6
Hardwood Lands NS 34 F2
Hardwood Ridge NB 31 F6
Hardwood Ridge NB 32 B4
Hardy NB 35 F2
Hardy SK 11 F5
Hardy Channel PE 35 C2-3
Hardy Inlet BC 1 C-D4
Hardy Lake NT 10 A8
Hardy Lake PP ON 18 E7-8
Hare Bay NL 36 B8
Hare Bay NL 36 D5
Hare Bay NL 37 B6
Hare Bay NL 37 D3
Hare Bay NL 38 B5
Hare Bay NL 38 E7
Hare Bay NL 39 D8
Hare Bay Islands Ecological Reserve NL 38 B5
Hare Fiord NU 42 B4
Hare Hill NL 36 B2-3
Hare Indian River NT 5 E7-8
Hares Islands NL 39 A6
Hargrave MB 11 E8
Hargrave MB 13 E1
Hargrave Lake MB 11 A8
Hargrave Lake MB 12 F8
Hargrave Lake MB 13 A2
Hargrave Lake MB 15 F2
Hargreen AB 8 C2
Harley ON 19 C6
Harley ON 20 E5
Harlowe ON 21 C5
Harmattan AB 6 C5
Harmattan AB 7 A3
Harmon Lake ON 13 E8
Harmon Lake ON 16 D5
Harmony NS 33 A6-7
Harmony NS 34 E2
Harmony PE 35 C2
Harmony Islands PMP BC 1 E6
Harmony Islands PMP BC 2 C3-4
Harmony Mills NS 33 D3
Haro Strait BC 2 F4
Harpellville NS 34 F5
Harper ON 21 C7
Harper ON 24 F1
Harper, Mount YT 5 F2
Harper Creek AB 9 C5
Harper Lake SK 9 A7
Harper Lake SK 12 A3
Harperville MB 14 C4
Harp Lake NL 39 A5
Harptree SK 11 F5
Harpurhey ON 19 A4
Harpurhey ON 20 D3
Harricana, rivière QC 23 A3 B4
Harricana, rivière QC 23 D-E4
Harricana, rivière QC 40 F4
Harricott NL 37 E7
Harrietsfield NS 32 F8
Harrietsfield NS 33 C6
Harrietsville ON 19 C5
Harrietsville ON 20 E4
Harrigan Cove NS 33 B8
Harrigan Cove NS 34 F4
Harrington ON 19 B5
Harrington ON 20 E4
Harrington PE 35 D4-5
Harrington QC 24 C4
Harrington, îles QC 39 E6
Harrington Harbour QC 39 E6
Harriott Lake SK 12 D-E6
Harriott Lake SK 15 D1
Harriott River SK 12 D6
Harriott River SK 15 D1
Harris SK 11 C3-4
Harris, lac QC 22 A6
Harris, lac QC 23 F6
Harris, lac QC 25 B1
Harris Bay ON 21 A-B4
Harrisburg ON 19 B6
Harrisburg ON 20 E5
Harris Hill ON 14 F8
Harris Lake ON 18 C6
Harrison, Cape NL 39 A7
Harrison, Cape NL 40 D8
Harrison Hot Springs BC 1 F7-8
Harrison Hot Springs BC 2 D6
Harrison Islands NU 41 B5
Harrison Islands NU 42 F4
Harrison Lake BC 1 F7-8
Harrison Lake BC 2 C-D6
Harrison Mills BC 1 F7-8
Harrison Mills BC 2 D6
Harrison River BC 2 D6
Harrisons Corner ON 24 E3
Harrison Settlement NS 32 D7
Harrison Settlement NS 33 A4
Harriston ON 19 A5
Harriston ON 20 C4
Harrogate BC 6 D4
Harrogate BC 7 B1
Harrop BC 6 F3
Harrop Lake MB 13 C4-5
Harrow ON 19 E1
Harrowby MB 11 D7-8
Harrowby MB 13 D1
Harrowby Bay NT 5 A6-7
Harrowsmith ON 21 D6
Harry Lake ON 21 A3
Harry Lake ON 22 F3
Harry Lake Aspen PP BC 1 D-E8
Harry Lake Aspen PP BC 2 A7
Harry's Harbour NL 38 E5
Harry's Harbour NL 39 F8
Hart SK 11 F5
Hart, Mount YT 4 A1
Harte MB 14 D2
Hartell AB 7 C4
Hartington ON 21 D6
Hart Jaune, rivière QC 39 D1
Hartland NB 31 F3
Hartland NB 32 B1
Hartlen Point NS 33 C6
Hartley ON 20 A8
Hartley ON 21 D2
Hartley Bay BC 1 B3
Hartleyville AB 7 F4
Hartney MB 11 F8
Hartney MB 13 F1-2
Hart Ranges BC 3 E-F7
Hart River YT 5 F3
Hartshorn AB 6 B7
Hartsmere ON 21 B4-5
Hartsville PE 35 D-E4
Harty ON 17 B5
Harvey NB 32 C2
Harvey NB 32 C6
Harvey, anse QC 30 A6
Harvey Lake NB 32 C2
Harvie Heights AB 6 D4-5
Harvie Heights AB 7 B2
Harwill MB 13 D3
Harwill MB 14 B4
Harwood ON 21 E3
Harwood Island BC 2 C2-3
Harwood Islands ON 18 A7
Hasbala Lake MB 12 A7
Hasbala Lake MB 15 A1-2
Haskett MB 13 F3
Haskett MB 14 F4
Haslam Lake BC 2 C3
Hassel Sound NU 42 B-C3 C4
Hassett NS 33 D1-2
Hasté, lac QC 39 C1
Hastings NS 32 C7
Hastings NS 34 D1
Hastings ON 21 D4
Hastings Arm BC 3 E3
Hatchet Cove NL 36 C8
Hatchet Cove NL 37 C6
Hatchet Lake SK 12 B6
Hatchet Lake SK 12 B-C6
Hatchet Lake SK 15 B1
Hat Creek BC 2 A7
Hatfield SK 11 D5
Hatfield Point NB 32 C4
Hatfield Point NB 33 A1-2
Ha'thayim PMP BC 2 B-C2
Hatley QC 27 F4
Hatton SK 6 E8
Hatton SK 11 E2
Hattonford AB 8 C3-4
Haultain AB 8 D7
Haultain Lake SK 12 D4
Haultain River SK 12 D-E4
Haut-Bouctouche NB 31 E8
Haut-Bouctouche NB 32 A6
Haute-Aboujagane NB 35 E1
Hautes-Gorges-de-la-Rivière-Malbaie, parc des QC 28 D7
Hautes-terres-du-Cap-Breton, PN des NS 34 A6-7 B6-7
Hauteurs-de-Queenston, LHN des ON 20 E8
Haut-Pokemouche NB 30 E2
Haut-Pokemouche NB 31 B7-8
Haut-Shippagan NB 31 B8
Havelock NB 31 F7
Havelock NB 32 B-C5
Havelock NS 33 D1-2
Havelock ON 21 D4
Havelock QC 24 E5
Havelock QC 27 F1
Havelock Lake ON 21 B3
Havre, île du QC 39 F4
Havre-Aubert QC 30 F7
Havre Aubert, île du QC 30 F7
Havre-aux-Maisons QC 30 F7
Havre aux Maisons, île du QC 30 F7
Havre Boucher NS 34 D5
Havre-Saint-Pierre QC 39 E3-4
Havre-Saint-Pierre QC 40 F7
Hawarden SK 11 D4
Hawke Harbour NL 39 C8
Hawke Hill Ecological Reserve NL 37 E7-8
Hawke Island NL 39 C8
Hawke River NL 39 C7-8
Hawke's Bay NL 38 C3
Hawke's Bay NL 39 E7-8
Hawkesbury ON 24 D4
Hawkesbury Island BC 1 A-B3
Hawkestone ON 18 F8
Hawkestone ON 20 A7
Hawkestone ON 21 D1
Hawkesville ON 19 A6
Hawkesville ON 20 D5
Hawkins Corner ON 18 F8
Hawkins Corner ON 20 A7
Hawkins Corner ON 21 C1
Hawkins Lake SK 12 A5
Hawk Junction ON 17 D4
Hawkrock River SK 12 B5
Hawks, Cape NU 42 B5
Hawks Creek BC 1 C7
Hawkshaw NB 32 C2
Hawthorne Cottage NHS NL 37 D-E7
Hawtrey ON 19 C6
Hawtrey ON 20 E5
Hay Bay ON 21 E5-6
Hay Camp AB 9 A6
Hay Camp AB 10 F8
Hay Camp AB 12 A2
Hay Cove NS 34 D7
Hay Island ON 18 E5
Hay Lake AB 9 B3
Hay Lake ON 21 B3
Hay Lakes AB 6 B6
Hay Lakes AB 8 D7
Hay River AB 9 A4
Hay River AB 10 F5-6
Hay River AB 41 E1
Hay River BC 3 B8
Hay River BC 9 B2
Hay River NT 10 E6
Hay River NT 41 E1
Hay River TP NT 10 E6
Hay River TP NT 41 E1
Haydon ON 20 B8
Haydon ON 21 E2
Hayes Bay ON 21 B6-7
Hayes Bay ON 24 D1
Hayes Creek BC 2 D8
Hayes Peak YT 4 E4-5
Hayes River MB 13 A4
Hayes River MB 15 E6
Hayes River MB 15 F4
Hayes River MB 40 C-D1
Hayes River NU 41 B-C5
Hayesville NB 31 E5
Hayesville NB 32 A3
Hayfield MB 14 E1
Haynes AB 8 F6
Haynes Point PP BC 6 F2
Hays AB 6 E7
Hays AB 7 D7
Hays AB 11 E1
Haysville ON 19 B5-6
Haysville ON 20 D4-5
Hayter AB 6 C8
Hayter AB 11 C2
Haywood MB 13 F3
Haywood MB 14 E4
Haywood Lake NT 10 B8
Hay-Zama Lakes Wildland PP AB 9 B2-3
Hazel MB 13 E4
Hazel MB 14 E6
Hazel Dell SK 11 C6
Hazel Hill NS 34 E6
Hazelbrook PE 35 E5
Hazeldean NB 31 D3
Hazeldean ON 24 E2
Hazelglen MB 13 E4
Hazelglen MB 14 D6
Hazell AB 7 E3
Hazelridge MB 13 E4
Hazelridge MB 14 D5-6
Hazelton BC 3 F4
Hazelton Mountains BC 3 E-F4
Hazen, Lake NU 42 A5
Hazenmore SK 11 F4
Hazen Strait NT 42 C2-3
Hazen Strait NU 42 C2-3
Hazlet SK 11 E3
Headingley MB 14 E5
Head Lake ON 20 A8
Head Lake ON 20 A8
Head Lake ON 21 C2
Head Lake ON 21 C2
Head of Amherst NS 34 D1
Head of Bay d'Espoir NL 36 D6
Head of Bay d'Espoir NL 37 D4
Head of Chezzetcook NS 33 C6-7
Head of Hillsborough PE 35 D6
Head of Jeddore NS 33 C7
Head of Loch Lomond NS 34 D7
Head of Millstream NB 32 C5
Head of St. Margarets Bay NS 32 F7-8
Head of St. Margarets Bay NS 33 C5
Headquarters CA ON 20 B4
Head River ON 20 A7-8
Head River ON 21 C1-2
Head-Smashed-In AB 6 F5-6
Head-Smashed-In AB 7 E4
Head-Smashed-In Buffalo Jump PHS AB 6 E5-6 F5-6
Head-Smashed-In Buffalo Jump PHS AB 7 E4
Healey Lake ON 18 D7
Heaman MB 12 E7
Heaman MB 15 E1-2
Hearne SK 11 E5
Hearne Lake NT 10 D7
Hearst ON 17 B4
Hearst ON 40 F2-3
Heart Lake AB 9 F7
Heart Lake AB 12 F1-2
Heart River AB 9 E4
Heart's Content NL 37 D7
Hearts Content Cable Station PHS NL 37 D7
Heart's Delight NL 37 D7
Heart's Delight-Islington NL 37 D7
Heart's Desire NL 37 D7
Hearts Hill SK 6 C8
Hearts Hill SK 11 C2
Heaslip MB 14 E1
Heaslip ON 17 D7-8
Heatburg AB 8 F7
Heath AB 6 B7
Heath AB 11 B2
Heath, pointe QC 30 B7
Heath, pointe QC 40 F8
Heathcote ON 18 F6
Heathcote ON 20 A5
Heather Beach PP NS 32 C8
Heather Beach PP NS 34 D1
Heather Beach PP NS 35 F3
Heatherbrae AB 8 D7
Heatherdale PE 35 F6
Heather-Dina Lakes PP BC 3 E-F6
Heatherdown AB 8 C5-6
Heatherton NL 36 C2
Heatherton NS 34 E5
Heath Steele NB 29 F7
Heath Steele NB 31 C5-6
Hebbs Cross NS 33 D4
Hebbville NS 33 D4
Hébécourt, lac QC 23 D2
Heber Down CA ON 20 C8
Heber Down CA ON 21 E2
Hébert NB 31 F8
Hébert NB 32 B6
Hébert, lac QC 23 E1-2
Hébert, lac QC 26 C3
Hebert, River NS 32 C-D7
Hébertville QC 28 C5
Hébertville-Station QC 28 C4-5
Hebron NL 40 C7
Hebron NS 33 E1
Hecate BC 1 E4
Hecate, détroit d' BC 1 B-C2 C3
Hecate Island BC 1 D4
Hecate Strait BC 1 A-B2
Heckman Pass BC 1 C5
Heckston ON 21 C8
Heckston ON 24 E2
Hecla MB 13 D4
Hecla MB 14 B5-6
Hecla, Cape NU 42 A5
Hecla and Griper Bay NT 42 C2
Hecla/Grindstone PP MB 13 D4
Hecla/Grindstone PP MB 14 B5-6
Hecla Island MB 13 D4
Hecla Island MB 14 B5-6
Hectanooga NS 33 E1-2
Heddery Lake SK 12 D4
Hedley BC 6 F1
Heffley Creek BC 2 A8
Heffley Creek BC 6 D1
Heidelberg ON 19 B6
Heidelberg ON 20 D5
Height of the Rockies PP BC 6 E4-5
Height of the Rockies PP BC 7 C-D2
Heinsburg AB 6 A7
Heinsburg AB 11 A2
Heisler AB 6 B-C6
Heisler AB 8 E8
Heisler AB 11 B1
Hekkla ON 18 D8
Hekkla ON 21 B1
Helena Island NU 42 C3
Helen Bay ON 18 B2
Helene Lake SK 11 B3
Helen Lake ON 16 E6
Helen Lake ON 17 C1
Helliwell PP BC 2 D3
Helmer Lake SK 9 A8
Helmer Lake SK 12 A4
Helston MB 14 D2
Hemaruka AB 7 A7
Hemer PP BC 2 E4
Hemford NS 32 F6
Hemford NS 33 C3-4
Heming Lake MB 12 F7-8
Heming Lake MB 15 F1-2
Hemlo ON 16 E-F8
Hemlo ON 17 C2
Hemmingford QC 24 E6
Hemmingford QC 27 F1
Hemphill, Cape NT 42 C2
Henday AB 8 F6
Henderson ON 21 C6
Henderson Corner YT 4 A2
Henderson Lake BC 1 F5-6
Henderson Lake BC 2 E2
Hendon SK 11 C6
Hendrickson Island NT 5 B5
Hendriksen Strait NU 42 C4
Hendrix Lake BC 1 C8
Hendrix Lake BC 6 C1
Heney, lac QC 22 E7
Heney, lac QC 24 C2
Hen Island ON 19 F1
Henley Harbour NL 39 D8
Hennepin Island ON 18 B1
Henri, rivière QC 27 C5
Henribourg SK 11 B5
Henrietta Island NL 39 B6-7
Henrietta Maria, Cape ON 40 D3
Henry House, LHN AB 8 D1
Henry House NHS AB 8 D1
Henry Island NS 34 D5
Henry Kater, Cape NU 41 A-B8
Henry Kater, Cape NU 42 E7
Henryville QC 24 E7
Henryville QC 27 F2
Hensall ON 19 B4
Hensall ON 20 D3
Henvey Inlet ON 18 B-C6
Henvey Inlet ON 18 B-C6
Hepburn SK 11 C4
Hepburn Lake SK 12 E5
Hepworth ON 18 F5
Hepworth ON 20 A4
Herald PP BC 6 D2
Herbert SK 11 E4
Herbert Inlet BC 1 F5
Herbert Inlet BC 2 D1
Herbert Lake SK 12 A5
Herbert Point BC 1 D3-4
Herb Lake MB 12 F8
Herb Lake MB 15 F2
Herb Lake Landing MB 12 F8
Herb Lake Landing MB 15 F2
Herblet Lake MB 12 F8
Herblet Lake MB 15 F2
Herchmer MB 15 C5-6
Herdman QC 24 E5
Hereford, mont QC 27 F5
Heriot Bay BC 1 E5
Heriot Bay BC 2 C2
Hermanville PE 34 B4
Hermitage PE 35 E6
Hermitage Bay NL 36 D5-6
Hermitage Bay NL 37 D3-4
Hermitage-Sandyville N 36 E5-6
Hermitage-Sandyville NL 37 E3-4
Hermon ON 21 B4
Hernando Island BC 2 C2
Heron, île NB 31 A5
Heron Bay ON 16 F8
Heron Bay ON 17 C2
Heron Island NB 29 D7
Heron Island NB 31 A5
Hérouxville QC 24 A8
Hérouxville QC 25 E8
Hérouxville QC 27 B3
Herrick Creek BC 1 A8
Herrick Creek BC 6 A1
Herrick Creek BC 9 F1
Herring Cove NS 32 F8
Herring Cove NS 33 C6
Herring Cove PP NB 32 E2-3
Herriot MB 12 D7
Herriot MB 15 D1
Herriot Creek MB 15 B5
Herronton AB 7 C5
Herschel SK 11 D3
Herschel Island YT 5 A3
Herschel Island TP YT 5 A3
Hertel, lac QC 26 A7
Hertzberg Island ON 18 D6
Hervey-Jonction QC 24 A8
Hervey-Jonction QC 25 E8
Hervey-Jonction QC 27 A-B3
Hesketh AB 7 A5
Hesquiat BC 1 F4-5
Hesquiat Lake PP BC 1 F5
Hesquiat Peninsula PP BC 1 F4
Hess Mountains YT 4 B5
Hesson ON 19 A5
Hesson ON 20 C-D4
Hess River YT 4 B4-5
Heward SK 11 F6
Heyden ON 17 F4
Heydon Lake BC 2 B1
Heywood Island ON 18 B4
Hiawatha ON 21 E3
Hibbard QC 25 B5
Hibbard QC 28 D1
Hibben Island BC 1 B1
Hibbs Cove NL 37 D7-8
Hibernia NS 33 D3
Hibou CA ON 18 F5
Hibou CA ON 20 A4
Hickey, lac QC 22 E6
Hickman's Harbour NL 37 C7
Hickory Corner ON 19 C4
Hickory Corner ON 20 E3
Hicks-Oke Bog, RNP ON 17 C6
Hicks-Oke Bog PNR ON 17 C6
Hickson ON 19 B5
Hickson ON 20 E4
Hickson Lake SK 12 D5
Hidden Bay SK 12 B6
Hidden Lake TP NT 10 C7
Higginsville NS 33 B7
Higginsville NS 34 F3
High Bank PE 34 D3
High Bank PE 35 F6
Highbank Lake ON 16 A8
High Beach NL 36 F6
High Beach NL 37 F4
High Bluff MB 13 E3
High Bluff MB 14 D4
High Falls ON 17 F6
High Falls ON 18 A4
Highgate ON 19 D3
Highgate ON 20 F2
Highgate SK 11 B3
High Hill Lake MB 15 E4-5
High Hill River MB 15 E5
High Lakes Basin PP BC 6 D1
Highland Creek ON 21 B5
Highland Grove ON 21 B3-4
Highland Lake NT 10 C3
Highland Valley BC 2 B7
Highlands BC 2 F4
Highlands NL 36 C1
High Level AB 9 B3
High Prairie AB 9 E4
Highridge AB 8 B5-6
High River AB 6 E5
High River AB 7 C4
Highrock MB 12 E8
Highrock MB 15 E2
Highrock Lake MB 12 E8
Highrock Lake MB 15 E2
Highrock Lake SK 12 D5
Highvale AB 8 C5
Highwater QC 24 E8
Highwater QC 27 F3-4
Highway AB 8 B4
Highwood House AB 7 D3
Highwood River AB 6 E5
Highwood River AB 7 C-D3
Hilbre MB 13 D3
Hilbre MB 14 A3
Hilda AB 6 E8
Hilda AB 11 E2
Hilden NS 33 A6
Hilden NS 34 E2
Hillandale NB 31 E3
Hillandale NB 32 A1
Hillcrest Mines AB 6 F5
Hillcrest Mines AB 7 E3
Hillgrade NL 38 E6
Hillgrove NS 32 F4
Hillgrove NS 33 C2
Hilliard AB 6 A6
Hilliard AB 8 C7-8
Hilliard AB 11 A1
Hilliard's Bay PP AB 9 E4
Hilliardton ON 17 D8
Hilliardton ON 23 F1
Hillier ON 21 E5
Hilliers BC 1 F6
Hilliers BC 2 D3
Hillman Marsh CA ON 19 E2
Hillmond SK 6 B8
Hillmond SK 11 B2
Hillsborough NB 32 C6
Hillsborough Bay PE 34 C2
Hillsborough Bay PE 35 E5
Hillsborough River PE 34 C2-3
Hillsborough River PE 35 E5
Hillsburgh ON 19 A7
Hillsburgh ON 20 C6
Hillsburn NS 32 F5
Hillsdale NB 32 D5
Hillsdale NB 33 A2
Hillsdale ON 18 F7
Hillsdale ON 20 A6
Hillside AB 8 D6
Hillside NB 32 C6
Hillside NS 34 C8
Hillside ON 21 B2
Hillside Beach MB 14 C5-6
Hillsport ON 16 E8
Hillsport ON 17 B3
Hillspring AB 6 F6
Hillspring AB 7 F4
Hillsvale NS 32 E8
Hillsvale NS 33 B5
Hillsvale NS 34 F1
Hilltop MB 14 C1
Hilltop Lake NT 10 B8
Hillview NL 36 C8
Hillview NL 37 C6
Hilton ON 21 E4
Hilton Beach ON 17 F4
Hilton Falls CA ON 19 B7
Hilton Falls CA ON 20 D6
Hinchcliffe SK 11 C6-7
Hinds Brook NL 36 A4
Hinds Brook NL 37 A2
Hinds Lake NL 36 B4
Hinds Lake NL 37 B2
Hines Creek AB 9 D3
Hinton AB 6 B3
Hinton AB 8 C1-2
Hippa Island BC 1 A1
Hirsch SK 11 F7
Hislop Lake NT 10 C5
Hitchcock SK 11 F6
Hitchcock Bay SK 11 D4
Hitchie Creek PP BC 2 E1
Hixon BC 1 B7
Hjalmarson Lake MB 12 C7
Hjalmarson Lake MB 15 C2
Hnausa MB 13 D4
Hnausa MB 14 B5
Hnausa PP MB 13 D4
Hnausa PP MB 14 B5
Hoadley AB 6 B5
Hoadley AB 8 D-E5
Hoards ON 21 D4
Hoare Bay NU 42 F8
Hobbema AB 6 B6
Hobbema AB 8 E6
Hobson Lake BC 6 C1-2
Hochfeld MB 13 F3
Hochfeld MB 14 F4
Hochstadt MB 14 E5
Hockin MB 15 E-F3
Hocking Lake SK 12 B4-5
Hockley ON 20 C6
Hockley Valley, RNP ON 20 C5-6
Hockley Valley PNR ON 20 C5-6
Hodge's Cove NL 37 C-D7
Hodges Hill NL 36 A6
Hodges Hill NL 37 A4
Hodges Hill NL 38 F5
Hodgeville SK 11 E4
Hodgson MB 13 D3-4
Hodgson MB 14 B4
Hodson NS 34 D3
Hoey SK 11 B5
Hoffer SK 11 F6
Hogan Lake ON 22 E3
Hogem Ranges BC 3 F5
Hogg, Mount YT 4 D5
Hogg Lake MB 15 C4
Hog Island PE 32 A8
Hog Island PE 34 B1
Hog Island PE 35 C3
Hokanson Point MB 14 B5
Holbein SK 11 B4-5
Holberg BC 1 E3-4
Holberg Inlet BC 1 E3-4
Holborn AB 8 C6
Holbrook ON 19 C5-6
Holbrook ON 20 E4-5
Holden AB 6 B6
Holden AB 8 D8
Holden AB 11 B1
Holdfast SK 11 D5
Hole-in-the-Wall PP BC 3 F7-8
Hole-in-the-Wall PP BC 9 E-F1
Holgar Lake SK 12 C5
Holiday Beach CA ON 19 E1
Holinshead Lake ON 16 D5
Holland MB 13 F2-3
Holland MB 14 E3
Holland Centre ON 18 F6
Holland Centre ON 20 A4-5
Holland Landing ON 20 B7
Holland Landing ON 21 E1
Holland Landing Prairie, RNP ON 20 B7
Holland Landing Prairie, RNP ON 21 E1
Holland Landing Prairie PNR ON 20 B7
Holland Landing Prairie PNR ON 21 E1
Holland River ON 20 B6-7
Holland River ON 21 E1
Hollow Lake AB 8 B7
Hollow Water MB 13 D4
Hollow Water MB 14 B6
Holly ON 20 B6
Holman NT 41 A2
Holman NT 42 E1
Holmes Lake MB 15 D4
Holmes River BC 6 B2
Holmesville NB 31 E3
Holmesville NB 32 A1
Holmesville ON 19 A4
Holmesville ON 20 C3
Holmfield MB 13 F2
Holmfield MB 14 F2
Holstein ON 20 B4-5
Holt ON 20 B7
Holt ON 21 E1
Holton NL 39 A7
Holton Island NL 39 A7
Holtville NB 31 E5
Holtville NB 32 A3
Holtyre ON 17 C-D7
Holyrood NL 37 E7-8
Holyrood ON 20 B3
Holyrood Pond NL 37 F7
Homards, baie des QC 39 F2
Homathko Estuary PP BC 1 D6
Homathko Estuary PP BC 2 A2-3
Homathko Icefield BC 1 D6
Homathko River BC 1 D6
Homathko River BC 2 A2
Homathko River-Tatlayoko PPA BC 1 D6
Home Bay NU 41 B8
Home Bay NU 42 E7
Homebrook MB 13 C2-3
Homebrook MB 14 A2-3

Homefield *SK* 11 D6
Homeglen *AB* 8 E6
Home Pond *NL* 36 A8
Home Pond *NL* 37 A6
Homestead-Motherwell, LHN du *SK* 11 E6
Homeville *NS* 34 C8
Homewood *MB* 13 F3
Homewood *MB* 14 E4
Homfray Channel *BC* 1 E6
Homfray Channel *BC* 2 B-C3
Hondo *AB* 9 F5
Hone *MB* 12 D7
Hone *MB* 15 D1-2
Honey Harbour *ON* 18 E7
Honeydale *NB* 32 D2
Honeymoon Bay *BC* 2 E3
Honeywell Corners *ON* 21 E5
Honeywood *ON* 20 B5
Honfleur *QC* 27 B6
Honguedo, détroit d' *QC* 30 A3-4
Honguedo, détroit d' *QC* 39 F3
Honguedo, détroit d' *QC* 40 F7
Honguedo, Strait of *QC* 39 F3
Honguedo, Strait of *QC* 40 F7
Honora *ON* 18 B3
Hood River *NU* 41 C2-3
Hooker Lake *ON* 13 E8
Hoole Canyon *YT* 4 D5
Hoole River *YT* 4 D5
Hooper Island *NT* 5 A4
Hooping Harbour *NL* 38 C4
Hoosier *SK* 6 C-D8
Hoosier *SK* 11 C-D2
Hootalinqua *YT* 4 D4
Hope *BC* 1 F8
Hope *BC* 2 D7
Hope Bay *ON* 18 E5
Hope Bay Forest, RNP *ON* 18 E5-6
Hope Bay Forest PNR *ON* 18 E5-6
Hopedale *NL* 39 A6
Hopedale *NL* 40 D7
Hopedale Mission NHS *NL* 39 A5-6
Hopedale Mission NHS *NL* 40 D7
Hopefield *PE* 35 F6
Hope Island *ON* 18 E7
Hope Mill CA *ON* 21 E3
Hope Town *QC* 30 D1
Hope Town *QC* 31 A7
Hopes Advance, cap *QC* 40 B5-6
Hopetown *ON* 21 B7
Hopetown *ON* 24 E1
Hopeville *ON* 20 B5
Hopewell *NS* 33 A7
Hopewell *NS* 34 E3
Hopewell Cape *NB* 32 C6
Hopewell Islands *NU* 40 C4
Hopewell Islands *NU* 41 F7-8
Hopewell Rocks PP *NB* 32 C6
Horburg *AB* 8 E4
Horen *AB* 8 C5
Horizon *SK* 11 F5
Hornaday River *AB* 9 A6
Hornaday River *AB* 10 F8
Hornaday River *AB* 12 A2
Hornaday River *NT* 41 B1
Hornby *ON* 19 A-B7
Hornby *ON* 20 D6
Hornby Island *BC* 1 F6
Hornby Island *BC* 2 D2-3
Hornby Island *BC* 2 D3
Hornby Lake *ON* 16 A2
Horndean *MB* 14 F4
Horne Lake *BC* 2 D2-3
Horne Lake PP *BC* 2 D2
Horneline Creek PP *BC* 3 D4
Hornell Lake *NT* 10 D4
Hornepayne *ON* 17 C3
Hornepayne *ON* 40 F7
Horner Creek *ON* 19 B-C6
Horner Creek *ON* 20 D-E5
Horne Settlement *NS* 32 E8
Horne Settlement *NS* 33 B6
Horne Settlement *NS* 34 F2
Hornes Road *NS* 34 C8
Horning's Mills *ON* 20 B5
Horn Lake *ON* 18 C8
Horn Lake *ON* 18 D8
Horn Lake *ON* 21 A1
Horn Lake *ON* 21 B1
Horn Lake *ON* 22 F1
Horn Mountains *NT* 10 D4
Horn Peak *YT* 4 D5-6
Horn River *NT* 10 D4-5
Horn River *NT* 41 D1
Horsefly *BC* 1 C8
Horsefly *BC* 6 C1
Horsefly Lake PP *BC* 1 C8
Horsefly Lake PP *BC* 6 C1
Horsefly Lake Reservoir *AB* 6 F7
Horsefly Lake Reservoir *AB* 7 E6-7
Horsefly Lake Reservoir *AB* 11 E1
Horsefly River *BC* 1 C8
Horsefly River *BC* 6 C1
Horse Island *MB* 13 B3
Horse Islands *NL* 38 D5

Horse Islands *NL* 39 E8
Horse Lakes *SK* 11 D6
Horse River *AB* 9 D6-7
Horse River *AB* 12 D1
Horseshoe Bay *BC* 6 A7
Horseshoe Bay *AB* 11 A1
Horseshoe Bay *BC* 1 F6-7
Horseshoe Bay *BC* 2 D4
Horseshoe Lake *AB* 8 F6
Horseshoe Lake *BC* 2 C3
Horseshoe Lake *ON* 13 C8
Horseshoe Lake *ON* 16 A4-5
Horseshoe Lake *ON* 18 A3
Horseshoe Lake *ON* 18 D7-8
Horseshoe Lake *ON* 21 C2
Horseshoe Slough Territorial Habitat Protection Area *YT* 4 B4
Horseshoe Valley *ON* 18 F8
Horseshoe Valley *ON* 20 A7
Horseshoe Valley *ON* 21 D1
Horsham *SK* 6 E8
Horsham *SK* 11 E2
Horton *NS* 32 E7
Horton *NS* 33 B4-5
Horton, rivière *QC* 29 D2-3
Horton Lake *NT* 41 B1
Horton River *NT* 5 B7-8
Horton River *NT* 41 A-B1
Horwood *NL* 38 F7
Horwood Lake *ON* 17 D5
Hoselaw *AB* 6 A7
Hoselaw *AB* 11 A2
Hoselaw *AB* 12 F2
Hosmer *BC* 6 F5
Hosmer *BC* 7 E3
Hôtel-Dalvay-by-the-Sea, LHN de l' *PE* 34 C2-3
Hôtel-Dalvay-by-the-Sea, LHN de l' *PE* 35 D5
Hotham Sound *BC* 1 E6
Hottah Lake *NT* 10 A4
Hottah Lake *NT* 41 C1
Hough Lake *ON* 18 A2-3
House Mountain *AB* 9 F4
House River *AB* 9 E6
House River *AB* 12 D-E1
Houseys Rapids *ON* 21 C1-2
Houston *BC* 1 A5
Houston Stewart Channel *BC* 1 C2
Howard *NB* 31 E6
Howard *NB* 32 A4
Howard, lac *QC* 22 D8
Howard, lac *QC* 24 A2
Howard, lac *QC* 25 E2
Howden *MB* 14 D2
Howdenvale *ON* 18 E4-5
Howe Bay *PE* 35 E7
Howe Bay *PE* 35 E7
Howe Island *ON* 21 D7
Howe Point *PE* 34 C4
Howe Point *PE* 35 E7
Howe Sound *BC* 1 F6-7
Howe Sound *BC* 2 D4
Howick *QC* 24 E5
Howick *QC* 27 F1
Howie *AB* 7 B7
Howie Centre *NS* 34 C7-8
Howlan *PE* 35 B1
Howley *NL* 36 A4
Howley *NL* 37 A2
Howley *NL* 38 F3
Howley *NL* 39 F8
Howse Pass *BC* 6 E3
Howse Pass NHS *AB* 6 C3-4
Howser *BC* 6 E3
Howser Creek *BC* 6 E3-4
Hoyle *ON* 17 C6
Hoyt *NB* 32 D3
H.R. Frink CA *ON* 21 D-E5
Huallen *AB* 9 F2
Huard, lac *QC* 26 C6
Huards, lac aux *QC* 26 B8
Huards, lac aux *QC* 28 A6
Hubbard *SK* 11 D6
Hubbard, Mount *YT* 4 E2
Hubbards *NS* 32 F7
Hubbards *NS* 33 C5
Hubbards *NS* 34 F1
Hubbards PP *NS* 33 C5
Hubberdeau *QC* 24 C4
Hubert Lake Wildland PP *AB* 8 A5
Hubert Lake Wildland PP *AB* 9 F5
Hubley *NS* 32 F8
Hubley *NS* 33 C5
Huddersfield, lac *QC* 22 E6
Hudson *ON* 13 E7
Hudson *ON* 16 D3
Hudson *QC* 24 D5
Hudson, baie d' *MB* 15 C7-8
Hudson, baie d' *NU* 41 F5-7
Hudson, baie d' 40 C2-3
Hudson, détroit d' *NU* 40 A-B5
Hudson, détroit d' *NU* 41 D8
Hudson Bay *MB* 15 B7

Hudson Bay *NU* 41 E5-7 F5-7
Hudson Bay *QC* 40 B2-3
Hudson Bay *SK* 11 B7
Hudson's Hope *BC* 9 E1
Hudson's Hope *BC* 3 E7
Hudson Strait *NU* 40 A-B5
Hudson Strait *NU* 41 D8
Hudwin Lake *MB* 13 B4-5
Hudwin Lake PP Reserve *MB* 13 B5
Hughenden *AB* 6 C7
Hughenden *AB* 11 C1-2
Hughes *ON* 23 E1
Hughes Brook *NL* 36 A-B3
Hughes Brook *NL* 37 A-B1
Hughes River *MB* 12 D7-8
Hughes River *MB* 15 D2
Hughton *SK* 11 D3
Huguenin, lac *QC* 25 A4
Huguenin, lac *QC* 26 E-F4
Hu Haven *AB* 8 B-C7
Huit, lac du *QC* 27 C-D6
Huit Chutes, lac des *QC* 28 B6
Hull *QC* 21 A8
Hull *QC* 24 D2
Humber Arm South *NL* 36 A-B2
Humber River *NL* 36 A-B3
Humber River *NL* 37 A-B1
Humber River *ON* 20 C6
Humber Village *NL* 36 B3
Humber Village *NL* 37 B1
Humboldt *SK* 11 C5
Hume *SK* 11 F6
Hume River *NT* 5 E-F6
Humphrey *ON* 18 D7-8
Humphrey Corner *NB* 31 F6
Humphrey Corner *NB* 32 B4
Humpy Lake *NT* 10 A6-7
Humqui, rivière *QC* 29 C4-5
Hungry Creek *YT* 5 E3-4 F3
Hungry Lake *ON* 21 C6
Hunta *ON* 17 C6
Hunter Bay *SK* 12 F5-6
Hunter Creek *SK* 12 B-C4
Hunter Island *BC* 1 C4
Hunter Island *ON* 16 F3-4
Hunter Lake *ON* 18 A4
Hunter Point *BC* 1 B1
Hunter River *PE* 34 C2
Hunter River *PE* 35 D4
Hunter River *PE* 35 D4
Hunters Mountain *NS* 34 C6
Hunters Point *QC* 17 E8
Hunter's Point *QC* 22 B2-3
Hunterstown *QC* 24 B7
Hunterstown *QC* 25 F7
Hunterstown *QC* 27 C2
Huntingdon *BC* 1 F7-8
Huntingdon *BC* 2 E6
Huntingdon *QC* 24 E5
Huntingdon Island *NL* 39 B7
Huntingdon Island *NL* 40 D8
Huntingford *ON* 19 B5
Huntingford *ON* 20 D4
Hunting River *MB* 15 D4
Huntingville *QC* 27 E4-5
Huntley *PE* 35 B2
Huntoon *SK* 11 F6
Hunt River *NL* 39 A5
Hunts Point *NS* 33 E4
Hunts Pond *NL* 36 B7
Hunts Pond *NL* 37 B5
Huntsville *ON* 18 D8
Huntsville *ON* 21 B1
Huntsville *ON* 21 B1-2
Hurd, Cape *ON* 18 D4
Hurds Lake *ON* 21 A6
Hurkett *ON* 16 E6
Hurley River *BC* 2 A-B5
Huron, lac *ON* 18 E2-3
Huron, lac *ON* 19 B3
Huron, lac *ON* 20 C1-2
Huron, Lake *ON* 18 D2-3
Huron, Lake *ON* 19 A2-3
Huron, Lake *ON* 20 B1-2
Huron, rivière *QC* 27 B5
Huron East *ON* 19 A4-5
Huron East *ON* 20 C3-4
Huron Heights *ON* 19 C3
Huron Heights *ON* 20 E2
Huron Park *ON* 19 B4
Huron Park *ON* 20 D3
Huron Ridge *ON* 18 E4
Huronas, rivière des *QC* 27 A5
Husavik *MB* 14 C5
Husky Channel *NT* 5 C4
Hussar *AB* 6 D6
Hussar *AB* 7 B5
Hutchison Bay *NT* 5 A5
Hutch Lake *AB* 9 B3-4
Hutton Heights *ON* 19 A4
Hutton Heights *ON* 20 C3
Huttonville *ON* 19 A7
Huttonville *ON* 20 C6
Huxley *AB* 6 C6
Huxley *AB* 8 F7
Huxley Island *BC* 1 C2
Hyas *SK* 11 C7
Hyas *SK* 13 C1
Hyde Park *ON* 19 C4
Hyde Park *ON* 20 E3
Hyland River *YT* 4 D-E7
Hyland River PP *BC* 3 A4
Hyland River PP *BC* 4 A7
Hylo *AB* 8 A8
Hylo *AB* 9 F6
Hylo *AB* 12 F1

Hymers *ON* 16 F5
Hyndford *ON* 21 A5-6
Hyndford *ON* 22 F5-6
Hyndman Lake *NT* 5 C5-6
Hyperite Point *NU* 42 C4
Hythe *AB* 9 E2

I

Ian Lake *BC* 1 A1
Iberville *QC* 24 E6-7
Iberville *QC* 27 F2
Iberville, lac d' *QC* 40 D5
Iberville, ZEC d' *QC* 28 B8
Iberville, ZEC d' *QC* 29 B1
Ibex Valley *YT* 4 E3
Iceberg Point *NU* 42 B4
Ice Lake *ON* 18 B3
Ice Mountain *BC* 1 A8
Ice Mountain *BC* 6 A1
Ice Mountain *BC* 9 F1
Iconoclast Mountain *BC* 6 D3
Ida *ON* 21 E3
Ida, lac *QC* 26 A5
Iddesleigh *AB* 6 D7
Iddesleigh *AB* 7 C7
Iddesleigh *AB* 11 D1
Ideal *NL* 38 A6
Iffley *SK* 11 B3
Igloolik (Iglulik) *NU* 41 B6
Igloolik (Iglulik) *NU* 42 F5-6
Igluligaarjuk (Chesterfield Inlet) *NU* 40 A2
Igluligaarjuk (Chesterfield Inlet) *NU* 41 D-E5
Iglulik (Igloolik) *NU* 41 B6
Iglulik (Igloolik) *NU* 42 F5-6
Ignace *ON* 13 F7
Ignace *ON* 16 E3-4
Ijiraliq, parc territorial *NU* 40 A2
Ijiraliq, parc territorial *NU* 41 E5
Ijiraliq TP *NU* 40 A2
Ijiraliq TP *NU* 41 E5
Ikeda Point *BC* 1 C2
Ikpiarjuk (Arctic Bay) *NU* 41 A5
Ikpiarjuk (Arctic Bay) *NU* 42 D-E5
Ilderton *ON* 19 C4
Ilderton *ON* 20 E3
Île-à-la-Brume, RNOM de l' *QC* 39 E5-6
Ile-à-la-Brume NMBS *QC* 39 E5-6
Île-à-la-Crosse *SK* 12 E3
Île-à-la-Crosse (IR) *SK* 12 E4
Île-à-la-Crosse, lac *SK* 12 E3-4
Île au Castor, lac de l' *QC* 38 A1
Île au Castor, lac de l' *QC* 39 D6
Île-aux-Canes, RNOM de l' *NL* 38 C5-6
Île aux Canes NMBS *NL* 38 C5-6
Île-Bizard *QC* 24 D5
Île-Bizard *QC* 27 E1
Île-Boot, RNF de l' *NL* 32 D7
Île-Boot, RNF de l' *NL* 33 B5
Île-Brion, refuge écologique de l' *QC* 30 E8
Île-Chantry, RNOM l' *ON* 18 F4
Île-Chantry, RNOM l' *ON* 20 A3
Ile-Corossol NMBS *QC* 39 F2
Île-d'Entrée *QC* 30 F7
Île-de-Carillon, RNF l' *QC* 24 D4-5
Île-de-Carillon National Wilderness Area *QC* 24 D4-5
Île-de-Salaberry *QC* 24 E5
Île-de-Salaberry *QC* 27 F1
Île-du-Corossol, RNOM de l' *QC* 39 F2
Île-Dupas *QC* 24 C7
Île-Dupas *QC* 27 C7
Île-du-Prince-Édouard, PN de l' *PE* 34 B3
Île-du-Prince-Édouard, PN de l' *PE* 34 B2-3
Île-du-Prince-Édouard, PN de l' *PE* 35 D4-5
Île-du-Prince-Édouard, PN de l' *PE* 35 D5-6
Île-Eleanor, RNF de l' *ON* 18 E8
Île-Eleanor, RNF de l' *ON* 21 C1
Île-Grassy, LHN de l' *NS* 34 E6-7
Île-Kendall, RNOM de l' *NT* 5 A3-4
Île-Machias-Seal, RNOM de l' *NB* 32 F2
Île-Mohawk, RNF de l' *ON* 19 D8
Île-Mohawk, RNF de l' *ON* 20 F7
Île-Navy, LHN de l' *ON* 20 E8
Île-Portage, RNF de l' *NB* 31 C7-8
Îles, lac des *SK* 9 F8

Îles, lac des *ON* 16 E5
Îles, lac des *QC* 22 D8
Îles, lac des *QC* 24 B2
Îles, lac des *QC* 24 C5
Îles, lac des *QC* 25 F2
Îles, lac des *QC* 26 A7
Îles, lac des *QC* 28 D5-6
Îles, lac des *SK* 11 A3
Îles, lac des *SK* 12 F3
Île-Sainte-Croix, lieu historique international de l' *NB* 32 E1-2
Île-Scotch-Bonnet, RNF de l' *ON* 21 F4-5
Îles-de-Boucherville, parc des *QC* 24 D6
Îles-de-Boucherville, parc des *QC* 27 D2
Îles-de-Contrecœur, RNF des *QC* 24 C6
Îles-de-Contrecœur, RNF des *QC* 27 D2
Îles-de-Contrecœur National Wilderness Area *QC* 24 C6
Îles-de-Contrecœur National Wilderness Area *QC* 27 D2
Îles-de-la-Baie-Georgienne, PN des *ON* 18 E6-7
Îles-de-la-Baie-Georgienne, PN des *ON* 18 E7
Îles-de-la-Madeleine, les *QC* 30 F7
Îles-de-l'Estuaire, RNF des *QC* 28 D8
Îles-de-l'Estuaire, RNF des *QC* 29 D1
Îles-de-l'Estuaire NWA *QC* 28 D8
Îles-de-l'Estuaire NWA *QC* 29 D1
Îles-du-Saint-Laurent, PN des *ON* 21 D-E7 D8
Île-Sea-Wolf, RNF de l' *NS* 34 B5-6
Île-Shepherd, RNOM de l' *NL* 38 C5-6
Îles-Monger *QC* 38 B1
Îles-Sainte-Marie, RNOM des *QC* 39 E-F6
Iles-Sainte-Marie NMBS *QC* 39 E-F6
Île Verte, lac de l' *QC* 28 A7
Ilford *MB* 15 E5
Ilfracombe *ON* 18 D8
Ilfracombe *ON* 21 A-B1
Îlots, lac aux *QC* 28 D7
Imperial *SK* 11 D5
Imperial Eagle Channel *BC* 2 E2
Imperial Mills *AB* 9 F6-7
Imperial Mills *AB* 12 F1
Imperial River *NT* 5 F7
Inchkeith *SK* 11 E7
Incomappleux River *BC* 6 D3
Inconnu, lac *QC* 26 A2
Independence *AB* 8 B6
Indian, lac *QC* 23 E7
Indian, lac *QC* 25 B1-2
Indian Arm *BC* 2 D5
Indian Arm PMP *BC* 2 D5
Indian Arm PP *BC* 2 D5
Indian Bay *MB* 14 E7-8
Indian Bay *NL* 36 A8
Indian Bay *NL* 37 A6
Indian Bay *NL* 38 F7-8
Indian Bay Pond *NL* 36 A7-8
Indian Bay Pond *NL* 37 A6
Indian Bay Pond *NL* 38 F7
Indian Brook *NS* 32 E8
Indian Brook *NS* 33 B6
Indian Brook *NS* 34 B7
Indian Brook *NS* 34 C5
Indian Brook *NS* 34 F2
Indian Cabins *AB* 9 A3-4
Indian Cabins *AB* 10 F5
Indian Creek *ON* 21 B6-7
Indian Creek *ON* 24 E1
Indian Gardens *NS* 33 D3
Indian Harbour *NL* 36 D2
Indian Harbour *NL* 39 A7
Indian Harbour *NS* 33 C5
Indian Harbour *NS* 34 F5
Indian Harbour Lake *NS* 34 F5
Indian Head *SK* 11 E6
Indian Head, RNOM d' *SK* 11 E6
Indian Head NMBS *SK* 11 E6
Indian Hill Lake *NT* 10 B-C8
Indian Island *NB* 31 E6
Indian Island *NB* 32 A6
Indian Lake *NS* 32 E6
Indian Lake *NS* 33 C5
Indian Lake *NS* 33 C5
Indian Lake *ON* 13 F7
Indian Lake *ON* 16 E3-4
Indian Line CA *ON* 20 C6
Indian Mountain Lake *NT* 10 C8
Indian Point *NS* 32 F7
Indian Point *NS* 33 D4-5
Indian Point PP *NS* 20 A8
Indian Point PP *NS* 21 D2
Indian Point Sand Hills *NS* 35 C1
Indian Pond *NL* 36 B3
Indian Pond *NL* 37 B1

Indian River *BC* 2 D5
Indian River *NL* 36 A5
Indian River *NL* 37 A3
Indian River *NL* 38 F4
Indian River *NL* 39 F8
Indian River *ON* 21 A5
Indian River *ON* 21 B6-7
Indian River *ON* 21 D3-4
Indian River *ON* 22 F5
Indian River *ON* 24 E1
Indian River *PE* 35 D3
Indian River *YT* 4 B2
Indian Tickle *NL* 39 B8
Indin Lake *NT* 10 B6
Indin River *NT* 10 A-B6
Indus *AB* 7 B4
Inférieur, lac *QC* 29 C4
Ingebright Lake *SK* 6 E8
Ingebright Lake *SK* 11 E2
Ingelow *MB* 14 D2
Ingenika River *BC* 3 D5-6
Ingersoll *ON* 19 C5
Ingersoll *ON* 20 E4
Ingleside *ON* 24 E3
Inglestrom Lake *ON* 13 A7
Inglewood *ON* 19 A7
Inglewood *ON* 20 C6
Inglisville *NS* 32 E5-6
Inglisville *NS* 33 C3
Ingoldsby *ON* 21 C3
Ingolf *ON* 13 F5
Ingolf *ON* 14 E8
Ingolf *ON* 16 D1
Ingomar *NS* 33 F3
Ingonish *NS* 34 A7
Ingonish Beach *NS* 34 A7
Ingonish Centre *NS* 34 B7
Ingonish Ferry *NS* 34 A7
Ingonish River *NS* 34 B7
Ingornachoix Bay *NL* 38 C3
Ingornachoix Bay *NL* 39 E7
Ingraham Bay *BC* 1 A1
Ingramport *NS* 32 F7-8
Ingramport *NS* 33 C5
Ingray Lake *NT* 10 B5
Ings River *NL* 38 A7
Inkaneep PP *BC* 6 F2
Inkerman *NB* 30 E2
Inkerman *NB* 31 B8
Inkerman *ON* 21 B8
Inkerman *ON* 24 E3
Inkerman Ferry *NB* 31 B8
Inkerman, pointe *QC* 28 F2
Inkster *SK* 11 D5
Inland *AB* 8 C8
Inland Lake *MB* 13 C2
Inner Bay *ON* 19 D6
Inner Bay *ON* 20 F5
Innerkip *ON* 19 B5-6
Innerkip *ON* 20 E4-5
Innes *SK* 11 F6
Innes Island *ON* 18 B3
Innisfail *AB* 6 C5
Innisfail *AB* 8 F6
Innisfil *ON* 20 B6-7
Innisfil *ON* 21 B1
Innisfil Heights *ON* 20 B6-7
Innisfil Heights *ON* 21 B1
Innisfree *AB* 6 B7
Innisfree *AB* 11 B1
Innismara *NL* 36 A2-3
Innismara *NL* 38 F2
Innisville *ON* 21 B7
Innisville *ON* 24 E1
Insinger *SK* 11 D6
Instow *SK* 11 E-F3
Intata Reach *BC* 1 B5
Intérieur, plaines de l' *BC* 3 C-D8
Intérieur, plaines de l' *BC* 9 C-D2
Intérieur, plateau de l' *BC* 1 B-C6
Interior Plains *BC* 3 B-C8
Interior Plains *BC* 9 B-C2
Interior Plateau *BC* 1 B6 C6-7
Interlake *AB* 7 B4
International Ridge PRA *BC* 2 E6
Intersection Mountain *AB* 6 A2
Intrepid Inlet *NT* 42 C4
Inukjuak *QC* 40 C4
Inukjuak *QC* 41 F8
Inuujivik TP *NU* 41 D4
Inuvik *NT* 5 C5
Inverarden House NHS *ON* 24 E4
Inverarity Lake *MB* 15 A3
Inverary *ON* 21 D7
Inverhaugh *ON* 19 B6
Inverhaugh *ON* 20 D5
Inverhuron *ON* 20 B3
Inverhuron PP *ON* 20 B3
Invermay *SK* 11 D6
Invermay *SK* 18 F5
Invermere *BC* 6 E4
Invermere *BC* 7 C1
Inverness *NS* 34 C5-6
Inverness *PE* 34 B1
Inverness *PE* 35 D3
Inverness *PE* 37 B-C1
Inverness *NS* 33 D4-5
Inverness *PE* 27 C5
Inwood *MB* 13 E3
Inwood *MB* 14 C4-5
Inwood *ON* 19 C3
Inwood *ON* 20 F2
Inzana Lake *BC* 3 F6

Iona *NS* 34 C6
Iona *ON* 19 C4
Iona *ON* 20 F3
Iona *PE* 34 C3
Iona *PE* 35 F6
Iona Station *ON* 19 C4
Iona Station *ON* 20 F3
Iosegun Lake *AB* 6 A3-4
Iosegun Lake *AB* 8 A2
Iosegun Lake *AB* 9 F3-4
Iosegun River *AB* 8 A2-3
Iosegun River *AB* 9 F3-4
Ipperwash Beach *ON* 19 B3
Ipperwash Beach *ON* 20 D-E2
Iqaluit *NU* 40 A5-6
Iqaluktuutiaq (Cambridge Bay) *NU* 41 B3
Iqaluktuutiaq (Cambridge Bay) *NU* 42 F3
Ira Lake PP *ON* 18 E4
Ireland *NS* 33 A8
Ireland *NS* 34 E4
Ireland's Eye *NL* 37 D7
Irène, lac *QC* 26 B4
Ireton *AB* 8 D6
Iris *PE* 34 D3
Iris *PE* 35 F6
Irish Cove *NS* 34 D7
Irish Cove PP *NS* 34 D7
Irish Lake *ON* 20 B5
Irishtown *NB* 31 F8
Irishtown *NB* 32 B6
Irishtown *NL* 36 B5
Irishtown *NL* 37 B1
Irma *AB* 6 B7
Irma *AB* 11 B1
Ironbound Islands *NL* 39 A6
Iron Bridge *ON* 17 F5
Iron Bridge *ON* 18 A1
Irondale *ON* 21 C3
Irondale River *ON* 21 C3
Iron Hill *QC* 24 E8
Iron Hill *QC* 27 F3
Iron Island *ON* 18 A7
Iron Mines *NS* 34 C6
Iron River *AB* 6 A7
Iron River *AB* 9 F7
Iron River *AB* 12 F2
Irons Creek *YT* 3 A4
Irons Creek *YT* 4 E7
Iron Springs *AB* 6 E6
Iron Springs *AB* 7 D5-6
Iroquois *ON* 24 F3
Iroquois, lac *QC* 22 E8
Iroquois, lac *QC* 24 C2
Iroquois, pointe *QC* 28 F2
Iroquois, rivière aux *NB* 29 E3
Iroquois, rivière aux *NB* 26 E8
Iroquois, rivière aux 28 C3
Iroquois Falls *ON* 17 C7
Iroquois River *NT* 5 C-D6
Irricana *AB* 6 D6
Irricana *AB* 7 B4
Irvine *AB* 6 E8
Irvine *AB* 11 E2
Irvine Creek *YT* 4 E5-6
Irvines Landing *BC* 1 F6
Irvines Landing *BC* 2 D3
Isaac Creek *YT* 4 B-C2
Isabel, lac *QC* 22 F7
Isabel, lac *QC* 24 C1
Isabella *MB* 11 E8
Isabella *MB* 13 E1
Isabella Lake *ON* 18 D7
Isachsen, Cape *NU* 42 B3
Isachsen Peninsula *NU* 42 B3
Isbister River *MB* 13 B5
Isham *SK* 11 D3
Ishkheenickh River *BC* 3 F3
Isidore, lac *QC* 28 A8
Isidore, lac *QC* 29 A1
Iskut *BC* 3 C3
Iskutewizaagegan (Kejick) *ON* 16 D1
Iskut Hot Springs PP *BC* 3 C3
Iskut River *BC* 3 D2-3
Iskwatam Lake *SK* 12 E6
Iskwatikan Lake *SK* 12 E5-6
Island Brook *QC* 27 E5
Island Cove *NL* 37 D6-7
Island Cove *NL* 38 F7
Island Falls *SK* 12 E7
Island Falls *SK* 15 E1
Island Grove *ON* 20 B7
Island Harbour *NL* 38 E7
Island Lake *AB* 8 F5
Island Lake *MB* 13 A5
Island Lake *MB* 13 A5
Island Lake *ON* 18 C7
Island Lake CA *ON* 20 C6
Island Lake PP *BC* 2 C3
Island Lake South *AB* 9 F5-6
Island of Ponds *NL* 39 B8
Island Pond *NL* 36 B-C3
Island Pond *NL* 37 B-C1
Island River *NT* 3 A8
Island River *NT* 10 F3
Islands, Bay of *NL* 36 A2
Islands, Bay of *NL* 38 F2

Islands, Bay of *NL* 39 A6
Islands, Bay of *NL* 40 F8
Islands, Bay of *ON* 18 B4
Islay *AB* 6 B7
Islay *AB* 11 B2
Isle aux Morts *NL* 36 D-E1
Isle Pierre *BC* 1 A6-7
Isle Valen *NL* 36 E8
Isle Valen *NL* 37 E6
Islington *NL* 37 D7
Ispas *AB* 9 F3
Ispatinow Island *SK* 12 C4
Issac Lake *BC* 1 B8
Issac Lake *BC* 6 A1
Issac's Harbour *NS* 20 D-E7
Issac's Harbour North *NS* 34 E-F5
Issoudun *QC* 27 B5
Italy Cross *NS* 33 D4
Itcha Ilgachuz PP *BC* 1 C5-6
Ithingo Lake *SK* 12 C4
Itomamo, lac *QC* 28 A7
Ittastoo *BC* 1 A5
Ittatsoo *BC* 2 E1-2
Ituna *SK* 11 D6
Ituna *SK* 21 D5
Ivanhoe *AB* 9 F5
Ivanhoe Lake ON 17 D5
Ivanhoe River *ON* 17 C5-D5
Ivry, lac *QC* 38 B1
Ivry, lac *QC* 39 E6-7
Ivry-sur-le-Lac *QC* 24 C4
Ivujivik *QC* 40 B4
Ivujivik *QC* 41 D7
Ivvavik, PN *YT* 5 B2
Ivvavik NP *YT* 5 A2-3 B2-3
Ivy *ON* 20 B6
Ivy Lea *ON* 21 D7
Ivy Lea, parc *ON* 21 D7
Ivy Lea Park *ON* 21 D7
Ixworth, sanctuaire d' *QC* 28 F8

J

Jacam *MB* 15 D5
Jackfish Lake *MB* 13 E2-3
Jackfish Lake *MB* 14 C3
Jackfish Lake *SK* 11 B3
Jackfish Lake *SK* 11 B3
Jackfish Lake *YT* 4 D5
Jackfish River *AB* 9 A-B5
Jackhead *MB* 13 C4
Jack Lake *ON* 21 C4
Jack Lake *ON* 21 C4
Jackman Flats PP *BC* 6 B2
Jackpine River *AB* 6 A-B2
Jackson *NS* 32 C8
Jackson *NS* 33 A5
Jackson *NS* 34 E1
Jackson *ON* 18 F5
Jackson *ON* 20 A4
Jackson Creek *SK* 11 F7-8
Jackson Creek *SK* 34 D5
Jackson Narrows PMP *BC* 1 C3-4
Jackson's Arm *NL* 38 D3-4
Jackson's Arm *NL* 39 F8
Jackson's Cove *NL* 38 E4-5
Jacksons Point *ON* 20 B7
Jacksons Point *ON* 21 D1
Jacksonville *NB* 31 F3
Jacksonville *NB* 32 B1
Jacques, lac à *NT* 5 E7
Jacques-Cartier, détroit *QC* 40 D7
Jacques-Cartier, détroit *QC* 39 F3-4
Jacques-Cartier, lac *QC* 28 F5
Jacques-Cartier, mont *QC* 29 D7
Jacques-Cartier, mont *QC* 40 F7
Jacques-Cartier, parc de la *QC* 28 F5
Jacques Cartier, Strait of *QC* 39 F4-5
Jacques Cartier, Strait of *QC* 40 F7
Jacques Cartier PP *PE* 34 A-B1
Jacques Cartier PP *PE* 35 B2
Jacques Fontaine *NL* 36 E7
Jacques Fontaine *NL* 37 E5
Jacquet River *NB* 29 E6-7
Jacquet River *NB* 29 E7
Jacquet River *NB* 31 B5
Jacquet River *NB* 31 A6
Jacquet River Gorge PPA *NB* 29 E6-7
Jacquet River Gorge PPA *NB* 31 B6
Jade City *BC* 3 B3
Jade *BC* 4 F6
Jaffray *BC* 6 F5
Jaffray *BC* 7 F2
Jaffray Melick *ON* 13 E5-6
Jaffray Melick *ON* 16 D1-2
Jake's Corner *YT* 4 E4
Jak TP *NT* 5 C3
J. Albert Bauer PP *ON* 21 A-B2
J. Albert Bauer PP *ON* 22 F2
Jalobert, lac *QC* 23 E8
Jalobert, lac *QC* 25 A2
Jalobert, lac *QC* 26 F2
Jalobert, lac *QC* 28 B7
James, baie *QC* 40 E3
James Bay *QC* 40 E3

James Chabot PP BC   6 E4
James Chabot PP BC   7 C1-2
James Creek AB   9 A4
James Lake MB   12 C8
James Lake MB   15 C2
James Lake NT   10 C5
Jameson, Cape NU   41 A7
Jameson, Cape NU   42 D-E6
James River NS   34 E4
James River Bridge AB   6 C5
James River Bridge AB   8 F5
James Ross Strait NU   41 B4
James Ross Strait NU   42 F4
James Smith SK   11 B5
Jamestown NL   37 C6-7
Jamet, rivière QC   24 A-B4
Jamet, rivière QC   25 F4
Jamie Lake MB   12 B8
Jamie Lake MB   15 B2
Jamière, lac QC   39 A3-4
Jamot ON   18 B6
Jamyn, lac QC   38 A2
Janet Lake YT   4 B3
Janetville ON   20 B8
Janetville ON   21 C7
Janeville NB   29 E8
Janeville NB   30 E1
Janeville NB   31 B7
Jan Lake SK   12 F6
Jans Bay SK   12 F3
Jansen SK   11 C5
Janvrin Island NS   34 E6
Jardins, lac des QC   22 C3
Jaro, ZEC QC   27 D7
Jaroslaw AB   14 B5
Jarratt ON   18 F8
Jarratt ON   20 A7
Jarratt ON   21 D1
Jarvie AB   6 A5
Jarvie AB   8 A6
Jarvie AB   9 F5
Jarvis ON   19 C7
Jarvis ON   20 F6
Jarvis Bay AB   8 E-F6
Jarvis Bay PP AB   6 C5
Jarvis Bay PP AB   8 E5-6
Jarvis River YT   4 D-E2
Jasmin SK   11 D6
Jasper AB   6 B3
Jasper AB   8 D1
Jasper ON   21 C7
Jasper ON   24 F2
Jasper, PN AB   6 C3
Jasper, PN AB   8 E1-2
Jasper House, LHN AB
  6 B2-3
Jasper House, LHN AB   8 D1
Jasper House NHS AB
  6 B2-3
Jasper House NHS AB   8 D1
Jasper NP AB   6 B2-3
Jasper NP AB   8 D1-2 E1-2
Jasper Park Information
  Centre NHS AB   8 D1
Jaux, lac QC   25 A3
Jaux, lac QC   26 F3
Jean, lac ON   17 B1
Jean Cote AB   9 E3
Jean, Lake ON   16 E6-7
Jean de Baie NL   36 E7
Jean de Baie NL   37 E5
Jeanette Bay NL   39 A7
Jean Maria River NT
  10 E3-4
Jeanne Mance NB   31 C7
Jeanne-Mance NB   29 F8
Jeanne-Mance NB   30 F1
Jeannettes Creek ON   19 E2
Jeannotte, ZEC QC   25 C8
Jeannotte, ZEC QC   28 F4
Jean-Péré, lac QC   22 B3-4
Jean-Péré, lac QC   25 D1
Jedburgh SK   11 D6
Jeddore Cape NS   33 C7
Jeddore Harbour NS   33 C7
Jeddore Lake NL   36 C6
Jeddore Lake NL   37 C4
Jeddore Oyster Pond NS
  33 C7
Jedediah Island PMP BC
  2 D3
Jeffrey AB   8 B6
Jeffrey's NL   36 C1-2
Jeffries Corner NB   32 C5
Jeffries Corner NB   33 A2
Jellicoe BC   2 C-D8
Jellicoe BC   6 E-F1
Jellicoe ON   16 D7
Jellicoe ON   17 B1
Jemseg NB   32 C4
Jennejohn Lake NT 10 C-D7
Jenner AB   6 D7
Jenner AB   7 C7
Jenner AB   11 D1
Jennings River BC   3 A2-3
Jennings River BC   4 F5-6
Jenny Lind Island NU
  41 B-C4
Jenny Lind Island NU 42 F3
Jenpeg MB   13 A3
Jenpeg MB   15 F3
Jens Munk Island NU 41 B6
Jens Munk Island NU
  42 F5-6
Jenssen, lac QC   26 E7
Jenssen, lac QC   28 C2
Jérôme, lac QC   25 D6
Jérôme, lac QC   27 A3
Jerrys Nose NL   36 C1
Jersey Cove QC   30 B3
Jersey Harbour NL   36 E6
Jersey Harbour NL   37 E4
Jersey Mills QC   27 C6-7

Jerseyside NL   36 E8
Jerseyside NL   37 E6
Jerseyville ON   19 B6-7
Jerseyville ON   20 E5-6
Jervis Inlet BC   1 E6
Jervis Inlet BC   2 C4
Jesmond BC   1 D7-8
Jessups Falls CA ON   24 D3
Jésuite, lac du QC   25 E8
Jésuite, lac du QC   27 A3
Jetait MB   12 E7
Jetait MB   15 E1
Jeune, lac QC   25 B3
Jewel Lake PP BC   6 F2
Jewellville ON   21 B5
Jewett Lake SK   12 E5
Jim, lac QC   22 E6
Jim's Cove NL   38 E-F5
Jimsmith Lake PP BC   6 F4
Jimsmith Lake PP BC   7 E1
Joannès, lac QC   23 E3
Job Lake ON   16 B1
Job's Cove NL   37 C7
Jocko Point ON   22 D1
Jocko River ON   22 C2
Jocko River PP ON   17 F8
Jock River ON   21 B7
Jock River ON   24 E1-2
Joe Batt's Arm NL   38 E7
Joe Batt's Arm-Barr'd
  Islands-Shoal Bay NL
  38 E7-8
Joe Creek YT   5 B2
Joe Glodes Pond NL   36 B5
Joe Glodes Pond NL   37 B3
Joe Lake ON   21 A2
Joe Lake ON   23 B1-2
Joffre AB   6 C6
Joffre AB   8 F6
Joffre Lakes PP BC   1 E7
Joffre Lakes PP BC   2 B5-6
Joggins NS   32 C7
Jog Lake ON   17 A3
Jogues ON   17 B4
John, Cape NS   34 D2
John Dean PP BC   2 F4
John D'or Prairie AB   9 B5
John D'or Prairie AB
  41 E-F1
John E. Pearce PP ON 19 D4
John E. Pearce PP ON
  20 F3
John Island ON   18 B2
John Osborn Lake MB
  12 A8
John Osborn Lake MB
  15 A3
John Richardson Bay NU
  42 B5
Johnny Hoe River NT 10 B3
John's Beach NL   36 A2
Johnson, lac QC   22 F7
Johnson, lac QC   24 C1
Johnson Creek YT   5 D3
Johnson River NT   10 B-C2
Johnson's Mills NB 32 C6-7
Johnsons Crossing YT   4 E5
Johnsons Landing BC
  6 E3-4
Johnstone Creek PP BC   6 F2
Johnstone Strait BC   1 E5
Johnstone Strait BC   2 B1
Johnston Harbour/Pine Tree
  Point PP ON   18 D-E4
Johnston Island SK   9 A8
Johnston Island SK   12 A3
Johnstown NS   34 D6-7
Johnstown ON   24 D2-3
Johnville NB   31 E3
Johnville NB   32 A1
Johnville QC   27 E-F5
Joint Lake MB   13 A5
Joint Lake MB   15 F5
Joinville, lac QC   24 B3
Joinville, lac QC   25 F3
Jo-Jo Lake YT   4 E3
Jolicure NB   32 C7
Jolicure NB   35 F1
Joliette QC   24 C6
Joliette QC   27 D1-2
Jolly Lake NT   10 B7
Joly QC   27 B-C5
Jonathan's Pond NL   36 A7
Jonathan's Pond NL
  37 A5-6
Jonathan's Pond NL   38 F7
Jonchée, lac QC   39 D5
Jones ON   13 E6
Jones ON   16 D2
Jones Falls ON   21 D7
Jones Sound NU   42 C4-5
Jonquière QC   28 C5
Jordan ON   19 C8
Jordan ON   20 E7
Jordan Bay NS   33 F3
Jordan Falls NS   33 E3
Jordan Lake MB   12 C8
Jordan Lake MB   15 C2
Jordan Lake NS   33 E3
Jordan River BC   2 F3
Jordan River NS   33 E3
Jordan River ON   21 C-D4
Jordan River SK   11 B6
Jordan Station ON   19 C8
Jordan Station ON   20 E7
Jordanville NS   34 F5
Joseph, lac NL   40 E7
Joseph, pointe QC   30 A6-7
Josephburg AB   6 A6
Josephburg AB   8 C7

Joseph Henry, Cape NU
  42 A5
Joseph Lake NL   40 E7
Jourimain, île NB   35 E2-3
Jourimain Island NB
  35 E2-3
Journois NL   36 C2
Joussard AB   9 E4
Joutel QC   17 B8
Joutel QC   23 A4
Joy, Mount YT   4 B5
Joy Bay QC   40 B5
Joy Bay QC   41 D8
Joyceville ON   21 D7
J.T. Cheeseman PP NL
  36 D1
Juan de Fuca, détroit de BC
  2 F2-3
Juan de Fuca, Strait of BC
  2 F3
Juan de Fuca PP BC   2 F3
Juan Perez Sound BC
  1 B-C2
Jubilee Island MB   13 A5
Jubilee Lake NL   36 C7
Jubilee Lake NL   37 C5
Jude Island NL   36 E7
Jude Island NL   37 E5
Judes Point PE   35 A2
Judge Daly Promontory NU
  42 A5
Judique NS   34 D5
Judith Island NT   5 F7
Judson AB   7 E6
Juillet, lac QC   39 A3-4
Julia Bay ON   18 B2
Jumonville, lac QC   26 A6
Jumpers Brook NL   36 A6
Jumpers Brook NL   37 A-B4
Junction Brook NL 36 A3-4
Junction Brook NL   37 A2
Junction Brook NL   38 F3
Junction Sheep Range PP
  BC   1 C7
Juniper NB   31 E3-4
Juniper NB   32 A2
Juniper Beach PP BC   1 D8
Juniper Beach PP BC   2 A7
Juniper Beach PP BC   6 D1
Juniper Station NB   31 E4
Juniper Station NB   32 A2
Juno MB   14 E7
Jupiter Bay NT   10 A3
Jura BC   2 D8
Jura BC   6 F1
Juskatla BC   1 A1
Justice MB   13 E2
Justice MB   14 D1-2

K

Kabamichigama Lake ON
  16 E7
Kabamichigama Lake ON
  17 C1
Kabania Lake ON   16 A6
Kabenung Lake ON   17 D3
Kabika River ON   17 B-C7
Kabika River ON   23 A-B1
Kabinakagami Lake ON
  17 C4
Kabinakagami River ON
  17 B-C4
Kabinakagamisis Lake ON
  17 C4
Kabitotikwia River, RNP ON
  16 D6
Kabitotikwia River PNR ON
  16 D6
Kaboni ON   18 C4
Kaegudeck Lake NL
  36 C6-7
Kaegudeck Lake NL
  37 C4-5
Kagawong ON   18 B3
Kagawong, Lake ON
  18 B-C3
Kagianagami Lake ON
  16 C7
Kagiano Lake ON   16 E8
Kagiano Lake ON   17 B2
Kaglik Lake NT   5 B6
Kahnawake SK   11 E7
Kahnawake QC   24 D5-6
Kahnawake QC   27 E1
Kahntah River BC   3 C8
Kahntah River BC   9 C1-2
Kahshe Lake ON   18 E8
Kahshe Lake ON   18 E8
Kahshe Lake ON   21 C1
Kahshe Lake ON   21 C1
Kahwin AB   8 B8
Kaiashk PP ON   16 E5
Kainairiktok Bay NL 39 A6
Kaipokok River NL 39 A5-6
Kakabeka Falls ON   16 F5
Kakabeka Falls ON   40 F1
Kakabeka Falls PP ON
  16 F5
Kakagi Lake ON   13 F6
Kakagi Lake ON   16 E2
Kakiddi Lake BC   3 C3
Kakisa NT   10 E5
Kakisa NT   41 E1
Kakisa Lake NT   10 E5
Kakisa Lake NT   41 E1
Kakisa River NT   10 E-F4
Kakisa River Bridge TP NT
  10 E5-6
Kakwa PP BC   1 A8
Kakwa PP BC   6 A1-2

Kakwa River AB   6 A2
Kakwa Wildland PP AB 6 A2
Kakweiken River BC   2 A1
Kaladar ON   21 C-D5
Kalamalka Lake BC   6 E2
Kaleden BC   6 F2
Kaleida MB   13 F3
Kaleida MB   14 F3
Kaleland AB   8 C8
Kalliecahoolie Lake MB
  13 A5
Kalone Peak BC   1 C4-5
Kalzas River YT   4 B4
Kama Hills, RNP ON   16 E7
Kama Hills, RNP ON   17 C1
Kama Hills PNR ON   16 E7
Kama Hills PNR ON   17 C1
Kamaniskeg Lake ON 21 B4
Kamatsi Lake SK   11 E6
Kamatsi Lake SK   15 D-E1
Kaminak Lake NU   40 A1
Kaministiquia QC   27 E8
Kaminuriak Lake NU 40 A1
Kaminuriak Lake NU 41 E4
Kamiskotia River ON
  17 C-D6
Kamloops BC   2 A8
Kamloops BC   6 D1-2
Kamloops Lake BC   1 E8
Kamloops Lake BC   2 A8
Kamloops Lake BC   6 D1
Kamouraska QC   28 E8
Kamouraska, îles de QC
  28 E8
Kamsack SK   11 D7
Kamsack SK   13 C1
Kamuchawie Lake SK
  12 D7
Kamuchawie Lake SK
  15 D1
Kanaaupscow, rivière QC
  40 D5 E4-5
Kanairiktok River NL 39 A5
Kanairiktok River NL
  39 A-B4
Kananaskis Village AB
  7 B-C2
Kanasuta, rivière QC 23 D2
Kanata ON   21 B7
Kanata ON   24 D7
Kandahar SK   11 C6 D5-6
Kane MB   13 F3
Kane MB   14 F4
Kangiqiniq (Rankin Inlet)
  NU   40 A1-2
Kangiqiniq (Rankin Inlet)
  NU   41 E5
Kangiqsualujjuaq QC 40 C6
Kangiqsujuaq QC   40 C6
Kangiqsujuaq QC   41 D-E8
Kangiqtugaapik (Clyde
  River) NU   41 A8
Kangiqtugaapik (Clyde
  River) NU   42 E7
Kangirsuk QC   40 B-C5
Kano Inlet BC   1 B1
Kaotisinimigo Lake ON
  22 C1
Kapikik Lake ON   13 D7
Kapikik Lake ON   16 B3
Kapikog Lake ON   18 D-E7
Kapikotongwa River ON
  16 C7
Kapikotongwa River ON
  17 A1-2
Kapiskau River ON 40 E2-3
Kapiskong Lake ON   17 D6
Kapkichi Lake ON   16 B4-5
Kap-Kig-Iwan PP ON 17 D7
Kap-Kig-Iwan PP ON 23 A7
Kaposvar Creek SK 11 D-E7
Kapuskasing ON   17 C8
Kapuskasing ON   40 F1
Kapuskasing Lake ON
  17 C-D5
Kapuskasing River ON
  17 B5
Kapuskasing River ON
  17 C5
Kapusta Lake MB   12 A8
Kapusta Lake MB   15 A3
Karagamac, lac QC 24 A5-6
Karagamac, lac QC 25 F5-6
Karagamac, lac QC   27 B1
Karalash Corners ON   17 F4
Karloske River MB 15 E5-6
Karlstad AB   8 A8
Kars ON   21 B8
Kars ON   24 E2
Karsakuwigamak Lake MB
  12 D8
Karsakuwigamak Lake MB
  15 D3
Karsdale NS   32 F4-5
Karsdale NS   33 C2
Kasabonika Lake NU   41 F3
Kaipokok River NL   39 A5-6
Kashabowie ON   16 F4
Kashabowie ON   17 D8
Kashabowie PP ON
  16 E4-5 F4-5
Kashagawigamog Lake ON
  21 C3
Kashaweogama Lake ON
  16 C-D4
Kashegaba Lake ON   18 C7
Kashishibog Lake ON 16 D5
Kashwakamak Lake ON
  21 C5-6
Kaskattama River MB
  15 D7
Kaskattama River MB
  40 C-D1
Kaskawulsh River YT   4 E2
Kaslo BC   6 E3

Kasmere Lake MB   12 A7
Kasmere Lake MB   15 A2
Kasshabog Lake ON 21 D4
Katannilik, parc territorial
  NU   40 A5
Katannilik TP NU   40 A5
Katannilik TP NU   41 D8
Katepwa Beach SK   11 E6
Katepwa Point PP SK   11 E6
Katherine SK   11 F2
Kathleen AB   9 E3-4
Kathleen Lake YT   4 E2-3
Kathryn AB   6 D5-6
Kathryn AB   7 B4
Katimik Lake MB   13 B2-3
Katrime MB   13 E2-3
Katrime MB   14 D3
Katrine ON   18 C6
Katrine ON   21 A1
Katrine ON   22 F1
Kattawagami Lake ON
  17 B7
Kattawagami River ON
  17 A7
Kavaksuatilik Island NU
  39 A6
Kavanagh AB   6 B6
Kavanagh AB   8 D6
Kawagama Lake ON   21 B3
Kawartha Highlands,
  réserve récréative
  provinciale de ON
  21 C-D3
Kawartha Highlands
  Provincial Recreation
  Reserve ON   21 C3
Kawartha Lakes ON
  20 A-B8
Kawartha Lakes ON
  21 C3
Kawartha Lakes ON
  21 D2-3
Kawartha Park ON   21 D3
Kawawachikamach QC
  39 A2
Kawawachikamach QC
  40 D6
Kawawaymog Lake ON
  22 E2
Kawaweogama Lake ON
  13 E8
Kawaweogama Lake ON
  16 D5
Kaweenakumik Lake MB
  13 B2-3
Kawene ON   13 F8
Kawene ON   16 E4
Kawigamog Lake ON
  18 B6-7 C7
Kawinogans River ON
  13 D8
Kawinogans River ON
  16 B4
Kawnipi Lake ON   16 F4
Kaybob AB   8 A2
Kay Point YT   5 B3
Kayville SK   11 F5
Kazabazua QC   22 E7
Kazabazua QC   24 C1-2
Kazabazua, rivière QC
  22 E-F7
Kazabazua, rivière QC
  24 C1
Kazan Lake SK   9 E8
Kazan Lake SK   12 E3
Kazan River NU   41 D-E4
Kazchek Lake BC   3 F6
Keady ON   18 F5
Keady ON   20 A4
Kearney ON   21 A1-2
Kearney ON   21 A2
Kearney ON   22 F1-2
Kearns ON   17 D8
Kearns ON   23 E1
Keating, lac QC   39 A2
Keatley ON   11 B4
Keats Island BC   1 F6-7
Keats Island BC   2 D4
Kebaowek QC   17 E8
Kebaowek QC   22 C2
Kechika Ranges BC   3 B4 C4-5
Kechika River BC   3 B4 C5
Kecil Lake ON   18 A3
Kedgwick NB   29 E5
Kedgwick NB   31 B3-4
Kedgwick, RF of NB
  29 D-E4
Kedgwick River NB   29 E4
Kedgwick River NB   31 B2
Kedgwick River NB   31 B3
Kedgwick River NB   31 B3
Kedgwick, unité provinciale
  d'aménagement de la
  faune NB   31 B3
Kedgwick Game Refuge NB
  29 E4
Kedgwick Provincial WMA
  NB   31 A-B3
Keefe Lake SK   12 C5
Keefers BC   1 E8
Keefers BC   2 A7
Keele Range YT   5 D1-2
Keele River NT   4 A-B7
Keelor Lake ON   18 A2
Keels NL   37 B7
Keene ON   21 D3
Keeper River ON   13 C-D5
Keeper River ON   16 A-B1
Keeseekoose SK   11 C7
Keeseekoose SK   13 C1
Keeseekoowenin MB 11 E8

Keeseekoowenin MB
  13 E1-2
Keeseekoowenin MB 14 C1
Keewatin ON   13 F5
Keewatin ON   14 E8
Keewatin ON   16 D1
Keewatin River MB 12 D7-8
Kee-way-win ON   13 B6-7
Keezhik Lake ON   16 B6
Kegaska QC   39 F5
Kegaska, lac QC   39 E-F5
Keg Lake SK   12 E6
Keg River AB   9 C3
Keg River AB   9 C3
Kegworth SK   11 E6-7
Keho Lake AB   6 E6
Keho Lake AB   7 D5
Keith Arm NT   41 C1
Keith Island NT   10 D8
Keith Lake SK   12 E5
Kejick ON   13 F5
Kejick (Iskutewizaagegan)
  ON   14 E8
Kejick (Iskutewizaagegan)
  ON   16 D1
Kejimkujik, LHN NS
  33 D2-3
Kejimkujik, PN NS   33 D3
Kejimkujik (annexe côtière),
  PN NS   33 E4-5
Kejimkujik Lake NS   33 D3
Kejimkujik NHS NS 33 D2-3
Kejimkujik NP NS   33 D3
Kejimkujik NP (seaside
  adjunct) NS   33 E4-5
Kekek, rivière QC
  23 D8 E7-8
Kekek, rivière QC   25 A2
Kekek, rivière QC   26 E-F2
Kekuli Bay PP BC   6 E2
Keld MB   14 B1
Keldon ON   20 B5
Kelfield SK   6 C8
Kelfield SK   11 C3
Kellet MB   15 C5
Kellett Strait NT   42 C2
Kelley Lake NT   10 B3
Keller Lake SK   12 E4
Kelley Cove NS   33 E1
Kelliher SK   11 D6
Kelloe MB   11 E8
Kelloe MB   13 E1
Kelly QC   29 D8
Kelly QC   30 D1
Kelly QC   31 A7
Kelly Lake BC   1 D8
Kelly Lake BC   2 A6
Kelly Lake BC   3 F8
Kelly Lake BC   9 E-F2
Kelly Lake NT   5 F7
Kellys Corner ON   21 A5-6
Kellys Cross PE   32 B8
Kellys Cross PE   34 C1
Kellys Cross PE   35 E4
Kelowna BC   6 E2
Kelp Point BC   1 B2
Kelsey AB   6 B6
Kelsey AB   8 D7
Kelsey MB   15 E4
Kelsey Bay BC   1 E5
Kelsey Bay BC   2 B1
Kelsey Creek MB   15 C6
Kelsey Lake MB   11 A-B7
Kelsey Lake MB   13 A1
Kelso SK   11 E7
Kelso SK   13 E1
Kelso CA ON   19 B7
Kelso CA ON   20 D6
Kelstern SK   11 E4
Kelvin ON   19 C6
Kelvin ON   20 E5
Kelvington SK   11 C6
Kelvin Grove PE   35 D3
Kelvin Island BC   16 D6
Kelwood MB   13 E2
Kelwood MB   14 C2
Kemano BC   1 B4
Kemble ON   18 E-F5
Kemble ON   20 A4
Kemnay MB   11 E8
Kemnay MB   13 E2
Kemnay MB   14 E1
Kemp River AB   9 C3
Kemp River AB   9 C3
Kempt NS   33 D3
Kempt, lac QC   25 C5
Kempt, rivière QC   29 D6
Kemptown NS   33 A6-7
Kemptown NS   34 E2-3
Kempt Shore NS   32 E7
Kempt Shore NS   33 B5
Kempt Shore NS   34 F1
Kemptville NS   33 D3
Kemptville ON   21 B8
Kemptville ON   24 E2
Kemptville Creek ON 21 C8
Kemptville Creek ON
  24 E-F2
Kenabeek ON   17 D-E7
Kenabeek ON   23 E1
Kenamu River NL   39 B-C6
Kendal ON   20 C8
Kendal SK   11 E6
Kendall, Cape NU   40 A3
Kendall, Cape NU   41 D6
Kendall Island BC   5 A4
Kendall Island NMBS NT
  5 A3-4

Keeseekoowenin MB
  13 E1-2
Keeseekoowenin MB 14 C1
Keeseekoowenin MB 14 E8
Keewatin ON   14 E8
Keewatin ON   16 D1
Keewatin River MB 12 D7-8
Kee-way-win ON   13 B6-7
Keezhik Lake ON   16 B6
Kegaska QC   39 F5
Kegaska, lac QC   39 E-F5
Keg Lake SK   12 E6
Keg River AB   9 C3
Keg River AB   9 C3
Kenilworth ON   20 C5
Kenmore ON   24 E3
Kennaway ON   21 B3
Kennebecasis River NB
  32 C-D4
Kennebec Lake ON 21 C5-6
Kennedy SK   11 E7
Kennedy, lac QC   38 A1
Kennedy, Mount   1 D5
Kennedy, Mount BC   2 A2
Kennedy, passage NU
  42 A5
Kennedy Bog PP BC   1 F5
Kennedy Bog PP BC   2 E1
Kennedy Channel NU 42 A5
Kennedy Lake BC   1 F5
Kennedy Lake BC   2 E1-2
Kennedy Lake PP BC   1 F5
Kennedy Lake PP BC 2 E1-2
Kennedy Lakes, APP NB
  31 D5
Kennedy Lakes PPA NB
  31 D5
Kennedy Lakes Wilderness,
  ZCP NB   31 D4-5
Kennedy Lakes Wilderness
  PCA NB   31 D4-5
Kennedy River BC   2 A8
Kennetcook NS   32 E8
Kennetcook NS   33 B5-6
Kennetcook NS   34 F1
Kennetcook River NS
  32 D-E8
Kennetcook River NS
  33 B5-6
Kennetcook River NS
  34 F1-2
Kenney, Mount BC   3 F3
Kenney Dam BC   1 B6
Kennisis Lake ON   21 B2
Kennisis Lake ON   21 B3
Kenny Forest, RNP ON
  17 F8
Kenny Forest, RNP ON
  22 C1
Kenny Forest PNR ON 17 F8
Kenny Forest PNR ON
  22 C1
Keno YT   4 A-B4
Kénogami, lac QC   28 C5
Kenogami Lake ON   17 D7
Kenogami River ON   17 A4
Kenogami River ON
  17 A3-4
Kenogami River ON   40 F2
Kenogamissi Lake ON
  17 D6
Kenora ON   13 F5
Kenora ON   14 E8
Kenora ON   16 D1
Kenosee Lake SK   11 E7
Ken Reid CA ON   20 A8
Ken Reid CA ON   21 D2
Kensington PE   32 A8
Kensington PE   34 C1
Kensington PE   35 D3
Kensington, lac QC   24 B2
Kensington, lac QC   25 F2
Kent BC   1 F8
Kent BC   2 D6-7
Kent Bridge ON   19 D3
Kent Bridge ON   20 F2
Kent Junction NB   31 E7
Kent Junction NB   32 A5
Kent Lake NB   31 E7
Kent Lake NB   32 A5-6
Kenton MB   11 E8
Kenton MB   13 E1
Kent Peninsula NU   41 B3
Kent Peninsula NU   42 F2
Kentucky-Alleyne PP BC
  2 C8
Kentucky-Alleyne PP BC
  6 E1
Kentvale ON   17 F4
Kentville NS   32 E6-7
Kentville NS   33 B4
Kenville MB   11 C7-8
Kenville MB   13 B1
Kenyon Lake MB   15 F6
Kenzieville NS   34 F4
Keoma AB   6 D6
Keoma AB   7 B4
Kepenkeck Lake NL   36 C7
Kepenkeck Lake NL   37 C5
Kepimits Lake NL   39 C3
Kerbodot, lac QC   39 B1
Keremeos BC   6 F1
Keremeos Columns PP BC
  6 F1-2
Kerrobert SK   6 C8
Kerrobert SK   11 C3
Kerry MB   14 E2
Kersey AB   8 B7
Kersley BC   1 B7
Kerwood ON   19 C3-4
Kerwood ON   20 E2-3
Kesagami Lake ON   17 A7
Kesagami Lake ON   40 F3
Kesagami PP ON   17 A7
Kesagami PP ON   40 E2-3
Keseechewun Lake SK
  12 A6
Keseechewun Lake SK
  15 A1
Keseekoose SK   13 C1

Keswick River NB   31 F4
Keswick River NB   32 B2
Ketchen SK   11 C6-7
Ketch Harbour NS   33 C6
Ketsall River BC   4 F3
Kettleby ON   20 B-C7
Kettleby ON   21 E1
Kettle Cove NL   38 E6
Kettle Creek ON   19 D4
Kettle Creek ON   20 E-F4
Kettle Lake AB   9 E5
Kettle Lakes PP ON   17 C6
Kettle Point ON   19 B3
Kettle Point ON   19 B3
Kettle Point ON   20 E2
Kettle Point ON   20 E2
Kettle Rapids MB   15 D5
Kettle River BC   6 F2
Kettle River NB   15 D8
Kettle River NB   15 E5
Kettle River PRA BC   6 F2
Kettle Stones PP MB 11 C8
Kettle Stones PP MB   13 C2
Kettle Valley BC   6 F2
Kevisville AB   8 F5
Key MB   11 C7
Key SK   13 C1
Keyano QC   40 E5
Keyes MB   14 D2
Key Lake Mine SK   12 D5
Key River ON   18 B6
Keyser ON   19 C3-4
Keyser ON   20 E2-3
Keystone AB   8 D5
Kezik Lake ON   16 B4
Khartum ON   21 B5
Khedive SK   11 F5-6
Khutzeymateen Inlet BC
  3 F3
Khutzeymateen PP BC   3 F3
Khutzeymateen Valley
  Grizzly Bear Sanctuary
  BC   3 F3
Kiamika QC   24 B3
Kiamika QC   25 F3
Kiamika, réservoir QC
  24 A3
Kiamika, réservoir QC
  25 E3
Kianuko PP BC   6 F4
Kianuko PP BC   7 F1
Kicking Horse Pass BC 6 D4
Kicking Horse Pass BC 7 A1
Kicking Horse Pass NHS AB
  7 A1
Kikiak (Rigolet) NL 39 B6-7
Kikino AB   6 A6
Kikino AB   8 B7
Kikino AB   9 F6
Kikino AB   9 F6
Kikiwissi, lac QC   22 B3
Kikkertavak Island NL
  39 A6-7
Kikomun Creek PP BC
  6 F4-5
Kikomun Creek PP BC   7 F2
Kikupegh Pond NL   36 C5
Kikupegh Pond NL   37 C3
Kilbride NL   19 B7
Kilbride NL   20 D6
Kilburn NB   31 E3
Kilburn NB   32 A1
Kilby PP BC   1 F7-8
Kilby PP BC   2 D-E6
Kildala Arm BC   1 A3-4
Kildala River BC   1 A3-4
Kildare PE   34 A1
Kildare PE   35 B2
Kildare, Cape PE   34 A1
Kildare, Cape PE   35 B2
Kildare Capes PE   34 A1
Kildare Capes PE   35 B2
Kildare River PE   35 B2
Kildonan BC   1 F6
Kildonan BC   2 E2
Kilekale Lake NT   5 D8
Kilian Island NU   41 A3
Kilian Island NU   42 F2
Killala Lake ON   17 B2
Killala Lake ON   17 C2
Killaloe ON   21 A5
Killaloe ON   22 F5
Killaly SK   11 D6-7
Killam AB   6 B6-7
Killam AB   8 D-E8
Killam AB   8 B1
Killarney MB   13 F2
Killarney MB   14 F1-2
Killarney ON   17 F8
Killarney ON   18 B4
Killarney ON   18 B4
Killarney ON   18 B4
Killarney Beach BC   6 E2
Killarney Coast and Islands
  PP ON   18 B4
Killarney Coast and Islands
  PP ON   18 B5
Killarney Lakelands and
  Headwaters PP ON
  17 F6-7
Killarney Lakelands and
  Headwaters PP ON
  18 B5
Killarney PP ON   17 F6
Killarney PP ON   18 B4
Killarney PP ON 18 B4-5
Killbear PP ON   18 D6-7
Killdeer SK   11 F4
Killiniq QC   40 B6
Killiniq Island NL   40 B6
Killock Bay SK   12 B6
Kilmar QC   24 C4

Kil-Lak

Kilmuir PE 34 C3
Kilmuir PE 35 F6
Kilsyth ON 18 F5
Kilsyth ON 20 A4
Kilwinning SK 11 B4
Kilworth ON 19 C4
Kilworth ON 20 E3
Kilworthy ON 18 E8
Kilworthy ON 21 C1
Kimball AB 7 F5
Kimberley BC 6 F4
Kimberley BC 7 E1
Kimberley ON 18 F6
Kimberley ON 20 A-B5
Kimiwan Lake AB 9 E4
Kimmirut (Lake Harbour) NU 40 B5-6
Kimowin River SK 9 D8
Kimowin River SK 12 D3
Kimsquit BC 1 B4
Kimsquit River BC 1 B4
Kinaskan Lake BC 3 C3
Kinaskan Lake PP BC 3 C3
Kinbasket Lake BC 6 C2-3
Kinbasket Lake BC 8 F1
Kin Beach PP BC 2 C2
Kinbrook Island PP AB 6 E6-7
Kinbrook Island PP AB 7 C6-7
Kinburn ON 19 A4
Kinburn ON 20 C3
Kinburn ON 21 A7
Kinburn ON 24 D1
Kincaid SK 11 F4
Kincardine NB 31 E3
Kincardine NB 32 A1
Kincardine ON 20 B3
Kindakun Point BC 1 B1
Kindersley SK 6 D8
Kindersley SK 11 D2
Kingaok (Bathurst Inlet) NU 41 C3
King Christian Island NU 42 C3
King City ON 20 C7
King City ON 21 E1
Kingcome Inlet BC 1 D4-5
Kingcome Inlet BC 1 D5
Kingcome Inlet BC 2 A1
Kingcome River BC 1 D5
Kingfisher BC 6 E2
Kingfisher Lake ON 13 B8
Kingfisher Lake ON 13 B8
King George, Mount BC 6 E4
King George, Mount BC 7 C2
King George IV Ecological Reserve NL 36 C3
King George IV Ecological Reserve NL 37 C1
King George IV Lake NL 36 C3
King George IV Lake NL 37 C1
King George Islands NU 40 C-D4
King George Islands NU 41 F8
King Island BC 1 C4
King Kirkland ON 17 D7
King Kirkland ON 23 D1
Kingkown Inlet BC 1 A-B2
King Lake NT 10 E8
Kingman AB 6 B6
Kingman AB 8 D7
Kingman's NL 37 F8
Kingnait Fiord NU 42 F8
King Peak YT 4 E1
King Point YT 5 B3
Kingross NS 34 B6
Kingsboro PE 34 B4
Kingsboro PE 35 D8
Kingsbridge ON 20 C2-3
Kingsburg NS 33 D5
Kingsbury QC 24 D8
Kingsbury QC 27 E4
Kings Castle PP PE 34 C-D3 C-D4
Kings Castle PP PE 35 F6-7
Kingsclear NB 32 C2
Kingsclear (IR) NB 32 C2-3
Kingscote Lake ON 21 B3
King's Cove NL 37 B7
King's Cove NL 38 E5
Kingscroft QC 27 F4
Kingsey Falls QC 27 D4
Kingsford SK 11 F6-7
Kingsgate BC 6 F4
Kingsgate BC 7 F1
Kingsley MB 14 F3
Kingsley NB 31 F4
Kingsley NB 32 B2-3
Kingsley Lake SK 12 B7
Kingsley Lake SK 15 B1
Kingsmere Lake SK 11 A4
King's Point NL 38 E4
King's Point NL 39 F8
Kingsport NS 32 E7
Kingsport NS 33 B4-5
Kingston NB 32 D4
Kingston NB 33 A1
Kingston NL 37 D7-8
Kingston NS 32 E6
Kingston NS 33 B3
Kingston ON 21 D6-7
Kingston ON 21 E6-7
Kingston PE 34 C2
Kingston PE 35 E4
Kingston Lake SK 12 B6
Kingston Lake SK 15 B1
Kingston Mountain YT 4 D3
Kingsvale BC 2 C7-8
Kingsville NS 34 D6
Kingsville ON 19 E1-2
Kingwell NL 36 D8
Kingwell NL 37 D6
King William Island NU 41 B4
King William Island NU 42 F3-4
Kinhuron ON 20 B3
Kinikinik AB 8 B4
Kinistin SK 11 C6
Kinistino SK 11 B5
Kinkora ON 19 B5
Kinkora ON 20 D4
Kinkora PE 32 B8
Kinkora PE 34 C1-2
Kinkora PE 35 D3
Kinley SK 11 C4
Kinloch Lake ON 16 B4
Kinloss ON 20 B3
Kinlough ON 20 B3
Kinmount ON 21 C2-3
Kinnear, rivière NB 35 E1
Kinnear River NB 35 E1
Kinnear's Mills QC 27 C5
Kinngait (Cape Dorset) NU 40 A4
Kinngait (Cape Dorset) NU 41 D7
Kinojévis, lac QC 23 E3
Kinojévis, rivière QC 23 D3
Kinojévis, rivière QC 23 E3
Kinoosao SK 12 D7
Kinoosao SK 15 D1
Kinosota MB 13 D3
Kinosota MB 14 B3
Kinross PE 35 E6
Kinsale ON 20 C8
Kinsale ON 21 E2
Kinsella AB 6 B7
Kinsella AB 11 B1
Kinsman Corner NS 32 E6
Kinsman Corner NS 33 B4
Kinsman Lake MB 12 B8
Kinsman Lake MB 15 B3
Kintail ON 20 C3
Kintore NB 31 E3
Kintore NB 32 A1
Kintore ON 19 C5
Kintore ON 20 E4
Kinusisipi MB 13 A3
Kinuso AB 9 E4
Kinwow Bay MB 13 C3-4
Kinwow Bay PP Reserve MB 13 C3-4
Kioshkokwi Lake ON 22 E2
Kiosk ON 17 F8
Kiosk ON 22 E2
Kiowana Beach ON 18 F6
Kiowana Beach ON 20 A5
Kipahigan Lake MB 12 E7
Kipahigan Lake MB 15 E1
Kipawa QC 17 E-F8
Kipawa QC 22 C2
Kipawa, lac QC 17 E8
Kipawa, lac QC 22 B2
Kipawa, ZEC QC 22 B3
Kipling SK 11 E7
Kippase BC 1 E4
Kippen ON 19 B4
Kippen ON 20 D3
Kippens NL 36 C2
Kirby ON 21 E3
Kirbys Corner ON 17 F4
Kirkcaldy AB 6 E6
Kirkcaldy AB 7 D5
Kirk Cove ON 21 C6
Kirkella MB 11 E7
Kirkella MB 13 E1
Kirkfield ON 20 A8
Kirkfield ON 21 D2
Kirkhill NS 32 D7
Kirkhill NS 33 A4
Kirkland QC 24 D5
Kirkland QC 27 E1
Kirkland Creek YT 4 D3
Kirkland Lake ON 17 D7
Kirkland Lake ON 23 D1
Kirkness Lake ON 13 D6
Kirkness Lake ON 16 B2
Kirkpatrick Lake AB 6 C7
Kirkpatrick Lake AB 11 C1
Kirkpatrick Lake ON 17 F5
Kirkton ON 19 B4
Kirkton ON 20 D3
Kirriemuir AB 6 C8
Kirriemuir AB 11 C2
Kisbey SK 11 F7
Kisgegas Peak BC 3 E4
Kishikas Lake ON 16 A4
Kishikas River ON 13 B-C7
Kiskatinaw PP BC 3 E8
Kiskatinaw PP BC 9 E2
Kiskatinaw River BC 3 E-F8
Kiskatinaw River BC 9 E-F2
Kiski Lake MB 15 F3
Kiskissink, lac QC 28 D4
Kiskitto Lake MB 13 A3
Kiskittogisu Lake MB 13 A3
Kispiox BC 3 F4
Kispiox River BC 3 E4
Kisseynew Lake MB 12 F7
Kisseynew Lake MB 15 F1
Kississing Lake MB 12 F7
Kississing Lake MB 15 E-F1
Kississing River MB 12 E7
Kississing River MB 15 E1-2
Kistigan Lake MB 15 F6
Kitamaat Village BC 1 A3-4
Kitchener BC 6 F4
Kitchener BC 7 F1
Kitchener ON 19 B6
Kitchener ON 20 D5
Kitchener Lake BC 3 D4
Kitchie Lake ON 16 A7-8
Kitigan ON 17 B5
Kitigan-Zibi QC 22 D7-8
Kitigan-Zibi QC 24 B2
Kitigan-Zibi QC 25 F2
Kitimat BC 1 A3
Kitimat Arm BC 1 A3
Kitimat Ranges BC 1 A-B3
Kitkatla BC 1 A2
Kitkiata Inlet BC 1 A3
Kitlope Heritage Conservancy Provincial Area BC 1 B4
Kitlope River BC 1 B4
Kitsakie SK 12 F5
Kitsault River BC 3 E3
Kitscoty AB 6 B7-8
Kitscoty AB 11 B2
Kitseguecla (Gitsegukla) BC 3 F4
Kitson Island PMP BC 1 A2-3
Kitsumkalum Lake BC 3 F3-4
Kitsumkalum PP BC 3 F3
Kitsumkalum River BC 3 F3
Kitsumkaylum BC 1 A3
Kitsumkaylum BC 3 F3
Kittigazuit NT 5 B5
Kitty Coleman PP BC 2 C2
Kitwancool BC 3 F4
Kitwanga BC 3 F4
Kitwanga Fort NHS BC 3 F3-4
Kitwanga Mountain PP BC 3 F3-4
Kivimaa-Moonlight Bay SK 6 A8
Kivimaa-Moonlight Bay SK 11 A3
Kiyiu Lake SK 11 D3
Klappan River BC 3 C3
Klashwun Point BC 1 A1
Klastline River BC 3 C3
Klawli River BC 3 F6
Klaza, Mount YT 4 C2-3
Klaza River YT 4 C2-3
Kleanza Creek PP BC 3 F4
Kleczkowski, lac QC 39 E4
Kledo Creek PP BC 3 B6
Kleefeld MB 13 F4
Kleefeld MB 14 E5
Kleena Kleene BC 1 C6
Kleinburg ON 19 A7-8
Kleinburg ON 20 C6-7
Klemka, lac QC 28 A7
Klemtu BC 1 C3
Klewnuggit Inlet PMP BC 1 A3
Klinaklini River BC 1 C-D5
Klinkit Creek BC 3 A2-3
Klinkit Creek BC 4 F5-6
Klin-se-za PP BC 3 E7
Klondike Historic Complex NHS YT 4 A2
Klondike River YT 4 A2-3
Kloo Lake YT 4 D2
Klotassin River YT 4 C2
Klotz, Mount YT 5 F2
Klotz Lake ON 16 D8
Klotz Lake ON 17 B3
Klua Lakes PPA BC 3 C7
Klua Lakes PPA BC 9 B1
Kluane YT 4 D2
Kluane, PN et réserve YT 4 E1-2
Kluane Lake YT 4 D2
Kluane NP and Reserve YT 4 D1-2 D-E2
Kluane Ranges YT 4 D1-2 D-E2
Kluane River YT 4 C-D2
Kluane Wildlife Sanctuary YT 4 D1
Kluane Wildlife Sanctuary YT 4 D2
Kluane Wildlife Sanctuary YT 4 E2-3
Kluane/Wrangell-St. Elias/ Glacier Bay/Tatshenshini-Alsek PN 4 F2-3
Kluane/Wrangell-St. Elias/ Glacier Bay/Tatshenshini-Alsek YT 4 E1-2
Kluayetz Creek BC 3 D4
Klueys Bay ON 18 E8
Klueys Bay ON 21 C1
Klukshu YT 4 E3
Klusha Creek YT 4 D3
Kluskoil Lake PP BC 1 B6
Kluskus BC 1 B6
Klutlan Creek YT 4 C-D1
Kluziai Island NT 10 C8
Kneehill AB 7 A5
Kneehills Creek AB 6 C5 D5-6
Kneehills Creek AB 7 A4-5
Knee Lake MB 15 F5
Knee Lake SK 12 E4
Knee Lake SK 12 E4
Knewstubb Lake BC 1 B6
Knife Lake ON 13 A7
Knight Inlet BC 1 E5
Knight Inlet BC 2 A1
Knights Cove NL 37 B7
Knightville NB 32 C5
Knorr Creek YT 5 F4-5
Knorr Range YT 5 F4
Knowlesville NB 31 E3-4
Knowlesville NB 32 A1-2
Knowlton QC 24 E8
Knowlton QC 27 F3
Knox, Cape BC 1 A1
Knox Lake NL 39 A3
Knox Lake ON 16 B2
Knoydart NS 34 D4
Knutsford BC 2 B8
Knutsford BC 6 E1
Knutsford PE 32 A7
Knutsford PE 35 C1
Koch Creek BC 6 F3
Koch Island NU 41 B7
Koch Island NU 42 E-F6
Kogaluc, rivière QC 40 C4
Kogaluc, rivière QC 41 E8
Kogaluk Bay QC 40 C4
Kogaluk Bay QC 41 F7-8
Kogaluk River NL 40 D7
Kohler ON 19 C7
Kohler ON 20 E6
Kohn Lake SK 12 A6
Kohn Lake SK 15 A1
Koidern YT 4 C1
Kokanee Creek PP BC 6 F3
Kokanee Glacier PP BC 6 E-F3
Kokish BC 1 E4
Koko Lake ON 18 A8
Koksilah River PP BC 2 F4
Koksoak, rivière QC 40 C6
Kola MB 11 E8
Kola MB 13 E1
Kolbec NS 32 C8
Kolbec NS 34 D1
Komakuk Beach YT 5 A2
Komarno MB 13 E3-4
Komarno MB 14 C5
Komoka ON 19 C4
Komoka ON 20 E3
Komoka PP ON 19 C4
Komoka PP ON 20 E3
Kondiaronk, lac QC 22 C6
Koocanusa, Lake BC 7 F2
Kookatsoon Lake Territorial Recreation Site YT 4 E3-4
Koona Lake MB 12 A7
Koona Lake MB 15 A2
Kootenay, PN BC 6 D4
Kootenay, PN BC 7 B1
Kootenay Bay BC 6 F3-4
Kootenay Lake BC 6 E3-4 F4
Kootenay Lake (Davis Creek) PP BC 6 E3
Kootenay Lake (Lost Ledge) PP BC 6 E3-4
Kootenay Lake (Midge Creek) PP BC 6 F4
Kootenay NP BC 6 D4
Kootenay NP BC 7 B1
Kootenay Pass BC 6 F3-4
Kootenay Ranges BC 6 D-E4
Kootenay Ranges BC 7 B-C1
Kootenay River BC 6 F3
Kootenay River BC 6 F4-5
Kootenay River BC 7 E-F2
Kopka River ON 16 D5
Kopka River PP ON 16 D5
Kopp's Kove SK 11 B3
Kormak ON 17 E5
Kortright CA ON 19 A8
Kortright CA ON 20 C6-7
Kortright CA ON 21 F1
Koshlong Lake ON 21 C3
Koskaecodde Lake NL 36 D6-7
Koskaecodde Lake NL 37 D4-5
Kotaneelee River NT 10 E-F2
Kotcho Lake BC 3 B7
Kotcho Lake BC 9 A-B1
Kotcho Lake Village Site PP BC 3 B8
Kotcho Lake Village Site PP BC 9 B1-2
Kouchibouguac NB 31 D7
Kouchibouguac, baie de NB 31 D8
Kouchibouguac, PN NB 31 D8
Kouchibouguac Bay NB 31 D8
Kouchibouguac NP NB 31 D8
Kouchibouguac River NB 31 D7-8
Kouchibouguasis River NB 31 E7
Kouchibouguasis River NB 32 A5
Koukdjuak River NU 40 A5
Koukdjuak River NU 41 C8
Koukdjuak River NU 42 F7
Kovik Bay QC 40 B4
Kovik Bay QC 41 E7
Krakow AB 8 C8
Kronau SK 11 E5-6
Kronsgart MB 14 F4
Krusenstern, Cape NU 41 B2
Krusenstern, Cape NU 42 F1
Krydor SK 11 B4
Ksi Hlginx BC 3 F3
Kugaluk River NT 5 B5-6
Kugluktuk (Coppermine) NU 41 B2
Kugluktuk (Coppermine) NU 42 F1
Kugmallit Bay NT 5 A5
Kukatush ON 17 D5-6
Kuklok (Bloody Falls) TP NU 41 B-C2
Kuklok (Bloody Falls) TP NU 42 F1
Kukukus Lake ON 13 E7
Kukukus Lake ON 16 D3-4
Kunga Island BC 1 B2
Kunghit Island BC 1 C2
Kuper Island BC 1 F6-7
Kuper Island BC 2 E4
Kuroki SK 11 C6
Kurtzville ON 19 A5
Kurtzville ON 20 C4
Kusawa Lake YT 4 E3
Kusawa Lake Territorial Recreation Site and Campground YT 4 E3
Kushog Lake ON 21 B2
Kustra Lake MB 12 C8
Kustra Lake MB 15 C2
Kutawagan Lake SK 11 D5
Kutcho Creek BC 3 B-C4
Kuujjuaq QC 40 C6
Kuujjuarapik QC 40 D4
Kwadacha PRA BC 3 C5
Kwadacha PWP BC 3 C5-6
Kwadacha River BC 3 C5-6
Kwanta Inlet BC 1 C4
Kwejinne Lake NT 10 B6
Kwokullie Lake BC 3 B8
Kwokullie Lake BC 9 A2
Kyaska Lake SK 12 D6
Kyaska Lake SK 15 D1
Kyklo Creek BC 3 B7-8
Kyklo Creek BC 9 B1-2
Kyle SK 11 D3
Kylemore SK 11 C6
Kynoch ON 18 A1
Kynoch Inlet BC 1 B4
Kyuquot BC 1 E4
Kyuquot Sound BC 1 E4

L

La Baie QC 28 C6
La Baleine QC 28 F7
L'Abbé, lac QC 26 E6
L'Abbé, lac QC 28 C1-2
Labelle NS 33 D4
Labelle QC 24 B4
Labelle QC 25 F4
Labelle, lac QC 24 B4
Labelle, lac QC 25 F4
Laberge, Lake YT 4 D4
La Biche River AB 9 F6
La Biche River AB 12 E-F1
La Biche River YT 10 E1 F2
La Biche River Wildland PP AB 9 F6
La Bostonnais QC 25 C7-8
La Bostonnais QC 28 E3
Labouchere Channel BC 1 C4
Labrador, mer du NL 39 A7-8
Labrador (océan Atlantique), mer du NL 37 A7-8
Labrador (océan Atlantique), mer du NL 38 C6-8
Labrador (océan Atlantique), mer du NL 40 B-C8
Labrador City NL 39 C2
Labrador City NL 40 E6
Labrador Sea NL 39 A7-8
Labrador Sea (Atlantic Ocean) NL 37 A7-8
Labrador Sea (Atlantic Ocean) NL 38 B6-8
Labrador Sea (Atlantic Ocean) NL 40 B7-8
La Branche QC 27 A5-6
Labrecque QC 28 B5
Labrecque, lac QC 28 B5
Labrieville QC 28 A8
Labrieville-Sud QC 29 A1-2
La Broquerie MB 13 F4
La Broquerie MB 14 E6
La Bruère, lac QC 25 A6
La Bruère, lac QC 26 E6
La Bruère, lac QC 28 C1
La Butte Creek AB 9 A6-7
La Butte Creek AB 12 A2
La Butte Creek Wildland PP AB 9 A6-7
La Butte Creek Wildland PP AB 10 F8
La Butte Creek Wildland PP AB 12 A2
Lac, île du QC 39 F6
Lac-à-Beauce QC 25 D7-8
Lac-à-Beauce QC 28 F3
Lacadena SK 11 D3
L'Acadie QC 24 E6
L'Acadie QC 27 E-F2
L'Acadie, rivière QC 24 E6
Lac-à-la-Croix QC 28 C5
Lac-à-la-Tortue QC 24 A7-8
Lac-à-la-Tortue QC 25 E7-8 F7-8
Lac-à-la-Tortue QC 27 B3
Lac-Allard QC 39 E4
Lac-Alouette QC 24 C5
Lac-Alouette QC 27 D1
La Canadienne, pointe ON 16 F8
La Canadienne, pointe ON 17 D2
Lac-au-Sable, ZEC du QC 28 D-E7
Lac-au-Saumon QC 29 C4-5
Lac-aux-Sables QC 24 A8
Lac-aux-Sables QC 25 E8
Lac-aux-Sables QC 27 A3-4 B3-4
Lac-Baker NB 29 F2
Lac-Baker NB 31 C1
Lac-Beauport QC 27 A5-6
Lac-Big-Glace-Bay, RNOM du NS 34 C8
Lac-Bouchette QC 28 C4
Lac-Brébeuf, ZEC du QC 28 D7
Lac Brochet (Northlands) MB 12 B7
Lac Brochet (Northlands) MB 15 B2
Lac-Brome QC 24 E8
Lac-Brome QC 27 F3
Lac-Castagnier QC 23 C5
Lac-Cayamant QC 22 E7
Lac-Cayamant QC 24 B1
Lac-Connelly QC 24 C5
Lac-Connelly QC 27 D1
Lac-Daigle QC 39 E2
Lac-de-la-Boiteuse, ZEC du QC 28 B5-6
Lac-de-l'Achigan QC 24 C5
Lac-de-l'Achigan QC 27 D1
Lac-Delage QC 27 A5
Lac-des-Aigles QC 29 D2
Lac-des-Aigles QC 31 A1
Lac-des-Commissaires QC 25 A8
Lac-des-Commissaires QC 26 F8
Lac-des-Commissaires QC 28 D4
Lac-des-Écorces QC 24 A3
Lac-des-Écorces QC 25 E-F3
Lac-Désert QC 24 B3
Lac-Désert QC 25 F3
Lac-des-Îles QC 22 D8
Lac-des-Îles QC 24 B2
Lac-des-Îles QC 25 F2
Lac-des-Loups QC 21 A7
Lac-des-Loups QC 22 F7
Lac-des-Loups QC 24 C-D1
Lac-des-Plages QC 24 C3
Lac-des-Seize-Îles QC 24 C4
Lac-Drolet QC 27 D6
Lac du Bois PP BC 1 D8
Lac du Bois PP BC 2 A8
Lac du Bois PP BC 6 D1
Lac du Bonnet MB 13 E4-5
Lac du Bonnet MB 14 C6-7
Lac du Bonnet MB 14 D6-7
Lac-du-Cerf QC 22 D8
Lac-du-Cerf QC 24 B2-3
Lac-du-Cerf QC 25 F2-3
Lac-Dufault QC 17 D8
Lac-Dufault QC 23 D2
Lac-Dufresne (Mai) QC 39 D2-3
Lac-Écho QC 24 C5
Lac-Écho QC 27 D1
Lac-Édouard QC 25 C8
Lac-Édouard QC 28 E4
Lac-Etchemin QC 27 C7
Lac-Frontière QC 27 B7-8
Lac-Gatineau QC 22 D8
Lac-Gatineau QC 24 A2
Lac-Gatineau QC 25 E2
Lac-Grosleau QC 24 C3
Lac-Haley, RNOM du NS 33 E3
Lachenaie QC 24 D6
Lachenaie QC 27 E1-2
Lachine QC 24 D5-6
Lachine QC 27 E1
Lac-Humqui QC 29 C4
Lachute QC 24 D5
Lac-John QC 39 A2
Lac-John QC 40 D6
Lac Joseph-Atikonak Wilderness Reserve NL 39 C-D3
Lac-Kénogami, centre touristique du QC 28 C5
Lac la Biche AB 9 F6
Lac la Biche AB 9 F6
Lac la Biche AB 12 F1
Lac la Biche AB 12 F1
Lac-Labrie QC 39 E2
Lac-La Grenouille, LHN du AB 6 A7-8
Lac-La Grenouille, LHN du AB 11 A2
Lac la Hache PP BC 1 C7-8
Lac la Nonne AB 8 B5-6
Lac La Ronge PP SK 12 F5
Lac-Last Mountain, RNF du SK 11 D5
Lac Le Jeune BC 2 B8
Lac Le Jeune BC 6 E1
Lac Le Jeune PP BC 2 B8
Lac Le Jeune PP BC 6 E1
La Cloche Creek ON 18 B3-4
La Cloche Lake ON 18 B3
La Cloche Mountains ON 18 B3-4
La Cloche PP ON 18 B3-4
Laclu ON 13 E-F5
Laclu ON 14 E8
Laclu ON 16 D1
Lac-Manitou-Sud QC 24 C4
Lac-Marois QC 24 C5
Lac-Mégantic QC 27 E6
Lac-Mississippi, réserve naturelle de faune du ON 21 B-C7
Lac-Mississippi, réserve naturelle de faune du ON 24 E1
Lac-Neely, RNOM du SK 11 B6-7
Lac-Noir QC 24 B6
Lac-Noir QC 25 F6
Lac-Noir QC 27 C1-2
Lac-Old Wives, RNOM du SK 11 E4-5
Lacolle QC 24 E6
Lacolle QC 27 F2
Lacombe AB 6 C5-6
Lacombe AB 8 E6
La Conception QC 24 B4
Lac-Opuntia, RNOM du SK 11 C3
La Corey AB 6 A7
La Corey AB 9 F7
La Corey AB 12 F2
La Corne QC 23 D4
Lacoste, lac QC 24 B4
Lacoste, lac QC 25 F4
La Coulee MB 14 E6
La Coupe Dry Dock NHS NB 32 C7
La Coupe Dry Dock NHS NB 35 F1-2
La Course, lac SK 11 C7
La Course, lac SK 13 C1
Lacoursière, lac QC 23 E8
Lacoursière, lac QC 25 A2
Lacoursière, lac QC 26 E-F2
Lac-Paré QC 24 B5
Lac-Paré QC 27 C1
Lac-Poulin QC 27 C6
Lac-Rapide QC 22 B6
Lac-Redberry, RNOM du SK 11 C4
La Crete AB 9 B-C4
Lac-Richardson, RNOM du AB 9 B7
Lac-Richardson, RNOM du AB 12 B2
La Croche QC 25 C7-8
La Croche QC 28 E3
Lacroix, lac QC 26 C-D3
Lacs, rivière des QC 22 B2
Lac-Saguay QC 24 A3
Lac-Saguay QC 25 F3
Lac-Saint-Charles QC 27 A5
Lac-Sainte-Marie QC 22 E7
Lac-Sainte-Marie QC 24 C2
Lac-Ste-Thérèse ON 17 B4
Lac-Saint-François, RNF du QC 24 E4-5
Lac St. François National Wilderness Area QC 24 E4-5
Lac-Saint-Joseph QC 27 A5
Lac-Saint-Paul QC 24 A3
Lac-Saint-Paul QC 25 E3
Lacs-Albanel-Mistassini-et-Waconichi, parc QC 40 F4-5
Lacs-Albanel-Mistassini-et-Waconichi, RF des QC 26 A5
Lac-Sergent QC 27 A4-5
Lacs-Guillaume-Delisle-et-à-l'Eau-Claire, parc QC 40 D4-5
Lac-Simon QC 23 E5
Lac-Simon QC 24 C3
Lac-Spiers, RNF du AB 6 C7
Lac-Spiers, RNF du AB 8 F7-8
Lac-Spiers, RNF du AB 11 C1
Lac-Supérieur QC 24 B4
Lac-Supérieur (projet), aire marine nationale de conservation du ON 17 C-D1
Lac-Supérieur (projet), aire marine nationale de conservation du ON 16 F6-7
Lacs-Waterton, PN des AB 6 F5
Lacs-Waterton, PN des AB 7 F4
Lac-Upper Roussay, RNOM du SK 11 D6-7
Lacusta Lake NT 12 A5
La Dauversière, lac QC 26 B5
Ladder Lake Beach SK 11 A4
Ladle Cove NL 38 E7
La Doré QC 26 D7-8
La Doré QC 28 B3
Ladue River YT 4 B1
La Durantaye QC 27 B6
Lady Cove NL 37 C6-7
Lady Douglas Island BC 1 C3
Lady Evelyn Falls NT 10 E5
Lady Evelyn Falls TP NT 10 E5
Lady Evelyn Lake ON 17 E7
Lady Evelyn-Smoothwater PP ON 17 E7
Lady Franklin Bay NU 42 A5
Lady Grey Lake NT 10 E8
Lady Lake SK 11 C7
Ladysmith BC 1 F6
Ladysmith BC 2 E3-4
Ladysmith QC 22 F7
Ladysmith QC 24 C1
Ladywood MB 13 E4
Ladywood MB 14 D6
Laferté QC 17 C8
Laferté QC 23 C-D3
Laferte River NT 10 D4-5
Laflamme, lac QC 28 B7
Laflamme, rivière QC 23 B-C5
Lafleche SK 11 F4
Lafond AB 6 A7
Lafond AB 11 A1
Lafond Creek AB 9 D4
Lafontaine ON 18 E7
Lafontaine ON 20 A6
Lafontaine QC 24 C5
Laforce QC 17 E8
Laforce QC 22 A3
Laforce QC 23 F3
Laforge-Deux QC 40 D-E5
Lafrenay, lac QC 26 E6
Lafrenay, lac QC 28 B-C1
Lagacéville NB 29 F8
Lagacéville NB 30 F1
Lagacéville NB 31 C7
La Galissonnière, lac QC 39 D4-5
Laganière, lac QC 26 A6
La Garde, lac QC 22 C3
Laggan ON 24 D4
La Glace AB 9 E2
Lagoon City ON 18 F8
Lagoon City ON 20 A7
Lagoon City ON 21 D1
Laguadeloupe QC 27 D6
LaHave NS 33 D4-5
La Have River NS 32 F6
La Have River NS 33 C3-4
La Hêtrière NB 31 F8
La Hêtrière NB 32 B6
La Hune, Cape NL 36 E4
La Hune, Cape NL 37 E2
Laidlaw BC 1 F8
Laidlaw BC 2 D7
Laird SK 11 B4
Laird Island SK 9 A7-8
Laird Island SK 12 A3
La Jannaye, lac QC 39 B1-2
Lajoie, lac QC 25 A4
Lajoie, lac QC 26 F4
Lajord SK 11 E6
Lajoue, lac QC 25 C3
La Justone, lac QC 39 C1
Lake Abitibi Island PP ON 17 C7-8
Lake Alma SK 11 F6
Lake Annis NS 33 E1
Lake Audy MB 14 C1
Lakeburn NB 31 F8
Lakeburn NB 32 B6
Lake Charlotte NS 33 C7
Lake Country BC 6 E2
Lake Cowichan BC 2 E3
Lake Creek YT 4 A3
Lake Creek YT 4 B3
Lake Dalrymple ON 20 A8
Lake Dalrymple ON 21 C-D2
Lake Edward NB 31 D3
Lake Errock BC 2 D-E6
Lakefield ON 21 D3
Lakefield QC 24 C5
Lake Francis MB 13 E3
Lake Francis MB 14 D4
Lake George NB 32 C2
Lake George NS 32 E6
Lake George NS 33 B4
Lake George NS 33 E1
Lake George PP NS 32 E6-7
Lake George PP NS 33 B4
Lake Harbour (Kimmirut) NU 40 B5-6
Lake Helen ON 16 E6
Lake Helen ON 17 C1
Lake Huron Highland ON 20 B3
Lakehurst ON 21 D3
Lakeland MB 13 E3
Lakeland MB 14 D3
Lakeland NS 32 E8
Lakeland NS 33 B5
Lakeland PP AB 9 F7
Lakeland PP AB 12 F1
Lakeland PRA AB 9 F7
Lakeland PRA AB 12 F1-2
Lakelands NS 32 D7
Lakelands NS 33 A4-5
Lake La Rose NS 32 F5
Lake La Rose NS 33 C2-3
Lake Laurentian CA ON 18 A5-6
Lake Lenore SK 11 C5
Lakelet ON 20 C4
Lake Louise AB 6 D4
Lake Louise AB 7 A1
Lakelse Lake BC 1 A3
Lakelse Lake BC 1 A3-4
Lakelse Lake PP BC 1 A3-4
Lake Majeau AB 8 B5
Lake Midway PP NS 32 F4
Lake Midway PP NS 33 C-D1
Lakenheath SK 11 F5
Lake Nipigon PP ON 16 E6
Lake Nipigon PP ON 17 B1
Lake Nipigon PP ON 40 F1-2
Lake O'Brien NL 36 A7
Lake O'Brien NL 37 A5
Lake O'Brien NL 38 F6
Lake of the Woods PP ON 13 F5-6
Lake of the Woods PP ON 16 E1
Lake O'Law PP NS 34 C6
Lake on the Mountain PP ON 21 E5-6
Lake Paul NS 32 E6-7
Lake Paul NS 33 C4

Lakeport ON **21** E4
Lake Ramsay NS **32** F7
Lake Ramsay NS **33** C4
Lake St. George PP MB
13 D3-4
Lake St. George PP MB
14 A4
Lake St. Peter ON **21** B3-4
Lake St. Peter PP ON **21** B4
Lakeshore ON **19** E2
Lakeside NB **32** D4
Lakeside NB **33** A2
Lakeside NS **32** F8
Lakeside NS **33** C5-6
Lakeside ON **19** B5
Lakeside ON **20** E4
Lakeside Beach ON **20** B8
Lakeside Beach ON **21** E2
Lake Stream NB **31** F7
Lake Stream NB **32** B5
Lake Superior National
Marine Conservation
Area (proposed) ON
16 F6-7
Lake Superior National
Marine Conservation
Area (proposed) ON
17 C-D1
Lake Superior PP ON
17 E3-4
Laketon NB **31** D7
Lake Uist NS **34** D7
Lakevale NS **34** D5
Lake Valley SK **11** E4
Lakeview AB **8** F6-7
Lakeview NL **37** E7
Lakeview NS **32** F8
Lakeview NS **33** C6
Lakeview QC **24** C4
Lakeview Heights ON
24 E3-4
Lakeville NB **31** F3
Lakeville NB **31** F8
Lakeville NB **32** B1
Lakeville NB **32** B6
Lakeville NS **32** E6-7
Lakeville NS **33** B4
Lakeville PE **34** B4
Lakeville PE **35** D8
Lakeville Corner NB
32 C3-4
Lake Whittaker CA ON
19 C5
Lake Whittaker CA ON
20 E4
Laliberté, lac QC **25** C5
Laliberté, rivière QC **29** A2
La Loche SK **9** D8
La Loche SK **12** D2-3
La Loche, lac SK **9** D7-8
La Loche, lac SK **12** D2-3
La Loche River NT **10** D8
La Loche River SK **9** D8
La Loche West SK **9** D7-8
La Loche West SK **12** D2-3
L'Alverne QC **29** D6
L'Alverne QC **31** A4-5
L'Amable ON **21** C4
La Macaza QC **24** B4
La Macaza QC **25** F4
La Malbaie QC **28** E7-8
La Malbaie QC **30** C3
Lamaline NL **36** F6
Lamaline NL **37** F4
La Manche NL **36** D8
La Manche NL **37** D6
La Manche NL **37** E8
La Manche PP NL **37** E8
Lamarche QC **28** B5
La Martre QC **29** A7
La Martre, lac NT **10** D7
La Martre, lac NT **41** D1
La Mauricie NP QC **24** A7
La Mauricie NP QC **25** E7
La Mauricie NP QC **27** B2
Lamb, lac QC **22** D5
Lambert, lac QC **22** A5
Lambert, lac QC **23** F1
Lambertville NB **32** E2
Lambeth ON **19** C4-5
Lambeth ON **20** E3-4
Lambton QC **27** C5
Lambton, Cape NT **41** A1
Lambton, Cape NT **42** E1
Lambton Shores ON
19 B-C3
Lambton Shores ON **20** D2
Lamèque NB **30** E2
Lamèque NB **31** B8
Lameque, île NB **31** B8
Lameque, île NB **30** E2-3
Lameque Island NB **30** E2-3
Lameque Island NB **31** B8
Lamerton AB **8** E7
La Minerve QC **24** B3-4
La Minerve QC **25** F3-4
La Minerve, lac QC **24** B3
La Minerve, lac QC **25** F3
Lamont AB **6** A6
Lamont AB **8** C7
Lamont AB **11** A1
La Morandière QC **23** D4-5
La Mothe, lac QC **28** B5-6
La Motte QC **23** D4
La Motte, lac QC **23** D4
La Motte Lake PP ON **17** D6
Lampman SK **11** F6-7
Lamprey MB **15** B5
La Muir, Lake QC **22** E2-3
Lamy QC **29** E2
Lanark ON **21** B7
Lanark ON **24** E1
Lancaster ON **24** E4

Lancaster Sound NU
42 D4-5
Lance, Point NL **36** F8
Lance, Point NL **37** F6
La Passe ON **22** F6
La Patrie QC **27** E6
La Pêche QC **21** A7
La Pêche QC **22** F7
La Pêche QC **24** C-D1
La Pêche, lac QC **21** A7
Lapêche, lac QC **22** F7
Lapêche, lac QC **24** D1
La Pérouse MB **15** F3
La Pérouse Bay MB **15** B6
Lapeyrère, lac QC **25** D8
Lapeyrère, lac QC **27** A3
Lapeyrère, lac QC **28** F3
Lapie River YT **4** D5
L'Ancienne-Lorette QC
27 B5
Landing SK **9** E8
Landing SK **12** E3
Landing Lake MB **15** E4
Landmark MB **13** F4
Landmark MB **14** E5-6
Landrienne QC **23** D4
Landron, lac QC **22** A7
Landron, lac QC **23** F7
Landron, lac QC **25** C1
Landry, lac QC **25** B4
Landry, lac QC **39** E5
LaPierre House Territorial
Historic Site YT **5** D3
Landry Creek NT **4** B-C8
Landry Creek NT **10** C1-2
Landseer MB **14** E3
Land's End NT **42** C1
Lanezi Lake BC **1** B8
Lanezi Lake BC **6** B1
Lanfine AB **7** A8
Lang ON **21** E3
Lang SK **11** E5-6
Langara Island BC **1** A1
Langara Point BC **1** A1
Langara Point BC **3** F1
Lang Bay BC **1** F6
Lang Bay BC **2** C3
Langdale BC **1** F6-7
Langdale BC **2** D4
Langdon AB **6** D6
Langdon AB **7** B4
L'Ange-Gardien QC **21** A8
L'Ange-Gardien QC **24** D2-3
L'Ange-Gardien QC **24** E7
L'Ange-Gardien QC **27** A5-6
Langenburg SK **11** D7
Langenburg SK **13** D1
Langford BC **2** F4
Langham SK **11** C4
Langlade QC **23** B8
Langlade QC **25** A2
Langlade QC **26** F2
Lang Lake ON **18** B4
Langley BC **1** F7
Langley BC **2** E5
Langley Island NT **5** B4
Langruth MB **13** E3
Langruth MB **14** C-D3
Langstaff ON **19** A8
Langstaff ON **20** C7
Langstaff ON **21** F1
Langton ON **19** D6
Langton ON **20** F5
Langton Bay NT **5** A-B7
Languedoc QC **17** C8
Languedoc QC **23** C3
Laniel QC **17** E8
Laniel QC **22** B2
Lanigan SK **11** C5
Lanigan Creek SK **11** C5
L'Annonciation QC **24** B4
L'Annonciation QC **25** F4
Lanoraie QC **24** C6
Lanoraie QC **27** D2
Lansdowne NS **33** A7
Lansdowne NS **34** E3
Lansdowne ON **21** D7
Lansdowne House ON
40 E2
Lansdowne House
(Neskantaga) ON
16 A6-7
Lansdowne Lake MB **12** C4
L'Anse-à-Beaufils QC **30** D3
L'Anse-à-Fugère QC **30** B3
L'Anse-à-Gilles QC **27** A7
L'Anse-à-la-Cabane QC
30 F6-7
L'Anse-à-la-Croix QC **29** B5
L'Anse-Amour NL **38** A3-4
L'Anse-au-Diable NL **38** A-B3
L'Anse-au-Griffon QC **30** B3
L'Anse-au-Loup NL **38** A3
L'Anse-au-Loup NL **39** D8
L'Anse-aux-Gascons QC
30 D2
L'Anse-aux-Gascons QC
31 A8
L'Anse aux Meadows NL
38 A5-6
L'Anse aux Meadows, LHN
de NL **38** A5-6
L'Anse aux Meadows, LHN
de NL **39** D8
L'Anse aux Meadows NL
38 A5
L'Anse aux Meadows NL
39 D8
L'Anse aux Meadows NHS
NL **38** A5-6
L'Anse aux Meadows NHS
NL **39** D8
L'Anse-à-Valleau QC
30 B2-3
L'Anse-de-Roche QC **28** C8
L'Anse-Pleureuse QC **29** A8
L'Anse-Saint-Jean QC **28** C7
Lansing River YT **4** B5
Lantier QC **24** B5

Lantz NS **33** B6
Lantz NS **34** F2
Lantzville BC **1** F6
Lantzville BC **2** D3
Lanz Island BC **1** D3
La Passe QC **22** F6
La Patrie QC **27** E6
La Plaine QC **24** C6
La Plaine QC **27** D1
Lapland NS **33** D4
LaPlante NB **31** B6
La Plonge QC **12** E-F4
La Plonge, lac SK **12** F4
La Pocatière QC **28** F8
La Poile NL **36** E-F5
La Poile Bay NL **36** D2
La Poile River NL **36** D2
Lapointe, lac QC **39** B1
Laporte QC **6** D8
Laporte SK **11** D2
La Potherie, lac QC **40** C5
Lappe ON **16** F5
La Prairie QC **24** D6
La Prairie QC **27** E2
La Présentation QC **24** D7
L'Archevêque NS **34** D7
Larchwood ON **18** A5
Lardeau River BC **6** E3
Larder Lake ON **17** D7-8
Larder Lake ON **23** E1
Larder Lake ON **23** E1
Larder River PP ON **17** D7-8
Larder River PP ON **23** E1
L'Ardoise NS **34** D7
Lareau, lac QC **25** A6
Lareau, lac QC **26** F6
Lareau, lac QC **28** D1
La Rédemption QC **29** C4
Laredo Channel BC **1** B3
Laredo Inlet BC **1** B3
Laredo Sound BC **1** C3
La Reine QC **17** C7-8
La Reine QC **23** C2
La Reine, rivière ON
23 B-C2
La Ribourde, lac QC **26** A3
Larive, lac QC **22** B5
La Rivière MB **13** F3
La Rivière MB **14** F3
Lark Harbour NL **36** A2
Lark Harbour NL **38** F1-2
Larkspur AB **8** A6
Larkspur AB **9** F5-6
La Rochelle MB **13** F4
La Rochelle MB **14** F5
La Romaine QC **39** F5
La Romaine QC **40** F8
La Ronde, lac QC **26** B3
La Ronge SK **12** F5
La Ronge, lac SK **12** F5
Larouche QC **28** C5
Larrey, lac QC **28** B7-8
Larrys River NS **34** E5-6
Larsen Sound NU **41** B4
Larsen Sound NU **42** E-F3
Larus Lake ON **16** B2
Larus Lake ON **18** B2
La Salette ON **19** C6
La Salette ON **20** E5
La Salle MB **13** F3-4
La Salle MB **14** E5
La Salle ON **19** E1
LaSalle QC **24** D6
LaSalle QC **27** E1
Lasalle, lac QC **28** F4
La Sarre QC **17** C8
La Sarre QC **23** C2
La Sarre, rivière QC **23** C2
La Saulx, lac QC **28** A7-8
La Scie NL **38** E5
La Scie NL **39** F8
Lashburn SK **6** B8
Lashburn SK **11** B2
Laskeek Bay BC **1** B2
La Société QC **29** D2
Lasqueti Island BC **1** F6
Lasqueti Island BC **2** D3
L'Assomption QC **24** C6
L'Assomption QC **27** D1-2
Lasswade ON **21** C4
Last Lake ON **18** C7
Last Mountain SK **11** D5
Last Mountain House
Provincial Historic Park
SK **11** E5
Last Mountain Lake SK
11 D5
Last Mountain Lake
National Wilderness
Area SK **11** D5
La Tabatière QC **38** C1
La Tabatière QC **39** E6-7

La Tabatière QC **40** E8
Latchford ON **17** E7
Latchford ON **22** A1
Latchford Bridge ON **21** B5
Laterrière QC **28** C6
Lathorn AB **7** C6
La Trinité-des-Monts QC
29 D3
La Trinité-des-Monts QC
31 A1
Latties Brook NS **32** D8
Latties Brook NS **33** A6
Latties Brook NS **34** F2
Latulipe QC **17** E8
Latulipe QC **22** A2
La Tuque QC **25** C7
La Tuque QC **28** F3
Lauder AB **11** F8
Lauder MB **13** F1
Launay QC **17** C8
Launay QC **23** C3
Launay, lac QC **25** D5
Launching PE **34** C4
Launching PE **35** E7
Launching Point PE **34** C4
Launching Point PE **35** E7
Launière, rivière QC
28 E-F5
Laura SK **11** C4
Lauréat, lac QC **25** C6
Lauréat, lac QC **28** E2
Laurel ON **20** C5
Laurel ON **24** C4
Laurel Creek CA ON **19** B6
Laurenceton NL **36** A6-7
Laurenceton NL **37** A4-5
Laurenceton NL **38** F6
Laurent, lac QC **28** C6
Laurentia Beach MB **14** C4
Laurentian Mountains QC
25 E7 F6-7
Laurentian Mountains QC
27 A5-6
Laurentian Mountains QC
27 B2 C1-2
Laurentian Mountains QC
28 E5-6
Laurentian Mountains QC
29 A2 B1
Laurentian Mountains QC
40 F6
Laurentides QC **24** C5-6
Laurentides QC **27** D1
Laurentides, les QC
25 E6 F5-6
Laurentides, les QC **27** A4-5
Laurentides, les QC **27** B1-2
Laurentides, les QC
28 D5-6 E5
Laurentides, les QC
29 A1-2 B1
Laurentides, RF des QC
28 D-E5
Laurie Lake SK **12** D7
Laurie Lake SK **15** D1
Laurie PP NS **32** E8
Laurie PP NS **33** B6
Laurier MB **13** D2
Laurier MB **14** B2
Laurier, Mount BC **3** D3
Laurie River MB **12** D8
Laurie River MB **15** D2
Laurier-Station QC **27** B5
Laurierville QC **27** C5
Laurus Lake ON **13** D5
Laurus Lake ON **14** A-B8
Laussedat, Mount BC **6** D3
La Vallee ON **16** F2
Lavallée Lake SK **11** A4
Lavaltrie QC **24** C6
Lavaltrie QC **27** D2
Lavant ON **21** B6
Lavender Peak BC **3** E3
Lavenham QC **13** E-F3
Lavenham MB **14** E3
L'Avenir QC **24** C8
L'Avenir QC **27** D4
La Vérendrye, RF QC
22 A5-6 B5-6
La Verendrye PP QC
16 F4-5
La Vernière QC **30** F7
La Visitation-de-Yamaska
QC **24** C7-8
La Visitation-de-Yamaska
QC **27** C3
Lavington BC **6** E2
Lavinia MB **11** E8
Lavinia MB **13** E1
La Visitation-de-Yamaska
QC **24** C7-8
Lavoie, lac QC **25** B6
Lavoie, lac QC **28** E1-2
Lavoie Bay SK **12** E4
Lavoy AB **6** B6-7
Lavoy AB **8** C8

Lavoy AB **11** A-B1
Lawford Lake MB **13** A4
Lawford Lake MB **13** A4
Lawford Lake MB **10** F8
Lawford River MB **13** A4
Lawford River MB **15** F4
Lawledge MB **15** D5
Lawn NL **36** F6
Lawn NL **37** F4
Lawn Bay NL **36** F6
Lawn Bay NL **37** F4
Lawn Point NL **36** F6
Lawn Point NL **37** F4
Lawn Point PP BC **1** E3-4
Lawrence Bay SK **12** A8
Lawrence Bay SK **15** D1
Lawrence Lake AB **9** F5
Lawrence Lake ON **16** E2
Lawrence Station NB **32** D2
Lawrencetown NS **32** E5-6
Lawrencetown NS **33** C3
Lawrencetown Beach PP NS
33 C6-7
Lawrenceville QC **24** D8
Lawrenceville QC **27** E4
Lawson SK **11** C4
Lawton AB **8** B5
Laxgalts'ap (Greenville) BC
3 F3
Lax Kw'alaams BC **3** F2
Layco SK **11** C-D6
Layland MB **13** E-F3
Layland MB **14** E3-4
Lazo BC **1** F6
Lazo BC **2** C-D2
Leach Island ON **17** E3
Lead Cove NL **37** C7-8
Leader SK **6** D8
Leader SK **11** C4
Leading Tickles NL **38** E-F5
Leaf Lake SK **11** B7
Leaf Lake SK **13** B1
Leaf Rapids MB **12** D8
Leaf Rapids MB **15** D2
Leahurst AB **8** E7-8
Leamington ON **19** E2
Leamside MB **14** D7
Leanchoil BC **6** D3-4
Leask SK **11** B6
Leaskdale ON **20** B7-8
Leaskdale ON **21** E2
Leavitt AB **6** F6
Leavitt AB **7** F5
Leavitt Bay SK **12** C-D4
Lebanon QC **25** A4
Lebel-sur-Quévillon QC
23 C6
Lébel-sur-Quévillon QC
23 B-C6
Leblanc NB **32** B7
Leblanc NB **35** E1
Leblanc, lac QC **25** A5
Leblanc, lac QC **26** F5
Le Blanc Lake SK **9** A8
Le Blanc Lake SK **12** A3
Lebret SK **11** D-E6
Le Breton, lac QC **28** B7
Lebrix Lake MB **13** A4
Leclercville QC **27** B4
Lecointre, lac QC **22** B8
Lecointre, lac QC **25** C2
Lecompte, lac QC **23** C6-7
Lecompte, lac QC **26** D1
Lecompte, rivière QC **23** C6
Le Croq, lac QC **39** C1
Le Doré, lac QC **39** D-E5
Le Gardeur QC **24** C6
Le Gardeur QC **27** D2
Legal AB **6** A5-6
Legal AB **8** B6
Legend AB **7** E7
Legend Lake AB **9** C6
Legend Lake AB **12** C1
Le Gentilhomme, lac QC
39 C2
Légerville NB **31** F7-8
Légerville NB **32** B6
Leggat Lake ON **21** C4
Le Goulet NB **30** E2
Le Goulet NB **31** F7
Leg Pond NB **38** C3-4
Lee AB **7** E3-4
Leeburn ON **17** F4
Leech NB **31** C7
Leedale AB **8** E5
Lee River MB **14** D7
Lee River Falls MB **14** D6-7
Lefaivre ON **24** D3-4
Lefebvre QC **24** D8
Lefebvre QC **27** D-E3
Le Fer, lac QC **39** A2
Lefroy ON **20** B7
Lefroy ON **21** E1
Leftrook Lake MB **15** E3
Legal AB **6** A5-6
Legal AB **8** B6

Lejeune QC **31** B1
Leland Lakes AB **9** A7
Leland Lakes AB **10** F8
Leluau, lac QC **25** C4
Lemain, lac QC **25** D3
Leman, lac QC **28** A8
Leman, lac QC **29** A1
Le Marié, lac QC **28** B7
Lemay, rivière QC **39** E1
Lemberg SK **11** D-E6
Lemieux ON **24** D3
Lemieux QC **24** B8
Lemieux QC **25** F8
Lemieux QC **27** C4
Lemieux Islands NU **40** A6
Leminster NS **32** E-F7
Leminster NS **33** C4-5
Lemoine, lac QC **23** E4
Lemsford SK **11** D2-3
Lena MB **13** F2
Lena MB **14** F1-2
Leney SK **11** C3-4
Lennox Island PE **34** B1
Lennox Island PE **35** C2-3
Lennox Island PE **35** C2-3
Lennox Passage PP NS
34 D6-7
Lennoxville QC **27** E4-5
Lenore MB **11** E8
Lenore MB **13** E1
Lenore Lake SK **11** C5
Lenore Lake, RNOM QC
11 C5
Lenore Lake NMBS SK
11 C5
Lenôtre, lac QC **22** B7
Lenôtre, lac QC **25** C2
Lenswood MB **11** C8
Lenswood MB **13** C1-2
Lenvale SK **11** B5
Leo AB **8** F8
Leo Creek BC **3** F5
Leonardville NB **32** E2
Leoville NB **11** A4
Léoville PE **35** B2
Lepage, lac QC **22** B7
Lepage, lac QC **26** E4
Le Pate, RNP ON **16** F6
Le Pate PNR ON **16** F6
L'Épiphanie QC **24** C6
L'Épiphanie QC **27** D2
Lepreau, Point NB **32** E3
Lepreau, Point NB **33** B1
Lepreau, ZPF de NB **32** D3
Lepreau PGA NB **32** D3
Lepreau River NB **32** D-E3
Le Précieux-Sang QC **24** B8
Le Précieux-Sang QC **27** C3
Lequille NB **32** F5
Lequille NS **33** C2
Le Rageois, lac QC **39** F1
Leross SK **11** D6
Le Royer, lac QC **26** B5
Léry QC **24** E5-6
Léry QC **27** E1
Lesage, lac QC **24** B3
Lesage, lac QC **25** F3
Les Boules QC **29** B4
Les Buissons QC **29** A3
Les Caps QC **30** F7
Lescarbot, lac QC **28** E4
Les Cèdres QC **24** E5
Lescot, lac QC **22** B3
Les Coteaux QC **24** E4-5
Les Éboulements QC **28** E7
Les Escoumins QC **29** C1-2
Les-Hauteurs QC **29** C3-4
Les Îlets-Jérémie QC
29 B2-3
Les Islets-Caribou QC
39 F1-2
Les Jardins de la République
PP NB **29** E2-3 F2-3
Les Jardins de la République
PP NB **22** F6
Les Méchins QC **29** B5
Leslie SK **11** D6
Leslieville AB **6** C5
Leslieville AB **8** D-E5
Les Méchins QC **29** B5
Lessard, lac QC **23** A8
Lessard, lac QC **26** B2-3
Lessard, lac QC **26** B2
Lesser Slave Lake AB **9** E4
Lesser Slave Lake PP AB
9 E5
Lesser Slave Lake Wildland
PP AB **9** E4-5
Lesser Slave River AB **9** F5
Lester Beach MB **14** C5-6
Lester-Garland Premises
PHS NL **37** C7-8
Le Sueur, ZEC QC **25** D3
Letang NB **32** E2-3
Le Tétang-du-Nord QC **30** F7
Letellier MB **13** F4
Letellier MB **14** F5
L'Etete NB **32** E2
Lethbridge AB **6** F6
Lethbridge AB **7** E5
Lethbridge NL **36** C6
Lethbridge NL **37** C6
Leitch Collieries PHS AB
7 E3
Letondal, lac QC **25** B5
Le Tort, lac QC **39** D5
Lett SK **11** C3
Letty Harbour NT **5** A8
Leumat Lake NT **5** B7
Levack ON **17** F6
Levasseur, lac QC **25** A5
Levasseur, lac QC **26** E5

Levasseur, lac QC **28** C1
Leven MB **15** E4
Lever Lake NT **10** A5
Leville NS **32** F7
Leville NS **33** C4
Levine MB **14** D1
Lévis QC **27** B6
Levis, lac NT **10** C5
Lewes PE **35** F6
Lewin's Cove NL **36** E6-7
Lewin's Cove NL **37** E4-5
Lewis MB **14** D6
Lewis, lac QC **23** A8
Lewis, lac QC **26** B2-3
Lewis Hills NL **36** B2
Lewis Hills NL **36** B2
Lewis Lake NS **32** E8
Lewis Lake NS **33** A6
Lewis Lake PP NS **32** F8
Lewis Lake PP NS **33** C5-6
Lewisporte NL **36** A7
Lewisporte NL **37** A5
Lewisporte NL **38** F6
Lewvan SK **11** E6
Lexington NS **34** D6
Leyond River MB **13** C-D4
Leyond River MB **14** A6
Leyson Point NU **40** A3
Leyson Point NU **41** D7
L'Heureux, lac QC **22** B6-7
L'Heureux, lac QC **25** D1
L'hutsaw Wetland Territorial
Habitat Protection Area
YT **4** C3
Liard Canyon Territorial
Recreation Site BC **3** A4
Liard Canyon Territorial
Recreation Site BC **4** F7
Liard River BC **3** A6
Liard River BC **3** B5
Liard River BC **4** F8
Liard River YT **3** A3-4
Liard River YT **4** E6
Liard River YT **4** E-F7
Liard River Corridor PP BC
3 A5-6
Liard River Crossing River
TP NT **10** D3-4
Liard River Hotsprings PP
BC **3** A5
Liard River Hotsprings PP
BC **4** F7
Libau MB **13** E4
Libau MB **14** D5
Lichen, lac QC **23** B8
Lichen, lac QC **26** B2
Liddon Gulf NT **42** D2
Liebenthal SK **6** D8
Liebenthal SK **11** E2
Liège, lac QC **25** B6
Liège, lac QC **28** E2
Liege River AB **9** C-D5
Lièvre, rivière du QC **22** F7
Lièvre, rivière du QC
24 C2 D2-3
Lièvre, ZEC de la QC
23 A7-8
Lièvre, ZEC de la QC **28** D8
Lièvres, île aux QC **28** E7
Lighthouse Cove ON **19** E2
Lighthouse Point PNR ON
19 F1-2
Lighthouse Point, RNP ON
19 F1-2
Ligne, lac de la QC **23** C7
Ligne, lac de la QC **26** C1
Likely BC **1** C8
Likely BC **6** B1
L'Île d'Entrée QC **30** F7
L'Islet QC **27** A7
L'Islet QC **28** F7
L'Islet-sur-Mer QC **27** A7
L'Islet-sur-Mer QC **28** F7
L'Isle-aux-Grues QC **27** A7
L'Isle-aux-Grues QC **28** F7
L'Isle-Verte QC **29** D1-2
Lismore NS **34** D4
Lister BC **6** F3
Lister BC **7** F1
Listen Lake ON **11** A4
Listen Lake SK **12** F4
Listowel ON **19** A5
Listowel ON **20** C4
Listuguj QC **29** D6
Listuguj QC **31** A4
Litchfield NS **32** F5
Litchfield NS **33** C2
Little Abitibi Lake ON **17** B7
Little Abitibi PP ON **17** B6-7
Little Abitibi River ON
17 A-B6
Little Andrews Bay PMP NL
1 A4-5
Little Anse NS **34** E6-7
Little Ausable River ON
19 B-C4
Little Ausable River ON
20 D-E3
Little Barachois Brook NL
36 C2-3
Little Barachois Brook NL
36 C3
Little Baraway NL **36** E8
Little Barasway NL **37** E6
Little Bay NL **36** D2
Little Bay NL **36** D5
Little Bay NL **37** E7
Little Bay NL **37** D3
Little Bay NL **38** E5
Little Bay East NL **36** E7
Little Bay East NL **37** E5
Little Bay Islands NL **38** E5
Little Bay West NL **36** E6
Little Bay West NL **37** E4

Little Bear Lake SK 11 A5
Little Bear Lake SK 12 F5
Little Bear River NT 4 A7-8
Little Bear River NT 10 A1
Little Beaver River MB 15 C4-5
Little Black Bear SK 11 D6
Little Bluff CA ON 21 E6
Little Bolton Lake MB 13 A4
Little Bona NL 36 E7-8
Little Bona NL 37 E5-6
Little Bone SK 11 D7
Little Bow PP AB 6 E6
Little Bow PP AB 7 D5
Little Bow River AB 6 E6
Little Bow River AB 7 C4 D4-5
Little Bras d'Or NS 34 C7-8
Little Brehat NL 38 A5
Little Britain ON 20 B8
Little Britain ON 21 D-E2
Little Brook NS 33 D1
Little Buffalo AB 9 D4
Little Buffalo NT 10 E-F7
Little Buffalo River NT 41 E1
Little Buffalo River Crossing TP NT 10 E7
Little Buffalo River Falls TP NT 10 F7
Little Burnt Bay NL 36 A7
Little Burnt Bay NL 37 A5
Little Burnt Bay NL 38 F6
Little Cadotte River AB 9 D4
Little Catalina NL 37 B7-8
Little Cataraqui Creek CA ON 21 D6
Little Chiblow Lake ON 18 A1-2
Little Churchill River MB 15 C5 D4-5
Little Clarke Lake SK 11 A4
Little Clarke Lake SK 12 F4
Little Cornwallis Island NU 42 D4
Little Cove, RNP ON 18 D4
Little Cove PNR ON 18 D4
Little Current ON 18 B4
Little Current River ON 16 C8
Little Current River ON 40 F2
Little Current River PP ON 16 C7-8
Little Current River PP ON 17 A2-3
Little Cygnet Lake MB 15 D5
Little Doctor Lake NT 10 D2
Little Dover NS 34 E6
Little Duck Lake MB 15 A4
Little Duck Post MB 15 A3
Little Falls NL 36 A4
Little Falls NL 37 A2
Little Falls NL 38 F3
Little Fishing Lake SK 11 A2-3
Little Fish Lake PP AB 6 D6-7
Little Fish Lake PP AB 7 A6
Little Fish Lake PP AB 11 D1
Little Flatstone Lake SK 12 E3-4
Little Fogo Islands NL 38 E7
Little Forehead Lake NT 10 A6-7
Little Fort BC 6 D1
Little French River ON 18 B7
Little Friars Cove NL 36 D1
Little Gander Pond NL 36 C6-7
Little Gander Pond NL 37 C5
Little Gem AB 7 A8
Little Grand Lake NL 36 B3
Little Grand Lake NL 37 B1
Little Grand Rapids MB 13 C5
Little Grand Rapids MB 16 A1
Little Grand Rapids (IR) MB 13 C5
Little Grand Rapids (IR) MB 16 A1
Little Greenwater Lake, RNP ON 16 F4-5
Little Greenwater Lake PNR ON 16 F4-5
Little Harbour NL 36 A3-4
Little Harbour NL 36 D8
Little Harbour NL 36 E7
Little Harbour NL 37 A1-2
Little Harbour NL 37 C7
Little Harbour NL 37 D6
Little Harbour NL 37 E5
Little Harbour NL 38 F3
Little Harbour NS 33 C7
Little Harbour NS 33 F3
Little Harbour NS 34 E3-4
Little Harbour PE 35 D-E8
Little Harbour Deep NL 39 E8
Little Harbour East NL 36 D7
Little Harbour East NL 37 D5
Little Hawk Lake ON 21 B2-3
Little Heart's Ease NL 37 C-D7
Little Hills SK 12 F5
Little Hyland River YT 4 C-D7
Little Jackfish River ON 16 C-D6
Little Jackfish River ON 17 A1
Little Joseph Lake NL 39 C3
Little Judique NS 34 D5
Little Keele River NT 4 A7
Little Keele River NT 5 F7
Little Key River ON 18 B-C6
Little Klappan River BC 3 C-D3
Little Lake ON 19 B6-7
Little Lake ON 20 D5-6
Little Lake CA ON 19 C6
Little Lake CA ON 20 E5
Little Limestone Lake MB 11 A8
Little Limestone Lake MB 13 A2
Little Limestone Lake MB 15 D5
Little Main Restigouche River NB 29 E4
Little Maitland River ON 19 A5
Little Maitland River ON 20 C4
Little Manitou Lake SK 11 D5
Little Marten Lake NT 10 A7
Little Mecatina River NL 39 C4-5
Little Missinaibi Lake ON 17 D4
Little Mississippi River ON 21 B4-5
Little Moose Island MB 14 A5
Little Nahanni River NT 4 C7
Little Narrows NS 34 C6
Little Paradise NL 36 E7-8
Little Paradise NL 37 E5-6
Little Partridge River MB 12 A7
Little Partridge River MB 15 A2
Little Pickerel River ON 18 B7-8 C7
Little Pic River ON 16 E8
Little Pic River ON 17 C2
Little Pine SK 6 B8
Little Pine SK 11 B3
Little Playgreen Lake MB 13 A3
Little Pond PE 34 C4
Little Pond PE 35 E7
Little Port l'Hébert NS 33 E3-4
Little Qualicum Falls PP BC 1 F6
Little Qualicum Falls PP BC 2 D-E3
Little Quill Lake SK 11 C6
Little Quirke Lake ON 18 A2-3
Little Rancheria River BC 3 A3
Little Rancheria River BC 4 F6
Little Rapids NL 36 A-B3
Little Rapids NL 37 A-B1
Little Rapids ON 17 F4
Little Rapids ON 18 A1
Little Red River SK 11 B4
Little Ridge NB 32 D-E1
Little River BC 1 F6
Little River BC 2 C2
Little River NB 29 F4
Little River NB 31 C3
Little River NB 31 F5
Little River NB 32 B3
Little River NB 32 C6
Little River NB 32 C6
Little River NS 32 C8
Little River NS 33 D1
Little River NS 34 D1
Little River Harbour NS 33 F1
Little Sachigo Lake ON 13 A7
Little St. Lawrence NL 36 F6
Little St. Lawrence NL 37 F4
Little Salmon Lake YT 4 C4
Little Salmon River Gorge, ZCP NB 32 D5-6
Little Salmon River Gorge, ZCP NB 33 A2-3
Little Salmon River Gorge PCA NB 32 D5-6
Little Salmon River Gorge PCA NB 33 A2-3
Little Sand Lake MB 15 C3
Little Sand Lake ON 14 D8
Little Sands PE 34 D3
Little Sands PE 35 F6
Little Saskatchewan MB 13 D3
Little Saskatchewan MB 14 A3
Little Seal River MB 15 A-B5
Little Seldom NL 38 E7
Little Shemogue NB 32 B7
Little Shemogue NB 34 C1
Little Shemogue NB 35 E2
Little Shemogue, havre de NB 35 E2
Little Shemogue Harbour NB 35 E2
Little Smoky AB 9 F3
Little Smoky River AB 9 F3
Little Southwest Miramichi River NB 31 D5
Little Stull Lake MB 15 F6
Little Sturgeon River ON 18 A8
Little Sturgeon River ON 22 C-D1
Little Tobique River NB 31 C4
Little Tobique River (Nictor Branch) NB 29 F5
Little Tomiko River ON 18 A8
Little Traverse Bay ON 14 F8
Little Trout Lake ON 13 D6
Little Trout Lake ON 16 C2-3
Little Turtle Lake ON 16 E3
Little Turtle River ON 16 E3
Little Vermilion Lake ON 13 D6
Little Vermilion Lake ON 16 B2
Little White River ON 17 F5
Little White River PP ON 17 F5
Livelong SK 6 A-B8
Livelong SK 11 B3
Lively ON 17 F6
Lively ON 18 A5
Liverpool NS 33 E4
Liverpool Bay NT 5 A6
Liverpool Bay NT 41 A1
Livingston NL 39 B2
Livingstone Cove NS 34 D4
Livingstone Creek YT 4 D4
Livingstone Lake ON 21 B2
Livingstone Lake SK 12 B4
Livingstone Point PP ON 16 D6
Livingstone Point PP ON 17 B1
Lizotte QC 25 B8
Lizotte QC 26 F8
Lizotte QC 28 D4
Llewellyn Glacier BC 3 A-B1
Lloyd Lake SK 9 C8
Lloyd Lake SK 12 C3
Lloydminster AB 6 B7-8
Lloydminster AB 11 B2
Lloyds Lake NL 36 C3
Lloyds Lake NL 37 C1
Lloyds River NL 36 C3-4
Lloyds River NL 37 C1-2
Lloydtown ON 20 C6
Lobo ON 19 C4
Lobo ON 20 E3
Lobster Cove NL 38 D-E4
Lobster Cove NL 38 E2
Lobster House NL 36 A4
Lobster House NL 37 A2
Lobster House NL 38 F3-4
Lobstick AB 6 A6
Lobstick AB 8 D8
Lobstick AB 11 A1
Lobstick Island SK 9 A7
Lobstick Island SK 12 A3
Lobstick Lake Provincial Reserve SK 11 A7
Lochaber NS 34 E4-5
Lochaber Lake NS 34 E4
Lochaber Mines NS 33 B7-8
Lochaber Mines NS 34 F3-4
Lochalsh ON 17 D4
Loch Alva NB 32 D3
Loch Alva, APP NB 32 D-E3
Loch Alva, APP NB 33 B1
Loch Alva PPA NB 32 D-E3
Loch Alva PPA NB 33 B1
Loch Broom NS 34 D-E3
Lochiel ON 24 D4
Lochiel Lake PP NS 34 E4-5
Lochinvar AB 8 E6
Lochlin ON 21 C3
Loch Lomond NB 32 D4
Loch Lomond NB 33 A2
Loch Lomond NS 34 D7
Loch Lomond NS 34 D7
Lockeport NS 33 F3
Lockhart AB 8 E5
Lockhart Beach PP BC 6 F4
Lockhart Creek PP BC 6 F4
Lockhart Lake NT 10 B7
Lockhart River NT 10 B8
Lock Leven NL 36 C1-2
Lockport MB 13 E4
Lockport MB 14 D5
Lock's Cove NL 36 D5
Lock's Cove NL 37 D3
Lockston NL 37 C7
Lockston Path PP NL 37 B7
Lockwood SK 11 D5
Lodge Bay NL 39 C8
Lodge Creek AB 6 F8
Lodge Creek AB 11 F2
Lodgepole AB 6 B4
Lodgepole AB 8 D4
Logan, mont QC 29 B6
Logan, Mount YT 4 E1
Logan Glacier YT 4 D1
Logan Island ON 16 D6
Logan Lake AB 9 F7
Logan Lake AB 12 E1-2
Logan Lake BC 1 E8
Logan Lake BC 2 B8
Logan Lake BC 6 E1
Logan Lake ON 21 C2
Logan Mountains YT 4 D7
Logans Point NS 34 D3
Loganville NS 34 E3
Loggieville NB 31 D7
Log Valley SK 11 D-E4
Logy Bay NL 37 D8
Logy Bay-Middle Cove-Outer Cove NL 37 D8
Lohbiee BC 1 D6
Lois, rivière QC 23 C2-3
Lois Lake BC 2 C3
Lokken, Mount YT 4 C-D4
Loks Land NU 40 B6
Lola Lake, RNP ON 16 D3
Lola Lake PNR ON 13 E7
Lola Lake PNR ON 16 D3
Lombardy ON 21 C7
Lombardy ON 24 F1
Lomond AB 6 E6
Lomond AB 7 D6
Londesborough ON 19 A4
Londesborough ON 20 C3
London ON 19 C4
London ON 20 E3
Londonderry NS 32 D8
Londonderry NS 33 A5-6
Londonderry NS 34 E1-2
Londonderry PP NS 33 A6
Londonderry PP NS 34 E2
Londonderry Station NS 32 D8
Londonderry Station NS 33 A6
Londonderry Station NS 34 E1-2
Lone Butte BC 1 D8
Lone Butte BC 6 D1
Lone Creek ON 22 E4
Lonely Bay NT 10 D6
Lonely Island ON 18 C4
Lonely Lake MB 13 D2
Lonely Lake MB 14 B2
Lonely Lake MB 14 B2
Lone Mountain YT 5 D2
Lone Pine AB 6 A5
Lone Pine AB 8 A-B4
Lone Prairie BC 3 E8
Lone Prairie BC 9 E1
Lone Ridge AB 8 D6
Lone Rock SK 6 B8
Lone Rock SK 11 B2
Lonesand MB 14 F6
Lone Spruce MB 14 C3
Long, lac QC 25 C4
Long, lac QC 28 C5
Long Bay ON 18 C3
Long Beach NL 37 D7-8
Long Beach NL 37 F8
Long Beach ON 19 C8
Long Beach ON 20 A8
Long Beach ON 20 F7
Long Beach ON 21 D2
Long Beach CA ON 19 C8
Long Beach CA ON 20 F7
Longbow Lake ON 13 F6
Longbow Lake ON 16 D2
Long Cove NL 37 D7
Long Creek NB 32 C4-5
Long Creek PE 35 E4
Long Creek SK 11 F6
Longford ON 18 F8
Longford ON 20 A7
Longford ON 21 C1
Long Harbour NL 36 D7
Long Harbour NL 37 D5
Long Harbour NL 37 E6-7
Long Harbour-Mount Arlington Heights NL 36 E8
Long Harbour-Mount Arlington Heights NL 37 E6
Long Island BC 2 D6
Long Island NL 36 D5-6
Long Island NL 36 D8
Long Island NL 37 D3-4
Long Island NL 37 D6
Long Island NL 38 E5
Long Island NL 33 D1
Long Island NU 40 D3-4
Longlac ON 16 D8
Longlac ON 17 B2
Longlac ON 40 F2
Long Lake MB 14 B7
Long Lake NB 31 D4
Long Lake NL 36 C4
Long Lake NL 37 C2
Long Lake NS 35 F2
Long Lake ON 16 E7
Long Lake ON 16 D7-8
Long Lake ON 17 B2
Long Lake ON 17 D7
Long Lake ON 17 B2
Long Lake ON 18 A5
Long Lake ON 18 C3
Long Lake ON 18 D8
Long Lake ON 21 A2
Long Lake ON 21 B1
Long Lake ON 22 F1
Long Lake YT 4 D3
Long Lake PP AB 6 A6
Long Lake PP AB 8 A7
Long Lake PP AB 9 F6
Long Lake PP AB 12 F1
Longlegged Lake ON 13 D6
Longlegged Lake ON 16 C2
Longlegged River ON 16 C2
Long Plain MB 13 E3
Long Plain MB 14 E3
Long Point MB 13 B3
Long Point MB 15 D3
Long Point NB 32 D4
Long Point NB 33 A2
Long Point NL 36 B2
Long Point NL 36 B1-2
Long Point NL 39 B6
Long Point NL 39 B7
Long Point NS 34 A7
Long Point NS 34 D5
Long Point ON 19 D6-7
Long Point ON 19 D6
Long Point ON 20 F5-6
Long Point ON 20 F5
Long Point ON 21 E6
Long Point ON 21 E6
Long Point, RNF de ON 20 F5-6
Long Point, RNF de ON 19 D6-7
Long Point Bay ON 19 D6-7
Long Point Bay ON 20 F5-6
Long Point NWA ON 19 D6-7
Long Point NWA ON 20 F5-6
Long Point PP NS 34 D5
Long Point PP ON 19 D6
Long Point PP ON 20 F5
Long Pond NL 36 D8
Long Pond NL 37 D6
Longrais, lac QC 39 B1
Long Range Mountains NL 36 C2-3 D2
Long Range Mountains NL 38 C3-4 D-E3
Long Range Mountains NL 39 E8 F7-8
Long Reach NB 32 D4
Long Reach NB 32 D4
Long Reach NB 33 A1
Long Reach NB 33 A1
Long River PE 35 D3
Long Sault ON 24 E3
Long Sault CA ON 20 B8
Long Sault CA ON 21 E2
Long Schooner Lake ON 21 B6
Longs Creek NB 32 C2
Longtom Lake NT 10 A5
Longue-Pointe QC 40 F7
Longue-Pointe-de-Mingan QC 39 F3
Longueuil QC 24 D6
Longueuil QC 27 E1-2
Longview AB 6 E5
Longview AB 7 C3-4
Longwoods Road CA ON 19 C4
Longwoods Road CA ON 20 E3
Longworth BC 1 A8
Longworth BC 6 A1
Lonira AB 8 B4
Looma AB 8 C7
Loomis SK 11 F3
Loon Bay NL 36 A7
Loon Bay NL 37 A5
Loon Bay NL 38 F6
Loonhaunt Lake ON 13 F6
Loonhaunt Lake ON 16 E2
Loonhead Lake MB 12 F7-8
Loonhead Lake MB 15 F2
Loon Lake AB 9 D4
Loon Lake NS 34 E5
Loon Lake NT 5 D-E6
Loon Lake ON 18 B1-2
Loon Lake ON 21 B-C3
Loon Lake SK 6 A8
Loon Lake SK 11 A3
Loon Lake SK 12 E7
Loon Lake SK 15 E1
Loon Lake PP BC 1 D8
Loon Lake PP BC 2 A7
Loon Lake PP BC 6 D1
Loon River AB 9 D4-5
Loon River MB 12 D-E7
Loon River MB 15 D-E1
Loos BC 1 B8
Loos BC 6 A1
Loranger Island SK 12 C6
Lord Creek YT 5 D2
Lords Cove NB 32 E2
Lord's Cove NL 36 F6
Lord's Cove NL 37 F4
Lord Selkirk PP PE 34 C2-3
Lord Selkirk PP PE 35 F5
Loreburn SK 11 D4
Lorens, lac QC 39 D5
Lorette MB 13 F4
Lorette MB 14 E5
Lorette, lac QC 25 B4
Lorette, lac QC 26 F4
Loretteville QC 27 B5
Loretto ON 20 B6
Lories NL 36 F5-6
Lories NL 37 F3-4
L'Orignal ON 24 D4
Lorimer Lake ON 18 C7
Loring ON 18 B7
Lorlie SK 11 D6
Lorne NB 29 E7
Lorne NB 31 B5
Lorne NS 33 A7
Lorne NS 34 E3
Lorne, Mount YT 4 E4
Lorne Beach ON 20 B3
Lorne C. Henderson CA ON 19 C2-3
Lorne C. Henderson CA ON 20 E2
Lornevale NS 32 D8
Lornevale NS 33 A5-6
Lornevale NS 34 E1
Lorne Valley PE 35 E6
Lorneville NB 32 E4
Lorneville NB 33 B1
Lorneville NS 32 B8
Lorneville NS 34 D1
Lorneville NS 35 F2
Lorneville ON 20 A8
Lorneville ON 21 D2
Lorraine QC 24 D6
Lorraine QC 27 E1
Lorrain Valley ON 17 E8
Lorrainville QC 17 E8
Lorrainville QC 22 A2
Lortie, lac QC 25 C5
Losier Settlement NB 30 F2
Losier Settlement NB 31 B8
Lost Channel ON 18 B6
Lost Lake ON 16 D3
Lost Reindeer Lakes NT 5 C5
Lost River QC 24 C4
Lotbinière QC 27 B4-5
Lots-Renversés QC 29 E2-3
Lots-Renversés QC 31 B1
Louden, lac QC 26 B4-5
Loudoun Channel BC 2 E2
Loughborough Inlet BC 1 E5
Loughborough Inlet BC 2 B2
Loughborough Lake ON 21 D6-7
Lougheed AB 6 B7
Lougheed AB 11 B1
Lougheed Island NU 42 C3
Louisa QC 24 C4-5
Louisa, Lake ON 21 A3
Louisa, Lake ON 22 F3
Louisbourg NS 34 C8
Louisbourg Harbour NS 34 C-D8
Louis Creek BC 6 D1-2
Louisdale NS 34 D6
Louise, lac QC 24 C4
Louise, lac QC 27 D5
Louise Falls NT 10 F6
Louise-Gosford, ZEC QC 27 E6-7
Louise-Gosford, ZEC QC 27 E-F6
Louise Island BC 1 B1
Louise Lake YT 4 E2
Louiseville QC 24 B7
Louiseville QC 25 F7
Louiseville QC 27 C2
Louis Head NS 33 E3-4
Louison, lac QC 23 D7
Louison, lac QC 26 D1
Louis-XIV, pointe QC 40 D-E3
Louis-S.-St-Laurent, LHN QC 27 F5
Louis S. St. Laurent NHS QC 27 F5
Louisville ON 19 D3
Lount Lake ON 13 E6
Loup, rivière du QC 24 A6-7 B7
Loup, rivière du QC 25 E6 F7
Loup, rivière du QC 27 B-C2
Loup, rivière du QC 29 E1
Loup Marin, lac au QC 29 A3
Loups, lac des QC 22 B3
Loups Marins, rivière aux QC 30 A7
Lourdes NL 36 B1
Lourdes-de-Blanc-Sablon QC 38 A-B3
Lourdes-de-Blanc-Sablon QC 39 D7
Lousana AB 6 C6
Lousana AB 8 F7
Loutre, rivière de la QC 22 A1-2
Loutres, lac aux QC 23 C8
Loutres, lac aux QC 26 D2
Louvicourt QC 23 E5
Love SK 11 B6
Loveland Bay PP BC 1 E5
Loveland Bay PP BC 2 C1-2
Lovering, lac QC 27 F4
Loverna SK 6 C8
Loverna SK 11 C2
Low QC 22 F7
Low QC 24 C2
Low, Cape NU 40 A3
Low, Cape NU 41 D6
Lowbanks ON 19 C8
Lowbanks ON 20 F7
Low Bush River ON 17 C7
Lowe Farm MB 13 F3
Lowe Farm MB 14 F4
Lowe Inlet PMP BC 1 A-B3
Lower Argyle NS 33 F2
Lower Arrow Lake BC 6 F3
Lower Barneys River NS 34 D4
Lower Bedeque PE 35 D3
Lower Beverley Lake ON 24 F1
Lower Branch NS 33 D4
Lower Caledonia NS 33 A8
Lower Caledonia NS 34 E4
Lower Cove NL 36 C1
Lower East Pubnico NS 33 F2
Lower Economy NS 32 D8
Lower Economy NS 33 A5
Lower Economy NS 34 E1
Lower Eel Brook NS 33 E2
Lower Five Islands NS 32 D7
Lower Five Islands NS 33 A5
Lower Five Islands NS 34 E1
Lower Fort Garry, LHN de MB 14 D5-6
Lower Fort Garry NHS MB 14 D5-6
Lower Foster Lake SK 12 D5
Lower Freetown PE 35 D3
Lower Gulf Shore NS 35 F3
Lower Hainesville NB 31 F4
Lower Hainesville NB 32 B2
Lower Hay Lake ON 21 A-B3
Lower Hay Lake ON 22 F3
Lower Island Cove NL 37 C8
Lower Jemseg NB 32 C4
Lower Lance Cove NL 37 C7
Lower Madawaska River PP ON 21 B5
Lower Manitou Lake ON 13 F6
Lower Manitou Lake ON 16 E3
Lower Middle River NS 34 C6
Lower Montague PE 35 E6-7
Lower Newtown PE 35 F5-6
Lower Nicola BC 1 E8
Lower Nicola BC 2 C7-8
Lower Nicola BC 6 E1
Lower Nimpkish PP BC 1 E4
Lower Ohio NS 33 E3
Lower Post BC 3 A4
Lower Post BC 4 F7
Lower Rockport NB 32 C6-7
Lower Sackville NS 32 F8
Lower Sackville NS 33 C5-6
Lower St. Esprit NS 34 D7
Lower Shinimicas NS 35 F2
Lower South Jaquet River NB 29 E7
Lower South River NS 34 D-E5
Lower Tsitika River PP BC 1 E4-5
Lower Twin Lake ON 16 D8
Lower Twin Lake ON 17 A2
Lower Wedgeport NS 33 F2
Lower West Pubnico NS 33 F2
Lower Windsor NB 31 E-F3
Lower Windsor NB 32 B1-2
Lower Woods Harbour NS 33 F2
Low Landing NS 33 D3
Low Point NL 37 C8
Lowther ON 17 B5
Lowther Island NU 42 D3-4
Lowville ON 19 B7
Lowville ON 20 D6
Loyalist PE 35 E4
Lozeau, lac QC 39 D3-4
Lubicon Lake AB 9 D4
Lubicon River AB 9 D4
Lucan ON 19 B4
Lucan ON 20 E3
Lucania, Mount YT 4 D1
Lucasville ON 19 C2-3
Lucasville ON 20 E1-2
Lucerne, lac QC 22 F7-8
Lucerne, lac QC 24 C2
Luceville QC 29 C3
Lucie, lac QC 17 A8
Lucien, lac QC 25 A6
Lucien, lac QC 26 E6
Lucien, lac QC 28 C2
Lucknow ON 20 C3
Lucky Lake SK 11 D4
Lucky Lake SK 11 D4
Lucky Man SK 11 B4
Ludger, lac QC 24 B5
Ludlow NB 31 E5
Ludlow NB 32 A3
Luke MB 15 D-E5
Luke's Arm NL 38 E6
Lumberton BC 7 F1
Lumby BC 6 E2
Lumsden NL 37 A7
Lumsden NL 38 F8
Lumsden SK 11 E5
Lumsden Pond PP NS 32 E7
Lumsden Pond PP NS 33 B4
Lund BC 1 E6
Lund BC 2 C2-3
Lundar MB 13 E3
Lundar MB 14 C4
Lundar Beach MB 14 C3
Lundar Beach PP MB 13 E3
Lundar Beach PP MB 14 C3
Lundbreck AB 6 F5
Lundbreck AB 7 E4
Lundy NS 34 E5
Lunenburg NS 32 F6-7
Lunenburg NS 33 C4
Lunenburg NS 33 D4-5
Lunenburg Fisheries Museum of the Atlantic NS 33 D5
Lunenburg Harbour NS 33 D5
Lurgan SK 11 B6
Lurgan Beach ON 20 B3
Luscar AB 8 D1-2
Luseland SK 6 C8
Luseland SK 11 C2-3
Lushes Bight NL 38 E5
Lushes Bight-Beaumont-Beaumont North NL 38 E5
Lusignan, lac QC 24 A5
Lusignan, lac QC 25 E5
Luskville QC 22 F7
Luskville QC 24 D1
Lutes Mountain NB 31 F8
Lutes Mountain NB 32 B6
Luther Lake ON 19 A6
Luther Lake ON 20 C5
Luther Marsh CA ON 19 A6
Luther Marsh CA ON 20 C5
Luton ON 19 D5
Luton ON 20 F4
Lutose AB 9 A3-4
Lutsel K'e NT 10 C8
Lutsel K'e NT 41 E2
Luxana Bay BC 1 C2
Luzan AB 8 B8
Lyal Island ON 18 E4
Lyalta AB 6 D6
Lyalta AB 7 B4
Lyddal MB 15 F3
Lydiatt MB 14 D6
Lyell Island BC 1 B1-2
Lyleton MB 11 F8
Lyleton MB 13 F1
Lymburn AB 9 E2
Lyn ON 21 D8
Lyn ON 24 F2
Lynch, lac QC 22 D5
Lynch, lac QC 24 A4
Lynch, lac QC 25 F4
Lynden ON 19 B6-7
Lynden ON 20 E5-6
Lynde Shores CA ON 20 C8
Lynde Shores CA ON 21 F2
Lyndhurst ON 21 D7
Lynedoch ON 19 D6
Lynedoch ON 20 F5
Lynn NS 32 D7
Lynn NS 33 A5
Lynn NS 34 E1
Lynn Lake MB 12 D7
Lynn Lake MB 15 D1-2
Lynnwood ON 19 D3
Lyn Valley CA ON 21 D8
Lynx Bay MB 13 C3-4
Lynx City YT 4 C2
Lynx Lake NT 41 E3
Lyon, Cape NT 5 A8
Lyon, Cape NT 41 A1
Lyons ON 19 C5
Lyons ON 20 F4
Lyons Brook NS 34 D3
Lyonshall MB 14 F1-2
Lyster QC 27 C5
Lyttleton NB 31 D6
Lytton BC 1 E8
Lytton BC 2 B7

M

Mabee's Corners ON 19 D6
Mabee's Corners ON 20 F5
Mabel Lake BC 6 E2
Mabel Lake PP BC 6 E2
Maberly NL 37 B7-8
Maberly ON 21 C6
Mabille, lac QC 39 D4
Mabou NS 34 C5
Mabou Harbour NS 34 C5
Mabou Harbour Mouth NS 34 C5
Mabou Mines NS 34 C5
Mabou PP NS 34 C5
McAdam NB 32 D2
Macallum Lake SK 9 F8
Macallum Lake SK 12 F3
MacAlpine Lake NU 41 C3
Macamic QC 17 C8
Macamic QC 23 C2-3
Macamic, lac QC 23 C2-3
Macamic, rivière QC 23 C3
McAras Brook NS 34 D4
McArthur Falls MB 13 E4-5
McArthur Falls MB 14 C6-7
McArthur Mills ON 21 B4
Macaulay Mountain CA ON 21 E5
McAuley MB 11 E7-8
McAuley MB 13 E1
Macaza, lac QC 24 B4
Macaza, lac QC 25 F4
McBean Harbour ON 18 B3
McBeth Fiord NU 41 B7-8
McBeth Fiord NU 42 E7
McBeth Point MB 13 C3-4
McBride BC 1 B8
McBride BC 6 B1
McBride Lake SK 11 C7
McBride River BC 3 C3
McCabe Creek YT 4 C3
McCallum NL 36 D5
McCallum NL 37 D3
McCallum Lake MB 12 E7
McCallum Lake MB 15 E1
McCallum Settlement NS 33 A6
McCallum Settlement NS 34 E2
MacCallums Point PE 35 D2
Maccan NS 32 C7
Maccan River NS 32 C7
McCarthy, lac QC 25 C8
McCarthy, lac QC 28 E4
McCauley Island BC 1 A2
McClarty Lake MB 11 A8
McClarty Lake MB 12 F8
McClarty Lake MB 13 A2
McClarty Lake MB 15 F2
McClelland Lake AB 9 C6-7
McClelland Lake AB 12 C2
Maccles Lake NL 36 B8
Maccles Lake NL 37 B6
M'Clintock MB 15 C5-6
M'Clintock Channel NU 41 A-B4
M'Clintock Channel NU 42 E3

M'Clintock Inlet *NU* 42 A4-5
M'Clintock River *YT* 4 E4
M'Clure Strait *NT* 42 D2
McConnell *MB* 11 E8
McConnell *MB* 13 E1-2
McConnell Lake PP *BC* 2 B8
McConnell Lake PP *BC* 6 E1
McConnell Range *NT* 10 B2
McConnell River *YT* 4 D5
McCord *NT* 11 F4
MacCormack PP *NS* 34 C6-7
McCoy Lake *ON* 13 C7
McCoy Lake *ON* 16 A3
McCracken, lac *QC* 22 D2-3
McCrackens Landing *NS* 21 D3-4
McCraney Lake *ON* 21 A2
McCrea Lake *ON* 13 D8
McCrea Lake *ON* 16 C5
McCrea River *NT* 10 B-C7
McCreary *MB* 13 D2
McCreary *MB* 14 C2
McCulloch *BC* 6 E2
Macculloch, Cape *NU* 41 A12
Macculloch, Cape *NU* 42 D6
McCusker Lake *ON* 14 A8
McCusker Lake *ON* 16 B1
McCusker Lake Provincial Ecological Reserve *SK* 9 E8
McCusker Lake Provincial Ecological Reserve *SK* 12 E-F3
McCusker River *SK* 9 E-F8
McCusker River *SK* 12 B4
Macdiarmid *ON* 16 E6
Macdiarmid *ON* 17 B1
Macdonald *MB* 13 E4
Macdonald *MB* 14 D3
McDonald, lac *QC* 24 C7
McDonald Bay *SK* 12 E4
McDonald Creek PP *BC* 6 E3
MacDonald Farm PHS *NB* 31 D7
McDonald Lake *NT* 10 D8
MacDonald Lake *SK* 12 A4
MacDonald Range *BC* 6 F5
MacDonald Range *BC* 7 F3
McDonalds Corners *ON* 21 C6
McDonalds Point *NB* 32 C4
McDonald Unit (Gulf Islands NPR) *BC* 2 F4
McDougal Creek *SK* 11 A5-6
MacDougall *NB* 31 F8
MacDougall *MB* 13 D2
McDougall Gulch *NL* 36 D1
McDougall Pass *NT* 5 C3-4
Macdowell *SK* 11 B4-5
McDowell *ON* 13 C6
McDowell *ON* 13 C3
MacDowell Lake *ON* 13 C7
MacDowell Lake *ON* 16 A3
MacDowell River 13 B-C7
MacDuff *ON* 17 C4
MacElmons Pond PP *NS* 32 D8
MacElmons Pond PP *NS* 33 A5-6
MacElmons Pond PP *NS* 34 E1-2
Maces Bay *NB* 32 E3
McEvoy, Mount *BC* 3 D4
McEvoy Lake *YT* 4 D6
McFarlane Lake *ON* 13 C6
McFarlane River *SK* 9 A-B8
McFarlane River *SK* 9 B8
MacFarlane River *SK* 12 B4
MacFarlane River *SK* 41 F2
McGavock Lake *MB* 12 D7
McGavock Lake *MB* 15 D1
McGee *SK* 11 D3
McGerrigle, monts *QC* 29 B7
McGillivray, lac *QC* 22 E5
McGillivray Range *BC* 6 F4
McGillivray Range *BC* 7 F1-2
McGivney *NB* 31 F5
McGivney *NB* 32 B3
McGowans Corner *NB* 32 C3
McGrath Cove *NS* 32 F8
McGrath Cove *NS* 33 C5
McGraw Brook *NB* 31 D5-6
MacGregor *MB* 13 E3
MacGregor *MB* 14 D3
McGregor *ON* 19 E1
McGregor, lac *QC* 21 A8
McGregor, lac *QC* 21 A8
McGregor, lac *QC* 22 C8
McGregor, lac *QC* 22 F8
McGregor, lac *QC* 24 D2
McGregor Bay *ON* 18 B4
McGregor Bay *ON* 18 B4
McGregor Lake *AB* 6 E6
McGregor Lake *AB* 7 C5
MacGregor Point PP *ON* 18 F4
MacGregor Point PP *ON* 20 A3
McGregor River *BC* 1 A7-8
McGregor River *BC* 6 A1

McGregor River *BC* 9 F1
Machawaian Lake *ON* 16 B6-7
Machias Seal Island NMBS *NB* 32 F2
Machichi River *MB* 13 E1-2
Machmell River *BC* 1 D4-5
McInnes Lake *ON* 13 C6
McInnes River *ON* 13 C6
McInnis Point *PE* 35 E-F5
McIntosh *ON* 13 E6
McIntosh *ON* 16 D2
McIntosh Lake *ON* 22 F2
McIntyre Bay *ON* 1 A1
MacIntyre Lake *SK* 12 C5
McIver's *NL* 36 A3
McIver's *NL* 37 A1
McIver's *NL* 38 F2
MacIvor River *BC* 1 A3
McIvor River *AB* 12 B-C1
McKague *SK* 11 C6
McKaskill Lake *ON* 21 A4
McKaskill Lake *ON* 21 A4
MacKay *AB* 6 A-B4
MacKay *AB* 8 C4
McKay Creek *ON* 22 F5
MacKay Lake *NT* 41 D2
Mackay Lake *NT* 10 B8
McKay Lake *NL* 39 B2-3
McKay Lake *ON* 16 D-E8
McKay Lake *ON* 17 B2
Mackay River *AB* 9 D6
Mackay River *AB* 12 D1
McKay's *NL* 36 C2
McKays Corners *ON* 19 D3
McKeand River *NU* 40 A5
McKeand River *NU* 41 C8
McKees Mills *NB* 31 E4
McKees Mills *NB* 32 A6
McKellar *ON* 18 C7
McKendrick *NB* 31 A5
Mackenzie *BC* 3 F6-7
Mackenzie, fleuve *NT* 4 B4
Mackenzie, fleuve *NT* 5 B4
Mackenzie, fleuve *NT* 10 A-B2
Mackenzie, fleuve *NT* 10 E4
Mackenzie, fleuve *NT* 41 D-E1
Mackenzie Bison Sanctuary *NT* 10 D6
MacKenzie Creek *ON* 19 C6-7
McKenzie Creek *ON* 20 E5-6
Mackenzie Delta *NT* 5 C4
McKenzie Island *ON* 13 D6
Mckenzie Island *ON* 16 B-C2
Mackenzie King Island *NT* 42 C2-3
McKenzie Lake *ON* 21 B4
Mackenzie Lake *SK* 11 A7
McKenzie Lake *SK* 12 C6
McKenzie Lake *SK* 13 A1
Mackenzie Lake *SK* 15 C1
McKenzie Lake *SK* 15 F1
Mackenzie Mountains *NT* 4 A6-7 B7-8 C8
Mackenzie Mountains *NT* 5 E-F4 F5-6
McKenzie River *NT* 4 A8
McKenzie River *SK* 5 D5-6
McKenzie River *NT* 10 A1
McKenzie River *NT* 10 D3-4
Mackenzie River 41 D-E1
McKerracher Lake *MB* 12 C8
McKerracher Lake *MB* 15 C3
McKerrow *ON* 17 F6
McKerrow *ON* 18 A4
Mackey *ON* 22 E4
McKiel Lake *NB* 31 E4
McKiel Lake *NB* 32 A2
McKillop, lac *QC* 22 C3
Mackin Creek *BC* 1 C7
McKinlay Lake *NT* 10 A1
McKinley Bay *NT* 5 A5-6
McKinleyville *NB* 31 D6-7
McKinnon TP *NT* 5 F7-8
McKinnon TP *NT* 10 A1
McKinnons Harbour *NS* 34 D6-7
Mack Lake *MB* 15 C5
Macklin *SK* 6 C8
Macklin *SK* 11 E2
McKnight Lake *MB* 12 E7
McKnight Lake *MB* 15 E2
McLachlan, lac *QC* 22 C3
McLaren, lac *QC* 25 D6
McLaren, lac *QC* 27 A2
McLaren, lac *QC* 28 F2
McLaughlin *AB* 6 B8
McLaughlin *AB* 11 B2
McLaughlin River *MB* 13 A4
McLean *SK* 11 E6
McLean Settlement *NB* 31 E7-8
McLean Settlement *NB* 32 A6
Maclean Strait *NU* 42 C3
McLeese Lake *BC* 1 C7
McLennan *AB* 9 E3-4

McLennan, lac *QC* 22 A8
McLennan, lac *QC* 25 C2
McLennan Lake *SK* 12 E5
McLeod Bay *NT* 41 D2
McLeod Lake *BC* 3 F7
McLeod Lake *BC* 3 F7
McLeod PP *ON* 16 D7
McLeod PP *ON* 17 B2
McLeod River *AB* 6 A4 B3-4
McLeod River *AB* 8 B-C3
McLeod River *AB* 8 C2
McLeod Valley *AB* 8 C3
McLure *BC* 2 A8
McLure *BC* 6 D1
McMahon *SK* 11 E3-4
McManus Hill, ZCP *NB* 32 C5-6
McManus Hill PCA *NB* 32 C6
McMaster Island, RNP *ON* 18 E4
McMaster Island PNR *ON* 18 E4
McMillan Lake *AB* 9 E6
McMillan Lake *AB* 12 E1
McMillan Lake *MB* 12 D7
McMillan Lake *MB* 15 D1
Macmillan Pass *YT* 4 B6
MacMillan PP *BC* 2 D-E3
Macmillan River *YT* 4 B4 C3-4
McMorran *SK* 11 D3
McMunn *MB* 13 F5
McMunn *MB* 14 E7
McMurdo *BC* 6 D3-4
McNab *AB* 7 F6
McNab Cove *NS* 34 D7
McNabs Island *NS* 33 C6
McNallie Creek TP *NT* 10 E5-6
McNamara, Mount *BC* 3 C4-5
McNamara Lake *ON* 16 E4
McNamee *NB* 31 E5
McNamee *NB* 32 A3
McNeil Lake *YT* 4 D5
McNeil River *YT* 4 D5
McNeills Mills *PE* 35 C2
MacNutt *SK* 13 D1
McNutt *NB* 11 D7
McNutt Island *NS* 33 F3
Macoun *SK* 11 F6
Macoun Lake *SK* 12 D6
Macpès, lac *QC* 29 C3
McPhadyen River *NL* 39 B2
McPhee Corner *NS* 32 E8
McPhee Corner *NS* 33 B6
McPhee Corner *NS* 34 F2
McPherson Lake *YT* 4 D6
McPhersons Mills *NS* 33 A8
McPhersons Mills *NS* 34 A8
McQuaby Lake *ON* 22 E1
McQuesten *YT* 4 B3
McQuesten Lake *YT* 4 A4
McQuesten River *YT* 4 B3
McRae *AB* 6 A7
McRae *AB* 8 A8
McRae *AB* 9 F7
McRae *AB* 11 A1
McRae *AB* 12 F1
MacRae *YT* 4 E4
McRae Point PP *ON* 18 F8
McRae Point PP *ON* 20 A7
McRae Point PP *ON* 21 D1
Macrorie *SK* 11 D4
Mactaquac *SK* 32 C2
Mactaquac PP *NB* 32 C2
McTaggart *SK* 11 F6
McTaggart Lake *SK* 9 B-C8
McTaggart Lake *SK* 12 C3
McTavish *ON* 16 E4-5
McTavish *MB* 14 E4-5
McTavish Lake *SK* 12 E5
MacTier *ON* 18 D7-8
Macton *ON* 19 A5-6
Macton *ON* 20 D4-5
McVeigh *MB* 12 D7
McVeigh *MB* 15 C3
McVicar Arm *NT* 10 A3-4
McVicar Arm *NT* 41 C1
McVitties *ON* 17 F7
McVitties *ON* 18 A5-6
McWatters *QC* 17 D8
McWatters *QC* 23 E2-3
Madame, île *QC* 27 A6
Madame, Isle *NS* 34 E6
Madawaska *ON* 21 A4
Madawaska *ON* 22 F3-4
Madawaska, rivière *QC* 31 B-C1
Madawaska Lake *ON* 21 B3
Madawaska River *ON* 21 A3-4
Madden *AB* 6 D5
Madden *AB* 7 A3-4
Maddox Cove *NL* 37 D-E8
Madeira Park *BC* 2 E3
Madeleine, cap de la *QC* 29 A8
Madeleine, cap de la *QC* 30 A1
Madeleine, îles de la *QC* 30 F7-8
Madeleine, lac *QC* 23 B6
Madeleine, rivière *QC* 29 A-B8
Madeleine, rivière *QC* 30 B1
Madeleine-Centre *QC* 29 A8

Madeleine-Centre *QC* 30 A1
Madge Lake *MB* 11 C-D7
Madge Lake *MB* 13 C1
Madison *SK* 11 D3
Madoc *ON* 21 D5
Madran *NB* 31 B6
Mad River *ON* 20 B6
Madsen *ON* 13 D6
Madsen *ON* 16 C2
Maelpaeg Reservoir *NL* 36 C5
Maelpaeg Reservoir *NL* 37 C5
Mafeking *MB* 11 B8
Mafeking *MB* 13 B1
Magaguadavic *QC* 32 C2
Magaguadavic Lake *NB* 32 C1
Magaguadavic River *NB* 32 D2
Maganasipi, lac *QC* 22 D3
Maganasipi, ZEC *QC* 22 D3
Magill Lake *ON* 15 F5
Magiss Lake *ON* 13 B7
Magna Bay *BC* 6 D2
Magnet *MB* 14 B2
Magnetawan *ON* 18 C7-8
Magnetawan *ON* 22 F1
Magnetawan River *ON* 18 C6-7
Magnetawan River *ON* 18 C7
Magnetawan River *ON* 18 C8
Magnetawan River *ON* 21 A1
Magnetawan River PP *ON* 18 C6-7
Magnolia *AB* 8 C5
Magog *AB* 24 E8
Magog *QC* 27 F4
Magog, lac *QC* 27 E-F4
Magpie *QC* 39 E-F3
Magpie, baie de *QC* 39 E-F3
Magpie, lac *QC* 39 E3
Magpie, lac *QC* 40 F7
Magpie, rivière *QC* 39 E3
Magpie Ouest, rivière *QC* 39 D3
Magpie River *ON* 17 D3-4
Magrath *AB* 6 F6
Magrath *AB* 7 F5-6
Magundy *NB* 32 C2
Magundy River *YT* 4 C4-5
Maguse Lake *NU* 40 A-B1
Maguse Lake *NU* 41 E4
Mahaska *AB* 8 B3
Mahekun Lake *MB* 12 C7
Mahekun Lake *MB* 15 C2
Mahers *NL* 37 E7
Mahone Bay *NS* 32 F7
Mahone Bay *NS* 33 C-D5
Mahone Bay *NS* 33 D4-5
Mahony Lake *NT* 5 E8
Mahood Falls *BC* 1 C8
Mahood Falls *BC* 6 C1
Mahood Lake *BC* 1 C8
Mahood Lake *BC* 6 C1
Maicasagi, rivière *QC* 26 A2
Maiden Point *NL* 38 B5
Maidstone *NL* 36 C1
Maidstone *ON* 19 E1
Maidstone *SK* 6 B8
Maidstone *SK* 11 B3
Main-à-Dieu *NS* 34 C8
Main Brook *NL* 38 B4
Main Brook *NL* 39 D8
Main Centre *SK* 11 E4
Main Channel *ON* 18 D4
Main Dam *NL* 36 A4
Main Dam *NL* 37 A2
Main Dam *NL* 38 F8
Main Duck Island *ON* 21 E6
Main Point *NL* 36 F7
Main Point *NL* 37 A5-6
Main Point *NL* 38 F7
Main River *NL* 38 E3
Main River *NL* 39 F7-8
Main Topsail *NL* 36 A5
Main Topsail *NL* 37 A3
Main Topsail *NL* 38 F4
Mair *NL* 11 E-F7
Mair *SK* 11 E7
Maison-Commémorative-Bethune, LHN de la *ON* 21 C1-2
Maison de Pierre, lac *QC* 25 E4
Maison-de-Pierre, ZEC *QC* 25 E4
Maison-de-Sir-John-Johnson, LHN de la *ON* 24 E4-5
Maison Green Gables *PE* 35 D4
Maison-Inverarden, LHN de la *ON* 24 E4
Maisonnette *NB* 30 E2
Maisonnette *NB* 20 C6-7
Maison-Riel, LHN de la *MB* 14 E5
Maitland *NS* 32 D8

Maitland *NS* 33 A6
Maitland *NS* 33 D4
Maitland *NS* 34 E-F2
Maitland *ON* 21 C8
Maitland *ON* 24 F2
Maitland Bridge *NS* 33 D3
Maitland Island *BC* 1 A3
Maitland Point *NT* 5 A6
Maitland River *ON* 19 A4-5
Maitland River *ON* 20 C3
Maitland River *ON* 20 C4
Major *SK* 6 C8
Major *SK* 11 C2
Major, lac *QC* 22 C8
Major, lac *QC* 24 A3
Major, lac *QC* 25 E3
Majorville *AB* 7 C5-6
Makamik *QC* 25 D4
Makaroff *MB* 11 D7
Makaroff *MB* 13 D1
Makepeace *AB* 7 B6
Makinak *MB* 13 D2
Makinak *MB* 14 B2
Makinsons *NL* 37 D7
Makkovik *NL* 39 A6
Makkovik *NL* 40 D8
Makkovik Bay *NL* 39 A6
Makkovik River *NL* 39 A6
Makobe Lake *ON* 17 E7
Makobe-Grays River *ON* 17 E7
Makokibatan Lake *ON* 16 B7
Makoop River *ON* 13 A7
Makwa *SK* 6 A8
Makwa *SK* 11 A3
Makwa Lake PP *SK* 6 A8
Makwa Lake PP *SK* 11 A2-3
Makwa-Sahfahcan *SK* 6 A8
Makwa-Sahgaican *SK* 6 A8
Makwa-Sahgaican *SK* 11 A3
Makwa-Sahgaiehcan *SK* 11 A3
Malachi *ON* 13 E5
Malachi *ON* 14 D8
Malachi *ON* 16 D1
Malagash *NS* 34 D2
Malagash Point *NS* 34 D2
Malagash Station *NS* 34 D2
Malagawatch *NS* 34 D6
Malahat *BC* 2 F4
Malakwa *BC* 6 D2
Malartic *QC* 23 E4
Malartic, lac *QC* 23 D4
Malaspina Strait *BC* 1 F4
Malaspina Strait *BC* 2 C-D3
Malauze *NB* 31 A4
Malay Falls *NS* 33 B8
Malay Falls *NS* 34 F4
Malbaie, lac *QC* 29 D1
Malbaie, rivière *QC* 28 D-E7
Malbaie, rivière *QC* 30 C2-3
Malcolm Island *BC* 1 E4
Malcolm Island *BC* 12 D7
Malcolm Island *SK* 15 D1
Malcolm River *YT* 5 A2
Malden *NS* 35 E2
Malden Centre *ON* 19 E1
Mâle, lac du *QC* 26 E3
Maleb *AB* 6 E7
Maleb *AB* 7 E7-8
Malfait, lac *NT* 10 A4-5
Malfait, lac *QC* 28 A4
Maliceet *NB* 31 D3
Malignant Cove *NS* 34 D4
Maligne Lake *AB* 6 B-C3
Maligne Lake *AB* 8 E1-2
Maligne River *AB* 6 B3
Maligne River *AB* 8 D1
Maligne River *ON* 16 F3-4
Maliotenam *QC* 39 E-F2
Mallaig *AB* 6 A7
Mallaig *AB* 11 A1
Mallaig *AB* 12 F1
Mallard *MB* 13 C2
Mall Bay *NL* 37 F7
Mallery Lake *NU* 41 D4
Mallorytown *ON* 21 D7-8
Mallorytown Landing PP *ON* 21 D8
Mallow *AB* 7 B-C6
Malmo *AB* 8 E7
Malo, lac *QC* 26 B5
Malone *ON* 21 D4-5
Malonton *MB* 13 E4
Malonton *MB* 14 C5
Malouin, rivière *QC* 17 A8
Malpeque *PE* 32 A8
Malpeque *PE* 34 B1
Malpeque *PE* 35 C3
Malpeque Bay *PE* 32 A8
Malpeque Bay *PE* 34 B1
Malpeque Bay *PE* 35 C2-3
Malpeque Harbour *PE* 35 C2
Maltais *QC* 29 D6
Maltais *NB* 31 A5
Maltempec *NS* 30 E1-2
Maltempec *NS* 31 B7
Malton *ON* 19 A7-8
Malton *ON* 20 C6-7
Malton *ON* 21 F1
Mamakwash Lake *ON* 16 B3
Mamawi Lake *AB* 9 B6
Mamawi Lake *AB* 12 B2
Mameigwess Lake *ON* 16 A6-7
Mameigwess Lake *ON* 16 D-E3
Ma-Me-O Beach *AB* 8 D6
Mamiegowish Lake *ON* 13 C-D6

Mamozekel River *NB* 29 F5
Mamozekel River *NB* 31 C4
Man of War Point *NL* 38 E5
Manawan *QC* 25 D4
Manawan Lake *SK* 12 E6
Manche-d'Épée *QC* 29 A8
Manche-d'Épée *QC* 30 A1
Manchester *ON* 20 B8
Manchester *ON* 21 E2
Mandanna Lake *YT* 4 D3-4
Mandaumin *ON* 19 C3
Mandaumin *ON* 20 E2
Manful Bight *NL* 38 E5
Manhattan Beach *MB* 14 F2
Manic-Cinq *QC* 39 E1
Manic-Deux, barrage *QC* 29 A3
Manic-Deux, réservoir *QC* 29 A3
Manicouagan *QC* 40 F6
Manicouagan, péninsule de *QC* 39 E1
Manicouagan, pointe de *QC* 29 A3-4
Manicouagan, réservoir *QC* 40 F6
Manicouagan, réservoir *QC* 39 D1
Manicouagan, rivière *QC* 39 E-F1
Manicouagan, rivière *QC* 40 F6
Manic-Un, barrage *QC* 29 A3
Manigotagan *MB* 13 D4
Manigotagan *MB* 14 B6
Manigotagan River *MB* 13 D5
Manigotagan River *MB* 14 B7
Manigotagan River PP Reserve *MB* 13 D4-5
Manigotagan River PP Reserve *MB* 14 B6
Manilla *ON* 20 B8
Manilla *ON* 21 D2
Manipogo PP *MB* 13 D2
Manipogo PP *MB* 14 A2
Manitoba, lac *MB* 13 D3
Manitoba, lac *MB* 13 E3
Manitoba, lac *MB* 14 C3 D3-4
Manitoba, Lake *MB* 13 D2-3
Manitoba, Lake *MB* 13 D-E3
Manitoba Lowlands NP (proposed) *MB* 13 D4-5
Manitoba Lowlands NP (proposed) (Black & Deer Island Section) *MB* 14 B6
Manitoba Lowlands NP (proposed) (Limestone Bay Section) *MB* 13 A3
Manitoba Lowlands NP (proposed) (Long Point Section) *MB* 13 B2-3
Manitou *MB* 13 F3
Manitou *MB* 14 E4
Manitou *QC* 39 E-F3
Manitou, lac *QC* 39 E3
Manitou, lac *QC* 18 C3-4
Manitou, rivière *QC* 39 E3
Manitou Beach *SK* 11 D5
Manitou Island *NT* 5 E6
Manitou Island *NT* 10 A3
Manitou Island PP *ON* 17 F7-8
Manitou Islands *ON* 18 A-B8
Manitou Islands *ON* 22 D1
Manitou Islands PP *ON* 18 B8
Manitou Islands PP *ON* 22 D1
Manitou River *ON* 18 C-D7
Manitouwabing Lake *ON* 18 C-D7
Manitouwadge *ON* 16 E8
Manitouwadge *ON* 17 C3
Manitouwadge *ON* 40 F6
Manitowaning *ON* 18 C4
Manitowaning Bay *ON* 18 B-C4
Manitowik Lake *ON* 17 D4
Maniwaki *QC* 22 D7
Maniwaki *QC* 25 F1-2
Mankota *SK* 11 F4
Manly *AB* 8 C5-6

Mannard, lac *QC* 26 B5
Manners Sutton *NB* 32 C2
Manneville *QC* 17 C8
Manneville *QC* 23 D3
Mannheim *ON* 19 B6
Mannheim *ON* 20 D5
Manning *AB* 9 D3
Manning, Cape *NT* 42 C1
Manning Park *BC* 2 E8
Manning Park *BC* 6 F1
Manning PP *BC* 1 F8
Manning PP *BC* 2 E8
Manning PP *BC* 6 F1
Mann Settlement *QC* 29 D5
Mann Settlement *QC* 31 A4
Mannville *AB* 6 B7
Mannville *AB* 11 B1-2
Manola *AB* 6 A5
Manola *AB* 8 B5
Manor *SK* 11 F7
Manotick *ON* 21 B8
Manotick *ON* 24 E2
Manotick Station *ON* 21 B8
Manotick Station *ON* 24 E2
Manouane, lac *QC* 25 C5
Manouane, lac *QC* 40 F5-6
Manseau *QC* 27 C4
Mansel Island *NU* 40 B4
Mansel Island *NU* 41 E7
Mansfield *NS* 32 C7-8
Mansfield *NS* 34 D1
Mansfield *ON* 20 B6
Mansfield *ON* 21 B7
Mansonville *QC* 24 E8
Mansonville *QC* 27 F4
Mansons Landing PP *BC* 2 C2
Mantagao Lake *MB* 14 A4
Mantagao River *MB* 13 D3
Mantagao River *MB* 14 A4
Mantario *SK* 6 D8
Mantario *SK* 11 D2
Manuel Lake *NT* 5 D6
Manuels *NB* 31 D8
Manvers *ON* 21 E2-3
Manyberries *AB* 6 F8
Manyberries *AB* 7 E8
Manyberries *AB* 11 F1-2
Many Island Lake *AB* 11 E2
Many Islands Lake *AB* 6 E8
Maple *ON* 19 A8
Maple *ON* 20 C7
Maple *ON* 21 F1
Maple Bay *BC* 2 E4
Maple Beach *MB* 14 A3
Maple Creek *SK* 6 E8
Maple Creek *SK* 11 E2
Maple Glen *NB* 31 D6
Maple Grove *NB* 31 E4-5
Maple Grove *NB* 32 A-B3
Maple Grove *ON* 24 E5-6
Maple Grove *ON* 27 E-F1
Maple Island *ON* 18 C7
Maple Lake *ON* 18 D7
Maple Lake *ON* 21 B2-3
Maple Lake *ON* 22 E2
Maple Lake Park *ON* 19 B6
Maple Lake Park *ON* 20 E5
Maple Leaf *ON* 21 B4
Maple Plains *PE* 35 E3
Maple Ridge *BC* 1 F7
Maple Ridge *BC* 2 E5-6
Maple Ridge *BC* 6 F1
Maple Ridge *NB* 31 F3-4
Maple Ridge *NB* 32 B2
Mapleton *NS* 32 C-D7
Mapleton *NS* 33 A5
Mapleton *NS* 34 C1
Mapleton *ON* 19 C5
Mapleton *ON* 20 F4
Maple Valley *ON* 20 B5
Maplewood *NS* 32 F6-7
Maplewood *NS* 33 C4
Maplewood *NS* 33 D2
Mapova *AB* 8 A-B7
Maquereau, pointe au *QC* 30 D2
Mar *ON* 18 E5
Mara *BC* 6 E2
Mara PP *BC* 6 D-E2
Mara PP *BC* 18 F8
Mara PP *ON* 20 A7
Mara PP *ON* 21 D1
Mara PP *ON* 22 D1
Maraiche Lake *SK* 11 A7
Maraiche Lake *SK* 12 D2
Maraiche Lake *SK* 15 F1
Marathon *ON* 16 F8
Marathon *ON* 17 C2
Marathon Village *ON* 21 B7
Marble Canyon PP *BC* 1 D7-8
Marble Island *NU* 40 A2
Marble Island *NU* 41 E5
Marble Lake *NL* 39 A-B2
Marble Mountain *NS* 34 D6
Marble Range PP *BC* 1 D8
Marble Range PP *BC* 2 A6
Marble River PP *BC* 1 E4
Marbleton *QC* 27 E5
Marceau, lac *QC* 39 D7
Marcelin *SK* 11 B4
Marchand *MB* 13 F4
Marchand *MB* 14 E6
Marches Point *NL* 36 C1

Marchington Lake *ON* 16 D4
March Water *PE* 35 C-D3
Marchwell *SK* 11 D7
Marchwell *SK* 13 D1
Marcil *QC* 30 D2
Marcil *QC* 31 A7
Marc Lake *NL* 39 C3-4
Marconi, LHN *NS* 34 C8
Marconi, Mount *BC* 6 E5
Marconi, Mount *BC* 7 D2
Marconi NHS *NS* 34 C8
Marden *ON* 19 A6
Marden *ON* 20 D5
Marécage, lac du *QC* 22 B3
Marengo *SK* 6 D8
Marengo *SK* 11 D2
Margaree *NL* 36 E1
Margaree Centre *NS* 34 B6
Margaree Forks *NS* 34 C6
Margaree Harbour *NS* 34 B6
Margaree River *NS* 34 C6
Margaree Valley *NS* 34 B6
Margaret *MB* 13 F2
Margaret *MB* 14 E-F1
Margaret, Cape *NU* 41 B5
Margaret, Cape *NU* 42 F4
Margaret Hamilton Lake *NL* 39 B2
Margaret Lake *AB* 9 B4
Margaret Lake *NT* 10 A-B5
Margaretsville *NS* 32 E5-6
Margaretsville *NS* 33 B3
Margate *PE* 35 D3
Margo *SK* 11 C6
Margot Lake *ON* 16 A3
Margry, lac *QC* 23 B8
Margry, lac *QC* 26 C2
Marguerite *BC* 1 C7
Marguerite, lac *QC* 22 B-C8
Marguerite, lac *QC* 25 D2
Marguerite River *AB* 12 C2
Marguerite River Wildland *AB* 41 F1-2
Marguerite River Wildland PP *AB* 9 C7
Marguerite River Wildland PP *AB* 12 C2
Maria *QC* 29 D7
Maria *QC* 31 A6
Maria-Chapdelaine, lac *QC* 28 A6-7
Maria Lake *MB* 12 B7
Maria Lake *MB* 15 B2
Maria Lake *ON* 13 B8
Mariana Lake *AB* 9 E6
Mariana Lake *AB* 12 E1
Marian Lake *NT* 5 D6
Marian River *NT* 10 B5
Marian River *NT* 10 D5
Mariapolis *MB* 13 F2-3
Mariapolis *MB* 14 F2-3
Maribelli Lake *SK* 12 D5-6 E5-6
Maricourt *QC* 24 D8
Maricourt *QC* 27 E4
Maricourt, lac *QC* 23 D7-8
Maricourt, lac *QC* 26 C2
Marie-Claire, lac *QC* 39 E5
Marie Joseph *NS* 34 F4-5
Marie Joseph *NS* 34 F4-5
Marie Lake *AB* 9 F7
Marie Lake *AB* 12 F2
Marie-Lefranc, lac *QC* 24 B3-4
Marie River *PE* 35 D6
Marie-Reine *AB* 9 E3-4
Marieval *SK* 11 E6-7
Marieville *QC* 24 D7
Marieville *QC* 27 E2
Mari Lake *SK* 12 F7
Mari Lake *SK* 15 E-F1
Marin, lac *QC* 22 C4
Marine (St. Clair Parkway), parc *ON* 19 D2
Marine (St. Clair Parkway), parc *ON* 20 F1
Marine Park (St. Clair Parkway) *ON* 19 D2
Marine Park (St. Clair Parkway) *ON* 20 F1
Marinette *NS* 33 B7
Marinette *NS* 34 F3
Maringouin, Cape *NB* 32 C6-7
Marion, lac *QC* 22 C4
Marion, lac *QC* 26 D6
Marion, lac *QC* 28 B2
Marion Bridge *NS* 34 C7-8
Marionville *ON* 24 E2-3
Mariposa Brook *ON* 20 B8
Mariposa Brook *ON* 21 D-E2
Markdale *ON* 20 B4-5
Markerville *AB* 6 C6
Markerville *AB* 8 F5
Markham *ON* 20 C7-8
Markham *ON* 21 F1-2
Markham Bay *NU* 40 A5
Markham Bay *NU* 41 E7
Markinch *SK* 11 D5-6
Markland *MB* 14 C4
Markland *NL* 37 E7
Mark S. Burnham PP *ON* 21 D3-4
Markstay *ON* 17 F7
Markstay *ON* 18 A6

Markstay-Warren ON **18** A6
Marktosis BC **1** F5
Marktosis BC **2** D1
Marlboro ON **21** D5
Marlboro AB **6** B4
Marlboro AB **8** C2
Marl Creek PP BC **6** D3
Marmion Lake ON **13** F8
Marmion Lake ON **16** E4
Marmora ON **21** D4
Marquette MB **13** E3
Marquette MB **14** D4
Marquette, lac QC **26** D5-6
Marquette, lac QC **28** B1
Marquis SK **11** E5
Marriott SK **11** C3
Marriotts Cove NS **32** F7
Marriotts Cove NS **33** C5
Mars, rivière à QC **28** C-D6
Marsac QC **22** C2
Marsboro QC **27** E6
Marsden SK **6** B8
Marsden SK **11** B2
Marshall SK **6** B8
Marshall SK **11** B2
Marshall Lake ON **16** C-D7
Marshall Lake ON **17** A1
Marshalltown NS **32** F4-5
Marshalltown NS **33** C2
Marshfield PE **35** E5
Marsh Lake NS **18** D7
Marsh Lake YT **4** E4
Marsh Lake YT **4** E4
Marshland Lake ON **18** A2
Marsh Point MB **15** D6-7
Marshville NS **34** D2-3
Marshy Hope NS **34** E4
Mars-Moulin, ZEC de QC
　　28 D6
Marsoui QC **29** A7
Marsoui QC **39** F2
Marsoui, rivière QC **29** A7
Marsville ON **19** A6
Marsville ON **20** C5
Marteau, lac du QC **25** A5
Marteau, lac du QC **26** F5
Marteau, lac du QC **28** C1
Martel BC **2** B7
Marten Beach AB **9** E5
Marten Falls ON **16** B8
Marten Lake ON **22** C1
Marten River ON **17** F7
Marten River ON **22** C1
Marten River PP ON
　　17 F7-8
Marten River PP ON **22** C1
Martensville SK **11** C4
Martha Creek PP BC **6** D3
Martin ON **13** F8
Martin ON **16** E4
Martin, lac QC **23** D6
Martin House NT **5** D5
Martin River NT **10** D-E3
Martindale QC **22** F7-8
Martindale QC **24** C2
Martineau River SK **9** F8
Martineau River SK **12** F2
Martinenda Lake ON **17** F5
Martinique Beach PP NS
　　33 C7
Martins Point NS **32** F7
Martins Point NS **33** C5
Martins River NS **32** F7
Martins River NS **33** C-D4
Martintown ON **24** E4
Martinvale PE **35** E6
Martin-Valin, ZEC QC
　　28 B-C7
Martock NS **27** F5
Martock NS **33** B5
Martock NS **34** F1
Martres, lac des QC
　　28 D-E6
Martres, ZEC des QC
　　28 E6-7
Marwayne AB **6** B7
Marwayne AB **11** B2
Mary Ann Lake NL **36** A6
Mary Ann Lake NL **37** A4
Mary Ann Lake NL **38** F5
Maryen, lac QC **39** D5-6
Maryfield SK **11** E7
Maryfield SK **13** E1
Maryhill ON **19** B6
Maryhill ON **20** D5
Mary Lake ON **18** D8
Mary Lake ON **21** B1
Marysburg SK **11** C5
Mary's Harbour NL **39** C8
Marys River ON **17** B-C6
Marystown NL **36** E6-7
Marystown NL **37** D5
Marysvale NL **37** D-E7
Marysville BC **7** E1
Marysville NB **31** F5
Marysville NB **32** C3
Marysville ON **21** E5
Marysville ON **21** E7
Maryville NS **34** D5
Mascouche QC **24** C-D6
Mascouche QC **27** D1
Mascouche, rivière QC
　　24 C-D5
Mascouche, rivière QC
　　27 D1
Masefield SK **11** F3
Maseres, lac QC **23** C8
Maseres, lac QC **26** D2
Mashkinonje PP ON **17** F7
Mashkinonje PP ON **18** B6
Mashteuiatsh QC **26** E8
Mashteuiatsh QC **28** C4
Masketsi, lac QC **25** D8

Masketsi, lac QC **27** A3
Maskinongé QC **24** B7
Maskinongé QC **25** F7
Maskinongé QC **27** C2
Maskinongé, lac QC **24** B6
Maskinongé, lac QC **25** F6
Maskinongé, lac QC **27** C2
Maskinonge Lake ON
　　17 E-F7
Mason Point NS **34** C6
Mason River NT **5** A7
Masquapit Lake NB **32** C3-4
Masquapit Lake NB **32** C3-4
Massawipi QC **27** F4
Massawippi, lac QC **27** F4
Masset BC **1** A1
Masset Inlet BC **1** A1
Massey ON **17** F6
Massey ON **18** A-B3
Massey Drive NL **36** B3
Massey Drive NL **37** B1
Massey Island NU **42** C3
Massey Sound NU **42** B-C4
Massie ON **18** F6
Massie ON **20** A4-5
Masson QC **22** F8
Masson QC **24** D2-3
Masson, lac QC **24** C5
Masson, lac QC **27** D1
Masstown NS **32** D8
Masstown NS **33** A6
Masstown NS **34** E2
Massueville QC **24** C7
Massueville QC **27** D3
Mastigou, lac QC **24** A6
Mastigou, lac QC **25** F6
Mastigou, lac QC **27** B1-2
Mastigouche, lac QC **24** B6
Mastigouche, lac QC **25** F6
Mastigouche, lac QC
　　27 B-C1
Mastigouche, RF QC **24** A6
Mastigouche, RF QC **25** E6
Mastigouche, RF QC
　　27 B1-2
Matachewan ON **17** D6-7
Matachewan (IR) ON
　　17 D6-7
Matagami QC **23** A5
Matagami QC **40** F4
Matago MB **15** E4
Matamec QC **39** E2
Matamec, lac QC **39** E2
Matane QC **29** B4
Matane, lac QC **29** B5
Matane, RF de QC **29** B5-6
Matane, rivière QC **29** B-C5
Matapédia QC **29** D5
Matapédia QC **31** A4
Matapédia, lac QC **29** C4-5
Matapédia, rivière QC
　　29 C-D5
Matapédia, rivière QC
　　31 A4
Matawatchan ON **21** B5
Matawatchan PP ON **21** B5
Matawin, lac QC **24** A5
Matawin, lac QC **25** E5
Matawin, rivière QC **27** A2
Matawin River PP ON
　　16 F4-5
Matchi-Manitou, lac QC
　　23 E6
Matchlee Bay BC **2** D1
Mates Corner NB **35** E2
Mather MB **13** F2
Mather MB **14** F1
Mathers Corners ON **21** E3
Matheson ON **17** C7
Matheson Island MB **13** C4
Matheson Island MB **14** A5
Mathieson Channel BC
　　1 B-C4
Mathieu, lac QC **26** D4
Matimek, ZEC QC **39** E2
Matimekosh QC **39** A2
Matimekosh QC **40** D6
Matinenda Lake ON **18** A2
Matlock MB **13** E4
Matlock MB **14** C5
Matson Creek YT **4** B1-2
Matsqui BC **2** E6
Mattagami Lake ON **17** D6
Mattagami River ON
　　17 A5-6
Mattagami River ON
　　17 B-C6
Mattawa ON **22** D2
Mattawa, rivière ON **22** D2
Mattawa River ON **22** D1-2
Mattawa River PP ON **17** F8
Mattawa River PP ON **22** D2
Mattawitchewan River ON
　　17 B-C6
Mattberry Lake NT **10** B6
Matthews NB **31** D6
Mattice ON **17** B5
Mattie Settlement NS
　　34 D-E5
Mattis Point NL **36** C2
Matty Island NU **41** B4
Matty Island NU **42** F4
Maude, lac QC **23** D7
Maude, lac QC **25** A1
Maude, lac QC **26** E1
Maugerville NB **32** C3
Maunoir, lac NT **5** C8
Maunoir, lac NT **41** B1
Maurice Point SK **9** A7
Maurice Point SK **12** A3

Mauricie, PN de la QC
　　24 A7
Mauricie, PN de la QC
　　25 E7
Mauricie, PN de la QC
　　27 A2-3 B2-3
Mauser, lac QC **25** B4
Mauves, lac des QC
　　24 B3-4
Mavillette NS **33** E1
Mavillette Beach PP NS
　　33 E1
Mawcroft SK **11** E5
Mawdesley Lake MB **11** A8
Mawdesley Lake MB **13** A2
Mawer SK **11** D-E4
Maxim SK **11** F6
Maxime, lac QC **22** B8
Maxime, lac QC **25** C2
Maximeville PE **35** D1-2
Maxstone SK **11** F4
Maxville ON **24** E3-4
Maxwell ON **20** B5
Maxwell Bay NU **42** D4-5
Maxwellton Station NS
　　33 D1-2
May, Mount AB **6** A2
May Inlet NU **42** C3
May Lake SK **12** D6
Maybelle River Wildland PP
　　AB **9** B7
Maybelle River Wildland PP
　　AB **12** B2
Mayberry SK **11** E5
Maycroft AB **7** E3-4
Mayerthorpe AB **6** A4-5
Mayerthorpe AB **8** B4-5
Mayfair SK **11** B4
Mayfield MB **14** D2
Mayfield PE **34** B-C2
Mayfield PE **35** D4
Maymont SK **11** C3-4
Maynard ON **21** C8
Maynard ON **24** F2
Maynard Lake ON **13** E6
Maynard Lake ON **16** C-D2
Maynard Lake, RNP ON
　　16 C2
Maynard Lake PNR ON
　　21 A8
Maynard Lake PNR ON
　　24 F2
Mayne Bay BC **2** E2
Mayne Island BC **2** E4
Maynooth ON **21** B4
Maynooth Station ON
　　21 B4
Mayo QC **21** A8
Mayo QC **22** F8
Mayo QC **24** D3
Mayo YT **4** B4
Mayo River YT **4** B3-4
Mayson Lake SK **12** C4
Mayton AB **7** A4
Mazana, lac QC **25** D4
Mazana, ZEC QC **25** D4
Mazenod SK **11** E4
Mazenod Lake NT **10** B5
Mazeppa AB **7** A4
Mazinaw Lake ON **21** C5
Meacham SK **11** C5
Meachen BC **6** F4
Meachen BC **7** E1
Mead ON **17** B4
Meadow Bank CE **17** B4
Meadow Brook NB **32** B6-7
Meadow Creek BC **6** E3-4
Meadow Lake SK **6** A8
Meadow Lake SK **11** A3
Meadow Lake SK **11** A3
Meadow Lake PP SK **9** F8
Meadow Lake PP SK
　　11 A2-3
Meadow Lake PP SK
　　12 F2-3
Meadow Lea MB **14** D4
Meadow Portage MB **13** C2
Meadow Portage MB **14** A2
Meadowlands MB **14** A2
Meadows MB **13** E3
Meadows MB **14** D4
Meadows NL **36** B3
Meadows NL **37** B1
Meadowside ON **18** A7
Meadowvale NB **14** E5-6
Meadowvale Village ON
　　19 A7
Meadowvale Village ON
　　20 D6
Meadowview AB **8** B5
Meadowville NS **34** D3
Meaghers Grant NS **33** B6-7
Meaghers Grant NS **34** F2-3
Mealy Mountains NL
　　39 B-C6
Mealy Mountains NL
　　40 D-E8
Meander River AB **9** B3
Meanook AB **8** A6
Meanook, RNF AB **6** A5-6
Meanook, RNF AB **8** A6
Meanook, RNF AB **9** F5-6
Meanook NWA AB **6** A5-6

Meanook NWA AB **8** A6
Meanook NWA AB **9** F5-6
Meares Island BC **1** F5
Meares Island BC **2** D1
Meat Cove NS **34** A7
Meath Park SK **11** B5
Mechamego, lac QC **26** B3
Mechanic Settlement NB
　　32 C5-6
Méchins, cap des QC **29** A5
Medard BC **15** F3
Médéra, lac QC **23** E8
Médéra, lac QC **25** A3
Médéra, lac QC **26** F3
Medford ON **32** E7
Medford NS **33** B4
Medicine Hat AB **6** E7-8
Medicine Hat AB **7** D8
Medicine Hat AB **11** E1-2
Medicine River AB **6** C5
Medicine River AB **8** E5
Medika MB **13** F4
Medika MB **14** E7
Medina ON **19** B5
Medina ON **20** E4
Medley AB **6** A7
Medley AB **9** F7
Medley AB **11** A2
Medley AB **12** F2
Medonnegonix Lake ON
　　36 D6
Medonnegonix Lake ON
　　37 D4
Medora MB **11** F8
Medora MB **13** F1
Medstead SK **11** B3
Meductic NB **32** C1
Meduxnekeag River NB
　　31 F3
Meduxnekeag River NB
　　32 B1
Medway Creek ON **19** C4
Medway Creek ON **20** E3
Medway Harbour NS **33** D4
Medway River NS **32** F5-6
Medway River NS **33** C-D3
Meek Lake BC **3** B3
Meeting Creek AB **6** B-C6
Meeting Creek AB **8** E7
Meeting Lake SK **11** B3-4
Meeting Lake SK **11** B4
Meetoos SK **11** A3
Meeyomot Lake AB **11** A5
Meeyomot Lake SK **12** F5
Mega River AB **9** B2
Mégantic, lac QC **27** E6
Mégantic, mont QC **27** E6
Megisan Lake ON **17** E4-5
Mégiscane, lac QC **23** D8
Mégiscane, lac QC **26** E2
Mégiscane, rivière QC
　　23 D-E6
Mégiscane, rivière QC
　　23 D7
Mégiscane, rivière QC
　　26 E1-2
Mehatl Creek PP BC **1** E7-8
Mehatl Creek PP BC **2** C6
Meighen Island NU **42** B3
Meikle River AB **9** C3
Meilleur, lac QC **26** D6
Meilleur, lac QC **28** B1
Meilleur River NT **4** D8
Meilleur River NT **10** E1
Meisners Section NS **32** F6
Meisners Section NS
　　33 C3-4
Meister River YT **4** E6
Mékinac, lac QC **25** D7-8
Mékinac, lac QC **27** A3
Melancon NS **32** E7
Melanson NS **33** B4-5
Melanson Settlement NHS
　　NS **32** F3-5
Melanson Settlement NHS
　　NS **33** C1-2
Melaval SK **11** F4
Melbourne MB **14** E2
Melbourne ON **19** C4
Melbourne ON **20** E3
Melbourne QC **24** D8
Melbourne QC **27** E4
Melbourne Blockhouse
　　NHS ON **21** C7-8
Melbourne Blockhouse
　　NHS ON **24** E1-2
Melbourne Island NU **41** B-C3
Melbourne Island NU **42** F3
Melchett Lake ON **16** C7
Melchett Lake ON **17** A2
Meldrum Bay ON **18** B1-2
Meldrum Bay ON **18** B1
Meleb MB **13** E4
Meleb MB **14** C5
Mélèzes, rivière aux QC
　　40 C-D5
Melford NS **34** D6
Melford NS **34** E6
Melfort SK **11** B5-6
Melissa ON **18** D8
Melissa ON **21** B1
Melissa ON **22** F1
Melita MB **11** F8
Melita MB **13** F1
Mellowdale AB **8** B5
Melmerby Beach PP NS
　　34 D-E4
Melnice MB **14** C5
Melocheville QC **24** E5
Melrose NS **32** B7-8
Melrose NB **34** C1
Melrose NB **35** E2
Melrose NL **37** B7-8
Melrose NL **38** E4-5
Melrose ON **19** C4
Melrose ON **20** E3

Melville ON **21** E5
Melville PE **34** D3
Melville PE **35** F6
Melville SK **11** D7
Melville, île de NT **42** D2-3
Melville, île de NU **42** D2-3
Melville, Lake NL **39** B6
Melville, Lake NL **40** D8
Melville Beach SK **11** F7
Melville Hills **41** A-B1
Melville Island BC **1** A2
Melville Island NT
Melville Island NU
　　42 C-D2-3
Melville Peninsula NU
　　41 B-C6
Melville Peninsula NU
　　42 F5
Melville Sound NU **41** C3
Melville Sound NU **42** F3
Melville Sound NU **18** E5
Melvin Lake MB **12** C8
Melvin Lake MB **15** C-D2
Melvin River AB **9** B3-4
Membertou NS **34** C8
Memesagamesing Lake ON
　　18 B7
Memewin, lac QC **22** D3
Memorial Island PP NL **2** F7
Memphrémagog, lac QC
　　24 E8
Memphrémagog, lac QC
　　27 F4
Memramcook NB **31** B8
Memramcook NB **32** B6
Memramcook NB **32** B7
Memramcook, rivière NB
　　35 E-F1
Memramcook-Est NB **32** B7
Memramcook River NB
　　35 E-F1
Menaik AB **8** E6
Menako Lake ON **13** C8
Menako Lake ON **16** A5
Ménascouagama, lac QC
　　39 D-E5
Mendham SK **6** D8
Mendham SK **11** D2
Meneset ON **19** A3-4
Meneset ON **20** C2-3
Menihek NL **39** A2
Menihek Lakes NL **39** B2
Menihek Lakes NL **40** E6
Menisino MB **13** F4
Menisino MB **14** F6
Menneval NB **29** E5
Menneval NB **31** B3-4
Méntstouc, lac NL **39** D7
Menzel Centennial, RNP ON
　　21 D5
Menzel Centennial PNR ON
　　21 D5
Menzie MB **11** E8
Menzie MB **13** E1-2
Meota SK **11** B3
Mephisto Lake ON **21** C4
Merasheen NL **36** E8
Merasheen NL **37** E6
Merasheen Island NL
　　36 D-E8
Merasheen Island NL
　　37 D-E6
Mercer's Cove NL **36** E6
Mercer's Cove NL **37** E4
Merchant Lake ON **22** E3
Mercier QC **24** E6
Mercier QC **27** E-F1
Mercoal AB **6** A3
Mercoal AB **8** D2
Mercutio Lake ON **16** A5
Mercy Bay NT **42** D1-2
Merid SK **6** D8
Merid SK **11** D2
Meridian Island NT **10** E5
Meridian River MB **13** D-E4
Merigomish NS **34** E4
Merlin ON **19** E3
Mermaid PE **34** C2-3
Mermaid PE **35** E5
Merrickville ON **21** C8
Merrickville ON **24** F2
Merrickville Blockhouse
　　NHS ON **21** C7-8
Merrickville Blockhouse
　　NHS ON **24** E1-2
Merrickville-Wolford ON
　　21 C8
Merrickville-Wolford ON
　　24 F2
Merrill, lac QC **26** B4
Merrill, Mount YT **3** A6
Merrill, Mount YT **10** F1
Merrill Lake ON **21** C5
Merritt BC **1** E8
Merritt BC **2** C5
Merritt BC **6** E1
Merritt's Harbour NL **38** E6
Mersey River NS **33** D1 E4
Meruimtcook, lac QC **29** E2
Méruimtcook, lac QC
　　31 C1
Merville BC **1** F5-6
Merville BC **2** C5
Mervin SK **6** B8
Mervin SK **11** B3
Mesa Lake NT **10** A6
Mesachie Lake BC **2** E3
Mesgouez, lac QC **40** F4
Meskanaw SK **11** B5
Mesomikenda Lake ON
　　17 E6
Mespark Lake NS **33** E2

Mesplet, lac QC **23** C8
Mesplet, lac QC **26** D2
Mess Creek BC **3** C2
Messines QC **22** D-E7
Messines QC **24** B1-2
Messines QC **25** F1-2
Meta Incognita Peninsula
　　NU **40** A5-6 B6
Meta Pond NL **36** C7
Meta Pond NL **37** C5
Métabetchouan QC **28** C4
Métabetchouane, lac QC
　　28 D4
Métabetchouane, rivière QC
　　28 C-E4
Métabetchouane Est, rivière
　　QC **28** E4-5
Metagama ON **17** F6
Metagama ON **18** A4
Métascouac, lac QC
　　28 E4-5
Metcalf Bay MB **12** D7
Metcalf Bay MB **15** D2
Metcalfe ON **21** B8
Metcalfe ON **24** E2-3
Metchin River NL **39** B4
Metchosin BC **2** F4
Metheny NS **33** D1
Meteghan NS **33** D1
Meteghan River NS **33** D1
Meteghan Station NS **33** D1
Methley AB **14** B2
Methley Beach MB **14** B2
Metinota SK **11** B3
Metionga Lake ON **13** E8
Métis-sur-Mer QC **29** B3-4
Metiskow AB **6** C7-8
Metiskow AB **11** C1
Metlakatla BC **1** A2
Metlakatla BC **3** C4-5
Mewassin AB **8** C5
Mewatha Beach AB **12** F1
Mewatha Beach AB **8** A7
Mewatha Beach AB **9** F6
Meyersburg ON **21** E4
Meyronne SK **11** F4
Meziadin Junction BC **3** E3
Meziadin Lake BC **3** E3
Meziadin Lake PP BC **3** E3
Miami MB **13** F3
Miami MB **14** F3-4
Mica Creek BC **6** C2-3
Mica Dam BC **6** C2
Mica Peak BC **3** D-E6
Michael, Lake NL **39** A6
Michael, Lake NL **40** E8
Michael, Lake SK **12** C6
Michael's Bay ON **18** C3
Michaels Harbour NL **36** A7
Michaels Harbour NL **37** A5
Michaels Harbour NL **38** F5
Michaud Point NS **34** D7
Michel BC **6** F5
Michel BC **7** E3
Michel SK **9** B8
Michel SK **12** E3
Michel, lac QC **22** D7-8
Michel, lac QC **24** B2
Michel, lac QC **25** F2
Michel, Lake NL **38** D3
Michenel AB **6** D6
Michenel AB **7** A6
Michener, Mount AB **6** C4
Michener, Mount AB **8** F3
Michichi AB **6** D6
Michichi AB **7** A6
Michikamats Lake NL
　　39 A3
Michikinabish Lake ON
　　15 F5
Michipicoten ON **17** C4
Michipicoten Island ON
　　17 D2-3
Michipicoten Island PP ON
　　17 E2-3
Michipicoten Post PP ON
　　17 D3
Michipicoten River ON
　　17 D3
Michwacho, lac QC **26** A4
Micksburg ON **21** A5-6
Micksburg ON **22** F5-6
Midale SK **11** F6
Middle Arm NL **36** A3
Middle Arm NL **37** A1
Middle Arm NL **38** F2
Middle Arm NL **38** F2
Middle Bay QC **38** A2-3
Middle-Bay QC **39** D7
Middlebro MB **13** F5
Middlebro MB **14** F7
Middlebro MB **16** E1
Middle Brook NL **36** B8
Middle Brook NL **37** B6
Middle Cape NS **34** C8
Middle Castor River ON
　　21 B8
Middle Channel NT **5** C4
Middlechurch MB **14** D5
Middle Clyde River ON
　　33 E2-3
Middle Cove NS **33** C5
Middle Cove NL **37** D8
Middle East Pubnico NS
　　33 F2
Middle Falls PP ON **7** F6
Middlefield NS **33** D3-4
Middle Fiord NU **42** B4
Middle Foster Lake SK
　　12 D5
Middle Head NS **34** B7
Middle Island ON **19** F2
Middle Lake SK **11** C5
Middle Lake NL **36** C-D3
Middle Lake NL **37** C-D1
Middle Maitland River ON
　　19 A5
Middle Maitland River ON
　　20 C4

Middlemiss ON **19** D4
Middlemiss ON **20** F3
Middle Musquodoboit
　　33 B7
Middle Musquodoboit NS
　　34 F2-3
Middle New Cornwall NS
　　32 F7
Middle New Cornwall NS
　　33 C-D4
Middle Ohio NS **33** E3-4
Middle Pond NL **36** C8
Middle Pond NL **37** C6
Middleport ON **19** C7
Middleport ON **20** E6
Middle Ridge Pond NL
　　36 C6-7
Middle Ridge Pond NL
　　37 C4-5
Middle Ridge Wildlife
　　Reserve NL **36** C6
Middle Ridge Wildlife
　　Reserve NL **37** C4
Middle River BC **3** F5
Middle River NB **29** E7
Middle River NB **31** B6
Middle River NS **34** B6
Middle Sackville NB **32** C7
Middle Sackville NB **35** F1
Middle Sackville NS
　　33 C5-6
Middlesex NB **31** F7-8
Middlesex NB **32** C5-6
Middle Stewiacke NS
　　33 A6-7
Middle Stewiacke NS **34** F2
Middle Thames River ON
　　19 C5
Middle Thames River ON
　　20 D-E4
Middleton NB **32** C6-7
Middleton NS **32** F8
Middleton NS **33** B3
Middleton PE **35** D3
Middleton Island SK **12** C4
Middleville ON **21** B7
Middleville ON **24** E1
Middlewood NS **33** D4
Midgell PE **35** D6
Midgic NB **32** B7
Midgic NB **35** F1
Midhurst ON **18** F7
Midhurst ON **20** A6
Midland ON **18** E-F7
Midland ON **20** A6
Midland PP AB **6** D6
Midland PP AB **7** A5-6
Midnight Lake SK **11** B3
Midway BC **6** F2
Mignault, lac QC **26** C5-6
Migration Lake NT **10** A8
Miguasha ON **29** D6
Miguasha ON **31** A5
Miguasha, parc de QC
　　31 A5
Miguasha, parc de QC
　　29 D6
Miguasha, pointe de QC
　　29 D7
Miguasha Ouest ON **31** A5
Miguasha-Ouest ON
　　29 D6-7
Miguels Lake NL **36** B6
Miguels Lake NL **37** B4
Mikado SK **11** D7
Mikisew PP ON **18** C8
Mikisew PP ON **22** E1
Mikkola ON **18** A5
Mikkwa River AB **9** C3
Mikkwa River AB **41** F1
Milan QC **27** E6
Milbanke Sound BC **1** C3
Milburn PE **35** D4
Milburn PE **35** E4
Milden SK **11** D3-4
Mildmay ON **20** B4
Mildred SK **11** B4
Mile Lake ON **21** B6
Miles Cove NL **38** E6
Mile Lake NL **21** B6
Milestone SK **11** E5-6
Milford NS **32** D8
Milford NS **33** A6
Milford NS **34** F2
Milford ON **21** E5-6
Milford Bay ON **18** E8
Milford Bay ON **21** B1
Milford Haven River NS
　　34 D5
Militia Point NS **34** D7
Milk River AB **6** F6-7
Milk River AB **7** F5
Milk River AB **6** F7
Milk River AB **11** F1-2
Milk River Ridge Reservoir
　　AB **7** F6
Mill Bay BC **2** F4
Mill Cove NB **32** C2
Mill Cove NS **32** F7-8
Mill Cove NS **33** C5
Mill Cove PE **34** C2-3
Mill Cove PE **35** D5
Mill Creek ON **20** B3
Mill Island NU **40** A4
Mill Island NU **41** D7
Mill Lake ON **18** D7
Mill of Kintail CA ON **21** B7
Mill of Kintail CA ON **24** E1
Mill Pond CA ON **21** C7

Mill Pond CA ON **24** F1
Mill River PE **35** B2
Mill River East PE **34** B1
Mill River East PE **35** B2
Mill River PP PE **35** B2
Mill Road NS **32** F7
Mill Road NS **33** C4
Mill Village NS **33** D4
Millar Hill ON **21** B2
Millar Hill ON **22** F2
Millarton ON **20** B3
Millarville AB **6** D-E5
Millarville AB **7** C3
Millbank ON **19** A5
Millbank ON **20** D4
Millbridge ON **21** C4
Millbrook NS **33** A6
Millbrook NS **34** E2
Millbrook ON **21** E3
Millburn PE **35** D6
Milldale ON **19** C6
Milldale ON **20** E5
Mille Îles, rivière des QC
　　24 D5-6
Mille Îles, rivière des QC
　　27 E1
Mille-Isles QC **24** C5
Mille Lacs, lac des ON
　　13 F8
Mille Lacs, lac des ON
　　40 F1
Mille Lacs, lac des ON
　　16 E4-5
Millerand ON **17** F7
Millerand ON **18** A7
Millerdale SK **6** C8
Millerdale SK **11** C2-3
Miller Lake ON **18** D4-5
Miller Lake ON **18** E4
Miller's Passage NL **36** E6
Miller's Passage NL **37** E4
Millerton NB **31** D6-7
Millertown NL **36** B5
Millertown NL **37** B3
Millertown Junction NL
　　36 A-B5
Millertown Junction NL
　　37 A-B3
Millet AB **6** B6
Millet AB **8** D6
Mill Farm Unit (Gulf Islands
　　NPR) BC **2** E4
Millgrove ON **19** B7
Millgrove ON **20** D6
Millhaven ON **21** E6
Millicent AB **6** D7
Millicent AB **7** C7
Millicent AB **11** D1
Milieu, rivière du QC **24** A5
Milieu, rivière du QC **25** E5
Milligan Hills PP BC **3** C8
Milligan Hills PP BC **9** C2
Milliken ON **19** A8
Milliken ON **20** C7
Milliken ON **21** F1
Million MB **15** D3
Mills Lake NT **10** E5
Mills Lake NT **41** D1
Millstream River NB **32** C5
Milltown NL **36** D6
Milltown NL **37** D4
Milltown Cross PE **34** C3
Milltown Cross PE **35** D5
Milltown-Head of Bay
　　d'Espoir NL **36** D6
Milltown-Head of Bay
　　d'Espoir NL **37** D4
Millvale PE **35** D4
Millview PE **34** C3
Millview PE **35** E5-6
Millville NB **31** F4
Millville NB **32** B2
Millville NL **36** D1
Millville NS **32** E6
Millville NS **33** B3-4
Millwood MB **11** F7
Millwood MB **13** D1
Milne Inlet NU **41** A6
Milne Inlet NU **42** E5
Milner Lake NL **39** B2
Milner Ridge MB **14** D6
Milnet ON **17** F6
Milnikek, rivière QC **29** D5
Milo AB **6** E6
Milo AB **7** C5
Milo PE **32** A7
Milo PE **35** C1
Milton NL **36** C8
Milton NL **37** C6
Milton NS **33** D4
Milton ON **19** B7
Milton ON **20** D6
Milton PE **34** C2
Milton PE **35** E4
Milverton ON **19** A5
Milverton ON **20** D4
Miminegash PE **35** B1
Miminegash Pond PE **35** B1
Miminiska Lake ON **16** B6
Minago River MB **13** A3
Minahico ON **13** F6
Minaki ON **16** E1-2
Minaki ON **13** F6
Minaki ON **14** D8
Minaki ON **16** D1
Minaret AB **7** A4
Minas Basin NS **32** D7
Minas Basin NS **33** A5
Minas Basin NS **34** E-F1
Minas Channel NS **32** D6-7

Minas Channel NS 33 A4
Minasville NS 32 D8
Minasville NS 33 A5
Minasville NS 34 F1
Minburn AB 6 B7
Minburn AB 11 B1
Mindemoya ON 18 C3
Mindemoya Lake ON 18 C3
Minden ON 21 C2
Mine Centre ON 16 E-F3
Mine Mile Lake ON 18 C-D7
Miner River NT 5 B-C5
Miner River YT 5 E2
Miners Bay ON 21 C2
Miners Range YT 4 D3
Mines, bassin des NS 32 D7-8
Mines, bassin des NS 33 A5
Mines, bassin des NS 34 E-F1
Mines, chenal des NS 32 D6-7
Mines, chenal des NS 33 A-B4
Minesing ON 18 F7
Minesing ON 20 A6
Minett ON 18 D8
Mineville NS 33 C6
Mingan QC 39 E3
Mingan QC 40 F7
Mingan, rivière QC 39 E4
Mingan Archipelago NPR QC 39 F3-4
Mingo Lake NU 40 A5
Mingo Lake NU 41 C8
Mingré, lac QC 39 B-C2
Ming's Bight NL 36 E6
Ming's Bight NL 39 E-F8
Miniac, rivière QC 23 C4
Miniota MB 11 E8
Miniota MB 13 E1
Minipi Lake NL 39 C-D5
Minipi River NL 39 C5
Minisinakwa Lake ON 17 E6
Miniss Lake ON 13 D8
Miniss Lake ON 16 C4
Miniss River ON 16 C4
Ministic, lac QC 25 B7
Ministic, lac QC 26 F7
Ministic, lac QC 28 D2
Ministic Lake ON 18 A4
Ministik AB 8 C7
Ministik Lake AB 8 C7
Ministikwan SK 6 A8
Ministikwan SK 11 A2
Ministikwan Lake SK 6 A8
Ministikwan Lake SK 11 A2
Minitonas MB 11 C8
Minitonas MB 13 C1
Mink Cove NS 33 D1
Mink Lake AB 9 D5-6
Mink Lake NT 10 D5
Mink Lake ON 21 A5
Mink Lake ON 22 F5
Minnedosa MB 11 E8
Minnedosa MB 13 E-F3
Minnedosa MB 14 D1-2
Minnewakan MB 14 C3-4
Minnewanka, Lake AB 6 D4-5
Minnewanka, Lake AB 7 B2
Minnitaki ON 13 E6
Minnitaki ON 16 D2
Minnitaki Kames PP ON 13 E7
Minnitaki Kames PP ON 16 D3
Minnitaki Lake ON 13 E7
Minnitaki Lake ON 16 D3
Minoachak SK 11 D7
Minomaquam, lac QC 25 C7
Minomaquam, lac QC 28 E3
Minstrel Island BC 1 E5
Minstrel Island BC 2 A-B1
Minto MB 11 F8
Minto MB 13 F2
Minto MB 14 E-F1
Minto NB 31 F6
Minto NB 32 B4
Minto ON 19 A5
Minto ON 20 C4
Minto ON 21 D5
Minto YT 4 C3
Minto, lac QC 40 D4
Minto, lac QC 41 F8
Minto Head NU 41 A4
Minto Head NU 42 D-E3
Minto Inlet NT 41 A2
Minto Inlet NT 42 E1
Minton SK 11 F5
Minudie NS 32 C7
Miquelon QC 23 B7
Miquelon Lake PP AB 6 B6
Miquelon Lake PP AB 8 D7
Mira NS 34 C8
Mira Bay NS 34 C8
Mirabel QC 24 C5
Miracle Beach PP BC 1 E6 F5-6
Miracle Beach PP BC 2 C2
Miracle Valley BC 2 D-E6
Mirage, lac au QC 25 B8
Mirage, lac au QC 26 F8
Mirage, lac au QC 28 D4
Miramichi NB 31 D6-7
Miramichi NB 31 D7
Miramichi, baie de NB 31 C7
Miramichi Bay NB 31 C7
Miramichi Lake NB 31 E4

Miramichi Lake NB 32 A2
Mirande, lac QC 23 E8
Mirande, lac QC 25 B2
Mirande, lac QC 26 F2
Mira River NS 34 C7-8 D7
Mira River PP NS 34 C8
Mira Road NS 34 C8
Mirepoix, lac QC 24 A6-7
Mirond Lake SK 12 F6-7
Mirond Lake SK 12 F6
Mirond Lake SK 15 F1
Mirond Lake SK 15 E1
Mirror AB 6 C6
Mirror AB 8 E7
Mirror Lake BC 6 E3
Mirror River SK 9 C8
Mirror River SK 12 C3
Misamikwash Lake ON 13 B8
Misaw Lake SK 12 A6
Misaw Lake SK 15 A1
Miscou, île NB 30 D2-3
Miscou, île NB 31 A8
Miscou Centre NB 30 E2
Miscou Centre NB 31 A8
Miscouche PE 32 A7-8
Miscouche PE 34 C1
Miscouche PE 35 D2
Miscou Harbour NB 30 E2-3
Miscou Island NB 30 D2-3
Miscou Island NB 31 A8
Misehkow River ON 16 B-C5
Misekumaw Lake SK 12 B6 F6
Misery Bay, RNP ON 18 C2
Misery Bay PNR ON 18 C2
Mishibishu Lake ON 17 D3
Mishkeegogamang (New Osnaburgh) ON 16 B4-5
Mishwamakan River ON 13 A-B8
Misikeyask Lake ON 13 A8
Misinchinka Ranges BC 3 E6-7 F7
Miskwabi Lake ON 21 B3
Mispec NB 32 E4
Mispec NB 33 B1-2
Misquamaebin Lake ON 13 A7-8 B7
Missanabie ON 17 D4
Missawai Lake AB 9 F6
Missawai Lake AB 12 F1
Missi Lake SK 12 D6
Missinaibi Lake ON 17 D4
Missinaibi PP ON 17 A5
Missinaibi PP ON 17 C4-5
Missinaibi PP ON 17 D4
Missinaibi River ON 17 A5-6
Missinaibi River ON 17 B-C5
Missinipe SK 12 E5
Mission BC 1 F7
Mission BC 2 E6
Mission-de-Hopedale, LHN de la NL 39 A5-6
Mission-de-Hopedale, LHN de la NL 40 C6-7
Missionnaire, lac QC 25 E8
Missionnaire, lac QC 27 A3
Mission-Saint-Louis, LHN de la ON 18 F7-8
Mission-Saint-Louis, LHN de la ON 20 A6-7
Missipuskiow River SK 11 A6
Missisa Lake ON 16 A8
Missisquoi Nord, rivière QC 24 E8
Missisquoi Nord, rivière QC 27 E-F4 F3-4
Mississagagon Lake ON 21 C5
Mississagi Bay ON 18 B1-2
Mississagi Delta PNR ON 18 B2
Mississagi Delta PNR ON 18 B2
Mississagi Delta, RNP ON 18 B2
Mississagi Delta, RNP ON 18 B2
Mississagi Island ON 18 B2
Mississagi PP ON 17 F5
Mississagi River ON 17 E5
Mississagi River ON 17 F4-5
Mississagi River ON 17 F5
Mississagi River ON 18 A1
Mississagi River ON 18 A2
Mississagi River PP ON 17 E5
Mississagi Strait ON 18 B1
Mississagua Lake ON 21 C3
Mississagua River ON 21 C-D3
Mississauga ON 19 A-B8
Mississauga ON 20 D7
Mississauga ON 21 F7
Mississippi Lake ON 21 B7
Mississippi Lake ON 24 E1
Mississippi Lake National Wildlife Reserve ON 24 E1
Mississippi Lake NWA ON 21 B-C7
Mississippi Mills ON 21 B7
Mississippi River ON 21 B7
Mississippi River ON 21 C6
Mississippi River ON 40 E6 F6-7

Mississippi Station ON 21 C6
Mista Lake MB 15 E6
Mistahayo Lake MB 15 D8
Mistaken Point Ecological Reserve NL 37 F7-8
Mistanipisipou, rivière QC 39 C3-4
Mistaouac, lac QC 17 B8
Mistaouac, lac QC 23 A3
Mistaouac, rivière QC 17 B8
Mistassibi, rivière QC 26 A8
Mistassibi, rivière QC 26 C8
Mistassibi, rivière QC 28 A4
Mistassini QC 28 B4
Mistassini, rivière QC 40 F5
Mistassini, rivière QC 26 B7-8 C8
Mistassini, rivière QC 40 F5
Mistatim NS 11 B6
Mistawasis SK 11 B5
Mistigougèche, lac QC 29 D4
Mistigougèche, lac QC 31 A2-3
Mistigougèche, rivière QC 29 C3-4
Mistikokan River MB 15 D7
Mistinic, lac QC 39 C1
Mistinikon Lake ON 17 D6-7
Mistissini QC 40 F5
Mistusinne SK 11 D4
Misty Icefield BC 1 E-F7
Misty Icefield BC 2 C5-6
Misty Lake MB 12 B7
Misty Lake MB 15 B2
Misty Lake ON 21 A2
Misty Lake ON 22 F2
Mitchell MB 13 F4
Mitchell MB 14 E5
Mitchell ON 19 B4-5
Mitchell ON 20 D3-4
Mitchell Lake BC 1 B8
Mitchell Lake BC 6 B1
Mitchell Lake ON 18 A8
Mitchell's Bay ON 19 D2
Mitchells Brook NL 37 E7
Mitchell's Corners ON 20 C8
Mitchell's Corners ON 21 E2
Mitchellton SK 11 E5
Mitchinamécus, lac QC 25 C3-4
Mitchinamécus, rivière QC 25 C4
Mitchinamécus, ZEC QC 25 C-D3
Mitford AB 7 B3
Mitis, rivière QC 29 C4
Mitishto River MB 12 F8
Mitishto River MB 13 A2
Mitishto River MB 15 F2
Mitlenatch Island PP BC 2 C2
Mittimatalik (Pond Inlet) NU 41 A6
Mittimatalik (Pond Inlet) NU 42 D-E6
Mizzen Topsail NL 36 A4
Mizzen Topsail NL 37 A2
Mizzen Topsail NL 38 F3-4
Moar Lake MB 13 C5
Moar Lake MB 16 A1
Moberly BC 6 D3-4
Moberly Lake BC 3 E7-8
Moberly Lake BC 9 E1
Moberly Lake PP BC 3 E7
Moberly Lake PP BC 9 E1
Moberly River BC 3 E7
Mobile NL 37 E8
Mobile Big Pond NL 37 E8
Mocassins, lac des QC 24 A4-5
Mocassins, lac des QC 25 E-F4
Mocaque de Canaan, APP NB 31 F7
Mocaque de Canaan, APP NB 32 B5
Mochelle NS 32 F5
Mochelle NS 33 C2-3
Mocodome, Cape NS 34 F5
Moe, rivière QC 27 F5
Moes River QC 27 F5
Moffat ON 19 B7
Moffat ON 20 D6
Moffat, lac QC 27 E5-6
Moffet QC 17 E8
Moffet QC 22 A2
Moffet QC 23 F2
Moha BC 2 A6
Mohawk Island NWA ON 19 D8
Mohawk Island NWA ON 20 F7
Mohawk Lake NT 10 B7
Mohawk Point ON 19 C8
Mohawk Point ON 20 F7
Moira ON 21 D5
Moira River ON 21 C4-5
Moira River ON 21 D5
Moira River ON 21 D5-6
Moisie QC 39 E-F2
Moisie QC 40 F7
Moisie, baie de QC 39 E2
Moisie, rivière QC 39 D-E2
Moisie, rivière QC 39 E2
Moisie, rivière QC 40 E6 F6-7

Mojikit Lake ON 16 C6
Mojikit Lake ON 17 A1
Molanosa SK 11 A5
Molanosa SK 12 F5
Molard, lac QC 26 E6
Molard, lac QC 28 B-C2
Molega NS 33 D3-4
Molega Lake NS 33 D4
Molesworth ON 19 A5
Molesworth ON 20 C4
Molliers NL 36 E-F6
Molly Ann Cove NL 36 B2
Mollyguajeck Lake NL 36 C7
Mollyguajeck Lake NL 37 C5
Molson MB 13 E4
Molson MB 14 D6
Molson Lake MB 13 A4
Molson Lake NL 39 B2
Molson River MB 13 A4
Moltke ON 20 B4
Molus River NB 31 E7
Molus River NB 32 A5
Momich Lakes PP BC 6 D2
Monaco, lac QC 26 C4
Monarch AB 6 E6
Monarch AB 7 E5
Monarch Icefield BC 1 C5
Monarch Mountain BC 1 C5
Monashee Mountains BC 6 C-D2
Monashee Mountains BC 6 E3 F2-3
Monashee PP BC 6 E3
Monastery NS 34 E5
Monchy NL 36 B7
Monchy NL 37 B5
Monchy SK 11 F3
Monck ON 20 C5
Monck PP BC 1 E8
Monck PP BC 2 B8
Monck PP BC 6 E1
Moncouche, lac QC 28 B6
Moncton NB 31 F8
Moncton NB 32 B6
Mondonac, lac QC 25 C5
Mondonac, lac QC 28 F1
Mondou SK 11 D3
Monet QC 23 E4
Monet QC 25 A2
Monet QC 26 F2
Monetville ON 17 F7
Monetville ON 18 B6-7
Money Creek YT 4 D6
Monger, îles QC 39 E7
Monitor AB 6 C7
Monitor AB 11 C2
Monkland ON 24 E3-4
Monkman PP BC 9 F1
Monkstown NL 36 D8
Monkstown NL 37 D6
Monkton ON 19 A5
Monkton ON 20 D4
Mono ON 20 B-C6
Mono Centre ON 20 B6
Mono Cliffs PP ON 20 B6
Mono Mills ON 20 C6
Mono Road ON 19 A7
Mono Road ON 20 C6
Monroe NL 37 C6-7
Montagnais, lac aux QC 28 D-E4
Montagnais Point NL 39 B6
Montague PE 34 C3
Montague PE 35 E6
Montague Harbour PMP BC 2 E4
Montague Lake SK 11 F5
Montague River PE 35 E-F6
Mont-Apica QC 28 D5
Montauban, lac QC 25 E8
Montauban, lac QC 27 A4
Montbeillard QC 17 D8
Montbeillard QC 23 E3
Montbeillard, lac QC 23 E2
Mont-Brun QC 23 D3
Mont-Carleton, APP NB 29 F6
Mont-Carleton, APP NB 31 C5
Mont-Carleton, PP NB 29 F6
Mont-Carleton, PP NB 31 C4
Mont-Carmel PE 32 A7
Mont-Carmel PE 34 C1
Mont-Carmel PE 35 D2
Mont-Carmel QC 28 E8
Montcerf QC 22 D7
Montcerf QC 24 A1-2
Montcerf QC 25 E-F1
Montcevelles, lac QC 39 E5-6
Montebello QC 24 D3
Monte Creek BC 6 E1-2
Monte Creek PP BC 6 E2
Monteith MB 14 E1
Monteith ON 17 C7
Monte Lake BC 6 E1-2
Monte Lake PP BC 6 E2
Montfort QC 24 C4
Mont-Gabriel QC 24 C5
Monticello PE 34 B3
Monticello PE 35 D7

Monticules-Linéaires, LHN des MB 11 F7-8
Monticules-Linéaires, LHN des MB 13 F1
Montjoie, lac QC 24 B3
Montjoie, lac QC 25 F3
Mont-Joli QC 29 C3
Mont-Laurier QC 22 D8
Mont-Laurier QC 24 A3
Mont-Laurier QC 25 F3
Mont-Lebel QC 29 C3
Mont-Louis QC 29 A8
Mont-Louis QC 39 F2
Mont-Louis QC 40 F7
Mont-Louis, rivière de QC 29 A7-8 B7
Montmagny QC 27 A6-7
Montmartre SK 11 E6
Mont-Mégantic, parc du QC 27 E6
Mont-Mégantic, parc du QC 28 F6
Montmorency, rivière QC 28 F6
Mont Nebo SK 11 B4
Montney BC 3 D8
Montney BC 9 D1
Mont-Orford QC 24 E8
Mont-Orford, parc du QC 24 D-E8
Mont-Orford, parc du QC 27 E4
Montpellier QC 24 C3
Montréal QC 24 D5-6
Montréal QC 27 E1
Montréal, lac QC 26 C7
Montréal, lac QC 28 A3
Montreal Island ON 17 E3
Montreal Lake SK 11 A5
Montreal Lake SK 11 A5
Montréal-Nord QC 24 D6
Montréal-Nord QC 27 E1-2
Montreal Point NB 13 B3
Montreal River ON 17 D-E7
Montreal River ON 17 E4
Montreal River ON 17 E3-4
Montreal River ON 22 A-B1
Montréal River SK 12 F5
Montreal River PP ON 17 E3
Mont-Revelstoke, PN du BC 6 D2-3
Mont-Riding, PN du MB 11 E-E7
Mont-Riding, PN du MB 11 D8
Mont-Riding, PN du MB 13 D1-2
Mont-Riding, PN du MB 14 C1-2
Mont-Rolland QC 24 C5
Montrose BC 6 F3
Montrose NS 32 D8
Montrose NS 33 A5
Montrose NS 33 A5-6
Montrose NS 34 E1
Montrose PE 34 A1
Montrose PE 35 B2
Mont-Saint-Bruno, parc du QC 24 D6
Mont-Saint-Bruno, parc du QC 27 E2
Mont-Sainte-Anne, parc du QC 27 A6
Mont-Sainte-Anne, parc du QC 28 F6
Mont-Saint-Grégoire QC 24 D6-7 E6-7
Mont-Saint-Grégoire QC 27 E2
Mont-Saint-Hilaire QC 24 D7
Mont-Saint-Hilaire QC 27 E2
Mont-Saint-Michel QC 24 A3
Mont-Saint-Michel QC 25 E3
Mont-Saint-Pierre QC 29 A7
Mont-Saint-Pierre, rivière de QC 29 A7
Monts-Torngat-et-de-la-Rivière-Koroc, parc des QC 40 C6
Monts-Valin, parc des QC 28 C6
Mont-Tremblant QC 24 B4
Mont-Tremblant, lac QC 23 E2
Mont-Tremblant, parc du QC 24 A4-5 B4-5
Mont-Tremblant, parc du QC 25 F4-5
Mont-Tremblant-Village QC 24 B4
Mont-Wright QC 39 C1-2
Monument-Lefebvre, LHN du NB 32 B7
Monument Lefebvre NHS NB 32 B7
Moodie Island NU 40 A6
Moon Island QC 18 D7
Moon Lake AB 6 A6
Moonlight Bay AB 8 B5-6
Moon River QC 18 E7
Moonshine Lake PP AB 9 E2
Moonstone ON 18 F7-8
Moonstone ON 20 A6
Moore Dale MB 14 B2
Moore Falls ON 21 C2
Moore Lake ON 21 A4
Moore Park MB 13 E2
Moore Park MB 14 D1
Moore, lac QC 22 A2
Moorefield ON 19 A5-6
Moorefield ON 20 C4-5

Mooresburg ON 20 B4
Moores Mills NB 32 D2
Mooretown ON 19 C2
Mooretown ON 20 F1
Mooring Cove NL 36 E6-7
Mooring Cove NL 37 E4-5
Moose, baie QC 27 D5
Moose Bay MB 14 A1-2
Moose Brook NS 32 D8
Moose Brook NS 33 A5
Moose Brook NS 34 F1
Moose Channel YT 5 B3-4
Moose Creek ON 24 E3
Moose Factory ON 40 F3
Moosehead NS 33 B8
Moosehern MB 13 D3
Mooseheorn MB 14 B3
Moose Horn River NT 4 B7
Moose Island MB 12 E-F7
Moose Island MB 13 C-D4
Moose Island MB 14 A5
Moose Island MB 15 E1
Moose Jaw SK 11 E5
Moose Jaw River SK 11 E5-6
Moose Lake MB 11 A8
Moose Lake MB 13 A2
Moose Lake MB 14 A5
Moose Lake MB 14 F7
Moose Lake MB 14 F7-8
Moose Lake ON 18 A8
Moose Lake (Mosakahiken) MB 11 A8
Moose Lake (Mosakahiken) MB 13 A2
Moose Lake PP AB 6 A7
Moose Lake PP AB 9 F7
Moose Lake PP AB 11 A1-2
Moose Lake PP MB 12 F1-2
Moose Lake PP MB 13 F5
Moose Lake PP MB 14 F7-8
Moose Lake PP MB 16 E1
Mooseland NS 33 B7
Mooseland NS 34 B7
Moose Mountain Creek SK 11 F6-7
Moose Mountain Lake SK 11 E6
Moose Mountain PP SK 11 F6-7
Moose Nose Lake MB 15 E4-5
Moose Point ON 18 E8
Moose Range SK 11 B6
Moose River NS 32 D7
Moose River NS 33 A8
Moose River NS 33 A5
Moose River NS 33 A8
Moose River NS 34 E4
Moose River NS 34 E4
Moose River NS 34 E1
Moose River ON 17 A6
Moose River ON 40 F3
Moose River Gold Mines NS 33 B7
Moose River Gold Mines NS 34 B7
Moose River Gold Mines PP NS 33 B7
Moose River Gold Mines PP NS 34 B7
Moose Valley SK 11 E7
Moose Valley PP BC 1 D7-8
Moose Woods SK 11 C4
Moosomin MB 11 D3
Moosomin SK 11 E7
Moosomin SK 13 E1
Moosonee ON 40 F3
Moraine Point NT 10 D6
Morass Point MB 13 C3
Moraviantown ON 19 D3
Moraviantown ON 20 F2
Morden MB 13 F3
Morden MB 14 F3-4
Morden NS 33 B3
Morden Colliery PP BC 2 E3-4
Morecambe AB 6 A7
Morecambe AB 11 A1
More Creek BC 3 D2-3
Moreland SK 11 F5-6
Morell PE 34 B-C3
Morell PE 35 D6
Morell (IR) PE 35 D6
Morell Bay SK 12 C6
Morell East PE 34 B-C3
Morell East PE 35 D6
Morell River PE 34 C3
Morell River PE 35 D-E6
Moresby, île BC 1 B1
Moresby Camp BC 1 B1
Moresby Island BC 1 B1
Moreton's Harbour NL 36 E6
Morewood ON 24 E3
Morgan Point BC 1 A1
Morganston ON 21 E4
Morganville NS 32 F5
Morganville NS 33 D2
Morice Lake BC 1 A4
Morice River NB 35 F1
Morice River BC 1 A4
Moricetown BC 3 F4
Morien, Cape NS 34 C8
Morin, lac QC 25 D8
Morin, lac QC 28 B8
Morin, lac QC 28 D4
Morin Heights QC 24 C4-5
Morin Lake MB 15 E1
Morin Lake SK 12 F5
Morinville AB 6 A5

Morinville AB 8 B-C6
Morisset-Station QC 27 C7
Morkill River BC 6 A1-2
Morley AB 6 D5
Morley AB 7 B3
Morley River YT 4 E5
Morley River Territorial Recreation Site YT 3 A2
Morley River Territorial Recreation Site YT 4 E-F5
Morleyville AB 7 B3
Morning Lake SK 12 E-F5
Morningside AB 6 C6
Morningside AB 8 E6
Morpeth ON 19 E3
Morrin AB 6 D6
Morrin AB 7 A5
Morris MB 13 F3-4
Morris MB 14 F5
Morris QC 30 B2
Morris Lake ON 16 B4
Morris Lake YT 4 E5
Morris River MB 13 C7-8
Morris Tract, RNP ON 19 A3-4
Morris Tract, RNP ON 20 C2-3
Morris Tract PNR ON 19 A3-4
Morris Tract PNR ON 20 C2-3
Morrisburg ON 24 F3
Morrisdale NB 32 D3-4
Morrisdale NB 33 A1
Morrison Lake ON 13 B2
Morrissey BC 7 F2-3
Morrissey PP BC 6 F5
Morrissey PP BC 7 F3
Morriston ON 19 B7
Morriston ON 20 D6
Morristown NS 32 E6
Morristown NS 33 B4
Morristown NS 34 D5
Morrisville ON 36 D6
Morrisville NL 37 D4
Morse SK 11 E4
Morson ON 13 F6
Morson ON 16 E1
Mort, lac du NT 10 C8
Mortier NL 36 E-F7
Mortier NL 37 E-F5
Mortlach SK 11 E4
Morton ON 21 C7
Morton Lake PP BC 1 E5
Morton Lake PP BC 2 B-C1
Morvan NS 33 A8
Morvan NS 34 E4
Morven ON 21 D6
Morweena MB 13 D3-4
Morweena MB 14 B4-5
Moscow ON 21 D6
Mose Ambrose NL 36 E6
Mose Ambrose NL 37 E4
Moser River NS 33 B8
Moser River NS 33 B8
Moser River NS 34 F4
Moser River NS 34 F4
Moses Inlet BC 1 C4
Mosher Lake NT 10 C6
Mosley Creek BC 1 D5-6
Mosque River BC 3 D4
Mosquic, lac QC 24 A4
Mosquic, lac QC 25 E4
Mosquito NL 36 D5
Mosquito NL 37 D3
Mosquito NL 37 F7
Mosquito Bay QC 40 B4
Mosquito Cove NL 36 D6-7
Mosquito Creek SK 18 A7-8
Mosquito-Grizzly Bear's Head-Lean Man SK 11 C3
Mossbank SK 11 E4
Moss Glen NB 32 D4
Moss Glen NB 33 A1
Mosside AB 8 B5
Moss Lake MB 12 C8
Moss Lake MB 15 C3
Mossleigh AB 6 E6
Mossleigh AB 7 C5
Mossley ON 19 C5
Mossley ON 20 E4
Moss Spur MB 14 D6
Mossy Point PE 35 C2
Mossy River SK 11 A4
Mostoos Hills SK 9 E8
Mostoos Hills SK 12 E3
Motase Peak BC 3 D4
Motherwell Homestead NHS SK 11 E6
Motion Head NL 37 E8
Mouat, Cape NU 42 C5
Mouche, rivière à la QC 38 A1
Moulin, lac QC 24 A4
Moulin, rivière du QC 29 D5
Moulin-Morneault NB 29 E3
Moulin-Morneault NB 31 C1-2
Mound AB 7 A3
Mountain ON 24 E2
Mountain Grove ON 21 C6
Mountain Lake ON 18 F5
Mountain Lake ON 20 A4
Mountain Lake ON 21 C2
Mountain Lake SK 12 E5

Mountain Park AB 6 B3
Mountain Park AB 8 D2
Mountain River NT 5 E6 F6-7
Mountain Road MB 13 E2
Mountain Road MB 14 C1
Mountainside MB 14 F1
Mountain View AB 6 F4
Mountain View AB 7 F4-5
Mountain View ON 21 E5
Mount Albert ON 20 B7
Mount Albert ON 21 E1
Mount Albion PE 35 E5
Mount Arlington Heights NL 36 E8
Mount Arlington Heights NL 37 E6
Mount Assiniboine PP BC 6 D4
Mount Assiniboine PP BC 7 B1-2
Mount Blanchet PP BC 3 F5
Mount Brydges ON 19 D4
Mount Brydges ON 20 E3
Mount Buchanan PE 34 C2-3
Mount Buchanan PE 35 F5
Mount Carleton PP NB 29 F6
Mount Carleton PP NB 31 C4
Mount Carleton PPA NB 29 F6
Mount Carleton PPA NB 31 C4
Mount Carmel NL 37 E7
Mount Carmel ON 19 B4
Mount Carmel ON 20 D3
Mount Carmel-Mitchell's Brook-St. Catherines NL 37 E7
Mount Carmel Pond NL 37 E8
Mount Chesney ON 21 D6-7
Mount Currie BC 1 E7
Mount Currie BC 2 B5
Mount Denson NS 32 D8
Mount Denson NS 33 B5
Mount Denson NS 34 F1
Mount Edziza PP BC 3 C2-3
Mount Edziza PRA BC 3 C2-3
Mount Elgin ON 19 C5-6
Mount Elgin ON 20 E4-5
Mount Elphinstone PP BC 2 D4
Mount Fernie PP BC 6 F4-5
Mount Fernie PP BC 7 E2
Mount Forest ON 20 B-C5 C4-5
Mount Hanley NS 33 B3
Mount Herbert PE 35 E5
Mount Hope ON 19 C7
Mount Hope ON 20 E6
Mount Judge Howay PP BC 2 D6
Mount Judge Howay PRA BC 1 F7-8
Mount Julian ON 21 D3
Mount Lorne YT 4 E4
Mount Maxwell PP BC 2 E4
Mount Mellick PE 35 E5
Mount Moriah NL 36 B2-3
Mount Pearl NL 37 E8
Mount Pelly (Uvajuq) TP NU 41 B3
Mount Pelly (Uvajuq) TP NU 42 F2
Mount Pleasant NB 32 A-B1
Mount Pleasant NS 32 C8
Mount Pleasant NS 34 D1
Mount Pleasant ON 19 C6
Mount Pleasant ON 20 E5
Mount Pleasant ON 21 E3
Mount Pleasant PE 34 B2
Mount Pleasant PE 34 B1
Mount Pleasant PE 35 C2
Mount Pope PP BC 1 A6
Mount Revelstoke PP NL 36 D2-3
Mount Richardson PP BC 2 D4
Mount Robson BC 6 B2
Mount Robson PP BC 6 B2
Mount Royal PE 35 E5
Mount St. Patrick ON 21 B6
Mount Salem ON 19 D5
Mount Salem ON 20 F4
Mount Savona PP BC 1 E8
Mount Savona PP BC 2 A-B8
Mount Savona PP BC 6 D-E1
Mount Seymour PP BC 1 F7
Mount Seymour PP BC 2 D5
Mount Stewart PE 34 C3
Mount Stewart PE 35 D5-6
Mount Terry Fox PP BC 6 B2
Mount Thom NS 33 A7
Mount Thom NS 34 E3
Mount Uniacke NS 33 B5
Mount Uniacke NS 34 F1
Mount Uniacke PP NS 32 E8
Mount Uniacke PP NS 33 B5-6
Mount Vernon ON 19 C6
Mount Vernon ON 20 E5
Mount View NB 35 F1

Mount Whatley NB 35 F1
Mourier, lac QC 23 E4
Mouton Island NS 33 E4
Mowachaht BC 1 F5
Mowachaht BC 2 C1
Mowbray MB 14 F3
Moyen, lac QC 39 A3-4
Moyie BC 6 F4
Moyie BC 7 F1-2
Moyie Lake PP BC 6 F4
Moyie Lake PP BC 7 F1
Moyie River BC 6 F4
Moyie River BC 7 F1
Moyre, lac QC 25 D5
Mozart SK 11 C6
Muchalat Inlet BC 1 F5
Muchalat Inlet BC 2 D1
Mud Island NS 33 F1
Mud Lake NL 39 C6
Mud Lake ON 18 C3
Mud Lake Delta PP BC 6 C2
Muddy Bay NL 39 B7
Muddy Hole Point NL 36 D3
Muddy Hole Point NL 37 D1
Muddy Lake SK 6 C8
Muddy Lake SK 11 C3
Mudge Bay ON 18 B3
Mudjatik River SK 12 D4
Mudzenchoot PP BC 3 F6
Muenster SK 11 C5
Muir MB 14 D3
Muirkirk ON 19 D3-4
Muirkirk ON 20 F2-3
Mukutuwa River MB 13 B4
Mulgrave NS 34 D5
Mulgrave, Lake NS 32 F5
Mulgrave, Lake NS 33 C2 D2-3
Mulhurst Bay AB 6 B5
Mulhurst Bay AB 8 D6
Mulligan Bay NL 39 B6
Mulligan River NL 39 B6
Mullingar SK 11 B4
Mullin Stream Lake NB 31 D5
Mulock Lake ON 18 A8
Mulvihill MB 13 D3
Mulvihill MB 14 B4
Mummery, Mount ON 6 C-D4
Muncey ON 19 C4
Muncey ON 20 F3
Muncho Lake BC 3 B5
Muncho Lake BC 3 B5
Muncho Lake BC 4 F8
Muncho Lake PP BC 3 B5
Mundare AB 6 B6
Mundare AB 8 C8
Mundare AB 11 A1
Munekun Lake ON 13 B7
Munk MB 15 E4-5
Munn Lake NT 10 B8
Munro Lake MB 15 F5
Munroe Lake MB 15 A-B3
Munsee-Delaware ON 19 C-D4
Munsee-Delaware ON 20 F3
Munson AB 6 D6
Munson AB 7 A5
Munster ON 21 B7-8
Munster ON 24 E2
Murchison Island ON 16 D6
Murchison Island ON 17 A1
Murchyville NS 33 B7
Murchyville NS 34 F3
Murdochville QC 29 B8
Murdochville QC 30 B1
Murdochville QC 40 F7
Murdock Lake MB 15 B3
Muriel Lake AB 6 A7
Muriel Lake AB 11 A2
Murillo ON 16 C5
Murky Lake NT 10 C-D8
Murphy, Mount YT 4 E4-5
Murphy Cove NS 33 C7
Murphys Point PP ON 21 C7
Murphys Point PP ON 24 F1
Murray, lac QC 25 D-E5
Murray, Mount YT 4 E7
Murray Beach PP NB 32 B7
Murray Beach PP NB 34 C1
Murray Beach PP NB 35 F7
Murray Corner NB 32 B7-8
Murray Corner NB 34 C1
Murray Corner NB 35 E2
Murray Harbour PE 34 C4
Murray Harbour PE 34 D3-4
Murray Harbour PE 35 F7
Murray Harbour PE 35 F7
Murray Harbour North PE 34 C4
Murray Harbour North PE 35 F7
Murray Head PE 34 C-D4
Murray Head PE 35 F7
Murray Islands PE 35 F7
Murray Lake MB 13 A5
Murray Lake MB 15 F5
Murray Lake SK 11 B3
Murray Lake, RNOM SK 11 B3
Murray Lake NMBS SK 11 B3
Murray River BC 3 E-F8
Murray River BC 9 E1
Murray River PE 34 D3
Murray River PE 35 F6
Murray River PE 35 F7
Murray Road NB 35 E2
Murray Road PE 35 C2
Murtle Lake BC 6 C2
Musclow Lake ON 13 D5

Musclow Lake ON 14 A7-8
Musclow Lake ON 16 B1
Muscote Bay ON 21 E5
Muscovite Lakes PP BC 3 E6
Musée-du-Parc-Banff, LHN du AB 7 B1-2
Musgrave Harbour NL 38 E7-8
Musgravetown NL 36 C8
Musgravetown NL 37 C6
Mushaboom NS 33 B8
Mush Lake YT 4 E2-3
Musidora AB 6 A7
Musidora AB 11 A1
Muskeg Lake ON 13 F8
Muskeg Lake ON 16 E5
Muskeg Lake SK 11 B4
Muskeg River NT 10 F2-3
Musket Island PMP BC 2 C-D3
Muskiki Lake SK 11 C5
Muskoday SK 11 B5
Muskoka, Lake ON 18 E8
Muskoka, Lake ON 21 B-C1
Muskoka Falls ON 18 E8
Muskoka Falls ON 21 C1
Muskosung Lake ON 18 A7
Muskowekwan SK 11 D-6
Muskowpetung SK 11 D5-6
Muskrat Dam ON 13 B7
Muskrat Dam Lake ON 13 B7
Muskrat Lake ON 21 A6
Muskrat Lake ON 22 F6
Muskwa-Kechika Management Area BC 3 B4 D6-7
Muskwa-Kechika Management Area BC 4 F7-8
Muskwa Lake AB 9 E5
Muskwa Ranges BC 3 C5 D5-6
Muskwa River AB 9 E5
Muskwa River BC 3 B-C6
Muskwesi Lake MB 15 C3
Muskwesi River MB 12 C8
Musquaro QC 39 F5
Musquaro, lac QC 39 E5
Musquaro, rivière QC 39 E5
Musquash NB 32 E3
Musquash NB 33 B1
Musquash Lake NB 32 C1
Musquodoboit Harbour NS 33 C7
Musquodoboit Harbour NS 33 C6-7
Musquodoboit River NS 33 B6-7
Musquodoboit River NS 34 F2-3
Musquodoboit Valley PP NS 33 B7
Musquodoboit Valley PP NS 34 F3
Mussel Inlet BC 1 B3-4
Musselman's Lake ON 20 B-C7
Musselman's Lake ON 21 E1-2
Mustard Lake NT 10 D4
Mutton Bay NL 37 F7
Mutton Bay QC 38 C1
Mutton Bay QC 39 E6
Muzon, Cape BC 3 F1
Mye, Mount YT 4 C5
Myers Cave ON 21 C5
Myles Bay ON 18 E4
Mynarski Lake MB 12 D8
Mynarski Lakes MB 15 D5
Myre Lake MB 15 D5
Myrnam AB 6 A7
Myrnam AB 11 A1-2
Myrtle MB 13 F3
Myrtle MB 14 F4
Myrtle ON 20 C8
Myrtle ON 21 E2
Myrtle Station ON 20 B8
Myrtle Station ON 21 E2
Mystery Lake AB 8 B4-5
Mystery Lake NT 10 D7
Mystic QC 24 E7
Mystic QC 27 F2-3

N
Nabel Lake MB 15 A4
Nabisipi, pointe QC 39 F5
Nabisipi, rivière QC 39 E4
Nachvak Fiord NL 40 C7
Nackawic NB 31 F3-4
Nackawic NB 32 C1-2
Nackawic Stream NB 31 F3-4
Nackawic Stream NB 32 B2
Nacmine AB 6 D6
Nacmine AB 7 A5
Naco AB 7 B8
Nadaleen Range YT 4 A4-5
Nadaleen River YT 4 A5
Naden Harbour BC 1 A1
Nadina Lake BC 1 A4
Nadina River BC 1 A4-5
Naelin Lake MB 15 B4
Nagagami Lake ON 17 B3
Nagagami Lake PP ON 17 B3
Nagagami River ON 17 B3-4

Nagagamisis Lake ON 17 B3-4
Nagagamisis PP ON 17 B3-4
Nagas Point BC 1 C1-2
Nahanni NT 4 D8
Nahanni NT 10 E1
Nahanni, RPN NT 4 D8
Nahanni, RPN NT 10 E1-2
Nahanni Butte NT 10 E2
Nahanni NPR NT 4 D8
Nahanni NPR NT 10 D-E1
Nahatlatch PP BC 1 E8
Nahatlatch PP BC 2 C6-7
Nahatlatch River BC 1 E7-8
Nahatlatch River BC 2 C6
Nahili Lake ON 12 A7
Nahili Lake MB 15 A2
Nahlin River BC 3 B2
Nahmint BC 1 F5-6
Nahmint BC 2 E2
Nahoni Range YT 5 E2
Naicam SK 11 C5-6
Naikoon PP BC 1 A1-2
Nail Pond PE 35 A2
Nail Pond PE 35 A2
Nain NL 40 C-D7
Nainlin Brook NT 4 A7
Nainlin Brook NT 10 B1
Nairn ON 20 E3
Nairn, lac QC 26 D5
Nairn Centre ON 17 F6
Nairn Centre ON 18 A4
Nairn Falls PP BC 1 E7
Nairn Falls PP BC 2 B5
Naiscoot River ON 18 C6
Najoua, lac QC 25 B5
Najoua, lac QC 26 F5
Nakamun AB 8 B5-6
Nakaneet SK 11 E-F2
Nakina ON 16 D7-8
Nakina ON 17 A2
Nakina ON 40 F2
Nakina Moraine, RNP ON 16 D7-8
Nakina Moraine, RNP ON 17 B2
Nakina Moraine PNR ON 16 D7-8
Nakina Moraine PNR ON 17 B2
Nakina River BC 3 A2
Nakina River BC 4 F5
Nakusp BC 6 E3
Namaka AB 7 B5
Namakan River ON 16 F3
Namao AB 6 A6
Namao AB 8 C6
Nameigos Lake ON 17 C3
Nameless Cove NL 38 B3-4
Nameless Lake SK 12 D4
Namew Lake SK 11 A7
Namew Lake SK 13 A1
Nampa AB 9 E3-4
Namu BC 1 C4
Namur QC 24 C3
Namur Lake AB 9 C6
Namur Lake AB 12 C1
Nanaimo BC 1 F6
Nanaimo BC 2 E3
Nanaimo River BC 1 F6
Nanaimo River BC 2 E3
Nancy Greene PP BC 6 F3
Nancy's Cellar NS 33 A7-8
Nancy's Cellar NS 34 E3
Nango Lake ON 16 A4
Nango River BC 13 B-C7
Nanika Lake BC 1 A4
Nanika River BC 1 A4
Nanisivik NU 41 A6
Nanisivik NU 42 D5
Nanoose Bay BC 1 F6
Nanoose Bay BC 2 D3
Nan Sdins, LHN de BC 1 C1-2
Nan Sdins NHS BC 1 C1-2
Nansen, Mount YT 4 C3
Nansen Sound NU 42 A-B4
Nantais, lac QC 40 B4-5
Nantais, lac QC 41 E8
Nantes QC 27 E6
Nanticoke ON 19 D7
Nanticoke ON 20 F6
Nanticoke Creek ON 19 C6-7
Nanticoke Creek ON 20 E5-6
Nanton AB 6 E5
Nanton AB 7 D4
Nantyr Park ON 20 B7
Nantyr Park ON 21 D-E1
Naococane, lac QC 40 B6-7
Naosap Lake MB 12 F7
Naosap Lake MB 15 F1
Napadogan NB 31 E4
Napadogan NB 32 A2
Napanee ON 21 E6
Napanee River ON 21 D6
Napatak SK 11 C7
Napetipi, lac QC 38 A-B2
Napetipi, rivière QC 39 D7
Napier ON 19 C3
Napier ON 20 E2
Napierville ON 24 E6
Napierville QC 27 F2
Napinka MB 11 F8
Napinka MB 13 F1
Naples AB 8 B5
Napoiak Channel NT 5 B-C4
Napoléon, lac QC 25 D4-5
Nappan NS 32 C7

Naramata BC 6 F2
Narcisse MB 13 E3
Narcisse MB 14 C4-5
Narcosli Creek BC 1 C7
Nardin Lake NT 10 B7
Narraway River BC 6 A1-2
Narrow Hills PP SK 11 A5
Narrows Inlet BC 1 E6
Narrows Inlet BC 2 C4
Nash Creek NB 29 D7
Nash Creek NB 31 A6
Nashwaak Bridge NB 31 F5
Nashwaak Bridge NB 32 B3
Nashwaak River NB 31 F4-5
Nashwaak River NB 32 B2-3
Nashwaak Village NB 31 F5
Nashwaak Village NB 32 B3
Nasigon, lac QC 25 C3
Naskaupi River NL 39 B4-5
Naskaupi River NL 39 B5
Naskaupi River NL 40 D7
Nasoga Gulf BC 3 F3
Nasonworth NB 32 C2-3
Nasparti Inlet BC 1 E4
Nass Bay BC 3 F3
Nass Camp BC 3 F3
Nass River BC 3 E3
Nastapoca, rivière QC 40 D4-5
Nastapoca, rivière QC 41 F8
Nastapoka Islands NU 40 D4
Nastapoka Islands NU 41 F8
Natal BC 7 E3
Natalkuz Lake BC 1 B5
Natashquan QC 39 F5
Natashquan QC 40 F8
Natashquan, rivière QC 39 D5
Natashquan, rivière QC 39 E5
Natashquan, rivière QC 40 E7-8 F8
Natashquan Est, rivière QC 39 D-E5
Natashquan River NL 39 C-D4
Nathorst, Cape NU 42 C3
National Mills MB 11 B7
National Mills MB 13 B1
Nation River BC 3 F6
Nation River YT 5 E1-2
Native Bay NU 40 A3
Native Bay NU 41 D6
Natla River NT 4 B6-7
Nat River ON 17 C6
Natuashish NL 40 D7
Naufrage PE 35 D7
Naufrage, baie du QC 30 A7
Naufrage Harbour PE 35 D7
Naughton ON 17 F6
Naughton ON 18 A5
Naujaat (Repulse Bay) NU 41 C5-6
Nautley SK 11 F6
Nauwigewauk NB 32 D4
Nauwigewauk NB 33 A2
Navan ON 21 A8
Navan ON 24 D3
Navin MB 14 E5
Navy Board Inlet NU 41 A6
Navy Board Inlet NU 42 D5
Navy Island NHS ON 20 E8
Nazco BC 1 B6
Nazko BC 1 B6
Nazko Lake PP BC 1 C6
Nazko River BC 1 B6 C7
Neapolis AB 7 A4
Neault, lac QC 23 E4
Neault, lac QC 25 A-B3
Neault, lac QC 26 F3
Neawagank Lake ON 16 A5
Nechako River BC 1 A6-7
Nechako River BC 1 A-B6
Nechako River NMBS BC 1 A6
Necoslie BC 1 A6
Necum Teuch NS 33 B8
Necum Teuch NS 34 F4
Neddy Harbour NL 38 E2
Nédélec QC 17 D8
Nédélec QC 23 F2
Neeb SK 11 A3
Needles BC 6 E2-3
Neelin MB 13 F2
Neelin MB 14 F2
Neepawa MB 13 E2
Neepawa MB 14 D2
Neerlandia AB 6 A5
Neerlandia AB 8 A5
Negagssa Lake MB 15 B3
Neguac NB 30 F1-2
Neguac, plage NB 30 F2
Neguac Beach NB 30 F2
Neguac Beach NB 31 C7-8
Negwazu Lake ON 17 D3
Neidpath SK 11 E4
Neiges, lac des QC 25 D3
Neiges, lac des QC 26 F3
Neiges, lac des QC 28 E6
Neiges, rivière des QC 28 F6
Neigette QC 29 C7
Neigette, rivière QC 29 C3
Neilburg SK 6 B8

Neilburg SK 11 B2
Neils Harbour NS 34 A7
Neiman Lake SK 9 A8
Neiman Lake SK 12 A4
Nejanilini Lake MB 15 A4
Nejanilini Lake MB 41 F4
Nekweaga Bay SK 12 C6
Nelles Corners ON 19 C7
Nelles Corners ON 20 E6
Nellie Lake ON 17 C6-7
Nelson BC 6 F3
Nelson, fleuve MB 15 D6
Nelson, fleuve MB 40 C1
Nelson, lac QC 26 D4
Nelson Forks BC 3 A6
Nelson House MB 15 E3
Nelson Island BC 1 F6
Nelson Island BC 2 D3
Nelson Lake MB 12 E8
Nelson Lake MB 15 E2
Nelson-Miramichi NB 31 D7
Nelson Range BC 6 F3
Nelson River NB 9 A1
Nelson River MB 15 D6
Nelson River MB 15 E-F4
Nelson River MB 40 C1
Nelway BC 6 F3
Nemaiah Valley BC 1 D6
Nemebien River SK 12 E-F5
Nemegos ON 17 D5
Nemegosenda Lake ON 17 D5
Nemegosenda River ON 17 D5
Nemegosenda River Wetlands PP ON 17 D5
Némégousse, lac QC 26 C4
Nemeiben Lake SK 12 C7
Nemio, rivière QC 26 E4
Némiscachingue, lac QC 25 C4-5
Nemiscau QC 40 F4
Nemiskam AB 7 E7
Nepean ON 21 B8
Nepean ON 24 D-E2
Nepewassi Lake ON 17 F7
Nepewassi Lake ON 18 A6
Nephton ON 21 D4
Nepisiguit, baie de NB 29 E8
Nepisiguit, baie de NB 30 B1
Nepisiguit, baie de NB 31 B6-7
Nepisiguit Bay NB 29 E8
Nepisiguit Bay NB 30 E1
Nepisiguit Bay NB 38 F5
Nepisiguit River NB 29 F6-7
Nepisiguit River NB 31 C5-6
Neptune SK 11 F6
Nerepis NB 32 D3
Nerepis NB 33 A1
Nerepis River NB 32 C-D3
Nerepis River NB 33 A1
Neroutsos Inlet BC 1 E4
Nesbitt MB 13 F2
Nesbitt MB 14 E1
Neskantaga (Lansdowne House) ON 16 A6-7
Nesle, lac QC 39 E6
Nesselrode, Mount BC 3 B1
Nesslin Lake SK 11 A4
Nestaocano, rivière QC 26 A-B6
Nesleton ON 20 B8
Nesleton ON 21 E2
Nesleton Station ON 20 B8
Nesleton Station ON 21 E2
Nestor Falls ON 13 F6
Nestor Falls ON 16 E2
Nestorville ON 17 F4
Nestow AB 6 A5
Nestow AB 8 B6
Netalzul Meadows PP BC 3 F4-5
Netherhill SK 11 D3
Net Lake ON 22 B1
Netley MB 13 E4
Netley MB 14 D4
Netley Creek PP MB 13 E4
Netley Creek PP MB 14 D5
Netley Lake MB 14 D5
Netson Creek BC 3 B5
Nettell Lake SK 9 A7
Nettell Lake SK 12 A3
Nettilling Fiord NU 41 F8
Nettilling Fiord NU 42 F7-8
Nettilling Lake NU 41 F8
Nettilling Lake NU 42 F7
Nettogami River ON 17 A7
Neubergthal MB 13 F3-4
Neubergthal MB 14 F4-5
Neudorf SK 11 E6-7
Neuf Milles, lac des QC 22 B5
Neuhorst SK 11 C4
Neustadt ON 20 B4
Neuville QC 27 B5
Neveton MB 31 C7
Neville SK 11 E3-4
Nevins Lake SK 9 A8
Nevins Lake SK 12 A4
Nevis AB 6 C6
Nevis AB 8 E-F7
Nevoir, lac QC 26 B6
Néwiska, lac QC 23 A3
New Aiyansh BC 3 F3
New Albany NS 32 F5-6
New Albany NS 33 C3
New Annan PE 35 D3
New Bandon NB 29 E8
New Bandon NB 30 E1

New Bandon NB 31 B7
New Bandon NB 31 E5
New Bandon NB 32 A3-4
New Bay Pond NL 36 A6
New Bay Pond NL 37 A4
New Bay Pond NL 38 F5
Newbliss ON 21 C7
Newbliss ON 24 F1-2
New Bonaventure NL 37 C7
Newboro ON 21 C7
Newboro ON 24 F1
Newboro Lake ON 21 D7
Newboro Lake ON 24 F1
New Bothwell MB 13 F4
New Bothwell MB 14 E5
New Bridge NL 37 E7
New Brigden AB 6 C7-8
New Brigden AB 7 A8
New Brigden AB 11 C2
New Brighton BC 1 F7
New Brighton BC 2 D4
New Brunswick (province)
Newbrook AB 6 A6
Newbrook AB 8 A7
Newbrook AB 9 F6
Newburg NB 31 F3
Newburg NB 32 B1
Newburne NS 32 F7
Newburne NS 33 C4
Newbury ON 19 D3
Newbury ON 20 F2
New Campbellton NS 34 B-C7
New Canaan NB 31 F7
New Canaan NB 32 B5
New Canaan NB 32 D7
New Canaan NB 33 A5
New Carlisle QC 29 D8
New Carlisle QC 30 D1
New Carlisle QC 31 A7
Newcastle ON 21 E-F3
Newcastle (Miramichi West) NB 31 D6
Newcastle Bridge NB 31 F6
Newcastle Bridge NB 32 B4
Newcastle Creek NB 31 F6
Newcastle Creek NB 32 B4
Newcastle Island PMP BC 1 F6
Newcastle Island PMP BC 2 E4
New Chelsea NL 37 C7
New Chester NS 33 B8
New Chester NS 34 F4
Newcombville NS 33 D4
New Credit ON 19 C7
New Credit ON 20 E6
Newdale MB 11 E8
Newdale MB 13 E2
Newdale MB 14 D1
New Dayton AB 6 F6-7
New Dayton AB 7 E-F6
New Denmark NB 31 D3
New Denver BC 6 E3
New Dominion PE 34 C2
New Dominion PE 35 E4
New Dublin ON 21 C8
New Dublin ON 24 F2
New Dundee ON 19 B6
New Dundee ON 20 D5
New Durham ON 19 C6
New Durham ON 20 E5
New Edinburgh NS 33 D1
Newell, Lake AB 6 E6-7
Newell, Lake AB 7 C6-7
Newellton NS 33 F2
New Elm NS 33 D4
New Ferolle NL 38 B3
New Ferolle NL 38 E7-8
New Ferolle Peninsula NL 38 B3
New Fish Creek AB 9 E-F3
Newfoundland T'Railway PP NL 36 A7 B7-8
Newfoundland T'Railway PP NL 36 C2 D1
Newfoundland T'Railway PP NL 37 A2-3
Newfoundland T'Railway PP NL 37 A-B5 B5-6
Newfoundland T'Railway PP NL 37 D6 E7
Newfoundland T'Railway PP NL 38 F3-4
Newgate BC 6 F4-5
Newgate BC 7 F2
New Germany NS 32 F6
New Germany NS 33 D3
New Glasglow QC 24 C5
New Glasgow QC 27 D1
New Glasgow NS 34 B3
New Glasgow ON 19 D4
New Glasgow ON 20 F3
New Glasgow PE 34 C2
New Glasgow PE 35 D4
New Grafton NS 33 D3
New Hamburg ON 19 B5
New Hamburg ON 20 D4
New Harbour NL 37 D7
New Harbour NS 34 F5-6
New Haven PE 34 C2
New Haven PE 35 E4
New Hazelton BC 3 F4
Newington ON 24 E3
New Liskeard ON 17 E7
New Liskeard ON 22 A1
New Liskeard ON 23 F2
New London PE 34 B1-2
New London PE 35 D3

New London Bay PE 35 D4
New Lowell ON 20 B6
New Lowell CA ON 20 B6
Newman Island NT 5 A7
Newmans Beach ON 20 B8
Newmans Beach ON 21 E2
Newmans Cove NL 37 B7
Newmarket NB 32 C2
Newmarket ON 20 B7
Newmarket ON 21 E1
New Maryland NB 32 C2-3
New Melbourne NL 37 C7
New Mills NB 29 D7
New Mills NB 31 A5
New Minas NS 32 E7
New Minas NS 33 A4
New Norway AB 6 B6
New Norway AB 8 D7
New Osgoode SK 11 B6
New Osnaburgh (Mishkeegogamang) ON 13 D8
New Osnaburgh (Mishkeegogamang) ON 16 B4-5
New Perlican NL 37 D7
New Perth PE 34 C3-4
New Perth PE 35 E6
Newport PE 34 C3-4
Newport PE 35 E7
Newport QC 30 D2
Newport, pointe de QC 30 D2
Newport Corner NS 32 E8
Newport Corner NS 33 B5
Newport Corner NS 34 F1
Newport Station NS 32 E7
Newport Station NS 33 B-C5
New Richmond QC 29 D7
New Richmond QC 30 D1
New River NB 32 D-E3
New River Beach NB 32 E3
New River Beach PP NB 32 E3
New Ross NS 32 F7
New Ross NS 33 C4
New Ross Road NS 33 B4
New Ross Road NS 33 C4
New Russell NS 32 F7
New Russell NS 33 C4
Newry ON 19 A5
Newry ON 20 C4
New Salem NS 32 D6
New Salem NS 33 A3-4
New Sarepta AB 6 B6
New Sarepta AB 8 D7
New Sarum ON 19 D5
New Sarum ON 20 F4
Newstead NL 36 A7
Newstead NL 37 A5
Newstead NL 38 F6
New Tecumseth ON 20 B7
Newton MB 14 D4
Newton ON 19 A5
Newton ON 20 D4
Newton PE 35 E4
Newton Lake NL 36 C7
Newton Lake NB 35 E1-2
Newton Lake SK 11 F3
Newton Mills NS 33 A7
Newton Mills NS 34 F3
Newton-Robinson ON 20 B6
Newtonville ON 21 E3
New Town NS 33 A8
New Town NS 34 F4
Newtown NB 32 C5
Newtown NL 37 A7
Newtown NL 38 F7
New Victoria NS 34 B-C8
Newville NS 38 E6
Newville Lake PP NS 32 E6
Newville Lake PP NS 33 A4-5
New Waterford NS 34 B-C8
New Westminster BC 2 E5
New-Wes-Valley NL 37 A6-7
New World Island NL 38 E6
New Yarmouth NS 33 D2
New Yarmouth NS 33 A3-4
New Zealand PE 34 D3
New Zealand PE 35 D7
New Zion NB 31 F5-6
New Zion NB 32 B4
Ney Lake ON 15 F7
Neys ON 16 E7-8
Neys ON 17 C2
Neys PP ON 16 E7-8
Neys PP ON 17 C2
Nezan ON 16 D7
Nezan ON 17 B1
Nez Croche, lac NT 10 B-C8
Niagara Escarpment ON 20 A-B5 B-C6
Niagara Falls ON 20 E7-8
Niagara Falls ON 20 E7-8
Niagara-on-the-Lake ON 20 E8
Niagara Peninsula ON 19 C8
Niagara Peninsula ON 20 E6-7
Niagara River ON 20 E8
Niapenco, Lake ON 19 C7
Niapenco, Lake ON 20 E6
Nibinamik (Summer Beaver) ON 16 A6
Nicabau, lac QC 26 C3
Nicabong QC 22 E5
Nicette, lac QC 29 A-B1

Nicholas-Denys NB 31 B7
Nichol Island NS 33 C7
Nicholson NT 5 A6
Nicholson Island NT 5 A6
Nicholson Island ON 21 E4-5
Nicholson Lake SK 9 A8
Nicholsville NB 36 A3
Nicholsville NL 37 A1
Nicholsville NL 38 F2-3
Nicholsville NS 33 B4
Nickel Plate PP BC 6 F1
Nicklin Lake MB 12 B8
Nicklin Lake MB 15 B2-3
Nicman QC 39 E2
Nicobi, lac QC 23 B8
Nicobi, lac QC 26 C2
Nicola BC 1 E8
Nicola BC 2 C8
Nicola BC 6 E1
Nicola Lake BC 2 C8
Nicola River BC 1 E8
Nicola River BC 2 C7-8
Nicola River BC 6 E1-2
Nicolas, lac QC 22 B5-6
Nicolas-Denys NB 29 E7
Nicolet QC 24 B7-8
Nicolet QC 25 F7-8
Nicolet, lac QC 27 C3
Nicolet, lac QC 27 D5
Nicolet, rivière QC 24 C3
Nicolet, rivière QC 30 D2
Nicolet, RNOM de QC 27 C3 A4
Nicolet, RNOM de QC 24 B7-8
Nicolet, RNOM de QC 27 C2-3
Nicolet NMBS QC 24 B7-8
Nicolet NMBS QC 27 C2-3
Nicolet Sud-Ouest, rivière QC 27 C-D3 D4-5 E5
Nicolson ON 20 B6
Nicolum River PP BC 1 E8
Nicolum River PP BC 2 D7
Nicolum River PP BC 6 F1
Nictau NB 29 F5
Nictau NB 31 C4
Nictaux Falls NS 32 E6
Nictaux Falls NS 33 B3
Nictaux River NS 32 F6
Nictaux River NS 33 C3
Nictaux South NS 32 E6
Nictaux South NS 33 C3
Nigadoo NB 29 E8
Nigadoo NB 31 B6
Nigadoo River NB 29 E8
Niger Sound NL 39 C-D8
Night Hawk Lake ON 17 D6-7
Nightingale AB 7 B4-5
Nikip Lake ON 13 B7
Nile ON 19 A4
Nile ON 20 C3
Niles, lac SK 35 E1-2
Niles Lake NB 35 E1-2
Nilestown ON 19 C5
Nilestown ON 20 E4
Nilgaut, lac QC 22 C5
Nilkitkwa Lake PP BC 3 F5
Nilkitkwa River BC 3 E4-5
Nimpkish Lake BC 1 E4
Nimpkish Lake PP BC 1 E4
Nimpkish River BC 1 E4-5
Nimpo Lake BC 1 C5
Nimpo Lake BC 1 C5-6
Nine Mile Creek PE 34 C2
Nine Mile Creek PE 35 E4-5
Nine Mile River NS 32 E8
Nine Mile River NS 33 B5
Nine Mile River NS 34 F2
Nine Mile River NS 20 C3
Ninette MB 13 F2
Ninette MB 14 F1
Ninevah NS 33 D3-4
Ninevah PP NS 33 D3-4
Ninga MB 13 F2
Ninga MB 14 F1
Ningunsaw PP BC 3 D3
Niobe AB 8 F6
Nipawin SK 11 B6
Nipekamew-Sand Cliffs PPA SK 11 B7
Nipew Lake SK 12 E5
Nipi, lac QC 29 A2
Nipigon ON 16 E6
Nipigon ON 40 F1-2
Nipigon, lac ON 16 D6
Nipigon, lac ON 17 B1
Nipigon, Lake ON 16 D6
Nipigon, Lake ON 17 B1
Nipigon, Lake ON 40 F1
Nipigon Bay ON 16 E6-7
Nipigon Bay ON 17 C1
Nipigon River ON 16 D6
Nipigon River ON 17 B-C1
Nipin River SK 9 E8
Nipin River SK 12 E3
Nipisi QC 39 E2
Nipishish Lake NL 39 B5
Nipisi River AB 9 E5
Nipissing ON 17 F8
Nipissing ON 18 B8
Nipissing, lac ON 22 D-E1
Nipissing, lac ON 17 F7-8
Nipissing, lac ON 18 A7-8
Nipissing, lac ON 22 D1
Nipissing, Lake ON 18 A7-8
Nipissing, Lake ON 22 D1

Nipissing, réserve de chasse de la Couronne ON 17 E-F8
Nipissing, réserve de chasse de la Couronne ON 22 B-C1
Nipissing Beach ON 18 B8
Nipissing Crown Game Preserve 17 E-F8
Nipissing Crown Game Reserve ON 22 C1
Nipissing Ouest ON 17 F7
Nipissing Ouest ON 18 A7
Nipissing River ON 22 E2
Nipissis, lac QC 39 E2
Nipissis, rivière QC 39 D-E2
Nipisso, lac QC 39 E2-3
Nippers Harbour NL 38 E5
Nippers Harbour NL 39 F8
Nippon, lac du QC 26 D6
Nippon, lac du QC 28 B1
Nisbet AB 8 F6
Nisga'a Memorial Lava Bed PP BC 3 F3
Niska Lake SK 9 E8
Niska Lake SK 12 E3
Niskonlith Lake PP BC 6 D1-2
Nisku AB 6 B6
Nisku AB 8 C-D6
Nisling Range YT 4 C-D2
Nisling River YT 4 D5
Nistocaponano, rivière QC 26 C7
Nistowiak Lake SK 12 E6
Nisutlin Lake YT 4 D5
Nisutlin River YT 4 D-E5
Nisutlin River Delta NWA YT 4 E5
Nisutlin River Territorial Recreation Site YT 4 E5
Nitainlaii TP NT 5 D4
Nitchequon QC 40 E5-6
Nith River ON 19 B6
Nith River ON 20 D5
Nithburg ON 19 B5
Nithburg ON 20 D4
Nitinat BC 1 F6
Nitinat BC 2 E3
Nitinat Lake BC 2 E-F2
Nitinat River BC 2 E3
Nitinat River PP BC 2 E2-3
Niton AB 8 C4
Niton Junction AB 6 B4
Niton Junction AB 8 C3-4
Niverville MB 13 F4
Niverville MB 14 E5
Niverville, lac QC 25 B4-5
Niwelin Lake NT 5 C7
Niwene ON 18 C6
Nixon ON 19 C6
Nixon ON 20 F5
Nizard, lac QC 22 B6
Njau, lac des QC 26 B6
Nobel ON 18 D7
Nobleford AB 6 E6
Nobleford AB 7 E5
Nobleton ON 19 A7
Nobleton ON 20 C6
Noeick River BC 1 C5
Noel NS 34 F1
Noell Lake NT 5 B-C5
Noel Road NS 32 D8
Noel Road NS 33 B5
Noel Road NS 34 F1
Noel Shore NS 32 D8
Noel Shore NS 33 A6
Noel Shore NS 34 E-F2
Noels Pond NL 36 B-C2
Noëlville ON 17 F7
Noëlville ON 18 B6
Noganosh Lake ON 18 C6-7
Nogies Creek ON 21 C-D3
Nogies Creek ON 21 D3
Noir, lac QC 28 A4
Noirclair, lac QC 39 E6
Noire, rivière QC 22 D5 E6
Noire, rivière QC 24 D7
Noire, rivière QC 24 D8
Noire, rivière QC 25 E8
Noire, rivière QC 27 A-B4
Noire, rivière QC 27 E5
Noisy Creek YT 5 E-F4
Noisy River, RNP ON 20 B5-6
Noisy River PNR ON 20 B5-6
Nojack AB 6 B4
Nojack AB 8 C4
Nokomis SK 11 D5
Nokomis Lake SK 12 D6
Nokomis Lake SK 15 D1
Nolalu ON 16 F5
Nominingue QC 24 B3
Nominingue QC 25 F3
Nominingue, lac QC 24 B3
Nominingue, lac QC 25 F3
Nonacho NT 41 E2
Nonsuch MB 15 E5
Nootka Island BC 1 F4
Nopiming PP MB 13 E5
Nopiming PP MB 14 C7
Nopiming PP MB 16 C1
Nora SK 11 C6
Nora, lac QC 23 D2
Norah Willis Michener Game Preserve YT 4 E8
Norah Willis Michener Game Preserve YT 10 E1
Noral AB 8 A7-8

Noralee BC 1 A5
Norbertville QC 27 C4-5
Norboro PE 35 D3
Norbuck AB 8 D5
Norbury Lake PP BC 6 F4-5
Norcan Lake ON 21 B6
Nord, rivière du QC 24 C-D5
Nordbye Lake SK 12 B6
Nordbye Lake SK 15 A1
Nordegg AB 6 C4
Nordegg Eiver AB 8 E3-4
Nordegg River AB 6 B4
Nordenskiold River YT 4 C-D3
Nordenskiold Wetland Habitat Protection Area YT 4 D3
Nordique, ZEC QC 28 B-C8
Nordique, ZEC QC 29 B-C1
Nord-Ouest, pointe QC 30 B3
Norembega ON 17 C7
Norfolk CA ON 19 D6
Norfolk CA ON 20 F5
Norfolk County ON 19 C6
Norfolk County ON 20 F5
Norgate MB 13 D-E2
Norgate MB 14 C2
Norge SK 11 F4
Norham ON 21 E4
Norland ON 20 A8
Norland ON 21 C2
Norma AB 8 C8
Norman ON 19 D5
Norman ON 20 F4
Norman Bay NL 39 C8
Norman, lac QC 25 D6-7
Normand, lac QC 27 A2
Normand, lac QC 28 F2
Normandale ON 19 D6
Normandale ON 20 F5
Normandie, ZEC QC 25 C4
Normandin QC 26 D8
Normandin QC 28 B3
Normandin, lac QC 26 D5
Norman Range NT 5 F7-8
Norman's Cove NL 37 D6-7
Norman Wells NT 5 F7
Norman Wells NT 10 A1
Normétal QC 17 C8
Normétal QC 23 B2
Norquay SK 11 C7
Norquay SK 13 C1
Norris Arm NL 36 A6-7
Norris Arm NL 37 A4-5
Norris Arm NL 38 F6
Norris Arm North Side NL 36 A6
Norris Arm North Side NL 37 A4
Norris Arm North Side NL 38 F6
Norris Lake MB 11 A-B8
Norris Lake MB 13 B2
Norris Lake MB 14 C4-5
Norris Lake PP MB 13 E3
Norris Lake PP MB 14 C4
Norris Point NL 38 E-F2
Norris Point NL 39 F7
Norris Point NL 40 F8
Norsemans Pond NL 36 C8
Norsemans Pond NL 37 C6
North, Cape NS 34 A7
Northam PE 35 C2
North Arm BC 1 B-C8
North Arm BC 6 B1
North Arm NL 36 A3
North Arm NL 37 A1
North Arm NL 38 F2
North Arm NT 10 D6-7
North Arm TP NT 10 C6
North Arm TP NT 41 D1
North Aspy River NS 34 A6-7
North Augusta ON 21 C8
North Augusta ON 24 F2
Northbank AB 8 B7
North Battleford SK 11 B3
North Bay NL 36 D5
North Bay NL 36 D2
North Bay NL 37 D3
North Bay ON 17 F8
North Bay ON 18 A8
North Bay ON 22 D1
North Bay SK 12 E5
North Bay Ingonish NS 34 A-B7
North Beach PP ON 21 E4-5
North Bedeque PE 35 D3
North Bend BC 1 E-F8
North Bend BC 2 C7
North Bentinck Arm BC 1 C4-5
North Big Salmon River YT 4 D4
North Branch NL 36 D1-2
North Branch ON 13 F6
North Branch ON 16 E2
North Branch Big Segovie River NB 29 F6-7
North Branch Big Segovie River NB 31 C5
North Branch Muskoka River ON 18 D-E8
North Branch Muskoka River ON 21 B1
North Branch Oromocto River NB 32 C2-3 D2
North Branch Renous River NB 31 D5

Northbrook ON 21 C5
North Brookfield NS 33 D3-4
North Bruce ON 18 F4
North Bruce ON 20 A3
North Buck Lake AB 8 A7
North Buck Lake AB 9 F6
North Buxton ON 19 E3
North Cape PE 34 A1
North Cape PE 35 A2
North Caribou Lake NT 5 C5
North Caribou Lake ON 13 B8
North Caribou Lake ON 16 A4
North Carleton PE 40 E1
North Carleton PE 32 B8
North Carleton PE 34 C1
North Carleton PE 35 E1
North Castor River ON 21 B8
North Castor River ON 24 E2
North Channel ON 18 B1-2
North Channel ON 21 E6
North Cobalt ON 17 E8
North Cobalt ON 22 A1
North Cobalt ON 23 F1
North Cooking Lake AB 8 C7
North Cowichan BC 2 F4
North Driftwood River PNR ON 17 B6
North Driftwood River, RNP ON 17 B6
North Duck River MB 11 C8
North Duck River MB 13 C1-2
North Earltown NS 34 E2-3
North East Arm NL 36 D4
North East Arm NL 37 D2
Northeast Cove NS 32 F7-8
Northeast Cove NS 33 C5
Northeastern Manitoulin and the Islands ON 18 B3-4
North East Harbour NS 33 F3
North East Margaree NS 34 A6
North East Margaree River NS 34 B6
North Enmore PE 35 C2
Northern Arm NL 36 A6
Northern Arm NL 37 A4
Northern Arm NL 38 F5
Northern Bathurst Island (Tuktusiuqvialuk) NP (proposed/projeté) NU 42 C3-4
Northern Bay NL 37 D7
Northern Bruce Peninsula ON 18 E4-5
Northern Indian Lake MB 15 C4
Northern Light Lake ON 16 F4-5
Northern Peninsula NL 38 C3-4
Northern Rocky Mountains PP BC 3 C4
North Etomami River MB 13 C4
Northfield NS 32 F5-6
Northfield NS 32 F6
Northfield NS 33 D3
Northgate SK 11 F7
North Gower ON 21 B8
North Gower ON 24 E2
North Grant NS 34 D4
North Gut St. Anns NS 34 C7
North Harbour NL 22 C1
North Harbour NL 37 D6
North Harbour NL 37 E7
North Harbour NS 34 A7
North Hatley QC 27 F4
North Head NB 32 F3
North Head NL 36 D5
North Head NL 38 F1-2
North Heart River AB 9 D-E4
North Kemptville NS 33 E2
North Kent Island NU 42 C4
North Kingston NS 32 E6
North Kingston NS 33 B3
North Klondike River YT 4 A2-3
North Knife Lake MB 15 C4
North Knife Lake MB 41 F1
North Knife River MB 15 B4-5
North Lake NB 32 C1
North Lake PE 34 B4
North Lake PE 35 D8
North Lake Provincial Campground NB 32 C1
North Lake, camping provincial NB 32 C1
North Lancaster ON 24 E4
Northleigh AB 8 C5
North Lochaber NS 34 E4-5
North McQuesten River YT 4 A-B3
North Milton PE 35 D-E4
Northminster SK 11 B2
North Monetville ON 17 F7
North Monetville ON 18 B6-7
North Moose Lake MB 11 A8

North Moose Lake MB 13 A2
North Moose Lake MB 32 E5-6
North Mountain NS 33 B3-4
North Nahanni NT 10 D1-2
North Noel Road NS 32 D8
North Noel Road NS 33 B5
North Noel Road NS 34 F1
North Pelham ON 19 C8
North Pelham ON 20 E7
North Pender Island BC 2 F4
North Perth ON 19 A5
North Perth ON 20 C4
North Pine BC 3 E8
North Pine BC 9 D1
North Pond NL 36 B7
North Pond NL 37 B5
Northport NS 32 C8
Northport NS 34 D1
Northport NS 35 F2-3
North Port ON 21 E5
Northport PE 35 C8
Northport (Alberton South) PE 35 B2
Northport Beach PP NS 32 C8
Northport Beach PP NS 34 D1-2
Northport Beach PP NS 35 F3
North Portage ON 21 B2
North Portal SK 11 F7
North Preston NS 33 C6
North Ridge ON 19 E1-2
North River MB 15 B5
North River NL 37 D7
North River NL 39 B7
North River NS 32 F6
North River NS 33 C4
North River NS 34 E2
North River ON 18 F8
North River ON 20 A7
North River ON 21 C1
North River ON 22 D1-2
North River Bridge NS 34 B-C7
North River PP NS 34 B6-7
North Rustico NB 34 D4
North Rustico PE 35 D4
North Saanich BC 2 F4-5
North Saskatchewan River AB 6 A7
North Saskatchewan River AB 6 B-C5
North Saskatchewan River AB 8 C5-6 D6
North Saskatchewan River AB 8 D4
North Saskatchewan River AB 11 A1
North Saskatchewan River SK 11 B2-3
North Saugeen River ON 20 A-B4
North Seal River MB 12 A8 B7-8
North Seal River MB 15 B2-3
North Shoal Lake MB 14 C4
North Shore NS 34 B7
North Shore NS 34 D2
North Shore Waterway PP ON 17 F5
North Spirit Lake ON 13 C6
North Spirit Lake ON 13 C6
North Spirit Lake ON 16 A3
North Spirit Lake ON 16 A2-3
North Spruce Lake ON 22 C1
North Star AB 9 D3
North Sydney NS 34 C7
North Tea Lake ON 22 E2
North Tetagouche NB 29 E7
North Tetagouche NB 31 B6
North Thames River ON 19 B-D5
North Thames River ON 20 D-E4
North Thompson Islands PP BC 6 D1-2
North Thompson Oxbows East PP BC 6 C2
North Thompson Oxbows Manteau PP BC 6 C2
North Thompson Oxbows-Jensen Island PP BC 2 A8
North Thompson River PP BC 2 A8
North Thompson River PP BC 6 C-D2
North Thompson River PP BC 6 D1-2
North Tryon PE 35 E3
North Tweedsmuir PP BC 1 B5
North Twillingate Island NL 38 E6
North Twin Island NU 40 E3-4
North Twin Lake NL 36 A5
North Twin Lake NL 37 A3-4
North Twin Lake NL 38 F5
Northumberland, détroit de NB 32 A-B7
Northumberland, détroit de NS 34 C-D4 C5

Northumberland, détroit de PE 35 F3-5 E4 F7-8
Northumberland PP NE 34 D3
Northumberland PP PE 35 F6
Northumberland Strait NB 32 A-B7
Northumberland Strait NS 34 D2-3
Northumberland Strait PE 35 D1-2 E7 F8
North Vancouver BC 1 F7
North Vancouver BC 2 D5
North Vermilion AB 9 B4
North Veuve River ON 18 A6
Northville ON 19 B3
Northville ON 20 E2
North Wabasca Lake AB 9 E5
Northwest Angle Inlet ON 14 E-F8
North West Arm NL 36 A8
North West Arm NL 37 A6
North West Arm NL 38 F7
Northwest Bay ON 13 F6
Northwest Bay ON 16 E2
North West Brook NL 36 C-D8
North West Brook NL 37 C-D6
Northwest Brook NL 37 F7
Northwest Gander River NL 36 B6-7 C6
Northwest Gander River NL 37 B4-5 C4
Northwest Miramichi River NB 29 F6-7
Northwest Miramichi River NB 31 C5-6
Northwest Passage TP NU 41 C4
Northwest Passage TP NU 42 F4
Northwest Point NT 10 D6
North West River NL 39 B5-6
North West River NL 40 E7-8
Northwest Upsalquitch River NB 29 E5-6
Northwest Upsalquitch River NB 31 B4
North Whirl ON 20 D4
North Wiltshire PE 34 C2
North Wiltshire PE 35 E4
North Wind Lake ON 16 D6-7
North Wind Lake ON 17 B1
North Woodslee ON 19 E1-2
North York ON 19 A8
North York ON 20 C7
North York ON 21 F1
Northwood ON 19 D3
Northwood ON 20 F2
Norton NS 32 C4
Norton NB 33 A2
Norton Lake MB 15 B6
Norton Shaw, Cape NU 42 C5
Norval ON 19 A7
Norval ON 20 C6
Norway PE 34 A1
Norway PE 35 A2
Norway Bay QC 21 A7
Norway Bay QC 22 F6-7
Norway Bay QC 24 D1
Norway House MB 13 A3
Norway Lake ON 21 B6
Norwegian Bay NU 42 C4
Norwich ON 19 C6
Norwich ON 20 E5
Norwood NS 33 E1
Norwood ON 21 D4
Nosbonsing ON 17 F8
Nosbonsing ON 18 B8
Nosbonsing ON 22 D1-2
Nosbonsing, Lake ON 22 D2
Notawassi, lac QC 22 B8
Notawassi, lac QC 25 D3
Notawassi, rivière QC 22 B-C8
Notawassi, rivière QC 25 D2
Notch Hill BC 6 D2
Notikewin AB 9 D3
Notikewin PP AB 9 C3-4 D3-4
Notikewin River AB 9 D3
Notre-Dame NB 31 F8
Notre-Dame NB 32 B6
Notre-Dame, baie de NL 38 E5
Notre-Dame, lac QC 24 C1
Notre-Dame, lac QC 27 B7
Notre-Dame, monts QC 27 A-B7 C6
Notre-Dame, monts QC 29 B6-7
Notre-Dame, monts QC 29 D2-3
Notre-Dame, monts QC 31 A1-2 B1
Notre Dame PP NL 38 E5
Notre Dame PP NL 37 A7
Notre Dame PP NL 38 F6
Notre-Dame-de-Ham QC 27 D4-5
Notre-Dame-de-la-Merci QC 24 B5
Notre-Dame-de-la-Merci QC 25 F5
Notre-Dame-de-la-Paix QC 24 C3-4

Notre-Dame-de-la-Salette QC 22 F8
Notre-Dame-de-la-Salette QC 24 C2
Notre-Dame-de-Lorette QC 26 C8
Notre-Dame-de-Lorette QC 28 A3-4
Notre Dame de Lourdes MB 13 F3
Notre Dame de Lourdes MB 14 E3
Notre-Dame-de-Lourdes NB 29 F4
Notre-Dame-de-Lourdes QC 31 C2-3
Notre-Dame-de-Lourdes QC 24 B-C6
Notre-Dame-de-Lourdes QC 27 C1-2
Notre-Dame-de-Lourdes QC 27 C4-5
Notre-Dame-de-Montauban-les-Mines QC 24 A8
Notre-Dame-de-Montauban-les-Mines QC 25 E8
Notre-Dame-de-Montauban-les-Mines QC 27 B4
Notre-Dame-de-Pierreville QC 24 B-C7
Notre-Dame-de-Pierreville QC 27 B4
Notre-Dame-de-Pontmain QC 22 D8
Notre-Dame-de-Pontmain QC 24 B2
Notre-Dame-de-Pontmain QC 25 F2
Notre-Dame-de-Portneuf QC 27 B4-5
Notre-Dame-des-Anges QC 24 A8
Notre-Dame-des-Anges QC 25 E8
Notre-Dame-des-Anges QC 27 A4
Notre-Dame-des-Bois QC 27 E6
Notre-Dame-des-Champs ON 21 A8
Notre-Dame-des-Champs ON 24 D2-3
Notre-Dame-des-Érables NB 29 E8
Notre-Dame-des-Érables NB 30 E1
Notre-Dame-des-Érables NB 31 B7
Notre-Dame-des-Monts QC 28 E7
Notre-Dame-des-Pins QC 27 D2
Notre-Dame-des-Prairies QC 24 C6
Notre-Dame-des-Prairies QC 25 F6
Notre-Dame-des-Sept-Douleurs QC 29 D1
Notre-Dame-de-Stanbridge QC 24 E7
Notre-Dame-de-Stanbridge QC 27 F2
Notre-Dame-du-Bon-Conseil QC 24 C8
Notre-Dame-du-Bon-Conseil QC 27 D4
Notre-Dame-du-Lac QC 29 E2
Notre-Dame-du-Laus QC 22 E8
Notre-Dame-du-Laus QC 24 B2
Notre-Dame-du-Mont-Carmel QC 24 B8
Notre-Dame-du-Mont-Carmel QC 24 E6
Notre-Dame-du-Mont-Carmel QC 25 E8
Notre-Dame-du-Mont-Carmel QC 27 B3
Notre-Dame-du-Mont-Carmel QC 27 F2
Notre-Dame-du-Nord QC 17 D-E8
Notre-Dame-du-Nord QC 22 A1-2
Notre-Dame-du-Portage QC 28 E8
Notre-Dame-du-Portage QC 29 E1
Notre-Dame-du-Rosaire QC 27 B7
Notre-Dame-du-Rosaire QC 28 B5
Notre Dame Junction NL 36 A7
Notre Dame Junction NL 37 A5
Notre Dame Junction NL 38 F6
Notre Dame PP NL 37 A7
Notre Dame PP NL 38 F6
Nottawa ON 18 F6-7
Nottawa ON 20 A5
Nottawaga Beach ON 18 F7
Nottawaga Beach ON 20 A6
Nottawasaga, baie ON 18 F6-7

Nottawasaga Bay ON 18 F6-7
Nottawasaga Bay ON 20 A5-6
Nottawasaga Lookout PNR ON 18 F6-7
Nottawasaga Lookout PNR ON 20 A5-6
Nottawasaga Lookout, RNP ON 18 F6-7
Nottawasaga Lookout, RNP ON 20 A5-6
Nottawasaga River ON 20 A-B6
Nottawasaga River ON 20 B-C6
Nottaway, rivière QC 40 F4
Nottingham Island 40 A4
Nottingham Island 41 D7
Notukeu Creek SK 11 E4
Nourse MB 14 D6
Nouveau, lac QC 39 B1
Nouveau-Québec (Chubb Crater), cratère du QC 40 B4-5
Nouveau-Québec (Chubb Crater), cratère du QC 41 D8
Nouvelle QC 29 D7
Nouvelle QC 31 A5
Nouvelle, rivière QC 29 C-D6
Nouvelle, rivière QC 31 A5
Nouvelle-France, cap de QC 40 B5
Nouvelle-France, cap de QC 41 D8
Novar ON 18 D8
Novar ON 21 A1
Novar ON 22 F1
Novellet, lac QC 23 B7
Novellet, lac QC 26 C1
Novra MB 11 C8
Novra MB 13 C1
Noyan QC 24 E6
Noyan QC 27 F2
Noyrot, lac QC 38 A-B1
Noyrot, lac QC 39 D6
Nuchatlitz Inlet BC 1 F4
Nuchatlitz PP BC 1 F4
Nueltin Lake NU 41 F1
Nukko Lake BC 1 A7
Nulki Lake BC 1 A7
Numabin Bay SK 12 D6
Numaykoos Lake MB 15 C5
Numaykoos Lake PP MB 15 C4
Numogate ON 21 C7
Numogate ON 24 E1
Nunalla MB 15 A5
Nungesser Lake ON 13 B2
Nungesser Lake ON 16 B2
Nunim Lake SK 12 A6-7
Nunim Lake SK 15 A1
Nunn Lake SK 12 E-F6
Nunsti PP BC 1 C-D6
Nutak NL 40 D7
Nut Lake SK 11 C6
Nut Mountain SK 11 C6
Nuttby NS 33 A6
Nuttby NS 34 E2
Nuttlude Lake SK 3 C3
Nutzotin Mountains YT 4 C1
Nuvorak Point NT 10 E-F7
Nyanza NS 34 C6
Nyarling River NT 10 E-F7
Nymphes, ZEC des QC 24 A-B6
Nymphes, ZEC des QC 25 F6
Nymphes, ZEC des QC 27 B-C1

O

Oakbank MB 13 E4
Oakbank MB 14 D5
Oak Bay BC 2 F4-5
Oak Bay NB 32 E2
Oak Bay QC 29 D6
Oak Bay QC 31 A4-5
Oak Bay PP NB 32 E2
Oak Bluff MB 14 E5
Oak Brae MB 14 A1
Oakburn MB 11 E8
Oakburn MB 13 E1
Oakdale ON 19 D3
Oakdale ON 20 F2
Oakfield PP NS 32 E8
Oakfield PP NS 33 B6
Oak Hill NB 32 D2
Oak Island NS 34 D2
Oak Lake MB 11 F8
Oak Lake MB 11 E-F8
Oak Lake ON 13 E6
Oak Lake ON 16 C2
Oak Lake (IR) MB 13 F1
Oak Lake PP MB 13 E-F1
Oak Lake PP MB 14 B3

Oakland ON 20 E5
Oakner MB 11 E8
Oakner MB 13 E1
Oak Orchard ON 21 D3
Oak Park NS 33 D4
Oak Point MB 13 E3
Oak Point MB 14 C4
Oak Point NB 32 D4
Oak Point NB 33 A1
Oak Ridges ON 19 A8
Oak Ridges ON 20 C7
Oak Ridges ON 21 E1
Oak River MB 11 E8
Oak River MB 13 E1-2
Oak River MB 13 E2
Oak River MB 14 D1
Oakshela SK 11 E6-7
Oakview MB 14 B3
Oakville MB 13 E3
Oakville MB 14 D4
Oakville ON 19 B7-8
Oakville ON 20 D6-7
Oakwood ON 20 B8
Oakwood ON 21 D2
Oastler Lake PP ON 18 D7-8
Oatfield MB 14 B3
Oba ON 17 C4
Obabcata, lac QC 23 E7-8
Obabcata, lac QC 25 B2
Obabcata, lac QC 26 F2
Obabika Lake ON 17 E1
Obabika River PP ON 17 E1
Obakamiga Lake ON 17 C3
Oba Lake ON 17 C4
Obalski, lac QC 23 C4
Oban SK 11 C3
Obaska QC 23 E8
Obatagamau, lac QC 26 B4
Obatanga PP ON 17 D3
Obed AB 8 C2
Obedjiwan QC 26 D4
Obed Lake PP AB 6 A-B3
Obed Lake PP AB 8 C2
Oberon MB 14 D2
Oblats, lac des QC 22 D7
Oblats, lac des QC 24 B1-2
Oblats, lac des QC 25 F1-2
Obonga Lake ON 16 D5-6
Obonga-Ottertooth PP ON 16 D5
O'Brien PP AB 9 F2
O'Brien's Landing ON 13 E8
O'Briens Landing ON 16 C1
Observatory Inlet BC 3 F3
Obustiga Lake ON 16 B5
Ocean Falls BC 1 C4
Ocean Man SK 11 E6-7
Ocean Pond NL 36 A8
Ocean Pond NL 37 A6
Ocean Pond NL 38 F7
Ochak Lake SK 12 A6
Ochapowace SK 11 E7
Ochiichagwe'babigo'ining ON 16 D1
Ochre Beach MB 14 B1-2
Ochre River MB 11 D8
Ochre River MB 13 D8
Ochre River MB 13 D2
Ochre River MB 14 B1
Ochre River NT 10 C2-3
Octave, rivière QC 23 B4 C3
Octopus Islands PMP BC 1 E-5-6
Octopus Islands PMP BC 2 B2
Odanak QC 24 C7
Odanak QC 27 D3
O'Day MB 15 C5
Odei River MB 15 E3-4
Odell MB 31 D3
Odell River NB 31 D-E3
Odell River NB 32 A1-2
Odessa ON 21 D-E6
Odessa SK 11 E6
Odhill MB 15 F3
Odin, Mount NU 41 D8
Odin, Mount NU 42 F8
O'Donel River BC 3 A1
O'Donnel River BC 4 F4-5
O'Donnell Point, RNP ON 18 E6-7
O'Donnell Point PNR ON 18 E6-7
O'Donnells NL 37 E7
Off Lake Corner ON 16 E2
Ogascanane, lac QC 22 B3
Ogden NS 34 E5
Ogden Mill NB 35 F1
Ogema SK 11 F5
Ogilvie MB 13 E2-3
Ogilvie MB 14 D2
Ogilvie Island NT 5 F7
Ogilvie Mountains YT 5 E-F2
Ogilvie River YT 5 F2
Ogoki, Lake ON 16 C7
Ogoki, Lake ON 17 A2
Ogoki Reservoir ON 16 C7
Ogoki Reservoir ON 17 A1
Ogoki River ON 16 B8 C7
Ogoki River ON 17 A1
Ogoki River ON 40 F1-2
Ogoki River ON 16 C7
O'Hara, lac QC 22 E8
O'Hara, lac QC 24 C2
Ohaton AB 6 B6

Ohaton AB 8 D7
Ohaton AB 11 B1
Ohio NS 33 A8
Ohio NS 33 E2-3
Ohio NS 34 E4
Ohio-du-Barachois NB 35 E1
Ohsweken ON 19 C7
Ohsweken ON 20 E6
Oies, cap aux QC 28 E7
Oies, île aux QC 27 A7
Oies, île aux QC 28 F7
Oil City ON 19 C3
Oil City ON 20 F2
Oil Springs ON 19 C-D3
Oil Springs ON 20 F2
Oiseau Point ON 16 F8
Oiseau Point ON 17 D2
Oiseaux, rochers aux QC 30 E8
Ojibway PP ON 13 E7
Ojibway PP ON 16 D3
Oka QC 24 D5
Oka, parc d' QC 24 D5
Okanagan Centre BC 6 E2
Okanagan Falls BC 6 F2
Okanagan Falls PP BC 6 F2
Okanagan Lake BC 6 E-F2
Okanagan Lake PP BC 6 F2
Okanagan Mountain PP BC 6 E-F2
Okane, lac QC 25 C6
Okane, lac QC 28 F2
Okanese SK 11 D6
Okeover Arm BC 2 C3
Okeover Arm PP BC 1 E6
Okeover Arm PP BC 2 C3
Okipwatsikew Lake SK 12 E7
Okipwatsikew Lake SK 15 E1
Okla SK 11 C6
Okno MB 14 B5
Okotoks AB 6 D5-6 E5-6
Okotoks AB 7 C4
Olalla BC 6 F1
Old Barns NS 33 A6
Old Barns NS 34 E2
Old Bonaventure NL 37 C7
Old Canoe Lake NT 10 B7-8
Old Crow YT 5 C2
Old Crow Flats Special Management Area YT 5 C2-3
Old Crow Range YT 5 C1-2
Old Crow River YT 5 C2
Old Fort Bay AB 9 B7
Old Fort Bay AB 12 B2
Old Fort Nelson BC 3 B7
Old Fort Nelson BC 9 B1
Old Fort River AB 9 B7
Old Fort River AB 12 B2
Old Harry QC 30 E8
Old Horton Channel NT 5 A7
Old Man Lake NT 5 B5
Old Mans Pond NL 36 A3
Old Mans Pond NL 37 A1
Old Mans Pond NL 38 F2
Old Perlican NL 37 C7-8
Old Shoes Lake ON 16 A2
Old Shop NL 37 D-E7
Old Town Lunenburg NS 33 D5
Old Wives SK 11 E4-5
Old Wives Lake SK 11 E4-5
Old Wives Lake NMBS SK 11 E4-5
Oldcastle ON 19 E1
Oldenberg MB 14 D6-7
Oldham NS 33 B6
Oldman Dam AB 6 F5-6
Oldman Dam AB 7 E4
Oldman Dam PRA AB 6 F5-6
Oldman Dam PRA AB 7 E4
Oldman Lake SK 9 A8
Oldman River AB 6 E7
Oldman River AB 6 E-F5 F6
Oldman River AB 7 D7
Oldman River AB 7 E4
Oldman River MB 15 C4
Oldman River SK 9 A8
Oldman River SK 12 A4
Oldman River Reservoir AB 7 E4
Olds AB 6 C5
Olds AB 7 A4
O'Leary PE 32 A7
O'Leary PE 35 C1
Olga, lac QC 23 A6
Olha MB 11 D-E8
Olha MB 13 D-E1
Oliphant ON 18 E-F5
Oliphant ON 20 A3-4
Oliva, lac QC 26 C4
Oliver BC 6 F2
Oliver NS 34 E2
Oliver ON 19 E1
Oliver Cove PMP BC 1 C3-4
Oliver Lake SK 12 D6
Olomane, rivière QC 39 E5-6
Oman Lake SK 12 A4
Ombabika River ON 16 D6-7
Ombabika River ON 17 A1
Omemee ON 21 D-E3
Omerville QC 27 F4
Omineca Mountains BC 3 C4 D4-5
Omineca PP BC 3 E6
Omineca River BC 3 E5-6
Ominicetla Creek BC 3 E5

Ommanney Bay NU 41 A4
Ommanney Bay NU 42 D-E3
Omo, lac QC 26 A3
Ompah ON 21 C6
Onamakawash Lake ON 16 D5
Onaman Lake ON 16 D7
Onaman Lake ON 17 B1-2
Onanole MB 11 E8
Onanole MB 13 E2
Onanole MB 14 C1
Onaping ON 17 F6
Onaping Lake ON 17 E6
Onatchiway, lac QC 28 A6
Onatchiway, ZEC QC 28 A6
One Arrow SK 11 B5
One Island Lake PP BC 3 F8
One Island Lake PP BC 9 E1-2
Onefour AB 6 F8
Onefour AB 11 F1-2
100 Mile House BC 6 C1
100 Mile House BC 6 C1
108 Mile House BC 1 C-D8
108 Mile House BC 6 C1
150 Mile House BC 1 C7-8
Onésime, lac QC 28 D7
Onhda Lake NT 5 D6
Onion Lake SK 11 A2
Onondaga ON 19 C7
Onondaga ON 20 E6
Onoway AB 6 A-B5
Onoway AB 8 C5-6
Onslow NS 33 A6
Onslow NS 34 E2
Onslow Corners QC 24 A7
Onslow Corners QC 22 F7
Onslow Corners QC 24 D1
Ontaratue River NT 5 D6 E5
Ontario, lac ON 19 B8
Ontario, lac ON 20 B8
Ontario, lac ON 21 F4-6
Ontario, Lake ON 19 B8
Ontario, Lake ON 20 C-D8
Ontario, Lake ON 21 F4-5
Onyota'aka ON 19 C4
Onyota'aka ON 20 F3
Oona River BC 1 A2
Ootsa Lake BC 1 A-B5
Ootsa Lake BC 1 A5
Opachuanau Lake MB 12 D8
Opachuanau Lake MB 15 D2-3
Opakopa Lake ON 13 B7
Opal AB 6 A6
Opal AB 8 B6-7
Opapimiskan Lake ON 13 B8
Opasatica, lac QC 23 E2
Opasatika ON 17 B5
Opasatika Lake ON 17 C5
Opasatika River ON 17 A-B5
Opaskwayak MB 11 A7
Opaskwayak MB 13 A1
Opasquia Lake ON 13 B6
Opasquia PP ON 13 B6
Opawica, lac QC 23 A8
Opawica, lac QC 26 B2
Opawica, rivière QC 26 B3
Opawica, rivière QC 26 C4
Opeepeesway Lake ON 17 D-E5
Opémisca, lac QC 26 A1
Open Bay NL 39 B8
Open Hall NL 37 B7
Openshaw ON 11 F7
Opeongo Lake ON 21 A3
Opeongo Lake ON 22 F3
Opeongo River ON 21 A3-4
Opeongo River ON 22 F3-4
Opeongo River PP ON 21 A4
Opeongo River PP ON 22 F4
Opescal Lake NT 12 A5
Ophir ON 17 F4
Opikeigen Lake ON 16 B6-7
Opikinimika Lake ON 17 E6
Opinaca, rivière QC 40 E4
Opiscotéo, lac QC 39 C1
Opiscotéo, lac QC 40 E1
Opiscotiche, lac QC 39 C1-2
Opitsat BC 1 F5
Opitsat BC 2 D-E1
Opocopa, lac QC 39 C2
Optic Lake MB 12 F7
Optic Lake MB 15 F1-2
Opuntia Lake SK 11 C3
Opuntia Lake NMBS SK 11 C3
Opuskiamishish River MB 15 E6-7
Or, Cape d' NS 32 D6
Or, Cape d' NS 33 A4
Orange Bay NL 39 E8
Orangedale NS 34 D6
Orangeville ON 20 C5-6
Orby Head PE 35 D4
Orcadia SK 11 D7
Orchre Pit Cove NL 37 D7-8
O'Regan's NL 36 D1
Oregon Jack PP BC 1 E8
Oregon Jack PP BC 2 B6-7
Orford, mont QC 27 F4
Orford River BC 2 A3 B2
Orient, rivière de l' QC 29 D3
Orient Bay ON 16 E6
Orient Bay ON 17 B1

Orignal, cap à l' QC 29 C2
Orignal, lac de l' QC 22 B4
Orillia ON 18 F8
Orillia ON 20 A7
Orillia ON 21 D1
Orion AB 6 F7
Orion AB 7 E8
Orion AB 11 F1
Orkney SK 11 F3
Orleans ON 21 A8
Orleans ON 24 D2-3
Orléans, île d' QC 27 A6
Ormes, rivière des QC 27 C4
Ormiston SK 11 F5
Ormsby ON 21 C4
Ormstown QC 24 E5
Ormstown QC 27 F1
Oro Beach ON 18 F8
Oro Beach ON 20 A7
Oro Beach ON 21 D1
Orok MB 11 A7-8
Orok MB 13 A1-2
Oro Lea Beach ON 18 F8
Oro Lea Beach ON 20 A7
Oro Lea Beach ON 21 D1
Oromocto NB 32 C3
Oromocto Lake NB 32 D2
Orono MB 20 C8
Orono ON 21 E2-3
Oro Station ON 18 F8
Oro Station ON 20 A7
Oro Station ON 21 D1
Orr Lake MB 15 E4
Orr Lake ON 18 F7
Orr Lake ON 18 F7
Orr Lake ON 20 A6
Orr Lake ON 20 A6
Orrville ON 18 D7-8
Ortell, Mount YT 4 A-B5
Orton AB 7 E5
Orton ON 19 A6-7
Orton ON 20 C5-6
Ortonville NB 31 D3
Orwell ON 19 D5
Orwell ON 20 F4
Orwell PE 34 C3
Orwell PE 35 E5-6
Orwell Bay PE 34 C3
Orwell Bay PE 35 E-F5
Orwell Corner Historic Village Provincial Heritage Site PE 35 E5
Orwell Cove PE 35 E5
Osaca ON 21 E3
Osage SK 11 E6
Osborne MB 13 F3-4
Osborne MB 14 E4-5
Osborne Corners ON 19 B6
Osborne Corners ON 20 E5
Osborne Lake MB 12 F8
Osborne Lake MB 15 F2
Osbourne Bay ON 13 F6-7
Oscar, lac QC 25 C6
Oscar, lac QC 28 E1-2
Oscar Peak BC 3 F3
Osceola ON 21 A5-6
Osceola ON 22 F5-6
Osgoode ON 21 B8
Osgoode ON 24 E2
Osgoode, rivière QC 27 C5
Oshawa ON 20 C8
Oshawa ON 21 F2
Osik Lake MB 12 E8
Osik Lake MB 15 E3
Osilinka River BC 3 E5-6
Oskélanéo QC 25 A3
Oskélanéo QC 26 B3
Oskélanéo, lac QC 25 A3
Oskélanéo, lac QC 26 B3
Osler SK 11 C4
Osnabruck Centre ON 24 E3
Osnaburgh Lake ON 13 D8
Osnaburgh Lake ON 16 B-C5
Osoyoos BC 6 F2
Osoyoos Lake BC 6 F2
Ospika River BC 3 D6
Ospringe ON 19 A6-7
Ospringe ON 20 C5-6
Ospwagan Lake MB 15 E3
Ossokmanuan Lake NL 39 B-C3
Ossossane Beach ON 18 F7
Ossossane Beach ON 20 A6
Ostaboningue, lac QC 17 E8
Ostaboningue, lac QC 22 B2-3
Ostenfeld MB 13 E-F4
Ostenfeld MB 14 E6
Osterwick MB 13 F3
Osterwick MB 14 F4
Ostrander ON 19 C5-6
Ostrander ON 20 E4-5
Ostrea Lake NS 33 C7
Ostryhon Corners ON 19 C8
Ostryhon Corners ON 20 E7
Oswald MB 14 D4
Oswald Point BC 1 B3
Oswego Creek ON 19 C7-8
Oswego Creek ON 20 E6-7
Otasawian River ON 17 A4 B3-4
Otatakan Lake ON 16 C3-4
Otherside River NT 12 B4
Otis, lac QC 28 C6-7
Otish, monts QC 40 F5-6

Otonabee River ON 21 D3
Otonabee River ON 23 F4-5
Otoskwin-Attawapiskat PP ON 16 A6 B5
Otoskwin River ON 16 B4
Otoskwin River ON 16 B5-6
Otoskwin River ON 40 E1-2
Otosquen SK 11 B7
Otosquen SK 13 B1
Ottawa ON 21 A8
Ottawa ON 24 D2
Ottawa ON 24 D2
Ottawa, cap QC 30 A4
Ottawa, lac QC 25 D5
Ottawa, lac QC 28 F1
Ottawa Islands NU 41 E-F7
Ottawa Islands NU 41 E-F7
Ottawa River ON 17 E-F8
Ottawa River ON 21 A6
Ottawa River ON 22 C2
Ottawa River QC 22 E-F6
Ottawa River QC 24 D3-4
Ottawa River QC 23 E-F3
Ottawa River QC 23 F4-5
Ottawa River PP ON 21 A6
Ottawa River PP ON 22 F6
Otter Bay BC 2 E4
Otter Brook NS 33 A7
Otter Brook NS 34 F3
Otterburne MB 13 F4
Otterburne MB 14 E5
Otterburn Park ON 24 D7
Otterburn Park QC 27 E2
Otter Creek ON 1 E-F8
Otter Creek BC 2 C-D8
Otter Creek BC 6 E-F1
Otter Creek YT 4 C6
Otter Falls Territorial Recreation Site YT 4 D3
Otter Island ON 16 F8
Otter Island ON 17 D2
Otter Lake NL 39 B5
Otter Lake ON 18 D7
Otter Lake ON 18 D7
Otter Lake ON 21 C7
Otter Lake QC 22 F6-7
Otter Lake QC 24 C1
Otter Lake SK 12 E5
Otter Lake YT 4 C6
Otter Lake PP BC 1 F8
Otter Lake PP BC 2 D8
Otter Lake PP BC 6 E-F1
Otter-Orloff Lakes Wildland PP AB 9 E5-6
Otter Point NL 36 D3
Otter Point NL 37 D1
Otter Point NL 37 D1
Ottertail Creek ON 22 C1
Otterville ON 19 C6
Otterville ON 20 E5
Otthon MB 11 D7
Otto MB 14 C4
Otto Fiord NU 42 A-B4
Otty Lake ON 21 C7
Otukamamoan Lake ON 13 F7
Otukamamoan Lake ON 16 B3
Ouapetec, rivière QC 39 D-E2
Ouareau, lac QC 24 B5
Ouareau, lac QC 25 F5
Ouareau, rivière QC 24 B5 C6
Ouareau, rivière QC 27 C-D1
Ouasiemsca, rivière QC 26 B-C7
Ouellette ON 17 F7
Ouellette ON 18 B6
Ouest, lac de l' QC 28 A4
Ouest, pointe de l' QC 30 D2
Ouest, pointe de l' QC 31 A7-8
Ouest, pointe de l' QC 40 F7
Ouimet Canyon, RNP ON 16 F5-6
Ouimet Canyon PNR ON 16 F5-6
Ouiscatis, lac QC 23 D8
Ouiscatis, lac QC 26 E2
Oungre SK 11 F6
Ours, lac à l' QC 39 E4
Ours, lac des QC 22 D4
Ours, lac des QC 24 B2
Ours, lac des QC 25 F2
Ours, rivière à l' QC 26 E8
Ours, rivière à l' QC 28 B-C3
Ours, rivière l' QC 22 D4
Ours Blanc, lac de l' QC 25 B4
Ours Blanc, lac de l' QC 26 F4
Ouse River ON 21 D4
Oustic ON 19 A6
Oustic ON 20 C5
Outaouais, lac des QC 22 A8
Outaouais, lac des QC 23 F8
Outaouais, lac des QC 25 B4
Outaouais, rivière des QC 21 A6-7
Outaouais, rivière des QC 22 C2
Outaouais, rivière des QC 23 E-F3

Outaouais, rivière des QC 23 F4-5
Outaouais, rivière des QC 24 D1
Outardes, baie aux QC 29 A3
Outardes, rivière aux QC 40 F6
Outer Cove NL 37 D8
Outer Duck Island ON 18 C2
Outer Island NS 33 F2
Outlet ON 21 D7
Outlet ON 21 F5
Outlook SK 11 D4
Outram NS 32 E5
Outram NS 33 B3
Outram SK 11 F6
Outram Lakes NT 10 B8
Overby Lake MB 15 B3
Overflow Bay MB 11 B8
Overflow Bay MB 13 B1-2
Overflowing River MB 11 B7
Overflowing River MB 13 B1
Overflowing River SK 11 B7
Overflowing River SK 13 B1
Overton MB 14 B3
Overton NS 33 E1
Owen, rivière QC 29 E3
Owen, ZEC QC 29 E3
Owen Channel ON 18 C4
Owendale AB 7 F5
Owen Sound ON 18 E-F5
Owen Sound ON 18 F5-6
Owen Sound ON 20 A4
Owen Sound ON 20 A4
Owikeno Lake BC 1 D4
Owl River AB 9 F6-7
Owl River AB 12 E-F1
Owl River MB 15 C6
Owl River MB 40 C1
Oxbow NB 31 D3
Oxbow SK 11 F7
Oxbow Creek ON 19 C4
Oxbow Creek ON 20 E3
Oxdrift ON 13 E6
Oxdrift ON 16 D3
Oxenden ON 18 E5
Oxford NS 32 C8
Oxford NS 34 D1
Oxford Centre ON 19 C6
Oxford Centre ON 20 E5
Oxford House MB 15 D5
Oxford Junction NS 32 C8
Oxford Junction NS 34 D-E1
Oxford Lake MB 15 F4-5
Oxford Mills ON 21 C8
Oxford Mills ON 24 E2
Oxley ON 19 F1
Oxtongue Lake ON 21 B2
Oxtongue Lake ON 21 B2
Oxtongue River ON 21 A2
Oxtongue River ON 22 F2
Oyama AB 6 E2
Oyen AB 6 D8
Oyen AB 7 A8
Oyen AB 11 D2
Oyster Bed Bridge PE 34 C2
Oyster Bed Bridge PE 35 D4
Oyster Cove PE 35 D3
Oyster River BC 2 C2
Ozema MB 14 C1
Ozhiski Lake ON 16 B6

P

Paarens Beach PP BC 1 A6
Pabineau NB 29 E8
Pabineau NB 31 B6
Pabos QC 30 C-D2
Pabos Mills QC 30 D2
Pachena Bay BC 2 F2
Pachena Point BC 2 F2
Pacific Ocean BC 1 D2-3
Pacific Ocean BC 3 F1
Pacific Ranges BC 1 D5
Pacific Ranges BC 2 A-B3
Pacific Rim, RPN BC 1 F4-5
Pacific Rim (archipel Broken Group), RPN BC 2 E1-2
Pacific Rim (plage Long), RPN BC 2 E1
Pacific Rim (sentier de la Côte-Ouest), RPN BC 2 F2
Pacific Rim NPR BC 1 F4-5
Pacific Rim NPR (Broken Group Islands) BC 2 E1-2
Pacific Rim NPR (Long Beach) BC 2 E1
Pacific Rim NPR (West Coast Trail) BC 2 F2
Pacifique, océan BC 1 E2-3 F2-3
Pacifique, océan BC 3 F1
Packers, Mount YT 4 D3-4
Packington QC 29 E2
Packington QC 31 C1
Packs Harbour NL 39 B7-8
Pacquet NL 38 D5
Pacquet NL 39 F8
Paddle Prairie AB 9 C5
Paddle River AB 6 A5
Paddle River AB 8 B5
Paddling Lake SK 11 B4
Paddockwood SK 11 B5
Padoue QC 29 C4

Pagato Lake SK 12 E6
Pagato Lake SK 15 D1
Pagato River SK 12 E7
Pagato River SK 15 E1
Page, Mount YT 5 A2
Pageant AB 7 F8
Pagwachuan River ON 16 D8
Pagwachuan River ON 17 B3
Pagwa River ON 17 B3
Paguchi Lake ON 13 F7-8
Paimpont, lac QC 39 E5
Pain Court ON 19 E2
Painted Bluffs PP BC 2 A7-8
Paint Lake MB 15 E3
Paint Lake PP MB 15 E3
Paisley ON 20 B4
Paix, rivière de la AB 12 A1
Paix, rivière de la AB 41 F1
Paix, rivière de la BC 3 E8
Pakashkan Lake ON 13 F8
Pakashkan Lake ON 16 E5
Pakenham ON 21 B7
Pakenham ON 24 D1
Pakowki Lake AB 6 F7
Pakowki Lake AB 7 E-F8
Pakowki Lake AB 11 F1
Pakuashipi QC 38 B1
Pakuashini QC 39 E6-7
Pakulak Lake MB 15 A4-5
Pakwa Lake MB 15 F3
Pakwash Lake ON 13 D-E6
Pakwash Lake ON 16 C2
Pakwash PP ON 13 D6
Pakwash PP ON 16 C2
Palermo ON 19 B7
Palermo ON 20 D6
Palgrave ON 20 C6
Palluau, lac QC 26 D5
Palluau, lac QC 28 B1
Palmarolle QC 17 C8
Palmarolle QC 23 C2
Palmer SK 11 E4
Palmer, rivière QC 27 A5-6
Palmer Rapids ON 21 B4-5
Palmer Road PE 35 B2
Palmerston ON 19 A5
Palmerston ON 20 C4
Palmerston, Cape NS 32 C8
Palmerston, Cape NS 33 C2
Palmerston/Canonto CA ON 21 B6
Palmerston Lake ON 21 B-C6
Palmyra ON 19 D3-4
Palo SK 11 C3
Palowki AB 7 E8
Palsen River MB 13 B5
Pambrun SK 11 E4
Pambrun, lac QC 26 C4
Pamialic Bay NL 39 A6
Pamiokit MB 15 F1
Pan Lake Fen, RNP ON 16 B8
Pan Lake Fen, RNP ON 17 C2
Pan Lake Fen PNR ON 16 B8
Pan Lake Fen PNR ON 17 C2
Panache, lac du QC 25 A4
Panache, lac du QC 26 F8
Panache, Lake ON 18 A-B5
Panache, rivière au QC 23 B-C8
Panache, rivière au QC 26 C2
Panache Lake ON 17 F6
Pancake Bay PP ON 17 E3
Panchia Lake NL 39 C3
Pandora Island NU 41 A4
Pandora Island NU 42 A4
Pangman SK 11 F5
Pangniqtuuq (Pangnirtung) NU 41 A6 B5
Pangnirtung (Pangniqtuuq) NU 42 A8
Panmure ON 21 B7
Panmure Island PE 34 C4
Panmure Island PE 34 C3-4
Panmure Island PE 35 E7
Panmure Island PE 35 E7
Panmure Island PP PE 34 C4
Panmure Island PP PE 35 F7
Panny River AB 9 C-D5
Panny River AB 12 A1
Panorama BC 6 E4
Panorama BC 7 C1
Pansy MB 14 F6
Pantagruel Creek PP ON 16 D5
Panther Mountain AB 6 D4
Panther Mountain AB 7 A2
Papanakies Lake NT 10 B-C8
Papinachois QC 29 A3
Papinachois, rivière QC 29 A2-3
Papineau, lac QC 24 C3
Papineau Creek ON 21 B4
Papineau-Labelle, RF de QC 24 B-C3
Papineau Lake ON 21 B4
Papineau Lake QC 22 D2-3
Papineauville QC 24 D3
Paquette Corners ON 19 E3
Paquetville NB 29 E8
Paquetville NB 30 E1
Paquetville NB 31 B7
Paradis QC 23 E7
Paradis QC 25 A1
Paradis QC 26 F1
Paradise NL 37 B7

Paradise NL 37 D8
Paradise NS 32 E5-6
Paradise NS 33 C3
Paradise Hill SK 6 A-B8
Paradise Hill SK 11 B2
Paradise Lake NS 32 F5-6
Paradise Lake NS 33 C4
Paradise Point ON 18 E7
Paradise River NL 36 D7-8
Paradise River NL 37 D5-6
Paradise River NL 39 C7
Paradise River NL 39 B7
Paradise Sound NL 36 D7-8 E7
Paradise Sound NL 37 D5-6 E5-6
Paradise Valley AB 6 B7-8
Paradise Valley AB 11 B2
Paradise Valley BC 2 C3
Paragon Lake MB 15 B4
Paramé, lac QC 38 A2
Paramé, lac QC 39 D7
Parent QC 25 B4
Parent QC 26 F4
Parent, lac QC 23 C6
Parham ON 21 C6
Paris ON 19 B-C6
Paris ON 20 E5
Parisville QC 27 B4
Park Court AB 8 C5
Park Head ON 18 F5
Park Head ON 20 A4
Park Lake PP AB 6 E6
Park Lake PP AB 7 E5
Parkbeg SK 11 E4
Parkdale NS 32 F6
Parkdale NS 33 C4
Parkhill ON 19 C4
Parkhill ON 20 C5
Parkhill Creek ON 19 B3-4
Parkhill Creek ON 20 E2-3
Parkindale NB 32 C6
Parkinson ON 17 F5
Parkinson ON 18 A1
Parkland AB 6 E6
Parkland AB 7 D4
Parkman SK 11 E6
Parks Creek ON 21 D5
Parkside NB 31 E5
Parksville BC 2 D3
Parlee Beach PP NB 32 B7
Parlee Beach PP NB 35 E1
Parrsboro NS 32 D7
Parrsboro NS 33 A4-5
Parry SK 11 F5
Parry, Cape NT 5 A8
Parry, îles de NT 42 C2-3
Parry, îles de NU 42 F5-6
Parry Bay NU 41 B-C6
Parry Bay NU 42 F5-6
Parry Island (Wasauksing) ON 18 D6-7
Parry Islands NT 42 C2-3
Parry Islands NU 42 C2-3
Parry Passage BC 1 A1
Parry Peninsula NT 5 A8
Parry Sound ON 18 D7
Parry Sound ON 18 D7
Parsnip River BC 3 F7
Parson BC 6 D3-4
Parsons Lake NT 5 B4-5
Parson's Pond NL 38 D2
Parson's Pond NL 39 B6
Parsons Pond NL 38 D2-3
Parsons Pond NL 39 B7
Partridge Bay NL 39 C8
Partridge Breast Lake MB 15 C-D3
Partridge Creek ON 21 C5
Partridge Point NL 39 E8
Pasadena NL 36 A3
Pasadena NL 37 A1
Pascagama, lac QC 23 D8
Pascagama, lac QC 26 E2
Pascagama, rivière QC 29 A2-3
Pascalis, lac QC 23 D-E5
Pas d'Eau Lake NL 39 C3
Pasfield Lake SK 12 B5
Pashkokogan Lake ON 13 D8
Pashkokogan Lake ON 16 C5
Paskwachai River ON 15 E-F7
Paskwachi Bay MB 12 C7
Paskwachi Bay MB 15 C1
Paspébiac QC 30 D2
Paspébiac QC 31 A7
Paspébiac, pointe de QC 31 A7
Pasqua SK 11 E5
Pasqua SK 11 E6
Pasquatchai River ON 15 E-F7
Pasquia Hills SK 11 B6

Pasquia River SK 11 A-B7
Pasquia River SK 13 A-B1
Passage Point NT 42 D2
Passamaquoddy Bay NB 32 E2
Pass Island NL 36 E3
Pass Island NL 37 E3
Pass Island NL 16 F6
Pass Peak YT 4 D5
Patapédia, rivière QC 29 D4
Patapédia, rivière QC 31 A3
Patch Lake MB 15 E6
Paterson MB 11 A8
Paterson MB 12 F8
Paterson MB 13 A2
Paterson MB 15 F2
Path End NL 37 F7
Pathlow SK 11 B-C5
Patricia AB 6 D7
Patricia AB 7 C7
Patricia AB 11 D1
Patricia Beach PP MB 13 E4
Patricia Beach PP MB 14 C5-6
Patrick's Cove NL 36 F8
Patrick's Cove NL 37 F6
Patten River ON 23 A2 B1
Patterson MB 32 D3
Patterson, lac QC 26 D5
Patterson, lac QC 28 B1
Patterson, Mount YT 4 A4
Patterson Lake SK 9 C8
Patterson Lake SK 12 A6
Patterson Lake SK 12 C3
Patterson Lake SK 15 A1
Patton ON 18 A1
Pattullo, Mount BC 3 E3
Patuanak SK 12 E3-4
Paudash ON 21 C4
Paudash Lake ON 21 C3-4
Paugh Lake ON 21 A4
Paugh Lake ON 22 F4
Pauingassi MB 13 C5
Pauingassi MB 16 A1
Paulatuk NT 5 B8
Paulatuk NT 41 A1
Pauline Cove YT 5 A3
Paul Island NL 40 C-D7
Paul Lake PP BC 6 D1
Paull Lake SK 12 E5
Paull River SK 12 E5
Paulson BC 6 F2-3
Pauquachin BC 1 D7-8
Pavilion BC 2 A6
Pawistik MB 15 E1-2
Pawistik MB 16 A1
Paynton SK 11 B2
Payne, lac QC 40 C5
Payne, lac QC 41 E8
Payne River ON 24 E3
Paynton SK 6 B8
Paynton SK 11 B2
Pays Plat ON 16 F7
Pays Plat ON 17 C1
Payuk MB 12 F7
Payuk MB 15 F1
Peace Arch Provincial/State Park BC 1 F6
Peace Point AB 9 A-B6
Peace Point AB 12 A1
Peace Reach BC 3 E7
Peace River AB 9 B5
Peace River AB 9 B3
Peace River BC 3 E7-8
Peace River BC 9 A3
Peace River AB 41 F1
Peace River Corridor PP BC 3 E7-8
Peace River Corridor PP BC 9 D-E1
Peace River Valley AB 9 E2
Peace River Wildland PP AB 9 E3
Peachland BC 6 E1-2
Peacock AB 6 B4
Peacock Hills NU 41 C2
Peacock Point ON 19 D7
Peacock Point ON 20 F6
Peacock Point ON 20 F6
Peakes PE 34 C3
Peakes PE 35 E6
Pearce AB 7 E5
Pearce Point NT 5 A8
Pearl Island NL 36 A4
Pearl Island NL 38 F2
Pearse Island BC 3 F2-3
Pearson Lake MB 15 D-E4
Pearsonville NS 32 C4
Peary Channel NU 42 B3
Peavey AB 8 B6
Peavine AB 8 B4-5
Peawanuck ON 40 D2
Pebble Bay SK 11 B4
Pebble Beach BC 2 C3
Pebble Beach MB 14 B3
Pebonishewi Lake ON

Pecten AB 7 F4
Pedley AB 8 C2
Peeagwon Lake ON 16 A4
Peebles SK 11 E6-7
Peel NB 31 F3
Peel NB 32 B1
Peel Channel NT 5 A4
Peel Point NT 41 A3
Peel Point NT 42 D2
Peel River YT 5 B4
Peel River Territorial Preserve NT 5 D-E5
Peel Sound NU 41 A4
Peel Sound NU 42 D-E4
Peerless SK 11 B4

Peerless *SK* **9** F8
Peerless *SK* **11** A3
Peerless *SK* **12** F3
Peerless Lake *AB* **9** D5
Peerless Lake *AB* **9** D5
Peers *AB* **6** B4
Peers *AB* **8** C3
Peesane *SK* **11** B6
Pefferlaw *ON* **20** B7
Pefferlaw *ON* **21** D1-2
Pefferlaw Brook *ON* **20** B7
Pefferlaw Brook *ON* **21** E1
Peggys Cove *NS* **32** F8
Peggys Cove *NS* **33** C-D5
Peguis *MB* **13** D3-4
   15 D-E6
Peguis *MB* **14** B4
Peguis *MB* **14** D5
Pekisko *AB* **7** C4
Pelé, cap *NB* **35** E1
Pelé Cape *NB* **35** E1
Pelee, Point *ON* **19** F2
Pelee Island *ON* **19** F2
Pelee Island *ON* **19** F1-2
Pelee Passage *ON* **19** F2
Pèlerins, les *QC* **28** E8
Pèlerins, les *QC* **29** E1
Pelham *ON* **19** C8
Pelham *ON* **20** E7
Pelican *AB* **9** E6
Pelican *AB* **12** E1
Pelican Bay *MB* **11** B8
Pelican Bay *MB* **13** B2
Pelican Cove *SK* **11** B8
Pelican Islands PP Reserve *MB* **13** C3-4
Pelican Lake *AB* **9** G-4
Pelican Lake *MB* **11** C8
Pelican Lake *MB* **13** A4
Pelican Lake *MB* **13** C2
Pelican Lake *MB* **13** F2
Pelican Lake *MB* **14** F2
Pelican Lake *SK* **11** A3
Pelican Lake *SK* **12** F6
Pelican Narrows *SK* **12** F6
Pelican Rapids *MB* **11** B8
Pelican Rapids *MB* **13** B2
Pelican River *AB* **9** E6
Pelican River *AB* **12** E1
Pellatt Lake *NT* **10** A8
Pelletier Lake *MB* **15** D4
Pelly *SK* **11** C7
Pelly *SK* **13** C1
Pelly Bay *NU* **42** F4
Pelly Bay (Arviligjuat) *NU*
   41 C5
   42 F4-5
Pelly Creek *BC* **3** D5
Pelly Crossing *YT* **4** C3
Pelly Island *NT* **5** A4
Pelly Mountains *YT*
   4 C4 D4-6
Pelly Point *NU* **41** B4
Pelly Point *NU* **42** F4-5
Pelly River *YT* **4** C3
Pelly River *YT* **4** C5 D5-6
Pemberton *BC* **1** E7
Pemberton *BC* **2** D3
Pemberton Icefield *BC* **1** E7
Pemberton Icefield *BC* **2** B4
Pemberton Meadows *BC* **2** B5
Pembina *AB* **8** D4
Pembina River *MB* **13** F3
Pembina River *MB* **14** F3
Pembina River PP *AB*
   16 C2-3 D2-3
   6 A-B5
Pembina River PP *AB* **8** C4-5
Pembina Valley PP *MB* **13** F3
Pembina Valley PP *MB* **14** F3-4
Pembridge *AB* **8** B5
Pembroke *NS* **33** A7
Pembroke *NS* **33** B5
Pembroke *NS* **34** F3
Pembroke *NS* **34** F1
Pembroke *ON* **22** F5
Pembroke, Cape *NU* **40** A-B3
Pembroke, Cape *NU* **41** D7
Pembroke Shore *NS* **33** A7
Pemichangan, lac *QC* **22** E8
Pemichangan, lac *QC* **24** C2
Pemichigamau Lake *MB* **12** D8
Pemichigamau Lake *MB* **15** D3
Pemmican Island PP Reserve *MB* **11** B8
Pemmican Island PP Reserve *MB* **13** B2
Pemmican Portage *SK* **11** A7
Pemmican Portage *SK* **13** A1
Pen Lake *ON* **21** A3
Pen Lake *ON* **22** F3
Pender Harbour *BC* **1** F6
Pender Harbour *BC* **2** D3
Pendleton *ON* **24** D3
Pendryl *AB* **8** D5
Penetanguishene *ON* **18** E7
Penetanguishene *ON* **21** D-E3
Penguin Islands *NL* **36** E4
Penguin Islands *NL* **37** E4
Penhold *AB* **6** C5
Penhold *AB* **8** F6
Peninsula Lake *ON* **21** B2
Peninsular Lake *ON* **16** B6
Péninsule-Bruce, PN de la *ON* **18** D4-5
Penn *SK* **11** A4

Pennant *NS* **32** F8
Pennant *NS* **33** C6
Pennant *SK* **11** E3
Pennant Bay *NS* **33** D6
Pennant Point *NS* **33** D6
Pennask Lake *BC* **6** E1
Pennask Lake PP *BC* **6** E1
Pennfield *NB* **32** E2-3
Pennfield Ridge *NB* **31** F5
Penniac *NB* **31** F5
Penniac *NB* **32** B3
Penny *BC* **1** A8
Penny *BC* **6** A1
Pennycutaway River *MB* **15** D-E6
Penny Strait *NU* **42** C1
Peno *AB* **8** B7
Penobsquis *NB* **32** C5
Penouille *QC* **30** B3
Penrhyn, Cape *NU* **41** C6
Penrhyn, Cape *NU* **42** F6
Penrose Island PMP *BC* **1** D4
Pense *SK* **11** E5
Pentecôte, lac *QC* **39** F1
Pentecôte, rivière *QC* **39** E-F1
Penticton *BC* **6** F2
Penzance *SK* **11** D5
Peonan Point *MB* **13** D3
Peonan Point *MB* **14** A2-3
Peoria *AB* **9** E3
Pepaw River *SK* **11** C7
Pepeekisis *SK* **11** D6
Perbeck *AB* **8** F7
Percé *QC* **30** C3
Percé, Cape *NB* **34** C8
Percé, rocher *QC* **30** C3
Perche, lac la *QC* **22** A5
Perch River *SK* **12** B5-6
Percival *SK* **11** E7
Percival River *PE* **35** E1
Percy Lake *ON* **16** C7-8
Percy Lake *ON* **17** A2
Percy Lake *ON* **21** B3
Percy Reach *ON* **21** E4
Perdrix Blanche, lac de la *QC* **26** B8
Perdue *SK* **11** C4
Péré, lac *QC* **39** A1
Pereau *NS* **32** E7
Pereau *NS* **33** B4
Peribonca, rivière *QC* **40** F5
Péribonka *QC* **28** B4
Péribonka, rivière *QC* **28** A5
Périgny, lac *QC* **23** C7
Périgny, lac *QC* **26** C1-2
Perigord *QC* **11** C6
Perivale *ON* **18** C3
Perkins *QC* **21** A8
Perkins *QC* **22** F8
Perkins *QC* **24** D2
Perkinsfield *ON* **18** F7
Perkinsfield *ON* **20** A6
Perlson Lake *NT* **10** C7
Péronne *QC* **23** E7-8
Péronne, lac *QC* **25** B2
Péronne, lac *QC* **26** F2
Perotte *NS* **32** F5
Perotte *NS* **33** C3
Perras, lac *QC* **22** D-E8
Perras, lac *QC* **24** B3
Perras, lac *QC* **25** F3
Perrault Falls *ON* **13** E6
Perrault Falls *ON* **16** C2-3 D2-3
Perrault Lake *ON* **16** D3
Perrier, lac *QC* **26** D4
Perrot, île *QC* **24** D5
Perrot, île *QC* **27** E1
Perry *ON* **17** D3-4
Perry Island *NT* **5** F7
Perry's Cove *NL* **37** D7-8
Perryvale *AB* **6** A6
Perryvale *AB* **9** A6-7
Perseus, Mount *BC* **1** C8
Perseus, Mount *BC* **6** C1
Perth *ON* **21** C7
Perth *ON* **24** F1
Perth-Andover *NB* **31** E3
Perth-Andover *NB* **32** A1
Perth Road *ON* **21** D6-7
Peskawa Lake *NS* **33** D2-3
Peskawesk Lake *NS* **33** D3
Petabec Lakes *SK* **11** A7
Petabec Lakes *SK* **13** A1
Petaigan *SK* **11** B6
Petawaga, lac *QC* **22** B7-8
Petawaga, lac *QC* **25** D2
Petawaga, ZEC *QC* **22** B7-8
Petawaga, ZEC *QC* **25** D2
Petawawa *QC* **22** F5
Petawawa *QC* **28** C3
Petawawa River *ON* **21** A2
Petawawa River *ON*
   22 E4-5
Petawawa Terrace PP *ON* **22** E5
Peter, lac *QC* **25** A5
Peter, lac *QC* **26** F5
Peterbell *ON* **17** C4-5
Peterborough *ON* **21** D-E3
Peterborough, réserve de chasse de la Couronne *ON* **21** C-D4
Peter Lake *SK* **12** C6
Peter Lougheed PP *AB* **6** E4-5
Peter Lougheed PP *AB* **7** C2

Peter Pond Lake *SK* **9** D-E8
Peter Pond Lake *SK* **12** E3
Petersburg *ON* **19** B6
Petersburg *ON* **20** D5
Peters Corners *ON* **19** B6-7
Peters Corners *ON* **20** D5-6
Petersfield *MB* **13** E4
Petersfield *MB* **14** D5
Petersville *NB* **32** D3
Petersville *NB* **33** A1
Peterview *NL* **36** A4
Peterview *NL* **37** A4
Peterview *NL* **38** F5
Peterville *PE* **35** A-B2
Pethei Peninsula *NT* **10** C8
Pethericks Corners *ON* **21** D4
Petherton *ON* **19** A6
Petherton *ON* **20** C5
Petit-Cap *NB* **32** B7
Petit-Cap *NB* **34** C1
Petit-Cap *QC* **35** E2
Petit-Cap *QC* **30** B3
Petitcodiac *NB* **32** C5
Petitcodiac River *NB* **31** F7-8
Petitcodiac River *NB* **32** B-C6
Petit-de-Grat Bridge *NS* **34** E6-7
Petit-de-Grat Island *NS* **34** E6-7
Petit-Matane *QC* **29** B4-5
Petit Mécatina, île *QC* **40** E-F8
Petit Mécatina, île du *QC* **39** E6
Petit Mécatina, rivière du *NL* **37** E7-8
Petit Mécatina, rivière du *QC* **39** D-E6
Petit Mécatina, rivière du *QC* **40** E7-8
Petitot River *AB* **9** A3
Petitot River *AB* **10** F5
Petitot River *BC* **3** A7
Petitot River *BC* **9** A1
Petitot River *BC* **10** F3
Petit Pabos *QC* **30** C2-3
Petit Pabos, rivière du *QC* **30** C2
Petit-Rivière-de-l'Île *NB* **30** E2
Petit-Rivière-de-l'Île *NB* **31** A8
Petit-Rocher *NB* **29** E7-8
Petit-Rocher *NB* **31** B6
Petit-Rocher-Nord *NB* **29** E7-8
Petit-Rocher-Nord *NB* **31** B6
Petit-Rocher-Sud *NB* **29** E7-8
Petit-Rocher-Sud *NB* **31** B6
Petit-Saguenay *QC* **28** C7-8
Petit-Shippagan *NB* **30** E2-3
Petit-Shippagan *NB* **31** A8
Petitsikapau Lake *NL* **39** A2
Petitsikapau Lake *NL* **40** D6
Petit-Témis, parc linéaire interprovincial *QC*
   29 D1 E1-2
Petit-Témis, parc linéaire interprovincial *QC*
   31 B-C1
Petit-Témis Interprovincial Linear Park *QC* **29** E2-3
Petit-Témis Interprovincial Linear Park *QC* **31** B-C1
Petley *NL* **37** C6-7
Petoweniki Lake *ON* **13** B7
Petpeswick Inlet *NS* **33** C7
Petre, Point *ON* **21** F5
Petrofka Bridge *SK* **11** B-C4
Petroglyphs PP *ON* **2** E3-4
Petroglyphs PP *ON* **21** D3-4
Petrolia *ON* **19** C3
Petrolia *ON* **20** E2
Pettapiece *MB* **14** D1
Petticoat Creek CA *ON* **20** C8
Petticoat Creek CA *ON* **21** F2
Petty Harbour *NL* **37** E8
Petty Harbour-Maddox Cove *NL* **37** E8
Pevensey *ON* **18** C8
Pevensey *ON* **21** A1
Pfister, lac *QC* **26** D4
Phare-de-l'Île-Bois Blanc, LHN du *ON* **19** E1
Phare-de-la-Pointe-Clark, LHN du *ON* **20** B2-3
Phare-de-Pointe-au-Père, LHN du *QC* **29** C2-3
Pheasant Rump *SK* **11** F7
Phelans *ON* **18** A4-5
Phelpston *ON* **18** F7
Phelpston *ON* **20** A6
Philip, River *NS* **34** D-E1
Philip, River *NS* **32** C8
Philip Edward Island *ON* **18** B5
Philipsburg *QC* **24** E7
Philipsburg *QC* **24** E7
Philipsburg, RNOM de *QC* **24** E7
Philipsburg National Wilderness Area *QC* **27** F2-3
Philipsburg National Wilderness Area *QC* **24** E7
Philipsburg, RNOM de *QC* **27** F2-3
Philips Harbour *NS* **34** E6
Philipsville *ON* **21** C7
Philipsville *ON* **24** F1
Phillips Arm *BC* **1** E5
Phillips Arm *BC* **2** B2
Phillips Bay *YT* **5** B3
Phillips Grove *SK* **11** A4
Phillips Head *NL* **36** A4
Phillips Head *NL* **37** A4
Phillips Head *NL* **38** F5-6
Phillips Inlet *NU* **42** A4
Phillips River *BC* **2** A-B2
Phinney Cove *NS* **32** E6
Phinney Cove *NS* **33** C2-3
Phippen *SK* **11** C3
Pian, lac *SK* **23** E2
Piapot *SK* **11** E2-3
Piapot *SK* **11** E5-6
Pibroch *AB* **6** A6
Pibroch *AB* **8** B6
Pic Chapman *QC* **27** E5
Pic Island *ON* **16** F8
Pic Island *ON* **17** C2
Pic Mobert South *ON* **16** F8

Pic Mobert South *ON* **17** C3
Pic River *ON* **16** E8
Pic River *ON* **16** F8
Pic River *ON* **17** C2
Pic River *ON* **17** C2
Picanoc, rivière *QC* **22** E6-7
Picanoc, rivière *QC* **24** C1
Picard, lac *QC* **25** D6
Picard, lac *QC* **28** F2
Piccadilly *NL* **36** B1
Pichogen River, RNP *ON* **17** C4
Pichogen River PNR *ON* **17** C4
Pickardville *AB* **6** A5
Pickardville *AB* **8** B6
Pickerel *ON* **18** B6
Pickerel Lake *MB* **13** C2
Pickerel Lake *ON* **16** F4
Pickerel Lake *ON* **18** C8
Pickerel Lake *ON* **18** C8
Pickerel Lake *ON* **21** A1
Pickerel Lake *ON* **21** A1
Pickerel Lake *ON* **22** E1
Pickerel Lake *ON* **22** F1
Pickerel Lake *ON* **22** F1
Pickerel River *ON* **18** B6
Pickerel River *ON* **18** B6-7
Pickerel River *ON* **18** C7-8
Pickerel River *ON* **18** B6
Pickering *ON* **20** C8
Pickering *ON* **21** F2
Pickering Village *ON* **20** C8
Pickering Village *ON* **21** F2
Pickhandle Lake Territorial Recreation Site *YT*
   4 C1-2
Pickle Lake *ON* **13** C8
Pickle Lake *ON* **13** D8
Pickle Lake *ON* **16** B5
Pickle Lake *ON* **40** E1
Picton *ON* **21** E5
Pictou *NS* **34** D3
Pictou Harbour *NS* **34** D3
Pictou Island *NS* **34** D3-4
Pictou Landing *NS* **34** D3
Picture Butte *AB* **6** E6
Picture Butte *AB* **7** E5-6
Pie Island *ON* **16** F6
Pied-du-Lac *QC* **29** E2
Pied-du-Lac *QC* **31** C1
Piedmont *QC* **24** C5
Pierce Lake *ON* **13** A6
Pierce Lake *SK* **9** F8
Pierce Lake *SK* **11** A2
Pierce Lake *SK* **12** F2
Pierceland *SK* **9** F8
Pierceland *SK* **11** A2-3
Pierceland *SK* **12** F2-3
Pierre, lac *QC* **25** C4
Pierrefonds *QC* **24** D5
Pierrefonds *QC* **27** E1
Pierrefonds, lac *QC* **23** B8
Pierrefonds, lac *QC* **26** C2-3
Pierreville *QC* **24** C7
Pierreville *QC* **27** D3
Pierriche, rivière *QC* **28** B7
Pierriche, rivière *QC* **28** D2
Pierson *MB* **11** F8
Pierson *MB* **13** F1
Pigeon Bay *ON* **19** F2
Pigeon Cove *NL* **38** B4
Pigeon Hill *NB* **30** E2-3
Pigeon Hill *NB* **31** A-B8
Pigeon Hill *QC* **24** E7
Pigeon Hill *QC* **27** F2-3
Pigeon Lake *AB* **6** B5
Pigeon Lake *AB* **8** D6
Pigeon Lake *MB* **14** D4
Pigeon Lake *ON* **21** D3
Pigeon Lake PP *AB* **6** B5
Pigeon Lake PP *AB* **8** D5-6
Pigeon River *MB* **13** C4-5
Pigeon River *ON* **16** F5
Pigeon River *ON* **20** B8
Pigeon River *QC* **21** E2
Pikangikum *ON* **13** C6
Pikangikum *ON* **16** B2
Pikangikum Lake *ON* **13** C5-6
Pikangikum Lake *ON* **16** B2
Pikauba, lac *QC* **28** E6
Pikauba, rivière *QC* **28** D5
Pike, Mount *YT* **4** C6
Pike Bay *ON* **18** E5
Pike Lake *ON* **18** B3-4
Pike Lake *SK* **11** C4
Pike Lake PP *SK* **11** C4
Pike River *QC* **24** E7
Pike River *QC* **27** F2
Pikes Arm *NL* **38** E6-7
Pikianikijuan, lac *QC* **22** A7
Pikianikijuan, lac *QC* **23** F7
Pikianikijuan, lac *QC* **25** D2
Pikitigushi River *ON* **16** C6
Pikogan *QC* **23** D4
Pikwitonei *MB* **15** C4
Pikwitonei Lake *MB* **15** C4
Pilger *SK* **11** C5
Pilley's Island *NL* **38** E-F5
Pilot Bay PP *BC* **6** F3-4
Pilot Butte *SK* **11** E5-6
Pilot Mound *MB* **13** F2-3
Pilot Mound *MB* **14** F3
Pilot Mount *YT* **4** D3
Pimodan, lac *QC* **24** B3
Pimodan, lac *QC* **25** F3
Pin, rivière du *QC* **28** B7
Pin, rivière du *QC* **39** D7-8
Pinafore Park NMBS *ON* **19** D4-5
Pinafore Park NMBS *ON* **20** F3-4

Pinafore Park, RNOM *ON*
   20 F3-4
Pinafore Park, RNOM *ON*
   19 D4-5
Pinantan Lake *BC* **6** D1-2
Pinawa *MB* **13** E4-5
Pinawa *MB* **14** D7
Pinawa Dam Provincial Heritage Park *MB* **13** E5
Pinawa Dam Provincial Heritage Park *MB* **14** D7
Pin Blanc, lac du *QC* **22** C4
Pincher *AB* **6** F5-6
Pincher *AB* **7** E4
Pincher Creek *AB* **6** F5-6
Pincher Creek *AB* **7** E4
Pinchi Lake *BC* **1** A6
Pinchi Lake *BC* **3** F6
Pincourt *QC* **24** D5
Pine, Cape *NL* **37** F7
Pine Bluff *SK* **11** A6
Pine Creek *AB* **9** F6
Pine Creek *AB* **12** F1
Pine Creek *MB* **11** C8
Pine Creek *MB* **13** C2
Pine Creek *NT* **10** C4
Pine Creek *YT* **5** D2-3
Pine Creek Station *MB* **14** D2-3
Pine Dock *MB* **13** D4
Pine Dock *MB* **14** A5
Pine Falls *MB* **13** E4
Pine Falls *MB* **14** C6
Pine Grove *ON* **19** B6
Pine Grove *ON* **20** F5
Pine Hill *SK* **24** C4
Pinehouse Lake *SK* **12** E4
Pinehouse Lake *SK* **12** E4
Pinehurst *NS* **33** C-D4
Pinehurst Lake *AB* **9** E7
Pinehurst Lake *AB* **12** F1
Pinehurst Lake CA *AB* **9** E7
Pinehurst Lake CA *AB*
   20 D-E5
Pineimuta Lake *ON* **16** A5-6
Pineimuta River *ON* **16** A5-6
Pineimuta River *ON* **16** A5-6
Pine Island *SK* **11** A7
Pine Island *SK* **13** A1
Pine Lake *AB* **6** C5-6
Pine Lake *AB* **8** F6-7
Pine LeMoray PP *BC* **3** F7
Pine Pass *BC* **3** F7
Pine Point *NT* **10** E6-7
Pine Point *NT* **10** E6
Pine Point *NT* **41** E1
Pine Portage *ON* **16** E6
Pine Ridge *MB* **13** D5
Pine Ridge *NB* **31** E7-8
Pine Ridge *NB* **32** A6
Pine River *BC* **3** E-8
Pine River *BC* **9** E1
Pine River *MB* **11** C8
Pine River *MB* **13** C1-2
Pine River *MB* **14** A1
Pine River *ON* **18** F6
Pine River *ON* **20** B6
Pine River *ON* **20** B3
Pine River Breaks PP *BC* **3** E8
Pine River Breaks PP *BC* **9** E1
Pine Tree Point *ON* **18** E4
Pinette *PE* **34** C3
Pinette *PE* **35** F5
Pinette Harbour *PE* **35** F5
Pinette PP *PE* **34** C-D3
Pinette PP *PE* **35** F5
Pineville *NB* **31** B6
Pinewood *AB* **8** B6
Pinewood *ON* **16** E1-2
Piney *MB* **13** F4
Piney *MB* **14** F7
Pingualuit, parc *QC* **40** B5
Pingualuit, parc *QC* **41** E6
Pinkerton *ON* **20** B3-4
Pinkham *SK* **11** D2
Pinkham *SK* **11** D2
Pink Mountain *BC* **3** C7
Pink Mountain *BC* **9** C-D1
Pink Mountain PP *BC* **3** C7
Pink River *SK* **12** D5-6
Pinnacles PP *BC* **1** B7
Pins Rouge, lac du *QC* **25** C4
Pins, rivière aux *QC* **29** D2
Pinsent's Arm *NL* **39** C8
Pintendre *QC* **27** B6
Pinware *NL* **38** A3-4
Pinware *NL* **39** C-D8
Pinware River *NL* **38** A3-4
Pinware River PP *NL* **38** A4
Pinware River PP *NL*
   39 D7-8

Pipestone PP *MB* **11** F7-8
Pipestone PP *MB* **13** F1
Pipestone River *ON* **13** D7-8
Pipestone River *ON* **16** A4
Pipestone River *ON* **16** A5
Pipestone River *ON* **16** A5
Pipestone River *ON* **40** E1
Pipestone River *SK*
   12 B5 C4
Pipestone River PP *ON* **13** C8
Pipestone River PP *ON*
   13 B-C8
Pipestone River PP *ON*
   16 A4 B4-5
Pipestone River *SK* **40** F5-6
Piprell Lake *SK* **11** B5
Pipun *MB* **15** F3
Pirates Cove PMP *BC* **1** F6-7
Pirates Cove PMP *BC* **2** E4
Piscatosine, lac *QC* **22** C8
Piscatosine, lac *QC* **25** E2-3
Pisew Falls PP *MB* **15** F3
Pisquid *PE* **35** E6
Pisquid River *PE* **35** E6
Piste-Chilkoot, LHN de la *BC*
   3 A1
Piste-Chilkoot, LHN de la *BC*
   4 F3-4
Pistolet Bay *NL* **38** A5
Pistolet Bay PP *NL* **38** A4-5
Pistolet Bay PP *NL* **39** D8
Pitaga *NL* **39** C2
Pitchimi Lake *AB* **9** B5
Pitman *BC* **3** C4
Pitman River *BC* **3** C4
Pit Siding *MB* **15** E4
Pitsutinu-Tugavik TP *NU* **42** F8
Pitt Island *BC* **1** A-B3
Pitt Lake *BC* **2** D2
Pitt Meadows *BC* **1** F7
Pitt Meadows *BC* **2** D-E5
Pittock CA *ON* **19** C5
Pittock CA *ON* **20** E4
Pitt River *BC* **1** F7
Pitt River *BC* **2** C-D5
Pitts Lake *NL* **36** E7
Pitts Ferry *NL* **21** D7
Pitts Lake *NL* **36** E7
Pittston *ON* **24** F2
Pitukopi Lake *ON* **17** A4
Piusville *PE* **35** B1
Pivabiska, Lake *ON* **17** B4
Pivabiska River *ON*
   17 A5 B4
Placentia *NL* **36** E8
Placentia *NL* **37** E6
Placentia Bay *NL* **36** E7-8
Placentia Bay *NL* **37** E5-6
Plages, lac des *QC* **24** C3
Plainfield *ON* **21** D5
Plaisance *QC* **24** D3
Plaisance, baie de *NL*
   36 E7-8 F7-8
Plaisance, baie de *NL*
   37 E5-6 F5-6
Plaisance, baie de *QC* **30** F7
Plaisance, rivière *QC*
   29 D1-2
Plamondon *AB* **9** F6
Plamondon *AB* **12** F1
Plantagenet *ON* **24** D3-4
Plantin, lac *QC* **22** C3
Plassez, lac *QC* **22** B-C4
Plaster Rock *NB* **31** D3-4
Plaster Rock-Renous PGA *NB* **31** D4
Plaster Rock-Renous, ZPF *NB* **31** D4
Plate Cove East *NL* **37** B7
Plate Cove West *NL* **37** B7
Plato *SK* **11** D3
Plattsville *ON* **19** B6
Plattsville *ON* **20** D5
Playgreen Lake *MB* **13** A4
Playgreen Lake *MB* **15** F4
Pleasant Bay *NS* **34** A6
Pleasant Camp *BC* **4** F3
Pleasant Corners *ON* **24** D4
Pleasant Creek *YT* **4** B5
Pleasantdale *SK* **11** C5
Pleasant Grove *PE* **35** C5
Pleasant Grove *PE* **35** D5
Pleasant Harbour *NS* **33** C7
Pleasant Hills *AB* **8** E6
Pleasant Home *MB* **14** C5
Pleasant Lake *NS* **33** E1-2
Pleasant Point *MB* **13** B2
Pleasant Point *ON* **20** A8
Pleasant Point *ON* **21** D2
Pleasant Ridge *NB* **31** E7
Pleasant Ridge *NB* **32** A5
Pleasant Ridge *NB* **32** D2
Pleasant River *NS* **33** D3-4
Pleasant Valley *NS* **33** B7
Pleasant Valley *NS* **33** D4
Pleasant Valley *PE* **35** D4
Pleasantview *NL* **36** A4
Pleasantview *NL* **37** A4
Pleasantville *NS* **33** D4
Pleasantville *ON* **20** B7
Pleasantville *ON* **21** E1
Pledger Lake *ON* **17** A3
Plenty *SK* **11** C3
Plessisville *QC* **27** C4-5
Plétipi, lac *QC* **40** E-F6
Plevna *ON* **21** C5-6

Plongeon, lac au *QC* **28** D7-8
Pluie, lac à la *ON* **13** F6
Pluie, lac à la *ON* **16** E2
Pluie, rivière à la *ON* **16** F2
Plumas *MB* **13** E2
Plumas *MB* **14** C-D2
Plum Coulee *MB* **13** F3
Plum Coulee *MB* **14** F4
Plum Lake *MB* **11** F8
Plum Lake *MB* **13** F1
Plummer *ON* **17** F4
Plumper Cove PMP *BC* **2** D4
Plum Point *NL* **38** B3-4
Plum Point *NL* **39** E8
Plunkett *SK* **11** C5
Plymouth *NS* **33** E1
Plymouth *NS* **34** E3
Plympton *NS* **32** F4
Plympton *NS* **33** D1-2
Plympton Station *NS* **33** D2
Plympton-Wyoming *ON* **19** C3
Plympton-Wyoming *ON* **20** E2
Pocahontas *AB* **6** B3
Pocahontas *AB* **8** D1
Pocket Knife Lake *NL* **39** A-B5
Pocknock, lac *QC* **22** D7
Pocknock, lac *QC* **24** B1
Pocknock, lac *QC* **25** F1
Pocologan *NB* **32** E3
Poe *AB* **6** B6
Poe *AB* **8** D8
Poe *AB* **8** B1
Pogamasing Lake *ON* **17** E6
Pohénégamook *QC* **29** E1-2
Pohénégamook, lac *QC*
   29 E1-2
Poigan, lac *QC* **22** D7
Poignan, lac *QC* **25** D1
Poincaré, lac *QC* **39** D7
Point Aconi *NS* **34** B7
Point Alexander *ON* **22** E4
Point Anne *ON* **21** D5
Point au Gaul *NL* **36** F6
Point au Gaul *NL* **37** F4
Point au Mal *NL* **36** B2
Point Clark *ON* **20** B2-3
Point Clark Lighthouse NHS *ON* **20** B2-3
Point Comfort *QC* **22** E8
Point Comfort *QC* **24** B-C2
Point Cross *NS* **34** B6
Point de Bute *NB* **32** C7
Point de Bute *NB* **35** F1
Pointe-à-Boisvert *QC* **29** B2
Pointe-à-la-Croix *QC* **29** D6
Pointe-à-la-Croix *QC*
   31 A4-5
Pointe-à-la-Frégate *QC*
   30 A2
Pointe-à-la-Garde *QC* **29** D6
Pointe-à-la-Garde *QC*
   31 A5
Pointe au Baril *ON* **18** C6
Pointe au Baril Station *ON*
   18 C6-7
Pointe-au-Chêne *QC* **24** D4
Pointe-au-Père *QC*
   29 D1-2
Pointe-au-Père, RNF de *QC* **29** C2-3
Pointe-au-Père Lighthouse NHS *QC* **29** C2-3
Pointe-au-Père NWA *QC* **29** C2-3
Pointe-aux-Anglais *QC* **39** F1-2
Pointe-aux-Loups *QC* **30** F7
Pointe-aux-Outardes *QC* **29** A3
Pointe-aux-Outardes, parc régional de *QC* **29** A3-4
Pointe aux Pins *ON* **17** F3-4
Pointe aux Pins *ON* **19** E3
Pointe-Calumet *QC* **24** D5
Pointe-Canot *NB* **31** B8
Pointe-Claire *QC* **24** D5
Pointe-Claire *QC* **27** E1
Pointe-de-l'Est, RNF de la *QC* **30** B8
Point de l'Est NWA *QC* **30** B8
Pointe-des-Cascades *QC* **24** D5
Pointe-des-Cascades *QC* **27** E1
Pointe-des-Monts *QC* **29** A5
Pointe du Bois *MB* **13** E5
Pointe du Bois *MB* **14** D7
Pointe-du-Chêne *NB* **32** B6-7
Pointe-du-Lac *QC* **24** B7
Pointe-du-Lac *QC* **25** F7-8
Pointe-du-Lac *QC* **27** D2
Point Edward *ON* **19** C2
Point Edward *ON* **20** E1
Pointe-Fortune *QC* **24** D4-5
Pointe-Jaune *QC* **30** B2-3
Pointe-Lebel *QC* **29** A3-4
Pointe-Parent *QC* **39** F5
Pointe-Pelée, PN de la *ON* **19** F2
Pointe-Pelée, PN de la *ON* **19** F2-3
Pointe-Prince-Edward, RNF de la *QC* **21** E-F6
Pointe-Saint-Pierre *QC* **30** C3
Pointe-Sapin *NB* **31** D8
Point Escuminac *NB* **31** D8

Pointe-Taillon, parc de la QC **28** B4
Pointe-Verte NB **29** E7-8
Pointe-Verte NB **31** B6
Point Farms PP ON **19** A3-4
Point Farms PP ON **20** C2-3
Point La Haye NL **37** F7
Point La Nim NB **29** A5
Point La Nim NB **31** A5
Point Lake NT **10** A7
Point Lake NT **41** C2
Point Lance NL **36** F8
Point Lance NL **37** F6
Point Leamington NL **36** A4
Point Leamington NL **37** A4
Point Leamington NL **38** F5
Point May NL **36** F5-6
Point May NL **37** F3-4
Point Michaud NS **34** D7
Point Michaud Beach PP NS **34** D7
Point of Bay NL **36** A6
Point of Bay NL **37** A4
Point of Bay NL **38** F5-6
Point Pelee NP ON **19** F2-3
Point Pelee NP ON **19** F2-3
Point Prim PE **34** C2-3
Point Prim PE **35** F5
Point Rosie NL **36** E6
Point Rosie NL **37** E4
Points North Landing SK **12** B6
Point Tupper NS **34** D6
Point Verde NL **36** E8
Point Verde NL **37** E6
Point Wolfe River Gorge PCA NB **32** D5
Point Wolfe River Gorge PCA NB **33** A2-3
Point Wolfe River Gorge, ZCP NB **32** D5
Point Wolfe River Gorge, ZCP NB **33** A2-3
Poissant QC **24** A3
Poissant QC **25** E3
Poisson Blanc, lac QC **22** F8
Poisson Blanc, lac QC **24** C2-3
Poisson Blanc, lac (réservoir) QC **22** E8
Poisson Blanc, lac (réservoir) QC **24** C2
Poissons River NL **39** C3
Poivre, lac au QC **28** A6
Pokei Lake-White River Wetlands PNR ON **17** C-D3
Pokei Lake-White River Wetlands, RNP ON **17** C-D3
Pokemouche NB **30** E2
Pokemouche NB **31** B8
Pokemouche River NB **29** E8
Pokemouche River NB **30** F1
Pokemouche River NB **31** B7
Pokeshaw NB **29** E8
Pokeshaw NB **30** E1
Pokeshaw NB **31** B7
Pokesudie NB **31** B8
Pokesudie, île NB **30** E2
Pokesudie Island NB **30** E2
Pokiok NB **32** C2
Poland ON **21** B6
Polar Bear PP ON **40** D2-3
Police Island NT **5** F8
Police Island NT **10** A2
Police Outpost PP AB **6** F6
Police Outpost PP AB **7** F4-5
Pollards Point NL **38** E3-4
Pollards Point NL **39** F8
Pollett River NB **32** C5
Pollock Point NS **33** D4
Pollockville AB **6** D7
Pollockville AB **7** B7
Pollockville AB **11** D1
Polonais, lac des QC **25** D3
Polonia MB **13** E2
Polonia MB **14** C2
Poltimore QC **22** F8
Poltimore QC **24** C2
Polwarth SK **11** B4
Pomeroy MB **14** F4
Pomeroy NB **32** D2
Pommeroy, lac QC **22** B3
Pomquet NS **34** D5
Pomquet Beach PP NS **34** D4-5
Ponask Lake ON **13** A6-7
Ponask River ON **13** A6
Ponass Lake SK **11** C6
Pond Cove NL **38** B3
Pond Inlet NU **41** A6-7
Pond Inlet NU **42** D6
Pond Inlet (Mittimatalik) NU **41** A6-7
Pond Inlet (Mittimatalik) NU **42** D-E6
Pondosy Lake BC **1** B4-5
Ponds NS **34** D4
Pondville Beach PP NS **34** E6-7
Ponemah MB **13** E4
Ponemah MB **14** C5
Ponhook Lake NS **32** E7-8 F7
Ponhook Lake NS **33** C5
Ponoka AB **6** B-C6
Ponoka AB **8** E6
Pontbriand QC **27** C5

Pont-de-Béton-en-Arc-du-Lac-Canal, LHN du ON **20** A8
Pont-de-Béton-en-Arc-du-Lac-Canal, LHN du ON **21** D2
Ponteix SK **11** F3-4
Pontgrave NB **31** C8
Pontiac QC **21** A7
Pontiac QC **22** F7
Pontiac QC **24** D1
Pontiac, ZEC QC **22** D6
Pont-Lafrance NB **30** F1-2
Pont-Lafrance NB **31** C7
Pont-Landry NB **30** F2
Pont-Landry NB **31** B7
Ponton MB **15** F3
Ponton River AB **9** B4
Pontypool ON **20** B8
Pontypool ON **21** E2-3
Poodiac NB **32** D5
Poodiac NB **33** A2
Poole ON **19** B5
Poole ON **20** D4
Poole's Corner PP PE **34** C2
Poole's Corner PP PE **35** E6
Pooley Island BC **1** B3-4
Pool's Cove NL **36** D6
Pool's Cove NL **37** D4
Pool's Island NL **37** A7
Pool's Island NL **38** F8
Poor Man SK **11** D5
Pope, lac QC **22** D8
Pope, lac QC **24** A2
Pope, lac QC **25** E2
Pope, RNF MB **11** E8
Pope, RNF MB **13** E1
Pope, NWA MB **11** E8
Pope, NWA MB **13** E1
Pope's Harbour NS **33** C8
Popham Bay NU **40** A6
Popkum BC **2** E6-7
Poplar ON **18** C2-3
Poplar Dale ON **17** F4
Poplarfield MB **13** D3-4
Poplarfield MB **14** B4
Poplar Grove PE **32** A7-8
Poplar Grove PE **34** B1
Poplar Grove PE **35** C2
Poplar Hill ON **13** C5-6
Poplar Hill ON **16** A2
Poplar Hill ON **19** C4
Poplar Hill ON **20** E3
Poplar/Nanowin Rivers PP Reserve MB **13** B4
Poplar Park MB **14** D5
Poplar Point MB **13** B3-4
Poplar Point MB **13** E3
Poplar Point MB **14** D4
Poplar Point PE **35** E7
Poplar Ridge AB **8** D4
Poplar River MB **13** B4 C5
Poplar River MB **13** B4
Poplar River NT **10** E3
Porc-Épic, lac au QC **28** D7
Porcher Island BC **1** A2
Porcupine ON **17** C6
Porcupine, Cape NL **39** C7
Porcupine Meadows PP BC **1** D8
Porcupine Meadows PP BC **2** A8
Porcupine Meadows PP BC **6** D1
Porcupine Plain SK **11** C6
Porcupine River NT **10** A2
Porcupine River SK **12** A5-6
Porcupine River YT **5** D3
Porphyry Island PP ON **16** F6-7
Porpoise Bay PP BC **2** C4
Porquis Junction ON **17** C6-7
Portage, lac du QC **27** D7
Portage, rivière du QC **30** C2-3
Portage Bay MB **13** D3
Portage Bay MB **14** A3
Portage Bay NT **10** B8
Portage-du-Fort QC **21** A6
Portage-du-Fort QC **22** F6
Portage Island NWA **31** C7-8
Portage Island NWA **31** C7-8
Portage la Prairie MB **13** D3
Portage la Prairie MB **14** D3
Portage Lake BC **36** C3
Portage Lake NL **37** C1
Portage Vale NS **32** C5
Port Alberni BC **1** F6
Port Alberni BC **2** D-E2
Port Alberni Inlet BC **2** C2
Port Albert NB **38** E7
Port Albert ON **19** A3-4
Port Albert ON **20** C2-3
Port Albion BC **1** F5
Port Albion BC **2** E1-2
Port Alice BC **1** E4
Port Alma ON **19** E2-3
Port Anne NL **36** E7
Port Anne NL **37** E5
Port Anson NL **38** E7
Port Anson ON **18** C8
Port Anson ON **21** A1
Portapique NS **32** D8
Portapique NS **33** A5-6
Portapique NS **34** E1-2
Port au Choix NL **38** C3
Port au Choix NL **39** E7
Port au Choix, LHN de NL **38** C2-3
Port au Choix, LHN de NL **39** E7

Port au Choix NHS NL **38** C2-3
Port au Choix NHS NL **39** E7
Port-au-Persil QC **28** E8
Port au Port NL **36** C2
Port au Port NL **40** F8
Port au Port Bay NL **36** B2
Port au Port East NL **36** C2
Port au Port Peninsula NL **36** B-C1
Port au Port Peninsula NL **40** F8
Port au Port West-Aguathuna-Felix Cove NL **36** C1-2
Port-aux-Quilles QC **28** D8
Port Bickerton NS **34** B5
Port Blandford NL **36** C8
Port Blandford NL **37** C6
Port Bolster ON **20** B7
Port Bolster ON **21** D1-2
Port Bruce ON **19** D5
Port Bruce ON **20** F4
Port Bruce PP ON **19** D5
Port Bruce PP ON **20** F4
Port Burwell ON **19** D5
Port Burwell ON **20** F4
Port Burwell PP ON **19** D5
Port Burwell PP ON **20** F4
Port Carling ON **18** D-E8
Port Carling ON **21** B1
Port Carmen ON **18** C8
Port Carmen ON **21** A1
Port Carmen ON **22** F1
Port-Cartier QC **39** F1-2
Port-Cartier QC **40** F6
Port-Cartier-Sept-Îles, RF de QC **39** E1-2
Port Clements BC **1** A1
Port Clyde NS **33** F2
Port Clyde NS **33** F2
Port Colborne ON **19** C8
Port Colborne ON **20** F7
Port Coquitlam BC **1** F7
Port Coquitlam BC **2** D5
Port Credit ON **19** B8
Port Credit ON **20** D7
Port Cunnington ON **21** B2
Port Dalhousie ON **19** B-C8
Port Dalhousie ON **20** E7
Port-Daniel QC **30** D1-2
Port-Daniel QC **31** A7-8
Port-Daniel, baie de QC **30** D2
Port-Daniel, RF de QC **30** D2
Port-Daniel Nord, rivière QC **30** D1-2
Port Darlington ON **21** F2-3
Port de Grave NL **37** D7-8
Port Douglas BC **2** C6
Port Dover ON **19** D6-7
Port Dover ON **20** F5-6
Port Dufferin NS **33** B8
Port Dufferin NS **34** F4
Port Edward BC **1** A2
Port Elgin NB **32** B7
Port Elgin NB **34** D1
Port Elgin NB **35** F2
Port Elgin ON **18** F4
Port Elgin ON **20** A3
Port Eliza BC **1** E4
Port Elmsley ON **21** C7
Port Elmsley ON **24** F1
Porter Cove NB **31** E5
Porter Cove NB **32** A3
Porter Creek YT **4** E3-4
Porter Lake SK **12** D4
Porters Lake NS **33** C6
Porters Lake PP NS **33** C6
Porterville NL **36** A6-7
Porterville NL **37** A4-5
Porterville NL **38** F6
Port Essington BC **1** A3
Port Felix NS **34** E6
Port Franks ON **19** B3
Port Franks ON **20** D2
Port George NS **32** E5
Port George NS **33** B3
Port Glasgow ON **19** D4
Port Glasgow ON **20** F3
Port Greville NS **32** D7
Port Greville NS **33** A4
Port Hardy BC **1** E4
Port Hastings NS **34** D6
Port Hawkesbury NS **34** D6
Port Hébert, RNOM de NS **33** E4-5
Port Hill PE **32** A8
Port Hill PE **34** B1
Port Hill PE **35** C2-3
Port Hillford NS **34** C5
Port Hood NS **34** C5
Port Hood Island NS **34** C5
Port Hood Station PP NS **34** C5
Port Hope ON **21** E3
Port Hope Simpson NL **39** C8
Port Howe NS **32** C8
Port Howe NS **34** D1
Portia MB **14** B2
Port Joli NS **33** E4
Port Joli Head NS **33** E4
Port Joli NMBS NS **33** E4-5
Port Joli, RNOM de NS **33** E4-5
Port Kirwan NL **37** F8
Port-la-Joye-Fort-Amherst, LHN de PE **34** C2-3
Port-la-Joye-Fort-Amherst, LHN de PE **35** E7

Port-la-Joye-Fort-Amherst, LHN de PE **35** E5
Port-la-Joye-Fort Amherst NHS PE **34** C2-3
Port-la-Joye-Fort Amherst NHS PE **35** E5
Port Lambton ON **19** D2
Port Lambton ON **20** F1
Portland NL **37** C6-7
Portland ON **21** C7
Portland ON **24** F1
Portland CA ON **21** D6
Portland Canal BC **3** F2-3
Portland Creek NL **38** D2
Portland Creek NL **39** E-F7
Portland Creek Pond NL **38** D3
Portland Creek Pond NL **39** E-F7
Portland Inlet BC **3** F2-3
Port La Tour NS **33** F2-3
Port Lewis QC **24** E5
Port l'Hébert NS **33** E3
Port l'Hébert NMBS NS **33** E3-5
Port Loring ON **18** B7
Port Lorne NS **32** E5
Port Lorne NS **33** B3
Port Louis BC **1** A1
Port Maitland NS **33** E1
Port Maitland ON **19** C8
Port Maitland ON **20** F7
Port Maitland Beach PP NS **33** E1
Port McNeill BC **1** E4
Port McNicoll ON **18** E-E7
Port McNicoll ON **20** A6
Port Malcolm NS **34** E6
Port Medway NS **33** D-E4
Port Mellon BC **1** F6
Port Mellon BC **2** D4
Port-Menier QC **39** F3
Port-Menier QC **40** F7
Port Moody BC **1** F7
Port Moody BC **2** D5
Port Morien NS **34** C8
Port Mouton NS **33** E4
Port Mouton NS **33** E3-4
Port Mouton Head NS **33** E4
Port Nelson ON **19** D6
Port Nelson MB **15** D6
Portneuf QC **27** B4
Portneuf, lac QC **28** A7
Portneuf, RF de QC **25** D8
Portneuf, RF de QC **28** B3-4
Portneuf, rivière QC **28** B8
Portneuf, rivière QC **29** B1
Port Neville BC **1** E5
Port Neville BC **2** B1
Port Neville BC **2** B1
Portobello Creek, RNF NB **32** C3
Portobello Creek National Wilderness Area NB **32** C3
Port of Big Beaver SK **11** F5
Port of Carievale SK **11** F7-8
Port of Carievale SK **13** F1
Port of Climax SK **11** F1
Port of Coronach SK **11** F5
Port of Estevan Hwy. SK **11** F6
Port of Oungre SK **11** F6
Port of Torquay SK **11** F6
Port Perry ON **20** B8
Port Perry ON **21** E2
Port Philip NS **32** C8
Port Philip NS **34** D1
Port Rexton NL **37** C7
Port Robinson ON **19** C8
Port Robinson ON **20** E7
Port Rowan ON **19** D6
Port Rowan ON **20** F5
Port Royal NS **32** F4-5
Port Royal NS **33** C2
Port Royal ON **19** D6
Port Royal ON **20** F5
Port-Royal, LHN de NS **32** F4-5
Port-Royal, LHN de NS **33** C1-2
Port-Royal NHS NS **32** F4-5
Port-Royal NHS NS **33** C1-2
Port Ryerse ON **19** D6-7
Port Ryerse ON **20** F5-6
Port-Saint-François QC **24** B7-8
Port-Saint-François QC **25** F7-8
Port-Saint-François QC **27** C5
Port San Juan BC **2** F3
Port Sandfield ON **18** D-E8
Port Sandfield ON **21** B1
Port Saunders NL **38** C3
Port Saunders NL **39** E7-8
Port Saxon NS **33** F2
Port Severn ON **18** E8
Port Severn ON **21** C1
Port Shoreham NS **34** E5-6
Port Shoreham Beach PP NS **34** E6
Port Stanley ON **19** D4-5
Port Stanley ON **20** F3-4
Port Stanton ON **18** E8
Port Stanton ON **21** C1
Port Sydney ON **21** B1-2
Portugal Cove NL **37** D8
Portugal Cove South NL **37** F7-8

Portuguese Cove NS **33** C6
Port Union NL **37** B7-8
Port Wade NS **32** F4
Port Wade NS **33** C2
Port Williams NS **32** E7
Port Williams NS **33** B4
Postville NL **39** A6
Postville NL **40** D8
Potherie Inférieur, lac QC **25** D5
Potherie Inférieur, lac QC **26** B4
Potherie Inférieur, lac QC **27** A1
Potherie Inférieur, lac QC **28** F1
Potherie Supérieur, lac QC **25** D6
Potherie Supérieur, lac QC **27** A1
Potherie Supérieur, lac QC **28** F1
Potholes, RNP ON **17** D4
Potholes PNR ON **17** D4
Potomac River ON **18** A1-2
Pottageville ON **20** C6-7
Pottageville ON **21** E1
Pottawatomi CA ON **18** F5
Pottawatomi CA ON **20** A4
Potters Landing ON **18** E7
Pottles Bay NL **39** A7
Potts Lake AB **9** A7
Potts Lake AB **12** A2-3
Pouce Coupe BC **3** E8
Pouce Coupe BC **9** E2
Pouce Coupe River AB **9** E2
Pouch Cove NL **37** D8
Pougnet, lac QC **26** C3-4
Poularies QC **17** C8
Poularies QC **23** C2-3
Poulin-de-Courval, lac QC **28** B7
Poulter, lac QC **22** B6
Pound Cove NL **37** A7
Pound Cove NL **38** F8
Poundmaker SK **11** B2-3
Poutret, lac QC **39** B2
Poutrincourt, lac QC **26** C5
Poutrincourt, lac QC **28** A1
Poverty Cape NL **35** F7
Povungnituk, rivière de QC **40** B4-5
Povungnituk, rivière de QC **41** E8
Povungnituk Bay **40** C4
Povungnituk Bay QC **41** E7-8
Powassan ON **17** F8
Powassan ON **18** B8
Powassan ON **22** E1
Powell ON **17** F5
Powell MB **13** B1
Powell Lake BC **1** E6
Powell Lake BC **2** C3
Powell Peak BC **1** A-B4
Powell River BC **1** E-F6
Powell River BC **2** C3
Powells Point PP NS **34** D3-4
Powerscourt QC **24** E5
Powerview ON **13** E4
Powerview MB **14** C6
Pownal PE **35** E5
Pownal Bay PE **35** E5
Prairie River SK **11** B6
Prairie River Mouth, RNP ON **16** E7-8
Prairie River Mouth, RNP ON **17** C2
Prairie River Mouth PNR ON **16** E7-8
Prairie River Mouth PNR ON **17** C2
Prairies, Lake of the SK **11** D7
Prairies, Lake of the SK **13** D1
Prairies, PN des SK **11** F3-4
Prairies, rivière des QC **24** D6
Prairies, rivière des QC **27** E1
Prairie Siding ON **19** E2
Prairie View SK **11** E4
Prarie Creek NT **10** D-E2
Pratt MB **14** E3
Prawda MB **13** F5
Prawda MB **14** E7
Preacher Davis River NL **36** A6
Preacher Davis River NL **37** A4
Preacher Davis River NL **38** F5
Preble Island NT **10** D7
Precious Corners ON **21** E3
Pré-d'en-Haut NB **31** F8
Pré-d'en-Haut NB **32** B-C6
Preeceville SK **11** C7
Preissac QC **17** C8
Preissac QC **23** D3-4
Preissac, lac QC **23** D3
Prelate SK **6** D8
Prelate SK **11** D2
Prelude Lake NT **10** C7
Prelude Lake TP NT **10** C6-7
Premier Lake BC **6** F4
Premier Lake PP BC **6** E4
Premier-Puits-de-Pétrole-de-l'Ouest-Canadien, LHN du NB **7** F3-4
Premio QC **39** E2
Prentiss AB **8** E-F6
Prescott ON **21** C8

Prescott ON **24** F2
Prescott Island BC **1** A2
Prescott Island NU **41** A4
Prescott Island NU **42** E4
Prés du lac Grand, APP NB **32** C3-4
Prespatou BC **3** D8
Prespatou BC **9** D1
Presqu'île NS **34** B6
Presqu'île, lac de la QC **26** B4
Presqu'île, lac QC **23** E6
Presqu'ile Point ON **21** E4
Presqu'ile PP ON **21** E4
Press QC **23** E6
Press Lake ON **13** E7-8
Press Lake ON **16** D4
Preston NS **33** C6
Preston, lac QC **24** B3
Preston Lake ON **20** C7
Preston Lake ON **21** E1
Preston Lake SK **9** C8
Preston Lake SK **12** C3
Pretty River Valley PP ON **18** F6
Pretty River Valley PP ON **20** A5
Prévost QC **24** C5
Prévost, lac QC **23** F2
Prevost Island Unit (Gulf Islands NPR) BC **2** E4-5
Prevost River YT **4** C6
Price QC **29** B-C3
Price Island BC **1** C3
Prices Corner ON **20** A7
Prices Corner ON **21** D1
Price Settlement NB **30** F1
Price Settlement NB **31** C7
Priceville NB **31** E5
Priceville NB **32** A3
Priceville ON **20** B5
Priddis AB **6** D5
Priddis AB **7** C3
Priest Pond PE **34** B4
Priest Pond PE **35** D8
Priestville NB **31** E5
Priestville NB **32** A3
Primate SK **6** C8
Primate SK **11** C2
Primeau Lake SK **12** E4
Primeau Lake SK **12** E4
Primeau, lac QC **23** E-E8
Primeau, lac QC **25** B2
Primeau, lac QC **26** F2
Prim Point NS **32** F4
Prim Point NS **33** C2
Primrose PE **35** E6
Primrose Lake SK **9** F8
Primrose Lake SK **12** F2
Primrose Lake YT **4** E3
Primrose Lake Provincial Ecological Reserve SK **9** F8
Primrose Lake Provincial Ecological Reserve SK **12** F2-3
Primrose River YT **4** E3
Prince SK **11** B3
Prince Albert ON **20** B8
Prince Albert ON **21** E2
Prince Albert SK **11** B5
Prince Albert, PN de SK **11** A4
Prince Albert NP SK **11** A4
Prince Albert Peninsula NT **41** A4
Prince Albert Peninsula NT **42** D1-2 E1
Prince Albert Sound NT **41** B-C7
Prince Albert Sound NT **42** E1-2
Prince Charles Island NU **41** B-C7
Prince Charles Island NU **42** F6
Prince-de-Galles, cap du QC **40** B5
Prince-de-Galles, île du NU **42** E3-4
Prince Edward Bay ON **21** E6
Prince Edward County ON **21** E5
Prince Edward Island NP PE **34** B2-3
Prince Edward Island NP PE **34** B3
Prince Edward Island NP PE **35** D4-5
Prince Edward Island NP PE **35** D5-6
Prince Edward Point NWA ON **21** E-F6
Prince George BC **1** A7
Prince Gustaf Adolf Sea NU **42** B-C3
Prince Leopold Island NU **42** D4
Prince of Wales NB **32** B3
Prince of Wales NB **33** B1
Prince of Wales Fort NHS MB **15** B5
Prince of Wales Fort NHS MB **40** C1
Prince of Wales Fort NP MB **15** E1
Prince of Wales Island NU **41** A4
Prince of Wales Island NU **42** D-E3

Prince of Wales Strait NT **41** A2
Prince of Wales Strait NT **42** D1
Prince Patrick Island NT **42** C2
Princeport NS **33** A6
Princeport NS **34** F2
Prince Regent Inlet NU **41** A5
Prince Regent Inlet NU **42** D-E4
Prince Rupert BC **1** A2-3
Princess Harbour MB **13** C4
Princess Louisa Inlet BC **1** E6
Princess Louisa Inlet BC **2** B-C4
Princess Louisa PMP BC **1** E6
Princess Louisa PMP BC **2** B-C4
Princess Marie Bay NU **42** B3
Princess Park NB **32** C4
Princess Royal Channel BC **1** B3
Princess Royal Island BC **1** B3
Princeton BC **1** F8
Princeton BC **2** D8
Princeton BC **6** F1
Princeton NL **37** C7
Princeton ON **19** C6
Princeton ON **20** E5
Princeville QC **27** C4-5
Prince William NB **32** C2
Principal, lac du QC **26** D4
Principe Channel BC **1** B2-3
Pringle Lake ON **16** B2
Prinsta, baie QC **30** A7
Prinsta, rivière QC **30** A6-7
Prior Centennial Unit (Gulf Islands NPR) BC **2** E4-5
Pritchard BC **6** E2
Procter BC **6** F3-4
Profits Point PE **34** B1
Profits Point PE **35** C3
Progress SK **3** E8
Progress BC **9** E1-2
Progress BC **40** C4
Prongua SK **11** B3
Pronto East ON **17** F5
Pronto East ON **18** B2
Prophet River BC **3** C7
Prophet River BC **3** C7
Prophet River BC **3** C7
Prophet River Hotsprings PP BC **3** C6
Prophet River Wayside PP BC **3** C7
Prospect NS **32** F8
Prospect NS **33** C5-6
Prospect ON **21** B7
Prospector MB **11** A7
Prospector MB **13** A1
Prospector, Mount YT **4** C2-3
Prosperous Lake NT **10** C6
Prosser Brook NB **32** C5
Proton Station ON **20** B5
Proulx, lac QC **28** A-B4
Proulx Lake ON **22** E-F3
Provancher, lac QC **28** A4
Providence, Lake NT **10** A7
Providence Bay ON **18** C3
Province House, LHN PE **34** C2
Province House, LHN PE **35** E5
Province House NHS PE **34** C2
Province House NHS PE **35** E5
Provost AB **6** C8
Provost AB **11** C2
Prud'homme SK **11** C5
Prudhomme Lake PP BC **1** A3
Ptarmigan Bay ON **14** E8
Ptarmigan Creek PP BC **1** B8
Ptarmigan Creek PP BC **6** B1
Pubnico NS **33** F2
Pubnico Harbour NS **33** F2
Puce ON **19** E1-2
Puff Island, RNP ON **16** F6-7
Puff Island, RNP ON **17** C1
Puff Island PNR ON **16** F6-7
Puff Island PNR ON **17** C1
Pugwash NS **32** C8
Pugwash NS **34** D1-2
Pugwash Harbour NS **35** F3
Pugwash Junction NS **32** C8
Pugwash Junction NS **34** D1-2
Pukaskwa, PN ON **16** F8
Pukaskwa, PN ON **17** D2-3
Pukaskwa NP ON **16** F8
Pukaskwa NP ON **17** D2-3
Pukaskwa River ON **16** F8
Pukaskwa River ON **17** D3
Pukaskwa River PP ON **17** D3
Pukatawagan MB **12** E7
Pukatawagan MB **15** E1-2
Pukatawagan (IR) MB **12** E7
Pukatawagan (IR) MB **15** E1
Pukatawagan Lake MB **12** E7
Pukatawagan Lake MB **15** E1

Pukeashun Mountain BC **6** D2
Pullen Island NT **5** A4-5
Pulp River MB **11** C8
Pulp River MB **13** C2
Pulp River MB **14** A1
Punnichy SK **11** D6
Puntchesakut Lake PP BC **1** B6-7
Puntledge River BC **2** D2
Puntzi Lake BC **1** C6
Purbeck's Cove NL **38** E4
Purcell Lake ON **16** B8
Purcell Mountains BC **6** E4
Purcell Mountains BC **7** C-D1
Purcell Wilderness Provincial Conservancy BC **6** E4
Purden Lake PP BC **1** A7
Purdon CA ON **21** C6
Purdy ON **21** B4
Pure Lake PP BC **1** A1
Purple Springs AB **6** E7
Purple Springs AB **7** E6-7
Purple Springs AB **11** E1
Purple Valley ON **18** E5
Purtuniq QC **40** B5
Purtuniq QC **41** D8
Purves MB **14** F3
Pushkin Hills, RNP ON **17** D7-8
Pushkin Hills, RNP ON **23** D1
Pushkin Hills PNR ON **17** D7-8
Pushkin Hills PNR ON **23** D1
Puskwakau River AB **9** E3
Puslinch ON **19** B7
Puslinch ON **20** D6
Pusticamica, lac QC **23** B7
Pusticamica, lac QC **26** C1-2
Putahow Lake MB **12** A7
Putahow Lake MB **15** A2
Putahow River MB **12** A7
Putahow River MB **15** A2
Putnam ON **19** C5
Putnam ON **20** E4
Puvirnituq QC **40** C4
Puvirnituq QC **41** E7-8
Puyjalon, lac QC **39** E4
Puzzle Lake PP ON **21** C5
Pynn's Brook NL **36** A3-4
Pynn's Brook NL **37** A1-2
Pynn's Brook NL **38** F3
Pyramid Falls PP BC **6** C2
Pyramid Mountain AB **6** B3
Pythonga, lac QC **22** B1
Pythonga, lac QC **24** B1
Pythonga, lac QC **25** F1

Q

Qamanit'uaq (Baker Lake) NU **41** D4-5
Qasuittuq (Resolute) NU **42** D4
Qaummaarviit, parc territorial NU **40** A5
Qaummaarviit TP NU **40** A5
Qaummaarviit TP NU **41** C-D8
Qikiqtarjuaq (Broughton Island) NU **42** E-F8
Qilaluqat TP NU **42** F6
Qilaluqat TP NU **42** D5-6
Qu'Appelle SK **11** E6
Qu'Appelle River SK **11** E6
Quaco Head NB **32** D5
Quaco Head NB **33** A2
Quadeville ON **21** B5
Quadra Island BC **1** E5
Quadra Island BC **2** B-C2
Qualche Lake BC **1** B5
Qualicum BC **2** D3
Qualicum Beach BC **1** F6
Qualicum Beach BC **2** D2
Qualicum NWA BC **2** D2
Qualicum NWA BC **2** D3
Qualicum NWA BC **2** D3-4
Quantock SK **11** F4
Quaqtaq NU **40** B5
Quaqtaq NU **41** B8
Quarry Bay ON **18** B1
Quarryville NB **31** D6
Quartz Lake ON **16** B8
Quathiaski Cove BC **1** E5-6
Quathiaski Cove BC **2** C2
Quatsino BC **1** E4
Quatsino PP BC **1** E4
Quatsino Sound BC **1** E4
Quatsino Subdivision BC **1** E4
Québec QC **27** B6
Québec QC **29** B6
Québec, arrondissement historique de QC **27** B6
Québec, Historic District of QC **27** B6
Queen Bess, Mount BC **1** D6
Queen Charlotte City BC **1** B1
Queen Charlotte Islands BC **1** B1
Queen Charlotte Sound BC **1** D3
Queen Charlotte Strait BC **1** D-E4

Queen Elizabeth Islands *NT* **42** A3-4 B2-3
Queen Elizabeth Islands *NU* **42** A3-4 B2-3
Queen Elizabeth PP *AB* **9** D-E3
Queen Elizabeth TP *AB* **10** F8
Queen Elizabeth TP *NT* **41** E1-2
Queen Elizabeth II Wildlands PP *ON* **21** C2
Queen Mary, Mount *YT* **4** E1
Queen Maud Gulf *NU* **42** F3
Queens *NS* **33** D3
Queensborough *ON* **21** D5
Queen's Cove *NL* **36** B4
Queen's Cove *NL* **37** D6
Queensland *NS* **32** F8
Queensland *NS* **33** C5
Queensland Beach PP *NS* **32** F7-8
Queensland Beach PP *NS* **33** C5
Queensport *NS* **34** E6
Queens Reach *BC* **2** C3-4
Queens Sound *BC* **1** C3
Queenston *ON* **20** E7-8
Queenston Heights NHS *ON* **20** E8
Queenstown *AB* **6** E6
Queenstown *AB* **7** C5
Queenstown *NB* **32** C3-4
Queensville *NS* **34** D6
Queensville *ON* **20** B7
Queensville *ON* **21** E1
Quenouilles, lac aux *QC* **24** B4
Quesnel *BC* **1** B7
Quesnel Lake *BC* **1** C8
Quesnel Lake *BC* **6** C-E1
Quesnel River *BC* **1** C7-8
Quetachou, baie *QC* **39** E-F4
Quetico Lake *ON* **16** F3
Quetico PP *ON* **16** F4
Quetico PP *ON* **40** F1
Quévillon, lac *QC* **23** B6
Quibell *ON* **13** E6
Quibell *ON* **16** D2
Quidi Vidi *NL* **37** D8
Quiet Lake *YT* **4** D-E5
Quiet Lake Territorial Recreation Site *YT* **4** D4-5
Quilchena *BC* **2** C8
Quilchena *BC* **6** E1
Quill Lake *SK* **11** C5-6
Quinan *NS* **33** E2
Quinn, lac *QC* **22** D8
Quinn, lac *QC* **24** A2
Quinn, lac *QC* **25** F2
Quinn Lake *MB* **15** B4
Quinn Lake *NL* **36** C4
Quinn Lake *NL* **37** C2
Quinsam *BC* **2** C2
Quinte, Bay of *ON* **21** E5
Quinte CA *ON* **21** E5
Quinte West *ON* **21** E4-5
Quinton *SK* **11** D5
Quinze, lac des *QC* **17** D8
Quinze, lac des *QC* **23** F2
Quirke Lake *ON* **17** F5
Quirke Lake *ON* **18** A3
Quirpon *NL* **38** A5
Quirpon Island *NL* **38** A5
Quisibis *NB* **29** F3-4
Quisibis *NB* **31** C2
Quisibis River *NB* **29** E-F3
Quispamsis *NB* **32** D4
Quispamsis *NB* **33** A1-2
Quoich River *NU* **41** D5
Quoin Inlet *BC* **1** A3
Quottoon Inlet *BC* **1** A3
Quttinirpaaq (Ellesmere Island) NP *NU* **42** A5
Quyon *QC* **21** A7
Quyon *QC* **22** F7
Quyon *QC* **24** D1

R

Raanes Peninsula *NU* **42** B-C4
Rabbabou Bay *SK* **12** B6-7
Rabbabou Bay *SK* **15** B1
Rabbit, lac *QC* **22** A3
Rabbit, lac *QC* **23** F3
Rabbit Island *NT* **5** A7-8
Rabbit Island *ON* **18** C4
Rabbit Lake *ON* **17** E8
Rabbit Lake *ON* **22** B1
Rabbit Lake *SK* **11** B3
Rabbit Lake Mine *SK* **12** B-C6
Rabbit Lake Mine *SK* **11** B3
Rabbit River *BC* **3** B4-5
Rabbit River *BC* **4** F8
Rabbitskin River *NT* **10** D4
Raccoon Lake *NT* **10** C5
Race Rocks, zone de protection marine de *BC* **2** F3-4
Race Rocks Marine Protected Area *BC* **2** F3-4
Racine *QC* **24** D8
Racine *QC* **27** E4
Racine de Bouleau, rivière de la *QC* **39** C-D1
Racine Lake *ON* **17** D5

Racing Island *NT* **5** A8
Racing River *BC* **3** B5-6 C6
Rackham *MB* **11** E8
Rackham *MB* **13** E2
Rackham *MB* **14** C1
Rackla River *YT* **4** A4
Radiant Lake *ON* **22** E3
Radilih Koe (Fort Good Hope) *NT* **5** E7
Radisson *QC* **40** E4
Radisson *SK* **11** C4
Radisson Lake *SK* **11** C4
Radium Hot Springs *BC* **6** E4
Radium Hot Springs *BC* **7** C1
Radville *SK* **11** F6
Radway *AB* **6** A6
Radway *AB* **8** B7
Rae *NT* **10** C6
Rae *NT* **41** D1
Rae Creek *YT* **4** A3
Rae-Edzo *NT* **10** C5-6
Rae Lake *NT* **10** B5
Rae Lakes *NT* **10** B5
Rae Lakes *NT* **41** D1
Rae Strait *NU* **41** B4-5 C4
Rafferty Dam *SK* **11** F6
Rafferty Dam Reservoir *SK* **11** F6
Raft Cove PP *BC* **1** E3
Rafter *MB* **12** E7
Rafter *MB* **15** E1-2
Ragged Falls/Oxtongue River PP *ON* **21** B2
Ragged Harbour *NL* **38** F7
Ragged Island *NL* **39** A7
Ragged Islands *NL* **39** A7
Ragged Lake *ON* **21** A2
Ragged Lake *ON* **22** F2
Raglan *ON* **20** B-C8
Raglan *ON* **21** E2
Ragueneau *QC* **29** A3
Ragueneau, rivière *QC* **29** A3
Raimbault, lac *QC* **39** B-C1
Raimbault, rivière *QC* **25** A7
Raimbault, rivière *QC* **26** E-F7
Raimbault, rivière *QC* **28** C-D3
Rain Lake *ON* **21** A2
Rainbow *AB* **7** A6
Rainbow Alley PP *BC* **3** F5
Rainbow Beach PP *MB* **13** D2
Rainbow Beach PP *MB* **14** B1-2
Rainbow Falls PP *ON* **16** E7
Rainbow Falls PP *ON* **17** C1-2
Rainbow Haven Beach PP *NS* **33** C6-7
Rainbow Lake *AB* **3** B8
Rainbow Lake *AB* **9** B2
Rainbow River *BC* **3** C5
Rainham Centre *ON* **19** C7
Rainham Centre *ON* **20** E7
Rainier *AB* **6** E6-7
Rainier *AB* **7** D6
Rainy Lake *ON* **13** F6
Rainy Lake *ON* **16** E2
Rainy Lake *ON* **18** C8
Rainy Lake *ON* **21** A1
Rainy River *ON* **16** E-F1
Rainy River *ON* **16** E-F1
Raisin River *ON* **24** E3-4
Raith *ON* **16** E5
Raleigh *NL* **38** A5
Raley *AB* **7** F5
Ralph *SK* **11** F6
Ralston *AB* **6** E7
Ralston *AB* **7** D7-8
Rama *SK* **11** C6
Rama Road *ON* **18** F8
Rama Road *ON* **20** A7
Rama Road *ON* **21** D1
Ramé, lac *QC* **22** C4
Ramea *NL* **36** E3-4
Ramea *NL* **37** E1-2
Ramea Islands *NL* **36** E4
Ramea Islands *NL* **37** E2
Rameau *QC* **30** C2-3
Ramore *ON* **17** D7
Rampart House Territorial Historic Site *YT* **5** C2
Ramparts River *NT* **5** E6
Ram River *NT* **10** D2
Ramsay Arm *BC* **2** B2
Ramsay Island *BC* **1** B2
Ramsey *ON* **17** E5
Ramsey Lake *ON* **17** E6
Ramusio, lac *QC* **39** A4
Ranch-Bar U, LHN du *AB* **6** E5-6
Ranch-Bar U, LHN du *AB* **7** C-D4
Rancheria *YT* **3** A3
Rancheria *YT* **4** E-F6
Rancheria Falls Territorial Recreation Site *YT* **3** A2-3
Rancheria Falls Territorial Recreation Site *YT* **4** E6
Rancheria River *YT* **3** A3
Rancheria River *YT* **4** E-F6
Randboro *QC* **27** E-F5
Randolph *MB* **14** E5
Random Island *NL* **37** C7
Rane, lac *QC* **26** B4
Ranfurly *AB* **6** B7

Ranfurly *AB* **11** B1
Rang-des-Bosse *NB* **31** C2
Ranger *SK* **11** B3
Ranger Lake *ON* **17** E4
Ranger Lake *ON* **17** E-F4
Rangeton *AB* **8** C4-5
Rangifer, Mount *YT* **4** D4
Rang-Saint-Georges *NB* **30** E1-2
Rang-Saint-Georges *NB* **31** B7
Rankin *ON* **21** A5
Rankin *ON* **22** F5
Rankin Inlet *NU* **40** A2
Rankin Inlet *NU* **41** E5
Rankin Inlet (Kangiqiniq) *NU* **40** A1-2
Rankin Inlet (Kangiqiniq) *NU* **41** E5
Rannoch *ON* **19** B4-5
Rannoch *ON* **20** D3-4
Rantem *NL* **37** D6-7
Raoul-Blanchard, mont *QC* **28** F6
Raper, Cape *NU* **41** A8
Raper, Cape *NU* **42** E7
Rapid City *MB* **11** E8
Rapid City *MB* **13** E2
Rapid City *MB* **14** D1
Rapide-Blanc *QC* **25** B7
Rapide-Blanc *QC* **28** E2
Rapide-Blanc-Station *QC* **25** C7
Rapide-Blanc-Station *QC* **28** E2-3
Rapide-Danseur *QC* **17** C7-8
Rapide-Danseur *QC* **23** D2
Rapide-des-Cèdres *QC* **23** C6
Rapide-Deux *QC* **17** D8
Rapide-Deux *QC* **23** F3
Rapide River *BC* **3** B4
Rapid River *BC* **3** B4
Rapid View *SK* **6** A8
Rapid View *SK* **9** F8
Rapid View *SK* **11** A3
Rapson Bay *ON* **13** A7
Rapson Bay *ON* **15** F7
Ratcliffe *SK* **11** F6
Rathouse Bay *ON* **13** B6
Rathtrevor Beach PP *BC* **1** F6
Rathtrevor Beach PP *BC* **2** D3
Rathwell *MB* **13** F3
Rathwell *MB* **14** E3
Rat Lake *MB* **12** D-E8
Rat Lake *MB* **15** E2
Rat Lake *MB* **15** F5
Rat Portage *ON* **13** F5
Rat Portage *ON* **14** E8
Rat River *MB* **12** D-E8
Rat River *MB* **13** F4
Rat River *MB* **14** F6
Rat River *MB* **15** E3
Rat River *NT* **5** C4
Rat River *NT* **10** E7-8
Rats, lac aux *QC* **25** A7-8
Rats, lac aux *QC* **25** C7
Rats, lac aux *QC* **26** C8
Rats, lac aux *QC* **26** E7-8
Rats, lac aux *QC* **28** A4
Rats, lac aux *QC* **28** C3
Rats, lac aux *QC* **28** E2
Rats, rivière aux *QC* **25** C-D7
Rats, rivière aux *QC* **26** D8
Rats, rivière aux *QC* **28** A-B4
Rats, rivière aux *QC* **28** C3
Ratting Brook *NL* **36** A6
Rattling Brook *NL* **37** A4
Rattling Brook *NL* **38** A4
Rattling Brook *NL* **37** F5-6
Ratz, Mount *BC* **3** C2
Raude, lac *QC* **39** A3
Raven *AB* **6** C5
Raven *AB* **8** F5
Raven Lake *NT* **5** C7
Raven Lake *ON* **18** B4
Raven Lake *ON* **21** B2
Ravenna *ON* **18** F6
Ravenna *ON* **20** A5
Ravenscliffe *ON* **18** D8
Ravenscliffe *ON* **21** B1
Ravenscliffe *ON* **22** F1
Ravenscrag *SK* **11** F2
Ravenshoe *ON* **20** B7
Ravenshoe *ON* **21** E1
Ravens Throat River *NT* **4** B7-8
Ravensview *ON* **21** D-E7
Ravenswood *ON* **19** B3
Ravenswood *ON* **20** E2
Ravine *AB* **7** C-D4
Rawalpindi Lake *NT* **10** A6
Rawdon *NS* **32** E8
Rawdon *NS* **33** B5
Rawdon *NS* **34** F1
Rawdon *QC* **24** C6
Rawdon *QC* **27** D1
Rawdon Gold Mines *NS* **32** E8
Rawdon Gold Mines *NS* **33** B5-6
Rawdon Gold Mines *NS* **34** F1-2
Rawebb *MB* **11** A8
Rawebb *MB* **12** F8

Rawebb *MB* **13** A2
Rawhide Lake *ON* **17** F5
Raymond *AB* **6** F6
Raymond *AB* **7** E6
Raymond *ON* **18** D8
Raymond *ON* **21** B1
Raymore *SK* **11** D5-6
Reaboro *ON* **20** B8
Reaboro *ON* **21** D2-3
Reaburn *MB* **14** D4
Reader Lake *MB* **11** A7
Reader Lake *MB* **13** A1
Read Island PP *BC* **2** C2
Readlyn *SK* **11** F5
Rearguard Falls PP *BC* **6** B1-2
Rebecca Spit PMP *BC* **2** C2
Rebesca Lake *NT* **10** A6
Reboul, rivière *QC* **29** C8
Reboul, rivière *QC* **30** C1
Red Bank *NB* **31** D6
Red Bay *NL* **38** A4
Red Bay *NL* **39** D8
Red Bay *ON* **18** E5
Red Bay, LHN de *NL* **38** A4
Red Bay, LHN de *NL* **39** D8
Red Bay NHS *NL* **38** A4
Red Bay NHS *NL* **39** D8
Red Bluff PP *BC* **3** F5
Red Brook *NL* **36** C1
Red Cliff *NL* **36** B6
Red Cliff *NL* **37** B4
Red Cliff *NL* **37** B7
Red Cross Lake *MB* **15** F6
Red Deer *AB* **6** C5-6
Red Deer *AB* **8** F6
Red Deer, RNOM de *AB* **6** C5-6
Red Deer, RNOM de *AB* **8** F6
Red Deer Hill *SK* **11** B4-5
Red Deer Lake *AB* **8** B7
Red Deer Lake *MB* **11** B7
Red Deer Lake *MB* **11** B8
Red Deer Lake *MB* **13** B1
Red Deer Lake *MB* **13** B1
Red Deer Lake *ON* **18** C8
Red Deer NMBS *AB* **6** C5-6
Red Deer NMBS *AB* **8** F6
Red Deer Point *MB* **11** C8
Red Deer Point *MB* **13** C2
Red Deer River *AB* **6** C6
Red Deer River *AB* **6** D4-5
Red Deer River *AB* **6** D7-8
Red Deer River *AB* **7** A2
Red Deer River *AB* **7** B6
Red Deer River *AB* **7** B7-8
Red Deer River *AB* **8** F6-7
Red Deer River *AB* **11** D1
Red Deer River *SK* **11** B6-7
Red Earth *SK* **11** A6
Red Earth Creek *AB* **9** D4-5
Red Earth Creek *AB* **41** F1
Red Earth Lake *SK* **11** B6
Red Harbour *NL* **36** E7
Red Harbour *NL* **37** E5
Red Head *NB* **32** E4
Red Head *NB* **33** B1-2
Red Head Cove *NL* **37** C8
Red Indian Lake *NL* **36** B4-5
Red Indian Lake *NL* **37** B2-3
Red Island *NL* **36** E8
Red Island *NL* **36** E8
Red Island *NL* **37** E6
Red Island *NL* **37** E6
Red Islands *NS* **34** D6-7
Red Jacket *SK* **11** E7
Red Lake *ON* **13** D6
Red Lake *ON* **13** D6
Red Lake *ON* **16** B-C2
Red Lake *ON* **16** C2
Red Lake Road *ON* **13** E6
Red Lake Road *ON* **16** D2
Red Lodge PP *AB* **6** D5
Red Lodge PP *AB* **8** F5-6
Red Mountain *YT* **4** A-B3
Red Pass *BC* **6** B2
Red Pheasant *SK* **11** C3
Red Pine Lake *ON* **21** B2
Red Point *NS* **34** D7
Red Point *PE* **34** C4
Red Point *PE* **35** C2-3
Red Point *PE* **34** C4
Red Point PP *PE* **34** C4
Red Point PP *PE* **35** D8
Red Rapids *NB* **31** D3
Red Rapids *NB* **32** A1
Red River *BC* **4** F7
Red River *MB* **14** E5
Red River *NS* **34** A6
Red Rock *BC* **1** A-B7
Red Rock *ON* **16** E6
Red Rock *ON* **17** C1
Red Rock Point *NL* **39** A7
Red Rocks *SK* **11** D1
Red Rose *MB* **13** D3
Red Rose *MB* **14** C2
Red Sucker Lake *MB* **13** A6
Red Sucker Lake *MB* **13** A6
Red Sucker Point, RNP *ON* **16** E8
Red Sucker Point, RNP *ON* **17** C2-3
Red Sucker Point PNR *ON* **16** E8
Red Sucker Point PNR *ON* **17** C2-3
Red Sucker River *MB* **15** E-F6

Red Willow *AB* **6** C6
Red Willow *AB* **8** E7-8
Red Wine River *NL* **39** B4-5
Redberry Lake *SK* **11** C4
Redberry Lake NMBS *SK* **11** C4
Redbridge *ON* **17** F8
Redbridge *ON* **18** A4
Redbridge *ON* **22** D2
Redcliff *AB* **6** E7
Redcliff *AB* **7** D8
Redcliff *AB* **11** E1
Redcliff Island *NT* **10** C-D8
Redcross Lake *SK* **36** C4
Redcross Lake *SK* **37** C2
Redditt *ON* **13** E5-6
Redditt *ON* **16** D1-2
Redfern-Keily Creek *BC* **3** D6
Redfield *SK* **11** B3-4
Redickville *ON* **20** B5
Redknife River *NT* **10** E-F4
Redland *AB* **7** B5
Rednersville *ON* **21** E5
Redonda Bay *BC* **1** E6
Redonda Bay *BC* **2** B2
Redonda Island *BC* **1** E6
Redrock Lake *ON* **22** E3
Redstone *BC* **1** C6
Redstone Flat *BC* **1** C6
Redstone Lake *ON* **21** B2-3
Redstone River *NT* **4** B8
Redstone River *NT* **10** B1-2
Redvers *SK* **11** F7
Redvers *SK* **13** F1
Redwater *AB* **6** A6
Redwater *AB* **8** B7
Redwood Meadows *AB* **6** D5
Redwood Meadows *AB* **7** B3
Reeces Corners *ON* **19** C3
Reeces Corners *ON* **20** E2
Reed Bay *ON* **21** E6-7
Reed Lake *MB* **12** F8
Reed Lake *MB* **15** F2
Reed Lake *SK* **11** E4
Reedy Creek *MB* **14** B3
Reef Icefield *BC* **6** B2
Reef's Harbour *NL* **38** B3
Reeve *NB* **14** C2
Reevecraig *ON* **21** B8
Refuge Cove *BC* **1** E6
Refuge Cove *BC* **2** C2-3
Refuge-du-Col-Abbot, LHN du *AB* **7** A-B1
Regent *MB* **11** F8
Regent *MB* **13** F1-2
Regent *MB* **14** F1
Regina *SK* **11** E5
Regina Beach *SK* **11** D-E5
Regina Beach PRS *SK* **11** D5
Reginaville *NL* **37** F7
Regway *SK* **11** F5-6
Reid Lake *BC* **1** A7
Reid Lake *NT* **10** B8
Reid Lake *NT* **41** C4
Reid Lake TP *NT* **10** C-D7
Reid Lake TP *NT* **41** D2
Reidville *NL* **36** A3-4
Reidville *NL* **37** A2
Reindeer Island *MB* **13** C3
Reindeer Lake *NT* **10** B7
Reindeer Lake *SK* **12** C7
Reindeer Lake *SK* **15** C1
Reindeer Lake *SK* **41** A7
Reindeer Mountain *YT* **4** B2
Reindeer River *SK* **12** E6
Reine-Charlotte, bassin de la *BC* **1** D3
Reine-Charlotte, îles de la *BC* **1** B1-2
Reine-Élisabeth, îles de la *AB* **42** A3-4 B2-3
Reine-Élisabeth, îles de la *NU* **42** A4 B2-3
Reine-Maud, golfe de la *NU* **41** C3-4
Reine-Maud, golfe de la *NU* **42** F3
Reinfeld *MB* **13** F3
Reinfeld *MB* **14** F4
Reinland *MB* **13** F3
Reinland *MB* **14** F4
Relais-Gabriel *QC* **39** D1
Relique, lac *QC* **23** A8
Relique, lac *QC* **26** B3
Remac *BC* **7** D2
Remblais-de-Southwold, LHN des *ON* **19** D4
Remblais-de-Southwold, LHN des *ON* **20** F3
Rembrandt *MB* **13** D3-4
Rembrandt *MB* **14** C5
Rémigny *QC* **17** D8
Rémigny *QC* **23** F2
Rémigny, lac *QC* **23** E-F2
Renard, baie du *QC* **30** A7
Renard, lac du *QC* **30** A7
Renards, pointe aux *QC* **32** A6-7
Rencontre, lac de la *QC* **28** E2
Rencontre East *NL* **36** D6-7
Rencontre East *NL* **37** D4-5
Rencontre West *NL* **36** D-E5
Rencontre West *NL* **37** D-E3

Rendezvous Island South PP *BC* **2** B2
Rene Brunelle PP *ON* **17** B5-6
Reneault *QC* **17** C8
Reneault *QC* **23** D2
Renews *NL* **37** F8
Renews-Cappahayden *NL* **37** F8
Renforth *NB* **32** D4
Renforth *NB* **33** A1
Renfrew *NS* **33** B6
Renfrew *NS* **34** F1-2
Renfrew *ON* **21** A6
Renne, rivière le *QC* **24** D8
Renne, rivière le *QC* **27** E3-4
Rennell Sound *BC* **1** A-B1
Rennie *MB* **13** E5
Rennie *MB* **14** E7
Rennison Island *BC* **1** B3
Reno *AB* **9** E3-4
Renommée, pointe à la *QC* **30** A-B2
Renous *QC* **24** D6-7
Renous River *NB* **31** D6
Renown *SK* **11** D5
Renton *BC* **19** C6-7
Renton *ON* **20** F5-6
Renwer *MB* **11** C8
Renwer *MB* **13** C1-2
Repentigny *QC* **24** D6
Repentigny *QC* **27** D2
Repos, lac du *QC* **25** D5
Repulse Bay (Naujaat) *NU* **41** C5-6
Reserve *SK* **11** C6-7
Reserve Mines *NS* **34** C8
Resolin, lac *QC* **22** D5
Resolute (Qasuittuq) *NU* **42** D4
Resolution Bay *NT* **10** E7
Resolution Island *NU* **40** B6
Resource *SK* **11** B5-6
Resthaven Icefield *AB* **6** B2
Resthaven Mountain *AB* **6** B2
Restigo, ZEC *QC* **22** C3
Restigouche River *NB* **29** D-E5
Restigouche River *NB* **29** E-F4
Restigouche River *NB* **31** B3-4
Restigouche River *NB* **31** B-C3
Reston *MB* **11** F8
Reston *MB* **13** F1
Restoule *ON* **17** F8
Restoule *ON* **18** B7-8
Restoule *ON* **22** E1
Restoule Lake *ON* **17** F7-8
Restoule Lake *ON* **22** E1
Restoule PP *ON* **17** F7-8
Restoule PP *ON* **18** B7
Restoule PP *ON* **22** E1
Restoule River *ON* **18** B7
Retty, lac *QC* **22** B6
Revelstoke *BC* **6** D3
Revelstoke, Lake *BC* **6** D2-3
Revelstone, lac *QC* **25** D-E4
Revenue *SK* **6** C8
Revenue *SK* **11** C3
Reward *SK* **6** C8
Reward *SK* **11** C2
Rexton *NB* **31** E8
Rexton *NB* **32** A6
Reykjavik *MB* **13** D3
Reykjavik *MB* **14** B2-3
Reynaud *SK* **11** C5
Rhéaume, lac *QC* **25** B6
Rhéaume, lac *QC* **28** D2
Rhein *SK* **11** D7
Rhineland *SK* **11** E3-4
Ribstone *AB* **6** B7-8
Ribstone *AB* **11** C1
Ribstone Creek *AB* **6** B-C7
Ribstone Creek *AB* **11** B2 C1
Rice Lake *ON* **17** D5
Rice Lake *ON* **21** E3
Rice Lake *SK* **11** C4
Rice Lake CA *ON* **21** E3
Rice Point *PE* **35** E4
Rice Point *PE* **35** E4
Rice River Provincial Reserve *SK* **11** B7
Rice River Provincial Reserve *SK* **13** A-B1
Riceton *SK* **11** E5-6
Riceville *ON* **24** D3
Rich, Cape *ON* **18** F6
Rich, Cape *ON* **20** A5
Richan *ON* **13** E6-7
Richan *ON* **16** D2
Richard *SK* **11** B3
Richard Collinson Inlet *NT* **5** B4
Richard Collinson Inlet *NT* **42** D2
Richard Point *PE* **35** E4
Richards Island *NT* **5** B4
Richards Lake *AB* **11** E5-6
Richards Landing *ON* **17** F4
Richardson Islands *NU* **40** D1
Richardson Islands *NU* **42** F2

Richardson Islands *NU* **42** F2
Richardson Lake *AB* **9** B7
Richardson Lake *AB* **12** B3
Richardson Lake NMBS *AB* **9** B7
Richardson Lake NMBS *AB* **12** B2
Richardson Mountains *YT* **5** C3 D3-4
Richardson River *AB* **9** B-C7
Richardson River *AB* **12** B-C2
Richardson River Dunes Wildland PP *AB* **9** B-C7
Richardson River Dunes Wildland PP *AB* **12** B-C2
Richdale *AB* **6** D7
Richdale *AB* **7** A7
Richdale *AB* **11** C1
Riche, Point *NL* **38** C3
Riche, Point *NL* **40** E8
Richelieu *QC* **24** D6-7
Richelieu *QC* **27** E2
Richelieu, rivière *QC* **24** C-D7
Richelieu, rivière *QC* **27** D-E2
Richer *MB* **13** F4
Richer *MB* **14** E6
Richfield *NS* **33** E1-2
Richibucto *NB* **31** E8
Richibucto *NB* **32** A6
Richibucto Cape *NB* **31** E8
Richibucto Cape *NB* **32** A6
Richibucto River *NB* **31** E7
Richibucto River *NB* **32** A5
Richibucto-Village *NB* **31** E8
Richibucto-Village *NB* **32** A6
Rich Lake *AB* **6** A7
Rich Lake *AB* **9** F7
Rich Lake *AB* **12** F1
Richlea *SK* **11** D3
Richmond *BC* **1** F6-7
Richmond *BC* **2** E4-5
Richmond *ON* **19** D5
Richmond *ON* **20** F4
Richmond *ON* **21** B8
Richmond *ON* **24** E2
Richmond *PE* **32** A7
Richmond *PE* **34** B1
Richmond *PE* **35** D2
Richmond *QC* **27** E4
Richmond Corner *NB* **31** E3
Richmond Corner *NB* **32** B1
Richmond Hill *ON* **19** A8
Richmond Hill *ON* **20** D8
Richmond Hill *ON* **21** F1
Richmound *SK* **6** E8
Richmound *SK* **11** E2
Rich Valley *AB* **6** A5
Rich Valley *AB* **8** B5
Riddell River *YT* **4** C5
Rideau, canal *ON* **21** B-C8
Rideau, canal *ON* **21** D7
Rideau, canal *ON* **24** F2
Rideau, RNOM de *ON* **21** C8
Rideau, RNOM de *ON* **24** F2
Rideau Canal *ON* **21** B-C8
Rideau Canal *ON* **21** D7
Rideau Canal *ON* **24** F1
Rideau Ferry *ON* **21** C7
Rideau Ferry *ON* **24** F1
Rideau NMBS *ON* **21** C8
Rideau NMBS *ON* **24** F2
Rideau River *ON* **21** B-C8
Rideau River *ON* **24** E2
Rideau River PP *ON* **21** B8
Rideau River PP *ON* **24** E2
Ridgedale *SK* **11** B5-6
Ridge River *ON* **17** A4
Ridgetown *ON* **19** D3
Ridgevalley *AB* **9** F3
Ridgeville *MB* **13** F4
Ridgeville *ON* **19** C8
Ridgeville *ON* **20** E7
Ridgeway *ON* **20** E8
Ridgewood *AB* **8** F6
Riding Mountain *MB* **11** B8
Riding Mountain *MB* **13** D1-2
Riding Mountain NP *MB* **11** D8
Riding Mountain NP *MB* **13** D1-2
Riding Mountain NP *MB* **14** B-C1
Riel House NHS *MB* **14** E5
Rigaud *QC* **24** D3
Right Serpentine River *NB* **29** F5
Right Serpentine River *NB* **31** C3-4
Rigolet *NL* **40** D8
Rigolet (Kikiak) *NL* **39** B6-7
Riley Brook *NB* **31** C3-4
Riley Lake *ON* **21** D5
Rimbey *AB* **6** C5
Rimbey *AB* **8** E5
Rimington *ON* **21** D5
Rimouski *QC* **29** C3
Rimouski, RF de *QC* **29** D3
Rimouski, RF de *QC* **31** A2

Rimouski, rivière *QC* **29** D3
Rimouski, rivière *QC* **29** D3
Rimouski, rivière *QC* **31** A1-2
Rimouski-Est *QC* **29** C3
Ringwood *QC* **20** C7
Ringwood *ON* **21** E1
Riondel *BC* **6** F3-4
Riou Lake *SK* **12** B4-5
Ripault, lac *QC* **28** E6
Ripley *ON* **20** B3
Ripon *QC* **24** C3
Ripples *NB* **31** F5
Ripples *NB* **32** C3
Riske Creek *BC* **1** C7
Rissers Beach PP *NS* **33** D4-5
Ristigouche, rivière *NB* **31** B3
Ristigouche, rivière *QC* **29** D5
Ristigouche, rivière *QC* **31** A3-4 B3
Rita, lac *QC* **25** A6
Rita, lac *QC* **26** F6
Rita, lac *QC* **28** D2
Ritchie *QC* **32** C1-7
Ritchie *SK* **11** F5
Rivard, lac *QC* **26** B7
River aux Sables PP *ON* **17** F5-6
River aux Sables PP *ON* **18** A3-4
Riverbank *NB* **31** E3
Riverbank *NB* **32** A1
Rivercourse *AB* **6** B8
Rivercourse *AB* **11** C1
River Bourgeois *NS* **34** D6
River Brook *NL* **36** C2
River Charlo *NB* **29** D7
River Charlo *NB* **31** A5
Rivercrest *MB* **14** D1
Riverdale *NS* **33** D2
Riverdale *PE* **35** E4
Riverdale *PE* **35** E4
River de Chute *NB* **31** E3
River de Chute *NB* **32** B1
River Denys *NS* **34** D6
River Drive Park *ON* **20** B7
River Drive Park *ON* **21** E1
Riverfield *QC* **24** E5-6
Riverfield *QC* **27** F1
River Glade *NB* **31** F7-8
River Glade *NB* **32** B5-6
Riverhead *NL* **37** D7
Riverhead *NL* **37** F7
River Hebert *NS* **32** C7
River Hills *MB* **13** E4-5
River Hills *MB* **14** D6-7
Riverhurst *SK* **11** D4
River John *NS* **34** D3
River of Ponds *NL* **38** C3
River of Ponds *NL* **39** E7-8
River of Ponds Lake *NL* **38** C3
River of Ponds Lake *NL* **39** E7
River Philip *NS* **32** C8
River Philip *NS* **34** E1
Riverport *NS* **33** D5
Rivers *MB* **13** E2
Rivers *MB* **14** D1
Rivers Inlet *BC* **1** D4
Rivers Inlet *BC* **1** C-D4
Rivers PP *MB* **11** E8
Rivers PP *MB* **14** D1
Rivers, Lake of the *SK* **11** E-F5
Riverside *NS* **33** A7
Riversdale *NS* **33** A7
Riversdale *NS* **33** D1
Riversdale *ON* **20** B3
Riverside *NS* **14** F4-5
Riverside-Albert *NB* **32** C6
Riverton *MB* **13** D4
Riverton *MB* **14** B5
Riverton *NS* **33** A7
Riverton *NS* **34** D3
Riverton *PE* **35** E6
Riverview *NB* **31** F8
Riverview *NB* **32** B6
Riverview *ON* **20** B5
Riverview Heights *ON* **21** C8
Riverview Heights *ON* **24** F2
Rivett Lake *NT* **10** B7-8 C7-8
Rivière-à-Claude *QC* **29** A7
Rivière-à-Pierre *QC* **27** A7
Rivière-au-Portage *NB* **31** D7-8
Rivière-au-Renard *QC* **30** B3
Rivière-au-Tonnerre *QC* **39** E-F3
Rivière-aux-Graines *QC* **39** E-F3
Rivière-aux-Rats *QC* **25** D7
Rivière-aux-Rats *QC* **27** A3
Rivière-aux-Rats, ZEC de la *QC* **26** C8
Rivière-aux-Rats, ZEC de la *QC* **28** A4
Rivière-Beaudette *QC* **24** E5
Rivière-Bersimis *QC* **29** B3
Rivière Black, APP *QC* **31** D7

Rivière-Blanche,
ZEC de la QC **28** F4
Rivière-Bleue QC **29** E2
Rivière-Bonaventure,
ZEC de la QC **29** B-C8
Rivière-Bonaventure,
ZEC de la QC **29** C8
Rivière-Bonaventure,
ZEC de la QC **29** C-D8
Rivière-Bonaventure,
ZEC de la QC **30** B-C1
Rivière-Bonaventure,
ZEC de la QC **30** C-D1
Rivière-Cap-Chat,
RF de la QC **29** B6
Rivière-Cap-Chat,
ZEC de la QC **29** A-B6
Rivière-Cascapédia,
RF de la QC **29** B-C7
Rivière-Cascapédia,
RF de la QC **29** C7
Rivière-Cascapédia,
RF de la QC **29** B6-7
Rivière-Dartmouth,
ZEC de la QC **30** B2
Rivière-de-la-Chaloupe QC
30 A5-6
Rivière-de-Sable,
RNOM de la NS **33** E3-5
Rivière des Escoumins, ZEC
de la QC **28** C8
Rivière des Escoumins, ZEC
de la QC **29** C1
Rivière-du-Loup QC **28** D8
Rivière-du-Loup QC **29** D1
Rivière-du-Portage NB
30 F2
Rivière-du-Portage NB
31 C8
Rivière-Éternité QC **28** C7
Rivière-Héva QC **23** E4
Rivière-la-Madeleine QC
29 A8
Rivière-la-Madeleine QC
30 A1
Rivière-Madeleine,
ZEC de la QC **29** A8
Rivière-Madeleine,
ZEC de la QC **30** A-B1
Rivière-Malbaie QC **28** E7
Rivière-Matane,
RF de la QC **29** B4-5
Rivière-Matane,
ZEC de la QC **29** B5
Rivière-Matapédia,
RF de la QC **31** A4
Rivière-Matapédia,
RF de la QC **29** C5
Rivière-Matawin,
RF de la QC **29** D5
Rivière-Matawin QC **25** E7
Rivière-Matawin QC **27** A3
Rivière-Moisie,
RF de la QC **39** E-F2
Rivière-Nechako,
RNOM de la BC **1** A6
Rivière-Ouelle QC
28 E7-8 F7-8
Rivière-Paspébiac QC
29 D8
Rivière-Paspébiac QC
30 D1
Rivière-Paspébiac QC **31** A7
Rivière-Patapédia,
RF de la QC **29** D4-5
Rivière-Pentecôte QC **39** F1
Rivière-Petit-Saguenay,
RF de la QC **28** D7
Rivière-Pigou QC **39** E2-3
Rivière Qui Barre AB **8** C6
Rivière-Ristigouche,
RF de la QC **31** A4
Rivière-Sainte-Anne,
RF de la QC **29** A-B6
Rivière-Sainte-Marguerite
QC **28** C8
Rivière Sainte-Marguerite,
ZEC de la QC **28** C7-8
Rivière-Saint-Jean QC
39 E-F3
Rivière-Saint-Jean,
RF de la QC **30** C2
Rivière-Saint-Jean,
RF de la QC **30** B-C2
Rivière-Saint-Paul QC
38 A2
Rivière-Saint-Paul QC
39 D7
Rivière-Saint-Paul QC
40 E8
Rivière-Trois-Pistoles QC
29 D1-2
Rivière-Verte NB **29** F3-4
Rivière-Verte NB **31** C2
Rivière-York,
ZEC de la QC **29** B8
Rivière-York,
ZEC de la QC **30** B1
Rivière-York,
ZEC de la QC **30** B2
Rivington QC **24** C4
Roachvale NS **34** E5
Roachville NS **32** C5
Road River YT **5** D4
Roaring River MB **11** C7-8
Roaring River MB **13** C1
Roaring River ON **16** D-E5
Robb AB **6** B3-4
Robb AB **8** D7
Robb Lake NT **10** A5-6
Robe Noire, lac de la QC
39 E4
Roberge, lac QC **25** D8
Roberge, lac QC **27** A3

Robert, lac QC **26** C5
Robert-Bourassa,
réservoir QC **40** E4
Robertine, lac QC **23** C8
Robertine, lac QC **26** D2
Robert's Arm NL **36** A6
Robert's Arm NL **37** A4
Robert's Arm NL **38** F5
Robert's Arm NL **39** F8
Robertson, lac QC **23** C3
Robertson, lac QC **39** E6
Robertson Lake AB **9** A6
Robertson Lake AB **12** A1
Robertsonville QC **27** C5-6
Roberts Peak BC **1** B8
Roberts Peak BC **6** B1
Robertville NB **29** E7
Robertville NB **31** B6
Roberval QC **26** E8
Roberval QC **28** C4
Robeson, détroit de NU
42 A5
Robeson Channel NU
42 A5
Robichaud NB **32** B7
Robichaud NB **35** E1
Robin, rivière QC **23** C6
Robinhood SK **11** B3
Robinson YT **4** E4
Robinsons NL **36** C1-2
Robinsons River NL **36** C2
Robinsonville NB **29** E5-6
Robinsonville NB **31** B4
Robitaille Lake ON **21** A4
Robitaille Lake ON **22** F4
Roblin MB **11** D7-8
Roblin MB **13** D1
Roblin ON **21** D6
Robsart SK **11** F2
Robson BC **6** F3
Robson, lac QC **23** F8
Robson, lac QC **25** B2
Robson, Mount BC **6** B2
Rocanville SK **11** E7
Rocanville SK **13** E1
Roc-Cousacouta, lac QC
25 D6
Roc-Cousacouta, lac QC
27 A1-2
Roc-Cousacouta, lac QC
28 F1-2
Roche, Pointe de NT **10** E6
Rochebaucourt QC **23** C5
Roche Lake PP BC **6** E1
Roche Percée SK **11** F7
Rocher, lac du NT **10** D-E7
Rocher River NT **10** D-E7
Rochers, rivière aux QC
39 E2
Rochers-aux-Oiseaux,
RNOM de QC **30** E8
Roches Point ON **20** B7
Roches Point ON **21** E1
Rochester AB **6** A6
Rochester AB **8** A6
Rochester AB **9** F6
Rochester, lac QC **23** B7
Rochester, lac QC **26** C1
Rocheuses, contreforts des
AB **6** B3 C3-4 D4
Rocheuses, contreforts des
AB **7** C3 D3-4 E4
Rocheuses, contreforts des
AB **8** D-E2 E-F3
Rocheuses, contreforts des
BC **1** A8
Rocheuses, contreforts des
BC **3** C6 D6-7
Rocheuses, montagnes AB
6 B2 C2-3
Rocheuses, montagnes AB
8 E1 F1-2
Rocheuses, montagnes BC
1 A-B8
Rocheuses, montagnes BC
3 D6 E6-7
Rocheuses, montagnes BC
7 C1-2 D2
Rocheuses, montagnes BC
6 D-E4 E-F5
Rocheuses, montagnes BC
7 C-E3
Rocheuses canadiennes,
parcs des montagnes AB
6 C3-4
Rocheuses canadiennes,
parcs des montagnes AB
7 A1-2
Rocheuses canadiennes,
parcs des montagnes AB
8 E1-2
Rocheuses canadiennes,
parcs des montagnes BC
7 B1-2
Rocheville NB **31** B7
Rochfort Bridge AB **6** A5
Rochfort Bridge AB **8** B4-5
Rochon Lake AB **13** A5-6
Rochon Sands AB **8** B8
Rochon Sands AB **8** E7
Rochon Sands PP AB **6** C7
Rochon Sands PP AB **8** E7
Rock Bay BC **1** E5
Rock Bay BC **2** B2
Rock Bay MPP BC **1** E5
Rock Bay MPP BC **2** B1-2
Rockburn QC **24** E5
Rockcliffe Park ON **21** A8
Rockcliffe Park ON **24** D2
Rock Creek BC **6** F2
Rockford ON **18** F5
Rockford ON **20** A4
Rock Glen CA ON **19** C3-4
Rock Glen CA ON **20** E2-3
Rockglen SK **11** F5
Rock Harbour NL **36** E7
Rock Harbour NL **37** E5
Rockhaven SK **11** B3

Rockingham ON **21** B5
Rock Island Lake AB **9** E6
Rock Lake MB **14** F2
Rock Lake ON **17** F4
Rock Lake ON **21** A3
Rock Lake ON **22** F3
Rock Lake-Solomon Creek
Wildland PP AB **6** B2-3
Rock Lake-Solomon Creek
Wildland PP AB **8** C1
Rockland NS **33** F3
Rockland ON **24** D3
Rocklin NS **33** A7
Rocklin NS **34** E3
Rocklyn ON **18** F6
Rocklyn ON **20** A5
Rock Point PP ON **19** D8
Rock Point PP ON **20** F7
Rockport NB **32** C7
Rockport NB **21** D7-8
Rock Ridge MB **13** C2
Rock River YT **4** E8
Rock River YT **5** D3
Rocksprings ON **21** C8
Rocksprings ON **24** F2
Rockton ON **19** B7
Rockton ON **20** D6
Rockwood ON **19** A7
Rockwood ON **20** D6
Rockwood, RNF de MB
14 D5
Rockwood CA ON **19** A7
Rockwood CA ON **20** D6
Rockwood NWA MB **14** D5
Rocky Bay NL **39** B8
Rocky Bay NL **16** E6
Rocky Bay NL **17** B1
Rocky Brook NB **31** D4 E5
Rocky Cove NL **39** A7
Rockyford AB **6** D6
Rockyford AB **7** B5
Rocky Harbour NL **38** E2
Rocky Harbour NL **39** F7
Rocky Inlet ON **16** E-F2
Rocky Island Lake ON
17 E5
Rocky Lake MB **11** A7
Rocky Lake MB **13** A1
Rocky Lane AB **9** B4
Rocky Mountain NS **33** A8
Rocky Mountain NS **34** E4
Rocky Mountain Foothills
AB **6** B3 C3
Rocky Mountain Foothills
AB **7** B2-3 C3
Rocky Mountain Foothills
AB **8** D-E2 E-F3
Rocky Mountain Foothills
BC **3** C6 D6-7
Rocky Mountain House AB
6 C4-5
Rocky Mountain House AB
8 E4-5
Rocky Mountain House,
LHN AB **6** C4-5
Rocky Mountain House,
LHN AB **8** F4-5
Rocky Mountain House NHS
AB **6** C4-5
Rocky Mountain House NHS
AB **8** F4-5
Rocky Mountains AB
8 E-F1
Rocky Mountains BC **1** A8
Rocky Mountains BC
3 B-C5
Rocky Mountains BC
6 B2 C2-3
Rocky Mountains BC
7 C1-2 D2
Rocky Point BC **2** F4
Rocky Rapids AB **6** B5
Rocky Rapids AB **8** D5
Rocky Ridge Pond NL
36 C-D3
Rocky Ridge Pond NL
37 C-D1
Rocky Saugeen River ON
20 B4
Roddick, lac QC **22** E7-8
Roddick, lac QC **24** B2
Roddick, lac QC **25** F2
Roddickton NL **38** C4
Roddickton NL **39** E8
Rodef AB **8** B7
Roderick Haig-Brown
PP BC **6** D2
Roderick Island BC **1** B-C3
Roderick Lake ON **13** D5
Roderick Lake ON **14** A8
Roderick Lake ON **16** B2
Rodgers Cove NL **36** A7
Rodgers Cove NL **37** A5
Rodgers Cove NL **38** F7
Rodin, lac QC **22** A6
Rodney ON **19** D4
Rodney ON **20** F3
Rodney Pond NL **36** B7
Rodney Pond NL **37** B5
Roe Lake MB **15** D3
Roe Lake SK **9** D8
Roe Lake SK **12** D3
Roes Welcome Sound NU
40 A2-3
Roes Welcome Sound NU
41 B6
Roger, lac QC **17** D8
Roger, lac QC **23** F2-3
Rogers MB **14** C1
Rogers SK **11** E4
Rogerson Lake NL **36** C4-5
Rogerson Lake NL **37** C2-3

Rogers Pass BC **6** D3
Rogers Pass BC **6** D3
Rogers Pass NHS BC **6** D3
Rogersville NB **31** D7
Rogersville NB **32** A5
Rognons, lac aux QC **25** C8
Rognons, lac aux QC **28** E4
Rognons, lac aux QC **28** F7
Rohault, lac QC **26** C5
Rokeby SK **11** D7
Roland NS **33** F3
Roland MB **14** F4
Rolfe Lake NT **10** C7-8
Rolla AB **3** E8
Rolla BC **9** E2
Rollet ON **17** D8
Rollet QC **23** E2
Rolley Lake PP BC **1** F7
Rolley Lake PP BC **2** D5-6
Rollingdam NB **32** D2
Rolling Hills AB **6** E7
Rolling Hills AB **7** D7
Rolling Hills AB **11** E1
Rolling Hills Lake AB **7** D7
Rolling River MB **11** E8
Rolling River MB **13** E2
Rolling River MB **14** C1
Rollo Bay PE **34** C4
Rollo Bay PE **35** E7
Rollo Bay PE **35** D7
Rolly View AB **6** B6
Rolly View AB **8** D6
Rolphton ON **22** E4
Romaine, rivière QC
39 C3-4
Romaine, rivière QC
39 D-E4
Romaine, rivière QC
40 E-F7
Romaines NL **36** B-C2
Romance SK **11** C5
Roman Valley NS **34** E5
Roméo, lac QC **26** C3
Rond, lac QC **26** C7
Rond, lac QC **28** A6
Rondeau Harbour ON **19** E3
Rondeau Park ON **19** E3
Rondeau PP ON **19** E3
Rondelet, lac QC **22** A2
Rondelet, lac QC **23** F2
Rooms NL **38** E3-4
Roosville BC **6** F5
Roosville BC **7** F2-3
Root, Mount BC **4** F2
Root Lake MB **11** A7
Root Lake MB **13** A1
Root River NT **10** C2
Rope Cove NL **36** B2
Roquemaure QC **17** C7-8
Roquemaure QC **23** C2
Rorey Lake NT **5** D6-7
Rorke Lake ON **15** F6-7
Rorketon MB **13** D2
Rorketon MB **14** A2
Rosa MB **13** F4
Rosa MB **14** F5
Rosaireville NB **31** D7
Rosalind AB **8** B6
Rosalind AB **8** E8
Rosalind AB **11** B1
Roscoe Bay PP BC **1** E6
Roscoe Bay PP BC **2** C2-3
Roscoe Inlet BC **1** C4
Rose NS **32** C8
Rose NS **33** A5
Rose NS **34** E1
Roseau River MB **13** F4
Roseau River MB **14** F6
Roseau River MB **14** F5-6
Rosebank MB **13** F3
Rosebank MB **14** F4
Rosebank PE **35** B2
Rosebary Lake ON **21** A2
Rose Bay NS **33** D5
Roseberry PE **35** F5-6
Roseberry River ON
13 B6-7 C7
Rosebery PP BC **6** E2
Rose Blanche NL **36** D2
Rose Blanche-Harbour
Le Cou NL **36** D-E2
Rosebud AB **6** D6
Rosebud AB **7** B5
Rosebud Creek YT **4** B3
Rosebud River AB **6** D6
Rosebud River AB **7** B4-5
Rosedale AB **6** D6
Rosedale AB **7** A6
Rosedale BC **2** E6
Rosedale ON **20** A8
Rosedale ON **21** D2
Rosedale ON **21** D6
Rosehall ON **21** E5
Roseisle MB **13** F3
Roseisle MB **14** E3
Roseland MB **14** E1
Rose Lynn AB **7** A7
Rosemary AB **6** D7
Rosemary AB **7** C6
Rosemary AB **11** D1
Rosemere QC **24** D5-6
Rosemere QC **27** E1
Rosemere QC **21** F1-2
Rosemont ON **20** B6
Rosenburg MB **14** B5
Roseneath ON **21** B3-4
Roseneath PE **34** C3
Roseneath PE **35** E6
Rosenfeld MB **13** F3-4
Rosenfeld MB **14** F4-5
Rosengart MB **13** F3

Rosengart MB **14** F4
Rosenhof SK **11** E3-4
Rosenort MB **13** F3
Rosenort MB **14** E4-5
Rose Point BC **1** A2
Rose Prairie BC **3** D8
Rose Prairie BC **9** D1-2
Roseray SK **11** E3
Rose River YT **4** D5
Rosetown MB **14** F4
Rosetown SK **11** D3
Rose Valley SK **11** C6
Rosevear AB **8** C3
Roseville ON **19** B6
Roseville ON **20** D5
Roseville PE **35** B1
Rosewall Creek PP BC
1 F5-6
Rosewall Creek PP BC **2** D2
Roseway NS **33** E3
Roseway NS **33** F3
Roseway River NS **33** E2-3
Rosewood AB **14** E5-6
Rosiers, cap des QC **30** B3
Rosiers, rivière aux QC
29 A2-3
Rosiers, rivière des QC
27 D4
Roslin ON **21** D5
Roslyn Lake ON **16** E7
Roslyn Lake ON **17** B-C1
Ross MB **13** F4
Ross, lac QC **25** A8
Ross, lac QC **26** E8
Ross, lac QC **28** C4
Ross Bay Junction NL **39** C2
Rossburn MB **11** D8
Rossburn MB **13** D-E1
Rosseau ON **18** D8
Rosseau ON **21** B1
Rosseau River ON **18** D8
Rosseau River ON **21** B1
Rosseau Road ON **18** D7
Rosseau, Lake ON **18** D8
Rosseau, Lake ON **21** B1
Rossendale MB **13** E3
Rossendale MB **14** E3
Rosser MB **13** E3
Rosser MB **14** D5
Ross Ferry NS **34** C7
Ross Ferry NS **34** C7
Rossfield NS **33** A8
Rossfield NS **34** E4
Rossignol, lac NS **33** D3
Rossignol, Lake NS **33** D3
Rossington AB **6** A5
Rossington AB **8** B6
Ross Island NB **13** A3
Ross Island NB **32** F3
Ross Lake NT **10** C7
Ross Lake PP BC **3** F4
Rossland BC **6** F3
Rossmore ON **21** E5
Ross Point NU **42** D2-3
Rosslyn Village ON **16** F5-6
Rossport ON **16** E7
Rossport ON **17** C1
Rossport, camping
provincial ON **16** E6-7
Rossport, camping
provincial ON **17** C1
Rossport Provincial
Campground ON **16** E6-7
Rossport Provincial
Campground ON **17** C1
Ross River YT **4** C6 C-D5
Ross River YT **4** D5
Rossville MB **13** A3-4
Rossville NB **31** F3-4
Rossville MB **32** B2
Rossway NS **32** F4
Rossway NS **33** C1-2
Rosswood BC **3** F3-4
Rosthern SK **11** B4
Rostock ON **19** B5
Rostock ON **20** D4
Rothesay NB **32** D4
Rothesay NB **33** A1
Rothsay NB **19** A6
Rothsay ON **20** C5
Roti Bay NL **36** D5-6
Roti Bay NL **37** D4
Rottenfish River ON
13 A-B7
Rouge, Cape NL **38** B-C5
Rouge, Cape NL **39** A7
Rouge, lac QC **25** E4
Rouge, lac QC **26** C3
Rouge, parc ON **19** A8
Rouge, parc ON **20** C7
Rouge, parc ON **21** F1-2
Rouge, rivière MB **14** F5
Rouge, rivière MB **14** F5
Rouge, rivière MB **14** E4
Rouge, rivière QC **25** E4
Rouge-Matawin, RF QC
24 A4
Rouge-Matawin, RF QC
25 E4
Rougemont QC **24** D7
Rougemont QC **27** E2-3
Rouge Park ON **19** A8
Rouge Park ON **20** C7
Rouge Park ON **21** F1-2
Rouge River ON **19** A8
Rouge River ON **20** C7
Rouge River ON **21** F1
Rouge River YT **4** B8
Roughrock Lake ON **14** D8
Rouillard, lac QC **23** E4
Roulante Lake NT **10** A6-7
Rouleau SK **11** E5

Roulier QC **17** D8
Roulier QC **23** F2
Roundabout NL **36** F6
Roundabout NL **37** F4
Round Bay NS **33** F3
Round Harbour NL **36** D5
Round Harbour NL **37** D3
Round Harbour NL **38** E5
Round Hill AB **6** B6
Round Hill AB **8** D7
Round Hill AB **11** B1
Round Hill NS **32** F5
Round Hill NS **33** C1
Round Island NS **34** C8
Round Island Lake ON
22 F3
Round Lake NS **35** F2
Round Lake ON **18** A5
Round Lake ON **21** A5
Round Lake ON **21** D4
Round Lake ON **22** F1
Round Lake ON **22** F4-5
Round Lake Centre ON
21 A4
Round Lake Centre ON
22 F4
Round Lake PP ON **18** C7
Round Pond NL **36** C5-6
Round Pond NL **37** C3-4
Round Valley AB **8** C-D5
Rounthwaite MB **13** F2
Rounthwaite MB **14** E1-2
Routhierville QC **29** D5
Routhierville QC **31** A4
Rouvray, lac QC **28** A6
Rouyn-Noranda QC **17** D8
Rouyn-Noranda QC
23 D2-3
Rouyn-Noranda QC **23** E2-3
Rowan Lake ON **13** F6
Rowan Lake ON **16** E2
Rowatt SK **11** E5
Rowdy Lake ON **13** E5
Rowdy Lake ON **14** C8
Rowena MB **31** D3
Rowley AB **6** C6
Rowley AB **7** A5
Rowley Island NU **41** B6
Rowley Island NU **42** F6
Rowley River NU **41** A-B7
Rowley River NU **42** E6
Roxboro PE **35** C2
Roxton Falls QC **24** D8
Roxton Falls QC **27** E3
Roxton Pond QC **24** D7-8
Roxton Pond QC **27** E3
Roxton-Sud QC **24** D8
Roxton-Sud QC **27** E3
Roy, lac QC **26** C4
Royal Geographical
Society Islands NU
41 B-C4
Royal Geographical
Society Islands NU
42 F3
Royal Park AB **8** C8
Royston BC **1** F6
Royston BC **2** D2
Ruaux, île aux QC **27** A6
Ruban, rivière QC **25** B5
Ruban, rivière QC **26** F5
Ruban, rivière QC **28** D1
Rubin Beach SK **11** B7
Ruby Lake PP ON **16** E6
Ruby Lake PP ON **17** C1
Ruby Range YT **4** D2
Rubyrock Lake PP BC **1** A5
Rubyrock Lake PP BC **3** F5
Ruckle PP BC **2** E4
Ruddell SK **11** C3
Ruddock MB **12** E7
Ruddock MB **15** E1-2
Rufus Lake NT **5** A6
Rugged Point PMP BC **1** E4
Ruis Lake AB **9** B5
Ruis Lake AB **12** B1
Ruisseau-à-Rebours QC
29 A7
Ruisseau-Big, RNF du QC
19 D6
Ruisseau-Big, RNF du QC
20 F5
Ruisseau-Castor QC
29 A6-7
Ruisseau-Vert QC **29** A3
Rumely SK **11** B6
Rumsey AB **6** C6
Rumsey AB **7** A5
Runciman SK **11** B6
Runnymede ON **29** D5
Runnymede SK **11** D7
Runnymede SK **13** D1
Runt Creek YT **5** D1-2
Rupert QC **21** A7
Rupert QC **22** F7
Rupert QC **24** C1-2
Rupert, baie de QC **40** F4
Rupert, lac QC **25** D4
Rupert, lac QC **25** F6
Rupert, rivière QC **25** E4
Rupert Creek MB **15** C6
Rusagonis NB **32** C3
Ruscom River ON **19** E2
Ruscom Station ON **19** E2
Rushing River PP ON **13** F6
Rush Lake ON **17** D5
Rush Lake SK **11** E4
Rushoon NL **36** E7
Rushoon NL **37** E5
Rushton's Beach PP NS
34 B7
Rushy Pond Siding NL
36 A-B6
Rushy Pond Siding NL
37 A-B4
Russel Bay NT **10** A3

Russel Island ON **18** D4
Sadene Lake NT **5** B7
Sadler Lake SK **12** E-F6
Sadowa ON **20** A7-8
Sadowa ON **21** C2
Sagamok ON **17** F5-6
Sagamok ON **18** D3
Saganaga Lake ON **16** F4
Saganaga Lake ON **16** F4
Saganaga Lake ON **40** F1
Saganagons Lake ON
16 F4
Saganash Lake ON **17** C5
Sagard QC **28** D7
Sagawitchewan Bay MB
13 A6
Sagehill SK **11** C4-5
Sagemace Bay MB **11** C8
Sagemace Bay MB **13** C2
Sagemace Bay MB **14** A1
Saglek Bay NL **40** C7
Saguenay, parc du QC
28 C7 C-D8
Saguenay, rivière QC
28 C6
Saguenay River QC **28** C7
Saguenay-Saint-Laurent,
parc marin du QC
28 C6-7 D8
Saguenay-Saint-Laurent,
parc marin du QC **29** D1
Saguenay-St. Lawrence
Marine Park QC
28 C7-8 D8
Saguenay-St. Lawrence
Marine Park QC **29** D1
Sahanatien ON **18** E7-8
Sahdoanah Creek NT **3** A8
Sahdoanah Creek BC
9 A1-2
Sahtaneh River BC **3** B7
Sahtaneh River BC **9** A-B1
Saindon, lacs QC **40** D5
Saint-Adalbert QC **28** A8
Saint-Adelme QC **29** B5
Saint-Adelphe QC **24** A8
Saint-Adelphe QC **25** E8
Saint-Adelphe QC **27** B3-4
Saint-Adelphe MB **13** F3
Saint-Adolphe MB **14** E5
Saint-Adolphe-de-Dudswell
QC **27** C6
Saint-Adolphe-d'Howard
QC **24** C4
Saint-Adrien QC **27** D5
Saint-Adrien-d'Irlande QC
27 C-D5
Saint-Agapit QC **27** B5
St. Agatha QC **19** B6
St. Agatha ON **20** D5
Saint-Aimé-des-Lacs QC
28 E7
St. Alban's NL **36** D5-6
St. Alban's NL **37** D3-4
Saint-Alban QC **27** B4
St. Albert QC **8** A5-6 B5-6
St. Albert AB **8** C8
St. Albert ON **24** E3
Saint-Albert QC **27** D4
Saint-Alexandre QC **24** E7
Saint-Alexandre QC **27** F2
Saint-Alexandre QC **28** E8
Saint-Alexandre QC **29** D8
Saint-Alexandre-des-Lacs
QC **29** C5
Saint-Alexis QC **24** C6
Saint-Alexis QC **27** D1
Saint-Alexis-de-Matapédia
QC **29** D5
Saint-Alexis-de-Matapédia
QC **31** A4
Saint-Alexis-des-Monts QC
24 B6-7
Saint-Alexis-des-Monts QC
25 F6-7
Saint-Alexis-des-Monts QC
27 B-C2
Saint-Alfred QC **27** C6
St. Almo NB **31** D3
St. Alphonse MB **13** F2
Saint-Alphonse MB **14** E2-3
St. Alphonse NS **33** E1
Saint-Alphonse QC **24** E7
Saint-Alphonse QC **27** F3
Saint-Alphonse QC **29** D8
Saint-Alphonse QC **30** D1
Saint-Alphonse-Rodriguez
QC **24** B5-6
Saint-Alphonse-Rodriguez
QC **27** C1
Saint-Amable QC **24** D6
Saint-Amable QC **27** E1
Saint-Amand NB **31** C3
St. Ambroise MB **13** E3
St. Ambroise MB **14** D4
St. Ambroise Beach PP MB
13 E3
St. Ambroise Beach PP MB
14 D3-4
Saint-Ambroise-de-Kildare
QC **24** C6
Saint-Ambroise-de-Kildare
QC **27** D1
Saint-Amour, lac QC **22** B7
Saint-Amour, lac QC
25 C-D1
Saint-Anaclet QC **29** C3
Saint-André QC **24** E8
Saint-André QC **31** D3
Saint-André QC **28** E8
Saint-André QC **29** E1

Saint-André-Avellin QC 24 C-D3
Saint-André-de-Restigouche QC 29 D5-6
Saint-André-de-Restigouche QC 31 A4
Saint-André-de-Shediac NB 35 E1
Saint-André-du-Lac-Saint-Jean QC 28 C4
Saint-André-Est QC 24 D4-5
St. Andrew, Lake MB 13 D3-4
St. Andrew, Lake MB 14 A4-5
St. Andrews MB 14 D5
St. Andrews NB 32 E2
St. Andrew's NL 36 D1
St. Andrews NS 34 E5
St. Andrews ON 34 C7
St. Andrews PE 35 D5-6
St. Andrews Blockhouse NHS NB 32 E2
St. Andrews Channel NS 34 C7
Saint-Anicet QC 24 E4-5
St. Ann PE 35 D4
Saint-Anne-du-Lac QC 27 D5-6
St. Ann Point NS 33 F2
St. Anns NS 34 C7
St. Anns ON 19 C8
St. Anns ON 20 E7
St. Anns Bay NS 34 B7
St. Anns PP NS 34 C7
Saint-Anselme NB 31 F8
Saint-Anselme NB 32 B6
Saint-Anselme QC 27 B6
St. Anthony NL 38 B5
St. Anthony NL 39 D8
St. Anthony Bight NL 38 B5
Saint-Antoine NB 32 A-B6
Saint-Antoine QC 24 C5
Saint-Antoine QC 27 D1
Saint-Antoine-Abbé QC 24 E5
Saint-Antoine-de-Tilly QC 27 B5
Saint-Antoine-sur-Richelieu QC 24 C6-7
Saint-Antoine-sur-Richelieu QC 27 D2
Saint-Antonin QC 29 E1
Saint-Apollinaire QC 27 B5
Saint-Armand NB 29 F4
Saint-Armand QC 24 E7
Saint-Armand QC 27 F2
Saint-Arsène QC 29 D1
Saint-Arthur NB 29 D-E6
Saint-Arthur NB 31 B4
Saint-Athanase QC 29 E1
Saint-Aubert QC 27 A7
Saint-Aubert QC 28 F7
Saint-Augustin QC 24 D5
Saint-Augustin QC 28 B4
Saint-Augustin QC 38 B1
Saint-Augustin QC 39 D6-7
Saint-Augustin QC 40 E8
Saint-Augustin, baie QC 39 E7
Saint-Augustin, rivière NL 40 E8
Saint-Augustin, rivière NL 38 A-B1
Saint-Augustin, rivière NL 39 D6-7
Saint-Augustin, RNOM de QC 38 B1-2
Saint-Augustin, RNOM de QC 39 E7
Saint-Augustin-de-Desmaures QC 27 B5
Saint-Augustin NMBS QC 38 B1-2
Saint-Augustin NMBS QC 39 E7
Saint-Augustin Nord-Ouest, rivière QC 39 D6
St. Barbe NL 38 B4
St. Barbe NL 39 D8
St. Barbe Bay NL 38 B3
Saint-Barnabé, île QC 29 C2-3
Saint-Barnabé-Nord QC 24 B7
Saint-Barnabé-Nord QC 25 F7
Saint-Barnabé-Nord QC 27 C2-3
Saint-Barnabé-Sud QC 24 D7
Saint-Barnabé-Sud QC 27 D2-3
Saint-Barthélemy QC 24 B6-7
Saint-Barthélemy QC 27 C2
Saint-Basile NB 29 F3
Saint-Basile NB 31 C2
Saint-Basile-de-Tableau QC 28 C7
Saint-Basile-le-Grand QC 24 D6-7
Saint-Basile-le-Grand QC 27 E2
Saint-Basile-Sud QC 27 B4
Saint-Benjamin QC 27 C6-7
St. Benedict SK 11 C5
Saint-Benoît QC 24 D5
Saint-Benoît-du-Lac QC 24 E8
Saint-Benoît-du-Lac QC 27 F4

Saint-Benoît-Labre QC 27 D6-7
St. Bernard NS 33 D1
Saint-Bernard QC 24 C7
Saint-Bernard QC 27 B5-6
Saint-Bernard QC 27 D2
Saint-Bernard, lac QC 24 A6
Saint-Bernard, lac QC 25 F6
Saint-Bernard, lac QC 27 B2
Saint-Bernard-de-Lacolle QC 24 E6
Saint-Bernard-de-Lacolle QC 27 F2
St. Bernardin ON 24 D3-4
St. Bernard's NL 36 E7
St. Bernard's NL 37 E5
St. Bernard's-Jacques Fontaine NL 36 E7
St. Bernard's-Jacques Fontaine NL 37 E5
Saint-Bernard-sur-Mer QC 28 E-F7
Saint-Blaise QC 24 E6
Saint-Blaise QC 27 F2
Saint-Bonaventure QC 24 C7
Saint-Bonaventure QC 27 D3
Saint-Boniface-de-Shawinigan QC 24 A-B7
Saint-Boniface-de-Shawinigan QC 25 F7
Saint-Boniface-de-Shawinigan QC 27 B2-3
St. Boswells SK 11 E4
St. Brendan's NL 37 B7
St. Bride, Mount AB 6 D4
St. Bride, Mount AB 7 A1
St. Bride's NL 36 F8
St. Bride's NL 37 F6
St. Brides AB 6 A7
St. Brides AB 11 A1
St. Brieux SK 11 C5
Saint-Bruno QC 28 C5
Saint-Bruno-de-Guigues QC 17 E8
Saint-Bruno-de-Guigues QC 22 A1
Saint-Bruno-de-Guigues QC 23 F1
Saint-Bruno-de-Kamouraska QC 28 E8
Saint-Bruno-de-Montarville QC 24 D6-7
Saint-Bruno-de-Montarville QC 27 E2
Saint-Cajetan QC 22 D7-8
Saint-Cajetan QC 24 A2
Saint-Cajetan QC 25 F2
Saint-Calixte QC 24 C5
Saint-Calixte QC 27 D1
Saint-Camille QC 27 E5
Saint-Camille-de-Lellis QC 27 B7-8
St. Canut QC 24 D5
St. Carols NL 38 B5
St. Casimir QC 27 B4
Saint-Cassien-des-Caps QC 28 F6-7
St. Catherine's NL 37 E7
St. Catharines ON 19 B8
St. Catharines ON 20 E7
Saint-Célestin QC 24 B8
Saint-Célestin QC 27 C3
Saint-Césaire QC 24 D7
Saint-Césaire QC 27 E2-3
St. Chads NL 37 B6-7
Saint-Charles NB 31 E7-8
Saint-Charles NB 32 A6
St. Charles ON 17 F7
St. Charles ON 18 A6
Saint-Charles, lac QC 27 A5
Saint-Charles-Borromée QC 24 C6
Saint-Charles-Borromée Q 27 C1
Saint-Charles-de-Bellechasse QC 27 B6
Saint-Charles-de-Bourget QC 28 C5
Saint-Charles-de-Drummond QC 24 C8
Saint-Charles-de-Drummond QC 27 D3-4
Saint-Charles-de-Mandeville QC 24 B6
Saint-Charles-de-Mandeville QC 25 F6
Saint-Charles-de-Mandeville QC 27 C2
Saint-Charles-Garnier QC 29 C4
Saint-Charles-sur-Richelieu QC 24 D7
Saint-Charles-sur-Richelieu QC 27 E2
Saint-Christophe-d'Arthabaska QC 27 D4-5
Saint-Chrysostome PE 32 A7
Saint-Chrysostome PE 35 C1-2
Saint-Chrysostome QC 24 E5-6
Saint-Chrysostome QC 27 F1
St. Clair, Lake ON 19 D2
St. Clair, Lake ON 20 F1
St. Clair Beach ON 19 E1

St. Clair NWA ON 19 E2
St. Clair River ON 19 C-D2
St. Clair River ON 20 E-F1
St. Clare Creek YT 4 D1
St. Claude MB 13 F3
St. Claude MB 14 E3
Saint-Claude QC 27 E4
Saint-Clément QC 29 D2
St. Clements ON 19 B5-6
St. Clements ON 20 D4-5
Saint-Cléophas QC 24 B6
Saint-Cléophas QC 25 F6
Saint-Cléophas QC 27 C2
Saint-Cléophas QC 29 C4
Saint-Clet QC 24 D-E5
Saint-Colomban ON 24 C5
St. Columban ON 19 B4-5
St. Columban ON 20 D3-4
Saint-Côme QC 24 B5-6
Saint-Côme QC 25 F5-6
Saint-Côme QC 27 C1
Saint-Côme-Linière QC 27 D7
Saint-Constant QC 24 D-E6
Saint-Constant QC 27 E1
St. Croix QC 32 D1-2
St. Croix Island International HS NB 32 E1-2
St. Croix PP NB 32 D1
Saint-Cuthbert QC 24 B6
Saint-Cuthbert QC 27 C2
Saint-Cyprien QC 27 C7
Saint-Cyprien QC 29 D2
Saint-Cyr QC 27 D4
Saint-Cyr, lac QC 23 C8
Saint-Cyr, lac QC 26 D2
St. Cyr, Mount YT 4 D5
Saint-Cyriac QC 28 C5
Saint-Cyrille-de-l'Islet QC 27 A7
Saint-Cyrille-de-Wendover QC 24 C8
Saint-Cyrille-de-Wendover QC 27 D3-4
St. Cyr Range YT 4 D5
Saint-Damase QC 24 D7
Saint-Damase QC 27 E2-3
Saint-Damase QC 29 B4
Saint-Damase-des-Aulnaies QC 27 F7-8
Saint-Damien QC 24 B6
Saint-Damien QC 25 F6
Saint-Damien QC 27 C2
Saint-Damien-de-Buckland QC 27 B6-7
Saint-Daniel QC 27 D5-6
Saint-David QC 24 C7
Saint-David QC 27 D2-3
St. David, Lake MB 13 C3
St. David, Lake MB 14 A4
Saint-David-de-Falardeau QC 28 B-C6
St. David's NL 36 C1-2
St. Davids ON 20 E7-8
Saint-Denis QC 24 C7
Saint-Denis QC 27 D2
Saint-Denis QC 28 E8
St. Denis SK 11 C4
St. Denis, RNF SK 11 C4
Saint-Denis-de-Brompton QC 27 E4
St. Denis National Wilderness Area SK 11 C5
Saint-Didace QC 24 B6-7
Saint-Didace QC 25 F6-7
Saint-Didace QC 27 C2
Saint-Dominique QC 24 D7
Saint-Dominique QC 27 E3
Saint-Dominique-du-Rosaire QC 23 C4
Saint-Donat QC 24 B5
Saint-Donat QC 25 F5
Saint-Donat QC 29 C3
Sainte-Adèle QC 24 C5
Sainte-Agathe MB 13 F4
Sainte-Agathe MB 14 E5
Sainte-Agathe QC 27 C5
Sainte-Agathe-des-Monts QC 24 C4-5
Sainte-Agnès QC 28 E7
Sainte-Agnès-de-Bellecombe QC 17 D8
Sainte-Agnès-de-Bellecombe QC 23 E2-3
Sainte-Agnès-de-Dundee QC 24 E4-5
Ste. Amelie MB 13 D2
Ste. Amelie MB 14 D2
Sainte-Anastasie QC 27 C5
Sainte-Angèle-de-Laval QC 24 B8
Sainte-Angèle-de-Laval QC 25 F8
Sainte-Angèle-de-Laval QC 27 C3
Sainte-Angèle-de-Mérici QC 29 C3-4
Sainte-Angèle-de-Monnoir QC 24 D-7
Sainte-Angèle-de-Monnoir QC 27 E2
Sainte-Angèle-de-Prémont QC 24 B7
Sainte-Angèle-de-Prémont QC 25 F7
Sainte-Angèle-de-Prémont QC 27 C2
Ste. Anne MB 13 F4
Ste. Anne MB 14 E6
Ste. Anne NB 31 B6
Ste. Anne, lac AB 6 A5
Ste. Anne, lac AB 8 C5

Ste. Anne, lac AB 8 C5
Sainte-Anne, lac QC 28 F8
Sainte-Anne, lac QC 39 E1
Sainte-Anne, mont QC 28 F6
Sainte-Anne, pointe QC 29 A6
Sainte-Anne, rivière QC 27 A5 B4
Sainte-Anne, rivière QC 28 F6
Sainte-Anne-de-Beaupré QC 27 A6
Sainte-Anne-de-Kent NB 31 E8
Sainte-Anne-de-Kent NB 32 A6
Sainte-Anne-de-la-Pérade QC 27 B4
Sainte-Anne-de-la-Rochelle QC 24 D8
Sainte-Anne-de-la-Rochelle QC 27 E3-4
Sainte-Anne-de-Madawaska NB 29 F4
Sainte-Anne-de-Madawaska NB 31 C2-3
Sainte-Anne-de-Portneuf QC 29 B2
Sainte-Anne-de-Prescott ON 24 D4
Sainte-Anne-des-Lacs QC 24 C5
Sainte-Anne-des-Monts QC 29 A6
Sainte-Anne-des-Monts QC 40 F6-7
Sainte-Anne-des-Plaines QC 24 C5-6
Sainte-Anne-des-Plaines QC 27 D1
Sainte-Anne-du-Lac QC 25 E3
Ste. Anne du Ruisseau NS 33 F2
Sainte-Apolline QC 27 B7
Sainte-Aurélie QC 27 D7
Sainte-Barbe QC 24 E5
Sainte-Béatrix QC 24 B6
Sainte-Béatrix QC 27 C1
Sainte-Blandine QC 29 C4
Sainte-Brigide-d'Iberville QC 24 D7
Sainte-Brigide-d'Iberville QC 27 E-F2
Sainte-Brigitte-de-Laval QC 27 A5-6
Sainte-Brigitte-des-Saults QC 24 C8
Sainte-Brigitte-des-Saults QC 27 D3
Sainte-Catherine QC 24 D6
Sainte-Catherine QC 27 E1
Sainte-Catherine-de-Hatley QC 27 F4
Sainte-Catherine-de-la-Jacques-Cartier QC 27 B4-5
Sainte-Cécile NB 30 E2
Sainte-Cécile NB 31 A-B8
Sainte-Cécile, mont QC 27 D-E6
Sainte-Cécile-de-Lévrard QC 27 B-C4
Sainte-Cécile-de-Masham QC 21 A7
Sainte-Cécile-de-Masham QC 22 F7
Sainte-Cécile-de-Masham QC 24 D1-2
Sainte-Cécile-de-Milton QC 24 D7
Sainte-Cécile-de-Milton QC 27 E3
Sainte-Cécile-de-Whitton QC 27 E6
Sainte-Christine QC 24 D8
Sainte-Christine QC 27 E3
Sainte-Christine-d'Auvergne QC 27 B4
Sainte-Claire QC 27 B6
Sainte-Claire, lac ON 19 D-E2
Sainte-Claire, lac ON 20 F1
Sainte-Claire, RNF ON 19 E2
Sainte-Clotilde-de-Beauce QC 27 C6
Sainte-Clotilde-de-Châteauguay QC 24 E6
Sainte-Clotilde-de-Châteauguay QC 27 F1
Sainte-Clotilde-de-Horton QC 24 C8
Sainte-Clotilde-de-Horton QC 27 D4
Sainte-Croix QC 27 B5
Sainte-Croix, lac NT 10 B5
Ste. Croix Cove NS 32 E5
Ste. Croix Cove NS 33 B2-3
Saint-Edgar QC 29 D2
Saint-Edgar QC 31 A6
Saint-Edmond QC 23 E4
Saint-Edmond QC 26 D8
Saint-Edmond QC 28 B3
Saint-Edmond-de-Grantham QC 24 C7
Saint-Edmond-de-Grantham QC 27 D3
Saint-Édouard QC 24 E6

Saint-Édouard QC 27 B4-5
Saint-Édouard QC 27 F1
Saint-Édouard-de-Frampton QC 27 B-C6
Saint-Édouard-de-Kent NB 31 E8
Saint-Édouard-de-Kent NB 32 A6
Saint-Édouard-de-Maskinongé QC 24 B7
Saint-Édouard-de-Maskinongé QC 25 F7
Saint-Édouard-de-Maskinongé QC 27 C2
St. Edward PE 35 B2
Sainte-Edwidge QC 27 F5
Sainte-Élisabeth QC 24 C6
Sainte-Élisabeth QC 27 C2
Sainte-Élisabeth-de-Proulx QC 28 B4
Sainte-Élisabeth-de-Warwick QC 27 D4
Sainte-Elizabeth MB 13 F3-4
Sainte-Elizabeth MB 14 F5
Sainte-Émélie-de-l'Énergie QC 24 B6
Sainte-Émélie-de-l'Énergie QC 25 F6
Sainte-Émélie-de-l'Énergie QC 27 C1
Sainte-Eulalie QC 24 C8
Sainte-Eulalie QC 27 C4
Sainte-Euphémie QC 27 B7
Sainte-Famille QC 27 A6
Sainte-Famille-d'Aumond QC 22 D7-8
Sainte-Famille-d'Aumond QC 24 A-B2
Sainte-Famille-d'Aumond QC 25 F2
Sainte-Félicité QC 27 A8
Sainte-Félicité QC 29 B5
Sainte-Flavie QC 29 B3
Sainte-Florence QC 29 C5
Sainte-Florence QC 31 A3-4
Sainte-Foy QC 27 B5
Sainte-Françoise QC 27 C4
Ste. Genevieve MB 13 F4
Ste. Genevieve MB 14 E6
Sainte-Geneviève-de-Batiscan QC 24 A8
Sainte-Geneviève-de-Batiscan QC 25 F8
Sainte-Geneviève-de-Batiscan QC 27 B3-4
Sainte-Germaine-Boulé QC 17 C8
Sainte-Germaine-Boulé QC 23 C2
Sainte-Germaine-Station QC 27 C7
Sainte-Gertrude QC 24 B8
Sainte-Gertrude QC 25 F8
Sainte-Gertrude QC 27 C2
Sainte-Gertrude-Manneville QC 23 D4
Sainte-Hedwidge QC 25 A8
Sainte-Hedwidge QC 26 E8
Sainte-Hedwidge QC 28 C3-4
Sainte-Hélène QC 24 B8
Sainte-Hélène QC 29 E1
Sainte-Hélène-de-Bagot QC 24 D7-8
Sainte-Hélène-de-Bagot QC 27 D-E3
Sainte-Hélène-de-Chester QC 27 D5
Sainte-Hélène-de-Mancebourg QC 17 C7-8
Sainte-Hélène-de-Mancebourg QC 23 C2
Sainte-Hénédine QC 27 B6
Sainte-Irène QC 29 C4
Sainte-Jeanne-d'Arc QC 28 B4
Sainte-Jeanne-d'Arc QC 29 C4
Sainte-Julie QC 24 D6
Sainte-Julie QC 27 C5
Sainte-Julie QC 27 E2
Sainte-Julienne QC 24 C5-6
Sainte-Julienne QC 27 D1
Sainte-Justine QC 27 C7
Sainte-Justine-de-Newton QC 24 D5
St. Eleanor's PE 32 A8
St. Eleanor's PE 34 C1
St. Eleanors PE 35 D3
Saint-Éleuthère QC 29 E1
St. Elias, Mount YT 4 E1
St. Elias Mountains YT 4 D1 E1-2
Saint-Élie QC 24 B7
Saint-Élie QC 25 F7
Saint-Élie-d'Orford QC 27 E4
Saint-Éloi QC 29 D1-2
Sainte-Louise QC 28 F7-8
Saint-Elphège QC 24 C7-8
Saint-Elphège QC 27 D3
Saint-Luce QC 29 C3
Sainte-Lucie-de-Beauregard QC 27 B7-8
Sainte-Lucie-de-Doncaster QC 24 B5
Saint-Elzéar QC 27 C6
Saint-Elzéar QC 29 D8
Saint-Elzéar QC 29 E2
Saint-Elzéar QC 30 D1
Saint-Esprit QC 24 C6
Saint-Esprit QC 27 D1

Saint-Elzéar QC 31 A7
Sainte-Madeleine QC 24 D7
Saint-Esprit, rivière QC 24 C6
Saint-Esprit, rivière QC 27 D1
Sainte-Madeleine-de-la-Rivière-Madeleine QC 29 A8
Sainte-Madeleine-de-la-Rivière-Madeleine QC 30 A1
Sainte-Marcelline-de-Kildare QC 24 C5-6
Sainte-Marcelline-de-Kildare QC 27 C1
Sainte-Marguerite QC 24 C5
Sainte-Marguerite QC 27 B6
Sainte-Marguerite QC 27 D1
Sainte-Marguerite QC 29 C5
Sainte-Marguerite Nord-Est, rivière QC 28 B7 C7-8
Sainte-Marguerite, mont QC 27 C6
Sainte-Marguerite, rivière QC 28 C7-8
Sainte-Marguerite, rivière QC 39 E2
Sainte-Marguerite, rivière QC 40 E-F6
Sainte-Marguerite-de-Lingwick QC 27 E5-6
Sainte-Marguerite-Marie QC 28 B4
Sainte-Marguerite-Station QC 24 C5
Sainte-Marie QC 27 C6
Sainte-Marie, lac QC 22 E7-8
Sainte-Marie, lac QC 24 C2
Sainte-Marie-de-Blandford QC 27 C4
Sainte-Marie-de-Kent NB 31 E8
Sainte-Marie-de-Kent NB 32 A6
Sainte-Marie-Saint-Raphaël NB 30 E2-3
Sainte-Marie-Saint-Raphaël NB 31 B8
Sainte-Marie-Salomé QC 24 C6
Sainte-Marie-Salomé QC 27 D1
Sainte-Marthe QC 24 D4-5
Sainte-Marthe-du-Cap QC 24 B8
Sainte-Marthe-du-Cap QC 25 F8
Sainte-Marthe-du-Cap QC 27 C3-4
Sainte-Marthe-sur-le-Lac QC 24 D5
Sainte-Martine QC 24 E5-6
Sainte-Martine QC 27 F1
Sainte-Mélanie QC 24 B6
Sainte-Mélanie QC 27 C1
Sainte-Monique QC 24 B8
Sainte-Monique QC 24 D5
Sainte-Monique QC 27 C3
Sainte-Monique QC 27 E1
Sainte-Odile QC 29 C3
Sainte-Paule QC 29 B4-5
Sainte-Perpétue QC 24 C8
Sainte-Perpétue QC 27 A8
Sainte-Perpétue QC 27 D3
Sainte-Pétronille QC 27 A6
Sainte-Praxède QC 27 D6
Ste. Rita MB 13 E4
Ste. Rita MB 14 E6
Sainte-Rita QC 29 D2
Sainte-Rita QC 31 A1
Sainte-Rosalie QC 24 D7
Sainte-Rosalie QC 27 E3
Sainte-Rose-de-Watford QC 27 C7
Sainte-Rose-de-Prescott ON 24 D3
Ste. Rose du Lac MB 13 D2
Ste. Rose du Lac MB 14 B2
Sainte-Rose-Gloucester NB 31 B8
Sainte-Sabine QC 24 E7
Sainte-Sabine QC 27 B7
Sainte-Sabine QC 27 F2
Sainte-Sabine-Station QC 27 B-C7
Sainte-Scholastique QC 24 D5
Sainte-Séraphine QC 24 C8
Sainte-Séraphine QC 27 D4
Sainte-Sophie QC 24 C5-6
Sainte-Sophie QC 27 D1
Sainte-Sophie-de-Lévrard QC 24 B8
Sainte-Sophie-de-Lévrard QC 27 D3 E4
Sainte-Thècle QC 24 A8
Sainte-Thècle QC 25 E8
Sainte-Thècle QC 27 B3
Sainte-Thérèse QC 24 D5
Sainte-Thérèse QC 27 E1
Sainte-Thérèse, lac NT 10 A-B3
Sainte-Thérèse-de-Gaspé QC 30 C3
Sainte-Thérèse-de-la-Gatineau QC 22 D8
Sainte-Thérèse-de-la-Gatineau QC 24 B2
Sainte-Thérèse-de-la-Gatineau QC 25 F2
Saint-Étienne-de-Beauharnois QC 24 E5
Saint-Étienne-de-Beauharnois QC 27 F1
Saint-Étienne-de-Bolton QC 24 E8
Saint-Étienne-de-Bolton QC 27 F4
Saint-Étienne-de-Lauzon QC 27 B5-6
Saint-Étienne-des-Grès QC 24 B7
Saint-Étienne-des-Grès QC 25 F7
Saint-Étienne-des-Grès QC 27 C3
St. Eugene ON 24 D4
Saint-Eugène QC 24 C7
Saint-Eugène QC 26 D8
Saint-Eugène QC 27 A7
Saint-Eugène QC 27 D1
Saint-Eugène QC 28 F7
Saint-Eugène-de-Chazel QC 23 C3
Saint-Eugène-de-Guigues QC 17 E8
Saint-Eugène-de-Guigues QC 22 A2
Saint-Eugène-de-Guigues QC 23 F2
Saint-Eugène-de-Ladrière QC 29 C2-3
Saint-Eugène-de-Ladrière QC 31 A1
Sainte-Ursule QC 24 B7
Sainte-Ursule QC 25 F7
Sainte-Ursule QC 27 C2
Saint-Eusèbe QC 29 E2
Saint-Eusèbe QC 31 B1
St. Eustache MB 13 E3
St. Eustache MB 14 D4
Saint-Eustache QC 24 D5
Saint-Évariste-de-Forsyth QC 27 D6
Sainte-Véronique QC 24 A3
Sainte-Véronique QC 25 F3
Sainte-Victoire QC 24 C7
Sainte-Victoire QC 27 D2
Saint-Fabien QC 29 C2
Saint-Fabien-de-Panet QC 27 B7-8
Saint-Fabien-sur-Mer QC 29 C2
Saint-Faustin-Lac-Carré QC 24 B4
Saint-Félicien QC 26 E8
Saint-Félicien QC 28 B3-4
St. Felix PE 35 B2
Saint-Félix-d'Otis QC 28 C6
Saint-Félix-de-Dalquier QC 23 C4
Saint-Félix-de-Kingsey QC 24 C8
Saint-Félix-de-Kingsey QC 27 D3-4
Saint-Félix-de-Valois QC 24 B6
Saint-Félix-de-Valois QC 27 C2
Saint-Ferréol-les-Neiges QC 27 A6
Saint-Ferréol-les-Neiges QC 28 F6
Saint-Fidèle-de-Mont-Murray QC 28 E8
Saint-Fidèle-de-Restigouche QC 29 D6
Saint-Fidèle-de-Restigouche QC 31 A4
Saintfield ON 20 B8
Saintfield ON 21 E2
St. Fintan's NL 36 C2
Saint-Flavien QC 27 B5
Saint-Fortunat QC 27 C6
St. Francis AB 6 B5
St. Francis AB 8 D5
St. Francis, Cape NL 37 D8
St. Francis Harbour NS 34 D5
St. Francis River NB 29 F2
Saint-François QC 27 A6
Saint-François, lac QC 24 E5
Saint-François, lac QC 27 D6
Saint-François, rivière QC 27 D3 E4
Saint-François, rivière QC 27 E5
Saint-François-d'Assise QC 29 D5

Saint-François-d'Assise QC 31 A3-4
Saint-François-de-Madawaska NB 29 F2
Saint-François-de-Madawaska NB 31 C1
Saint-François-de-Masham QC 21 A7
Saint-François-de-Masham QC 22 F7
Saint-François-de-Masham QC 24 D1
Saint-François-de-Sales QC 25 A8
Saint-François-de-Sales QC 26 E8
Saint-François-de-Sales QC 28 C4
Saint-François-du-Lac QC 24 C7
Saint-François-du-Lac QC 27 D2-3
St. François Xavier MB 13 E3-4
St. François Xavier MB 14 D4
Saint-François-Xavier-de-Brompton QC 27 E4
Saint-François-Xavier-de-Viger QC 29 D1-2
Saint-Frédéric QC 27 C6
St. Front SK 11 C5-6
Saint-Fulgence QC 28 C6
Saint-Gabriel QC 24 B6
Saint-Gabriel QC 25 F6
Saint-Gabriel QC 27 C2
Saint-Gabriel QC 29 C3-4
Saint-Gabriel-de-Kamouraska QC 28 F8
Saint-Gabriel-de-Valcartier QC 27 B5
Saint-Gédéon QC 27 D7
Saint-Gédéon QC 28 C4-5
St. George NB 32 E2
St. George ON 19 B6
St. George ON 20 D-E5
St. George, Cape NL 36 C1
St. George, Lake MB 13 C3-4
St. George, Lake MB 14 A4
St. Georges MB 14 C6
St. George's NL 36 C2
St. Georges PE 34 C3-4
St. Georges PE 35 E7
St. Georges QC 24 A8
St. Georges QC 25 E8
St. Georges QC 27 B3
St. Georges QC 27 C7
Saint-Georges, baie de NS 34 B5
St. George's Bay NL 36 C1
St. George's Bay NL 40 F8
St. Georges Bay NS 34 C5
St. Georges Channel NS 34 D6
Saint-Georges-de-Cacouna QC 29 D1
Saint-Georges-de-Clarenceville QC 24 E6-7
Saint-Georges-de-Clarenceville QC 27 F2
Saint-Georges-de-Malbaie QC 30 C3
Saint-Georges-de-Windsor QC 27 E4-5
St. George's Hill SK 9 E8
St. George's Hill SK 12 E3
Saint-Gérard-de-Berry QC 23 C4
Saint-Gérard-des-Laurentides QC 24 A7
Saint-Gérard-des-Laurentides QC 25 E-F7
Saint-Gérard-des-Laurentides QC 27 B3
Saint-Gérard-Majella QC 24 C6
Saint-Gérard-Majella QC 27 C7
Saint-Gérard-Majella QC 27 D1-2
Saint-Gérard-Majella QC 27 D3
Saint-Germain QC 28 E8
Saint-Germain, lac QC 22 F7-8
Saint-Germain, lac QC 24 C2
Saint-Germain, rivière QC 24 C-D8
Saint-Germain, rivière QC 27 D3-4 F4
Saint-Germain-de-Grantham QC 24 C8
Saint-Germain-de-Grantham QC 27 D3
Saint-Germains, lac QC 28 C6-7
Saint-Gervais QC 27 B6
Saint-Gilbert PE 32 A7
Saint-Gilbert PE 34 B1
Saint-Gilbert PE 35 D2
Saint-Gilbert QC 27 B4
Saint-Gilles QC 24 E5
Saint-Godefroi QC 30 D1-2
Saint-Godefroi QC 31 A7
Saint-Grégoire QC 25 F8
Saint-Grégoire QC 27 E5
Saint-Grégoire-de-Greenlay QC 27 E4
St. Gregor SK 11 C5

St. Gregory, Cape NL 36 A2
St. Gregory, Cape NL 38 F1-2
St. Gregory, Mount NL 36 A2-3
St. Gregory, Mount NL 38 F2
Saint-Guillaume QC 24 C7
Saint-Guillaume QC 27 D3
Saint-Guillaume-de-Granada QC 17 D8
Saint-Guillaume-Nord QC 24 A5
Saint-Guillaume-Nord QC 25 E-F5
Saint-Guy QC 29 D2
Saint-Guy QC 31 A1
St. Helens ON 19 A4
St. Helens ON 20 C3
Saint-Henri QC 27 B6
Saint-Henri-de-Taillon QC 28 B4-5
Saint-Hermas QC 24 D5
Saint-Herménégilde QC 27 F5
Saint-Hilaire NB 29 F3
Saint-Hilaire NB 31 C1-2
Saint-Hilaire-de-Dorset QC 27 D6
Saint-Hilarion QC 28 E7
Saint-Hippolyte QC 24 C5
Saint-Hippolyte QC 27 D1
Saint-Honoré QC 27 D6
Saint-Honoré QC 28 C6
Saint-Honoré QC 29 E2
Saint-Hubert QC 24 D6
Saint-Hubert QC 27 E2
Saint-Hubert QC 29 D-E2
St. Hubert Mission SK 11 E7
Saint-Hugues QC 24 C7
Saint-Hugues QC 27 D2-3
Saint-Hyacinthe QC 24 D7
Saint-Hyacinthe QC 27 E3
Saint-Ignace NB 31 E7
Saint-Ignace NB 32 A5
Saint-Ignace-de-Loyola QC 24 C6-7
Saint-Ignace-de-Loyola QC 27 D2
Saint-Ignace-de-Stanbridge QC 24 E7
Saint-Ignace-de-Stanbridge QC 27 F2-3
Saint-Ignace-du-Lac QC 25 E5-6
Saint-Ignace-du-Lac QC 27 B1
St. Ignace Island ON 16 E6-7 F6-7
St. Ignace Island ON 17 C1
Saint-Irénée NB 30 F1-2
Saint-Irénée NB 31 B7
Saint-Isidore QC 28 E7
St. Isidore AB 9 E3-4
Saint-Isidore NB 30 F2
Saint-Isidore NB 31 B7
St. Isidore ON 24 D3-4
Saint-Isidore QC 24 E6
Saint-Isidore QC 27 B6
Saint-Isidore QC 27 F1
Saint-Isidore QC 30 C2-3
Saint-Isidore-d'Auckland QC 27 F5
Saint-Isidore-de-Bellevue SK 11 B4-5
St. Jacobs ON 19 B6
St. Jacobs ON 20 D5
Saint-Jacques NB 29 F3
Saint-Jacques NB 31 C1-2
St. Jacques NL 36 E6
St. Jacques NL 37 E4
Saint-Jacques QC 24 C6
Saint-Jacques QC 27 D1-2
St. Jacques-Coombs Cove NL 36 E6
St. Jacques-Coombs Cove NL 37 E4
Saint-Jacques-de-Leeds QC 27 C5-6
Saint-Jacques-le-Majeur-de-Wolfestown QC 27 D5
Saint-Jacques-le-Mineur QC 24 E6
Saint-Jacques-le-Mineur QC 27 F2
St. James, Cape BC 1 C2
Saint-Janvier QC 24 D5
Saint-Janvier QC 27 D1
Saint-Jean QC 27 A6
Saint-Jean, fleuve NB 29 F3
Saint-Jean, fleuve NB 31 D3
Saint-Jean, fleuve NB 32 C2
Saint-Jean, lac QC 26 E8
Saint-Jean, lac QC 28 B-C4
Saint-Jean, rivière QC 28 D7
Saint-Jean, rivière QC 30 B-C2 C1
Saint-Jean, rivière QC 39 E3
St. Jean Baptiste MB 13 F3-4
St. Jean Baptiste MB 14 F5
Saint-Jean-Baptiste QC 24 D7
Saint-Jean-Baptiste QC 27 E2
Saint-Jean-Baptiste-de-Restigouche NB 29 E5
Saint-Jean-Baptiste-de-Restigouche NB 31 B4

Saint-Jean-Chrysostome QC 27 B6
Saint-Jean-de-Brébeuf QC 27 C5
Saint-Jean-de-Cherbourg QC 29 B5
Saint-Jean-de-Dieu QC 29 D2
Saint-Jean-de-la-Lande QC 27 D6-7
Saint-Jean-de-la-Lande QC 29 E-F2
Saint-Jean-de-la-Lande QC 31 C1
Saint-Jean-de-Matapédia QC 29 D5
Saint-Jean-de-Matapédia QC 31 A3-4
Saint-Jean-de-Matha QC 24 B6
Saint-Jean-de-Matha QC 25 F6
Saint-Jean-de-Matha QC 27 C1
Saint-Jean-des-Piles QC 24 A7
Saint-Jean-des-Piles QC 25 E7
Saint-Jean-des-Piles QC 27 B3
Saint-Jean-Port-Joli QC 28 F7
Saint-Jean-sur-le-Lac QC 22 D8
Saint-Jean-sur-le-Lac QC 24 A2
Saint-Jean-sur-le-Lac QC 25 F2
Saint-Jean-sur-Richelieu QC 24 E6
Saint-Jean-sur-Richelieu QC 27 F2
Saint-Jérôme QC 24 C5
Saint-Jérôme QC 27 D1
St. Joachim ON 19 E2
Saint-Joachim QC 27 A6
Saint-Joachim-de-Courval QC 24 C8
Saint-Joachim-de-Courval QC 27 D3
Saint-Joachim-de-Shefford QC 24 D8
Saint-Joachim-de-Shefford QC 27 E3
Saint-Jogues QC 29 D8
Saint-Jogues QC 30 D1
Saint-Jogues QC 31 A7
St. John NB 32 D4
St. John, Cape NL 38 D5
St. John, Lake NL 36 C7
St. John, Lake NL 37 C5
St. John Bay NL 38 C3
St. John Bay NL 39 E7
St. John Harbour NB 32 E4
St. John Harbour NB 33 B1
St. John Harbour NL 36 E4
St. John Harbour NL 37 E4
St. John Island NL 38 C3
St. John Island NL 39 E7
St. John River NB 31 C2
St. John River NB 31 F3
St. John River NB 32 B-C1
St. John's NL 37 D8
St. Jones Within NL 37 C7
St. Jones Without NL 37 D6-7
Saint-Joseph MB 13 F3-4
Saint-Joseph NB 14 F4-5
Saint-Joseph NB 31 F8
Saint-Joseph NB 32 C6
St. Joseph NS 33 A8
St. Joseph NS 33 D1-2
St. Joseph NS 34 E4
St. Joseph ON 19 B3-4
St. Joseph ON 20 D2-3
St. Joseph, lac QC 24 C4-5
Saint-Joseph, lac QC 27 C5
St. Joseph, Lake ON 16 C4-5
St. Joseph, Lake ON 40 F1
Saint-Joseph-de-Beauce QC 27 C6
Saint-Joseph-de-Cléricy QC 17 D8
Saint-Joseph-de-Kamouraska QC 28 E8
Saint-Joseph-de-Kamouraska QC 29 E1
Saint-Joseph-de-la-Rive QC 28 E7
Saint-Joseph-de-Lepage QC 29 C3
Saint-Joseph-de-Madawaska NB 31 C2
Saint-Joseph-de-Mékinac QC 25 E7-8
Saint-Joseph-de-Mékinac QC 27 A3
Saint-Joseph-de-Sorel QC 24 C6-7
Saint-Joseph-de-Sorel QC 27 D2
St. Joseph du Moine NS
St. Joseph Island ON 17 F4
St. Joseph's NL 36 E7
St. Joseph's NL 37 E5
St. Joseph's NL 37 E7

St. Joseph's Cove NL 36 D5-6
St. Joseph's Cove NL 37 D3-4
St. Joseph's Island, RNOM ON 17 F4
St. Joseph's Island NMBS ON 17 F4
Saint-Jovite QC 24 B4
Saint-Jude QC 24 C7
Saint-Jude QC 27 D2-3
St. Judes NL 36 A3-4
St. Judes NL 37 A1-2
St. Judes NL 38 F3
Saint-Jules QC 27 C6
Saint-Jules QC 29 D7
Saint-Jules QC 31 A6
Saint-Julien QC 27 D5
St. Julien's NL 38 B5
St. Julien's NL 39 D-E8
Saint-Just-de-Bretenières QC 27 B7-8
Saint-Juste-du-Lac QC 29 E2
Saint-Juste-du-Lac QC 31 B1
Saint-Justin QC 24 B7
Saint-Justin QC 25 F7
Saint-Justin QC 27 C2
St. Kyran's NL 36 E7-8
St. Kyran's NL 37 E5-6
St. Labre MB 13 F4-5
St. Labre MB 14 F6-7
Saint-Lambert QC 17 C7-8
Saint-Lambert QC 23 B2
Saint-Lambert QC 24 D6
Saint-Lambert QC 27 E2
Saint-Lambert-de-Lauzon QC 27 B5-6
St. Laurent MB 13 E3
St. Laurent MB 14 E4
Saint-Laurent QC 24 D5-6
Saint-Laurent QC 27 A6
Saint-Laurent QC 27 E1
Saint-Laurent, cap NB 35 F2-3
Saint-Laurent, Cape NB 35 F2-3
Saint-Laurent, fleuve ON 21 C-D8
Saint-Laurent, fleuve ON 24 B7 C6-7
Saint-Laurent, fleuve ON 24 E4-5
Saint-Laurent, fleuve QC 25 F8
Saint-Laurent, fleuve QC 27 C2-3 D2
Saint-Laurent, fleuve QC 28 E7-8 F7
Saint-Laurent, fleuve QC 29 B2-4
Saint-Laurent, fleuve QC 39 F2
Saint-Laurent, fleuve QC 40 F6-7
Saint-Laurent, golfe du NB 31 C8
Saint-Laurent, golfe du NL 36 A1-2
Saint-Laurent, golfe du NL 38 D1-2
Saint-Laurent, golfe du PE 32 A7
Saint-Laurent, golfe du PE 34 A3-5
Saint-Laurent, golfe du PE 35 B4-6
Saint-Laurent, golfe du QC 28 F7-8
Saint-Laurent, golfe du QC 30 D5-6
Saint-Laurent, golfe du QC 39 F6
St. Lawrence NL 36 F6-7
St. Lawrence NL 37 F4-5
St. Lawrence PE 35 B1-2
St. Lawrence, Bay NS 34 A7
St. Lawrence, Cape NS 34 A7
St. Lawrence, Gulf of NB 31 C8
St. Lawrence, Gulf of NL 36 A1-2
St. Lawrence, Gulf of NL 38 D1-2
St. Lawrence, Gulf of PE 32 A8
St. Lawrence, Gulf of PE 34 A3-5
St. Lawrence, Gulf of PE 35 B4-6
St. Lawrence, Gulf of QC 30 D5-6 E5-6
St. Lawrence, Gulf of QC 39 F5-6
St. Lawrence, Gulf of QC 40 F7-8
St. Lawrence Bay NS 34 A7
St. Lawrence Islands NP ON 21 D-E7 D8
St. Lawrence River ON 21 D8
St. Lawrence River ON 24 F2-3
St. Lawrence River QC 25 F8
St. Lawrence River QC 27 B-C4
St. Lawrence River QC 27 D2
St. Lawrence River QC 28 E8
St. Lawrence River QC 29 A4 B3-4

St. Lawrence River QC 39 F2
St. Lawrence River QC 40 F6-7
Saint-Lazare MB 11 E7-8
Saint-Lazare MB 13 E1
Saint-Lazare QC 24 D5
Saint-Lazare-de-Bellechasse 27 B6-7
Saint-Léandre QC 29 B4
Saint-Léolin NB 29 E8
Saint-Léolin NB 30 E1
Saint-Léolin NB 31 B7
St. Leon MB 13 F4
St. Leon MB 14 F3
Saint-Léon QC 28 B5
Saint-Léonard NB 29 F4
Saint-Léonard NB 31 C2-3
Saint-Léonard QC 24 D6
Saint-Léonard QC 27 A4
Saint-Léonard QC 27 E1
Saint-Léonard-d'Aston QC 24 C8
Saint-Léonard-d'Aston QC 27 C-D3 C4
Saint-Léonard-Parent NB 29 F4
Saint-Léonard-Parent NB 31 C2-3
St. Leonards NL 36 E8
St. Leonards NL 37 E6
Saint-Léon-de-Standon QC 27 B7
Saint-Léon-le-Grand QC 24 B7
Saint-Léon-le-Grand QC 25 F7
Saint-Léon-le-Grand QC 27 C3
Saint-Léon-le-Grand QC 29 C4-5
St. Lewis NL 39 C8
St. Lewis River NL 39 C7-8
Saint-Liboire QC 24 D7
Saint-Liboire QC 27 E3
Saint-Liguori QC 24 C6
Saint-Liguori QC 27 D1
Saint-Lin QC 24 C6
Saint-Lin QC 27 D1
St. Lina AB 6 A7
St. Lina AB 9 F7
St. Lina AB 11 A1
St. Lina AB 12 F1
St. Louis PE 35 B2
Saint-Louis QC 24 C7
Saint-Louis QC 27 D2
St. Louis SK 11 B5
Saint-Louis, lac QC 24 B4
Saint-Louis, lac QC 24 E6
Saint-Louis, lac QC 25 F4
Saint-Louis, lac QC 27 E1
Saint-Louis-de-Blandford QC 27 C4
Saint-Louis-de-France QC 24 B7-8
Saint-Louis-de-France QC 25 F7-8
Saint-Louis-de-France QC 27 C3
Saint-Louis-de-Gonzague QC 24 E5
Saint-Louis-de-Gonzague QC 27 C7
Saint-Louis-de-Gonzague QC 27 F1
Saint-Louis-de-Kent NB 31 D8
Saint-Louis-de-Kent NB 32 A6
Saint-Louis-de-l'Isle-aux-Coudres QC 28 E7
Saint-Louis-du-Ha! Ha! QC 29 E1-2
St. Louis Mission NHS ON 18 F7-8
St. Louis Mission NHS ON 20 A6-7
Saint-Luc QC 24 D-E6
Saint-Luc QC 27 B7
Saint-Luc QC 27 E2
Saint-Luc QC 29 B5
Saint-Luc-de-Vincennes QC 24 A-B8
Saint-Luc-de-Vincennes QC 25 F8
Saint-Luc-de-Vincennes QC 27 B3-4
Saint-Lucien QC 24 C8
Saint-Lucien QC 27 D4
Saint-Ludger QC 27 D6-7
Saint-Lunaire QC 38 B4
St. Lunaire NL 38 A5
St. Lunaire-Griquet NL 38 A5
St. Lupicin MB 14 E3
Saint-Magloire QC 27 B7
Saint-Majorique QC 30 B2
Saint-Majorique-de-Grantham QC 24 C7-8
Saint-Majorique-de-Grantham QC 27 D3
Saint-Malachie QC 27 B6-7
St. Malo MB 13 F4
St. Malo MB 14 F5
St. Malo PP MB 13 F4
St. Malo PP MB 14 F5
Saint-Marc QC 23 D4
Saint-Marc-de-Latour QC 28 E8
Saint-Marc-des-Carrières QC 29 A4 B3-4

Saint-Marc-du-Lac-Long QC 29 F2
Saint-Marc-du-Lac-Long QC 31 C1
Saint-Marcel QC 27 A8
Saint-Marcel-de-Richelieu QC 24 C7
Saint-Marcel-de-Richelieu QC 27 D2-3
Saint-Marcellin QC 29 C3
Saint-Marc-sur-Richelieu QC 24 D6-7
Saint-Marc-sur-Richelieu QC 27 E2
St. Margarets NB 31 D7
St. Margarets PE 35 B4
St. Margarets PE 35 D7
St. Margaret's Bay NL 38 B3
St. Margaret's Bay NS 33 C5
St. Margaret Village NS 34 A7
St. Martin MB 13 C-D3
St. Martin MB 14 A3
Saint-Martin QC 24 D7
St. Martin, Lake MB 13 D3
St. Martin, Lake MB 14 A3
Saint-Martin-de-Restigouche NB 29 E5
Saint-Martin-de-Restigouche NB 31 B3-4
St. Martin Junction MB 13 C-D3
St. Martin Junction MB 14 A3
St. Martins NB 32 D5
St. Martins NB 33 A2
St. Martins NS 33 D1
St. Mary, Cape NS 33 E1
St. Mary Reservoir AB 6 F6
St. Mary Reservoir AB 7 F5
St. Mary River BC 6 F4
St. Mary River BC 7 E1
St. Marys NS 32 C3
St. Marys NS 34 F4
St. Marys ON 19 B5
St. Marys ON 20 D4
St. Mary's, Cape NL 36 F8
St. Marys, Cape NL 37 F6
St. Marys, Cape NS 34 F5
St. Mary's Alpine PP BC 6 E-F4
St. Mary's Alpine PP BC 7 E1
St. Mary's Bay NL 37 F7
St. Mary's Bay NS 33 D1
St. Mary's Bay PE 35 E-F7
St. Mary's River NS 34 E-F4 F5
St. Mary's River NS 34 F4-5
St. Marys Road PE 34 C3
St. Mary's Road PE 35 F6
Saint-Mathias-de-Bonneterre QC 27 E5-6 F5
Saint-Mathias-sur-Richelieu QC 24 D6-7
Saint-Mathias-sur-Richelieu QC 27 E2
Saint-Mathieu QC 24 A7
Saint-Mathieu QC 24 E6
Saint-Mathieu QC 25 F7
Saint-Mathieu QC 27 B3
Saint-Mathieu QC 27 F1
Saint-Mathieu QC 29 D2
Saint-Mathieu QC 31 A1
Saint-Mathieu, lac QC 29 D2
Saint-Mathieu-d'Harricana QC 23 D4
Saint-Maure NB 31 A5
Saint-Maurice NB 24 B8
Saint-Maurice QC 25 F8
Saint-Maurice QC 27 C3
Saint-Maurice, RF du QC 25 D7
Saint-Maurice, RF du QC 27 A2
Saint-Maurice, rivière QC 25 A-B6
Saint-Maurice, rivière QC 25 D7
Saint-Maurice, rivière QC 28 C-D1 E2
Saint-Maurice-de-Dalquier QC 23 C-D4
Saint-Maurice-de-l'Échouerie QC 30 B2-3
Saint-Maxime-du-Mont-Louis QC 29 A8
Saint-Médard QC 29 D2
Saint-Médard QC 31 A1
Saint-Méthode QC 26 D8
Saint-Méthode QC 28 B3
Saint-Méthode-de-Frontenac QC 27 D6
St. Michael AB 6 A6
St. Michael AB 8 B7
St. Michael AB 11 A1
St. Michael's Bay NL 39 C8
Saint-Michel QC 24 E6
Saint-Michel QC 27 F1
Saint-Michel, bras QC 27 B6
Saint-Michel-de-Bellechasse QC 27 A6
Saint-Michel-des-Saints QC 24 A5
Saint-Michel-des-Saints QC 25 E5

Saint-Michel-des-Saints QC 27 B1
Saint-Michel-de-Wentworth QC 24 C4
Saint-Modeste QC 29 D1
Saint-Moise QC 29 C4
Saint-Narcisse QC 24 A8
Saint-Narcisse QC 25 F8
Saint-Narcisse QC 27 B3-4
Saint-Narcisse QC 27 B6 C5-6
Saint-Narcisse-de-Rimouski QC 27 E2
Saint-Nazaire QC 24 C-D8
Saint-Nazaire QC 27 D3
Saint-Nazaire-de-Berry QC 27 D3-4
Saint-Nazaire-de-Buckland QC 27 B7
Saint-Nérée QC 27 B6-7
Saint-Nicéphore QC 24 C8
Saint-Nicéphore QC 27 D3-4
Saint-Nicholas QC 32 A7
Saint-Nicholas PE 34 C1
Saint-Nicholas PE 35 D2
Saint-Nicolas QC 27 B5
Saint-Noël QC 29 C4
St. Nora Lake ON 21 B2
Saint-Norbert MB 14 E5
Saint-Norbert NB 31 E8
Saint-Norbert NB 32 A6
Saint-Norbert QC 24 B6-7
Saint-Norbert QC 27 C5
Saint-Norbert-d'Arthabaska QC 27 D4-5
Saint-Norbert-du-Mont-Brun QC 17 C-D8
Saint-Norbert Provincial Heritage Park MB 14 E5
Saint-Octave-de-Métis QC 29 B-C4
Saint-Odilon QC 27 C6-7
St. Ola ON 21 C4
Saint-Omer QC 27 A8
Saint-Omer QC 28 F8
Saint-Omer QC 29 D7
Saint-Omer QC 31 A5
Saint-Onésime QC 28 F8
Saint-Ours QC 24 C7
Saint-Ours QC 27 D2
Saint-Ours, canal de QC 24 C7
Saint-Ours, canal de QC 27 D2
Saint-Ours Canal QC 24 C7
Saint-Ours Canal QC 27 D2
Saint-Pamphile QC 27 A8
Saint-Pancrace, pointe QC 29 A4
St. Pascal ON 24 D3
Saint-Pascal QC 28 E8
Saint-Patrice QC 28 D8
Saint-Patrice QC 29 D1
Saint-Patrice, lac QC 22 D5
Saint-Patrice, ZEC QC 22 D-E5
Saint-Patrice-de-Beaurivage QC 27 C5-6
St. Patrick's Channel NS 34 C6
St. Patricks NL 38 E4-5
St. Patricks Channel NS 34 C6
St. Paul AB 6 A7
St. Paul AB 11 A1-2
Saint-Paul NB 31 F7
Saint-Paul NB 32 B5-6
St. Paul NS 33 A7-8
St. Paul NS 34 E3
Saint-Paul QC 24 C6
Saint-Paul QC 27 D2
Saint-Paul, lac QC 24 A3
Saint-Paul, lac QC 25 E3
Saint-Paul, lac QC 28 D4
Saint-Paul, rivière NL 40 E8
Saint-Paul, rivière QC 38 A2
Saint-Paul, rivière QC 39 D7
Saint-Paul-d'Abbotsford QC 24 D7
Saint-Paul-d'Abbotsford QC 27 E3
Saint-Paul-de-la-Croix QC 28 C-D1 E2
Saint-Paul-de-l'Île-aux-Noix QC 24 E6
Saint-Paul-de-l'Île-aux-Noix QC 27 F2
Saint-Paul-de-Montminy QC 27 B7
Saint-Paul-du-Nord QC 29 B-C2
Saint-Paulin QC 24 B7
Saint-Paulin QC 25 F7
Saint-Paulin QC 27 C2-3
St. Paul River NL 39 D7
St. Pauls NL 38 E2
St. Pauls NL 39 F7
St. Paul's Bay NL 40 F8
St. Pauls Inlet NL 38 E2
St. Pauls Inlet NL 39 F7
St. Pauls Station ON 19 B5
St. Pauls Station ON 20 D4
Saint-Père, lac QC 24 B7
Saint-Père, lac QC 27 C2
St. Peter's NS 34 D6
St. Peters PE 34 B3
St. Peters PE 35 D6
St. Peters Bay PE 34 B3
St. Peters Bay PE 35 D6

St. Peters Canal NHS NS 34 D6-7
St. Peters Harbour PE 35 D6
St. Peters Island PE 34 C2
St. Peters Island PE 35 E4-5
St. Peters Lake PE 35 D6
Saint-Philémon QC 27 B7
Saint-Philibert QC 27 C7
Saint-Philippe NB 31 F8
Saint-Philippe NB 32 B6
Saint-Philippe PE 35 D7
Saint-Philippe QC 24 D-E6
Saint-Philippe QC 27 F2
Saint-Philippe-d'Argenteuil QC 24 D4
Saint-Philippe-de-Néri QC 28 E8
St. Philips SK 11 C-D7
St. Philips SK 13 C1
St. Phillip's NL 37 D8
Saint-Pie QC 24 D7
Saint-Pie QC 27 E3
Saint-Pie-de-Guire QC 24 C7-8
Saint-Pie-de-Guire QC 27 D3
Saint-Pierre QC 24 C6
Saint-Pierre QC 27 A6
Saint-Pierre QC 27 D1-2
Saint-Pierre QC 27 F1
Saint-Pierre, lac QC 24 B7
Saint-Pierre, lac QC 27 C3
Saint-Pierre-Baptiste QC 27 C6
Saint-Pierre-de-Broughton QC 27 C6
Saint-Pierre-de-Lamy QC 29 E2
Saint-Pierre-de-Sorel QC 24 C7
Saint-Pierre-de-Sorel QC 27 D2
Saint-Pierre-de-Wakefield QC 21 A8
Saint-Pierre-de-Wakefield QC 22 F8
Saint-Pierre-de-Wakefield QC 24 C-D2
Saint-Pierre-Jolys MB 13 F4
Saint-Pierre-Jolys MB 14 F5
Saint-Pierre-les-Becquets QC 27 B4
Saint-Pierre-Montmagny QC 27 A7
Saint-Placide QC 24 D5
Saint-Placide-de-Charlevoix QC 28 F6-7
Saint-Polycarpe QC 24 E4-5
Saint-Prime QC 26 E8
Saint-Prime QC 28 B-C4
Saint-Prosper QC 24 A8
Saint-Prosper QC 25 E8
Saint-Prosper QC 27 B4
Saint-Prosper QC 27 C7
Saint-Quentin NB 29 E4-5
Saint-Quentin NB 31 B3-4
Saint-Raphaël PE 35 D2
Saint-Raphaël QC 27 B6-7
St. Raphael PP ON 16 C4
St. Raphaels ON 24 E4
St. Raymond MB 14 E6
Saint-Raymond QC 27 A4
Saint-Redempteur QC 24 D4-5
Saint-Rédempteur QC 27 B5
Saint-Rémi QC 24 E6
Saint-Rémi QC 27 F1
Saint-Rémi-d'Amherst QC 24 C4
Saint-Rémi-de-Tingwick QC 27 D5
Saint-René QC 27 C7
Saint-René-de-Matane QC 29 B5
Saint-Robert QC 24 C7
Saint-Robert QC 27 D2
Saint-Robert-Bellarmin QC 27 D7
St. Roch PE 34 A1
St. Roch PE 35 B2
Saint-Roch QC 17 D8
Saint-Roch QC 23 E2-3
Saint-Roch-de-l'Achigan QC 24 C6
Saint-Roch-de-l'Achigan QC 27 D1-2
Saint-Roch-de-Mékinac QC 24 A7-8
Saint-Roch-de-Mékinac QC 25 E7-8
Saint-Roch-de-Mékinac QC 27 B3
Saint-Roch-de-Richelieu QC 24 C7
Saint-Roch-de-Richelieu QC 27 D2
Saint-Roch-des-Aulnaies QC 28 F7
Saint-Romain QC 27 D6
Saint-Romuald QC 27 B6
Saint-Rosaire, rivière QC 27 C4
St. Rose NS 34 B-C6
Saint-Rose-du-Nord QC 28 C6-7
Saint-Samuel QC 24 C8
Saint-Samuel QC 27 D4
Saint-Samuel-Station QC 27 D6

Saint-Sauveur NB 30 F1
Saint-Sauveur NB 31 B7
Saint-Sauveur-des-Monts QC 24 C5
Saint-Sébastien QC 24 E7
Saint-Sébastien QC 27 D6
Saint-Sébastien QC 27 F2
Saint-Sébastien, mont QC 27 D6
Saint-Sévère QC 24 B7
Saint-Sévère QC 27 C2-3
Saint-Séverin QC 24 A6
Saint-Séverin QC 25 E4
Saint-Séverin QC 27 B3
Saint-Séverin QC 27 C6
St. Shotts NL 37 F7
Saint-Siméon QC 28 D8
Saint-Siméon QC 29 D8
Saint-Siméon QC 31 A6
Saint-Simon NB 30 E2
Saint-Simon NB 31 B8
Saint-Simon QC 24 C-D7
Saint-Simon QC 27 D3
Saint-Simon QC 29 C2
Saint-Simon-les-Mines QC 27 C7
Saint-Sixte QC 24 D3
Saints-Martyrs-Canadiens QC 27 D5
Saint-Stanislas QC 24 A8
Saint-Stanislas QC 25 E8
Saint-Stanislas QC 26 D8
Saint-Stanislas QC 27 B3
Saint-Stanislas QC 28 A4
Saint-Stanislas-de-Kostka QC 24 E5
St. Stephen NB 32 E2
St. Stephens NL 37 F7
St. Sulpice QC 24 C6
St. Sulpice QC 27 D2
Saint-Sylvère QC 24 B8
Saint-Sylvère QC 25 F8
Saint-Sylvère QC 27 C4
Saint-Sylvestre QC 27 C6
Saint-Télesphore QC 24 E4-5
St. Teresa NL 36 C2
St. Teresa PE 34 C3
St. Teresa PE 35 E6
Saint-Tharcisius QC 29 C5
Saint-Théodore-d'Acton QC 24 D7-8
Saint-Théodore-d'Acton QC 27 E3
Saint-Théophile QC 27 D6
St. Theresa Point MB 13 A5
St. Thomas NB 31 E8
St. Thomas NB 32 A6
St. Thomas NL 37 D8
St. Thomas ON 19 C-D5
St. Thomas ON 20 F4
Saint-Thomas QC 24 C6
Saint-Thomas QC 27 D2
Saint-Thomas, lac QC 25 D6-7
Saint-Thomas, lac QC 27 A2-3
Saint-Thomas, lac QC 28 F2-3
St. Thomas Bay BC 1 B4-5
Saint-Thomas-d'Aquin QC 24 D7
Saint-Thomas-d'Aquin QC 27 E3
Saint-Thomas-de-Caxton QC 24 B7
Saint-Thomas-de-Caxton QC 25 F7
Saint-Thomas-de-Caxton QC 27 C3
Saint-Thomas-Didyme QC 26 D7
Saint-Thomas-Didyme QC 28 B3
Saint-Thuribe QC 24 A8
Saint-Thuribe QC 25 E8
Saint-Thuribe QC 27 B3
Saint-Timothée PE 34 A1
Saint-Timothée PE 35 B2
Saint-Timothée QC 24 E5
Saint-Timothée QC 27 F1
Saint-Tite QC 24 A8
Saint-Tite QC 25 E8
Saint-Tite QC 27 B3
Saint-Tite-des-Caps QC 27 A6-7
Saint-Tite-des-Caps QC 28 F6
Saint-Ubalde QC 24 A8
Saint-Ubalde QC 25 E8
Saint-Ubalde QC 28 B4
Saint-Ulric QC 29 B4
Saint-Urbain QC 28 E6-7
Saint-Urbain-Premier QC 24 E6
Saint-Urbain-Premier QC 27 F1
Saint-Valentin QC 24 E6
Saint-Valentin QC 27 F2
Saint-Valère QC 24 D7-8
Saint-Valérien QC 27 E3
Saint-Valérien QC 29 C3
Saint-Vallier QC 27 A6
Saint-Venant-de-Paquette QC 27 F5
St. Veronica's NL 36 D5-6
St. Veronica's NL 37 E4
Saint-Vianney QC 29 C4-5
Saint-Viateur QC 24 B6-7
Saint-Viateur QC 27 C1

Saint-Victor QC 27 C6
St. Victor SK 11 F5
Saint-Victor, rivière QC 27 C-D6
St. Victor's Petroglyphs Provincial Historic Park SK 11 F4-5
St. Vincent AB 6 A7
St. Vincent AB 11 A1-2
St. Vincent's NL 37 F7
St. Vincent's-St. Stephen's-Peter's River NL 37 F7
St. Walburg SK 6 A8
St. Walburg SK 11 A2-3
Saint-Wenceslas QC 24 B8
Saint-Wenceslas QC 27 C3-4
Saint-Wilfrid NB 31 C7
St. Williams ON 19 D6
St. Williams ON 20 F5
Saint-Yvon QC 30 A2
Saint-Zacharie QC 27 C7
Saint-Zénon QC 24 A5
Saint-Zénon QC 25 F5
Saint-Zénon QC 27 B1
Saint-Zéphirin-de-Courval QC 24 C8
Saint-Zéphirin-de-Courval QC 27 D3
Saint-Zotique QC 24 E5
Sainville River NT 5 E5
Sairs, lac QC 22 C3
Sakami QC 40 E4
Sakami, lac QC 40 E4
Sakami, rivière QC 40 E5
Sakimay SK 11 E6-7
Sakwaso Lake ON 13 B7
Sakwatamau River AB 6 A4
Sakwatamau River AB 8 A3 B4
Sakwesew Lake MB 15 E6
Salaberry-de-Valleyfield QC 24 E5
Salem NS 32 C7
Salem NS 34 D1
Salem ON 19 A6
Salem ON 20 C5
Salem ON 21 E4
Salem Road NS 34 D7
Salford ON 19 C5
Salford ON 20 E4
Salisbury NB 31 F7-8
Salisbury NB 32 B6
Salisbury Island NU 40 A4
Salisbury Island NU 41 D7
Salk, lac QC 26 C5
Salliq (Coral Harbour) NU 40 A3
Salliq (Coral Harbour) NU 41 D6-7
Salluit QC 40 B4
Salluit QC 41 D8
Sally's Beach PP PE 35 E7
Sally's Cove NL 38 E2
Sally's Cove NL 39 F7
Sallysout Creek BC 3 E4
Sally's Pond PP PE 34 C4
Salmo BC 6 F3
Salmon Arm BC 6 E2
Salmon Bay QC 38 A-B3
Salmon Beach NB 29 E8
Salmon Beach NB 30 E1
Salmon Beach NB 31 B6-7
Salmon Cove NL 36 B1
Salmon Cove NL 37 D7-8
Salmon Creek NB 31 F6
Salmon Creek NB 32 B4
Salmon Fork YT 5 D1-2
Salmon Inlet BC 1 F6
Salmon Inlet BC 2 D4
Salmon Lake ON 21 C3
Salmon Point ON 21 F5
Salmon River BC 1 A6-7
Salmon River BC 1 E5
Salmon River BC 2 B1
Salmon River NB 29 F4
Salmon River NB 31 C3
Salmon River NB 31 E7 F6
Salmon River NB 32 B4-5
Salmon River NL 36 D5
Salmon River NL 37 D3
Salmon River NL 38 B4
Salmon River NL 39 D-E8
Salmon River NS 33 A6-7
Salmon River NS 33 E1
Salmon River NS 34 E2
Salmon River ON 21 D5-6
Salmon River ON 21 D-E5
Salmon River Lake NS 34 E5
Salmon River Road NS 34 D7
Salmonier NL 36 F6-7
Salmonier NL 37 E7
Salmonier NL 37 F4-5
Salmonier Provincial Nature Park NL 37 E7
Salon-de-Thé-des-Chutes-Twin, LHN du BC 7 A1
Salone, lac QC 25 C5
Salone, lac QC 28 F1
Salsman PP NS 34 E5
Salt Harbour Island NL 38 E6-7
Salt Lake SK 11 F5
Salt Point MB 11 B8
Salt Point MB 13 B1
Salt Point MB 14 A1
Salt Pond NL 36 E6-7
Salt Pond NL 37 E4-5
Salt Prairie AB 9 E4
Salt River AB 9 A6
Salt River AB 10 F8
Salt River AB 12 A2
Salt River NT 9 A6
Salt River NT 10 F8
Salt River NT 41 E1-2
Salt Springs NS 33 A7
Salt Springs NS 34 E3
Salt Springs NS 34 E4-5
Salt Springs PP NS 33 A7
Salt Springs PP NS 34 E2-3
Saltair BC 2 E4
Saltcoats SK 11 D7
Salter SK 11 C3
Saltery Bay BC 1 F6
Saltery Bay BC 2 C3-4
Saltery Bay PP BC 1 E-F6
Saltery Bay PP BC 2 C3
Saltford ON 20 C3
Saltspring Island BC 2 E4
Salutation Cove PE 35 D2-3
Salvador SK 6 C8
Salvador SK 11 C2
Salvage NL 37 B7
Salvail, rivière QC 24 C-D7
Salvail, rivière QC 27 D2-3
Sam Lake ON 13 E7
Sam Lake ON 16 D3
Samaqua, rivière QC 26 B-C8
Sambaa Deh Falls TP NT 10 E4
Sambo Creek YT 4 E6
Sambo Lake YT 4 E6
Sambro NS 32 F8
Sambro NS 33 C6
Sambro, Cape NS 33 C-D6
Sampson Lake ON 16 A3
Samson, rivière QC 27 D-E7
Samuel de Champlain PP ON 17 F8
Samuel de Champlain PP ON 22 D2
Sanca BC 6 F4
San Clara MB 11 D7-8
San Clara MB 13 D1
Sanctuary SK 11 D2
Sandbanks PP NL 36 D3
Sandbanks PP NL 37 D1
Sandbanks PP ON 21 E-F5
Sandbar Lake PP ON 13 F7-8
Sandbar Lake PP ON 16 D-E4
Sand Beach NS 33 E1
Sandeau, lac QC 22 B4
Sandfield ON 18 C3-4
Sandfly Lake SK 12 E4-5
Sandford NS 33 E1
Sandford ON 20 B7
Sandford ON 21 E1-2
Sandford Island ON 18 B2
Sandford Lake ON 13 F7
Sandgren SK 11 D2
Sandhill ON 19 A7
Sandhill ON 20 C6
Sand Hill Cove NL 39 B8
Sand Hill River NL 39 B7-8 C7
Sand Hills Beach PP NS 33 F2
Sandhurst ON 21 E6
Sandilands MB 13 F4
Sandilands MB 14 F6
Sand Lake ON 13 E5
Sand Lake ON 16 D1
Sand Lake ON 18 B8
Sand Lake ON 18 C8
Sand Lake ON 21 A1
Sand Lake ON 21 C5
Sand Lake ON 21 D7
Sand Lake ON 21 A1-2
Sand Lake ON 22 D1
Sand Lake ON 22 F1
Sand Lake ON 24 F1
Sand Lakes PP MB 15 C3
Sand Lakes PP MB 41 F4
Sandon BC 6 E3
Sand Point NS 34 E6
Sandpoint Island PP ON 16 F2-3
Sand Pond NWA NS 33 E2
Sandridge MB 13 E3
Sandridge MB 14 C4-5
Sandringham NL 36 B8
Sandringham NL 37 B6
Sand River AB 9 F7
Sand River AB 12 E-F2
Sand River NS 32 D6
Sand River NS 33 A4
Sandspit BC 1 B1-2
Sandville NS 34 D2
Sandwell PP BC 2 E4
Sandwich Bay NL 39 B7
Sandwich Bay NL 40 D8
Sandy, pointe NB 30 E2-3
Sandy Bar MB 13 C4
Sandy Bay MB 13 E3
Sandy Bay MB 14 C3
Sandy Bay SK 9 A7
Sandy Bay SK 11 A-B4
Sandy Bay SK 12 A3
Sandy Bay SK 12 E7
Sandy Bay SK 15 E1
Sandy Beach AB 6 A5
Sandy Beach AB 8 B-C6
Sandy Beach QC 30 B3
Sandybeach Lake ON 13 E7
Sandy Cove NL 37 B6-7
Sandy Cove NL 38 B4
Sandy Cove NL 38 E7
Sandy Cove NS 32 F4
Sandy Cove NS 33 D1
Sandy Cove ON 20 B7
Sandy Cove ON 21 D1
Sandy Harbour River NL 36 D7-8
Sandy Harbour River NL 37 D5-6
Sandy Hook MB 13 E4
Sandy Hook MB 14 C5
Sandy Island ON 18 B7
Sandy Island ON 18 D6-7
Sandy Island PMP BC 1 F5-6
Sandy Island PMP BC 2 D2-3
Sandy Islands, RNP ON 17 F3
Sandy Islands PNR ON 17 F3
Sandy Lake AB 6 A5
Sandy Lake AB 8 B6
Sandy Lake AB 9 E6
Sandy Lake AB 9 E5
Sandy Lake MB 11 E8
Sandy Lake MB 13 E2
Sandy Lake MB 14 C1
Sandy Lake NL 36 A4
Sandy Lake NL 37 A2
Sandy Lake NL 38 F3
Sandy Lake NL 39 F8
Sandy Lake NT 5 C5
Sandy Lake ON 13 B6
Sandy Lake ON 13 B6
Sandy Lake ON 40 E1
Sandy Lake ON 40 E1
Sandy Narrows SK 12 F6
Sandy Point NB 30 E2-3
Sandy Point NB 31 A8
Sandy Point NL 39 B6
Sandy Point NS 33 F3
Sandy Point ON 20 A8
Sandy Point ON 21 D2
Sanford MB 13 F3
Sanford MB 14 E4-5
Sangsues, lac aux QC 22 D4
Sangudo AB 6 A5
Sangudo AB 8 B4-5
Sanikluaq QC 40 D4
Sanirajak (Hall Beach) NU 41 B6
Sanirajak (Hall Beach) NU 42 F6
San Josef BC 1 E3-4
San Josef Bay BC 1 E3
San Juan River BC 2 F3
Sanmaur QC 25 B6
Sanmaur QC 28 D1
Sans Souci ON 18 D7
Santa Boca PP BC 1 F4
Santein, lac QC 39 E6
Santoy Lake ON 16 E7
Santoy Lake ON 17 C2
Saoyue and Ehdacho HS (Saoyue Unit) NT 10 A3-4
Saoyue HS NT 41 C1
Sapawe ON 13 F7-8
Sapawe ON 16 E4
Saprae Creek Estates AB 9 D7
Saprae Creek Estates AB 12 D2
Sapton MB 14 D5-6
Sarah Island BC 1 B3
Sarah Lake NT 10 B5
Saratoga Beach BC 1 E5-6
Saratoga Beach BC 2 C2
Sarcee AB 7 A5
Sardis BC 1 F8
Sardis BC 2 E6
Sargeant Bay PP BC 2 D4
Sarita BC 2 E2
Sarnia ON 19 C2
Sarnia ON 20 E1
Sarsfield ON 24 D3
Sarto MB 13 F4
Sarto MB 14 E-F5
Sasaginnigak Lake MB 13 D5
Sasaginnigak Lake MB 14 A7
Sasaginnigak Lake MB 16 B1
Saseginaga, lac QC 22 B3
Saskatchewan, rivière SK 11 A6
Saskatchewan Beach SK 11 D5-6
Saskatchewan Landing PP SK 11 E3
Saskatchewan Nord, rivière AB 6 B4-5 C5
Saskatchewan Nord, rivière AB 8 B8
Saskatchewan Nord, rivière AB 8 E4
Saskatchewan Nord, rivière AB 11 A1-2
Saskatchewan Nord, rivière SK 6 B8
Saskatchewan Nord, rivière SK 11 B-C4
Saskatchewan Point MB 13 C3
Saskatchewan River SK 11 B5
Saskatchewan River Crossing AB 6 C3-4
Saskatchewan River Crossing AB 8 F2
Saskatchewan Sud, rivière AB 6 D-E8
Saskatchewan Sud, rivière AB 7 C-D8
Saskatchewan Sud, rivière AB 11 D2 E1-2
Saskatchewan Sud, rivière SK 11 C-D4
Saskatoon SK 11 C4-5
Saskatoon Island PP AB 9 E-F2
Saskatoon Lake, RNOM de AB 9 E-F2
Saskatoon Lake NMBS AB 9 E-F2
Saskeram Lake MB 11 A7
Saskeram Lake MB 13 A1
Sasquatch PP BC 1 F8
Sasquatch PP BC 2 D6-7
Sass River NT 10 F7
Satah Mountain BC 1 C6
Satah River YT 5 D4
Satellite Bay NT 42 C2
Saturna BC 2 E4-5
Saturna Island BC 2 E-F5
Sauble Beach ON 18 F4-5
Sauble Beach ON 20 A3-4
Sauble Beach North ON 18 F4-5
Sauble Beach North ON 20 A3-4
Sauble Beach South ON 18 F4-5
Sauble Beach South ON 20 A3
Sauble Falls ON 18 F4-5
Sauble Falls ON 20 A3-4
Sauble Falls PP ON 18 F4-5
Sauble Falls PP ON 20 A3-4
Sauble River ON 18 F5
Sauble River ON 20 A4
Saubles, lac aux QC 22 A3
Saugeen Bluffs CA ON 20 B3-4
Saugeen River ON 20 A3 B4
Saugeen River ON 20 B4-5
Saugeen Shores ON 18 F4
Saugeen Shores ON 20 A3
Saugstad, Mount BC 1 C5
Saulnierville NS 33 D1
Sault-au-Mouton QC 29 C2
Sault au Mouton, rivière du QC 28 B-C8
Sault au Mouton, rivière du QC 29 B-C1
Sault aux Cochons, lac du QC 28 A8
Sault aux Cochons, rivière du QC 28 A-B8
Sault aux Cochons, rivière du QC 29 A-B1
Saulteaux SK 11 B3
Saulteaux River AB 9 F5
Sault Ste. Marie ON 17 F3-4
Saumon, cap au QC 28 E8
Saumon, rivière au QC 27 E5-6
Saumons, rivière aux QC 30 A6
Saumur, lac QC 39 E4
Saunders Cove NL 36 B8
Saunders Cove NL 37 B6
Sautauriski, lac QC 28 F5-6
Sauterelles, lac aux QC 39 D3-4
Sauvage, lac du NT 10 A8
Sauvage, lac du QC 26 A4
Sauvage, pointe QC 29 C1
Sauvageau, lac QC 25 A6-7
Sauvageau, lac QC 26 F6-7
Sauvageau, lac QC 28 C2
Savage Cove NL 38 B3-4
Savage Harbour PE 34 B3
Savage Harbour PE 35 D6
Savage Harbour PE 35 D6
Savage Lake ON 18 A3
Savane, lac de la QC 24 A-B4
Savane, lac de la QC 25 F4
Savant Lake ON 13 E8
Savant Lake ON 13 E8
Savant Lake ON 16 C5
Savant Lake ON 16 D4
Savary, lac QC 22 C7
Savary, lac QC 24 A1
Savary, lac QC 25 E1
Savary Island BC 1 E6
Savary Island BC 2 C2
Savary Island BC 2 C2
Savary PP NS 32 F4
Savary PP NS 33 C1-2 D2
Savona BC 1 D-E8
Savona BC 2 A8
Savona BC 6 D1
Sawbill NL 39 B2
Sawbill Lake NL 39 B2
Sawlog Bay ON 18 E7
Sawyer Glacier BC 3 C1-2
Sawyerville QC 27 E5
Sayabec QC 29 C4
Saymo-Aubinadong-Gong PP ON 17 E4
Sayward BC 1 E5
Sayward BC 2 B1
Scandia AB 6 E6-7
Scandia AB 7 D6
Scandinavia MB 14 C1-2
Scanlon Creek CA ON 20 B7
Scanlon Creek CA ON 21 E1
Scapa AB 8 F8
Scarborough ON 19 A8
Scarborough ON 20 C7
Scarborough ON 21 F1
Scarth MB 11 F8
Scarth MB 13 E-F1
Scaterie Island NS 34 C8
Scatter River Old Growth PP BC 3 A6
Scent Grass, RNOM SK 11 B3
Scent Grass NMBS SK 11 B3
Sceptre SK 6 D8
Sceptre SK 11 D2
Schade Lake ON 13 B8
Schade River ON 13 B7-8
Schanzenfeld MB 13 F3
Schanzenfeld MB 14 F4
Schefferville NL 39 A2
Schefferville NL 40 D6
Schipa River BC 3 B-C5
Schist Lake MB 12 F7
Schist Lake MB 15 F1
Schmitt, rivière QC 30 A6
Schoenfeld SK 11 E3
Schoen Lake PP BC 1 E5
Schoenwiese MB 14 F4
Schomberg ON 20 B-C6
Schoolhouse Lake PP BC 1 C8
Schoolhouse Lake PP BC 6 C1
Schreiber ON 16 E7
Schreiber ON 17 C1
Schreiber Channel, RNP ON 16 F7
Schreiber Channel, RNP ON 17 C1
Schreiber Channel PNR ON 16 F7
Schreiber Channel PNR ON 17 C1
Schuler AB 6 E8
Schuler AB 11 E2
Schultz Lake NU 41 D4
Schumacher ON 17 C6
Schutt ON 21 B5
Schwandt River SK 12 A6
Schwandt River SK 15 A1
Schwartz QC 22 F6-7
Schwartz QC 24 C1
Schyan, lac QC 22 D5
Schyan, rivière QC 22 E5
Scollard AB 8 F7
Scone ON 20 B4
Scot Bay ON 14 D8
Scotch Bay MB 14 C3
Scotch Bonnet Island NWA ON 21 F4-5
Scotch Creek BC 6 D2
Scotchfort PE 35 D5
Scotch Line ON 21 C7
Scotch Line ON 24 F1
Scotch Ridge NB 32 D1
Scotch River ON 24 D3 E4
Scotch Settlement ON 18 F4-5
Scotch Settlement ON 20 A3
Scotchtown NB 32 C4
Scotchtown NS 34 C7-8
Scotch Village NS 32 E8
Scotch Village NS 33 B5
Scotch Village NS 34 F1
Scotfield AB 6 D7
Scotfield AB 7 A7
Scotfield AB 11 C-D1
Scotia ON 18 C8
Scotia ON 21 A1
Scotia ON 22 F1
Scotland ON 19 C6
Scotland ON 20 E5
Scots Bay NS 33 A4
Scots Bay PP NS 32 D7
Scots Bay PP NS 33 A4
Scotsburn NS 34 E3
Scotsguard SK 11 F3
Scotstown QC 27 E6
Scotsville NS 34 C6
Scott QC 27 B6
Scott SK 11 C3
Scott, Cape BC 1 D3
Scott, lac QC 26 A4
Scottie Creek YT 4 B-C1
Scott Islands BC 1 D3
Scott Islands PP BC 1 D-E3
Scott Lake SK 12 A4
Scott Settlement ON 21 B4
Scotts Lake NL 36 C-D3
Scotts Lake NL 37 C-D1
Scottsville ON 19 C4
Scottsville ON 20 E3
Scoudouc NB 31 F8
Scoudouc NB 32 B6-7
Scout Lake SK 11 F4
Scraggy Lake NS 33 B7
Scraggy Lake NS 34 F3
Scroggie Creek YT 4 B2
Scudder ON 19 F2
Scugog ON 20 B8
Scugog ON 21 E2
Scugog, Lake ON 20 B8
Scugog, Lake ON 21 E2
Scugog River ON 20 B8
Scugog River ON 21 D-E2
Scurvy Creek YT 4 E6
Seabright NS 32 F8
Seabright NS 33 C5
Seacliffe ON 19 E2
Seacow Head PE 32 B8
Seacow Head PE 34 C1
Seacow Head PE 35 D2-3
Seacow Pond PE 34 A1
Seacow Pond PE 35 A2
Seafoam NS 34 D3
Seaforth NS 33 C6-7
Seaforth ON 19 A-B4
Seaforth ON 20 D3
Seager Wheeler Lake SK 11 A6
Seager Wheeler Lake Provincial Ecological Reserve SK 11 A6
Seagram Lake SK 6 B8
Seagram Lake SK 11 C2
Seagrave ON 20 B8
Seagrave ON 21 E2
Seagrove NS 35 F2
Seahorse Lake NT 10 B8
Seahorse Point NU 40 A4
Seahorse Point NU 41 D7
Seal Bay NL 36 A6
Seal Bay NL 37 A4
Seal Bay NL 38 B4-5
Seal Bay NL 38 F5
Seal Bight NL 39 C8
Seal Cove NB 32 F2
Seal Cove NL 36 E5
Seal Cove NL 37 E3
Seal Cove NL 38 E4
Seal Cove NL 39 F8
Seal Harbour NS 34 F5
Seal Inlet BC 1 A1
Seal Island NS 33 F1
Seal Islands Harbour NL 39 B-C8
Seal Lake NL 39 B5
Seal Point PE 35 B1
Seal River MB 15 B4-5
Seal River MB 41 F4
Seal Rocks NL 36 C2
Searchmont ON 17 F4
Searletown PE 32 B8
Searletown PE 34 C1
Searletown PE 35 E3
Searston NL 36 D1
Searsville NB 32 C4
Sea Side NB 31 A5-6
Seattle, Mount YT 4 E2
Sea View PE 32 A8
Sea View PE 34 B1-2
Sea View PE 35 C3
Sea Wolf Island NWA NS 34 B5-6
Seba Beach AB 6 B5
Seba Beach AB 8 C5
Sebaskachu River NL 39 B5-6
Sébastien, lac QC 26 B4
Sebastopol ON 19 B5
Sebastopol ON 20 D4
Sebright ON 20 A7
Sebright ON 21 C1-2
Sebringville ON 19 B5
Sebringville ON 20 D4
Sechelt BC 1 F6
Sechelt BC 2 D4
Sechelt Inlet BC 2 D4
Sechelt Inlets MPP BC 1 F6
Sechelt Inlets MPP BC 2 D4
Sechelt Peninsula BC 1 F6
Sechelt Peninsula BC 2 D4
Sec Lake ON 22 E4
2nd Burnt Pond NL 36 B7
2nd Burnt Pond NL 37 B5
Second Eel Lake NB 32 C1
Second Lac NB 29 E3
Second Peninsula NS 33 D5
Second Peninsula PP NS 33 D5
Secord ON 17 F7
Secord ON 18 A5-6
Secretan SK 11 E4
Sedalia AB 6 C7
Sedalia AB 7 A8
Sedalia AB 11 C1-2
Seddons Corner MB 13 E4
Seddons Corner MB 14 D6
Sedgewick AB 6 B7
Sedgewick AB 11 B1
Sedgman Lake PP ON 16 C7
Sedgman Lake PP ON 17 A1
Sedgwick, Mount YT 5 B2-3
Sedley SK 11 E6
Seebe AB 6 D5
Seebe AB 7 B3
Seeber Lake ON 13 A6
Seeber River ON 13 A6
Seech MB 14 C1
Seeley Lake PP BC 3 F4
Seeleys Bay ON 21 D7
Seffernville NS 32 F7
Seffernville NS 33 C4-5
Segise Lake ON 16 D2
Séguin, lac QC 22 B7
Séguin, lac QC 25 C-D2
Seguin Lake ON 22 F1
Seguin River ON 18 D7
Seibert Lake AB 9 F7
Seibert Lake AB 12 F1
Seignelay, rivière QC 39 C1
Seigs Corner MB 14 D6
Seine River ON 16 E-F3
Seine River Village ON 16 F3
Seize Îles, lac des QC 24 C4
Sekulmun Lake YT 4 D2
Selbaie QC 17 B8
Selby ON 21 D6
Seldom NL 38 E7
Selenite Point Provincial Ecological Reserve SK 12 F4
Self Lake NT 10 A5
Seline River ON 16 E4
Selkirk MB 13 E4
Selkirk MB 14 D5
Selkirk ON 19 C7
Selkirk ON 20 F6
Selkirk PE 35 D7
Selkirk Mountains BC 6 D3
Selkirk PP ON 19 D7
Selkirk PP ON 20 F6
Seller Lake MB 15 F5
Sellwood Bay NT 5 A7-8
Selma NS 32 D8
Selma NS 33 A6
Selma NS 34 E2
Selous, Mount YT 4 C5
Selwyn ON 21 D3
Selwyn YT 4 C2
Selwyn CA ON 21 D3
Selwyn Lake NT 41 E-F3
Selwyn Lake SK 12 A5
Selwyn Mountains YT 4 A5-6 C6-7
Semans SK 11 D5
Semenof Hills YT 4 D4
Semmens Lake MB 15 F5-6
Semple Lake MB 15 F5
Senate SK 6 F8
Senate SK 11 F2
Senlac SK 6 C8
Senlac SK 11 C2
Senneterre QC 23 D5-6
Senneville, lac QC 23 E4-5
Sentinel Peak BC 3 F7
Sentinel Peak BC 9 F1
Separation, Point NT 5 C4-5
Separation Lake ON 13 E6
Separation Lake ON 16 D2
Sept Frères, lac des QC 24 B3
Sept Frères, lac des QC 25 F3
Sept Îles, lac QC 27 A5
Sept Îles, lac des QC 30 D2
Sept-Îles QC 39 E-F2
Sept-Îles QC 40 F6
Sept Milles, lac QC 22 C4-5
Sequart Lake NL 39 C-D4
Serath SK 11 D5
Sérigny, rivière QC 40 D6
Serpent, lac QC 22 E8
Serpent, lac QC 23 E7
Serpent, lac QC 24 B2-3
Serpent, lac QC 25 A2
Serpent, lac QC 26 E2
Serpent, rivière QC 23 D8 E7-8
Serpent, rivière QC 25 A2
Serpent, rivière QC 26 E2
Serpentine Lake NL 36 B2
Serpent River ON 13 D6-7
Serpent River ON 17 F5
Serpent River ON 18 A3
Serpent River ON 18 A3 B2
Serpent River ON 18 A2-3
Seseganaga Lake ON 16 D5
Sesegonago Lake ON 13 E8
Sesekinika ON 17 D7
Sesikinaga Lake ON 13 D7
Sesikinaga Lake ON 16 B-C3
Seton Lake BC 1 E7
Seton Lake BC 2 A-B6
Seton Portage BC 1 E7
Seton Portage BC 2 A6
Seton Portage Provincial Historic Park BC 1 E7
Seton Portage Provincial Historic Park BC 2 A-B6
Settee Lake MB 15 D4
Setting Lake MB 15 F3
Seul, lac ON 13 E7
Seul, lac ON 13 E7
Seul, lac ON 16 C-D3
Seul, lac ON 16 D3
Seven Persons AB 6 E7
Seven Persons AB 7 D-E8
Seven Persons AB 11 E1
Seven Persons Creek AB 6 F7-8
Seven Persons Creek AB 7 E8
Seven Persons Creek AB 11 E-F1
Seven Sisters Falls MB 13 E4-5
Seven Sisters Falls MB 14 D6-7
Seven Sisters PP BC 3 F4
70 Mile House BC 1 D8
70 Mile House BC 6 D1
Severn Bridge ON 18 E8
Severn Bridge ON 21 C1
Severn Falls ON 18 E8
Severn Falls ON 21 C1
Severn Lake ON 13 A7-8
Severn River ON 13 B6
Severn River ON 13 B7
Severn River ON 15 F8
Severn River ON 18 E8
Severn River ON 21 C1
Severn River ON 40 D1-2
Severn River PP ON 13 A8
Severn Sound ON 18 E7
Sevestre, lac QC 39 C1
Sevogle NB 31 D6
Seward Glacier YT 4 E1
Sewell MB 14 F5
Sewell Inlet BC 1 B1
Sexsmith AB 9 E2-3
Sextant Rapids, RNP ON 17 A6
Sextant Rapids PNR ON 17 A6
Seymour Arm BC 6 D2
Seymour Inlet BC 1 D4
Seymourville MB 13 D4
Seymourville MB 14 B6
SG̲aang Gwaii (Anthony Island) BC 1 C1-2
SG̲aang Gwaii (île Anthony) BC 1 C1-2
Shabaqua Corner ON 16 F5
Shabo NL 39 B-C2
Shabogamo Lake NL 39 C2
Shabogamo Lake NL 40 E6
Shabumeni Lake ON 16 B3
Shabuskwia Lake ON 16 B6
Shackleton SK 11 D-E3
Shad Bay NS 32 F8
Shad Bay NS 33 C5-6
Shadd Lake SK 12 E5
Shadow Lake ON 20 A8
Shadow Lake ON 21 C2
Shaftesbury AB 9 E3
Shag, île QC 30 F7
Shag Harbour NS 33 F2
Shagwenaw Lake SK 12 E3-4
Shakespeare ON 19 B5
Shakespeare ON 20 D4
Shakespeare Island ON 16 D6
Shakespeare Island ON 17 B1
Shalalth BC 1 E7
Shalalth BC 2 A6
Shaler Mountains NT 41 A2-3
Shaler Mountains NT 42 E2
Shallop Cove NL 36 C2
Shalloway Cove NL 36 B8
Shalloway Cove NL 37 B6
Shallow Bay NT 5 B4
Shallow Lake ON 18 F5
Shallow Lake ON 20 A4
Shallow River, RNP ON 17 C7
Shallow River PNR ON 17 C7
Shamattawa MB 15 E7
Shamattawa MB 40 D1
Shamblers Cove NL 37 A6-7
Shamblers Cove NL 38 F8
Shamrock ON 21 B6
Shamrock PE 35 D3
Shamrock SK 11 E4
Shandro AB 8 B8
Shanklin NB 32 D4-5
Shanklin NB 33 A2
Shanly ON 21 C8
Shanly ON 24 F2
Shannon NB 32 C4
Shannon QC 27 A5
Shannon, lac QC 23 E8
Shannon, lac QC 25 B2
Shannon, lac QC 26 F2
Shannon Falls PP BC 1 F6-7
Shannon Falls PP BC 2 D5
Shannon Lake MB 12 A7-8
Shannon Lake MB 15 A2
Shannon Lake ON 17 B5
Shannonville ON 21 E5
Shanty Bay ON 18 F8
Shanty Bay ON 20 A7
Shanty Bay ON 21 D1
Shantz AB 7 A3
Shapio Lake NL 39 A5
Sharbot Lake ON 21 C6
Sharbot Lake ON 21 C6
Sharbot Lake PP ON 21 C6
Sharon ON 20 B7
Sharon ON 21 E1
Sharpe Lake MB 13 A6
Sharpe Lake MB 15 F6
Sharpes Creek ON 19 A4
Sharpes Creek ON 20 C3
Sharpewood MB 14 B4
Sharples Lake NT 10 B7
Sharp Mountain YT 5 D3
Sharpstone Lake ON 13 C5
Sharun Lake NT 10 D5
Shaughnessy AB 6 E6
Shaughnessy AB 7 E5-6
Shaunavon SK 11 F3
Shaw, lac à QC 25 B8
Shaw, lac à QC 28 E3
Shawanaga ON 18 C6-7
Shawanaga Inlet ON 18 C-D6
Shawanaga Island ON 18 C6
Shawanaga Lake ON 18 C7
Shawinigan QC 24 A7-8
Shawinigan QC 25 F7-8
Shawinigan QC 27 B3
Shawinigan, lac QC 24 A7
Shawinigan, lac QC 25 E7
Shawinigan, lac QC 27 B2
Shawinigan-Sud QC 24 A7-8
Shawinigan-Sud QC 25 F7-8
Shawinigan-Sud QC 27 B3
Shaw Lake SK 12 D6
Shaw Lake SK 15 D1
Shawnigan Lake BC 2 F4
Shawshe (Dalton Post) Territorial Historic Site YT 4 E2-3
Shawville QC 21 A6-7
Shawville QC 22 F6-7
Shawville QC 24 D1
Shearwater BC 1 C4
Sheaves Cove NL 36 B-C1
Shebandowan ON 16 F5
Shebandowan Lake ON 16 F5
Shebeshekong River ON 18 D6-7
Shedden ON 19 D4
Shedden ON 20 F3
Shedden Lake ON 18 A3
Shediac NB 31 F8
Shediac NB 32 B6-7

Shediac, baie de NB 32 B6-7
Shediac, baie de NB 35 D-E1
Shediac Bay NB 31 F8
Shediac Bay NB 32 B6-7
Shediac Bay NB 35 D-E1
Shediac Bridge NB 31 F8
Shediac Bridge NB 32 B6
Shediac Cape NB 31 F8
Shediac Cape NB 32 B6
Shediac Ridge NB 31 D7
Sheemahant River BC 1 C-D5
Sheenboro QC 22 E5
Sheep River AB 6 E5
Sheep River AB 7 C3
Sheep River PP AB 6 E5
Sheep River PP AB 7 C3
Sheerness AB 6 D7
Sheerness AB 7 A7
Sheerness AB 11 D1
Sheet Harbour NS 33 B8
Sheet Harbour NS 33 B8
Sheet Harbour NS 34 F4
Sheet Harbour Road NS 33 B7
Sheet Harbour Road NS 34 F3
Sheffield NB 32 C3
Sheffield ON 19 B6-7
Sheffield ON 20 D5-6
Sheffield CA ON 21 D5
Sheffield Lake NL 36 A5
Sheffield Lake NL 37 A3
Sheffield Lake NL 38 F4
Sheffield Mills NS 32 E7
Sheffield Mills NS 33 B4
Sheguiandah ON 18 B4
Sheho SK 11 D6
Sheila NB 30 F2
Sheila NB 31 C7-8
Shekak River ON 17 B4 C3-4
Shekatika QC 38 B1-2
Shekilie River BC 3 B8
Shekilie River BC 9 A-B2
Shelagyote Peak BC 3 E4
Shelburne NS 33 E3
Shelburne NS 33 E-F3
Shelburne ON 20 B5
Shelburne Harbour NS 33 F3
Sheldon, Mount YT 4 C6
Sheldon Creek ON 20 B6
Sheldrake QC 39 E-F3
Shell Brook SK 11 B4
Shellbrook SK 11 B4
Shelley BC 1 A7
Shell Lake SK 11 B4
Shellmouth MB 11 D7
Shellmouth MB 13 D1
Shell River MB 11 D7-8
Shell River MB 13 D1
Shelter Bay BC 6 E3
Shelter Inlet BC 2 D1
Shelter Point BC 2 C2
Shemogue NB 32 B7
Shemogue NB 35 E1-2
Shemogue, havre de NB 35 E2
Shemogue Harbour NB 35 E2
Shemogue Head NB 35 E2
Shepard AB 7 B4
Shepherd Bay NU 41 C5
Shepherd Bay NU 42 F4
Shepherd Island NMBS NL 38 C5-6
Shepody, RNF NB 32 C6
Shepody Bay NB 32 C6-7
Shepody NWA NB 32 C6
Sheppard Peak BC 3 C2
Sheppardville NL 36 A5
Sheppardville NL 37 A3
Sheppardville NL 38 F4
Sherard, Cape NU 42 D5
Sherborne Lake ON 21 B2
Sherbrooke NS 34 F4-5
Sherbrooke PE 35 D3
Sherbrooke QC 27 E4-5
Sherbrooke QC 27 F4-5
Sherbrooke Lake NS 32 F7
Sherbrooke Lake NS 33 C4
Sherbrooke PP NS 34 F4-5
Shergrove MB 13 D2-3
Shergrove MB 14 B2
Sheridan Lake BC 1 D8
Sheridan Lake BC 6 D1
Sherkston ON 19 C8
Sherkston ON 20 F7
Sherman Basin NU 41 C4
Sherridon MB 12 F7-8
Sherridon MB 15 F2
Sherrington QC 24 E6
Sherrington QC 27 F1
Sherritt Junction MB 12 F7
Sherritt Junction MB 15 F1-2
Sherwood MB 14 C6
Sherwood NS 32 F7
Sherwood NS 33 C5
Sherwood Lake ON 13 E-F5
Sherwood Lake ON 14 E8
Sherwood Lake ON 16 D1
Sherwood Park AB 6 B6
Sherwood Park AB 8 C6-7
Sherwood River ON 21 A4
Sherwood River ON 22 F4
Sheshatshiu NL 39 B5-6
Shesheeb Bay, RNP ON 16 F6-7
Shesheeb Bay, RNP ON 17 C1
Shesheeb Bay PNR ON 16 F6-7
Shesheeb Bay PNR ON 17 C1
Sheshegwaning ON 18 B2
Sheslay River BC 3 C2
Shethanei Lake MB 15 B3-4
Shetland ON 19 D3
Shetland ON 20 F2
Shetland CA ON 19 D3
Shetland CA ON 20 F2
Shields SK 11 C4
Shigawake QC 30 D1-2
Shigawake QC 31 A7
Shikag Lake ON 13 E-F8
Shikag Lake ON 16 D4
Shillington ON 17 C6-7
Shilo MB 13 E2
Shilo MB 14 E2
Shingle Point YT 5 B3
Shinimicas Bridge NS 32 C7-8
Shinimicas Bridge NS 34 D1
Shinimicas Bridge NS 35 F2
Shinimicas PP NS 32 C8
Shinimicas PP NS 34 D1
Shining Tree ON 17 E6
Ship Cove NL 36 C1
Ship Cove NL 36 E8
Ship Cove NL 37 E6
Ship Cove NL 38 A5
Ship Cove NL 39 D8
Ship Harbour NL 36 E8
Ship Harbour NL 37 E6
Ship Harbour NS 33 C7-8
Ship Harbour NS 33 B-C7
Ship Harbour East NS 33 C7
Shipiskan Lake NL 39 A4-5
Shipka ON 19 B4
Shipka ON 20 D3
Shipman SK 11 B5
Shippagan NB 30 E2
Shippagan NB 31 B8
Shipshaw QC 28 C5
Shipshaw, rivière QC 28 B6 C5
Shipton QC 27 D4
Shirley Lake ON 21 A3
Shirley Lake ON 22 F3-4
Shoal Arm NL 38 E4-5
Shoal Bay NL 37 E8
Shoal Bay NL 38 E7
Shoal Brook NL 36 A3
Shoal Brook NL 37 A1
Shoal Brook NL 38 F2
Shoal Cove NL 38 B3
Shoal Harbour NL 36 C8
Shoal Harbour NL 37 C6
Shoal Lake MB 11 E8
Shoal Lake MB 13 E1-2
Shoal Lake ON 13 F5
Shoal Lake ON 14 E8
Shoal Lake ON 16 D1
Shoal Lake SK 11 B7
Shoal Lakes MB 13 E3
Shoal River (Sapotaweyak) MB 11 B8
Shoal River (Sapotaweyak) MB 13 B2
Shoalwater Bay YT 5 B3-4
Shoe Cove NL 37 D8
Shoe Cove NL 38 E5
Shoe Cove Point NL 37 A7
Shoe Cove Point NL 38 F8
Shonts AB 8 C7
Shoreacres BC 6 F3
Shores Cove NL 37 E8
Shorewood MB 14 C5
Shorncliffe MB 13 D4
Shorncliffe MB 14 B5
Short Hills PP ON 19 C8
Short Hills PP ON 20 E7
Shortdale MB 11 D8
Shortdale MB 13 D1
Shouldice AB 7 C5
Shrewsbury ON 19 E3
Shubenacadie NS 33 B6
Shubenacadie NS 34 F2
Shubenacadie Grand Lake NS 32 E8
Shubenacadie Grand Lake NS 33 B6
Shubenacadie Grand Lake NS 34 F2
Shubenacadie Provincial Wildlife Park NS 33 B6-7
Shubenacadie Provincial Wildlife Park NS 34 F2-3
Shubenacadie River NS 33 A-B6
Shubenacadie River NS 34 F2
Shulie NS 32 C6-7 D6-7
Shulie NS 33 A4
Shunacadie NS 34 C7
Shuswap BC 6 E4
Shuswap BC 7 C1
Shuswap Falls BC 6 E2
Shuswap Lake BC 6 D2
Shuswap Lake MPP BC 6 D2
Shuswap Lake PP BC 6 D2
Shuswap River BC 6 D-E3
Shuswap River BC 6 E2
Sibbald AB 6 D8
Sibbald AB 11 D2
Sibbald Point PP ON 20 B7
Sibbald Point PP ON 21 E1
Sibbeston Lake NT 10 D3
Sibley Peninsula ON 16 F6
Sibleys Cove NL 37 C7
Sicamous BC 6 D2
Sidewood SK 11 E3
Sidney BC 2 F4
Sidney MB 13 E2-3
Sidney MB 14 E2
Sidney Bay ON 18 E5
Sidney Spit Unit (Gulf Islands NPR) BC 2 F4-5
Siegas NB 31 C2
Siffleur Provincial Wilderness Area AB 8 F3
Siffleur Wilderness Area AB 6 C4
Sifton MB 11 D8
Sifton MB 13 D2
Sifton MB 14 A1
Sifton Beach MB 14 A-B1
Sifton Range YT 4 D3
Siglunes MB 14 B3
Signal Hill, LHN de NL 37 D8
Signal Hill NHS NL 37 D8
Sikanni Chief BC 3 D7
Sikanni Chief River BC 3 C-D7
Sikanni Chief River BC 9 C1
Sikanni Old Growth PP BC 3 C7
Sikanni Old Growth PP BC 9 B1
Sik-e-dakh BC 3 F4
Silcox MB 15 C-D5
Silcox Creek MB 15 C-D6
Silent Lake PP ON 21 C4
Sillikers NB 31 D6
Siloam ON 20 B7
Siloam ON 21 E1
Silsby Lake MB 15 E5
Silton SK 11 D5
Silver MB 13 D4
Silver MB 14 C5
Silver Bay MB 14 B3
Silver Beach PP BC 6 D2
Silverberry River NT 4 B8 C7
Silver Creek BC 2 D7
Silver Creek BC 6 E2
Silver Creek ON 21 A5
Silver Dollar ON 13 E8
Silver Dollar ON 16 D4
Silver Falls MB 13 E4-5
Silver Falls MB 14 C6
Silver Falls PP ON 16 E-F5
Silver Hill ON 19 D6
Silver Hill ON 20 F5
Silver Islet ON 16 F6
Silver Lake ON 13 E5-6
Silver Lake ON 16 D2
Silver Lake ON 18 B2
Silver Lake ON 20 A8
Silver Lake ON 20 A8
Silver Lake ON 21 C2
Silver Lake ON 21 D2-3
Silver Lake PP BC 1 F8
Silver Lake PP BC 2 D7
Silver Lake PP ON 21 C6
Silver Park SK 11 C5-6
Silver Plains MB 14 E5
Silver Ridge MB 13 D3
Silver Ridge MB 14 C3
Silver Star PP BC 6 E2
Silverthrone Glacier BC 1 D5
Silverthrone Mountain BC 1 D5
Silverton BC 6 E3
Silverton MB 11 D8
Silverton MB 13 D1
Silver Valley AB 9 E2
Silver Water ON 18 B2
Simard, lac QC 17 D8
Simard, lac QC 22 A3
Simard, lac QC 23 F3
Simcoe ON 19 C6
Simcoe ON 20 F5
Simcoe, Lake ON 18 F8
Simcoe, Lake ON 20 A7
Simcoe, Lake ON 21 D1
Simcoe Island ON 21 E6
Simcoeside ON 18 F8
Simcoeside ON 20 A7
Simcoeside ON 21 D1
Similkameen River BC 6 F1-2
Simmie SK 11 E3
Simmons Peninsula NU 42 C4
Simon, lac QC 24 B4
Simon, lac QC 24 C3
Simon, lac QC 26 A4-5
Simonds NB 31 F3
Simonds NB 32 B1
Simonette River AB 6 A3
Simonette River AB 8 A1
Simonhouse MB 11 A7
Simonhouse MB 12 F7
Simonhouse MB 13 A1
Simonhouse MB 15 F1
Simonhouse Lake MB 11 A7-8
Simonhouse Lake MB 12 F7-8
Simonhouse Lake MB 15 F1-2
Simon Peak BC 6 C2-3
Simpson SK 11 D5
Simpson Island ON 16 E-F7
Simpson Island ON 17 C1
Simpson Islands NT 10 D7
Simpson Lake NT 5 C7
Simpson Lake YT 4 E7
Simpson Peak BC 3 A2-3
Simpson Peak BC 4 F5-6
Simpson Peninsula NU 41 B5
Simpson Peninsula NU 42 F4-5
Simpsons Corner NS 32 F6
Simpsons Corner NS 33 C3-4
Simpson Strait NU 41 C4
Simpson Strait NU 42 F3-4
Sims Lake NL 39 B2
Simson PP BC 2 D3-4
Sincennes, lac QC 25 C5-6
Sincennes, lac QC 28 E1
Sinclair MB 11 F8
Sinclair MB 13 F1
Sinclair, lac QC 22 F7
Sinclair, lac QC 24 C1
Sinclair Mills BC 1 A7-8
Sinclair Mills BC 6 A1
Singhampton ON 20 B5
Sinnett SK 11 C5
Sintaluta SK 11 E6
Sioux Lake MB 12 B8
Sioux Lake MB 15 B3
Sioux Lookout ON 13 E7
Sioux Lookout ON 16 D3
Sioux Lookout ON 40 F1
Sioux Narrows ON 13 F6
Sioux Narrows ON 16 E2
Sioux Narrows PP ON 13 F6
Sioux Narrows PP ON 16 E2
Sioux Valley MB 11 E8
Sioux Valley MB 13 E1
Sipanok Channel SK 11 A-B6
Sipiwesk MB 15 E4
Sipiwesk Lake MB 15 F4
Sir Alexander, Mount BC 1 A8
Sir Alexander, Mount BC 6 A1
Sir Alexander Mackenzie PP BC 1 C4
Sirdar BC 6 F4
Sirdar Mountain AB 6 B3
Sirdar Mountain AB 8 D1
Sir Douglas, Mount AB 6 E4-5
Sir Douglas, Mount BC 7 C2
Sir James Macbrien, Mount NT 4 C7
Sir John Johnson House NHS ON 24 E4-5
Sirmilik NP NU 41 A6
Sirmilik NP NU 42 D5
Sir Richard Squires Memorial PP NL 36 A4
Sir Richard Squires Memorial PP NL 37 A2
Sir Richard Squires Memorial PP NL 38 F3
Sir Richard Squires PP NL 39 F7-8
Sir Sandford, Mount BC 6 C-D3
Sir Wilfrid Laurier, Mount BC 6 B2
Sir Wilfrid Laurier NHS QC 24 C5-6
Sir Wilfrid Laurier NHS QC 27 D1
Sir Winston Churchill PP AB 9 F6
Sir Winston Churchill PP AB 12 F1
Sir-Wilfrid, mont QC 22 C8
Sir-Wilfrid, mont QC 24 A2
Sir-Wilfrid, mont QC 25 E2
Sir-Wilfrid-Laurier, LHN de QC 24 C5-6
Sir-Wilfrid-Laurier, LHN de QC 27 D1
Sisib Lake MB 13 C2
Sisipuk Lake MB 12 E7
Sisipuk Lake MB 15 E1
Sissiboo Falls NS 33 D2
Sisson Branch Reservoir NB 29 F5
Sisson Branch Reservoir NB 31 C3
Sisson Ridge NB 31 D3
Sitdown Pond NL 36 C5
Sitdown Pond NL 37 C3
Sitidgi Lake NT 5 B-C5
Siwash Creek YT 3 A5
Siwash Creek YT 4 E8
Six Mile Lake PP ON 18 E7-8
60th Parallel TP NT 9 A4
60th Parallel TP NT 10 F5-6
60th Parallel TP NT 41 E1
Sixty Mile River YT 4 A1-2 B1-2
Skagit River BC 2 E7
Skagit Valley PP BC 1 F8
Skagit Valley PP BC 2 E7
Skagit Valley PP BC 6 F1
Skaha Lake BC 6 F2
Skaro AB 8 B7
Skead ON 17 F7
Skedans Point BC 1 B2
Skeena Mountains BC 3 D3-4 E4
Skeena River BC 1 A3
Skeena River BC 3 E4
Skeetchestn BC 1 D8
Skeetchestn BC 2 A7
Skeetchestn BC 6 D1
Skeleton Lake ON 18 D8
Skeleton Lake ON 21 B1
Skelu Bay BC 1 A1
Skerryvore ON 18 C6
Skidegate BC 1 B1
Skidegate Inlet BC 1 B1-2
Skiff AB 6 F7
Skiff AB 7 E7
Skiff AB 11 F1
Skiff Lake NB 32 C1
Skiff Lake NB 32 C1
Skihist Mountain BC 1 E7-8
Skihist Mountain BC 2 B-C6
Skihist PP BC 1 E8
Skihist PP BC 2 B7
Skihist PP BC 6 E1
Skincuttle Inlet BC 1 C2
Skinner Lake ON 13 B8
Skinners Pond PE 35 A2
Skir Dhu NS 34 B7
Skoki Ski Lodge NHS AB 6 D4-5
Skoki Ski Lodge NHS AB 7 A1-2
Skookumchuck BC 2 C6
Skookumchuck BC 6 E4
Skookumchuck BC 7 E1-2
Skookumchuck Creek BC 6 E4
Skookumchuck Creek BC 7 D1
Skookumchuck Narrows PP BC 2 C4
Skootamatta Lake ON 21 C5
Skootamatta River ON 21 C-D5
Skownan MB 13 C2
Skukum, Mount YT 4 E3-4
Skylake MB 14 B4-5 C4-5
Sky Lake ON 18 E5
Slabtown ON 21 A5
Slate Falls ON 13 D7
Slate Falls ON 16 B-C4
Slate Island PP ON 16 F7
Slate Island PP ON 17 C2
Slate Islands ON 16 F7
Slate Islands ON 17 C2
Slate Lake ON 16 C3
Slave Bay NT 10 E6
Slave Lake AB 9 F5
Slave Point NT 10 E6
Slave River AB 9 A6
Slave River AB 10 F8
Slave River AB 12 A2
Slave River NT 10 E7
Slave River NT 41 E1 F2
Slavey Creek AB 9 A-B3
Sled Lake SK 11 A4
Sled Lake SK 11 A4
Sled Lake SK 12 F4
Sled Lake SK 12 F4
Sled River SK 12 F4
Sleeman ON 16 E1
Sleeper Islands NU 40 C3-4
Sleeper Islands NU 41 F7
Sleeping Giant PP ON 16 F6
Slemon Lake NT 10 C5-6
Slesse Park BC 2 E6-7
Sliammon BC 1 E6
Sliammon BC 2 C3
Slim Creek PP BC 1 A-B8
Slim Creek PP BC 6 A1
Slims River YT 4 D-E2
Slocan BC 6 E-F3
Slocan Park BC 6 F3
Slocan River BC 6 E-F3
Sloko River BC 3 A-B1
Sloko River BC 4 F4
Sloop Cove NHS MB 15 B5
Small Inlet PP BC 2 B2
Small Lake MB 15 C4
Small Point NL 37 D7-8
Small Point-Broad Cove-Blackhead-Adam's Cove NL 37 D7-8
Small River Caves PP BC 6 B2
Smallwood Reservoir NL 39 B3-4
Smallwood Reservoir NL 40 D-E7
Smeaton SK 11 B5
Smelt Bay PP BC 1 E5-6
Smelt Bay PP BC 2 C2
Smelt Brook NS 34 A7
Smiley SK 6 C8
Smiley SK 11 C-D2
Smiley's PP NS 32 E8
Smiley's PP NS 33 B5
Smiley's PP NS 34 F1
Smith AB 9 F5
Smith, détroit de NU 42 B5
Smith, lac QC 22 C2
Smith Arm NT 41 B-C1
Smith Bay NU 42 C4
Smith Bay ON 18 C4
Smith Creek ON 19 A5
Smith Creek ON 20 C-D4
Smithers BC 3 F4
Smithers Landing BC 3 F5
Smithfield NS 33 A8
Smithfield NS 34 E4
Smithfield ON 21 E4
Smith Hill MB 14 F2
Smith Inlet BC 1 D4
Smith Island NU 40 B4
Smith Island NU 41 E7
Smith River BC 3 A5
Smith River BC 3 A5
Smith River BC 4 E-F8
Smith River BC 4 F8
Smith River BC 10 F1
Smiths Corner NB 31 E7
Smiths Corner NB 32 A5
Smiths Corner NS 32 F7
Smiths Corner NS 33 B4-5
Smiths Cove NS 32 F4-5
Smiths Cove NS 33 C2
Smiths Creek NB 32 C5
Smiths Falls ON 21 C7
Smiths Falls ON 24 F1-2
Smith's Harbour NL 38 E5
Smith Sound BC 1 D4
Smith Sound NU 42 B5
Smithville NS 33 F2-3
Smithville ON 19 C8
Smithville ON 20 E7
Smoke Lake ON 21 A2-3
Smoke Lake ON 22 F2
Smokey NL 39 A7
Smokey, Cape NS 34 B7
Smokey Head-White Bluff, RNP ON 18 D-E5
Smokey Head-White Bluff PNR ON 18 D-E5
Smoky Falls ON 17 B5-6
Smoky Lake AB 6 A6
Smoky Lake AB 8 B7-8
Smoky Lake AB 11 A1
Smoky Lake AB 12 F1
Smoky River AB 6 A2-3
Smoky River AB 8 A2
Smoky River AB 9 E3
Smoky River ON 18 A7-8
Smooth Rock Falls ON 17 B-C6
Smooth Rock Falls ON 40 F3
Smoothrock Lake ON 16 C5
Smoothstone Lake SK 12 F4
Smoothstone River SK 12 F4
Smuggler Cove PMP BC 2 D3-4
Smuggler Cove PP BC 1 F6
Smugglers Cove PP NS 33 D1
Smuts SK 11 C4-5
Snag YT 4 C1
Snag Creek YT 4 C1
Snake Creek ON 20 A3-4 B4
Snake Creek ON 21 B5
Snake Falls ON 13 D6
Snake Falls ON 16 C2
Snake Indian River AB 6 B2-3
Snake River ON 22 F5
Snake River YT 5 F5
Snakes Bight NL 36 D1
Snare Lake NT 10 B6-7
Snare Lake SK 9 B8
Snare Lake SK 12 B4
Snare River NT 10 A-B7
Snare River NT 10 B6
Snare River NT 41 D1-2
Snare River SK 12 B-C4
Snegamook Lake NL 39 A5
Snelgrove ON 19 A7
Snelgrove ON 20 C6
Snelgrove Lake NL 39 A2-3
Sniatyn AB 8 B7-8
Snipe Lake AB 9 F4
Snipe Lake SK 11 D3
Snooks Arm NL 38 E5
Snook's Harbour NL 36 C8
Snook's Harbour NL 37 C6
Snowball ON 20 C7
Snowball ON 21 E1
Snowbird Lake NT 41 E3
Snowden SK 11 B5
Snowdrift River NT 41 D-E2
Snowflake MB 13 F3
Snowflake MB 14 F3
Snow Lake MB 12 F8
Snow Lake MB 15 F2
Snow Road Station ON 21 C6
Snowshoe Island SK 12 B6
Snowshoe Lake ON 16 C1
Snowshoe Peak YT 4 E2
Snug Harbour NL 39 C8
Snug Harbour ON 18 D6
Snug Harbour ON 20 A8
Snug Harbour ON 21 D2-3
Snyder ON 20 E8
Snyder Lake MB 12 A7
Snyder Lake MB 15 A1
Sober Island NS 33 B8
Sober Island NS 33 B8
Soda Creek BC 1 C7
Soda Creek (IR) BC 1 C7
Sointula BC 1 E4
Solace PP ON 17 E7
Soldiers Cove NS 34 D7
Solina ON 20 C8
Solina ON 21 E2
Solmesville ON 21 E5
Solsgirth MB 11 E8
Solsgirth MB 13 E1
Sombra ON 19 D2
Sombra ON 20 F1
Somerset MB 13 F3
Somerset MB 14 E-F3
Somerset NS 32 E6
Somerset NS 33 B4
Somerset, île NU 41 A4-5
Somerset, île NU 42 D4
Somerset, île NU 42 E4
Somerset Island NU 41 A4-5
Somerset Island NU 42 D4
Somerville NB 31 F3
Somerville NB 32 B1
Somerville Island BC 3 F2-3
Somme SK 11 C6
Sommerfeld MB 13 F3-4
Sommerfeld MB 14 F4-5
Sonningdale SK 11 C3
Sonora NS 34 F5
Sonora Island BC 1 E5
Sonora Island BC 2 B2
Sonya ON 20 B8
Sonya ON 21 E2
Sooke BC 2 F4
Sooke Basin BC 2 F4
Sooke Potholes PP BC 2 F4
Soperton ON 21 D7
Soperton ON 24 F1
Sop's Arm NL 38 E3-4
Sop's Arm NL 39 F8
Sop's Island NL 38 E4
Sop's Island NL 39 F8
Sorcier, lac au QC 24 A6
Sorcier, lac au QC 25 E6
Sorcier, lac au QC 27 B2
Sorel QC 24 C7
Sorel QC 27 D2
Sorrento BC 6 D2
Soufflets River NL 38 C-D4
Soufflot, lac QC 22 A3
Soulier Lake SK 9 A8
Soulier Lake SK 12 A3
Soulis Pond NL 36 B8
Soulis Pond NL 37 B6
Soul Lake MB 13 B2
Sounding Creek AB 6 C-D7
Sounding Creek AB 7 A7
Sounding Creek AB 11 C1
Sounding Lake AB 6 C7-8
Sounding Lake AB 11 C2
Sound Island NL 36 D8
Sound Island NL 37 D6
Soup Harbour ON 21 F5
Sourd, lac du QC 24 B3
Souris MB 11 F8
Souris MB 13 F2
Souris MB 14 E1
Souris PE 34 C4
Souris PE 35 D7-8
Souris Beach PP PE 34 C4
Souris Beach PP PE 35 E7
Souris Line Road PE 35 D7-8
Souris River MB 11 F8
Souris River MB 13 F1-2
Souris River MB 14 E1
Souris River PE 35 D7
Souris River PE 35 D7
Souris Valley SK 11 F6
Sour Spring ON 19 C6-7
Sour Spring ON 20 E5-6
South Allan SK 11 C4
South Alton NS 32 E6-7
South Alton NS 33 B4
Southampton NS 32 C-D7
Southampton NS 33 A4
Southampton ON 18 F4
Southampton ON 20 A3
Southampton PE 35 D6-7
Southampton, Cape NU 40 B3
Southampton, Cape NU 41 E6
Southampton, île NU 40 A3
Southampton, île NU 41 D6
Southampton Island NU 40 A3
Southampton Island NU 41 D6
South Arm NL 36 A6
South Arm NL 37 A4
South Arm NL 38 F6
South Arm ON 21 A3
South Arm ON 22 F3
South Atikaki PP MB 13 D5
South Atikaki PP MB 14 B7
South Aulatsivik Island NL 40 C7
Southbank BC 1 A5
South Bar NS 34 C8
South Bay MB 12 D8
South Bay MB 15 D3
South Bay ON 13 D7
South Bay ON 16 C3
South Bay ON 18 B8
South Bay ON 18 C4
South Bay ON 18 E7
South Bay SK 12 E4
South Bay Ingonish NS 34 B7
South Bay PP ON 17 F7-8
South Bay PP ON 18 B7-8
South Bay PP ON 22 D1
South Baymouth ON 18 C3
South Beach MB 14 C5
South Beach ON 21 D3
South Bentinck Arm BC 1 C4-5
South Big Salmon River YT 4 D4
South Bolton QC 24 E8
South Bolton QC 27 F4
South Branch NB 31 E8
South Branch NB 32 A6
South Branch NL 36 D1-2
South Branch NS 33 B7
South Branch NS 34 F3
South Branch Benjamin River NB 29 D7 E6
South Branch Big Segovie River NB 31 D5-6
South Branch Muskoka River ON 21 B2 C1-2
South Branch Nepisiguit River NB 29 F6
South Branch Oromocto River NB 32 D3
South Branch Renous River NB 31 D-E5
South Brook NL 36 A5
South Brook NL 36 A5
South Brook NL 37 A3
South Brook NL 37 A3
South Brook NL 38 F4
South Brook NL 38 F4
South Brook NL 39 F8
South Brook NS 32 D7
South Brook NS 33 A5
South Brookfield NS 33 D3
South Bruce ON 20 B4
South Bruce Peninsula ON 18 F5
South Bruce Peninsula ON 20 A4
South Buxton ON 19 E3
South Castor River ON 21 B8
South Castor River ON 24 E2-3
South Cayuga ON 19 C7
South Cayuga ON 20 F6
South Charlo River NB 29 D-E6
South Charlo River NB 31 A-B5
South Cooking Lake AB 6 B6
South Cooking Lake AB 8 C6-7
South Dildo NL 37 D-E7
Southeast Bay MB 12 A8
Southeast Bay MB 15 A2-3
South East Bight NL 36 E7
South East Bight NL 37 E5-6
Southeast Upsalquitch River NB 29 E6
Southeast Upsalquitch River NB 31 B5
Southend SK 12 D6
Southend (IR) SK 12 D6
Southern Bay NL 37 C6-7
Southern Harbour NL 36 D8
Southern Harbour NL 37 D6
Southern Indian Lake MB 15 C-D3
Southey SK 11 D5-6
South Fork SK 11 F2-3
South Freetown PE 35 D3
Southgate River BC 1 D-E6
Southgate River BC 2 A3
South Gillies ON 16 F5
South Gloucester ON 21 B8
South Gloucester ON 24 E2
South Granville PE 35 D4
South Gut St. Anns NS 34 C7
South Harbour NS 34 A7
South Hazelton BC 3 F4
South Head NL 37 B7-8
South Heart River AB 9 E4
South Henik Lake NU 40 A1
South Henik Lake NU 41 E4
South Huron ON 19 B4
South Huron ON 20 D3
South Indian Lake MB 15 D3
South Junction MB 13 F5
South Junction MB 14 F7
South Kedgwick River NB 29 D3-4
South Knife Lake MB 15 B-C4
South Knife River MB 15 B4-5
South La Cloche Mountains ON 18 B4-5
South Lake PE 35 D8
South Lake PE 35 D8
South Lake Ainslie NS 34 C6
South Macmillian River YT 4 C5-6
South Maitland NS 32 D8
South Maitland NS 33 A6
South Maitland NS 34 F2
South Maitland River ON 19 A4
South Maitland River ON 20 C3
South McQuesten River YT 4 A3-4 B3
South Melville PE 35 E4
South Middleton ON 19 D6
South Middleton ON 20 F5
South Milford NS 32 F5
South Milford NS 33 C3
South Monaghan ON 21 E3
South Moose Lake MB 11 A8
South Moose Lake MB 13 A2
South Mountain NS 32 E6
South Mountain NS 33 B3-4
South Mountain ON 21 B-C8
South Mountain ON 24 E2-3
South Nahanni River NT 4 C7 D8
South Nation River ON 21 C8
South Nation River ON 24 D-E3
South Ohio NS 33 E1
South Pender Island BC 2 F5
South Pine River ON 20 B3
South Porcupine ON 17 C-D6-7
Southport MB 13 E3
Southport MB 14 D3-4
Southport NL 37 C7
South Range NS 33 D2
South Rawdon NS 32 E8
South Rawdon NS 33 B5-6
South Rawdon NS 34 F1
South River NL 37 D7
South River NS 34 E5
South River ON 18 B8
South River ON 18 C8
South River ON 18 C8
South River ON 22 E1-2

South River ON 22 E1
South River Lake NS 34 E5
South Rushbrook Old Pine PP ON 17 F6
South Rustico PE 35 D4
South Saskatchewan River AB 6 E7
South Saskatchewan River AB 7 D7-8
South Saskatchewan River AB 11 E1
South Saskatchewan River SK 11 D3
South Saugeen River ON 20 B5 C4
South Seal River MB 15 B-C3
South Shoal Lake MB 14 D4
South Side NS 33 F2
Southside Antigonish Harbour NS 34 D5
South Slocan BC 6 F3
South Tetagouche NB 29 E7
South Tetagouche NB 31 B6
South Tweedsmuir PP BC 1 B-C5
South Twillingate Island NL 38 E6
South Twin Island NU 40 E3-4
South Twin Lake NL 36 A6
South Twin Lake NL 37 A4
South Twin Lake NL 38 F5
South Uniacke NS 32 E8
South Uniacke NS 33 B5-6 C5-6
South Victoria NS 32 C8
South Victoria NS 34 D1
Southview BC 2 C2-3
Southville NS 33 D2
South Wabasca Lake AB 9 E5
South Wellington BC 1 F6
South Wellington BC 2 E3-4
Southwest Gander River NL 36 B6-7
Southwest Gander River NL 37 B5
Southwest Head NB 32 F2
South West Lot 16 PE 35 D2
Southwest Margaree NS 34 C6
Southwest Margaree PP NS 34 C6
Southwest Miramichi River NB 31 D-E6
Southwest Miramichi River NB 31 E4-5
Southwest Miramichi River NB 32 A2-4
South West Port Mouton NS 33 E4
Southwest River NL 36 C6
Southwest River NL 37 C6
Southwest River PE 35 D3-4
Southwold ON 19 C-D4
Southwold ON 20 F3
Southwold Earthworks NHS ON 19 D4
Southwold Earthworks NHS ON 20 F3
South Wolf Island NL 39 B8
Southwood ON 18 E8
Southwood ON 21 C1
South Woodslee ON 19 E2
Sovereign SK 11 D3
Sovereign Lake SK 12 A5
Sowchea Bay PP BC 1 A6
Sowden Lake ON 13 E8
Sowden Lake ON 16 E4
Sowerby ON 17 F4-5
Sowerby ON 18 A1
Spaffordton ON 21 D6-7
Spalding SK 11 C5-6
Spallumcheen BC 6 E2
Spaniard's Bay NL 37 D7
Spanish ON 17 F5
Spanish ON 18 B3
Spanish River ON 17 E-F6
Spanish River ON 17 F6
Spanish River ON 18 A4
Spanish River ON 18 A4
Spanish River ON 18 A4 B3
Spanish River PP ON 17 E-F6
Spanish River PP ON 18 A4
Spanish Room NL 36 E7
Spanish Room NL 37 E6
Spanish Ship Bay NS 34 F4
Spar Island ON 16 F5
Sparkling Lake ON 13 E8
Sparrow Lake ON 18 E8
Sparrow Lake ON 21 C1
Sparta ON 19 D5
Sparta ON 20 F4
Sparwood BC 6 F5
Sparwood BC 7 E2-3
Spatsizi Headwaters PP BC 3 D3
Spatsizi Plateau PWP BC 3 C3-4
Spatsizi River BC 3 C-D4
Spear, cap NB 35 F3
Spear, Cape NB 35 F3
Spear Harbour NL 39 C8
Spearhill MB 13 D3
Spearhill MB 14 B3
Spear Lake NS 9 D8
Spear Lake SK 12 D3
Spectacle Lake PP BC 2 F4
Spector Lake MB 15 E7-8
Spectre Peak BC 3 C5

Spedden AB 6 A6-7
Spedden AB 8 B8
Spedden AB 11 A1
Spedden AB 12 F1
Spednic Lake NB 32 C-1
Spednic Lake, APP NB 32 C1
Spednic Lake PPA NB 32 B2-3
Spednic Lake Provincial Campground NB 32 C1-2
Speed River ON 19 A6
Speed River ON 20 C5
Speers SK 11 B-C4
Spence Lake MB 13 D2
Spence Lake MB 14 A2
Spencer, Cape NB 32 E4
Spencer, Cape NB 33 B2
Spencer Lake AB 9 F7
Spencer Lake AB 12 F1-2
Spencers Island MB 11 B8
Spencers Island NS 33 A4
Spencerville ON 21 C8
Spencerville ON 24 F2
Spences Bridge BC 1 E8
Spences Bridge BC 2 B7
Spence Settlement NB 32 B7-8
Spence Settlement NB 34 C1
Spence Settlement NB 35 E2
Sperling MB 13 F3
Sperling MB 14 E4
Speyside ON 19 A7
Speyside ON 20 D6
Spider Lake ON 18 D7
Spider Lake PP BC 2 D2-3
Spiers Lake NWA AB 6 C6-7
Spiers Lake NWA AB 8 F7-8
Spiers Lake NWA AB 11 C1
Spillans Cove NL 37 B7-8
Spiller Channel BC 1 C3-4
Spiller Inlet BC 1 C4
Spillimacheen BC 6 D4
Spillimacheen BC 7 B1
Spillimacheen River BC 6 D3-4
Spillway NL 36 A3-4
Spillway NL 37 A1-2
Spillway NL 38 F3
Spipiyus PP BC 2 D4
Spirit River AB 9 E2
Spirit Rock CA ON 18 E5
Spirit Wood Acres SK 11 B4
Spiritwood SK 11 B4
Spius Creek BC 1 E8
Spius Creek BC 2 C7
Spius Creek BC 6 E1
Split, Cape BC 32 D6-7
Split, Cape NS 33 A4
Split Lake MB 15 E4
Split Lake MB 15 E4-5
Split Lake (IR) MB 15 E4-5
Spoonbill Lake ON 16 B1
Spoon Lake ON 18 B5
Sporting Mountain NS 34 D6
Spotted Island NL 39 B8
Spragge ON 17 F5
Spragge ON 18 A2
Sprague MB 13 F5
Sprague MB 14 F7
Spray Lakes Reservoir AB 7 B-C2
Spray Valley PP AB 6 D5
Spray Valley PP AB 7 B-C2
Springbank, parc ON 20 E3
Springbank Park ON 20 E3
Spring Bay ON 18 C3
Spring Brook ON 21 D4-5
Springbrook PE 32 A8
Springbrook PE 34 B2
Springbrook PE 35 D4
Spring Coulee AB 6 F6
Spring Coulee AB 7 F5
Spring Creek ON 18 B7
Springdale AB 8 E5-6
Springdale NL 38 F4-5
Springfield NB 31 F4
Springfield NB 32 C2
Springfield NB 32 C4
Springfield NS 32 F6
Springfield NS 33 C3
Springfield ON 19 C5
Springfield ON 20 F4
Springfield PE 32 A8
Springfield PE 34 C2
Springfield PE 35 D3
Springfield West PE 35 C1
Springford ON 19 C5-6
Springford ON 20 E4-5
Springhill NS 32 F7-8
Springhill NS 34 E1
Springhill PE 32 A7
Springhill PE 34 B1
Springhill PE 35 C2
Springhill Junction NS 32 F7
Springhill Junction NS 34 E1
Springhouse BC 1 C7-8
Spring Lake AB 18 C7-8
Spring Lake ON 22 E1
Springmount ON 18 D7
Springmount ON 20 A4
Spring Point AB 7 E4
Springside ON 11 D6-7
Springstein MB 13 F3-4
Springstein MB 14 E4
Springtown ON 21 B6
Springvale ON 19 C6-7

Springvale ON 20 E5-6
Springvale PE 35 E4
Spring Valley ON 21 C8
Spring Valley ON 24 F2
Spring Valley PE 32 A8
Spring Valley PE 34 B1-2
Spring Valley PE 35 D3
Spring Valley SK 11 E5
Springville NS 33 A7-8
Springville NS 34 E3-4
Springville ON 21 E3
Springwater SK 11 C3
Springwater CA ON 19 D5
Springwater CA ON 20 F4
Springwater PP ON 18 F7
Springwater PP ON 20 A6
Spring Well MB 14 D6
Sproat Lake BC 1 F6
Sproat Lake BC 2 D2
Sproat Lake BC 2 D2
Sproat Lake PP BC 1 F6
Sproat Lake PP BC 2 D2
Sprott Lake MB 12 B8
Sprott Lake MB 15 B2
Sproule, lac QC 25 D4
Sproule Peninsula NT 42 C2
Spruce Beetle Trail Territorial Recreation Site YT 4 E2
Spruce Brook NL 36 B2
Spruce Creek MB 14 B1
Sprucedale ON 18 D8
Sprucedale ON 21 A1
Sprucedale ON 22 F1
Sprucefield AB 8 B7
Spruce Grove AB 6 B5
Spruce Grove AB 8 C6
Spruce Home SK 11 B5
Spruce Island MB 11 B8
Spruce Island MB 13 B2
Spruce Island NT 5 E6
Spruce Islands, RNP ON 16 E1-2
Spruce Islands PNR ON 16 E1-2
Spruce Lake SK 6 A-B8
Spruce Lake SK 11 B3
Spruce Pond NL 36 C3
Spruce Pond NL 37 C1
Spruce River ON 14 A-B5
Spruce River SK 11 B4-5
Spruce View AB 6 C5
Spruce View AB 8 F5
Sprucewoods MB 13 E2
Sprucewoods MB 14 E2
Spruce Woods PP MB 13 E-F2
Spruce Woods PP MB 14 E2
Spry Bay NS 33 C8
Spry Bay NS 33 B8
Spry Bay PP NS 33 B7-8
Spry Cove PE 35 E7
Spry Harbour NS 33 B7-8
Spry Lake ON 18 E5
Spry Point PE 35 E7
Spudgels Cove NL 38 D2-3
Sputinow AB 6 A7-8
Sputinow AB 11 A2
Sputinow AB 12 F8
Spuzzum BC 2 D7
Spy Hill SK 11 E7
Spy Hill SK 13 E1
Squally Channel BC 1 B3
Squamish BC 1 F7
Squamish BC 2 D4-5
Squamish River BC 1 E7
Squamish River BC 2 B-C4
Squamish River BC 2 C4
Squanga Lake YT 4 A4
Square, lac NB 35 E1
Square Forks, rivière QC 29 C6-7
Square Islands NL 39 C8
Square Lake MB 35 E1
Squatec QC 29 D5
Squatec QC 31 B1
Squatec, rivière QC 29 D-E2
Squatec, rivière QC 31 B1
Squaw Island ON 18 C4
Squaw Lake YT 4 A4
Squilax BC 6 D2
Squinas BC 1 C5
Squire ON 18 F5
Squire ON 20 A4
Squirrel Creek CA ON 21 E3
Squitty Bay PP BC 1 F6
Squitty Bay PP BC 2 D3
S.S. Klondike, LHN YT 4 E4
S.S. Klondike NHS YT 4 E4
Stackler, lac QC 26 C7
Stackler, lac QC 28 A2
Staffa ON 19 B4
Staffa ON 20 D3
Stafford River BC 1 D5
Stafford River BC 2 A2
Stagg Lake NT 10 C6
Stag Harbour NL 38 E7
Stagleap PP BC 6 F3
Stait of Honguedo QC 30 A3-4 B4
Stalwart, Cape NU 42 A4
Stalwart SK 11 D5
Stalwart, RNF de SK 11 D5
Stalwart National Wilderness Area SK 11 D5
Stamp River PP BC 1 F5-6
Stamp River PP BC 2 D2
Stampville ON 24 F2-3
Stanbridge East QC 24 E7
Stanbridge East QC 27 F3
Stanbridge Station QC 24 E7
Stanbridge Station QC 27 F2

Stanburn NS 32 F6
Stanburn NS 33 C4
Stanchel PE 35 D-E4
Standard AB 6 D6
Standard AB 7 B5
Standing Buffalo SK 11 D6
Stand Off AB 6 F6
Stand Off AB 7 E-F5
Stanger AB 8 C5
Stanhope NL 36 A6-7
Stanhope NL 37 A4-5
Stanhope NL 38 F6
Stanhope PE 34 C2-3
Stanhope PE 35 D5
Stanhope QC 27 F4-5
Stanley NB 31 F4
Stanley NB 32 B2-3
Stanley NS 32 E8
Stanley NS 33 B5
Stanley ON 34 F1
Stanley ON 16 F5
Stanley SK 12 E5
Stanley Bridge PE 32 A8
Stanley Bridge PE 34 B2
Stanley Bridge PE 35 D4
Stanley Cove NL 36 D5
Stanley Cove NL 37 D3
Stanley Mission SK 12 E5
Stanley Mission (Holy Trinity Anglican Church) PHS SK 12 E5-6
Stanley River PE 35 D4
Stanleyville ON 21 C7
Stanleyville ON 24 F1
Stanmore AB 7 A7
Stanstead QC 27 F4
Stanwell-Fletcher Lake ON 41 A4-5
Stanwell-Fletcher Lake NU 42 A4
Staples ON 19 E2
Star AB 6 A6
Star AB 8 B7
Star AB 11 A1
Star Blanket SK 11 D6
Starbuck MB 13 E-F3
Starbuck MB 14 E4
Star City SK 11 B5-6
Starfish Lake NT 10 A7
Starkville ON 21 E3
Star Lake NL 36 B4
Star Lake NL 37 B2
Starratt-Olsen ON 13 D6
Starratt-Olsen ON 16 C2
Starvation Lake NT 10 A7
State Mount YT 4 D-E4
Stauffer AB 6 C5
Stauffer AB 8 F5
Stave Falls BC 2 D-E6
Stave Lake BC 1 F7
Stave Lake BC 2 D6
Stavely AB 6 E6
Stavely AB 7 D4
Stave River BC 2 D5
Stawamus Chief PP BC 1 F7
Stawamus Chief PP BC 2 C-D5
Stayner ON 18 F7
Stayner ON 20 A6
Stead MB 13 E4
Stead MB 14 C6
Steady Brook NL 36 B3
Steady Brook NL 37 B1
Steamboat Mountain YT 4 A4
Steel Lake ON 16 E7
Steel Lake ON 17 C2
Steel Lake ON 17 C2
Steel Narrows Provincial Historic Park SK 6 A8
Steel River ON 16 E7
Steel River ON 17 C2
Steel River PP ON 16 E7
Steel River PP ON 17 B-C2
Steele Narrows Provincial Historic Park SK 11 A2-3
Steelhead PP BC 1 D8
Steelhead PP BC 2 A8
Steelhead PP BC 6 D1
Steelman SK 11 F7
Steels Ferry MB 14 F5
Steen River AB 9 A3
Steen River AB 9 A3
Steensby Inlet NU 41 B7
Steensby Inlet NU 42 B7
Steepbank River AB 9 D7
Steepbank River AB 9 D7
Steephill Lake SK 12 E6
Steep Rock MB 13 D3
Steep Rock MB 14 A3
Steep Rock Junction MB 14 A3
Steeprock Lake PP MB 13 B-C7
Steeprock Lake PP MB 13 B1
Steeves Mountian NB 31 F7-8
Steeves Mountian NB 32 B5-6
Stefansson Island NU 41 A3
Stefansson Island NU 42 D3
Steinbach MB 13 F4
Steinbach MB 14 E6
Stein Mountain BC 1 E7-8
Stein Mountain BC 2 B6
Stein River BC 1 E7-8
Stein River BC 2 B6
Stein Valley Nlaka'pamux PP BC 1 E7-8
Stein Valley Nlaka'pamux PP BC 2 B6

Stelcam SK 11 E5
Stella ON 21 E6
Stellako BC 1 A5-6
Stellarton NS 33 A7-8
Stellarton NS 34 E3
Stemwinder PP BC 2 D8
Stemwinder PP BC 2 B8
Stenen SK 11 C7
Stephansson House PHS AB 6 C4-5
Stephansson House PHS AB 8 F5-6
Stephenfield MB 14 E3-4
Stephenfield MB 13 F3
Stephenfield PP MB 14 E3
Stephens Island BC 1 B2
Stephens Lake MB 15 D5
Stephenville NL 36 B2
Stephenville Crossing NL 36 C2
Sterlet Lake NT 10 A8
Stettler AB 6 C6
Stettler AB 8 E-F7
Steven Creek ON 21 B8
Steven Creek ON 24 E2
Stevens ON 16 D-E8
Stevens ON 17 B2-3
Stevens Lake MB 12 B8
Stevens Lake MB 15 B2
Stevenson, Mount BC 1 B-C8
Stevenson, Mount BC 6 B1
Stevenson Lake MB 13 A4-5
Stevenson River MB 13 A5
Stevensville ON 20 E7-8
Steveston NL 37 C7
Stewardson Inlet BC 1 F5
Stewart BC 3 E3
Stewart, Mount YT 4 B2
Stewart Crossing YT 4 B3
Stewartfield AB 8 B5
Stewart Hall ON 21 E3
Stewart Lake NT 4 A8
Stewart Lake NT 10 B1-2
Stewart Lake YT 4 E7
Stewart Property PNR ON 21 A-B6
Stewart Property, RNP ON 21 A-B6
Stewart River YT 4 A5
Stewart River YT 4 C2
Stewart River YT 4 B4
Stewarttown ON 19 A7
Stewarttown ON 20 D6
Stewart Valley SK 11 D3
Stewiacke NS 33 B6
Stewiacke NS 34 F2
Stewiacke Cross Road NS 33 A7
Stewiacke Cross Road NS 34 F3
Stewiacke East NS 33 B6-7
Stewiacke East NS 34 F2
Stewiacke River NS 33 A-B7
Stewiacke River NS 34 F2-3
Stickney NB 31 E3
Stickney NS 32 A-B1
Stikine BC 3 D2
Stikine Ranges BC 3 B-C4
Stikine River BC 3 C3-4
Stikine River BC 3 D2
Stikine River PP BC 3 C3
Still River ON 18 C6
Still River ON 21 A1
Stillwater BC 1 F6
Stillwater BC 2 C3
Stillwater NS 34 F5
Stirling AB 6 F6
Stirling AB 7 E6
Stirling ON 21 D5
Stirling Creek ON 18 C8
Stirling Creek ON 21 A1
Stirling Creek ON 22 F1
Stirlingville AB 7 F6
Stirton ON 19 A5-6
Stirton ON 20 C4-5
Stitt MB 13 E4
Stittsville ON 21 B7-8
Stittsville ON 24 E2
Stivens, Point NT 5 A7
Stobart AB 7 B5
Stock Cove NL 37 D7
Stockdale ON 21 E4
Stockholm AB 8 F6
Stockholm SK 11 E7
Stockport MB 13 F2
Stockton MB 14 E2
Stoco ON 21 D5
Stoco Fen PP ON 21 D5
Stoco Lake ON 21 D5
Stoke, rivière QC 27 E4-5
Stokes Bay ON 18 E4
Stokes Bay ON 18 E5
Stokes Point YT 5 A-B3
Stone BC 1 C7
Stonecliffe ON 22 D4
Stoneham QC 27 A5
Stonehaven NB 29 E8
Stonehaven NB 30 E1
Stonehaven NB 31 B7
Stonehouse NS 32 C8
Stonehouse NS 34 D2
Stonehurst West NS 33 D5
Stone Lake ON 16 C7
Stone Lake ON 17 A1
Stone Mountain PP BC 3 B5-6
Stoner BC 1 B7

Stone's Cove NL 36 D-E7
Stone's Cove NL 37 D-E5
Stone Valley NL 36 D5
Stone Valley NL 37 D3-4
Stoneville NL 38 F6-7
Stonewall MB 13 E4
Stonewall MB 14 D5
Stoney Creek ON 19 B7-8
Stoney Creek ON 20 E6-7
Stoney Point ON 19 E2
Stoney Point Beach MB 14 B1-2
Stony Creek NT 5 D4
Stony Hill NL 14 C4
Stony Island NL 39 C8
Stony Lake MB 12 B8
Stony Lake MB 15 B3
Stony Lake NL 36 B6
Stony Lake NL 37 B4
Stony Lake ON 21 D3-4
Stony Lake SK 12 A5
Stony Mountain MB 13 E4
Stony Mountain MB 14 D5
Stony Mountain Wildland PP AB 9 D7
Stony Mountain Wildland PP AB 12 D1-2
Stony Plain AB 6 B5
Stony Plain AB 8 C6
Stony Rapids SK 12 F7
Stony Rapids SK 41 F2-3
Stonyridge ON 21 D4
Stor Island NU 42 B4
Storkerson Peninsula NU 41 A3
Storkerson Peninsula NU 42 C2
Storm, Cape NU 42 C4
Stormont NT 34 E-F5
Stormy Lake ON 13 F7
Stormy Lake ON 16 E3
Stormy Lake ON 18 B7-8
Stormy Lake ON 22 D-E1
Stornoway QC 27 D6
Stornoway SK 11 C7
Storthoaks SK 11 F7-8
Storthoaks SK 13 F1
Stouffville ON 20 C7
Stouffville ON 21 E1-2
Stoughton SK 11 F6-7
Stout Lake ON 13 C5
Stout Lake ON 16 A1-2
Strabane ON 19 B7
Strabane ON 20 D6
Straffordville ON 19 D5
Straffordville ON 20 F4
Straight River SK 12 A4-5
Straitsview NL 38 A5
Strand Bay NU 42 B4
Strangmuir AB 7 C5
Stranraer SK 11 C3
Strasbourg SK 11 D5
Stratford ON 19 B5
Stratford ON 20 D4
Stratford PE 34 C2-3
Stratford PE 35 D5
Stratford QC 27 D5
Strathallen SK 11 F4
Strathburn ON 19 D4
Strathburn ON 20 F3
Strathclair MB 11 E8
Strathclair MB 13 E2
Strathclair MB 14 C1
Strathcona ON 21 D6
Strathcona PE 35 E6
Strathcona PP BC 2 C-D1
Strathcona-Westmin PP BC 2 D1-2
Strathcona-Westmin PP BC 1 F5
Strathgartney PP PE 34 C2
Strathgartney PP PE 35 E4
Strathlorne NS 34 C5-6
Strathmore AB 6 D6
Strathmore AB 7 B5
Strathnaver BC 1 B7
Strathroy ON 19 C4
Strathroy ON 20 E3
Stratton ON 16 E2
Strawberry Island ON 18 B6
Streak, Mount YT 4 E4
Streamstown AB 6 B7-8
Streamstown AB 11 B2
Streatfield Lake ON 16 A8
Streatfield River ON 16 A8
Streets Ridge NS 32 C8
Streets Ridge NS 34 D2
Streetsville ON 19 A7-8
Streetsville ON 20 D6-7
Strome AB 6 B6-7
Strome AB 8 D-E8
Strome AB 11 B1
Strongfield SK 11 D4
Stroud ON 20 B7
Stroud ON 21 D1
Struan SK 11 C4
Stry AB 8 B8
Stuartburn MB 13 F4
Stuartburn MB 14 F6
Stuart Channel BC 2 E4
Stuart Island BC 1 E5-6
Stuart Island BC 2 B2-3
Stuart Lake BC 1 A6
Stuart Lake PP BC 1 A6
Stuart River BC 1 A6-7
Stuart River PP BC 1 A6-7
Stubbs, lac QC 22 E6
Stuie BC 1 C5
Stukely Lake QC 27 F3
Stukely-Sud QC 27 F3
Stull Lake MB 15 F6
Stull Lake ON 13 A6

Stull Lake ON 15 F6
Stull River MB 15 F6
Stum Lake BC 1 C7
Stump Lake BC 2 B8
Stump Lake BC 2 B8
Stump Lake PP BC 6 E1
Stump Pass BC 3 B6
Sturgeon PE 35 F7
Sturdies Bay BC 2 E4-5
Sturgeon PE 35 D2
Sturgeon Point PE 35 D2
Sturgeon Bay MB 13 C3
Sturgeon Bay ON 18 F7-8
Sturgeon Bay ON 20 A6
Sturgeon Bay PP ON 18 C6
Sturgeon Bay PP Reserve MB 13 C3
Sturgeon Bay PP Reserve MB 14 A4
Sturgeon Falls ON 17 F7-8
Sturgeon Falls ON 18 A7
Sturgeon Heights AB 9 F3
Sturgeon Lake AB 9 F3
Sturgeon Lake ON 13 E8
Sturgeon Lake ON 16 D4
Sturgeon Lake ON 20 A8
Sturgeon Lake ON 21 D2
Sturgeon Lake SK 11 B4-5
Sturgeon Landing SK 12 F7
Sturgeon Landing SK 13 A1
Sturgeon Landing SK 15 F1
Sturgeon Point ON 20 A8
Sturgeon Point ON 21 D2
Sturgeon River ON 13 E7
Sturgeon River ON 14 C8
Sturgeon River ON 15 E7-8
Sturgeon River ON 17 E7
Sturgeon River ON 18 A7
Sturgeon River ON 18 F7-8
Sturgeon River ON 20 A6
Sturgeon River PP ON 17 E7
Sturgis SK 11 C7
Styx River ON 20 B4
Success SK 11 E3
Sucker Creek ON 18 B3
Sucker River SK 12 E5
Sud, pointe du QC 30 B6
Sud, rivière du QC 24 E7
Sud, rivière du QC 27 A6-7
Sud, rivière du QC 27 B6-7
Sud, rivière du QC 27 F2
Sudbury ON 17 F7
Sudbury ON 18 A5
Sudeten PP BC 3 E8
Sudeten PP BC 9 E1-2
Sud-Ouest, cap du QC 30 F7
Sud-Ouest, rivière du QC 29 C2
Suffield AB 6 E7
Suffield AB 7 D8
Suffield AB 11 E1
Suffolk PE 35 E5
Sugarbowl-Grizzly Den PP BC 1 A7-8
Sugarbowl-Grizzly Den PP BC 6 A1
Sugar Lake BC 6 E2-3
Sugarloaf PP NB 29 D6
Sugarloaf PP NB 31 A5
Suggi Lake SK 11 A6
Suggi Lake SK 12 F6
Sukunka Falls PP BC 3 F7
Sukunka Falls PP BC 9 E1
Sukunka River BC 3 E-F7
Sukunka River BC 9 E1
Suley Ann's Cove NL 38 E4
Sullivan QC 23 E4
Sullivan Bay BC 1 D4
Sullivan Lake AB 6 C6-7
Sullivan Lake AB 8 E8
Sullivan Lake AB 11 C1
Sully QC 29 E2
Sulphur Bay NT 10 E6
Sulphur Passage PP BC 1 F5
Sulphur Passage PP BC 2 D1
Sulphur Point NT 10 E6
Sultan ON 17 E5
Sulte, lac QC 25 A4
Sulte, lac QC 26 E-F4
Summer Beaver (Nibinamik) ON 16 A6
Summerberry SK 11 E6-7
Summerfield PE 35 D3-4
Summerford NL 38 E6
Summerland BC 6 F1-2
Summers Corners ON 19 D5
Summers Corners ON 20 F4
Summerside NL 36 B3
Summerside NL 37 B1
Summerside PE 32 A8
Summerside PE 34 C1
Summerside PE 35 D2-3
Summerside Harbour PE 35 D2-3
Summerstown ON 24 E4
Summerstown Station ON 24 E4
Summerville NL 37 C7
Summerville NS 33 A1
Summerville NS 34 F1
Summerville PE 35 E6
Summerville Beach PP NS 33 E4

Summerville Centre NS 33 E3-4
Summit Lake BC 1 A7
Summit Lake BC 1 A7
Summit Lake BC 2 B8
Summit Lake PP BC 6 E3
Summit Pass BC 3 B6
Sunbury ON 21 D7
Sunbury Cove PE 35 D2
Sunbury Point PE 35 D2
Sundance MB 15 D5
Sundance MB 40 C1
Sundance Beach AB 6 B5
Sundance Beach AB 8 C5-6
Sundance PP AB 6 A3-4
Sundance PP AB 8 C2
Sunday Inlet BC 1 E8
Sunderland ON 20 B8
Sunderland ON 21 E2
Sunderland Channel BC 2 B1
Sundown MB 13 F4
Sundown MB 14 F6
Sundre AB 6 C5
Sundre AB 7 A3
Sundridge ON 18 C8
Sundridge ON 21 A1
Sundridge ON 22 E1
Sunnidale Corners ON 18 F7
Sunnidale Corners ON 20 A6
Sunny Brae NS 33 A8
Sunny Brae NS 34 6 D2
Sunnybrae PP NS 6 D2
Sunnybrook AB 8 D5-6
Sunny Corner NB 31 D6
Sunny Glen SK 11 C2-3
Sunny Lake NT 5 C5
Sunnynook AB 6 D7
Sunnynook AB 7 B7
Sunnynook AB 11 D1
Sunnyside NB 29 E7
Sunnyside NB 31 B5-6
Sunnyside NL 36 D8
Sunnyside NL 37 D6
Sunnyslope AB 7 A4
Sunnyville AB 8 D6-7
Sun-Oka Beach PP BC 6 F1-2
Sunset Beach AB 8 D4
Sunset Beach AB 9 F5
Sunset House AB 9 F3-4
Sunset Prairie BC 3 E8
Sunset Prairie BC 9 E1
Sunset, lac QC 25 E4
Sun Valley SK 11 E5
Sunville MB 16 F5
Suomi ON 16 C8
Superb SK 11 C2
Superb Mountain BC 1 D-E6
Superb Mountain BC 2 A3
Supérieur, lac QC 16 F7-8
Supérieur, lac ON 17 D-E1 E1-2
Supérieur, lac QC 29 C-D4
Supérieur, lac QC 31 A3
Supérieur, lac ON 16 F7-8
Superior, Lake ON 17 D1-2 D-E2
Superior, Lake ON 16 F7-8
Superior Junction ON 13 E7
Superior Junction ON 16 D4
Supreme SK 11 C5
Surbiton SK 11 F6
Surette Island NS 33 E-F2
Surf Inlet BC 1 B3
Surge Narrows BC 1 E5-6
Surge Narrows BC 2 B2
Surge Narrows PP BC 2 B2
Surprise Creek YT 5 C2
Surprise Lake BC 3 A1-2
Surprise Lake 4 F4-5
Surprise, lac QC 26 D5
Surprise, lac QC 29 C4
Surprise, lac de la QC 26 C4
Surrey BC 1 F7
Surrey BC 2 E5
Surveyor Point PE 35 D8
Suskwa River BC 3 F4
Sussex NB 32 C5
Sussex Corner NB 32 C5
Sustut PP BC 3 E4-5
Sustut River BC 3 E5
Sutherland, RNOM SK 11 C4
Sutherland NMBS SK 11 C4
Sutherland River PP NL 1 A5-6
Sutherlands River NS 34 E4
Sutil, Cape BC 1 D3-4
Sutton ON 21 D1
Sutton ON 24 E8
Sutton QC 27 F3
Sutton QC 27 F3
Sutton, monts QC 24 E8
Sutton, monts QC 27 F3
Sutton Junction QC 24 E8
Sutton Junction QC 27 F3
Sutton Ridges ON 40 E2-3
Suwannee Lake MB 12 E8
Suwannee Lake MB 15 E2
Svendsen Peninsula NU 42 B4
Sverdrup, îles NU 42 B3-4
Sverdrup Islands NU 42 B3-4
Sverre, Cape NU 42 B4
Swale Island NL 37 B6-7
Swalwell AB 6 D6
Swalwell AB 7 A5
Swan Bay SK 12 C6
Swan Bay SK 15 C1
Swanger Cove NL 36 D5-6
Swanger Cove NL 37 D3-4

Swan Hills AB 8 A3
Swan Hills AB 8 A4
Swan Hills AB 9 F4
Swan Hills AB 9 F4
Swan Lake AB 9 D4
Swan Lake BC 3 E3
Swan Lake MB 11 C8
Swan Lake MB 11 C8
Swan Lake MB 13 B-C2
Swan Lake MB 13 C1-2
Swan Lake MB 13 F3
Swan Lake MB 14 F3
Swan Lake MB 14 E-F3
Swan Lake ON 13 A7
Swan Lake ON 14 D8
Swan Lake SK 15 F7
Swan Lake ON 16 D1
Swan Lake Kispiox River PP BC 3 E3-4
Swan Lake PP BC 9 E2
Swan Lakes SK 12 F4
Swannell Ranges BC 3 D4-5 E5
Swan Plain SK 11 C7
Swan Plain SK 13 C1
Swan River AB 9 F4
Swan River MB 11 C7-8
Swan River MB 13 C1
Swanson SK 11 C-D4
Swartz Bay BC 2 F4
Swastika ON 17 D7
Sweaburg ON 19 C5-6
Sweaburg ON 20 E4-5
Sweet Bay NL 37 B-C4
Sweet Grass SK 11 B3
Swift Current NL 36 D8
Swift Current NL 37 D6
Swift Current SK 11 E3-4
Swift Current Creek SK 11 E3
Swift Rapids ON 18 E8
Swift Rapids ON 21 C1
Swift River BC 1 B7-8
Swift River BC 3 A2
Swift River BC 4 F5
Swift River BC 3 A2
Swift River YT 4 F5
Swinburne, Cape NU 41 B4
Swinburne, Cape NU 42 E3
Swindle Island BC 1 C3
Swinton Park ON 20 B5
Swords ON 18 D7-8
Swords ON 19 C-D4
Sybouts SK 11 F5-6
Sydenham ON 21 D6
Sydenham Lake ON 21 D6-7
Sydenham River ON 18 F5
Sydenham River ON 19 C3-4
Sydenham River ON 19 D2-3
Sydenham River ON 20 A4
Sydenham River ON 20 E2
Sydenham River ON 20 F1
Sydenham River ON 20 F1-2
Sydney NS 34 C8
Sydney Forks NS 34 C8
Sydney Harbour NS 34 B8
Sydney Inlet BC 1 F5
Sydney Inlet PP BC 1 F5
Sydney Lake ON 13 E5
Sydney Lake ON 14 C8
Sydney Lake ON 16 C1
Sydney Mines NS 34 C7-8
Sydney River NS 34 C7
Sydney River NS 34 C7
Sylvan MB 13 F3
Sylvan MB 14 B4-5
Sylvan ON 19 C3-4
Sylvan ON 20 E2-3
Sylvan Glen AB 8 A6
Sylvania SK 11 B6
Sylvan Lake AB 6 C5
Sylvan Lake AB 8 E5-6 F6
Sylvan Lake AB 8 F6
Sylvan Lake PP AB 6 C5
Sylvan Lake PP AB 8 F5-6
Sylvester NS 34 E3
Sylvia, Mount BC 3 C6
Sylvia Grinnell, parc territorial NU 40 A5-6
Sylvia Grinnell TP NU 40 A5-6
Symons Valley AB 7 B3-4
Syringa Creek BC 6 F3
Syringa PP BC 6 F3
Syroga, lac QC 25 B6
Syroga, lac QC 26 F6
Syroga, lac QC 28 D2

T

Taber AB 6 E-F7
Taber AB 7 E6
Table, cap de la QC 30 A7
Table Bay NL 39 B8
Table Head NL 39 D8
Table Island NU 42 C4
Table Mountain NL 36 D1
Table Point Ecological Reserve NL 38 D2-3
Tabusintac NB 30 F2
Tabusintac NB 31 C7-8
Tabusintac Lagoon NB 30 F2
Tabusintac River NB 29 F8
Tabusintac River NB 30 F1
Tabusintac River NB 31 C7

Taché, lac NT 10 B4
Taché, lac QC 29 C3
Tachick Lake BC 1 A6
Tachie BC 3 F6
Tachie BC 1 A6
Tachie River BC 3 F6
Tadek Lake NT 5 D7
Tadenac Lake ON 18 E7
Tadenet Lake NT 5 B7
Tadmore SK 11 C7
Tadoule Lake MB 12 B8
Tadoule Lake MB 15 B3
Tadoule Lake MB 15 B3
Tadoule Lake MB 41 F4
Tadoule Lake MB 41 F4
Tadoussac SK 28 D8
Tadoussac QC 29 D1
Taff Creek BC 3 D3
Taghum BC 6 F3
Tagish YT 4 E4
Tagish Bridge Territorial Recreation Site YT 4 E4
Tagish Lake YT 4 E-F4
Tahsis BC 1 E4
Tahsish-Kwois PP BC 1 E4
Tahsis Inlet BC 1 F4-5
Tahtsa Lake BC 1 A4
Tahtsa Reach BC 1 A4
Taizie NL 39 B2
Taka Lake NT 10 B5
Takhini YT 4 E3
Takhini Hotspring YT 4 E3-4
Takhini River YT 4 E3-4
Takijug Lake NT 41 C2
Takipy MB 12 E7
Takipy MB 15 E1-2
Takla Lake BC 3 F5
Takla Lake PMP BC 3 F5
Takla Landing BC 3 E-F5
Taku River BC 3 B1
Taku River BC 4 D2
Taksie Lake BC 1 A5
Talbot Arm YT 4 D2
Talbot Creek YT 4 D2
Talbot Lake MB 11 A8
Talbot Lake BC 13 A2
Talbot Lake ON 20 A8
Talbot Lake ON 21 C2
Talbot River ON 21 D2
Talbotville Royal ON 19 C-D4
Talbotville Royal ON 20 F3
Tallman SK 11 B4
Tall Pines SK 11 C7
Tally Pond NL 36 B5
Tally Pond NL 37 B3
Talmage SK 11 F6
Talon, lac QC 27 B7
Talon, lac ON 17 F8
Talon, Lake ON 22 D2
Taloyoak NL 41 B5
Taloyoak NU 42 F4
Taltpin Lake NT 1 A5
Taltson River NT 10 E7-8
Taltson River NT 41 E2
Talunkwan Island BC 1 B1-2
Tamarac, lac QC 23 E8
Tamarac, lac QC 25 A2-3
Tamarac, lac QC 25 A2-3
Tamarac, lac QC 26 F2-3
Tamarack ON 19 A7
Tamarack ON 20 C6
Tamarack Island MB 13 C4
Tamworth ON 21 D5-6
Tancook Island NS 32 F7-8
Tancook Island NS 33 D5
Tancredia QC 21 A6
Tancredia QC 22 F6
Tangamong Lake ON 21 C4
Tangent AB 9 E3
Tangier NS 33 B-C7
Tangier Grand Lake NS 33 B7
Tangier Grand Lake NS 34 F3
Tangier River NS 33 B7
Tangier River NS 34 F3
Tanquary Fiord NU 42 A5
Tansleyville ON 16 D7
Tansleyville ON 17 B1
Tantallon NS 32 F8
Tantallon NS 33 C5
Tantallon SK 11 E7
Tantallon SK 13 E1
Tantalus PP BC 1 E-F7
Tantalus PP BC 2 C4
Tantramar, rivière NB 35 F1
Tantramar River NB 35 F1
Tanu Island BC 1 B1
Tanzilla River BC 3 B-C3
Tapani, lac QC 25 E3
Tappen BC 6 D2
Taquanyah CA ON 19 C7
Taquanyah CA ON 20 E6
Tara ON 18 F5
Tara ON 20 A4
Tarbotvale NS 34 B7
Tarnopol SK 11 B-C5
Tarpon Lake NT 10 A8
Tarzwell ON 17 D7
Tarzwell ON 23 E1
Taschereau QC 17 C8
Taschereau QC 23 C-D5
Taschereau, rivière QC 23 C-D5
Taseko Lakes BC 1 D6-7
Taseko River BC 1 C-D6
Taseko River BC 2 A4
Tasiujaq QC 40 C5

Tasseriuck Lake NT 5 B8
Tasso Lake ON 21 A2
Tasu Sound BC 1 B1
Tatachikapika River ON 17 D6
Ta Ta Creek BC 6 F4
Ta Ta Creek BC 7 E1
Tatagwa Lake SK 11 F6
Tatalrose BC 1 A5
Tatamagouche NS 34 D2
Tatamagouche Bay NS 34 D2
Tatamagouche PP NS 34 D2
Tatchu Point BC 1 E4
Tatchun Hills YT 4 C4
Tate SK 11 D5
Tate Lake NT 4 A8
Tate Lake NT 10 A-B2
Tathlina Lake NT 10 F5
Tathlina Lake NT 41 E1
Tatla Lake BC 1 C6
Tatla Lake BC 1 C6
Tatlatui Lake BC 3 C4-4
Tatlatui PP BC 3 D4
Tatlayoko Lake BC 1 D6
Tatlayoko Lake BC 1 D6
Tatlow, Mount BC 1 D6
Tatnam, Cape MB 15 C7
Tatnam, Cape MB 40 C1
Tatogga BC 3 C2
Tatonduk River YT 5 F2
Tatowaycho Lake MB 12 A7
Tatowaycho Lake MB 15 A2
Tatsamenie Lake BC 3 B2
Tatshenshini-Alsek PWP BC 4 F2-3
Tatshenshini River BC 4 E-F3
Tatuk Lake BC 1 B6
Taunton ON 20 C8
Taunton ON 21 E2
Tauraue, réservoir QC 24 A6
Tauraue, réservoir QC 25 E6
Tauraue, réservoir QC 27 B1
Tavistock ON 19 B5
Tavistock ON 20 F3
Tawachiche, ZEC QC 25 D8
Tawachiche, ZEC QC 27 A3
Tawatinaw AB 6 A6
Tawatinaw AB 8 A6
Taweel PP BC 1 C-D8
Taweel PP BC 6 C1
Taxis River NB 31 E4-5
Taxis River NB 31 E5
Taxis River NB 32 A2-3
Taxis River NB 32 A3
Tay, canal ON 21 C7
Tay, canal ON 24 F1
Tay Canal ON 21 C7
Tay Canal ON 24 F1
Tay Creek NB 32 B2
Taye Lake YT 4 D-E3
Tay Lake YT 4 C5
Taylor BC 3 E8
Taylor BC 9 D1-2
Taylor, lac QC 23 A7
Taylor, lac QC 26 B1-2
Taylor, Mount BC 6 F5
Taylor, Mount BC 7 E3
Taylor Arm PP BC 1 F5
Taylor Arm PP BC 2 D2
Taylor Corners ON 20 B8
Taylor Corners ON 21 D2
Taylor Head PP NS 33 C8
Taylor Lake ON 24 E1
Taylor Landing PP BC 3 E8
Taylor Landing PP BC 9 E2
Taylor River BC 3 D-E8
Taylor's Bay NL 36 F6
Taylor's Bay NL 37 F4
Taylors Head NS 33 C8
Taylorville AB 7 F5
Taymouth NB 31 F5
Taymouth NB 32 B3
Tay River YT 4 C4-5
Tazin Lake SK 9 A7-8
Tazin Lake SK 12 A3
Tazin Lake SK 41 E2
Tazin River SK 9 A7
Tazin River SK 12 A4
Tchaneta River NT 5 D7
Tchendfери Lake NT 5 D7
Tchentlo Lake BC 3 F5-6
Tchesinkut Lake BC 1 A5
Tchesinkut Lake BC 1 A5
Tchitogama, lac QC 28 B5
Tea Cove NL 36 B1-2
Tea Hill PE 35 E5
Teepee Creek AB 9 E3
Teepee Mountain BC 6 E-F4
Teepee Mountain BC 7 E2
Tees AB 6 C6
Tees AB 8 E6-7
Teeswater ON 20 B3
Teeswater River ON 20 B3
Teeterville ON 19 C6
Teeterville ON 20 E5
Tehek Lake NU 41 D4
Tehkummah ON 2 A4
Telegraph Cove BC 1 E4-5
Telegraph Creek BC 3 C2
Telegraph Range BC 1 B6

Telford MB 14 E7
Telfordville AB 6 B5
Telfordville AB 8 D5-6
Telkwa BC 3 F4
Telkwa River BC 3 F4
Tellier QC 39 E2
Temagami ON 17 E7
Temagami ON 22 B1
Temagami, Lake ON 17 E7
Temagami, Lake ON 22 B1
Temagami River ON 17 F7
Temagami River PP ON 17 F7
Témiscaming QC 17 F8
Témiscaming QC 22 C2
Témiscamingue QC 17 D8
Témiscamingue QC 22 A1-2
Témiscamingue, lac QC 23 F1-2
Témiscamingue, lac QC 17 E8
Témiscamingue, lac QC 22 A1-2
Témiscamingue, lac QC 23 F1-2
Témiscouata, lac QC 29 E2
Témiscouata, lac QC 31 B1
Temperance Vale NB 31 F3-4
Temperance Vale NB 32 B1-2
Tempest AB 7 E6
Temple NB 32 C1
Templeman NL 37 A6-7
Templeman NL 38 F8
Templeman, Mount BC 6 E3
Ten Mile Lake NL 36 A7
Ten Mile Lake NL 38 A3
Ten Mile Lake NL 38 B4
Ten Mile Lake NL 38 A6
Ten Mile Lake BC 1 B7
Ten Mile Lake PP NS 33 D3-4
Ten Mile Pond NL 36 A8
Ten Mile Pond NL 37 A6
Ten Mile Pond NL 38 F7
Tenby MB 13 E2
Tenby MB 14 C2
Tenlen Lake NT 5 C6
Tennycape NS 32 D8
Tennycape NS 33 A5
Tennycape NS 34 F1
Tent Island NT 5 B4
Tepee Lake AB 9 D5
Terence MB 14 E1
Terence Bay NS 32 F8
Terence Bay NS 33 D6
Terrace BC 1 A3
Terrace BC 3 F3
Terrace Bay ON 16 E-F7
Terrace Bay ON 17 C2
Terrace Bay ON 40 F2
Terra Cotta ON 19 A7
Terra Cotta ON 20 C6
Terra Cotta CA ON 19 A7
Terra Cotta CA ON 20 C6
Terra Nova NL 36 B-C8
Terra Nova NL 37 B-C6
Terra Nova NL 20 B6
Terra-Nova, PN NL 36 B8
Terra Nova Lake NL 37 B6
Terra Nova Lake NL 36 B8
Terra Nova NP NL 36 B8
Terra Nova NP NL 37 B6-7
Terrasses, lac des QC 23 D8
Terrasses, lac des QC 26 D-E2
Terrebonne QC 24 D5-6
Terrebonne QC 27 D-E1
Terrenceville NL 36 D7
Terrenceville NL 37 D5
Terrien, lac QC 27 A7-8
Terror Point BC 1 B2-3
Teslin YT 4 E5
Teslin Lake YT 4 E5
Teslin River BC 3 A-B2
Teslin River BC 4 F5
Teslin River YT 4 D-E4
Tessier SK 11 C4
Tessier, lac QC 25 A3
Tessier, lac QC 26 F3
Tessik Lake NU 40 A4
Tessik Lake NU 41 C7
Tetachuck Lake BC 1 B5
Tetagouche River NB 29 E7
Tetagouche River NB 31 B5-6
Tetcho Lake NT 10 F3-4
Tête, lac de la QC 23 D8
Tête, lac de la QC 26 E3
Tête-à-la-Baleine QC 39 E6
Tête d'Ours, lac NT 10 B8
Tête Jaune Cache BC 6 B2
Tetlit Gwinjik TP NT 5 D4
Tetlit Zheh (Fort McPherson) NT 5 D4
Tetrahedron PP BC 2 D4
Tetsa River PP BC 3 B6
Têtu, lac QC 28 A6
Tetu Lake ON 16 D1
Teulon MB 13 E4
Teulon MB 14 C-D5
Teviotdale ON 19 A5-6
Teviotdale ON 20 C4-5
Tewkesbury QC 27 A5
Texada Island BC 1 F6
Texada Island BC 2 D3
Texas Creek BC 2 B6
Tezzeron Creek BC 3 F6
Tezzeron Lake BC 3 F6
Tha-anne River NU 40 A-B1
Tha-anne River NU 41 E4

Thackeray, RNP ON 17 C-D7
Thackeray, RNP ON 23 D1
Thackeray PNR ON 23 D1
Thackeray PNR ON 17 C-D7
Thaddeus Lake ON 16 D5-6
Thaïs, lac QC 26 D5-6
Thaïs, lac QC 28 B1
Thalberg MB 13 E4
Thalberg MB 14 C-D6
Thames River ON 19 B-C5
Thames River ON 19 D3
Thames River ON 20 E4
Thames River ON 20 F2
Thamesford ON 19 C5
Thamesford ON 20 E4
Thamesville ON 19 D3
Thamesville ON 20 F2
Thanet Lake ON 21 C4
Thaumur, lac QC 25 B3
The Anchorage PP NB 32 F2-3
The Arches PP NL 38 D2
The Arches PP NL 39 E-F7
The Backway NL 38 B3
The Banks Fishery—The Age of Sail NHS NS 33 D5-6
The Battlefords PP SK 11 B3
The Beaches NL 38 E4
The Beaches NL 39 F8
The Big Ridge NS 34 C6 D5
The Blue Mountains ON 18 F6
The Blue Mountains ON 20 A5
The Dalles ON 13 E5
The Dalles ON 14 D8
Thedford ON 19 B3
Thedford ON 20 E2
The Falls NS 34 E2
The Fundy Isles NB 32 E3
The Glades NB 32 C6
The Great Sand Hills SK 11 E2-3
The Gut CA ON 21 C4
The Hawk NS 33 F4
The Hiscock House PHS NL 37 C7-8
The Islands PP NS 33 E2-3
The Ledge NB 31 D3-4
The Massasauga PP ON 18 D7
The Middle Sand Hills AB 6 D8 E7
The Middle Sand Hills AB 7 C8
The Middle Sand Hills AB 11 D1-2 E1
Thémines, rivière QC 39 C-D1
The Mockbeggar Property & Cape Bonavista Lighthouse Provincial Historic Sites NL 37 B7-8
The Narrows MB 13 C3
The Narrows MB 14 A3
The Narrows MB 14 A8
Théo, rivière QC 23 A2
Theodore SK 11 D6
The Old Settler BC 1 F8
The Old Settler BC 2 D7
The Pas MB 11 A7
The Pas MB 13 A1
The Pas MB 11 A-B7
The Pas SK 11 A7
The Pinery PP ON 19 B3
The Pinery PP ON 20 D2
The Porcupine Hills MB 11 C1
The Porcupine Hills MB 13 C1
The Porcupine Hills MB 11 C7
The Porcupine Hills MB 13 C1
The Queen Elizabeth The Queen Mother M'Nidoo M'Nissing PP ON 18 B2
The Ranee AB 6 B2-3
The Range NB 31 F6
The Range NB 32 B4
Theriau Lake SK 12 B5
Therien AB 6 A7
Therien AB 8 A7
Therien AB 11 A1
Therien AB 12 F1
Three Mile Plains NS 32 F7
The Shoals PP ON 17 D4
Thessalon ON 17 F4-5
Thessalon ON 18 A1
Thessalon Point ON 18 A1
The Tablelands NL 36 A3
The Tablelands NL 37 A1
The Tablelands NL 38 F2
Thetford Mines QC 27 C5
Thetis Bay YT 5 A3
Thetis Island BC 1 F6-7
Thetis Island BC 2 E4
Thetis Lake NT 10 B7
Thetlaandoa Creek BC 3 A7 B7-8
Thetlaandoa Creek BC 9 A1
The Two Rivers SK 12 E6
Thévet, lac QC 39 D3
Thibault AB 11 A7
Thicke Lake SK 12 A4
Thicket Portage MB 15 F3-4
Thickwood Hills SK 11 B4
Thinahtea Lake BC 3 A8
Thinahtea Lake BC 9 A2
Thinahtea PPA BC 3 A8

Thinahtea PPA BC 9 A2
Third Lac NB 29 E3
Thirty Mile Lake YT 4 E5
Thirty Thousand Islands ON 18 C-D6
Thistlethwaite Lake NT 10 C7
Thlewiaza River NU 41 E-F4
Thluicho Lake SK 9 A7
Thluicho Lake SK 12 A3
Thoa River NT 41 E2
Thode SK 11 C4
Thoen, Mount BC 3 F4
Thomas Bay ON 18 C3-4
Thomasburg ON 21 D5
Thomas H. Raddall PP NS 33 D5-6
Thomas Hubbard, Cape NU 42 A4
Thomas Lake MB 15 D4
Thomas River NL 39 B5
Thomaston Corner NB 32 C2
Thomasville NS 33 F2
Thompson MB 15 E3-4
Thompson Island, RNP ON 16 F6
Thompson Island PNR ON 16 F6
Thompson Lake ON 22 D-E2
Thompson Landing NT 10 C8
Thompson Point MB 15 B6
Thompson River BC 1 D-E8
Thompson River BC 2 A-B7
Thompson River BC 6 D-E1
Thompson Sound BC 1 E5
Thompson Sound BC 1 D-E5
Thompson Sound BC 2 A1
Thompson Sound BC 2 A1
Thomsen River NT 42 D1
Thomson Lake SK 12 B4-5
Thomson Station SK 32 C8
Thomson Station NS 34 E1
Thonokied Lake NT 10 A8
Thorah Island ON 18 F8
Thorah Island ON 20 A7
Thorah Island ON 21 D1
Thorburn SK 11 A8
Thorburn NS 34 E3-4
Thorburn Lake NL 36 C8
Thorburn Lake NL 37 C6
Thorhild AB 6 A6
Thorhild AB 8 B7
Thormanby Island BC 1 F6
Thornbury ON 18 F6
Thornbury ON 20 A5
Thornby QC 22 F6
Thorndale ON 19 C5
Thorndale ON 20 E4
Thorne ON 18 F8
Thorne ON 22 C2
Thorne River ON 15 F7
Thornhill MB 13 F3
Thornhill MB 14 F3
Thornhill ON 19 A8
Thornhill ON 20 C7
Thornhill ON 21 F1
Thornlea NL 37 D7
Thornloe ON 17 D7-8
Thornloe ON 23 F1
Thornton ON 20 B6
Thorold ON 19 C8
Thorold ON 20 E7
Thorold South ON 19 C8
Thorold South ON 20 E7
Thorsby AB 6 B5
Thorsby AB 8 D6
Thorsteinson Lake MB 15 C3-4 D3-4
Three Brooks NB 31 D3
Three Day Lake NT 5 F7
Three Day Lake NT 10 A1
Three Hills AB 6 C6
Three Hills AB 7 A5
Three Mile Bay ON 21 B6
Three Mile Lake ON 18 D8
Three Mile Lake ON 21 B1
Three Mile Lake ON 22 E2
Three Mile Lake ON 22 F1
Three Mile Plains NS 32 F7
Three Mile Plains NS 33 B-C5
Three Mile Rock NL 37 D4
Three Mile Rock NL 38 D-E2
Threepoint Lake MB 15 E3
Three Rock Cove NL 36 A3
Three Sisters Lakes PP BC 1 B7
Three Valley BC 6 D2
Throat River ON 13 C6
Throat River ON 16 A3
Throne AB 6 C7
Throne AB 11 C1
Thrums BC 6 F3
Thubun Lakes NT 10 D8
Thubun River NT 10 D7-8
Thultue Lake AB 9 A5
Thultue Lake AB 10 F7
Thultue Lake AB 12 A1
Thunder Bay ON 16 F6
Thunder Beach ON 18 F7
Thunder Brook NL 36 B5-6
Thunder Brook NL 37 B3-4
Thunder Cape ON 16 F6
Thunderchild SK 11 B3
Thundercloud Creek NT 4 C7-8

Thundercloud Creek NT 10 C-D1
Thunder Creek SK 11 E4
Thunder Hill PP BC 6 E4
Thunder Hill PP BC 7 D1
Thunder Hills SK 12 F4
Thunder Lake PP AB 6 A5
Thunder Lake PP AB 8 B5
Thunder Mountain BC 1 C4-5
Thurso QC 24 D3
Thurston Bay PMP BC 1 E5
Thurston Bay PMP BC 2 B2
Thutade Lake BC 3 D4-5
Thurston Lake AB 9 A3
Thurston Lake AB 10 F5
Thuycholeen Lake MB 12 B7
Thuycholeen Lake MB 15 B2
Thwart Island NL 36 A6
Thwart Island NL 37 A4-5
Thwart Island NL 38 F6
Tian Head BC 1 A1
Tiblemont, lac QC 23 E5
Tice Lake MB 12 A7
Tice Lake MB 15 A2
Tichborne ON 21 C6
Tichfield SK 11 D4
Tickle Beach NL 36 D7
Tickle Beach NL 37 D5
Tickle Cove NL 37 B7
Tickle Harbour NL 36 D8
Tickle Harbour NL 37 D6
Tickle Harbour Point NL 37 D7
Ticouapé, rivière QC 26 D8
Ticouapé, rivière QC 28 B3
Tidal MB 15 B5
Tidd, Mount YT 4 C5-6
Tiddville NS 33 D1
Tide Head NB 29 D6
Tide Head NB 31 A4
Tide Lake AB 6 E7
Tide Lake AB 7 C7
Tide Lake AB 11 D-E1
Tide Lake, RNP ON 16 C1-2
Tide Lake PNR ON 13 E6
Tide Lake PNR ON 16 C1-2
Tides Point NL 36 E7
Tides Point NL 37 E5
Tidney River NS 33 D3
Tidnish NS 34 D1
Tidnish NS 35 F2
Tidnish Bridge NS 32 B-C7
Tidnish Bridge NS 34 D1
Tidnish Bridge NS 35 F2
Tidnish Dock PP NS 32 B7-8
Tidnish Dock PP NS 34 D1
Tidnish Dock PP NS 35 F2
Tidnish Head NS 35 F2
Tiger Lake AB 8 B5
Tiger Lily AB 6 A5
Tiger Lily AB 8 B5
Tignish PE 34 A1
Tignish PE 35 E1
Tignish River PE 35 A-B2
Tignish Shore PE 35 A1
Tignish Shores PE 34 A1
Tika QC 39 E2
Tikamaganda Lake ON 17 E6
Tikirarjuaq (Whale Cove) NU 40 A-B2
Tikirarjuaq (Whale Cove) NU 41 E5
Tilbury ON 19 E2
Tilden Lake ON 17 F8
Tilden Lake ON 18 A8
Tilden Lake ON 18 A8
Tilden Lake ON 22 C1
Tilden Lake ON 22 C1
Tilley NB 31 D3
Tilley AB 6 E7
Tilley AB 7 C6
Tilley AB 11 E1
Tilley Road NB 31 B7
Tilley NB 31 D3
Tilston MB 11 F8
Tilston MB 13 F1
Tilt Cove NL 38 E5
Tilting NL 38 E7
Tilton NL 37 D7
Timber Bay SK 11 A5
Timber Island ON 21 D1
Timber Island PNR ON 21 B1
Timber Island, RNP ON 21 B6
Timberlea NS 32 F8
Timberlea NS 33 C6
Timber River NB 35 E-F2
Timeu AB 8 A5
Timiskaming, Lake ON 22 A1
Timiskaming, Lake ON 23 F1
Timiskaming, Lake ON 17 E8
Timmins ON 17 C-D6
Tim River ON 22 E-F2
Tincap ON 21 C-D8
Tincap ON 24 F2

Tinchebray AB 8 E8
Tincup Lake YT 4 C-D2
Tingwick QC 27 D4
Tintamarre, RNF NB 32 B-C7
Tintamarre, RNF NB 35 F1-2
Tintamarre NWA NB 32 B-C7
Tintamarre NWA NB 35 F1-2
Tin Town MB 14 D4
Tiny MB 11 C-D7
Tipahaskayo Lake MB 15 E6
Tip Top Mountain ON 16 F8
Tip Top Mountain ON 17 D2-3
Tisdale SK 11 B6
Titusville NB 32 D4-5
Titusville NB 33 A2
Tiverton ON 20 B3
Tizzard's Harbour NL 38 E6
Tlell BC 1 A1
Tlogotsho Range NT 10 E1-2
Toad River BC 3 B5-6
Toad River BC 3 B5
Toad River Hotsprings PP BC 3 B6
Toanche ON 18 E7
Tobacco Lake ON 18 B3
Toba Inlet BC 1 E6
Toba Inlet BC 2 B3
Toba River BC 1 E6
Toba River BC 2 B3-4
Tobeatic Lake NS 33 D3
Tobeatic Wilderness Area NS 33 D2
Tobeatic Wilderness Area NS 33 E2-3
Tobeatic WMA NS 33 D2-3
Tobermory ON 18 D4
Tobin Lake SK 11 B6
Tobin Lake SK 11 B6
Tobique Narrows NB 31 C4
Tobique River NB 31 C4 D3
Toby, Mount BC 6 E4
Toby, Mount BC 7 D1
Toby Creek BC 7 D1
Tochcha Lake BC 3 F5
Tod, Mount BC 6 D1-2
Todagin South Slope PP BC 3 C3
Tod Creek AB 7 E3-4
Tod Lake MB 15 D1
Tod Lake MB 15 D1
Tofield AB 6 B6
Tofield AB 8 C7
Tofino BC 1 F5
Tofino BC 2 E1
Tofino Inlet BC 1 F5
Tofino Inlet BC 2 E1
Togo SK 11 D7
Togo SK 13 D1
Toker Point NT 5 A5
Toledo ON 21 C7
Toledo ON 24 F1-2
Tolman AB 7 A5
Tolmie Channel BC 1 B3
Tolsmaville ON 18 B1
Tolstoi MB 13 F4
Tolstoi MB 14 F5
Tomahawk AB 6 B5
Tomahawk AB 8 C6
Tomasine, lac QC 22 C7
Tomasine, lac QC 24 A1
Tomasine, lac QC 25 E1
Tom Browne Lake BC 2 A-B1
Tombstone TP YT 4 A2
Tombstone TP YT 5 F2
Tomifobia QC 24 E8
Tomifobia QC 27 F4
Tomifobia, rivière QC 27 F4
Tomiko ON 18 A8
Tomiko ON 18 A8
Tomiko Lake ON 17 F8
Tomiko Lake ON 18 A7
Tomiko Lake ON 18 A8
Tomiko Lake ON 22 C1
Tomiko Lake ON 18 A7-8
Tom Luscombe Brook NL 39 B6-7
Tomney, lac QC 23 E8
Tomney, lac QC 25 B2
Tomney, lac QC 26 F2
Tomogonops River NB 29 F7
Tomogonops River NB 31 C6
Tompkins NL 36 D1
Tompkins SK 11 E3
Tomslake BC 3 E8
Tomslake BC 9 E2
Tomstown ON 17 D7-8
Tomstown ON 23 E1
Toney River NS 34 D3
Tonkin SK 11 D7
Toodoggone River BC 3 D4-5
Toogood Arm NL 38 E6-7
Toosey BC 1 C6
Topaze Harbour BC 2 B2
Top of the World PP BC 6 E4-5
Top of the World PP BC 7 E2
Topley BC 1 A5
Topley Landing BC 3 F5
Topley BC 3 F5
Top Pond NL 36 D3
Top Pond NL 37 D1
Toquart Bay BC 2 E2
Torbay NL 37 D8
Tor Bay NS 34 E-F6

Tor Bay NS 34 F6
Tor Bay PP NS 34 E6
Torbrook SK 32 E6
Torbrook NS 33 B3
Torch River SK 11 A5 A-B6
Torch River SK 11 C3
Tormentine, cap NB 35 E3
Tormentine, Cape NB 32 B8
Tormentine, Cape NB 34 C1
Tormentine, Cape NB 35 E3
Tornado Mountain AB 6 E5
Tornado Mountain AB 7 D3
Torngat Mountain NP (proposed/projeté) NL 40 C6-7
Torngat Mountains NL 40 C6-7
Toronto ON 19 A8
Toronto ON 20 C-D7
Toronto ON 21 F1-2
Toronto Islands ON 19 A8
Toronto Islands ON 20 D7
Toronto Islands ON 21 F1
Torquay SK 11 F6
Torrance ON 18 E8
Torrance ON 21 C1
Torrance Lake MB 15 D3
Torrington AB 6 C5-6
Torrington AB 7 A4
Tors Cove NL 37 E6
Tortue, lac à la QC 22 D7
Tortue, lac à la QC 24 A-B1
Tortue, lac à la QC 25 F1
Tortue, rivière à la QC 24 E6
Tortue, rivière à la QC 27 F1
Tory Hill ON 21 C3
Toslow NL 36 E8
Toslow NL 37 E6
Totnes NL 11 D3
Totogan Lake 16 A5-6
Tottenham ON 20 B-C6
Touchwood Hills SK 11 D5-6
Touchwood Hills Post Provincial Historic Park SK 11 D5-6
Touchwood Lake AB 9 F7
Touchwood Lake AB 12 F1
Touchwood Lake MB 13 A5
Touchwood Lake MB 15 F5
Touladi, lac QC 29 E2
Touladi, lac QC 31 B1
Toulnustouc, rivière QC 39 E-F1
Tourbis, lac QC 25 D5
Tourelle QC 29 A6
Tourilli, lac QC 28 F5
Tour-Martello-de-Carleton, LHN de la NB 32 E4-5
Tour-Martello-de-Carleton, LHN de la NB 33 B1-2
Tourond MB 14 E5
Tourouvre, lac QC 25 D7
Tourouvre, lac QC 28 E3
Tourville QC 27 A8
Tourville QC 28 F8
Toussaint, rivière QC 26 D4
Toutes Aides MB 13 D2
Toutes Aides MB 14 A2
Townsend ON 19 C6-7
Townsend ON 20 E5-6
Tracadie NB 30 F2
Tracadie NB 31 B8
Tracadie NS 34 D5
Tracadie Bay PE 34 C3
Tracadie Bay PE 35 D5
Tracadie Cross PE 34 C3
Tracadie Cross PE 35 D5
Tracadie-Sheila NB 30 F2
Tracadie-Sheila NB 31 B8
Tracadigache, pointe QC 29 D7
Tracadigache, pointe QC 31 A5-6
Tracey Mills NB 31 E3
Tracey Mills NB 32 A1
Tracy NB 32 C3
Tracy QC 24 C7
Tracy QC 27 D2
Trade Lake SK 12 E6
Trafalgar NS 33 A7-8
Trafalgar NS 34 E3
Trail BC 6 F3
Trail River YT 5 D-E4
Traîne, lac de la QC 25 D6
Traîne, lac de la QC 27 A2
Traîne, lac de la QC 28 F2
Train Lake SK 12 A4
Trainor Lake NT 10 F4
Tramore ON 21 A5
Tramore ON 22 F5
Tramping Lake SK 6 C8
Tramping Lake SK 11 C3
Tramping Lake SK 11 C3
Tranquil Creek PP NL 1 F5
Tranquil Creek PP BC 2 D1
Tranquille BC 2 A8
Tranquille BC 6 D1
Trappist Monastery PP MB 14 E5
Travaillant Lake NT 5 C-D5
Travaillant River NT 5 C-D5
Travellers Rest PE 35 D3
Travers AB 7 D6
Travers, lac de QC 25 D8
Travers, lac de QC 27 A3-4
Travers, lac de QC 28 F3-4
Travers, Lake ON 22 E4
Traverse, lac de la QC 26 A7
Traverse Bay MB 13 E4
Traverse Bay MB 14 C6

Traverse Bay MB 14 C6
Traverspine River NL 39 C5-6
Travers Reservoir AB 6 E6
Travers Reservoir AB 7 D5
Traynor SK 11 C3
Traytown NL 36 B8
Traytown NL 37 B6
Tree River NT 5 D5
Treesbank MB 13 F2
Treesbank MB 14 E2
Tregarva SK 11 E5
Treherne MB 13 F3
Treherne MB 14 E3
Tremaine MB 14 D1
Tremaudan MB 11 A7-8
Tremaudan MB 13 A1-2
Tremblant, lac QC 24 B4
Tremblant, lac QC 25 F4
Tremblant, mont QC 24 B4
Tremblant, mont QC 25 F4
Tremblay QC 31 B6
Tremblay, lac QC 28 C6
Tremblay, lac QC 28 B7
Trembleur Lake BC 3 F5-6
Trembleur Lake PP BC 3 F6
Tremblowla MB 11 D8
Tremblowla MB 13 D2
Tremblowla MB 14 B1
Tremont NS 32 E6
Tremont NS 33 B3
Trenche, lac QC 26 E6
Trenche, lac QC 28 B2
Trenche, rivière QC 25 A-B7
Trenche, rivière QC 26 E-F7
Trenche, rivière QC 28 C2 D3
Trenholm QC 24 D8
Trenholm QC 27 E4
Trenholme, lac QC 26 B4
Trentham MB 14 F6
Trent Canal ON 20 A8
Trent Canal ON 21 D4
Trente et Un Milles, lac des QC 22 E8
Trente et Un Milles, lac des QC 24 B2
Trente et Un Milles, lac des QC 25 F2
Trenton NS 34 E3
Trenton ON 21 E4-5
Trent River ON 21 E4
Trent River ON 21 D4
Trent-Severn, voie navigable ON 18 E8
Trent-Severn, voie navigable ON 21 C1
Trent-Severn, voie navigable ON 21 D2-3
Trent-Severn, voie navigable ON 21 D-E4
Trent-Severn Waterway ON 18 E8
Trent-Severn Waterway ON 21 C1
Trent-Severn Waterway ON 21 D2-3
Trent-Severn Waterway ON 21 D-E4
Trepassey NL 37 F7
Trepassey Bay NL 37 F7
Très Rocheux, lac QC 26 B5
Trévet, lac QC 23 E7
Trévet, lac QC 25 A2
Trévet, lac QC 26 F2
Trévet, rivière QC 23 E7-8
Trévet, rivière QC 25 A2
Trévet, rivière QC 26 E-F2
Trewdale SK 11 F6
Triangular Lake ON 16 B6-7
Tribune SK 11 F6
Tribune Bay PP BC 2 D3
Tribune Channel BC 1 D-E5
Trillium Woods PP ON 19 C5-6
Trillium Woods PP ON 20 E4-5
Trilsbeck Lake ON 13 E7
Tring-Jonction QC 27 C6
Trinity NL 36 A8
Trinity NL 37 A6
Trinity NL 37 C7
Trinity Bay NL 37 D7
Trinity East NL 37 C7
Triquet, lac QC 39 E6
Tristram AB 8 E7
Triton NL 38 E5
Triton Brook NL 36 B7
Triton Brook NL 37 B5
Triton-Jim's Cove-Card's Harbour NL 38 E5
Trochu AB 6 C6
Trochu AB 7 B6
Trois Caribous, lac des QC 28 E4
Trois-Lacs QC 27 D4-5
Trois-Pistoles QC 29 D1-2
Trois-Rivières QC 24 B7-8
Trois-Rivières QC 25 F7-8
Trois-Rivières QC 27 C3
Trois-Rivières-Ouest QC 24 B7-8
Trois-Rivières-Ouest QC 25 F7-8
Trois-Rivières-Ouest QC 27 C3
Trois-Ruisseaux NB 35 E1-2
Trois-Saumons QC 25 D6
Trois-Saumons QC 27 F7
Trois Saumons, lac QC 27 A7

Trois Saumons, lac QC 28 F7
Troitsa Lake BC 1 B4
Trophy Mountain BC 6 C2
Trossachs SK 11 F5-6
Trousers Lake NB 31 D4
Trout Brook NB 31 C6
Trout Brook NB 34 C6
Trout Brook NS 34 C8
Trout Brook PP NS 34 C6
Trout Cove NS 32 F4
Trout Cove NS 33 C1
Trout Creek ON 18 B8
Trout Creek ON 22 E1
Troutly Lake ON 16 B6
Trout Lake AB 9 D5
Trout Lake BC 6 E3
Trout Lake BC 6 E3
Trout Lake MB 12 C8
Trout Lake MB 15 C3
Trout Lake NT 10 F3
Trout Lake NT 10 F3
Trout Lake ON 13 D6
Trout Lake ON 16 B2
Trout Lake ON 17 F7
Trout Lake ON 18 A8
Trout Lake ON 18 B6
Trout Lake ON 18 C7
Trout Lake ON 18 D7
Trout Lake ON 21 A2
Trout Lake ON 21 A4
Trout Lake ON 21 B5
Trout Lake ON 22 D1
Trout Lake ON 22 F2
Trout Lake ON 22 F4
Trout Lake PP ON 13 D6
Trout Lake PP ON 16 B-C2
Troutlake River ON 13 D6
Trout River AB 9 D5
Trout River NL 38 F2
Trout River NL 39 F7
Trout River NT 10 E3-4
Trout River PE 35 C1-2
Trout River Pond NL 36 A2-3
Trout River Pond NL 37 A1
Trout River Pond NL 38 F2
Trouty NL 37 C7
Trowbridge ON 19 A5
Trowbridge ON 20 C4
Troy NS 34 D5
Troy ON 19 B6-7
Troy ON 20 E5-6
Troyes, lac QC 25 D5
Truax SK 11 E5
Trudeau Airport QC 24 D5-6
Trudeau Airport QC 27 E1
Trudel NB 31 B7
Truemanville NS 32 C7-8
Truemanville NS 34 C6
Truite, lac à la QC 22 B3-4
Truite, lac à la QC 26 B7
Truite, rivière à la QC 29 B-C5 B6
Truitt Peak YT 4 C4
Truman Dagnus Locheed PP BC 7 C3-4
Trunmore Bay NL 39 B7
Truro NS 33 A6
Truro NS 34 E2
Truro Heights NS 33 A6
Truro Heights NS 34 E2
Trutch BC 3 C7
Trutch Creek BC 3 C7
Trutch Creek BC 9 C1
Tryon PE 32 B8
Tryon PE 34 C2
Tryon PE 35 E3
Tryon Head PE 35 E3
Tsacha Lake BC 1 B6
Tsalwor Lake SK 9 A7
Tsalwor Lake SK 12 A3
Tsar Mountain BC 6 C3
Tsar Mountain BC 8 F1
Tsawwassen BC 2 E4-5
Tsea River BC 3 A7
Tsea River BC 9 A1
Tseepantee Lake NT 10 C3
Tseeteli Lake MB 12 B7-8
Tseeteli Lake MB 15 B2
Tsiigehtchic (Arctic Red River) NT 5 D4-5
Ts'il-os PP BC 2 A3-4
Tsinstikeptum BC 2 A8
Tsintsunko Lakes PP BC 2 A8
Tsintsunko Lakes PP BC 6 D1
Tsintu River NT 5 E7
Tsitsutl Peak BC 1 B-C5
Tsoko Lake NT 5 C7-8
Tsu Lake NT 10 E8
Tsulquate BC 1 D-E4
Tsuniah Lake BC 1 D6
Ts'yl-os PP BC 1 D6
Tuberose NT 5 D6
Tuchialic Bay NL 39 A7
Tuchitua YT 4 E6-7
Tuchitua River YT 4 D6
Tucho River BC 3 C4
Tuchodi River BC 3 C6
Tudor AB 7 B5
Tudyah Lake PP BC 3 F6-7
Tuffnell SK 11 D6
Tugaske SK 11 D4
Tugate AB 9 B3
Tuillé, lac QC 23 D7
Tuillé, lac QC 26 E1
Tuktoyaktuk NT 5 B5
Tuktusiuqvialuk (Northern Bathurst Island) NP (proposed/projeté) NU 42 C3-4
Tuktut Nogait, PN NT 5 B8

Tuktut Nogait NP NT 5 B8
Tuktut Nogait NP NT 41 B1
Tulameen BC 1 F8
Tulameen BC 2 D8
Tulameen BC 6 F1
Tulameen River BC 1 F8
Tulameen River BC 2 D8
Tulameen River BC 6 F1
Tulita NT 5 F8
Tulita NT 10 A1-2
Tulliby Lake AB 6 A8
Tulliby Lake AB 11 A2
Tulsequah BC 3 B1
Tulugay River YT 5 B2-3
Tumbledown Dick Island NL 39 B7
Tumbler Ridge BC 3 F8
Tumbler Ridge BC 9 E-F1
Tumeka Lake BC 3 D3
Tummel MB 11 D7
Tummel MB 13 D1
Tummel River YT 4 C4
Tunago Lake NT 5 E8
Tungsten NT 4 C-D7
Tunis ON 17 C6-7
Tunkwa PP BC 1 F8
Tunkwa PP BC 2 A7 B7-8
Tunkwa PP BC 6 D-E1
Tunnel Lake ON 18 A1
Tunstall SK 11 E2
Tunungayualok Island NL 40 D7
Tununuk NT 5 B4
Tupper BC 3 E8
Tupper BC 9 E2
Tupper Lake NS 33 D3
Tupperville NS 32 F5
Tupperville NS 33 C3
Tupperville ON 19 D2
Tupperville ON 20 F1
Tuque, lac la QC 25 C7
Tuque, lac la QC 28 E-F2
Turbine ON 18 A4
Turcotte, lac QC 25 C7
Turcotte, lac QC 28 F3
Turgeon, lac QC 23 B3
Turgeon, rivière QC 17 B8
Turgeon, rivière QC 23 A2
Turin AB 6 E6
Turin AB 7 D6
Turkey Point ON 19 D6
Turkey Point ON 19 D6
Turkey Point ON 20 F5
Turkey Point ON 20 F5
Turkey Point PP ON 19 D6
Turkey Point PP ON 20 F5
Turmoil Lake NT 10 A5
Turnagain River BC 3 B4
Turnavik Island NL 39 A6
Turnberry MB 11 B7
Turnberry MB 13 B1
Turnbull MB 12 F8
Turnbull MB 13 A2-3
Turnbull MB 15 F2-3
Turnbull, lac QC 25 C4
Turnbull Island ON 18 B2
Turner's Bight NL 39 B7
Turner Valley AB 6 E5
Turner Valley AB 7 F4
Turner Valley Gas Plant PHS AB 7 C3-4
Turnor Lake SK 9 D8
Turnor Lake SK 9 D8
Turnor Lake SK 12 D3
Turnor Lake SK 12 D3
Turnour Island BC 1 E5
Turtle Creek NB 31 F8
Turtle Creek NB 32 C6
Turtleford SK 6 B8
Turtleford SK 11 A3
Turtle Lake ON 18 C4
Turtle Lake SK 11 A3
Turtlelake River SK 6 B8
Turtlelake River SK 11 B3
Turtle Lake South Bay SK 6 A-B8
Turtle Lake South Bay SK 11 B3
Turtle Mountain PP MB 11 F8
Turtle Mountain PP MB 13 F2
Turtle Mountain PP MB 14 F1
Turtle River MB 13 D2
Turtle River MB 14 B-C2
Turtle River ON 16 B3
Turtle River ON 16 E3
Turtle River PP ON 13 F7
Turtle River PP ON 16 E3
Turton Lake NT 5 E7
Tusket NS 33 E1-2
Tusket Island NS 33 F1
Tusket Lake NS 33 E1
Tusket River NS 33 D-E2
Tutshi Lake BC 3 A1
Tutshi Lake BC 4 F4
Tutsieta Lake NT 5 D6
Tuxford SK 11 E5
Tuya Lake BC 3 B3
Tuya Mountains PP BC 3 B2-3
Tuya River BC 3 B2-3
Tway SK 11 B5
Tway Lake, RNF SK 11 B5
Tway Lake National Wilderness Area SK 11 B5
Tweed ON 21 D5
Tweed Island NL 36 A2
Tweed Island NL 38 F1

Tweed Lake NT 5 D8
Tweedside NB 32 C-D2
Tweedsmuir SK 11 B5
Tweedsmuir Glacier BC 4 F2
Tweedsmuir North PRA BC 1 B4
Tweedsmuir South PRA BC 1 B-C5
Twelve Mile Bay ON 18 E7
Twelve Mile Lake SK 11 F4
Twenty Mile Creek ON 19 C7-8
Twenty Mile Creek ON 20 E6-7
Twigge Lake SK 11 A6
Twigge Lake SK 12 F6
Twillingate NL 38 E6
Twin Butte BC 6 F5-6
Twin Butte AB 7 F4
Twin Falls NL 39 B3
Twin Falls Gorge TP NT 10 F6
Twin Falls Gorge TP NT 41 E1
Twin Falls Tea House NHS BC 7 A1
Twin Lakes AB 9 C3
Twin Lakes Beach MB 14 D4
Twin Mount YT 4 A6-7
Twitya River NT 4 A6-7 B6
Twoforks River SK 12 F4-5
Two Hills AB 6 A6-7
Two Hills AB 8 C8
Two Hills AB 11 A1
Two River Lake AB 13 A7
Two Rivers, Lake of ON 21 A3
Two Sheds NS 32 F6
Two Sheds NS 33 C3
Two Spring PPA BC 2 A6-7
Tyaughton Creek BC 2 A5
Tyendinaga ON 21 E5
Tyers River YT 4 D7
Tyhee Lake PP BC 3 F4-5
Tyndall MB 13 E4
Tyndall MB 14 D6
Tyner SK 11 D3
Tyne Valley PE 32 A7
Tyne Valley PE 34 B1
Tyne Valley PE 35 C2
Tyrconnell ON 19 D4
Tyrconnell ON 20 F3
Tyrone ON 20 C8
Tyrone ON 21 E2
Tyrrell MB 15 F3
Tyson Lake ON 18 B5
Tyvan SK 11 E6

U

Uchi Lake ON 16 C3
Ucluelet BC 1 F5
Ucluelet BC 2 E1
Udney ON 20 A7
Udney ON 21 D1-2
Udora ON 20 B7
Udora ON 21 E1
Uffington ON 21 C1-2
Ufford ON 18 D8
Ufford ON 21 C1
Ugjoktok Bay NL 39 A5-6
Uhlman Lake MB 15 D3
Uisage Bahn Falls PP NS 34 C6-7
Uist, Lake NS 34 D7
Ukalta AB 8 B7
Ukkusiksalik (Wager Bay) NP NU 41 C-D5
Ukraina MB 11 D8
Ukraina MB 13 D2
Ukraina MB 14 A1
Ullswater ON 18 D8
Ullswater ON 21 B1
Ulverton QC 24 D8
Ulverton QC 27 D4
Umfreville ON 13 E7
Umfreville ON 16 D4
Umfreville Lake ON 13 E5
Umfreville Lake ON 14 D8
Umfreville Lake ON 16 C1
Umiujaq QC 40 D4
Umiujaq QC 41 F8
Uncas AB 8 C7
Uncha Lake BC 1 A5
Uncha Mountains-Red Hills PP BC 1 A5
Underhill MB 11 F8
Underhill MB 13 F1-2
Underhill MB 14 E1
Underwood ON 20 B3
Ungava, baie d' QC 40 C6
Ungava, péninsule d' QC 40 B4-5 C4-5
Ungava, péninsule d' QC 41 E8
Ungava Bay QC 40 B-C6
Union NS 34 E2-3
Union ON 19 D4-5
Union ON 20 F3-4
Union Bay BC 1 F5-6
Union Bay BC 2 D2
Union Corner PE 35 D2
Union Corner PP PE 32 A-B7
Union Corner PP PE 34 C1
Union Corner PP PE 35 D2
Union Island BC 1 E4

Union Island NT 10 D8
Union Lake SK 6 A8
Union Passage PMP BC 1 B3
Union Road PE 35 D-E5
Union Road PE 35 E6
Union Square NS 32 F6-7
Union Square NS 33 C4
Unionville PE 35 C1-2
Unionville ON 19 A8
Unionville ON 20 C7
Unionville ON 21 F1
Unity SK 6 C8
Unity SK 11 C2-3
Unmingmaktok NU 41 C3
Unmingmaktok NU 42 F2
Unuk River BC 3 D-E2
Unwin SK 11 B2
Upham NB 32 D4-5
Upham NB 33 A2
Uphill ON 20 A8
Uphill ON 21 C2
Upper Adams River PP BC 6 D2
Upper Arrow Lake BC 6 E3
Upper Beaver River NT 5 E5
Upper Beverley Lake ON 21 C-D7
Upper Big Tracadie NS 34 E5
Upper Blackville NB 31 E6
Upper Blackville NB 32 A4
Upper Branch NS 33 D4
Upper Brockway NB 32 D2
Upper Campbell Lake BC 2 C1-2
Upper Cape NB 32 B8
Upper Cape NB 34 D1
Upper Cape NB 35 F2
Upper Carp Lake NT 10 B-7
Upper Clements NS 32 F5
Upper Clements NS 33 C2
Upper Clements PP NS 32 F5
Upper Clements PP NS 33 C2-3
Upper Clyde River NS 33 D4
Upper Cumins Lake SK 9 E8
Upper Cumins Lake SK 12 E3
Upper Dorchester NB 32 C7
Upper Economy NS 32 D8
Upper Economy NS 33 A5
Upper Economy NS 34 E1
Upper Ferry NL 36 D1
Upper Foster Lake SK 12 D5
Upper Fraser BC 1 A7
Upper Fraser BC 6 A1
Upper Gagetown NB 32 C3
Upper Goose Lake ON 13 C7
Upper Goose Lake ON 16 B3
Upper Granville NS 32 F5
Upper Granville NS 33 C2-3
Upper Gulf Shore NS 34 E5
Upper Hainesville NB 31 F4
Upper Hainesville NB 32 B1
Upper Hammonds Plains NS 32 F7-8
Upper Hammonds Plains NS 33 C5
Upper Humber River NL 38 F3
Upper Humber River NL 39 F7-8
Upper Indian Pond NL 36 A5
Upper Indian Pond NL 37 A3
Upper Indian Pond NL 38 F4
Upper Island Cove NL 37 D7-8
Upper Kennetcook NS 32 D-E8
Upper Kennetcook NS 33 B6
Upper Kennetcook NS 34 F3
Upper Kent NB 31 E3
Upper Kent NB 32 A1
Upper LaHave NS 33 D4
Upper Lakeville NS 33 C7
Upper Lawrencetown NS 33 C6
Upper Liard YT 3 A4
Upper Liard YT 4 F7
Upper Lillooet PP BC 1 E6-7
Upper Lillooet PP BC 2 A-B4
Upper Linden NS 32 B2-3
Upper Madawaska River PP ON 21 A3-4
Upper Madawaska River PP ON 22 F3-4
Upper Manitou Lake ON 13 F6-7
Upper Manitou Lake ON 16 E3
Upper Margaree NS 34 C6
Upper Maugerville NB 32 C2
Upper Middle River NS 34 C6
Upper Mills NB 32 E1-2
Upper Musquodoboit NS 33 B7
Upper Musquodoboit NS 34 F3
Upper Nine Mile River NS 32 E8
Upper Nine Mile River NS 33 B6

Upper Nine Mile River NS 34 F2
Upper Northfield NS 33 C4
Upper Northfield NS 34 F1
Upper Ohio NS 33 E3
Upper Point de Bute NB 35 F1-2
Upper Rawdon NS 32 E8
Upper Rawdon NS 33 B6
Upper Rawdon NS 34 F1-2
Upper Rideau Lake ON 24 F1
Upper River Denys NS 34 D6
Upper Rockport NB 32 C7
Upper Roussay River NMBS SK 11 D6-7
Upper Sackville NB 32 F8
Upper Sackville NS 33 C5-6
Upper Salmon Reservoir NL 36 C5
Upper Salmon Reservoir NL 37 C3
Upper Scotch Lake ON 13 F8
Upper South River NS 34 E5
Upper South West Mabou NS 34 D5-6
Upper Stewiacke NS 33 A-B7
Upper Stewiacke NS 34 F1
Upper Tantallon NS 32 F8
Upper Tantallon NS 33 C5-6
Upper Tracy NB 32 C3
Upper Twin Lake ON 16 D8
Upper Twin Lake ON 17 A-B2
Upper Windigo Lake ON 13 C7
Upper Windigo Lake ON 16 A4
Upper Woods Harbour NS 33 F2
Upper Woodstock NB 31 F3
Upper Woodstock NB 32 B1
Upsala ON 13 F8
Upsala ON 16 E4-5
Upsalquitch NB 29 E5-6
Upsalquitch NB 31 B4
Upsalquitch River NB 29 E5-6
Upsalquitch River NB 31 B4
Upton PE 35 D-E6
Upton ON 20 D7-8
Upton ON 21 D1
Upton QC 27 E3
Uqsuqtuuq (Gjoa Haven) NU 41 B-C4
Uqsuqtuuq (Gjoa Haven) NU 42 F3-4
Uranium City SK 9 A8
Uranium City SK 12 A3
Uranium City SK 41 F2
Urbainville PE 35 D2
Urbania NS 33 B6
Urbania NS 34 F2
Uren SK 11 E4
Urquhart Lake NT 5 B5
Ursula Channel BC 1 B3
Ursula Lake NT 10 A8
Usam Island SK 12 B6
Usam Island SK 15 B1
Usborne, lac QC 22 E6
Usherville SK 11 C6-7
Usk BC 3 F3-4
Usona AB 8 E6
Utica ON 20 B8
Utica ON 21 E2
Utikuma Lake AB 9 E4
Utikuma River AB 9 E4-5
Utopia, Lake NB 32 E2-3
Utopia PGA NB 32 E2-3
Utterson ON 18 D8
Utterson ON 21 B1
Uvajuq (Mount Pelly) TP NU 41 B3
Uvajuq (Mount Pelly) TP NU 42 F3
Uxbridge ON 20 B7
Uxbridge ON 21 E1-2

V

Vachon, rivière QC 27 C-D7
Vadzaih Van Tshik TP NT 5 C5
Vail Point ON 18 F6-7
Vail Point ON 20 A4
Val-Alain QC 27 C5
Val-Barrette QC 24 A3
Val-Barrette QC 25 F3
Val-Brillant QC 29 C4-5
Val-Caron QC 17 F6-7
Val-Comeau NB 30 F2
Val-Comeau NB 31 C8
Val-Comeau PP NB 31 B-C8
Val Côté ON 17 A4
Val-David QC 24 B5
Val-des-Bois QC 22 E-F8
Val-des-Bois QC 24 C2
Valdes Island BC 2 E4

Val-des-Lacs QC 24 B5
Val-des-Monts QC 21 A8
Val-des-Monts QC 22 F8
Val-des-Monts QC 24 C1
Val-d'Espoir QC 30 C3
Val-d'Or QC 23 C4-5
Val-Doucet NB 29 E8
Val-Doucet NB 30 E-F1
Val-Doucet NB 31 B7
Valemount BC 6 B2
Valens CA ON 19 B6-7
Valens CA ON 20 D5-6
Valentia ON 20 B8
Valentia ON 20 B8
Valentia ON 21 E2
Valetta ON 19 E2
Val Gagné ON 17 A-C7
Valhalla Beach MB 14 C5
Valhalla Centre AB 9 E2
Valhalla PP BC 6 E3
Valin QC 28 C6
Val-Jalbert QC 28 C4
Val-Jalbert, village historique de QC 25 A8
Val-Jalbert, village historique de QC 26 E8
Val-Jalbert, village historique de QC 28 C3-4
Val-Joli QC 27 E4
Vallard, lac QC 39 C1
Vallée-Jonction QC 27 C6
Vallentyne ON 20 B7-8
Vallentyne ON 21 E2
Valley NS 34 E2
Valley Bay NL 39 B6
Valley Centre SK 11 F3
Valley Mills NS 34 D6
Valleyfield NL 37 A6-7
Valleyfield NL 38 E8
Valleyfield PE 34 C3
Valleyfield PE 35 E6
Valley Pond NL 38 E6
Valley River MB 11 D8
Valley River MB 11 D8
Valley River MB 13 D1
Valley River MB 13 D2
Valley River MB 14 B1
Valley River (Tootinaowaziibeeng) MB 11 D8
Valley River (Tootinaowaziibeeng) MB 13 D1-2
Valleyview AB 9 E2
Valleyview PP NS 32 E5
Valleyview PP NS 33 C2-3
Vallican BC 6 F3
Val-Limoges QC 22 D8
Val-Limoges QC 24 A2
Val-Limoges QC 25 E2
Val Marie SK 11 F3
Val Marie Reservoir NMBS SK 11 F3
Val-Morin QC 24 C5
Valmy, lac QC 23 D7
Valmy, lac QC 25 A1
Valmy, lac QC 26 E1
Val-Paradis QC 17 C8
Val-Paradis QC 23 B2
Valparaiso SK 11 B6
Val-Racine QC 27 E6
Val Rita ON 17 B5
Val-Saint-Gilles QC 17 C8
Val-Saint-Gilles QC 23 B2
Val-Senneville QC 23 E5
Val Therese ON 17 F6
Val-Viger QC 24 A3
Val-Viger QC 25 E3
Vananda BC 1 F6
Vananda BC 2 C3
Vanastra ON 19 A4
Vanastra ON 20 D3
Vance SK 11 C3
Vancouver BC 1 F6-7
Vancouver BC 2 D4-5
Vancouver, île de BC 1 F6-7
Vancouver, île de BC 2 D4-5
Vancouver Island BC 1 F6-7
Vancouver Island BC 2 D1-2
Vancouver Island Ranges BC 2 E3 F3-4
Vancouver Island Ranges BC 2 B-C1 D3 E2-3
Vandekerckhove Lake NT 12 D7
Vandekerckhove Lake MB 15 D1-2
Vanderhoof BC 1 A6
Vandorf ON 20 C7
Vandorf ON 21 E1
Vandry QC 25 B6
Vandry QC 28 D1-2
Vandura SK 11 E7
Vanel, lac QC 28 A6-7
Vanessa ON 19 C6
Vanessa ON 20 E5
Vanguard SK 11 E4
Vanier QC 27 B5
Vanier, île NU 42 D4
Vanier, lac QC 25 A5
Vanier, lac QC 26 E5
Vankleek Hill ON 22 E8
Van Koenig Point NU 41 B6
Van Koenig Point NU 42 E4
Vankoughnet ON 21 C2

Vanscoy SK 11 C4
Van Scoy Lake SK 11 C3-4
Vansittart Island NU 41 C6
Vantage SK 11 E4-5
Varennes QC 24 D6
Varennes QC 27 E2
Vargas Island BC 1 F5
Vargas Island BC 2 D1
Vargas Island PP BC 1 F4-5
Vargas Island PP BC 2 E1
Varna NB 19 B4
Varna ON 20 D3
Varna ON 20 B4
Varney ON 20 B4
Vars ON 24 D3
Varty Lake ON 21 D6
Vaseau Lake, RNOM BC 6 F1-2
Vaseux Lake NMBS BC 6 F1-2
Vaseux Lake PP BC 6 F1-2
Vasey ON 20 A6
Vassan QC 23 E4
Vassar MB 13 F4-5
Vassar MB 14 F7
Vaudray, lac QC 23 E3
Vaudreuil-Dorion QC 24 D5
Vaudreuil-Dorion QC 27 E1
Vaudreuil-sur-le-Lac QC 24 D5
Vaughan NS 32 F7
Vaughan NS 33 C5
Vaughan ON 19 A8
Vaughan ON 20 C7
Vaughan ON 21 F1
Vauquelin, baie QC 23 E6
Vauxhall AB 6 E7
Vauxhall AB 7 D6
Vavenby BC 6 D2
Vawn SK 11 B3
Vega AB 6 A5
Vega AB 8 A5
Vega AB 9 F5
Vegreville AB 6 B6-7
Vegreville AB 8 C8
Vegreville AB 11 A1
Veillardville SK 11 B7
Vendée QC 24 C4
Venice AB 8 A8
Venise-en-Québec QC 24 E7
Venise-en-Québec QC 27 F2
Venison Islands NL 39 C8
Venlaw NB 11 D8
Venlaw MB 13 D1-2
Venn SK 11 D5
Vennachar ON 21 B5
Vennachar Junction ON 21 B5
Venosta QC 22 E-F7
Venosta QC 24 C1
Ventadour, lac QC 26 D5
Ventadour, lac QC 28 E4
Ventnor ON 21 C8
Vents, lac des QC 26 B4
Vents River BC 3 A-B5
Vents River BC 4 F8
Vera SK 11 C2-3
Verchères QC 24 C6
Verchères QC 27 D2
Verdun QC 24 D6
Verdun QC 27 E1
Veregin SK 11 D7
Verlo SK 11 E3
Vermette Lake SK 9 E8
Vermette Lake SK 12 E3
Vermeulle, lac QC 39 A1
Vermilion AB 6 B7
Vermilion AB 11 B2
Vermilion Bay ON 13 E6
Vermilion Crossing BC 6 D3
Vermilion Crossing BC 7 B1
Vermilion Hills ON 11 E4
Vermilion Lake ON 16 D3
Vermilion Lake ON 18 A5
Vermilion Pass BC 6 D3
Vermilion Pass BC 7 B1
Vermilion PP AB 6 B7
Vermilion PP AB 11 B1-2
Vermilion River AB 6 B7
Vermilion River AB 11 A1 B1-2
Vermilion River MB 11 D8
Vermilion River MB 13 D2
Vermilion River MB 14 B1
Vermilion River ON 16 C4
Vermilion River ON 17 E6-7
Vermilion West ON 18 A4-5
Vermillion Bay ON 16 D2
Vermillon, lac QC 25 D6
Vermillon, lac QC 28 F2
Vermillon, rivière QC 25 C6
Vermillon, rivière QC 26 D6-7
Vermillon, rivière QC 28 A-B2
Vermillon, rivière QC 28 E-F2
Vermilyea Lake 13 A5
Vermilyea Lake MB 15 F5
Vermont, lac QC 28 B6
Verner ON 17 F7
Verner ON 18 A7
Verneuil, lac QC 26 B4
Vernon BC 6 E2
Vernon ON 21 B8
Vernon ON 24 E2-3
Vernon, Lake ON 18 D8
Vernon, Lake ON 21 B1
Vernon Bridge PE 35 E5-6
Vernon Lake BC 1 E4-5
Vernon River PE 34 C3
Vernon River PE 35 E6
Vernonville ON 21 E4

Verona ON 21 D6
Verret NB 29 F3
Verret NB 31 C1-2
Versailles Lake SK 12 E6
Verschoyle ON 19 C5
Verschoyle ON 20 E4
Vert, lac QC 22 E8
Vert, lac QC 24 C2
Vert, lac SK 11 C5-6
Verte, baie NB 32 B7-8
Verte, baie QC 35 F2
Verte, baie NS 32 B7-8
Verte, baie NS 34 D1
Verte, île QC 29 D1
Verte, pointe QC 30 C3
Verte, rivière NB 29 E3
Verte, rivière NB 31 B2
Verte, rivière SK 29 D-E1
Vert Island ON 16 E6-7
Vert Island ON 17 C1
Verton, lac QC 39 D6
Verwood SK 11 F5
Vesuvius BC 1 F6-7
Vesuvius BC 2 E4
Veteran AB 6 C7
Veteran AB 11 C1
Vezina Lake NL 39 A3
Vibank SK 11 E6
Viceroy SK 11 F5
Vicomte-de-Melville, détroit du NT 42 D2-3
Vicomte-de-Melville, détroit du NU 42 D2-3
Victoire SK 11 B4
Victor AB 7 A6
Victor, lac QC 39 E5
Victoria AB 6 A6
Victoria AB 8 B7-8
Victoria AB 11 A1
Victoria BC 2 F4
Victoria NL 37 D7
Victoria ON 19 A7
Victoria ON 20 C6
Victoria PE 32 B8
Victoria PE 34 C2
Victoria PE 35 E3
Victoria, île NT 41 B2-3
Victoria, île NT 42 E2-3
Victoria, île NU 41 B2-3
Victoria, île NU 42 E2-3
Victoria Beach MB 13 E4
Victoria Beach MB 14 C5-6
Victoria Beach NS 32 F4
Victoria Beach NS 33 C2
Victoria Bridge NS 34 D7
Victoria Corner NB 31 F3
Victoria Corner NB 32 B1
Victoria Cove NL 36 A7-8
Victoria Cove NL 37 A5-6
Victoria Cove NL 38 F7
Victoria Cross PE 34 C3
Victoria Cross PE 35 E6
Victoria Harbour NS 32 F4
Victoria Harbour NS 33 B3
Victoria Harbour ON 18 E7
Victoria Head NU 42 F8
Victoria Island NT 41 A2-3
Victoria Island NT 42 E2-3
Victoria Island NU 41 A2-3
Victoria Island NU 42 E1-3
Victoria Lake BC 1 E4
Victoria Lake NL 36 C3-4
Victoria Lake NL 37 C1-2
Victoria Lake ON 21 A3-4
Victoria Lake ON 22 F4
Victoria Lake ON 23 D1
Victoria Peak BC 1 E5
Victoria Peak BC 2 C1
Victoria PP PE 32 B8
Victoria PP PE 34 C2
Victoria PP PE 35 E3-4
Victoria River NL 36 B-C4
Victoria River NL 37 B-C2
Victoria Road ON 20 A8
Victoria Road ON 21 D2
Victoria Settlement PHS AB 6 A6
Victoria Settlement PHS AB 8 B8
Victoria Settlement PHS AB 11 A1
Victoria Strait NU 41 B4
Victoria Strait NU 42 F3
Victoria Vale NS 32 E6
Victoria Vale NS 33 B3
Victoriaville QC 27 D4-5
Victoria West PE 35 C2
Victor Lake PP BC 6 D3
Victory Lake NT 10 C7
Vidal Bay ON 18 B2
Vidir MB 14 B5
Vidora SK 6 F8
Vidora SK 11 F2
Vieillard, lac du QC 22 A4
Vieille, lac de la QC 22 C7
Vieille, lac de la QC 24 A1
Vieille, lac de la QC 25 C1
Vienna ON 19 D5
Vienna ON 20 F4
Vieux, Bay de NL 36 D-E4
Vieux, Bay de NL 37 D-E2
Vieux-Fort QC 38 A2
Vieux-Fort QC 39 D7
Vieux Fort, île du QC 38 D2
Vieux Fort, île du QC 39 D7
Vieux Lunenburg, le NS 39 F5
Vieux Poste, pointe du QC 39 F5
Viewfield SK 11 F6-7
View Royal BC 2 F4
Vignal, lac QC 39 B1
Vigneault, lac QC 39 E4-5

Vignerod, lac QC 25 D6
Vignerod, lac QC 28 F2
Viking AB 6 B6-7
Viking AB 8 D8
Viking AB 11 B1
Villa-Bellevue, LHN de la ON 21 E6-7
Village Bay BC 2 E4-5
Village Cove NL 38 E-F6
Village-des-Aulnaies QC 28 F7
Villa Marie NL 37 E6-7
Villa Nova ON 19 C6
Villa Nova ON 20 E5
Villa Marie QC 22 A1-2
Villebois QC 23 B2
Villebois QC 23 C7
Villejouin, lac QC 23 C7
Villejouin, lac QC 26 C1
Ville-Marie QC 17 E8
Ville-Marie QC 22 A1-2
Villemontel QC 23 C3
Villeneuve AB 6 A-B5
Villeneuve AB 8 C6
Villeroy QC 27 C4
Villier, lac QC 25 D5
Villier, lac QC 27 A1
Villier, lac QC 28 F1
Villiers ON 21 E4
Vilna AB 6 A6
Vilna AB 8 B8
Vilna AB 11 A1
Vilna AB 12 F1
Vimont, lac QC 22 B8
Vimont, lac QC 25 C2
Vimont, lac QC 26 B5
Vimy AB 9 A5-6
Vimy AB 8 B6
Vimy-Ridge QC 27 D5
Vin, Bay du NB 31 D7
Vincent Lake ON 13 D-E8
Vineland ON 19 C8
Vineland ON 20 E7
Vineland Station ON 19 C8
Vineland Station ON 20 E7
Vinemount ON 19 C7
Vinemount ON 20 E6
Vingt-Deuxième Mille, lac du QC 39 E4
Vinoy QC 24 C3
Vinsulla BC 2 A8
Vinton QC 22 F6
Violet ON 21 D-E6
Violet Grove AB 6 B5
Violet Grove AB 8 D4
Violet Hill ON 20 B6
Virago Sound BC 1 A1
Virden MB 11 E8
Virden MB 13 E1
Virgil ON 19 B8
Virgil ON 20 E7
Virgin Arm NL 38 E6
Virginia ON 20 B7
Virginia ON 21 D1
Virginia Falls NT 4 D8
Virginia Falls NT 10 D1
Virginiatown ON 17 D8
Virginiatown ON 23 E1
Virgin River SK 9 C8
Virgin River SK 12 C-D4
Viscount ON 11 C5
Viscount Island BC 2 A1
Viscount Melville Sound NT 42 D2-3
Viscount Melville Sound NU 42 D2-3
Vista MB 11 E8
Vista MB 13 D-E1
Vita MB 13 F4
Vita MB 14 F6
Vittoria ON 19 D6
Vittoria ON 20 F5
Vittrekwa River YT 5 D4
Vivian ON 19 A8
Vivian ON 20 B7
Vivian MB 14 D-E6
Vogar MB 13 D3
Vogar MB 14 B3
Voglers Cove NS 33 D4
Voisey's Bay NL 40 D7
Volant, rivière QC 29 A1-2
Volga AB 14 A1
Volmer AB 8 C6
Voltigeurs, parc des QC 24 C7-8
Voltigeurs, parc des QC 27 D3
Vonda SK 11 C4-5
Voyageur PP ON 24 D4
Vulcan AB 6 E6
Vulcan AB 7 C-D5
Vulcan, PN YT 5 C2-3
Vuntut, PN YT 5 B2
Vuntut NP YT 5 B2

W

Waasagomach MB 13 A5
Waasis NB 32 C3
Waba ON 21 B6-7
Wababimiga Lake ON 16 D8
Wababimiga Lake ON 17 A2
Wabagishik Lake ON 18 A4
Wabakimi Lake ON 13 D8
Wabakimi Lake ON 16 E5
Wabakimi PP ON 16 C5
Wabakimi PP ON 40 F1
Wabamun AB 6 B5
Wabamun AB 8 C5
Wabamun Lake PP AB 6 B5
Wabamun Lake PP AB 8 C5

Wabana NL 37 D8
Wabano, rivière QC 26 E5
Wabano, rivière QC 28 B-C1
Wabasca-Desmarais AB 9 E5
Wabasca River AB 9 C4
Wabasca River AB 9 D-E5
Wabasca River AB 41 F1
Wabash ON 19 D3
Wabash ON 20 F2
Wabaskang Lake ON 13 E6
Wabaskang Lake ON 16 C2
Wabasseemoong (Whitedog) ON 16 D1
Wabassi River ON 16 B7
Wabatongushi Lake ON 17 C4
Wabauskang ON 13 E6
Wabauskang ON 16 C2
Wabigoon ON 13 E-F7
Wabigoon ON 16 D3
Wabigoon Lake ON 13 E6 F7
Wabigoon Lake ON 13 F7
Wabigoon Lake ON 16 D3
Wabigoon River ON 13 E6
Wabimeig Lake ON 16 B8
Wabiskaw AB 9 E5
Wabos ON 17 F4
Wabowden MB 15 F3
Wabu Creek ON 24 D1
Wabuk Point ON 40 D2-3
Wabush NL 39 C2
Wabush NL 40 E6
Wabush Lake NL 39 C2
W.A.C. Bennett Dam BC 3 E7
Wachigabau, lac QC 23 A8
Wachigabau, lac QC 26 B2
Waco QC 39 D2-3
Waconichi, lac QC 26 A5
Wacouno, rivière QC 39 D2-3
Waddington, Mount BC 1 D5-6
Wade, Mount BC 4 F2
Wade Lake NL 39 B3
Wadena SK 11 D6
Wade's Landing ON 18 B8
Wadham Islands NL 38 E7
Wadin Lake SK 9 C4
Wadsworth Lake ON 21 A4
Wagarville ON 17 C-D6
Wager Bay NU 41 D5
Wager Bay (Ukkusiksalik) NP NU 41 C-D5
Waglisla-McLoughlin Bay BC 1 C3-4
Wagmatcook NS 34 C6
Wagosh Bay ON 18 B1
Wahgoshig (Abitibi) ON 17 C7
Wahleach Lake ON 2 E7
Wahnapitae ON 17 F7
Wahnapitae ON 18 A6
Wahnekewaning Beach ON 18 F7
Wahnekewaning Beach ON 20 A5-6
Wahpeton SK 11 B4-5
Wahwashkesh ON 18 C7
Wahwashkesh Lake ON 18 C7
Wainfleet ON 19 C8
Wainfleet ON 20 E7
Wainwright AB 6 B7
Wainwright AB 11 B2
Waiparous AB 6 D5
Waiparous AB 7 B3
Wakami Lake ON 17 E5
Wakami Lake PP ON 17 E5
Wakaw SK 11 C5
Wakaw Lake SK 11 B-C5
Wakaw Lake SK 11 C5
Wakefield QC 21 A7-8
Wakefield QC 22 F7-8
Wakefield QC 24 D2
Wakeham QC 30 B2
Wakeman River AB 9 C4
Wakeman Sound BC 1 D5
Wakes Cove PP BC 2 E4
Wakomata Lake ON 17 F5
Wakopa MB 13 F2
Wakopa MB 14 F1
Wakwayowkastic River ON 17 A6-7
Waldeck SK 11 E3
Waldemar ON 19 A6
Waldemar ON 20 C5
Walden NS 32 F7
Walden NS 33 C4
Waldersee MB 14 C2-3
Waldheim SK 11 C4
Waldo BC 6 F4-5
Waldron SK 11 D7
Waldron River NT 10 C8
Walesback Channel NS 18 B2-3
Wales Island BC 1 B3
Wales Island NU 40 B5
Wales Island NU 41 C5-6
Wales Island NU 41 B8
Wales Island NU 42 F5
Walford ON 17 F5-6
Walford ON 18 A-B3
Walhachin BC 1 D-E8
Walhachin BC 2 A7
Walhachin Oxbows PP BC 1 D8
Walhachin Oxbows PP BC 2 A7-8

Walhachin Oxbows PP BC 6 D1
Walker, lac QC 39 E1-2
Walker Creek SK 12 D5
Walker Lake MB 15 F4
Walker Lake SK 12 A6
Walkers Point ON 20 B4
Walkers Point ON 21 C1
Walkerton ON 20 B4
Walkleyburg MB 14 D5-6
Wallace NS 34 D2
Wallace ON 19 A5
Wallace ON 20 C4
Wallace Bay, RNF de NS 34 D2
Wallace Bay NWA NS 34 D2
Wallaceburg ON 19 D2
Wallaceburg ON 20 F1
Wallace Island PMP BC 2 E4
Wallace Lake PP MB 13 D5
Wallace Lake PP MB 14 B7
Wallace Mountain AB 9 F4
Wallace Ridge NS 32 C8
Wallace Ridge NS 34 D2
Wallace River NS 34 E1-2 D2
Wallace Station NS 32 C8
Wallace Station NS 34 D2
Wallacetown ON 19 D4
Wallacetown ON 20 F2
Wallenstein ON 19 A5-6
Wallenstein ON 20 D4-5
Wall Island ON 18 C4
Walloper Lake PP BC 1 E8
Walloper Lake PP BC 2 B8
Walloper Lake PP BC 6 E1
Walpole SK 11 E7
Walpole SK 13 E1
Walpole Island ON 19 D2
Walpole Island ON 20 D1
Walpole Island ON 20 F1
Walpole Island ON 20 F1
Walsh AB 6 E8
Walsh AB 11 E2
Walsh ON 19 D6
Walsh ON 20 F5
Walsh Cove PP BC 2 B2
Walsh Creek YT 4 C-D4
Walsh Lake SK 12 B6
Walsh Lake SK 15 B1
Walsingham ON 19 D6
Walsingham ON 20 F5
Walter Cook Upland Caves PP Reserve MB 11 B8
Walter Cook Upland Caves PP Reserve MB 13 B2
Walters Falls ON 18 F6
Walters Falls ON 20 A5
Waltham QC 22 E6
Walton NS 32 D7-8
Walton NS 33 A-B5
Walton NS 34 F1
Walton ON 19 A4-5
Walton ON 20 C3-4
Walton River NS 32 D8
Walton River NS 33 B5
Walton River NS 34 F1
Wampum MB 13 F4-5
Wampum MB 14 F7
Wanapitei Lake ON 17 F7
Wanapitei PP ON 17 E-F7
Wanapitei River ON 17 E6-7
Wanapitei River ON 18 A4-5 B5
Wanasing Beach MB 14 C6
Wandering River AB 9 E6
Wandering River AB 9 F6
Wandering River AB 12 E1
Wandering River AB 12 E1
Waneta BC 6 F3
Wanham AB 9 E3
Wanipigow River MB 13 D4-5
Wanipigow River MB 14 B6-7
Wanless MB 11 A7
Wanless MB 13 A1
Wanup ON 17 F7
Wanup ON 18 A6
Wapah MB 13 E2
Wapaseese River ON 15 F7-8
Wapata Lake SK 12 B5
Wapekeka ON 13 A8
Wapella NS 19 B6
Wapella ON 20 D5
Wapesi Bay ON 13 E7
Wapesi Lake ON 13 E7
Wapesi Lake ON 16 C3
Wapesi River ON 13 D-E7
Wapikaimaski Lake ON 16 D5
Wapikani River MB 15 E-F7
Wapisu Lake MB 15 D4
Wapisu Lake MB 15 E2-3
Wapiti Lake PP BC 1 A8
Wapiti Lake PP BC 9 F1
Wapiti Mountain AB 6 C-D4
Wapiti Mountain AB 7 A2
Wapiti River BC 9 F2

Wapiyao Lake SK 12 A6
Wapiyao Lake SK 15 A1
Wapske NB 31 D3
Wapus, rivière QC 22 B8
Wapus, rivière QC 25 C-D2
Wapusk, PN MB 15 C6
Wapusk, PN MB 40 F5
Wapusk NP MB 15 B-C6
Wapusk NP MB 40 C1
Wapusk NP MB 41 F5
Wapus Lake MB 15 F4
Wapus Lake SK 12 D7
Wapus Lake SK 15 D1
Wapuspimiskunow Lake MB 15 E6
Wapustagamau, lac QC 39 D6
Warburg AB 6 B5
Warburg AB 8 D5
Warburton AB 21 D7
Warburton Bay NT 10 B7
Ward NB 35 F1
Ward, baie QC 27 D5
Ward, lac QC 22 B6
Warden AB 8 F7
Warden QC 24 D8
Warden QC 27 E3
Wardlow AB 6 D7
Wardlow AB 7 B7
Wardlow AB 11 D1
Wardner BC 6 F4
Wardner BC 7 F2
Wardner PP BC 6 F4
Wardner PP BC 7 F2
Ward's Brook NS 32 D6
Ward's Brook NS 34 E1
Wardsville ON 19 D3-4
Wardsville ON 20 F2-3
Wareham NL 36 A8
Wareham NL 37 A6
Wareham NL 38 F7-8
Warfield BC 6 F3
Warina ON 24 E3
Warkworth ON 21 E4
Warkworth Lake MB 15 B5-6
Warman SK 11 C4
Warminster ON 18 F8
Warminster ON 20 A7
Warminster ON 21 D1
Warneford River BC 3 C5-6
Warner AB 6 F6-7
Warner AB 7 F6
Warpath River MB 13 C3
Warren AB 9 E3
Warren MB 14 D4
Warren ON 17 F7
Warren ON 18 A6
Warren Grove PE 35 E4
Warren Landing MB 13 A3
Warren Point NT 5 A5
Warspite AB 6 A6
Warspite AB 8 B7
Warspite AB 11 A1
Warspite AB 12 F1
Wartburg ON 19 B5
Wartburg ON 20 D4
Wartime SK 11 D3
Wart Lake ON 17 E4
Warwick AB 6 A6-7
Warwick ON 19 C3
Warwick ON 20 E2
Warwick QC 27 D4
Warwick CA ON 19 C3
Warwick CA ON 20 E2
Wasa BC 6 F4
Wasa BC 7 E2
Wasaga Beach ON 18 F7
Wasaga Beach ON 20 A6
Wasaga Beach PP ON 18 F7
Wasaga Beach PP ON 20 A6
Wasagaming MB 13 E2
Wasagaming MB 14 C1
Wasa Lake PP BC 6 F4
Wasa Lake PP BC 7 E2
Wasca BC 6 F4
Waseca SK 11 B2
Wasekamio Lake SK 9 D8
Wasekamio Lake SK 12 D3
Wasel AB 8 B8
Washabuck Centre NS 34 C6-7
Washademoak Lake NB 32 C4
Washago ON 18 E-F8
Washago ON 20 A7
Washago ON 21 C1
Washburn Lake NU 41 B3
Washburn Lake NU 42 E7-8
Washi Lake ON 16 B7
Washington ON 19 B6
Washington ON 20 D5
Washow Bay MB 13 D4
Washow Bay MB 14 B5
Wasi Lake ON 18 D7
Wasi Lake ON 22 D-E2
Waskada MB 11 F8
Waskada MB 13 F1
Waskaganish QC 40 F4
Waskaiowaka Lake MB 15 D4
Waskatenau AB 6 A6
Waskatenau AB 8 B7
Waskatenau AB 11 A1
Waskesiu Lake SK 11 A4
Waskesiu Lake SK 12 A4
Waskesiu River SK 11 A4-5
Waskwei Island SK 12 D3
Waspison Lake SK 12 B6-7

Waspison Lake SK 15 B1
Wastina AB 7 A7-8
Waswanipi QC 23 A8
Waswanipi QC 23 A7
Waswanipi QC 26 B1-2
Waswanipi, lac QC 23 A7
Waswanipi, lac QC 26 B1
Waswanipi, rivière QC 23 A7
Waswanipi, rivière QC 26 B1-2
Watabeag Lake ON 17 D7
Watapi Lake SK 9 E8
Watapi Lake SK 12 E2
Watchorn PP MB 13 D3
Watchorn PP MB 14 B3
Water's Edge AB 8 C5
Waterborough NB 32 C4
Waterbury Lake SK 12 C5
Waterdown ON 19 B7
Waterdown ON 20 D6
Waterford NS 32 F4
Waterford NS 33 C1
Waterford ON 19 C6
Waterford ON 20 E5
Waterford PE 35 A1-2
Waterford CA ON 19 C6
Waterford CA ON 20 E5
Waterfound River SK 12 B5-6
Waterhen MB 11 C8
Waterhen MB 13 C2
Waterhen (IR) MB 13 C2
Waterhen Lake MB 13 C2
Waterhen Lake SK 9 E8
Waterhen Lake SK 12 E3
Waterhen Lake SK 11 A3
Waterhen Lake SK 12 F3
Waterhen Marsh MB 11 B5
Waterhen River SK 9 E8
Waterhen River SK 11 A3
Waterhen River SK 12 F3
Waterloo NS 33 D4
Waterloo ON 19 B6
Waterloo ON 20 D5
Waterloo ON 24 E8
Waterloo QC 27 E3
Waterloo, lac QC 25 D4
Waterloo Lake ON 22 C5
Waterloo Lake SK 9 A7-8
Waterloo Lake SK 12 A3
Waternish NS 34 F4
Waterside NB 32 C6
Waterside Beach PP NS 34 D3
Waterton ON 21 D7
Waterton-Glacier AB 7 F4
Waterton-Glacier, parc international de la paix AB 7 F4-5
Waterton-Glacier International Peace Park AB 7 F4-5
Waterton Lakes NP AB 6 F5
Waterton Lakes NP AB 7 F4
Waterton Park AB 6 F5
Waterton Park AB 7 F4
Waterton Reservoir AB 7 F4
Watervale NS 33 A7
Watervale NS 34 E3
Watervale PE 35 E5
Water Valley AB 6 D5
Water Valley AB 7 A3
Waterville NB 31 F3
Waterville NB 32 B1
Waterville NS 32 D2
Waterville NL 37 C6-7
Waterville NL 38 E-F7
Waterville ON 33 B4
Waterville QC 27 F4-5
Watford ON 19 C3
Watford ON 20 E2
Watham Lake SK 12 D5-6
Wathaman River SK 12 D5-6
Watino AB 9 E3
Watopeka, rivière QC 27 E4-5
Watrous SK 11 D5
Watshishou, lac QC 39 E4
Watshishou, rivière QC 39 E4
Watshishou, RNOM QC 39 F4-5
Watshishou NMBS QC 39 F4-5
Watson SK 11 C5-6
Watson, lac QC 22 B3
Watson Lake YT 3 A4
Watson Lake YT 4 E3
Watson Lake YT 4 E7
Watson Lake Campground TP YT 3 A4
Watson Point AB 15 B6
Watson River YT 4 E3-4
Watta Lake NT 10 D7
Watson Section NS 33 B8
Watt Section NS 34 F4
Watts Point Calcareous Ecological Reserve NL 38 A4
Waubamik ON 18 D7
Waubaushene ON 18 E8
Waubaushene ON 20 A6-7
Waubaushene ON 21 C1

Waubaushene Beaches, RNP ON 18 E-F8
Waubaushene Beaches, RNP ON 21 C1
Waubaushene Beaches PNR ON 18 E-F8
Waubaushene Beaches PNR ON 21 C1
Waubuno Channel ON 18 B3-4
Waubuno Creek ON 19 C5
Waubuno Creek ON 20 E4
Wauchope SK 11 F7
Wauchope SK 13 F1
Waugh AB 8 B6
Waugh MB 13 F5
Waugh MB 14 E7
Waugh MB 16 D1
Waugh Creek YT 5 F3
Waupoos ON 21 E6
Waupoos Island ON 21 E6
Wauquimakog Lake ON 18 B-C7
Wauzhushk Onigum ON 16 D1
Wavell ON 17 D7
Waverley NS 32 E4
Waverley NS 33 C6
Waverley ON 18 F7
Waverley ON 20 A6
Waverley Game Sanctuary NS 33 C6
Wavy Lake ON 17 D3-4
Wawa ON 17 D3-4
Wawagosic, rivière QC 17 B8
Wawagosic, rivière QC 23 A-B3
Wawanesa MB 13 F2
Wawanesa MB 14 E2
Wawang Lake ON 13 F8
Wawang Lake ON 16 E4
Wawanosh CA ON 19 A4
Wawanosh CA ON 20 D-E2
Waweig NB 32 F2-E2
Wawota SK 11 E7
Wayagamac, lac QC 25 D8
Wayagamac, lac QC 28 F3
Way Bay NL 39 B3
Wayerton NB 29 F7
Wayerton NB 31 C6
Wayne AB 6 D6
Wayne AB 7 A5-6
Wayow Lake SK 12 A6
Ways Mills QC 27 F4
Weagamow Lake ON 13 B7
Weagamow Lake ON 13 B7
Weagamow Lake ON 40 F8
Weald AB 8 C2
Weasel Creek AB 8 B7
Weatherall Bay NU 42 C3
Weaver Lake AB 13 B4
Weaver Settlement NS 33 D1-2
Weaver Siding NB 31 E6
Weaver Siding NB 32 A4
Webb SK 11 E3
Webber Cove PE 35 D3
Webber Lake AB 13 A6
Webber Lake MB 15 F6
Webbwood ON 17 F7
Webbwood ON 18 A3-4
Webeck Island NL 39 A7
Weber, Mount BC 3 F3
Wecho Lake NT 10 B6-7
Wecho River NT 10 B-C6
Wedding, rivière QC 23 B6
Wedge Mountain BC 1 E6
Wedge Mountain BC 2 C5
Wedgeport NS 33 F2
Weectigo, lac QC 25 B5
Weectigo, lac QC 26 C1
Weed Creek ON 27 E5
Weedon ON 20 E5
Weedon Centre QC 27 D-E5
Weekes SK 11 C6-7
Weequed Lake ON 18 A4
Weeskinisht Peaks BC 3 F4
Weeteeam Bay BC 1 C3
Weiden AB 14 A1-2
Weir QC 24 C4
Weirdale SK 11 B5
Weir River MB 15 D5-6
Weir River MB 15 D5-6
Weirs Pond NL 36 A8
Weirs Pond NL 37 A6
Weirs Pond NL 38 F7
Weitzel Lake SK 12 C5
Wekusko MB 12 B8
Wekusko MB 13 A3
Wekusko MB 15 A2
Wekusko Falls PP MB 12 B8
Wekusko Falls PP MB 15 F2
Wekusko Lake MB 12 B8
Wekusko Lake MB 15 F2
Wekweti NT 5 B6
Wekweti NT 41 D1-2
Welcome ON 21 E3
Weldon NB 32 C6
Weldon SK 11 B5
Welland ON 19 C8
Welland ON 20 E7
Welland Canal ON 19 C8
Welland Canal ON 20 E7
Wellandport ON 19 C8
Wellandport ON 20 E7
Welland River ON 19 C7-8
Welland River ON 20 E6-7
Wellbore Channel BC 2 B1
Wellburn ON 19 B5
Wellburn ON 20 E4
Wellers Bay National Wilderness Area ON 21 E4-5

Witchekan Lake *SK* **11** B4
Witch Lake *BC* **3** F6
Witegoo River *ON* **15** F8
Withers Lake *ON* **13** A7
Withers Lake *ON* **15** F7
Withrow *AB* **8** E5
Witless Bay *NL* **37** E8
Witless Bay Ecological
 Reserve *NL* **37** E8
Wittenburg *NS* **33** B6-7
Wittenburg *NS* **34** F2
Wivenhoe *MB* **15** E5
Wiwa Hill *SK* **11** E4
W.J.B. Greenwood PP *ON* **17** E7
W.J.B. Greenwood PP *ON* **22** A1
Woburn *QC* **27** E6
Woking *AB* **9** E2
Wolf Bay *QC* **39** E-F6
Wolf Creek *AB* **6** B4
Wolf Creek *AB* **8** C3
Wolf Creek *AB* **8** C3
Wolfe *SK* **11** C3
Wolfe Island *ON* **21** E7
Wolfe Lake *ON* **21** C6
Wolf Island PP *ON* **21** D3
Wolf Lake *AB* **9** F7
Wolf Lake *AB* **12** F2
Wolf Lake *NL* **36** C4-5
Wolf Lake *NL* **37** C2-3
Wolf Lake *ON* **21** C3
Wolf Lake *YT* **4** E5
Wolf River *AB* **9** F7
Wolf River *AB* **12** F2
Wolf River *BC* **2** C1
Wolf River *ON* **18** B7
Wolf River *YT* **4** E5
Wolfville *NS* **32** E7
Wolfville *NS* **33** B4-5
Wôlinak *QC* **24** B8
Wôlinak *QC* **25** F8
Wôlinak *QC* **27** C3-4
Wollaston, Cape *NT* **41** A2
Wollaston, Cape *NT* **42** E1
Wollaston, lac *SK* **12** C6
Wollaston, lac *SK* **15** C1
Wollaston, lac *SK* **41** F3
Wollaston Lake *ON* **21** C4
Wollaston Lake *SK* **12** B6
Wollaston Lake *SK* **12** C6
Wollaston Lake *SK* **15** B1
Wollaston Lake *SK* **15** B-C1
Wollaston Lake *SK* **41** F3
Wollaston Lake *SK* **41** F3
Wollaston Lake Landing *SK* **12** C5-6

Wollaston Peninsula *NU* **41** B2
Wollaston Peninsula *NU* **42** E1
Wolseley *SK* **11** E6
Wolseley Bay *ON* **17** F7
Wolseley Bay *ON* **18** B7
Wolseley Bay *ON* **18** B7
Wolseley River *ON* **18** B6
Wolsey, Lake *ON* **18** B-C2
Wolverine Lake *NT* **10** C7-8
Wolverine Lake *YT* **4** D6
Wolverine River *AB* **9** C4
Wolverine River *MB* **15** A-B4
Wolverine River *NT* **5** C6
Wolverton *ON* **19** B6
Wolverton *ON* **20** D5
Woman Lake *ON* **13** D6
Woman Lake *ON* **16** B3
Woman River Forest PP *ON* **17** E5
Wonowon *BC* **3** D7
Wonowon *BC* **9** D1
Wood, Mount *YT* **4** D1
Wood Bay *NT* **5** A6
Woodbridge *ON* **19** A7-8
Woodbridge *ON* **20** C6-7
Wood Buffalo *AB* **9** A6
Wood Buffalo *AB* **9** B6
Wood Buffalo *AB* **9** C-D7
Wood Buffalo *AB* **10** F7
Wood Buffalo *AB* **12** A1
Wood Buffalo *AB* **12** C2
Wood Buffalo, PN *AB* **9** B-C6
Wood Buffalo, PN *AB* **10** F7
Wood Buffalo, PN *AB* **12** B1
Wood Buffalo NP *AB* **9** A5-6
Wood Buffalo NP *AB* **12** A1
Wood Buffalo NP *AB* **41** E1
Wood Buffalo NP Fort
 Chipewyan Visitors
 Centre *AB* **9** B6-7
Wood Buffalo NP Fort
 Chipewyan Visitors
 Centre *AB* **12** B2
Wood Buffalo NP Fort Smith
 Visitors Centre *AB* **9** A6-7
Wood Buffalo NP Fort Smith
 Visitors Centre *AB* **12** A2
Woodburn *ON* **19** C7
Woodburn *ON* **20** E6
Woodfibre *BC* **1** F6-7
Woodfibre *BC* **2** D4

Woodford *ON* **18** F5-6
Woodford *ON* **20** A4
Woodham *ON* **19** B4
Woodham *ON* **20** D3
Woodhouse *AB* **7** D4-5
Woodington *ON* **18** D8
Woodington *ON* **21** B1
Wood Islands *PE* **34** D3
Wood Islands *PE* **35** F6
Wood Islands PP *PE* **34** D3
Wood Islands PP *PE* **35** F6
Wood Lake *MB* **15** C3
Wood Lake *ON* **21** B-C2
Wood Lake *SK* **12** E-F6
Woodland Beach *ON* **18** F7
Woodland Beach *ON* **20** A6
Woodland Caribou PP *ON* **13** C4
Woodland Caribou PP *ON* **13** D5
Woodland Caribou PP *ON* **14** B8
Woodland Caribou PP *ON* **16** B-C1
Woodlands *MB* **13** E3
Woodlands *MB* **14** D4
Woodley *SK* **11** F6-7
Woodmore *MB* **14** F5
Wood Mountain *SK* **11** F4
Wood Mountain (IR) *SK* **11** F4
Wood Mountain Post
 Provincial Historic Park
 SK **11** F4
Woodnorth *MB* **11** E8
Woodnorth *MB* **13** E1
Woodridge *MB* **13** F4-5
Woodridge *MB* **14** F6
Woodrow *SK* **11** F4
Woods, Lake of the *ON* **13** F5-6
Woods, Lake of the *ON* **14** E-F8
Woods, Lake of the *ON* **16** D1
Woods, Point of the *MB* **15** B5
Woods Bay *ON* **18** D7
Woods Harbour *NS* **33** F2
Woodside *MB* **13** E2-3
Woodside *MB* **14** D3
Woodside *MB* **35** E2
Woodside *NB* **35** E2
Woodside, LHN *ON* **19** B6
Woodside, LHN *ON* **20** D5
Woodside NHS *ON* **19** B6
Woodside NHS *ON* **20** D5

Woodside River *YT* **4** C6
Woods Island *NL* **36** A2-3
Woods Island *NL* **38** F2
Woods Lake *NL* **39** A3
Woodstock *NB* **31** F3
Woodstock *NB* **32** B1
Woodstock *NL* **38** E5
Woodstock *ON* **19** C5
Woodstock *ON* **20** E4
Woodstock (IR) *NB* **31** F3
Woodstock (IR) *NB* **32** B1
Woodview *ON* **21** D3-4
Woodville *ON* **20** A8
Woodville *ON* **21** D2
Woodville Mills *PE* **35** E7
Woodwards Cove *NB* **32** F3
Woody Island *NL* **36** D8
Woody Lake *SK* **12** E-F6
Woody Point *NL* **38** F2
Woody Point *NL* **39** F7
Woody River *SK* **11** C7
Woody River *SK* **13** C1
Wooler *ON* **21** E4
Woolford PP *AB* **6** F6
Woolford PP *AB* **7** F5
Woosey Lake *MB* **12** F8
Woosey Lake *MB* **15** F2
Wopmay Lake *NT* **10** A5
Wopmay River *NT* **10** A5
Worby *MB* **14** E2
Worcester *MB* **11** E-F6
Wordsworth *SK* **11** F7
Work Channel *BC* **3** F2-3
Worsley *AB* **9** D2
Worthington *ON* **17** F6
Worthington *ON* **18** A4
Woss *BC* **1** E4
Woss Lake *BC* **1** E4
Woss Lake PP *BC* **1** E4-5
Wostok *AB* **6** A6
Wostok *AB* **8** B7-8
Wostok *AB* **11** A1
Wotton *QC* **27** D5
Wottonville *QC* **27** D5
Woyenne *BC* **1** A5
Wreck Cove *NL* **36** D1
Wreck Cove *NL* **36** E6
Wreck Cove *NL* **37** E4
Wreck Cove *NS* **34** B7
Wreck Cove Lakes *NS* **34** B7
Wrentham *AB* **6** F7
Wrentham *AB* **7** E6
Wright *QC* **22** E7
Wright *QC* **24** B1-2
Wright Bay *NT* **5** A7-8
Wright Lake *ON* **16** B4

Wrigley *NT* **10** C2
Woods Island *NL* **36** A2-3
Wrigley Creek *NT* **4** C-D8
Wrigley Creek *NT* **10** D1
Wrigley Lake *NT* **4** A-B8
Wrigley Lake *NT* **10** B1
Wrigley River *NT* **10** C2
Writing-On-Stone PP *AB* **6** F7
Writing-On-Stone PP *AB* **7** F7
Writing-On-Stone PP *AB* **11** F1
Wrong Lake *MB* **13** C4
Wroxeter *ON* **19** A5
Wroxeter *ON* **20** C4
Wroxton *SK* **11** D7
Wroxton *SK* **13** D1
Wunnummin Lake *ON* **40** E1
Wuskwatim Lake *MB* **15** E3
Wycliffe *BC* **6** F4
Wycliffe *BC* **7** E1
Wyebridge *ON* **18** F7
Wyebridge *ON* **20** A6
Wyecliff *AB* **8** C7
Wyevale *ON* **18** F7
Wyevale *ON* **20** A6
Wylie Lake *AB* **9** A7
Wylie Lake *AB* **12** A2
Wymark *SK* **11** E3
Wymbolwood Beach *ON* **18** F7
Wymbolwood Beach *ON* **20** A6
Wyndham-Carseland PP *AB* **6** D6
Wyndham-Carseland PP *AB* **7** C5
Wynndel *BC* **6** F4
Wynniatt Bay *NT* **41** A3
Wynniatt Bay *NT* **42** D-E2
Wynyard *SK* **11** C-D6
Wyoming *ON* **19** C3
Wyoming *ON* **20** E2
Wyse Corner *NS* **33** B6
Wyse Corner *NS* **34** F2
Wyvern *NS* **33** A5
Wyvern *NS* **34** E1

X Y

Xhlawit (Alder Peak) *BC* **3** F3
Yahk *BC* **6** F4

Yahk *BC* **7** F1
Yahk Mountain *BC* **6** F4
Yahk Mountain *BC* **7** F2
Yahk PP *BC* **6** F4
Yahk PP *BC* **7** F1
Yakoun River *BC* **1** A-B1
Yale *BC* **1** F8
Yale *BC* **2** D7
Yamachiche *QC* **24** B7
Yamachiche *QC* **25** F7
Yamachiche *QC* **27** C2-3
Yamaska *QC* **24** C7
Yamaska *QC* **27** D2-3
Yamaska, parc de la *QC* **24** D8
Yamaska, parc de la *QC* **27** E3
Yamaska, rivière *QC* **24** C-D7
Yamaska, rivière *QC* **27** D2-3
Yamaska-Est *QC* **24** C7
Yamaska-Est *QC* **27** D2-3
Yamba Lake *NT* **10** A7-8
Yankeetown *NS* **32** F8
Yankeetown *NS* **33** C5
Yarbo *SK* **11** E7
Yarbo *SK* **13** D1
Yard Creek PP *BC* **6** D2
Yarker *ON* **21** D6
Yarmouth *NS* **33** E1-2
Yarmouth *NS* **33** E1
Yarrow *BC* **2** E6
Yates *AB* **8** C3
Yates River *AB* **9** A4
Yathkyed Lake *NU* **40** A1
Yathkyed Lake *NU* **41** E4
Yatton *ON* **19** A6
Yatton *ON* **20** C-D5
Yehiniko Creek *BC* **3** C2
Yellow Creek *SK* **11** B5
Yellow Grass *SK* **11** F5-6
Yellowhead *BC* **6** B2-3
Yellowhead Pass *AB* **6** B3
Yellowhead Pass NHS *AB* **6** B2-3
Yellowknife *NT* **10** D6
Yellowknife *NT* **41** D1
Yellowknife Bay *NT* **10** D6
Yellowknife River *NT* **10** B-C6
Yellowknife River *NT* **41** D2
Yellowquill *SK* **11** C6
Yeltea Lake *NT* **5** D6
Yelverton Bay *NU* **42** A4
Yeoford *AB* **8** D5

Yeo Island *BC* **1** C4
Yeo Island *ON* **18** D4
Ymir *BC* **6** F3
Yoho, PN *BC* **6** D4
Yoho, PN *BC* **7** B1
Yoho NP *BC* **6** D4
Yoho NP *BC* **7** A1
Yolakom River *BC* **1** D7
Yolakom River *BC* **2** A5-6
Yonge Mills *ON* **21** D8
Yonker *SK* **11** B2
York *ON* **19** A8
York *ON* **19** C7
York *ON* **20** C7
York *ON* **20** E6
York *ON* **21** F1
York *PE* **34** C2
York *PE* **35** E5
York, lac *QC* **29** B8
York, lac *QC* **30** B1
York, rivière *QC* **30** B1-2
York-Baillargeon, ZEC *QC* **30** B2
York Centre *QC* **30** B2
York Factory *MB* **15** D6
York Factory, LHN *MB* **15** D6-7
York Factory, LHN *MB* **40** C1
York Factory NHS *MB* **15** D6-7
York Factory NHS *MB* **40** C1
York Harbour *NL* **36** A2
York Harbour *NL* **38** F1
York Landing *MB* **15** E4
York Mills *NB* **32** C2
York Point *PE* **35** E4-5
York River *MB* **13** A6
York River *ON* **21** B4
Yorkton *SK* **11** D7
Youbou *BC* **2** E3
Youghall *NB* **29** E8
Youghall *NB* **31** B6
Young *SK* **11** C5
Young Lake *SK* **12** A5
Youngs Cove *NB* **32** C2
Young's Cove *NS* **33** C2
Youngs Cove Road *NB* **32** C4
Youngs Point *ON* **21** D3
Young's Point PP *AB* **9** F3
Youngstown *AB* **6** D7
Youngstown *AB* **7** A7-8
Youngstown *AB* **11** C-D1
Youngstown *ON* **21** D3

Yser, lac *QC* **23** F6
Yukon, fleuve *YT* **5** F1-2
Yukon/Northwest
 Territories Border TP *YT* **5** D3-4
Yukon River *YT* **4** B-C2
Yukon River *YT* **4** C-D4
Yuquot *BC* **1** F4
Yusezyu River *YT* **4** C-D6

Z

Zakwaski Mountain *BC* **1** E8
Zakwaski Mountain *BC* **2** C7
Zakwaski Mountain *BC* **6** E1
Zama City *AB* **9** A-B3
Zama Lake *AB* **9** B2-3
Zangeza Bay *SK* **12** C7
Zangeza Bay *SK* **15** B-C1
Zawale *AB* **8** B7-8
Zayas Island *BC* **3** F2
Zbaraz *MB* **13** D3-4
Zbaraz *MB* **14** B4-5
Zealand *NB* **31** F4
Zealand *NB* **32** B2
Zealandia *SK* **11** D3
Zeballos *BC* **1** E4
Zebulon Lake *NT* **10** A5
Zebulon River *NT* **10** A5
Zed Lake *MB* **12** D7
Zed Lake *MB* **15** D1-2
Zed Lake PP *MB* **12** D7
Zed Lake PP *MB* **15** D1-2
Zehner *SK* **11** E5
Zelana *MB* **14** A1
Zelma *SK* **11** C5
Zeneta *SK* **11** D-E7
Zengle Lake *SK* **12** C6-7
Zengle Lake *SK* **15** C1
Zenon Park *SK* **11** B6
Zephyr *ON* **20** B7
Zephyr *ON* **21** E1
Zeta Lake *NU* **41** B3
Zeta Lake *NU* **42** E2-3
Zhoda *MB* **13** F4
Zhoda *MB* **14** F6
Zinto Lake *NT* **10** B5
Zionz Lake *ON* **13** D7
Zionz Lake *ON* **16** B4
Zoria *MB* **14** A1
Zurich *ON* **19** B4
Zurich *ON* **20** D3